NETWORKING with WINDOWS™ 2000 and 2003

SECOND EDITION

Patrick Regan

Institute of Technology
Sacramento, CA

PEARSON

Prentice
Hall

Upper Saddle River, New Jersey
Columbus, Ohio

Library of Congress Cataloging-in-Publication Data

Regan, Patrick E.
   Networking with Windows 2000 and 2003 / Patrick Regan.
      p. cm.
   ISBN 0-13-112462-5 (alk. paper)
      1. Computer networks. 2. Microsoft Windows (Computer file) 3. Microsoft .NET. I. Title.

TK5105.5.R44523 2004
005.4′4769—dc21   2003043371

Editor in Chief: Stephen Helba
Assistant Vice President and Publisher: Charles E. Stewart, Jr.
Assistant Editor: Mayda Bosco
Production Editor: Kevin Happell
Design Coordinator: Diane Ernsberger
Cover Designer: Bryan Huber
Cover image: Digital Vision
Production Manager: Matthew Ottenweller
Marketing Manager: Ben Leonard

This book was set in Times Roman by Carlisle Communications Ltd. It was printed and bound by Courier-Kendallville, Inc. The cover was printed by the Lehigh Press, Inc.

Active Directory, ActiveX, FrontPage, Hotmail, Microsoft, MS-DOS, MSDN, Outlook, PowerPoint, Visual Basic, Visual C++, Visual J++, Win32, Win32s, Windows, Windows NT, Windows Server, and Windows Server System are either registered trademarks or trademarks of Microsoft Corporation in the United States and/or other countries. Microsoft products are the intellectual property of Microsoft Corporation and are protected by copyright laws and one or more U.S. and foreign patents and patent applications.

Pearson Education Ltd.   Pearson Education Australia Pty. Limited
Pearson Education Singapore Pte. Ltd.   Pearson Education North Asia Ltd.
Pearson Education Canada, Ltd.   Pearson Educación de Mexico, S.A. de C.V.
Pearson Education—Japan   Pearson Education Malaysia Pte. Ltd.

10 9 8 7 6 5 4 3 2 1
ISBN 0-13-112462-5

This book is dedicated to my best friend, Jessica. She has always been there for me and has always been supportive of what I do.

Preface

Since I first got involved in local area networks and earned my first certification as a Novell Certified Network Engineer and a Novell Certified Network Instructor, I have learned how complex networking can be. As the Internet was introduced to the general public, new technology has also been introduced at a staggering pace. As I maintain the Novell certifications, gain Microsoft certifications, and work as a network administrator, it is evident that essential topics in many books are skipped; and often topics that are included are incomplete and lack the ability to challenge me. Because I often encounter gaps in this information, it takes a great deal of effort to piece it all together.

This book is designed to help you learn the basic concepts of networking, starting with the basic hardware components that affect server performance and reliability. The first part of this book introduces the process of how to build a simple LAN by connecting the PCs with the various wiring and topology. The second part of the book describes Windows 2000 and Windows Server 2003 as PC operating systems and as network operating systems. The third part of the book focuses on today's basic features of a network server including DNS and DHCP services, directory services (Active Directory), disk and file management, and print management. The book's fourth unit covers network topics such as remote access, WAN technology, routing between networks, and web servers.

Although this book does not hold all the answers, it will give you the basic foundations that you need to succeed as a network administrator and to complete some beginning certifications, including Comptia's Network + Exam and the four core Microsoft MSCE exams.

To reflect my method of teaching any of the PC or networking classes, each chapter in this book often repeats material that is related to basic, yet essential, concepts. In addition, each chapter includes review questions and hands-on exercises to reinforce those basic skills and to immediately apply what you are reading. Lastly, I always try to use real-world examples so that you can see how basic skills are applied and to show how to take those basic skills to the next level of learning.

ACKNOWLEDGMENTS

I would like to thank the following reviewers for their invaluable feedback: Mike Awwad, DeVry University–North Brunswick, NJ; Larry Knupp, DeVry University–Kansas City, MO; Darrell G. Kohr, Renton Technical College, Renton, WA; Rick Miller, Ferris State University, Big Rapids, MI; and David Oliver, Johnston Community College, Smithfield, NC.

ABOUT THE AUTHOR

Patrick Regan has been a PC technician and network administrator/engineer for the past 12 years. He has also taught many computer and networking technology classes at Sacramento local colleges (Heald Colleges and Institute of Technology), conducted considerable formal and informal training while an IT administrator (Heald Colleges) and a product support engineer for the Intel Corporation's customer service, and participated in and led many projects (Heald Colleges and Intel). For his teaching accomplishments, he received the Teacher of the Year award from Heald Colleges; in addition, he received several recognition awards from Intel. Currently, he holds many certifications, including Microsoft's MCSE, MCSA, and MCT; COMPTIA's A+, Network+, Server+, Linux+, Security+, and CTT+; Cisco's CCNA; and Novell's CNE.

You can write with questions and comments to the author at patrick_regan@hotmail.com. (Because of the high volume of mail, every message may not receive a reply.)

Brief Contents

Contents

CHAPTER **3**

The OSI Model   72

CHAPTER 13 **Managing Computers, Users, and Groups   458**

UNIT IV   ADVANCED NETWORK TOPICS   643

CHAPTER 18 **Understanding WAN Technology   644**

UNIT I

NETWORK BASICS

CHAPTER 1

Introduction to Networks

Topics Covered in This Chapter

Introduction

A network is a group of computers connected by cables or some method of wireless technology. In today's business world, a network is an important tool for many businesses. It allows users to access large databases, centralized files, and expensive equipment.

Objectives

- Define *network*.
- Define common networking terms for LANs and WANs.
- List the components that compose a network.
- Compare a file-and-print server with an application server.
- Compare a client-server network with a peer-to-peer network.
- List and define the various network services.
- Define *protocols*.

- List the benefits of networks.
- Differentiate between client-server and peer-to-peer networks.
- List and explain the different server roles.
- Differentiate between LANs, MANs, and WANs.
- Define a NOS and explain how it relates to the LAN.
- List the responsibilities of the network administrator.

1.1   NETWORK BEGINNINGS

Early computers were called **mainframes,** which were large centralized computers used to store and organize data. To access a mainframe, you used a **dumb terminal,** which consisted of a monitor to display the data and a keyboard to input the data. The dumb terminal did not process the data; instead, all processing was done by the mainframe computer (centralized computing).

Eventually, as computers became smaller and less expensive, the **personal computer (PC)** was introduced. Unlike the mainframe computer, a PC is meant to be used by one person and contains its own processing capabilities. As PCs became more popular, the need for people to move data from one computer to another became a reality. This process was initially performed with "sneaker net," in which a person would hand-carry the data from computer to computer via a floppy disk. Unfortunately, this method was relatively expensive and time consuming when the disk had to be transported over a long distance.

As the need to share data between different computers grew, distributed computing was developed, which consists of taking several computers and connecting them by cable. Different from centralized computing, the processing in a distributed computing system is done by the individual PCs. In fact, the distributed computing system is typically more powerful than the centralized computing system, because the sum of the processing power of the individual PCs is more than a single mainframe.

1.2   NETWORK DEFINED

A **network** is two or more computers connected to share resources such as files or a printer. A common device used to connect computers is a hub. See Figure 1.1. To function, a network requires a service to share or access a common medium or pathway and thus connect the computers. To bring it all together, protocols give the entire system common communication rules.

3

Figure 1.1   Computer network consisting of computers connected together with a hub

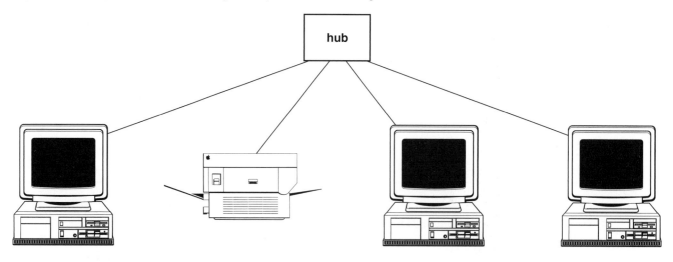

1.2.1   Network Services

The two most common services provided by a network are file sharing and print sharing. **File sharing** allows a user to access files on another computer without using a floppy disk or other forms of removable media. To ensure that files are secure, most networks can limit access to a directory or file and the type of access (permissions or rights) a user or users may have. For example, if you have full access to your home directory (personal directory on the network to store files), you can list, read, execute, create, change, and delete files in your home directory. Depending on the contents of the directory or file, you could specify who has access to it and what permissions or rights those users have over it. In this way, you may specify one group of people who will not be able to see or execute the file, and give a second group of people the ability to see or execute the file but not change or delete the file. Lastly, you may give rights to a third group of users to see, execute, and change the file.

Print sharing allows several people to send documents to a centrally located printer in the office, so not everyone requires a personal laser printer. Much like files, networks can limit who has access to the printer. For example, if you have two laser printers (a standard laser printer and an expensive, high-resolution, color laser printer), you can assign everyone access to the standard laser printer but only a handful of people access to the expensive printer.

Internet services provide important tools to business. E-mail and the World Wide Web (WWW) are two popular services. **Electronic mail, or e-mail,** is a powerful, sophisticated tool that allows users to send text messages and file attachments (documents, pictures, sound, and video) to another e-mail address. See Figure 1.2.

Like mail from the post office, e-mail is delivered to a mailbox (delivery location or holding area for electronic messages). An Internet mail address includes the user name, followed by the @ symbol and the name of the mail server. When users connect to the network, they can access their e-mail messages. Other features may include return receipt (to verify that the e-mail was read or delivered) and reply. To reply to an e-mail message, click on the reply button or option, thereby sending the e-mail message to several people simultaneously or forwarding the message to someone else.

Because the Internet is essentially a huge network, it is possible to make a single network part of the Internet or to provide a common connection to the Internet for many users. For example, you can create your own web page on the Internet to provide products and services to the public or you can perform research on the Internet.

1.2.2   Network Media

When users share a file or printer, they must have a pathway to access the network resource. Computers connect to the network by using a special expansion card called a **network interface card (NIC).** The network card communicates by sending signals through a cable (twisted pair, coaxial, or fiber optic)

Figure 1.2   E-mail with Microsoft Outlook

or by using wireless technology (infrared wavelengths, microwaves, or radio waves). The role of the network card is to prepare and send data to another computer, receive data from another computer, and control the data flow between the computer and the cabling system. See Figure 1.3.

1.2.3   Protocols

Protocols are the rules or standards that allow computers to connect to one another and enable computers and peripheral devices to exchange information with as little error as possible. Common protocol suites are Transmission Control Protocol/Internet Protocol (TCP/IP), Internetwork Packet Exchange (IPX), and NetBIOS Extended User Interface (NetBEUI). A **suite** is a set of protocols that work together.

1.3   NETWORK CHARACTERISTICS

All networks can be characterized by the following:

- Client-server network or peer-to-peer network
- Area network (LAN, MAN, or WAN)

1.3.1   Servers, Clients, and Peers

A network computer can either provide or request services. A **server** is a service provider that provides access to network resources, and a **client** is a computer that requests services. A network of servers and clients is called a **client-server network,** which is typically used on medium or large networks. A server-based network is the best network for sharing resources and data, as it provides network security for such information. Windows NT, Windows 2000, Windows Server 2003, and Novell NetWare networks are primarily client-server networks.

Figure 1.3   A network card with an unshielded twisted-pair (UTP) cable attached to an RJ-45 connector and an unused BNC connector

A **peer-to-peer network,** sometimes referred to as a **workgroup,** has no dedicated servers. Instead, all computers are equal; thus, they both provide and request services. By keeping resources on their own machines, users manage their own shared resources. Windows 95, Windows 98, and Windows Millennium can be used to form a peer-to-peer network.

In discussions of server and server applications, you may hear the terms *front end* and *back end.* In client-server applications, the client part of the program is often called the **front end** and the server part is called the **back end.** The front end is the interface that is provided to a user or another program; it is the part that a user or program sees and with which it interacts. The back end consists of services provided by the server. All that a user and program need to know is that they perform a request using the front end, and the front end provides a response. A user does not need to be concerned about what happens in the back end to get the response. For example, when you access a website, you type in a web address (called a uniform resource locator, or **URL**) in a browser and the web page is displayed. You did not worry that the computer had to first contact a DNS server to get an IP address for that website, and you did not have to set up a connection with that web server to download the html instructions to display the web page.

1.3.2   Server Roles

Because companies have different needs for their networks, servers can assume several different roles. A single server also could have several roles. These roles are as follows:

- **File server**—Manages user access to files stored on a server. When a file is accessed on a file server, the file is downloaded to the client's RAM. For example, if you are creating a report on a word processor, the word-processing files will be executed from your client computer and the report will be stored on the server. As you access the report from the server, it will be downloaded or copied onto the RAM of the client computer. Note that all processing on the report is done by the client microprocessors. Other advantages of a file server are that it allows easy access to the data files from any computer and it allows for easy backup of data files on the server.

- **Print server**—Manages user access to printer resources connected to the network, allowing one printer to be used by many people
- **Application server**—Is similar to a file-and-print server, but also does some of the processing
- **Mail server**—Manages electronic messages (e-mail) between users
- **Fax server**—Manages fax messages sent into and out of the network through a fax modem
- **Communication server**—Handles data flow and e-mail messages from one network to another using modems or other dial-up technology
- **Web server**—Runs WWW and FTP (File Transfer Protocol) services for access via the intranet or Internet
- **Proxy server**—Provides local intranet clients with access to the Internet while keeping the local intranet free from intruders
- **Directory services server**—Locates information about the network such as domains (logical divisions of the network) and other servers

1.3.3   Area Networks

Modern networks are broken into three main categories: **local area network (LAN), metropolitan area network (MAN),** and **wide area network (WAN).** A LAN consists of computers that are connected within a geographically close network such as a room, building, or group of adjacent buildings. A MAN is designed for a town or city, and uses high-speed connections such as fiber optics. A WAN uses long-range telecommunication links to connect the network computers over long distances and often consists of two or more smaller LANs. See Figure 1.4. Typically, LANs are connected through public networks (e.g., the public telephone system).

A WAN can be either an enterprise WAN or a global WAN. An **enterprise WAN** is owned by one company or organization. A **global WAN** is not owned by any one company and may cross national boundaries. The best known example of a global WAN is the Internet, which connects millions of computers. The Internet has more than 490 million users in over 100 countries, and the number of users is growing rapidly. See Figure 1.5.

Figure 1.4   A wide area network (WAN)

Figure 1.5   The Internet

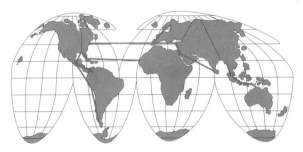

1.4   NETWORK SOFTWARE

A **network operating system (NOS)** includes special functions for connecting computers and devices into a LAN, to manage the resources and services of the network and provide network security for multiple users. The most common client-server network operating systems are Windows NT Server family, Novell NetWare, and UNIX/Linux. Some operating systems such as Windows 9X, Windows 2000 Professional, Windows XP, and Windows NT Workstation also can provide network resources as file and printer access, although they are not servers.

The workstations that are attached to the network communicate through the use of **client software** called **shells, redirectors,** or **requesters.** While the network protocol enables data transmission across the LAN, the client software resides on top of the network protocol so that it can communicate with other network computers. In Windows 9X, Windows NT Workstation, Windows 2000 Professional, and Windows XP the client software is installed and configured using the network dialog box accessed by clicking on the network applet in the control panel or by accessing the shortcut menu of the Network Neighborhood and selecting the Properties option.

1.4.1   UNIX

UNIX, a popular multiuser, multitasking operation, is the grandfather of network operating systems. It was developed at Bell Laboratories in the early 1970s. Although UNIX is a mature, powerful, reliable operating system, it has been traditionally known for its cryptic commands and its general lack of user friendliness. It is designed to handle high usage loads while providing support for common Internet services such as web server, FTP server, terminal emulation (Telnet), and database access. In addition, it can use the network file system (NFS), which allows various network clients running different operating systems to access shared files stored on a UNIX machine.

OTHER NETWORK TERMS

Enterprise—Any large organization that utilizes computers, usually multiple LANs.

Internetwork—A network consisting of several LANs linked together. The smaller LANs are known as **subnetworks** or **subnets.**

Intranet—A network based on the TCP/IP protocol—the same protocol used by the Internet. Unlike the Internet, the intranet belongs to a single organization and is accessible only by that organization's members. An intranet's websites look and act like any other websites, but they are isolated by a firewall to stop illegal access. Note that an intranet could have access to the Internet, but does not require it.

Small office/home office (SOHO)—Small networks used primarily in home offices that might be part of a larger corporation but yet remain apart from it. SOHO networks are usually peer-to-peer networks.

Value-added network (VAN)—A network with special services such as electronic data interchange (EDI) or financial services such as credit card authorization or ATM transactions.

In contrast to other network operating systems, UNIX is produced by many manufacturers. The two main dialects of UNIX are AT&T's System V and Berkeley University's BSD4.x. Popular manufactured versions include Digital Equipment Corporation

UNIX, Hewlett-Packard HP-UX, SCO OpenServer, and Sun Microsystems Solaris. Another popular NOS, Banyan Vines, is based on a highly modified UNIX System V core. The official trademarked UNIX is now owned by The Open Group, an industry standards organization that certifies and brands UNIX implementations.

POSIX is a set of standards of the Institute of Electrical and Electronic Engineers (IEEE) and the International Organization for Standardization (ISO) that defines an interface between programs and UNIX. By following the POSIX standard, developers have some assurance that their software can be easily ported or translated to a POSIX-compliant operating system. The POSIX standard is now maintained by an arm of the IEEE called the Portable Applications Standards Committee (PASC).

1.4.2   Linux

Linux (pronounced LIH-nuhks with a short "i") is an UNIX-like operating system that was designed to provide personal computer users a free, or very low-cost, operating system comparable to traditional and usually more expensive UNIX systems. Linux comes in versions for all major microprocessor platforms, including the Intel, PowerPC, Sparc, and Alpha platforms. Because it conforms to the POSIX standard user and programming interfaces, developers can write programs that can be ported to other platforms running Linux (or UNIX, which also conforms to the POSIX standard).

The Linux kernel acts as a mediator for your programs and your hardware. Like the UNIX kernel, the Linux kernel is designed to do one thing well. It handles low-level operations such as managing memory, files, programs that are running, networking, and various hardware devices. For example, Linux arranges for memory management for all of the running programs (processes) and makes sure that they all get a fair share of the processor clock cycles. In addition, it provides a nice, fairly portable interface for programs to talk to your hardware. Think of the kernel as a police officer directing traffic. Unlike Windows, Linux does not include a windowing system or graphical user interface (GUI). Instead, Linux users can choose among a number of X servers and Windows managers.

By the time Linux version 1.0 was released, several Linux distributors had begun packaging the Linux kernel with basic support programs, the GNU utilities and compilers, the X Window System, and other useful programs. In 1995, the Linux 1.2 kernel was released; it supported kernel modules, the peripheral component interconnect (PCI) bus, kernel-level firewalls, and non-TCP/IP networking protocols. By this time, Linux had become as stable as any commercial version of UNIX on the Intel x86 platforms.

Since Linux is often used as a server, it has a complete implementation of TCP/IP networking software, including drivers for the popular Ethernet cards and the ability to use serial line protocols such as the Serial Line Internet Protocol (SLIP) and Point-to-Point Protocol (PPP) to provide access to a TCP/IP network via a modem. With Linux, TCP/IP, and a connection to the network, you can communicate with users and machines across the Internet via electronic mail, USENET news, file transfers, and more.

In fact, Linux owes its versatility to the wide availability of software that runs on it. Understanding what software to use to solve what problems is key to maximizing the utility of Linux:

- **Web server**—Apache (http://www.apache.org) is the most popular web server.
- **Web proxy**—To better control web use and to allow for caching of frequently accessed pages, Squid (http://www.squid-cache.org) is used.
- **File sharing**—Linux can be made to look like a Windows NT server with respect to file and print sharing. Samba (http://www.samba.org) is the software that does this.
- **E-mail**—Linux excels at handling e-mail. Sendmail (http://www.sendmail.org) is the most widely used mail transfer agent (MTA). Qmail (http://www.qmail.org) and PostFix (http://www.postfix.org) are alternatives.
- **Domain name server**—This server provides mappings between names and IP addresses, along with distributing network information (i.e., mail servers). BIND (http://www.isc.org/products/BIND/) is the most widely used name server.

1.4.3   Novell NetWare

Several years ago, **Novell NetWare** was the standard LAN-based network operating system. It was one of the primary players to bring networking to the PC arena; it helped replace the dumb terminals with PCs and thus allowed a much easier way to share data files, applications, and printers. Novell NetWare

Table 1.1   Various NetWare versions

	Default Protocol	Type of Server-based Access	Interface	Comments
NetWare 3.11	IPX (Ethernet uses 802.3 frame)	Bindery (single-server database)	Command interface	
NetWare 3.12/3.2	IPX (Ethernet uses 802.2 frame)	Bindery (single-server database)	Command interface	
NetWare 4.11/4.2	IPX (Ethernet uses 802.2 frame)	NDS (distributed replicated database)	Command interface	Introduced directory services
NetWare 5.0/5.1	TCP/IP	NDS (distributed replicated database)	Command/GUI interface	Added many Internet and Windows NT-like utilities and allowed management of network resources at the server
NetWare 6.0	TCP/IP	NDS (distributed replicated database)	Command/GUI interface	Added CIFS, AFP, and NFS

is known as a strong file and print server. Unlike the other primary network operating systems, Novell NetWare runs as a dedicated stand-alone server.

Novell NetWare lost its dominance because Windows GUI interface became more popular than NetWare's command/menu interface. In addition, Novell users cannot perform common administrative tasks such as creating users and giving a user access to a network resource at the server, rather than at a client computer. Lastly, Novell initially missed key opportunities during the development of the Internet.

Early versions of NetWare (NetWare 3.11, 3.12, and 3.2) use the NetWare Bindery for security. The Bindery is a flat-based database that resides on a single server and contains profiles of the network users for that server. See Table 1.1.

Newer versions of NetWare use **Novell Directory Services (NDS),** a global, distributed, replicated database that tracks users and resources and provides controlled access to network resources. NDS is global because it spans an enterprise or multiple server network. It is distributed because the database is kept close to the users rather than in a single, central location, and it is replicated to several servers to provide fault tolerance. Since the database exists for multiple servers, a user has to be created only once and has to log in to access all servers. Within the NDS design, the network objects such as users, printers, and storage units are grouped into containers (used to organize the network objects) much like files are divided into subdirectories or folders on a user's hard drive.

NetWare 5 and 6 come with support for both Novell's own IPX network protocol and the Internet's TCP/IP protocol. NetWare has integrated its own NDS with the TCP/IP's Domain Name System (DNS) protocol, Dynamic Host Configuration Protocol (DHCP), and application-level support for a web server. In addition, NetWare 5 and 6 support Java applications and include an enhanced file system, enhanced printing services, and advanced security.

NetWare 6 incorporates Novell iFolder, a unique Net services solution that enables you to access personal files from anywhere, at anytime, through virtually any Web-enabled device. When you use Novell iFolder, you don't have to worry about e-mailing critical presentation files from your corporate desktop to your laptop. Anything that you save in iFolder on one machine will be seamlessly synchronized in iFolder on all of your other machines. You can work online, offline, at home, in the office, or on the road, and iFolder will ensure that you always have the most recent version of your file. Moreover, iFolder provides powerful security for your data; your files are always protected from prying eyes.

To further extend your network's boundaries, NetWare 6 supports various file protocols, such as Appletalk Filing Protocol for Macintosh (AFP), Network File System (NFS), and Common Internet File System (CIFS), and systems application architecture (SAA) for mainframes and AS/400. CIFS is the same protocol that allows you to create, view, and access shared drives, directories, and printers with Microsoft Windows. NetWare's support for these diverse protocols eliminates the need for client software; communication is accomplished over TCP/IP and native applications are run over the network. This protocol support also enables you to seamlessly leverage the power of eDirectory through virtually any third-party system, including Windows, Macintosh, and UNIX for central administration and file access.

1.4.4   OS/2

OS/2 was one of the first 32-bit GUI operating systems originally developed by IBM and Microsoft (before Microsoft's Windows NT), but it is now owned and controlled by IBM. It uses the same domain concept used by Windows NT. Domain controllers are used to store the network user and group database, which is replicated from a primary domain controller (PDC) to one or more backup domain controllers (BDCs). OS/2 uses NetBEUI as its native protocol, but supports TCP/IP as well. It is compatible with DOS, all Windows versions, Macintosh, and OS/2 clients.

1.4.5   Windows NT Family

Microsoft's early attempt at a network operating system began as a combined effort between Microsoft and IBM as OS/2. After some disagreement, Microsoft abandoned OS/2 to develop Windows NT. **Windows NT** (NT stands for new technology) is an advanced, high-performance network operating system, which is robust in features and services, security, performance, and upgradeability. Windows NT provides a good file and print server, and it makes an excellent application server.

The early versions of Windows NT (such as Windows NT 3.51) used the Windows 3.xx Program Manager Interface. Newer versions of Windows NT use the popular Windows 95 or the Internet Explorer Active Desktop interface.

The next version of Windows NT was **Windows 2000** (NT 5.0). There are four versions of Windows 2000: Windows 2000 Professional (workstation version), Windows 2000 Server, Windows 2000 Advanced Server, and Windows 2000 Datacenter Server. Windows 2000 servers provide the following:

- **File and print sharing**—In all Microsoft operating systems since Windows 95. Supports file and print sharing through File and Print Sharing for Microsoft Networks and Clients for Microsoft Networks services.
- **Internet Information Server (IIS)**—Provides web services (Hypertext Transfer Protocol, or HTTP, and FTP).
- **SQL server**—Provides database services.
- **Microsoft Exchange**—Provides e-mail services.
- **NT File System (NTFS)**—Provides a robust, flexible file system that provides file security
- **Active Directory (AD)**—Similar to NDS in NetWare, uses the "tree" concept for managing resources on a network. Its benefits will especially be realized in Enterprise applications where network administration and management will be almost painless. Everything is treated as an object that can be moved or edited across servers and domains.
- **Internet Connection Sharing (ICS)**—In all Microsoft Windows since Window 98SE. Allows a single dial-up connection to be shared across the network. This has great implications for SOHOs and home users with multiple machines who no longer will need to purchase an application to provide this feature.
- **Kerberos security**—A security protocol that is used for distributed security within a domain tree/forest. Allows for transitive trusts and a single logon to provide access to all domain resources.
- **Clustering**—In Windows 2000 Advanced Server and Windows 2000 Datacenter Server. Enables two or more servers to work together to keep server-based applications available.

.NET is a Microsoft operating system platform that incorporates distributed applications. This platform brings users into the next generation of the Internet by overcoming the deficiencies of the first generation and by giving users a more enriched experience in using the web for both personal and business applications. It proposes to integrate web applications with the desktop PC seamlessly by "hosting" desktop applications (primarily) on the "Net." So instead of having an application like Microsoft Word installed on an end-user's computer, it is, in theory, "housed" on the web. Microsoft's .NET strategy revolves around using the Internet as a pseudo-operating system by storing data "on the Net" instead of on a PC. Developers can thus create programs that theoretically "live" on the Net, and end-users can accordingly use these applications with their own personal data, from anywhere.

From the perspective of the user, there are four main principles of .NET:

■ It erases the boundaries between applications and the Internet. Instead of interacting with an application or a single website, .NET connects the user to an array of computers and services that exchange and combine objects and data.
■ Software is rented as a hosted service over the Internet instead of purchased from a store shelf. Essentially, the Internet will be housing all of a user's applications and data.
■ Users have access to their information on the Internet from any device, anytime, anywhere.
■ New ways are provided to interact with application data, for example, speech and handwriting recognition.

.NET allows you to move from one site to another and not worry about multiple user names and passwords. It remembers your preferences and delivers the appropriate data at the appropriate time to any device that you choose, including PCs and handheld devices such as cellular phones. In addition, it provides services that let you manage your personal information and control access to it.

.NET uses the **XML language**, which is designed for web pages, to enable the definition, transmission, validation, and interpretation of data between applications and between organizations. Using the XML in a modular approach, .NET attempts to remove barriers to data sharing and software integration. Businesses can benefit because the modular approach allows them to expand their online applications by adding modules as needed and to move data from module or application to another as needed. Therefore, many applications can easily interface with each other and share information.

With the introduction of .NET, Microsoft released a new family—Windows Server 2003—which includes four editions: Web Server, Standard Server, Enterprise Server, and Datacenter Server. Windows Server 2003 is based on much of the same code used in Windows 2000, especially in the deployment and administration of Active Directory. In addition, IIS version 6.0 is said to be up to 30% faster than IIS version 5.0. In addition, all .NET servers include the .NET Framework, a run-time environment for XML-based web services.

The client released as part of the Windows Server 2003 family is Windows XP, the long-awaited merger of Microsoft's consumer and business operating systems. Windows XP introduced the interface that is also used in Windows Server 2003. The interface is different from that of Windows 2000; it is a cleaner default desktop and a more intuitive interface. Yet, it contains the 32-bit kernel and driver set from Windows NT and Windows 2000. In addition, it is the first Windows for consumers that includes

■ A personal firewall
■ Remote assistance that lets you invite someone to connect to your computer and help you with problems
■ Remote desktop connection, which allows you to connect to a computer's desktop from a remote location and run applications as if you were sitting at its console

Windows XP comes in two versions, home and professional. The professional version supports up to two processors and can connect to a Microsoft Windows domain. The home version supports only one processor and cannot connect to a Microsoft Windows domain. (Domains will be explained later in this book.)

1.5   NETWORK ADMINISTRATOR

Networks are typically found only within companies and organizations. An information technology (IT) department usually maintains these networks, and the person who is responsible for maintaining them is the **administrator.** Job responsibilities include the following:

■ Install and configure the server
■ Install and configure the network clients

- Establish and maintain a network security system to protect the network resources
- Document the network, including the server configuration, the cabling architecture, and the network problems and solutions. Network documentation is a valuable tool in troubleshooting network problems
- Establish backup systems and back up important data files on a regular basis
- Minimize the number and severity of network failures
- Monitor network performance to determine trends, foresee network failure, and provide troubleshooting

Although the previous list summarizes the network administrator's duties, this person's primary responsibility is to fulfill the needs of the network clients. This means the administrator must make the network resources available to the user and make access easy, while keeping the network secure. Lastly, the network administrator must be effective in time and priority management.

1.6   INTRODUCTION TO TROUBLESHOOTING

In comparison to PC problems, network problems can have a much more devastating effect on network users. This is because users in corporations tend to store many of their documents on the network, and they require access to many network services such as file and print sharing and e-mail. In addition, a network problem can affect many users, not just one. Problems can be related to a server, a network, a client, or a user. The only way to get good at troubleshooting computer and network problems is to practice, practice, practice.

When encountering a problem, you should follow certain guidelines. First, your mind must be clear and rested. You must be able to concentrate on the problem. If not, you may overlook something that is obvious, such as the power cord not being plugged in.

Next, don't panic, don't get frustrated, and allow enough time to do the job right. If you panic, you may do something that will make the situation worse. If you start to get frustrated, take a break. Five or ten minutes away from the problem will clear your mind and allow you to look at the problem a little differently. Lastly, make sure that you have enough time to properly analyze the problem, fix the problem, and properly test the system after the repair. Again, if you rush a job, you may make the problem worse or you may overlook something simple.

1.6.1   Computer Problems

Everything that applies to a PC problem also applies to a server or client problem. The problem could be a hardware failure, incompatibility, improper configuration, a software glitch, an environmental factor, or user error. See Table 1.2. A component such as a hard drive, floppy drive, power supply, cable, or modem, could be faulty. In addition, problems can be caused by a virus, software that is not compatible with a screen saver, BIOS setup program settings, power management features, Control Panel settings, software drivers, hardware settings, power fluctuations, or electromagnetic interference.

1.6.2   Network Problems

Network problems include trouble with the media that connect a server and/or client to the network and anything else the media connects to. For example, most computers are connected to a network through a cable that is connected to a hub. The smaller networks can be connected together to form a larger network by using routers. Therefore, the cables, the hub, or the router could be faulty, a cable may not be connected properly, or a hub or router may not be configured properly.

For a computer and a server to operate properly, the computer's protocol has to be configured properly. In addition, users must have proper permissions to use a network resource, and the network may require services provided by other servers. For example, a DNS server may provide name resolution for the network to function properly; when you enter http://www.acme.com, a DNS server looks up the IP address for the www.acme.com so that it knows how to contact that web server. Also, network communications can be interrupted by external environmental factors such as electromagnetic interference.

Table 1.2 Computer problem classifications

Reason for Failure	Description
Hardware Failure	One or more components fail inside the computer.
Hardware Incompatibility[1]	A component is not compatible with another component.
Improper Hardware Configuration[1]	Harware has not been installed or configured properly. This happens often when the user does not read the manual or does not have the knowledge to make use of the manual.
Improper Software Configuration[1]	Software (operating system or application) is not installed or configured properly. This happens often when the user does not read the manual or does not have the knowledge to make use of the manual.
Software Failure	A glitch occurs in the software. This can range from corrupted data to a flaw in the programming.
Software Compatibility[1]	The software may not be compatible with the hardware or other software.
Environment	The location of the computer and its environment (e.g., room temperature, air flow, electromagnetic interference, magnetic fields) may affect the reliability of the PC and has a direct impact on the PC's life.
User Error	A common situation where the user hits the wrong keys or is not familiar with the computer and/or software. It could be something as simple as hitting the zero (0) key rather than the letter O.

[1]May appear to be a hardware failure.

1.6.3 General Troubleshooting Strategy

COMPTIA, the organization responsible for the A+, Network+, and Server+ exams use a general troubleshooting strategy that consist of the following eight steps:

1. Establish symptoms.
2. Identify the affected area.
3. Establish what has changed.
4. Select the most probable cause.
5. Implement a solution.
6. Test the result.
7. Recognize the potential effects of the solution.
8. Document the solution.

Before trying to fix the problem, you need to gather information. You need to clarify exactly what is happening. Determine if the problem is localized to one machine or a small group of machines, or if it extends throughout the network. Make sure that you can duplicate the problem, and verify that the user is not part of the problem. In addition, determine if the problem is always repeatable or if it is intermittent. If it is an intermittent problem, ask if the problem follows a certain pattern (such as when the computer is on for a while) or if it occurs completely randomly.

The more difficult problems are the intermittent ones. Since the intermittent errors do not happen on a regular basis, something may be fine when you stop to test it, but fail when you get back to work. When dealing with intermittent problems, after you make a change that might fix the system, you must thoroughly test the system over a period of time to see if the problem actually goes away.

After the problem has been repeated and verified, you need to test the system further to see the extent of the problem. For example, if your system doesn't boot properly, can you boot from a floppy drive and access the hard drive? If you can't print from a program, can you print using another program? If the mouse doesn't work in one environment such as Windows, does it work using DOS? Is the problem exhibited on one computer or several computers on the network? If several computers have the same problem, what is common with those computers that is not common with the computers that do work?

You can gather additional information by trying to use software utilities to test your system; use a digital multimeter (DMM) and cable testing equipment. Some utilities include software to test the computer components, check for viruses, look for formatting errors on a disk, or check software and protocol configuration.

When gathering information about the problem, also find out what has changed recently on the computer and the network. Many times servicing or changes can cause other problems.

After you have gathered as much information as you can, you are ready to make the repair or fix. Sometimes you will know exactly what to change or replace. Other times you will have the problem narrowed down to several causes, which requires you to isolate the problem. If you suspect a faulty component, replace the component with a known good component. If the system works with the new component, the problem was the item that you just removed. Note: When a new item is taken off the shelf, it does not mean that the item is good. In addition, you can try "reverse swapping," which is trying a suspected component in a second working system.

Other solutions including reconfiguring the software or hardware; reloading the operating system, application software, or drivers; making changes to the BIOS setup program; or reconfiguring the software. Whatever course of action that you choose, make one change at a time. If the problem still exists, then make another change; follow this pattern until the problem no longer exists. When determining which item to check or swap, first try to check items that are likely to cause the problem and are the easiest and quickest to check. Always check the obvious first. For example, if the hub is not working at all and there are no lights, make sure that the AC adapter is plugged in.

After you fix the problem, you should always thoroughly test the computer and/or network. This will ensure that the problem did go away and that you did not cause another problem when fixing the first problem. With networking, it is important to realize what other problems your solution may cause, so that you can select the best solution.

Keep a log of changes made to a system and list any problems and their solutions. The log lets you know if the system has gone through any changes recently; this is especially important if you work for a department that has several PC support people. In addition, the log will help you spot trends so that you can make plans to minimize problems and to have the resources available when a problem occurs.

1.6.4   Where To Get Help

Many times when you get an error message or you research a network problem, you are told to contact your system administrator to get the problem straightened out. Unfortunately, *you* are the system administrator and you don't have a clue about what to do. There are several places where you can get help:

- Documentation
- Resource kits
- Microsoft websites
- Microsoft's TechNet and Microsoft's Knowledge Base
- Internet

Anything that deals with computers involves lots of documentation (hardware and software), which generally provides a wealth of information and tips or warnings that solve many problems. Microsoft and a few other companies offer resource kits for their operating systems and other software packages. For example, Microsoft has resources for DOS, Windows 3.xx (3.0, 3.10, and 3.11), Windows 95, Windows 98, Windows Millennium, Windows NT, Windows 2000, Windows XP, Windows Server 2003, and Microsoft Office. These packages offer more in-depth help than manuals and address many issues that deal with networking.

When documentation and resource kits do not help, try the Internet. Excellent websites that have a wealth of troubleshooting information are Microsoft's TechNet and Microsoft's Knowledge Base. If you order Microsoft's TechNet on CD, you will receive monthly updates. After you become a Microsoft Certified Engineer, you receive TechNet free for a year. When all else fails, administrators must go to any search engine on the Internet and perform a basic search to find worthwhile information that someone else may have gathered.

USEFUL NETWORKING URLS

Microsoft can be found at:

http://www.microsoft.com

Other useful Microsoft URLs:

Search	http://search.microsoft.com/advanced_search.asp
Microsoft Servers	http://www.microsoft.com/servers
Windows Family	http://www.microsoft.com/windows/default.asp
Important Windows Download	http://www.microsoft.com/downloads/
Training and Certification	http://www.microsoft.com/train_cert/
Microsoft TechNet	http://www.microsoft.com/technet/

Good reference websites

Webopedia Online Dictionary	http://www.webopedia.com/
Whatis knowledge exploration tool	http://www.whatis.techtarget.com
Protocols.com	http://www.protocols.com

Magazines

Network Magazine	http://www.networkmagazine.com/
Windows & .NET Magazine	http://www.winnetmag.com
ZDNet	http://www.zdnet.com
CNET	http://www.cnet.com/

When troubleshooting computer problems, note that help is available in your PC, your server, and many of your networking components such as routers. Most of these produce log files that you can analyze and gain insight to a problem. So before giving up, be sure to utilize whatever resources are available.

SUMMARY

1. Large, centralized computers used to store and organize data are called mainframes, which were accessed by dumb terminals (a monitor to display data and a keyboard to input data).
2. A personal computer (PC) is meant to be used by one person and contains its own processing capabilities.
3. Distributed computing consists of taking several computers (computers that do their own processing) and connecting them by cable.
4. A distributed computing system is typically more powerful than a centralized computing system.
5. A network is two or more computers that are connected to share resources.
6. For a network to function, it requires network service (something to share), common media (pathways for contacting each other), and protocol (common communication rules).
7. File sharing allows users to access files, which are on another computer, without using a floppy disk or other forms of removable media.
8. Print sharing allows several people to send documents to a centrally located printer in the office.
9. Electronic mail (e-mail) is a powerful, sophisticated tool that allows users to send text messages and file attachments.
10. Computers connect to the network by using a special expansion card called a network interface card (NIC).
11. Protocols are the rules or standards that allow computers to connect to one another.
12. A server is a service provider that provides access to network resources.
13. A client is a computer that requests services.
14. A network that consists of servers and clients is a client-server network.
15. A peer-to-peer network, or workgroup, has no dedicated servers.
16. A file server manages user access to files stored on a server.
17. A print server manages user access to printer resources connected to the network, thus allowing one printer to be used by many people.
18. An application server is similar to a file-and-print server but also does some of the processing.
19. A mail server manages electronic messages (e-mail) between users.
20. A directory services server is used to locate information about the network such as domains (logical divisions of the network) and other servers.
21. A local area network (LAN) has computers that are connected within a geographically close network.
22. A wide area network (WAN) uses long-range telecommunication links to connect the network computers over long distances and often consists of two or more smaller LANs.

23. An enterprise WAN is owned by one company or organization.

24. A global WAN is not owned by any one company and may cross national boundaries.

25. An internetwork consists of several LANs, which are linked together. The smaller LANs are known as subnetworks or subnets.

26. An intranet is a network based on the TCP/IP, the same protocol used by the Internet, usually belonging to a single organization and accessible only by that organization's members.

27. A network operating system (NOS) includes special functions for connecting computers and devices into a LAN, to manage the resources and services of the network and provide network security for multiple users.

28. The most common client-server network operating systems are Windows NT Server, Novell NetWare, and UNIX.

29. Workstations that are attached to the network communicate through client software called shells or requesters.

30. The information technology (IT) department maintains networks and computers for a company.

31. An administrator is an individual who is responsible for maintaining the network.

32. The network administrator should fulfill the needs of the network clients.

33. In comparison to PC problems, network problems can have a much more devastating effect on users.

34. The only way to get good at troubleshooting computers and networks is to practice, practice, practice.

35. COMPTIA, the organization responsible for the A+, Network+, and Server+ exams uses a general troubleshooting strategy that consists of the following eight steps:
    - Establish symptoms.
    - Identify the affected area.
    - Establish what has changed.
    - Select the most probable cause.
    - Implement a solution.
    - Test the result.
    - Recognize the potential effects of the solution.
    - Document the solution.

QUESTIONS

1. A network needs all of the following components except
   _____.
   a. a protocol
   b. media
   c. services
   d. a dedicated server

2. The _____ is used to connect to a network's media.
   a. hard drive controller
   b. motherboard
   c. SCSI card
   d. network card

3. What are the rules or standards that allow computers to communicate with each other?
   a. media
   b. services
   c. client software
   d. protocols

4. Which type of network is made for a single building or a campus?
   a. LAN
   b. MAN
   c. global WAN
   d. enterprise WAN

5. A _____ is a network that uses long-range telecommunication links to connect the network computers over long distances.
   a. LAN
   b. MAN
   c. WAN
   d. NOS

6. An operating system that includes special functions for connecting computers and devices into a local area network (LAN), to manage the resources and services of the network and provide network security for multiple users, is a _____.
   a. client
   b. server
   c. NOS
   d. WAN

7. You are the IT administrator for a small company. You currently have 15 users with plans to hire another 10 users. You have files that need to be located by all 15 users and you must maintain different security requirements for the users. What type of network would you implement?
   a. peer-to-peer network
   b. server-based network
   c. workgroup network
   d. client-server network with each computer acting as both a client and a server

8. A peer-to-peer network can sometimes be a better solution than a server-based network. Which of the following statements best describes a peer-to-peer network?
   a. It requires a centralized and dedicated server.
   b. It provides extensive user and resource security.
   c. It provides each user the ability to manage his or her own shared resources.
   d. It requires at least one administrator to provide centralized resource administration.

9. In a client-server environment, tasks are divided between the client computer and the server. Which role does the server play in a client-server environment?
   a. The server satisfies requests from the client computer for data and processing resources.
   b. The server stores data for the client, but all data processing occurs on the client computer.
   c. The server stores data and performs all data processing so that the client computer functions primarily as an intelligent display device.
   d. The server satisfies requests from the client for remote processing resources, but data are stored on the client computer.

10. Which one of the following statements is true of peer-to-peer networks?
    a. They are also called workgroups.
    b. They are best suited for sharing many resources and data.
    c. They can support thousands of users in different geographical areas.
    d. They provide greater security and more control than server-based networks.

11. Most networks operate in the client-server environment. Which of the following is an example of client-server computing?
    a. a terminal accesses information in a mainframe database
    b. a workstation application accesses information in a remote database
    c. a workstation application accesses information in a database on the local hard drive
    d. a workstation application processes information obtained from a local database

12. Which of the following is *not* a NOS?
    a. Windows NT   d. Novell NetWare
    b. UNIX   e. Windows 98
    c. Windows 2000   f. Linux

13. For an operating system to connect to a network resource, the PC must _____.
    a. load the appropriate server driver
    b. share a drive or directory
    c. be an administrator or server operator
    d. load the appropriate client software

14. Patrick works for a large Internet bookseller. Patrick's manager has directed him to install a computer on the company's local area network (LAN) that will provide customers with the company's e-commerce web pages. Which type of network node should Patrick install?
    a. a bridge   c. a client
    b. a workstation   d. a server

15. Which network node provides file and printer services?
    a. a workstation   c. a server
    b. a router   d. a hub

16. What term can be used to describe multiple networks that are connected?
    a. LAN   c. WAN
    b. transnetwork   d. internetwork

17. Which of the following are indicative of a client-server environment as opposed to a peer-to-peer environment? (Select two answers.)
    a. Backups are centralized.
    b. Client machines often take the role of a server.
    c. Security and administration are managed at the server level.
    d. A router is required.

18. Which of the following is *not* a function of a NOS?
    a. management of printer and file resources
    b. data backup to tape
    c. server performance monitoring
    d. management of user directory
    e. All of the above choices *are* functions.

19. What is the function of a print server?
    a. to advertise print jobs on the LAN
    b. to provide print sharing on the network
    c. to give a printer the ability to render high-quality graphics on the network
    d. to give a printer the ability to be locally connected to a computer

20. You have five network printers that each need to function as an independent node, allowing multiple workstations access to each. What device on the network provides this functionality?
    a. print server   c. printer hub
    b. print router   d. printer data link

21. In network terminology, what is the back end?
    a. the workstation component in a client-server configuration
    b. the network core
    c. the backbone
    d. the server component in a client-server configuration

22. True or False. The eight troubleshooting steps, in order, are
    • Verify the symptoms. See if you can repeat them
    • Identify the area(s) of trouble (entire network or only one workstation, etc.).
    • Determine if anything has been changed (network settings, ports, cabling, software, etc.).
    • Deduct the most likely cause.
    • Engage a solution.
    • Test the results of the solution.
    • See if the solution has any side effects.
    • Write down the solution.

23. What should be your first step when troubleshooting a network problem?
    a. Select the most probable cause.
    b. Establish what has changed.
    c. Establish symptoms.
    d. Implement the result.

24. What three items are included in the basic troubleshooting model?
    a. Apply all of the latest service packs.
    b. Test the results.
    c. Develop a plan to correct the problem.
    d. Establish symptoms and duplicate the problem.
    e. Replace all questionable hardware.

25. Maintaining documentation as you progress through the troubleshooting process _____. (Select two answers.)
    a. is not as useful as doing all the documentation after the problem has been resolved
    b. helps organize the identification and isolation process
    c. helps in identifying the root problem and not just the symptoms
    d. is usually not cost justifiable
    e. adds too much time to the project

26. What is the first thing you need to determine when a failure occurs on the network?
    a. whether it is server or workstation related
    b. whether it is hardware or software
    c. whether it is a cable problem or a computer problem
    d. whether it is an isolated problem or network wide

27. You have intermittent problems on the network. Which would *not* generally be one of the things you would check for first?
    a. exposed network cable
    b. electromagnetic interference
    c. crashed server
    d. virus on the server

CHAPTER 2

PC Fundamentals

Topics Covered in This Chapter

Introduction

Because networks consist of two or more computers, having a good understanding of the personal computer is a necessity. A computer is a machine composed of electronic devices that are used to process data. The performance of the server is partly based on its hardware, how the hardware is configured, the function of the server, and the load of the server.

Objectives

- List and describe each of the major components of the microprocessor.
- Describe the 386 protection mechanism.
- Install and uninstall RAM.
- Describe how virtual memory affects the server.
- List the functions of the system ROM BIOS.
- List and describe the types of expansion slots.
- List and describe the resources of an expansion card.
- Given an expansion card, install it into a system.
- Compare and contrast the IDE and SCSI hard drives.
- Given a hard drive, install it into a system and prepare it for use.
- Install a CD-ROM drive and its drivers.

2.1 UNDERSTANDING THE PC

When choosing the hardware components for Windows, ensure that they are listed in the Microsoft Hardware Compatibility List (HCL) to avoid compatibility problems and much grief. For example, certain network interface cards (NICs) work with DOS, Windows 3.xx, Windows 95, and Novell NetWare, yet do not work for Windows NT or Windows 2000. The hardware items that are not listed on the HCL may still be compatible, as many devices emulate more common devices. For example, many sound cards emulate the Sound Blaster card and many network cards emulate the NE2000 network card.

2.2 MICROPROCESSORS

The **microprocessor,** also known as the central processing unit (CPU), is an integrated circuit that acts as the brain of the computer. It is made from a silicon wafer consisting of many transistors that act like tiny on–off switches. Unlike most integrated chips, the microprocessor is programmable, so it can be made to perform many tasks. The older 8088 and 8086 microprocessors had 29,000 transistors; the newer Pentium III microprocessor has 9.5 million transistors (not including the L2 cache).

Typically, the speed of the processor is determined by its clock speed, which is measured in megahertz (MHz)—1 MHz equals 1 million cycles per second and 1 gigahertz (GHz) equals 1 billion cycles per second. The faster the clock speed, the more instructions the microprocessor can execute per second. The original IBM PC had a clock speed of 4.77 MHz. Today's machines exceed 1 GHz.

A **register** is a high-speed internal storage area that acts as the microprocessor's short-term memory and work area. For a microprocessor to manipulate data, the data must be put in a register before they are processed. For example, if two numbers are to be added, both numbers are put in two different registers, added, and the result stored back into one of the two registers. The result can then be used for other processing or stored in the RAM.

The number of registers and the size of each register (word size or number of bits) help determine the power and speed of the microprocessor. For example, a 32-bit microprocessor, such as the 386DX or 486, has 32-bit registers, which can manipulate 32 bits of data. If the software is not written to use the entire register or the extra registers, the microprocessor will not perform at its peak.

The **data bus** carries the instructions and data into and out of the CPU. The size of the data bus is measured in bits. Each bit on the bus is a wire that allows one piece of information to flow into or out

The HCL is located on the Windows installation CD or can be located at the following Microsoft website:

http://www.microsoft.com/hcl/default.asp

To find a readiness analyzer program, product compatibility search, and Windows 2000 system requirements, go to the following website:

http://www.microsoft.com/windows2000/upgrade/compat/default.asp

of the microprocessor. A microprocessor with a data bus size of 32 bits has 32 wires connected to it for data transfer. If a microprocessor has more wires, it can transfer more data at the same time, making the microprocessor faster. The Intel 8088 microprocessor used in the IBM PC has an 8-bit data bus while the Intel Pentium, Pentium Pro, Pentium II, Pentium III, and Pentium 4 have 64-bit data buses.

Today, the processor is the fastest component on the system. Since the other components could not keep up, the data bus that connects to the RAM runs at one speed and the processor runs at a faster speed (multiple of the data bus speed).

The signals of the **address bus,** controlled by the address control unit, define where the data bus signals are going to or coming from. Similar to the data bus, the address bus is measured in bits. For every wire or bit added, the amount of RAM that is addressable by the microprocessor is doubled. Therefore, the amount of RAM the address bus can access is determined by the following equation:

$$\text{Amount of RAM} = 2^{\text{Size of Address Bus}}$$

Example 1:

If you have a 20-bit address bus, the largest binary number that you can access is 1111111111 1111111111. If this figure is converted to decimals, then it is equivalent to 1048575 bytes (1 megabyte, MB) of RAM. For a 20-bit address, the highest address that can be accessed is 1,048,575—not 1,048,576—because there are 1,048,576 bytes altogether, but the numbering of bytes begins at 0, not 1.

Note that usually the motherboard (not the microprocessor) limits the amount of RAM that a system can recognize.

While all processors are integer (whole number) processors, all modern processors also include a floating-point processor. This type of processor specializes in performing calculations on float-point numbers (numbers that have a decimal number or an exponent).

The microprocessor is the fastest component within the computer. For example, the microprocessor is several times faster than the motherboard's system bus and RAM. To help bridge the speed gap, the computer uses a level 1 (L1) and level 2 (L2) RAM cache (a form of high-speed RAM). Since most programs access the same data and instructions over and over, RAM cache improves performance by keeping as much of this information as possible. When the processor needs to access the slower RAM, it will first look in the faster L1 cache in the hope of finding the needed instruction or data. If it fails to find it in the L1 cache, it will then look in the L2 cache. If it finds the needed information in the cache, the information is retrieved faster than if the processor went to the slower RAM. L1 cache is typically kept very small [8 kilobytes (KB) to 64 KB] and is always kept inside all modern processors. The larger L2 cache (128 KB to 2 MB) is typically kept inside the processor, but some older systems may have it located on the motherboard.

2.2.1 Superscalar Architecture

In 1993, Intel introduced the Pentium microprocessor (see Figure 2.1). The Pentium processor is the minimum processor needed to load Windows 2000. It is based on an advanced superscalar architecture that allows the processor to execute two instructions simultaneously. To keep the processor working at full capacity, the processor uses an assembly-line approach in which it starts processing another instruction before finishing the current instruction. In addition, when it reaches a point in the program where it needs to decide on which direction to take, the processor uses dynamic branch prediction in an attempt to keep the processor working instead of waiting for the rest of the processor to catch up.

Figure 2.1   A motherboard with the Pentium processor, two PCI slots (center), and three ISA slots (bottom left). (Courtesy of Intel Corporation)

2.2.2   P6 Architecture

The P6 architecture uses a longer pipeline than the Pentium processor. The pipeline is divided into three units: the in-order front unit, the out-of-order execution unit, and the in-order retirement unit. The in-order front unit brings and decodes the instructions in the correct program sequence. The execution unit determines the optimal order and executes the instructions. The retirement unit then saves the results of the instruction in the correct order.

To make the processor work more efficiently than previous processors, P6 architecture uses advanced algorithms (multiple-branch prediction, data flow analysis, and speculative execution) and a dual independent bus (DIB) architecture. The advanced algorithms are designed to keep the assembly lines working while they wait for certain parts of the processor to catch up. The DIB uses two buses (one from the processor to the RAM and one from the processor to the L2 cache) that can be accessed simultaneously. With these features, P6 architecture has approximately 50% higher performance than a Pentium of the same clock speed. The Pentium Pro, Pentium II, Pentium III, and Intel Celeron processors are based on P6 architecture.

The Pentium Pro processor is constructed with a dual-cavity pin grid array (PGA) package, which includes an internal 256 KB or 512 KB, L2 RAM cache running at the full speed of the processor core.

Pentium processors with MMX technology and the Pentium II/III processors use 57 new instructions specifically designed to manipulate and process video, audio, and graphical data. They are oriented to the highly parallel, repetitive sequences often found in multimedia operations. In addition, they can use single instruction, multiple data (SIMD) that reduce the number or repetitive actions by loading several pieces of data into the microprocessor and performing the same command on them simultaneously. For example, if the microprocessor has several 16-bit numbers that need to have the same action performed on them, a Pentium can load four 16-bit numbers ($4 \times 16 = 64$ bits) and perform the same action on all four numbers at the same time.

The Pentium II processor uses the same P6 architecture as the Pentium Pro and includes MMX technology. It includes 512 KB of cache that runs at half the speed of the processor core. Instead of using a PGA package, it uses a single-edge contact (SEC) package, which has a single-edge connector that is inserted into slot 1 on the motherboard.

Intel's previous mainstream family of microprocessors is the Pentium III, which starts at 450 MHz and extends beyond 1 GHz, which equals 1 billion cycles per second. The biggest performance increase comes from the new Internet streaming SIMD extensions, which are 70 multimedia instructions used in the chip to improve performance of three-dimensional graphics, video performance, audio performance, and speech recognition. The Pentium III processor can be found in the SECC2 package and the flip-chip PGA (FCPGA) package. See Figure 2.2.

The flagship of the Pentium II and III processor families includes the Pentium II Xeon and Pentium III Xeon processors. See Figure 2.3. The Xeon processor incorporates an L2 cache ranging from 256 KB to 2 MB, which operates at the same speed as the processor core. In addition, it has a 36-bit address that can allow the processor to address up to 64 GB of RAM. Different from the Pentium II and III processors, Xeon processors connect to the motherboard via slot 2. Today's Xeon processors are typically found in high-power workstations or servers and so contain additional management features that make it easier to monitor performance and reliability of the processor.

The Intel Celeron processor is Intel's value processor. Usually Intel's value processors are "cut-down" versions of its main line of processors and they are not designed for multiprocessor systems. Although Intel Celeron processors are ideal for learning networking, and they are cost-effective for small servers, they are not recommended for busy servers.

Early Intel Celeron processors used the SEPP and PPGA packages, no cache, and a 66-MHz system bus. The SEPP package is similar to a SECC or SECC2 package, but it has no covering. The second version of the Intel Celeron processor is similar to the Pentium II processor, but the Celeron processor has 128 KB of L2 cache running at full speed and a 66-MHz system bus. The third version is similar to the Pentium III processor in the FCPGA package, but the Celeron processor has 128 KB of L2 cache running at a full speed and a 66-MHz or 100-MHz system bus. The newest version of the Intel Celeron processor uses the Intel NetBurst microarchitecture, which is explained in the next section.

2.2.3   Intel NetBurst Microarchitecture

Intel's first all-new chip architecture since the Pentium Pro is called NetBurst microarchitecture and it is used by the Pentium 4 and Intel Xeon processor. The Pentium 4 processor started out at 1.3 GHz, 1.4 GHz, and 1.5 GHz, but it has the ability to scale much higher. The Intel Xeon processor is similar to a Pentium 4 processor but is multiprocessor capable.

The NetBurst microarchitecture refers to a technology that rearranges the way data are processed within the chip. Characteristics of this architecture follow:

- Hyperpipelined technology that uses a 20-stage pipeline (double that of the Pentium III) increases processor frequency and hence performance.
- Rapid-execution engine can execute arithmetic instructions in half a clock cycle, effectively doubling the core frequency and reducing latency for those functions.
- A 400-MHz system bus gives the processor a transfer rate of 3.2 GB/s.
- Execution trace cache, which is an intelligent caching system, stores decoded microoperations in the order of program execution. As a result, it makes more efficient use of cache memory and reduces latency.
- Advanced dynamic execution processes data more efficiently by choosing from 126 instructions in the execution buffer (triple the Pentium III processor) and predicting program flow more accurately.
- Advanced transfer cache optimizes data transfer to the processor core. The advanced transfer cache consists of a 256-bit (32-byte) interface that transfers data on each core clock. As a result, the Pentium 4 processor, 1.5 GHz, can deliver a data transfer rate of 48 GB per second. This compares to a transfer rate of 16 GB per second on the Pentium III processor at 1 GHz.
- Enhanced floating-point and multimedia unit accelerates processor-intensive tasks such as streaming video, voice recognition, video and audio encoding, and image processing.
- The SSE2 consists of 144 new instructions to accelerate video and encryption/decryption and support the next generation of Internet applications. It also supports newer, more computationally intensive, graphics.

Figure 2.2   Pentium III processor (SECC2 and FCPGA packages)

As was the case when the Pentium Pro processor was introduced with P6 architecture, software has to be optimized for the Intel NetBurst microarchitecture. If you are using older software that is not optimized for the Pentium 4 family, the programs (including software that measures software) may actually run slower than with the Pentium III processor.

In newer versions of Pentium 4 and Xeon processors, Intel introduced hyperthreading. Hyperthreading allows the processor to act like two virtual processors, so that it can use the processor

Figure 2.3 Pentium III Xeon processor

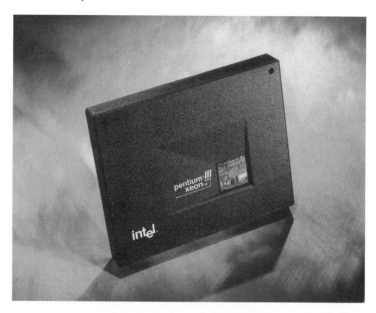

resources more efficiently and improve performance. Programs would have to support multiple threads to take advantage of hyperthreading.

Systems based on the Pentium 4 processor must use chassis that comply with the ATX specification (revision 2.01 or later) and must have the Pentium 4 processor-specific mounting support. Power supplies must comply with the ATX12V design guidelines and supply additional current on the 12-V power rail through a new 2 × 2 connector. Also, additional 3.3-V and 5-V current is supplied through a separate 1 × 6 connector.

2.2.4   IA-64 Architecture

Intel has introduced its first 64-bit processor based on the IA-64 processor, which is based on the IA-64 architecture. We already have processors with a 64-bit external data bus and registers, but the IA-64 processors also have a 64-bit address bus that will allow the processor to access 2^{64} = 18,466,744,073, 709,551,616 bytes of RAM.

The Itanium is a new processor family and architecture, designed by Intel and Hewlett-Packard for high-end server and workstation computing. It is designed for fast, parallel instruction execution. The Itanium should contain more than 10 million transistors using .18-micron technology.

The Itanium uses four-way associative, 16-KB, L1 on-die instruction cache and a four-way associative, 16-KB, integer-only L1 on-die data cache. It also has a six-way associative, 96-KB, of L2 on-die cache with a 256-bit bus. Lastly, the Itanium processor has a 2-MB or 4-MB four-way set, associative, off-die L3 cache.

The IA-64 architecture differs from IA-32 in several ways. Rather than variable-length instructions, IA-64 uses fixed-length, 4 byte instructions bundled in sets of three "long instruction words." It uses 256 registers for integer and floating-point operations compared with 16 in IA-32. IA-64 employs a technique known as predication, in which both sides of a branch instruction are executed in parallel. When the correct branch is determined, the results for the incorrect side are discarded. With IA-64, compilers have to be more intelligent, because they place codes into the instruction bundles that tell the CPU how to execute instructions in parallel. They also have to place instructions in interleaved order for predication. If predication is not set up, the CPU will perform traditional branch predication, whereby it attempts to guess the outcome of a branch and executes instructions in parallel.

IA-64 also supports speculative loading, whereby data are loaded into registers before the instructions actually need to process the data. Explicitly Parallel Instruction Computing (EPIC) is Intel's brand name for its new parallel architecture. Therefore, although x86-based software (IA-32 software) will run intact on IA-64 machines, programs have to be recompiled in order to take full advantage of the new architecture.

2.2.5   AMD Processors

Although Intel processors are considered the de facto standard, Intel is not the only company that produces PC processors. Two other manufacturers are Advanced Micro Devices (AMD) and Cyrix. Both companies offer processors similar to Intel's, but at a lower cost.

With the release of the Athlon (code name, K7), AMD has become a major player in the processor market. Early versions of Athlon are manufactured in .25-micron technology and consist of no less than 22 million transistors. Currently, the newer Athlon processor is manufactured on a .18-micron processor and uses approximately 37 million transistors on 120-mm^2 die. In addition, the newer Athlon processors use copper metal technology, a first in the PC processor business. Eventually all other processors will follow, as copper interconnects allow for lower power consumption and faster operation.

The AMD Athlon has a nine-issue, superpipelined, superscalar x86 processor microarchitecture designed for high-clock frequencies. It includes multiple, parallel x86 instruction decoders; three out-of-order, superscalar, fully pipelined, floating-point execution units, which execute x87 (floating point) MMX and 3DNow! instructions; three out-of-order, superscalar, pipelined integer units; and three out-of-order, superscalar, pipelined address calculation units. Therefore, it can start up to nine instructions on each tick of the clock. The chip's floating-point unit can add and multiply at the same time, just like many digital signal processors. In addition to the 3DNow! and Enhanced 3D Now! instructions, AMD has added instructions that are specifically designed for signal processing. The company hopes the chip will be used in software modems, speech recognition, and similar applications.

Athlon processors have 128 KB of L1 cache. Early Athlon processors had 512 KB of L2 cache, on the package running at one half, two fifths, or one third the clock speed of the processor. The newer versions have 256 KB of integrated, on-chip, L2 cache running at full speed.

The Athlon processor was AMD's first product to drop any attempt at pin compatibility with Intel chips. The first Athlon processor used an SEC package called slot A that was mechanically compatible but not pin compatible with slot 1. Later versions of the Athlon were built for socket A, which can access 200-MHz and 266-MHz system buses based on Alpha EV6 bus protocol.

Traditionally, the biggest disadvantage of AMD processors is that they consume more power and dissipate much more heat than their Intel counterparts. Therefore, they need a higher-level cooling solution. In addition, if the cooling solution fails, typically the processor will burn. Recently, AMD processors have been designed to run cooler.

AMD has introduced new versions of the Athlon processors that are capable of dual processing. Unfortunately, they require a large-capacity power supply. In addition, AMD chose to use a proprietary power supply which many power supply manufacturers may not build and may cost more than one of the ATX or ATX2 power supplies.

For the value market, AMD manufactures the Duron processor. The Duron processor is similar to the Athlon processor, but it only has a 64-KB, full-speed, 16-way set-associative L2 cache. The Duron uses the same 100-MHz double-pumped (so, 200-MHz) front-side bus that the Athlon has always used.

AMD's processors of the future will use x86-64 technology, which provides the traditional x86 32-bit compatibility of today's applications while providing 64-bit technology. In contrast to Intel's IA-64 architecture, AMD's technology can preserve companies' investment in 32-bit applications while allowing a seamless transition to 64-bit computing.

The AMD Opteron, which will use the x86-64 technology, is designed to be scalable, reliable, and compatible, which can result in lower total cost of ownership. Key innovations of the AMD Opteron processor include an integrated memory controller, which reduces memory bottlenecks, and Hyper-Transport technology, which increases overall performance by removing or reducing I/O bottlenecks, increasing bandwidth, and reducing latency.

2.2.6   386 Protection Mechanism

Processors since the time of the 386 processor have the **386 protection mechanism,** which assigns data and instructions to a privilege ring or level. See Figure 2.4. The four privilege levels are 0, 1, 2, and 3. The privilege level 0 is the highest and level 3 is the lowest. Programs in ring 0 can access programs in all rings, but programs in ring 3 cannot access the programs in rings 0, 1, and 2. Today, some operating

Figure 2.4 386 Protection mechanism

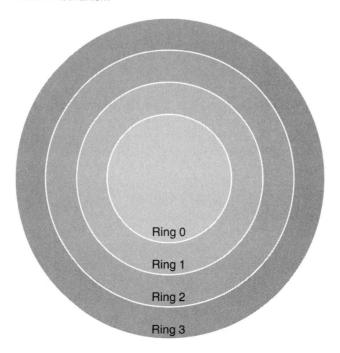

systems such as Windows NT, Windows 2000, Windows XP, and Windows Server 2003 assign the operating system to level 0 and other programs to level 3. If a program becomes corrupt in ring 3, then the program will not affect the operating system.

2.2.7 Symmetric Multiprocessing

Symmetric multiprocessing (SMP) involves a computer that uses two or more microprocessors that share the same memory. If software is written to use the multiple microprocessors, then several programs can be executed simultaneously, or multithreaded applications can be executed faster. A multithreaded application is broken into several smaller parts and executed simultaneously. For example, Microsoft Word uses a thread to respond to keys typed on the keyboard by the user to place characters in a document. Other threads are used to check spelling, paginate the document as it is typed, and spool a document to the printer in the background. The ability of an operating system to use additional microprocessors is known as multiprocessing scalability.

To determine if processors will work for your multiprocessing system, you must first determine if the processors will support multiprocessing and if the processors will work with each other. As a general rule, the processors must be multiprocessor capable; must have identical frequency, bus speed, and cache size; and must have compatible steppings.

Much like software, hardware often has errata (bugs). Processors are revised and new versions are released. In addition, processors may go through some form of enhancement such as a die shrink or a voltage change. Such changes are not widely publicized. Often people do not realize that there are many different versions of popular processors on the market, with newer ones often fixing problems in the older ones.

Some companies (e.g., Cyrix) use an explicit version number with their chips. Intel, instead, uses a term called a *stepping*. Essentially, a stepping number is the same as a revision number. The word itself comes from the name of the machine that is used to make the chip, which is called a "stepper." The stepping can be identified by the CPU identification number, information in the support website, the specification update guide, and the Frequency ID utility (an Intel utility that can identify your processor). When considering multiprocessing, make sure that processor steppings are compatible with other processors used in the same system.

2.3   RANDOM ACCESS MEMORY

Random access memory, more commonly referred to as **RAM,** consists of electronic memory chips, which store information inside the computer. It is called random access memory because the information is accessed nonsequentially. In a reel of storage tape, a user begins a search at one end and proceeds sequentially. In contrast, information in RAM can be accessed directly without looking at the preceding information.

RAM is **volatile memory,** which means it loses its contents when the power is turned off. Much like a blackboard, information can be stored and overwritten. In addition, RAM is temporary memory, because when power is no longer supplied to the RAM, the contents of the RAM is lost. This explains why the user must save the contents of RAM to a disk.

RAM is considered the main memory or the primary memory, because it is the memory that the microprocessor accesses directly. This means the program instruction that the CPU is executing must be first copied to RAM from a device such as a disk. In addition, the data such as letters, reports, and charts, which are generated by programs, must be in RAM to be manipulated. Therefore, it is the amount of RAM that determines how many programs can be executed at one time and how much data can be available to a program. In addition, the amount of memory is a major factor in determining how fast the computer will operate.

2.3.1   DRAM

The most common RAM chips are dynamic RAM (DRAM) chips, which use a storage cell consisting of a tiny solid-state capacitor and a MOS transistor. A capacitor is a simple electrical device, similar to a battery, which is capable of storing a charge of electrons. The charge or lack of charge represents a single bit of data. If it is charged, it has a logic state of 1. If it is discharged, it has a logic state of 0. The storage cells are organized into a large, two-dimensional array or table of rows and columns.

At the time of the early PCs, the typical access speed for a DRAM chip was 120 nanoseconds (ns) or slower. Newer machines (up through 1995), used **fast-page mode RAM (FPM RAM),** which had typical speeds of 70 ns or 80 ns. A lower number indicates a faster speed.

The FPM RAM works in a similar way to the normal DRAM chip except it tries to reduce the number of wait states. A wait state is a period of time during which the microprocessor has to wait for the RAM chips to catch up. If data are accessed in the same row (sometimes referred to as a page) as the preceding data, time is saved by not deactivating the row after the first piece of data and reactivating it for the second piece of data. Ideally, a read from a 70-ns FPM memory can achieve a burst cycle timing of 5-3-3-3, down from 5-5-5-5. The 5-3-3-3 indicates that it takes the RAM five clock cycles to access the first piece of data in a row. After that row is activated, it takes an additional three clock cycles each for the next three pieces of data contained within the same row.

Extended data output RAM, or **EDO RAM,** takes the fast-page mode RAM one step further. To make it even faster, EDO DRAM uses a two-stage pipeline, which lets the memory controller read data off the chip while it is being reset for the next operation. Instead of deactivating the column and turning off the output buffer, EDO RAM keeps the output data buffer on. If the data to be transferred are sequential to the data just sent, the EDO RAM will do it more efficiently. As a result, the burst cycle timing is reduced to 5-2-2-2, giving EDO RAM approximately 10% to 15% better performance over FPM RAM. Therefore, the speed of an EDO RAM chip is either 50 ns or 60 ns.

A faster form of EDO RAM is **burst extended data output (BEDO) RAM.** It is faster because it allows the page-access cycle to be divided into two components. To achieve faster access time, data are read from the memory array at the same time that data are being transferred through the data bus. In addition, a counter on the chip keeps track of the next address so that sequential data can be accessed faster. As a result, EDO RAM offers an average of 15 to 25% increase in efficiency over FPM RAM and reduces the transfer of sequential data transfer to one clock (5-1-1-1).

Although EDO RAM and BEDO RAM are faster than FPM RAM, their popularity has already decreased, because they do not work well with bus speeds higher than 66 MHz, which some motherboards are already using. Instead, you will find synchronous dynamic RAM (SDRAM), double data rate–synchronous DRAM (DDR–SDRAM), synchronous link DRAM (SLDRAM), and rambus DRAM (RDRAM). A brief overview of each follows.

2.3.2   SDRAM

Synchronous dynamic RAM (SDRAM) runs in synchronization with the memory bus. SDRAM delivers information in very high-speed bursts using a high-speed, clocked interface. SDRAM removes most of the latency involved in asynchronous DRAM because the signals are already in synchronization with the motherboard clock.

These chips work with bus speeds up to 133 MHz. SDRAM is usually expressed in 2-2-2 or 1-1-1. With the exception of using the external clock speed, it is similar to the other forms of DRAM and, therefore, still has latency. The fast 12, 10, and 8 ns numbers that everyone talks about refer only to the second, third, and fourth accesses in a four-access burst. The first access is still a relatively slow five cycles. Therefore, SDRAM has a burst cycle timing of 5-2-2-2 or 5-1-1-1.

SDRAM is also expresed by MHz rating, such as 100 MHz or 133 MHz. So they are called 83-MHz or 100-MHz SDRAMs, for example. Because SDRAMs are synchronous, they must be fast enough for the system in which they are being used. The whole point of the technology is to be able to run with zero wait states. In order to do this, memory must be fast enough for the bus speed of the system. Users run into trouble when they take the reciprocal of the nanosecond rating of the module and conclude that the module can run at that speed. For example, the reciprocal of 10 ns is 100 MHz, so people assume that 10-ns modules will be able to run on a 100-MHz system. The problem is that absolutely no room is allowed for slack. In practice, you want memory rated slightly higher than what is required, so 10-ns modules are really intended for 83-MHz operation. A 100-MHz system requires faster memory.

The Joint Electron Device Engineering Council (JEDEC) developed the PC100 specification (see Table 2.1). PC66 SDRAM is designed to run on a 66-MHz bus, PC100 SDRAM is designed to run on a 100-MHz bus, and PC133 SDRAM is designed to run on a 133-MHz bus.

To keep SDRAM working at full capacity at all times, SDRAM uses internal pipelining and interleaving. Internal pipelining brings additional data in while the previous data is being processed to improve throughput.

Banks of SDRAM operate in parallel, performing the same sequence of commands required for reading and writing data. Some **dual inline memory modules** (DIMMs) may actually have two banks on a single DIMM. One bank populates each face of the module, but only one bank can transmit or receive data at a time.

Interleaving means two banks of memory chips are working together to service a bus. When one bank is getting ready for access, the other bank is being accessed. DIMMs can have up to four banks, regardless of their size. Therefore, two 512-MB DIMMs of SDRAM will outperform a single 1-GB DIMM because of the increased number of banks.

Most motherboards now require the use of special SDRAM modules that include a **serial presence detect (SPD)** chip. This is an electrical erasable programmable ROM (EEPROM) that contains speed and design information about the module. The motherboard queries the chip for information about the module and makes adjustments to system operation based on what it finds.

Table 2.1   SDRAM timing: actual speed and rated speed

Timing	Actual Speed	Rated Speed
15 ns	66 MHz	PC66
10 ns	100 MHz	PC66
8 ns	125 MHz	PC100
7.5 ns	133 MHz	PC133

2.3.3   DDR-SDRAM

Double data rate SDRAM (DDR-SDRAM) is similar in function to regular SDRAM, but it doubles the bandwidth of memory by transferring data twice per cycle—on both the rising and falling edges of the clock signal. The clock signal transitions from 0 to 1 and back to 0 each cycle; the first is called the *rising edge* and the second is called the *falling edge*.

Currently, two forms of DDR system memory are popular, each with a variety of names. The first is DDR1600, or DDR200, which runs at 100-MHz DDR for an equivalent of 200 MHz of bandwidth. On a 64-bit wide memory bus, the memory bandwidth is 1,600 MB/s hence the name DDR1600. The second system used today is DDR2100/DDR266, which runs on a 133 MHz for an equivalent of 266 MHz of bandwidth. On a 64-bit wide memory bus, the theoretical peak is about 2,100 MB/s of memory bandwidth, hence the name DDR2100. Two other forms of DDR are DDR2700/DDR333 and DDR3200/DDR400.

The long-term successor of DDR memory will be DDR-II. DDR-II uses a lower voltage of 1.8 V, with speeds of 400 and 533 MHz. As part of the preliminary specification, JEDEC approved 400- and 533-MHz DDR chips. Comparable DDR memory modules would carry the PC3200 nomenclature for a 3.2-GB bandwidth using the 400-MHz chip, and PC4300 with a bandwidth of 4.3 GB for the 533-MHz chip.

2.3.4   RDRAM

Rambus DRAM (RDRAM), also known as direct Rambus DRAM (DRDRAM), takes DRAM technology and rethinks it from the ground up in regard to how it should be integrated into a system. It is a new memory design that involves changes to the bus structure and to how signals are carried. RDRAM was developed by Rambus Incorporated.

RDRAM is based on the Rambus channel, a high-speed, 16-bit bus running at a clock rate of up to 533 MHz. The Rambus channel is routed through the **Rambus inline memory modules** (RIMM) and is terminated on the motherboard after the last RIMM module. The Rambus channel requires that all sockets be populated with either a RIMM or a continuity RIMM so that the channel remains continuous with the termination resistors.

As with DDR-SDRAM, transfers are accomplished on the rising and falling edges of the clock. The effective theoretical bandwidth is approximately 1.6 GB for a single Rambus channel and 3.2 GB for dual Rambus channels running at 400 MHz, or 2.1 GB for a single Rambus channel and 4.2 GB for a dual Rambus channel running at 533 MHz. It may seem counterproductive to narrow the channel, because that reduces bandwidth; however, the channel is then capable of running at much higher speeds than would be possible if the bus were wide.

To get the bus speed high, the motherboard has to be manufactured to a high standard of quality in order to reduce noise, stray capacitance, variations in line impedance, and other problems associated with rising bus speeds. In some cases, more layers may be added to the motherboard just to provide a clean enough signal.

In an SDRAM system, each module is only a few inches from the memory controller, so commands and data do not have to travel far to reach their destination. The Rambus channel gets longer as more RDRAM devices are added to it, which means that the amount of time that commands and data must travel to reach the outermost device can get pretty high. What makes the situation worse is that the read latency of the entire system can be only as fast as that farthest (and, by extension, slowest) RDRAM.

To reduce the latency for RDRAM, Rambus uses a high number of banks. Each individual RDRAM chip can hold up to 32 banks of memory. In an ideal world, you could keep a row active in each of those 32 banks to maximize the odds that you are going to be able to get data from an active row. In reality, though, you can only have 16 banks open at once, or half the number of banks on the chip.

Since the RDRAM devices further along on the bus need more time to send a signal, the RDRAM devices closer to the memory controller need to have a longer amount of delay so that the memory sent can arrive at the memory controller at the same time. Therefore, during the boot-up process, the Rambus system goes through an elaborate initialization ritual to determine the amount of delay for each device. Note: As with SDRAM, RDRAM makes use of an SPD chip to tell the motherboard certain characteristics of the RDRAM module when the system is booted.

As more devices are added to a Rambus system, the entire system has higher and higher read latency (access time). An individual RDRAM chip might have a read latency of 20 ns, which is about the same read latency as some SDRAMs. Once RDRAM chips are placed in a system with three full RIMMs, however, the overall system latency will be either slightly better or significantly worse than the system latency for an SDRAM system.

Memory requests in a Rambus system are typically burst like; that is, they tend to appear in groups followed by quiet periods with no requests. So although the average memory bandwidth required by a program may be low, during periods of activity with bursts, bandwidth required can be much higher. The high bank count, and separate row and column address buses, make RDRAMs much better suited to communication involving bursts than other memory technologies.

> **Question:** Which RAM is the best RAM to use, DDR-SDRAM or RDRAM?
>
> **Answer:** This is one of the huge debates in today's PC markets. Although Rambus modules have the ability to transfer data faster, RDRAM appears to have higher latency than DDR-SDRAM. In other words, the first data item transfer in a Rambus transaction takes longer to initiate than the first data item moved in a DDR-SDRAM system. In an environment where data transactions involve lengthy streams of data (e.g., gaming or workstation environments), Rambus performs outstandingly. If a computer does many small transactions regularly (e.g., server), DDR-SDRAM would be a better choice. However, RDRAM has never become popular because of its extra expense and the introduction of faster DDR-RAM.

2.3.5   RAM Chip Packaging

Many modern PCs use a **single inline memory module,** or **SIMM.** A SIMM uses a small circuit board consisting of several soldered dual inline pin (DIP) chips. To connect to the motherboard, the SIMM has a row of tin or gold metal plates (contacts) along the bottom of the module. As they are inserted into the motherboard, metal pins make contact with the metal plates.

SIMMs are available in a wide range of capacities (from 256 KB to 64 MB and beyond) and come in two pin configurations: 30 pin (8/9 bits) and 72 pin (32/36 bits). If a 30-pin SIMM uses parity for error control, it will have 9 bits; if it does not use parity, it will have 8 bits. If a 72-pin SIMM uses parity, it will have 36 bits; if not, it will have 32 bits.

The 72-pin SIMM is approximately 25% larger than the 30-pin SIMM and it includes a notch in the center to prevent connecting a 30-pin SIMM into a 72-pin socket. Both SIMMs have notches to prevent a SIMM from being connected backwards. In addition, 4 of the 72 pins are used to indicate the speed rating of the chips.

Today, new machines use DIMMs or RIMMs. DIMMs contains SDRAM or DDR-SDRAM chips and RIMMs contain RDRAM chips. **DIMMs** closely resemble (SIMMs). See Figure 2.5. Similar to SIMMs, DIMMs are installed vertically into memory expansion sockets. One difference between SIMMs and DIMMs is that the SIMMs' opposing pins on both sides of the circuit board are connected as one, whereas the pins of the DIMMs are electrically isolated to form two separate contacts. Another difference is that DIMMs support 64-bit pathways (72 bits with parity). As with 72-pin SIMMs, 168-pin SDRAM DIMMs include electrical provisions for telling a PC the speed ratings of the module. The module connector provides 8 pins for signaling this information. DDR-SDRAM DIMMs use 184 pins and DDR-II SDRAM DIMMs use 232 pins to connect to the motherboard.

Figure 2.5   A DIMM

Figure 2.6   A RIMM

The **RIMM** conforms to the standard DIMM form factor (184 pins), but is not pin compatible. See Figure 2.6. Its architecture is based on the electrical requirements of the direct rambus channel. Since the RAM runs at a faster speed than the DIMMs, RIMMs typically include a heat spreader to help dissipate heat faster. The motherboards will support two or more RIMMs. Since the RIMMs fit into a channel, low-cost continuity modules must be used to maintain channel integrity in systems having less than three RIMM modules.

To help avoid inserting a DIMM or RIMM in an incorrect socket or inserting the DIMM or RIMM incorrectly into the socket, DIMMs and RIMMs have notches known as keys on the bottom of the circuit board. SDRAM DIMMs have two notches, DDR-SDRAM DIMMs have one notch, and RIMMs have two notches.

2.3.6   Virtual Memory

Virtual memory is disk space pretending to be RAM, which allows the operating system to load more programs and data. For all programs and data to be accessed, parts of each are constantly swapped back and forth between RAM and disk. As far as the programs are concerned, the virtual memory looks and acts like regular RAM, which is beneficial to the user because disk memory is far cheaper than RAM. Unfortunately, a disk is a thousand times slower than RAM, and since the disk consists of mechanical parts and pieces, the disk has a higher failure rate than RAM.

The Intel microprocessors use **demand paging,** which swaps data between the RAM and disk only on the demand of the microprocessor. It does not try to anticipate the needs of the microprocessor.

RAM and virtual memory are divided into chunks of information called **pages,** which are monitored by the operating system. When the RAM becomes full, the virtual memory system copies the least recently used programs and data to the virtual memory. Since this frees part of the RAM, it then has room to copy something from virtual memory, load another program, or load more data. Windows 3.xx and Windows 9x virtual memory take the form of an ordinary file called a *swap* file, whereas Windows NT, Windows 2000, Windows XP, and Windows Server 2003 call virtual memory a *paging* file.

2.3.7   Memory Error Control

RAM chips are found in a set of either 8 or 9 bits. In older systems, 8 of the 9 bits were used for the data while bit 9 was used for parity to provide an error check for the other 8 bits. The DIPs used in the IBM PC, IBM XT, and IBM AT were arranged in neat rows of nine chips. Some SIMMs and DIMMs use bit 9 for parity.

Parity chips ensure accurate reading and writing of data, particularly on systems released prior to the introduction of Pentium motherboards. When a PC uses parity checking, it is using odd parity checking. As the 8 individual bits in a byte are stored in memory, a parity generator/checker, which is either part of the microprocessor or is located in a special chip on the motherboard, evaluates the data bits by counting the number of 1s in a byte. If an even number of 1s is in the byte, the parity generator/checker creates a 1 and stores it in the parity bit. This makes the total sum for all 9 bits an odd number. If the original sum of the 8 data bits is an odd number, the parity bit created is 0, again keeping the 9-bit sum an odd number. The value of the parity bit is always chosen so that the sum of all 9 bits is an odd number.

When the system reads memory, it checks the parity information. If the 9 bits equal an even number of bits, that byte must have an error. When a parity-check error is detected, the motherboard parity-checking circuits generate a **nonmaskable interrupt (NMI),** which halts processing and diverts the system's attention to the error. The NMI causes a routine in the system ROM BIOS chip (discussed in Section 2.4) to be executed. The routine clears the screen and then displays a message such as *Parity Error* or *Parity Check 1* in the upper-left corner of the screen.

There are two disadvantages of using parity for error control. First, RAM will only discover errors when bits 1, 3, 5, or 7 have changed. It will not discover a problem if 2 bits have been changed, since the 2 bits cancel each other out. Second, RAM detects errors but does not correct them.

Newer systems do not use parity checking, but rather **error checking and correcting (ECC) memory.** When data are stored in memory, this code is responsible for generating check bits, which are stored with the data. When the contents of a memory location are referenced, the ECC memory logic uses the check bit information and the data to generate a series of "syndrome bits." If these syndrome bits are all zeros, then the data are valid and the operation continues. If any bits are 1s, then the data have an error and the ECC memory logic isolates any errors and reports them to the operating system. In the case of a correctable error, the ECC memory scheme can detect single and double bit errors and correct single bit errors. For example, you need 1 bit for every 8 bits for parity, whereas you need 7 bits to check 32 bits using ECC.

2.4   MOTHERBOARDS

The **motherboard,** also referred to as the **main board** or the **system board,** is the primary printed circuit board located within the PC. It includes connectors for attaching additional boards (expansion slots) and additional devices (ports). It also contains the microprocessor, the RAM chips, the RAM cache, several ROM BIOS chips, CMOS RAM, the real-time clock, and several support chips. The CMOS RAM is a low-power RAM that holds basic PC configuration. It is powered by a battery, so its contents are not lost when the PC is off.

2.4.1   Chipsets

The **chipset** is a number of integrated circuits designed to perform one or more related functions. Chipsets control the flow of bits between the processor, system memory, and the motherboard bus. Efficient data transfers, fast expansion bus support, and advanced power management features are just a few of the system chipset's responsibilities. It is the chipset that determines the functionality and capabilities of the motherboard. The common Intel chipset includes the 440BX and the 810, 815, 820, 830, 840, and 850 chipsets.

The advanced configuration and power interface (ACPI) is a relatively new power management specification that was developed by Intel, Microsoft, and Toshiba. Before ACPI, there was advanced power management (APM). It controls the amount of power given to each device attached to the computer. With ACPI, the operating system can turn off peripheral devices such as a controller card or network card, when they are not in use. As another example, ACPI will enable manufacturers to produce computers that automatically power up at the touch of the keyboard.

2.4.2   ROM BIOS Chips

Computer ROM chips provide instructions and data to the microprocessor. The instructions and data kept in the ROM chip that control the boot process and hardware are known as the **basic input/output system (BIOS),** or sometimes known as **firmware.**

Every PC has several BIOS chips including the system ROM BIOS, the keyboard ROM, and the video ROM BIOS. The **system ROM BIOS,** which is located on the motherboard, directs the boot-up and allows basic control of the majority of the hardware. The **keyboard ROM BIOS,** which is also found on the motherboard, controls the keyboard. The **video ROM BIOS,** located on the video card or on the motherboard if the video card is built into the motherboard, controls the video systems.

Other ROM chips, which are often found on expansion cards, supplement the instructions of the system ROM BIOS. They include instructions used to control new or nonstandard hardware that is not included in the system ROM BIOS. They include small computer systems interface (SCSI) controller cards, enhanced integrated drive electronics (IDE) controller cards, sound cards, proprietary CD-ROM drive controller cards, and network cards.

2.4.3   System ROM BIOS

The primary ROM BIOS chip is the system ROM BIOS, which has the following functions:

1. Controls the boot-up procedure
2. Performs a series of diagnostic tests known as the power-on self-test (POST) during boot-up
3. Generates hardware error (audio and video) codes if a problem is found during boot-up
4. Finds other ROM BIOS chips from the expansion cards
5. Finds boot sector/boot files to boot an operating system
6. Provides the most basic commands to control hardware
7. Provides the compatibility between the operating system and the hardware
8. Contains the CMOS setup program

During this time, the system ROM BIOS has instructions to search for additional ROM BIOS chips. Because the system ROM BIOS cannot possibly hold instructions for every piece of hardware or include instructions for new pieces of hardware, which are introduced every day, there was a need for additional instructions to control hardware. The additional hardware instructions are located in the other ROM BIOS chips found on the expansion cards.

The last function that the system ROM BIOS chip performs during boot-up is to find a boot device to load the operating system. If all goes well, the system will finish with a prompt waiting to input a command (DOS or UNIX) or will display a GUI interface (Windows).

Today, several companies specialize in developing compatible IBM system ROM BIOS chips. See Table 2.2. The most popular are American Megatrends Incorporated (AMI), Phoenix, and Award. After a system ROM BIOS is developed, companies license their own ROM BIOS chips to a motherboard manufacturer. The motherboard manufacturer then matches the hardware to a chosen system ROM BIOS or has one developed specifically for its motherboard.

2.4.4   ROM BIOS Shortcomings

Although all PCs are compatible to the ROM BIOS level, ROM BIOS chips have two shortcomings. First, the BIOS cannot hold every instruction for every hardware device or predict devices based on new technology. To overcome this shortcoming, PC designers use the following techniques to supplement the standard ROM BIOS:

■ Use additional ROM BIOS chips located on expansion cards to supplement the instructions of the system ROM BIOS

Table 2.2   Popular BIOS manufacturers

BIOS Manufacturer	Description
IBM	IBM represents today's personal computer standard. All other ROM BIOSs need to be compatible with the IBM BIOS if they wish to be truly IBM compatible.
AMI	AMI is the most popular BIOS. Its success is due to its many features and enhancements.
Award	Award is unique among BIOS because it sells its BIOS code to other vendors and allows that vendor to customize the BIOS for its own particular system.
Phoenix	Phoenix was one of the first BIOS to design its own IBM-compatible BIOS and has been the standard for IBM-compatible BIOS. Phoenix ROM BIOS is efficient and reliable.

Note: IBM, AMI, Award, and Phoenix are by far the most popular, but many other companies sell their own BIOS. These BIOS are proprietary or compatible with common ROM BIOS. Some of the more popular are DTK, Epson, Hewlett-Packard, NCR, Compaq, Wang, and Zenith.

■ Obtain software that is written to access and control the hardware directly
■ Use device drivers to enhance the BIOS instructions and terminate-stay resident programs (TSRs) to modify the interrupt vector table

Question: Is every system ROM BIOS the same?

Answer: No. First, when a company makes an IBM-compatible ROM BIOS chip, it must do so from scratch, because the IBM ROM BIOS program code is copyrighted. Second, the ROM BIOS codes have been curtailed for the hardware. Third, some BIOSs are better optimized for hardware than other BIOSs which allows the PC to operate faster. Lastly, only some ROM BIOS chips include instructions to handle newer hardware.

The second shortcoming of ROM BIOS chips is occasionally you may need to upgrade the system ROM BIOS. Reasons to upgrade the system are as follows:

■ New hardware is introduced and the system ROM BIOS does not know how to work with the new hardware.
■ There are programming glitches or compatibility issues.
■ The newer system ROM BIOS runs more efficiently than the older system BIOS.

To upgrade a BIOS, access the website of the motherboard manufacturer and download the BIOS upgrade program. Then follow the instructions from the motherboard manufacturer or the downloaded files. *Be sure to have the most current version of the BIOS before installing Windows.*

2.5   EXPANSION SLOTS AND CARDS

The **expansion slot,** also known as the **input/output (I/O) bus,** extends the reach of the microprocessor so that it can communicate with peripheral devices. Expansion slots are so named because they allow the user to expand the system by inserting circuit boards called expansion cards. They are essential for the computer because a basic system cannot satisfy everyone's needs. In addition, the expansion cards allow the system to use new technology as it becomes available.

The expansion slots consist of connectors and metal traces that carry signals from the expansion card to the rest of the computer, specifically the RAM and CPU. These connections are used for power, data, addressing, and control lines.

The primary purpose of these slots is to carry data between the expansion cards and the CPU and RAM. The **data bus** carries the actual data between the expansion card, the RAM, and the CPU. The size (width) of a bus is the amount of data that can be transmitted at one time. For example, a 32-bit bus can transmit 32 bits of data over 32 traces or wires.

2.5.1   Hardware Interrupts

When a device (such as a modem, mouse, keyboard, hard drive controller, floppy drive controller, sound card, or network card) needs the attention of the microprocessor, it sends a signal through an interrupt line within the expansion bus to the interrupt controller. The interrupt controller then signals the microprocessor so that the microprocessor can stop what it is doing to service the device. When the microprocessor is done servicing the device, it returns to its original task.

A single expansion card is set to use a single interrupt. When the device needs to interrupt the CPU, it sends a signal through the selected interrupt. If two devices are set to use the same interrupt, the cards will function improperly because the microprocessor will not know which device needs its attention. Computers since the IBM AT (286 microprocessor) have 16 interrupts (15 which are usable because IRQ 2 and IRQ 9 are cascaded). See Table 2.3.

With the wide assortment of devices available, it is possible to run out of interrupts; therefore, some bus designs are allowed for interrupt sharing. Interrupt sharing allows two different devices to use the same interrupt. The interrupt-handling software/firmware distinguishes for the microprocessor which

Table 2.3 AT default interrupt assignments

IRQ[1]	Default Use	Bus Slot
0	System timer	No
1	Keyboard controller	No
2	2nd IRQ controller (cascade)	No
3	Serial port 2 (COM2)	Yes (8 bit)
4	Serial port 1 (COM1)	Yes (8 bit)
5	Parallel port 2 (LPT2)	Yes (8 bit)
6	Floppy disk controller	Yes (8 bit)
7	Parallel port 1 (LPT1)	Yes (8 bit)
8	Real-time clock	No
9	Available	Yes (8/16 bit)
10	Available	Yes (8/16 bit)
11	Available	Yes (8/16 bit)
12	Bus mouse (or available)	Yes (8/16 bit)
13	Math coprocessor	No
14	Primary IDE	Yes (8/16 bit)
15	Secondary IDE (or Available)	Yes (8/16 bit)

[1]IRQ = interrupt request

device is making the request. Note that unless you have no other choice in sharing interrupts and the two devices are made to be shared with each other, it is best not to have two devices use the same interrupt.

2.5.2   Direct Memory Address

Direct memory address (DMA) channels are used by high-speed communication devices that must send and receive large amounts of information at high speed (e.g., sound cards, some network cards, and some SCSI cards). The DMA controller takes over the data bus and address lines to bring data from an I/O device to the RAM without any assistance or direction from the CPU. Since the CPU can perform other tasks while the data transfer is taking place, the PC performance will be greater. See Table 2.4.

A device using a DMA address is similar to a device using an IRQ (Interrupt). Each DMA line goes from the DMA controller to each of the expansion slots. When a device uses DMA to transfer data using a DMA channel, it first sends a signal along a single DMA channel to the DMA controller. The DMA controller then sends a request to the CPU. When the CPU acknowledges the request, the DMA controller takes control of the data bus and the address bus. The DMA controller then sends another signal to the device, which tells the device to start sending information (up to 64 KB of data). After the transfer is done, the DMA controller will release the data bus and address bus back to the CPU.

2.5.3   Bus Mastering

Bus mastering occurs when an expansion card with its own processor takes temporary control of the data and address bus to move information from one point to another. Consequently, the PC is faster. This differs from DMAs in which the DMA controller takes control of the buses. If you have several

Table 2.4 AT default DMA assignments

DMA	Default Use	Bus Slot
0	Unused	Yes (8 bit)
1	Unused	Yes (8 bit)
2	Floppy disk controller	Yes (8 bit)
3	Unused	Yes (8 bit)
4	First DMA controller	No
5	Unused	Yes (16 bit)
6	Unused	Yes (16 bit)
7	Unused	Yes (16 bit)

devices trying to use the data and address bus at the same time, the data being transferred would become corrupted. To prevent two devices from taking over the buses at the same time, the bus is managed by integrated system peripheral (ISP) chips.

Much like IRQs and DMAs, the devices that use the bus are prioritized as follows:

1. RAM refresh
2. DMA transfers
3. CPU
4. Bus master expansion cards

Extended Industry Standard Architecture (EISA), Micro-Channel Architecture (MCA), and Peripheral Component Interconnect (PCI) expansion slots support bus mastering.

2.5.4   I/O Addresses

As the microprocessor communicates with a device, it will use either an OUT command or an IN command. The OUT command is an assembly language command used to send data or a command to an I/O device. The IN command is used to read data from the device or to check the status of a device. In either case, the IN and OUT commands must include the **I/O address,** sometimes called **base I/O port address,** which will identify the device. To ensure that the PC does not confuse an I/O address with a RAM address, a special signal accompanies the I/O address.

Each device is configured to respond to a range of addresses known as **ports.** Generally, a device will respond to a range of addresses. For example, the COM1 port responds to addresses 03F8 to 03FF. The address 03F8 handles all data. Four addresses are used to configure the line (speed and parity), control the telephone (hang-up and begin), check modem status, and perform other housekeeping tasks. (Note: The addresses are expressed in hexadecimal form.)

Therefore, the I/O address is a memory address used to identify the input/output (I/O) device much like a street address identifies a house or building. Similarly, no two devices can be set to use the same I/O address or range of addresses.

Intel designed its microprocessors with 65,536 I/O ports, each address being 16 bits long. The engineers did not think they would use all available ports, so they limited the addresses to 1024. See Table 2.5.

2.5.5   Memory Addresses

Many expansion cards use a range of **memory addresses,** or **base memory addresses,** in the reserve memory between 640 KB and 1 MB of RAM. The reserve memory will either be used as a working area for the expansion card or by the ROM BIOS chips.

Table 2.5   Common IBM PC AT I/O addresses

Hex 000-0FF for System I/O Board		Common Expansion Cards and Ports	
000–01F	DMA controller 1	1F0–1F8	Fixed disk
020–03F	Interrupt controller 1	200–207	Game port
040–05F	Timer	278–27F	Parallel port 2 (LPT2)
060–06F	Keyboard	2F8–2FF	Serial port 2 (COM2)
070–07F	Real-time clock, NMI mask	378–37F	Parallel printer port 1(LPT1)
0A0–0BF	Interrupt controller 2	3B0–3BF	Monochrome display and
0C0–0DF	DMA controller 2		printer adapter
0F8–0FF	Math coprocessor	3C0–3CF	Enhanced graphics adapter
		3D0–3DF	CGA monitor adapter
		3F0–3F7	Diskette controller
		3F8–3FF	Serial port 1 (COM1)

2.6   TYPES OF EXPANSION SLOTS

Through the years there have been several types of expansion slots. The original IBM PC used the 8-bit PC slot and the original IBM AT used the 16-bit **Industry Standard Architecture (ISA)** slot. Later, the Micro-Channel Architecture (MCA) and the Extended Industry Standard Architecture (EISA) were introduced for use within 386 machines. Today's desktop computers use a combination of ISA slots and local bus slots (VESA and PCI, to be discussed later in the chapter) while notebooks use a PC slot/CardBus slot. This chapter will only focus on the ISA, VESA, PCI, and PC slots. See Table 2.6.

2.6.1   ISA Slot

In the early 1980s, most technology used for personal computers was based on 8-bit technology. Therefore, IBM chose the 8088 microprocessor, which had an external 8-bit data bus. This became known as the **PC slot** or the **8-bit ISA bus.**

In 1984, Intel released the 286 microprocessor. The 286 used an external 16-bit data bus and a 24-bit address bus, which allowed the microprocessor to see up to 16 MB of RAM. This gave IBM two choices. First, IBM could choose to develop a new motherboard from scratch to take advantage of the new technology. Unfortunately, this meant that the large base of 8-bit cards could not be used. The second choice was to somehow modify the older design to use both the 8-bit cards and the new 16-bit cards.

IBM's solution was introduced as the original IBM AT. The AT motherboard still used the older 8-bit connector to accommodate the 8-bit cards. To accommodate a 16-bit card, the 8-bit slots were extended by adding a second 36-pin connector. The second connector contained the additional data and address lines. In addition, there were five more interrupt lines and four additional DMA channels added.

By 1987, an IEEE committee approved the AT bus as the Industry Standard Architecture (ISA). Although the ISA slot is considered old technology, even the most advanced motherboards contain some ISA slots. Other names include the classic bus, the AT bus, or the Legacy bus.

The ISA bus did not have a significant change until 1993 when Intel and Microsoft introduced the **plug-and-play (PNP) ISA.** The PNP ISA bus allows a PNP ISA card to be inserted and its resources automatically assigned without any need to use jumpers or DIP switches to configure the card. ISA cards that are not plug-and-play are called **Legacy cards.**

Instead of physically changing the ISA slot, a plug-and-play manager (software) identifies the card and assigns its needed resources. This is made possible because the PNP cards contain a ROM chip,

Table 2.6   Common expansion slots

Name	Date	Bus Width	Operating Speed	Maximum Bandwidth	Comments
PC Bus	1981	8	4.77 MHz	2.385 MB/s	Used in IBM PC and XT
ISA	1984	16	8.33 MHz	8.33 MB/s	Used in IBM AT
MCA	1987	32	10 MHz	20 MB/s	Used in PS/2
EISA	1988	32	8.33 MHz	16.6 MB/s	Created to compete against MCA
VL Bus	1992	32	33 MHz	105.6 MB/s	Used mostly in 486 computers
PCI*[1]	1992	32	33 MHz	66.6 MB/s or higher (nonburst mode) 133 MB/s (burst mode)	Used in 486 and some Pentium machines
PCI*	1992	64	66 MHz (or higher)	264 MB/s or higher (nonburst mode) 528 MB/s (burst mode)	Used in Pentium machines
PC Card	1990	16	8 MHz	16 MB/s	Used in notebook computers
CardBus	1994	32	33 MHz	133 MB/s	Used in notebook computers
AGP	1996	32	66 MHz (or higher)	1X–266 MB/s 2X–533 MB/s 4X–1.07 GB/s 8X–2.14 GB/s	First used in newer Pentium systems
PCI-X	1998	64	133 MHz	1,066 MB/s	Update to the PCI

[1]As the PCI bus matured, the bus speed increased and is still being increased today.

which contains a number. Since the number identifies the card, not its model number, several of the same cards can be used within the same system, such as two network cards or two hard drive controllers. After the card is identified, the plug-and-play manager assigns the needed resources (I/O and memory addresses, IRQs, and DMAs) to the card.

2.6.2   MCA and EISA Slots

By 1985, the 386DX was introduced. It ran at 16 MHz and used a 32-bit data bus. Again, IBM was faced with designing a computer that would utilize all features of the new microprocessor. In addition, as programs incorporated graphics, it was becoming evident that video performance was a major concern in PC performance. Lastly, IBM tried to regain its dominance in the PC market back from companies such as Compaq.

As a result, IBM introduced the PS/2. On the outside, it was a sleek, modern-looking PC. On the inside, it was redesigned to accommodate the new features of the 386DX and overcome some of the limitations established by the original IBM PC. It integrated the display adapter, diskette controller, serial port, parallel port, and mouse port onto the motherboard. In addition, it used the 3.5-inch diskette drive and it introduced the new VGA graphics adapter standard. Lastly, it introduced the Micro-Channel Architecture (MCA). To avoid the use of jumpers and DIP switches to configure the MCA expansion cards, cards used a PS/2 reference disk to configure the card.

The MCA was a 32-bit expansion bus. Its standard operating speed was 10 MHz, but had the capability of increasing speed to match the top speed of the card up to the speed of the microprocessor. To improve performance, MCA increased the speed of the DMA channel up to 2.5 times, and it used a form of bus mastering called central arbitration point. This allowed the microprocessor to complete additional jobs while other devices used the data and address lines. IBM also used a burst mode that allowed a device to send a steady flow of data up to 12 milliseconds (ms).

Unfortunately, the PS/2 and MCA had three disadvantages. First, the MCA did not accommodate the older 8-bit and 16-bit ISA cards. Second, IBM tried to charge heavy licensing fees to companies that wanted to use the new technology, which in turn drove them away. Third, although the expansion slots were faster, system performance was not increased significantly. Therefore, customers did not want to pay the extra money for such a small increase in performance.

Since companies were not in favor of IBM's hefty licensing fees, several of them formed the "gang of nine" to design a bus to compete against the MCA. The gang was led by Compaq and consisted of AST Research, Epson, Hewlett-Packard, NEC, Olivetti, Tandy, Wyse, and Zenith Data Systems. The newly developed bus was the **Extended Industry Standard Architecture (EISA)**.

The EISA consists of two slots in one. The 16-bit slot, used by ISA cards, exists on top while the 32-bit slot exists on the bottom. Because the ISA card connectors are shorter and thicker, they only go part way into the slot. The EISA cards are longer and thinner, so they can be inserted to make contact with the 32-bit bus. Although the EISA slot initially ran at 8 MHz, newer technology increased the performance of the slots. First, instead of only reacting when the clock signal rose, EISA cards would lock their address when the clock signal rose and transfer data when the clock signal fell. In addition, much like the MCA, the EISA offered bus mastering.

EISA systems were an early attempt to produce a plug-and-play system. To avoid IRQ and I/O address conflicts, the EISA setup software would automatically configure the expansion cards. Unfortunately, not many EISA cards were developed, because many companies believed they did not have to develop such cards for a machine that already supported their ISA cards. In addition, instead of designing a complete line of EISA cards, companies waited to see if the EISA standard would become successful. As a result, only a handful of EISA cards was created, mostly for network servers (disk array controllers and network cards).

2.6.3   Local Bus Slot (VESA and PCI)

The **local bus** is a modern bus similar to one used in the original PC. To maximize performance, it has the same data path size of the microprocessor, which connects directly to the microprocessor, running at the same speed. After some early attempts, two standards emerged: the VESA local bus and the PCI local bus.

The first widely accepted local bus was the VESA local bus (VL bus). It was created by the Video Electronics Standards Association (VESA), which originally formed to standardize super VGA (variable graphics array) monitors. Its interest in developing a local bus was to improve video performance.

The VESA local bus was built around the 486 microprocessor, aimed at supplementing the existing slots (ISA, EISA, or MCA). When coupled with the ISA slot, the VESA slot was mounted directly in line with the ISA slot on the system board. Because it was built around the 486, it used a 32-bit data bus to match the microprocessor and ran at the same speed as the microprocessor.

The local bus can run in a faster **burst mode,** in which sequential data are transferred faster by specifying one memory address followed by transferring up to four pieces of data. Thus, when the bus is in burst mode running at 33 MHz, it could transfer up to 105.6 MB/s while nonburst mode can only transfer up to 66 MB/s. In either case, both speeds are far greater than the ISA's 8.33 MB/s. In addition, VESA supports bus mastering.

VESA provided improvements over ISA of bus mastering and speeds of up to 66 MHz. However, its direct connection to the 486 processor led to losses in data integrity and introduced timing problems. As a result, the maximum speed was usually 33 MHz for up to three devices (video, disk controller, and network card).

Today, when you hear the term *local bus,* it probably refers to the **peripheral component interconnect (PCI)** local bus. The PCI slot was developed by Intel and was designed to eventually replace the older bus designs. Unlike the VESA, the PCI local bus is not an extension of any other slot; it is mounted on the system board offset from the normal ISA, MCA, or EISA connector. The PCI design provides between three and five slots. To increase performance, the PCI bus has a built-in burst mode.

While in burst mode, the transfer rate is 132 MB/s for the 32-bit PCI design and 264 MB/s for the 64-bit PCI design.

PCI supports plug-and-play technology. Different from other expansion bus designs, the expansion cards have their own storage space to store the cards' configuration information. Therefore, most PCI cards are not configured using jumpers or DIP switches, but are configured using software or a true plug-and-play system.

A newly developed high-performance PCI standard is the Compact PCI, which uses the rugged Eurocard packaging with a high-quality 2-mm metric pin and socket connector. The new Compact PCI supports hot swap capabilities, which allow inserting and extracting the card while the system is turned on.

In 1998, Compaq, Hewlett-Packard, and IBM announced their intention to expand on the PCI design to increase I/O bandwidth. The bandwidth can be used in industry standard servers that run enterprise applications such as Gigabit Ethernet, Fibre Channel, Ultra3 SCSI, and Cluster Interconnects.

This new specification, called **PCI-X,** defines two frequency design points for PCI-X adapters: PCI-X 66 MHz and PCI-X 133 MHz. When operating in PCI-X mode, PCI-X 66-MHz adapters have actual clock frequencies ranging from 50 to 66 MHz, and PCI-X 133-MHz adapters have clock frequencies ranging from 50 to 133 MHz. To support more adapter slots on the PCI-X bus, system designers can lower the bus frequency to a minimum of 50 MHz. For example, a PCI-X bus segment with two expansion slots would typically operate at 100 MHz, rather than at the full 133 MHz. A PCI-X bus segment with four expansion slots would typically operate at 66 MHz. Like conventional PCI adapters, PCI-X adapters can implement a 64-bit interface or a 32-fit interface. A 64-bit adapter running at 133 MHz gives a bandwidth of 1066 MB/s.

A PCI-X adapter can operate in a conventional PCI system, and vice versa. If the adapter and system both support PCI-X, the new PCI-X adapter can immediately take advantage of the higher operating frequencies of a PCI-X system. When the PCI-X adapter is put in a conventional 33-MHz PCI system, the adapter functions at 33-MHz. If a conventional PCI device is installed on a PCI-X bus, the bus clock remains at a frequency acceptable to the conventional adapter, and the other adapters on that bus segment run at the same speed. PCI-X systems do not require operating system or device-driver updates to work, but if you want to take advantage of the new PCI-X features, you will need new device drivers.

If a PCI-X bus segment includes only PCI-X devices, the bus operates in PCI-X mode. A PCI-X system automatically adjusts the bus frequency to match the frequency of the slowest adapter on that bus segment. For example, if the bus includes a 66-MHz PCI-X adapter, the maximum clock frequency of the bus segment is 66 MHz. PCI-X supports up to 256 bus segments, and each segment is initialized separately so that different operating frequencies can be used.

In addition to the faster bus speed, design improvements (e.g., eliminating wasted clock cycles that PCI uses as wait states, supporting split transactions that eliminate polling across the bus, transferring predetermined transaction byte counts) permit PCI-X devices to perform up to 10 times as fast as 32-bit 33-MHz PCI devices. Real-time audio and video applications benefit from relaxed ordering, which lets PCI bridges handle transactions from multiple PCI-X devices in the most efficient order, rather than in the first in/first out (FIFO) order that earlier PCI protocols enforce. Non-cache-coherent transaction support lets the PCI device driver tell the system cache controllers not to "snoop" the processors, thereby reducing processor bus utilization and increasing system efficiency. (Snooping is a technique used by cache memory controllers to monitor the system buses to detect an access to main memory that might cause a cache consistency problem.)

PCI cards and slots are keyed by voltage (i.e., 5 V or 3.3 V). Although universal PCI cards are notched for both 5 V and 3.3 V, PCI slot connectors can be keyed for only one voltage. PCI 2.1 and 2.0 specifications permitted both 5-V and 3.3-V signaling; PCI 2.2 favored 3.3-V signaling but also supported 5 V signaling. (PCI 2.2 cards can be 5 V, 3.3 V or universal; vendors have designed most PCI 2.2 cards as universal cards.) When PCI cards and slots use 5-V signaling, they operate at a maximum speed of 33 MHz; only 3.3-V PCI slots can support higher bandwidths. Therefore, all PCI-X slots are 3.3-V slots. PCI-X slots work with universal PCI cards and 3.3-V cards but do not work with 5-V only cards. Universal PCI-X cards operate at 33 MHz in a 5-V slot, at speeds as fast as 66 MHz in a 3.3-V PCI 2.2 slot, and at speeds as fast as 133 MHz in a 3.3-V PCI-X slot. As when you mix SCSI devices of different speeds, mixing PCI and PCI-X cards on the same bus causes the speed of the PCI-X bus and all other cards on the bus to operate at the slowest card's speed.

2.7   CONFIGURING EXPANSION CARDS

When an expansion card is inserted into a system, it must be configured to use the proper resources. The resources include I/O addresses (including COMx/LPT), IRQs, DMAs, and memory addresses. When configuring a card, one general rule should apply: No two devices can use the same resource. Therefore, two expansion cards should not be set to use the same DMA channel or the same I/O address. If two devices are using the same setting, the devices will either not work properly or not work at all. To determine the available resources, use diagnostic software such as QA Plus or Checkit Pro or use Utilities, which comes with the operating system such as Windows Device Manager located within the control panel. It is possible to share an IRQ among more than one device, but only under limited conditions. If you have two devices that are seldom used, and that you never use simultaneously, you may be able to have them share an IRQ. Unfortunately, this can lead to more problems if you are not careful.

After determining which resources the card can use, the card itself can be configured one of three ways:

1. DIP switches and/or jumpers
2. Software setup program
3. Plug and play (PNP)

DIP switches are found on many older computers, either on the motherboard or on the expansion card. They consist of a bank of tiny on–off switches. See Figure 2.7.

A **jumper** is a small, plastic-covered metal clip that is used to connect two pins protruding from an expansion card. The jumper (same as an on switch) connects the pins, which closes the circuit and allows current to flow. The two types of pins that need to be jumped are the 2-pin configuration and the 3-pin configuration. See Figure 2.8.

The 2-pin configuration will have a jumper that either connects both pins or not. If the jumper is placed over the two pins, the documentation will say "On," "Closed," or show a small line diagram of where the jumper should be placed. If the jumper is not to be placed over the two pins, the documentation will say "Off," "Open," or show a small line diagram of where the jumpers should not be placed. Jumpers that are not in use can be placed over one pin to avoid losing them.

The 3-pin configuration has a high/low capability. If the documentation says "High," you will jumper the two pins on the side indicated with an *H*. If the documentation says "Low," you will jumper the two pins on the side indicated with an *L*.

To determine which resources the card can use and how to select the resources, you most likely need the expansion board documentation. Most documentation is written in a manual, but some is silk-screened on the card itself or placed within a file on a disk.

After the expansion card is installed, it may require a software driver to function. DOS drivers are typically loaded by running the install program from disks that come with the expansion card or by copying the appropriate files to the hard drive and modifying the CONFIG.SYS and AUTOEXEC.BAT files.Windows drivers are typically loaded by running the Add New Hardware Driver icon or by using the installation disks that come with the expansion card.

With no documentation, installation will usually require much trial and error before figuring out the correct settings. If the documentation or drivers become lost, look in the following places for help:

■ Internet
■ Manufacturer of the device
■ Microhouse Technical Library/Online Service

Figure 2.7   DIP switches

Figure 2.8 NE2000–compatible card with jumpers

Two good resources are the Internet, on which companies post their documentation for quick and easy access, and the manufacturer of the device. Another option is to contact Microhouse Incorporated, which publishes a technical library (book/CD-ROM and online service) of motherboard and hard drive documentation and expansion cards.

2.8   UNIVERSAL SERIAL BUS AND IEEE 1394 (FIREWIRE)

The universal serial bus (USB) is an external port that allows connection of external PC peripheral devices in series. The USB connector accepts any USB peripheral device, including mice, keyboards, printers, modems, and external disk drivers. Seven devices can be connected directly using the standard 4-pin connector. These seven devices can then be connected to others, to a total of 127 devices, by connecting external hubs (each hub accommodates another seven devices) in a chain (hence, the term *daisy chain* for this type of serial connection). One of the biggest advantages of the USB interface is that it only requires a single interrupt from the PC for all 127 devices. Note that although USB can support up to 127 devices, it is usually limited by bus speed and power limitations.

A USB port or hub can provide power to the attached peripherals. A hub recognizes the dynamic attachment of a peripheral and provides at least 0.5 W per peripheral during initialization. Under control of the host PC driver software, the hub may provide more device power, up to a maximum of 2.5 W, for peripheral operations. Typically, if you have a device more than 0.5 W, the device must have an external power source such as an AC adapter.

When you attach a USB device on a Windows system that supports USB, you may receive a "USB Hub Power Exceeded" error message containing the following text:

```
The hub does not have enough power available to operate the
device driver name. Would you like assistance in solving this
problem? If you click No, the device may not function properly.
```

When this happens, the USB device mentioned in the error message does not work properly and the device listing (in the system properties of the Device Manager properties window for the device) appears with the following error message:

```
A USB device has requested more power than the hub can provide.
Windows cannot enable the device. Remove the device and restart
your computer.
```

To resolve this issue, replace the passive USB hub with an active (powered) hub, or disconnect the affected device from the passive hub and connect it directly to the USB host controller's hub (in the back of the computer), or attach an AC adapter if one is available.

USB 1.1 offers a data transfer rate of up to 12 megabits per second. For low-speed peripherals such as pointing devices and keyboards, the USB also has a slower 1.5 Mbit/s subchannel. Maximum cable length between two full-speed (12 Mbit/s) devices or a device and a hub is 5 meters using twisted-pair, shielded cable with 20-gauge wire. Maximum cable length for low speed (1.5 Mbit/s) devices, using non-twisted-pair wire, is 3 meters. These distance limits are shorter if small-gauge wire is used.

Two different connectors are specified for USB, called series A and series B. The series A connector is designed for devices where the cable remains permanently attached, such as hubs, keyboards, and mice. The USB ports on most motherboards are also normally a series A connector. Series B connectors are designed for devices that require detachable cables, such as printers, scanners, modems, telephones, and speakers. The physical USB plugs are smaller than the series A connector.

USB 2.0 is similar to USB 1.1 except that it runs up to 480 Mbit/s, yet remains backward-compatible. It uses the same cables, connectors, and software interfaces. The support of higher-speed USB 2.0 peripheral devices requires a USB 2.0 hub. You can still use older USB 1.1 hubs on a 2.0 bus, but any peripherals or additional hubs connected downstream from a 1.1 hub will operate at the slower speed of 1.5 Mbit/s.

To take advantage of USB 2.0 hardware, users must upgrade their current USB 1.1 systems with USB 2.0-compliant PCI cards or purchase motherboards with built-in USB 2.0 support. On the software side, operating systems with full USB 2.0 support will continue to work with USB 1.1 peripherals and will be able to recognize USB 2.0 hardware. The system software will be able to optimize performance in a mixed environment where USB 1.1 and USB 2.0 hardware are connected concurrently to a USB 2.0 bus. If the system detects a USB 2.0 peripheral attached to a USB 1.1 system, it will notify the user of detection of a sub-optimal configuration and recommend a better configuration for attaching the device.

Another external bus standard is **IEEE 1394**, sometimes called **FireWire.** IEEE 1394 supports data transfer rates of up to 400 Mbit/s. A single 1394 port can connect up to six external devices. It can deliver data at a guaranteed rate, which makes it ideal for devices that need to transfer large amounts of data in real-time, such as video cameras and other video devices. Like USB, 1394 supports plug-and-play and hot swapping operations. IEEE 1394 port uses a tree topology (physical layout), whereby any device can be connected to any other device as long as there are no loops. Unfortunately, IEEE 1394 costs a lot more than USB.

IEEE 1394 is defined as part of the SCSI-3 family of related standards, and at one point it was sometimes called "serial SCSI." It is, in fact, a type of SCSI, that is based on the broad coverage of SCSI-3, which goes beyond regular SCSI to cover several similar, "SCSI-like" technologies. In terms of signaling and some aspects of operation, IEEE 1394 really can be thought of as "serial SCSI." Yet, IEEE 1394 is better considered USB.

IEEE 1394 still has not become popular as a storage interface within the PC. Some systems, however, are now equipped with this interface, and a variety of storage devices are made for it, so it is a viable option if your system supports it or if you wish to add support for it. IEEE 1394 is growing in popularity in a variety of specialty markets, especially digital video. It may well become the next significant interface standard for consumer electronics devices such as camcorders and VCRs.

2.9   HARD DRIVES

Hard drives are half electronic and half mechanical devices, that use magnetic patterns to store information onto rotating platters. They are considered long-term storage devices because they do not forget their information when power is disconnected. They are also considered the primary mass storage system, because they hold all programs and data files, which are fed into RAM. The first hard drive used in the PC had a capacity of only 5 MB. Today, hard drives can be larger than 100 GB.

Hard drives are sometimes referred to as *fixed disks* because they usually are not removed from the PC as easily as a floppy disk. Today, this term does not describe all hard drives because there are external (disks that rest outside of the case) hard drives and removable hard drives. Hard drives communicate with the rest of the computer via a cable connected to a controller card. The controller card could be an expansion card or could be built on the motherboard.

2.9.1   Hard Drive Performance

Because programs and data files are larger than ever, hard drives are required to store greater amounts of information. Therefore, the overall performance of the PC is partially dependent on how long it takes to get information from the hard drive into RAM so that it can be processed by the microprocessor. Hard drive performance can be measured by access time (consisting of seek time and latency period), data transfer rate, drive RPMs, and PC data handling. See Figure 2.9.

Access time is the average amount of time it takes to move the read/write head to the requested sector. It is the sum of seek time and latency period. **Seek time** is the average time it takes the read/write heads to move to the requested track—usually to move one-third of the way across the platter. The **latency period** is the time, after the read/write heads move to the requested track, for the requested sector to spin underneath the read/write head. The latency period is usually half the time required for a single revolution of the disk platter. All times are measured in milliseconds (ms). The **disk transfer rate** is the speed at which data are transferred to and from the platters, which is usually measured in bits per second (bps) or bytes per second.

The host transfer rate is defined by the method of data transfered through the hard drive interface (IDE, EIDE, SCSI, and so on; see following sections). IDE hard drives use either a processor input/output mode or a direct memory address (DMA) mode while SCSI drives use either SCSI I, SCSI II, or SCSI III. The different versions of SCSI are explained later in this chapter.

The PC data handling occurs after the data have been transferred to the controller card. It is the time it takes for the data to be transferred to the RAM. It is not necessarily a factor of the hard drive, but rather of the PC itself. It is dependent on the type and speed of the microprocessor, the speed and amount of RAM, the speed and amount of RAM cache, and the speed of the hard drive controller card (expansion card).

Another way to increase disk performance is to use some form of software disk cache such as DOS's SMARTDRV.EXE or Windows 9X VCACHE. The software disk cache sets a cache area in RAM to store

Figure 2.9   Hard drive performance factors

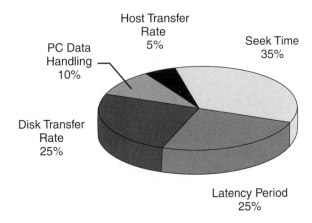

both data and instructions. One method is to keep a copy of information that has been recently accessed. If it has already been accessed, then it probably will be accessed again. Another method reads additional sectors after a sector has been accessed before those sectors are requested. Regardless of the method, when the disk needs to be accessed, it will look in the cache area first. If it cannot find what it is looking for, the disk will access the slower hard drive. The time to search the cache area (RAM) is almost negligible compared with the time required to access the hard drive. Therefore, if it finds the needed information in the RAM, PC performance will be greatly increased. Since servers are providing files for use by the server's clients, any RAM not being used by an application will normally be used to cache the disk.

Another form of cache is the hardware cache located on the hard drive controller card or the hard drive logic board. This cache is not to be confused with the L1 or L2 cache used to buffer the microprocessor and the RAM. Much like its software counterparts, it fulfills the same functions as the software disk cache. Instead of using a hard drive software interrupt, the controller card physically completes the task. Hard drive controllers with cache are quite common for servers.

2.9.2   IDE Hard Drives

Today, there are two main types of hard drives, IDE and SCSI. The **integrated drive electronics (IDE)** interface was developed in 1988 as a fast, low-cost hard drive interface. The IDE hard drive connects to a controller card (via an expansion card or built into the motherboard) using a 40-pin cable. For example, the Ultra DMA-66 and ultra DMA-100 mode require a special 40-pin cable that has 80 wires, 40 pins for the signal, and 40 ground pins to reduce noise. The newest IDE interface supports up to four IDE devices by using two IDE cables. In addition to hard drives, it supports nondisk peripherals, which follow the Advanced Technology Attachment Packet Interface (ATAPI). The ATAPI is the protocol used on the enhanced IDE devices (IDE CD-ROM drives, IDE tape backup drives, and other IDE storage devices).

When connecting the ribbon cable, be sure the cable has the correct orientation. Pin 1 of the cable (marked with a red or blue stripe along one edge) must be connected to pin 1 of the drive and to pin 1 of the cable connector on the motherboard or expansion card. Pin 1 of the drive is designated by a small number 1 or 2 printed on the drive's circuit board. Pin 1 of the expansion card/motherboard connector can be identified with a small number 1 or 2 printed on the circuit board or will use a square solder (other pins use a round solder). Some drives and cables have a notch, which prevents the cable from being inserted incorrectly. If the cable is connected incorrectly, the hard drive may cause a short, which then causes the computer not to boot.

Up to two hard drives can be connected to one IDE cable. See Figures 2.10 and 2.11. If one drive is installed, then the drive is known as a stand-alone drive. If two hard drives are installed, then the first physical drive is the master drive (drive C) and the second physical drive is the slave drive (drive D). The master drive got its name because the controlling electronics on the logic board of the master drive control both the master drive and the slave drive. The stand-alone, master, and slave drives are

Figure 2.10 IDE hard drive connected to a controller card

Figure 2.11 Connector ribbon cable and power connector (Courtesy of Seagate Corporation)

determined with jumpers on the hard drive. It does not matter where the drive and controller card is connected to the cable. The most common jumpers that are used to determine a drive as a stand-alone, master, and slave device are the Master (M/S) and the Slave Present (SP) jumpers.

The two methods in transferring data are **processor input/output (PIO)** and **direct memory access (DMA).** Depending on the transfer mode, a hard drive transfer rate can reach 100 MB/s. In PIO mode, transfers are directly controlled by the processor; the DMA drives use a form of bus mastering. See Tables 2.7 and 2.8

After the hard drive is configured and physically installed, the next step is to enter the CMOS setup program and input the proper hard drive parameters for the installed hard drive (such as the number of cylinders, the number of read/write heads, and the number of sectors/track or selecting the appropriate

Table 2.7   PIO modes used with EIDE devices

PIO Mode	Average Transfer Rate	Flow Controlled	Specification
0	3.3 MB/s	No	ATA
1	5.2 MB/s	No	ATA
2	8.3 MB/s	No	ATA
3	11.1 MB/s	Yes	ATA-2
4	16.6 MB/s	Yes	ATA-2

Table 2.8   DMA modes used with EIDE devices

DMA Mode	Average Transfer Rate	Requirements	Specifications
0—Single word	2.08 MB/s		ATA
1—Single word	4.16 MB/s		ATA
2—Single word	8.33 MB/s		ATA
0—Multiword	4.16 MB/s	Local bus controller	ATA
1—Multiword	13.33 MB/s	Local bus controller	ATA-2
2—Multiword	16.6 MB/s	Local bus controller	ATA-3
3—Multiword	33.3 MB/s	Local bus controller	Ultra DMA-33
4—Multiword	66.6 MB/s	Local bus controller and 40-pin/80 conductor cable	Ultra DMA-66
5—Multiword	100.0 MB/s	Local bus controller and 40-pin/80 conductor cable	Ultra DMA-100

mode as Large or LBA). Some CMOS setup programs have an Auto Detect feature that automatically determines the hard drive parameters; others have an Auto choice, which automatically determines the hard drive parameters during boot-up.

Ultra DMA-66 has a transfer rate of 66 MB/s and Ultra DMA-100 has a transfer rate of 100 MB/s. Unfortunately, the original 40-conductor IDE cable could not handle the faster data rate. Therefore, starting with Ultra DMA-66, a 40-pin conductor, 80-conductor IDE/ATA cable was introduced. Forty conductors or wires carry the data and 40 ground conductors or wires reduce "crosstalk" between adjacent wires.

Since no changes have been made to the connector, the new cable is pin-compatible with older IDE drives. Therefore, the 80-conductor cable can be used in systems of up to 33.3 MB/s, but it is required for Ultra DMA-66 and higher.

On the standard 40-pin/40-conductor IDE interfaces, pin 34 was not grounded, but on the newer 40-pin/80-conductor IDE interface, pin 34 is grounded. By sending a signal on pin 34, the hard drive controller can tell if the system is using the older cable or the newer cable. Therefore, on systems that can use Ultra DMA-66 or Ultra DMA-100, if you connect an Ultra DMA-100 drive, it will detect the drive, detect the type of cable, and automatically configure for the appropriate data transfer rate.

On the newer IDE drives, the connectors on the cable define which connector goes with which device. The blue connector attaches to the controller. The gray connector is in the middle of the cable and goes to any slave drive (if present). The black connector is at the opposite end from the controller connector and goes to the master drive, or a single drive if only one is used. (This was done because if you connect a single drive to the middle connector of the ribbon cable, the unconnected cable can cause signaling problems.)

An alternative to the standard master/slave jumpering system used in most IDE systems is the cable select (CS) system. By connecting the drives to a specific connector on the cable, the system determines which device is master and which is slave. Since pin 28 is grounded at the host's connector, which is connected to the master, it detects the end drive as the master and the middle drive, which is not connected with pin 28, becomes the slave drive.

Therefore, instead of setting the master and slave jumpers, the jumpers are set to CS; when connected to the appropriate connector, the drives will be assigned to the appropriate master or slave designation. Unfortunately, most people do not know of this option, and it was never accepted in the industry. Most drives are already jumpered, by default, as a master or slave drive. Therefore, you would have to change the jumper to enable this feature.

The current IDE/ATA standard is a parallel interface; this means that multiple bits of data are transmitted at one time. In the case of ATA, 16 bits are moved across the interface simultaneously during each transfer. The advantage of a parallel interface is that it allows for high throughput; the disadvantage is that as the frequency of the interface is increased, signaling problems and interferences between signals become common.

A new IDE standard, known as **serial ATA interface**, is based on 1 signal instead of 16 parallel signals. Because signaling problems are largely eliminated, a serial interface enables much higher speeds than are possible from a parallel implementation. The serial ATA interface will start at 150 MB/s and will be able to be expanded to 600 MB/s.

Parallel ATA allows up to two devices to be connected to a single port using a master/slave communication technique. Both devices are daisy-chained together via one ribbon cable that is an unterminated multidrop bus. It eliminates the +5 V power requirement, which allows for lower power consumption. The transmit signal on the interface cable consists of differential signals so that it has improved tolerance to electrical noise. (Differential signaling is explained in the following section.) The cable can be up to 1 meter in length. In addition, adapters can be used to connect regular IDE hard disks to a serial ATA controller.

2.9.3   SCSI Hard Drives

Another popular hard drive and system interface is the small computers system interface (SCSI, pronounced "skuzzy"), which evolved from Shugart Associates standard interface (SASI). Much like the IDE devices, SCSI is a much more advanced interface than ATA/ATA-2 and is ideal for high-end computers, including network servers. It is capable of supporting multiple devices in and out of the computer.

SCSI interfaces that have an 8-bit data bus, referred to as narrow, allow up to 7 devices (hard drives, tape drives, CD-ROM drives, removable drives/disks, and scanners) to be connectd to one SCSI adapter/controller (8 devices if you count the controller card). SCSI interfaces with a 16-bit data bus, referred to as wide, allow up to 15 devices (16 devices including the controller card). See Table 2.9.

Like any other expansion card, you may need to configure the card's resources. Standard SCSI I/O address range is 0330 to 0333. The IRQs for the SCSI interface are typically assigned to the unused IRQs, such as IRQ 11, or they will be plug-and-play. Today, the cards typically do not use DMAs.

With a SCSI host adapter, the BIOS on the adapter is used to control SCSI hard disk drives and perform the boot function. The BIOS also intercepts all hardware Interrupt 13 calls (read and write to disk) and passes the non-SCSI interrupt to the system ROM BIOS. The SCSI host adapter then translates these Interrupt 13 commands into SCSI commands for the SCSI disk drives.

The SCSI standard (SCSI-1) was approved in 1986 by the American National Standards Institute (ANSI). SCSI-1 defined the basics of the first SCSI buses, including cable length, signaling characteristics, commands, and transfer modes. It specified an 8-bit bus with a transfer rate of 5 MB/s. It supported single-ended transmission with passive termination (these terms will be explained later in this section). Unfortunately, the standard only included the hardware connection and did not specify the driver specification/Common Command Set required to communicate with the SCSI hard drive. Therefore, manufacturers used their own communication standards, which led to many compatibility problems between different devices, drivers, and adapters.

SCSI-1 is now obsolete, and the standard has been withdrawn by ANSI. In most cases, devices that adhere to the SCSI-1 standard can be used with host adapters and other devices that use the higher

Table 2.9 Types of SCSI devices and interfaces

Transfer Mode	SCSI Spec	Bus Width[1] (bits)	Throughput (MB/s)	Cabling	Signaling Method[2]	Maximum Devices per Bus	Maximum Cable Length (m)
"Regular" SCSI (SCSI-1)	SCSI-1/ SCSI-2	8	5	50-pin	SE	8	6
					HVD	8	25
Wide SCSI	SCSI-2	16	10	50-pin	SE	16	6
					HVD	16	25
Fast SCSI (also known as Fast Narrow)	SCSI-2	8	10	50-pin	SE	8	3
					HVD	8	25
Fast Wide SCSI (also known as Fast SCSI)	SCSI-2	16	20	68-pin	SE	16	3
					HVD	16	25
Ultra SCSI (also known as Ultra Narrow or Ultra Fast-20 SCSI)	SCSI-3/ SP1	8	20	50-pin	SE	8	1.5
						4	3
					HVD	8	25
Wide Ultra SCSI (also known as Fast Wide 20)	SCSI-3/ SP1	16	40	68-pin	SE	8	1.5
						4	3
					HVD	16	25
Ultra2 SCSI	SCSI-3/ SPI-2	8	40	50-pin	LVD	8	12
						2	25
					HVD	8	25
Wide Ultra2 SCSI	SCSI-3/ SPI-2	16	80	68-pin	LVD	16	12
						2	25
					HVD	16	25
Ultra3 SCSI (also known as Ultra 160 SCSI)	SCSI-3/ SPI-3	16	160	68-pin	LVD	16	12
						2	25
Ultra320 SCSI	SCSI-3	16	320	68-pin	LVD	16	12
						2	25
Serial SCSI (fiber channel SCSI I)	SCSI-3	Serial	100 MB/s	126	NA	10,000	N/A
Serial SCSI (fiber channel SCSI II)	SCSI-3	Serial	200 MB/s	126	NA	10,000	N/A

[1]Narrow = 8 bits and wide=16 bits.

[2]SE = single ended. LVD = low-voltage differential. HVD = high-voltage differential.

transfer rates of the more advanced SCSI-2 protocols, but they will still function at their original slow speed. (Note: Since all SCSI-1 devices are single ended, they may cause performance degradation if placed onto a multimode LVD SCSI bus. If you want to run LVD devices to their full potential, avoid mixing them with single-ended devices.)

To overcome some of the shortcomings of the SCSI-1 interface, ANSI approved the SCSI-2 standard in 1992. It included a set of 18 basic SCSI commands called the Common Command Set (CCS) that supported different peripheral devices, including CD-ROM drives, tape drives, removable drives/ disks, and scanners. In addition, SCSI-2 used command queuing. **Command queuing** allows a device to accept multiple commands and execute them in an order that is efficient, rather than in the order received. Think of command queuing as similar to driving a bus of people. You can drive to each person's stop in the order that they entered the bus, or you can try to figure out the most efficient way to drop off these passengers. For example, if two people live close to one another, you would drop them off one after the other. For SCSI hard drives, this method increases the performance of computers running multitasking operating systems and makes it ideal for servers.

SCSI-2 also established faster SCSI variations, such as Fast Wide SCSI, which increased the data path from 8 bits to 16 bits and increased data transfer to 20 MB/s. On buses that run with Wide SCSI, 16 devices are supported (as opposed to 8 with regular SCSI). To achieve improved bandwidth, SCSI-2 used a large number of different cables and connectors. For example, SCSI-2 defined new higher-density connections, extending the basic 50-pin connectors defined in SCSI-1. It also defined the use of active termination, which provides more reliable termination of the bus, and differential signaling to allow longer cable lengths. Differential signaling was later renamed high-voltage differential (HVD) to distinguish it from low-voltage differential (LVD) signaling.

As SCSI-3 was being developed, it was becoming a huge specification with a large number of different technologies, command sets, and features. Such a huge specification would have required many people to work on it, and the development of hardware would have been slow. Therefore, the SCSI-3 specification was broken into sub-specifications, so that impatient companies would not start developing their own proprietary extensions. The most implemented form of SCSI became the SCSI-3 Parallel Interface (SPI). There are now several versions of SPI, each defining new features and transfer speeds for conventional, parallel SCSI devices.

SCSI-3 specifies a high-speed synchronous transfer called Ultra SCSI and Wide Ultra SCSI, which allow a type A cable (8-bit data bus) and Ultra Fast-20 SCSI, which allows the P cable (16-bit data bus). SCSI-3 allows a data transfer rate of up to 320 MB/s and allows up to 16 devices using the same cable.

Another SCSI interface is the Serial SCSI (fiber channel SCSI). The fiber channel SCSI is a serial connection made of fiber or coaxial cable in lengths of up to 10,000 m, and it supports up to 126 devices. This interface can support 100 MB/s and a data transfer rate of 200MB/s. Although SCSI has not been used in mainstream SCSI, it has found a niche in storage area networks (SANs) in which the hard drives are shared among several systems that act as redundancy for each other. Therefore, if one computer goes down, other computers fill in for it. The hard drives are centrally located so that they can access the same data.

Traditional SCSI used single-ended (SE) signaling, which is similar to signaling used for most other interfaces and buses within the PC. A positive voltage is a "1" and a zero voltage is a "0." This signaling is relatively simple compared to today's more advanced methods, and it is inexpensive to implement. As SCSI became faster, problems arose with bouncing signals, interference, degradation over distance, and cross talk from adjacent signals. In addition, the length of a single-ended SCSI cable is rather limited.

To get around these problems, differential signaling was used. For a logical 0, zero voltage is sent on both wires. For a logical 1, the first wire of each signal pair contains a positive voltage, similar to the signal on an SE bus, but not necessarily at the same voltage. The second wire contains the electrical opposite of the first wire. The circuitry at the receiving device takes the difference between the two signals sent, and thus sees a relatively high voltage for a 1 and a zero voltage for a 0. Because differential signals are more expensive and use more power than those for single-ended SCSI, and because a single-ended SCSI was good enough for most users, differential signaling never became popular.

As SE signaling could not handle faster speeds and the cost of differential signaling was considered too high, another form of differential signaling was created. Low-voltage differential (LVD), which was defined in SPI-2, took the best attributes of SE and HVD signaling. Lower voltage reduced cost and power requirements. LVD devices function on a single-ended SCSI bus. LVD signaling is required for

Ultra2 or Wide Ultra2 SCSI (unless HVD is used) and is required for any SCSI method faster than Ultra2. As you might imagine, LVD has become very popular.

> *NOTE:* Since SE and HVD SCSI use very different voltage levels, they are incompatible at the electrical level. Do not mix SE or LVD devices with HVD SCSI devices on the same bus. If you do, you may damage the SE or LVD devices.

Some LVD devices can automatically switch between LVD and SE operation by detecting whether the other devices on the chain are running in SE or LVD mode. These devices are called multimode LVD devices or LVD/SE or LVD/MSE (M for multimode). Note: As soon as multimode LVD devices begin running as single-ended signaling, all the rules and restrictions of SE operations apply, including cable length.

In addition, to following the usual SCSI rules, LVD operations must meet these requirements:

- All devices on the chain must be capable of LVD; if even one device is only SE, all devices "drop down" and run as single ended.
- All devices must not be set to run in SE mode; some multimode devices have a jumper to force SE operation, which will make the entire SCSI chain unable to work in LVD.
- LVD (or multimode LVD/SE) terminators must be used.
- Singling does not support bus speeds over 20 MHz. Therefore, if you use a faster LVD/MSE device on an SE chain, it will run at a maximum of only 40 MB/s.

Currently, there are many types of SCSI cables available. Since each SCSI cable must meet the specific electrical requirements associated with the SCSI signaling speeds and signaling methods, the design of any SCSI cable is based on a combination of attributes chosen to implement a particular kind of SCSI bus. Some characteristics of the cable include the number of pins, the type of cable (internal or external), the connector type, the length of the cable, the number of connectors, spacing of the connectors on the cable, and the overall quality of the cable. In addition, some cables have a built-in terminator at the end of the cable, whereas others require the addition of a separate terminator.

Narrow cables, officially called "A" cables, are used for all narrow (8-bit) SCSI transfer modes. These are also sometimes called 50-conductor or 50-pin cables after the number of wires in the cable and pins in its connectors. They are organized into 25 pairs of two wires each. Traditionally, each pair generally consists of a signal and a signal return, which is the same as a ground line. Wide cables, officially called "P" cables, are used for 16-bit SCSI transfer modes. These are also sometimes called 68-conductor or 68-pin cables after the number of wires in the cable or pins in its connectors. Wide cables are organized into 34 pairs.

Cables are classified as single ended or low-voltage differential. LVD narrow cables are similar to SE cables, except that on LVD cables each pair consists of a positive and negative complement of the signal. In addition, one cable conductor is used to control the differential signaling. Although the SE and LVD cables use the same connectors, the LVD connectors are typically of much higher quality to accommodate the faster speeds used in LVD signaling. Therefore, it is not wise to use an SE cable for an LVD implementation. To determine if a cable is an SE cable or an LVD cable, you must look at the connectors for the appropriate icons, at written material that states, the type of cable, or at the cable itself.

External cables should be specifically rated for LVD use. Such cables have been designed and tested for LVD applications, even if they look the same as their single-ended cousins. As with regular wide cables, they may have either high-density or very-high-density connectors. Internal LVD cables are very different from SE cables. To improve signal integrity, internal LVD cables typically do not use regular flat-ribbon cabling. Instead, they use so-called twist-n-flat cabling in which adjacent pairs of wires are twisted between the connectors, and the wires "flatten out" where the connectors attach.

SCSI cables come in two distinct varieties, external and internal. External cables are used to connect SCSI devices that do not reside inside the PC; instead, they have their own enclosures and power supplies. Internal cables connect SCSI devices installed within the PC case. Internal cables are flat-ribbon cables like the cables of IDEs or floppy disk drives.

Since external cases are more affected by environmental factors such as an electromagnetic interface, external cables are shielded to protect the data from being corrupted. For example, twisted-pair wiring is used; the two wires are twisted around each other to reduce the affects of crosstalk. Crosstalk can occur if two copper wires are next to each other; the signal will induct, or transfer, from one wire to the other. By twisting the wires around each other, the electromagnetic fields cancel each other, thereby greatly reducing the crosstalk. So an external narrow cable with 50 wires actually contains 25 pairs and a 68-wire cable has 34 pairs. To reduce noise and interference, wires are shielded, or wrapped, with a metal such as aluminum or copper foil or braid. These cables are not simple to manufacture, so external SCSI cables are expensive compared with internal cables.

Even with internal cables, there are differences in construction, such as thickness of the wire and the insulation that goes over the wires. Better cables generally use Teflon as an insulation material, while cheaper ones may use polyvinyl chloride or vinyl. Regular flat cables are typically used for single-ended SCSI applications up to Ultra speeds (20 MHz). For Ultra2 or faster internal cables that use LVD signaling, the newer wires are twisted pairs, but they maintain the shape of a flat ribbon where the connectors are located.

Connectors, whether internal or external, are the physical devices that are used to attach SCSI cables to SCSI devices. There are several different types of internal connectors:

- **Regular density**—A SCSI-1 standard-defined connector for internal narrow (8-bit) devices. The regular-density cable is similar to an IDE cable connector except it is a 2-row, 50-pin connector. It is most often seen in older devices and some newer, slower drives. See Figure 2.12.
- **High density**—A SCSI-2 standard-defined connector that comes in 50-pin and 68-pin versions. Pins are spaced half the distance between the pins of the regular-density so they are much smaller. High-density connectors are the most common internal SCSI connectors used today.
- **Single connector attachment (SCA)**—An 80-contact connector typically used in RAID systems or hot-swappable drives where the drive is slid into a drive bay. Different from all of the other connectors, the SCA also includes the power for the device.

These are also different types of external connectors:

- **D-shell (D-Sub, DD)**—The earliest SCSI standard, SCSI-1, defined a 3-row, 50-pin D-shell (similar to a parallel port except for the number of rows and number of pins) for narrow SCSI implementations. This connector type was very large and cumbersome and it never became popular.
- **Centronics**—For early external connections, Centronics was defined by the SCSI-1 standard as a 50-pin connector, similar to what would be used to connect to the printer from the parallel port. In Centronics connectors, instead of thin pins, two rows of flat contracts are used. Two latches on either side are used to hold the connector in place. See Figure 2.13.
- **High-density (HD)**—SCSI-2 replaced the D-shell connectors with a high-density shielded connector. These are not much different from the older D-shell connectors, but the space between

Figure 2.12 Single-ended 50-pin SCSI ribbon cable with regular-density internal connectors (in front) and 68-pin low-voltage differential with high-density internal connectors and built-in termination

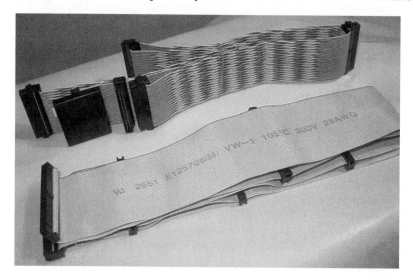

Figure 2.13   Typical SCSI connectors (Centronics and mini-SCSI port with very-high-density cable interconnect

pins was reduced, which made the connectors smaller, cheaper to make, and easier to use. These connectors use a squeeze-to-release latching mechanism.

■ **Very-high-density cable Interconnect (VHDCI)**—These 68-pin connectors are similar to Centronics connectors, but the contacts are smaller and closer together. Two of these connectors can be squeezed within the width of a single SCSI host adapter's back edge (expansion slot insert). See Figure 2.13.

As mentioned earlier, the standard SCSI interface allows up to 7 devices connected to one SCSI adapter/controller (8 devices counting the controller card). Newer SCSI interfaces allow up to 15 devices (16 devices including the controller card). Each device, including the adapter/controller card, is numbered with a SCSI identification number (ID) from 0 to 7. The numbers are selected with jumpers, DIP switches, or a thumb wheel. The SCSI adapter is usually set to ID 7. The primary SCSI hard drive or any other boot device is set to ID 0. The SCSI ID numbers do not have to be in order, nor do they have to be sequential. Of course, no two devices within the same chain can use the same SCSI ID number.

The priority that a device has on the SCSI bus is based on its ID number. For the first eight IDs, higher numbers have higher priority, so 7 is the highest and 0 the lowest. Therefore, if two devices need to be communicating on the SCSI bus, the device with the highest priority will go first and lower-priority device will wait. For Wide SCSI, the additional IDs from 8 to 15 give the highest number the highest priority, but the entire sequence is lower in priority than the numbers from 0 to 7. So the overall priority sequence for Wide SCSI is 7, 6, 5, 4, 3, 2, 1, 0, 15, 14, 13, 12, 11, 10, 9, 8.

In high-traffic settings, you typically want to set the slower devices (e.g., scanners, tape drives) to the higher-priority IDs to ensure that they are not crowded off the bus by the faster devices like hard disks. For best performance, you might consider moving the slow devices to their own SCSI controller card, as they may significantly degrade the performance of the bus. If you have devices that absolutely cannot tolerate delays in receiving their stream of data (e.g., CD recording drive or video encoder), give these devices top priority on the bus.

For older host adapters, the host adapter is the highest-priority device on the bus, which is why the host adapter stays at the default SCSI ID of 7. In addition, some older host adapters insist on having the boot device on ID 0. These older adapters also only recognized SCSI hard drives configured as SCSI ID 0 and SCSI ID 1 without loading some drivers. Typically, these types of adapters have been done away with in newer hardware.

Today, most SCSI devices use jumpers to configure the SCSI ID numbers. For a narrow bus, three jumpers are required to set the SCSI ID. To represent the SCSI ID, numbers are derived from the binary representation of the jumpers. For example, setting all three ID jumpers "off" is a binary number of 0 0 0, which would translate to an ID of 0. A binary setting of 0 0 1 equals ID 1, a setting of 0 1 0 equals 2, a setting of 0 1 1 equals 3, and so on. Of course, 1 1 1 would be 7. Unfortunately, the jumper can appear either forward or backward, depending on how the manufacturer set them up. See Tables 2.10 and 2.11.

Table 2.10 SCSI ID jumper setting with the most significant bit to the left for narrow SCSI

SCSI ID	Jumper Settings		
	4	2	1
0	0 (off)	0 (off)	0 (off)
1	0 (off)	0 (off)	1 (on)
2	0 (off)	1 (on)	0 (off)
3	0 (off)	1 (on)	1 (on)
4	1 (on)	0 (off)	0 (off)
5	1 (on)	0 (off)	1 (on)
6	1 (on)	1 (on)	0 (off)
7	1 (on)	1 (on)	1 (on)

Table 2.11 SCSI ID jumper setting with the most significant bit to the right for narrow SCSI

SCSI ID	Jumper Settings		
	1	2	4
0	0 (off)	0 (off)	0 (off)
1	1 (on)	0 (off)	0 (off)
2	0 (off)	1 (on)	0 (off)
3	1 (on)	1 (on)	0 (off)
4	0 (off)	0 (off)	1 (on)
5	1 (on)	0 (off)	1 (on)
6	0 (off)	1 (on)	1 (on)
7	1 (on)	1 (on)	1 (on)

Each SCSI device can have a number of subdevices contained within itself. The most common example is one of the new SCSI CD-ROMs that handle more than one disk at a time. Each CD is addressed as a logical unit number (LUN) of that particular device. But most devices—such as hard disks and tape drives—are only one device and will be assigned to a LUN of 0.

The two SCSI devices at either end of the chain must be terminated; the other devices should not be terminated. If only an internal cable is used, the adapter card and the device at the end of the cable need to be terminated, but the other devices in between should not be terminated. If an internal cable and an external cable are used, the two devices located at the end of each cable should be terminated. To terminate or not terminate a device, the terminators are inserted/removed or enabled/disabled with jumpers or DIP switches. Some SCSI devices can be automatically terminated. See Figures 2.14, 2.15, and 2.16.

Figure 2.14 Internal daisy chain

Terminate   Do Not   Do Not   Terminate
                   Terminate   Terminate

Figure 2.15 External daisy chain

Terminate   Do Not   Do Not   Do Not   Terminate
              Terminate   Terminate   Terminate

Figure 2.16   Internal and external daisy chain

Question: What is a terminating resistor?

Answer: Terminating resistors control the signal in the SCSI pathway. Termination is needed because when signals reach the end of a cable segment, they have a tendency to bounce back and collide with new data packets. Termination dampens these signals. It also reduces noise on the lines.

Several kinds of termination, which differ in electrical circuitry, are used on SCSI buses. Better forms of termination make for more reliable SCSI chains. The better the termination, the fewer problems (all else being equal) with the bus, although cost is generally higher. In general terms, slower buses are less particular about the kind of termination used, whereas faster buses have more demanding requirements. In addition, buses using differential signaling (either HVD or LVD) require special termination.

- **Passive terminator**—The classic, or standard, terminator is the passive terminator. The passive terminator uses special electrical resistors (220-and 330-ohm resistors for each bus line) to act as voltage dividers. Since they help ensure that the chain has the correct impedance load, these resistors prevent signals from reflecting or echoing when the signals reach the end of the chain. Passive terminating resistors work well for chains of short distances (2 to 3 feet) and slower speeds (SCSI-1 specification). The chain should never exceed 6 m. The passive terminator is for single-ended SCSI buses only, and it should only be used in narrow (8-bit) SCSI buses running at 5 MHz.
- **Active termination**—Active termination acts as voltage regulator (using 110-ohm resistors) to maintain a stable voltage through the chain by utilizing the termination power lines to compensate for voltage drops. Since active termination helps reduce noise, it allows for longer cable lengths and faster speeds. In fact, active termination is the minimum required for any of the faster-speed, single-ended SCSI buses. The chain should never exceed 18 m. Active termination is for single-ended SCSI buses only.
- **Forced perfect terminator**—The forced perfect termination (FTP) diode clamps are added to circuitry to automatically match line impedance by forcing the termination to the correct voltage, thereby allowing "perfect" termination. It is for single-ended SCSI buses only and should be used for single-ended applications that experience high levels of electrical noise.
- **High-voltage differential**—Buses using HVD signaling require use of special HVD terminators.
- **Low-voltage differential**—Newer buses using LVD signaling also require their own special type of terminators. In addition, there are special LVD/SE terminators designed for use with multimode LVD devices; these terminators can function in either LVD or SE modes. When the bus is running

in single ended mode, these terminators behave like active terminators. Note: Many internal cables have a built-in LVD terminator at the end of the cable.

NOTE: LVD/SE multimode terminators are available. They function as LVD types on an LVD bus and as active types on an SE bus. If there is any SE device on the bus, the terminator will function in SE mode and never use LVD mode, thereby severely limiting bus length and performance. If any SE-only terminators or SE devices are on the bus, the bus will default into SE mode.

While IDE drives are controlled by the system ROM BIOS, the SCSI devices are controlled by an SCSI ROM chip located on the SCSI controller card or the motherboard, if the SCSI is built into the motherboard. During boot-up, the SCSI BIOS searches and activates the individual SCSI devices, which is shown during boot-up before the operating system is loaded.

As the SCSI BIOS activates the individual SCSI devices, it usually displays a message to press a key or key combination to enter a SCSI setup program. Most of these setup programs allow you to configure the SCSI card (setting the host adapters SCSI ID, enable/disable SCSI parity checking, and host adapter SCSI termination), configure the SCSI devices (setup sync negotiation, maximum sync transfer rate, enable disconnection, and so on), and configure SCSI disk utilities (low-level format SCSI hard drives and verify disk media).

Adaptec is probably the de facto standard for SCSI adapters. This adapter works well and comes with all the necessary formatting and operating software. In addition, Windows 9x and Windows 2000 have built-in support for Adaptec SCSI adapters. For Adaptec SCSI controllers, you press Ctrl+A when instructed to do so during the POST to enter the SCSI BIOS program called SCSISelect. Note: The Adaptec host adapters are often abbreviated as AHA.

Software Interrupt 19 handles the boot function. The boot code is typically handled by the motherboard's BIOS, but it can be handled by the host adapter BIOS with some host adapters. If a host adapter does not have a BIOS or have the BIOS enabled, then hard disk drives controlled by that host adapter cannot be used to boot the system. Instead, you will have to boot from floppy disk, IDE, or another SCSI host adapter.

The hard drive can consume three or four times more power during the first few seconds after power is turned on than during normal operations. If several drives are drawing all this power at the same time, the power supply may be overloaded, which can cause the system to have intermittent start problems or to constantly reboot. Therefore, nearly all SCSI drives provide a way to delay drive spinning so that this problem does not occur. When enabled, the SCSI drive waits until it gets a command from the SCSI host adapter before spinning. It actually does this in order from highest to lowest priority. Note: This is not necessary for external hard drives because they get their power from an external power source.

SCSI parity is a limited form of error checking that helps ensure that all data transfers are reliable. Virtually all host adapters support SCSI parity checking, so this option should be enabled on every device. The only reason that you disable this feature is if some older host adapter or SCSI does not work with SCSI parity or does not have SCSI parity. Much like RAM, SCSI parity is useful but limited in its effectiveness, especially for very high transfer rates. It cannot detect if two bits changed. Therefore, starting in SPI-3, cyclic redundancy checking (CRC) was introduced to SCSI. Unlike parity that checks each byte, CRC checks an entire block of data by performing a mathematical calculation on the data to be sent.

The terminators at each end of the SCSI bus require power from at least one device on the bus. In most cases, the host adapter supplies this terminator power. If no device supplies terminator power, the bus will not be terminated correctly and will not function properly. To ensure that this is not a problem, some users configure all devices to supply terminator power.

Many SCSI adapters have a setting for the sync transfer rate (synchronous transfer rate). This determines the maximum synchronous data transfer rate that the SCSI card supports. It is usually recommended to leave the maximum (default value) of the card.

The SCSI bus can run in two modes: asynchronous (default) and synchronous. The bus actually switches modes during transfers through a protocol called synchronous negotiation. Before data are transferred across the SCSI bus, the sending device and the receiving device negotiate how the transfer will take place. If both devices support synchronous transfers, they will discover this fact through the negotiation, and the transfer will take place at the faster synchronous rate. By default, all devices today should support synchronous transfer. Unfortunately, some older devices do not respond to a request for synchronous transfer and this request can actually disable the device. Therefore, both the host adapter and devices that support synchronous negotiation usually have a jumper that can disable this feature so that it can work with older devices.

Some cards have an Initiate Wide Negotiation option. By default, the option is set to Yes, which allows 16-bit data transfers. When set to No, the SCSI card uses 8-bit data transfers, unless the SCSI device requests wide negotiation. Typically, you would want this feature enabled; you would disable it if one of your 8-bit SCSI devices causes the system to exhibit performance problems with the 16-bit data transfer rate.

The Enable Disconnection option, when set to Yes, allows the SCSI device to disconnect from the SCSI bus. Typically, you want to leave the setting at Yes if two or more SCSI devices are connected to the SCSI card. If only one SCSI device is connected, changing the setting to No results in slightly better performance.

Some adapters can support devices identified with their logical unit number (LUN). If the adapter has the BIOS Multiple LUN Support option, the default will be set to No. If the device does have multiple LUNs, then you can set this option to Yes; the SCSI card BIOS provides boot support for a SCSI device with multiple LUNs (e.g. a CD juke box contains multiple CDs that can be accessed simultaneously). You can define which device to boot from using the Boot LUN Number option. Note: If the SCSI device is old or poorly designed, it might not handle being probed and the result may be the SCSI device locking up or taking the entire SCSI bus down.

2.9.4   Hot Swappable Hard Drives

A new type of hard drive is the **hot swappable drive,** which can be removed or installed while the computer is running. The ability to hot swap a disk drive is beneficial for those computers that cannot be shut off for even a few minutes, such as network servers. Currently, SCSI drives are the only drives available that are hot swappable.

2.9.5   Partitioning and Formatting a Hard Drive

The last two steps in installing a hard drive are to partition and format the hard drive. **Partitioning** is to define and divide the physical drive into logical volumes called *partitions*. Each partition functions as if it were a separate hard disk. See Figure 2.17. The physical drive is actually installed and configured, whereas the logical drive is only a drive that the system thinks it has. Every drive must include at least one partition. The reasons to partition hard drives are to overcome operating system size limits, to use a driver more efficiently, to have multiple operating systems, and to isolate data areas.

Figure 2.17   Partitioning (before and after)

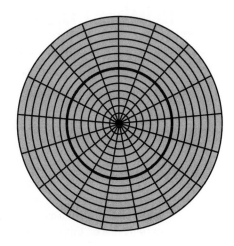

Example 2:

> You are installing and configuring a 4-GB hard drive. The first steps are to install the controller card, connect the cable, configure the hard drive, and set the CMOS setup program. If the drive requires a low-level format, it must be done with the proper software. The drive is then partitioned into two hard drives, C and D. Although one hard drive was installed, the operating system, including File Manager/Explorer, recognizes drives C and D.

The information about how a hard drive is partitioned is stored in the master boot record (MBR), which is located in the first sector of the disk. The MBR contains a small program that reads the partition table, checks which partition is active (the partition to boot from), and reads the first sector of the bootable partition.

The most common utility to partition a hard drive is the FDISK utility, which is found in DOS and Windows 9X. FDISK can create both primary and extended partitions. The primary partitions are the drives, which can be made active. The extended partitions can be used to designate logical drives, which are actually assigned the drive letter. Note that if you desire to change the partition size, then you will have to delete the partitions and re-create them. Unfortunately, all data are lost during this process. Also, Windows NT family includes a GUI program called Disk Manager or Disk Administrator.

The primary partition on the first hard drive is assigned as drive C. Any other primary partitions are assigned drive letters followed by any logical partitions. The assigned drive letters are not permanent, so, for example, if you install another hard drive and define a primary partition on that drive, it will grab the next drive letter after the first primary partition. The logical drives also are reassigned new drive letters. Unfortunately, programs configured to look under a certain drive letter to find a particular directory and/or file will not be found thus, numerous software execution errors occur.

After the drive has been partitioned, it must then be formatted. **High-level formatting** is the process of writing the file system structure (e.g., FAT, FAT32, or NTFS) on the disk so that it can be used to store programs and data. This includes creating a file allocation table (an index listing all directories and files and where they are located on the disk) and a root directory. In addition, formatting creates a volume boot sector, which is used to store the boot files of an operating system. If you format a disk (high-level format), which already has files and a directory, you will usually re-create the file allocation tables; and without the index used to find the files, the previous information is inaccessible.

During high-level formatting, the partition can be made bootable by copying the operating system's boot files such as DOS's IO.SYS, MSDOS.SYS, and COMMAND.COM. High-level formats are usually performed with the FORMAT.COM command. If the disk was not made bootable during formatting, it will have to be reformatted, which of course will lose all data on the partition, or formatting will have to be done with a special operating system utility/command such as the SYS command.

Much of the installation can be simplified with the operating system's installation disks (or CD-ROM). If no partitions are created, then the installation program will usually partition the drive. If the partitions are not formatted, then it will format them individually. In addition, it will transfer the boot files to the disk, making it bootable, and copy the operating system files to the hard drive.

2.10   COMPACT DISKS

The **compact disk (CD)** is a 4.72-inch encoded platter, which is read by laser. A CD drive is required to read a CD. Because they can hold large amounts of information (680 MB) and are inexpensive, CDs are used to distribute programs, including these:

- Operating systems (such as Windows)
- Applications software (Office, Adobe Photoshop, various encyclopedias, and most games)
- Device drivers
- Multimedia libraries (pictures, sound clips, and video clips)

Through the years, there have been different kinds of compact disks available in the market. The more common ones include the audio CD, CD-ROM, CD-R and CD-W, and DVD.

Internal CD drives are half-height devices designed to fit into a standard 5.25-inch open drive bay. Like other drives, this one is typically held in place with four screws. External drive bays sit outside of the computer. Today, most CD drives use an IDE or SCSI interface. For example, if your drive uses an IDE interface, configure the drive as either a stand-alone, master, or slave. If it uses the SCSI interface, configure the drive's SCSI ID number and its terminating resistor.

After the drives are physically installed and configured, the final steps to activating the CD drive are to load the device drivers and to configure the operating system so it recognizes the CD drive. These steps are usually done with an installation disk that comes with the CD drive and/or controller card. Some operating systems install the proper drivers automatically during installation.

Today, some system ROM BIOS chips support a bootable CD drive (El Torito standard) without loading any CD drivers. For example, you can insert a bootable compact disk in the drive and if the CMOS setup program is set to search the CD drive for a bootable disk, it will boot like a bootable A drive or C drive.

For DOS and Windows 9X machines, EIDE CD drives require a device driver to be loaded in the CONFIG.SYS, while SCSI drives usually require a device driver for the controller card and a device driver for the CD-ROM drive. The device drivers allow the operating system to control the CD-ROM drive. There are many drives available on the market, so be sure that the driver matches the CD-ROM drive.

Another driver needed to activate the CD drive is a file system extension. The file system extension enables the operating system to identify and use data from CDs that are attached to the system. For DOS, the file system extension is the Microsoft Compact Disk Extension (MSCDEX.EXE), which is loaded in the AUTOEXEC.BAT. For newer versions of Windows, the file system extension is built into the operating system. If a user boots a Windows 95 or 98 machine to Windows DOS mode, the CONFIG.SYS will have necessary device drivers but will not have the file system extension (MSCDEX.EXE) loaded. Therefore, it needs to be executed at the command prompt.

2.11   DISKLESS WORKSTATIONS

Diskless computers that have no floppy drives or disk drives are known as **diskless workstations.** Because the computer does not have a hard drive, it boots by loading the instructions within a special ROM chip on the network card, which connects to the network and loads all necessary files from it. The most obvious advantage of using a diskless workstation is its low cost compared with a fully equipped machine. Another reason to use a diskless workstation is for security. A person cannot copy sensitive files to a floppy disk or insert a floppy disk with a virus or a utility that could be used to bypass the network security.

2.12   SERVER OPTIMIZATION

When selecting components, a good starting point is to look at the minimum requirements needed to install the Windows 2000 Server or Windows Server 2003 Standard Edition on an Intel-based computer. They are as follows:

- Pentium processor running at 133 MHz or higher
- 128 MB of RAM (256 MB or higher recommended for most network environments)
- 1 GB of free disk space on the partition that contains the system files (1.5 GB for Windows Server 2003)
- VGA video card (PCI super VGA recommended) and monitor
- 3.5-inch floppy disk drive
- A CD-ROM drive (12X or faster recommended) Note: Windows 2000 could be installed over the network.
- Network card and cabling (if connected to the network)
- Microsoft mouse or other pointing device

To increase the performance of the server, look at the following components:

- Speed and number of microprocessors
- Speed and amount of RAM
- Speed of the disk subsystem
- Type and speed of the network card (discussed in Chapter 4)

Any of the previous components can cause a bottleneck. Sometimes relieving one bottleneck will cause another to occur. For example, when there is a relatively small number of clients, a 256-MB RAM configuration holds its own; but as the number of clients increases, the available cache shrinks and the file server starts to rely heavily on the disk subsystem. Adding RAM will increase the available file cache and let the server get the most out of its single processor. If the processor is saturated, however, there will be no significant improvement in performance by adding RAM. For example, if the hard drive is causing the bottleneck and you add a second processor, you only make matters worse by inundating the already overworked disk with more requests. No matter how many processors and how much RAM you add, you will not be able to increase server performance until you replace the disk subsystem with a faster one. When a server becomes overworked, an additional option would be to install another server and move some of the services from one server to the other.

How many processors and how much RAM is enough? Unfortunately, the answer depends on too many factors to provide a simple answer. Some factors include the number of clients, the type of server and type of services offered by the server, the type of files being accessed, and how the files are being accessed.

Therefore, when first installing a server, perform a best guess on hardware requirements based on prior experience. After the server is installed, keep monitoring the performance of the server to determine if any part needs to be upgraded. To monitor the server, most have intensive utilities that can help determine the server's performance and bottlenecks. For Windows 2000 and Windows Server 2003, it is Performance Monitor and Network Monitor and for Novell NetWare, it is the Monitor NLM and Novell's Lanalyzer. The Windows utilities will be discussed in detail later in this book.

For beginners and those with little experience, the author recommends the following hardware requirements for the Windows Server as a good starting point to service a moderate LAN of under 100 users:

- A minimum of a Pentium III processor running at 800 MHz or better if the main function of the server is a file-and-print server, and two Pentium III processors running at 1 GHz or better if it is a busy application server
- 1 GB of RAM (SDRAM or better). Additional RAM can increase performance since it will be used to cache local request, network request, and the file system and it will reduce the use of virtual memory.
- 4 GB of free disk space plus a generous amount for the actual files that need to be stored on disk. The disks are connected to a fast PCI SCSI controller card.
- PCI or AGP Super VGA video card and monitor
- A sufficient power supply (300 watts or larger depending on the number of drives and processors)
- 3.5-inch floppy disk drive
- CD-ROM drive (Windows could be installed over the network.)
- PCI network card and cable
- Microsoft mouse or other pointing device

To learn Windows, beginners do not need such a powerful system. When choosing equipment for a server, also avoid the newest or the fastest equipment. Buyers want to choose items that offer good performance, but it is also important to choose items that are reliable and have a good track record. Remember that a primary goal of a network is to minimize downtime.

SUMMARY

1. A computer is a machine made of electronic devices that are used to process data.
2. The performance of the server is partly based on hardware choices, hardware configuration, server function, and server load.
3. When choosing hardware components for Windows, make sure they are listed in the Microsoft Hardware Compatibility List (HCL).
4. A microprocessor, also known as the central processing unit (CPU), is an integrated circuit that acts as the brain of the computer. The clock speed is the speed at which the microprocessor executes instructions.
5. Clock speeds (frequency) are expressed in megahertz (MHz); 1 MHz is equal to 1 million cycles per second.
6. The faster the clock speed, the more instructions the microprocessor can execute per second.
7. Symmetric multiprocessing (SMP) is a computer consisting of two or more microprocessors that share the same memory.

8. Random access memory, or RAM, consists of electronic memory chips which store information inside the computer. It is so named because the information is accessed nonsequentially.

9. ROM chips in the computer provide instructions and data to the microprocessor.

10. The system ROM BIOS that controls the boot process and hardware is known as the basic input/output system (BIOS), or firmware.

11. It is important to update the system ROM BIOS before installing Windows.

12. Virtual memory is disk space pretending to be RAM, which allows the operating system to load more programs and data.

13. Virtual memory in Windows NT family is called a paging file.

14. The expansion slot, also known as the I/O bus, extends the reach of the microprocessor so that it can communicate with peripheral devices. They are called expansion slots because they allow the user to expand the system by inserting circuit boards called expansion cards.

15. When a device needs the attention of the microprocessor, it sends a signal through an interrupt line within the expansion bus to the interrupt controller.

16. The DMA controller takes over the data bus and address lines to bring data from an I/O device to the RAM without any assistance or direction from the CPU.

17. Bus mastering occurs when an expansion card with its own processor takes temporary control of the data and address bus to move information from one point to another.

18. Each device is configured to respond to a range of addresses known as ports or I/O addresses.

19. Many expansion cards use a range of memory addresses, also known as the base memory address, in the reserve memory between 640 KB and 1 MB of RAM.

20. When an expansion card is inserted into a system, it must be configured to use the proper resources. The resources include I/O addresses (including COMx/LTPx), IRQs, DMAs, and memory addresses.

21. After determining which resources the card can use, the card itself can be configured by DIP switches and/or jumpers; electronically, using a software setup program; or by using the plug-and-play (PNP) method.

22. Hard drives are half electronic and half mechanical devices, which use magnetic patterns to store information onto rotating platters. They are considered long-term storage devices because they do not forget their information when power is disconnected.

23. Hard drive performance can be measured by the access time (consisting of seek time and latency period), data transfer rate, drive RPMs, and PC data handling.

24. To increase the performance of the server, you must look at the speed and number of microprocessors, the speed and amount of RAM, the speed of the disk subsystem, and the type and speed of the network card.

25. Each IDE channel has up to one drive (stand-alone drive) or two drives (the master and slave drive).

26. When configuring SCSI drives, you must configure a unique SCSI ID number for each daisy chain and you must terminate both ends of the daisy chain.

QUESTIONS

1. Another term for microprocessor is _____.
   a. motherboard   c. CPU
   b. system unit   d. RAM

2. The main integrated chip around which the PC is built is the _____.
   a. UART   d. real-time clock
   b. processor   e. system ROM BIOS
   c. RAM

3. Computer clock speeds are expressed in _____. (Select two answers.)
   a. gigahertz   c. hertz
   b. megahertz   d. kilohertz

4. Which of the following uses a single-edge connector?
   a. Pentium   c. Pentium Pro
   b. Pentium with MMX   d. Pentium II

5. Microprocessors since the 386 microprocessor use the Intel Protection model. Which ring allows the greatest access to the CPU?
   a. 0   d. 3
   b. 1   e. 7
   c. 2

6. RAM is considered volatile memory. Which of the following best describes volatile memory?
   a. UV light is used to erase the contents of the chip.
   b. Data in RAM are permanent and cannot be erased.

   c. Data in RAM are lost when system is shut off.
   d. Data are maintained by a small battery when the power is shut off.

7. Virtual memory is _____ .
   a. extended memory pretending to be expanded memory
   b. ROM chips pretending to be memory
   c. extended memory being used for video RAM
   d. a disk pretending to be RAM

8. A small circuit board consisting of several DRAM chips and small metal contact plates, which are inserted into the motherboard, is known as a _____ . (Select two answers.)
   a. DIPP   d. SRAM
   b. SIPP   e. DIMM
   c. SIMM   f. FIMM

9. Cache memory is _____.
   a. spare storage
   b. virtual memory
   c. ultrafast memory, which buffers the microprocessor with the slower RAM
   d. shadow RAM

10. RAM cache inside the microprocessor is known as _____ .
    a. L1 cache   c. local cache
    b. fast cache   d. extended cache

11. COM1 is usually assigned which interrupt?
    - a. IRQ 1
    - b. IRQ 2
    - c. IRQ 3
    - d. IRQ 4
    - e. IRQ 9

12. The DMA channel used for the floppy controller is _____ .
    - a. DMA-1
    - b. DMA-2
    - c. DMA-3
    - d. DMA-5

13. After installing a new sound card, the system fails to boot. Which of the following could be causing the problem?
    - a. The operating system does not support the sound card.
    - b. The cables to the sound card are incorrectly connected.
    - c. There is an IRQ conflict.
    - d. None of the above

14. How many hardware interrupts does a Pentium PC have?
    - a. 4
    - b. 8
    - c. 12
    - d. 16

15. Bus mastering is similar to (a) _____ .
    - a. I/O address
    - b. IRQ
    - c. DMA
    - d. memory address
    - e. none of the above

16. The most common expansion slot found on new and old machines is _____.
    - a. MCA
    - b. EISA
    - c. ISA
    - d. PC
    - e. PCI
    - f. VESA

17. Which type of slot is the fastest?
    - a. ISA
    - b. EISA
    - c. MCA
    - d. PCI local bus
    - e. PCMCIA

18. Which of the following are *not* possible conflicts when installing an expansion card?
    - a. port conflict
    - b. I/O address conflict
    - c. IRQ conflict
    - d. power conflict
    - e. memory conflict

19. You are suspecting an IRQ conflict when installing a sound card. How would you check to see which IRQs are free?
    - a. Reboot the computer.
    - b. Install the operating system.
    - c. Run software diagnostic such as QA Plus or MSD.
    - d. Enter the CMOS setup program.

20. Which of the following describes IRQs?
    - a. an address that points to an input or output device
    - b. a line that allows access to memory without using the CPU
    - c. a line that allows the user to temporarily stop the CPU from doing something so that it can give its attention somewhere else
    - d. a line that supplies power to an interface card

21. Which of the following describes a DMA?
    - a. an address that points to an input or output device
    - b. a line that allows access to memory without using the CPU
    - c. a line that allows users to temporarily stop the CPU from doing something so that it can give its attention somewhere else
    - d. a line that supplies power to an interface card

22. The device I/O address _____ .
    - a. must be unique and correspond to a port or device
    - b. must be the same for each device
    - c. is not needed for some devices
    - d. is only needed for devices that do not require or use a DMA

23. Expansion boards are configured in which of the following ways? (Choose all that apply.)
    - a. The board may have jumpers that need to be set.
    - b. The board may have DIP switches that need to be set.
    - c. The board may require a special preprogrammed ROM chip.
    - d. The board may be configured with software.

24. When installing an expansion board, what is the best method of determining the current settings?
    - a. Run MSD to view the IRQs after the board is installed.
    - b. Consult the documentation for the board.
    - c. Systematically change the DIP switch settings on the board.
    - d. Remove all jumpers on the expansion card and reinstall them one by one until the board functions.

25. What is the standard I/O address for parallel port 1?
    - a. 3F8–3FF
    - b. 2F8–2FF
    - c. 3F0–3F7
    - d. 278–27F
    - e. 378–37F

26. What is the standard I/O address for serial port 1?
    - a. 3F8–3FF
    - b. 2F8–2FF
    - c. 3F0–3F7
    - d. 278–27F
    - e. 378–37F

27. What is meant by the term *memory address* in relation to expansion boards?
    - a. an area above 640 KB that a device can use exclusively for its operations
    - b. an address in RAM that flags the CPU to an expansion board's presence
    - c. a unique number assigned to a device to identify the expansion card to the computer
    - d. ROM memory that specifies what drivers are needed

28. An NE2000 compatible card is configured to use IRQ 3 and I/O address: 0x300. With which device would the card most likely conflict?
    - a. COM1
    - b. COM2
    - c. LPT1
    - d. LPT2

29. Pat has just installed a network adapter card in his computer, but the operating system is unable to detect the network adapter card. Which of the following is the most likely cause of the problem?
    - a. wrong protocol
    - b. resource conflict such as an IRQ or DMA conflict
    - c. faulty cable
    - d. faulty terminating resistor

30. You want to install an NE2000 network card. Which of the following IRQs is most likely free?
    - a. IRQ 3
    - b. IRQ 4
    - c. IRQ 7
    - d. IRQ 11
    - e. IRQ 14

31. A ribbon cable has a red stripe along one edge. What does this mean?
    a. This is the positive lead.
    b. This is the negative lead.
    c. The cable carries hazardous voltage.
    d. The conductor with the stripe connects to pin 1 of the connector.

32. The time it takes for the hard drive to find data is called the _____.
    a. rotational latency period   c. data transfer rate
    b. access time   d. seek time

33. The time required to position the head over the proper track is the _____ .
    a. seek time   c. latency period
    b. access time   d. data transfer rate

34. Which of the following should be done *before* replacing a hard drive?
    a. Back up the hard drive.
    b. Run the CMOS setup program.
    c. Run CHKDSK.
    d. Erase the hard drive.

35. Which program partitions a hard drive?
    a. SCANDISK   d. FDISK
    b. DISKCOPY   e. SETUP
    c. FORMAT

36. When configuring a system with preloaded software, formatting the primary hard disk will _____.
    a. improve system performance
    b. erase the partitions

    c. compress preloaded programs
    d. provide additional partition and format options

37. When replacing an IDE hard drive, you must _____ .
    a. set the ID jumper on the drive
    b. set the master/slave jumper on the drive
    c. set the speed jumper on the drive
    d. set the speed jumper on the motherboard

38. How many devices does EIDE support?
    a. 2   c. 7
    b. 4   d. 8

39. Which of the following IRQs would probably be free so that it can be used by a SCSI card if the system has a standard IDE controller card? (Choose two answers.)
    a. IRQ 7   d. IRQ 14
    b. IRQ 6   e. IRQ 15
    c. IRQ 10

40. When installing a SCSI CD-ROM drive, you must configure the drive's _____. (Choose all that apply.)
    a. terminating resistors
    b. SCSI ID number
    c. stand-alone, master, or slave jumpers
    d. frequency modulation

HANDS-ON EXERCISES

Exercise 1: Identify the CPU

Note: When performing this exercise, follow an ESD program and use an ESD-grounded strap.

1. What kind of CPU do you have?
2. Look to see how pin A1 is designated on the motherboard and on the CPU.
3. If the microprocessor has a heat sink, carefully remove it.
4. If the microprocessor is not soldered onto the motherboard, carefully remove it from the motherboard. Be careful to not bend or mangle the pins of the microprocessors.
5. Reinsert the microprocessor, reinstall the heat sink, and test the system.

Exercise 2: Identify the Ram Chips and Ram Cache Chips

Note: When performing this exercise, follow an ESD program and use an ESD-grounded strap.

1. Open your computer.
2. Remove the RAM chips.
3. Identify the size and speed of each RAM chip.
4. Reinsert the RAM chips.
5. Identify the RAM cache on the motherboard (if any).
6. Identify the microprocessor on the motherboard. Does the microprocessor have any internal L1 or L2 RAM cache? If yes, how much cache memory does the microprocessor have?

Exercise 3: Using Diagnostic Software

Using diagnostic software, such as QA Plus or Checkit Pro, answer the following questions.

1. Which device is actually using IRQ 4?
2. Which device is actually using IRQ 5?
3. Which device is actually using IRQ 7?
4. Which device is actually using IRQ 11?
5. Which device is actually using DMA-2?
6. Which device is actually using DMA-3?

Exercise 4: Using the Operating System Internal Software

Using DOS's Microsoft Diagnostic (MSD), Windows 95/98's system icon within the control panel, or Windows NT's Microsoft Diagnostic software, answer the following questions.

1. Which device is actually using IRQ 4?
2. Which device is actually using IRQ 5?
3. Which device is actually using IRQ 7?
4. Which device is actually using IRQ 11?
5. Which device is actually using DMA-2?
6. Which device is actually using DMA-3?

Exercise 5: Configuring a Modem or I/O Card

Note: When performing this exercise, follow an ESD program and use an ESD-grounded strap.

1. Make sure the computer is off. If your system has a modem, remove it.
2. By looking at the back of the computer, how many serial ports does your system have?
3. Turn on the computer. If you have a COM1 and a COM2, by running some form of diagnostic software that shows hardware resources, what are the IRQs for COM1 and COM2?
4. Install the mouse to COM1 and load the mouse driver in the appropriate configuration file.
5. Test the mouse to make sure that it is working properly.
6. Shut off the computer. By looking at the modem's documentation, set the modem to COM1 and insert the modem card into an available expansion slot.
7. Turn on the computer. Test the mouse. Does the mouse work? If not, what is the problem?
8. Shut off the computer. Using the I/O controller card documentation or the motherboard documentation if the serial ports are part of the motherboard, disable COM2. Note: If the serial ports are part of the motherboard, it is probably done with the CMOS setup program.
9. If possible, use the modem documentation to change the modem to COM2 and use the same IRQ as the mouse. Remember that the mouse is plugged into COM1.
10. Turn on the computer. Test the mouse. Does the mouse work? If not, what is the problem?
11. Shut off the computer. Using the modem documentation, change the modem's IRQ to an available one. Hint: Use the IRQ that is standard for COM2.
12. Turn on the computer. Test the mouse again. Does the mouse work?
13. Shut off the computer and remove the modem.
14. Enable COM2 on the I/O controller card and reinsert the card into the expansion slot.
15. Turn on the computer and test the mouse to make sure it is working properly.

Exercise 6: Installing a Network Card

Note: When performing this exercise, follow an ESD program and use an ESD-grounded strap.

1. By using some form of software diagnostic, determine which I/O address, IRQs, DMAs, and memory address are available to install the network card.
2. By reading the network card documentation, configure the card to an available I/O address, IRQ, DMA, and memory address (if needed).
3. Insert the card in the expansion slot.
4. Turn on the computer. Did it boot?
5. If the card is plug-and-play, determine what resources the card is using.

Exercise 7: Install an IDE Hard Drive

Note: When performing this exercise, follow an ESD program and use an ESD-grounded strap.

1. Ensure that the computer can boot to drive C.
2. With the CMOS setup program, record the drive type, number of tracks, number of read/write heads, number of sectors per track, and hard drive mode (if any).
3. Using the FDISK utility, view the partitions (option 4). Look for the number and the type of partitions.

```
                        Microsoft Windows 98
                      Fixed Disk Setup Program
                 (C)Copyright Microsoft Corp. 1983-1998


                          FDISK Options


Current fixed disk drive: 1

Choose one of the following:

1. Create DOS partition or Logical DOS Drive
2. Set active partition
3. Delete partition or Logical DOS Drive
4. Display partition information

Enter choice: [4]

Press Esc to exit FDISK
```

```
                   Display Partition Information

Current fixed disk drive: 1

Partition      Status      Type      Volume Label      MB      System      Usage
C: 1           A           PRI DOS                      1039    FAT16       50%
   2                       EXT DOS                      1024    FAT32       50%

Total disk space is 2067 MB (1 MB = 1048576 bytes)

The Extended DOS Partition contains Logical DOS Drives.
Do you want to display the logical drive information (Y/N)......?[Y]

Press Esc to return to FDISK Options
```

4. Using the FDISK utility, delete all partitions (option 3) by deleting any logical partitions, then deleting the extended partition, and then deleting the primary partition. Lastly, delete any non-DOS partitions.

```
               Delete DOS Partition or Logical DOS Drive

Current fixed disk drive: 1

Choose one of the following:

1. Delete Primary DOS Partition
2. Delete Extended DOS Partition
3. Delete Logical DOS Drive(s) in the Extended DOS Partition
4. Delete Non-DOS Partition

Enter choice: [3]

Press Esc to return to FDISK Options
```

5. After the partitions are deleted, press the ESC key several times until it asks to insert a system disk.
6. If the drive is set to a type 47, type 48, or user-definable type, set the number of tracks, number of read/write heads, and number of sectors per track to zero.
7. Go into the CMOS setup program and set the drive C to Type 1.
8. Save the changes to the CMOS setup program and shut down the computer.
9. Shut off the computer. Disconnect the power cable and remove the hard drive, cable, and controller card from the system. Look to see how the cable, particularly pin 1, is connected to the card and the drive.
10. Reinstall the hard drive, cable, and controller into the system and connect the power to the hard drive.
11. Set the proper CMOS settings for the hard drive.
12. Try to boot the computer with the C drive. Record the error message.
13. Boot the computer with the A drive.
14. Run FDISK to create (option 1) a primary DOS partition. Do not maximize the partition and do not make it active. Specify the size of the primary DOS partition to be 75%. Note: You must include the % sign or it will create the partition of 75 MB instead of 75%.

```
                    Create DOS Partition or Logical DOS Drive

Current fixed disk drive: 1

Choose one of the following:

1. Create Primary DOS Partition
2. Create Extended DOS Partition
3. Create Logical DOS Drive(s) in the Extended DOS Partition

Enter choice: [1]

Press Esc to return to FDISK Options
```

15. Go back to the main menu. Notice the warning at the bottom of the screen.
16. Use the rest of the free disk space to create an extended DOS partition. Assign one logical drive (drive D).
17. Press the ESC key until it asks to insert a system disk.
18. Boot the computer using drive C. Record the error message.
19. Using FDISK, make the primary DOS partition active (option 2).
20. Boot the computer using drive C. Record the error message.
21. Boot the computer using drive A. Switch over to the C drive. Perform a DIR command. Record the error message.
22. Use the Abort/Fail option to move back to the A drive.
23. Boot the computer using drive A. Format the hard drive, but do not make it bootable.
24. Boot the computer using drive C and record the error message.
25. Boot the computer using drive A. Make the hard drive bootable with either a FORMAT command or a SYS command.
26. Format the D drive.
27. Boot the computer using drive C.
28. Using the CMOS setup program, reduce the number of cylinders by 50% and double the number of read/write heads. Note: You may need to use a user-definable type if you are not already doing so. Save the changes.
29. Boot the computer using drive C. Record any error messages or if it fails to boot.
30. Using the CMOS setup program, put back the original settings.
31. Boot the computer to drive C.
32. Shut off the computer. Remove the cable connector from the hard drive and place it on backwards.
33. Boot the computer using drive C. Record any error messages or if it fails to boot.
34. Shut off the computer. Reconnect the cable properly.
35. Disconnect the gray ribbon cable.
36. Boot the computer to drive C. Record any error messages or if it fails to boot.
37. Shut off the computer. Reconnect the gray ribbon cable and disconnect the power connector.
38. Boot the computer to drive C. Record any error messages or if it fails to boot.
39. Shut off the computer. Reconnect the power cable.
40. Go into the CMOS setup program and set the drive D to a Type 1 drive.
41. Boot the computer to drive C. Record any error messages or if it fails to boot.
42. Go into the CMOS setup program and disable the drive D.
43. Ensure that the computer boots properly.

Exercise 8: Install a Second IDE Hard Drive

Note: When performing this exercise, follow an ESD program and use an ESD-grounded strap.

1. Ensure that the computer can boot to drive C.
2. With the CMOS setup program, record the drive type, number of tracks, number of read/write heads, and number of sectors per track.
3. Shut off the computer. Remove the hard drive, which is already in the computer. Examine the jumpers on the hard drive. It should be set to a stand-alone hard drive.
4. Set the jumpers on the original hard drive to master and on the second hard drive as slave.
5. Connect both hard drives to the cable and connect the power cables.
6. Set the CMOS parameters for drives C and D.
7. Boot the computer using drive C.
8. Using FDISK, switch to the second hard drive (option 5). Create a primary DOS partition (option 1).
9. Press the ESC key until it asks to insert a system disk.
10. Boot the computer using drive C. Change over to the D drive. Remember that all primary partitions are given drive letters first.
11. Use the Abort/Fail option to move back to the A drive. Format the D drive.
12. Change to the E drive, which should be the extended DOS partition on the first hard drive.
13. Remove the second hard drive.
14. Change the first drive back to a stand-alone drive.
15. Disable the drive D in the CMOS setup program.
16. Ensure that the computer boots properly.

Exercise 9: Installing a SCSI Hard Drive

Note: When performing this exercise, follow an ESD program and use an ESD-grounded strap.

1. Remove any IDE drives from your system.
2. Disable the drive C in the CMOS setup program.
3. Set the resources of the SCSI expansion card. Use the card's documentation and software diagnostic to determine I/O addresses, IRQs, and DMA.
4. Locate the terminating resistors on the SCSI expansion card. Make sure that they are installed and enabled.
5. If the SCSI controller card has a floppy disk drive controller and one already exists in the computer, disable the one on the SCSI controller card.
6. Install the SCSI controller.
7. Using the drive's documentation, set the boot drive to SCSI ID 0. Make sure that the terminating resistor is installed and enabled.
8. Install the boot drive to the end of the chain (cable) and connect the power.
9. Using the drive's documentation, set a second SCSI hard drive or an SCSI CD-ROM to SCSI ID 5.
10. Disable or remove the terminating resistor on the second drive.
11. Connect the second drive to the middle of the chain and connect the power.
12. Boot the computer using drive A.
13. Create a primary DOS partition. Use the entire drive for the partition and make it active.
14. Format the hard drive and make it bootable.
15. Using the correct software, low-level format the first SCSI hard drive.
16. Remove all SCSI drives including the controller card.
17. Reinstall the IDE hard drive.
18. Enter the correct parameters in the CMOS setup program.
19. Ensure that the computer boots properly.

Exercise 10: Installing an IDE CD-ROM Drive

Note: When performing this exercise, follow an ESD program and use an ESD-grounded strap.

1. Configure the IDE CD-ROM drive as either a master, slave, or stand-alone, as appropriate.
2. If the system already has an IDE device, configure the device as either a master, slave, or stand-alone, as appropriate.
3. Connect the CD to the appropriate IDE channel.
4. Boot the system and install the appropriate drivers for the CD drive.

5. Insert a CD into the drive and test it.

6. Remove the CD-ROM drive and reconfigure the system.

Exercise 11: Installing a SCSI CD-ROM Drive

Note: When performing this exercise, follow an ESD program and use an ESD-grounded strap.

1. Configure the SCSI drive's SCSI ID number and terminating resistors.

2. Connect the CD to the appropriate SCSI connector.

3. Boot the system and install the appropriate drivers for the CD drive.

4. Insert a CD into the drive and test it.

5. Remove the CD-ROM drive and reconfigure the system.

Exercise 12: Motherboard BIOS Upgrade

1. Go to the motherboard manufacturer's website.

2. Find and download the newest BIOS update program or file to update the motherboard system ROM BIOS.

3. Find the instructions on how to update/flash the BIOS and update the BIOS. Note: when updating the BIOS, it is very important that you do not shut off the computer or interrupt the computer in any way until the update is complete. If not, the motherboard will not boot and you would have to replace the BIOS chip or motherboard.

Exercise 13: Internet Research

1. Find the CMOS parameters for the Western Digital Caviar AC33200 (3.2-GB EIDE) hard drive.

2. Find the jumper settings to make the Western Digital Caviar AC33200 (3.2-GB EIDE) a master drive.

3. Find the jumper settings to make the Western Digital Caviar AC33200 (3.2-GB EIDE) a slave drive.

4. Find the jumper settings to make a Seagate ST-11900N (1.7-GB SCSI hard drive) SCSI ID 0.

5. Find the jumper settings to make a Seagate ST-11900N (1.7-GB SCSI hard drive) SCSI ID 5.

6. Find how to terminate the resistance on a Seagate ST-11900N (1.7-GB SCSI hard drive).

7. Find and download the software to make a Seagate Medallist Pro hard drive to overcome certain system BIOS and operating system limitations.

8. Find and download the Windows NT driver for the AHA-2940 SCSI card.

9. Find and download the installation guide for the Adaptec 2940 Ultra SCSI card.

CHAPTER **3**

The OSI Model

Topics Covered in This Chapter

Introduction

In the early days of networking, networking software was created in a haphazard fashion. When networks grew in popularity, the need to standardize the by-products of network software and hardware became evident. Standardization allows vendors to create hardware and software systems that can communicate with one another, even if the underlying architecture is dissimilar. For example, you can run the TCP/IP protocol to access the Internet on either an IBM-compatible PC that is running Windows or on an Apple Macintosh that is running System 8.

Objectives

- Explain the need for standardization in networks.
- List the differences between the de jure and the de facto standard.
- Describe the OSI model and how it relates to networks.
- List and define the layers of the OSI model.
- Define the communication devices that communicate at each level of the OSI model.
- Describe the various addresses and ports and how they relate to networks.
- Define a virtual circuit.
- Define a session and explain how it relates to networks.

- List and define the types of dialogs.
- List and define the 802 Project standards.
- Given a network device, specify the layer of the OSI model that the device works at.
- Define *signaling, modulation,* and *encoding.*
- Define *bandwidth* and compare baseband and broadband.
- List and describe the different connection services.
- Compare the implications of using connection-oriented communications with connectionless communications.

3.1   THE NEED FOR STANDARDIZATION

To overcome compatibility issues, hardware and software often follow **standards** (dictated specifications or the most popular specifications). Standards exist for operating systems, data formats, communication protocols, and electrical interfaces. If a product does not follow a popular standard, it usually will not be widely accepted in the computer market and will often cause problems within a PC. As far as the user is concerned, standards help determine what hardware and software to purchase, and they allow the user to customize a network made of components from different manufacturers.

As new technology is introduced, manufacturers are usually rushing to get their products out so that their products have a better chance of becoming the standard. Often, competing computer manufacturers introduce similar technology at the same time. Until one is designated as the standard, other companies and customers are sometimes forced to take sides. Since it is sometimes difficult to determine what will emerge as the true standard, and the technology sometimes needs time to mature, it is best to wait and see what happens.

There are two main types of standards. The first is called the de jure standard. The **de jure standard,** or the bylaw standard, is dictated by an appointed committee such as the International Organization for Standardization for (ISO). Some common standard committees are shown in Table 3.1. The second type is the de facto standard. The **de facto standard** or "from the fact" standard is accepted by the industry because of its commonality. Such standards are not recognized by a standard committee. For example, the de facto standard for microprocessors is produced by Intel and the de facto standard for sound cards is produced by Creative Labs.

Table 3.1   Common standard committees

American National Standards Institute (ANSI) http://www.ansi.org	ANSI is primarily concerned with software. ANSI has defined standards for several programming languages including C Language and the SCSI interface.
International Telecommunications Union (ITU) http://www.itu.int/	ITU defines international standards, particularly communications protocols, and was formerly called the Comité Consultatif Internationale Télégraphique et Téléphonique (CCITT).
Institute of Electrical and Electronic Engineers (IEEE) http://www.ieee.org	IEEE sets standards for most types of electrical interfaces including RS-232C (serial communication interface) and network communications.
International Organization for Standardization (ISO) http://www.iso.ch/	ISO is an international standard for communications and information exchange.
Electronic Industry Alliance (EIA) http://www.eia.org	EIA is a Trade Organization composed of representatives from electronics manufacturing firms across the United States. EIA is divided into several subgroups: Telecommunications Industry Association(TIA); Consumer Electronics Manufacturers Association(CEA); Joint Electron Device Engineering Council(JEDEC); Solid State Technology Association, the Government Division; and Electronic Information Group (EIG).

When a system or standard has an **open architecture,** it indicates that the specification of the system or standard is public. This includes both approved standards and privately designed architecture whose specifications are made public by the designers. The advantage of an open architecture is that anyone can design products based on the architecture and can design add-on products for it. This type also allows other manufacturers to duplicate the product, however.

The opposite of an open architecture is a proprietary system. A **proprietary system** is privately owned and controlled by a company and has not divulged specifications that would allow other companies to duplicate the product. Proprietary architectures often do not allow mixing and matching products from different manufacturers and may cause hardware and software compatibility problems.

3.2   OSI REFERENCE MODEL

With the goal of standardizing the network world, the **International Organization for Standardization (ISO)** began development of the **Open Systems Interconnection (OSI) reference model**. The key reason that ISO released the OSI model was so that different vendor networks could work with each other. Since the ISO model separated the various functions, the vendor did not have to write an entire protocol stack. A vendor can write device drivers for its device and not worry about higher layers, and the work can be contained and modularized. Thus, the process of bringing a product to market is faster, as it minimizes code that a vendor needs to write. The OSI reference model was completed and released in 1984.

Today, the OSI reference model is the world's prominent networking architecture model. It is a popular tool for learning about networks. The OSI protocols, on the other hand, have had a long "growing up period." While OSI implementations are not unheard of, the OSI protocols have not yet attained the popularity of many proprietary and de facto standards.

The OSI reference model adopts a layered approach in which a communication subsystem is broken down into seven layers, each one of which performs a well-defined function. The OSI reference model defines the functionality that needs to be provided at each layer, but it does not specify actual services and protocols to be used at each one of these layers. From this reference model, actual protocol architecture can be developed. See Figure 3.1 and Table 3.2.

Figure 3.1   The OSI reference model

OSI Reference Model

Application
Concerned with the support of end-user application processes

- Supports the local operating system via a redirector/shell
- Provides access for different file systems
- Provides common application programming interfaces (APIs) for file, print, and message services
- Defines common data syntax and semantics
- Converts to format required by computer via data encoding and conversion functions

Presentation
Provides for the representation of the data

Session
Performs administrative tasks and security

- Establishes sessions between services
- Handles logical naming services
- Provides checkpoints for resynchronization

Transport
Ensures end-to-end error-free delivery

- Break up blocks of data on send or reassembles on receive
- Has end-to-end flow control and error recovery
- Provides a distinct connection for each session

Network
Responsible for addressing and routing between subnetworks

- Forms internetwork by providing routing functions
- Defines end-to-end addressing (logical – Net ID + Host ID)
- Provides connectionless datagram services

Data Link
Responsible for the transfer of data over the channel

- Sends frames on network; turns received bits into frames
- Defines the station address (physical); provides link management
- Provides error detection across the physical segment

Physical
Handles physical signaling, including connectors, timing, voltages, and other matters

- Provides access to the media
- Defines voltages and data rates for sending binary data
- Defines physical connectors

Table 3.2   Common technologies as they relate to the OSI model

OSI Model	TCP/IP	Novell NetWare	Microsoft Windows
Application	FTP, SMTP, Telnet	NDS	SMB
Presentation	ASCII, MPEG, GIF, JPEG	NCP	NetBIOS
Session		SAP	NetBEUI
Transport	TCP, UDP	SPX	NetBEUI
Network	IP	IPX	NetBEUI
Data Link	Ethernet, 802.3, 802.5, FDDI, Frame Relay, ISDN	Ethernet, 802.3, 802.5, FDDI, Frame Relay, ISDN	Ethernet, 802.3, 802.5, FDDI, Frame Relay, ISDN
Physical	10BaseT, 100BaseT, UTP 4/16 Unshielded Twisted Pair, SONET	10BaseT, 100BaseT, UTP 4/16 Unshielded Twisted Pair, SONET	10BaseT, 100BaseT, UTP 4/16 Unshielded Twisted Pair, SONET

ISO has defined internationally standardized protocols for each one of the seven layers. The seven layers are divided into three separate groups: application-oriented layers (upper layers), an intermediate layer, and network-oriented (lower) layers.

When a computer needs to communicate with another computer, it starts with a network service, which is running in the application layer. The actual data that need to be sent are generated by the

An easy way to remember the order of the OSI Reference Model involves mnemonics:						
Bottom to top						
Please	Do	Not	Take	Sales	Peoples	Advice
Physical	Data Link	Network	Transport	Session	Presentation	Application
Top to bottom						
All	People	Seem	To	Need	Data	Processing
Application	Presentation	Session	Transport	Network	Data Link	Physical

Figure 3.2 Layer interaction of the OSI reference model

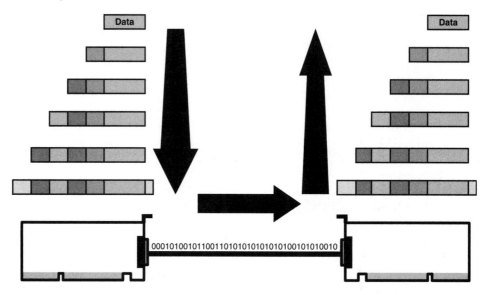

software and are sent to the presentation layer. The presentation layer then adds its own control information, called a header, which contains the presentation layer's requests and/or information. The data packet then is sent to the session layer where another header is added. The data packet keep going down the OSI model until it reaches the physical layer, which means that the data are sent on the network media by the network interface card (NIC). See Figure 3.2. The concept of placing data behind headers (and before trailers) for each layer is called **encapsulation.**

When the data packet gets to the destination computer, the NIC sends the data packet to the data link layer. The data link layer then strips the first header off. As it goes up the model, each header is stripped away until it reaches the application layer. At this time, only the original data are left and they are processed by the network service.

What is so great about this OSI system is that it allows you to communicate with different computer systems. For example, a Windows NT server can send information to a UNIX server or an Apple Macintosh client.

Let's follow the steps of communication between two computers from initial contact to data delivery. A computer wants to request a file. The process starts with a network application on the client computer. Before the request can be made, the client has to first determine the address of the computer. Therefore, it sent a request out to resolve a computer name to a network address.

If the client already knows the server's network address, it makes its request in the form of a data packet and sends it to a presentation layer protocol. The presentation protocol encrypts and compresses the packet and sends it to a session layer protocol, which establishes a connection with the server. During this time, the packet includes the type of dialog, such as half-duplex connection (discussed later in this chapter), and determines how long the computer can transmit to the server. The session protocol then sends the packet to the transport layer, which divides the packet into smaller packets so that they can be sent over the physical network. The transport layer protocol then sends the packets to the network layer where the source network and destination network addresses are added. It then sends the packets to a data link layer so that it can add the source and destination address and the port number that identifies the service requested and prepare the packets to be sent over the media. As you can see in Figure 3.2, the packet is bigger than when it started. The packet is then converted to electrical or electromagnetic signals that are sent on the network media.

When the packets get to the destination server, the NIC sees the signals and interprets the signals as 0s and 1s. It takes the bits and groups them together into frames. The NIC then determines the destination address of the packet to see if the packet was meant for the server. After the server has determined that it was, it removes the data link header and sends the packet up to the network layer. The network layer sends the packet to the transport layer. If the data packets have reached the server out of order, the transport layer protocol puts them back into proper order, merges them into one larger packet, and sends the packet to the appropriate session layer protocol. The session layer protocol authenticates the user and sends the packet to the presentation layer protocol. The presentation layer protocol decompresses, decrypts, and reformats the packet so that it can be read by the application layer protocol. The application layer protocol reads the request and takes the appropriate steps to fulfill the request.

Before the packet is actually sent, the sending computer must determine if the packet is to go to another computer within the same network or to a computer in another network. If it is a local network, the packets are sent to the computer. If it has to go to another network, the packet is sent to a router. The router determines the best way to get the packet to its destination and sends the packet from one router to another until it gets to the destination network. If one network route is congested, the router can reroute the packet another way, and if it detects errors, it can slow down the transmission of the packets in the hope that the link will become more reliable.

In reality, encapsulation does not occur for all seven layers. Layers 5 through 7 use headers during initialization, but in most data flows, there is no specific layer 5, 6, or 7 header. This is so because there is no new information to exchange for every flow of data. Therefore, layers 5, 6, and 7 can be grouped together, and the layers actually used can be simplified into 5 layers: application (equivalent to the application, presentation, and session layers), transport, Internet (equivalent to the network layer), network interface (equivalent to the data link layer), and physical layer. See Figure 3.3.

When encapsulation with TCP/IP is used, the order in which information blocks are created is data, segments, packets, frames, and bits. The user application creates the data and a variety of parameters and passes the segment to the network layer. The network layer places the destination network address in a header, puts the data behind it, and transmits a packet, or datagram, to the data link layer. The data link layer creates the data link header, which includes the destination media access control (MAC) address. The datagram is converted to a frame and is passed to the physical layer. The physical layer transmits the bits. See Figure 3.4.

Figure 3.3   Encapsulation that actually occurs on today's networks

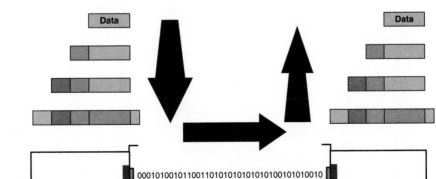

Figure 3.4 Information blocks associated with the simplified OSI model

| Application Layer |
| Transport Layer |
| Network Layer |
| Data Link Layer |
| Physical Layer |

User Data

Flow Control, Sequencing, and Error Checking Information

Segments

Logical Addressing Information

Packets/Datagrams

Data Framing and Physical Addressing Information — Error Control

Frames

0101010110101 Bits

Figure 3.5 A network request going through the simplified OSI model

Data — Word Processor Application open file request to server — Local File System Services — Data

Client/Redirector — Server Service (File and Print Sharing)

Network Protocol — Network Protocol

NIC Driver — NIC Driver

0001010010110011010101010101010100101010010

Many protocols have the destination computer send back an acknowledgment stating that the packet arrived intact. If the source computer does not receive an acknowledgement after a certain amount of time, it resends the packet.

Example 1:

Let's say you are running a word processor and decide to access a file that is located on a remote computer's shared directory. A shared directory is a directory on a computer that provides the directory to clients over the network. You click on the open button so that you can view the files of the remote computer. The word processor initiates the entire process by generating a network request. The request is sent through a client/redirector, which forwards the request to the network protocol, such as TCP/IP. The data packet is then forwarded to the NIC driver and sent out through the network card where it is send through the network to the remote computer. Of course, as the request is being sent from the word processor to the network card, the request becomes bigger as the packet is encapsulated. See Figure 3.5.

When the packet is received at the remote computer, it is processed by the driver on the remote computer. It is then forwarded to the network protocol, which forwards it to the server service (file and print sharing). The server service uses the local file system services to access the file. As the packet goes from the network card to the local file system services, the packet is stripped back to the original request. The file is then sent back to the requesting computer.

3.3   BITS AND BYTE

The most commonly used numbering system is the **decimal number system.** In a decimal numbering system, each position contains 10 different possible digits. Since there are 10 different possible digits, the decimal number system consists of numbers with base 10. These digits are 0,1, 2, 3, 4, 5, 6, 7, 8 and 9. In order to count values larger than 9, each position away from the decimal point in a decimal number increases in value by a multiple of 10. See Table 3.3.

Example 2:

Decimal number: 234

2	3	4
2×10^2	3×10^1	4×10^0
200	30	4

Therefore, the value is $200 + 30 + 4 = 234$.

3.3.1   Binary Number System

The **binary number system** is another way to count. The binary system is less complicated than the decimal system because it has only two digits, a zero (0) and a one (1). A computer represents a binary value with an electronic switch known as a transistor. If the switch is on, it allows current to flow through a wire or metal trace to represent a binary value of one (1). If the switch is off, it does not allow current to flow through a wire, representing a value of zero (0). See Table 3.4. The on switch is also referred to as a high signal, while the off switch is referred to as a low signal.

If you use two wires to represent data, the first switch can be on or off and the second switch can be on or off, which gives you a total of four combinations, or four binary values. See Table 3.5. If you use four wires to represent data, you can represent 16 different binary values. See Table 3.6.

Each switch represents two values, so each switch used doubles the number of binary values. Therefore, the number of binary values can be expressed with the following equation:

$$\text{Number of Binary Numbers} = 2^{\text{Number of Binary Digits}}$$

One wire allows $2^1 = 2$ binary numbers, 0 and 1. Two wires allow $2^2 = 4$ binary numbers, 0,1, 2, and 3. Four wires allow $2^4 = 16$ binary numbers.

> **Question:** How many values does 8 bits represent?
>
> **Answer:** Since a byte has 8 binary digits, a byte can represent $2^8 = 256$ characters.

Much like decimal numbers, binary digits have placeholders that represent certain values, as shown in Table 3.7.

Table 3.3   Decimal number system

7th Place	6th Place	5th Place	4th Place	3rd Place	2nd Place	1st Place
10^6	10^5	10^4	10^3	10^2	10^1	10^0
1,000,000	100,000	10,000	1,000	100	10	1

Table 3.4   One-digit binary number

Wire 1	Binary Equivalent	Decimal Equivalent
Off	0	0
On	1	1

Table 3.5   Two-digit binary number

Wire 1	Wire 2	Binary Equivalent	Decimal Equivalent
Off	Off	00	0
Off	On	01	1
On	Off	10	2
On	On	11	3

Table 3.6   Four-digit binary number

Wire 1	Wire 2	Wire 3	Wire 4	Binary Equivalent	Decimal Equivalent
Off	Off	Off	Off	0000	0
Off	Off	Off	On	0001	1
Off	Off	On	Off	0010	2
Off	Off	On	On	0011	3
Off	On	Off	Off	0100	4
Off	On	Off	On	0101	5
Off	On	On	Off	0110	6
Off	On	On	On	0111	7
On	Off	Off	Off	1000	8
On	Off	Off	On	1001	9
On	Off	On	Off	1010	10
On	Off	On	On	1011	11
On	On	Off	Off	1100	12
On	On	Off	On	1101	13
On	On	On	Off	1110	14
On	On	On	On	1111	15

Table 3.7   Binary number system

8th Place	7th Place	6th Place	5th Place	4th Place	3rd Place	2nd Place	1st Place
2^7	2^6	2^5	2^4	2^3	2^2	2^1	2^0
128	64	32	16	8	4	2	1

Example 3:

Convert the binary number 11101010 to a decimal number.

1	1	1	0	1	0	1	0
1×2^7	1×2^6	1×2^5	0×2^4	1×2^3	0×2^2	1×2^1	0×2^0
128	64	32	0	8	0	2	0

Therefore, the binary number of 11101010 is equal to the decimal number of 128+64+32+8+2=234.

Example 4:

Convert the decimal number 234 to a binary number. Referring to Table 3.7, you can see that the largest power of 2 that subtracts from 234 is 2^7 (128). This leaves the value of 234 –128 = 106. The largest power of 2 that subtracts from 106 is 2^6 (64). This leaves a value of 106–64 = 42. The largest power of 2 that subtracts from 42 is 2^5 (32), which gives 42–32 = 10. The largest power of 2 that subtracts from 10 is 2^3 (8), which gives 10–8 = 2. The largest power of 2 that fits into 2 is 2^1 (2), which gives 2–2 = 0.
Therefore, the binary equivalent is 11101010:

$$
\begin{array}{rl}
234 & \\
-128 & 2^7 \\
\hline
106 & \\
-64 & 2^6 \\
\hline
42 & \\
-32 & 2^5 \\
\hline
10 & \\
-8 & 2^3 \\
\hline
2 & \\
-2 & 2^1 \\
\hline
0 &
\end{array}
$$

1	1	1	0	1	0	1	0
2^7	2^6	2^5	2^4	2^3	2^2	2^1	2^0

In computers, one switch is known as a **bit**. When several bits are combined together, they can signify a letter, a digit, a punctuation mark, a special graphical character, or a computer instruction. Eight bits make up a **byte**. Since bytes are small units, they are measured as Kilobytes (KB), megabytes (MB), and gigabytes (GB), and terabytes (TB). The prefix *kilo* indicates a thousand, *mega* indicates a million, *giga* indicates a billion, and *tera* indicates a trillion. With computers, the measurement is not exact. A kilobyte is actually 1024 bytes, not 1000. This is because 2^{10} is equal to 1024. A megabyte is 1024 kilobytes, a gigabyte is 1024 megabytes, a terabyte is 1024 gigabytes.

> 1 kilobyte = 1024 bytes
> 1 megabyte = 1024 kilobytes = 1,048,576 bytes
> 1 gigabyte = 1024 megabytes = 1,048,576 kilobytes = 1,073,741,824 bytes
> 1 terabyte = 1024 gigabytes = 1,048,576 megabytes
>   = 1,073,741,824 kilobytes = 1,099,511,627,776 bytes

3.3.2   Hexadecimal Number System

The **hexadecimal number system** has 16 digits. One hexadecimal digit is equivalent to a 4-digit binary number (4 bits or a nibble) and 2 hexadecimal digits represent a byte (8 bits). Thus, it is easy to translate between the hexadecimal and binary systems. The hexadecimal system is used primarily as a "shorthand" way of displaying binary numbers. See Table 3.8. To designate a number as a hexadecimal, the letter "H" is often used at the end. To count values larger than 15, each position away from the decimal point in a decimal number increases in value by a multiple of 16. See Table 3.9.

> **Question:** What is the hexadecimal number of the binary number of 1001 1010?
> **Answer:** Since 1001 is equivalent to 9 and 1010 is equivalent to A, the hexadecimal equivalent is 9AH.

Table 3.8 Hexadecimal digits

Decimal	Binary	Hexadecimal
0	0000	0
1	0001	1
2	0010	2
3	0011	3
4	0100	4
5	0101	5
6	0110	6
7	0111	7
8	1000	8
9	1001	9
10	1010	A
11	1011	B
12	1100	C
13	1101	D
14	1110	E
15	1111	F

Table 3.9 Hexadecimal number system

7th Place	6th Place	5th Place	4th Place	3rd Place	2nd Place	1st Place
16^6	16^5	16^4	16^3	16^2	16^1	16^0
16777216	1048576	65536	4096	256	16	1

To convert a hexadecimal number to decimal number, you first could convert the hexadecimal number to binary, then convert the binary number to decimal. Another way to convert is to multiply the decimal value of each hexadecimal digit by its weight, then take the sum of these products.

Example 5:

To convert EAH to a decimal number, multiply the A by the 1s and E by 16, then add them up.

E	A
$Ex16^1$	$Ax16^0$
$14x16^1$	$10x16^0$
14x16	10x1
224	10

Therefore, the hexadecimal number of EA is equal to the decimal number of 224 + 10 = 234.

Example 6:

To convert the decimal number 234 to a hexadecimal number, refer to Table 3.9 to see that the largest power of 16 that fits into 234 is 16^1 (16). 16 goes into 234, 14 (E) times, leaving a 10 (A).

16^1	16^0
14×16^1	10×16^0
E	A

$$234/16 = \mathbf{14}.625$$
$$234 - (\mathbf{14} \times 16) = 10$$
$$14 = \mathbf{EH}$$

Today, TCP/IP addresses (IPv4) are based on 32 bits divided as four groups of 8 bits. The groupings of 8 bits is sometimes referred to as an **octet**. Of course, since a hexadecimal digit consists of 4 bits, it takes 2 hexadecimal digits to express an octet.

3.3.3   ASCII Character Set

In order to communicate, we need numbers, letters, punctuation, and other symbols. An alphanumeric code represents these characters and various instructions necessary for conveying information. One commonly used alphanumeric code is the **ASCII (American Standard Code for Information Interchange)** character set. ASCII is based on 8 bits, so there is a total of 256 different combinations of 0s and 1s ($2^8 = 256$ different characters). A partial listing of the ASCII characters is shown in Table 3.10. For example, if a byte had the following binary code, 01000001, the byte would represent the letter "A"(see Figure 3.6) and 01100001 would represent "a".

3.4   PHYSICAL LAYER

The network-oriented lower layers of the OSI model are concerned with the protocols associated with the actual physical part of the network that allows two or more computers to communicate. The **physical layer** is responsible for the actual transmission of the bits sent across a physical medium. It allows signals, such as electrical signals, optical signals, or radio signals, to be exchanged among communicating machines. Therefore, it defines the electrical, physical, and procedural characteristics required to establish, maintain, and deactivate physical links. The physical layer is concerned about how the bits (0s and 1s) of data are represented and transmitted. It is not concerned with how many bits make up each unit of data, nor is it concerned with the meaning of the data being transmitted. In the physical layer, the sender simply transmits a signal and the receiver detects it.

The physical layer is also responsible for the physical topology or actual network layout. The physical layer includes the network cabling, hubs, repeaters, and NIC. Note: Most network problems occur at the physical layer, whether it is a failed NIC, cable, transceiver, router, or switch port, interference (electromagnetic or radio frequency) or just a loose connection.

3.4.1   Signaling

Signaling is the method for using electricity, light energy, or radio waves to communicate. The process of changing a signal to represent data is often called **modulation** or **encoding.** The two forms of signaling are digital signaling and analog signaling.

Digital signals (the language of computers) are based on a binary signal system produced by pulses of light or electric voltages. The site of the pulse is either on/high or off/low to represent 1s and 0s. **Binary digits (bits)** can be combined to represent different values.

A digital signal can be measured in two ways. The **current state** method periodically measures the digital signal for the specific state. The **transition state** method represents data by how the signal

Table 3.10   Partial list of the ASCII character set

DEC	BIN	HEX	ASCII	DEC	BIN	HEX	ASCII	DEC	BIN	HEX	ASCII
32	00100000	20	space	64	01000000	40	@	96	01100000	60	'
33	00100001	21	!	65	01000001	41	A	97	01100001	61	a
34	00100010	22	"	66	01000010	42	B	98	01100010	62	b
35	00100011	23	#	67	01000011	43	C	99	01100011	63	c
36	00100100	24	$	68	01000100	44	D	100	01100100	64	d
37	00100101	25	%	69	01000101	45	E	101	01100101	65	e
38	00100110	26	&	70	01000110	46	F	102	01100110	66	f
39	00100111	27	'	71	01000111	47	G	103	01100111	67	g
40	00101000	28	(	72	01001000	48	H	104	01101000	68	h
41	00101001	29	)	73	01001001	49	I	105	01101001	69	i
42	00101010	2A	*	74	01001010	4A	J	106	01101010	6A	j
43	00101011	2B	+	75	01001011	4B	K	107	01101011	6B	k
44	00101100	2C	,	76	01001100	4C	L	108	01101100	6C	l
45	00101101	2D	-	77	01001101	4D	M	109	01101101	6D	m
46	00101110	2E	.	78	01001110	4E	N	110	01101110	6E	n
47	00101111	2F	/	79	01001111	4F	O	111	01101111	6F	o
48	00110000	30	0	80	01010000	50	P	112	01110000	70	p
49	00110001	31	1	81	01010001	51	Q	113	01110001	71	q
50	00110010	32	2	82	01010010	52	R	114	01110010	72	r
51	00110011	33	3	83	01010011	53	S	115	00111011	73	s
52	00110100	34	4	84	01010100	54	T	116	01110100	74	t
53	00110101	35	5	85	01010101	55	U	117	01110101	75	u
54	00110110	36	6	86	01010110	56	V	118	01110110	76	v
55	00110111	37	7	87	01010111	57	W	119	01110111	77	w
56	00111000	38	8	88	01011000	58	X	120	01111000	78	x
57	00111001	39	9	89	01011001	59	Y	121	01111001	79	y
58	00111010	3A	:	90	01011010	5A	Z	122	01111010	7A	z
59	00111011	3B	;	91	01011011	5B	[	123	01111011	7B	{
60	00111100	3C	<	92	01011100	5C	\	124	01111100	7C	¦
61	00111101	3D	=	93	01011101	5D	]	125	01111101	7D	}
62	00111110	3E	>	94	01011110	5E	^	126	01111110	7E	~
63	00111111	3F	?	95	01011111	5F	_	127	01111111	7F	Delete

Figure 3.6   A byte representing an ASCII character

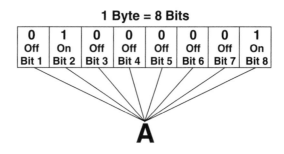

Figure 3.7   Measuring data bits by using current state and state transition

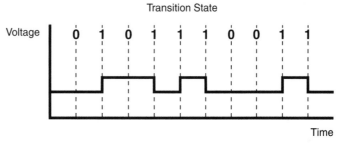

transitions from high to low or low to high. A transition indicates a binary 1 and the absence of a transition indicates binary 0. See Figure 3.7.

An **analog signal** is the opposite of a digital signal. Instead of having a finite number of states, an analog signal has an infinite number of values, which is constantly changing. Analog signals are typically sinusoidal waveforms, that are characterized by its amplitude and frequency. The **amplitude** represents the peak voltage of the sine wave. The **frequency** indicates the number of times that a single wave repeats over any period. It is measured in hertz (Hz) or cycles per second. Another term related to modulation is its *time reference,* or *phase.* A **phase** is measured in degrees. Phase can be measured in 0°, 90°, 180°, and 270° or 0°, 45°, 90°, 135°, 180°, 225°, 270°, 315°, and 360°. See Figure 3.8.

By varying amplitude, frequency, and phase, data are sent over telephone lines. The earliest form of encoding data over telephone lines was frequency shift keying (FSK), which was very similar to frequency modulation used with FM radio stations. FSK sends a logical 1 at one particular frequency (usually 1750 Hz) and a logical 0 at another frequency (often 1080 Hz). FSK was typically used with 300-baud modems.

Phase shift keying (PSK) involves varying the phase angle (0°, 90°,180°, and 270°) to represent data. Since the phase has four different values, it represents 2 bits of data. See Table 3.11. A 1200-baud modem using PSK can transmit data at 2,400 bps.

Much like digital signals, analog signals can be measured as current state or state transition. For example, an analog signal can measure amplitude at set intervals or it can measure the transition from one amplitude to another.

Noise is interference or static that destroys the integrity of signals. Noise can come from a variety of sources, including radio waves, nearby electrical wires, lightning and other power fluctuations, and bad connections. For example, you are talking on the telephone and you hear static on the line, or you hear another conversation on your phone line.

Figure 3.8 A sine wave showing amplitude, frequency (cycles per second), and phase

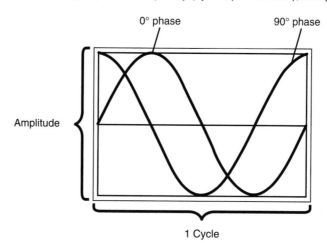

Table 3.11 Data bits interpreted from phase signals

Phase	Data Bits
0°	0 0
90°	0 1
180°	1 0
270°	1 1

Analog signals are not optimal for data transmission because they are more prone to errors than data signals. This is because as analog signals are amplified so that they can travel longer distances, noise is also amplified. Since digital signals are discrete values (a bit being either a 0 or a 1), the signal is regenerated with a repeater. Therefore, every time the signal goes through a repeater, the signal starts out fresh, with no noise.

3.4.2 Synchronous and Asynchronous Connection

Data bits are encoded on a network medium and the receiving network card interprets the signal by taking measurements of the signal. Therefore, the receiving network card must use a clock or a timing method to determine when to measure and decode the signal and to decode the data bits. The two timing methods are synchronous and asynchronous.

Synchronous devices use a timing or clock signal to coordinate communications between the two devices. If the sending and receiving devices were both supplied by exactly the same clock signal, then transmission could take place forever with the assurance that the signal sampling at the receiver was always in perfect synchronization with the transmitter.

In synchronous communications, data are not sent in individual bytes but as frames of large data blocks. For example, frame sizes vary from a few bytes to many bytes. Ethernet uses 1500-byte packets. The clock is embedded in the data stream encoding, or is provided on a separate clock line so that the sender and receiver are always in synchronization during a frame transmission.

Asynchronous signals are intermittent signals; they can occur at any time and at irregular intervals. They do not use a clock or timing signal. As the data frame is sent, the data frame consists of a start signal, a number of data bits, and a stop signal. The start signal is sent to notify the other end that data are coming, and the stop signal is sent to indicate the end of the data frame. Although asynchronous signals are simpler electronic devices, asynchronous signals are not as efficient as synchronous signals because of the extra overhead of the start and stop signal. An example of an asynchronous device is a modem.

3.4.3   Bandwidth

Bandwidth refers to the amount of data that can be carried on a given transmission medium. Larger bandwidth means greater capabilities of data transmission. Bandwidth is typically expressed in bits per second. Since bits is such a small unit, you usually see kilobits per second, megabits per second, and gigabits per second. Kilobits per second may be expressed as Kbits/second or Kbps (contrasted with kilobytes per second: Kbytes/second or KB/s).

Bandwidth uses schemes based on the availability and utilization of channels. A channel is a part of the medium's total bandwidth. It can be created by using the entire bandwidth for one channel or by splitting up multiple frequencies to accommodate multiple channels. For example, if a medium can support 10 megabits per second (Mbps), two channels can be created at 5 Mbps each.

Baseband systems use the transmission medium's entire capacity for a single channel. Baseband networks can use either analog or digital signals, but digital is more common.

A **broadband** system uses the transmission medium's capacity to provide multiple channels by adopting **frequency division multiplexing (FDM).** Each channel uses a carrier signal, which runs at a different frequency than the other carrier signals used by the other channels. Data are embedded within the carrier channel. As data are sent onto the transmission channel, one multiplexer (mux) sends several data signals at different frequencies. When the various signals reach the end of the transmission media, another multiplexer separates the frequencies so that the data can be read.

Although a baseband system can support only one signal at a time, it can be made into a broadband system through time division multiplexing. **Time-division multiplexing (TDM)** divides the single channel into short time slots, which allows multiple devices to be assigned time slots. The TDM method works well in many cases, but it does not always account for the varying data transmission needs of different devices or users. Regardless of the needs of the devices that transmit data, the same duration of time to transmit or receive data is allocated. A derivative of TDM is **statistical time-division multiplexing (SDTM),** which analyzes the amount of data that each device needs to transmit and determines on-the-fly how much time each device should be allocated for data transmission on the cable or line. As a result, SDTM uses bandwidth more efficiently.

3.4.4   Point-to-Point and Multipoint Connection

All physical topologies are variations of two fundamental methods of connecting devices, point-to-point and multipoint. See Figure 3.9. **Point-to-point** topology connects two nodes directly together, for example, two computers connected together using modems, a PC communicating with a printer using a parallel cable, or WAN links connected together. In a point-to-point link, the two devices monopolize the communication medium between the two nodes. Because the medium is not shared, nothing is needed to identify the two nodes. Whatever data are sent from one device, are sent to the other device.

Multipoint connection links three or more devices together through a single communication medium. Because multipoint connections share a common channel, each device needs a way to identify itself and the device to which it wants to send information. The method used to identify senders and receivers is called **addressing.** SCSI devices connected on a single-ribbon cable are identified with their SCSI identification numbers. Network cards connected on a network are identified with their media access control (MAC) address.

Figure 3.9   Point-to-point and multipoint connections

3.5 DATA LINK LAYER

The **data link layer** of the OSI model is responsible for providing error-free data transmission and establishes local connections between two computers or hosts. It divides data it receives from the network layer into distinct frames that can then be transmitted by the physical layer, and it packages raw bits from the physical layer into blocks of data called frames. A **frame** is a structured package for moving data that includes not only the raw data, or "payload," but also the sender's and receiver's network addresses and error checking and control information. The control information provides necessary synchronization and flow control. The error checking information includes a checksum (cyclic redundancy check, or CRC) or some other form of error control information. Since a package contains the data and destination address, each packet travels the network independent from other packets.

The data link layer is divided into two sublayers, the **logical link control (LLC)** sublayer (IEEE 802.2) and the **media access control (MAC)** sublayer. The MAC sublayer is the lower sublayer that communicates directly with the network adapter card. It defines the network logical topology, which is the actual pathway (ring or bus) of the data signals being sent. In addition, the MAC sublayer allows multiple devices to use the same medium, and it determines how the network card gets access or control of the network medium so that two devices don't trample over each other. It also maintains the physical device address, known as MAC address, which is used to identify each network connection. Lastly, the MAC sublayer builds frames from bits that are received from the physical layer. Some examples of MAC sublayer protocols are CSMA/CA, CSMA/CD, token passing, and demand priority.

The LLC sublayer manages the data link between two computers within the same subnet. A **subnet** is a simple network or smaller network that is used to form a larger network. In addition, if we were operating a multiprotocol LAN, each network layer protocol would have its own **service access point (SAP),** which is used by the LLC to identify the protocol. For example, the TCP/IP, IPX/SPX, and NetBIOS systems would each have a different SAP, so that the LLC can identify each. When a packet is received by the network card, the LLC checks the destination MAC address in the frame. If it matches the host, the host system accepts the frame. If it does not match, the host system ignores the frame. If a destination LLC receives a bad frame, it discards it and does not send an acknowledgement that it received the frame. Since the sending LLC does not receive the acknowledgement, it resends the frame.

3.5.1 Physical Device Addressing

Many network devices share the same transmission channel; therefore, the data link layer must have some way to identify itself from the other devices. The physical device address, or **media access control (MAC) address**, is a unique hardware address (unique on the LAN/subnet) burned onto a ROM chip assigned by the hardware vendors or selected with jumpers or DIP switches. Much like a street address within a city, you cannot have two network cards or nodes with the same MAC address on the same network. You can have the same MAC address on two separate networks. For Ethernet and Token Ring cards, the MAC address is embedded onto the ROM chip on the card. See Figure 3.10.

The MAC address is 48 bits, or 6 bytes, in length and is usually represented in a particular format. The first 24 bits of a MAC address are referred to as the organizationally unique identifier (OUI). OUIs are sold and assigned to network hardware vendors by the IEEE. The last 24 bits are assigned by the individual vendor. A MAC address is ordinarily expressed as six pairs of hexadecimal characters, separated by colons. An example of a MAC address is 00:53:AD:B2:13:BA, or 00-53-AD-B2-13-BA.

3.5.2 Media Access Methods

The set of rules defining how a computer puts data onto the network cable and takes data from the cable is called the **access method.** The access method is sometimes referred to as **arbitration.** Although multiple computers share the same cable system, only one device can access a cable at a time. If two devices do use the same cable at the same time, both data packets sent by the card become corrupted. The typical cable access methods are contention, token passing, polling, and demand priority.

Figure 3.10 Three networks connected together with a router. Each computer is identified by its 8-hexadecimal digit MAC address. Note that the MAC address 22-33-A3-34-43-43 is used repeatedly, but on different networks

NETWORK A

22-33-A3-45-23-32   22-33-A3-47-23-42   22-33-A3-34-43-43

Router

C3-5F-29-87-A4-8C

C3-5F-29-11-8D-CC

C3-5F-29-43-43-B2

22-33-A3-45-23-32

22-33-A3-64-87-34   **NETWORK B**   **NETWORK C**

22-33-A3-AA-BD-54

22-33-A3-B4-63-23

22-33-A3-34-43-43

22-33-A3-5B-AC-76   22-33-A3-34-63-12

Contention occurs when two or more devices contend (compete) for network access. Any device can transmit whenever it needs to send information. To avoid data collisions (two devices sending data at the same time), specific contention protocols were developed that require a device to listen to the cable before transmitting data.

The most common form of contention is the **carrier-sense multiple access (CSMA)** network. Even though each station listens for network traffic before it attempts to transmit, it remains possible for two transmissions to overlap on the network or to cause a collision. As a result of collisions, access to a CSMA network is somewhat unpredictable, and CSMA networks are referred to as random or statistical access networks. To avoid collisions, CSMA networks use one of two specialized methods of collision management: collision detection (CD) and collision avoidance (CA).

The collision detection approach listens to the network traffic as the card is transmitting. By analyzing network traffic, it detects collisions and initiates retransmissions. **Carrier-sense, multiple access with collision detection (CSMA /CD)** is the access method utilized in Ethernet and IEEE 802.3. Collision avoidance uses time slices to make network access smarter and avoid collisions. **Carrier-sense, multiple access with collision avoidance (CSMA/ CA)** is the access mechanism used in Apple's LocalTalk network. When a collision occurs, the logical link control sublayer of the data link layer retransmits a frame, if it does not receive an acknowledgement from the destination LLC.

Contention is a simple access method that has low administrative overhead requirements, but high traffic levels cause many collisions. Thus, a lot of retransmitting occurs, which causes even slower network performance.

Token passing uses a special authorizing packet of information to inform devices that they can transmit data. These packets, called tokens, are passed around the network in an orderly fashion from one device to the next. Devices can transmit only if they have control of the token, which distributes access control among all the devices. The Token Ring and FDDI systems use a ring topology in which each station passes the token to the next station in the ring. ARCnet uses a token passing bus as it passes the token to the next higher hardware address (MAC address), regardless of its physical location on the network.

Token passing is deterministic, because you can calculate the maximum time before a workstation can grab the token and begin to transmit. In addition, you can assign priorities to certain network devices that use the network more frequently. If a workstation has equal or higher priority than the priority value in the token, it can take possession of the token.

Polling has a single device (sometimes referred to as a channel-access administrator) such as a mainframe front-end processor designated as the primary device. The primary device polls, or asks, each of the secondary devices (known as slaves) if they have information to be transmitted. Only when it is polled does a secondary computer have access to the communication channel. To make sure that a slave does not hog all of the bandwidth, each system has rules pertaining to how long each secondary computer can transmit data.

The newest access method is called demand priority. In **demand priority,** a device makes a request to the hub and the hub grants permission. High-priority packets are serviced before any normal-priority packets. To effectively guarantee bandwidth to time-sensitive applications such as voice, video, and multimedia applications, the normal-priority packets are promoted to a high-priority after 200 to 300 ms.

3.6   THE 802 PROJECT MODEL

In the 1970s, when LANs first began to emerge as a valuable business tool, the IEEE realized that there was a need for certain LAN standards, specifically for the physical and data link layer of the OSI reference model. To accomplish this, IEEE launched Project 802, which was named for the year and month it began (1980, February). These standards have several areas of responsibility, including the network card, components of the LAN, and media components. See Table 3.12 and Figure 3.11.

Probably the two most popularly discussed 802 standards are 802.3 (CSMA/CD LAN [Ethernet]) and 802.5 (token ring). When these two standards were originally created, the 802.3 standard showed better performance on smaller networks and the 802.5 standard showed better performance on larger networks. Both networks slow down as more computers are added because of the increased traffic, but the 802.5 network runs more efficiently, as the number of collisions increases with the 802.3 network. Fortunately,

Figure 3.11   The IEEE standards as they relate to the OSI model

	LLC Sublayer	802.2					802.7	802.8	802.9	802.10	802.11
Data Link Layer	**Mac Sublayer**	802.3	802.4	802.5	802.6	802.12					
	Physical Layer										

Table 3.12   802 project standards

Standard	Category
802.1	Overview and architecture of internetworking, including bridging and virtual LAN (VLAN)
802.2	Logical link control (LLC), which is the data link layer sublayer
802.3	Carrier-sense, multiple access with collision detection (CSMA/CD) LAN (Ethernet)
802.4	Token bus LAN
802.5	Token ring LAN
802.6	Metropolitan area network (MAN), which includes the Distributed Queue Dual Bus (DQDB)
802.7	Broadband LANs
802.8	Fiber-Optic Technical Advisory Group covering fiber optic LANs and MANs, which include FDDI and 10BaseFL
802.9	Integrated voice/data networks, including ISDN and DSL lines
802.10	Network security, including virutal private network (VPN)
802.11	Wireless networks
802.12	Demand priority access LAN, 100Base, VG-AnyLAN
802.14	Coaxial and fiber cables such as those found on cable television to support two-way communication

Table 3.13   Popular 802 standards

Technology	Speed(s)	Access Method	Topologies	Media[1]
Ethernet (IEEE 802.3)	10,100, or 1000 Mbps	CSMA/CD	Logical bus	Coaxial cable or UTP
Token Ring (IEEE 802.5)	4 or 16 Mbps	Token passing	Physical star, logical ring	STP or UTP
FDDI (IEEE 802.8)	100 or 200 Mbps	Token passing	Physical star, logical ring	Fiber optic or UTP (implemented as CDDI)
Wireless (IEEE 802.11)	1 or 11 Mbps	CSMA/CA	Cellular	Wireless

[1] UTP=unshielded twisted pair; STP=shielded twisted pair; CDDI=copper data distribution interface.

802.3 network performance has been improved with increased bandwidth and enhanced with switches. Note: Recently the 802.3u working group updated 802.3 to include Ethernet 100BaseT implementation, and 802.3z described the Gigabit Ethernet. Another standard that has becomes more popular recently is 802.11, which covers wireless networks. See Table 3.13.

3.7   NETWORK LAYER

The **network layer** of the OSI model is concerned with the addressing and routing necessary to move data (known as packets or datagrams) from one network (or subnet) to another. This function includes establishing, maintaining, and terminating connections between networks, making routing decisions, and relaying data from one network to another. The OSI model classifies a **host** as the computer or device that connects to the network and is the source or final destination of data . Routers (intermediate systems) perform routing and relaying functions that link the individual networks. Therefore, routers are network layer devices.

3.7.1   Network Addressing

For each network to operate on an internetwork and to identify itself to another, each network must be assigned a network ID. At the network layer, therefore, networks are identified by a unique **network address.** This means that every computer on an individual LAN must use the same network address. Of course, if the LAN is connected to other LANs, its address must be different from that of all the other LANs. Physical device (MAC address) and logical network addresses are used jointly to move data between devices on an internetwork.

When planning a network, assign logical addresses to each host. For example, when you use the TCP/IP protocol, the administrator assigns IP addresses to each computer. The IP address contains the network address for the subnet that the host is on and a host address to represent the host on the subnet.

As a packet is sent to a remote host several networks away, it is sent to the first router. The router looks at the packet's destination by looking at the logical address. It then determines which way to send the packet, strips off and rebuilds the data link layer source and destination addresses information, and sends the packet to the next router. When the packet gets to the next router, the router reads the logical address to determine its destination. It then determines which way to send the packet, strips off and rebuilds the data link layer source and destination address information, and sends it to the next router. Routers keep working until the packet gets to the destination network, then a router sends it to the destination computer.

Remember, the data link layer provides for the transmission of frames within the same LAN, and the network layer provides for the much more complex task of transmitting packets between two network computers or devices in the network, regardless of how many data links/routers exist between the two. Examples of network layer protocols that connect the network together include IP and IPX; examples of protocols that determine which route to take are the Routing Information Protocol (RIP) and Open Shortest Path First (OSPF) protocol.

A network computer or other networked device can perform several roles simultaneously. The term *entity* identifies the hardware and software, that fulfill each individual role. Every entity must have its service address so that it can send and receive data. This address is usually referred to as a **port** or **socket,** which is used to identify a specific upper-layer software process or protocol. Multiple service addresses can be assigned to any computer on which several network applications are running. For example, when you try to read a web page, the packet from the Internet is routed to your computer using a TCP/IP network. Since today's operating systems are multitasking environments, they can be running or accessing several different network services. The port, which is included in the packet, is used to identify the type of packet so that the system knows which software on the host is needed for the packet.

A network computer can handle multiple conversations with other computers at the same time; therefore, the system must be able to keep track of the different conversations. The two methods of distinguishing conversations are connection identifier and transaction identifier.

When dealing with Windows and networking, you will become familiar with Windows socket, or WinSock. A Windows socket is a Windows implementation of the University of California Berkeley Sockets Application Programming Interface, which is used in TCP/IP protocols to connect to the appropriate TCP/IP service such as HTTP, FTP, or Telnet. The WINSOCK.DLL file is the Microsoft Windows interface for the TCP/IP protocol.

3.7.2   Data Switching Techniques

Large internetworks can have multiple paths linking source and destination devices. Information is switched as it travels through the various communication channels. Data switching techniques can be either circuit switching or packet switching. **Circuit switching** is a technique that connects the sender and the receiver by a single path for the duration of a conversation. Once a connection is established, a dedicated path exists between both ends; this path is always consuming network capacity, even when there is no active transmission taking place (such as when a caller is put on hold). Once the connection

Figure 3.12 Circuit switching

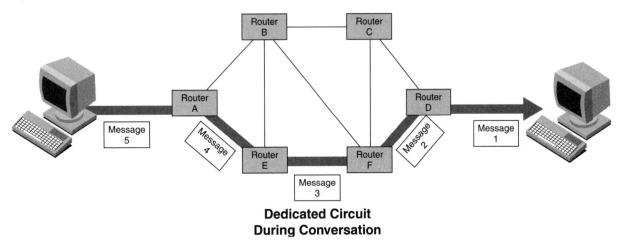

Dedicated Circuit
During Conversation

Figure 3.13 Packet switching

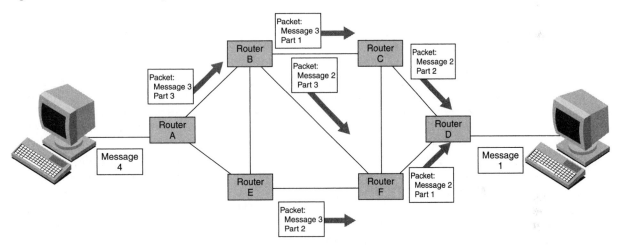

has been made, the destination device acknowledges that it is ready to carry on a transfer. When the conversation is complete, the connection is terminated. See Figure 3.12. Therefore, circuit switching networks are sometimes called connection-oriented networks. Examples of circuit switching include phone systems and data that need to be transmitted in live video and sound.

In **packet switching** methods, messages are broken into small parts called packets. Each packet is tagged with source, destination, and intermediary node addresses as appropriate. Packets can have a defined maximum length and can be stored in RAM instead of hard disk. Packets can take a variety of possible paths through the network as the system attempts to keep the network connections filled. However, because the message is broken into multiple parts, sending packets via different paths adds to the possibility that packet order could get scrambled. Therefore, a sequencing number is added to each packet.

Packets are sent over the most appropriate path. Each device chooses the best path at that time for every packet. If one path is too busy, the device can send the packet through another path. Since some packets may be delayed, which causes the packets to arrive out of order, the device reorders them by sequence number to reconstruct the original message. See Figure 3.13. The Internet is based on a packet switching protocol. Other protocols are Asynchronous Transfer Mode (ATM), Frame Relay, Switched Multimegabit Data Service (SMDS), and X.25. Message switching is typically used to support services such as e-mail, web pages, calendaring, or workflow information.

Connections between two hosts in a packet switching network are often described as a virtual circuit. A **virtual circuit** is a logical circuit created to ensure reliable communication between two network devices. A bidirectional communications path is established from one device to another and is uniquely identified by some type of identifier. A number of virtual circuits can be multiplexed into a single physical circuit for transmission across the network. This capability often can reduce the equipment and network complexity required for multiple-device connections.

A virtual circuit can pass through any number of intermediate devices or switches located within the virtual circuit. In these cases, the two hosts can communicate as though they have a dedicated connection, even though the packets might actually travel very different routes before arriving at their destination. Although the paths may vary, the computers do not know this nor do they need to know.

Virtual networks are sometimes depicted as a cloud, because a user does not worry about the path taken through the cloud. The user is only worried about entering the cloud and exiting the cloud. A virtual circuit acts as a direct connection, even though it may not be directly connected. See Figure 3.14.

> *NOTE:* A switch in a network is a device that filters and forwards packets between LAN segments, which operate at the data link layer of the OSI reference model. A switch (layer 2 switch) can also be referred to as a routing switch (layer 3 switch), which performs routing operations much like a router. The routing switch performs many of the functions found in the network layer of the OSI model. Since the routing switch has its routing capabilities implemented with hardware and not software, it is faster. Routing switches, however, are not as powerful as full-fledged routers.

Virtual circuits can be either **permanent virtual circuits (PVCs)** or **switched virtual circuits (SVCs ;** also known as temporary virtual circuits). A PVC is a permanently established virtual circuit of one mode: data transfer. PVCs are used in situations in which data transfer between devices is constant. PVCs decrease bandwidth use associated with the establishment and termination of virtual circuits, but they increase costs due to constant availability. Of course, PVCs are efficient for connections between hosts that communicate frequently. PVCs play a central role in Frame Relay and X.25 networks.

SVCs are virtual circuits that are dynamically established on demand and are terminated when transmission is complete. Communication over an SVC consists of three phases: circuit establishment, data transfer, and circuit termination. The establishment phase involves creating the virtual circuit between the source and destination devices. Data transfer involves transmitting data between the devices over the virtual circuit, and the termination phase involves tearing down the virtual circuit between the source and destination devices. SVCs are used in situations in which data transmission between devices is sporadic, largely because SVCs increase bandwidth use as a result of the circuit establishment and termination phases. SVCs do decrease the cost associated with constant availability of virtual circuits.

Figure 3.14   Virtual circuit as a cloud

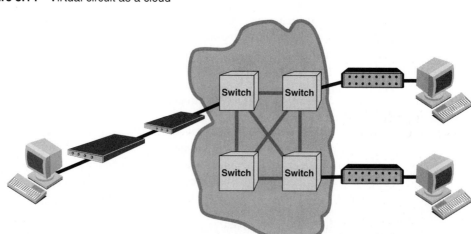

When you lease a PVC or SVC end-to-end circuit, you pay monthly whether you send data or not. If you choose not to lease the line but sign up with a network provider, the provider bills you only for the amount of data packets you send and the distance the packets travel. Of course, cost will also be based on the technology used, and often there is a minimum charge per call.

3.7.3   Routing Protocols

To determine the best route, the routers use complex algorithms, that take into account a variety of factors, including speed of the transmission media, number of network segments, and the network segment that carries the least amount of traffic. Routers share status and routing information with other routers so that they can provide better traffic management and bypass slow connections. In addition, routers provide functions such as the ability to filter messages and forward them to different places based on various criteria. Most routers are multiprotocol routers; that is, they can route data packets using many different protocols.

A metric is a standard of measurement, such as hop count, which is used by routing algorithms to determine the optimal path to a destination. A hop is the trip a data packet takes from one router to another router or from a router to another intermediate point in the network. On a large network, the number of hops a packet takes toward its destination is called the **hop count.** When a computer communicates with another computer, and the computer has to go through four routers, the hop count is four. With no other factors taken into account, a metric of 4 would be assigned. If a router had a choice between a route of 4 metrics and a route of 6 metrics, it would choose the route of 4 metrics. If you want the router to choose the route of 6 metrics, you can overwrite the 4-metric route.

To keep track of the various routes in a network, routers create and maintain routing tables. The routers communicate with one another to maintain their routing tables through a routing update message. The routing update message can consist of all or a portion of a routing table. By analyzing routing updates from all other routers, a router can build a detailed picture of network topology.

Various routing protocols use different metrics, including path length, hop counts, routing delay, bandwidth, load, reliability, and cost. Path length is the most common routing metric. Some routing protocols allow network administrators to assign arbitrary costs to each network link. In this case, path length is the sum of the costs associated with each link traversed. Other routing protocols define hop counts.

Routing algorithms can be differentiated based on several key characteristics. The capability of the routing algorithm to choose the best route is very important. One routing algorithm may use the number of hops and the length of delays, but it may weigh the length of delay more heavily in the calculation. To maintain consistency and predictability, routing protocols use strict metric calculations.

Routing algorithms are designed to be as simple as possible. In other words, the routing algorithm must offer efficiency with a minimum of software and utilization overhead. While being efficient, however, the routing algorithm must be robust so that it can quickly change routes when a route goes down because of hardware failure or a route has a high load (high amount of traffic). When such a situation occurs, the routing algorithm must be stable.

Routing algorithms must converge rapidly. **Convergence** is the process of agreement by all routers about which routes are the optimal ones. When a route goes down, routers distribute the new routes by sending routing update messages. The time that it takes for all routers to get new routes on which they all agree should be quick. If not, routing loops or network outages can occur. A routing loop occurs when a packet is sent back and forth between several routers without ever getting to its final destination.

3.8   TRANSPORT LAYER

The **transport layer** of the OSI model can be described as the middle layer that connects the lower and upper layers. In addition, it is responsible for reliable, transparent transfer of data (known as segments) between two end points. Since the transport layer provides end-to-end recovery of lost and corrupted packets and flow control, it deals with handling errors, dividing messages into smaller packets, numbering messages, and repackaging messages. In addition, if packets arrive out of order at the destination, the transport layer is responsible for reordering the packets back to the original order. Examples of transport layer protocols are Sequenced Packet Exchange (SPX), Transmission Control Protocol (TCP), User Datagram Protocol (UDP), and NetBEUI.

Computers and network devices often use long strings of numbers to identify themselves. The transport layer is responsible for name resolution, whereby it takes a more meaningful name and translates it to a computer or network address. Examples of name resolution protocols are Domain Name System (DNS) and Windows Internet Naming Service (WINS).

3.8.1   Connection Services

Networks can be connection-oriented or connectionless-oriented networks. In a **connection-oriented network,** you must establish a connection using an exchange of messages or must have a preestablished pathway between a source point and a destination point before you can transmit packets. Establishing a connection before transmitting packets is similar to making a telephone call. You must dial a number, the destination telephone must ring, and someone must pick up the telephone receiver before you can begin speaking. An example of a connection-oriented protocol is TCP.

Connection-oriented services provide flow, error, and packet sequence control through acknowledgments. An **acknowledgment (ACK)** is a special message that is sent back when a data packet makes it to its destination. Think of a letter sent at the post office with a return receipt request; the return receipt is forwarded to the sender to indicate that the letter arrived at its destination.

TCP is a connection-oriented network because a set of three messages must be completed before data are exchanged. SPX is also connection oriented. Frame Relay, when using PVCs, does not require any messages be sent ahead of time, but it does require predefinition in the Frame Relay switches to establish a connection between two attached devices. ATM protocol PVCs are connection oriented for similar reasons.

The disadvantage of using a connection-oriented network is that it takes time to establish a connection before transmitting packets. The advantage of using a connection is that the connection can reserve bandwidth for specific connections. As a result, connection-oriented networks can guarantee a certain **quality of service (QoS)**. By using QoS to guarantee bandwidth, connection-oriented networks can provide sufficient bandwidth for audio and video, without jitters or pauses, and transfer of important data within a timely manner. A connection-oriented network can also better manage network traffic and prevent congestion by refusing traffic that it cannot handle.

Connectionless-oriented networks do not require an exchange of messages with the destination host before data transfer begins, nor do they make a dedicated connection, or virtual circuit, with a destination host. Instead, connectionless protocols rely upon upper-level, not lower-level, protocols for safe delivery and error handling. Since data are segmented and delivered in the order the data are received from the upper OSI layers, connectionless protocols do not sequence data segments. Connectionless protocols are best suited for situations where high data transfer rate and low data integrity is needed. An example of a connectionless protocol is UDP.

The exchange of messages before data transfer begins is called a call setup or a three-way handshake:

- The first "connection agreement" segment is a request for synchronization.
- The second and third segments acknowledge the request and establish connection parameters (the rules) between hosts.
- An acknowledgment notifies the destination host that the connection agreement has been accepted and that the actual connection has been established.

Data are then transferred. When the transfer is finished, call termination takes place to tear down the virtual circuit.

The data link layer, network layer, and transport layer offer some form of connection services, which define how two devices form a connection. The connection services determine the level of error detection, recovery, and flow control that are used in communicating data between two network devices. The data link layer is concerned with connection services from one device to another device within the LAN, whereas the network layer is concerned with connection services from one device to another device on different LANs. The transport layer is concerned with an end-to-end connection service (a type of overall quality assurance). Note: To speed communication, most network layer protocols are connectionless; they do not bother with the sending or receiving of acknowledgments. Instead, they let the transport layer handle acknowledgments and provide the error control.

3.8.2   Error Control

Error control refers to the notification of lost or damaged data frames. Possible errors include these:

- The destination does not receive the data packet.
- The checksum does not match. A checksum value is mathematically generated before the data packet is sent and attached to the data packet. When the data packet gets to its destination, the same mathematical calculation is performed. If the result matches the value that was sent, the data are assumed intact.
- The packet size does not configure to a minimum or maximum size requirement for the frame type used.
- Noise, interference, and distortion occur, which scramble the data.
- The capacity of a channel or network device is exceeded, which causes a buffer overflow.

Error detection and error recovery are different. Any header or trailer with a frame check sequence (FCS) or similar file can be used to detect bit errors in a protocol data unit. In error detection, if the FCS detects error, the protocol data unit is discarded. Error recovery implies that the protocol reacts to the lost data and somehow causes the data to be retransmitted. Regardless of which protocol specification performs the error recovery, all work in basically the same way. The transmitted data are labeled or numbered. After receipt, the receiver signals back to the sender that the data were received, using the same label or number to identify the data. If the data were not received, the receiver tells the sender to resend the data. If no acknowledgment was received, the sender assumes that data were not received and resends the data.

3.8.3   Flow Control

Flow control is the process of controlling the rate at which a computer sends data. Depending on the particular protocol, both the sender and the receiver of the data (as well as any intermediate routers, bridges, and switches) might participate in the process of controlling the flow from sender to receiver.

Flow control is needed because data are discarded when congestion occurs. A sender of data might be sending the data faster than the receiver can accept the data, so the receiver discards the data. Or, the sender might be sending the data faster than the intermediate switching devices (switches and routers) can forward the data, which also causes discarding of data. Packets can be lost due to transmission errors as well. This happens in every network, sometimes temporarily and sometimes regularly, depending on the network and the traffic patterns. A receiving computer may have insufficient buffer space to receive the next incoming frame, or the processor may be too busy to process the incoming frame. Intermediate routers might need to discard the packets because of a temporary lack of buffers (holding space).

Flow control attempts to reduce unnecessary discarding of data. Flow-control protocols do not prevent the loss of data due to congestion; the protocols simply reduce the amount of lost data, which in turn reduces the amount of retransmitted traffic, which reduces overall congestion. With flow control, the sender is artificially slowed, or throttled, so the sender submits data less quickly than it could without flow control.

There are three methods of implementing flow control:

- Buffering
- Congestion avoidance
- Windowing

Buffering simply means that the computer reserves enough buffer space in memory so that a burst of incoming data can be held until processing. No attempt is made to actually slow the transmission rate of the sender of data. In fact, buffering is such a common method of dealing with changes in the rate of arrival of data that most of us would probably just assume that it is happening.

In the congestion avoidance method, the computer receiving the data notices that its buffers are filling. This causes either a separate protocol data unit or file in a header to be sent to the sender, signaling the sender to stop transmitting. A preferred method might be to get the sender to simply slow down instead of stopping altogether. This method would still be considered congestion avoidance, but instead of signaling the sender to stop, the signal would be to slow down.

The third flow-control method is called windowing (also called sliding windows). A window is the maximum amount of data the sender can send without getting an acknowledgment. When you have configured a window size of 1, the sending machine waits for acknowledgment for each data segment it transmits before transmitting another. If you have configured a window size of 3, the sending machine is allowed to transmit three data segments before an acknowledgment is received. This cuts down on the amount of traffic, because the number of acknowledgments is reduced. If your network is stable, use a higher number for the window. If the network is not stable, it is best to use a low number to focus more on reliability than performance.

3.8.4   Multiplexing

Some protocols for the transport-layer use a technique called multiplexing and demultiplexing. This technique allows data from different applications to share a single data stream. When multiplexing occurs, the only way to tell one application from another is by identifying each unit of data with a transition mechanism, such as a port number and sequence number. Sequence numbers ensure proper reassembly, while port numbers ensure appropriate destination for the application. Demultiplexing occurs when the destination computer receives the data stream and separates and rejoins the application's segments.

3.9   SESSION LAYER

The application-oriented layers of the OSI model are concerned with the protocols that provide user network applications and services. The **session layer** allows remote users to establish, manage, and terminate a connection (sessions). A **session** is a reliable dialog between two computers. In addition, the session layer enables two users to organize and manage their data exchange and to implement dialog control between the source and destination network devices, including the type of dialog (simplex, half duplex, full duplex) and the length of time a computer transmits. (Simplex, half duplex, and full duplex are explained in the next paragraph.) When establishing sessions, the session layer creates checkpoints in the data streams. If a transmission fails, only the data after the last checkpoint have to be retransmitted. The session layer also implements security, such as validation of user names (commonly known as authentication) and passwords. Examples of session layer protocols are in SQL, NFS, RPC, NetBIOS, FTP, NCP, and Telnet.

Data can flow in one of three ways: simplex, half duplex, full duplex. See Figure 3.15. Simplex dialog allows communication on the transmission channel to occur in only one direction. Essentially, one device is allowed to transmit and all of the other devices receive. This type of communication is

Figure 3.15   Simplex, half-duplex, and full-duplex communication

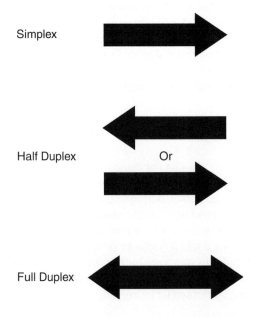

Simplex

Half Duplex   Or

Full Duplex

often compared to a public address system in which the speaker talks to an audience, but the audience does not talk back to the speaker.

Half-duplex dialog allows each device to both transmit and receive, but not at the same time. Therefore, only one device can transmit at a particular time. This method is often compared to a CB radio or a walkie-talkie. A full-duplex dialog allows every device to both transmit and receive simultaneously. The network media channels consist of two physical channels, one for receiving and one for transmitting.

3.10   PRESENTATION LAYER

The **presentation layer** of the OSI model ensures the information sent by an application layer protocol of one system will be readable by the application layer protocol of the remote system. This layer, unlike lower layers, is simply concerned with the syntax and the semantics of the information transmitted. Therefore, it acts as the translator between different data formats, protocols, and systems. It also provides encryption/decryption, compression/decompression of data, and network redirectors. Examples are NCP and SMB.

The presentation layer also deals with translation of character sets. Not all computer systems use the same table to convert binary numbers into text. Most standard computer systems use ASCII. Mainframe computers and some IBM network systems use the Extended Binary Coded Decimal Interchange Code (EBCDIC). These codes are totally different, but protocols at the presentation layer can translate between the two.

Another form of translation performed by the presentation layer involves byte order. In big-endian architectures, which are used by PCs with Intel processors, the leftmost bytes are considered the most significant. In little-endian architectures (used by systems based on Motorola processors), the rightmost bytes are significant. For example, big-endian architecture represents a 16-bit binary number as 1111111101010101, while little-endian architecture represents the same 16-bit binary number as 0101010111111111. To allow both of these types of systems to connect to the same network, the presentation layer translates from one format to the other.

3.11   APPLICATION LAYER

The **application layer** represents the highest layer of the OSI reference model. This layer initiates communication requests. It is responsible for interaction in the operating system and provides an interface to the system. It provides the user interface to a range of network-wide distributed services, including file transfer, printer access, and electronic mail. (Note that the application layer does not include software applications such as word processors and spreadsheets.) Since the application layer provides the user interface to the network services, when the transport layer notifies the upper-layer protocols that a nonrecoverable data error has been detected, the application layer notifies the user via error messages. Some examples of upper layer protocols are File Transfer Protocol (FTP), Simple Mail Transfer Protocol (SMTP), AppleTalk, and Network File System (NFS).

Directory services identify all resources on a network and make those resources accessible to users and applications. Resources can include e-mail addresses, computers, and peripheral devices (such as printers). Ideally, the directory service should make the physical network, including topology and protocols, transparent to users on the network. Users should be able to access any resources without knowing where or how they are physically connected.

The most common directory service is **X.500**, which uses a hierarchical approach, in which objects are organized similar to files and folders on a hard drive. At the top of the structure is the root container (percent), and "children" are organized under it. X.500 is part of the OSI model; however, it does not translate well into a TCP/IP protocol environment. Therefore, many of the protocols that are based on the X.500 do not fully comply with it.

Lightweight Directory Access Protocol (LDAP) is a set of protocols for accessing information directories. LDAP is based on the standards contained within the X.500 standard, but it is significantly simpler. Unlike X.500, LDAP supports TCP/IP, which is necessary for any type of Internet access.

Because it is a simpler version of X.500, LDAP is sometimes called X.500-lite. Microsoft's Active Directory and Novell Directory Services (NDS) use LDAP.

3.12   CONNECTIVITY DEVICES

To connect networks together, several devices can be used; these include network cards, repeaters, hubs, bridges, routers, brouters, and gateways. See Table 3.14.

3.12.1   Network Cards and Cables

The network cards that allow computers to connect to the network, and the cables that they connect, work at the physical OSI layer and data OSI layer. To communicate on LANs, a **network card,** or **network interface card (NIC),** found as an expansion card or integrated into the motherboard, uses **transceivers** (devices that both transmit and receive analog or digital signals) to send packets.

To get a better idea of the function of the network card, consider how data are sent from one computer to another. Data are generated by the microprocessor and sent to the network card using the computer's parallel data bus. At this point, the data consists of alphanumeric characters represented as a series of on (1) and off (0) signals.

Within the network card, the data are processed and converted so they can be transmitted on the network media. If they are being sent on a cable, the data are turned into a serial bit stream, amplified, and sent through the cable. The electrical signals that travel over the network cable must follow specific rules on how to gain sole access to the cable and what specific signals are sent to represent the data onto the cable.

The network card on the receiving computer sees the packet and reads part of the packet to determine if the packet was meant for it. The network card then converts the data into digital signals and sends the data to the microprocessor to be processed.

Cables, which also work at the physical layer of the OSI model, carry electrical or light signals between computers and networks. Most computers connect to the network using cables, and cables connect most networks.

Table 3.14   Connectivity devices and their associated OSI layer

OSI Layer	Device
Application	Gateways
Presentation	Gateways
Session	Gateways
Transport	Gateways
Network	Routers Brouters Layer 3 switches
Data Link	Bridges Layer 2 switches
Physical	Network interface cards Transceivers Repeaters Hubs Multistation access units Cables

Figure 3.16   A repeater

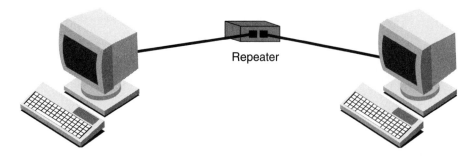

3.12.2   Repeaters

A **repeater,** which works at the physical OSI layer, is a network device used to regenerate or replicate a signal or to move packets from one physical medium to another. Note that a repeater cannot connect different network topologies or access methods. A repeater can regenerate analog or digital signals distorted by transmission loss, on the length of a cable connection. Analog repeaters usually can only amplify the signal (including distortion), whereas digital repeaters can reconstruct a signal to near its original quality. See Figure 3.16.

3.12.3   Hubs and MSAUs

A **hub** (also known as a concentrator), which works at the physical OSI layer, is a multiported connection point used to connect network devices via a cable segment. When a PC needs to communicate with another computer, it sends a data packet to the port, to which the device is connected. When the packet arrives at the port, it is forwarded, or copied, to the other ports so that all network devices can see the packet. In this way, all of the stations "see" every packet just as they do on a bus network. A standard hub is not very efficient on networks with heavy traffic, because it causes a lot of collisions and retransmitted packets. See Figure 3.17. See Chapter 4 for more information on hubs.

The **multistation access unit (MSAU or MAU)** is a physical layer device unique to token ring networks. The MSAU resembles a hub. Yet while token ring networks use a physical star topology, MSAUs use a logical ring topology. While a hub defines a logical bus, the MSAU defines a logical ring. Topologies, token rings, and MSAUs are discussed in Chapter 5.

Figure 3.17   A hub

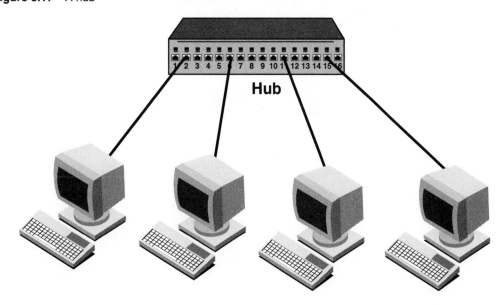

3.12.4   Bridge and Switching Hub

A **bridge,** which works at the data link OSI layer, is a device that connects two LANs and makes them appear as one, or a device used to connect two segments of the same LAN. The two LANs being connected can be alike or dissimilar such as an Ethernet LAN connected to a token ring LAN. Note: Bridges can connect dissimilar network types (e.g., token ring and Ethernet) as long as the bridge operates at the LLC sublayer of the data link layer. If the bridge operates only at the lower sublayer (the MAC sublayer), the bridge can connect only similar network types (token ring to token ring and Ethernet to Ethernet).

Unlike a repeater or hub, a bridge analyzes the incoming data packet and forwards the packet if its destination is on the other side of the bridge. Today, many bridges filter and forward packets with very little delay, which makes them good for networks with high traffic. See Figure 3.18.

There are two kinds of bridges, basic and learning. A basic bridge is used to interconnect LANs using one (or more) of the IEEE 802 standards. Packets received on one port may be retransmitted on another port. Unlike a repeater, a bridge does not start retransmission until it has received the complete packet. As a consequence, stations on both sides of a bridge can transmit simultaneously without causing collisions.

A **switching hub** (sometimes referred to as switch or a layer 2 switch) is a fast, multiported bridge that builds a table of the MAC addresses of all connected stations. It then reads the destination address of each packet and forwards the packet to the correct port. A learning bridge, also known as a transparent bridge, examines the source field of every packet it sees on each port and builds up a picture of which addresses are connected to which ports. Ideally, it will only forward through the port where the destination computer is located. If it does not know the location, it will forward the packet to all ports, except for the port from which the packet originated.

A major advantage of a switching hub is that it allows one computer to open a connection to another computer (or LAN segment).While those two computers communicate, other connections between the other computers (or LAN segments) can be opened. Therefore, several computers can communicate at the same time through the switching hub. As a result, the switches are used to increase performance of a network by segmenting large networks into several smaller, less congested LANs, while providing necessary interconnectivity between them. Switches increase network performance by providing each port

Figure 3.18   A bridge

with dedicated bandwidth, without requiring users to change any existing equipment, such as NICs, hubs, wiring, or any routers or bridges that are currently in place.

Many switching hubs also support load balancing, so that ports are dynamically reassigned to different LAN segments based on traffic patterns. In addition, some include fault tolerance, which can reroute traffic through other ports when a segment goes down.

3.12.5   Routers and Brouters

A **router,** which works at the network OSI layer, is a device that connects two or more LANs and enables LAN-to-LAN communication. In addition, a router can break a large network into smaller, more manageable subnets. As multiple LANs are connected, multiple routes are created to get from one LAN to another. Routers share status and routing information with other routers, so that they can provide better traffic management and bypass slow connections. In addition, routers provide functions such as the ability to filter messages and forward them to different places based on various criteria. Most routers are multiprotocol routers, because they can route data packets using many different protocols (including TCP/IP and IPX). See Figure 3.19. Note: Routers cannot pass nonroutable protocols such as NetBEUI.

Broadcasting is a method of sending unaddressed packets to everyone on the network. Routers control broadcast "storms" by filtering the packets and stopping the broadcast from traveling to the other networks connected by the router.

A **brouter** (short for bridge router) is a device that functions as both a router and a bridge. A brouter understands how to route specific types of packets (routable protocols), such as TCP/IP packets. For other specified packets (nonroutable protocols), it acts as a bridge; that is, it simply forwards the packets to the other networks.

When you send a packet from one computer to another computer, a brouter first determines if the packet is sent locally to another computer on the same LAN, or if the packet is sent to a router so that it can be routed to the destination LAN. If the packet is meant to go to a computer on another LAN, it is sent to the router(or gateway). The router then determines what is the best route to take and forwards the packet to that route. The packet then goes to the next router and the entire process repeats itself until the packet gets to the destination LAN. The destination router forwards the packet to the destination computer.

A newer type of switch, the **layer 3 switch,** switches packets based on logical addresses (layer 3), such as IP addresses. A layer 3 switch does many things that a traditional router does: It determines the forwarding path based on the layer 3 network layer information; it validates the integrity of the layer 3 header via checksum; it verifies packet expiration and updates accordingly; and it applies security controls if required. Since the layer 3 switch has been optimized for high-performance LAN support, it typically is much faster than a router. However, the layer 3 switch is not meant to service wide area connections.

3.12.6   Gateways

A **gateway** is hardware and/or software that links two different types of networks by repackaging and converting data from one network to another network or from one network operating system to another. An example of a gateway is a computer or device that connects a PC to a mainframe computer or minicomputer, such as an AS400 midrange computer. Connection can be done by (1) adding an Ethernet card or Token Ring card to the AS400 computer and adding software to the client computers, (2) adding a special expansion card to the PC so that it can communicate with the AS400 directly, or (3) by using a gateway computer to act as a translator between the AS400 network and client networks. Note: A gateway can be used at any layer of the OSI reference model, but it is usually identified with upper layers, because they must communicate with an application, establish and manage sessions, translate encoded data, and interpret logical and physical addressing data.

Gateways can reside on servers, microcomputers, mainframes, or routers. They are typically more expensive than routers because of their vast capabilities, and they are almost always application-specific. Since they require more processing for their tasks, gateways transmit data more slowly than bridges or routers.

Figure 3.19   A Router

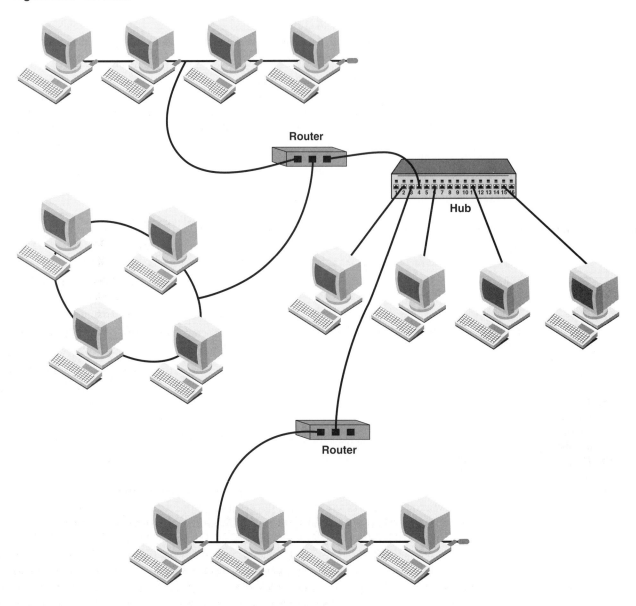

There are three different types of gateways:

- **Protocol gateway**—Functions like a router in that it connects networks that use different protocols. This is the most common type of gateway
- **Address gateway**—Connects networks with different directory structures and file management techniques
- **Format gateway**—Connects networks using different data format schemes (For example, a format gateway might connect two networks, one using ASCII and another using EBCDIC.)

The most common gateways in today's networks are listed next:

- **E-mail gateway**—A gateway that translates messages from one type of system to another
- **IBM host gateway**—A gateway that establishes and manages communication between a PC and an IBM mainframe computer

■ **Internet gateway**—A gateway that allows and manages access between LANs and the Internet. An Internet gateway can restrict the kind of access LAN users have to the Internet and vice versa.

■ **LAN gateway**—A gateway (usually a router or a server) that allows segments of a LAN running different protocols or different network models to communicate with each other. The LAN gateway category might also include remote access servers that allow dial-up connectivity to a LAN.

SUMMARY

1. To overcome compatibility issues, hardware and software often follow standards (dictated specifications or most popular specifications).

2. The de jure (by law) standard is a standard that has been dictated by an appointed committee.

3. The de facto (from the fact) standard is a standard that has been accepted by the industry just because it was most commonly followed.

4. When a system or standard has an open architecture, the specification of the system or standard is public.

5. A proprietary system is privately owned and controlled by a company that has not divulged specifications that would allow other companies to duplicate the product.

6. The Open Systems Interconnection (OSI) reference model is the world's prominent networking architecture model.

7. The concept of placing data behind headers (and before trailers) for each layer is called encapsulation.

8. The physical layer is responsible for the actual transmission of the bits sent across physical media.

9. Signaling is the method of using electricity, light energy, or radio waves to communicate.

10. The process of changing a signal to represent data is often called modulation or encoding.

11. Digital signals (the language of computers) are based on a binary signal system produced by pulses of light or electric voltages. The site of the pulse is either on/high or off/low to represent 1s and 0s.

12. An analog signal is the opposite of a digital signal. Instead of having a finite number of states, it has infinite number values, which are constantly changing.

13. Synchronous devices use a timing or clock signal to coordinate communication between the two devices.

14. Asynchronous signals are intermittent signals; they can occur at any time and at irregular intervals. They do not use a clock or timing signal.

15. Bandwidth refers to the amount of data that can be carried on a given transmission medium.

16. Baseband systems use the transmission medium's entire capacity for a single channel.

17. A broadband system uses the transmission medium's capacity to provide multiple channels.

18. Point-to-point topology connects two nodes directly together.

19. Multipoint connection links three or more devices together through a single communication medium. Because multipoint connections share a common channel, each device needs a way to identify itself and the device to which it wants to send information. The method used to identify senders and receivers is called addressing.

20. The data link layer is responsible for providing error-free data transmission and establishes local connections between two computers.

21. The media access control (MAC) sublayer is the lower sublayer that communicates directly with the network adapter card.

22. The logical link control (LLC) sublayer manages the data link between two computers within the same subnet.

23. The physical device address or media access control (MAC) address is a unique hardware address (unique on the LAN/subnet).

24. Topology describes the appearance or layout of the network. Depending on how you look at the network, topology can be physical or logical.

25. The physical topology (part of the physical layer) describes how the network actually appears.

26. The logical topology (part of the data link layer) describes how data flows through the physical topology (the actual pathway of the data).

27. The set of rules defining how a computer puts data onto the network cable and takes data from the cable is called the access method. The access method is sometimes referred to as arbitration.

28. Contention occurs when two or more devices contend (compete) for network access. Any device can transmit whenever it needs to send information. To avoid data collisions (two devices sending data at the same time), specific contention protocols were developed that require the device to listen to the cable before transmitting data.

29. The most common form of contention is the carrier-sense multiple access (CSMA) network.

30. Carrier-sense multiple access with collision detection (CSMA/CD) is the access method used in Ethernet and IEEE 802.3.

31. Token passing uses a special authorizing packet of information to inform devices that they can transmit data.

32. Polling has a single device, such as a mainframe front-end processor, designated as the primary device.

33. The network layer is concerned with the addressing and routing necessary to move data (known as packets or datagrams) from one network (or subnet) to another.

34. Networks are identified by a unique network address.

35. A port or socket is used to identify a specific upper-layer software process or protocol.

36. Circuit switching is a technique that connects the sender and the receiver by a single path for the duration of a conversation.

37. In packet switching methods, messages are broken into small parts called packets.

38. A virtual circuit is a logical circuit created to ensure reliable communication between two network devices.

39. To determine the best route, routers use complex algorithms that take into account a variety of factors, including speed of the transmission media, number of network segments, and the network segment that carries the least amount of traffic.

40. The transport layer can be described as the middle layer that connects the lower and upper layers. In addition, it is responsible for reliable transparent transfer of data (known as segments) between two end points.

41. Flow control is the process of controlling the rate at which a computer sends data.

42. The session layer allows remote users to establish, manage, and terminate a connection (sessions).

43. A session is a reliable dialog between two computers.

44. The presentation layer ensures that information sent by an application layer protocol of one system will be readable by the application layer protocol on a remote system.

45. The application layer represents the highest layer of the OSI reference model.

46. Directory services identify all resources on a network and make those resources accessible to users and applications.

47. A repeater, which works at the physical OSI layer, is a network device used to regenerate or replicate a signal or to move packets from one physical medium to another.

48. A hub, which works at the physical OSI layer, is a multiported connection point used to connect network devices via a cable segment.

49. A bridge, which works at the data link OSI layer, is a device that connects two LANs and makes them appear as one or that is used to connect two segments of the same LAN.

50. A switching hub (sometimes referred to as a switch or a layer 2 switch) is a fast, multiported bridge that builds a table of the MAC addresses of all the connected stations. It then reads the destination address of each packet and forwards the packet to the correct port.

51. A router, which works at the network OSI layer, is a device that connects two or more LANs. In addition, it can break a large network into smaller, more manageable subnets.

52. A brouter (short for bridge router) is a device that functions as both a router and a bridge.

53. A gateway is hardware and/or software that links two different types of networks by repackaging and converting data from one network to another network, or from one network operating system to another.

QUESTIONS

1. Which standard is used because it is the most common?
   a. de jure standard
   b. de facto standard
   c. a company standard
   d. the standard most preferred

2. Which model is the most well-known model for networking architecture and technologies?
   a. OSI model
   b. client-server model
   c. peer-to-peer model
   d. IEEE model

3. Which describes the correct order of the OSI model layers from bottom to top?
   a. physical, data link, network, transport, session, presentation, and application
   b. data link, physical, network, transport, session, presentation, and application
   c. physical, data link, network, transport, presentation, session, and application
   d. application, presentation, session, transport, network, data link, and physical

4. Which one of the following connectivity devices typically works at the physical layer of the OSI model?
   a. routers
   b. bridges
   c. repeaters
   d. gateways

5. What happens to the data link layer source and destination addresses when packets are passed from router to router?
   a. They are stripped off and then recreated.
   b. They are stripped off and replaced with MAC (hardware) addresses.
   c. They are stripped off and replaced with NetBIOS names.
   d. They are reformatted according to the information stored in the routing table.

6. Which layer of the OSI model determines the route from the source to the destination computer?
   a. transport layer
   b. session layer
   c. network layer
   d. physical layer

7. Bridges are often called media access control bridges because they work at the media access control sublayer. In which OSI layer does the media access control sublayer reside?
   a. transport layer
   b. physical layer
   c. network layer
   d. data link layer

8. Which layer of the OSI model provides synchronization between user tasks by placing checkpoints in the data stream?
   a. transport layer
   b. session layer
   c. network layer
   d. physical layer

9. Which layer of the OSI model adds header information that identifies the upper-layer protocols sending the frame?
   a. presentation layer
   b. network layer
   c. MAC sublayer
   d. LLC sublayer

10. Which layer of the OSI model defines how cable is attached to a network adapter card?
    a. cable layer
    b. connection layer
    c. hardware layer
    d. physical layer

11. Many applications use compression to reduce the number of bits to be transferred on the network. Which layer of the OSI model is responsible for data compression?
    a. application layer
    b. session layer
    c. network layer
    d. presentation layer

12. Which of the following connectivity devices typically works at the data link layer of the OSI model?
    a. routers
    b. bridges
    c. repeaters
    d. gateways

13. Which layer of the OSI model packages raw data bits into data frames?
    a. physical layer
    b. network layer
    c. presentation layer
    d. data link layer

14. Which layer of the OSI model is responsible for translating the data format?
    a. application layer
    b. network layer
    c. presentation layer
    d. data link layer

15. Which layer of the OSI model provides flow control and ensures messages are delivered error free?
    a. transport layer
    b. session layer
    c. network layer
    d. physical layer

16. The data link layer of the OSI model is responsible for what tasks?
    a. creating, maintaining, and ending sessions, and encryption
    b. reliable delivery of data and error control
    c. transferring and routing of packets on the network
    d. addressing and reassembling frames

17. The IEEE Project 802 divides the data link layer into two sublayers. Which sublayer communicates directly with the network adapter card?
    a. logical link control sublayer
    b. logical access control sublayer
    c. media access control sublayer
    d. data access control sublayer

18. What is the term for two computers acting as if there is a dedicated circuit between them even though there is not?
    a. virtual circuit
    b. physical circuit
    c. gateway
    d. dialog path

19. The Project 802 model defines standards for which layers of the OSI model?
    a. physical layer and data link layer
    b. network layer and data link layer
    c. transport layer and network layer
    d. application layer and presentation layer

20. Who developed the various pieces to the 802 models?
    a. Institute of Electrical Engineers
    b. Institute of Electronic Engineers
    c. Institute of Engineering Electricians
    d. Institute of Electrical and Electronic Engineers

21. Which Project 802 model specification describes Ethernet?
    a. 802.2
    b. 802.3
    c. 802.5
    d. 802.10

22. Which Project 802 model specification adds header information that identifies the upper-layer protocols sending the frame and specifies destination processes for data?
    a. 802.2
    b. 802.3
    c. 802.5
    d. 802.10

23. What does the 802.5 specification specify?
    a. Ethernet
    b. token ring
    c. fiber optics
    d. ARCnet

24. Which system is based on a binary signal system produced by pulses of light or electric voltages?
    a. analog
    b. digital
    c. signal propagation
    d. synchronous

25. Which of the following provides multiple channels on a network medium?
    a. baseband
    b. broadband
    c. broadbase
    d. multiband

26. Which of the following allows for two devices to communicate at the same time?
    a. simplex
    b. half duplex
    c. full duplex
    d. complex

27. Which of the following allows for two devices to communicate to each other, but not at the same time?
    a. simplex
    b. half duplex
    c. full duplex
    d. complex

28. The address that identifies a network card to the network is known as the_____.
    a. MAC address
    b. MAC identity
    c. port address
    d. I/O address

29. When different networks are not physically separated, you must have a unique configuration for each network. What has to be unique besides the node address on the network to tell the networks apart?
    a. network ID
    b. computer name
    c. IP address
    d. workgroup or domain name

30. Connection-oriented and connectionless communication are the two ways that communication can be implemented on a network. Which of the following is often associated with connectionless communication?
    a. fast but unreliable delivery
    b. error-free delivery
    c. fiberoptic cable
    d. infrared technology

31. The two ways to implement communication on networks are connection-oriented and connectionless communication. Which of the following is associated with connection-oriented communication?
    a. fast but unreliable delivery
    b. assured delivery
    c. fiberoptic cable
    d. infrared technology

32. What type of communication ensures reliable delivery from a sender to receiver without any user intervention?
    a. communication oriented
    b. connection oriented
    c. connectionless
    d. physical

33. Which of the following are connection-oriented protocols? (Choose all that apply.)
    a. TCP
    b. IP
    c. IPX
    d. SPX

34. Why does the transport layer assign port numbers to data segments?
    a. so each segment can be reassembled in order
    b. so each segment can be checked for errors
    c. so each segment can be sent to its appropriate application
    d. None of the choices apply.

35. Which OSI layer provides for multiple applications to use the same data stream?
    a. transport
    b. application
    c. network
    d. session

36. At what OSI layer is data merely a stream of bits (ones and zeros)?
    a. network
    b. datalink
    c. transport
    d. physical

37. What part of the OSI model is responsible for physical addressing?
    a. media access control
    b. network layer
    c. logical link control
    d. physical layer

38. What is another name for a switch that implements layer 2 and layer 3 technology?
    a. bridge
    b. brouter
    c. repeater
    d. router

39. At what layer of the OSI model does a router function?
    a. data link
    b. network
    c. transport
    d. physical

40. Pat is the network administrator for a meat-packing plant in Sacramento, California. He has installed a Microsoft Exchange Server version 5.5 computer on the Windows NT 4.0 local area network (LAN) at the plant. He tries to send an e-mail message outside the LAN to test the computer. The e-mail message never reached its destination. Brett discovers that the IBM mainframe that uses Simple Mail Transfer Protocol (SMTP) to transmit e-mail messages over the Internet did not process the e-mail message. Which device can Brett install to ensure that the meat-packing plant's Windows NT 4.0 LAN will be able to communicate with the IBM mainframe e-mail server?
    a. a router
    b. a brouter
    c. a gateway
    d. a hub

41. A hub (multiport repeater) operates at what OSI layer?
    a. physical
    b. transport
    c. network
    d. application

42. NICs operate at what layer of the OSI model?
    a. datalink
    b. network
    c. transport
    d. physical

43. On one network segment a router is allowing only IPX packets to pass. On another segment a router is allowing only IP packets to pass. How can network nodes on both segments communicate with each other?
    a. by bridge
    b. by router
    c. by brouter
    d. by gateway

44. What device will enable a mainframe computer to talk to a PC?
    a. bridge
    b. router
    c. brouter
    d. application gateway

45. Which of the following network devices do *not* examine packets as they pass through them?
    a. routers
    b. bridges
    c. switches
    d. repeaters

46. Your network suffers data loss due to attenuation. What device, at a minimum, must you install?
    a. bridge
    b. router
    c. brouter
    d. repeater

47. What is the binary number for the decimal value of 6?
    a. 00000101
    b. 00001111
    c. 00000111
    d. 01010101
    e. 00000110

48. What is the binary number for the decimal value of 68?
    a. 10101010
    b. 00001111
    c. 01000010
    d. 11110000
    e. 01010101
    f. 01000100

49. What is the decimal number for the binary value of 10101010?
    a. 170
    b. 165
    c. 224
    d. 128

50. What is the binary number for the hexadecimal value of FH?
    a. 1000
    b. 1110
    c. 1111
    d. 1010
    e. 0001

CHAPTER **4**

Media and Topologies

Topics Covered in This Chapter

Introduction

One of the primary components of a network is the common media that connect individual computers into a network through a network card. To enable the computers to communicate with each other, there are many options in cable types, cable layout, and protocols.

Objectives

- Recognize common media connectors (RJ-11, RJ-45, AUI, BNC, ST, and SC) and describe their uses.
- Choose the appropriate media types and connectors to add a client to an existing network.
- Identify the main characteristics of VLANs.
- Given a wiring task, select the appropriate tool (e.g., wire crimper, media tester/certifier, punch-down tool, tone generator, optical tester).
- Given a network scenario, interpret visual indicators (e.g., link lights, collision lights) to determine the nature of the problem.
- Build and test a UTP cable.

- Build and test a coaxial (Thinnet) cable.
- Explain the purpose of the plenum cable.
- Explain the role of a MAC address.
- List and compare the different connectivity devices.
- List the different devices used for cable management.
- Identify a network troubleshooting scenario involving a wiring/infrastructure problem; identify the cause of the problem (e.g., bad media, interference, malfunctioning network hardware).

4.1   DATA AND THE NETWORK

To communicate on LANS, **network cards,** or **network interface cards (NICs),** which are found on an expansion card or are integrated into the motherboard, use transceiver (devices that both transmit and receive analog or digital signals). To get a better idea of the function of the network card, consider how data are sent from one computer to another. The data are generated by the microprocessor and sent to the network card using the computer's parallel data bus. At this point, the data consist of alphanumeric characters represented as a series of on (1) and off (0) signals.

Within the network card, the data are processed and converted so that they can be transmitted on network media. If data are being sent on a cable, the data are turned into a serial bit stream, amplified, and sent on to the cable. The electrical signals that travel over the network cable must follow specific rules on how to gain sole access to the cable and learn what specific signals to send to represent the data on the cable.

The network card on the receiving computer sees the packet and reads part of the packet to determine if the packet was meant for it. The network card then converts the data into digital signals and sends the data to the microprocessor to be processed.

4.2   TOPOLOGIES

Topology describes the appearance or layout of the network. Depending on how you look at the network, topology is physical or logical. The **physical topology** (part of the physical layer of the OSI reference model) describes how the network actually appears. The **logical topology** (part of the data link layer) describes how the data flow through the physical topology—the actual pathway of the data. While the physical topology is easy to recognize, the logical topology is not.

Table 4.1   Physical topologies

Topology	Installation	Expansion/Reconfiguration	Troubleshooting	Medium Failure
Bus	Relatively easy	Moderately difficult	Difficult	Break in the bus prevents transmission
Ring	Moderately easy	Moderately difficult	Easy	Break in the ring prevents transmission (partial for dual rings)
Star	Easy but time consuming	Easy	Easy	Break in one cable only affects one computer
Mesh	Difficult	Difficult	Easy	Very low
Cellular	Easy	Easy	Moderately easy	Very low

4.2.1   Physical Topology

The physical topology describes how devices on a network are wired or connected together. Five types of physical topologies used in networks:

- Bus
- Ring
- Star
- Mesh
- Cellular

See Table 4.1.

A **bus topology** looks like a line where data are sent along a single cable. The two ends of the cable do not meet and the two ends do not form a ring or loop. See Figure 4.1. All **nodes** (devices connected to the computer, including networked computers, routers, and network printers) listen to the traffic on the network, but they only accept the packets that are addressed to them. The single cable is sometimes referred to as a **segment, backbone cable,** or **trunk.** Since all computers use the same backbone cable, the bus topology is easy to set up and install, and the cabling costs are minimal. Unfortunately, traffic builds up easily on this topology, so it is not a recommended topology for large networks. An example of a bus topology is Ethernet (10Base2 and 10Base5).

Typically with a bus topology network, the two ends of the cable must be terminated. This is done because when signals get to the end of a cable segment, they have a tendency to bounce back and collide with new data packets. If there is a break anywhere, or if one system does not pass the data along correctly, the entire network will go down. A break divides the cable trunk into two pieces, each with an end that is not terminated. These problems are difficult to troubleshoot, because a break causes the entire network to go down with no indication of where the break occurred.

In **ring topology** all devices are connected to one another in a closed loop. See Figure 4.2. Each device is connected directly to two other devices. Typically in a ring, each node checks to see if the packet was addressed to it and acts as a repeater (duplicates the data signal, which helps keep the signal from degrading) for the other packets. This allows the network to span large distances. Although it might look inefficient, a ring topology sends data very quickly, because each computer has equal access to communicate on the network.

When a client loses connectivity in a large multiring environment, the first task is to isolate the ring. Traditionally, a break in the ring causes the entire network to go down, and the break can be difficult to isolate. Today, some networks have overcome this pitfall by using dual rings to establish fault tolerance and by having a computer act as a beacon if it notices a break in the ring. Since each node in a ring is a repeater, the ring topology tends to be more expensive than the other topologies. IBM's Token Ring and Fiber Distributed Data Interface (FDDI) are examples of ring topologies.

Figure 4.1 Bus topology

The **star topology** is the most popular topology in use. It has each network device connect to a central point such as a hub, which acts as a multipoint connector. Other names for a hub are concentrator, multipoint repeater, and media access unit (MAU). See Figure 4.3.

Star networks are relatively easy to install and manage. Installation may be time consuming, however because each computer requires a cable that runs back to the central point. If a link fails (hub port or cable), the remaining workstations are not affected like those in the bus or ring topology. Unfortunately, bottlenecks can occur because all data must pass through the hub. Examples are Ethernet (10BaseT and 100BaseTX).

Another topology is the **mesh topology** in which every computer is linked to every other computer. While this topology is not very common in LANs, it is common in WANs, where it connects remote sites over telecommunication links. This topology is the hardest to install and reconfigure, since the number of cables increases geometrically with each computer that is added. Note: Some networks use

Figure 4.2   Ring topology

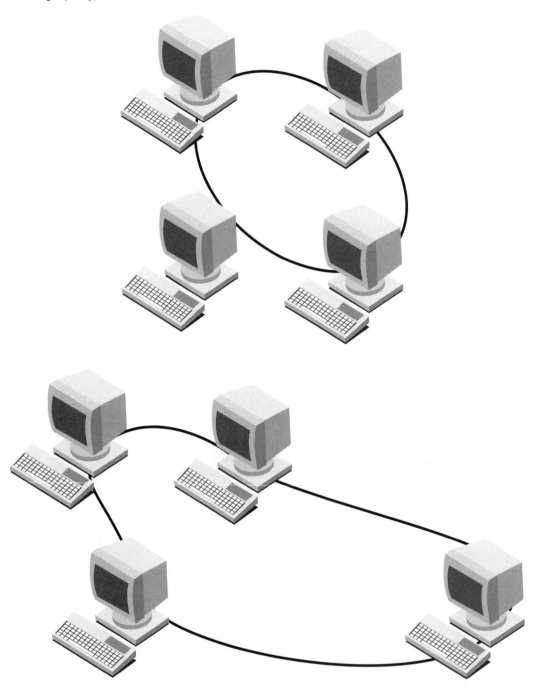

a modified mesh topology, which has multiple links from one computer to another but does not necessarily have each computer linked to every other computer. See Figure 4.4.

Many technologies that are wireless use a **cellular topology,** in which an area is divided into cells. A broadcast device is located at the center and broadcasts in all directions to form an invisible circle (cell). All network devices located within the cell communicate with the network through the central station or hub, which is connected with the rest of the network infrastructure. If cells are overlapped, devices may roam from cell to cell while maintaining connection to the network. See Figure 4.5. The best-known example of cellular topology is cellular phones.

Figure 4.3   Star topology

Figure 4.4   Mesh topology and modified mesh topology

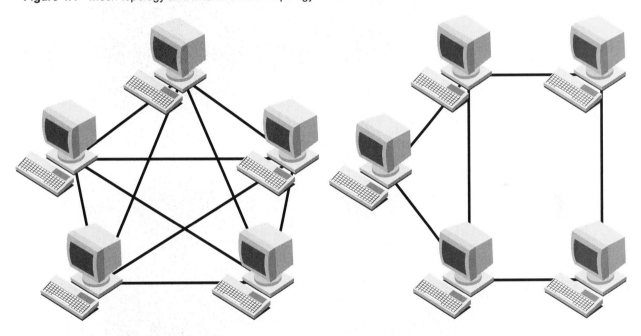

A **hybrid topology** combines two of the traditional topologies, usually to create a larger topology. A hybrid topology allows you to use the strengths of the various topologies to maximize the effectiveness of the network. Examples of the hybrid topology are the bus star topology and the star ring topology. See Figure 4.6.

4.2.2   Logical Topology

Physical topology describes how the network actually appears, while logical topology describes how the data flows through the physical topology—the actual pathway of the data. The two logical topologies are bus and ring.

Consider Ethernet using a backbone cable. Here, you have a network that physically is a bus topology. The pathway of the signals, or the logical topology, is also a bus topology. Now consider

Figure 4.5 Cellular topology

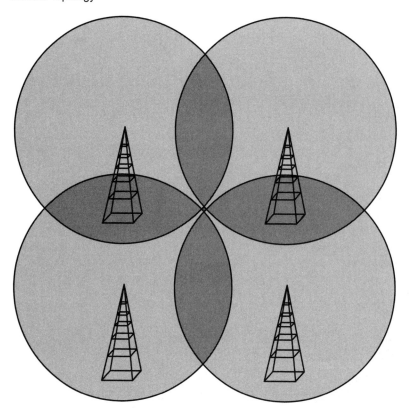

Figure 4.6 Hybrid topology (bus star and star ring)

Figure 4.7   Logical bus topology

Figure 4.8   Logical ring topology

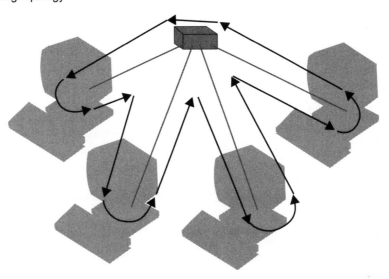

an Ethernet network using a star topology. The physical network is a star topology, yet the pathway, or logical topology, is a bus. This is so because each cable attached to the hub has two wires. One wire carries data from the hub to the network device, and the other wire carries data from the network device to the hub. The hub then connects the pairs of wires with each other, thereby creating a large bus pathway. Of course, the bus has two ends, which are contained within the hub. See Figure 4.7.

As another example, consider IBM's Token Ring network. While this network has a physical star topology, the pathway, or logical topology, is a ring. The Ethernet hub contains two cable ends, but the IBM Token Ring MAU connects the two ends to form a ring. See Figure 4.8.

4.2.3   Segment and Backbone

A segment could be a single cable, such as a backbone cable, or a cable that connects a hub and a computer. A logical segment contains all the computers on the same network and each of the computers has the same network address. Examples are networks with a backbone cable or hub used in a logical bus topology.

A backbone can be used as a main cable segment, such as that found in a bus topology network. Such a backbone would include a long, single cable with patch cables used to attach these computers, or smaller cables connected together with barrel and T-connectors. A backbone can be the main network connection through a building, campus, WAN, or the Internet.

Table 4.2   Cable types

Cable Type	Cable Cost	Ease of Installation	Installation Cost	EMI Sensitivity	Data Bandwidth	Comments
UTP	Lowest	Very simple	Lowest	Highest	Lowest to high	Used in more than 99% of LANs
STP	Medium	Simple to moderate	Moderate	Moderately Low	Moderate	Usually found in older networks
Coaxial	Medium	Simple	Moderate	Moderate	High	Often used as a backbone cable
Fiber Optic	Highest	Difficult	Highest	None	Very high	Uses light instead of electrical signal

4.3   CABLING

The cabling system used in networks form the veins of the network that connect all of the computers and allow them to communicate with each other. The common types of cabling are unshielded twisted pair (UTP), shielded twisted pair (STP), coaxial, and fiber optic. See Table 4.2.

Frequency (bandwidth) is the number of cycles that are completed per unit of time and is generally expressed in hertz (cycles per second). Data cabling is typically rated in kilohertz (KHz) or megahertz (MHz). The more cycles per second, the more interference the cable generates and the more susceptible the cable is to data loss.

The data rate (or information) capacity is defined as the number of bits per second (bps) that move through a transmission medium. When you choose a cable, you must choose one that will handle your current network traffic and allow for some growth.

With traditional cabling, there is a fundamental relationship between the number of cycles per second that a cable can support and the amount of data that can be pushed through the cable. For example, category 5 and category 5e cables are rated at 100 MHz. To implement a 100BaseTX network, you use category 5 cabling, because cable must support a frequency of 100 MHz. During each digital cycle, a single bit is pushed through. Although this is a good way to think of the relationship between information rate and cable bandwidth, the IEEE recently approved the 803.3ab standard (1000BaseT), which deals with running Gigabit Ethernet over category 5 cabling. Category 5 does not operate at 1 GHz. Instead, the cable uses four data pairs to transmit the data and sophisticated encoding (multiplexing) techniques to send more bits of data over the wire during each cycle.

In copper wiring, a signal loses energy during its travel because of electrical properties at work in the cable. The opposition to the flow of current through a cable or circuit is expressed in impedance. Impedance is a combination of resistance, capacitance, and inductance and is expressed in ohms. A typical UTP cable is rated at between 100 and 120 ohms. All category 3, 4, 5, and 5e cables are rated at 100 ohms.

Attenuation occurs when the strength of a signal falls off with distance over a transmission medium. This loss of signal strength is caused by several factors; for example, the signal converted to heat due to the resistance of the cable and the energy was reflected as the signal encountered impedance changes throughout the cable. Low decibel values of attenuation are desirable, since that means that less of the signal is lost on its way to the receiver.

Interference occurs when undesirable electromagnetic waves affect the desired signal. **Electromagnetic interference (EMI)** is caused by large electromagnets used in industrial machinery, motors, fluorescent lighting, and power lines. **Radio frequency interference (RFI)** is caused by transmission sources such as a radio station. Another term used to describe instability in a signal wave is called **jitter,** which is caused by signal interference.

Besides analyzing the capacity and electrical characteristics of the cable, you need to look at two other factors when choosing a cable. First, consider cost. If you are installing a large network within a building, the cabling system can cost thousands of dollars. Note: The cost of installing the cable (planning and hourly wages) is many times the cost of the cable itself. Therefore, make sure that you have the financial resources available to install such a system.

Figure 4.9   Twisted pair cable

Second, consider ease of installation of the cabling system, since this affects labor costs and can indirectly affect the reliability of the network. In addition, look at the ease of troubleshooting, including how the cable is affected by media faults and if the cable system offers any fault tolerance.

4.3.1   Unshielded Twisted-Pair (UTP) Cable

A **twisted pair** consists of two insulated copper wires twisted around each other. While each pair acts as a single communication link, twisted pairs are usually bundled together into a cable and wrapped in a protective sheath. See Figure 4.9.

> **Question:** Why are the wires twisted around each other?
>
> **Answer:** They are twisted because copper wire does not constrain electromagnetic signals well. So if two copper wires are next to each other, the signal will induct (law of induction), or transfer, from one wire to the other. This phenomenon is called **cross talk.**
>
> The circuits that send data on the cable are differential amplifiers. Twisted wires ensure that the noise is the same on each wire. The common noise is then canceled at the differential amplifier. Since the data are inverted on the second wire, the data are not canceled. Therefore, by using a twisted pair, the cross talk is canceled.

A twisted pair can be an **unshielded twisted pair (UTP)** or a shielded twisted pair (STP). The UTP cable is the type of cable used with telephones, and it is the most common cable used in networks. See Figure 4.10. UTP cable consists of four pairs of wires. In each pair, the wires are twisted about each other and used together to make a connection. Compared with other cable types, UTP is inexpensive and is the easiest to install. The biggest disadvantages of UTP are its limited bandwidth of 100 meters and its susceptibility to interference and noise. Traditionally, UTP has had a limited network speed, but now UTP can be used in networks running between 4 Mbps and 1 Gbps. Some companies, such as Hewlett-Packard, are working on a 10 Gbps network standard.

In 1995, UTP cable was categorized by the Electronic Industries Alliance (EIA) based on the quality and number of twists per unit. The UTP categories are published in EIA-568-A. See Table 4.3.

Early networks that used UTP cable typically used category 3, while today's high-speed networks typically use category 5 or enhanced category 5 cabling. Category 3 has three to four twists per foot and can operate up to 16 MHz. Category 5 uses three to four twists per inch, contains Teflon insulation, and can operate at 100 MHz. Enhanced category 5 is a higher-quality cable designed to reduce cross talk even further and support applications that require additional bandwidth. Category 7 has not been approved yet. Therefore, no vendor can promise complete compatibility for future networks.

Figure 4.10   UTP cable

Table 4.3   Unshielded twisted-pair cable categories for networks

Cable Type	Bandwidth (MHz)	Function	Attenuation (dB)[1]	Impedance (ohms)	Network Usage
Category 3	16	Data	11.5	100	10baseT (10 Mbps), IBM Token Ring (4 Mbps), ARCnet, 100VG-AnyLAN (100 Mpbs)
Category 4	20	Data	7.5	100	10baseT (10 Mbps), IBM Token Ring, ARCnet, 100VG-AnyLAN (100 Mpbs)
Category 5	100	High-speed data	24.0	100	10baseT (10 Mbps), IBM Token Ring, Fast Ethernet (100 Mbps), Gigabit Ethernet (1000 Mbps), ATM (155 Mbps)
Category 5E (Enhanced)	100	High-speed data	24.0	100	10baseT (10 Mbps), IBM Token Ring, Fast Ethernet (100 Mbps), Gigabit Ethernet (1000 Mbps), ATM (155 Mbps)
Category 6	250	High-speed data	19.8	100	10baseT (10 Mbps), IBM Token Ring, Fast Ethernet (100 Mbps), Gigabit Ethernet (1000 Mbps), ATM (155 Mbps)
Category 6E (Enhanced)	250	High-speed data	19.8	100	10baseT (10 Mbps), IBM Token Ring, Fast Ethernet (100 Mbps), Gigabit Ethernet (1000 Mbps), ATM (155 Mbps)
Category 7 (Not Yet Approved)	600	High-speed data			

[1]dB = decibel.

As network applications increased network traffic, there was a need for faster networks. One way to increase the performance of the network is to use more expensive, faster electronic devices. A cheaper way is to increase the amount of usable bandwidth by using all four pairs of the UTP cable instead of two pairs.

Question: If you are planning a network, what type of cable should you use?

Answer: Standard category 5 will handle standard network technologies for the next 5 years, including Fast Ethernet/100BaseTX and Gigabit Ethernet 1000BaseTX. If you are planning to support gigabit technology now or in the future, you should select enhanced category 5.

A telephone uses a cable with two pairs (four wires) and an RJ-11 connector; a computer network uses a cable with four pairs (eight wires) and an RJ-45 connector. See Figure 4.11. In a simple network, one end of the cable attaches to the network card on the computer and the other end attaches to a hub (multiported connection). With UTP wiring, you must be careful about the quality of the RJ-45 connector crimping. Bad crimping can lead to intermittent connections or pulled out wires. You also must make sure that the pairs stay twisted right down to the connector.

In a larger network, one end of the cable connects the network card of the computer to a wall jack. The wall jack is connected to the back of a patch panel kept in a server room or wiring closet. A cable is attached to the patch panel and connected to a hub. The cable that connects the computer to the wall jack, and the cable that connects the patch panel and the hub, are called patch cables.

Figure 4.11 UTP cable with an RJ-45 connector and a UTP cable with a RJ-11 connector

UTP cable is commonly available in 22, 24, and 26 AWG (American wire gauge) and can be either solid or stranded. **Solid cable** is typically used for cabling that exists throughout a building. This includes cables that lead from the wall jacks to the server room or wiring closet. **Stranded cable** is typically used as patch cables between patch panels and hubs and between computers and wall jacks. Since stranded wire is not as firm as solid wire, it is a little easier to work with. Unfortunately, stranded cable has 20% more attenuation than solid wire.

4.3.2 Building UTP Cable

There are two types of Ethernet cables: a straight-through cable and a crossover cable. The **straight-through cable,** which can be used to connect a network card to a hub, has the same sequence of colored wires at both ends of the cable. A **crossover cable,** which can be used to connect one network card to another network card or one hub to another hub, reverses the transmit and receives wires. See Tables 4.4, 4.5, and 4.6.

Two wiring standards are available: 568A and 568B. The 568B wiring is used in almost 90% of installations. The pin numbers refer to an RJ-45 telephone-type connector. Pin 1 is on the left when you hold the tab down with the wire facing you, as you would plug it in. Pin 2 is the next one on the right, and pin 8 is the one all the way to the right. The 568A wiring is used when compatibility to telephone wiring systems (USOC) is needed. It is not recommended, as parts are not as commonly available.

A good way of remembering how to wire a crossover Ethernet cable is to wire one end using the 568A standard and the other end using the 568B standard. Another way of remembering the color coding is to simply switch the green set of wires in place with the orange set of wires. Specifically, switch the solid green (G) with the solid orange, and switch the green/white with the orange/white.

To create a category 5 UTP patch cable, you will need the following items:

- Category 5 stranded cable
- Two RJ-45 round wire connectors
- Small wire-cutter
- RJ-45 crimping tool

Step 1   Measure and cut the needed length of the cable. Cut the cable about 3 inches longer than the final patch cable length.

Step 2   Take one end of the wire and remove the outer sheathing to reveal about 3/4-inch twisted wires.

Step 3   Untwist all of the exposed wires and straighten them out as much as you can. Rearrange the wires in a flat manner, as close together as possible in the proper color order. See Tables 4.4 and 4.5.

Step 4   Take all of the wires and cut them to the same length of approximately 1/2 inch exposed. Note: Today, most connectors can act as a vampire tap, since they can bite into the cable to get to the copper core. Therefore, when using these types of connectors, this step can be skipped.

4.3.3   Shielded Twisted-Pair Cable

Shielded twisted pair (STP) cabling is similar to UT Pair, except that STP is usually surrounded by a braided shield that reduces EMI sensitivity and radio emissions. See Figure 4.12. Shielded twisted-pair cable was required for all high-performance networks until a few years ago and is still commonly used

Step 5	Hold an RJ-45 connector and insert the wires from the bottom, making sure to keep the right color order. Each wire should slide into separate grooves toward the tip of the connector. Push the wires in as far as they will go. In addition, make sure that the outer sheathing is up into the opening and that the outer sheathing is under the crimping tab.	
Step 6	Insert the RJ-45 connector into the crimping tool and crimp the connector.	
Step 7	Repeat steps 2 through 6 for the other end of the cable.	
Step 8	Using a cable tester or digital multimeter, test the cable. (For more information, see Section 4.5.)	

Table 4.4   Standard color scheme for UTP, RJ-45 cables

Wire No.	Pair No.	EIA/TIA 568A Color Standard	AT&T 258A or EIA/TIA 568B Color Standard	
Pin 1	**Pair 2**	White with green strip	White with orange strip	
Pin 2	**Pair 2**	Green	Orange	
Pin 3	**Pair 3**	White with orange strip	White with green strip	
Pin 4	**Pair 1**	Blue	Blue	
Pin 5	**Pair 1**	White with blue strip	White with blue strip	
Pin 6	**Pair 3**	Orange	Green	
Pin 7	**Pair 4**	White with brown strip	White with brown strip	
Pin 8	**Pair 4**	Brown	Brown	

in IBM Token Ring networks (see Figure 4.13) and Apple's LocalTalk network. STP is relatively expensive compared to UTP, and is more difficult to work with.

The STP cables used by IBM networks are shown in Table 4.7. Unlike other connectors, IBM connectors are hermaphroditic, which means they are not male or female. Therefore, if the cable does not connect properly, just turn it around.

Table 4.5 Ethernet crossover cable pinouts

End 1	End 2
Pin 1 (white with green strip)	Pin 1 (white with orange strip)
Pin 2 (green)	Pin 2 (orange)
Pin 3 (white with orange strip)	Pin 3 (white with green strip)
Pin 4 (blue)	Pin 4 (blue)
Pin 5 (white with blue strip)	Pin 5 (white with blue strip)
Pin 6 (orange)	Pin 6 (green)
Pin 7 (white with brown strip)	Pin 7 (white with brown strip)
Pin 8 (brown)	Pin 8 (brown)

Table 4.6 Pins used in RJ-45 connector for various technologies[1]

Application	Pins 1/2	Pins 3/6	Pins 4/5	Pins 7/8
Analog Voice	—	—	Tx/Rx	—
ISDN	Power	Tx	Rx	Power
10BaseT (802.3)	Tx	Rx	—	—
IBM Token Ring (802.5)	—	Tx	Rx	—
100BaseTX (802.3u)	Tx	Rx	—	—
100BaseT4 (802.3u)	Tx	Rx	Bi	Bi
100BaseVG (802.12)	Bi	Bi	Bi	Bi
FDDI (TP-PMD)	Tx	Optional	Optional	Rx
ATM User Device	Tx	Optional	Optional	Rx
ATM Network Equipment	Rx	Optional	Optional	Tx
1000BaseT (802.3ab)	Bi	Bi	Bi	Bi

[1]Tx=transmit; Rx=receive; Bi=bidirectional; Optional=may be required by some vendors.

Figure 4.12 Shielded twisted-pair cable

Shielding

Figure 4.13   IBM shielded twisted-pair cable

4.3.4   Coaxial Cable

Coaxial cable, sometimes referred to as coax, is a cable that has a center wire surrounded by insulation, then a grounded shield of braided wire (mesh shielding). See Figure 4.14. The copper core carries the electromagnetic signal, and the braided metal shielding acts as both a shield against noise and a ground for the signal. The shield minimizes electrical and radio frequency interference and provides a connection to ground. Coaxial cable is the primary type of cable used by the cable television industry and is widely used for computer networks.

For computer networks, coaxial cables are usually used for the backbone cable for Ethernet networks. The network devices are attached by cutting the cable and using a T-connector or by applying a vampire tap (a mechanical device that has conducting teeth to penetrate the insulation and attach directly to the wire conductor). To maintain the correct electrical properties of the wire, you must terminate both ends of the cable and you must ground one end of the cable. The termination dampens signals that bounce back or reflect at the end of the cable. The ground completes the electrical circuit. Not grounding at all can lead to an undesirable charge in the coaxial cable. Grounding at both ends can lead to a difference in ground potential, which can cause an undesirable current on the cable, especially if it is located between two buildings.

BNC connector is short for British Naval Connector, Bayonet Nut Connector, or Bayonet Neill Concelman. It is a type of connector used with coaxial cables such as the RG-58 U/A cable used with the 10Base2 Ethernet system. The basic BNC connector is a male type that is mounted at each end of a cable. This connector has a center pin connected to the center cable conductor and a metal tube connected to the outer cable shield. A rotating ring outside the tube locks the cable to any female connector. **BNC T-connectors** (used with the 10Base2 system) are female devices for connecting two cables to a network interface card. See Figure 4.15. A **BNC barrel** connector allows two cables to be connected together.

> **Question:** You have two Ethernet hubs that you need to link together as one network. Each hub contains a single BNC connector, which allows you to connect the hubs together. Therefore, you take a coaxial cable and connect it directly from the BNC connector to the other BNC connector. Unfortunately, the hubs do not function together. What is the problem?
>
> **Answer:** The problem is, anytime that you use a coaxial cable with Ethernet, you must always connect network devices using a T-connector. In addition, the two ends must be terminated with the proper terminating resistor.

Table 4.7 IBM cabling system

IBM Type	Standard Label	Description
Type 1	Shielded twisted pair (STP)	Two pair of 22-AWG shielded wires surrounded by an outer braided shield. Used for computers and MAUs. Impedance of type 1 cable is 150 ohms and is rated at 20 Mbps. Typically used in token ring applications
Type 1A	Shielded twisted pair (STP)	Same as type 1, except the cable is rated at 100 Mbps.
Type 2	Voice and data cable	A voice and data shielded cable with two twisted pairs of 22-AWG wires for data, an outer braided shield, and four twisted pairs of 26-AWG for voice (unshielded). Impedance of type 1 cable is 150 ohms. The shielded pairs are rated at 20 Mbps and the unshielded pairs are rated at 4 Mbps.
Type 2A	Shielded twisted pair (STP)	Same as type 2, except the cable is rated at 100 Mbps.
Type 3	Voice grade cable	Consists of four solid, unshielded twisted pair 22 or 24-AWG cables. The type 3 cable is rated up to speeds of 4 Mbps and impedance is 100 ohms.
Type 4	Not yet defined	
Type 5	Fiber optic cable	Two 62.5/125-micron multimode optical fibers (the industry standard)
Type 6	Data patch cable	Considered a thinner and more flexible version of a type 1 cable. Two 26-AWG twisted pair stranded cables with a dual foil and braided shield. It is rated for speeds up to 20 Mbps and has an impedance of 150 ohms. Unfortunately, it has 1.33 times the loss of a type 1 cable. Typically used in token ring applications.
Type 7	Not yet defined	A single-pair version of type 6. Impedence of 150 ohms and is rated for speeds up to 20 Mbps.
Type 8	Carpet cable	Housed in a flat jacket for use under carpets. Two shielded twisted pair 26-AWG cables. Limited to half the distance of type 1 cable. Type 8 cable has twice the loss of a type 1 cable.
Type 9	Plenum	Fire safe. Two shielded twisted pair cables with an impedance of 150 ohms and rated up to 20 Mbps.

Figure 4.14 Coaxial cable

Insulation

Grounded
Shield

Inner
Conductor

Figure 4.15   A network card attached to a coaxial cable and terminator using a T-connector. Since this is the end of the bus, a terminator is required.

Table 4.8   Coaxial cable commonly used today

RG Rating	Popular Name	Ethernet Implementation	Type of Cable	Center Wire Gauge (AWG)	Resistance Value (ohms)
RG-6/U	Thicknet	10Base5	Solid copper	18	75
RG-8U	Thicknet	10Base5	Solid copper	10	50
RG-58/U	NA	None	Solid copper	20	50
RG-58/AU	Thinnet	10Base2	Stranded copper	20	50
RG-59	Cable TV	None	Solid/stranded copper	20	75
RG-62	ARCnet	NA	Solid copper	22	93

Several coaxial cable standards are applicable to computer networking. See Table 4.8.

4.3.5   Building a Coaxial Cable

To create a coaxial 10Base2 Ethernet cable, you need the following:

- RG-58/AU coaxial cable
- Two RG-58/U BNC connectors
- Racheting coaxial crimping tool
- Two-step rotating stripper
- Cable cutter (straight cut)

Step 1   Cut the coaxial cable (straight cut) to the core wire using the cable cutter. Adjust the stripper to meet the desired cable diameter and stripping requirements. For best results, the stripper should be adjusted to expose 1/4 inch of the conductor and 1/4 inch of the insulation. Insert the coaxial cable into the coaxial wire stripper. Strip the ends of the cable using a rotary motion (three to five full turns with the coax stripper). Always turn the stripper in the same direction. Do not cut completely through the jacket, to avoid nicking the shield. Flex the jacket to complete the separation. Pull the coaxial cable out of the stripper and inspect the cable for stripping quality. Make sure the center conductor is not nicked or scored and that the braid is pushed away from the conductor.

Step 2   Seat the center pin of the BNC connector on the exposed conductor. Crimp the center pin to the end of the center conductor using the small-diameter, pin crimp die on the ratchet crimping tool. Ensure that all strands of the center conductor are in the hole in the center pin before crimping.

Step 3   Slide the sleeve ferrule over the pin and exposed insulation. Place the BNC connector body on the cable end. Align the connector body on the cable end so that its shaft fits over the pin and between the braid and the insulation.

Step 4   Slip the connector body under the braided shield as far as it will go. Check for stray strands and push them out of the way. Ensure that the pin flange rests on the exposed insulation and that the top of the pin is flush with the top of the BNC body. Slide up the crimp ferrule sleeve to cover the exposed braided shield up to the BNC body shoulder.

Step 5	Ensure that the ratcheting crimping tool is fitted with the proper hex die. Place the crimping tool over the ferrule sleeve and squeeze it to evenly and completely crimp the ferrule to the BNC body.	
Step 6	Inspect the neatness and tightness of the conductor. Pull and flex firmly on the BNC connector to make sure it is crimped tightly to the cable.	
Step 7	Repeat steps 1 through 6 for the other end of the cable.	
Step 8	Test the cable with a cable tester or digital multimeter. For more information, see Section 4.5.	

4.3.6   Fiber Optic Cable

A **fiber optic** cable consists of a bundle of glass or plastic threads, each of which is capable of carrying data signals in the forms of modulated pulses of light. Although glass can carry the light pulses (several kilometers) further than plastic can, plastic is easier to work with. Since each thread can carry a signal in only one direction, a cable consists of two threads in separate jackets, one to transmit and one to receive. The fiber optic cable has cladding surrounding the fiber core; this helps reflect light back to the core and ensures that little of the light signal is lost. The cable also contains Kevlar strands to provide strength.

The light signals used in fiber optic cables are generated by light emitting diodes (LEDs) or by injection laser diodes (ILDs). ILDs are similar to LEDs but produce laser light. Laser light is purer than normal light, so it can increase both data rates and transmission distances. Signals are received by photodiodes, solid-state devices that detect variations in light intensity.

Fiber optic cables come in single-mode fiber and multimode fiber. **Multimode fiber (MMF)** is capable of transmitting multiple modes (independent light paths) at various wavelengths or phases. Unfortunately, the greater diameter of the fiber's core makes light more likely to bounce off the sides of the core; the results are dispersion and limitation of the bandwidth to 2.5 Gbps and of transmission distance between repeaters. MMF is usually used with networking applications such as 10BaseFL, 10BaseF, FDDI, ATM, and other applications that require fiber optic cable as horizontal cable and backbone cable. Multimode cabling typically uses an orange sheath.

Single-mode fiber (SMF) can transmit light in only one mode, but the narrower diameter of the fiber core yields less dispersion, which results in longer transmission distances. SMF is most commonly used by telephone companies and in data installations as backbone cable. Single-mode cabling typically uses a yellow sheath.

The types of fiber optic cable are differentiated by mode, composition (glass or plastic), and core/cladding size. The size and purity of the core determines the amount of light that can be transmitted. Common types of fiber optic cables include the following:

- 8.3-micron core/125-micron cladding single-mode
- 62.5-micron core/125-micron cladding multimode
- 50-micron core/125-micron cladding multimode
- 100-micron core/140-micron cladding multimode

The typical multimode fiber optic cable consists of two strands of fiber (duplex). The core is 62.5 microns in diameter, and the cladding is 125 microns in diameter. Often these dimensions are expressed as 62.5/125-micron. The newest version of the TIA/EIA 568 standard also recognizes the use of 50/125-micron multimode fiber optic cable. A typical indoor fiber optic cable consists of a core/cladding surrounded by a 250-micron acrylate coating. A 900-micron buffer surrounds the cladding, and this buffer is surrounded by Kevlar strands.

Over the past 5 years, fiber optic cables have found their way into cable television networks where they increase reliability, provide a greater bandwidth, and reduce costs. In the LAN, fiber cabling has become the primary medium for campus and building backbones, offering high-speed connections between diverse LAN segments.

Fiber optic cable has the largest bandwidth (up to 10 GHz) of any medium available. It can transmit signals over the longest distance (20 times farther than copper segments) at the lowest cost, with the fewest repeaters and the least amount of maintenance. In addition, since it has such a large bandwidth, it can support up to 1000 stations and it can support the faster speeds that will be introduced during the next 15 to 20 years.

Fiber optic cable is extremely difficult to tap, which makes it secure and highly reliable. Since fiber does not use electrical signals that run on copper wire, interference does not affect traffic; as a result, the number of retransmissions is reduced and network efficiency is increased.

To transmit data, two fibers are required. One strand of fiber is used to send and the other is used to receive. Fiber optic cables can be divided into three categories based on the number of optical fibers:

- Simplex
- Duplex
- Multifiber

A simplex fiber optic cable has only one optical fiber inside the cable jacket. Because simplex cables have only one fiber inside them, there is usually a larger buffer and a thicker jacket to make the cable easier to handle. Duplex cables have two optical fibers inside a single jacket. The most popular use for duplex fiber optic cable is as LAN backbone cable. Duplex cables are perfect because all LAN connections need a transmission fiber and a reception fiber. Multifiber cable has from three to several hundred optical fibers in it, typically in a multiple of two.

The disadvantage of simplex connectors is that you have to keep careful track of polarity. In other words, you must make sure that the plug on the send fiber is always connected to the send jack and that the receive plug is always connected to the receive jack. In duplex plugs and jacks, color-coding and keying ensures that the plug will be inserted only one way in the jack and will always achieve correct polarity.

Fiber optic cables use several connectors but the two most popular and recognizable connectors are the straight-tip (ST) and subscriber (SC) connectors. See Figure 4.16. The ST connector, developed by AT&T, is probably most common. It has a BNC attachment mechanism similar to the Thinnet connector mechanism. The SC connector (sometimes known as the square connector) is typically a latched connector. It is impossible for the connector to be pulled out without releasing the latch (usually by pressing some kind of button or release).

A new connector, called the MT-RJ, is similar to an RJ-45 connector. It is a small form-factor, two-fiber connector that is lower in cost and smaller than the duplex SC interface.

The main disadvantage of fiber optic cables is that they are expensive to install and require special skills and equipment for splitting or splicing. In addition, they are more fragile than wire. Now, as fiber optic products are more mass produced, the cost gap between them and the high grades of UTP has closed significantly, and there are many premade products available.

Figure 4.16   Fiber optic cable and common connectors (ST, SC, and MT-RJ)

4.4   CABLE MANAGEMENT

In a physical star topology used in Ethernet networks, all of the cables lead and connect to a hub or a set of hubs. Although a small network uses only one or two hubs, a network consisting of a few hundred computers uses a few hundred cables. In such situations, it is important to establish some form of cable management.

4.4.1   TIA/EIA 568-A Wiring Standard

A large network needs a horizontal wiring and/or backbone wiring system. The **horizontal wiring system** has cables that extend from wall outlets throughout a building to the wiring closet or server room. **Backbone wiring,** which often is designed to handle a higher bandwidth, consists of cables used to interconnect wiring closets, server rooms, and entrance facilities (telephone systems and WAN links from the outside world). Backbone wiring is sometimes referred to as the **vertical cabling system.** Vertical connections between floors are known as **risers.** A horizontal wiring system could be category 5 UTP (or better), while the backbone wiring system could be category 5 UTP (or better), coaxial or fiber optic. Note: Horizontal wiring and backbone wiring are usually done by a wiring contractor.

In 1991, TIA and EIA released their joint 568 Commercial Building Wiring Standard, also known as structured cabling, for uniform, enterprise-wide, multivendor cabling systems. Structured cabling suggests how networking media can best be installed to maximize performance and minimize upkeep. The cabling infrastructure is described as follows:

- **Work area**—The work area includes the station equipment, patch cable, and adapters. The maximum recommended patch cable is 3 meters.
- **Telecommunications closet**—The telecommunications closet is considered to be the floor-serving facility for horizontal cable distribution and can be used for intermediate and main cross-connects. The closet must be designed with minimal cable stress from bends, cable ties, and tensions (as defined in the ANSI/EIA/TIA 569-A standard).
- **Equipment room**—The equipment room is the area in a building where telecommunications equipment is located and the cabling system terminates.
- **Horizontal cabling**—The horizontal cabling covers the area from the work area receptacle to the horizontal cross-connect in the telecommunications closet. It includes the receptacle and optional transition connector (such as under-carpet cable connecting to round cable). The maximum length of a horizontal cable should be 90 meters.

Figure 4.17 EIA/TIA 568-A wiring summary

- **Backbone cabling**—The backbone cabling provides interconnections between telecommunications closets, equipment rooms, and entrance facilities and includes the backbone cables, intermediate and main cross-connects, terminations, and patch cables for backbone-to-backbone cross-connections. Cabling should be 30 meters or less for connection equipment to the backbone. If there are no intermediate cross-connects, a maximum of 90 meters is allowed. Hierarchical cross-connections cannot exceed two levels.
- **Entrance facility**—The entrance facility is where the outside telecommunications service enters the building and interconnects with the building's telecommunications systems. In a campus or multibuilding environment, it may also contain the building's backbone cross-connections.

See Figure 4.17.

Two outlets are required at the work area:

- 100-ohm unshielded twisted pair (UTP)
- 100-ohm shielded twisted pair (STP-A) or 62.5/125-micron multimode fiber.

The two outlets allow for a data and voice connection. Grounding needs to conform to applicable building codes.

The characteristic impedance is 100 ohms $\pm 15\%$ from 1 MHz to the highest referenced frequency (16, 20, or 100 MHz) of a particular category. The recognized shielded twisted pair cables are IBM type 1A for backbone and horizontal distribution and IBM type 6A for patch cables with two-pair, and 22-AWG solid with a characteristic impedance of 150 ohms $\pm 10\%$ (3 MHz to 300 MHz). The fiber optic medium for horizontal cabling is 62.5/125-micron multimode optical cable with a minimum of two fibers, and for backbone cabling it is 62.5/125-micron multimode and single-mode optical fiber.

4.4.2   Plenum

Most cables contain halogens, chemicals that give off toxic fumes when they burn. These fumes release acid gases that sear the eyes, nose, mouth, and throat. The person who is exposed to the gases may experience severe respiratory damage or may become disoriented and unable to escape from the fire.

In buildings, the **plenum** is the space above the ceiling and below the floors used to circulate air throughout the workplace. It can also be found in some walls. If there is a fire, the plenum circulates the toxic fumes generated by burning of cabling. Some international governments have already developed standards to achieve zero-halogen cabling. The U.S. National Electrical Code, which serves as the basis for local standards in most states, recommends use of halogen-sheathed cabling in the plenum of office buildings.

A **plenum cable** is a special cable that gives off little or no toxic fumes when burned. Whether a building's wiring includes plenum cabling depends on the building's fire code. Plenum cable is not required if cabling exists in a special sealed conduit that would prevent toxic fumes from escaping into the open air. The major disadvantage of using plenum cable is that it is significantly more expensive than other cabling.

Riser cable is intended for use in vertical shafts that run between floors. Many buildings have a series of equipment rooms that are placed vertically in a reinforced shaft for the purpose of enclosing power distribution equipment; heating, ventilation, and air conditioning (HVAC) units; telephone distribution; and other utility services throughout the building. Cable placed in these shafts must not contribute to the spreading of fire from floor to floor. Since the shafts are not plenums, the riser rating is less stringent than the plenum rating.

4.4.3   Wall Jacks

As an information technology administrator, you may have to decide where to place the wall jacks that lead to the patch panel in the server room or wiring closet. If you are planning the location of wall jacks while a building is under construction, include jacks for office computers (remember that some offices will be using two or more computers) that connect to the wall jacks directly or for any hubs (used to connect multiple computers using a single wall jack) that connect to the wall jacks directly. In addition, add additional wall jacks for any network printer that needs to be connected to the network. Since the network cabling system is being built as the building is being built, it is best to plan for growth by adding extra jacks throughout the building.

4.4.4   Punch-Down Blocks

Punch-down blocks or patch panels help manage the hundreds of cables that may enter a wiring closet or server room. A **punch-down block** connects several cable runs to each other without going through a hub. Rather than using RJ-45 ports, the block is attached (or punched) directly to the exposed wires by using a **punch-down tool.** Punch-down blocks are typically used for permanent wire connections. For example, if you have category 5 cabling, you have four pairs, or eight wires. Each wire would connect to a row of connectors on the punch-down block. You can connect additional wires from other cables by using the same connectors in a row. See Figures 4.18 and 4.19.

The most common punch-down blocks are the 110 blocks (commonly referred to as insulation displacement connection, or IDC) and 66 block. The 110 blocks are the termination of choice in category 5, high-bandwidth environments, while the 66 block is used mostly with telephone systems.

4.4.5   Patch Panels

Patch panels fill the same needs as punch-down blocks. Wall jacks are connected to the back of the patch panel via individual RJ-45 ports, which are numerous. Note: The ports are labeled similarly to the corresponding wall jack. You can use patch cables to connect the port in the front of the patch panel to a

Figure 4.18 A 66 punch-down block

Figure 4.19 66 and 110 punch-down connectors

computer or a hub. As a result, you can connect multiple computers with a hub located in the wiring closet or server room. Compared to the punch-down block, the patch panel is easier to work with, allows for easier troubleshooting, makes temporary connection much easier to establish, and offers a much cleaner look. Therefore, patch panels are more common in LANs than punch-down blocks. See Figures 4.20 and 4.21.

Figure 4.20 Patch panel front view (a) and back view (b)

Figure 4.21 Patch panel allows for easy connection of computers

Figure 4.22 Basket system

4.4.6 Cable Ties and Basket Systems

Cable ties and basket systems are tools to manage the cables anywhere throughout a building. The **cable ties** are used to bundle cables traveling together and to pull the cables off the floor so that they will not get trampled or run over by office furniture. When installing or laying cable, handle the cable with care. Do not step on cables, pinch tightly with the cable ties, or make sharp bends or kinks in the cable. **Basket systems** consist of baskets or trays placed on the back of office furniture to hold and hide network cables without using cable ties. See Figure 4.22.

4.4.7 Server Rooms

Many cables come together in server rooms and wiring closets. Although a single cable doesn't weigh much, many cables together add up quickly, and the weight causes a lot of stress to the cables. Some type of tray, conduit, trough, or ladder will help to reduce stress.

Remember that cable has bend radius limitations. **Bend radius** is the radius of the maximum arc into which you can loop a cable before you impair data transmission. Generally, a cable bend radius is less than four times the diameter of the cable. (Be careful not to exceed it.)

The server room is the work area of the information technology department where the servers and most of the communication devices reside. The room should be secure, and only a handful of people should have access to it. In addition, the server should be secure. Follow these rules:

■ Lock the computer when it is not in use.
■ Always require user names and passwords.

Note: When dealing with a small number of cables or large number of cables, it is very important to always label both ends of the cables, especially those that are part of the backbone or horizontal wiring system. This will become essential in quickly troubleshooting cable faults and to make your job easier in the future. In addition, it is very important that you document the cable system such as having a blueprint showing where and how the cables are connected.

- Always log out when the server is not being used.
- Restrict accounts so that they cannot log on directly (interactive) to the server.
- Enable security monitoring such as auditing.

Since the computers and telecommunication systems can generate a lot of heat, and a dry room is susceptible to electrostatic discharge that can damage electronic components, consider separate environmental controls for the server room. **Electrostatic discharge (ESD)** is electricity generated by friction, such as when your arm slides on a tabletop or when you walk across a carpet. To reduce ESD, implement the following suggestions:

- Develop an ESD prevention program. Include use of ESD wrist straps when opening computers and handling computer components. Install an antistatic flooring and/or place the servers on an antistatic mat.
- Keep humidity low (less than 50%).
- Install an uninterruptible power supply (UPS) to protect your system against power fluctuations, including outages.
- Keep your system cool (room temperature or less).
- Have a tape backup system or some other method to back up all important data files.

For the best results with, and longevity of, the system, ensure that the server room is clean and has access to clean air. Most office environments are clean enough that computer equipment only needs to be cleaned annually or biannually as part of a regular preventive maintenance program.

If the server room is in an industrial environment or the air is dusty or full of pollutants, you should move the server to a better location. If that is not an option, at least maintain a regular cleaning schedule to keep the server and the server room free of air problems. One easy preventive measure is to use an air cleaner in the server room. You can also buy special cases and enclosures for server hardware that are designed for industrial environments to prevent damage from dirt and pollutants. If you find that dust is continually causing the server to heat up and shut down, initiate a weekly, or at least monthly, preventive maintenance schedule that includes cleaning the cooling system elements and the interior of the system case.

If you have several servers, consider a **server rack** or **rack-mounted cabinet** to hold the servers. In addition, you can purchase a switch box to connect a single keyboard, mouse, and monitor to several servers. This will allow for less equipment and for a more organized work environment. As the Internet grew, there was a need to have many servers in a small amount of space. Therefore, manufacturers developed server racks that follow the Network Equipment Building Specification (NEBS), the same specification that is used in the telecommunications industry. The servers use the following form-factors:

- 4U (7 inches high)
- 2U (3.5 inches high)
- 1U (1.75 inches high)

When you stack these servers on top of one another, you can easily put a large number in a small area. Remember, though, that all of these servers require special electrical and cooling requirements. The cabinet should have exhaust fans over each bay to pull the heat up and away from the servers and other devices, to maximize the cooling systems. Make sure that the ventilation fans are operating properly.

Rack-mounted cabinets can also be equipped with surge-suppressor power strips. In most situations, however, it is better to install a UPS (uninterruptible power supply) in the bottom of the rack and use it to power the devices mounted in the rack.

When purchasing a server cabinet, look for a cabinet that has locking doors. Such doors form a vital part of the server's security. Avoid cabinets that use the same keys, for the doors on every bay. And of course, for the lock to serve its purpose, remember to keep the cabinet locked.

A **server blade** is a single circuit board populated with components such as processors, memory, and network connections that are usually found on multiple boards. Server blades are designed to slide into existing servers (known as a **blade server**) much like an expansion slot is plugged into a PC. Server blades allow many computers to be placed in a small area. Server blades are more cost-efficient and smaller and consume less power than traditional box-based servers.

4.5   TESTING CABLE SYSTEMS

Now that you have studied how cables are connected and how signals travel through the cable system, you are ready to learn how to troubleshoot cable problems. This subject is more important than you might think, because cables cause the most problems in a network. The best method for addressing a faulty cable installation is to avoid it in the first place by purchasing high-quality components and installing them carefully. No matter how careful you are, though, problems do arise.

Troubleshooting your network's cable system involves many of the common-sense skills that are part of any troubleshooting task. First, you try to isolate the cause of the problem by asking questions like the following:

- Has the cable *ever* worked properly?
- When did the malfunctions start?
- Do the malfunctions occur at specific times?
- Is the cable brand-new or has it been used for a while?
- What has changed since the cable functioned properly?

Once you have gathered all the information you can, the general troubleshooting process consists of steps such as the following:

1. Split the system into its logical elements.
2. Locate the element that is most likely the cause of the problem.
3. Test the element or install a substitute to verify it as the cause of the problem.
4. If the suspected element is not the cause, move on to the next likely element.
5. After locating the cause of the problem, repair or replace it.

Thus, you might begin troubleshooting by determining for sure that the cable is the source of the problem. You can do this by connecting different devices to both ends of the cable to see if the problem continues to occur. Once you verify that the cable is at fault, you can logically break it down into its component elements. For example, a typical cable run might consist of two patch cables, a wall plate, a punch-down block or patch panel, and the permanently installed cable itself. In this type of installation, the easiest thing to do is test the patch cables, either by replacing them or by testing them with a cable scanner. Replacing components can be a good troubleshooting method, as long as you know that the replacements are good. The most accurate method is to test the individual components with some form of cable tester.

Several types of problems can occur with cables:

- **Open**—A conductor with a break in it or wires that are unconnected, which prevents electricity to flow
- **Short**—When a circuit has zero or an abnormally low resistance path between two points, resulting in excessive current. In networking cables, a short is an unintentional connection made between two conductors (such as wires) or pins/contacts.
- **Crossed pairs**—When two wires are connected improperly causing the two wires to be crossed
- **Split pair**—Incorrect pinouts that cause data-carrying wires to be twisted together, resulting in additional crosstalk. Split pairs can be the result of mistakes during installation. The solution is to reattach the connectors at both ends using either the T568-A or T568-B pinouts.
- **Excessive length**—Cables that are longer than the recommended maximum for the network protocol you plan to use. Note: Don't be overly concerned if the maximum length for a cable segment is 100 meters and you have a run that is 101 meters long. Most protocols have some leeway built into them that permits a little excess.
- **Excessive attenuation**—Excessive loss of signal typically caused by excessive length or by use of a cable that is inferior or not designed for a particular network standard or speed. Attenuation can also be caused by faulty or substandard connectors, punch-down blocks, and patch panels.
- **Excessive NEXT**—Excessive near-end crosstalk (NEXT) typically caused by inferior cable, inferior components, improper patch cables, split pairs, loose twisting, or sharing cables for other signals such as voice communication.
- **Excessive noise**—Can be caused by AC power lines, light fixtures, electric motors, and other sources of EMI and RFI. Cabling should be routed away from these items.

Another problem is a jabbering Ethernet network card. **Jabbering** occurs when garbled bits of data are emitted within the frame sequence in a continuous transmission fashion. The packet length is usually more than 1518 bytes. Jabbering can be identified by a protocol analyzer as a CRC error. When nodes detect collisions they emit a normal jam signal on the network segment to clear transmission. Sometimes certain nodes attempt to keep jamming the network due to excessively high collision rates; this also can be captured as high CRC or late collision error rate. The cause can be overloaded traffic levels. If the bandwidth utilization levels are normal or low for the particular Ethernet segment, it is possible that the collision-detection pair of a jamming node's NIC or transceiver cannot hear the network signal and may not know that a collision has stopped. If this occurs, the node continues to jam the network. If a certain node on an Ethernet segment emits a lot of jabber, the node's NIC and transceiver should be checked through replacement and reanalysis. Note: If you use a protocol analyzer, you can capture the packets being transmitted and analyze them to determine which network interface is faulty.

As you will see, there are many tools and devices that can test cables. Some are simple and inexpensive, whereas others are elaborate and expensive. Some are easy to use because they supply easy-to-read pass/fail test results or simple numeric values; others provide results that need to be analyzed. These tools also can be used during installation to verify the installation and components.

4.5.1   Network Card Diagnostics

Today, most network cards come with diagnostic software that can be used to verify that the network card is functioning correctly. Diagnostic software falls into two categories: hardware and software. Note: If you can log into the network, generally speaking, the network card is functioning.

Hardware diagnostics examine the individual parts of the network card and verify the functions of each component. If there is a problem, the diagnostics will report it. Unfortunately, most diagnostics for UTP-based network cards cannot determine whether the network card is transmitting or receiving data successfully without a device known as a hardware loopback.

A hardware loopback is a special connector for Ethernet 10BaseT network cards. It functions similarly to a crossover cable, except that it connects the transmit pins directly to the receive pins (pin 1 connected to pin 3 and pin 2 connected to pin 6). It can then be used by the software diagnostics of the network card to test transmission and reception capabilities. The hardware loopback is no bigger than a single RJ-45 connector, with a few small wires on the back. You plug the loopback into the RJ-45 connector on the back of the network card, start the diagnostic software, and start the diagnostic routine that requires the loopback. As a result, you will be able to tell if the network card can send and receive data.

Software diagnostics test the higher-level functions of the network card such as network communication without stations. These programs typically consist of a sender and receiver portion. Each portion is run on one of a pair of computers connected to the network. The sender sends a test packet out to the receiver, and when the receiver receives the packet, it immediately sends a response. Similar tools are available with protocol suites such as TCP/IP or IPX, but these diagnostic tests are protocol independent.

4.5.2   Crossover Cables

As introduced earlier in this chapter, a crossover cable can be used to connect two hubs. You can also use the crossover cable to test communication between two Ethernet stations without using a hub. A crossover cable allows you to connect a portable computer directly to a server's network card using the cable. After you configure the network cards and logical addresses, you should be able to log into the server.

4.5.3   Voltmeter and Ohmmeter

Since the computer is a sophisticated electronic device, a voltmeter and ohmmeter can be used to test certain aspects of it. A **voltmeter** determines if a device is generating the correct voltage output or signal. An **ohmmeter** checks wires and connectors and measures the resistance of an electronic device. A **digital multimeter (DMM)** combines the functions of several measuring devices, including a voltmeter and an ohmmeter.

The ohmmeter tests wire in the following way: Since a wire or fuse is a conductor, essentially you should measure no resistance (0 ohms), which means that there is no break in the wire or fuse. This is known as a **continuity check.**

4.5.4   Cable Testers

Before looking at cable testers, remember that most cables have only two conductors, such as those found in a coaxial cable or in a cable that contains several pairs of wires such as the UTP cable. Unfortunately, since the pinouts of the UTP cable vary depending on implementation, the cable becomes more complicated to test.

The simplest type of cable tester performs continuity testing, which is designed to check a copper cable connection for basic installation problems (e.g., opens, shorts, and crossed pairs). A continuity tester consists of two separate units that are connected to each end of the cable to be tested. In many cases, the two units can snap together for storage and easy testing of patch cables. These testing devices usually cannot detect more complicated twisted-pair wiring faults such as split pairs, but they are sufficient for basic testing, especially for coaxial cables.

The more sophisticated form of cable tester is the wire map tester. This device transmits signals through each wire in a copper twisted-pair cable to determine if it is connected to the correct pin at the other end. Wire mapping is the most basic test for twisted-pair cables because the eight separate wire connections involved in each cable run are a common source of installation errors. Wire map testers detect transposed wires, opens, and shorts.

A wire map tester consists of a remote unit that you attach to the far end of a connection and the battery-operated, handheld main unit that displays the results. See Figure 4.23. Typically, the tester displays various codes or a series of lights to describe the type of faults it finds. In some cases, you can purchase a tester with multiple remote units that are numbered, so that one person can test several connections without constantly traveling back and forth from one end of the connection to the other to move the remote unit.

One problem that a wire map tester cannot detect is split pairs, because even though the pinouts are incorrect, the cable is still wired straight through. To detect split pairs, you must use a device that tests the cable for the near-end crosstalk that split pairs cause.

Figure 4.23   Cable tester

4.5.5   Tone Generators

Another type of tester for copper cables is a two-piece unit called a tone generator and probe, sometimes referred to as a "fox and hound" wire tracer. One unit is connected to a cable with a standard jack or an individual wire with alligator clips, which transmits a signal over the cable or wire. The other unit is a penlike probe that emits an audible tone when touched to the other end of the cable or wire or even the insulating sheath.

A tone generator is most often used to locate a specific connection in a punch-down block. For example, some installers prefer to run all of the cables for a network to the central punch-down block without labeling the cables; then they use a tone generator to identify which block is connected to which wall plate and label the punch-down block accordingly. You can also use the device to identify a particular cable at any point between the two ends. Since the probe can detect the cable containing the tone signal through its sheath, you can locate one specific cable out of a bundle in a ceiling conduit or other type of raceway by connecting the tone generator to one end and touching the probe to each cable in the bundle until you hear the tone.

By testing the continuity of individual wires using alligator clips, you can use a tone generator and probe to locate opens, shorts, and miswires. An open wire produces no tone at the other end, a short produces a tone on two or more wires at the other end, and an improperly connected wire produces a tone on the wrong pin at the other end. Unfortunately, this process is extremely time consuming and is prone to errors, especially if the tester is not systematic and thorough. In the testing process you have to continually travel from one end of the cable to the other to move the tone generator unit, or you have to work with a partner to test each connection, keeping in close contact by phone, radio, or some other means of communication to avoid confusion. When you consider the time and effort involved, you will probably find that testing with a wire map is a more practical solution than testing with a tone generator.

4.5.6   Time Domain Reflectometers

A **time domain reflectometer (TDR)** is the primary tool used to determine the length of a copper cable and to locate impedance variations that are caused by opens, shorts, damaged cables, and interference from other systems. The TDR, which works much like radar, transmits a signal on a cable with the opposite end left open and measures the amount of time that it takes for the signal's reflection to return to the transmitter. When you obtain this elapsed time measure, called the nominal velocity of propagation (NVP), and you know the speed at which electrons move through the cable, you can determine the length of the cable.

The NVP for a particular cable is usually provided by its manufacturer, measured as a percentage of light. Some manufacturers provide the NVP as a percentage, such as 75%, while others express it as a decimal value multiplied by the speed of light (c), such as 0.75c. Many cable testers compute the length internally, based on the results of the TDR test and an NVP value that is either preprogrammed or that the tester specifies for the cable being tested. Since NVP values for various cables can range from 60% to 90%, the margin of error for the cable length results can be up to 30% if the wrong value is used.

Two basic types of TDRs are available, those that display their results as a waveform on an LCD or CRT screen and those that use a numeric readout to indicate the distance to a source of impedance. The numeric readout provides less detail, but it is easy to use and relatively inexpensive. Waveform TDRs are not often used for field testing these days, because they are much more expensive than the numeric type and require a great deal more expertise to use effectively.

You can use a TDR to test any kind of cable that uses metallic conductors, including the coaxial and twisted-pair cables used to construct LANs. A high-quality TDR can detect a large variety of cable faults, for example, open conductors, shorted conductors, loose connectors, sheath faults, water damage, and crimped, cut, or smashed cables. In addition, a TDR can measure the length of the cable and the distance to any of these faults.

4.5.7   Visual Fault Locators

The light that carries signals over fiber optic cable is invisible to the naked eye, which makes it difficult to ensure that installers have made the proper connections. A visual fault locator (sometimes called a cable tracer) provides a quick and easy way to test the continuity of a fiber cable connection by sending visible light over a fiber optic cable. A typical fault locator is essentially a flashlight that applies its LED or incandescent light source to one end of a cable, which is visible from the other end. Thus, you can locate a specific cable out of a bundle and ensure that a connection has been established.

More powerful units that use laser light sources can actually show points of high loss in the cable, such as breaks, kinks, and bad splices, as long as the cable sheath is not completely opaque. For example, the yellow- or orange-colored sheaths commonly used on a single-mode cable or multimode cables, respectively, usually emit enough of the light energy lost by major cable faults to make them detectable from the outside.

4.5.8   Fiber Optic Power Meters

A fiber optic power meter is a device that measures the intensity of the signal being transmitted over a fiber optic cable. The meter is similar in principle to a multimeter that measures electrical current, except that it works with light instead of electricity. The meter uses a solid-state detector to measure signal intensity. There are different meters for different fiber optic cables and applications, such as those for short wavelength systems and those for long wavelength systems. More expensive units can measure both long and short wavelength signals.

To measure the strength of an optical signal, there must be a signal source at the other end of the cable. Although you can use a fiber optic power meter to measure the signal generated by your actual network equipment, accurate measurement of the signal loss on a cable requires a consistent signal generated by a fiber optic test source. The test source, which is provided in a fiber optic tool kit, is also designed for use with a particular type of network. Sources typically use LEDs for multimode fiber or lasers for single-mode fiber to generate a signal at a specific wavelength. Choose a unit that simulates the type of signals used by your network equipment.

4.5.9   Optical Time Domain Reflectometers

An **optical time domain reflectometer (OTDR)** is the fiber optic equivalent of the TDR that is used to test copper cables. The OTDR transmits a calibrated signal pulse over the cable to be tested and monitors the signal that returns back to the unit. Instead of measuring signal reflections caused by electrical impedance as a TDR does, however, the OTDR measures the signal returned by **backscatter,** a phenomenon that affects all fiber optic cables.

As with a TDR, the condition of the cable causes variances in the amount of backscatter returned to the OTDR, which is displayed on an LCD or CRT screen as a waveform. By interpreting the signal returned, it is possible to identify cable faults of specific types and other conditions. Like a TDR, an OTDR can locate splices and connectors and measure their performance; identify stress problems caused by improper cable installation; and locate cable breaks, manufacturing faults, and other weaknesses. Knowing the speed of the pulse as it travels down the cable, the OTDR can use the elapsed time between the pulse's transmission and reception to pinpoint the location of a specific condition of the cable.

You should not use OTDRs to measure a cable's signal loss or locate faults on LANs. To measure signal loss, you should use a power meter and light source, which are designed to simulate the actual conditions of the network. In addition, although it is possible to use an OTDR to compute a cable's length based on backscatter, it is far from accurate in the short lengths of a LAN environment. Therefore, the OTDR is used primarily on long-distance connections, such as those used by telephone and cable television networks.

To interpret an OTDR waveform requires a good deal of training and experience. Another disadvantage is that full-featured OTDR units are quite expensive.

4.5.10   Fiber Optic Inspection Microscopes

The fiber used in fiber optic cabling is extremely thin compared with any copper cable. Splicing and attaching connectors to fiber optic cables require great precision. The best way to inspect cleaved fiber ends and polished connection ferrules is with a microscope. Fiber optic inspection microscopes are designed to hold cables and connectors in precisely the correct position for examination so that dirty, scratched, or cracked connectors can be detected and so that cables are cleaved in preparation for splicing. Good microscopes typically provide at least 100 power magnification, have a built-in light source (not a fiber optic light source, but a source of illumination for the object under the scope), and are able to support various types of connectors.

4.5.11   Multifunction Cable Scanners

Multifunction cable scanners, sometimes called certification tools, are available for both copper and fiber optic networks. The scanners perform a series of tests on a cable run, compare the results against either preprogrammed standards or parameters that you supply, and display the outcome as a series of pass or fail ratings. Most units perform the basic tests called for by the most commonly used standards, such as wire mapping, length, attenuation, and NEXT for copper cables, and optical power and signal loss for fiber optic cables. Many of the copper cable scanners go beyond the basics to perform a comprehensive battery of tests, including propagation delay, delay skew, various versions of crosstalk, and return loss.

The primary advantage of this type of device is that anyone can use it. You simply connect the unit to a cable, press a button, and read off the results after a few seconds. Many units can store the results of many individual tests in memory, download them to a PC, or output them directly to a printer.

4.5.12   Protocol Analyzers

Sometimes when you have to troubleshoot network problems, you need to take a good look at what is being sent through your network. This is where **protocol analyzers** come in. A protocol analyzer, also known as a network analyzer, is software or a hardware/software device that captures, or receives, every packet on your media, stores it in a trace buffer, and shows a breakdown of each of the packets by protocol in the order that they appeared. Thus, you can analyze all levels of the OSI model to determine the cause of the problem. Network analysis is the art of listening in on network communications to examine how devices communicate and determine the health of that network. An example of a protocol analyzer is Microsoft's Network Monitor.

The operation of a protocol analyzer is actually quite simple:

- Receive a copy of every packet on a piece of wire by operating in a promiscuous capture mode (a mode that captures all packets on the wire, not just broadcast packets and packets addressed to the analyzer's adapter)
- Time-stamp the packets
- Filter out the stuff that is not of interest
- Show a breakdown of the various layers of protocols, bit by bit.

These packet traces can be saved and retrieved for further analysis. Once a packet is captured from the wire, the analyzer breaks down the headers and describes each bit of every header in detail.

It is easy to capture the packets and time-stamp the packets, so often people have the tendency to capture every packet on a segment when trying to troubleshoot a specific problem. The problem is that you will be amazed at how much traffic is sent through a wire. When you analyze the packets, you can easily become overwhelmed. Therefore, by setting up filters and doing some basic statistical analysis, you can isolate the problem with more ease and less time. For example, if the problem affects only users communicating with a certain server, put an analyzer on that segment and filter traffic to and from that server. If the problem affects only users who go through a router, start by putting an analyzer on one of the routed segments and filter traffic to and from the router's MAC addresses. If you are troubleshooting a slow login process, start analyzing from the client's segment and put a filter on the client's MAC address.

Protocol analyzers can be used for more than just troubleshooting. You can use them to monitor your network performance and head off problems before they occur, and you can determine when your network is becoming too congested. Thus, you can update your network hardware or subdivide your network, so that network performance does not become a problem. You can also find out what is using the bandwidth of your network, so that you can optimize or tweak your network.

A protocol analyzer enables you to determine the baseline throughput of a particular application. In other words, you can determine how much traffic the application is causing. This is particularly important if you can actually test the application before purchasing it, thereby establishing if your current network can handle the additional traffic. Try to determine how much traffic is generated when you log on to the new application or server, query and update a database, and transfer files.

If you analyze your network when everything is working properly, it will be easier to identify packet anomalies, and you can compare the difference in performance when you update or replace drivers, network interfaces, platform upgrades, and so forth. Concrete numbers can be used in reports to management to justify equipment costs and upgrades.

A good protocol analyzer should include alerts/alarms that notify you of unusual or faulty traffic patterns. Useful alarms should include these elements:

- **Utilization percentage**—Shows percentage of bandwidth that is used up. On Ethernet networks especially, performance degrades significantly when the utilization rate is above 40%. Watch the collision/fragment error count in relationship to utilization.
- **Packets per second**—Shows number of packets seen per second on the network. This number gives an idea of how many packets an interconnecting device (such as a router or switch) needs to process per second.
- **Broadcasts per second**—Tells how much broadcast (processed by all devices, regardless of their operating system or protocol) is on the network. Excessive broadcast slows a network dramatically.
- **Server/router down**—Indicates when the server and/or router goes down
- **MAC layer errors**—Shows errors in per-second increments. MAC (media access control) layer errors are defined as layer 1 and 2 errors that corrupt packet formats or make access to the network impossible.

The analyzer should also be able to build trend graphs to illustrate current and long-term traffic patterns (such as utilization and packets per second). In order to make the communications information useful to you, the analyzer decodes, or interprets, the actual packet information received.

4.6   WIRELESS LANs

The earth's atmosphere can act as a medium to transport data over networks. For decades, radio and television stations have used the atmosphere to transport information via analog signals. The atmosphere is also capable of carrying digital signals. Networks that transmit signals through the atmosphere are known as wireless networks. Wireless networks typically use infrared or radio frequency signaling. See Table 4.9. These wireless networks are suited to very specialized network environments that require mobility, long distances, or isolated locations. Note: Radio and infrared signals are considered unbound media because they are not carried or bound with a physical cable.

A wireless LAN (WLAN) is a local area network without wires. WLANs have been around for more than a decade, but they are just beginning to gain momentum because of falling costs and improved standards. WLANs transfer data through the air using radio frequencies instead of cables. They can reach a radius of 500 feet indoors and 1000 feet outdoors, but antennas, transmitters, and other access devices can be used to widen that area. WLANs require a **wire access point** (a special type of hub) that plugs all the wireless devices into the wired network.

Wireless LAN systems provide LAN users with access to real-time information anywhere in their organization. Installing a wireless LAN system can be fast and easy and can eliminate the need to pull cable through walls and ceilings. In addition, wireless technology allows the network to go where wire cannot go. Thus, WLANs combine data connectivity with user mobility, and through simplified configuration, enable movable LANs.

4.6.1   Radio Systems

Radio Frequency (RF) resides between 10 KHz to 1 GHz of the electromagnetic spectrum. It includes shortwave radio, very high frequency (VHF) and ultra-high frequency (UHF). Radio frequencies are

Table 4.9   Wireless technology

Media	Frequency Range[1]	Cost	Ease of Installation	Capacity Range	Attenuation	Immunity for Interference and Signal Capture
Low-power Single Frequency	Entire RF, high GHz is most common	Moderate (depends on equipment)	Simple	<1 to 10 Mbps	High	Extremely low
High-power Single Frequency	Entire RF, high GHz is most common	Moderately expensive	Difficult	<1 to 10 Mbps	Low	Extremely low
Spread Spectrum Radio	Entire RF, 902 to 928 MHz in United States, 2.4 GHz band is most common	Moderate (depends on equipment)	Simple to moderate	2 to 6 Mbps	High	Moderate
Terrestrial Microwave	Low GHz, 4 to 6 or 21 to 23 is most common	Moderate to high (depends on equipment)	Difficult	<1 to 10 Mbps	Variable	Low
Satellite Microwave	Low GHz, 11 to 14 GHz most common	High	Extremely difficult	<1 to 10 Mbps	Variable	Low
Point-to-point Infrared	100 GHz to 1000 THz	Low to moderate	Moderate to difficult	<1 to 16 Mbps	Variable	Moderate
Broadcast Infrared	100 GHz to 1000 THz	Low	Simple	≤1 Mbps	High	Low

[1] RF = radio frequency. THz = tera-hertz.

either regulated or unregulated bandwidths. Users of regulated frequencies must get a license from the regulatory bodies that have jurisdiction over the desired operating are (the FCC in the United States and CDC in Canada). Although the licensing process can be difficult, licensed frequencies typically guarantee clear transmission within a specific area.

In unregulated bandswidths, users must operate at regulated power levels (under 1 W in the United States) to minimize interference with other signals. Of course, if a device broadcasts using less power, the effective area will be smaller. The FCC (Federal Communications Commission) allocated the following bands for unregulated broadcast: 902 to 928 MHz, 2400 to 2483.5 MHz, and 5752.5 to 5850 MHz. Although you don't require a license from the FCC to use these frequencies, you must meet FCC regulations, which include power limits to minimize interference (antenna gain of 6 decibel interference and 1 W of radiated power).

In radio network transmissions, a signal is transmitted in one or multiple directions, depending on the type of antenna that is used. The wave is very short in length with a low transmission strength (unless the transmission operator has a special license for a high-wattage transmission), which means it is best suited to short-range, line-of-sight transmissions. A line-of-sight transmission is one in which the signal goes from point to point, rather than bouncing off the atmosphere over great distances. Line-of-sight transmissions are limited because they are interrupted by land masses such as mountains.

A **band** is a contiguous group of frequencies, that are used for a single purpose. Commercial radio stations often refer to the band of frequencies they are using as a single frequency. However, typical radio transmissions actually cover a range of frequencies and wavelengths. Because most tuning equipment is designed to address the entire bandwidth at the kilohertz or megahertz level, the distinction between one frequency and a band is often overlooked.

A **narrow-band radio system** transmits and receives user information on a specific radio frequency. Narrow-band radio keeps the radio signal frequency as narrow as possible, just to pass the information. Undesirable crosstalk between communication channels is avoided by carefully coordinating different users on different channel frequencies. In a radio system, privacy and noninterference are accomplished by the use of separate radio frequencies. The radio receiver filters out all radio signals except the ones on its designated frequency. Depending on the power and frequency of the radio signal, the range could be a room, an entire building, or long distances. A low-power (1 to 10 W), single-frequency signal has a data capacity in the range of 1 to 10 Mbps.

Spread-spectrum signals are distributed over a wide range of frequencies, then collected onto their original frequency at the receiver. Unlike narrow-band signals, spread-spectrum signals use wider bands, which transmit at a much lower spectral power density (measured in watts per hertz). Unless the receiver is not tuned to the right frequency or frequencies, a spread-spectrum signal resembles noise, which makes the signals harder to detect and harder to jam. As an additional bonus, spread-spectrum and narrow-band signals can occupy the same band, with little or no interference. There are two types of spread-spectrum signals: direct sequence and frequency hopping. Spread-spectrum frequency ranges are very high, in the range of 902 to 928 MHz and higher, and typically send data at a rate of 2 to 6 Mbps.

Direct-sequence, spread-spectrum (DSSS) signals generate a redundant bit pattern for each bit to be transmitted. This bit pattern is called a chip (or chipping code). The intended receiver knows which specific frequencies are valid and deciphers the signal by collecting valid signals and ignoring spurious signals. The valid signals are then used to reassemble the data. Because multiple subsets can be used within any frequency range, direct-sequence signals can coexist with other signals. Although direct-sequence signals can be intercepted almost as easily as other RF signals, eavesdropping is ineffective, because it is quite difficult to determine which specific frequencies make up the bit pattern, retrieve the bit pattern, and interpret the signal. Because of modern error detection and correction methods, the longer the chip, the greater the probability that the original data can be recovered, even if one or more bits in the chip are damaged during transmission.

Frequency hopping quickly (many times each second) switches between predetermined frequencies. Both the transmitter and receiver must follow the same pattern and maintain complex timing intervals to be able to receive and interpret the data being sent. Intercepting the data being sent is extremely difficult unless the receiver knows the signals to monitor and the timing pattern. Dummy signals can be added to increase security and confuse eavesdroppers. The length of time that the transmitter remains on a given frequency is known as the dwell time.

4.6.2   Microwave Signals

Microwave communication is a form of electromagnetic energy that operates at a higher frequency (low GHz frequency range) than radio wave communication. Since it provides higher bandwidths than those available using radio waves, it is currently one of the most popular long-distance transmission technologies.

Microwave signals propagate in straight lines and are affected very little by the lower atmosphere. In addition, they are not refracted or reflected by ionized regions in the upper atmosphere. The attenuation of microwave systems is highly dependent on atmospheric conditions; for example, both rain and fog can reduce the maximum distance possible. Higher-frequency systems are usually affected most by such conditions. The systems are not particularly resistant to EMI, and protection from eavesdropping can only be achieved by encryption techniques.

There are two types of microwave systems:

■ Terrestrial systems are often used where cabling is difficult or cost is a prohibitive factor. Relay towers are used to provide an unobstructed path over an extended distance. These line-of-sight systems use unidirectional, parabolic dishes that must be aligned carefully.

■ Satellite systems provide far bigger areas of coverage than can be achieved using other technologies. The microwave dishes are aligned to geostationary satellites that can either relay signals between sites directly or via another satellite. The huge distances covered by the signal result in propagation delays of up to 5 seconds. The costs of launching and maintaining a satellite are enormous; consequently, customers usually lease the services from a provider.

4.6.3   Infrared Systems

Another form of wireless technology is **infrared (IR) systems,** which are based on infrared light (light that is just below the visible light in the electromagnetic spectrum). Similar to your TV or VCR remote controls, infrared links use LEDs or ILDs to transmit signals and photodiodes to receive signals. IR systems transmit in light frequency ranges of 100 GHz to 1000 THz. Unfortunately, IR systems only transmit up to 1 Mbps for omnidirectional communication and 16 Mbps for directional communication.

Since IR is essentially light, it cannot penetrate opaque objects. Infrared devices work using either directed or diffused technology. **Directed IR** technology uses line-of-sight or point-to-point methods. **Diffused** (also known as **reflective** or **indirect**) IR technology spreads light over an area to create a cell. Since IR light can bounce off walls, ceilings, and any other objects in its path, indirect IR is not confined to a specific pathway. Since it is not confined to a specific pathway, transmission of data is not secure. IR signals are not capable of penetrating walls or other opaque objects and they are diluted by strong light sources; therefore, an IR system is most useful in small or open indoor environments.

4.6.4   Configurations

WLAN configurations vary from simple, independent, peer-to-peer connections between a set of PCs, to more complex, intrabuilding infrastructure networks. There are also point-to-point and point-to-multipoint wireless systems. A point-to-point system is used to bridge between two LANs and to provide an alternative to cable between two geographically distant locations (up to 30 miles). Point-to-multipoint systems connect several, separate locations to one single location or building. Both point-to-point and point-to-multipoint can be based on the 802.11b standard or on more costly infrared-based systems that provide throughput rates up to 622 Mbps (optical carrier [OC]-12 speed).

4.7   NETWORK CARDS

Network cards are media dependent, media-access-method dependent, and protocol independent. This means that all of the network cards on the network must use the same type of cable and must gain access to the cable the same way. In addition, it means that it does not matter what protocol you use. In fact, you can even use several protocols at the same time.

For example, let's say you are installing a network and you decide to start with a Novell NetWare 5.1 server. In this server, you choose an NE2000 (a popular ISA network card) network card connected to a twisted-pair cable running at 10 Mbits, running a protocol called IPX. If you install a second server such as a Windows 2000 server, you must choose a network card that also connects to a twisted-pair cable that supports a speed of 10 Mbits. You could choose an Intel E100B (one of today's popular PCI network cards) card, which supports both 10-Mbits and 100 Mbits speed. The Windows 2000 server is using the TCP/IP protocol. While the Novell server can communicate with any computer on the network using the IPX protocol, and the Windows 2000 server can communicate with any computer on the network using the TCP/IP protocol, the two servers cannot communicate with each other, even though they are using the same cabling system.

4.7.1   Characteristics of a Network Card

When selecting a network card, first look at the type of network to which you are connecting. See Figure 4.24. For example, is the network Ethernet, IBM Token Ring, or ARCnet, or are you connecting your computer using a WAN connection? Next, look at the speed of the network. Are you going to be transmitting at 4 Mbps, 10 Mbps, 16 Mbps, 100 Mbps, or 1 Gbps? In addition, make sure that the network card has the proper network connector. If you are using UTP cable, you will most likely use an RJ-45 connector. If you are connecting to a 10Base2 coaxial cable, you will most likely use

Figure 4.24   A typical network card with a 10base-2/BNC and 10base-T/RJ-45 connection

a BNC T-connector, or if you are connecting to a 10Base5 coaxial cable, you will connect to an external transceiver using an **AUI (attachment unit interface)** connector, a female 15-pin D connector. The AUI connector is also known as DIX (Digital-Intel-Xerox) connector.

Next, select a card based on the type of expansion bus (ISA, MCA, EISA, VESA, PCI, PCI-X, PC-Card, or CardBus) available in your computer. Since the ISA slot can transfer up to 8.33 MB/s and the PCI card can transfer 264 MB/s, the PCI slot is needed for today's high-speed networks. Note: If you are using a network card for a Windows NT machine, you should make sure that the card appears on the Windows NT Compatibility List (HCL). After you have evaluated the basic characteristics of a network card, you can consider the card's advanced features, for example, how much processing the network card will do so that it alleviates some of the work of the microprocessor.

Some cards offer various forms of fault tolerance such as using two cards on the same network link. If one network card or connection fails, the other card still transmits and receives packets. Some cards offer port aggregation—asymmetric port aggregation or symmetric port aggregation. Asymmetric port aggregation is the capability to evenly distribute outbound LAN traffic among multiple NICs while inbound traffic passes through a single NIC. Symmetric port aggregation is similar to the asymmetric port aggregation except that it combines the bandwidth of multiple NICs for both incoming and outgoing traffic to provide a single link of up to 800 Mbps.

4.7.2   MAC Address

A **media access control (MAC)** address is a hardware address that identifies a node on the network, much like a street address identifies a house or building within a city. You cannot have two network cards or nodes with the same MAC address on the same network. You can have the same MAC address on two separate networks. Note: The MAC address is also called the hardware address, physical address, IBM or the Ethernet address. The MAC address is protocol independent. For Ethernet and IBM Token Ring cards, the MAC address is embedded onto the ROM chip on the card.

The MAC address itself is 6 bytes (12-digit hexadecimal number). Each byte (two digits) is separated by colons: 03:34:A4:B3:74:2D. Note: The broadcast address to all MAC addresses is FF:FF:FF:FF:FF:FF.

4.7.3   Installing a Network Card

Installation of a network card is not much different from that of other expansion cards. First, configure the card's I/O address, IRQ, DMA, memory addresses, and any options that are specific to the type of network card that you selected. This is done with jumpers, DIP switches, or configuration software or by the plug-and-play system. After the card is physically installed and the network cable is attached, load the appropriate driver and client software. (The driver is included with the operating system or on a disk that comes with the network card, or it will have to be downloaded from the Internet.) Depending on the type of the card, the driver may need to have the hardware resources specified (I/O address, IRQ, DMA, and memory address). Of course, these resources need to match the settings of the card. Make sure that the LED for the expansion card is active.

In addition, you must **bind** the protocol stack to the network card and install any additional network software needed. If you are going to bind multiple protocols to an NCI, for the best performance, the most used protocol on the network should be listed first on the binding list. To reduce unnecessary packet traffic and to improve bandwidth for the protocols that are being used, you should unbind protocols for an NIC that are not being used.

NDIS (network device interface specification developed by Microsoft) and **ODI** (open data link interface developed by Apple and Novell) are sets of communication standards for protocols and network card drivers. Both allow multiple protocols to use a single network adapter card.

4.7.4   Diskless Workstations

A **diskless workstation** is a computer that does not have its own disk drive. Instead, the computer stores files on a network file server. Diskless workstations can reduce the overall cost of a LAN because one large-capacity disk drive at the server is usually less expensive than several low-capacity drives at workstations. In addition, workstations can provide an extra level of security, because a user cannot infect the network by inserting a virus-infected disk, a user cannot use a snooper disk to bypass network security, and a user cannot save confidential/secure information to a floppy disk. The disadvantage of using a diskless workstation is that if the network is down, the workstation does not function.

To enable a diskless workstation to connect to the network and to boot an operating system, you must have a network card that has a PROM chip inserted into a socket located on the network card. A PROM, short for programmable ROM, is a memory chip on which data can be written only once. Once a program has been written onto a PROM chip, it remains there forever. Unlike RAM, PROMs retain their contents when the computer is turned off. The type of PROM chips used today on network cards are electrical erasable PROMs, or EEPROMs.

The PROM chip includes enough instructions to attach the network and to read the necessary boot files from the network. For a TCP/IP network the bootstrap protocol (BOOTP) enables a diskless workstation to discover its own IP address, the IP address of a BOOTP server on the network, and a file to be loaded into memory to boot the machine.

A special type of diskless computer is called the Net PC, which was designed cooperatively by Microsoft and Intel. Unlike most other diskless workstations, a Net PC has a small hard disk that is used as a temporary cache to improve performance rather than to permanently store data. The Net PC is designed to be an inexpensive computer and to discourage users from configuring the machines themselves. Configuration and management of a Net PC is performed through a network server and Microsoft's Zero Administration Windows (ZAW) system.

4.8   HUBS

As mentioned in Chapter 3, a **hub,** which works at the physical OSI layer, is a multiported connection point used to connect network devices via a cable segment. When a PC needs to communicate with another computer, it sends a data packet to the port, to which the device is connected. When the packet arrives at the port, it is forwarded, or copied, to the other ports so that all network devices can see the packet. In this way, all of the stations "see" every packet just as they do on a bus network. Of course,

Figure 4.25 A hub

Hub

a standard hub is not efficient on networks with heavy traffic, because it causes many collisions and retransmitted packets. See Figure 4.25.

4.8.1 Types of Hubs

Hubs can be categorized as passive hubs or active hubs. A passive hub serves as a simple, multiple connection point; it does not act as a repeater for the signal. An active hub, which always requires a power source, acts as a multiported repeater for the signal. Note: When installing an active hub, if the hub has a fan (which provides cooling), make sure that the fan is operating.

The most advanced hub is called the intelligent hub (also known as a manageable hub). An intelligent hub includes additional features that enable an administrator to monitor the traffic passing through the hub and to configure each port in the hub. For example, you can prevent certain computers from communicating with other computers, or you can stop certain types of packets from being forwarded. In addition, you can gather information on a variety of network parameters, such as the number of packets that pass through the hub and each of its ports, types of packets, whether the packets contain errors, and how many collisions have occurred. Note: All intelligent hubs are active hubs.

4.8.2 Parts of the Hub

Hubs have several basic elements:

- **Ports**—Receptacles where patch cables connect workstations or other devices to the hub. The number of ports (typically RJ-45 ports) on a hub generally ranges from 4 to 24, not including the uplink port.
- **Uplink port**—The port used to connect one hub to another hub. Even though an uplink port may look like any other port, it should only be used to interconnect hubs. Note: Many hubs designate one of the normal ports as the uplink port; you must use a push button to change from a normal port to an uplink port. If you do not have an uplink port, or if you need to connect additional hubs through the other ports, you will need to use a crossover cable.
- **Backbone port**—The port used to connect a hub to the network's backbone. For the 10BaseT networks, this type of connection is often made with short lengths of Thinnet coaxial cabling. Today, hubs usually use a fast RJ-45 connection or fiber optic cable for the backbone.

- **Port for management console**—A port used to connect a console (a desktop or portable PC) that enables you to view the hub's management information, such as the traffic load or number of collisions. Note: Since not all hubs are intelligent hubs, not all hubs offer ports for the management consoles.
- **Link LED**—The light on a port that indicates whether it is in use. If a connection is live, this light should be solid green. If you think you have everything connected properly and that the connection should be live, but the light is not on, you need to check connections and transmission speed settings for the hub and network device. In addition, make sure that the hub has power and that the network card has the correct driver loaded.
- **Collision LED**—A light on a hub or port, found on Ethernet hubs, that indicates when a collision occurs. If the light is always on, there are too many collisions.
- **Traffic (transmit or receive) LED**—The light on a port that indicates that traffic is passing through the port. Under normal data traffic situations, this light should blink. Traffic LEDs are normally adjacent to the link LEDs beside each data port.
- **Power supply**—The device that provides power to the hub. Active hubs typically have a power-on light. If the power-on light is not lit, the hub has lost power.
- **Ventilation fan**—Fan used to cool the device's internal circuitry. To function properly, hubs must cool their circuitry with a ventilation fan. When installing or moving hubs, be careful not to block or cover the air-intake vents.

4.8.3 Installing a Hub

Hubs can be broken down into three types: stand-alone, stackable, and modular. Stand-alone hubs serve a workgroup of computers that are isolated from the rest of the network. They may be connected to another hub by a coaxial, fiber optic, or twisted-pair cable. Stand-alone hubs are best suited to small, independent departments, home offices, or test lab environments. Stand-alone hubs do not contain a standard number of ports, but usually have 4, 8, 12, or 24 ports. A small, stand-alone hub that contains 4 ports may be called a "hubby," "hublet," or a "minihub."

Stackable hubs resemble stand-alone hubs, but they are physically designed to be linked with other hubs in a single telecommunications closet. Stackable hubs linked together logically represent one large hub to the network. Although many stackable hubs use Ethernet uplink ports, some use a proprietary high-speed cabling system to link the hubs together for better interhub performance.

Modular hubs provide a number of interface options within one chassis, which makes them more flexible than either stackable or stand-alone hubs. Similar to a PC, a modular hub contains a system board and slots into which you can insert different adapters that contain various types of ports.

To install a hub, you must connect and plug in the hub and turn it on; then make sure that the hub's power light goes on. Most hubs perform self-tests when turned on. Blinking lights indicate that these tests are in progress. When the tests are completed, attach the hub to the network by connecting a patch cable from it to the backbone or to a switch or router. Next, connect patch cables from the computer or patch panel. Once the computer connects to the network through the newly installed hub, verify that the link and traffic lights act as they should. If you are installing a stackable hub or a rack-mounted hub, you need to use the screws and clamps that came with the hub to secure it to the rack or connect it to the other hub. If it is an intelligent hub, you need to configure the hub using the software that is built into the hub's firmware. For example, you may need to assign an IP address to the hub. Always check the documentation that comes with the hub before you start.

4.9 BRIDGES

A bridge, which is a layer 2 device, breaks larger network segments into smaller segments. It works much like a repeater, but because a bridge works solely with layer 2 protocols and layer 2 MAC sub-layer addresses, it operates at the data link layer.

Some bridges can also connect dissimilar network types (e.g., IBM Token Ring and Ethernet) as long as the bridge operates at the LLC sublayer of the data link layer. If the bridge operates only at the lower sublayer (the MAC sublayer), the bridge can connect only similar network types (Token Ring to Token Ring and Ethernet to Ethernet).

Several kinds of bridging have proven important as internetworking devices. Transparent bridging is found primarily in Ethernet environments, while source-route bridging occurs primarily in Token Ring environments. Translational bridging provides translation between the formats and transit principles of different media types (usually Ethernet and Token Ring). Source-route transparent bridging combines the algorithms of transparent bridging and source-route bridging to enable communication in mixed Ethernet and Token Ring environments.

4.9.1   Basic Bridges

There are two kinds of bridges, basic and learning. A basic bridge is used to interconnect LANs using one (or more) of the IEEE 802 standards. Packets received on one port may be retransmitted on another port. Unlike a repeater, a bridge will not start retransmission until it has received the complete packet. As a consequence, stations on both sides of a bridge can transmit simultaneously without causing collisions. Bridges, like repeaters, do not modify the contents of a packet in any way and forward all broadcasts.

4.9.2   Transparent Bridges

Transparent bridging, the type used in Ethernet and documented in IEEE 802.1, is based on the concept of a spanning tree. A transparent bridge (also referred to as a learning bridge) is called transparent because the end-point devices do not need to know that the bridge exists. In other words, computers attached to the LAN do not behave any differently in the presence or absence of transparent bridges.

The transparent bridge builds up its routing table by cataloging the network nodes that send out messages. A bridge examines the MAC address of a message's source or sending node. If this address is new to the bridge, it adds it to the routing table along with the network segment from which it originated. The bridge's routing table is stored in its RAM and just like a PC's RAM, it is dynamic. Therefore, if the power goes off, it goes away. When the power is restored, the bridge rebuilds the table. Because most network nodes send and receive packets continuously, it doesn't take long to completely rebuild the routing table.

The bridge operates with its Ethernet interfaces in promiscuous mode, where it receives all frames sent on the network segments. The bridge "learns" by looking at the source (port the frame came from) and destination addresses (port to send the frame to) of the frames sent on each network segment and builds a forwarding database (FDB).

The bridge applies three simple rules to an incoming frame:

- If its source and destination addresses are the same, ignore the frame.
- Find the destination address of the incoming frame in the FDB and send the frame to the port listed in the FDB for that destination address.
- If the destination address is not in the FDB (it is unknown), send the frame to all ports (flood) except the port it came in on.

Note that broadcasts and multicast frames are forwarded by a bridge.

Transparent bridges use several switching methods:

- Store-and-forward operation
- Cut-through processing
- FragmentFree processing

The store-and-forward operation is common in transparent bridging devices and is Cisco's primary LAN switching method. When in store-and-forward mode, the bridge or LAN switch copies the entire frame onto its onboard buffers and conducts a cyclic redundancy check (CRC). Because an entire frame is received before being forwarded, additional latency is introduced (as compared to a single LAN segment). The frame is discarded if it contains a CRC error, if it's too small (known as runts—less than 64 bytes including the CRC), and if it is too large (known as giants—over 1518 bytes including the CRC).

If the frame does not contain any errors, the LAN switch looks up the destination hardware address in its forwarding or switching table to find the correct outgoing interface. If a given address has not been heard from in a specified period of time, the address is deleted from the address table. To create a loop-free environment with other bridges, use the spanning-tree protocol (see Section 4.9.3).

With cut-through processing, the first bits of the frame are sent out the outbound port before the last bit of the incoming frame is received, instead of waiting for the entire frame to be received. In other words, as soon as the switching port receives enough of the frame to see the destination MAC address, the frame is transmitted out the appropriate outgoing port to the destination device. This reduces latency in comparison with store-and-forward and FragmentFree processing. The unfortunate side effect is that because the frame check sequence (FCS) is in the Ethernet trailer, the forwarded frame may have bit errors that the switch would have noticed with store-and-forward logic. If the outbound port is busy, the switch stores the frame until the port is available. Very few switches use cut-through processing.

FragmentFree processing performs like cut-through processing, but the switch waits for 64 bytes to be received before forwarding the first bytes of the outgoing frame. According to Ethernet specifications, collisions should be detected during the first 64 bytes of the frame; frames in error due to collision are not forwarded. As with cut-through processing, the FCS cannot be checked.

4.9.3   Spanning Tree Algorithm

Complex topology can cause multiple loops to occur. For example, to make your network more fault tolerant, you may have multiple bridge (or switch) connections from one segment to another. When a computer sends a message and the bridge does not know the destination computer, it forwards the message to all of the ports, except for the port from which the message came. The problem develops when the message gets to the other segment and the bridge does not know where the computer is: It forwards the message to all of the ports (except for the port from which the message came), including the other connections to the other segment. So in reality, the message looped back to the other segment and will keep on looping. Since layer 2 has no mechanism to stop the loop, the spanning tree protocol was created. See Figure 4.26.

The **spanning tree algorithm (STA)** was developed by Digital Equipment Corporation, revised by IEEE 802 committee, and published in the IEEE 802.1d specification. Note: The Digital algorithm and the IEEE 802.1d algorithm are not compatible. The STA designates a loopfree subset of the network's topology by placing those bridge ports that, if active would create loops, into a standby (blocking condition) mode. Blocking bridge ports can be activated in the event of the primary link failure, thereby providing a new path through the internetwork. See Figure 4.27.

4.9.4   Source-Route Bridging

Token ring networks use source-route bridging (SRB). In this bridging method, the responsibility of determining the path to the destination node is placed on the sending node, not on the bridge. In an SRB environment, these steps are taken:

1. Token ring devices send out a test frame to determine whether the destination node is on the local ring.
2. If no answer is forthcoming, which means the destination node is not on the local ring, the sending node sends out a broadcast message, which is called an explorer frame.
3. The bridge forwards the explorer frame across the network through the network's bridges. Each bridge adds its ring number and bridge number to the frame's routing information field (RIF), so it can retrace its route later.
4. The destination device, if it exists, receives and responds to the explorer frame. The sending node gets this response.
5. The sending node initiates communication between the two devices with each intermediate bridge using the RIF value to determine the path between the two nodes.

Because SRB uses RIF information to determine its routes, no bridging table is created.

Figure 4.26   Problem with complex topology is that a nonstopping loop can occur for packets destined for unknown computers.

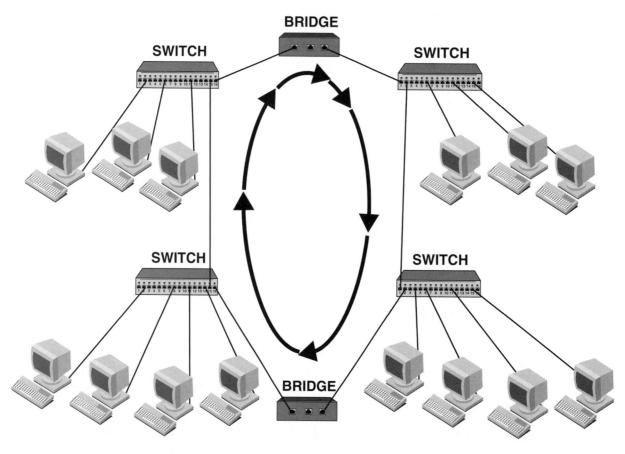

4.10   SWITCHES

In the most basic type of network found today, nodes are simply connected together using hubs. As a network grows, these problems can occur with this configuration:

- **Scalability**—In a hub network, limited shared bandwidth makes it difficult to accommodate significant growth without sacrificing performance.
- **Latency**—The amount of time that it takes a packet to get to its destination is called latency. Since each node in a hub-based network has to wait for an opportunity to transmit in order to avoid collisions, latency can increase significantly as more nodes are added. If someone is transmitting a large file across the network, all of the other nodes are waiting for an opportunity to send their own packets.
- **Network failure**—In a typical network, one device on a hub can cause problems for other devices attached to the hub as a result of incorrect speed settings (100 Mbps on a 10-Mbps hub) or excessive broadcasts. Switches can be configured to limit broadcast levels.
- **Collisions**—A network with a large number of nodes on the same segment often experiences many collisions; therefore, the network is a large collision domain.

A **switching hub** (sometimes referred to as switch or a layer 2 switch) is a fast, multiported bridge. Like a transparent bridge, a switch builds a table of the MAC addresses of all the connected stations. It then reads the destination address of each packet and forwards the packet to the correct port. Switches can be used to segment a large network into several smaller, less congested segments (breaking up collision domains) while providing necessary interconnectivity between them. Switches increase network performance by providing each port with dedicated bandwidth, without requiring

Figure 4.27   The spanning tree algorithm prevents looping of packets destined to unknown computers.

users to change any existing equipment, such as NICs, hubs, wiring, or any routers or bridges that are in place.

A major advantage of using a switch is that it allows one computer (or LAN segment) to open a connection to another computer (or LAN segment). While those two computers communicate, other connections between the other computers (or LAN segments) can be opened at the same time. Therefore, several computers can communicate at the same time through the switching hub. In addition, if the Ethernet connections that connect to the switch are full duplex, a computer can send data to one computer and receive data from another computer at the same time. Note: Remember that to transmit and receive simultaneously, full-duplex Ethernet requires a switch port, not a hub. This sets up a point-to-point connection, which also eliminates collisions.

LAN switches rely on packet switching. The switch establishes a connection between two segments just long enough to send the current packet. Incoming packets are saved to a temporary memory area known as a buffer. The MAC address contained in the frame's header is read and then compared with a list of addresses maintained in the switch's lookup table. In an Ethernet-based LAN, an Ethernet frame contains a normal packet as the payload of the frame, with a special header that includes the MAC address information for the source and destination of the packet.

While switches work much like a bridge does, there are some important differences:

- Layer 2 switching is hardware based, which means it uses the MAC addresses from the host's NIC cards to filter the network. Unlike bridges that use software to create and manage a filter table, switches use application-specific integrated circuits (ASICs) to build and maintain their filter tables. As a result, switches are faster than bridges.

- Bridges can only have one spanning tree instance per bridge, whereas switches can have many.
- Bridges can have a maximum of 16 ports. Switches can have hundreds.

Since LAN switches review the MAC addresses of a frame, unfortunately, there is a small amount of latency added before the frame can be forwarded to the correct port.

4.11   VLANs

As networks have grown in size and complexity, many companies have turned to virtual local area networks (VLANs) to provide a way for structuring this growth logically. Basically, a VLAN is a collection of nodes that are grouped together in a single broadcast domain that is based on something other than physical location. A VLAN is a switched network that is logically segmented on an organizational basis—by functions, project teams, or applications—rather than on a physical or geographical basis. In a VLAN, member hosts can communicate as if they were attached to the same wire, when in fact they can be located on any number of physical LANs. Because VLANs form broadcast domains, members enjoy the connectivity, shared services, and security associated with physical LANs. Reconfiguration of the network can be done through software rather than by physically unplugging and moving devices or wires.

In a traditional network with a hub connected to a router, the network might be divided by function. For example, let's say that the second floor of your building contains all of the sales people and their computers and the third floor contains all of the marketing people and their computers. The computers on the second floor are connected to hubs, which are connected to a router, and the computers on the third floor are connected to different hubs, which are also connected to a router. You run out of space on the second floor and you add sales people to the third floor. If you connect their computers into the hubs used by the third floor, the sales people on the third floor go through a slower router to get to the resources that have been assigned to the second floor. In addition, the system will see all of the broadcasts meant for the marketing people. As you can see, security issues and performance issues arise.

Some older applications have been rewritten to reduce their bandwidth needs. But today, there is a new generation of multimedia applications that consume more bandwidth than ever before. These applications use broadcast and multicasts extensively. In addition, faulty equipment, inadequate segmentation, and poorly designed firewalls only compound the problem that these broadcast-intensive applications create. All of these factors have added a new dimension to network design. Making sure the network is properly segmented in order to isolate one segment's problems and keep those problems from propagating throughout the internetwork is imperative. The most effective way of doing this is through strategic switching and routing.

A broadcast domain is a set of NICs for which a broadcast frame sent by one NIC will be received by all other NICs in the domain. While a bridge and switch isolate collision domains on the same subnet, a VLAN (defined using a switch) isolates broadcast domains. Note: Since routers typically do not allow broadcasts, they also define broadcast domains. See Figures 4.28 and 4.29.

Just as switches isolate collision domains for attached hosts and only forward appropriate traffic out a particular port, VLANs provide for complete isolation between VLANs. A VLAN is a bridging domain and all broadcast and multicast traffic is contained within it. Therefore, a VLAN can be thought of as a broadcast domain that exists within a defined set of switches. Since switches have become more cost-effective, many companies are replacing their hub networks with a switched network and VLAN environment. See Figure 4.30.

VLANs improve security by isolating groups. High-security users can be grouped into a VLAN, possibly on the same physical segment, and no users outside that VLAN can communicate with them. Thus, administrators can control each port and whatever resources that port can access. This prevents a user from plugging a workstation into any switch port and gaining access to network resources. To increase flexibility, servers can be members of multiple VLANs, so that the users can access the resources that they need.

Figure 4.28 A broadcast domain

SUMMARY

1. To communicate on LANS, network cards, or network interface cards (NICs), which found on an expansion card or are integrated into the motherboard, use transceivers (devices that both transmit and receive analog or digital signals).

2. Topology describes the appearance or layout of the network. Depending on how you look at the network, its topology is physical or logical.

3. The physical topology (part of the physical layer of the OSI reference model) describes how the network actually appears.

4. The logical topology (part of the data link layer) describes how the data flow through the physical topology—the actual pathway of the data.

5. A bus topology looks like a line where data are sent along a single cable. The two ends of the cable do not meet and the two ends do not form a ring or loop.

6. Typically with a bus topology network, the two ends of the cable must be terminated.

7. In a bus topology, if there is a break anywhere, or if one system does not pass the data along correctly, the entire network goes down.

8. A ring topology has all devices connected to one another in a closed loop.

9. Traditionally, a break in the ring causes the entire network to go down, and the break can be difficult to isolate.

10. A star topology is the most popular topology in use. In it, each network device connects to a central point such as a hub, which acts as a multipoint connector.

11. In a star topology, if a link fails (hub port or cable), the remaining workstations are not affected as they are in the bus and ring topologies.

12. Another topology is the mesh topology in which every computer is linked to every other computer. While this topology is not common in LANs, it is common in WANs where it connects remote sites over telecommunication links.

13. Many technologies that are wireless use a cellular topology in which an area is divided into cells. A broadcast device is located at the center and broadcasts in all directions to form an invisible circle (cell).

14. A hybrid topology combines two of the traditional topologies, usually to create a larger topology.

15. The cabling system used in networks forms the veins of the network; cables connect all of the computers and allow them to communicate with each other.

16. Attenuation means the strength of a signal falls off with distance over a transmission medium.

17. Interference occurs when undesirable electromagnetic waves affect the desired signal.

18. A twisted pair consists of two insulated copper wires twisted around each other.

19. Cables in a twisted pair are twisted to reduce crosstalk.

20. Crosstalk means a signal inducts, or transfers, from one wire to the other.

21. Unshielded twisted-pair (UTP) cable was categorized by the EIA based on the quality and number of twists per unit.

22. Early networks that used UTP typically used category 3; today's high-speed networks typically use category 5 or enhanced category 5 cabling.

23. While your telephone uses a cable with two pairs (four wires) and an RJ-11 connector, computer networks use a cable with four pairs (eight wires) and an RJ-45 connector.

24. The straight-through cable, which can be used to connect a network card to a hub, has the same sequence of colored wires at both ends of the cable.

Figure 4.29 A broadcast domain is defined by routers

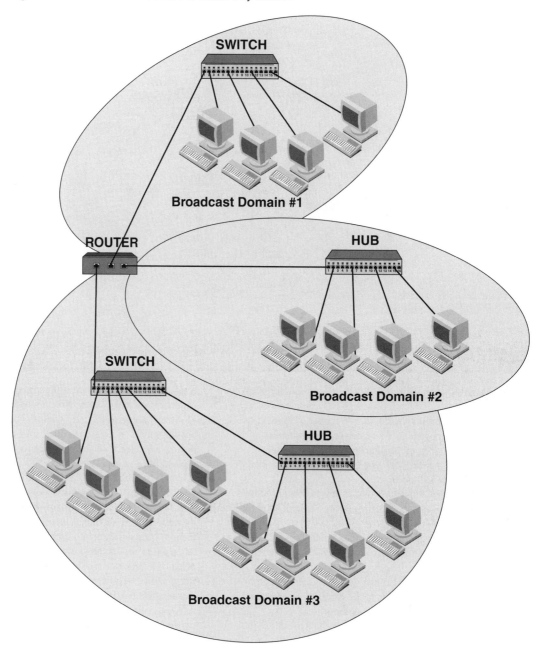

25. A crossover cable, which can be used to connect from one network card to another network card or from a hub to a hub, reverses the transmit, and receives wires.
26. Shielded twisted-pair (STP) cable is similar to UTP cable, except that STP cable is usually surrounded by a braided shield that reduces both EMI sensitivity and radio emissions.
27. Coaxial cable, sometimes referred to as coax, has a center wire surrounded by insulation and a grounded shield of braided wire (mesh shielding).
28. The BNC connector is used with coaxial cables; an example is the RG-58/AU cable used with the 10Base2 Ethernet system.

29. BNC T-connectors (used with the 10Base2 system) are female devices for connecting two cables to a network interface card.
30. A BNC barrel connector allows two cables to be connected together.
31. A fiber optic cable consists of a bundle of glass or plastic threads, each of which is capable of carrying data signals in the form of modulated pulses of light.
32. Fiber optic cables use several connectors, but the two most popular and recognizable connectors are the straight-tip (ST) and subscriber (SC) connectors.

Figure 4.30   A sample network using VLANs

33. A horizontal wiring system has cables that extend from wall outlets throughout the building to a wiring closet or server room.

34. Backbone wiring, which often is designed to handle a higher bandwidth, consists of cables that interconnect wiring closets, server rooms, and entrance facilities (telephone systems and WAN links from the outside world). Backbone wiring is sometimes referred to as the vertical cabling system.

35. Vertical connections between floors are known as risers.

36. TIA and EIA released their joint 568 Commercial Building Wiring Standard, also known as structured cabling, for uniform, enterprise-wide, multivendor cabling systems.

37. Most cables contain halogens, chemicals that give off toxic fumes when they burn.

38. The plenum is the space above the ceiling and below the floors that is used to circulate air throughout the workplace.

39. A plenum cable is a special cable that gives off little or no toxic fumes when burned. Whether a building's wiring includes plenum cabling depends on the building's fire code. Plenum cable is not required if cable exists in a special sealed conduit that would prevent toxic fumes from escaping into the open air.

40. Riser cable is intended for use in vertical shafts that run between floors.

41. A punch-down block connects several cable runs to each other without going through a hub.

42. To connect wires to the punch-down block, you use a punch-down tool.

43. A patch panel is a panel with many RJ-45 ports. The wall jacks are connected to the back of the patch panel, to individual RJ-45 ports. You can use patch cables to connect the port in the front of the patch panel to a computer or a hub. As a result, you can connect multiple computers with a hub located in the wiring closet or server room.

44. Cable ties and basket systems are tools used to help manage the cables anywhere in a building.

45. If you have several servers, you should consider a server rack or rack-mouned cabinet to hold the servers.

46. A wireless LAN (WLAN) transfers data through the air using radio frequencies instead of cables.

47. A band is a contiguous group of frequencies that are used for a single purpose.

48. Network cards are media dependent, media-access-method dependent, and protocol independent.

49. A media access control (MAC) address is a hardware address that identifies a node on the network.

50. You must bind the protocol stack to the network card and install any additional network software needed.

51. NDIS (network device interface specification developed by Microsoft) and ODI (open data link interface developed

by Apple and Novell) are sets of communication standards for protocols and network card drivers. Both allow multiple protocols to use a single network adapter card.

52. A diskless workstation is a computer that does not have its own disk drive.

53. A hub, which works at the physical OSI layer, is a multiported connection point used to connect network devices via a cable segment.

54. A bridge, which is a layer 2 device, breaks larger network segments into smaller network segments.

55. A switching hub (sometimes referred to as switch or a layer 2 switch) is a fast, multiported bridge.

56. A virtual LAN (VLAN) is a collection of nodes that are grouped together in a single broadcast domain that is based on something other than physical location.

57. A router, which works at the network ISO layer, is a device that connects two or more LANs. As multiple LANs are connected together, multiple routes are created to get from one LAN to another.

QUESTIONS

1. What basic terminology describes the low-level rules of communication that each network node must use?
   a. logical protocol
   b. physical topology
   c. physical protocol
   d. logical topology

2. You are a network administrator for the Acme Corporation, and you need to design a network for the corporate office in New York City. You design a network with category 5 unshielded twisted-pair cables arranged in a star topology. Which layer of the Open Systems Interconnection (OSI) model is associated with these design components?
   a. the transport layer
   b. the data link layer
   c. the network layer
   d. the physical layer

3. What is a point-to-point connection?
   a. a link that exists only between two devices
   b. a link that exists between multiple devices
   c. a secure channel on a TCP/IP link
   d. a baseband wireless connection

4. Because each node must be wired to a central point, this physical topology usually requires more cable runs than a topology with serially connected nodes.
   a. star
   b. bus
   c. ring
   d. mesh

5. As nodes are added to a network, an interface must be added to each existing node until it is impractical to add any more. What kind of topology is this?
   a. bus
   b. star
   c. ring
   d. mesh

6. The last node is connected to the first. Each node is connected to two neighboring nodes. These two statements are characteristic of what physical topology?
   a. star
   b. bus
   c. mesh
   d. ring

7. Network nodes connected in point-to-point links to a central device is characteristic of what physical topology?
   a. bus
   b. mesh
   c. ring
   d. star

8. Nodes connected to central devices in point-to-point links, where the central devices are connected in a serial fashion, is characteristic of what physical topology?
   a. ring
   b. mesh
   c. bus
   d. star-bus

9. What is the physical topology in which all the nodes are serially connected to each other?
   a. bus
   b. star-bus
   c. star
   d. mesh

10. Which of the following physical topologies has all its nodes interconnected?
    a. bus
    b. ring
    c. star
    d. mesh

11. Your network consists of four servers. Each server has three NICs. Server A is connected to servers B,C, and D. Server B is attached to C and D. Server C is attached to server D. No hub is used. All cabling is category 3 UTP crossover cables. What is your physical topology?
    a. star
    b. bus
    c. ring
    d. mesh

12. Your network consists of a 24-port bridge, two servers, and 15 workstations. Each computer interfaces with the bridge using its own segment of category 5 twisted-pair cable, which is terminated at both ends with RJ-45 connectors. What type of physical topology do you have?
    a. mesh
    b. bus
    c. ring
    d. star

13. Your network's physical topology is that of a star configuration. From time to time each workstation holds a packet called a token, during which time it transmits data, then passes the token along to the next workstation. What is the logical topology of your network?
    a. bus
    b. star
    c. mesh
    d. ring

14. Pat is the network engineer for the Acme Corporation, a nationwide bank. He needs to design a wide area network (WAN) that will connect offices in Dallas, San Francisco, Denver, and Tallahassee. The WAN that Pat designs should provide redundancy to ensure that if a link malfunctions, critical account data will not be lost. Which WAN topology should Pat design for Acme?
    a. ring
    b. bus
    c. star
    d. mesh

15. Which type of network topology uses terminators?
    a. star
    b. bus
    c. ring
    d. mesh

16. The network segment that provides the primary path for data flow is called _____ .
    a. primary link
    b. primary segment
    c. data link
    d. backbone

17. The physical topology that typically uses the least amount of cabling is _____ .
    a. star
    b. ring
    c. bus
    d. mesh

18. The following advantages are characteristic of what typology: easy to troubleshoot due to having a central point to isolate faults, and the ability to be organized in a hierarchical structure.
    - a. ring
    - b. bus
    - c. mesh
    - d. star

19. A single fault bringing down the entire network segment is characteristic of what physical topology?
    - a. ring
    - b. star
    - c. mesh
    - d. bus

20. Which of the following is used to connect two pieces of cable on a linear bus topology?
    - a. a BNC terminator
    - b. a network adapter card
    - c. a BNC barrel connector
    - d. a medium attachment unit

21. Crosstalk and other types of interference can affect network performance and security. Which type of cable is most susceptible to crosstalk?
    - a. RG-58/AU
    - b. STP
    - c. RG-58/U
    - d. category 5 UTP

22. Which type of problem is most likely to be caused by increasing cable lengths?
    - a. attenuation
    - b. beaconing
    - c. crosstalk
    - d. jitter

23. Twisted-pair cables use different connection hardware than coaxial cables. Which type of connector is commonly used by twisted-pair cables?
    - a. BNC
    - b. DIX
    - c. AUI
    - d. RJ-45

24. What term means a signal jumps from one wire to an adjacent wire?
    - a. attenuation
    - b. jitter
    - c. crosstalk
    - d. beaconing

25. Which cable is most common in networks?
    - a. UTP
    - b. STP
    - c. coaxial
    - d. fiber optic

26. When planning a network, you must be concerned about fire. What type of cable emits little or no toxic fumes when it burns?
    - a. polling
    - b. plenum
    - c. plastic
    - d. glass

27. Your company has offices in two separate buildings. Each office is networked. You are responsible for connecting the two separate networks. The distance between the two buildings is approximately 450 meters. The current capacity for each network is 10 Mbps. You could use 10Base5 cable to connect the two networks. What is one reason to consider using fiber optic cable instead?
    - a. Fiber optic cable is light and flexible and is easier to install than the heavy and inflexible coaxial cable used by 10Base5.
    - b. Fiber optic cable supports higher digital transmission rates and can provide additional capacity for future network expansion without the need to run new cable.
    - c. Fiber optic cable is the most widely used network cabling and is usually cheaper than plenum-grade coaxial cable.
    - d. Fiber optic cable is better suited for broadband transmission and provides a relatively inexpensive way to increase network capacity in the future.

28. You have been given the task of installing cables for an Ethernet network in your office building. The network cable will have to share the existing conduit with telephone cables. Cable segments will be up to 95 meters in length. Which cable is best suited for this installation?
    - a. fiber optic
    - b. category 3 UTP
    - c. category 1 UTP
    - d. Thicknet coaxial

29. What type of connector is normally used by a Thicknet cable for connection to the network adapter card?
    - a. BNC T-connector
    - b. RJ-45 connector
    - c. AUI connector
    - d. BNC barrel connector

30. What type of connector is used by Thinnet for connection to the network adapter card?
    - a. AUI connector
    - b. BNC T-connector
    - c. RJ-45 connector
    - d. BNC barrel connector

31. Plenum cable has which of the following characteristics?
    - a. It costs less than non-plenum cables.
    - b. It transmits data faster than other cables.
    - c. It is a military version of cable, which contains more shielding.
    - d. It meets fire codes.

32. Which of the following has the highest possible throughput?
    - a. STP
    - b. UTP
    - c. coax
    - d. fiber optic

33. An RJ-45 connector should be wired with _____ pairs when used on a category 5 UTP cable.
    - a. 1
    - b. 2
    - c. 4
    - d. 8

34. Which network installation tool can be used to connect UTP cable to a 110 block?
    - a. cable tester
    - b. wire crimper
    - c. punch-down tool
    - d. media installer

35. Which of the following is *not* an unbound network medium?
    - a. fiber optic cable
    - b. infrared pulses
    - c. radio waves
    - d. None of the above is an unbound network medium.

36. Where is the plenum located in a building?
    - a. in the ceilings
    - b. in the walls
    - c. in the elevator shaft
    - d. in the basement

37. What network cabling has four pairs of wires?
    - a. coaxial
    - b. twisted pair
    - c. fiber optic
    - d. none of the choices listed

38. What network medium uses a single copper conductor covered by an insulating layer, which is in turn covered by a conductive mesh and then a tough plastic skin?
    - a. fiber optic
    - b. twisted pair
    - c. stranded pair
    - d. coaxial

39. You are put in charge of building a network in a small power plant, which is full of EMI and RFI interference. There will be 20 servers and 500 workstations. The physical topology will be star-bus and the logical topology you have selected is Ethernet. You've drawn out the design and found that the longest cable segment you'll need to run is 85 meters. Now that it's time to order the cable, what do you select?
    - a. twisted pair
    - b. coaxial
    - c. fiber optic
    - d. STP

40. What cable uses a glass thread core?
    a. STP
    b. twisted-pair
    c. fiber optic
    d. coaxial

41. Some of the NICs in your network have only a single port that accepts an RJ-45 plug. What cable type will attach to these NICs?
    a. STP
    b. coaxial
    c. fiber optic
    d. UTP

42. Which media connector on an NIC is a D-shell 15-pin female interface? (Select two answers.)
    a. Thinnet
    b. DIX
    c. BNC
    d. AUI

43. Which cable connector looks like a large phone plug?
    a. BNC
    b. DB-15
    c. RJ-45
    d. RJ-11

44. What is the maximum length allowed for a segment of twisted-pair cabling? (Select two answers.)
    a. 425 feet
    b. 100 meters
    c. 115 meters
    d. 328 feet

45. RG-8 and RG-11 coaxial cabling is commonly called what?
    a. cable net
    b. Thinnet
    c. fiber net
    d. Thicknet

46. RG-58 cabling is commonly called what?
    a. Thinnet
    b. cable net
    c. fiber net
    d. Thicknet

47. Your boss wants you to recommend a cable type that will support Fast Ethernet. He said the cost to buy the cabling doesn't matter that much. There are no EMI or RFI issues where the cable is to run. What is the best choice?
    a. coaxial
    b. fiber optic
    c. STP
    d. UTP

48. You have an NIC with only a single AUI connector. What is needed to connect it to the network?
    a. vampire tap transceiver
    b. RJ-45 plug
    c. twisted-pair cable
    d. BNC-T connector

49. What are ST and SC connectors used for? (Select two answers.)
    a. multimode fiber
    b. optiplexed fiber
    c. single-mode fiber
    d. stranded copper cabling

50. Network transmission of data via radio, laser, infrared, or microwave is said to be sent on what?
    a. switching media
    b. bound media
    c. pulse media
    d. unbounded media

51. What physical medium requires the greatest expertise to install?
    a. coaxial
    b. fiber optic
    c. infrared
    d. copper wire

52. Which part of a coaxial cable carries the data?
    a. wire mesh shielding
    b. core
    c. plenum
    d. none of the choices listed

53. In an Ethernet network, what device should you use to connect two hubs?
    a. a crossover cable
    b. a tone generator
    c. a hardware loopback
    d. a tone locator

54. Pat is not able to access network resources from her computer. When she plugs her Ethernet cable into a coworker's machine, she is able to access the network without any problems. Which of the following network components is causing the problem?
    a. the server
    b. the cable
    c. the router or gateway
    d. the network adapter

55. You want to have a 10BaseT segment that is greater than 300 meters. Which device is required?
    a. a repeater
    b. a multiplexer
    c. an amplifier
    d. an RJ-45 connector

56. VLANs are a feature primarily of which type of network device?
    a. hubs
    b. switches
    c. routers
    d. NICs
    e. cables

57. What is the primary purpose of a VLAN?
    a. testing all router links on a network
    b. simulating a network
    c. segmenting a network inside a switch.
    d. connecting a LAN to another LAN

58. Which part of a network interface card identifies whether there is basic connectivity from the station to a hub or switch?
    a. link light
    b. port
    c. collision light
    d. jumper

59. You are installing a network interface card (NIC) on your computer. The NIC has a 15-pin attachment unit interface (AUI) connector. Which device do you need to attach to the NIC to connect your computer to a LAN and allow your computer to communicate with other computers on the LAN?
    a. a hub
    b. a transceiver
    c. a patch panel
    d. a router

60. Due to rapid growth of the company, your supervisor asks you to help her find a good switch that will break up the network into at least three different subnets, each with a different network identifier. You need what type of switch?
    a. multiplexing
    b. layer 3
    c. token passing
    d. layer 2

61. What is the main reason to use dynamic routing rather than static routing?
    a. Dynamic routing involves less administrative overhead.
    b. Actually, static routing is the preferred method.
    c. Dynamically routed packets use less bandwidth.
    d. Routers operate faster with dynamic routing.

62. The ABC company and the XYZ company are in the same building but on different floors. One day they decide to merge into a single company, called AXBYCZ. Each company has been running a simple local area network, the first using IBM Token Ring, and the second using Ethernet. To combine both networks, what devices are needed? (Choose two answers.)
    a. bridge
    b. gateway
    c. router
    d. layer 2 switch

63. You wish to set up a LAN in a star configuration. However, you want each node to have full bandwidth on its port. What device do you need?
    a. layer 2 switch
    b. router
    c. active hub
    d. brouter

64. A layer 2 switch is also known as a _____ .
   - a. brouter
   - b. router
   - c. repeater
   - d. bridge

65. Building tables based on MAC addresses is the job of what device?
   - a. bridge
   - b. gateway
   - c. router
   - d. switch

66. What switching mode causes the least amount of latency?
   - a. store-and-forward
   - b. FragmentFree
   - c. port switching
   - d. cut-through

67. Which devices forward all network traffic? (Choose all that apply.)
   - a. bridge
   - b. gateway
   - c. repeater
   - d. router

68. Which of the following is not a characteristic of a layer 2 switch?
   - a. builds a MAC address table
   - b. creates multiple collision domains
   - c. operates at the data link layer
   - d. routes packets based on IP address (layer 3)

69. Building tables based on network addresses is the job of what device?
   - a. bridge
   - b. gateway
   - c. repeater
   - d. router

70. What is another name for a layer 3 switch?
   - a. bridge
   - b. brouter
   - c. router
   - d. repeater

71. Why should unused protocols be unbound from NICs on a network? (Choose two answers).
   - a. to reduce unnecessary packet traffic
   - b. to improve bandwidth for the protocols that are used
   - c. to prevent lost packets
   - d. it is not necessary to unbind them.

72. A media converter that enables connecting an NIC to various cable types is called a _____ .
   - a. transceiver
   - b. dataplexer
   - c. receiver
   - d. multiplexer

73. When multiple protocols are bound to an NIC, the most used protocol on the network should be where in the binding list?
   - a. doesn't matter
   - b. always last
   - c. depends on the protocol
   - d. always first

74. Some NICs have a chip that allows a computer without an operating system to boot and attach to the network, and that is software configurable. What sort of chip is this?
   - a. EPROM
   - b. CPU
   - c. BIOS
   - d. EEPROM

75. You want to link two computers together without using a hub. Both computers have network cards. Which of the following would be best to use?
   - a. serial cable
   - b. coaxial cable
   - c. parallel cable
   - d. crossover cable

76. Suddenly none of the members in your peer-to-peer star topology network can access each other's computers. What would be the first thing you would check?
   - a. whether a cable terminator has loosened
   - b. whether one of the cables is crimped
   - c. whether one of the computer's NICs have failed
   - d. whether the power light on the hub is off

77. The onboard serial port on your PC is set to use IRQ 4 and I/O port 3f8. Your internal modem is using the standard resources used by Com port 3. You cannot dial out. What is the problem?
   - a. Your modem is using IRQ 4, which conflicts with the onboard serial port.
   - b. Your modem is using I/O port address 3f8, which conflicts with the onboard serial port.
   - c. You cannot configure an internal modem to be used as Com port 3.
   - d. Your modem is defective.

78. An NIC card's EEPROM can store all but which of the following?
   - a. IRQ
   - b. DMA channel
   - c. I/O address
   - d. network data

79. You need to prepare a 10-foot run of patch cable that will have two RJ-45 connectors on each end. What tool do you have to put the RJ-45s on?
   - a. C-clamp
   - b. flat-head screwdriver
   - c. pulse generator
   - d. wire crimper

80. What are BNC connectors used for?
   - a. to connect Thinnet Token Ring cabling to network devices
   - b. to connect twisted pair cabling to hubs
   - c. to connect Thicknet Ethernet cable to network devices
   - d. to connect Thinnet Ethernet cable to network devices

81. NDIS and ODI are specifications that define interfaces for communication between the data link layer and protocol drivers. Which need do NDIS and ODI fulfill?
   - a. the need to dynamically bind a single protocol to multiple MAC drivers
   - b. the need to bind multiple protocols to a single network adapter card
   - c. the need for monolithic protocols to conform to the OSI model
   - d. the need for monolithic protocols to be loaded into the upper memory area

82. Open data link interface (ODI) is a specification defined by Novell and Apple to simplify driver development. Which of the following statements is true of ODI?
   - a. ODI specifies cable and network architecture standards.
   - b. ODI specifies network topology standards.
   - c. ODI provides support for multiple protocols on a single network adapter card.
   - d. ODI provides support for multiple network topologies in a single networking environment.

83. Which of the following tools can be used to check for cable breaks?
   - a. digital voltmeters
   - b. time domain reflectometers
   - c. advanced cable testers
   - d. multiplexers

84. You connect the leads from a digital multimeter (DMM) to each of the conductors in a twisted-pair cable. Which of the following settings should you use on the DMM to see if there is a short?
   - a. resistance
   - b. DC voltage
   - c. current
   - d. capacitance
   - e. AC voltage

85. Which of the following tools can you use to trace the path of a cable through a physical network?
- a. a hardware loopback
- b. a tone generator
- c. a protocol analyzer
- d. a tone locator

86. Your company uses a large electric drill press as part of its manufacturing process. Occasionally, the 10BaseT local area network (LAN) stops responding when the operator uses the drill press. Which of the following could cause this problem? (Choose two answers.)
- a. electromagnetic interference
- b. power sag
- c. electrostatic discharge
- d. radiomagnetic interference

87. A surge of EMI that could corrupt network data could be caused by _____ .
- a. fluorescent lighting
- b. sonic energy wave
- c. electric motors
- d. crimped cable

88. Pat uses a Windows 2000 Professional computer that is connected to a 100BaseTX local area network (LAN). She attempts to use My Network Places to browse the computers on the LAN, but the Windows 2000 Professional computer displays the error message "Unable to Browse the Network. The Network is Not Accessible." Pat was able to connect to the network the last time she used the Windows 2000 Professional computer. What should Pat check first to determine the cause of this problem?
- a. the link light on her computer's network interface card (NIC)
- b. the power switch on the NIC
- c. the cable that connects the NIC to the wall outlet in her office
- d. the power switch on the hub in the wiring closet that connects the NIC to the rest of the network

89. In addition to testing for cable faults, which of the following can also test for excessive packet collisions, as well as cable voltage?
- a. protocol analyzer
- b. TDR
- c. SRT
- d. advanced cable tester

90. Which of the following tools can test voltage, resistance, and current, as well as continuity?
- a. advanced cable tester
- b. TDR
- c. voltmeter
- d. digital multimeter

91. What is a "fox and hound"?
- a. multiport fluke
- b. packet sniffer
- c. serial/parallel translator
- d. tone generator/locator

92. One of your servers is not accessible by anyone on the LAN. You go to the server and note that no error messages are being displayed. Also, there are no error messages in the event log. What is the next thing you should check?
- a. the server's NIC link light
- b. the server's network cable
- c. the server's port in the wirecloset
- d. the server's disk drives

93. One day your boss points at an unused RJ-45 jack near the bottom of a wall and asks, "Where does the other end of that cable come out?" What network tool would you use to help answer this question?
- a. fox and hound
- b. wire crimper
- c. media tester
- d. some other tool not listed here

CHAPTER 5

Networking Technologies

Topics Covered in This Chapter

Introduction

In Chapter 4, you read about the building blocks of a network These building blocks, including cables and connection devices, form the network. In this chapter, you will look at the different LAN technologies such as Ethernet, token ring, and 802.11 wireless networks.

Objectives

- Specify the main features (speed, access, method, topology, and media) of Ethernet and token ring networks.
- Specify the characteristics, including speed, length, topology and cable type, for these Ethernet standards: 10BaseT, 100BaseTX, 10Base2, 10Base5,100BaseFX, and Gigabit Ethernet.

- Specify the main features and characteristics of the 802.11 standard for wireless LANs.
- Given a troubleshooting scenario involving a network failure, identify the cause of the failure.
- Build a coaxial (Thinnet) Ethernet network.
- Build a UTP Ethernet network.
- Explain how to build a token ring network.

5.1   ETHERNET

Currently, there are three LAN technologies being used: Ethernet, token ring, and ARCnet. LAN technology includes topologies, packet structures, and access methods that can be used together on a segment. Of the three, **Ethernet** is the most widely used. It offers good balance between speed, price, reliability, and ease of installation. More than 85% of all LAN connections installed are Ethernet. All popular operating systems and applications are Ethernet-compatible, as are upper layer protocol stacks as TCP/IP, IPX, and NetBEUI.

The original Ethernet network was developed by Digital, Intel, and Xerox in the early 1970s; currently, Ethernet II is in use. The Ethernet standard is defined by the IEEE in a specification commonly known as **IEEE 802.3**. The 802.3 specification covers rules for configuring Ethernet LANs, types of media that can be used, and interaction of the elements of the network. See Table 5.1.

Ethernet was traditionally used on light-to medium-traffic networks, and it performs best when a network's data traffic is sent in short bursts. Recently, newer and faster Ethernet standards, combined with switches, have significantly increased the performance of the network.

Ethernet networks can be configured in either a star topology using unshielded twisted-pair cable connected to a hub, or as a bus topology using a coaxial cable acting as a backbone. Of the two, UTP cabling is by far the most commonly used. Ethernet cards can have one, two, or possibly all three of the following connectors:

- DIX (Digital, Intel, Xerox)/AUI connectors support 10Base5 external transceivers.
- BNC (British Naval Connector) connectors support 10Base2 coaxial cabling.
- RJ-45 connectors support 10baseT/100BaseTX (UTP) cabling.

When a network device wants to access the network, the access method used is carrier-sense multiple access with collision detection (CSMA/CD). When a computer wants to send data over the network, it listens to see if there is any traffic on the network. If the network is clear, it broadcasts. Unfortunately, it is possible for two network devices to listen and try to send data at the same time. As a result, a collision occurs and both data packets are corrupted. Each of the network devices waits a different, random amount of time and tries again. If the network is heavily congested, the network will have more collisions, which results in more traffic, and the entire network is slowed even more.

To maintain an efficient Ethernet network, collisions must be kept to a minimum. To accomplish this, you need to (1) keep wiring distances and repeater counts (see the 5-4-3 rule discussed later in this

Table 5.1 Various Ethernet standards

Ethernet Name	Cable Type	Maximum Speed	Maximum Transmission Distance	Notes
10Base5	Coaxial	10 Mbps	500 meters	Also called Thicknet
10Base2	Coaxial	10 Mbps	185 meters	Also called Thinnet
10BaseT	UTP	10 Mbps	100 meters	
100BaseT	UTP	10 Mbps	100 meters	
100BaseVG	UTP	100 Mbps	213 meters (category 5) or 100 meters (category 3)	100VG-AnyLAN
100BaseT4	UTP	100 Mbps	100 meters	Requires four pairs of category 3, 4, or 5 UTP cable
100BaseTX	UTP or STP	100 Mbps	100 meters	Two pairs of category 5 UTP or type 1 STP
10BaseFL	Fiber (multimode)	10 Mbps	2000 meters	Ethernet over fiber optic implementation; connectivity between network interface card and fiber optic hub
100BaseFX	Fiber (multimode)	100 Mbps	2000 meters	100 Mbps Ethernet over fiber optic implementation
1000BaseTX (Gigabit Ethernet)	UTP	1000 Mbps	100 meters	Uses same connectors as 10BaseT; requires category 5 or better
1000BaseSX	Fiber (multimode)	1000 Mbps	260 meters	Uses SC fiber connectors; designed for workstation to hub implementation
1000BaseLX	Fiber (single mode)	1000 Mbps	550 meters	Uses longer backbone wavelength laser than 1000BaseSX; typically used for backbone implementation
1000BaseCX	STP Type 1	1000 Mbps	25 meters	Typically used for equipment interconnection such as clusters
1000BaseT	UTP	1000 Mbps	100 meters	Requires category 5 or better

chapter) in any given path to a minimum and (2) optimize your applications and protocols to keep the average frame size up.

Within an Ethernet network, you are limited to 1024 nodes identified by their MAC addresses, which are burned into the ROM chip on the network card. IEEE assigns the first three bytes of the

6-byte address to the network card vendors. The vendor is then responsible for assigning the rest of the address to make sure that the MAC address is unique.

5.1.1   Ethernet Encoding Method

Although many methods are used for encoding signals Manchester Signal Encoding, which is used on an Ethernet medium, is the most common. When a device driver receives a data packet from the higher-layer protocols such as an IP or IPX packet, it constructs a frame (much like an envelope) with the appropriate Ethernet header information and with a frame check sequence at the end for error control. The circuitry on the adapter card then takes the frame and converts it into an electrical signal.

Data are measured as a transition state that occurs in the middle of each bit-time. To represent a binary 1, the first half of the bit-time is a low voltage, and the second half is always the opposite of the first half. To represent a binary 0, the first half of the bit-time is a high voltage and the second half is a low voltage. See Figure 5.1.

5.1.2   Ethernet Frame Types

When a packet is transmitted, information about the sender, receiver, and upper layer protocols is attached to the data. The format for the completed packet is called the frame type. There are four Ethernet frame types. Think of Ethernet as a language and the four different frame types as dialects of the language. The dialects are similar, yet there are differences. The four frame types started with Novell, when it decided it could not wait for the emerging Ethernet standard to be ratified by IEEE. See Table 5.2.

The Ethernet packet starts with the preamble, which consists of 8 bytes of alternating 1s and 0s, ending in 11. A station on an Ethernet network detects the change in voltage that occurs when another station begins to transmit and uses the preamble to "lock on" to the sending station's clock signal. When it reads the 11 at the end, it knows the preamble has ended. Next, the MAC address of the target (destination) computer is sent, followed by the MAC address of the source of the sending computer. Note: The target address could be represented in a multicast message (address sent to multiple computers). In addition, most Ethernet adapters can be set in promiscuous mode, whereby they receive all frames that appear on the LAN whether addressed to them or not. If this poses a security problem, a new generation of smart hub devices can filter out all frames with private destination addresses belonging to another station.

Depending on the Ethernet frame type, a type field or a length field is sent. For Ethernet 802.2, the length field describes the length of the data field, including the LLC and SNAP (Subnetwork Access Protocol) headers. The data field can be between 64 and 1500 bytes. The LLC header is used to identify the process/protocol that generated the packet and the process/protocol for which the packet is intended. The data field is between 43 and 1497 bytes, which include the TCP/IP or IPX packet. The last 4 bytes that the adapter reads is the frame check sequence (FCS) or CRC for error control. See Figure 5.2. Ethernet 802.3 is an incomplete implementation of the IEEE 802.3 specification, sometimes called Ethernet Raw. Novell implemented the 802.3 header but not the fields defined in the 802.2 specification. Instead, the IPX packet begins immediately after the 802.3 fields. The Novell frame type Ethernet 802.2 is a complete implementation; that is, it includes the 802.3 and

Figure 5.1   Ethernet using transition state to encode data

Table 5.2 Ethernet frame types

Novell Name	CISCO Name	Ethernet Type
Novell Ethernet 802.3	LLC	Also known as Ethernet Raw. Default Ethernet frame type of Novell NetWare 3.11 or earlier. Supports IPX.
Novell Ethernet II	ARPA	Used for IPX and TCP/IP
IEEE 802.2	Novell	Default Ethernet frame type of Novell NetWare 3.12 or later and Windows. Used for IPX.
IEEE 802.2 SNAP	SNAP	Used for IPX, TCP/IP, and AppleTalk

Figure 5.2 Ethernet packet

DSAP = destination service access point, SSAP = source service access point.

802.2 fields. Ethernet II is the standard frame type for TCP/IP networks. Ethernet SNAP includes the 802.3, 802.3, and SNAP fields.

5.1.3 10Base5

The original Ethernet was called **10Base5** or **Thicknet**. The name 10Base5 describes a 10-Mbps baseband network that can have cable segments up to 500 meters long. The network uses a 50-ohm RG-8 and RG-11 coaxial cable as backbone cable. 10Base5 uses physical and logical bus topology. Most network devices connected to the network have an external transceiver that uses a 4-pair **AUI cable** (sometimes referred to as a drop cable) via a **DIX connector** (2-row, 15-pin female connector). Other network devices can connect to the backbone cable via a vampire tap, which uses teeth that make contact with the inner conductor, or via a BNC barrel connector. See Figure 5.3.

When building a 10Base5 network, follow these rules:

- The minimum cable distance between transceivers must be 8 feet (2.5 meters).
- The AUI cable may be up to 164 feet (50 meters).
- You may not go beyond the maximum network segment length of 1640 feet (500 meters).
- The entire network cabling scheme cannot exceed 8200 feet (2500 meters).
- All unused ends must be terminated with 50-ohm terminating resistors.
- One end of the terminated network segment must be grounded.
- The maximum number of nodes per network segment, including repeaters, is 100.
- A signal quality error (SQE) test, which is present on some boards, must be turned off when repeaters are used.

5.1.4 10Base2

The **10Base2 (Thinnet)** network is a simplified version of the 10Base5 network. The name describes a 10-Mbps baseband network with a maximum cable segment length of approximately 200 meters (actually 185 meters). Instead of having external transceivers, the transceivers are on the network card, which attaches to the network using a BNC T-connector. The cable used is 50-ohm RG-58/AU coaxial cable. Different from the 10Base5 network, the 10Base2 does not use a drop cable. See Figure 5.4.

Figure 5.3   10base5 network

When building a 10Base2 network, follow these rules:

- The minimum cable distance between workstations must be 1.5 feet (0.5 meters).
- You may not go beyond the maximum network segment limitation of 607 feet (185 meters, not the 200 meters commonly stated).
- The entire network cabling scheme cannot exceed 3035 feet (925 meters).

Figure 5.4   10Base2 network

- The maximum number of nodes per network segment is 30 (this includes workstations and repeaters).
- All unused ends must be terminated with 50-ohm terminating resistors.
- A grounded terminator must be used on only one end of the network segment.
- You can connect 10Base5 networks to 10Base2 networks using special boards.

Figure 5.5 10BaseT network

0.6 Meter
Minimum/
100 Meters
Maximum

5.1.5   10BaseT

Different from 10Base2 and 10Base5, a **10BaseT** network uses UTP, which costs less, is smaller, and is easier to work with than coaxial cable. While Ethernet is a logical bus topology, 10BaseT is a physical star topology in which the network devices are connected to a hub (or switch). It uses a category 3 (or greater cable) with two pairs of wires (pins 1, 2, 3, and 6) connected with RJ-45 connectors. See Figure 5.5.

When building a 10BaseT network, follow these rules:

■ The maximum number of network segments or physical LAN is 1024.
■ The minimum unshielded cable segment length is 2 feet (0.6 meters).
■ The maximum unshielded cable segment length is 328 feet (100 meters).
■ To avoid EMI, you must route UTP cable no closer than 5 feet to any high-voltage (power) wiring or fluorescent lighting.

One advantage of using 10BaseT is that if you need to add another workstation, you just run an additional cable to the hub and plug it in. If there is a break in the cable, the hub has its own intelligence that routes traffic around the defective cable segment. As a result, the entire network is not affected.

> **Note:** Since most networks use category 5 twisted-pair cabling (or enhanced category 5 twisted-pair cabling) in a star topology, you should choose the same, unless you have an overwhelming reason to choose differently.

5.1.6   Fast Ethernet

Fast Ethernet is an extension of the 10BaseT Ethernet standard. Fast Ethernet transports data at 100 Mbps yet still uses the CSMA/CD protocol used by 10-Mbps Ethernet. The first type of Fast Ethernet is **100BaseTX**, which uses two pairs of the standard category 5 UTP cable. The second type is **100BaseT4**, which runs over existing category 3 UTP cable by using all four pairs; three pairs to transmit simultaneously and the fourth pair is used for collision detection. Note: If category 5 cable is used for backbone for Fast Ethernet, it should not exceed 5 meters. The third type is **100BaseFX**, which operates over multimode fiber optic cabling.

100VG-AnyLAN was developed by Hewlett-Packard as a 100-Mbps, half-duplex transmission network; it allows 100 Mbps on a four-pair category 3 cabling system and allows for **voice over IP (VoIP)**. Different from previous Ethernet standards, it uses the Demand Priority Protocol instead of the Ethernet CSMA/CD. The Demand Priority Protocol allows different nodes and data types to be assigned a priority. Unfortunately for the 100VG-AnyLAN network, Fast Ethernet has gained a greater market acceptance because it has been standardized by the original IEEE committee.

5.1.7   Gigabit Ethernet

Gigabit Ethernet has been demonstrated to be a viable solution for increased bandwidth requirements in growing networks, as it is used for high-speed backbones and specialized needs. The Gigabit Ethernet standards include 1000BaseSX (short wavelength fiber), 1000BaseLX (long wavelength fiber), 1000BaseCX (short run copper), and 1000BaseTX (100-meter, four-pair category 5 UTP cable).

The Gigabit Ethernet CSMA/CD method has been enhanced in order to maintain a 100-meter collision at gigabit speeds. Without this enhancement, minimum-sized Ethernet packets could complete transmission before the transmitting station senses a collision, thereby violating the CSMA/CD method. To resolve this issue, both the minimum CSMA/CD carrier time and the Ethernet slot time have been extended from their present value of 64 bytes to a value of 512 bytes. Note that the minimum packet length of 64 bytes has not been affected. Packets smaller than 512 bytes have an extra carrier extension. Packets longer than 512 bytes are not extended. These changes, which can impact small-packet performance, have been offset by incorporating a new feature called packet bursting into the CSMA/CD algorithm. Packet bursting allows serves, switches, and other devices to send bursts of small packets in order to fully utilize available bandwidth.

5.1.8   5-4-3 Rule

When creating and expanding an Ethernet network, always follow the **5-4-3 rule**: An Ethernet network must not exceed five segments connected by four repeaters. Of these segments, only three can be populated by computers. This means that the distance of a computer cannot exceed five segments and four repeaters when communicating with other computers on the network. See Figures 5.6, 5.7, and 5.8.

Propagation delay is the amount of time that passes between the time a signal is transmitted and the time it is received at the opposite end of the copper or optic cable. When an Ethernet adapter needs to communicate on the wire, it listens, and if no other adapter is already communicating, it sends its packets on the wire. If two adapters listen at the same time, both cards transmit at the same time, which results in a collision. When you combine Ethernet segments, each segment has a propagation delay. Therefore, when one adapter is communicating, it takes longer for those packets to be transmitted to all the computers on the LAN. If you don't follow the 5-4-3 rule and you don't adhere to the maximum cable lengths allowed by the Ethernet specifications, your network will have an increased propagation delay. As a result, a higher number of collisions occur, which makes the network run less efficiently. Note: If you use switches instead of hubs, you will reduce collisions because packets are only forwarded to their destination instead of to ports on the hub.

5.2   PLANNING AN ETHERNET NETWORK

Let's consider two network examples. In the first example, there are 10 computers in a room. This simple network needs network cards for each computer, one or more hubs, and enough UTP cabling to connect all of the network cards. The hub is located somewhere within the room and cables are stretched from each computer to the hub. Depending on the function of the network, standard 10-Mbps Ethernet using category 3 cabling (or better) will probably suffice.

The second example of a larger network is more complicated. First, a server (or servers) is located in a server room where it can be secured and have proper ventilation. Cables are then stretched from wall jacks throughout the building and lead to a patch panel located in the server room or in a wiring closet along with the hub (or hubs). The cables in the walls are eight-wire, four-pair category 5 or better solid wire cabling. Note: Depending on the fire code, some or all of the cabling will need to be plenum cabling.

Figure 5.6 The 5-4-3 rule for an Ethernet coaxial network

Figure 5.7 The 5-4-3 rule for an Ethernet UTP network

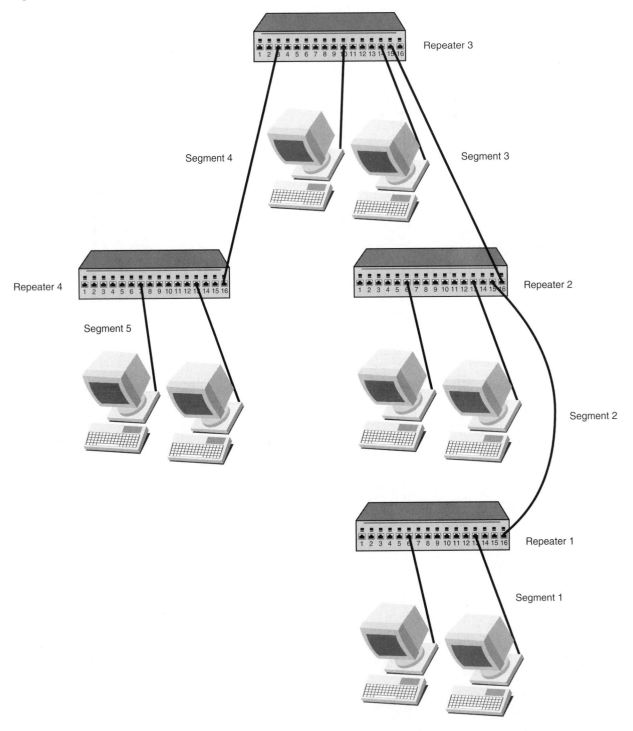

Figure 5.8   The 5-4-3 rule for an Ethernet UTP/coaxial network

Patch cables are then made using eight-wire, four-pair category 5 or better stranded cabling. The cables are used to connect the individual computers to the wall jacks. The port of the patch panel that connects to the wall jack is connected with another patch cable to the hub. The patch panel is a convenient way to connect the network together. In addition, it allows for easy reconfiguration. Depending on the function and load of the network, you have one of two options:

- The entire network could be 1 Gbps or 100 Mbps.
- You could install a backbone of 1 Gbps connected to 100-Mbps switches to connect the computers.

To help you design and document your network, consider diagramming software such as Microsoft Visio. Diagramming software is a specialized draw program that allows you to easily draw outlines of your buildings or offices and to specify the location of all cables.

5.3   TOKEN RING

Another major LAN technology in use today is token ring. **Token Ring** rules are defined in the IEEE 802.5 specification. The physical topology of a token ring is a star but the logical topology is a ring. Therefore, this network is actually implemented in what can best be described as a collapsed ring. In Token Ring LANs, each station is connected to a token ring wiring concentrator called a **multistation access unit (MSAU or MAU)** using STP or UTP cabling. Like Ethernet hubs, MSAUs are usually located in a wiring closet.

Figure 5.9 Token Ring frame

Start Delimiter	Access Control	Frame Control	Destination Address	Source Address	Data	Frame Check Sequence	End Delimiter	Frame Status

Figure 5.9 depicts a typical Token Ring frame. Some of its characteristics are similar to those of the Ethernet frame, but significant differences arise in how the control information is handled. The following list describes the components of the typical token ring frame:

- **Start delimiter (SD)**—Signifies the beginning of the packet
- **Access control (AC)**—Contains information about the priority of the frame
- **Frame control (FC)**—Defines the type of frame; used in the frame check sequence
- **Destination address**—Contains the address of the destination node
- **Source address**—Contains the address of the originating node
- **Data**—Contains data transmitted from the originating node. May also contain routing and management information.
- **Frame check sequence (FCS)**—Checks the integrity of the frame
- **End delimiter (ED)**—Indicates the end of the frame
- **Frame status (FS)**—Indicates whether the destination node recognized and correctly copied the frame, or whether the destination node was not available.

The access method used on token ring networks is called **token passing**. In token passing, a network device only communicates over the network when it has the token (a special data packet that is generated by the first computer that comes online in a Token Ring network). The token is passed from one station to another around a ring. When a station gets a free token and transmits a packet, the packet travels in one direction around the ring, passing all of the other stations along the way.

Each node acts as a repeater that receives tokens and data frames from its nearest active upstream neighbor (NAUN). After a frame is processed by the node, the frame is passed, or rebroadcast, downstream to the next attached node. Each token makes at least one trip around the entire ring. It then returns to the originating node. Workstations that have problems send a beacon to identify an address of the potential failure. If a station has not heard from its upstream neighbor in 7 seconds, it sends a packet down the ring that contains its address and the address of its NAUN. The token ring can then reconfigure itself to avoid the problem area.

Token Ring NICs can run at 4 Mbps or 16 Mbps. The 4-Mbps cards can run only at the data rate. However, 16-Mbps cards can be configured to run at 4 or 16 Mbps. All cards on a given network ring must be running at the same rate. To run at 4 Mbps, you should use category 3 UTP cabling or better; 16 Mbps requires category 4 cable or higher or type 4 STP cable or higher.

Like Ethernet cards, the node address on each NIC is burned in at the manufacturer on a ROM chip and is unique to each card. For fault tolerance purposes, a maximum of two token ring cards can be installed in any node; each card is defined as the primary or alternate token ring card. The token ring card uses two types of connectors, one is equipped with a female (DB-9) 9-pin connector (in which only 4 pins are used), while the second is an RJ-45 connector. MSAUs repeaters, and most other equipment use a special IBM type 1 unisex data connector. Note: To connect multiple MSAUs, the ring out (RO) port of each MSAU must be connected to the ring in (RI) port of the next MSAU to form a larger ring. See Figure 5.10. In a token ring network, you can have up to 33 MSAUs chained together.

When building a token ring network, follow these rules:

- The maximum cable length between a node and an MSAU is 330 feet (100 meters) for type 1 and 2 cables, 220 feet (66 meters) for type 6 and 9 cable, and 150 feet (45 meters) for a category 3 UTP cable.
- Nodes must be separated by a minimum of at least 8 feet (2.5 meters).

Figure 5.10   MSAUs connected together. Notice the cables attached to the ring in (RI) and the ring out (RO) ports are connected to form a larger ring.

- The maximum ring length is 660 feet (200 meters) for type 1 and 2 cable, 400 feet (120 meters) for a type 3 cable, 140 feet (45 meters) for type 6 cable, and 0.6 mile (1 kilometer) for a fiber optic segment.
- IEEE 802.5 specifies a maximum of 250 nodes, if using a small, movable token ring cable system; IBM STP cable specifies a maximum of 96 nodes and 12 MSAUs (IBM Model 8228) using IBM type 6 cable.
- IEEE 802.5 specifies a maximum of 250 nodes, if using a large, nonmovable token ring cable system; IBM STP and UTP cable specify a maximum of 260 nodes and 33 MSAUs.
- IEEE 802.5 specifies a maximum of 250 nodes; IBM UTP specifies 72 nodes.
- To run at 4 Mbps, use category 3 UTP cabling or better; at 16 Mbps, use category 4 cable or higher or type 4 STP cable or higher.
- Use a media filter to convert from type 1 (STP) cable to type 3 (UTP) cable or the reverse.

5.4   LOCALTALK

The Apple network architecture is called AppleTalk, which has been included in Apple Macintosh computers for several years. By using the computer's built-in network interface, you usually connect the Apple computers and printers using STP cable, but you could also use UTP and fiber optic cable. **LocalTalk** is Apple's own network interface and cable system. Since AppleTalk can operate at only 230 Kbps, it is not commonly used. Instead, Macintosh computers usually use EtherTalk or TokenTalk to communicate with larger and faster networks.

LocalTalk uses a "bus topology" in which each device in the network is directly connected to the next device in a daisy chain. For its access method, LocalTalk uses CSMA/CA. On a Macintosh or Apple IIgs, a small box with a "pigtail" connector is plugged into the printer port; the pigtail on LocalTalk boxes comes in two variations to support computers with either DIN or 9-pin D printer ports. It is often assumed that the LocalTalk box is only used with a DIN-style printer port, so be careful to purchase the right one for your computer.

The LocalTalk box is equipped with two other DIN sockets so that it can take its place in the daisy chain. The pigtail connector from the LocalTalk box plugs into the printer port, and a length of cable connects the LocalTalk box to the next box on the daisy chain. For the LocalTalk boxes at each end of the chain, only one of the DIN sockets is used. The two ends of the chain should not be joined together. Apple LocalTalk boxes are self-terminating, therefore, you do not have to provide external terminators.

In addition to being used with the Apple cabling system, LocalTalk is often used with PhoneNet cabling. A PhoneNet box, which is used in place of the LocalTalk box, is equipped with RJ-11 telephone-style jack connectors for connecting to the network. PhoneNet normally uses a bus topology, although some vendors manufacture hubs to support a variety of star topologies. In bus topology, PhoneNet requires a terminator at each end of the chain, and network performance is reduced without the terminators. The terminator is simply an RJ-11 connector with a suitable resistor across two of the pins.

5.5   802.11 WIRELESS STANDARD

The 802.11 standard for wireless local area networks (WLANs) can be compared to the IEEE 802.3 standard for Ethernet for wired LANs. A new standard issued by the IEEE called 802.11b or **Wi-Fi** (for wireless fidelity), is making WLAN use faster and easier, and the market is growing quickly. The number of users of IEEE 802.11b grew from almost zero in early 2001 to more than 15 million at the end of the year 2002. That still isn't much compared with cell phones and wired Ethernet, but growth will likely continue.

5.5.1   Physical Layer and Architecture

The 802.11 standard defines three physical layers for WLANs: two radio frequency (RF) specifications (direct sequence and frequency hopping spread spectrum) and one infrared (IR). Most WLANs operate in the 2.4-GHz, license-free frequency radio band and have throughput rates up to 2 Mbps. Note: The 2.4-GHz band is particularly attractive because it enjoys worldwide allocations for unlicensed operations. The 802.11b standard is direct sequence only and provides throughput rates up to 22 Mbps. The new standard, 802.11a, will operate in the 5-GHz license-free frequency band and is expected to provide throughput rates up to 54 Mbps in normal mode or 75 Mbps in turbo mode. The newest standard is the 802.11g standard, which has a nominal maximum throughput of 54 Mbps, but because it is using the 2.4-GHz frequency band, its products should be compatible with 802.11b products.

Two operation modes are defined in IEEE 802.11: infrastructure mode and ad hoc mode. The **ad hoc network**, also referred to as the **independent basic service set (IBSS)**, stands alone and is not connected to a base. Wireless stations communicate directly with each other without using an access point or any connection to a wired network. This basic topology is useful to quickly and easily set up a wireless network anywhere a wireless infrastructure does not exist (e.g., a hotel room, a convention center, or an airport).

In **infrastructure mode**, also known as extended service set (ESS), the wireless network consists of at least one **access point (AP)** connected to the wired network infrastructure and a set of wireless end stations. See Figure 5.11. An AP controls encryption on the network and may bridge or route the wireless traffic to a wired Ethernet network (or the Internet.) Access points that act as routers can also assign an IP address to PCs using DHCP services. APs can be compared to a base station used in cellular networks.

An ESS consists of two or more basic service sets (BSSs) forming a single subnetwork. Traffic is forwarded from one BSS to another to facilitate movement of wireless stations between BSSs using cellular topology. Almost always, the distribution system that connects these networks is an Ethernet LAN. Since most corporate WLANs require access to the Wired LAN for services (file servers, printers, Internet links), they operate in infrastructure mode.

One of the requirements of IEEE 802.11 is that it be used with existing wired networks; 802.11 solved this challenge with the use of a portal. A **portal** is the logical integration between wired LANs and 802.11 WLANs. A portal also can serve as the access point to the Distribution System. All data going to an 802.11 LAN from an 802.X LAN must pass through a portal. Thus, the portal functions as a bridge between wired and wireless networks.

The 802.11a standard still has some issues to work out, particularly in the area of compatibility. Currently, its products are not backward-compatible with 802.11b products, which clearly dominate the market. Although all 802.11a products use the same chipset, implementation by each manufacturer differs enough to make them incompatible. Until an interoperability standard is established, 802.11a products from one company may not communicate with those of another.

Figure 5.11   Wireless end station and wireless access point

The Wireless Ethernet Compatibility Alliance (WECA) is an industry consortium that tests from interoperability. Those 802.11b products that pass WECA's tests are given the wireless fidelity (Wi-Fi) seal of approval. WECA is working on an 802.11a certification called Wifi5.

5.5.2   Framing

Frame formats are specified for wireless LAN systems by the 802.11 standard. Each frame consists of a MAC header, a frame body, and a frame check sequence (FCS). The MAC header consists of seven fields and is 30 bytes long. The fields are frame control, duration, address 1, address 2, address 3, sequence control, and address 4. The frame control field is 2 bytes long and is comprised of 11 subfields.

The duration field is 2 bytes long. It contains the data on the duration value for each field, and for control frames it carries the associated identity of the transmitting station. The address fields identify the basic service set, the destination address, the source address, and the receiver and transmitter addresses. Each address field is 6 bytes long. The sequence control field is 2 bytes and is split into two subfields, fragment number and sequence number. Fragment number, which is 4 bits, tells how many fragments the MAC service data unit (MSDU) is broken into. The sequence number field is 12 bits, which indicates the sequence number of the MSDU. The frame body is a variable length field of from 0 to 2312; this is the payload. The frame check sequence is a 32-bit cyclic redundancy check, which ensures there are no errors in the frame.

5.5.3   Medium Access Control Protocol

Most wired LANs products use carrier-sense multiple access with collision detection CSMA/CD as the MAC protocol. Carrier sense means that the station listens before it transmits. If there is already a transmission underway, the station waits and tries again later. If no one is transmitting, the station goes ahead and sends what it has. When two stations send at the same time, the transmissions collide and the information is lost. This is where collision detection comes into play. The station listens to ensure that its

Figure 5.12   Hidden node problem

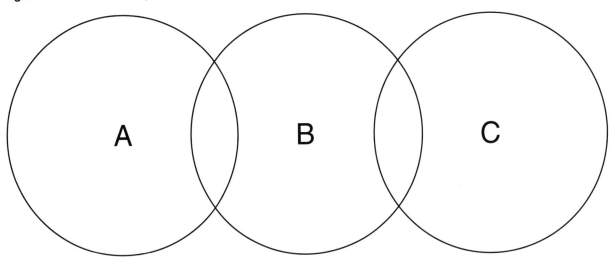

transmission made it to the destination without collisions. If a collision occurred, the station waits and tries again later. The time the station waits is determined by a random amount of time. This technique works great for wired LANs, but wireless topologies can be a problem for CSMA/CD. The problem is the hidden node.

The hidden node problem is shown in Figure 5.12. Node C cannot hear node A. So if node A is transmitting, node C will not know and may transmit as well. The result is a collision. The solution to this problem is carrier-sense multiple access with collision avoidance (CSMA/CA). In CSMA/CA, the station listens before it sends. If someone is already transmitting, the station waits for a random period and tries again. If no one is transmitting, it sends a short message called the ready-to-send message (RTS). This message contains the destination address and the duration of the transmission. Other stations now know that they must wait that long before they can transmit. The destination then sends a short message, which is the clear-to-send message (CTS). This message tells the source that it can send without fear of collisions. Each packet is acknowledged. If an acknowledgment (ACK) is not received, the MAC layer retransmits the data. This entire sequence is called the four-way handshake as shown by Figure 5.13. This is the protocol selected for the 802.11 standard.

5.5.4   Security

With traditional wired LANs, you controlled access to your network by housing it within your office. Tapping into the network remotely was somewhat difficult. But with a WLAN, your network communications are broadcast via radio waves past your office walls, through your neighbor's walls, out into the parking lot, and beyond. Unless you implement proper security, anyone with the right equipment and a little knowledge can see your network traffic.

Follow these minimum steps to protect your network:

- Change the default network name, ESS ID, and the default password that is needed to sign on to a WLAN on your access points. Each manufacturer's default settings are commonly known by hackers.
- Disable the ESS ID broadcast in the access point beacon. By default access points periodically transmit their ESS ID values. Wireless utilities, including those with Windows XP and those that are freeware, can capture these values and present them as a list of available networks to the user. Disabling this broadcast makes it more difficult for intruders to recognize your network.
- Enable wired equivalent privacy (WEP). Without encryption, your data are transmitted in readable form. Anyone within radio range using a wireless protocol analyzer or a promiscuous-mode network adapter may capture the data without joining the network. WEP employs RC4 encryption, the

Figure 5.13   The four-way handshake

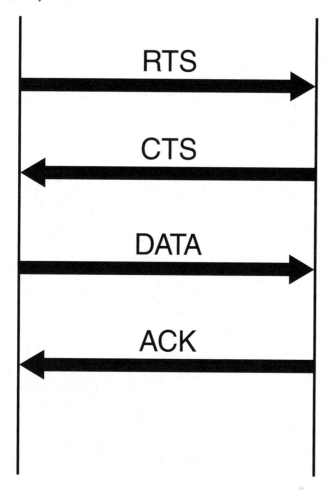

same algorithm used for secure online shopping. WEP encryption can generally be 64 bit or 128 bit; of course, use the 128-bit variety if available.

■ Change your encryption keys periodically. Although WEP is reasonably strong in time, the algorithm can be broken. The longer a key is used, the greater the chance to break the algorithm. So WEP allows changing of the key to prevent brute force attack of the algorithm. Note: WEP can be implemented in hardware or in software. WEP is optional because encryption cannot be exported from the United States. Thus, 802.11 can be a standard outside the United States, albeit without encryption.

■ Enable MAC filtering on your access point. Each wireless PC card has a unique identifier known as the MAC address. Many access points let you build a list of MAC addresses that are allowed on the network. Those not listed are denied.

WEP is probably adequate for most home use. Corporate administrators, however, should add strong encryption to the WLAN. Virtual private networks (VPNs) allow use of IPSec or PPTP encryption over the wireless segment. (See Chapter 23 for more information.)

A number of third-party manufacturers have stepped into the breach to offer a new class of hardware-based VPN products designed specifically for wireless networks. In addition, IEEE formed a task group, TGi, specifically to tighten up WLAN security in a nonproprietary, systematic format.

TGi proposed a stopgap measure called the Temporary Key Integrity Protocol (TKIP), which is intended to work with existing and legacy hardware. WLAN provider may add this feature through a firmware revision. TKIP uses a mechanism called fast-packet rekeying, which changes the encryption keys frequently.

In addition, TGi ratified the use of **802.1X.** This standard requires a WLAN client to initiate an authorization request to the access point, which authenticates the client with an Extensible Authentication Protocol (EAP)-compliant RADIUS server. The RADIUS server may authenticate either the user (via passwords) or the machine (by MAC address). In theory, the wireless client is not allowed to join the network until the transaction is complete.

One form of EAP that was created by Cisco and is supported by Microsoft is PEAP. PEAP, short for Protected Extensible Authentication Protocol, is a form of EAP that is combined with transport layer security (TLS) to create a TSL-encrypted channel between client and server. To provide mutual authentication, PEAP uses Microsoft Challenge Authentication Protocol (MS-CHAP), version 2. Because the challenge/response packets are sent over a TLS-encrypted channel, the password and the key are not exposed to offline dictionary attacks.

5.6   BLUETOOTH

Bluetooth refers to a short-range radio technology aimed at simplifying communication among network devices and between devices and the Internet. It also aims to simplify data synchronization between network devices and other computers. Bluetooth is similar to many other specifications already in use and it borrows many features from these specifications. The Bluetooth standard is becoming more and more of a short-time network between devices for a small amount of information.

At present, Bluetooth has a nominal link range of 10 centimeters to 10 meters, which can be extended to 100 meters with increased transmitting power. Bluetooth operates in the 2.4-GHz industrial-scientific-medical (ISM) band and uses a frequency hop, spread spectrum technology in which packets are transmitted in defined time slots on defined frequencies. A full-duplex information interchange rate of up to 1 Mbps may be achieved in which a time division duplex (TDD) scheme is used. The second generation of Bluetooth supports up to 2 Mbps.

Work on the Bluetooth specification is primarily the responsibility of the Bluetooth Special Interest Group (SIG). This is an industry group consisting of leaders in telecommunications and computing industries. The promoter group within the SIG currently consists of 3Com, Ericsson, IBM, Intel, Lucent Technologies, Microsoft, Motorola, Nokia, and Toshiba.

A Bluetooth system essentially has the following four major components:

- **Radio unit**–A radio transceiver that provides the radio link between Bluetooth devices
- **Baseband unit**—Hardware consisting of flash memory and a CPU. This interfaces with the radio unit and the host device electronics
- **Link management software**—Driver software of firmware that enables the application software to interface with the baseband unit and radio unit
- **Application software**—Programs that implement the user interface and are the applications that can run on wireless devices. For example, chat software that allows two laptop users in a conference hall to talk to each other using wireless technology

Each Bluetooth device has a unique 48-bit address based on the IEEE 802 standard. In addition, a frequency hop scheme allows devices to communicate even in areas with a great deal of electromagnetic interference. Bluetooth includes built-in encryption and verification.

One Bluetooth standard is **HomeRF SWAP** (SWAP means Shared Wireless Access Protocol). This standard is designed specifically for wireless networks in homes; in contrast, the 802.11 standard was created for use in businesses. HomeRF networks are designed to be more affordable to home users than other wireless technologies. HomeRF networks are based on frequency hopping and use of radio frequency waves for the transmission of voice and data with a range of up to 150 feet.

SWAP works together with the public switched telephone networks (PSTNs) and the Internet through existing cordless telephone and wireless LAN technologies to (1) enable voice-activated home electronic systems (2) access the Internet from anywhere in the home, and (3) forward fax, voice, and e-mail, messages. SWAP uses the Time Division Multiple Access protocol for interactive data transfer and CSMA/CA for high-speed packet transfer. SWAP operates in the 2400-MHz band at 50 hops per second to provide a data rate between 1 Mbps and 2 Mbps.

SUMMARY

1. Ethernet is the most widely used LAN technology in use today.
2. Today, the Ethernet standard is defined by the Institute of Electrical and Electronics Engineers (IEEE) in a specification commonly known as IEEE 802.3.
3. Ethernet networks can be configured in either a star topology using unshielded twisted-pair cable connected to a hub, or as a bus topology using a coaxial cable acting as a backbone.
4. When a network device wants to access the network, the access method used is carrier-sense multiple access with collision detection (CSMA/CD).
5. The original Ethernet was called 10Base5, or Thicknet. The name 10Base5 describes a 10-Mbps baseband network that can have cable segments up to 500 meters long. The network uses a 50-ohm terminator and RG-8 and RG-11 as backbone cable.
6. Most network devices connected to the network have an external transceiver that uses a 4-pair AUI cable (sometimes referred to as a drop cable) via a DIX connector (2-row, 15-pin female connector).
7. The 10Base2 (Thinnet) network is a simplified version of the 10Base5 network. The name describes a 10-Mbps baseband network with a maximum cable segment length of approximately 200 meters (actually 185 meters).
8. A 10BaseT network uses UTP cable, which costs less, is smaller, and is easier to work with than coaxial cable. 10BaseT is a physical star topology in which the network devices are connected to a hub (or switch).
9. Fast Ethernet, an extension of the 10BaseT Ethernet standard, transports data at 100 Mbps yet still uses the CSMA/CD protocol used by 10-Mbps Ethernet.
10. 100VG-AnyLAN was developed by Hewlett-Packard as a 100-Mbps, half-duplex transmission network; it allows 100 Mbps on a four-pair category 3 cabling system and allows for voice over IP (VoIP).
11. Gigabit Ethernet has been demonstrated to be a viable solution for increased bandwidth requirements in growing networks, as it is used for high-speed backbones and specialized needs.
12. The 5-4-3 rule states that an Ethernet network must not exceed five segments connected by four repeaters. Of these segments, only three can be populated by computers.
13. Propagation delay is the amount of time that passes between the time when a signal is transmitted and the time when it is received at the opposite end of the copper or optic cable.
14. Token ring rules are defined in the IEEE 802.5 specification.
15. In token ring LANs, each station is connected to a token ring wiring concentrator called a multistation access unit (MSAU) using STP or UTP cabling.
16. The access method used on token ring networks is called token passing.
17. LocalTalk is Apple's own network interface and cable system. Since AppleTalk can only operate at only 230 Kbps, it is not commonly used. LocalTalk uses a "bus topology" in which each device in the network is directly connected to the next device in a daisy chain. For its access method, LocalTalk uses CSMA/CA.
18. The 802.11 standard is the wireless standard that can be compared to the IEEE 802.3 standard for Ethernet for wired LANs.
19. The ad hoc network stands alone and is not connected to a base. The wireless stations communicate directly with others without using an access point or any connection to a wired network.
20. In infrastructure mode, the wireless network consists of at least one access point (AP) connected to the wired network infrastructure and a set of wireless end stations.
21. An access point controls encryption on the network and may bridge or route the wireless traffic to a wired Ethernet network (or the Internet). Access points that act as routers can also assign an IP address to PCs using DHCP services.
22. A portal is the logical integration between wired LANs and 802.11 WLANs.
23. Bluetooth is a radio technology specification for short-range, point-to-multipoint voice and data transfer.
24. HomeRF SWAP is a specification aimed at a small network of devices in the home environment.

QUESTIONS

1. A network interface card has only a single DB-9 female connector. What type of network is it used for?
   a. token ring
   b. FDDI
   c. Ethernet
   d. none of the choices listed
2. A network interface card has a DB-15 female connector and an RJ-45 connector. What type of card is this?
   a. token ring
   b. Ethernet
   c. FDDI
   d. all three listed
3. Carrier-sense multiple-access collision detection is a feature of what LAN technology?
   a. FDDI
   b. token ring
   c. ATM
   d. Ethernet
4. Which of the following networks has the greatest bit throughput?
   a. 100VG-AnyLAN
   b. 100Base TX
   c. 100Base FX
   d. They are all the same.

5. In a campus area network, you need to run a network cable between two buildings that are 250 meters apart. You need to make sure that you do not introduce a problem with attenuation, and you need to provide for high bandwidth capability. You decide to run thicknet coaxial cable. What is the result?
   a. You solve the first problem, but not the second.
   b. You solve the second problem, but not the first.
   c. You solve both problems.
   d. You don't solve either problem.
6. In your network you have five active hubs connected in a serial configuration. Three of the hubs are populated with 10 workstations each. How many unique network IDs do you need?
   a. 5
   b. 3
   c. 30
   d. 1

7. What technology was developed for VoIP?
   a. 100VG-AnyLAN   c. 100Base Tx
   b. 100BaseFx   d. 10Base5

8. What do Thicknet and Thinnet have in common?
   a. Both support 100-Mbps data transmission speeds.
   b. Both can be run up to 500 meters.
   c. Both support token ring.
   d. Both use coaxial cabling.

9. You are troubleshooting a newly installed network to determine why it is slow. On one side of a 24-port bridge is category 5 UTP cabling, which is run to the workstations. On the other side, a segment of RG –58 coaxial cabling is run to the network server. All network cards support 100 Mbps, but the network is only running at 10 Mbps. The company's owner will pay you enough to retire if you can get this network up and running at 100 Mbps. What do you do?
   a. Make sure "full duplex" is selected on the switch.
   b. Replace the RG-58 cable with a category 5 cable.
   c. Replace the category 5 cable with RG-58 cable.
   d. Replace the RG-58 cable with an RG-59 cable.

10. What is the maximum overall length of a 10-Mbps Ethernet network?
    a. 3000 feet   c. 3000 meters
    b. 5500 feet   d. 6000 meters

11. What is the maximum allowable length of a segment of cabling used for a 100BaseFX network? (Select two answers.)
    a. 500 meters   c. 1000 meters
    b. 1.2 miles   d. 2000 meters

12. What is the 5-4-3- rule?
    a. 5 repeaters, 4 segments, maximum of 3 populated segments
    b. 5 bridges, 4 segments, 3 repeaters
    c. 5 routers, 4 bridges, 3 repeaters
    d. 5 segments, 4 repeaters, maximum of 3 populated segments

13. What is the maximum number of stations that a single Thinnet segment can handle?
    a. 50   c. 60
    b. 40   d. 30

14. 100BaseTX Ethernet uses how many pairs of wires?
    a. 2   c. 4
    b. 6   d. 8

15. The maximum allowable length of a single Thinnet cable segment is
    a. 185 feet   c. 601 meters
    b. 601 feet   d. 185 meters

16. Which technology standard does not utilize CSMA/CD?
    a. 100VG-AnyLAN   c. 100BaseTx
    b. 10Base2   d. 10Base5

17. What is a BNC T-connector used for?
    a. to connect a workstation to a server
    b. to connect 10Base5 segments
    c. to terminate a coaxial segment
    d. to connect stations using Thinnet to the network

18. You need to run a single network cable between two buildings that are 650 meters apart. What cable type must you use?
    a. Thinnet coaxial   c. fiber optic
    b. twisted pair   d. Thicknet coaxial

19. If a workstation fails, its downsteam neighbor sends out a special packet called a beacon. Which technologies use beaconing? (Choose two answers.)
    a. Ethernet   c. ATM
    b. FDDI   d. token ring

20. What is the specification for running Fast Ethernet over fiber cable?
    a. 10Base5   c. 100BaseFX
    b. 100BaseTX   d. 10BaseT

21. Your boss asks you to recommend an inexpensive cable type and connector that are compatible with the 802.3 IEEE standard and will support 100 Mbps throughput. What do you suggest?
    a. category 7 UTP, BNC   c. Coaxial, BNC
    b. STP, R-J45   d. category 5 UTP, RJ-45

22. Which of the following is completely true of 100BaseTX?
    a. Requires coaxial cable,100 Mbps, 500-meter maximum cable segment
    b. Requires category 5 UTP cable, 1000 Mbps, 100-meter maximum cable segment
    c. Requires coaxial cable, 100-Mbps, 100-meter maximum cable segment
    d. Requires category 5 UTP cable, 100-Mbps, 100-meter maximum cable segment

23. Which of the following is completely true of 10Base5?
    a. Requires coaxial cable, 10 Mbps, 500-meter maximum cable segment, 1000 stations per segment
    b. Requires coaxial cable, 10 Mbps, 185-meter maximum cable segment, 500 stations per segment
    c. Requires coaxial cable, 10 Mbps, 500-meter maximum cable segment, 50 stations per segment
    d. Requires coaxial cable, 10 Mbps, 500-meter maximum cable segment, 500 stations per segment

24. A token ring hub is also known as a _____.
    a. VAX   c. BTU
    b. TPU   d. MSAU

25. Which media connectors on an NIC are a D-shell, 15-pin female interface?
    a. thinnet   c. BNC
    b. DIX   d. AUI

26. Most 16-Mbps token ring networks use what type of cabling?
    a. UTP   c. coaxial
    b. fiber optic d. STP

27. Which of the following is completely true of 100BaseFX?
    a. requires fiber optic cable, 100 Mbps, 1-kilometer maximum cable segment
    b. requires fiber optic cable, 10 Mbps, 2-kilometer maximum cable segment
    c. requires coaxial cable, 100 Mbps, 2-kilometer maximum cable segment
    d. requires fiber optic cable, 100 Mbps, 2-kilometer maximum cable segment

28. Which of the following is completely true of 10Base2?
    a. requires coaxial cable, 10 Mbps, 185-meter maximum cable segment, 30 stations maximum per segment
    b. requires coaxial cable, 10 Mbps, 500-meter maximum cable segment, 30 stations maximum per segment

c. requires category 5 UTP cable, 10 Mbps, 185-meter maximum cable segment, 30 stations maximum per segment

d. requires coaxial cable, 10 Mbps, 185-meter maximum cable segment, 50 stations maximum per segment

29. Which of the following is completely true of 10BaseT?
   a. Requires category 5 UTP cable, 100 Mbps, 100-meter maximum cable segment
   b. Requires category 3 UTP cable, 100 Mbps, 100-meter maximum cable segment
   c. Requires category 5 UTP cable, 10 Mbps maximum speed, 100-meter maximum cable segment
   d. Requires category 3 UTP cable, 10 Mbps maximum speed, 100-meter maximum cable segment

30. Token ring networks can operate at what speeds? (Choose two answers.)
   a. 24 Mbps
   b. 16 Mbps
   c. 100 Mbps
   d. 4 Mbps

31. The amount of time required for a packet to travel through a switch is called _____ .
   a. latency
   b. signal oscillation
   c. attenuation
   d. frequency

32. What is an AUI?
   a. attachment user interlink
   b. application user interface
   c. application user interlink
   d. attachment user interface

33. What is the maximum cable length used on a Gigabit Ethernet segment, which uses fiber optic media?
   a. 2 kilometers
   b. 5000 feet
   c. 3500 meters
   d. 5 kilometers

34. Which two Ethernet standards use fiber optic cabling?
   a. 100BaseT
   b. 1000BaseSX
   c. 10Base2
   d. 100BaseFX

35. What is the maximum speed of a gigabit network?
   a. one million bits per second
   b. one trillion bits per second
   c. one billion bits per second
   d. one million bytes per second

36. Which two high-speed Ethernet standards are commonly used as backbones?
   a. 10Base5
   b. Gigabit
   c. 100BaseT
   d. 100BaseFX

37. What is the maximum cable segment length for cable used in 100Base-FX (100 million bits per second)?
   a. 2 miles
   b. 1500 feet
   c. 5000 meters
   d. 2 kilometers

38. What is the maximum data transfer speed on a 100BaseFX network?
   a. 100 million bits per second
   b. 100 billion bits per second
   c. 1000 million bits per second
   d. 100 kilobits per second

39. Which of the following is an AppleTalk protocol?
   a. MegaTalk
   b. MacTalk
   c. RemoteTalk
   d. LocalTalk

40. In the 802.3 IEEE standard, what category UTP cable is required to support 10 Mbps?
   a. category 4
   b. category 5
   c. category 7
   d. category 3

41. In the 802.3 IEEE standard, what category UTP cable is required to support 100 Mbps?
   a. category 3
   b. category 5
   c. category 4
   d. category 7

42. A category 5 UTP cable from your wirecloset's patch panel to the workstation's patch panel is exactly 100 meters in length. The patch cable at the workstation is 3 meters long, and the patch cable in the wirecloset is 5 meters long. Your network is a 100BaseTX Ethernet network. Which statement below is the most accurate for this configuration?
   a. Category 5 supports 100BaseTX, so everything is configured properly.
   b. This configuration is correct, because the patch cables do not exceed 5 meters in length.
   c. As long as the patch cables are terminated properly, this configuration is correct.
   d. The total cable length exceeds UTP specifications for 100BaseTX.

43. What is an MSAU used for?
   a. as an FDDI ring.
   b. as a token ring hub.
   c. as a WAN link.
   d. as an Ethernet hub.

44. 100BaseTx requires, at a minimum, what category level of UTP?
   a. 4
   b. 5
   c. 7
   d. 3

45. What is propagation delay?
   a. routing table assimilation delay
   b. protocol switching time
   c. NIC buffer response time
   d. period of time for signal change to traverse the cable

46. Your network consists of 5 servers, 20 workstations, and 1 printer. Each device has a Thinnet coaxial cable going from it to a transceiver with a vampire tap that is tapped into a single run of 10Base5 cabling. The 10Base5 cable is terminated on both ends with a 50-ohm terminator, and one end of it is grounded. What is your physical topology?
   a. bus
   b. ring
   c. star
   d. mesh

47. Your WAN consists of the following: a local area network in Atlanta with a Cisco 2500 router and a local area network in Brisbane with a Cisco 4000 router. What is the least number of unique network IDs you need?
   a. 2
   b. 4
   c. 3
   d. 5

48. Which is the proper configuration for installing coaxial cable used by Ethernet?
   a. both ends terminated, both ends grounded
   b. one end terminated, one end grounded
   c. one end terminated, both ends grounded
   d. both ends terminated, one end grounded

49. You administer a LAN that uses the 10BaseT Ethernet standard. You have connected a Windows 95 computer to your network, but this computer cannot contact the network. You used a 10-meter cable to connect the network interface card to the wall outlet. A 90-meter drop cable connects the wall outlet to a patch panel in the wiring closet, and a 5-meter cable connects the patch

to an Ethernet hub. What should you do to allow the Windows 95 computer to contact the network?
a. Replace the 10-meter cable between the Windows 95 computer and the wall outlet with a 20-meter cable.
b. Replace the 10-meter cable between the Windows 95 computer and the wall outlet with a 5-meter cable.
c. Replace the 90-meter UTP cable between the wall outlet and the patch panel with a 90-meter fiber optic cable.
d. Replace the 5-meter UTP cable between the patch panel and the Ethernet hub with a 5-meter fiber optic cable.

50. The best cable choice for linking a few computers in a small office using a bus Ethernet network is cable with a _____ designation.
a. RG-47   c. RG-59
b. RG-58   d. RG-62

51. You have a Thinnet bus network, which has been in use for about a year. You have just added three new client computers to the network. When you test the network after installation, none of the computers on the network can access the server. Which of the following can be preventing the network from functioning?
a. The bus network is not properly terminated.
b. A client computer on the network has failed.
c. The new cables added to service the new computers are not compatible with the existing cable type.
d. The network adapter cards in the new computers are not compatible with the network adapter cards in other computers.

52. What is the distance limitation of a 10BaseT network?
a. 100 meters   c. 185 meters
b. 500 meters   d. 1 kilometer

53. What type of connector is used by Thinnet for connection to the network adapter card?
a. an AUI connector   c. an RJ-45 connector
b. a BNC T-connector   d. a BNC barrel connector.

54. Ethernet uses a special type of data format called frames. Which of the following statements is true of Ethernet frames?
a. All Ethernet frames are 1518 bytes long.
b. All Ethernet frames contain preambles that mark the start of the frame.
c. All Ethernet frames contain starting and ending delimiters.
d. All Ethernet frames contain CRC fields that store source and destination addresses.

55. Which type of media access methods used by IBM–based LANs with MSAUs?
a. token passing   c. demand priority
b. CSMA/CD   d. CDMS/CA

56. Pat is a network engineer for the Acme Corporation. The architects in the Sacramento branch office want to connect their Windows 98 SE computers and their laser printers in a network for file and printer sharing. They ask Pat to design the network for them. She tells the architects that a 10BaseT Ethernet network is inexpensive and relatively easy to install, and the architects agree to allow Pat to design this type of network. Which physical topology will Pat implement in designing the network for the architects in Sacramento?
a. bus   c. star
b. ring   d. mesh

57. Which of the following are characteristics of a token ring network? (Select all the correct answers.)
a. logical ring   c. physical star
b. token passing   d. demand priority access

58. Your company has just upgraded its category 5 Ethernet network from 10 Mbps to 100 Mbps. After the upgrade, the 20 Windows 2000 Professional computers in the marketing department can no longer connect to the network. However, the remaining 80 Windows 2000 computers in the company can connect. Your company uses NWLink (IPX) as the only network protocol. You need to connect the computers in the marketing department to the network. What must you do?
a. Configure the NWLink frame type of the network adapters to be Ethernet 802.3.
b. Configure the NWLink frame type of the network adapters to be Ethernet II.
c. Replace the network adapters with 10/100 BNC adapters.
d. Replace the network adapters with 10/100 UTP network adapters.

59. Chris has been contracted to build a network for a multimedia development firm that currently uses a 10-Mbps Ethernet network. The company requires a high bandwidth network for the multimedia team, which constantly views and manipulates large files across the network. The company is expecting moderate growth. Chris is to come up with a solution that *must* increase network bandwidth. Optionally, the solution can support the growth potential of this company, and improve server response time.

Required result:
• Increase network bandwidth

Optional result:
• Support future growth
• Improve server response time

Proposed solution:
• Install category 5 UTP cable in a star topology with the existing hub.
• Upgrade the workstation's adapter cards to support 100 Mbps.
• Increase the amount of RAM in the server.

Critique this proposal.
a. achieves the required result and both optional results
b. does not achieve the required result but achieves both optional results
c. does not achieve the required result but does achieve one of the optional results
d. achieves the required result but cannot achieve either of the optional results
e. achieves neither the required result nor either of the optional results

60. Suppose the following situation exists: You are the senior network administrator for the Acme Corporation. Pat,

the technology officer, has asked you to design a network for a new branch office in Russia. He would like you to use the following specifications in your design.

Required result:
- The Russian network must use category 5 UTP cable.

Optional desired results:
- Support a physical star topology.
- Transmit data at 1 Gbps.

Proposed solution:
- You design the Russian network using the 100BaseT standard.

Which results does the proposed solution produce?

a. The proposed solution produces the required result and both of the optional desired results.
b. The proposed solution produces the required result and only one of the optional desired results.
c. The proposed solution produces only the required result.
d. The proposed solution produces only the two optional desired results.

61. Your company is a medium-sized firm and leases two buildings. The two buildings are 800 meters apart. Each building has a 100BaseT Ethernet network.

Required result:
- Connect the two separate networks

Optional results:
- Support a transmission rate of 1000 Mbps
- Make the network immune to interference

Proposed solution:
- Implement fiber optic Ethernet

Which results does the proposed solution produce?

a. achieves the required result and both optional results
b. does not achieve the required result but does achieve both optional results
c. does not achieve the required result but does achieve one of the optional results
d. achieves the required result but cannot achieve either of the optional results
e. achieves neither the required result nor either of the optional results

CHAPTER 6

Common Protocol Suites

Topics Covered in This Chapter

Introduction

Up to now, we have discussed the physical part of the network. We have not considered the software, in particular the protocols that make the network run. It is essential that any IT administrator understand these protocols to be able to configure and troubleshoot the network.

Objectives

- Given an RFC number, find the RFC document on the Web.
- List the protocols that can connect to a TCP/IP network.
- List and describe each of the TCP/IP protocols.
- Given an IP address, determine its class and default subnet mask.
- Given an IP address and subnet mask, determine the network address and host address.
- Given a network situation, determine a subnet mask that can be used for the network.
- List and describe the ways to translate from the NetBIOS and host names to IP addresses.

- Differentiate between ports and sockets.
- Explain how classless interdomain routing differs from classful IP.
- List the differences between IPv4 and IPv6.
- Diagnose and troubleshoot a given IP problem.
- Configure and troubleshoot the TCP/IP protocol.
- Explain the difference between IPX and SPX.
- Diagnose and troubleshoot a given IPX problem.
- Explain how NetBEUI and NetBIOS relate to each other and how they can relate to TCP/IP and IPX protocols.
- Describe DLC and AppleTalk protocols.

6.1 PROTOCOL AND PROTOCOL SUITE

A **protocol** is a set of rules or standards designed to enable computers to connect with one another, and peripheral devices to exchange information with as little error as possible. A **protocol stack,** sometimes referred to as a **protocol suite,** is a set of protocols that works together to provide a full range of network services.

6.2 TCP/IP AND THE INTERNET

The Internet that we know today began as a U.S. Department of Defense (DOD)-funded experiment to interconnect DOD-funded research sites in the United States. In December 1968, the Advanced Research Projects Agency (ARPA) awarded a grant to design and deploy a packet switching network (messages divided into packets, transmitted individually, and recompiled into their original forms). In September 1969, the first node of the ARPANET was installed at UCLA. By 1971, the ARPANET spanned the continental United States and had connections to Europe by 1973.

Over time, the initial protocols used to connect the hosts proved incapable of keeping up with the growing network traffic load. Therefore, a new TCP/IP protocol suite was proposed and implemented. By 1983, the popularity of the TCP/IP protocol grew as it was included in the communications kernel for the University of California's UNIX implementation, 4.2BSD (Berkeley Software Distribution) UNIX. Today, the TCP/IP protocol is the primary protocol used on the Internet and is supported by Novell NetWare, Microsoft Windows NT, Microsoft Windows 2000, Windows Server 2003, UNIX, and other network operating systems.

The standards for TCP/IP are published in a series of documents called **Requests for Comments (RFC).** An RFC can be submitted by anyone. Eventually, if it gains enough interest, the submittal may evolve into an Internet standard. Each RFC is designated by an RFC number. Once published, an RFC never changes. Modifications to an original RFC are assigned a new RFC number.

RFCs are classified as one of the following: approved Internet standards, proposed Internet standards (circulated in draft form for review), Internet best practices, or For Your Information (FYI) documents. Administrators should always follow approved Internet standards.

For more information on RFCs, visit the following websites:

http:/www.rfc-editor.org/

http://www.cis.ohio-state.edu/hypertext/information/rfc.html

6.2.1 IP, TCP, and UDP Protocols

With the TCP/IP protocol suite, TCP/IP does not worry about how the hosts (computers or any other network connection) connect to the network. Instead, TCP/IP was designed to operate over nearly any underlying local or wide area network. See Figure 6.1. This would include the following:

- LAN protocols: Ethernet, Token Ring, and ARCnet networks
- WAN protocols: ATM, Frame Relay, and X.25
- Serial line protocols: Serial Line Internet Protocol (SLIP) and Point-to-Point Protocol (PPP)

When users send or receive data, the data are divided into little chunks called **packets.** Each of these packets contains both the sender's TCP/IP address and the receiver's TCP/IP address. When the packet must go to another computer on another network, it is then sent to a gateway computer, usually a router. The gateway understands the networks to which it is connected directly. The gateway computer reads the destination address to determine in which direction the packet needs to be forwarded. It then forwards the packet to an adjacent gateway. The packet is then forwarded from gateway to gateway until it gets to the network to which the destination host belongs. The last gateway forwards the packet directly to the computer whose address is specified. See Figure 6.2.

The lowest protocol within the TCP/IP suite is the **Internet protocol (IP),** which is primarily responsible for addressing and routing packets between hosts. IP is a connectionless protocol, which means that there is no established connection between the end points that are communicating. Each packet (also known as a datagram) that travels through the Internet is treated as an independent unit of data. Therefore, a packet is not affected by other data packets. In addition, IP does not guarantee any deliveries; packets can get lost, be delivered out of sequence, or be delayed. Instead, IP must rely on TCP to determine that the data arrived successfully at their destination and to retransmit the data if they did not. When a packet is received from the TCP, IP inserts its own header in the datagram. The main contents of the IP header are the source and destination addresses, the protocol numbers, and a checksum.

The protocols that work on top of the IP protocol are TCP and UDP. The **Transmission Control Protocol (TCP)** is a reliable, connection-oriented delivery service that breaks data into manageable packets, wraps them with the information needed to route them to their destination, and reassembles the pieces at the receiving end of the communication link. It establishes a virtual connection between the two hosts or computers so that they can send messages back and forth for a period of time. A virtual connection appears to be always connected, but in reality it is made of many packets being sent back and forth independently.

The most important information in the header are the source and destination port numbers, a sequence number for the datagram, and a checksum. The source port number and destination port number ensure that the data are sent back and forth to the correct process (or program) running on each computer. The sequence number allows the datagram to be rebuilt in the correct order in the receiving computer, and the checksum allows the protocol to check whether the data sent are the same as the data received.

The TCP uses acknowledgements to verify that the data were received by the other host. If an acknowledgment is not sent, the data are resent.

Another transport layer protocol is the **User Datagram Protocol (UDP).** Unlike the TCP, which uses acknowledgments to ensure data delivery, UDP does not. Therefore, the UDP is considered

Figure 6.1 TCP/IP protocol suite

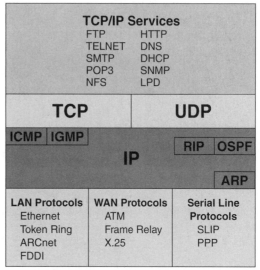

INTERNET PROTOCOLS

Routes data packets between different hosts or networks.

- **Internet Protocol (IP)**—Connectionless protocol primarily responsible for addressing and routing packets between hosts. (RFC 791)
- **Address Resolution Protocol (ARP)**—Used to obtain hardware addresses (MAC addresses) of hosts located on the same physical network. (RFC 826)
- **Internet Control Message Protocol (ICMP)**—Sends messages and reports errors regarding the delivery of a packet. (RFC 792)
- **Internet Group Management Protocol (IGMP)**—Used by IP hosts to report host group membership to local multicast routers. (RFC 1112)
- **Router Information Protocol (RIP)**—Distance vector route discovery protocol where the entire routing table is periodically sent to the other routers. (RFC 1723)
- **Open Shortest Path First (OSPF)**—Link State Route Discovery protocol where each router periodically advertises itself to other routers. (RFC 1245, 1246, 1247, and 1253)

HOST-TO-HOST PROTOCOLS

Maintains data integrity and sets up reliable, end-to-end communication between hosts.

- **Transmission Control Protocol (TCP)**—Provides connection/oriented, reliable communications for applications that typically transfer large amounts of data at one time or that require an acknowledgment for data received. (RFC 793)
- **User Datagram Protocol (UDP)**—Provides connectionless communications and does not guarantee that packets will be delivered. Applications that use UDP typically transfer small amounts of data at one. Reliable delivery is the responsibility of the application. (RFC 768)

PROCESS/APPLICATION PROTOCOLS

Acts as the interface for the user. Provides applications that transfer data between hosts.

- **File Transfer Protocol (FTP)**—Allows a user to transfer files between local and remote host computers. (RFC 959)
- **Telecommunication Network (Telnet)**—A virtual terminal protocol (terminal emulation) allowing a user to log on to another TCP/IP host to access network resources. (RFC 854)
- **Simple Mail Transfer Protocol (SMTP)**—The standard protocol for the exchange of electronic main over the Internet. It is used between e-mail servers on the Internet or to allow an e-mail client to send mail to a server. (RFC 821 and 822)
- **Post Office Protocol (POP)**—Defines a simple interface between a user's mail client software and e-mail server. It is used to download mail from the server to the client and allows users to manage their mailboxes. (RFC 1460)
- **Network File System (NFS)**—Provides transparent remote access to shared files across networks. (RFC 1094)
- **Hypertext Transfer Protocol (HTTP)**—The basis for exchange over the World Wide Web (WWW). Web pages are written in the hypertext markup language (HTML), an ASCII-based, platform-independent formatting language. (RFC 1945 and 1866)
- **Domain Name System (DNS)**—Defines the structure of Internet names and their association with IP addresses. (RFC 1034 and 1035)
- **Dynamic Host Configuration Protocol (DHCP)**—Used to automatically assign TCP/IP addresses and other related information to clients. (RFC 2131)
- **Simple Network Management Protocol (SNMP)**—Defines procedures and management information databases for managing TCP/IP-based network devices. (RFC 1157 and 1441)
- **Line Printer Daemon (LPD)**—Provides printing on a TCP/IP network.
- **Network Time Protocol (NTP)**—An Internet standard protocol that assures accurate synchronization to the millisecond of computer clock times in a network of computers. (RFC 1305)

Figure 6.2 TCP/IP packet

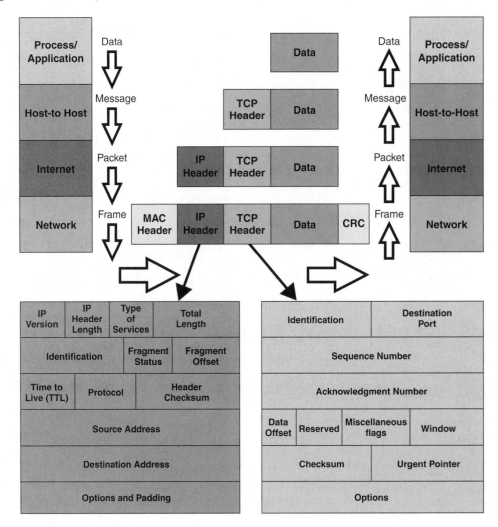

unreliable, "best effort" delivery. Since it is considered unreliable, UDP is used for protocols that transmit small amounts of data at one time or for broadcasts (packets sent to everyone). Being unreliable, however, does not mean that the packets will not be delivered; rather, there is no guarantee or check to ensure that they get to their destination.

6.2.2 IPv4 Addressing

The current version of the IP protocol is version 4: IPv4. Each connection on a TCP/IP address (logical address) is called a **host** (a computer or other network device that is connected to a TCP/IP network) and is assigned a unique **IP address** by IP. A host is any network interface, including each network interface card, or a network printer that connects directly onto the network. The format of the IP address is four 8-bit numbers (octet) divided by periods(.). Each number can be 0 to 255. For example, a TCP/IP address could be 131.107.3.1 or 2.0.0.1.

IP addresses are manually assigned and configured (**static IP addresses**) or dynamically assigned and configured by a DHCP server (**dynamic IP addresses**). Since the address is used to identify the computer, no two connections can use the same IP address. Otherwise, one or both of the computers would not be able to communicate, and you will usually see a message stating "IP address conflict."

Communications on a TCP/IP network can be classified as unicast, multicast, or anycast. **Unicast** means a single sender communicates with a single receiver over the network. **Multicast** is communication between a single sender and multiple receivers, and **anycast** is communication between any sender and the nearest of a group of receivers in a network. A broadcast means packets are sent to every computer on the network or a subnet. Note: Broadcasts are not normally forwarded by routers.

When connecting to the Internet, a corporation or business is assigned a network number. If the first number is between 1 and 126 (first bit is a 0), the network is a class A. If the first number is between 128 and 191 (first two bits are 1 0), the network is a class B. If the first number is between 192 and 223 (first three bits are 1 1 1), the network is a class C. See Table 6.1. Every computer on a TCP/IP network must have the same network number.

Because Internet addresses must be unique and because space on the Internet is limited, there is a need for some organization to control and allocate address number blocks. IP number management was formerly a responsibility of the Internet Assigned Numbers Authority (IANA), which contracted with Network Solutions Inc. for the actual services. If you go to the following website, you will see exactly what blocks are assigned to what purposes: http://www.iana.org/assignments/ipv4-address-space. Some of the class A blocks are staked out by corporations or government departments.

In December 1997, IANA turned over the responsibility of managing the world's Internet address assignment and allocation to the following organizations:

■ American Registry for Internet Numbers (ARIN)—North and South America, the Caribbean, and sub-Saharan Africa.
■ Réseaux IP Européens Network Coordination Centre (RIPE NCC)—Europe, the Middle East, and parts of Africa and Asia.
■ Asia Pacific Network Information Centre (APNIC)—Asia Pacific region

Domain name management is still the separate responsibility of Network Solution Inc. and a number of other registrars accredited by the Internet Corporation for Assigned Names and Numbers (ICANN).

Two additional classes are used for special functions only and are not commonly assigned to individual hosts. Class D addresses may begin with a value between 224 and 239, and are used for IP multicasting. Class E addresses begin with a value between 240 and 255, and are reserved for experimental use.

Since TCP/IP addresses are scarce for the Internet, a series of addresses have been reserved to be used by **private networks** (networks not connected to the Internet).

Class A—10.x.x.x (1 class A addresses)
Class B—Between 172.16.x.x and 172.31.x.x (16 class B addresses)
Class C—192.168.0.x and 192.168.255.x (256 class C addresses)

If you are not connected to the Internet or are using a proxy server, it is recommended that you use private addresses to prevent a renumbering of your internet work when you eventually connect to the Internet.

The TCP/IP address is broken down into a network number and a host number. The network number identifies the entire network while the host number identifies the computer or connection on the specified network. If it is a class A network, the first octet describes the network number while the last three octets describe the host address. If it is a class B network, the first two octets describe the network

Table 6.1   Standard IP classes for the IP address of w.x.y.z

Class Type	First Octet	Network Number[1]	Host Number	Default Subnet Mask	Comments
A	1–126	w	x.y.z	255.0.0.0	Supports 16 million hosts on each of 126 networks.
B	128–191	w.x	y.z	255.255.0.0	Supports 65,000 hosts on each of 16,000 networks.
C	192–223	w.x.y	z	255.255.255.0	Supports 254 hosts on each of 2 million networks.

[1]The w.x.y.z is a typical IP address where w,x,y, and z can be any number from 0 to 255. The w.x.y.z can be broken down to a network number based on its class type.

number while the last two octets describe the host address. If it is a class C, the first three octets describe the network number while the last octet describes the host number.

Example 1:

You have the following network address:

131.107.20.4

The 131 is between 128 and 191, identifying the address as a class B network. Therefore, the 131.107 identifies the network and the 20.4 identifies the host or computer on the 131.107 network.

Example 2:

You have the following network address:

208.234.23.4

The 208 is between 192 and 223, identifying the address as a class C network. Therefore, the 208.234.23 identifies the network and the 4 identifies the host or computer on the 208.234.23 network.

Several address values are reserved and/or have special meaning. The network number 127 is used for loopback testing, and the specific host address 127.0.0.1 refers to the **local host,** or the actual host or computer currently in use.

Usually when defining the TCP/IP for a network connection, IT managers also specify a subnet mask. The **subnet mask** is used to define which bits describe the network number and which bits describe the host address. Like the network address, every computer on a network must have the same subnet mask. The default subnet mask for a class A network is 255.0.0.0. Converting this to a binary equivalent gives 11111111.00000000.00000000.00000000, showing that the first 8 bits (first octet), marked with ones, is used to define the network address, while the last 24 bits, marked with zeros, are used to define the host address. The default subnet mask for a class B network is 255.255.0.0 (11111111.11111111.00000000.00000000) and the default subnet mask for a class C network is 255.255.255.0 (11111111.11111111.11111111.00000000). To convert decimal to binary numbers, see chapter 3.

If an individual network is connected to another network and users must communicate with any computers on the other network, they must also define the **default gateway,** which specifies the local address of a router. If the default gateway is not specified, users will not be able to communicate with computers on other networks. If the LAN is connected to more than two networks, users must specify only one gateway, because when a data packet is sent, the gateway will first determine if the data packet needs to go to a local computer or onto another network. If the data packet is meant to be sent to a computer on another network, the gateway will forward the data packet to the router. The router will then determine the best direction that the data packet must go to reach its destination. Occasionally, it will have to go back through the network to get to another gateway. See Figure 6.3.

Broadcasts are used to reach all devices on a network or subnetwork. The broadcast address is used when a machine wants to send the same packet to all devices on the network. There are two types of broadcasts, all-nets broadcast and subnet broadcast. While broadcasts are not forwarded by most routers, broadcasts can take up valuable bandwidth and processing power in the receiving devices. All-net broadcast packets are addressed to 255.255.255.255 in the IP header. Literally, the packets are addressed to all networks. Subnet broadcasts contain the subnet address in the broadcast packet and all 1s for the host address, and are aimed at all computers within the subnet. To get your broadcast address, you set the device or host portion of the IP address to 255. Therefore, if you have the IP address 129.23.123.2 (a class C with a mask of 255.255.255.0), your broadcast address is 129.23.123.255. Your network address is 129.23.123.0.

6.2.3   Subnetting the Network

The subnet mask can be changed to take a large network and break it into small networks called **subnets.** This explains why the subnet mask must be defined, so that the network can calculate which bits represent the network address and which bits represent the host address. All subnets on a network

Figure 6.3 IP network with addresses and subnet masks. Notice the multihomed computer (computer with two network cards connected to two subnets)

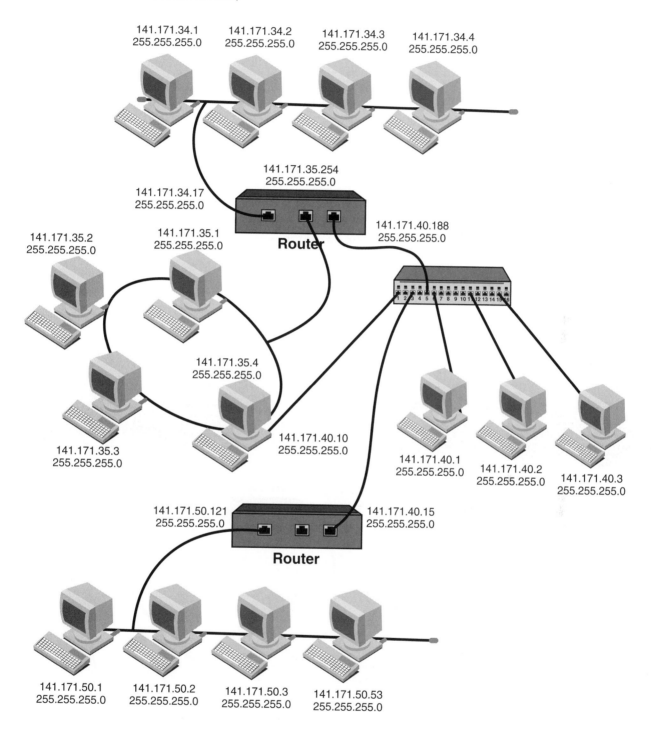

must use the same network address. For a subnet, the subnet network number and the subnet mask must be the same for all computers. See Figure 6.4.

Example 3:

Figure 6.5 shows two networks connected by a router. Every node (computer and router link) on LAN A has a network address of 141.171.50.0 with the subnet mask of 255.255.255.0. In addition, every node on LAN B has a network address of 132.11.0.0 with the subnet mask of 255.255.0.0. Note: A network address is expressed like an IP address, but the host bits are zeros. For example, the 141.171.50.0 with the subnet mask of 255.255.255.0 indicates that the first three octets define the network address and the last octet defines the host address. Therefore, every computer must begin

Figure 6.4   By changing the default subnet mask, you split the host number into a subnet number and a host number

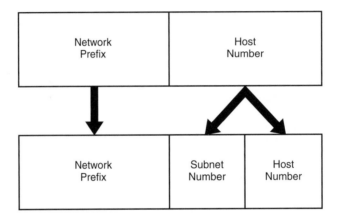

Figure 6.5   Two TCP/IP networks connected to a router

with 141.171.50. The router is actually a member of both networks. While every computer is not required to have the same gateway (router), since there is only one router connection on each network, the router link that is connected to the network is the gateway. If there were two routers connected to the network, then specify either one. Lastly, notice that the router does not use a default gateway because it *is* the gateway.

Example 4:

Your network is assigned a network number of 161.13.0.0. Since it is a class B network, it already has a default subnet mask of 255.255.0.0. Therefore, any network interface card that belongs to this network has a TCP/IP address beginning with 161.13. Since it is a class B network, it uses 16 bits to define the host address, which allows the network up to 65,534 computers. It's hard to imagine a single LAN with that many computers.

    The network administrator could take this large network and divide it into several smaller subnets. For example, if 161.13 defines the entire corporation network, the third octet could be used to define a site network or individual LAN while the last octet defines the host address.

    Therefore, if you have three individual LANs, use the third octet to define them. For example, the first building would have a network address of 161.13.1.0, the second building an address of 161.13.2.0, and the third building an address of 161.13.3.0. Since the last octet is used to define the host number and there are 8 bits to do so, there can be 254 hosts for each LAN. To let the network know that the 161.13.0.0 network is subnetted, the mask would have to be changed from 255.255.0.0 to 255.255.255.0 (11111111.11111111.11111111.00000000) to indicate that the first 24 bits are the network address.

To calculate the maximum number of subnets, use the following equation:

$$\text{Number of subnets} = 2^{\text{number of masked bits}} - 2$$

To calculate the maximum number of hosts, use the following equation:

$$\text{Number of hosts} = 2^{\text{number of unmasked bits}} - 2$$

The −2 is necessary because you cannot use a network number, subnet number, or host number of all zeros and all ones. For example, if you had an address of 131.107.3.4, then 131.107.0.0 is the network address and 3.4 is the host address. If you send a packet to the 131.107.0.0 (host address is all zeros), then you are sending the packet to the network itself, not to the individual computer on the network. If you send it to 131.107.255.255 (host address is all ones), then you are doing a broadcast to all computers on network 131.107. If you use the address of 0.0.3.4 (network number is all zeros), then it assumes 3.4 is on the current or local network.

Example 5:

In Example 3, you have 8 bits that are used to define the subnet/site number and 8 bits to define the host number. Therefore, the following equations apply:

$$\text{Number of subnets} = 2^{\text{number of masked bits}} - 2 = 2^8 - 2 = 254 \text{ subnets or sites}$$
$$\text{Number of hosts } = 2^{\text{number of unmasked bits}} - 2 = 2^8 - 2 = 254 \text{ hosts for each subnet}$$

Example 6:

Your network is assigned an address of 207.182.15. You choose to subnet your network into several smaller networks. Your largest network will have 25 computers. Therefore, how many bits can you mask to provide the largest number of subnets or sites?

    First, you have only the 8 bits that were used for the host address. The easiest method is to use the formula that calculates number of hosts. To determine how many unmasked bits allow 25 or more computers, use the following calculations:

$$\text{Number of hosts} = 2^{\text{number of unmasked bits}} - 2 = 2^1 - 2 = 0$$
$$= 2^{\text{number of unmasked bits}} - 2 = 2^2 - 2 = 2$$

$$= 2^{\text{number of unmasked bits}} -2 = 2^3 - 2 = 6$$
$$= 2^{\text{number of unmasked bits}} -2 = 2^4 - 2 = 14$$
$$= 2^{\text{number of unmasked bits}} -2 = 2^5 - 2 = 30$$

Since we used 5 of the 8 bits for the host number, we have 3 bits left that are masked, which gives us the following:

$$\text{Number of subnets} = 2^{\text{number of masked bits}} -2 = 2^3 - 2 = 6$$

Lastly, the subnet mask would be 11111111.11111111.11111111. 11100000, which is equivalent to 255.255.255.224.

Example 7:

Using the network discussed in Example 5, what is the range of TCP/IP addresses for the second subnet?

The network number is 207.182.15 with a subnet mask of 255.255.255.224, which describes the first 3 bits of the forth octet used for the subnet number. The possible subnet numbers (in binary) are as follows:

0 0 0
0 0 1
0 1 0
0 1 1
1 0 0
1 0 1
1 1 0
1 1 1

You cannot use 0 0 0 or 1 1 1, which leaves six possible subnets.

Using binary counting, the second subnet is defined by 0 1 0. Since there are 5 bits left, they can range from 0 0 0 0 1 (remember, not all zeros) to 1 1 1 1 0 (remember, not all ones). Therefore, the last octet will be 0 1 0 0 0 0 0 1 to 0 1 0 1 1 1 1 0. If you translate these to decimals, the last octet will be 65 to 94. Therefore, the address range is 207.182.15.65 to 207.182.15.94 with a subnet mask of 255.255.255.224.

Example 8:

You are the IT administrator for the Acme Corporation, whose main product is widgets. It is your responsibility to plan and implement the IP addresses for your company. You currently have 35 sites throughout the country with plans to add 5 more sites within the next three years. Currently, the largest site has 275 people, but it may add another 25 to 75 employees over the next two years. In addition, the corporate building has 10 web servers there and 15 corporate servers that also need IP addresses. ARIN has assigned 182.24.0.0 to your corporation.

1. How would you subnet your network so that you can get the maximum number of people per site?
2. What is the number of sites that your network can have with this configuration?
3. What is the maximum number of people that your network can have with this configuration?
4. What would the subnet mask be for your corporation?
5. The primary site (which is also the largest site) is the corporate office. If you assign this site as your first subnet, what would the extended network prefix be for the corporate office site?
6. What would the range of addresses be for this site?
7. What is the broadcast address for this site?

Let's take the first question and determine how would you subnet your network to get the maximum number of people per site. We know that we have a 182.24 (10110110.00011000) assigned by ARIN. Since it starts with 182, we know that it is a class B network with a default subnet mask of 255.255.0.0 (11111111.11111111.00000000.00000000). This tells us that the first 16-bits are locked for us and the last 16-bits are ours to assign. We know that we will have 40 (35 + 5) sites to plan for with a maximum number of 375 hosts (275 + 75 + 10 + 15). Since we want to maximize the number of hosts, let's figure out how many bits it would take to assign the 40 sites.

$$\begin{aligned}
\text{Number of subnets} &= 2^{\text{number masked bits}} - 2 = 2^1 - 2 = 0 \\
&= 2^{\text{number masked bits}} - 2 = 2^2 - 2 = 2 \\
&= 2^{\text{number masked bits}} - 2 = 2^3 - 2 = 6 \\
&= 2^{\text{number masked bits}} - 2 = 2^4 - 2 = 14 \\
&= 2^{\text{number masked bits}} - 2 = 2^5 - 2 = 30 \\
&= 2^{\text{number masked bits}} - 2 = 2^6 - 2 = 62
\end{aligned}$$

Therefore, it would take 6 bits to define the subnets. As you can see, if we use 6 bits, we can actually grow to 62 sites (answer to question 2). This leaves 10 bits (16–6) to define our hosts. Use the following equation:

$$\text{Number of hosts} = 2^{\text{number masked bits}} - 2 = 2^{10} - 2 = 1022$$

You can have up to 1022 hosts per site (answer to question 3). Note: If this number were smaller than what you needed, you would have to come up with another solution to get enough addresses for each site. You would have several options:

- Assign multiple subnets per site.
- Acquire a class A network from ARIN (highly unlikely).
- Use a proxy server or a network address translation solution so that you can use one set of IP addresses for internal traffic (private network) and second set of addresses for external traffic (IP addresses assigned by ARIN).

Since we are going to use 6 bits to define the subnets, the new subnet mask is (answer to question 4):

11111111.11111111.**111111**00.00000000

This is equivalent to

255.255.252.0

which would have to be assigned to every host on every subnet.

Looking at the 6 bits that define the subnets, number your subnets as follows:

Site Number (Decimal)	Site Number (Binary)	Extended Network Number (Binary)	Extended Network Number (Decimal)
0*	000000	10110110.00011000.000000XX.XXXXXXXX	182.24.0.0
1	000001	10110110.00011000.00001XX.XXXXXXXX	182.24.4.0
2	000010	10110110.00011000.00001XX.XXXXXXXX	182.24.8.0
3	000011	10110110.00011000.000011XX.XXXXXXXX	182.24.12.0
4	000100	10110110.00011000.000100XX.XXXXXXXX	182.24.16.0
5	000101	10110110.00011000.000101XX.XXXXXXXX	182.24.20.0
6	000110	10110110.00011000.000110XX.XXXXXXXX	182.24.24.0
7	000111	10110110.00011000.000111XX.XXXXXXXX	182.24.28.0
8	001000	10110110.00011000.001000XX.XXXXXXXX	182.24.32.0
.	.	.	.
.	.	.	.
.	.	.	.
62	111110	10110110.00011000.111110XX.XXXXXXXX	182.24.248.0
63*	111111	10110110.00011000.111111XX.XXXXXXXX	182.24.252.0

*Remember that a subnet number cannot be all 0s or all 1s.

Every host on the first site(the corporate site) will start with the following bits:

10110110.00011000.000001 XX.XXXXXXXX

To calculate the extended network number in decimal, assign 0s to the host bits. Therefore, the extended network number is

10110110.00011000.000001**00.00000000**

which gives an extended network number of 182.24.4.0 (answer to question 5). Note: This is the reason that we cannot use all 0s for the host, since it is used to define the network numbers.
The Xs define the hosts (101100110.00011000.000001**XX.XXXXXXXX**) on that site. Remember, you have 10 bits to assign to hosts. The first host will be assigned

10110110.00011000.000001**00.000000001**

which is equivalent to

182.24.4.1

The last host at this site would be

10110110.000110000.000001**11.11111110**

which is equivalent to

182.24.7.254

So as you can see, the range of addresses for the first subnet is 182.24.4.1 to 182.24.7.254 (answer to question 6). Remember, the host bits cannot be all 0s or 1s.

Host Number (Binary)	Host Number (Decimal)	IP Address (Binary)	IP Address (Decimal)
~~00.00000000*~~	~~0.0~~	~~10110110.00011000.00000100.00000000~~	~~182.24.4.0~~
00.00000001	0.1	10110110.00011000.000001**00.00000001**	182.24.4.1
00.00000010	0.2	10110110.00011000.000001**00.00000010**	182.24.4.2
00.00000011	0.3	10110110.00011000.000001**00.00000011**	182.24.4.3
00.00000100	0.4	10110110.00011000.000001**00.00000100**	182.24.4.4
00.00000101	0.5	10110110.11100111.000001**00.00000101**	182.24.4.5
00.00000110	0.6	10110110.00011000.000001**00.00000110**	182.24.4.6
00.00000111	0.7	10110110.00011000.000001**00.00000111**	182.24.4.7
00.00001000	0.8	10110110.00011000.000001**00.00001000**	182.24.4.8
00.00001001	0.9	10110110.00011000.000001**00.00001001**	182.24.4.9
.	.	.	.
.	.	.	.
.	.	.	.
11.11111110	3.254	10110110.00011000.000001**11.11111110**	182.24.7.254
~~11.11111111*~~	~~3.255~~	~~10110110.00011000.000001**11.11111111**~~	~~182.24.7.255~~

*Remember that a subnet number cannot be all 0s or all 1s.

The broadcast address is calculated by assigning all host bits as 1. This is the reason that we cannot use all 1s for the host bits assigned to a host address. The broadcast address for the entire network is (answer to question 7)

10110110.00011000.**11111111.11111111**

which is equivalent to 182.24.255.255.
The broadcast address for the corporate subnet (site 1) is

10110110.00011000.000001**11.11111111**

which is equivalent to 182.24.7.255.

6.2.4   Networking Address Translation and Proxy Servers

Because IP addresses are a scarce resource, most Internet service providers (ISPs) allocate only one address to a single customer. In most cases this address is assigned dynamically, so every time a client connects to the ISP a different address is provided. Big companies can buy more addresses, but for small businesses and home users, the cost of doing so is prohibitive. Because such users are given only one IP address, they can have only one computer connected to the Internet at one time. **Network address translation (NAT)** is a method of connecting multiple computers to the Internet (or any other IP network) using one IP address. With a NAT gateway running on this single computer, it is possible to share that single address among multiple local computers and connect them all at the same time. The outside world is unaware of this division and thinks that only one computer is connected.

To combat certain types of security problems, a number of firewall products are available, which are placed between the user and the Internet to verify all traffic before allowing it to pass through. This means, for example, that no unauthorized user would be allowed to access a company's file or e-mail server. The problem with firewall solutions is that they are expensive and difficult to set up and maintain, which puts them out of reach for home and small business users. Note: Recently, personal firewalls have become popular and are available in Windows XP and Linux to protect individual computers that surf the Internet.

NAT automatically provides firewall-style protection without any special setup. The basic purpose of NAT is to multiplex traffic from the internal network (private network) and present it to the Internet (public network) as if it was coming from a single computer having only one IP address. The TCP/IP protocols include a multiplexing facility, so that any computer can maintain multiple, simultaneous connections with a remote computer. For example, an internal client can connect to an outside FTP server; however, an outside client cannot connect to an internal FTP server because it would have to originate the connection, and NAT will not allow that. It is possible to make some internal servers available to the outside world via inbound mapping, which maps certain well-known TCP ports (e.g., 21 for FTP) to specific internal addresses, thereby making services such as FTP or the Web available in a controlled way.

To multiplex several connections to a single destination, client computers label all packets with unique port numbers. Each IP packet starts with a header containing the source and destination addresses and port numbers. This combination of numbers completely defines a single TCP/IP connection. The addresses specify the two machines at each end, and the two port numbers ensure that each connection between this pair of machines can be uniquely identified.

Each separate connection is originated from a unique source port number in the client. All reply packets from the remote server for this connection contain the same number as their destination port, so that the client can relate them back to their correct connection. In this way, for example, it is possible for a web browser to ask a web server for several images at once and to know how to put all the parts of all the responses back together.

A modern NAT gateway must change the source address on every outgoing packet to be its single public address. Therefore, the gateway also renumbers the source ports to be unique, so that it can keep track of each client connection. The NAT gateway uses a port mapping table to remember how it renumbered the ports for each client's outgoing packets. The port mapping table relates the client's real, local IP address and source port plus its translated source port number to a destination address and port. The NAT gateway can, therefore, reverse the process for returning packets and route them back to the correct clients.

When any remote server responds to a NAT client, incoming packets arriving at the NAT gateway will all have the same destination address, but the destination port number will be the unique source port number that was assigned by the NAT. The NAT gateway looks in its port mapping table to determine which "real" client address and port number a packet is destined for, and replaces these numbers before passing the packet on to the local client. This process is completely dynamic. When a packet is received from an internal client, NAT looks for the matching source address and port in the port mapping table. If an entry is not found, a new one is created, and a new mapping port is allocated to the client. A summary of the process follows:

- Incoming packet received on non-NAT port
- Look for source address and port in the mapping table
- If found, replace source port with previously allocated mapping port
- If not found, allocate a new mapping port
- Replace source address with NAT address; replace source port with mapping port

Packets received on the NAT port undergo a reverse translation process:

- Incoming packet received on NAT port
- Look up destination port number in port mapping table
- If found, replace destination address and port with entries from the mapping table
- If not found, the packet is not for us and should be rejected

Many higher-level TCP/IP protocols embed client addressing information in the packets. For example, during an "active" FTP transfer the client informs the server of its IP address and port number and waits for the server to open a connection to that address. NAT has to monitor these packets and modify them speedily to replace the client's IP address (which is on the internal network) with the NAT address. Since this changes the length of the packet, the TCP sequence/acknowledge numbers must be modified as well.

A **proxy** is any device that acts on behalf of another. A web proxy acts as a "halfway" web server; network clients make requests to the proxy, which then makes requests on their behalf to the appropriate web server. Proxy technology is often seen as an alternative way to provide shared access to a single Internet connection. The other aspect of proxy servers is to improve performance. This capability is usually called proxy server caching. In simplest terms, the proxy server analyzes user requests and determines which, if any, should have the content stored temporarily for immediate access. A typical corporate example would be a company's home page located on a remote server. Many employees may visit this page several times a day. Since this page is requested repeatedly, the proxy server would cache it for immediate delivery to the web browser. Cache management is a big part of many proxy servers, and it is important to consider how easily the cache can be tuned and for whom it provides the most benefit.

Unlike NAT, web proxying is not a transparent operation. It must be explicitly supported by its clients. As a result of early adoption of web proxying, most browsers, including Internet Explorer and Netscape Communicator, have built-in support for proxies, but manually this function must be configured on each client machine and can be changed by the naive or malicious user.

A proxy server operates above the TCP level and uses the machine's built-in protocol stack. For each web request from a client, a TCP connection has to be established between the client and the proxy machine, and another connection must be established between the proxy machine and the remote web server. This puts a lot of strain on the proxy server machine; in fact, since web pages are becoming more and more complicated, the proxy itself may become a bottleneck on the network. In contrast, NAT operates on packet level and requires much less processing for each connection.

6.2.5   Variable Length Subnet Mask and Classless Interdomain Routing

One of the major problems with the earlier limitations of IP addresses is that once the mask was selected across a given network prefix, the organization was locked into a fixed number of fixed-sized subnets. For example, assume that a network administrator decided to configure the 130.5.0.0 network with a default mask of 255.255.0.0 with a subnet mask of 255.255.252.0 (6 bits used for the subnet number). This permits 8 subnets ($2^{number\ masked\ bits}=8$), each of which supports a maximum of 1022 hosts ($2^{number\ unmasked\ bits}-2 = 2^{10}-2$). If you have some subnets that are small (maybe 20 or 30 hosts), you would waste approximately 1000 IP host addresses for each small subnet deployed.

In 1987, TCP/IP was modified with RFC 1009, which specified how a subnetted network could use more than one subnet mask. When an IP network is assigned more than one subnet mask, it is considered a network with **variable length subnet masks (VLSMs),** since the extended network prefixes have different lengths. There are two advantages of having more than one subnet mask assigned to a given IP network number:

- Multiple subnet masks permit more efficient use of an organization's assigned IP address space.
- Multiple subnet masks permit route aggregation, which can significantly reduce the amount of routing information at the "backbone" level within an organization's routing domain.

As class B network IDs would be depleted, and because for most organizations a class C network does not contain enough host IDs to provide a flexible subnetting scheme, IP addresses are no longer given out under the class A, B, or C designation. Instead, a method called classless internetwork domain routing (or CIDR, which is usually pronounced like the work *cider*) is used. Routers that support CIDR do not make assumptions on the first 3 bits of the address, but they rely on the prefix length information. Prefix length is described as slash x (/x) Where *x* represents the number of network bits. Note: Allocation can also be specified using the traditional dotted-decimal mask notation.

Under IPv4 addressing, a class C address (example 198.23.27.32) uses a subnet mask of 255.255.255.0 (which was equivalent to 11111111.11111111.11111111.00000000), which represented the first 24-bits as the network bits and the last 8 bits are the host bits. In CIDR addressing, the same address would be indicated as 198.23.27.32/24. The 24 represents that the first 24 bits indicate the network bits.

CIDR eliminates the traditional concept of class A, class B, and class C network addresses. CIDR supports the use of arbitrarily sized networks rather than the standard 8-bit, 16-bit, or 24-bit network numbers associated with addressing by class. Therefore, with CIDR, addresses that were wasted for the class A and class B networks are reclaimed and redistributed.

Prefixes are viewed as bitwise contiguous blocks of IP address space. For example, all prefixes with a /20 represent the same amount of address spaces ($2^{12}-2$ or 4094 host addresses). Examples for the traditional class A, class B, and class C follow:

Traditional class A	10.23.64.0/20	**00001010.00010111.0100**0000.00000000
Traditional class B	140.5.0.0/20	**10001100.00000101.0000**0000.00000000
Traditional class C	200.7.128.0/20	**11001000.00000111.1000**0000.00000000

Table 6.2 provides information about the most commonly used CIDR address blocks.

Much like VLSMs, CIDR allows you to take a single network ID and subdivide the network into smaller segments, depending on network requirements. While VLSM divides the addresses on the private network, CIDR divides the addresses according to the Internet registration: high-level ISP, mid-level ISP, low-level ISP, or private organization.

When subnetting was first defined in RFC 950, it prohibited the use of all 0s and all 1s for the subnet, which is why we use −2 when we calculate the number of subnets. This was done so that it would not confuse a classful router. Today, a router can be both classless and classful at the same time. But a classless router requires that each routing table update include the *route/<prefix-length>* pair to differentiate between a route to the all-0s subnet and a route to the entire network. The same can be said for the all-1s subnet. Since it indicates the number of bits for the network and for the host, you can use all 0s and all 1s for the subnet mask.

Table 6.2   CIDR address blocks

CIDR Prefix Length	Dotted Decimal	No. of Individual Addresses	No. of Classful Networks[1]
/13	255.248.0.0	512 K	8 Bs or 2048 Cs
/14	255.252.0.0	256 K	4 Bs or 1024 Cs
/15	255.254.0.0	128 K	2 Bs or 512 Cs
/16	255.255.0.0	64 K	1 B or 256 Cs
/17	255.255.128.0	32 K	128 Cs
/18	255.255.192.0	16 K	64 Cs
/19	255.255.224.0	8 K	32 Cs
/20	255.255.240.0	4 K	16 Cs
/21	255.255.248.0	2 K	8 Cs
/22	255.255.252.0	1 K	4 Cs
/23	255.255.254.0	510	2 Cs
/24	255.255.255.0	254	1 C
/25	255.255.255.128	126	1/2 C
/26	255.255.255.192	62	1/4 C
/27	255.255.255.224	30	1/8 C

[1]B = class B and C = class C.

Like VLSMs, CIDR plays an important role in controlling the growth of the Internet's routing tables. The reduction of routing information requires that the Internet be divided into addressing domains. Within a domain, detailed information is available about all of the networks that reside in the domain. Outside of an addressing domain, only the common network prefix is advertised. This allows a single routing table entry to specify a route to many individual network addresses.

Supernetting is the process of combining multiple IP address ranges into a single IP network, such as combining several class C networks. For example, rather than allocating a class B network ID to an organization that has up to 2000 hosts, the InterNIC allocates a range of eight class C network IDs. Each class C network ID accommodates 254 hosts, for a total of 2032 host IDs. Although this technique helps conserve class B network IDs, it creates a new problem. Using conventional routing techniques, the routers on the Internet now must have eight class C network ID entries in their routing tables to route IP packets to the organization. To prevent Internet routers from becoming overwhelmed with routes, CIDR is used to collapse multiple network ID entries into a single entry corresponding to all of the class C network IDs allocated to that organization.

Example 9:

Consider the following block of contiguous 32-bit addresses (192.32.0.0 through 192.32.7.0 in decimal notation). The supernet address (network address) for this block is 192.32.0.0 (11000000 00100000 00000000 00000000); the 21 upper bits (/21) are shared by the 32-bit addresses. The mask for the supernet address in this example is 255.255.248.0 (11111111 11111111 11111000 00000000).

192.32.0.0
192.32.1.0
192.32.2.0
192.32.3.0 /24   ⟹   192.32.0.0 /21

192.32.4.0
192.32.5.0
192.32.6.0
192.32.7.0

Example 10:

To list the individual network numbers defined by CIDR block 198.35.64.0/20, first express the CIDR block in binary format:

198.35.64.0/20   **11000110.00100011.0100** 0000.00000000

The /20 mask is 4 bits shorter than the natural mask for a traditional /24. This means that the CIDR block identifies a block of 16 (or 2^4) consecutive /24 network numbers. The range of /24 network numbers defined by the CIDR block 198.35.64.0/24 includes these:

Net 0:	11000110.00100011.0100**0000**.xxxxxxxx	198.35.64.0/20
Net 1:	11001000.00111000.0100**0001**.xxxxxxxx	198.35.65.0/20
Net 2:	11001000.00111000.0100**0010**.xxxxxxxx	198.35.66.0/20
Net 3:	11001000.00111000.0100**0011**.xxxxxxxx	198.35.67.0/20
Net 4:	11001000.00111000.0100**0100**.xxxxxxxx	198.35.68.0/20
Net 5:	11001000.00111000.0100**0101**.xxxxxxxx	198.35.69.0/20
Net 6:	11001000.00111000.0100**0110**.xxxxxxxx	198.35.70.0/20
Net 7:	11001000.00111000.0100**0111**.xxxxxxxx	198.35.71.0/20
Net 8:	11001000.00111000.0100**1000**.xxxxxxxx	198.35.72.0/20
Net 9:	11001000.00111000.0100**1001**.xxxxxxxx	198.35.73.0/20
Net 10:	11001000.00111000.0100**1010**.xxxxxxxx	198.35.74.0/20
Net 11:	11001000.00111000.0100**1011**.xxxxxxxx	198.35.75.0/20
Net 12:	11001000.00111000.0100**1100**.xxxxxxxx	198.35.76.0/20
Net 13:	11001000.00111000.0100**1101**.xxxxxxxx	198.35.77.0/20
Net 14:	11001000.00111000.0100**1110**.xxxxxxxx	198.35.78.0/20
Net 15:	11001000.00111000.0100**1111**.xxxxxxxx	198.35.79.0/20

Note: Unlike classful addressing, CIDR can have all 0s and all 1s for the extended network prefix. Aggregating the 16 IP /24 network addresses to the highest degree gives 198.35.64.0

6.2.6   IPv6

Since the TCP/IP protocol and the Internet became popular, the Internet has grown and continues to grow at an exponential rate. Eventually the Internet will run out of network numbers. Therefore, a new IP protocol called IPv6 previously known as IP Next Generation (IPng), is being developed to replace IPv4.

The IPv6 header has a simplified format that reduces the processing requirements and includes fields. Thus, the packets can be identified for real-time traffic used in multimedia presentations, so that routers can handle real-time traffic differently. See Figure 6.6.

In addition, IPv6 introduces the Extension Header, which is described by a value in the IPv6 Next Header field. Routers can view the Next Header value and independently and quickly decide if the Extension Header holds useful information. These headers carry much of the information that contributed to the large size of the IPv4 header. The information supports authentication, data integrity, and confidentiality, which should eliminate a significant class of network attacks (e.g., host masquerading attacks).

IPv6 has security built into it. Although it is not bulletproof security, it is enough to resist many of the common crippling problems that plagued IPv4. In IPv4, IPSec was optional; in IPv6, it is mandatory. IPSec, short for IP security, is a set of protocols to support secure exchange of packets at the IP level. In an IPv6 packet's authentication header, fields specify IPv6 parameters.

IPv4 is based on 32-bit addresses, which allow a little more than 4 billion hosts. IPv6 uses 128 bits for its addresses, which can have up to 3.4×10^{38} hosts. Thus, IPv6 can handle all of today's IP-based

Figure 6.6   IPv6 IP header

machines without using NAT and is prepared for future growth and for handling IP addresses for mobile devices such as personal digital assistants (PDAs) and cell phones.

An IPv6 address is usually divided into groups of 16 bits, written as 4 hex digits; the groups are separated by colons. Here is an example:

    FE80:0000:0000:0000:02A0:D2EF:FEA5:E9F5

Leading zeros within a group can be omitted; therefore, the address can be abbreviated as follows:

    FE80:0:2A0:D2FF:FEA5:E9F5

You can also drop any single grouping of zero octets (as in the number above) between numbers as long as you replace them with a double colon (::) and they are complete octets. You cannot use the zero compression rule to drop more than one grouping of zero octets. For example, the address can be further abbreviated as follows:

    FE80::2A0:D2FF:FEA5:E9F5

Because there must always be a certain number of bytes in the address, IPv6 can intelligently determine where the zeros are through this scheme.

To make addresses manageable, they are split in two parts: (1) the bits that identify the network a machine is on and (2) the bits that identify a machine on a network or subnetwork. The bits are known as *net bits* and *host bits*. In both IPv4 and IPv6, the net bits are the left, or most significant bits of an IP number; the host bits are the right, or least significant bits. In IPv4, the border is drawn with the aid of the net mask, which can be used to mask all net bits and host bits. In CIDR routing, the borders between net bits and host bits were no longer 8-bit boundaries; the /x designation was used, for example, /64 to indicate 64 bits as net bits. The same scheme is used in IPv6. IPv6 addresses can come with prefixes, which replace the "subnet mask" convention from IPv4. Prefixes are shown with a slash:

    2180:FC::/48

In this example, the /48 is a routing prefix. A /64 would be a subnet prefix. Usually though, you have an address such as

    FE80:0000:0000:0000:02A0:D2FF:FEA5:E9F5/64

which tells us that in this address the first (leftmost) 64 bits are used as the network address, and the last (rightmost) 64 bits are used to identify the machine on the network.

Even though 128 bits are available for addressing in IPv6, the scheme commonly used is the same, but the fields are wider. Providers usually assign /48 networks, which leaves 16 bits for subnetting and 64 host bits. This means that for your corporation or organization, you can have up to 65,536 subnets, and each subnet could have 18,446,744,073,709,551,616 hosts.

The idea behind having fixed-width, 64-bit-wide host identifiers is that addresses are not assigned manually as in IPv4. Instead, IPv6 host addresses are built from the so-called EUI64 addresses (EUI means extended unique identifier). The EUI64 addresses are 64-bits wide and derived from the MAC address of the network interface card. If the MAC address is

```
01:23:45:67:89:ab
```

an FF:FE is inserted in the middle of the MAC (which extends the 48-bit MAC address to a 64-bit host address) to become

```
01:23:45:FF:FE:67:89:AB
```

Therefore, the host bits of the IPv6 address are

```
:0123:45FF:FE67:89AB
```

These host bits can now be used to automatically assign IPv6 addresses to hosts. All that is needed to get a complete v6 IP number are the net and subnet bits, which can be assigned automatically.

An IPv4-mapped IPv6 address is the address of an IPv4-only node represented as an IPv6 address. The IPv4 address is stored in the low-order 32-bits. The high-order 96 bits bear the prefix 0:0:0:0:0:0. The address of any IPv4-only node may be mapped into the IPv6 address space by adding the prefix 0:0:0:0:0:0 to its IPv4 address. Note: The IPv4-mapped IPv6 addresses always identify IPv4-only nodes; they never identify IPv6/IPv4 or IPv6-only nodes.

IPv4-compatible IPv6 address is an address, assigned to an IPv6 node, that can be used in both IPv6 and IPv4 packets. An IPv4-compatible IPv6 address holds an IPv4 address in the low-order 32-bits. The high-order 96 bits bear the prefix 0:0:0:0:0:FFFF. The entire 128-bit address can be used when sending IPv6 packets. The low-order 32-bits can be used when sending IPv4 packets.

As with IPv4, there are several addresses in IPv6 that are reserved for special uses. The IPv6 address ::/0 is the default address for a host (like 0.0.0.0 in IPv4). The address ::1/128 (0:0:0:0:0:0:0:1) is reserved for the local loopback (like 127.0.0.1 in IPv4).

To support autoconfiguration, the Neighbor Discovery Protocol is used to discover local nodes, routers, and of the link layer addresses and to maintain reachability information based on them. The aim of autoconfiguration is to make connecting machines to the network as easy as possible. In many cases it actually allows you to plug your machine into the network and start using it immediately.

Each interface has at least one globally unique unicast address and one link-local address. The link-local address is used to provide addressing on a single link for the purpose of address autoconfiguration, neighbor discovery, and internal routing. The unicast address is used to establish hierarchical boundaries for the operation of routing protocols.

The long-term plans for IPv6 extend for the next 10 to 15 years. While Windows XP and Linux support it, for instance, this support is nowhere near complete. The protocol stacks for operating systems are still being tested and revised. Getting IPv6 to the average person on the desktop is going to be a long and involved procedure.

Any time a computer needs to communicate with a local computer, it first looks in the ARP cache in memory to see if it already knows the MAC address of a computer with the specified IP address. If the address is not in the ARP cache, it tries to discover the MAC address by broadcasting an ARP request packet. The station on the LAN recognizes its own IP address and sends an ARP response with its own MAC address. Then both the sender of the ARP reply and the original ARP requester record each other's IP address and MAC address as an entry in ARP cache for future reference. See Figure 6.8

If a computer needs to communicate with another computer that is located on another network, it will do the same except it will send the packet to the local router. Therefore, it will search for the MAC address of the local port of the router or it will send a broadcast looking for it.

Reverse Address Resolution Protocol (RARP) is a TCP/IP protocol that permits a physical address, such as an Ethernet address, to be translated into an IP address. Hosts such as diskless workstations often only know their hardware interface addresses, or MAC address, when booted but not their IP addresses. They must discover their IP addresses from an external source, usually a RARP server. RARP is defined in RFC 903.

Figure 6.7 TCP/IP address and MAC addresses

6.2.7 ARP and Address Resolution

Early IP implementations ran on hosts commonly interconnected by Ethernet LANs. Every transmission on these LANs contains the MAC address of the source and destination nodes. Since there is no structure to identify different networks, routing cannot be performed.

When a host needs to send a data packet to another host on the same network, the sender application must know both the IP and MAC addresses of the intended receiver, because the destination IP address is placed in the IP packet and the destination MAC address in the LAN's protocol frame (such as Ethernet or token ring). If the destination host is on another network, the sender will look instead for the MAC address of the default gateway or router. See Figure 6.7.

Unfortunately, the sender's IP process may not know the MAC address of the intended receiver on the same network. Therefore, the **Address Resolution Protocol (ARP)** (RFC 826) provides a mechanism so that a host can learn a receiver's MAC address when knowing only the IP address.

Figure 6.8   Name and address resolution done on an IP Network. WINS = Windows Internet Naming Service (WINS)

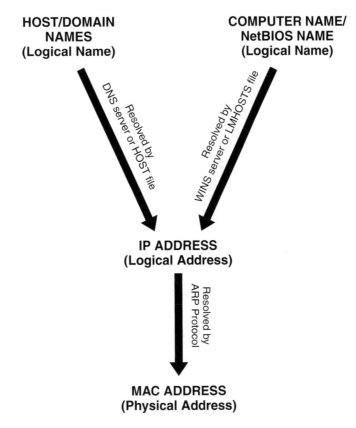

6.2.8   Navigating a TCP/IP Network

Fully qualified domain names (FQDNs), sometimes referred to as simply *domain names,* are used to identify computers on a TCP/IP network. Examples include Microsoft.com and Education.Novell.com.

While IP addresses are 32 bits in length, most users do not memorize the numeric addresses of the hosts to which they attach. Instead, people are more comfortable with host names. Most IP hosts, then, have both a numeric IP address and a host name. Although this is convenient for people, the name must be translated back to a numeric address for routing purposes, by using either a HOSTS file or a DNS server.

The **HOSTS file** is a text file that lists the IP address followed by the host name. Each entry should be kept on an individual line. In addition, the IP address should be placed in the first column followed by the corresponding host name. A # symbol is used as a comment or REM statement, which means that anything after the # symbol is ignored. See Figure 6.9.

When a computer is using the host table shown in Figure 6.9, if rhino.acme.com is entered into a browser such as Internet Explorer or Netscape Navigator, it will find the equivalent address of 102.54.94.97 to connect to it. The HOSTS file is kept in the ETC directory on most UNIX machines, in the WINDOWS directory in Windows 9x machines, and in *%systemroot%*\SYSTEM32\DRIVERS\ETC directory in Windows 2000 and Windows Server 2003 machines.

Figure 6.9   Sample HOSTS file

```
102.54.94.97          rhino.acme.com          # source server
38.25.63.10           x.acme.com              # x client host
127.0.0.1             localhost
```

Another way to translate the FQDN to the IP address is to use a DNS server. DNS is a distributed database (contained in multiple servers) containing host name and IP address information for all domains on the Internet. For every domain there is a single, authoritative name server that contains all DNS-related information about the domain.

For example, if you type in the web address "Microsoft.com" in your browser, your computer will then communicate with your local area network's DNS server. If the DNS server does not know the address of Microsoft.com, another DNS server will be asked. This search will continue until it finds the address of Microsoft.com or it determines that the host name is not listed and will then reply back with "No DNS Entry."

When you share a directory, drive, or printer on PCs running Microsoft Windows or Linux machines running Samba, you access these resources by using the Uniform Naming Convention (UNC) to specify the location of the resources. UNC follows this format:

```
\\computer_name\shared-resource-pathname
```

So to access the shared directory called *data* on the server1 computer, type the following:

```
\\server1\data
```

The computer name can actually be the IP address of the PC or the NetBIOS name. If you use the NetBIOS name, that name needs to be translated to the IP address. It could broadcast onto the network asking for the IP address of the computer. In that case, you would have to connect the TCP/IP address with the computer name (NetBIOS name). Microsoft Networks can use an LMHOSTS file (see Figure 6.10) or a WINS server.

A Windows Internet Naming Service (WINS) server contains a database of IP addresses and NetBIOS (computer names) that update dynamically. For a client to access the WINS server, the client must know the address of the WINS server. Therefore, the WINS server needs to have a static address—one that does not change. When the client accesses the WINS server, the client does not broadcast; instead the client sends a message directly to the WINS server. When the WINS server gets the message, it knows what computer sent the request and can reply directly to the originating IP address. The WINS database stores the information and makes it available to other WINS clients.

When a WINS client starts up, it registers its name, IP address, and type of services in the WINS server's database. Since WINS was only made for Windows operating systems, other network devices and services (such as a network printer and UNIX machines) cannot register with a WINS service. Therefore, these addresses have to be added manually.

6.2.9 TCP/IP Ports and Sockets

Every time a TCP/IP host communicates with another TCP/IP host, it uses the IP address and port number to identify the host and service/program running on the host. A TCP/IP port number is a logical connection placed by client programs to specify a particular server program running on a computer on the network defined at the transport layer. See Figure 6.11. The source port number identifies the application that sent the data, and the destination port number identifies the application that received the data. Port numbers range from 0 to 65536. Additionally, there are two types of ports, TCP and User Datagram Protocol (UDP).

Figure 6.10 Sample LMHOSTS file

102.54.94.97	rhino	#PRE	#DOM:networking	#File Server
182.102.93.122	MISSERVER	#PRE		#MIS Server
122.107.9.10	SalesServer			#Sales Server
131.107.7.29	DBServer			#Database Server
191.131.54.73	TrainServ			#Training Server

Figure 6.11   TCP/IP ports

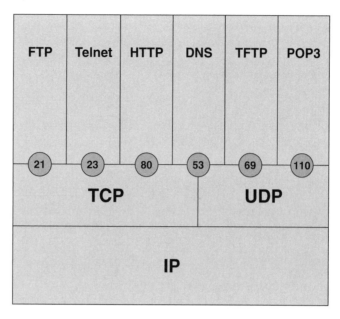

Today, the existence of ports and their numbers is typically transparent to the users of the network, as many ports are standardized. Thus, a remote computer will know which port it should connect to for a specific service. IANA divides port numbers into three groups:

- **Well-known ports**—These are the most commonly used TCP/IP ports; they range in number from 0 through 1023. These ports can be used by system processes or privileged programs. Well-known ports are TCP ports, but they are usually registered to UDP as well. Some of the well-known protocols are shown in Table 6.3.

Table 6.3   Popular TCP/IP services and their default assigned
port numbers

Network Program/Service	Default Assigned Port Number
FTP data transfer	TCP port 20
FTP control	TCP port 21
Telnet	TCP port 23
Simple Mail Transfer Protocol (SMTP)	TCP port 25
Domain Name Server (DNS)	UDP port 53
Hypertext Transfer Protocol (HTTP)	TCP/UDP port 80
Post Office Protocol (POP3)	TCP port 110
Network News Transport Protocol (NNTP)	TCP port 119
Network Time Protocol	TCP/UDP port 123
NetBIOS Name Service	UDP port 137
NetBIOS Session Service	UDP port 139
Simple Network Management Protocol (SNMP)	UDP port 161
Secure web traffic (HTTPS)	TCP/UDP port 443

■ **Registered ports**—These are the ports in the range of 1024 though 49252. On most systems, user programs use registered ports to create and control logical connections between proprietary programs.

■ **Dynamic (private) ports**—These ports range from 49152 through 65535. These ports are unregistered and can be used dynamically for private connections. In a multiuser system, a program can define a port, or ports, as needed or automatically if more than one user requires access to the same service at the same time.

Consider this example. When using your browser to view a web page, the default port to indicate the HTTP service is identified as port 80 and the FTP service is identified as port 21. Other application processes are given port numbers dynamically for each connection so that a single computer can run several services. When a packet is delivered and processed, the TCP protocol (connection-based services) or UDP protocol (connectionless-based services) read the port number and forward the request to the appropriate program.

A socket identifies a single network process in terms of the entire Internet. An application creates a socket by specifying three items: the IP address of the host, the type of service, and the port the application is using. Note: For Windows, it is the Windows socket (WinSock) that provides the interface between the network program or service and the Windows environment.

> For a complete list of registered well-known port numbers, go to the following website:
>
> http://www.isi.edu/in-notes/rfc1700.txt

By default, when using a web page browser, port 80 is the default port. But if a website is using a different port, you can override that default by specifying the URL followed by a colon and the port number. For example, to specify port 2232, you would use:

```
http://www.acme.com:2232
```

6.2.10   Troubleshooting a TCP/IP Network

Several utilities can be used to test and troubleshoot the TCP/IP network. To verify the TCP/IP configuration, use either the IP configuration program (WINIPCFG.EXE) command (available in Windows 9x) or the IPCONFIG.EXE command (available in Windows 98, Windows NT, Windows 2000, and Windows Server 2003). In addition, the ARP and TRACERT commands may be used. The utilities are as follows:

■ WINIPCFG or IPCONFIG
■ PING 127.0.0.1 (loopback address)
■ PING IP Address of the Computer
■ PING IP Address of Default Gateway (Router)
■ PING IP Address of Remote Host

Both IPCONFIG.EXE and WINIPCFG.EXE display addressing and settings of the TCP/IP. The PING utility can be used to verify a TCP/IP connection, while the TRACERT shows all router addresses as it connects to another computer. The ARP protocol can be used to display the MAC address. See Table 6.4 for TCP/IP commands that are available in Windows 2000 and Windows Server 2003 for troubleshooting TCP/IP networks.

To execute the Windows IP configuration utility, type WINIPCFG.EXE from the Windows Command prompt or from the Run option located on the Start button. See Figure 6.12. When there is more than one network interface, select the appropriate adapter from the pulldown menu and view the IP address, the subnet mask, and the default gateway/router for that interface. By clicking on the More Info. >>button, you can view other information such as addresses and configurations of the WINS, DNS, and DHCP servers. See Figure 6.13.

The IPCONFIG.EXE command can only be executed at the Command prompt. See Figure 6.14. Much like the IP configuration utility, it also shows the IP address, the subnet mask, and the default gateway/router address. To see additional information, type in IPCONFIG/ALL.

To make the address assignments easier, users can automatically assign the IP addresses to the computers using a DHCP server. To release the address assigned by the DHCP server, click on the IP Configurations Renew or Renew All button or type in IPCONFIG/RELEASE. To request new addresses

Table 6.4   Windows 2000 and Windows Server 2003 troubleshooting TCP/IP commands

Commands	Description
ARP	Displays and modifies the IP-to-MAC address translation tables used by the Address Resolution Protocol (ARP). See Chapter 10.
IPCONFIG	Displays all current TCP/IP configuration, including the IP address. This command is of particular use on systems that run DHCP, allowing users to determine which TCP/IP configuration values have been configured by DHCP. See this chapter.
PATHPING	The PATHPING command is a route-tracing tool that combines features of the PING and TRACERT commands with additional information that neither of those tools provides. See Chapter 10.
PING	Verifies connections to a remote computer or computers by verifying configurations and testing IP connectivity. See this chapter.
TRACERT	Traces the route that a packet takes to a destination and displays the series of IP routers that are used in delivering packets to the destination. If the packets are unable to be delivered to the destination, the TRACERT command displays the last router that successfully forwarded the packet. See this chapter.
NBTSTAT	Displays the local NetBIOS name table, which is a table of user-friendly computer names mapped to IP addresses. See Chapter 11.
NETDIAG	Command line, diagnostic tool that helps isolate networking and connectivity problems by performing a series of tests to determine the state of the network client used in TCP/IP and IPX networks. See Chapter 10.
NETSTAT	Displays protocol statistics and current TCP/IP network connections. See this chapter.

Figure 6.12   WINIPCFG utility. If there is more than one network adapter, the various cards can be selected from the pulldown box

from the DHCP server, click on the Renew or Renew All button. The Release All and Renew All buttons have all settings, including the WINS and DNS server addresses.

If you are using the IP configuration utility or the IPCONFIG.EXE command and are having trouble connecting to the network, verify the IP address (to make sure it is on the correct subnet), the subnet mask, and the router. If the address is not in the correct subnet, you will not be able to communicate with any other computer on the network. If the subnet mask is wrong, you may not be able to communicate with other computers. If the gateway address is wrong, you can communicate with computers on your subnet, but not on other subnets.

Another useful command to verify a network connection is PING.EXE. It sends three packets to a host computer and receives a report on the round trip. For example, if you ping the loopback address of

Figure 6.13 WINIPCFG utility in detailed mode

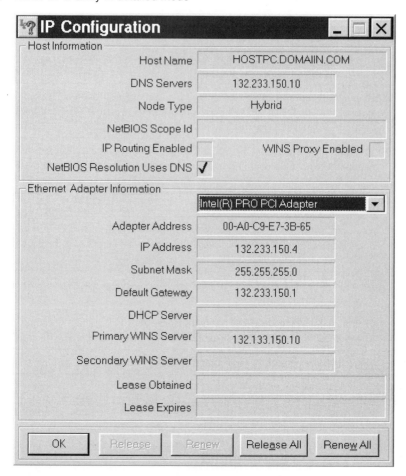

127.0.0.1 and the ping fails, verify that the TCP/IP software is installed correctly. If you ping your own IP address and it is unsuccessful, check the IP address. If you cannot ping the IP address of the default gateway/router, verify the IP address (make sure the address is in the correct subnet) and subnet mask. If you cannot ping a remote computer on a different subnet or network, verify the IP address of the default gateway/router, make sure the remote host/computer is functional, and verify the link between routers. See Figure 6.15.

Examples:

PING 127.0.0.1
PING 137.23.34.112

The PING command can also be used to ping a host/computer by the NetBIOS (computer) name or host/DNS name. For example, if you ping by address but not by name, the computer tells you that the TCP/IP is running fine but the name resolution is not working properly. Therefore, you must first check the LMHOSTS file and the WINS server to resolve computer names and then the HOSTS file and the DNS server to resolve domain names.

Examples:

PING FS1
PING WWW.MICROSOFT.COM

Figure 6.14   IPCONFIG command

```
C:\>ipconfig

Windows 98 IP Configuration

0 Ethernet adapter:

        IP Address.....................: 132.233.150.4
        Subnet Mask...................: 255.255.255.0
        Default Gateway...............: 132.233.150.1
```

```
C:\>IPCONFIG/ALL

Windows 98 IP Configuration
        Host Name...................: HOSTPC.DOMAIN.COM
        DNS Servers.................: 132.233.150.10
        Node Type...................: Hybrid
        NetBIOS Scope ID............:
        IP Routing Enabled...........: No
        WINS Proxy Enabled..........: No
        NetBIOS Resolution Uses DNS. : Yes

0   Ethernet adapter :
        Description..................: Intel (R) PRO PCI Adapter
        Physical Address.............: 00-A0-C9-E7-3B-65
        DHCP Enabled...............: No
        IP Address..................: 132.233.150.4
        Subnet Mask.................: 255.255.255.0
        Default Gateway..............: 132.233.150.1
        Primary WINS Server..........: 132.133.150.10
        Secondary WINS Server....... :
        Lease Obtained.............. :
        Lease Expires................:
```

Figure 6.15   PING Command

```
C:\>ping 132.233.150.4

Pinging 132.233.150.4 with 32 bytes of data:

Reply from 132.233.150.4: bytes=32 time, <0ms TTL=128
Reply from 132.233.150.4: bytes=32 time, <0ms TTL=128
Reply from 132.233.150.4: bytes=32 time, <0ms TTL=128
Reply from 132.233.150.4: bytes=32 time, <0ms TTL=128

Ping statistics for 132.233.150.4
        Packets: Sent = 4, Received = 4, Lost = 0 (0% loss),
Approximate round trip times in milliseconds:
        Minimum = 0ms, Maximum = 0ms, Average = 0ms
```

A time of 200 milliseconds (ms) is considered very good. A time between 200 and 500 ms is considered marginal and a time is over 500 ms is unacceptable. A request timed out indicates total failure, as shown in Figure 6.16.

Another useful command is TRACERT.EXE, which sends out a packet of information to each hop (gateway/router) individually a total of three times. Therefore, the TRACERT command can help determine where the break is in a network. See Figure 6.17 and Table 6.5.

Viewing the current configuration (IPCONFIG), pinging the loopback address (PING 127.0.0.1), and pinging the IP address of your computer will verify that the TCP/IP protocol is

Figure 6.16 PING command showing total failure

```
C:\>ping 132.233.150.2

Pinging 132.233.150.2 with 32 bytes of data:

Request timed out.
Request timed out.
Request timed out.
Request timed out.

Ping statistics for 132.233.150.2:
        Packets: Sent = 4, Received = 0, Lost = 4 (100% loss),
Approximate round trip times in milli-seconds:
        Minimum = 0ms, Maximum = 0ms, Average = 0ms
```

FIGURE 6.17 TRACERT command

```
C:\>tracert www.novell.com

Tracing route to www.novell.com [137.65.2.11]
over a maximum of 30 hops:

  1   97 ms    92 ms   107 ms   tnt3-e1.scrm01.pbi.net [206.171.130.74]
  2   96 ms    98 ms   118 ms   core1-e3-3.scrm01.pbi.net [206.171.130.77]
  3   96 ms    95 ms   120 ms   edge1-fa0-0-0.scrm01.pbi.net [206.13.31.8]
  4   96 ms   102 ms    96 ms   sfra1sr1-5-0.ca.us.ibm.net [165.87.225.10]
  5  105 ms   108 ms   114 ms   f1-0-0.sjc-bb1.cerf.net [134.24.88.55]
  6  107 ms   112 ms   106 ms   atm8-0-155M.sjc-bb3.cerf.net [134.24.29.38]
  7  106 ms   110 ms   120 ms   pos1-1-155M.sfo-bb3.cerf.net [134.24.32.89]
  8  109 ms   108 ms   110 ms   pos3-0-0-155M.sfo-bb1.cerf.net [134.24.29.202]
  9  122 ms   105 ms   115 ms   atm8-0.sac-bb1.cerf.net [134.24.29.86]
 10  121 ms   120 ms   117 ms   atm3-0.slc-bb1.cerf.net [134.24.29.90]
 11  123 ms   131 ms   130 ms   novell-gw.slc-bb1.cerf.net [134.24.116.54]
 12    *         *        *     Request timed out.
 13  133 ms   139 ms   855  ms  www.novell.com [137.65.2.11]

Trace complete.
```

Table 6.5 TRACERT Options

Options	Description
–d	In the event a name resolution method is not available for remote hosts, users can specify the –d option to prohibit the utility from trying to resolve host names as it runs. If not using this option, TRACERT will still function, but it will run very slowly as it tries to resolve these names.
–h	By specifying the –h option, users can specify the maximum number of hops to which a route can be traced.
Timeout_value	Used to adjust the timeout value. The value determines the amount of time in milliseconds the program will wait for a response before moving on. If you raise this value and the remote devices respond whereas they did not respond previously, then a bandwidth problem may be indicated.
–j	Known as loose source routing, TRACERT –j<router name><local computer>allows TRACERT to follow the path to the router specified and return to the user's computer.

properly functioning on the PC. By pinging the IP address of the default gateway or router, as well as other local IP computers, you determine if the computer is communicating on the local network. If it cannot connect to the gateway or any other local computer, either you are not connected properly or the IP protocol is misconfigured (IP address, IP subnet mask, or gateway address). If you cannot connect to the gateway but you can connect to other local computers, then check your IP address, IP subnet mask, and gateway address. Also check if the gateway is functioning by using the PING command at the gateway to connect to your computer and other local computers on your network as well as pinging the other network connections on the gateway/router or pinging computers on other networks. If you cannot ping another local computer, but you can ping the gateway, most likely the other computer is having problems and you need to restart this procedure at that computer. If you can ping the gateway, but you cannot ping computers on another gateway, then check the routers and pathways between the two computers by using the PING or TRACERT commands.

You also can use the NETSTAT command to display protocol statistics and current TCP/IP connections. The NETSTAT–A command displays all connections, and NETSTAT–R displays the route table plus active connections. The NETSTAT–E command displays Ethernet statistics, and NETSTAT–S displays per-protocol statistics. If you use NETSTAT–N, addresses and port numbers are not converted to names. For more information, see Windows Help.

6.3   IPX PROTOCOL SUITE

The **Internetwork Packet Exchange (IPX)** is a networking protocol suite used by Novell NetWare, Windows NT, and Windows 2000. Windows refers to the IPX protocol as NWLink (NDIS-compliant version of the IPX protocol which is fully compatible with the Novell IPX/SPX protocol). IPX is the fastest routable network protocol suite available. See Figure 6.18.

Similar to the TCP/IP network, users can connect to an IPX network by using one of several interfaces, including Ethernet, Token Ring, and ARCnet. For a Novell NetWare network, the software used to connect to an IPX network first loads a **multiple link interface driver (MLID),** which is basically the driver to control the network card. Unlike previous software interfaces used by early versions of IPX and other protocols, the MLID complies with the Novell open data link interface (ODI) architecture that allows a network driver to communicate with multiple protocol stacks such as TCP/IP and IPX.

Figure 6.18   IPX protocol

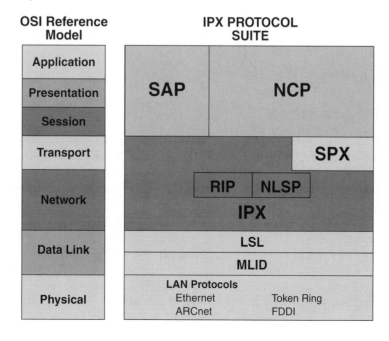

Table 6.6   Frame types

Topology	Supported Frame Type
Ethernet	Ethernet II, 802.3, 802.2, and subnetwork access protocol (SNAP), which defaults to 802.2
Token Ring	802.5 and SNAP
Fiber Distributed Data Interface (FDDI)	802.2 and 802.3

Since the MLID supports multiple protocols, software is needed to identify the packets that come through the network card and then route to the proper protocol stack. This software is called Link Support Layer (LSL).

6.3.1   Frame Types

When installing IPX on Windows consider setting the frame type. The frame type defines the way in which the network adapter formats data to be sent over a network. See Table 6.6.

On Ethernet networks, the standard frame type for NetWare 2.2 and NetWare 3.11 is 802.3. Starting with NetWare 3.12, the default frame type was changed to 802.2. Users can choose to automatically detect or manually configure the frame type; however, the frame type is automatically detected when NWLink is loaded. If multiple frame types are detected in addition to the 802.2 frame type, NWLink defaults to the 802.2 frame type. One big problem when connecting to an IPX network is using the wrong frame type, so if users have multiple frame types, they must manually configure the operating system to load them simultaneously.

6.3.2   IPX and Sequenced Packet Exchange

IPX is a networking protocol used to interconnect networks. It is a connectionless protocol and therefore does not require a connection to set up before packets are sent to a destination.

Another worthwhile protocol is the **Sequenced Packet Exchange (SPX).** Different from the IPX protocol, the SPX protocol uses packet acknowledgments to guarantee delivery of packets. SPX provides segmentation, reassembly, and segment sequencing of data streams that are too large to fit into the frame size. SPX uses virtual circuits referred to as connections. These connections are assigned specific connection identifiers as defined in the SPX header. Multiple connection IDs can be attached to a single socket.

6.3.3   IPX Addressing

When assigning addresses within the IPX network, there are two types of addresses, the internal and the external IPX network numbers. The **internal IPX network number,** an eight-digit (4-byte) hexadecimal number, is used to identify a server. Unlike TCP/IP, clients are not assigned internal network numbers, but instead use their MAC addresses. The **external IPX address** is used to identify the network (physical network and frame type). Therefore, all servers and routers on the same physical network must be assigned the same external IPX number. When assigning both the internal and external network numbers, all numbers must be unique. This includes numbers assigned to the network or to the individual servers. See Figure 6.19. Note: If a network is using two different frame types, a unique external IPX address will be assigned to the network with the first frame type and another unique external IPX address will be assigned to the network with the other frame type.

Much like the TCP/IP protocols, IPX also uses port numbers in order to identify to which network software the packet is sent. Some examples are shown in Table 6.7.

Figure 6.19   IPXROUTE CONFIG command

```
NWLink IPX Routing and Source Routing Control Program v2.00

Num     Name                        Network      Node          Frame
==========================================================================
1.      IpxLoopbackAdapter          1234cdef     000000000002  [802.2]
2.      Local Area Connection       00000000     00c0f056bb98  [802.2]
3.      Local Area Connection 2     00000000     00a0c9e73b65  [802.2]
4.      NDISWANIPX                  00000000     7ab920524153  [EthII]-

Legend
==========================================================================
- down wan line
```

Table 6.7   Common IPX Network Services

Port Number	Network Services
0×0451	NetWare Core Protocol (NCP)
0×0452	Service Advertising Protocol (SAP)
0×0453	Routing Information Protocol (RIP)
0×0455	Novell NetBIOS
0×9001	NetWare Link Services Protocol (NLSP)

6.3.4   Service Advertising and NetWare Core Protocols

The Service Advertising Protocol (SAP) is used to advertise the services of all known servers on the network, including file servers and print servers. Servers periodically broadcast their service information while listening for SAPs on the network, then store the information. Clients then access the service information table when they need a network service.

The NetWare Core Protocol (NCP) consists of the majority of network services offered by a Novell NetWare server. This includes but is not limited to file services, print services, Novell Directory Services (NDS), and message services.

6.3.5   Troubleshooting IPX Networks

To help troubleshoot the IPX protocol in Windows 2000, Windows Server 2003, and Windows XP, use the IPXROUTE command. This command can determine computer settings and perform diagnostic tests to resolve communication problems. At the prompt, type

```
IPXROUTE CONFIG
```

The current IPX status will be displayed including the network number, MAC address, interface name, and frame type. If you type

```
IPXROUTE RIPOUT network_number
```

you will learn if there is connectivity to a specific network. The *network_number* is the external IPX number representing the network. See Figure 6.20.

Figure 6.20   IPX network

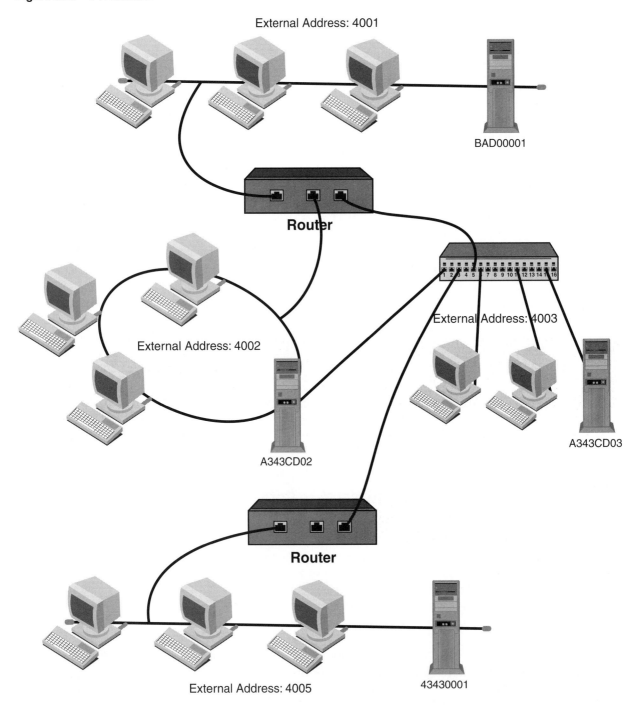

External Address: 4001

BAD00001

Router

External Address: 4002

A343CD02

External Address: 4003

A343CD03

Router

External Address: 4005

43430001

6.4   NETBIOS AND NETBEUI

The **network basic input/output system (NetBIOS)** is a common program that runs on most Microsoft networks. Originally created for IBM for its early PC networks, it was adopted by Microsoft and has since become a de facto industry standard. NetBIOS is a session-level interface used by applications to communicate with NetBIOS-compliant transports such as NetBEUI, IPX, or TCP/IP. It is responsible for establishing logical names (computer names) on the network, establishing a logical connection between the two computers, and supporting reliable data transfer between computers that have established a session.

6.4.1   SMB Protocol

Once a logical connection is established, computers can exchange data in the form of NetBIOS requests or in the form of a **server message block (SMB).** The SMB protocol, which was jointly developed by Microsoft, Intel, and IBM, defines a series of commands used to pass information between networked computers. Clients connected to a network using NetBIOS over TCP/IP, NetBEUI, or IPX/SPX can send SMB commands. Note: Microsoft refers to NetBIOS over TCP/IP as NBT.

SMB can be broken into four message types: session control, file, printer, and message. The session control consists of commands that start and end a redirector connection to a shared resource at the server. The file SMB messages are used by the redirector to gain access to files at the server. The printer SMB messages are used by the redirector to send data to a print queue at a server and to get status information about the print queue. The message SMB allows an application to send messages or to receive messages from another workstation. When you share a drive, directory, or printer on a Microsoft Windows computer, you are using the SMB protocol.

6.4.2   Common Internet File System

Common Internet File System (CIFS) is a standard protocol that lets programs make requests for files and services on remote computer on the Internet. CIFS is a public or open variation of the SMB protocol used by Microsoft Windows and is currently used by Linux with Samba, Novell Netware 6.0, and Apple TalkIP. A client program makes a request of a server program (usually in another computer) for access to a file or to pass a message to a program that runs in the server computer. The server takes the requested action and returns a response. This allows Microsoft Windows computers to access these files on Linux and NetWare 6.0 in the same way as accessing files on another Windows computer, and it allows Linux computers to access the files on the Microsoft Windows computers.

6.4.3   Using SMB/CIFS to Share

When using the SMB/CIFS protocol to share a directory, drive, or printer, these resources are accessed using the **Uniform Naming Convention (UNC):**

```
\\computer_name\shared-resource-pathname
```

The *computer_name* could be a NetBIOS name or an IP address.

6.4.4   Name Resolution with the NetBIOS Protocol

To navigate an SMB network, computers are identified with computer names (NetBIOS names), no matter what protocol (TCP/IP, IPX, or NetBEUI) is being used. The NetBIOS computer names are up to 15 characters long. To connect the TCP/IP address with the computer name (NetBIOS name), SMB networks use an LMHOSTS file or a WINS server.

An **LMHOSTS file** is a text file similar to a HOSTS file. Each entry should be kept on an individual line. The IP address should be placed in the first column, followed by the corresponding computer name. The address and the computer name should be separated by at least one space or tab. Again, like the HOSTS file, the # character is generally used to denote the start of a comment. See Figure 6.21 and Table 6.8.

A **WINS (Windows Internet Naming Service)** server determines the IP address with the computer's NetBIOS name. WINS uses a distributed database that is automatically updated with the names of computers available and the IP address assigned to each one. Note: UNIX machines do not use NetBIOS names. Therefore, if you want to use name resolution for these machines, you must use HOSTS files/DNS servers.

Figure 6.21 Sample LMHOSTS file

```
102.54.94.97      rhino         #PRE    #DOM:networking    #File server
182.102.93.122    MISSERVER     #PRE                       #MIS Server
122.107.9.10      SalesServer                              #Sales Server
131.107.7.29      DBServer                                 #Database Server
191.131.54.73     TrainServ                                #Training Server
```

Table 6.8 LMHOSTS special entries

Predefined Keywords	Description
#PRE	Defines which entries should be initially preloaded as permanent entries in the name cache. Preloaded entries reduce network broadcasts, because names are resolved from cache rather than from broadcast or by querying the LMHOSTS file. Entries with a #PRE tag are loaded automatically when TCP/IP initializes, or manually by typing NBTSTAT–R at a command prompt.
#DOM: [domain_name]	Facilitates domain activity, such as logon validation over a router, account synchronization, and browsing
#NOFNR	Avoids using NetBIOS-directed name queries for older LAN manager UNIX systems
#INCLUDE	Loads and searches NetBIOS entries in a separate file from the default LMHOSTS file. Typically the #INCLUDE file is a centrally located shared LMHOSTS file. Refer to the #INCLUDE file by using a universal naming convention (UNC) path. Any computer referred to in the UNC path must also have a name–to–IP address mapping in the LMHOSTS file. This enables Windows to resolve a computer's NetBIOS name when it reads the #INCLUDE file.
#BEGIN_ALTERNATE **#END_ALTERNATE**	Defines a redundant list of alternate locations for LMHOSTS files. When you include multiple #INCLUDE lines between #BEGIN_ALTERNATE and #END_ALTERNATE, Windows includes the first file that it can locate in the list.
#MH	Adds multiple entries for a multihomed computer. A multihomed computer is a computer that contains the IP addresses that belong to different networks.

Note: The NetBIOS name cache and file are always read sequentially. Add the most frequently accessed computers to the top of the list. Add the #PRE-tagged entries near the bottom, because they are loaded when TCP/IP initializes and are not accessed again.

Notes:

- If you need to connect to the Internet, use TCP/IP.
- If you need to communicate between two networks, use TCP/IP or IPX on all servers and client computers.
- You can use the NetBEUI protocol on the servers and then use NetBEUI on client boot disks so that you can perform downloads and installations over the network.

6.4.5   **NetBEUI Protocol**

NetBEUI is short for NetBIOS enhanced user interface, which provides the transport and network layers for the NetBIOS protocol, usually found on Microsoft networks. NetBEUI is a protocol used to transport data packets between two nodes. Although NetBEUI is smaller than TCP/IP or IPX and is extremely quick, it only sends packets within the same network. Unfortunately, NetBEUI is not a routable protocol, which means that it cannot send a packet to a computer on another network.

6.5   **OTHER PROTOCOLS**

Windows is designed to work with a wide variety of protocols at the same time. Although Windows includes the most common protocols, it also has the ability to install other protocols from disks. Some protocols with the Windows 2000 and Windows Server 2003 installation CD include the Data Link Control (DLC) and AppleTalk protocols.

The **DLC** protocol is a special, nonroutable protocol which enables computers that are running Windows to communicate with computers that are running DLC protocol stacks such as IBM mainframes, IBM AS/400 computers, and Hewlett-Packard network printers that are connected directly to the network using older HP JetDirect network cards. When using the DLC protocol to connect to a network printer, the DLC protocol must be installed and running on the print server for the printer. The protocol does not need to be installed on the computers that send print jobs to the print server.

The **AppleTalk protocol** allows Apple Macintosh computers to communicate with each other. For example, if the AppleTalk protocol is running on the Windows server, it can share its files and printers with other Apple Macintosh clients.

SUMMARY

1. A protocol is a set of rules or standards that are designed to enable computers to connect with one another, and peripheral devices to exchange information with as little error as possible.

2. A protocol stack, sometimes referred to as a protocol suite, is a set of protocols that works together to provide a full range of network services.

3. The standards for TCP/IP are published in a series of documents called Requests for Comments (RFCs).

4. The lowest protocol within the TCP/IP suite is the Internet protocol (IP). It specifies the format of the packets (also called datagrams) and worries about the delivery of the packets.

5. The protocols that work on top of the IP are TCP and UDP. The transport control protocol (TCP) is a reliable, connection-oriented delivery service that breaks data into manageable packets.

6. Each connection on a TCP/IP address is called a host (a computer or other network device that is connected to a TCP/IP network) and is assigned a unique IP address.

7. The format of the IP address is four 8-bit numbers separated by a period (.). Each number can be 0 to 255.

8. Every computer on a TCP/IP network must have the same network number.

9. When connecting to the Internet, network numbers are assigned to a corporation or business.

10. The subnet mask is used to define which bits describe the network number and which bits describe the host address.

11. Network number 127 is used for loopback testing, and the specific host address 127.0.0.1 refers to the local host or the actual host or computer currently in use.

12. If an individual network is connected to another network and a user must communicate with any number of computers on the other network, the user must also define the default gateway, which specifies the local address of a router.

13. All subnets on a network must use the same network address. The subnet network number and the subnet mask must be the same for all computers.

14. In supernetting, when the address is assigned, the network number and host number are not made along the standard octet boundaries; but instead, they are made from a specific number of bits from the beginning of the address. A supernet is a group of networks identified by contiguous network addresses. IP service providers can assign to customers blocks of contiguous addresses in order to define supernets as needed.

15. Classless interdomain routing (CIDR) collapses multiple network ID entries into a single entry.

16. The new IP protocol, IPv6, consists of 128 bits to allow for more addresses and includes other enhancements to the current 32-bit IP address.

17. The Address Resolution Protocol (ARP) provides a mechanism so that a host can learn a receiver's MAC address when knowing only the IP address.

18. Fully qualified domain names (FQDNs), sometimes referred to as simply *domain names,* are used to identify computers on a TCP/IP network.

19. The FQDN must be translated to a numeric address by either a HOSTS file or by using a DNS server.
20. Every time a TCP/IP host communicates with another TCP/IP host, it uses the IP address and port number to identify the host and service/program running on the host.
21. A TCP/IP port number is a logical connection placed by client programs to specify a particular server program that is running on a computer on the network defined at the transport layer.
22. The Internetwork Packet Exchange (IPX) is a fast routable networking protocol used by Novell NetWare and Windows.
23. Windows refers to the IPX protocol as NWLINK (NDIS-compliant version of the IPX protocol that is fully compatible with the Novell IPX/SPX protocol).
24. A frame type used in IPX networks defines the way in which the network adapter formats data to be sent over a network.

25. The internal IPX network number, an eight-digit (4-byte) hexadecimal number, is used to identify a server, while the external IPX address is used to identify the network.
26. NetBIOS enhanced user interface (NetBEUI) provides the transport and network layers for the NetBIOS protocol, usually found on Microsoft networks.
27. An LMHOSTS file is a text file that is used to resolve NetBIOS names to IP addresses.
28. The Data Link Control (DLC) is a special, nonroutable protocol which enables computers that are running Windows protocol to communicate with computers that are running DLC protocol stacks, such as IBM mainframes, IBM AS/400 computers, and Hewlett-Packard network printers that are connected directly to the network using older HP JetDirect network cards.
29. The AppleTalk protocol allows Apple Macintosh computers to communicate with each other.

QUESTIONS

1. The protocol used by the Internet is _____.
   a. TCP/IP
   b. IPX
   c. NetBEUI
   d. AppleTalk
2. To connect to a TCP/IP network, you must configure which of the following? (Choose two answers.)
   a. TCP/IP address
   b. gateway
   c. IPX address
   d. subnet mask
   e. DNS server address
3. To connect to a TCP/IP network that contains several subnets, which of the following must be configured? (Select all that apply.)
   a. TCP/IP address
   b. gateway
   c. IPX address
   d. subnet mask
   e. DNS server address
4. What is the default subnet mask for a class B network?
   a. 255.0.0.0
   b. 255.255.0.0
   c. 255.255.255.0
   d. 255.255.255.255
   e. 127.0.0.1
5. What does the 127.0.0.1 address represent?
   a. broadcast address
   b. network address
   c. loopback address
   d. subnet address
6. _____ means you take a large network and divide it into smaller networks.
   a. Subnetting
   b. Broadcasting
   c. Gatewaying
   d. Hosting
7. Which of the following must you consider when deciding which subnet mask to apply to a TCP/IP network? (Choose all that apply.)
   a. IP address class
   b. types of computers used on the network
   c. number of subnets
   d. potential for network growth
8. Your company is assigned the network address 150.50.0.0. You need to create seven subnets on the network. A router on one of the subnets will connect the network to the Internet. All computers on the network will need access to the Internet. What is the correct subnet mask for the network?

   a. 0.0.0.0
   b. 255.255.0.0
   c. 255.255.240.0
   d. the subnet mask assigned by InterNIC
9. A company with the network ID 209.168.19.0 occupies four floors of a building. You create a subnet for each floor. You want to allow for the largest possible number of host IDs on each subnet. Which subnet mask should you choose?
   a. 255.255.255.192
   b. 255.255.255.224
   c. 255.255.255.240
   d. 255.255.255.248
10. The Acme Corporation has been assigned the network ID 134.114.0.0. The corporation's eight departments require one subnet each; however, each department may grow to over 2500 hosts. Which subnet mask should you apply?
   a. 255.255.192.0.
   b. 255.255.224.0.
   c. 255.255.240.0.
   d. 255.255.248.0.
11. All IP addresses are eventually resolved to NIC addresses. Which of the following is used to map an IP address to an NIC address?
   a. WINS
   b. DHCP
   c. DNS
   d. ARP
12. The enhanced version of the IP (IPv4) is _____.
   a. IPv6
   b. IPX
   c. IPv5
   d. IPING
13. There are several UNIX computers and mainframes on your Windows NT network. You want to standardize the network protocol used on all computers and provide access to the Internet. Which protocol would you choose for your network?
   a. TCP/IP
   b. NWLINK
   c. NetBEUI
   d. IPX/SPX
14. If you are running Windows NT and want to know the MAC address of the network card in your server, you would type _____ at the command prompt.
   a. IPCONFIG /ALL
   b. WINIPCFG /ALL
   c. MACCFG /ALL
   d. CONFIG /ALL

15. What is the default assigned to ports used by a web server browser?
    a. 21   c. 119
    b. 80   d. 139

16. What is the default assigned to ports for a computer that uses the POP3 protocol to check for e-mail?
    a. 21   c. 80
    b. 110   d. 139

17. What is the default assigned to ports for an FTP server?
    a. 21   c. 80
    b. 119   d. 139

18. What two types of names can be resolved in a Windows TCP/IP platform? (Select two answers.)
    a. host   c. network name
    b. computer   d. NetBIOS name

19. What is used to resolve host names such as Microsoft.com? (Select two answers.)
    a. DNS server   c. LMHOSTS files
    b. HOSTS files   d. WINS server

20. You are troubleshooting a workstation and find the following information:

    IP address: 132.123.140.14
    Subnet mask: 255.255.255.0
    Default gateway: 131.123.140.200
    DNS servers: 130.13.18.3
                             140.1.14.240
    Router's IP address: 131.123.140.1

    What is the reason why the workstation cannot get to the Internet?
    a. The subnet mask is invalid for this network.
    b. There can only be one IP address for DNS servers.
    c. The IP address of the DNS should match the default gateway address.
    d. The IP address and subnet mask of the workstation are wrong.
    e. The default gateway should match the router's address.

21. Which of the following are transport layer protocols? (Choose all that apply.)
    a. TCP   c. SPX
    b. IP   d. IPX

22. Which one of the following protocols is an NDIS-compliant version of the Internetwork packet exchange protocol?
    a. IP   c. NetBEUI
    b. NWLINK   d. SMB

23. You have static IP addresses assigned to your workstation. If you have two workstations that are assigned the same IP address, what would happen as far as communication with these two workstations?
    a. The second workstation will take over communication when it boots.
    b. The first workstation to boot and log in will communicate.
    c. Both workstations will be okay.
    d. Neither workstation will be able to communicate on the network.

24. One computer on your IPX/SPX network cannot connect to the network. What is the most likely cause of the problem?
    a. incorrect frame type

b. protocol mismatch
c. upper memory area conflicts
d. faulty connectivity devices

25. There is a frame type mismatch on your Novell NetWare network. It is only affecting one computer. Which of the following needs to be reconfigured?
    a. frame type on the client machine
    b. frame type on the server machine
    c. frame binding setting on the client machine
    d. frame binding setting on the server machine

26. Which of the following uses 15-character names to identify computers on a network?
    a. TCP/IP   c. NetBIOS
    b. IPX/SPX   d. AppleTalk

27. Which of the following protocols are network layer protocols? (Choose all that apply.)
    a. IP   c. IPX
    b. TCP   d. SPX

28. Transport protocols provide for communication sessions between computers. Which of the following is a transport protocol?
    a. SNMP   c. IP
    b. NetBEUI   d. IPX

29. NetBEUI is the extended user interface of NetBIOS. Which of the following statements is true of NetBEUI? (Choose all that apply.)
    a. NetBEUI is a small, fast, and efficient transport layer protocol used primarily with Microsoft networks.
    b. NetBEUI is a small, fast, and efficient session layer protocol, but it is limited to Novell NetWare networks.
    c. NetBEUI does not support routing.
    d. NetBEUI is a relatively large protocol, which can cause problems in MS-DOS-based clients.

30. Which nonroutable protocol fits in both at the network and transport layers of the OSI model?
    a. TCP/IP   c. IPX/SPX
    b. AppleTalk   d. NetBEUI

31. What file is used to resolve a host name to an IP address?
    a. LMHOSTS   c. HOSTS.SAM
    b. HOSTS   d. LMHOSTS.SAM

32. Which of the following protocols are routable? (Choose all that apply.)
    a. TCP/IP   c. AppleTalk
    b. IPX/SPX   d. NetBEUI

33. The purpose of a WINS server in a network is to _____.
    a. keep a database of host names and corresponding IP addresses
    b. keep communication flowing on a TCP/IP network by assigning IP addresses dynamically to each workstation as it logs in
    c. keep a database of NetBIOS names and corresponding IP addresses
    d. authenticate each workstation as it logs in and determine the MAC address and corresponding IP address of each workstation

34. Routers interconnect networks and provide filtering functions. Which one of the following protocols can be used with a router?
    a. IPX/SPX   c. NetBEUI
    b. TCP/IP   d. AppleTalk

35. What is the primary protocol used with Novell NetWare 4.x?
    a. TCP/IP
    b. IPX/SPX
    c. NetBEUI
    d. DLC

36. You are using a computer with NetBEUI, but you cannot connect to a computer located on another LAN, although you can connect to the computers that are on the same LAN. What is the problem?
    a. You are using the wrong MAC address.
    b. You are using the wrong NetBEUI name.
    c. You are using the wrong gateway address.
    d. NetBEUI is a nonroutable protocol.

37. You have a Windows 95 workstation that is dynamically being assigned an IP address and you want to find out the current IP address. How do you do this?
    a. Click the Network properties and go to the IP address tab.
    b. Run the IPCFG utility.
    c. Run the WINIPCFG utility.
    d. Double-click on the My Computer icon, double-click on the Control Panel icon, and then double-click on the System applet.

38. Which operating systems use NetBIOS names? (Choose all that apply.)
    a. UNIX
    b. Linux
    c. Windows NT Server
    d. Windows 98

39. UNIX workstations resolve addresses on the Internet by using_____.
    a. WINS
    b. SMTP
    c. SNMP
    d. DNS

40. What protocol provides reliable, connection-based delivery?
    a. TCP
    b. UDP
    c. IP
    d. ARP

41. Several users are complaining that they cannot access one of your Windows NT file servers, which has an IP address that is accessible from the Internet. When you get paged, you are not in the server room but at another company in a friend's office that only has a UNIX workstation available, which also has Internet access. What can you do to see if the file server is still functioning on the network?
    a. Use PING from the UNIX workstation.
    b. Use ARP from the UNIX workstation.
    c. Use WINS from the UNIX workstation.
    d. Use DNS from the UNIX workstation.

42. When configuring a client computer, what information is required for the computer to operate in a TCP/IP environment? (Choose two answers.)
    a. IP address
    b. subnet mask
    c. default gateway
    d. DNS server address
    e. WINS server address

43. When configuring a client computer, what information is required for the computer to operate in a TCP/IP WAN environment? (Choose three answers.)
    a. IP address
    b. subnet mask
    c. default gateway
    d. DNS server address
    e. WINS server address

44. What tool can you use to see the path taken from a Windows XP system to another network host?
    a. PING
    b. IPCONFIG
    c. WINIPCFG
    d. SNMP
    e. TRACERT

45. Which bits of a subnet mask correspond to the network ID?
    a. ones
    b. zeros
    c. both ones and zeros
    d. neither ones nor zeros

46. You are troubleshooting the network connectivity for one of the client systems at your company, but you do not know the IP address for the system. You are at the client system and you want to make sure that the system can communicate with itself using TCP/IP. How can you accomplish this?
    a. Ping 127.0.0.1.
    b. Ping 255.255.0.0.
    c. Ping 255.255.255.255.
    d. Ping 0.0.0.0.

47. How are the network ID and the host ID for an IP address determined?
    a. subnet mask
    b. unicast mask
    c. range mask
    d. multicast mask

48. What are the TCP/IP addresses available for multicast transmissions?
    a. 128.0.0.0 to 191.255.0.0
    b. 192.0.0.0 to 223.255.255.0
    c. 224.0.0.0 to 239.255.255.255
    d. 240.0.0.0 to 247.255.255.255

49. At one of your company's remote locations, you have decided to segment your class B address down, since the location has three buildings and each building contains no more than 175 unique hosts. You want to make each building its own subnet and utilize your address space the best way possible. Which subnet mask meets your needs in this situation?
    a. 255.0.0.0
    b. 255.255.0.0
    c. 255.255.255.0
    d. 255.255.255.240

50. You have successfully obtained a class C subnet for your company. What is the default subnet mask?
    a. 255.255.255.0
    b. 255.255.0.0
    c. 255.0.0.0
    d. 255.255.240.0

51. A Windows 2000 Server computer, named SERVER1, resides on a remote subnet. Pat cannot ping SERVER1 using its IP address. He can successfully ping his default gateway address and the addresses of other computers on the remote subnet. What is the most likely cause of the problem?
    a. Pat's computer is set up with an incorrect default gateway address.
    b. Pat's computer is set up with an incorrect subnet mask.
    c. SERVER1 is not WINS enabled.
    d. The IP configuration on SERVER1 is incorrect.
    e. The LMHOSTS file on Pat's computer has no entry for SERVER1.

52. Pat is planning to set up an intranet web server at his company. Employees will be able to access the web server using the server's host name. Which one of the following services should Pat install on his intranet to provide name resolution?
    a. DHCP
    b. FTP
    c. DNS
    d. WINS

53. Pat fails repeatedly to access a Windows 2000 Server computer on a remote subnet. Using Network Monitor to troubleshoot the problem, he finds that every time he tries to connect to the server, his workstation broadcasts an ARP request for the IP address of the remote Windows

2000 server computer. No other users on the TCP/IP network have trouble accessing the server. What is the most likely cause of Pat's problem?

a. The workstation is not set up to use DNS.

b. The workstation is not set up to use WINS.

c. The workstation is set up with a duplicate IP address.

d. The workstation is set up with an incorrect subnet mask.

54. Pat connects to a remote UNIX computer using its IP address. He knows TCP/IP is properly installed on this computer. How should he determine if the router is working correctly?

a. Ping 127.0.0.1.

b. Ping the far side of the router.

c. Ping the local server.

d. Ping the near side of the router.

55. A Windows 2000 Professional computer user complains that he cannot connect to any other computers on his network. The network uses both a DHCP and a DNS server. Seated at his workstation, you ping 127.0.0.1 and fail to get a response. What is the most probable cause of the problem?

a. TCP/IP is not properly installed on the workstation.

b. The default gateway address on the workstation is incorrect.

c. The subnet mask on the workstation is incorrect.

d. The workstation is not set up for DHCP.

e. The workstation is not set up for DNS.

56. Which switch would you use if you want to prohibit the TRACERT utility from resolving names as it runs?

a. –r   c. –h

b. –n   d. –d

57. What value determines the amount of time in milliseconds the program will wait for a response before continuing?

a. hops   c. wait

b. timeout   d. time to live

58. Which type of proxy below hides internal IP addresses from the public Internet?

a. HTTP   c. FTP

b. DNS   d. NAT

59. Which of the following is an example of an IPv6 subnet mask?

a. 255.255.255.0

b. A119BBC01E48

c. 0AC9:0101:09A8:BBCD

d. 0AC9:0101:09A8:BBCD:921F:AE3C:1968:C00C

60. You administer a LAN. You have added several users to the LAN, and you notice that Internet access has become considerably slower. What can you use to improve the speed of Internet access from the LAN?

a. firewall   c. HTTP

b. an IP proxy   d. FTP

61. You are a network engineer who is implementing a network that consists of approximately 150 Windows 2000 workstations and five Windows 2000 servers. You have multiple sites located in the same city that are connected through a PSTN. Your manager wants you to ensure fast communication by implementing the proper protocol. Each site has a router that is already configured by the telephone company. The workstations are running Windows 98.

Required result:

• Use a routable protocol to ensure connectivity between sites.

Optional results:

• Ensure communication between the Windows 2000 servers.

• Log in to all the servers without maintaining multiple logins.

Proposed solution:

• Implement NetBEUI as your protocol and use the same user names on all servers, but different passwords for security purposes.

a. Achieves the required result and both optional results.

b. Does not achieve the required result but achieves both optional results.

c. Does not achieve the required result but does achieve one of the optional results.

d. Achieves the required result but cannot achieve either of the optional results.

e. Achieves neither the required result nor either of the optional results.

62. Which of the following entries in a HOSTS file residing on a Windows 2000 Server computer will connect to the UNIX server SERVER1?

a. 132.132.11.53 #SERVER1 #corporate server

b. 132.132.11.53 SRV1 #corporate server

c. 132.132.11.53 SERVER1 #corporate server

d. 132.132.11 #SERVER1 #corporate server

63. Pat oversees a network with five subnets: Subnet1, Subnet2, Subnet3, Subnet4, and Subnet5. A Windows 2000 computer user on Subnet4 complains that he can connect to local servers, but not to a Windows 2000 Server computer on Subnet1. Other users on Subnet4 have no trouble connecting to the Subnet1 server. Pat runs IPCONFIG on the workstation and notes the following output:

```
Ethernet Adapter Local Area Connection:

Connection-specific DNS Suffix:
IP Address . . . .  : 132.132.223.19
Subnet Mask . . . .  : 255.255.224.0
Default Gateway. . . : 132.132.224.1
```

What is the reason why the workstation cannot connect to the remote server?

a. The default gateway is incorrect.

b. The IP address must fall between 132.132.224.1 and 132.132.255.254.

c. The subnet mask must be 255.255.192.0.

d. The subnet mask must be 255.255.255.224.

64. You are a network engineer who is implementing a network that consists of approximately 150 Windows 2000 workstations and five Windows 2000 servers. You have multiple sites located in the same city that are connected through a PSTN. Your manager wants you to ensure fast communication by implementing the proper protocol. Each site has a router that is already configured by the telephone company. The workstation are running Windows 98.

Required result:

• Use a routable protocol to ensure connectivity between sites.

Optional results:

• Ensure communication between the Windows 2000 server.

• Log in to all the servers without maintaining multiple logins.

Proposed solution:

Implement TCP/IP as your protocol and use the same usernames on all servers, but different passwords for security purposes.

a. Achieves the required result and both optional results

b. Does not achieve the required result but achieves both the optional results

c. Does not achieve the required result but does achieve one of the optional results

d. Achieves the required result but cannot achieve either of the optional results

e. Achieves neither the required result nor either of the optional results

65. You are a network engineer who is implementing a network that consists of approximately 150 Windows NT workstations and five Windows NT servers. You have multiple sites located in the same city that are connected through a PSTN. Your manager wants you to ensure fast communication by implementing the proper protocol. Each site has a router that is already configured by the telephone company. The workstations are running Windows 98.

Required result:

• Use a routable protocol to ensure connectivity between sites.

Optional results:

• Ensure communication between the Windows NT servers.

• Log into all the servers without maintaining multiple logins.

Proposed solution:

• Implement TCP/IP as your protocol and use the same usernames and passwords on all servers.

a. Achieves the required result and both optional results.

b. Does not achieve the required result but achieves both optional results.

c. Does not achieve the required result but does achieve one of the optional results.

d. Achieves the required result but cannot achieve either of the optional results.

e. Achieves neither the required result nor either of the optional results.

66. Look at the following figure. The first number of each host is the IP address, the second number is the subnet mask, and the last number is the default gateway. What is the problem with the TCP/IP network?

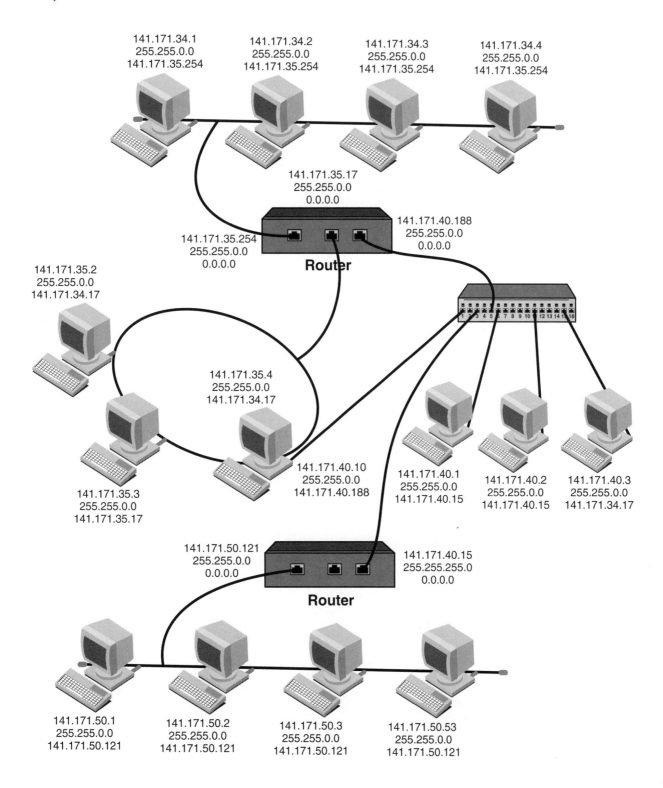

67. Look at the following figure. The first number of each host
is the IP address, the second number is the subnet mask,
and the last number is the default gateway. What are the
two problems with the TCP/IP network?

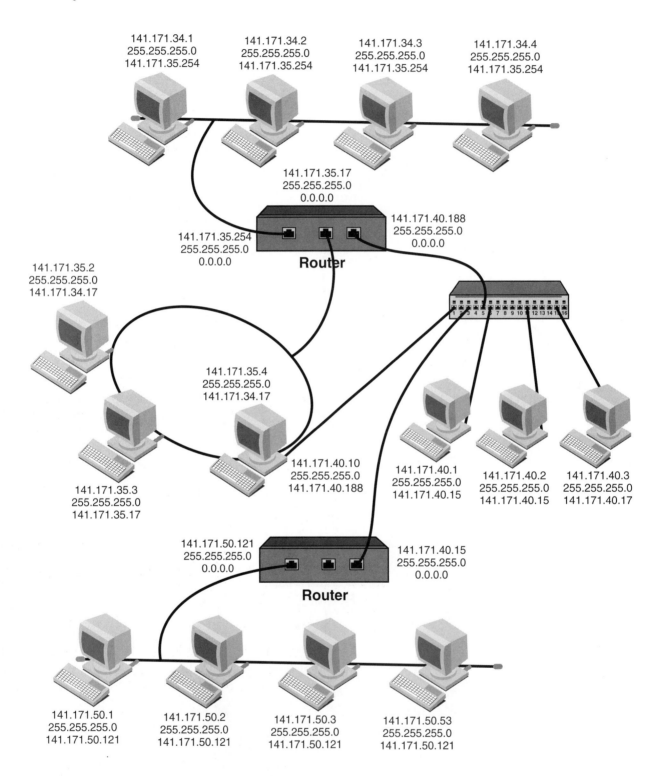

68. Look at the following figure. What is the problem with the
IPX network?

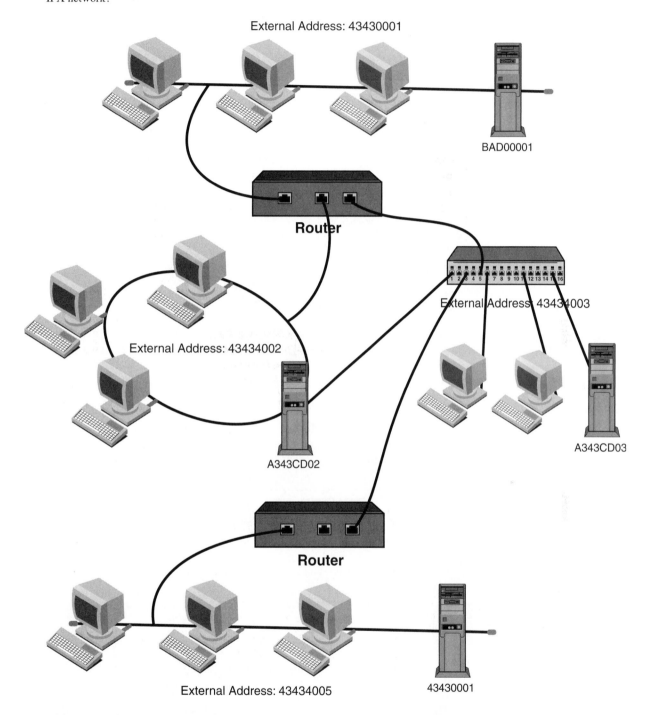

69. You are the administrator of a Windows 2000 network. You need to assign network ID numbers and host addresses to the computers in one of your company's branch offices. A single route to the branch office is advertised as 192.168.16.0/21. The branch office has 150 computers on a single subnet of 192.168.16.0/24. However, the company wants to be able to add up to another 2000 computers to the branch office. You want to be able to accommodate all computers in the branch office, while taking advantage of route summarization. Which steps should you take to achieve this goal? (Choose all that apply.)

a. In the branch office, add another route advertised as 192.168.32.0/22.

b. In the branch office, add additional network ID numbers 192.168.33.0/24 through 192.168.39.0/24.

c. In the branch office, add additional network ID numbers 192.168.17.0/24 through 192.168.23.0/24.

d. In the branch office, add additional network ID numbers 192.168.24.0/24 through 192.168.31.0/24.

e. Change the advertisement of the branch office to 192.168.16.0/20.

70. You have just been hired as the network administrator for a Windows 2000 network. The network uses TCP/IP exclusively and is not connected to the Internet. The 190.30.0.0 address range is used. When the company was first started several years ago, the network infrastructure was not planned and default settings were used. Now that the company and network have both grown considerably, a network plan needs to be created. Network traffic has been steadily rising and performance has become an issue. You need to develop a plan to improve performance and accommodate network growth. Over the next 3 years the projected growth of the network is 60 subnets with 750 hosts per subnet. Which CIDR-notation network IP address should you use to meet both current and future needs?

a. 190.30.0.0/20   c. 190.30.0.0/22

b. 190.30.0.0/21   d. 190.30.0.0/23

71. You are the administrator of a Windows 2000 network. You administer the routers in your network. Your Internet Service Provider (ISP) has assigned your network the network ID 172.24.8.0/22 (see following figure). You assign blocks of IP addresses to other administrators in your company when they request them. All of the routers in your network use either Open Shortest Path First (OSPF) or RIP version 2. You want to create two subnets that will each have approximately 75 computers. Your company expects the number of computers on these subnets to remain at 75. To create the subnets that will accommodate 75 computers, you want to use the most specific number of bits in your subnet mask. You also want to use the first two available network ID numbers. For the two subnets you need to create, what would the network ID numbers be? (Choose two answers.)

a. 172.24.12.0/22   d. 172.24.8.128/25

b. 172.24.16.0/22   e. 172.24.9.0/25

c. 172.24.24.0/22   f. 172.24.16.0/25

CHAPTER 7

Networking with Windows 9X

Topics Covered in This Chapter

Introduction

Windows 95 is a complete operating system designed to replace DOS and Windows 3.xx. The most obvious difference between Windows 95 and Windows 3.xx is that Windows 95 has a better, more intuitive user interface that supports long file names. Behind the interface, Windows 95 is a preemptive, multi-threading, multitasking environment. It is primarily a 32-bit operating system that is not limited by the conventional memory restrictions, yet provides compatibility for most DOS and Windows 3.xx device drivers and applications. It supports plug-and-play technology and has built-in multimedia and network capability. Windows 98 and Windows Millineum (Me) followed Windows 95. Note: Windows 95, Windows 98, and Windows Me can be grouped together and referred to as Windows 9X.

Objectives

- Configure the TCP/IP, IPX, and NetBEUI protocols on a Windows 9X computer.
- Share a drive or directory on a Windows 9X machine.
- Share a printer on a Windows 9X machine.
- Use Network Neighborhood in Windows 9X to navigate to a network resource.

7.1 LOADING AND CONFIGURING THE NETWORKING SOFTWARE

In Windows 9X, network components are installed and configured using the network dialog box, which is accessed by clicking on the Network applet in the control panel or by accessing the shortcut menu of the Network Neighborhood icon and selecting the Properties option. See Figure 7.1. The Network Neighborhood icon does not show on the desktop unless some network components are installed.

To get full access to the network, install the following network software through the Configuration tab:

- A client software choice such as Client for Microsoft Networks or Client for NetWare Networks
- A network adapter driver or dial-adapter driver (such as a modem)
- A protocol stack such as TCP/IP, IPX/NWLINK, or NetBEUI

7.1.1 Client Software

Client software often uses redirectors and designators. A **redirector** is a small section of code in the network operating system that intercepts requests in the computer and determines if they should be left alone to continue in the local computer's bus or redirected out to the network to another server. For example, when you request a file from the server or send a print job to a network printer, the request is intercepted by the redirector and forwarded out onto the network. A **designator** keeps track of which drive designations are assigned to network resources. For example, when you attach or map to a network drive, you and the software applications may see a drive letter, such as drive M or drive P, as on any other local drive. When these drives are accessed, a redirector routes the request to the network.

The **Client for Microsoft Networks** provides the redirector (VREDIR.VXD) to support all Microsoft networking products that use the SMB protocol. This includes support for connecting computers to and accessing files and printers on Windows for Workgroups, Windows 9X, Windows NT, Windows 2000, Windows XP, and Windows Server 2003 computers.

If the Client for Microsoft Networks is the primary network logon client, the Microsoft network usually consists of Windows NT, Windows 2000 servers, and Windows Server 2003. These could be

Figure 7.1   Windows 95 network dialog box

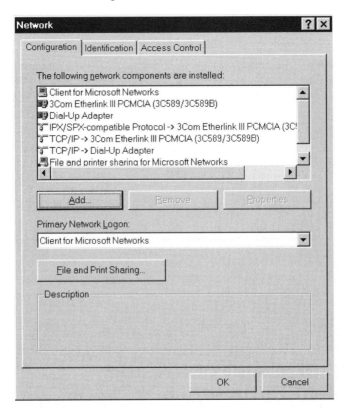

used to download system policies and user profiles. System policies and user profiles are used to control and manage the computers across the network. For example, you can restrict access to the control panel options and what users can do from the desktop, customize parts of the desktop, or configure network settings.

Under the properties of the Client for Microsoft Networks, users can specify a domain name to log on to and specify the network logon options. See Figure 7.2a. A **domain** is an organization unit consisting of computers, which uses one or more domain controllers to hold the centralized security account information. When a user logs on to a workstation/client computer on the network, the password is validated by one of the domain controllers and access is granted to the assigned network resources.

Client for NetWare Networks, run with the IPX protocol, is used to process login scripts, support all NetWare 3.xx command line utilities and most 4.x command line utilities, connect and browse to NetWare servers, access printers on the NetWare server, and process login scripts on the NetWare server. See Figure 7.2b. In addition, if you decide to install Client for NetWare, you will need to load a network card driver that supports the ODI protocol. To get full access to all utilities, you should load the client software provided by Novell.

7.1.2   Protocol Stacks

Since Windows 9X can use NDIS- and ODI-compatible network card drivers, it is possible to have one or more protocol stacks on the system. For example, you can load TCP/IP, IPX/SPX-compatible protocol, NetBEUI, and many others.

If users load the TCP/IP protocol, they must then configure it. If they highlight the TCP/IP protocol and click on the Properties button, the screen shows seven tabs. See Figure 7.3. For example, within the IP Address tab, you either assign the IP address or select to obtain an IP address automatically from a DHCP server. The gateway or address of the routers is set within the Gateway tab. The WINS

Figure 7.2   Client for microsoft and NetWare networks properties

Figure 7.3   TCP/IP Properties

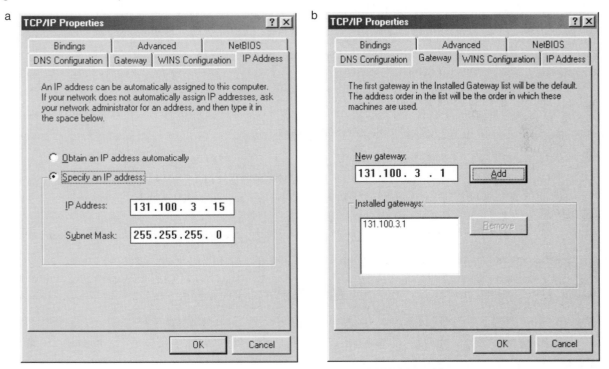

Configuration and DNS Configuration tabs are used to assign the addresses of the DNS and WINS servers, which are used for name resolution.

The IPX and NetBEUI protocols are not as complicated to configure as the TCP/IP protocol and usually require no configuration. See Figures 7.4 and 7.5. Within the properties of the IPX protocol, select the IPX frame types and enable NetBIOS over IPX/SPX. In either case, TCP/IP, IPX, and NetBEUI all have the option to become the default protocol.

Figure 7.4   IPX/SPX protocol properties

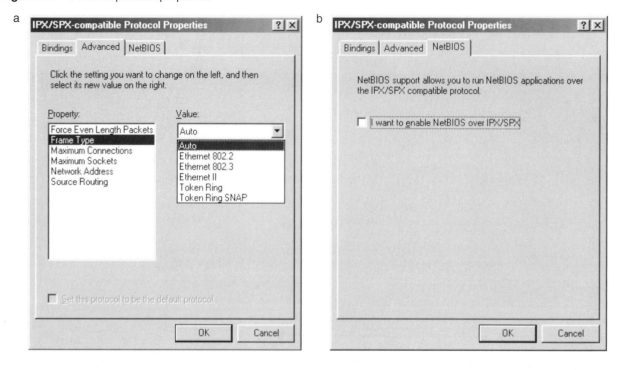

Figure 7.5   NetBEUI protocol properties dialog box

7.1.3   Network Card Drivers

The network card or adapter is the hardware device that allows users to connect to the network, but it requires a software driver before it can be used. If the driver is not listed, then use the Have Disk button and indicate where the installation files are located for the driver that is to be installed. See Figure 7.6.

If the card is a Legacy card, it will go into the properties of the network card and specify the card's resources such as IO address and IRQ. See Figure 7.7a. While most protocols are automatically bonded

Figure 7.6   Adding a network card/adapter driver

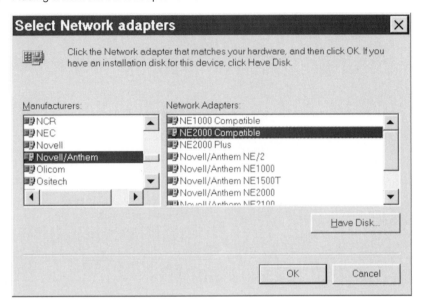

Figure 7.7   Network card/Adapter properties dialog box

to the network card, this can be configured in its properties dialog box under the Bindings tab. See Figure 7.7b. In addition, if a card has advanced features, it will usually be configured using the adapter properties dialog box.

7.1.4   Identification and Access Control

The Identification tab is used to assign the NetBIOS computer name. Much like the MAC addresses, no two computers can have the same computer name on the same workgroup or domain. You can then use utilities such as Network Neighborhood to access the computer and its network

Figure 7.8   Network dialog box

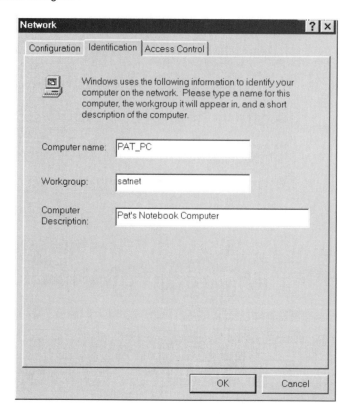

resources by using its computer name. The computer name is a maximum of 15 characters. See Figure 7.8.

The last tab in the Network dialog box is Access Control. The share-level security is used in Windows 9X to share resources and is secured with a single password for each resource. The user-level security uses the user accounts on a Windows server to give access to the network resources. Although there is security when accessing a shared resource from a remote computer (a computer elsewhere on the network), there is no security to files and directories when accessing a Windows 9X locally (when sitting at the actual computer).

7.2   SHARING DRIVES AND DIRECTORIES

File-and-print sharing for Microsoft networks gives users the ability to share files or printers with Windows computers. See Figure 7.9. Note that even though you enable file-and-print sharing for an individual computer, you still must share a drive, directory, or printer before it can be accessed through the network.

If users enable file sharing on a Windows 9X or Windows NT computer, they can share any drive or directory by right-clicking the drive or directory and selecting the Sharing option from the File menu or by selecting the Sharing option from the shortcut menu of the drive or directory. Users would then provide a **share name,** the name seen by other clients, and type of access that users can have. See Figure 7.10. A shared drive and directory will be indicated with a hand under the drive or directory. See Figure 7.11.

The shared drive or directory can then be accessed in one of three ways:

1. Using Network Neighborhood and accessing the resources under the server
2. Specifying the **UNC** using the Run option under the Start button. The UNC format is specified as \\COMPUTERNAME\SHARENAME.
3. Selecting the Map Drive button on the toolbar of Network Neighborhood or Microsoft Explorer on machines using Active Desktop

Figure 7.9   File and Print Sharing dialog box

Figure 7.10   Sharing drive/directory

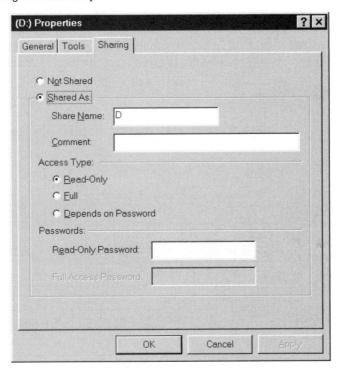

Figure 7.11   The hand indicates a shared drive or directory

7.3 SHARING PRINTERS

Sharing a printer that is connected to a Windows 9X machine makes it available to other people. Sharing a printer is similar to sharing files. For example, you first install the print driver using the Add Printer icon in the Printer folder. You then select the printer and choose the Sharing option. After assigning the printer share name and option password, click on the OK button and a hand will appear under the printer to indicate that it is shared. You then go to the client computers and run the Add Printer wizard. Instead of choosing the local printer option, choose the network printer option. You will then be prompted for the UNC name (//COMPUTERNAME/SHARENAME) of the printer. When you print to this printer, the print job will be automatically redirected to the Windows 9X machine and sent to the printer.

7.4 USING NETWORK NEIGHBORHOOD

Network Neighborhood is a **browser service** that shows the available network resources in a graphical environment and allows easy access to them. See Figure 7.12. After installing the appropriate network software (client software, network card driver, and protocol), the Network Neighborhood is automatically placed on the desktop. For example, when you double-click on the icon, it will open a window that displays computers that have network resources available. By double-clicking on one of the computers listed in Network Neighborhood, a new window will open and display the network resources (mostly shared drives, directories, and printers) that are provided by that computer. See Figure 7.13.

Figure 7.12 Network Neighborhood showing a computer with network resources

Figure 7.13 Network shares shown for a computer on the network

SUMMARY

1. In Windows 9X, network components are installed and configured using the Network dialog box, which is accessed by clicking on the Network applet in the control panel or by accessing the shortcut menu of the Network Neighborhood icon and selecting the Properties option.
2. To get full access to the network, install a network client software package, a network adapter driver or dial-adapter driver, and a protocol stack.
3. A redirector is a small section of code in the network operating system that intercepts requests in the computer and determines if they should be left alone to continue in the local computer's bus or redirected out to the network to another server.
4. A designator keeps track of which drive designations are assigned to network resources.
5. The Identification tab in the Network dialog box is used to assign the NetBIOS computer name.

6. No two computers can have the same computer name on the same workgroup or domain.
7. File-and-print sharing for Microsoft networks gives users the ability to share files or printers with Windows computers.
8. A shared drive and directory is indicated with a hand under the drive or directory.
9. The shared drive or directory can be accessed by using Network Neighborhood, by specifying the universal naming convention (UNC) using the Run option under the Start button, or by selecting the Map Drive button on the toolbar of Network Neighborhood or Microsoft Explorer on machines using Active Desktop.
10. The UNC format is specified as \\COMPUTERNAME\ SHARENAME.
11. Network Neighborhood is a browser service that shows the available network resources in a graphical environment and allows easy access to them.

QUESTIONS

1. When installing the network components in Windows 9X, which of the following components are required to connect to the network? (Choose all that apply.)
   a. network client software
   b. network protocol
   c. network service
   d. network card driver
2. To connect to a Windows NT network, install _____.
   a. Client Software for Microsoft
   b. Client Software for NetWare
   c. Client Software for UNIX
   d. Client Software for Linux
3. In Windows 98, to display the network resources that are available on the network, use _____.

   a. Internet Explorer
   b. Network Service Indexer
   c. Network applet in the control panel
   d. Network Neighborhood
4. A hand under a drive or directory indicates the drive or directory is _____.
   a. password protected
   b. virus protected
   c. shared
   d. invisible to the public
5. A drive letter that is assigned to a directory or drive on a remote computer is known as a _____.
   a. map
   b. pointer
   c. share
   d. ping

6. You are the system administrator for a company. The company's network consists of Windows NT servers, Windows NT workstations, and Windows 95/98 clients. Pat, who you recently hired, needs to configure a new Windows 98 client for a static IP address. You have given her the IP address 132.132.1.1. Pat is not sure where to input the IP address on the system, so you tell Pat to input it in the IP address tab of the _____.

a. Network properties   c. Client properties
b. TCP properties   d. TCP/IP properties

7. When installing and configuring networking components, you are asked to provide identification information for each network computer. Which of the following required names does *not* have to be unique?

a. network name   c. workgroup name
b. computer name   d. IP address

8. Paul wants to share resources with other users on the network. Which service should Paul install?

a. File and Printer Sharing
b. Administrator Tools
c. Microsoft Remote Administration
d. Peer Resource Sharing

9. You and your friend Jerry are working on a financial report. You open a shared folder on Jerry's computer by using _____.

a. System Monitor   c. Network Neighborhood
b. Remote Network   d. Briefcase

10. _____ intercepts requests in the computer and determines if the request should be sent to another server.

a. Redirector   c. Interceptor
b. Designator   d. Security manager

11. When you map a drive letter to a shared directory, you are using a(n) _____ to point to the shared directory.

a. redirector   c. interceptor
b. designator   d. security manager

HANDS-ON EXERCISES

Exercise 1: Partition and Format the Hard Drive

1. Delete all partitions on your drive.
2. Create a 800-MB primary partition and make it active.
3. Create an extended partition of at least 3.2 GB. Leave at least 200 MB of undesignated space to use in Windows 2000.
4. In the extended partition, create two logical drives, each at least 1.6 GB.
5. Format the C drive and make it bootable.
6. Format the D and E drives.
7. Install the DOS CD-ROM drivers so that the CD drive is active.

Exercise 2: Installing Windows 9X

Insert the Windows 9X installation CD in the CD drive and execute the SETUP.EXE file.
- When you get to the Choose Directory dialog box, install Windows in the C:\WINDOWS directory.
- When you get to the Setup Options dialog box, select Typical option.
- When you get to the Analyzing Your Computer dialog box, select Yes (recommended) option so that the setup program can automatically detect hardware devices.
- When you get to the Network Configuration dialog box, do *not* install any network components. This will be done in later exercises.

Exercise 3: Creating an Unshielded Twisted-Pair Ethernet

1. Determine the type of network card by looking at the card and using its documentation. Include the following:
   - Type of connection
   - Type of expansion slot
   - Speed of the network connection
   - Method of configuration (plug-and-play, software configurable, or jumper/DIP switches)
2. Configure the card for your system.
   a. Plug-and-play card
      - Physically install the card into the system.
   b. Software configurable
      - Start Windows 9X.
      - Using the Windows 9X device manager, determine what resources (IRQ, DMA, IO addresses, and memory addresses) are available. The device manager can be accessed by right-clicking on the My

Computer icon and selecting the Properties option or double-clicking on the System applet from within the control panel. The resources are shown by highlighting the computer shown at the top of the device manager and clicking on the Properties button.
- Reboot the computer to the command prompt. This can be done by selecting the Shut Down option from the Start button menu and selecting the Restart in MS-DOS mode.
- Insert the configuration disk that comes with the network card.
- Determine the executable file that configures the card and execute it.
- Within the configuration program, set the resources for the card so that there is no conflicts with any other device.
- If required, select the card's network speed and connection,
- Exit the configuration program and shut down the computer.
- Physically install the card into the computer.

c. Configuring a legacy card (jumpers/DIP switches)
- Start Windows 9X.
- Using the Windows 95/98 device manager, determine what resources (IRQ, DMA, IO addresses, and memory addresses) are available. The device manager can be accessed by right-clicking on the My Computer icon and selecting the Properties option or double-clicking on the System applet from within the control panel. The resources are shown by highlighting the computer shown at the top of the device manager and clicking on the Properties button.
- Looking at the card's documentation, set the resources for the card so that there is no conflict with any other device.
- If required, select the card's network speed and connection.
- Close Windows and shut down the computer.
- Physically install the card into the computer.

3. Connect the unshielded twisted-pair cable made in Chapter 4 to the hub and the network card.

Exercise 4: Installing the Network Software

To build an actual network, you will need access to two computers, Computer A and Computer B.

1. Open the control panel.
2. Double-click on the Network applet.
3. If there are any network components installed, remove them by highlighting them and clicking on the Properties button.
4. Select the Add button.
5. Select the Client option and click on the Add button.
6. Select the Microsoft option from the Manufacturers list and select Client for Microsoft Networks from the Network Clients list. Click on the OK button.
7. Select the card's manufacturer from the Manufacturers list and select the model of the card from the Models list. Click on the OK button. If the card is not listed, insert the driver disk and use the Have Disk button and browse to the appropriate director on the floppy disk.

> **Note:** It is often recommended to use the newest driver available. These drivers are usually found on the Internet.

8. If the TCP/IP protocol is not listed, click on the Add button and select Protocol from the list and click on the Add button. Then select Microsoft from the Manufacturers list and TCP/IP from Network Protocols. Click on the OK button.
9. From within the Network dialog box, select TCP/IP from the list of installed network components and click on the Properties button.
10. Since we do not have a DHCP server installed that automatically assigns TCP/IP addresses, we manually assign the addresses. Therefore, click on the Specify an IP Address option and enter the following address (unless your instructor specifies differently) and subnet mask.

- Computer A:
  IP Address: 132.132.1.1
  Subnet Mask: 255.255.255.0
- Computer B:
  IP Address: 132.132.2.2
  Subnet Mask: 255.255.255.0

11. Click on the OK button.
12. Click on the Identification tab.
13. Unless your instructor specifies differently, enter the following computer name:
    - Computer A: PC1
    - Computer B: PC2
14. Unless your instructor specifies differently, enter "Workgroup" as your name.
15. Click on the OK button.
16. If asked to do so, insert the Windows 9X installation CD in the CD drive or direct the program to the location of the installation files.
17. If asked to restart the computer, click on the OK button.

Exercise 5: TCP/IP Utilities

1. Perform WINIPCFG command. Notice the MAC address, the IP address, and the subnet mask.
2. If you are using Windows 98, click on the Start button, select the Programs option, and select the MS-DOS prompt option. Execute the IPCONFIG command. Again, notice the MAC address, the IP address, and the subnet mask.
3. Ping the loopback address (127.0.0.1).
4. Ping the computer's IP address.
5. Ping the IP address of another computer on the same subnet.
6. Ping the computer name of another computer on the same subnet.

Exercise 6: File-and-Print Sharing

1. From the desktop, select the Network Neighborhood icon and right-click on it. Select the Properties option. You also could open the network dialog box by opening the Network applet in the control panel.
2. Click on the File and Print Sharing button and select the options: I want to be able to give others access to my files and I want to be able to give others access to my printer(s). Click on the OK button.
3. Click on the OK button; and click on the Yes button if asked to reboot the computer.
4. From the desktop, double-click on the My Computer icon.
5. Right-click on the C drive and select the Sharing option.
6. Click on the Shared As: option, and then on the OK button.
7. In the C drive, create a folder called LEVEL1.
8. In the LEVEL1 folder, create a folder called LEVEL2.
9. In the LEVEL2 folder, create a folder called LEVEL3.
10. In the LEVEL1 folder, create a text file called FILE1.TXT. Put your name in the file. You can use EDIT or NOTEPAD.
11. In the LEVEL3 folder, create a text file called FILE3.TXT. Put your name in the file. You can use EDIT or NOTEPAD.
12. From within the C drive, select the LEVEL1 folder. Right-click the folder and select the Sharing option.
13. Select the Shared As: option and leave the Read-Only Access Type option selected. Click on the OK button.
14. From within the LEVEL2 folder, right-click the folder and select the Sharing option.
15. Select the Shared As: option and the Full Access Type option. Then click on the OK button.
16. From another computer on the same subnet and workgroup, double-click on Network Neighborhood.
17. If the computer shows in Network Neighborhood, double-click on it to see the shares. If the computer does not show in Network Neighborhood, click on the Start button and select the Run option. In the Run dialog box, type \\COMPUTERNAME of the other computer and click on the OK button. For example, if you are Computer A, type \\COMPUTERB. If you are Computer B, type \\COMPUTERA.
18. As you can see, the C, LEVEL1, and LEVEL3 shares are displayed, although they are located at different levels on the drive.
19. Open each of the shares.
20. Map a drive letter to the other computer's shared resource by taking the following steps:
    - Start Windows Explorer.
    - Select the Map Network Drive option from the Tools menu.
    - For the Drive pulldown option, select the G drive.
    - For the Path: text box, type \\PCX\LEVEL1, where X is the computer number. For example, if you are using PC2, type \\PC1\LEVEL1 (\\COMPUTERNAME\SHARENAME).
21. Go to the desktop and double-click on the My Computer icon. Double-click on the G drive.

Exercise 7: IPX Protocol

1. Display the network dialog box by right-clicking on the Network Neighborhood icon.
2. Click on the Add button, click on the Protocol option from the list, and then click on the Add button.
3. Select Microsoft from the Manufacturers list and IPX/SPX-compatible Protocol from Network Protocols. Click on the OK button.
4. From within the Network dialog box, select IPX/SPX-compatible Protocol from the list of installed network components and click on the Properties button.
5. Click on the Advanced tab and view the Frame Type (choices include Auto, 802.2, 802.3, II, and SNAP) option and the network address (external network address).
6. Click on the OK button.
7. Click on the TCP/IP option, and then click on the Remove button.
8. Click on the OK button.
9. From another computer on the same subnet and workgroup, double-click on Network Neighborhood.
10. If the computer shows in Network Neighborhood, double-click on it to see the shares. If the computer does not show in Network Neighborhood, click on the Start button and select the Run option. In the Run dialog box, type \\COMPUTERNAME, and click on the OK button.
11. As you can see, the C, LEVEL1, and LEVEL3 shares are displayed, although they are located at different levels on the drive.
12. Open each of the shares.

Exercise 8: NetBEUI Protocol

1. Display the Network dialog box by right-clicking on the Network Neighborhood icon.
2. Click on the Add button, click on the Protocol option from the list, and then click on the Add button.
3. Select Microsoft from the Manufacturers list and NetBEUI from Network Protocols. Click on the OK button.
4. From within the Network dialog box, select IPX/SPX-compatible Protocol from the list of installed network components and click on the Properties button.
5. Click on the IPX/SPX-compatible Protocol option, and click on the Remove button.
6. Click on the OK button.
7. From another computer on the same subnet and workgroup, double-click on Network Neighborhood.
8. If the computer shows in the Network Neighborhood, double-click on it to see the shares. If the computer does not show in Network Neighborhood, click on the Start button and select the Run option. In the Run dialog box, type \\COMPUTERNAME, and click on the OK button.
9. As you can see, the C, LEVEL1, and LEVEL3 shares are displayed, although they are located at different levels on the drive.
10. Open each of the shares.

Exercise 9: Troubleshooting TCP/IP Network

1. Remove the NetBEUI protocol.
2. Install the TCP/IP network with the following address (unless specified differently by your instructor).

   Computer A:
   IP Address: 132.132.1.1
   Subnet Mask: 255.255.255.0
   Computer B:
   IP Address: 132.132.2.2
   Subnet Mask: 255.255.255.0

3. Try to ping the other computer.
4. Change the address of Computer B to the following addresses:

   IP Address: 132.132.2.201
   Subnet Mask: 255.255.255.0

5. Try to ping the other computer. It should work.

Exercise 10: Connecting to the Internet

1. Install the appropriate software to connect to the Internet. You may need to use the Dial-Up Networking program.
2. Install Microsoft Internet Explorer and Netscape Communicator.
3. Connect to the Internet.
4. If you are using a modem to connect to the Internet, execute WINIPCFG or IPCONFIG to view your IP settings.
5. If you are using a modem to connect to the Internet, click on the Details button if using WINIPCFG or execute the IPCONFIG /ALL to see all IP settings.
6. Ping ZDNET.COM.
7. Perform the TRACERT command.
8. Find, download, and install the Adobe Acrobat Reader program and plug in from WWW.ADOBE.COM.
9. Access the IOMEGA.COM site and access one Adobe Acrobat Reader document.

Exercise 11: Building a Coaxial Ethernet Network

1. Remove the network components such as the Microsoft Client software, TCP/IP protocol, and network card driver.
2. Uninstall the UTP network.
3. Attach a T-connector to the network card.
4. Attach a coaxial segment between two T-connectors.
5. Put T-connectors on the two ends of the coaxial chain.
6. Install the Microsoft Client software, the appropriate network driver, and the TCP/IP protocol and File Sharing.
7. Test the network by trying to access the shared network resources.

Exercise 12: Connecting Multiple Hubs

1. Disassemble the network.
2. Connect two hubs to a central hub by using either a crossover cable or by using designated ports that allow connection to another hub.
3. If necessary, uninstall the network driver and install the appropriate network card driver. In addition, install any network components that need to be installed.
4. Test the network by trying to access the shared network resources.

Exercise 13: Gateways (Optional)

1. Connect the computer to a larger network.
2. Configure the TCP/IP address and subnet mask that is appropriate to the classroom.
3. Try to ping a computer on another network.
4. Configure the IP gateway (address of the router).
5. Try to ping a computer on another network. It should work.
6. For the IP gateway, put in the address of another computer.
7. Try to ping the other computer.

UNIT II

WINDOWS BASICS

CHAPTER 8

Introduction to Windows Architecture

Topics Covered in This Chapter

Introduction

Previous chapters have focused on connecting a network and getting the network to function. This chapter is the first to specifically discuss the Windows 2000 family. The chapter begins with the various methods of installing Windows, followed by an overview of the operating system architecture. Installing the operating system is an important step in learning how to support it. The architecture involves certain terms and concepts, as discussed in this chapter, that will be used throughout the rest of the book.

Objectives

- Install Windows from the installation CD or a network drive.
- List the system requirements for the various Windows operating systems.
- Given a scenario, recommend which Windows operating system to use.
- Upgrade to Windows 2000 or Windows Server 2003.
- Perform an attended installation of Windows 2000 Professional and Windows 2000 Server.
- Perform (1) an unattended installation of Windows and a Windows server, including use of a server remote installation service (RIS) and a system preparation tool; and (2) an unattended installation of answer files by using Setup Manager to automate the installation of Windows.
- Upgrade from a previous version of Windows to Windows 2000 or Windows Server 2003.
- Apply update packs to installed software applications.
- Deploy service packs.
- Implement, manage, and troubleshoot input and output (I/O) devices.

- Given a scenario, recommend which of the two types of licensing should be used.
- Given a common installation problem, determine and fix the cause of that problem.
- Update drivers.
- Monitor and configure multiple processing units.
- Given a scenario, recommend a method to complete automated installations.
- Compare the two major layers of Windows, user mode and kernel mode.
- Describe threads and processes and how they relate to each other.
- Given an application, describe how Windows will run the program.
- Describe real memory and virtual memory and how they relate to each other.
- List and describe the boot sequence.
- Open and modify the BOOT.INI file.
- Troubleshoot and fix common boot errors.
- Demonstrate how to use the Windows Security dialog box and Task Manager.
- Set priorities and start and stop processes.

8.1   THE WINDOWS FAMILY

Unlike Windows 9X, the Windows NT, Windows 2000, and Windows Server 2003 families, run on an architecture based on the architecture that was introduced with Windows NT. This architecutre was designed from the ground up as a revolutionary operating system to overcome some of the limitations of DOS/Windows 3.xx environment and Windows 9X operating system. The new architecture was designed as an advanced, high-performance network operating system, which is robust in features and services, security, performance, and upgradeability.

8.1.1   Windows NT 4.0 Family

Windows NT 4.0 includes three versions. Windows NT 4.0 Workstation is the client operating system for the Windows NT 4.0 family. The other two versions of Windows NT 4.0 are Windows NT 4.0 Server and Windows NT 4.0 Server Enterprise. Windows NT 4.0 Server Enterprise is similar to Windows NT

4.0 Server, except that it can address more RAM and use more processors and it offers two-server clustering. Clustering provides high availability or redundancy by providing duplicate servers. Windows NT Server 4.0, Terminal Server Edition, is an extension of the Windows NT server product line that delivers Windows using terminal emulation.

8.1.2   Windows 2000 Family

The Windows 2000 architecture uses an improved version of the Windows NT architecture to provide a more stable and reliable platform than Windows 9X, yet provide better performance and better security. Unfortunately, to achieve these benefits, Windows 2000 (like Windows NT) is not 100% backward compatible with all hardware and software. Windows 2000 offers four versions. For the client, there is Windows 2000 Professional. For the server, there are three possibilities: Windows 2000 Server, Windows 2000 Advanced Server, and Windows 2000 Datacenter Server. The Windows 2000 Server is meant to replace Windows NT 4.0 Server and Windows 2000 Advanced Server is meant to replace Windows NT 4.0 Server Enterprise.

Table 8.1 shows the system requirements for Windows 2000 family. Note these important characteristics:

- Windows 2000 Professional supports up to 2 processors and up to 4 GB of RAM.
- Windows 2000 Server supports up to 4 processors and 4 GB of RAM.
- Windows 2000 Advanced Server supports up to 8 processors and 8 GB of RAM.
- Windows 2000 Datacenter supports up to 32 processors and 64 GB of RAM.

Table 8.1   System requirements for Windows 2000

	Windows 2000 Professional — Intel-Based Machine	Windows 2000 Server— Intel-Based Machine	Windows 2000 Advanced Server— Intel-Based Machine
Processor	• Pentium 133 MHz (or higher) • Supports up to two processors	• Pentium 133 MHz (or higher) • Supports up to four processors	• Pentium 133 MHz (or higher) • Supports up to eight processors
RAM	• A minimum of 64 MB • 128 MB or higher recommended • 4 GB maximum	• A minimum of 128 MB • 256 MB or higher recommended for most network environments • 4 GB maximum	• A minimum of 128 MB • 256 MB or higher recommended for most network environments • 8 GB maximum
Disk Space	• 2-GB hard disk with a minimum of 685 MB free space (Additional free hard disk space is required if installing over a network.)	• 2-GB hard disk with a minimum of 1.0-GB free space (Additional free hard disk space is required if installing over a network.)	• 2-GB hard disk with a minimum of 1.0-GB free space (Additional free hard disk space is required if installing over a network.)
Display	• VGA or higher	• VGA or higher	• VGA or higher
Input Devices	• Keyboard and pointing device (e.g., mouse, trackball, or glide pad)	• Keyboard and pointing device (e.g., mouse, trackball, or glide pad)	• Keyboard and pointing device (e.g., mouse, trackball, or glide pad)
Networking	• Network card if you need network connectivity	• Network card if you need network connectivity	• Network card if you need network connectivity
Other	• CD-ROM (or network card for installation over the network)	• CD-ROM (or network card for installation over the network)	• CD-ROM (or network card for installation over the network)

Note: A version called Windows 2000 Datacenter Server supports up to 64 GB of memory and 32 processors. In addition it requires a minimum of eight processors.

Besides the amount of hardware that the different versions can support, all versions of Windows 2000 include the following:

- **File and print sharing**—Like all Microsoft operating systems since Windows 95, supports file and print sharing through these services: File and Print Sharing for Microsoft Networks and Client for Microsoft Networks
- **DNS, WINS, and DHCP services**—Provides name resolution and automatic TCP/IP configuration
- **Internet Information Services (IIS)**—Provides web services (HTTP and FTP)
- **NT File System (NTFS)**—Provides a robust, flexible file system that provides file security
- **Active Directory (AD)**—Similar to NDS in NetWare, AD uses the "tree" concept for managing resources on a network. Its benefits will especially be realized in Enterprise applications where network administration and management will be almost painless. Everything is treated as an object that can be moved or edited across servers and domains.
- **Remote access server**—Allows clients to dial into or provide access into your network.
- **Internet connection sharing (ICS)**—Like all Microsoft Windows since Windows 98SE, allows a single dial-up connection to be shared across the network. This has great implications for SOHOs and home users with multiple machines who no longer will need to purchase an application to provide this feature.
- **Terminal services**—Provides the Windows graphical user interface to remote devices over a network, wide area network (WAN) connection, or Internet connection. It is ideal for providing desktop users with access to limited, nonstandard, or infrequently used applications. Because all application and data processing takes place on the server, clients do not require significant amounts of RAM or processing power. Therefore, terminal services can help an organization reduce total cost of ownership (TCO) by using existing client hardware and lower-cost equipment, such as Windows-based terminals or handheld devices, and by providing centralized management and control of applications.
- **Kerberos security**—A security protocol that is used for distributed security within a domain tree/forest. This allows for transitive trusts and a single logon to provide access to all domain resources.

In addition, Windows 2000 Advanced Server and Windows 2000 Datacenter offer clustering.

8.1.3   Windows Server 2003 Family

The Windows Server 2003 family takes the best of Windows 2000 server technology and makes it easier to deploy, manage, and use. Windows Server 2003 includes all the functionality customers expect from a mission-critical Windows server operating system, such as security, reliability, availability, and scalability. In addition, Microsoft has improved and extended the Windows server operating systems to enable an organization to experience the benefits of Microsoft .NET software for connecting information, people, systems, and devices.

Windows Server 2003 includes Windows Server 2003 Standard Edition, Windows Server 2003 Enterprise Edition, and Windows Server 2003 Datacenter to replace the previous server versions of Windows 2000. In addition, there is a Windows Server 2003 Web Edition that is provided for building and hosting web applications, web pages, and XML web services. Thus, you do not have to purchase a more expensive server version that may include many network services you would not use. See Table 8.2 for system requirements.

The client used with the Windows Server 2003 is Windows XP. Windows XP is a merger of consumer (Windows 9X) and business (Windows 2000) operating systems. While Windows 2000 Professional used the same interface as Windows 2000 Server, the interface of Windows XP and Windows Server 2003 is quite different. It provides a cleaner default desktop and more intuitive interface. Yet , it contains the 32-bit kernel and driver set from Windows NT and Windows 2000. To protect your computer while you access the Internet, Windows XP includes a personal firewall.

Windows XP was introduced with two versions, Windows XP Home Edition and Windows XP Professional Edition. The Professional Edition allows you to connect to a large network (Windows domain) and to use the encrypting file system (EFS), and it includes the Internet Information Services (IIS). In addition, it provides more robust options for backing up and restoring data than the Home Edition, supports up to two processors, and supports multiple languages. The Professional

Table 8.2 Windows Server 2003

	Windows Server 2003 Web Edition	Windows Server 2003 Standard Edition	Windows Server 2003 Enterprise Edition
Processor	• Pentium 133 MHz (or higher) • 550 MHz or better • Supports up to two processors	• Pentium 133 MHz (or higher) • 550 MHz or better • Supports up to two processors	• Pentium 133 MHz (or higher) • 733 MHz or better • Supports up to eight processors
RAM	• 128 MB • 256 MB recommended • 2 GB maximum	• 128 MB • 256 MB recommended • 4 GB maximum	• 128 MB • 256 MB recommended • 32-GB maximum for x86-based computers • 64-GB maximum for Itanium-based computers
Disk Space	• 1.5 GB of free space	• 1.5 GB of free space	• 1.5 GB of free space for x86-based computers • 2.0 GB of free space for Itanium-based computers
Display	• VGA or higher	• VGA or higher	• VGA or higher
Input Devices	• Keyboard and pointing device (e.g., mouse, trackball, or glide pad)	• Keyboard and pointing device (e.g., mouse, trackball, or glide pad)	• Keyboard and pointing device (e.g., mouse, trackball, or glide pad)
Networking	• Network card if you need network connectivity	• Network card if you need network connectivity	• Network card if you need network connectivity
Other	• CD-ROM (or network card for installation over the network)	• CD-ROM (or network card for installation over the network)	• CD-ROM (or network card for installation over the network)

Note: Another version called Windows Datacenter Server 2003 supports up to 64 GB (x86-based computers) of memory or 128 GB (Itanium-based computers). It requires a minimum of 8 processors (400 MHz) and supports up to 32 processors. In addition, Microsoft also offers 64-bit versions of Windows.

Edition also provides Remote Assistance, which lets you invite someone to connect to your computer and help you with problems, and it provides Remote Desktop Connection, which allows you to connect to a computer's desktop from a remote location and run applications as if you were sitting at its console. See Table 8.3 for the Windows XP system requirements.

> Note: Don't worry if you don't understand all of these terms. They will all be explained throughout the book.

8.2   INSTALLING WINDOWS 2000

Although listed in the Windows 2000 documentation, the requirements in Table 8.1 offer slow and sometimes unreliable operations. For acceptable performance and reliability, Windows 2000 Professional should have an Intel Pentium II or III processor or better with a minimum of 128 MB of RAM; a Windows 2000 Server should have a Pentium II or III processor or better with a minimum of 256 MB of RAM.

To ensure hardware compatibility with Windows, Microsoft offers users a Hardware Compatibility List (HCL) of devices that have been tested and approved to work with Windows. The list is

Table 8.3   System requirements for Windows XP

	Windows XP Home Edition	**Windows XP Professional**
Processor	• 233 MHz or higher • Recommended 300 MHz or higher • Supports one processor	• 233 MHz or higher • Recommended 300 MHz or higher • Supports up to two processors
RAM	• A minimum of 64 MB • 128 MB or higher recommended • 4 GB maximum	• A minimum of 64 MB • 128 MB or higher recommended • 4 GB maximum
Disk Space	• Minimum of 1.5-GB available hard disk space	• Minimum of 1.5-GB available hard disk space
Display	• Minimum of VGA • SVGA (800×600) or higher video adapter and monitor recommended	• Minimum of VGA • SVGA (800×600) or higher video adapter and monitor recommended
Input Devices	• Keyboard and pointing device (e.g., mouse, trackball, or glide pad)	• Keyboard and pointing device (e.g., mouse, trackball, or glide pad)
Networking	• Network card if you need network connectivity	• Network card if you need network connectivity
Other	• CD-ROM (or network card for installation over the network) • Sound card and speakers or headphones recommended	• CD-ROM (or network card for installation over the network) • Sound card and speakers or headphones recommended

available at http://www.microsoft.com/hcl/default.asp. Therefore, users must check this list before installing Windows or purchasing a system. In addition to ensuring hardware compatibility, users should update to the newest system ROM BIOS for their motherboards.

8.2.1   Installation Process

Windows 2000 can be installed from the installation CD or from a network server. Although most Microsoft programs use SETUP.EXE to install their software, Windows 2000 uses WINNT.EXE file or WINNT32.EXE (both of which are located in the I386 directory on the Windows 2000 installation CD).

WINNT.EXE should be used for a clean installation on a computer that is running Microsoft MS-DOS or Microsoft Windows 3.xx (upgrades of these operating systems are not supported). **WINNT32.EXE** should be used on a clean installation or upgrade on a computer that is running Microsoft Windows NT 4.0 or Microsoft Windows 9X. WINNT32 can be executed from within the Windows 9X or Windows NT/2000 command prompt. The upgrade paths are shown in Table 8.4

Before running the installation program or during the installation process, create and size only the partition on which you will install Windows 2000. After installing Windows 2000, you can then use Disk Management to partition and format the remaining hard drive space. While Windows 2000 requires a minimum of 685 MB of disk space, Microsoft recommends that you install Windows 2000 on a 1-GB partition or larger. A 2-GB partition allows growth if needed. When installing other applications and setting up data file storage, then, create them on other partitions.

Windows 2000 supports file allocation table (FAT), FAT32, and NTFS. If you need file and folder security, disk compression, disk quotas (disk space limits for users), or encryption, use NTFS. If you need to dual boot between the first version of Windows 95, use FAT. If you need to dual boot between the later versions of Windows 95 and Windows 98, use FAT or FAT32. Note: The first version of Windows 95 does not support FAT32.

When executing the WINNT.EXE, the WINNT.EXE programs will copy the installation files from the installation CD or the network drive to a temporary directory (Win_nt.~ls) on the destination hard

Table 8.4   Upgrade paths to Windows 2000

Current Operating System	Upgrade to
Windows 95	Windows 2000 Professional
Windows 98	Windows 2000 Professional
Windows NT Workstation	Windows 2000 Professional
Windows NT Server	Windows 2000 Server
Windows NT Terminal Server Edition	Windows 2000 Server Advanced Server
Windows NT Server Enterprise	Windows 2000 Advanced Server, Datacenter
Windows 2000 Advanced Server	Windows 2000 Datacenter

Note: There is no upgrade path from Windows 3.xx.

drive. The system will then reboot and continue with the installation from the installation files in the temporary directory.

The Windows 2000 installation process is broken into four parts: running the setup program, running the Windows 2000 setup wizard, installing Windows 2000 networking components, and completing the installation. The WINNT allows you to select the partition on which to install Windows 2000 and select the file system for the new partition, and it gives you the option to format the new partition.

When the computer reboots, the setup wizard (GUI-based program) runs. The setup wizard sets the regional settings, licensing mode, computer name, password, and optional Windows 2000 components such as IIS, DHCP, DNS, and display settings.

A **software license** is the legal permission for an individual or group to use a piece of software. For Windows 2000, you should have a license to run the Windows 2000 Server and a client access license for each computer that connects to the server. There are two kinds of **client access licenses (CALs)**—per-seat licensing and per-server licensing. The **per-seat licensing** gives a license to access any Windows 2000 server for every specific computer (seat). For example, if you have several servers used by the clients, use the per-seat licensing. The **per-server licensing** gives the maximum number of clients that will connect to that server at any one point in time. For example, if you have multiple servers, ensure that you have sufficient licenses for all connections to all servers. The per-server mode is most economical in a single-server situation or with servers that are only used occasionally. Client access licenses are not required for anonymous or authenticated access to a computer that is running Windows 2000 Server with IIS or some other web server application. In addition, CALs are not needed for Telnet, IIS/WWW, or FTP connections.

During installation, you need to specify the type of network security group to join: a workgroup or a domain. If you want a computer to join an existing workgroup, assign the name of an existing workgroup. Adding the computer does not give it access to any domain. To join a domain during setup, you must have a computer account in the domain you want to join. If you're upgrading from Windows NT, Setup uses your existing computer account. Otherwise, you'll be asked to provide a new computer account. You would then ask your network administrator to create a computer account during Setup and join the domain. To join a domain during Setup, you need to provide the user name and password of which has the necessary rights to create a computer account. If you do not have a computer account created and you do not have the rights to add a computer to the domain, finish the installation. Add the computer to the domain later by starting the network and dial-up connections applet in the control panel. Select the network identification hypertext and click the Properties button. For more information about workgroups and domains, see Chapter 12. For more information about creating computer accounts, see Chapter 13.

During the installation of Windows 2000 networking components, load the Client for Microsoft Networks, detect and load the network card driver, install protocols, and load the file-and-print sharing for Microsoft networks. The setup wizard program will copy the necessary files to the hard disk and configure Windows 2000. During the last phase of installation, it will save the configuration, remove any temporary files, and restart the computer. See Exercise 8.1 at the end of the chapter.

8.2.2   Windows 2000 Setup Disks

Users can prepare for the possibility of a system failure on a computer that cannot be started from the CD-ROM drive by creating a set of four Windows 2000 Setup floppy disks so they can start the setup program, start the recovery console, and start the emergency repair process. The best method is to always try safe mode before booting with the floppy disks. For more information on safe mode and repair options, see Chapter 17.

The Windows 2000 Setup floppy disks must match the operating system on the computer that is to be started. Windows 2000 Setup floppy disks that are created from the Windows 2000 Professional setup CD cannot be used to start a computer that is running Windows 2000 Server or vice versa.

To create the four setup disks, perform the following steps:

1. Insert a blank, formatted, 3.5-inch, 1.44-MB disk into the floppy disk drive.
2. Insert the Windows 2000 CD-ROM into the CD-ROM drive.
3. Click on the Start button and select the Run option.
4. In the Open box, type *d:*\BOOTDISK\MAKEBOOT A: or *d:*\BOOTDISK\MAKEBT32.EXE A: (where *d:* is the drive letter assigned to the CD-ROM drive) and then click the OK button. MAKE-BOOT.EXE runs under DOS and Windows 3.xx, Windows 95, and Windows 98; MAKEBT32.EXE runs under Windows NT and Windows 2000.
5. Eventually, prompts will instruct to insert disks 2, 3, and 4.

8.2.3   WINNT.EXE and WINNT32.EXE Switches

Switches are customization options added to WINNT.EXE or WINNT32.EXE commands to modify the network installation. To use a switch, first type the command, followed by a space, followed by the switch. Some switches require additional information after the command. For example, to force Windows 2000 to install on drive D instead of drive C, type the WINNT /T:D command at the command prompt. If you execute WINNT /? at the prompt, the information displayed in Figure 8.1 will be shown. The /CHECKUPGRADEONLY switch used with the WINNT32.EXE command checks the system for incompatibilities that will prevent a successful upgrade (same as running chkupgrd.exe utility from Microsoft site). The /SYSPART:*drive_letter* specifies users to copy the Setup startup files to a hard disk and mark the disk as active, which can then be installed from the disk onto another computer and will automatically start the next phase of the setup.

8.2.4   Mass Storage Drivers and Hardware Abstraction Layers

As an IT manager, if you have a mass storage controller such as an SCSI or RAID controller for your hard disk, in which the driver does not come with Windows, you must tell Windows where it can locate the third-party driver. Shortly after the first reboot, during the early part of setup, a line at the bottom of the screen will prompt you to press F6 if you need to install a third-party SCSI or RAID driver. When you press the F6 key at this time, it will further prompt you to specify the location of the driver. Before using such a controller, however, check if the controller is on the HCL. If the controller is not supported and you proceed with the installation, an error message will indicate the problem as "inaccessible boot device."

The **hardware abstraction layer (HAL)** is a library of hardware manipulating routines that hides the hardware interface details. It contains the hardware-specific code that handles I/O interfaces, interrupt controllers, and multiprocessor operations so that it can act as the translator between specific hardware architectures and the rest of the Windows 2000 software. As a result, programs written for Windows 2000 can work on other architectures, making those programs portable. Therefore, when loading Windows 2000, be sure to load the appropriate HAL. See Table 8.5.

During setup, typically the correct HAL is loaded. If not, specify which HAL gets installed by pressing the F5 key at the same time that you would press the F6 key as mentioned previously. If you select the wrong HAL, unexpected results may occur, including an inability to boot the computer.

Figure 8.1 WINNT /?

```
Sets up Windows 2000 Server or Windows 2000 Professional.
WINNT  [/s[:sourcepath]] [/t[:tempdrive]]
       [/u[:answer file]] [/udf:id[,UDF_file]]
       [/r:folder] [/r[x]:folder] [/e:command] [/a]
/s[:sourcepath]
  Specifies the source location of the Windows 2000 files. The
  location must be a full path of the form x:[path] or
  \Servershare[path].
/t[:tempdrive]
  Directs Setup to place temporary files on the specified Drive
  and to install Windows 2000 on that drive. If you do not
  specify a location, Setup attempts to locate a drive for you.
/u[:answer file]
  Performs an unattended Setup using an answer file (requires
  /s). The answer file provides answers to some or all of the
  prompts that the end user normally responds to during setup.
/udf:id[,UDF_file]
  Indicates an identifier (id) that Setup uses to specify how a
  Uniqueness Database File (UDF) modifies an answer file (see
  /u). The /udf parameter overrides values in the answer file,
  and the identifier determines which values in the UDF file are
  used. If no UDF_file is specified, Setup prompts you to insert
  a disk that contains the $Unique$.udb file.
/r[:folder]
  Specifies an optional folder to be installed. The folder
  Remains after Setup finishes.
/rx[:folder]
  Specifies an optional folder to be copied. The folder is
  Deleted after Setup finishes.
/e Specifies a command to be executed at the end of GUI-mode Setup.
/a Enables accessibility options.
```

Table 8.5 Various HALs available in Windows 2000

HAL	Description
ACPI MultiProc	Use for multiprocessor ACPI systems.
ACPI UniProc	Use for ACPI multiprocessor board but with a single processor installed.
Advanced Configuration Power Interface PC	Use for single-processor motherboard with single-processor ACPI system.
Compaq Systempro	Use for Compaq Systempro computers.
MPS Uniprocessor PC	Use on non-ACPI systems dual-processor motherboard with a single processor installed.
MPS Multiproc PC	Use on non-ACPI systems with a dual processor running.
Standard PC	Use on any standard PC, non-ACPI, or non-MPS.

Note: ACPI = advanced configuration and power interface.

MPS = multiprocessor specification.

Figure 8.2   Changing the HAL in Device Manager

If Windows 2000 was originally installed on a computer with a single processor and you change your system to use multiple processors, then the HAL on your computer must be updated so that it will recognize and use the multiple processors. To change the HAL, take the following steps:

1. Click on the Start Button. Select Control Panel and then select System.
2. Click the Hardware tab and click on the Device Manager button. (The Device Manager will be explained in more detail in Chapter 9.) See Figure 8.2.
3. Double-click the Computer branch to expand it. Note your type of current support.
4. Double-click the computer type listed under the Computer branch, click the Drivers tab, click Update Driver, and then click Next.
5. Click "Display a list of known drivers for this device," then click "Show all hardware of this device class."
6. Click the appropriate computer type (one that matches your current type, except for multiple processors), click Next, and then click Finish.

Use this procedure only to upgrade from a single-processor HAL to a multiple-processor HAL. If you use this procedure to change from a standard HAL to an ACPI HAL (e.g., after a BIOS upgrade) or vice versa, unexpected results may occur, including an inability to boot the computer.

Table 8.6   Common troubleshooting problems

Problem	Troubleshooting Assistance
Media Errors	There is an error reading the installation files. If it is a CD, try cleaning the CD and the drive. If this fails to work, try a replacement CD. If installing over the network, check the integrity of the disk and files.
Nonsupported CD-ROM Drive	The CD drive is not compatible. Replace the CD-ROM with one that is supported or try installing over the network.
Insufficient Disk Space	The destination does not have enough space to install Windows NT. Delete some files from the destination drive, reformat the destination drive, or delete and re-create larger partitions.
Failure of Dependency Service to Start	The network services could not start. In the Windows 2000 Setup Wizard, return to the Network Settings dialog box and verify the protocol and network card settings.
Inability to Connect to the Domain Controller	The computer cannot connect to the domain controller. Verify that the domain name is correct and check protocol and network card settings. If you cannot locate a domain controller, install the computer into a workgroup and join the domain after the installation.
Failure of Windows 2000 to Install or Start	A hardware device on the computer has failed, which prevents Windows 2000 from installing or starting. Verify that Windows 2000 is detecting all hardware and the hardware is on the HCL.

8.2.5   Troubleshooting Installation Problems

Some common troubleshooting problems are listed in Table 8.6. For more information, refer to Windows 2000 Server Help files.

8.2.6   Installing Windows 2000 Over a Network

To install Windows 2000 from a network is very similar to installing it from a CD, except the location of the source file is on a distribution server (a server with a shared drive or directory with a copy of the installation files, particularly the contents of the i386 folder). To be able to perform the installation, you will need a FAT partition with at least an 850-MB (2 GB or larger recommended) partition on the target computer. Once the partition is set, install a network client on the client computer. If the client does not have an operating system, you need to boot from a disk that includes a network client, which enables the operating system to connect to the distribution server. After connecting to the distribution server and accessing the shared drive or directory with the installation files, start the WINNT or WINNT32 command.

To create a distribution server, follow these steps:

1. Log on to the server as administrator.
2. Create a folder on the server.
3. Copy the i386 folder and its contents from the Windows CD-ROM to the folder you just created.

If you create an OEM subfolder, you can place additional applications, drivers, or utilities in the subfolder and Setup will copy those to the target computer. You can also create a Cmdlines.text file that will contain a list of commands that Setup carries out during its GUI mode, so that you can run an application installation command (.INF file), use the SYSDIFF.EXE, or execute any other executable file. For example, the administrator can add the command line to run the Microsoft Office setup by including the command line for office setup.

Plug-and-play device drivers that are not included on the Windows installation CD can easily be added by first creating a $1 subfolder in the OEM subfolder. The $1 subfolder is equivalent to the

SystemDrive environment variable. If you install the operating system on drive C, \$OEM$\$1 refers back to drive C. The use of a variable makes it possible to rearrange drive letters without creating errors in applications that point to a hard-coded drive letter.

For mass storage devices that are not already supported by Windows, such as those used on some SCSI or RAID hard drive controllers to be added to the installation folder, you must create a Textmode subfolder in the \OEM subfolder. You would then copy the drivers (*.sys, *.dll, *.inf, *.cat, and the Txtsetup.oem files) to the Textmode subfolder and the PnPdrvrs subfolder. Note: If you have any HAL files, copy the files that you receive from the device vendor to the Textmode subfolder.

Then, to install Windows 2000 over the network, follow these steps:

1. On the target computer, boot from the network client. If you are booting with an MS-DOS boot disk, make sure disk caching software (e.g., smartdrv) is loaded.
2. After you start the network client on the target computer, connect to the shared folder on the distribution server that contains the Windows 2000 installation files.
3. Run WINNT.EXE or WINNT32. EXE located in the \\servername\sharename\i386\ folder to start the setup program. It creates the Win_nt.~ls temporary folder on the target computer and copies the Windows 2000 installation files from the shared folder on the distribution server to the Win_nt.~ls folder on the target computer.
4. Finish installing Windows 2000.

See the http://www.bootdisk.com website to learn how to create a network boot disk.

8.2.7   Automating Installations by Using Windows 2000 Setup Manager Wizard

When numerous computers will be running Windows 2000 and they all have to be installed, the Windows 2000 Setup Manager is of great help. The **Windows 2000 Setup Manager** wizard allows users to create an **answer file, uniqueness database file (UDF),** and a batch file that launches the Windows 2000 setup program with the answer file as the command-line argument, which can be used as scripts when using the WINNT command. The answer file is used as a generic script for many installations, whereas the UDF is used to supply unique information for an installation such as network settings or a computer name. The UDF (an ASCII text file created with a text editor such as Notepad) will identify the part of the answer file that data will be merged or replaced in the answer file.

Example 1:

> You plan to install Windows 2000 server on 25 new computers on your company's network. The computers have identical hardware and software configuration. To simplify the process, you want the Windows 2000 Setup Manager to create an Unattend.txt.file. You would then create a UDF file that identifies the names of the new computers. Lastly, you would begin the installation by running the WINNT command with the /s /u and /udf switches.

To automatically create answer files, you can use the Setup Manager wizard. The Setup Manager wizard, SETUPMGR.EXE is one of the files found in the Deploy.cab file located in the \Support\Tools folder on the Windows 2000 CD. It can be accessed directly from the Windows 2000 CD, or it can be extracted to your hard drive. To extract the SETUPMGR.EXE file and additional deployment files from the Deploy.cab file, perform the following steps:

1. Create a folder at the root of C.
2. Select all files in the Deploy.cab file, right-click any selected file, and then click Extract.
   The Setup Manager wizard extracts all the selected files.
3. In the Browse for Folder dialog box, select the folder you created, then click OK.

To start the Setup Manager wizard, double-click SETUPMGR.EXE. When it starts, the wizard presents you with three options:

- Create a new answer file.
- Create an answer file that duplicates the current computer's configuration.
- Modify an existing answer file.

If you create a new answer file, you need to choose the type of answer file to create. The Setup Manager wizard can create an answer file for a Windows 2000 unattended installation, a Sysprep install, or remote installation services.

If you choose to create an answer file for a Windows 2000 unattended installation and you select either Windows 2000 Professional or Windows 2000 Server, the Setup Manager wizard asks you to specify a level of user interaction. You can set the level of user interaction to one of five levels:

- **Provide Defaults**—The answers that you supply in the answer file are the default answers, and Windows Setup Manager prompts the user to review them. The user may change any answers that you supply.
- **Fully Automated**—Windows Setup Manager does not prompt the user for any answers. You supply all required answers in the answer file.
- **Hide Pages**—If you supplied all the answers on a Windows setup wizard page, Setup Manager hides the wizard page from the user.
- **Read only**—If a Windows setup wizard page is not hidden from the user, the user may not change any answers that you supplied in the answer file.
- **GUI attended**—Only the text-mode portion of Windows setup is automated.

If you are installing Windows 2000 from a CD, you can create an answer file that is designed to automatically provide answers for the installation. In the Setup Manager wizard, specify the installation folder, select "No, this answer file will be used to install from a CD on the Distribution Folder page," and then save the file to disk as Winnt.sif.

If your system supports bootable CDs, you can use unattended installations to perform a clean installation. This is quite useful for computers at remote sites with slow links and no local IT department. To use a bootable CD, the following criteria must be met:

- Your computer must have E1 Torito No Emulation support for bootable CDs.
- The answer file must contain a [Data] section with the required keys:
    UnattendedInstall =Yes
    MSDosInitiated=0
    AutoPartition=1
- The answer file must be called Winnt.sif and must be located on a floppy disk.

To install Windows 2000 Server by using a bootable CD, follow these steps:

1. Start the system from the Windows 2000 Server CD.
2. When the blue text-mode screen with "Windows 2000 Setup" appears, place the floppy disk containing the Winnt.sif file into the floppy disk drive.
3. Once the computer reads from the floppy disk drive, remove the floppy disk. Setup searches for the Winnt.sif file when you start the computer from the CD-ROM drive and perform the installation as specified in the file.

You can use the advanced options to store additional applications, drivers, and utilities in the OEM subfolder so that they can be copied to the temporary folder on each new computer's hard disk. If you don't use the wizard, you must add the OEMPreinstall=Yes parameter in the [Unattended] section of the answer file.

As nice as the wizard is in simplifying the installation process, the wizard does not contain every option that is available. Instead, you have to manually create or modify the answer file. All of the options that are available in the answer file are in the document titled Microsoft Windows 2000 Guide to Unattended Setup, which is the Unattend.doc file located in the Deploy.cab file mentioned earlier. Some of the more useful options are described in the next few paragraphs.

For a fully unattended installation to complete, the ProductID or product registration key must be specified in the UserData section of the answer file. The syntax of this key is ProductId = "XXXXX-XXXXXXXXXX-XXXXX-XXXXX." If this key is missing and your system requires one, you will get this message: "Unattended setup is unable to continue because a setup parameter specified by your system administrator or computer manufacturer is missing or invalid." Note: This parameter is not required for customers who are using Select CDs. Also be aware that this parameter assigns the same Product ID to all computers; this may cause some difficulty when you try to receive support on multiple computers with the same Product ID.

The OemSkipEula=Yes option in the [Unattended] section will automatically accept the Microsoft license agreement (previously known as the end user license agreement, or EULA) included with Windows 2000. Of course, setting this parameter to Yes implies that the person performing the installation has read and agreed to the contents of the license agreement included with the product. It also implies that the end user on whose behalf Windows is being installed has agreed to the license agreement. Note: Original equipment manufacturers (OEMs) must not use this key to bypass the Microsoft license agreement, because end users are required to see and accept it.

The Repartition=yes option in the [Unattended] section specifies whether all partitions on the first drive on the client computer should be deleted and the drive reformatted with the NTFS. Note: Repartition is only valid when performing an unattended installation by booting the computer from the Windows 2000 CD.

The ExtendOemPartition option in the [Unattended] section is used to extend the partition on which you are installing Windows. ExtendOemPartition=1 extends the partition to fill out the hard disk and ExtendOemPartition=*extra_size_in_MB* has Setup Manager increase the current partition size by the amount specified. Note: Only NTFS partitions can be extended. If the destination partition you plan to extend is FAT or FAT32, set FileSystem=ConvertNTFS to convert the partition during text-mode setup.

After you create the answer files, you should test the unattended installation, especially if you have set it up for other people to use. Sometimes there may be an additional parameter that might be required, or you may have to correct certain parameters. For example, as you run the Setup Manager wizard, you can establish parameters for your display. When the Setup file is created, these settings will be in the [Display] section and will include the following settings:

- Number of bits per pixel (BitsPerPel=BB)
- Valid refresh rate (Vrefresh=VV)
- Valid X resolution (X resolution=XXX)
- Valid Y resolution (Y resolution=YYY)

If you select parameters that your video system cannot handle, your screen will be unreadable.

8.2.8   Installing Windows XP and Windows Server 2003

Installing Windows XP and Windows Server 2003 is similar to installing Windows 2000. If you are installing from a CD or a distribution folder, you use the WINNT.EXE and WINNT32.EXE.

The following operating systems can be upgraded directly to Windows XP Professional:

- Windows 98
- Windows Millennium Edition
- Windows NT 4.0 Workstation with service pack 5 (SP5)
- Windows 2000 Professional

If you are using Windows earlier than Windows 98 and Windows NT 4.0 with SP5, you will have to perform an intermediate upgrade to the previous operating system before upgrading to Windows XP Professional.

The following operating systems can be upgraded to Windows Server 2003 Standard Edition:

- Windows NT 4.0 Server with SP5 or later
- Windows NT Server 4.0 Terminal Server Edition, with SP5 or later

■ Windows 2000 Server, on a computer with one or two processors. If you want to upgrade from Windows 2000 Server on a computer with three or four processors, you must choose Windows Server 2003 Enterprise Edition.

■ If you have Windows NT 4.0 Server Enterprise, you can upgrade to Windows Server 2003 Enterprise Edition, but not Windows Server 2003 Standard Edition. Before upgrading from Windows NT 4.0, you must apply SP5 or later.

You can upgrade to Windows Server 2003 Enterprise Edition from the following versions of Windows:

■ Windows NT 4.0 Server with SP5 or later
■ Windows NT Server 4.0, Terminal Server Edition, with SP5 or later
■ Windows NT 4.0 Server Enterprise with SP5 or later
■ Windows 2000 Server
■ Windows 2000 Advanced Server
■ Windows Server 2003 Standard Edition

NOTE: If you have a version of Windows NT earlier than 4.0, you cannot upgrade directly to a product in the Windows Server 2003 family. You must first upgrade to Windows NT 4.0 and apply SP5 before upgrading to a product in the Windows Server 2003 family.

Windows XP has an option to uninstall Windows after a successfully completed upgrade, which must include the creation of the Windows XP uninstallation files (Backup.cab and Boot.cab) during the initial upgrade. To uninstall Windows XP, follow these steps:

1. Restart your computer in Safe mode. To do so, press the F8 key while Windows is starting.
2. Log on using the Administrator account.
3. Click Start, click Control Panel, and then double-click Add or Remove Programs.
4. In the list of installed programs, double-click Uninstall Windows XP. Note: If Uninstall Windows XP is not in the list of installed programs, you must manually reinstall Windows 98 or Windows Me. If this is the case, make sure to back up all of your critical data before you reinstall.
5. You will receive this message: "Are you sure you want to uninstall Windows XP and restore your previous operating system?" Click Yes to start the Windows XP uninstallation process.
6. After the Windows XP uninstallation process is finished, your computer will shut down, restart, and then boot to the previously installed operating system.

8.2.9   Licenses and Product Activation for the Windows Server 2003 Family

Before purchasing Windows XP and Windows Server 2003, you need to understand that Microsoft has different types of licensing available for Windows:

■ **Original equipment manufacturer (OEM) licensing** — For products, such as Windows operating systems, that come installed when you purchase a new computer
■ **Full packaged product (FPP), retail, licensing**—For physical, shrink-wrapped boxes of licensed products that can be purchased in a local retail store or any local software retailer
■ **Volume licensing for organizations**—For organizations that acquire multiple products, Microsoft offers several volume licensing options, and the savings may be significant.

Recently, Microsoft initiated a change in its volume licensing called software assurance (SA). SA is meant to simplify how volume-license customers acquire and administer licenses for Microsoft products and streamline how volume-license customers obtain the newest releases.

The SA program replaces the array of upgrade licenses offered previously. Under the new program, customers acquire the right to install any new release of products covered in the agreement during the term of their coverage. Microsoft claims that the SA program has several benefits:

■ **Comprehensive technology protection**—Customers can install any new release for licensed products enrolled in SA that become available during the covered period.

■ **Predictable budgeting**—Customers can spread license payments over a three-year period when products are purchased through the Select License or Enterprise Agreement programs. In addition, customers avoid the financial spikes associated with varying product release schedules.

■ **Better license management**—Customers can standardize software versions throughout the organization and maintain competitiveness through the latest products and technologies.

■ **Cost savings**—Customers save because SA coverage is priced at 29% of the license price per year for eligible application products and at 25% for eligible Microsoft server products.

For more information on Microsoft licensing, visit the following websites:

Licensing

http://www.microsoft.com/licensing/default.asp

Volume licensing 101

http://www.microsoft.com/licensing/resources/overview.asp

Volume licensing overview

http://www.microsoft.com/licensing/programs/

Software assurance and volume licensing 6.0 programs

http://www.microsoft.com/licensing/programs/sa/

Software assurance overview

http://www.microsoft.com/licensing/programs/sa/sadefined.asp
For more information on Microsoft product activation, visit the following websites:

Description

http://support.microsoft.com/default.aspx?scid=KB;EN-US;Q302806&

Frequently asked questions

http://www.microsoft.com /piracy/basics/activation/mpafaq.asp

Volume licensing

http://www.microsoft.com/piracy/basics/activation/mpavlfaq.asp

How to activate Windows XP using an Unattend.txt file

http://support.microsoft.com/default.aspx?scid=KB;EN-US;Q291997&

Unless you are using volume licensing, you will need to activate your copy of Windows XP or Windows Server 2003. Product activation is an antipiracy measure that will be included in all future Microsoft software applications. The first time that a user logs onto a computer running Windows, the Activate Windows dialog box appears and the user is prompted to activate the installed copy of Windows. A user can choose not to activate the software, in which case reminders to activate will appear periodically until the user activates the software. The easiest way to activate the software is to select this option: Yes, let's activate Windows over the Internet now. Then click Next. If the computer is not connected to the Internet, the user can instead select the Telephone option and follow the directions for activating Windows over the telephone.

Users must activate Windows within 30 days of installation. If not activated within 30 days, users are prevented from gaining access to Windows until activation occurs. Note: The clock for Windows product activation for OEM installations begins its countdown the first time Windows starts. Keep in mind that if you change enough hardware on your PC, you need to reactivate your Windows. In that case, you may need to contact a Microsoft customer service representative by telephone.

8.2.10   Remote Installation Service

The **remote installation service (RIS)** is used to remotely install Windows; thus, the topic fits in this chapter that describes various ways of installing Windows. Unfortunately, some of the utilities and services that enable RIS to function are not explained until later in the book, so refer back to this section after learning those utilities and services.

RIS ships as part of the Windows 2000 Server and Windows Server 2003 operating systems (excluding Windows Server 2003 Web Edition). RIS enables client computers to connect to a server during the initial start-up phase and remotely install Windows. This reduces the time that administrators spend visiting all computers on a network, thereby reducing the cost of deploying Windows. Unlike a standard network installation performed by running WINNT.EXE, a remote installation does not require users to know where the installation source files are stored or what information to supply during the setup program. RIS that ships as part of the Windows 2000 Server operating system can be used to install Windows 2000 Professional. RIS that ships as part of the Windows Server 2003 can be used to install any of the following:

- Windows XP Professional
- Windows Server 2003 Web Edition
- Windows Server 2003 Standard Edition
- Windows Server 2003 Enterprise Edition
- 64-Bit version of Windows Server 2003 Enterprise Edition (RIS setup only)
- Windows 2000 Professional
- Windows 2000 Server
- Windows 2000 Advanced Server

Although any Windows server since Windows 2000 can host RIS, there are some prerequisites to be met before using RIS. They are as follows:

- RIS requires DNS, DHCP, and active directory somewhere on the network. See Chapters 11, 12, and 13.
- The drive on the server where RIS is installed must be formatted with the NTFS. See Chapter 14.
- RIS cannot be installed on the same drive or partition as Windows Server (boot partition).
- Since RIS requires a significant amount of disk space, the chosen drive must contain enough free space to hold the images of files to be installed. Free space is a minimum of 800 MB.

To install RIS, follow these steps:

1. On a Windows server, click the Start button, select the Settings option, and select Control Panel.
2. Double-click the Add/Remote Programs applet and double-click the Add/Remove Windows Components option.
3. Scroll down and select Remote Installation Services and click on the Next button.
4. Insert the Windows server CD-ROM into the CD drive and click the OK button. The necessary files are copied to the server. After the CD is entered, a dialog box asks if you want to upgrade to the operating system. Click No and exit this screen.
5. Click the Finish button to end the wizard.
6. When prompted to restart your computer, click the Yes button.

To configure RIS, follow these steps:

1. Click the Start button, select the Run option, and type RISETUP.EXE and click on the OK button. This starts the RIS setup wizard.
2. The Welcome screen appears, indicating some of the requirements to successfully install RIS. Click the Next button.
3. The next screen prompts you to enter the server drive and directory where you would like to install the RIS files. The default drive and directory will be the largest nonsystem, nonboot, NTFS-formatted drive. Click the Next button. The drive on which you choose to install RIS must be formatted with the NTFS file system. RIS requires a significant amount of disk space and cannot be installed on the same drive or partition on which Windows server is installed. Ensure that the chosen drive contains enough free disk space for at least one full Windows—a minimum of approximately 800 MB to 1 GB.
4. The setup wizard prompts you to either enable RIS at the end of setup or disable the service to allow modification of specific server options before servicing client computers. These options are as follows:

- *Respond to client computers requesting service.* This option controls whether this RIS server responds to client computers that are requesting service at the end of setup. If this option is checked, the server will respond to clients and provide them with operating system installation options. If unchecked, this RIS server will not respond to clients that are requesting service.
- *Do not respond to unknown client computers.* This option controls whether this server responds to unknown client computers that are requesting a remote installation server. A client computer is known if a managed computer account object exists for it within the active directory. This allows the administrator to offer only authorized—that is, prestaged within the active directory—computers the operating system installation options from this RIS server. **Prestaging** can be used to provide a measure of security (unauthorized clients cannot receive RIS images), customization (certain clients automatically receive certain images), and load balancing (server can be designated to service only certain clients). This setting also provides support for multiple remote boot or install servers from different vendors on one physical network. For example, if another vendor's remote install/boot server exists on the same network as the RIS server, you cannot control which server answers the client computer's request. Setting this option and prestaging client computers ensures that this RIS server will service only prestaged client computers.

5. If you select "Respond to client computers requesting service" and click the Next button, the setup wizard prompts you for the location of the Windows installation files. Insert the Windows CD into the server's CD drive and type the drive letter containing the CD (or browse to a network share that contains the installation source files). Click the Next button.

6. The wizard prompts you to enter the directory name that will contain the files on the RIS server. This directory is created beneath the directory specified in step 3. The directory name should reflect its contents.

7. You are prompted for a friendly description and help text that describes this operating system image. The friendly description and help text is displayed to users during the client installation wizard (OSChooser) at initial start-up on a remote client. The help text is displayed when the user selects the description within the client installation wizard. As an IT manager, make sure you provide clear help text to your users, to ensure that they choose the correct operating system option at installation time. Click Next to accept the default name.

8. At this point, you are presented with a summary screen indicating the choices you have made. Click the Finish button to confirm your choices. Once the installation wizard completes, you are ready to either service client computers or additionally configure the RIS settings.

9. Wait while the wizard installs the service and settings you have selected. This takes several minutes.

10. When the installation is done, click on Done.

NOTE: By default, a RIS server is not configured to begin servicing client computers immediately after the installation of the RIS server is completed. To configure RIS, you must authorize RIS servers, set RIS server properties, set RIS client installation options, and set RIPrep image permissions.

To administer the majority of the RIS configuration settings, you will use the Active Directory Users and Computers console. To start this console, click Start, select the Programs option, select the Administrative Tools, and then select the Active Directory Users and Computers. On the tree in the left pane, right-click the RIS and select properties. The Remote Install tab determines how this RIS responds to client computers that request service. Then click on the Advanced Settings button to specify the ways in which client computers are installed and to manage the images. See Figure 8.3

An **image** is a copy of all files of an operating system. It is not a disk image such as those used with Disk Image or Ghost. The Images tab is used for managing the client operating system images that are installed on a RIS server. Its options allow an administrator to add, remove, or modify the properties of an operating system image. There are two types of images that can be displayed on the Images tab:

- A CD image is a copy of all Windows installation files with answer files. It is not a disk image. When you install RIS, you will begin with the RISTANDARD.SIF answer file. You can then configure the RISTANDARD.SIF file or you can create additional answer files by using the Setup Manager wizard.
- Remote installation preparation (RIPrep) images are created by using the wizard on a source computer that has both Windows and its applications already configured.

Figure 8.3 Configuring Windows 2000 RIS

Upon start-up, RIS client computers can connect to a RIS server to install Windows remotely or to run diagnostic and maintenance utilities. The only client computers that support remote installation are as follows:

- Network PC (net PC)
- A network adapter with a PXE-based boot ROM (version .99c or higher) that allows the computer to remotely start the computer with the network card
- A supported network adapter and a remote installation start-up disk (Note: One of the disadvantages of using RIS to install Windows is that the list of supported network adapters is not very extensive. The most popular interfaces are interfaces that are produced by Intel and 3COM.)

The remote installation boot disk can be used with computers that do not contain a remote boot-enabled ROM on the network card. The boot disk is designed to simulate the PXE boot process for computers that lack support DHCP PXE-based remote boot ROM. The boot disk generator utility is called RBFG.EXE, which is located within the \RemoteInstall\admin directory on the RIS.

8.2.11 System Difference Tool

Another useful tool for installing many computers is the **system difference tool (SYSDIFF.EXE),** which is also available in the resource kit. The system difference tool enables users to automatically distribute and install applications and limited hardware devices during or after the Windows setup.

To use the system difference tool, run SYSDIFF.EXE /SNAP SNAP_FILE on a reference computer to take a snapshot of the computer before installation of the applications. After the applications have been installed, then use the SYSDIFF /DIFF SNAP_FILE DIFF_FILE to create the difference file that will contain only the changes that occurred during the installation of the applications. Then use the SYSDIFF.EXE /APPLY \\SETUPSERVER\W2K\DIFF_FILE to add or apply the difference file to the other computers.

8.2.12 Disk Image Software

Another way to quickly install Windows on computers that have identical hardware is to use **disk copying/disk cloning software,** where the software creates a file containing the disk image of the hard drive. You can then place the image file to a central location and use the disk cloning software to copy the image to other computers. Popular disk cloning software packages include Symantec Ghost Professional and Microhouse ImageCast Deluxe.

Windows uses a **security identifier (SID)** to uniquely identify the computer, even if the computer name has been changed. Because it can identify a computer, it can stop someone from installing a Windows computer with the same computer name to impersonate a server. The problem when using a disk image software package is the package also copies the SID to the other computer. Therefore, all the computers have the same SID.

Windows has the **system preparation tool (SYSPREP.EXE)** that will remove the security identifiers and all other user-specific or computer-specific information from a Windows-prepared system. You would then use the disk image software to create and distribute the disk images. New security identifiers will be created when the new computers are restarted.

The System Preparation Tool has the following syntax:

SYSPREP.EXE [/QUIET] [/NOSIDGEN] [/PNP]

/QUIET—Runs SYSPREP in the silent mode where no messages are displayed

/NOSIDGEN—Runs SYSPREP.EXE without generating a SID. Normally each computer must have an individual SID or security identifier. Use this option only to make a clone of a computer as a backup or to allow the end user to customize the computer.

/PNP—Forces plug-and-play to refresh when the computer reboots to redirect all the hardware devices in the computer.

/REBOOT—Reboots the computer after SYSPREP.EXE runs.

8.2.13   Installing Service Packs and Hot Fixes

After installing Windows, check to see if Microsoft has released any fixes or patches and apply them to the Windows system. By adding fixes and patches, you will keep Windows stable and secure. If there are many fixes or patches, Microsoft releases them together as a **service pack**. Look for the most recent service pack and install that before continuing. In addition, if you make any major changes including adding services to the computer, you should reinstall the service pack. To obtain information about service packs, refer to http://support.microsoft.com/support/downloads.

In earlier versions of Windows, if you applied a service pack to your computer, each time you changed the system state by adding or removing components, you had to reapply any service packs. Now Windows automatically recognizes that a service pack has been applied to the system and which files have been replaced or updated. Whenever you add or remove components from a computer running Windows, the system copies the required files from either the Windows installation files or from the service pack install location, so you don't have to reapply the service pack.

Microsoft has produced the http://windowsupdate.microsoft.com website, which is a catalog of fixes, updates, and enhancements to Windows and many programs that work with Windows. To get to the website, if you have a newer version of Internet Explorer, open the Tools menu and select Windows Update. When you go to this website, Windows will scan your system to see what you have installed and give you a list of suggested components. This system check assures that you will get the most up-to-date and accurate versions of anything you choose to download from the site. Additionally, you won't waste time downloading components you have already installed. When the list of components appears on the page, you can browse it, decide which components you want, and download them to your computer. It is highly recommended to download any Critical Updates recommended for your system. Critical Updates fix known problems (such as security issues) specific to your computer. Now you can download drivers from the Product Updates catalog.

To help users with the Windows update website, Windows systems starting with Windows XP include Dynamic Update and Auto Update. **Dynamic Update** is a new feature built into Windows Setup that automatically checks for new drivers, compatibility updates, and security fixes while Windows is being installed. All that is required is that you have a working connection to the Internet. During installation you can choose to have Dynamic Update check for updates. It automatically downloads any device or application updates and uses these replacement files instead of the files on the installation CD, thereby ensuring that you have the latest updates available. By updating your installation files as needed, Windows can quickly integrate new, certified device drivers, critical security fixes, and compatibility updates. These updates ensure that the system you install does not immediately need to be patched and that your new video card is recognized and supported as soon as there are certified drivers available for it.

After you install Windows, you can use **Auto Update** to ensure that critical security and compatibility updates are made available for installation automatically, without significantly affecting your regular use of the Internet. Auto Update works in the background when you are connected to the Internet to identify when new updates are available and to download them to your computer. The download is managed so that it does not affect your surfing the Web, and it picks up where it left off if the download is interrupted. When you install Windows, you will be prompted to set up Auto Update, and you can choose from these options:

- Automatically download the updates, then prompt you to install them. This is the default and is recommended for most users.
- Notify you before downloading, then notify you again after they are downloaded before installing. This option makes sense for users who travel and want to control when they perform the download.
- Disable AutoUpdate.

When the download is completed, you will be notified and be prompted to install the update. You can install it then, get more details about what is included in the update, or let Windows remind you about it later. Some installations may require you to reboot, but some do not. Click the Details button to see what is in the update and if a reboot is required. Even if a reboot is required for the update to be activated, you control when the reboot happens.

Starting with Windows 2000, you can perform **slipstreaming,** which gives you the ability to add service packs directly to the operating system's distribution share. When you install Windows from the modified distribution share, the service pack will already be included in the installation. You can also create new installation CDs that include the service packs. You must capture the boot sector from a Windows installation CD by using a program such as WinISO, then burn the boot sector and distribution share files (including any additional drivers and HALs that you might have applied) to a CD. To apply a new service pack, download the service pack and extract the service pack (usually by using the –x parameter). Then execute the UPDATE.EXE –s:folder_name command to copy over the existing Windows files with the updated service pack files.

Besides doing a manual installation of the service pack or using the http://windowsupdate. microsoft.com there are several other ways to automatically install and deploy service packs and other patches and fixes:

- **Microsoft Systems Management Server (SMS)**—Provides a variety of tools to help you deploy the service pack in your organization. With the SMS version 2.0 software distribution feature, you can simultaneously upgrade all of the SMS client computers in your site with the new service pack. You can allow your users to run the service pack installation whenever they like, or you can schedule the service pack installation to run at a specific time. You can also schedule it to run on SMS client computers at a time when no users are logged on to the network.
- **Microsoft Windows Installer Service**—A Windows component that standardizes the way you install software programs, such as the service pack on multiple computers. This system-resident installation service enables you to manage program installation, modification, repair, and removal. It provides consistent deployment, thereby enabling you to manage shared resources, customize installation processes, make decisions about application usage, and resolve configuration problems.
- **Unattend.txt**—A file that identifies how Windows 2000 Setup should interact with distribution folders and files you create, and it supplies information about your preinstallation requirements. You can create or modify the Unattend.txt answer file by using a text editor or through Setup Manager.
- **Cmdlines.txt**—File that contains a list of the commands that run during Windows GUI-mode Setup. These commands can, for example, run an application setup command (SYSDIFF.EXE) or another executable file. You can create the Cmdlines.txt file by using a text editor or through Setup Manager.
- **Microsoft System Preparation Tool (SYSPREP.EXE)**—A utility that enables you to perform legal imaging, disk duplication, automation of mini-setup, and auditing.
- **SYSDIFF.EXE**—A utility that enables you to distribute and install applications automatically during or after Windows 2000 Setup and to distribute files or make application configuration changes during the setup process.

> For more information on deploying service packs, visit the following website:
>
> **Microsoft Windows 2000 Service Pack Installation and Deployment Guide**
>
> http://www.microsoft.com/technet/treeview/default.asp?url=/technet/prodtechnol/windows2000serv/support/spdeploy.asp

In keeping your computers up-to-date, there are a few more programs or services that may be helpful. One is the **Microsoft Software Update Services (SUS),** which is designed to greatly simplify the process of keeping IT systems current with the latest critical updates (Windows Critical Updates, Windows Critical Security Updates, and Windows Security Roll-ups, but not service packs). SUS enables administrators to quickly and reliably deploy critical updates to Windows 2000 with service pack 2, Windows XP, and the Windows Server 2003 family computers. In addition, it works inside the corporate firewall so that users do not have to use the Internet to download the updates. SUS functions as follows:

- The SUS server component regularly polls the Windows Update Service site and downloads all new updates.
- SUS notifies the administrator of new updates.
- The administrator tests the new updates and, once approved, adds them to the distribution set.
- SUS clients are configured to poll the SUS server for new updates. If an update is available, the SUS clients download it, and the Windows Update icon appears in the notification area.
- If a user is present, he or she can open the Windows Update notification dialog box and initiate the installation.
- If no user is present or the user fails to manually initiate the installation at the defined installation time, the system displays a 5-minute warning. At the end of the 5-minute countdown, the update is installed and the system is rebooted.

> For more information about the Microsoft SUS and to download the SUS server and client components, visit the following websites:
>
> **Microsoft Software Update Services (SUS)**
>
> http://www.microsoft.com/windows2000/windowsupdate/sus/
>
> **Software Update Services Deployment White Paper**
>
> http://www.microsoft.com/windows2000/windowsupdate/sus/susdeployment.asp

8.3   WINDOWS ARCHITECTURE

Windows 2000, Windows .NET Server 2003, and Windows XP are modular operating systems that have many small, self-contained software components that work together to perform various operating system tasks. Each component provides a set of functions that acts as an interface to the rest of the system. See Figure 8.4.

8.3.1   User Mode

The Windows architecture can be divided into two major layers, user mode and kernel mode (also referred to as privileged mode). The **user mode** programs run in ring 3 of the **Intel 386 microprocessor protection model,** and are protected by the operating system. It is a less-privileged processor mode that has no direct access to hardware and can only access its own address space. Programs running in ring 3 have very little privilege compared with programs running in ring 0 (kernel mode), so the programs in user mode should not be able to cause problems with components in kernel mode. Since most of the user's applications run in ring 3, an application can be terminated without causing problems

Figure 8.4 Windows architecture

with the other applications that are running on the computer. In addition, programs executed in user mode do not have direct access to hardware. If a program tries to access the hardware directly, the program will be terminated; thus, the system can maintain reliability and security.

The user mode layer contains the environment and integral subsystems. The **environment subsystem** provides the application programming interfaces (APIs) for the programs and converts them to the proper calls for Windows. APIs are a set of routines, protocols, and tools for building software applications. In the Windows environment, APIs provide building blocks, which a program can then use, and a common interface. For example, when a Win32-based application such as Microsoft Word 97 asks the operating system to do something, the Win32 subsystem captures that request and converts it to commands that Windows can understand. The environment subsystems include the following:

- **32-bit Windows-based system (Client Server Runtime Subsystem—CSRSS.EXE)**—Handles windows and graphic functions for all subsystems. It provides a working environment for Win32, Win16, and DOS-based applications.
- **OS/2 subsystem**—Provides APIs for 16-bit character mode (DOS mode or bounded) OS/2 applications.
- **POSIX subsystem**—Provides API for POSIX-compatible UNIX applications.

The 32-bit Windows-based subsystem controls the I/O between subsystems so that all applications have a consistent user interface.

The **integral subsystem** performs essential operating system functions such as the security subsystem, the workstation service, and the server service. The security subsystem tracks rights and permissions associated with user accounts, tracks which system resources are audited, and performs login authentication. The workstation services allow access to the network, and the server service provides API to access the network server.

8.3.2   Kernel Mode

The **kernel mode** components run in ring 0 of the Intel 386 (I386) microprocessor protection model. Whereas user mode components are protected by the operating system, kernel mode components are protected by the microprocessor. It has direct access to all hardware and all memory including the address space of all user mode processes. It includes the Windows Executive, hardware abstraction layer (HAL), and the Microkernel.

The **Windows Executive** services consist of managers and device drivers. They include the I/O Manager, Object Manager, Security Reference Monitor, Virtual Memory Manager (VMM), Win32K Window Manager and graphical device interface (GDI), local procedure call facility, hardware device drivers, and graphics device drivers. See Table 8.7.

A **kernel** is the central module of an operating system. It is the part of the operating system that loads first and it remains in RAM. Because it stays in memory, a kernel must be as small as possible but still provide all the essential services required by other parts of the operating system and applications. Typically, the kernel is responsible for memory management, process and task management, and disk management.

The **Microkernel** is the central part of Windows, which coordinates all I/O functions and synchronizes the activities of the Executive services. Much like the other kernels in Windows 3.xx and Windows 9X, the Microkernel determines what is to be performed and when it is to be performed, while handling interrupts and exceptions. It is designed to keep the microprocessor(s) busy at all times.

Device drivers are programs that control a device. They each act like a translator between the device and programs that use the device. Each device has its own set of specialized commands that only its driver knows. While most programs access devices by using generic commands, the driver accepts the generic commands from the program and translates them into specialized commands for the device.

Table 8.7   Windows Executive

Component	Function
I/O Manager	Manages input from and delivers output to the file systems, device drivers, and software cache
Security Reference Monitor	Enforces security policies on the local computer
Interprocess Communication (IPC) Manager	Manages communications between clients and servers. It includes the following: • Local procedure call (LPC)—Manages communication when clients and servers exist on the same computer • Remote procedure call (RPC)—Manages communications when clients and servers exist on separate computers
Virtual Memory Manager (VMM)	Implements and controls memory (physical and virtual)
Process Manager	Creates and terminates processes and threads
Plug-and-Play Manager	Maintains central control of the plug-and-play process. It communicates with device drivers so that drivers can be directed to add and start devices.
Power Manager	Controls power management APIs, coordinates power events, and generates power management requests
Window Manager and graphical device interface (GDI)	A device driver (WIN32K.SYS) that manages the display system and contains the Window Manager and GDI. The Window Manager controls window displays, manages screen output, and receives input from devices such as the keyboard and mouse. The GDI contains the functions that are required for drawing and manipulating graphics.
Object Manager	Creates, manages, and deletes objects that represent operating system resources such as processes, threads, and data structures

Device drivers are installed into the Executive services section of Windows. Many drivers utilized by Windows have the **Windows Driver Model (WDM).**

8.3.3   Windows Processing

A **program,** sometimes referred to as a **process,** is an executable framework that follows a sequence of steps. A program consists of initializing code and data, a private memory address space, system resources (such as files, communication ports, and Windows resources), and one or more threads.

A **thread** is part of a program that can execute independently of other parts. Operating systems that support multithreading enable programmers to design programs whose threaded parts can execute concurrently. This can enhance a program by allowing multitasking, improving throughput, enhancing responsiveness, and aiding background processing. For example, Microsoft Word uses a thread to respond to keys typed on the keyboard by the user to place characters in a document. Other threads are used to check spelling and to paginate the document as the user types. If the user prints, another thread spools or feeds a document to the printer in the background. When a program uses multithreading, the programmer must carefully design the program in such a way that all the threads can run at the same time without interfering with each other.

Windows is a **preemptive** multitasking operating system, which means the system assigns time slices to threads, tasks, and applications. Threads, tasks, and applications with a higher priority get a larger time slice. At the end of the time slice, the kernel can take back control of the computer without permission from the thread or program. See Figure 8.5.

Win16-based applications (used by Windows 3.xx applications) use cooperative multitasking. Cooperative multitasking depends on applications that cooperate with each other. Since Windows 3.xx uses cooperative multitasking, the application uses the microprocessor and voluntarily gives control back for other programs. Poorly written software applications that do not give up control can cause problems for other applications.

Win16-based applications in Windows 2000, Windows Server 2003, or Windows XP cannot take advantage of preemptive multitasking. Instead, they share the same memory area or **virtual machine (VM)** and will all be assigned a single time slice. Unfortunately, if a program causes problems, it can cause all Win16-based applications to crash; however, all Win16-based applications are run preemptive with Windows 32-based applications and other Windows processes to improve the performance of Win16-based applications.

When the Windows kernel controls access to the microprocessor, Windows assigns 32 different priorities to each process, numbered 0 to 31. The levels are divided as follows:

Figure 8.5   Programs under Windows

- Levels 0–15 are used for user mode components.
- Levels 16–31 are reserved for kernel mode components.

The Windows kernel assigns each process a base priority level as well as each thread that executes within that process. The base priority for a thread can be adjusted by the kernel by two levels below to two levels above the one initially assigned. For example, if a thread were assigned a priority level of 8, the range would be from 6 to 10. If the thread is accepting user input, the kernel might raise the thread's priority level and if the thread requires computations, the kernel might assign it a lower priority.

To change the priority of an application, which will in turn modify the system resources allocated to the application, you would execute the following command using the Run option or from a command prompt:

```
Start /prioritylevel Application
```

The priority level offers several options:

/low — Starts an application in the idle priority class (priority 4)
/normal — Starts an application in the normal priority class (priority 8)
/high — Starts an application in the high priority class (priority 13)
/realtime — Starts an application in the real-time priority class (priority 24)
/abovenormal — Starts an application in the above-normal priority class (priority 10)
/belownormal — Starts an application in the below-normal priority class (priority 6)

You can also use the Task Manager to change priorities. In Task Manager, click the Processes tab and right-click a process name. When its menu appears, click Set Priority, then click a new base priority. Note: The change in priority is effective at the next Task Manager update; you need not restart the process.

A change in an application's priority from /normal to /high or to /real-time can cause severe degradation of performance of other tasks. In addition, if multiple processes are running at the high priority class level, problems can arise. Setting a processor-bound application to real-time priority could cause the computer to stop responding. Windows includes a Process Viewer (PVIEWER.EXE), which lets you monitor process and thread priority and change the base priority class of a process. It can be found in the Windows Support Tools on the Windows operating system CD.

8.3.4   Windows Memory Model

Physical memory refers to the actual RAM in the system. Virtual memory is disk pretending to be RAM, thereby allowing for the use of more RAM than what users physically have. Since the disk is much slower than RAM, virtual memory is much slower than physical RAM. The advantage of virtual memory is that it allows users to run more programs than would have been possible with only the physical memory. The file that makes up virtual memory in Windows NT, Windows 2000, Windows Server 2003, and Windows XP is called a paging file (PAGEFILE.SYS). If a system has multiple hard disks, create a paging file for each disk to increase paging performance.

The Windows NT, Windows 2000, Windows Server 2003, and Windows XP memory model is based on a flat, linear, 32-bit address space, which is managed by the Virtual Memory Manager (VMM). Remember that a 32-bit address (11111111 11111111 11111111 11111111) is the largest binary number that a 32-bit address can form, which equates to 4 GB of memory.

Whatever memory the system has, the VMM groups all physical and virtual memory together and assigns memory addresses to every byte. As processes (programs) request memory resources, the VMM assigns the memory resources to the process and protects them so that another program does not interfere with the memory space of another process.

Recall from Chapter 2 that the Intel microprocessors use demand paging, which swaps data between the RAM and disk only on the demand of the microprocessor. Since the processor does not try to anticipate what data will be needed from the hard drive, the code and data that are stored on disk as virtual memory will remain on disk until they are needed.

In Windows, the physical and virtual memory are grouped into 4-KB blocks called pages. The process of moving data in and out of physical memory is called paging. When physical memory becomes full and a thread needs access to code, or data are not currently in physical memory, the VMM moves some pages from physical memory to a storage disk called a page file. Since this frees RAM, there is now room to load the requested code or data into RAM.

The kernel divides memory into two pools, nonpaged pool and paged pool. Items that are in the nonpaged pool memory must stay in physical memory, whereas items in paged pool can be paged to disk if necessary.

When running programs, Windows uses dynamic memory allocation so that it can use the RAM more efficiently. Dynamic memory allocation gives a program memory when it needs it and takes it away when the program is not using it.

Windows Advanced Server, Enterprise Server, and Datacenter can recognize 8 GB and 64 GB, respectively. These servers are based on the Intel Physical Address Extension (PAE). The PAE is based on a 36-bit address that supports up to 64 GB of physical memory. Applications using Microsoft Address Windowing Extension (AWE) APIs can create data caches that are 16 times as large as the cache sizes used in the 32-bit model.

Each process has a 4-GB virtual address space. The 4-GB space is divided into two areas. The lower addresses (user mode) map to data and code that are private to the process or program. The upper addresses (kernel mode) map to system data and code (operating system, device drivers, and file system cache) that are common to all processes. By default, the lower address is 2 GB and the upper address is 2 GB. In Windows 2000, Windows Server 2003, and Windows XP the boundary can be moved with a switch in the BOOT.INI so that the programs have access to 3 GB and the system can access 1 GB.

By default, the system reserves about 50% of physical memory for the file system cache, but the system trims the cache if it is running out of memory. A server running a web server (specialized file server) such as IIS needs to have a large and effective file system cache to maintain efficiency in operation.

8.3.5   Interprocess Communication

Applications that split processing between networked computers are called distributed applications. A client-server application that uses distributed processing has its processes divided between a workstation and a more powerful server (application server). Typically, the client portion formats requests and sends them to the server for processing and the server runs the request and passes the result back to the client.

Interprocess communication (IPC) allows bidirectional communication between clients and servers using distributed applications. IPC is a mechanism used by programs and multiprocesses. IPCs allow concurrently running tasks to communicate between themselves on a local computer or between the local computer and a remote computer. Windows 2000 provides many different IPC mechanisms, including local procedure calls, remote procedure calls, named pipes, and mailslots.

Local procedure calls (LPCs) are used to transfer information between applications on the same computer. **Remote procedure calls (RPCs)** are used to transfer information between applications that are on separate computers. The Microsoft RPC mechanism is unique in that it uses other IPC mechanisms, such as named pipes, NetBIOS, or WinSock to establish communications between the client and the server. Since the RPCs are already defined, a programmer can send a message to another server with the appropriate arguments and the server returns a message containing the results of the program that was executed.

Named pipes and mailslots are high-level IPC mechanisms used by network computers. Unlike the other mechanisms, both are written as file system drivers. A **named pipe** is connection-oriented messaging via pipes that set up a virtual circuit between the two points to maintain reliable and sequential data transfer. A pipe connects two processes so that the output of one can be used as input to the other. A **mailslot** is connectionless messaging, which means that messaging is not guaranteed. Connectionless messaging is useful for identifying other computers or services on a network, such as the browser service offered in Windows. Connection to a named pipe and mailslot is done through the **CIFS** redirector. A redirector intercepts file I/O requests and directs them to a drive or resource on another computer. The redirector allows a CIFS client to locate, open, read, write, and delete files on another network computer that is running CIFS.

8.3.6   COM, COM+, and DCOM

Component object model (COM) is an object-based programming model designed to promote inter-operability by allowing two or more applications or components to easily cooperate with one another, even if they were written by different vendors, at different times, in different programming languages, or if they are running on different computers running different operating systems. COM is the foundation technology upon which broader technologies can be built, such as object linking and embedding (OLE) technology and ActiveX.

COM+ is an extension of the component object model. COM+ is both an object-oriented programming architecture and a set of operating system services. It adds to COM a new set of system services for application components while they are running, such as notifying them of significant events or ensuring they are authorized to run. COM+ is intended to provide a model that makes it relatively easy to create business applications that work well with the Microsoft Transaction Server (MTS) in a Windows NT system.

Distributed component object model (DCOM) is a set of Microsoft concepts and program interfaces in which client program objects can request services from server program objects in other network computers. Since DCOM uses TCP/IP and HTTP, it can work with a TCP/IP network or the Internet. For example, you can create a page for a website that contains a script or program that can be processed before being sent to a requesting user by a more specialized server in the network. Using DCOM interfaces, the web server site program, which is now acting as a client, forwards an RPC to the specialized server. The specialized server provides the necessary processing and returns the result to the web server. It passes the result on to the web page viewer.

8.4   WINDOWS BOOT SEQUENCE

During boot-up, the first Windows file to be read is **NTLDR (NT Loader),** which switches the microprocessor from real mode to protected mode and starts the appropriate minifile system drivers (built into NTLDR) so that it can read the VFAT/FAT16, FAT32, or NTFS file systems.

Next, NTLDR reads the **BOOT.INI** (if one is available) and displays the Boot Loader Operating System Selection menu. See Figure 8.6. NTLDR then loads the operating system (such as Windows NT, Windows 2000, Windows 9X, or DOS) as selected from the menu. If you do not select an entry before the timer reaches zero, NTLDR loads the default operating system specified in the BOOT.INI file. If the BOOT.INI file is not present, NTLDR tries to load Windows from the Windows directory (typically the Windows 2000 family uses the C:\WINNT directory and the Windows Server 2003 family uses C:\WINDOWS). In addition, the menu will not be displayed if you only have the one operating system.

Figure 8.6   Windows 2000 Boot Loader Operating System Selection menu

```
Please select the operating system to start:

    Microsoft Windows 2000 Advanced Server
    Microsoft Windows 2000 Professional
    Windows 98

Use ↑ and ↓ and to move the highlight to your choice.
Press Enter to choose.
Seconds until highlighted choice will be started automatically: 30




For troubleshooting and advanced startup options for Windows 2000, press F8.
```

NTLDR runs NTDETECT.COM, which attempts to detect the bus/adapter type, serial ports, floating-point coprocessor, floppy disks, keyboard, mouse/pointing device, parallel ports, SCSI adapters, and video adapters. If you have a system that has an SCSI hard disk, for which the BIOS on the SCSI adapter is disabled, NTLDR will load NTBOOTDD.SYS to access the SCSI devices during boot-up.

After NTLDR collects the hardware information, it gives you an option to press the spacebar to invoke the Hardware Profile/Configuration Recovery menu. This menu lists the hardware profiles that you have saved on your drive and lists the Last Known Good Configuration option.

The NTLDR finally loads the NTOSKRNL followed by the hardware abstraction layer (HAL.DLL). It then loads the HKEY_LOCAL_MACHINE\SYSTEM registry key from systemroot\system32\ CONFIG\SYSTEM directory. Note that the registry and hive are described in Chapter 9. The SYSTEM hive specifies which device drivers are to load during boot-up. When the device drivers are loaded, a hardware list is made and stored in the registry. Lastly, the Session Manager (SMSS.EXE) is loaded, which loads the appropriate services needed for Windows to function. The NTLDR initializes the NT kernel (NTOSKRNL.EXE) and takes control of the boot process.

The active partition that contains the NTLDR and BOOT.INI file is known as the **system partition.** The partition that contains the Windows operating system files is called the **boot partition.** If a system has only one partition with the initial boot files and the Windows directory, then the partition is both the system partition and the boot partition.

> **Note:** The %*systemroot*% or *systemroot* indicates the folder into which Windows 2000 is installed, which is located on the boot partition. By default, the Windows 2000 system root directory is C:\WINNT and the Windows Server 2003 family directory is C:\WINDOWS.

DOS and Windows 9X use a different volume boot sector. In addition, Windows NT, Windows 2000, and Windows Server 2003 start with NTLDR whereas DOS and Windows 9X start with IO.SYS. If DOS or Windows 9X boot files are already on a partition when you install Windows, then the old boot sector gets copied into a file called **BOOTSECT.DOS.** Therefore, when you select the old operating system from the boot menu, NTLDR loads BOOTSECT.DOS and passes control to it. The operating system then starts up as normal. When dual booting between Windows 2000 or Windows Server 2003 and DOS or Windows 9X, neither DOS nor Windows 9X can read NTFS partitions. See Figure 8.7.

8.4.1   BOOT.INI Files

During boot-up, the BOOT.INI file provides a Boot Loader Operating System Selection menu, which allows selection between multiple operating systems. The BOOT.INI file is a read-only, hidden system text file located in the root directory of the system partition. See Figure 8.8. The BOOT.INI file is divided into two sections, [boot loader] (see Table 8.8) and [operating systems]. The entries in the [boot loader] section configure the time (in seconds) that the Boot Loader Operating System Selection menu appears on the screen and that the default operating system is loaded.

Figure 8.7   The BOOT.INI/Boot menu allows two pathways during boot-up

Figure 8.8   Typical BOOT.INI File

```
[boot loader]
timeout=30
default=multi(0)disk(0)rdisk(0)partition(1)\WINNT
[operating systems]
multi(0)disk(0)rdisk(0)partition(1)\WINNT="Microsoft Windows 2000
Advanced Server" /fastdetect
multi(0)disk(0)rdisk(1)partition(1)\WINNT="Microsoft Windows 2000
Professional" /fastdetect
C:\="Windows 98"
```

Table 8.8   Settings in the [Boot Loader] section of the BOOT.INI file

Entries	Description
Timeout=XX	Specifies the number of seconds the user has to select an operating system from the boot loader screen before NTLDR loads the default operating system. If the value is zero, NTLDR immediately starts the default operating system without displaying the boot loader screen.
Default=	The ARC path to the default operating system.

Table 8.9   Optional parameters found in the BOOT.INI file

Entries	Descriptions
/3GB	Changes the standard of allocating 2 GB for each process and 2 GB for the system to 3 GB for each process and 1 GB for the system.
/BASEVIDEO	Specifies that Windows NT uses the standard VGA video driver.
/fastdetect=[comxl comx,y,z]	Disables serial mouse detection. Without a port specification, this switch disables peripherals detection on all COM ports.
/maxmem:n	Specifies the amount of RAM that Windows uses. Use this switch if you suspect memory is bad.
/noguiboot	Boots the computer without displaying the graphical boot status screen.
/SOS	Displays the device driver names while they are being loaded.
/PAE	Enables Physical Address Extension (PAE) so Windows can use up to 64 GB of RAM. Available in Windows 2000 Server (Advanced Server or Datacenter) and Windows Server 2003 (Enterprise or Datacenter).

The [operating systems] section contains the list of available operating systems. Each entry includes an ARC path to the boot partition for the operating system, the string to display in the boot loader screen, and optional parameters. The optional parameters are shown in Table 8.9.

An **advanced RISC (reduced instruction set computer) computing (ARC) path** is used to specify the location (partition) of an operating system. It follows the format:

```
multi(x)disk(y)rdisk(z)partition(a)\directory="description"
```

or

```
scsi(x)disk(y)rdisk(z)partition(a)\directory="description"
```

or

```
signature (abcdefgh) disk (y) rdisk (z) partition (a)
\directory="description"
```

The Multi syntax is used for disks that use INT13 (software interrupt 13), and the system BIOS usually identifies only one disk adapter. For this reason, you can only use the Multi syntax to start Windows from either of the two disks on the primary IDE or SCSI device or on the secondary IDE or SCSI device. The use of the Multi syntax depends on the type of adapter that your computer uses, for example:

- On IDE adapters, the Multi syntax works for up to four disks: two on primary and two on secondary IDE channels.
- On SCSI adapters, the Multi syntax works for the first two disks on the first SCSI adapter (the adapter whose BIOS loads first).
- With both SCSI and IDE adapters, the Multi syntax works for only the IDE disks on the first adapter.

Table 8.10 shows the meaning of the parameters used with the Multi syntax.

The SCSI syntax is used for an SCSI disk with its BIOS disabled. Different from Multi, SCSI tells Windows to load an SCSI device driver to access the boot partition. Table 8.11 defines the parameters used in the SCSI syntax.

The Signature syntax is equivalent to the SCSI syntax, but it is used to support the plug-and-play architecture in Windows. Because Windows 2000 and Windows Server 2003 family operating systems are plug-and-play operating systems, the SCSI controller number instance might vary each time you start Windows, especially if you add new SCSI controller hardware after setup. The Signature syntax instructs NTLDR to locate

Table 8.10 Multi Syntax Parameter Variables

Parameter	Multi Parameter Definitions
multi(x)	The number of the adapter, usually 0
disk(y)	Always 0
rdisk(z)	Number for the disk on the adapter, usually between 0 and 3
partition(a)	Partition number. All partitions that are in use receive a number. Primary partitions are numbered before logical drives. The first valid number for a is 1.

Table 8.11 SCSI Syntax Parameters

Parameter	SCSI Parameter Definitions
scsi(x)	The controller that is found
disk(y)	Number of the physical disk attached to the computer
rdisk(z)	SCSI logical unit number (LUN) of the disk that contains the boot partition. This is typically 0.
partition(a)	Partition number. All partitions that are in use receive a number. Primary partitions are numbered before logical drives. The first valid number for z is 1.

the drive with a disk signature that matches the value in the parentheses, regardless of which SCSI controller number the driver is connected to. The Signature syntax is used only if one of the following conditions exists:

- The partition on which you installed Windows is larger than 7.8 GB in size, or the ending cylinder number is higher than 1024 for that partition, and the system BIOS or boot controller BIOS does not support Extended INT13.
- The drive on which you installed Windows is connected to an SCSI controller whose BIOS is disabled, so INT13 BIOS calls cannot be used during the start-up process.

The Signature value is extracted from the MBR. This unique hexadecimal number is either written to the MBR during the text-mode portion of Setup or by a previous installation of Windows NT 4.0 or earlier.

When booting from a computer that does not use the correct ARC path, you may get one of the following error messages:

```
BOOT: Couldn't find NTLDR. Please insert another disk.
NT could not start because the following file is missing or corrupt:
\winntroot\system32\ntoskrnl.exe.
NTDETECT V1.0 Checking Hardware. . .
NTDETECT failed/missing
```

NOTE: Since primary partitions are numbered before logical drives, if you add primary partitions on a drive after establishing logical drives, the partition number for the logical drives will change. You then have to modify any ARC paths that point to the logical drives.

8.4.2   Advanced Boot Options

If you press F8 while the Windows Boot menu is listed, it will display the Advanced Boot menu. The Advanced Boot menu options are listed in Table 8.12 and displayed in Figure 8.9.

After you reboot the computer and log on, the kernel copies the configuration information to the Last Known Good control that is set in the registry. If you install a driver and the driver causes problems

Table 8.12   Advanced Boot Menu Options

Advanced Boot Option	Description
Safe Mode	Similar to Windows 9X safe mode. Windows will load and use basic files and drivers, including the mouse, VGA monitor, keyboard, hard drive, and default system services. However, no network components are loaded.
Enable Boot Logging	Logs the loading and initialization of drivers and services into an NTBTLOG.TXT text file in the Windows NT directory (usually WINNT). The text file can then be used for troubleshooting boot problems.
Enable VGA Mode	Starts Windows with basic VGA drivers (resolution of 640×480 at 16 colors).
Last Known Good Configuration	Starts Windows using the last saved configuration stored in the registry.
Directory Services Restore Mode	Allows to boot the computer into a mode that lets you restore the active directory (AD) of a domain controller from backup media. This option is not available for Windows that are not domain controllers.
Debugging Mode	Turns on debugging. Debugging information can be sent across a serial cable to another computer that is running a debugger. This mode is configured to use COM2. See Chapter 17 for more information.

Note: In Windows 2000, all options, except the Last Known Good Configuration, create the NTBTLOG.TXT file and uses the VGA driver (resolution of 640×480 at 16 colors).

Figure 8.9   Windows 2000 Advanced Boot menu options

```
┌─────────────────────────────────────────────────────────────────────────┐
│ Windows 2000 Advanced Options Menu                                        │
│ Please Select an option:                                                  │
│                                                                           │
│   Safe Mode                                                               │
│   Safe Mode with Networking                                               │
│   Safe Mode with Command Prompt                                           │
│                                                                           │
│   Enable Boot Logging                                                     │
│   Enable VGA Mode                                                         │
│   Last Known Good Configuration                                           │
│   Directory Services Restore Mode (Windows 2000 domain controllers only)  │
│   Debugging Mode                                                          │
│                                                                           │
│   Boot Normally                                                           │
│   Return to OS Choices Menu                                               │
│                                                                           │
│ Use ↑ and ↓ and to move the highlight to your choice.                     │
│ Press Enter to choose.                                                    │
└─────────────────────────────────────────────────────────────────────────┘
```

during boot, you can then activate the Last Known Good Configuration. This can be executed at the F8 during the boot menu or by pressing the spacebar when it says to open the OS Loader Recovery menu.

Safe mode loads Windows with the minimum number of device drivers and services necessary to boot successfully. Networking enabled safe mode adds network drivers and services to that of standard safe mode. Safe mode with the command prompt is identical to standard safe mode, except that Windows runs the command prompt application (CMD.EXE) instead of the Windows Explorer as the shell when the system switches into GUI mode. To keep track of which device drivers and services are part of the standard and networking enabled safe boots, the system uses HKEY_LOCAL_MACHINE\SYSTEM\CurrentControl\Set\Control\SafeBoot registry key. (Registry is explained in Chapter 9). When any of the safe modes are selected, the NT Loader (NTLDR) passes the /SAFEBOOT parameter to the NTOSKRNL.EXE so that the kernel can specify to only load these drivers and services.

8.5   WINDOWS START-UP FLOPPY DISK

After installing and configuring Windows 2000 or Windows Server 2003 family operating systems, make a Windows start-up floppy disk. A start-up floppy disk is used to access a drive with a faulty start-up sequence, such as a corrupted boot sector, corrupted MBR, a virus infection, missing or corrupt NTLDR or NTDETECT.COM, or an incorrect NTBOOTDD.SYS file. In addition, the disk can be used to start a computer after the primary disk of a mirrored volume. (A mirrored volume is volumes or partitions located on two different hard drives with duplicate information.) If one hard drive fails, the computer does not go down because the information can be read from the second disk. The start-up disk cannot be used for incorrect or corrupted device drivers or start-up problems that occur after NTLDR.

To create a boot disk, follow these steps:

1. Format a disk on a computer running Windows 2000 or Windows Server 2003 family operating systems. Since DOS and Windows 9X use different formats and boot sections, do not format with DOS or Windows 9X.
2. For an Intel machine, save NTLDR, NTDETECT.COM, NTBOOTDD.SYS (if you have an SCSI controller without an SCSI BIOS), and BOOT.INI file from the system partition to the floppy disk.
3. Test the boot files.

If using a mirrored volume, you should have two start-up floppy disks, one on which the ARC path points to the first disk and the second on which the ARC path points to the second disk. Therefore, after creating the second disk, you will need to modify the BOOT.INI file manually using a text editor such as EDIT or Notepad.

8.6   SHUTDOWN EVENT TRACKER

Shutdown Event Tracker provides a simple and standard mechanism you can use to consistently document the reasons for shutting down or restarting your computer. You can use this information to analyze the root causes of shutdowns and develop a more complete understanding of your system environment. The Shutdown Event Tracker is available in the Windows Server 2003 family operating systems and is enabled by default for the servers.

To record a shutdown or restart reason, enter it into the Shut Down Windows dialog box. The Shut Down Windows dialog box is displayed as part of the shutdown sequence, or when restarting a system after a sudden shutdown. Windows provides predefined reason options. You can also add customized reasons. The information you provide here is recorded in the system log in Event Viewer.

To enable or disable Shutdown Event Tracker, you can edit the registry or use the Group Policies feature. When editing the registry, change the HKEY_LOCAL_MACHINE\SOFTWARE\Microsoft\ Windows\CurrentVersion\Reliability\ShutdownReasonUI to 1 to enable and 0 to disable. To enable it using the local group policy, you need to execute the GPEDIT.MSC command. You then navigate to the Display Shutdown Event Tracker policy (under Local Policy, open Computer Configuration, open Administrative Templates, and select System) and double-click it. From there, you can enable or disable it. You can also enable or disable Shutdown Event Tracker on a domain or organizational unit using other group policies. The registry will be explained in Chapter 9 and group policies will be explained in Chapter 13.

A related command-line tool, Shutdown (SHUTDOWN.EXE) enables you to shut down the computer from the command line. By using the –d parameter, Shutdown also enables you to record shutdown reasons to the System log. Another related tool, Event Query (EVENTQUERY.VBS) enables you to search the System log on one or more computers for shutdown information, and save the output to a file for further evaluation. For more information about Shutdown Event Tracker and the Shutdown command-line tool, click Tools in Help and Support Center.

8.7   WINDOWS LOGON

To log on to a computer that is running Windows 2000 or Windows Server 2003, a user provides a user name and password. See Figure 8.10. Windows authenticates the user during the logon process to verify the identity of the user. Only valid users can gain access to resources and data on a

Figure 8.10   Logon dialog box

FIGURE 8.11   Security dialog box

computer or the network. In addition, depending on the situation, you can specify the domain name or computer name in the "Log on to:" text box. Note that the user name is not case sensitive, but the password is case sensitive.

There are two forms of logging on, logging on locally to the computer (sometimes known as interactively) and logging on remotely to another computer. A user can log on locally to a computer that is a member of a workgroup or to a computer that is a member of a domain, but is not a domain controller, and if it selects the computer name in the "Log on to:" text box. A domain controller does not maintain a local security database; therefore, local user accounts are not available on domain controllers, and a user cannot log on locally to one.

8.8   WINDOWS SECURITY DIALOG BOX

The Security dialog box provides information such as the user account currently logged on and the domain or computer to which the user is logged on. To access the Windows Security dialog box, press the Ctrl+Alt+Delete keys. See Figure 8.11. As shown, the screen indicates who you are logged as and when you logged on.

On the dialog box are six buttons. The Log Off button allows you to log off the system without restarting or shutting down the computer. The Shutdown button allows you to shut down or reboot the computer. The Log Off button and the Shutdown button close all running programs. The Lock Workstation button allows you to secure the computer without logging off. All programs remain running. For security reasons, if you are leaving your computer alone, either lock your workstation or log off. The Task Manager button brings up the Task Manager dialog box. See Figures 8.12 and 8.13. **Task Manager** provides a list of the current programs that are running and the overall CPU (including number of threads and processes) and memory usage (including the amount of physical memory, size of the file cache, paged memory, and nonpaged memory). Task Manager also switches between programs and stops a program that is not responding. A new feature of Windows server, called kill process tree utility, is its ability to end all processes related to the one being terminated by the administrator.

Figure 8.12 Task Manager showing applications and processes running in memory

Figure 8.13 Performance tab of the Task Manager showing processor utilization and memory, utilization, including the system cache

8.9   RUNNING PROGRAMS

Windows will run Win32 applications (such as Microsoft Office 97 and Office 2000), Win16 applications (programs written for Windows 3.xx), and DOS applications.

8.9.1   DOS Applications

DOS programs run in a special Win32-based application called the NT Virtual DOS machine (NTVDM). The NTVDM provides a simulated MS-DOS environment for MS-DOS–based applications. In addition, since each NTVDM has a single thread and its own address space, if one NTVDM fails, no other NTVDM is affected.

To customize an NTVDM for an MS-DOS–based application, go to the application file name and select Properties from the shortcut menu to create a program information file (PIF) for the MS-DOS application. The PIF describes how the DOS program will run under the Windows environment. These settings include specifying memory settings, screen settings, and customized CONFIG.NT and AUTOEXEC.NT files for DOS applications. See Figures 8.14, 8.15, and 8.16.

To create customized CONFIG.NT and AUTOEXEC.NT files, follow these steps.

1. Use a text edit such as Notepad or EDIT to edit the CONFIG.NT or AUTOEXEC.NT files located in the systemroot\SYSTEM32 directory.
2. Save each file with a new name.
3. Right-click on the MS-DOS–based program shortcut and select the Properties option.
4. Click on the Program tab and select Advanced button.
5. Under Custom MS-DOS–based program initialization files, type the new name for your custom start files.

If Windows displays an error message concerning the CONFIG.NT or AUTOEXEC.NT or if you have problems running MS-DOS–based programs, check the CONFIG.NT or AUTOEXEC.NT files for the particular program that you are trying to run.

You can switch between a full screen or DOS window by pressing the Alt+Enter keys. If an application cannot run in a DOS VM because the application requires full access to the computer's resources or the application has video problems, you would run the application in DOS mode.

Figure 8.14   Modifying the PIF settings of a DOS program

Figure 8.15 Screen and Misc tab within the properties of a DOS program in Windows 2000

Figure 8.16 Memory settings for a DOS program

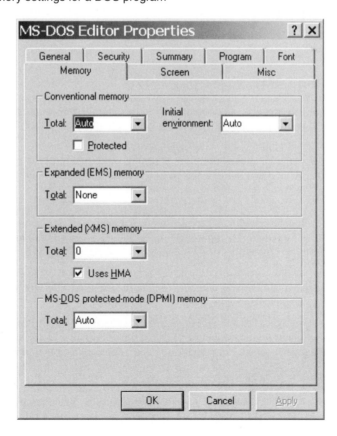

If you're trying to free up a lot of lower memory for a DOS program, specify different AUTOEXEC.BAT and CONFIG.SYS commands for each application by using the Advanced button in the Program tab.

If the DOS application that you are running appears scrambled while running Windows, remember that some legacy DOS applications can only run in 256-color mode. Therefore, set the video adapter to 256 colors. In addition, you can try to run the DOS application in full-screen mode.

8.9.2   Win16-Based Applications

Win16-based applications are executed by Win16 on Win32 (WOW) which translates, or thunks, 16-bit calls to 32-bit calls. Since Win16-based applications use cooperative multitasking, Win16-based applications in Windows cannot take advantage of preemptive multitasking. Instead, by default, the Win16-based applications share the same memory area and will all be assigned a single time slice. Unfortunately, if a program causes problems, it can cause all Win16-based applications to crash. However, all of the Win16-based applications are run preemptive with Windows 32-based applications and other Windows processes, which improves the performance of Win16-based applications.

To start a Win16-bit application in its one separate memory space, you can do one of the following:

- At the command prompt, type START /SEPARATE filename.
- On the Start menu, select the Open option from the Start button and select the Run in Separate Memory Space option.
- Create a shortcut and select the Run command in Separate Memory Space option found on the Properties shortcut tab.
- In Windows NT Explorer, select Options from the View menu, select the File Types tab, and click on the Win16 applications to be edited. Click on Edit and double-click on Open. Edit the open line to include the separate switch using the following syntax:

```
Cmd /c start /separate path\application_executable %1
```

While running multiple NTVDMs for 16-bit applications, there are some disadvantages. First, starting Win16 applications in their own memory spaces introduces additional overhead. In addition, if Win16-based applications do not follow the OLE and DDE specifications, they cannot communicate with other NTVDMs.

8.9.3   Sharing Data

To share data between documents, Windows applications can use dynamic data exchange (DDE) or object linking and embedding (OLE). DDE was introduced with Windows 3.0 to allow users to copy data between applications while maintaining a link. Whenever data were changed at the source, they were also changed at the target. For example, you could insert an Excel chart into a Word document. As the spreadsheet data changes, the chart in the document changes. Although DDE is still used by many applications, it is, slowly being replaced by OLE.

OLE (enhanced version of DDE) is a compound document standard developed by Microsoft. It allows you to create objects with one application and then link or embed objects into another application. Embedded objects keep their original format and link to the application that created them. For example, you could insert an Excel chart into a Word document. To make changes to the chart, you would double-click on the chart from within the Word document and Excel would run from within the Word document. This would allow you to make changes without going to the Program Manager and starting Excel in its own window.

A common way to move data between applications or documents is to use the clipboard. When you highlight the text or select a picture and you use the Copy or Cut function from the Edit menu in the source application, the text and picture go into RAM, specifically to the clipboard.

When you move to the target document, choose Paste from the Edit menu. The source application copies the data in the clipboard into the current document using the first available format. If you choose Paste Special from the Edit menu, a dialog box appears, which lists the formats from which you can choose for pasting the data. If you choose Paste Link, the application tries to make an OLE link to the source document. If the ObjectLink format is not available, a DDE link is created instead.

If you press the Print Screen button on your keyboard, you can place a bitmap picture of the entire screen to the clipboard. If you press Alt+Print Screen, the active bitmap picture is placed onto the clipboard.

8.9.4   Program Compatibility Wizard

Most programs run properly on the Windows 2000 and Windows Server 2003 families. The exceptions are some older games and other programs that were written specifically for an earlier version of Windows. Starting with Windows XP and extended to the Windows Server 2003 family, Windows has a Program Compatibility wizard to configure Windows to run a program under an older Windows environment. For example, say you have a program for Windows 95 that will run under Windows 9X, but will not run under Windows 2000 or Windows XP. Under Windows XP and the Windows Server 2003 family, you can configure Windows to run that program under the Windows 95 environment. The wizard also allows you to try different settings, such as switching the display to 256 colors and the screen resolution to 640×480 pixels. See Figure 8.17.

To start the Program Compatibility wizard, right-click the executable file that you are using to start the program, select Properties, and select the Compatibility tab. Enable the "Run this program in compatibility mode for:" option, and select the appropriate operating system environment.

Figure 8.17   Windows Program Compatibility wizard

SUMMARY

1. Windows 2000 and Windows Server 2003 operating systems that can function as a desktop operating system, network file print server, or application server.

2. Windows 2000, Windows Server 2003, and Windows XP use a different architecture, which offers higher performance and greater reliability and provides better security than DOS/Windows 3.xx and Windows 9X. Unfortunately, to achieve these benefits Windows 2000, Windows Server 2003, and Windows XP are not 100% backward compatible with all hardware and software.

3. To install Windows 2000 Professional, you should have a minimum of 133 MHz, 64 MB of RAM, and 650 MB of free disk space running on a Pentium processor.

4. To install Windows 2000 Server, you should have a minimum of 133 MHz, 128 MB of RAM, and 1 GB of free disk running on a Pentium processor.

5. Windows 2000 Professional supports up to 2 processors and 4 GB of RAM.

6. Windows 2000 Server supports up to 4 processors and 4 GB of RAM.

7. Advanced Server supports up to 8 processors and 8 GB of RAM.

8. Windows 2000 Datacenter supports up to 32 processors and 64 GB of RAM.

9. To make sure that you know what hardware is compatible with Windows 2000, you should only use devices that are on Microsoft's Hardware Compatibility List (HCL).

10. Windows Server 2003 includes four editions: Standard, Enterprise, Datacenter, and Web.

11. The client for the Windows Server 2003 is Windows XP.

12. There are two versions of Windows XP: Windows XP Home and Windows XP Professional.

13. To install or upgrade Windows 2000, use WINNT.EXE file or WINNT32.EXE, both of which are located in the I386 directory on the Windows 2000 installation CD.

14. WINNT.EXE should be used for a clean installation on a computer running Microsoft DOS or Microsoft Windows 3.xx.

15. WINNT32.EXE should be used on a clean installation or upgrade on a computer running Microsoft Windows NT version 4.0, Microsoft Windows 95, or Microsoft Windows 98.

16. Windows 2000, Windows Server 2003, and Windows XP support FAT, FAT32, and NTFS.

17. A software license typically allows an individual or a group to use a piece of software.

18. There are two kinds of client access licenses (CAL): per-seat licensing and per-server licensing.

19. After installing Windows, you should check to see if Microsoft has released any fixes, patches, or service packs. Be sure to apply those fixes or patches to the Windows system.

20. To prepare for the possibility of a system failure on a computer that cannot be started from the CD-ROM drive, you need to create a set of Windows setup floppy disks so you can start the setup program, the recovery console, and the emergency repair process.

21. To create the Windows 2000 setup floppy disk, use MAKEBT32.EXE, which is located in the BOOTDISK directory on the installation CD.

22. Switches are customization options added to WINNT.EXE or WINNT32.EXE commands to modify the network installation.

23. The hardware abstraction layer (HAL) is a library of hardware manipulating routines that hide the hardware interface details.

24. The Windows Setup Manager wizard allows you to create an answer file and uniqueness database file (UDF), which can be used as scripts when using the WINNT command to do automated installations.

25. The remote installation service (RIS) enables client computers to connect to a server during the initial start-up phase and remotely install Windows.

26. To install and use RIS, you must have DNS, DHCP, and Active Directory on the network. The drive on the server must be formatted with NTFS in which case you cannot install RIS on the same drive or partition as the Windows server.

27. The System Difference (SYSDIFF.EXE) tool enables you to automatically distribute and install applications and limited hardware devices during or after the Windows setup.

28. Windows uses a security identifier (SID) to uniquely identify the computer, even if the computer name has been changed.

29. Windows has the System Preparation Tool (SYSPREP.EXE) that will remove the security identifiers and all other user-specific or computer-specific information so that you can install disk images on several systems without them all having the same SID.

30. User mode programs run in ring 3 of the Intel 386 microprocessor protection model are protected by the operating system. It is a less privileged processor mode that has no direct access to hardware and can only access its own address space.

31. The kernel mode components (sometimes referred to as privileged mode) run in ring 0 of the Intel 386 microprocessor protection model. The kernel mode components are protected by the microprocessor.

32. A kernel is the central module of an operating system.

33. The Microkernel is the central part of Windows, which coordinates all I/O functions and synchronizes the activities of the executive services.

34. Device drivers are programs that control a device. A device driver acts as a translator between the device and programs that use the device.

35. Most drivers used by Windows 2000 use the Windows Driver Model (WDM), which is also compatible with Windows 98.

36. A program, sometimes referred to as a process, is an executable program that follows a sequence of steps.

37. A thread is part of a program that can execute independently of other parts.

38. Windows is a preemptive multitasking operating system.

39. Preemptive multitasking occurs when the operating system assigns time slices to threads, tasks, and applications.

Threads, tasks, and applications with a higher priority get a larger time slice.

40. The file that makes up virtual memory in Windows NT, Windows Server 2003, and Windows XP Windows 2000 is called a paging file (PAGEFILE.SYS).

41. The Windows NT, Windows 2000, Windows Server 2003, and Windows XP memory model is based on a flat, linear 32-bit address space, which is managed by the Virtual Memory Manager (VMM).

42. The process of moving data in and out of physical memory is called paging.

43. Interprocess Communication (IPC) allows bidirectional communication between clients and servers using distributed applications. IPC is a mechanism used by programs and multiprocesses.

44. During boot up, the first Windows file read is NTLDR, which switches the microprocessor from real mode to protected mode and starts the appropriate minifile system drivers.

45. NTLDR reads the BOOT.INI (if one is available) and displays the Boot Loader Operating System Selection menu.

46. NTLDR runs NTDETECT.COM, which attempts to detect the bus/adapter type, serial ports, floating-point coprocessor, floppy disks, keyboard, mouse/pointing device, parallel ports, SCSI adapters, and video adapters.

47. The active partition that contains the NTLDR and BOOT.INI file is known as the system partition.

48. The partition that contains the Windows operating system files is called the boot partition.

49. The default directory for Windows 2000 is C:\WINNT and the default directory for Windows Server 2003 is C:\WINDOWS.

50. An ARC (advanced RISC computing) path is used to specify the location (partition) of an operating system.

51. If you press the F8 key while the Windows boot menu is listed, the advanced boot menu displays.

52. Windows authenticates the user during the logon process to verify the identity of the user. Only valid users can gain access to resources and data on a computer or the network.

53. There are two forms of logging on: logging on locally to the computer (sometimes known as interactively) and logging on remotely to another computer.

54. Windows can run WIN16, WIN32, DOS, OS/2, and POSIX applications.

55. To share data between documents, Windows applications can use dynamic data exchange (DDE) or object linking and embedding (OLE).

56. Windows XP and Windows Server 2003 include a Program Compatibility wizard so that Windows can run software that was made to run under an older version of Windows.

57. A Windows start-up floppy disk is used to access a drive with a faulty start-up sequence.

QUESTIONS

1. What are the minimum requirements to run Windows 2000 Professional?
   a. Pentium processor—133 MHz, 32 MB of RAM, and 650 of free disk space
   b. Pentium processor—133 MHz, 64 MB of RAM, and 1 GB free disk space
   c. Pentium processor—166 MHz, 64 MB of RAM, and 650 MB of free disk space
   d. Pentium processor—233 MHz, 128 MB of RAM, and 1 GB of free disk space
   e. Pentium II processor—233 MHz, 128 MB of RAM, and 2 GB of free disk space

2. What are the minimum requirements to run Windows 2000 Server?
   a. Pentium processor—133 MHz, 64 MB of RAM, and 650 of free disk space
   b. Pentium processor—133 MHz, 128 MB of RAM, and 1 GB free disk space
   c. Pentium processor—166 MHz, 64 MB of RAM, and 650 MB of free disk space
   d. Pentium processor—233 MHz, 128 MB of RAM, and 1 GB of free disk space
   e. Pentium II processor—233 MHz, 256 MB of RAM, and 2 GB of free disk space

3. Which of the following statements are not true? (Choose all that apply.)
   a. Windows 2000 Professional can support only 1 processor.
   b. Windows 2000 Server can support up to 4 processors.
   c. Windows 2000 Advanced Server can support up to 8 processors.
   d. Windows 2000 Datacenter can support up to 16 processors.

4. You just installed Windows 2000 on a computer on which Windows NT was installed. Unfortunately, some of the components are not being detected by Windows 2000. What should you do?
   a. Try to install it again.
   b. Make sure that the hardware devices are on the compatibility list.
   c. Reformat the system and reinstall.
   d. Make sure that you have the newest BIOS.

5. To install Windows 2000, you would use the _____ command.
   a. INSTALL   c. WINNT
   b. SETUP   d. START

6. Which of the following statements are true. (Select all that apply.)
   a. If you have Windows 98, you can upgrade to Windows 2000 Professional.
   b. If you have Windows 98, you can upgrade to Windows 2000 Server.
   c. If you have Windows NT Server Enterprise edition, you can upgrade to Windows 2000 Advanced Server.
   d. If you have Windows NT Server, you can upgrade to Windows 2000 Advanced Server.
   e. If you have Windows 2000 Server, you can upgrade to Windows 2000 Advanced Server.

7. If you have many servers for your workplace with over 200 users, you should choose which type of license?
   a. per server
   b. per seat
   c. single
   d. multiple

8. True or False: You just bought a copy of Windows 2000 Server and you cannot wait to get it installed. Since it is brand-new, you don't have to worry about fixes, patches, or service packs.

9. To repair your computer, you sometimes need to use the four Windows 2000 Setup disks. How do you make the setup disks?
   a. Use the /B command with the WINNT command.
   b. Use the /OX command with the WINNT command.
   c. Use the BOOTDISK.EXE command.
   d. Use the MAKEBOOT.EXE command.
   e. Use the Add/Remove software applet in the Control Panel.

10. Which of the following procedures will allow you to install Windows 2000 Professional over the network onto an MS-DOS computer?
    a. booting the MS-DOS computer from the network installation start-up disk and running SETUP.EXE from the command prompt
    b. connecting to the network directory that contains the Windows NT installation files and running WINNT.EXE
    c. connecting to the network directory that contains the Windows 2000 installation files and running SETUP.EXE
    d. connecting to the network directory that contains the Windows 2000 installation files and running WINNT32.EXE

11. When using the WINNT32 command, which switch would you use to check your system for incompatibilities that might prevent a proper installation?
    a. /HELP
    b. /CHECKUPGRADE-ONLY
    c. /C
    d. /MAKELOCAL-SOURCE

12. What acts as a translator between hardware and the Windows 2000 operating system specific to the computer architecture?
    a. device drivers
    b. TSRs
    c. ACPI
    d. HAL
    e. Kernel
    f. Microkernel

13. If you get an Inaccessible Boot Device error, what is most likely the cause of the problem?
    a. Your controller is not supported because you do not have the proper driver specified.
    b. There is a read error from the installation CD.
    c. There is a write error on the installation target.
    d. You do not have enough disk space in your installation target.

14. If you get a media error during installation of Windows 2000, what is most likely the cause of the problem?
    a. Your controller is not supported because you do not have the proper driver specified.
    b. There is a read error from the installation CD.
    c. There is a write error on the installation target.
    d. You do not have enough disk space for your installation target.

15. What do you use to create the answer files and UDFs so that you can do automated installations?
    a. WINNT /U:namefile1 /UDF:*id*
    b. Use the Add/Remove software applet in the Control Panel.
    c. Use the Windows 2000 Setup Manager wizard from the Windows NT installation CD.
    d. Use the Windows 2000 Setup Manager wizard from the Resource Kit.

16. You would like to use RIS to install Windows 2000 Professional on a client computer. How would you create a network boot disk?
    a. WINNT/B
    b. WINNT32/R
    c. RBFG.EXE
    d. RISDISK.EXE
    e. RISETUP.EXE

17. Which of the following services are needed to use RIS? (Choose all that apply.)
    a. DHCP
    b. WINS
    c. DNS
    d. active directory
    e. NetBIOS

18. You want to automate the installation of Windows NT workstation on 200 identical laptop computers and 50 identical desktop computers. What is the minimum number of answer files and UDF files required to complete this installation?
    a. 1 answer file and 2 UDF files
    b. 2 answer files and 1 UDF file
    c. 2 answer files and 250 UDF files
    d. 250 answer files and 2 UDF files

19. Suppose you are responsible for installing Windows 2000 Professional on 75 identical desktop computers and 25 identical laptop computers. Your company's network consists of a single domain, Corp.

    Required result:
    You must automate the installation of Windows 2000 Professional on the 100 computers.

    Optional desired results:
    You want to automate the installation of a standard suite of Win32-based applications. You want to configure all computers to join the Acme domain during the installation of Windows 2000 Workstation.

    Proposed solution:
    Create two answer files, one for each hardware platform. Add "OemPreinstall=Yes" to the [Unattended] section. Add "JoinDomain=ACME" to the [Network] section. Create a UDF with a section for each computer that specifies the user name and computer name. Install Windows 2000 Professional on a reference computer. Run SYSDIFF.EXE /SNAP to take a snapshot of the reference computer. Install the applications on the reference computer, then run SYSDIFF.EXE /DIFF to create the difference file. Add the command SYSDIFF.EXE /APPLY to the OEM\Cmd-lines.Txt file. Start installation of Windows NT Workstation on the computers by specifying the appropriate answer file and the UDF in the WINNT.EXE command.

    Which result does the proposed solution produce?
    a. The proposed solution produces the required result and produces both of the optional desired results.

b. The proposed solution produces the required result and produces only one of the optional desired results.

c. The proposed solution produces the required result but does not produce either of the optional desired results.

d. The proposed solution does not produce the required result.

20. You want to use a disk imaging software package to create several Windows 2000 computers with the same configuration. What command will allow you to do that?

a. SYSDIFF   c. WINN32 /WALKER

b. WINDIFF   d. SYSPREP

21. Which of the following types of applications does Windows 2000 *not* support?

a. bounded OS/2 applications

b. Macintosh applications

c. WIN32 applications

d. DOS applications

e. POSIX applications

22. _____ is a less-privileged mode that has no direct access to hardware and can only access its own address space.

a. User mode   c. Isolated mode

b. Protected mode   d. Kernel mode

23. What is the central part of the operating system?

a. kernel   c. device drivers

b. boot files   d. compilers

24. Another name for a process is a_____.

a. thread   c. task

b. program   d. suite of programs

25. Which of the following best describes the relationship between processes and threads?

a. Each process consists of at least a single thread.

b. Each process consists of only one thread.

c. Each process consists of two or more threads.

d. Each process consists of two threads—one for input, the other for output.

26. What is the smallest unit that can be scheduled with the Microkernel?

a. thread   c. queue

b. process   d. segment

27. All memory in Windows 2000 is managed by the

a. kernel   c. VMM

b. Microkernel   d. process manager

28. Windows 2000 primarily uses _____ multitasking.

a. cooperating   c. task switching

b. preemptive   d. context switching

29. Windows 2000 Server supports only _____ of RAM.

a. 2 GB   d. 16 GB

b. 4 GB   e. 32 GB

c. 8 GB

30. To speed disk access, the _____ , which is a subset of the physical memory, is set aside to retain recently used information.

a. virtual memory   c. L2 cache

b. system cache   d. IPC

31. Which statement best describes how 16-bit Windows applications are run by default on a Windows NT Workstation computer?

a. 16-bit Windows applications are run as a single thread in a single NTVDM with a shared address space.

b. 16-bit Windows applications are run as a single thread in a single NTVDM with separate address spaces.

c. 16-bit Windows applications are run as separate threads in a single NTVDM with a shared address space.

d. 16-bit Windows applications are run as separate threads in a single NTVDM with separate address spaces.

e. 16-bit Windows applications are run as separate threads in separate NTVDMs with separate address spaces.

32. What function do the AUTOEXEC.NT and CONFIG.NT files serve?

a. They contain the set of commands that need to be executed to start Windows NT.

b. They contain the set of commands that need to be executed to start the Win16 NTVDM.

c. They provide a location to load files required to run Windows 16-bit applications.

d. They act as backup files for the AUTOEXEC.BAT and CONFIG.SYS files used to boot Windows NT.

33. Your friend Pat has a computer with Windows 2000 Professional that will not start. You format a blank disk using Windows 2000 and copy NTLDR, NTDETECT.COM, NTBOOTDD.SYS, and BOOT.INI from your computer that has Windows 2000 Professional to the floppy disk. Your computer has Windows 2000 load from your D drive. When you try to boot Pat's computer using this disk, you receive the following error message:

```
Windows NT could not start because the
following file is missing or corrupt:
\Winnt Root\System32\Ntoskrnl.Exe.
Please reinstall a copy of the above
file.
```

What should you do to correct this problem?

a. Use Windows 2000 Backup program to restore the registry on Pat's computer.

b. Copy the NTOSKRNL.EXE file from the bootable floppy to the root directory on Pat's computer.

c. Copy NTLDR, NTDETECT.COM, NTBOOTDD.SYS, and BOOT.INI from the bootable floppy to the root directory of the primary partition on Charlie's computer.

d. Edit the BOOT.INI file on the bootable floppy to specify the correct ARC path name to the Windows 2000 boot partition on Pat's computer.

34. Which one of the following statements describes limitations of MS-DOS applications running on Windows NT?

a. They cannot share memory space.

b. They cannot be preemptively multitasked.

c. They cannot be started with different priorities other than NORMAL.

d. They cannot be selectively terminated using Task Manager.

35. Your computer is configured to dual boot between Windows 2000 Professional and Windows 98. You are trying to boot to Windows 98, and you receive the following error message:

```
Non-System disk or disk error
Replace and press any key when ready.
```

Which one of the following is the most likely cause of the problem?

a. The NTLDR file is missing.

b. The NTDETECT.COM file is missing.

c. The BOOTSECT.DOS file is missing.

d. The BOOT.INI file is missing.

e. The BOOT.INI file is using the wrong ARC path.

36. Your Windows NT Server computer contains two IDE disks on the same controller card. Each disk contains only one primary partition. The Windows NT Server operating system is located on the first hard disk, and the boot files are located on the second hard disk. Which of the following is the correct ARC name for the system partition?

a. multi(0)disk(1)rdisk(0)partition(1)

b. multi(0)disk(0)rdisk(1)partition(1)

c. multi(0)disk(0)rdisk(0)partition(0)

d. multi(1)disk(1)rdisk(1)partition(1)

e. multi(1)disk(1)rdisk(0)partition(0)

37. Which of the following ARC names correctly indicates that the Windows NT boot files are located on the third partition on an SCSI disk with BIOS disabled, whose target ID is zero on the first SCSI controller?

a. scsi(0)disk(0)rdisk(0)partition(2)

b. scsi(0)disk(0)rdisk(0)partition(3)

c. scsi(0)card(0)disk(0)partition(2)

d. scsi(1)card(1)disk(1)partition(3)

38. The system and boot partitions have failed on the PDC. Fortunately, you are using disk mirroring on the PDC. How do you now modify the BOOT.INI file on your boot floppy disk so that the system will be started from the mirror partition?

a. Add the /2 switch to the end of the appropriate line in the [Boot Loader] section.

b. Modify the NTFS drive path and file name specifications in the [Boot Loader] section.

c. Modify the ARC path name specifications in the [Operating Systems] section.

d. The BOOT.INI file does not need to be modified as NTDETECT.COM will detect the change.

39. Your computer is configured to dual boot between Windows 98 and Windows 2000 Professional. However, your computer is only able to boot to Windows 98 and the boot menu never appears on the screen when you start the computer. What is the most likely cause of the problem?

a. The NTLDR file is corrupt.

b. The master boot record on the disk has been overwritten.

c. The timeout value in the BOOT.INI file is set to zero.

d. An entry has been added to the CONFIG.NT file to force the system to boot to Windows 98.

40. What allows us to use specialized programs to create a document by using objects from one program and inserting them into another program?

a. OLE   c. networks

b. multitasking   d. IFSHLP.SYS

41. Within the Windows 2000 architecture, user mode is made of which two components? (Select two answers.)

a. environment subsystems   c. integral subsystem

b. internal subsystems   d. VMM

42. Windows 2000 uses what type of multitasking?

a. symmetric   c. asymmetric

b. 32 bit   d. 64 bit

43. Which WINNT32 switch would you use if you wanted to mark the installation partition as active after the copying has finished?

a. /ACTIVE   c. BOOTSECTOR

b. /SYSPART   d. /SYSTEM

44. Which of the following components are installed by default on Windows 2000 Server? (Choose all that apply.)

a. Internet information server (IIS)

b. MicroSoft Script Debugger

c. certificate services

d. terminal services

45. You need to install Windows 2000 Professional on 300 computers for a customer company called the Acme Corporation. The computers have different manufacturers and different hardware abstraction layers (HALs). You plan to use a Windows 2000 Server computer running RIS to perform the installation. After the installation is complete for the first 25 computers, users of those computers report problems. You discover that the latest Windows 2000 service pack resolves those problems. You want to apply the service pack to the remaining 275 computers during the installation. What should you do?

a. Install the service pack on a reference Windows 2000 Professional computer, then run the RIPREP command on that computer. Use the resulting image for RIS.

b. Install the service pack on the RIS server, then run the RIPREP command on that server. Use the resulting image for RIS.

c. Copy the service pack to the CD-based image shared folder used by RIS.

d. Slipstream the service pack into a new i386 distribution shared folder, then run the RISETUP command to create a new CD-based image for the RIS server.

46. Which of the following is *not* required to use RIS to install a system?

a. DNS

b. DHCP

c. WINS

d. Active Directory

e. RIS must be installed on an NTFS partition.

f. RIS must not be installed on the same drive or partition as Windows.

47. Your are the administrator for your company's network. You are deploying Windows 2000 on your network of 10,500 users. There are 15 departments in your company. Each department needs to use specific features of Windows 2000 and customize third-party applications. You want to minimize the administrative time required to set up the clients' computers. You also want to provide customized software installations to the users. What should you do?

a. Install and configure a RIS server on your network. Use RIPREP.EXE to create multiple images for each department. Connect the client computers to the RIS server and deploy the custom images.

b. Install and configure a RIS server on your network. Create different installation script files for each department. Deploy the computers by using RIS.

c. Create a shared folder on one of the servers. Copy the source files from Windows 2000 Professional CD-ROM to the shared folder. Perform unattended installations from a shared folder by using script files, then install the third-party applications.

d. Create a shared folder on one of the servers. Copy the source files from Windows 2000 Professional CD-ROM to the shared folder. Perform attended installations from the shared folder, and then select only the components you need for each department.

48. Your company is deploying Windows 2000 Professional on a network of 300 computers. The network has two Windows 2000 server computers. You have only enough Windows 2000 Professional licenses for 250 users. You need to restrict the department so that Windows 2000 Professional can be installed only on the licensed computers. You will need to minimize user intervention during the deployment and centralize the installation files. What should you do?

a. Create a shared folder on one of the servers. Copy the source files from the Windows 2000 Professional CD-ROM to the shared folder. Allow users to perform attended installations from the shared folder only on the licensed computers.

b. Install RIS on one of the servers. Create user accounts for all the licensed users. Configure the RIS server to accept the connections from only known computers. Perform unattended installations for all connecting computers.

c. Create a shared folder on one of the servers. Restrict access to the share so that only 250 users can connect. Copy the source files from the Windows 2000 Professional CD-ROM to the shared folder. Allow users to perform unattended installation from the shared folder.

d. Install RIS on one of the servers. Create computer accounts in the domain for only the licensed computers. Configure the RIS server to accept connections from only known computers. Perform unattended installations from the shared computers.

49. Your company's network consists of a single Windows 2000 domain. You are a member of the domain admins group. You install a Windows 2000 member server and then install RIS on the member server. You enable the RIS server to respond to client computers. You successfully load a CD-based image on the server. You attempt to initiate a RIS session on your first PXE-compliant client computer, but your RIS server does not respond to the request. You want to ensure that the RIS server responds to client computers. What should you do?

a. Install DNS on the RIS server.

b. Install WINS on the RIS server.

c. Authorize the RIS server.

d. Assign the RIS server an address by means of DHCP.

e. Add a reservation for each client computer on the DHCP server.

50. You are using RIS to deploy Windows 2000 Professional on 1500 computers split between two subnets divided with a router. You have four RIS servers. You have deployed 100 computers. Some of the RIS servers are overworked and respond too slowly for the timely deployment of your

computers. You need more consistent performance results before you deploy the remaining computers. What should you do?

a. Create computer accounts for all the computers. Complete the Managed By property for each account.

b. Create one organizational unit (OU) for each segment. Add user accounts for all the users to the appropriate OUs. Specify the appropriate RIS server in the Log On To property for each user's account.

c. Create prestaged computer accounts for all the computers. Specify which RIS server will control each computer.

d. Create one site for each segment. Move two RIS servers to each site.

51. You are the administrator of a Windows 2000 domain named the Acme Corporation. You install RIS on the server. You are using RIS to install 35 new client computers. When you start a test client computer, the Client Installation wizard does not appear. You are using network adapter cards that are not PXE-compliant. You want to connect to the RIS server. What should you do next?

a. From a command prompt, run RBFG.EXE to create RIS a boot disk.

b. Identify the globally unique identifier (GUID) of each client computer.

c. Set up a DHCP Relay Agent.

d. Install Windows 2000 on the test client computer. Run RIPREP.EXE from a network share on the RIS server.

52. You need to install Windows 2000 Professional on 30 new computers. You also need to deploy a Windows 2000 Professional service pack during the installation. First, you create a network distribution folder named Install-Files. You copy the i386 folder from the Windows 2000 Professional CD to the InstallFiles folder. What should you do next?

a. Copy the service pack files to the InstallFiles\Misc folder.

b. Copy the service pack files to the InstallFiles\OEM folder.

c. From an existing client computer, run the update –u command from the service pack to the InstallFiles folder.

d. From an existing client computer, run the Update –s: InstallFiles command from the service pack to the InstallFiles folder.

53. You are a help desk technician for your company, which is in the process of deploying Windows XP Professional to all client computers. You upgrade Pat's Windows 98 portable computer to Windows XP Professional. After the upgrade, Pat reports that some of his older software applications no longer work properly. Also, one of the hardware devices on his computer is not currently supported by Windows XP Professional. Pat requests that you reinstall Windows 98 and all of his applications so that he can use his computer normally. You need to restore Pat's computer to its preupgraded state while retaining all of the applications, documents, and personal data on the computer. You want to accomplish this task in the minimum amount of time. What should you do?

a. Copy Pat's documents and personal data to a shared folder on the network. Reinstall Windows 98 and

Pat's applications. Copy the documents and personal data to the My Documents folder on Pat's computer.

b. On Pat's computer, run SETUP.EXE from a Windows 98 installation CD.

c. On Pat's computer, use the Add or Remove Programs wizard to remove the Windows XP Professional installation item.

d. On Pat's computer, use a third-party, disk-imaging software utility to apply a disk image that contains Windows 98 and Pat's applications.

54. You need to install Windows 2000 Professional on 35 new computers on the company LAN. First, you create a distribution folder on the network server. Then you create a network boot disk to install Windows 2000 Professional from the distribution folder. Now you need to create a batch file, which the network boot disk will execute to start the installation. You must specify a source path and temporary drive for the installation files. You also need to install the accessibility options within the batch file. The batch file must execute a hardware-specific application to run after the GUI-mode setup has completed. Which command must you specify in the batch file?

a. Z:\i386\winnt/s:z:\i386/t:d/a/e:z:\hardware\setup.exe

b. Z:\i386\winnt/s:z:\i386/rwinnt.tmp/a/e:z \hardware\setup.exe

c. Z:\i386\winnt32/s:z:\i386/tempdrive:d/cmd:z\ hardware\setup.exe

d. Z:\i386\winnt32/s:z:\i386/cmdcons:z:\ hardware\setup/makelocalsource

55. You are preparing to install Windows 2000 Professional on 100 MPS-compliant computers. Each computer has two 750 MHz processors. The computers are configured identically. You want to use one of the computers as a reference computer for deploying Windows 2000 Professional to the remaining computers. You install Windows 2000 Professional on the reference computer. You view the Device Manager and notice that the drivers for the second processor are not installed. You want to add support for the second processor and the remaining 99 computers. You want to do this with least amount of administrative effort. What should you do?

a. Use Setup Manager to configure the reference computer, then create a disk image.

b. Use the system preparation tool with the -pnp parameter to set up the reference disk, then create the disk image.

c. Use Device Manager to add the appropriate hardware abstraction layer to the reference computer to support the second processor, then create a disk image.

d. After imaging the reference computer, restart the reference computer in safe mode and add the driver for the second processor.

56. Your Windows 2000 Professional computer is configured to support two monitors. You install a DOS-based application on your computer. The application uses the Windows 2000 Professional default settings AUTOEXEC.NT and CONFIG.NT. Your primary and secondary video adapters are both set to 16-bit color, 1024×768 resolutions and default refresh rates. You create a shortcut for the DOS-application on the secondary monitor and use the default PIF settings. You attempt to run the DOS-based application on the primary monitor. The application opens, but the display area is scrambled. You then attempt to run the DOS-based application on the secondary monitor. The application does not open. Both monitors function correctly when you run Windows-based applications. What should you do?

a. Change the color setting for both video adapters to 256 colors. Reconfigure the shortcut properties to run the DOS-based application in full-screen mode.

b. Change the refresh rate setting to optimal for both video adapters. Reconfigure the PIF settings for the DOS-based application to start in the window.

c. Change the drivers for the secondary video adapter from WDM-compliant drivers to DOS drivers. Reconfigure the PIF settings to run the DOS-based application in full-screen mode.

d. Update the drivers for the primary video adapter. Change the secondary video adapter to use 640×480 resolution and 256 colors.

57. Every afternoon, you run Microsoft Excel locally on your Windows 2000 Server computer to update a performance spreadsheet. Users report that, during this time, the server's response to file requests appears to slow down. What should you do to resolve the problem?

a. Run the Start/normal CSRSS.EXE command before you start Excel.

b. Run the Start/normal EXCEL.EXE command to start Excel.

c. Use Task Manager to set the priority for CSRSS.EXE process to AboveNormal.

d. Use Task Manager to set the priority for EXCEL.EXE process to Low.

58. You are the desktop administrator for your company. All users have Windows XP Professional or Windows 2000 Professional computers. Users in the accounting department run an application that requires several hours to process financial and accounting data. Users in the accounting department report that when they run this application, the performance of other business applications becomes significantly slower. You need to allow the accounting application to run with the least amount of performance impact on the other business applications. How should you configure the users' applications?

a. Configure all other business applications to have high priority.

b. Configure all other business applications to have real-time priority.

c. Configure the accounting application to have Above-Normal priority.

d. Configure all accounting applications to have Below-Normal priority.

59. You are the desktop administrator for the Acme Corporation corporate office. You need to install Windows XP Professional on 100 client computers. Your company has a volume licensing agreement with Microsoft Corporation that includes Windows XP Professional. You receive a volume license product key from Microsoft that must be used to install Windows XP Professional on the 100 client computers. However, you do not have access to the Windows XP Professional CD-ROM that Microsoft provided your company. You purchase a copy of Windows XP Professional at a local computer store. You begin installing Windows XP Professional on two client computers by using the attended installation method. When Setup prompts you for a product key, you type your company's volume license product key. However, Setup displays the following error message: "Invalid product key". You need to complete the Windows XP Professional installation on all 100 computers. What should you do?

a. Use the product key that is printed on the back of the CD case for the retail copy of Windows XP Professional that you purchased.

b. Contact a Microsoft activation center to obtain a product activation key.

c. Cancel Setup. Obtain a volume license version of the Windows XP Professional CD-ROM from Microsoft. Rerun Setup from the CD-ROM.

d. Cancel Setup. Create an unattended installation answer file that contains your company's volume license product key, and use the answer file to perform an unattended installation of Windows XP Professional.

HANDS-ON EXERCISES

Note: This book covers, Windows 2000 Professional, Windows 2000 Server, Windows XP, and Windows Server 2003. The hands-on exercises are written for Windows 2000 Professional and Windows 2000 Server, or Windows XP and Windows Server 2003. In either case, you will need a 10-GB drive or larger. Some exercises can only be done with Windows XP and Windows Server 2003.

Exercise 1: Installing Windows 2000 Professional

1. Start FDISK. When it asks you to support large disks, answer Yes. Create a 4-GB (4096 MB) active primary partition on the hard drive.
2. Format the 4-MB primary partition and make it bootable.
3. Reboot the computer with the proper DOS CD-ROM drivers. You can also boot with a bootable network disk and connect to a network drive to load the Windows 2000 files.
4. Load the Windows 2000 Professional CD or go to the network drive/directory where the Windows 2000 installation files are located.
5. Change into the I386 directory by using the CD I386 command.
6. Type in WINNT and press enter.
7. When Windows 2000 Setup needs to know where the Windows 2000 files are located, press Enter. Windows 2000 will copy the installation files over the C drive. Be patient, this will take a few minutes.
8. When the MS-DOS–based portion of the setup is complete, remove any floppy disks from the A drive and press Enter to restart the computer.
9. Windows 2000 will welcome you to Setup. To set up Windows now, press Enter.
10. When the license agreement appears, press the F8 key to continue.
11. When Windows shows the partitions, select the C drive. Press the Enter key to install.
12. Setup will install Windows 2000 on partition C. Select "Leave the current file system intact (no changes)" and press Enter. Windows 2000 will copy more files. The system will reboot again.
13. When the system reboots and starts a graphical interface, it will automatically detect and install the hardware devices. Next it will ask for the regional settings. Select the appropriate regional settings and click on the Next button.
14. To personalize your software, enter your name and your company's or school's name. Click on the Next button.
15. If it asks, enter the product key provided with the CD and click the Next button.

> **Note:** To get the most out of this book, you will need to work with a partner or a second computer. The computer on the left will be designated as Computer A and the computer on the right will be Computer B.

16. The next screen shows a random computer name. Change the computer name to WS2000-xxy, where *xx* represents your two-digit partner number in the class and *y* represents A if you are Computer A or B if you are Computer B. If you are not doing this in class, use 01. For example, if you are the first set of partners and are

using the computer on the left, use WS2000-01A. If you are the first set of partners and are using the computer on the right, use WS2000-01B. Lastly, for the password, enter "password" in the Administrator password and confirm password text boxes. Click on the Next button.

17. If your computer has a modem, a modem dialing information box will appear. Enter your area code and type in the appropriate options for your computer. Click on the Next button.
18. For the date and time settings, enter the proper information and click on the Next button.
19. Windows 2000 will configure the network settings. Select typical settings and click on the Next button. If the network settings dialog box does not appear, it is probably because Windows did not detect the network interface on your machine. You will need to load the driver for the network interface after the installation.
20. The next window asks if you want to be a member of a workgroup or a computer domain. For now, select No and click on the Next button. It will then copy some files and perform final tasks.
21. When the Windows 2000 Setup wizard is complete, click on the Finish button and the computer will reboot.
22. The Welcome to the Network Identification wizard begins. Click on the Next Button.
23. It will ask, "Who can log on to this computer?" Since we will assume that this is going to be a secure environment, select users must enter a user name and password to use this computer. Click on the Next button, then on the Finish button.
24. Press the Ctrl+Alt+Del keys and log on as the administrator. Right-click the My Computer applet and select Properties. Click the Hardware tab and click the Device Manager button. Look to see if any drivers did not load and load those drivers according to the instructions that come with them.
25. If you are connected to the Internet, start Internet Explorer, open the Tools menu, and select the Windows Update option to go to Microsoft's website to search for updates. Download and install any updates that are needed.

Exercise 2: Installing Windows 2000 Server (or Windows 2000 Advanced Server)

1. Start Windows 2000 Professional.
2. Click on the Start button, select the Settings option and select Control Panel.
3. Double-click Administrative Tools applet.
4. Double-click the Computer Management icon.
5. In the left pane, select the Disk Management option located under Storage.
6. Right-click Unallocated space and select Create Partition. Click the Next button.
7. Select Primary partition and click the Next button.
8. For the size of the partition, specify 4096 MB and click the Next button.
9. With the default drive letter, click the Next button.
10. Specify an NTFS format, select "Enable file and folder compression" and click the Next button.
11. Click the Finish button.
12. Reboot the computer with the proper DOS CD-ROM drivers. You can also boot with a bootable network disk and connect to a network drive to load the Windows 2000 files.
13. Load the Windows 2000 Server CD or go to the network drive/directory where the Windows 2000 installation files are located.
14. Change into the I386 directory by using the CD I386 command.
15. Type in WINNT and press Enter.
16. When Windows 2000 Setup needs to know where the Windows 2000 files are located, press Enter. Windows 2000 will copy the installation files over the C drive. Be patient, this will take a few minutes.
17. When the MS-DOS–based portion of setup is complete, remove any floppy disks from the A drive and press Enter to restart the computer.
18. When the boot menu appears, select the Windows 2000 Installation/Upgrade and press the Enter key.
19. Windows 2000 will welcome you to Setup. To setup up Windows now, press Enter.
20. When the license agreement appears, press the F8 key to continue.
21. When Windows shows the partitions, select Partition 2 and press the Enter key.
22. Select "Leave the current file system intact" and press the Enter key.
23. When the system reboots and starts a graphical interface, it will automatically detect and install the hardware devices. Next it will ask for the regional settings. Select the appropriate regional settings and click on the Next button.
24. To personalize your software, enter your name and your company's name. Click on the Next button.
25. If it asks, enter the product key provided with the CD and click the Next button.
26. In the next screen, select the per-server licensing mode and enter 50 connections. Click on the Next button.
27. The next screen shows a random computer name. Change the computer name to Server2000-xxy, where *xx* represents your two-digit partner number in the class and *y* represents A if you are Computer A or B if you are

> **Note:** To get the most out of this book, you will need to work with a partner or a second computer. The computer on the left will be designated as Computer A and the computer on the right as Computer B.

Computer B. If you are not doing this in class, use 01. For example, if you are the first set of partners and are using the computer on the left, use Server2000-01A. If you are the first set of partners and are using the computer on the right, use Server2000-01B. Lastly, for the password, enter "password" in the Administrator password and confirm password text boxes. Click on the Next button.

28. The Installation wizard will ask you to add or remove components of Windows 2000. Since there is nothing that we want to add at this time, click on the Next button.

29. If your computer has a modem, a modem dialing information box will appear. Enter your area code and type in the appropriate options for your computer. Click on the Next button.

30. For the date and time settings, enter the proper information and click on the Next button.

31. Windows 2000 will configure the network settings. Select Custom Settings and click on the Next button. If the network settings dialog box does not appear, it is probably because Windows did not detect the network interface on your machine. You will need to load the driver for the network interface after the installation.

32. The network components chosen by default are Client for Microsoft Networks, file-and-print sharing for Microsoft networks, and Internet protocol (TCP/IP). Click on the Internet protocol and click on the Properties button.

33. In the Internet protocol (TCP/IP) properties dialog box, click on the "Use the following IP address" option and input as follows:

IP address: 192.168.1.1xx
Subnet mask: 255.255.255.0

where *xx* is the computer number assigned. If you are working at home, use 01. Therefore, the address would be 192.168.1.101. In addition, if your network has a gateway or DNS server, specify them. Click on the OK button and then on the Next button.

34. The next window asks if you want to be a member of a workgroup or a computer domain. For now, select No and click on the Next button. It will then copy some files and perform final tasks.

35. When the Windows 2000 Setup wizard is complete, click on the Finish button and the computer will reboot.

36. When the boot menu appears, select the Windows 2000 Server.

37. Press the Ctrl+Alt+Del keys and log on as the administrator. Right-click the My Computer applet and select Properties. Click the Hardware tab and click the Device Manager button. Look to see if any drivers did not load and load those drivers according to the instructions that come with the drivers.

38. If you are connected to the Internet, start Internet Explorer, open the Tools menu, and select the Windows Update option to go to Microsoft's website to search for updates. Download and install any updates that are needed.

39. Go to the www.adobe.com website and download the newest version of Adobe Acrobat reader.

40. Go to the www.winzip.com website and download the evaluation copy of the newest version of WinZip.

41. Install both Acrobat reader and WinZip on your server.

Exercise 3: Loading Windows XP

1. Start FDISK. When it asks you to support large disks, answer Yes. Create a 4-GB (4096 MB) active primary partition on the hard drive.

2. Format the 4-MB primary partition and make it bootable.

3. Boot with the Windows XP CD. If you cannot boot from the CD-ROM, reboot the computer with the proper DOS CD-ROM drivers. Change into the I386 directory by using the CD I386 command. Type in WINNT and press Enter. When the Windows XP Setup needs to know where the Windows XP files are located, press Enter. Windows XP will copy the installation files over to the C drive. Be patient, this will take a few minutes. When the MS-DOS–based portion of the setup is complete, remove any floppy disks from the A drive and press Enter to restart the computer.

4. Windows XP will welcome you to Setup. To set up Windows now, press Enter.

5. When the license agreement appears, press the F8 key to continue.

6. When Windows shows the partitions, select the Windows XP partition and press Enter.

7. Setup will install Windows XP on the partition. Select "Leave the current file system intact (no change)" and press Enter. Windows XP will copy more files. The system will reboot again.

8. When the system reboots and starts a graphical interface, it will automatically detect and install the hardware devices. Next it will ask for the regional settings. Select the appropriate regional settings and click on the Next button.

9. To personalize your software, enter your name and your company's or school's name. Click on the Next button.
10. If it asks, enter the product key provided with the CD and click the Next button.

> **Note:** To get the most out of this book, you will need to work with a partner or a second computer. The computer on the left will be designated as Computer A and the computer on the right will be Computer B.

11. The next screen shows a random computer name. Change the computer name to WSXP-xxy, where *xx* represents your two-digit partner number in the class and *y* represents A if you are Computer A or B if you are Computer B. If you are doing this in class, use 01. For example, if you are the first set of partners and are using the computer on the left, use WSXP-01A. If you are the first set of partners and are using the computer on the right, use WSXP-01B. Lastly, for the password, enter "password" in the Administrator password and confirm password text boxes. Click on the Next button.
12. If your computer has a modem, a modem dialing information box will appear. Enter your area code and type in the appropriate options for your computer. Click on the Next button.
13. For the date and time settings, enter the proper information and click on the Next button.
14. Windows XP will configure the network settings. Select typical settings and click on the Next button. If the network settings dialog box does not appear, it is probably because Windows did not detect the network interface on your machine. You will need to load the driver for the network interface after the installation.
15. The next window asks if you want to be a member of a workgroup or a computer domain. For now, select No and click on the Next button. It will then copy some files and perform final tasks.
16. When the Windows Setup wizard is complete, click on the Finish button and the computer will reboot.
17. When the Display Settings dialog box appears, click the OK button.
18. Select the appropriate monitor settings, then click the OK button.
19. When the Welcome to Microsoft Windows screen appears, click the Next button.
20. When Windows asks "Who will use this computer?" type "admin" under your name and "user1" for the second user. Click the Next button.
21. Click on the Finish button.
22. To begin, select the Admin account by clicking on it.
23. Click on the Start button and click on the Control Panel.
24. Click on User Accounts.
25. Click on the "Change the ways users log on and off."
26. Unselect the "Use Welcome screen option." Click the Apply option button.
27. Close the dialog box and Control Panel.
28. Click the Start button and log off.
29. Log in as Admin.
30. Open the Control Panel and select the User Accounts option.
31. Click on the Admin account.
32. Click create password and type "password" for the password and confirm password. Click the Create password button.
33. Do the same for user1.
34. Right-click the My Computer applet and select Properties. Click the Hardware tab and click the Device Manager button. Look to see if any drivers did not load and load those drivers according to the instructions that come with the drivers.
35. If you are connected to the Internet, start Internet Explorer, open the Tools menu, and select the Windows Update option to go to Microsoft's website to search for updates. Download and install any updates that are needed.

Exercise 4: Installing Windows Server 2003

1. Start Windows XP.
2. Click on the Start button and select Control Panel.
3. Double-click Administrative Tools applet.
4. Double-click the Computer Management icon.
5. In the left pane, select the Disk Management option located under Storage.
6. Right-click the Unallocated space and select Create Partition. Click the Next button.
7. Select the Primary partition and click the Next button.
8. For the size of the partition, specify 4096 MB and click the Next button.
9. With the default drive letter, click the Next button.
10. Specify an NTFS format, select "Enable file and folder compression," and click the Next button.

11. Click the Finish button.
12. From Windows XP, insert CD in the drive.
13. Click the Install Windows Server option.
14. When it gives you a warning that it cannot upgrade Windows XP to Windows Server, click the OK button.
15. When the Welcome to Windows Setup screen appears, select New Installation (Advanced) and click on the Next button.
16. Click the "I accept the agreement" option and click the Next button.
17. If it asks, enter the product key provided with the CD and click the Next button.
18. Select the appropriate language and click the Next button.
19. Select "Use the NTFS file system" and click the Next button.
20. Click "No, Skip this step," when it asks to automatically update files.
21. When the computer reboots, select the Setup option from the boot menu.
22. When the Welcome to Setup screen appears, press the Enter Key.
23. Select Partition 2 and press Enter.
24. After the computer reboots, and starts a graphical interface, it will automatically detect and install the hardware devices. Next it will ask for the regional settings. Select the appropriate regional settings and click on the Next button.
25. To personalize your software, enter your name and your company's or school's name. Click on the Next button.
26. In the next screen, select the per-server licensing mode and enter 50 connections. Click on the Next button.
27. The next screen shows a random computer name. Change the computer name to SERV-*xxy*, where *xx* represents your two-digit partner number in the class and *y* represents A if you are Computer A and B if you are Computer B. If you are not doing this in class, use 01. For example, if you are the first set of partners and are using the computer on the left, use SERV-01A. If you are the first set of partners and are using the computer on the right, use SERV-01B. Lastly, for the password, enter "password" in the Administrator password and confirm password text boxes. Click on the Next button.
28. If it asks you to continue because password is not a strong password, click the Yes button.
29. If your computer has a modem, a modem dialing information box will appear. Enter your area code and type in the appropriate options for your computer. Click on the Next button.
30. For the date and time settings, enter the proper information and click on the Next button.
31. Windows XP will configure the network settings. Select Custom Settings and click on the Next button. If the network settings dialog box does not appear, it is probably because Windows did not detect the network interface on your machine. You will need to load the driver for the network interface after the installation.
32. The network components chosen by default are Client for Microsoft Networks, file-and-print sharing for Microsoft networks, and Internet protocol (TCP/IP). Click on the Internet protocol and click on the Properties button.
33. In the Internet protocol (TCP/IP) properties dialog box, click on "Use the following IP address" option and input the following:

    IP address: 192.168.1.1*xx*
    Subnet mask: 255.255.255.0

    where *xx* is the computer number assigned. If you are working at home, use 01. Therefore, the address would be 192.168.1.101. In addition, if your network has a gateway or DNS server, specify them. Click on the OK button and then on the Next button.
34. The next window asks if you want to be a member of a workgroup or a computer domain. For now, select No and click on the Next button. It will then copy some files and perform final tasks.
35. When the Windows Setup wizard is complete, click on the Finish button and the computer will reboot.
36. When the Display Settings dialog box appears, click the OK button.
37. Right-click the My Computer applet and select Properties. Click the Hardware tab and click the Device Manager button. Look to see if any drivers did not load and load those drivers according to the instructions that come with the drivers.
38. If you are connected to the Internet, start Internet Explorer, open the Tools menu, and select the Windows Update option to go to Microsoft's website to search for updates. Download and install any updates that are needed.
39. Go to the www.adobe.com website and download the newest version of Adobe Acrobat reader.
40. Go to the www.winzip.com website and download the evaluation copy of the newest version of WinZip.
41. Install both Acrobat reader and WinZip on your server.

Exercise 5: Booting Windows 2000

1. Press the Ctrl+Alt+Del keys and click on the Shut Down button. Select Restart from the pulldown menu and click on the OK button.

2. During the reboot, study what is displayed during boot-up, specifically the boot menu.
3. Start a Command Prompt window by clicking on the Start button, clicking on the Accessories option, and clicking on the Command Prompt option.
4. The C:\> prompt should be showing. Type in the DIR command and press Enter.
5. The directory listing shows the WINNT, Documents and Settings, Program Files, and Inetpub folder. Type in the DIR /AH and press Enter.
6. The directory listing shows the BOOTSECT.DOS, NTLDR, NTDETECT.COM, BOOT.INI files. Type EDIT BOOT.INI and press Enter.
7. The BOOT.INI displays the boot menu that appears during boot-up.
8. Type EXIT and press Enter.
9. Reboot the computer again. When the boot menu appears, press a left arrow key.
10. Note at the bottom of the screen the "For troubleshooting and advanced startup options for Windows, press F8" message. Press the F8 key.
11. The Windows Advanced Options menu appears. Select Safe Mode and press Enter. Make sure the Windows Server option is highlighted and press Enter.
12. Press the Ctrl+Alt+Del keys to log on as the administrator. Then perform another reboot. Again, go into the Windows Advanced Options menu. Select Safe Mode with Command Prompt. Select the Windows Server and press Enter.
13. Log on as administrator. Close the Command Prompt window. Press the Ctlr+Alt+Del keys and perform another reboot.

Exercise 6: Exploring the Windows 2000 Security Dialog Box and Windows Task Manager

1. Press the Ctrl+Alt+Del keys to open the Windows Security dialog box.
2. Click on the Lock Computer option.
3. Unlock the computer.
4. Open the Windows Security dialog box and click on the Change Password button. Change the password to today.
5. Change the password back to password.
6. Open the Windows Security dialog box and select Task Manager. Click on the Process tab. After you study the Process tab, click the Performance tab.
7. At the bottom of the Windows Task Manager window, notice the number of processors and the CPU usage. In addition, notice the amount of system cache, which is located beneath the graphs.
8. Go back to the Processes tab and check for a NOTEPAD.EXE listing. Don't spend too much time on this.
9. Open the WordPad program. It can be opened by clicking on the Start button, selecting the Accessories option, and selecting the WordPad option.
10. Notice that there is a WORDPAD.EXE listed in the Processes tab and a Document-WordPad listed in the Application tab.
11. In the Application tab, click on the Document-WordPad listing and click on the End Task button.
12. Close the Task Manager.

Exercise 7: Creating Windows Start-up Floppy Disks

1. Insert a blank floppy disk in drive A.
2. Double-click My Computer to open it.
3. Right-click the A drive and select the Format option.
4. When the Format A:\ dialog box appears, click on the Start button. Click on the OK button to format the disk.
5. When the format is complete, click on the OK button and close the Format A:\ window.
6. Double-click on the C: icon to open it.
7. To show the hidden files, open the Tools menu and select the Folder Options option. Click on the View tab and click on "Show hidden files and folders." In addition, click on the "Hide protected operating system files (Recommended)" option and the "Hide file extensions for known file types" option to take off the check mark. Click on the Yes button when "Deleting or editing the protected operating system files can make your computer inoperable" warning appears. Click on the OK button.
8. While pressing the Ctrl key down, click on the following files.

NTLDR.EXE
NTDETECT.COM
NTBOOTDD.SYS (if available)
BOOT.INI

9. While these files are still highlighted, right-click on one of them and select the Send To option. Select the 3 1/2 floppy (A) option.

10. Close all windows.

11. Another way to do a shutdown is to click on the Start button and select the Shut Down option.

12. With the disk still in drive A, select the Restart option and click on the OK button.

13. Although the menu is identical to the previous boot menu, the difference is it is being executed from the floppy disk. Select the Windows Server option and press Enter.

14. Open a window for the A drive.

15. Delete the NTLDR.EXE file from the A drive. You can delete the file by right-clicking on the file and selecting the Delete option. If it asks if you are sure, click Yes. Make sure it is the A drive and not the C drive.

16. Close all windows and reboot the computer again with the disk in drive A.

17. You can see that an NTLDR is missing. Normally, when this happens you would expect something has happened to the NTLDR file in the C drive (boot drive). Of course, we are using the floppy disk instead.

18. Remove the disk in drive A. Use the Ctrl+Alt+Del keys to reboot the computer into the server.

19. Log on as administrator.

20. Double-click on the My Computer icon, then double-click on the C: drive icon.

21. Insert the disk. To open a second window, double-click on My Computer, then double-click on the A drive.

22. Position the windows to view both of them.

23. Drag the NTLDR file from the C drive window to the A drive window. Because the windows represent two different drive letters, the file is copied (a duplicate is made and placed in the A drive). If the two windows represented the same drive letter, but different directories/folders, then the file would be moved. In this particular case, if this file is moved, then the system would not boot, which is one reason why we are making the Windows boot disk.

24. Remove the disk and label the outside of the disk as the Windows Start-up floppy disk. If you modify the BOOT.INI file, save it to the disk after the changes have been made and tested.

25. To test the start-up disk, insert the disk in drive A and reboot the computer from the floppy disk.

Exercise 8: Looking at the BOOT.INI File

1. Double-click on My Computer to open a My Computer window.

2. Double-click on the C drive to open a C:\ window.

3. If you cannot see the BOOT.INI file and the other boot files (NTLDR and NTDETECT.COM), open the Tools menu and select the Folder option. Select the View tab.

4. If the option is not already enabled, under Advanced Settings, select the "Show hidden files and folders" option.

5. Under the Advanced Settings, deselect the "Hide file extension for known file types and Hide protected operating system files (Recommended)." Click on the OK button.

6. When it asks if you are sure you want to display these files, click on the Yes button.

7. Right-click the BOOT.INI file and select the Properties option. Deselect the "Read-only in the Attributes section" and click on the OK button.

8. Right-click the BOOT.INI file and select the Open With option. Select Notepad and click on the OK button.

9. As you can see, the default timeout is 30 seconds. Change the 30 to a 15.

10. Open the file menu and save the file.

11. Click on the Start button and reboot Windows. Notice that the timer is now 15 seconds instead of 30 seconds. Select the Windows Server.

12. Open the BOOT.INI file with Notepad again. For the default entry, change the partition from 1 to 2.

13. Save the changes for the BOOT.INI file. Again, click on the Start button and reboot Windows.

14. When the timer begins, let the time run out so that it will pick the Default menu option. Notice that while it selected the correct menu option, Windows Professional or Windows XP loaded because the ARC path indicated partition 2 and not partition 1.

15. From Windows Professional, we could use Notepad. Instead, click on the Start button, select the Accessories option, and select the Command prompt.

16. Switch to the C:\. If you do not know how, type in C: followed by pressing the Enter key and typing in CD\ followed by the Enter key.

17. At the C:\> prompt, type in EDIT BOOT.INI and press Enter.

18. Change the partition back to 1 for the ARC path for the default entry.

19. Press the Alt key and hold it down. While the Alt key is down, press the F key. Use the arrow keys to select the Save option.

20. Open the File menu again by using the Alt+F keys and select the Exit option.

21. Type EXIT at the prompt and then press Enter.

22. Restart Windows to test if the Default menu option brings up Server.

CHAPTER 9

Windows Basics

Topics Covered in This Chapter

Introduction

Once you have Windows installed, it is time to start using it. This chapter discusses how to operate and configure Windows as an operating system, not as a network operating system. When creating and configuring Windows 2000 and Windows Server 2003, you will find them quite similar to Windows 98 and Windows NT. However, when you start getting into more of the advanced features of Windows 2000 and Windows Server 2003, you will start seeing some major differences in these newer versions.

Objectives

- Demonstrate how to configure Windows taskbar.
- Demonstrate common file and directory management tasks.
- Demonstrate how to configure Windows using the Control Panel.
- Given common hardware problems, troubleshoot and fix such problems.
- Implement, manage, and troubleshoot display devices.
- Configure multiple-display support.
- Install, configure, and troubleshoot a video adapter.
- Manage and troubleshoot driver signing.
- Given a computer, optimize the performance of the paging files.
- Manage hardware profiles.

- Configure advanced power management (APM).
- Configure, manage, and troubleshoot the Task Scheduler.
- Given a UPS, configure Windows to communicate with the UPS.
- Starting with an empty MMC, create a custom console and save it in one of four MMC modes.
- Compare the four MMC modes.
- Use the Services console to enable, stop, or pause various services.
- Demonstrate using the Task Scheduler to schedule a maintenance task such as disk defragmenter or ScanDisk.
- Given a key and its location in the registry, find and make the correct changes.

9.1   WINDOWS 2000 INTERFACE

The Windows 2000 interface is based on the desktop, which is the graphical space on the screen from which all control and display presentations begin. On the desktop, you will find the My Computer icon, the Recycle Bin, a My Documents shortcut, and the taskbar (with the Start button). In addition, you may have a My Network Place icon to access network resources (files, applications, and printing) and an Inbox to receive electronic mail and various folders (directories) and shortcuts to programs and documents. See Figure 9.1.

The **My Computer** icon represents your computer. It includes all disk drives and the control panel. From within the My Computer icon, you can access and manage all files on your drives.

The **Recycle Bin** is used as a safe delete. When you delete a file using the GUI interface, Windows stores the file in the Recycle Bin. It will remain there until you empty it or you start running out of disk space (Windows will recycle the oldest files first). If you delete a file and decide that you want to undelete it, then open the Recycle Bin and drag it to any location or choose the Restore option from the File menu.

The **My Documents** shortcut points to a My Documents folder. By default, the My Documents folder is stored in the C:\Documents and Settings*user_login_name* folder. Users can change the target folder location of their My Documents folder by right-clicking the My Documents icon on the desktop, selecting the Properties option, and specifying a new location on the Target tab. See Figure 9.2.

The **taskbar** is located at the bottom of the screen. See Figure 9.3. You can configure the taskbar to be always visible or to auto hide, so that it appears only when you move the mouse pointer to the bottom of the screen. Auto hide can be used to give you more free area on the desktop.

Figure 9.1 Windows 2000 interface

Figure 9.2 Properties of My Documents

Figure 9.3 The taskbar

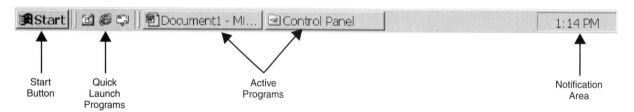

The taskbar is divided into four areas: the Start button, the notification area, the active program buttons, and quick launch programs. The **Start button** is used to start programs. In addition, you can open recently accessed documents, access the Control Panel and printer folder and find files, and get help for Windows 2000. The Start button is a series of shortcuts to programs.

The **notification area,** located on the right side of the taskbar, is used for the clock and for any programs running in the background such as printers and modems. The rest of the taskbar is blank or holds the active program buttons, which can be used to switch between open programs.

When a window is open, it will usually contain a Minimize button, a Maximize/Restore button, and a Close button in the top right corner and a Control Menu icon in the top left corner. In addition, most program windows include a menu and many include one or more toolbars.

Like Windows 95, Windows 98, and Windows NT, Windows 2000 uses **shortcut menus** (also referred to as context menus), which are accessed by clicking the secondary mouse button (usually the right mouse button). Shortcut menus contain common commands that you can use on the item that you clicked. For example, if you click a file with the right mouse button, then you can choose to open the file, copy the file, delete the file, or show the properties of the file. If you click the disk drive in My Computer with the right mouse button, you can open the disk, format the disk, or show the properties of the disk. If you highlight some text in a word processor such as Microsoft Word and click on the text with the right mouse button, you can choose the Cut, Copy, or Paste options or change the formatting of the text.

As stated, the desktop contains the My Computer and Recycle Bin icons. In addition, it can hold folders, files, and shortcuts. To create a folder or a shortcut, simply use the desktop's shortcut menu and select the New option. Note that content visible on the desktop is kept in C:\Documents and Settings*user_login_name*\Desktop folders.

The taskbar can be configured by using the Properties button (Taskbar Options) on the taskbar's shortcut menu or by using Taskbar in the Settings option under the Start button. In the Taskbar Options tab, specify the following:

- If the taskbar auto hides when not in use
- If the taskbar will show the time
- If the Start menu will use small icons or large icons

From the Start Menu Programs tab, add, remove, or reorganize the programs listed under the Start button or clear the Documents menu. See Figure 9.4.

Personalized Menus keep the Programs menu clean by hiding items you have not used recently, while keeping all of your programs easily accessible. When Personalized Menus is turned on, Windows keeps track of which programs you use each time you use your computer and hides the programs you have not used in a long time. You can still gain access to hidden programs by clicking Start, pointing to Programs, and then clicking the down arrow at the bottom of the menu.

In Windows 2000, to turn on Personalized Menus, click Start, point to Settings, click Taskbar & Start Menu, and then select Use Personalized Menus on the General tab. In Windows XP or Windows Server 2003, personalized menus are used with the Classic Start menu. To turn on Personalized Menus, right-click the Start button, then click Properties. On the Start Menu tab, click Classic Start menu, then click Customize. Under Advanced Start menu options, select the Use personalized menus check box.

9.2   WINDOWS XP INTERFACE

Most of the Windows XP and Windows Server 2003 interface is the same as in Windows 2000. Yet, the Windows XP and Windows Server 2003 interface is modified enough to give Windows a new look with a simple-to-use design. In addition, the new interface is designed to make the desktop and taskbar less cluttered.

The new Start menu is smarter and provides more customization options. It shows who is logged on, and it automatically adds the most frequently used programs to the top-level menu. It also enables

Figure 9.4   Taskbar properties

you to move any programs you want to the Start menu. Items such as the My Pictures and My Documents folders and Control Panel are available from the Start menu.

When many document and program windows are open, grouping creates more available space on the taskbar. For example, if you have 10 windows open and 3 of them are Wordpad documents, the 3 Wordpad document taskbar buttons will group together into one button named "Wordpad." Click this button, then click one of the documents to view it.

To reduce taskbar clutter, icons in the notification area (next to the clock) are hidden from view when they have not been used in a while. Click the arrow (<) to temporarily display the hidden icons. If you click one of these icons, it is displayed again.

9.3   FILE MANAGEMENT

Since Windows 2000 is an operating system, become familiar with how to accomplish common tasks such as managing files and disks, running programs, and configuring the Windows NT environment. Disk and file management is usually done with My Computer or **Windows Explorer.** See Figure 9.5. You can start Windows Explorer by clicking on the Start button; then select the Programs option, select the Accessories option, and select Windows Explorer. The most common actions are shown in Table 9.1.

If you want to move, delete, or copy several files or folders at the same time, use the Ctrl and Shift keys to select multiple files. For example, if you press and hold down the Ctrl key, you can select any file or folder within the same drive or folder. If you press the Shift key and keep it down, you can select two files or folders and everything listed between the two will be selected. After the file, or directories, have been selected, you can then copy, delete, or move them as one.

To start a DOS session to perform DOS commands at a prompt, click on the Start button, select the Programs option, select the Accessories option, and select the Command Prompt option.

Figure 9.5   Windows Explorer

9.4   RUNNING PROGRAMS

Windows will run Win16-based applications (Windows 3.xx), Win32-based applications (Windows 9X and Windows NT), DOS applications, and OS/2 bounded applications. To run a program, select the program by using the Program option in the Start button. In addition, you can start an executable file by following these steps:

1. Click on the file (or data document) using Windows Explorer or My Computer.
2. Create a shortcut on the desktop or in any folder.
3. Use the Run option in the Start button. See Figure 9.6.
4. Type the name of the executable file in an MS-DOS command session.

Since Windows is a multitasking environment, it allows you to start several programs simultaneously. You can then change between different programs as follows:

■ Press and hold down the Alt key and repeatedly press the Tab key until you get the desired application.
■ Use the Alt + Esc keys to move to the next application.
■ Select the Application button on the taskbar.
■ Use the Task Manager.

Table 9.1   Common disk and file management actions

Task	Action
To create a folder (directory) on the desktop, in the root directory, or in another folder	Select New from the File menu or New from the shortcut menu (right mouse button) and select the Folder option.
To delete a file or directory	Select the file or folder by clicking on it and dragging it to the Recycle Bin. Pick the Delete option from the shortcut or file menu or press the Del key on the keyboard.
To format a disk	Select the Format option from the drive's shortcut menu or select the Format option from the My Computer's file menu.
To copy a floppy disk	Select the Copy Disk option from the drive's shortcut menu or from the My Computer file menu.
To copy a file or directory from one drive to another	Drag the file (click on the file and keep the left mouse button clicked while moving the mouse) to its new destination. Another way is to first select the file or directory and select the Copy option from the shortcut menu or the Edit menu (Explorer or any disk or folder window). Then go to your destination and select the Paste option from the shortcut menu or Edit menu.
To move a file or directory to a different folder within the same drive	Press the Ctrl key while dragging the file to its new destination. If you do not press the Ctrl key, it will make a shortcut to the file or directory instead of moving the file. Another way is to first select the file or directory and select the Cut option from the shortcut menu or the Edit menu (Explorer or any disk or folder window). Then go to your destination and select the Paste option from the shortcut menu or Edit menu.
To rename a file	Select the file and choose the Rename option in the file menu or in the shortcut menu. Another way is to click once on the file name.
To view or change the directory or file attributes (read-only, hidden, or system)	Select the folder or file and select the Properties from the File menu or shortcut menu.

Note: Many 32-bit Windows applications also allow you to cut, copy, delete, and rename by using the shortcut menu from within some dialog boxes including the Open, Save, and Save As dialog boxes.

Figure 9.6   Run option under the Start button

9.4.1   Removing a Windows Application

During installation, a Windows program often adds or modifies information to the registry. To remove these entries and program files on the hard drive, many programs include an additional uninstall program or have an uninstall option within the installation program. In addition, if the program follows the Windows 2000 API standards, it can be removed by using the Add/Remove Programs applet in the Control Panel. Even when you uninstall a program, some of its files may remain on the hard drive.

Figure 9.7   Registered files shown in the Folder options dialog box

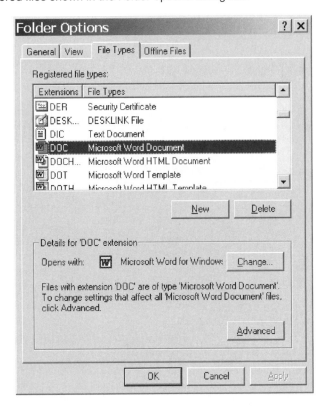

9.4.2   Windows Associations

When you double-click on a document in Windows 2000, it will recognize the file name extension and start the appropriate program to open the file. Associating an extension with a program is known as registering a file. The information identifying the file name extensions is located in the registry and can be accessed and modified by selecting Options under the View menu in the My Computer, disk, or folder window and clicking on the File Type tab or by opening the Folder Option applet in the Control Panel. See Figure 9.7.

9.5   CONTROL PANEL

There are several utilities used to configure Windows. The main utilities are the Control Panel and Registry Editor. The Windows Control Panel is a graphical tool to configure the Windows environment and hardware devices. See Figure 9.8. It can be accessed by using the Start button or by opening My Computer. In addition, there are various shortcuts to directly access certain Control Panel applets (icons). The most commonly used applets are the System applet, the Display applet, the Add/Remove applet, and the Add New Hardware applet.

While the Windows 2000 Control Panel is very similar to the Control Panel used in Windows 95 or Windows 98, there are some differences worth noting with Windows XP and Windows Server 2003. The Control Panel in Windows XP is configured to use Category view, which was designed to be more intuitive for the end user. To change into Classic view, click on the Classic view option located in the top left part of the screen. See Figure 9.9

Windows Server 2003 is primarily accessed through the Start menu. When you select the Control Panel, a submenu appears with all of the Control Panel applets. Right-click the Control Panel option and select the open option to open a Control Panel window. By default, the applets may look different because the Control Panel starts in Details view. You can easily open the View menu and select the Icons view.

Figure 9.8 Windows XP Control panel in category view

Figure 9.9 Control panel

9.5.1   **System Applet**

The System applet has five tabs: General, Network Identification, Hardware, User Profiles, and Advanced. See Figure 9.10. The General tab shows the user name and company entered during installation, the type of processor, and the amount of RAM in the system, as shown in Figure 9.10a. The Network Identification tab shows the full computer name. (This tab will be discussed in Chapter 10.)

The Hardware tabs allow access to the Hardware wizard, the Device Manager, and Hardware profiles. The Hardware wizard helps you install, uninstall, repair, eject, and configure your hardware. See Figure 9.10b.

The **Device Manager** lists all hardware devices on your computer and allows you to change the properties of any device. If you open the View menu and select Resources by Type, you will see the IRQ, DMA, I/O address, and memory areas used by the different hardware components. See Figure 9.11.

If you open the View menu and select Devices by Type or Devices by Connection, you see all hardware devices organized in a tree structure. When a red X appears through an icon this means the hardware device has been disabled. A yellow circled exclamation point through the icon means the hardware device has a problem. The problem could be a resource conflict (IRQ, DMA, I/O address, or memory address) or the drivers are not loaded properly. See Figures 9.12 through 9.15.

When viewing device information on your Windows-based computer using Device Manager, you may see an unknown device listed next to a yellow question mark. Determining the cause of this unknown device can be difficult, because there are few indications of what could be creating it. The unknown device may also cause a conflict when trying to install a driver for another device.

The most common reasons Device Manager may list a device as unknown are as follows:

- The Device Manager does not have a device driver.
- You are using a Windows 9X device driver.
- A device ID is not present.
- Windows does not recognize the device ID.
- The device is created by software.
- The system has faulty hardware or firmware.

Figure 9.10   Opening the System applet in the Control Panel displays the System Properties dialog box. Within the dialog box are five tabs: General, Network Identification, Hardware, User Profiles, and Advanced

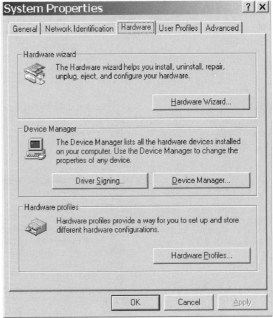

Figure 9.11 Device Manager showing the resources used by various devices within the computer

Figure 9.12 Device Manager showing all devices on the computer

Figure 9.13 Extended Capabilities Port (ECP) Printer Port properties as accessed through the Device Manager, including drivers and resources used

When a device driver for a device is not available, Device Manager displays the device as unknown and places it in the Other Devices folder. This commonly occurs with universal serial bus (USB) and IEEE 1394 composite devices. A status of "Error Code 1" or "Error Code 10" also may be displayed when you view the properties of the device in Device Manager.

You cannot use virtual device driver (.vxd) files common to Windows 9X drivers with Windows 2000 and Windows Server 2003, and attempting to install them may cause the device to be listed as unknown in Device Manager. This usually occurs when the device driver manufacturer does not properly differentiate between the two drivers, or assumes that Windows 2000 or Windows Server 2003 is capable of using Windows 9X .vxd files.

Every hardware device has a special identifier used by plug-and-play (PNP). This identifier can consist of several different types, such as vendor ID, device ID, subsystem ID, subsystem vendor ID, or revision ID. If a device ID is not present, or your Windows-based computer does not recognize the device ID, Device Manager may list the device as unknown.

Figure 9.14 If a device is not working properly, you can find more information about the problem by showing the properties of the device in the Device Manager

Figure 9.15 You can enable or disable a device by using the properties for the device in the Device Manager

Virtual devices that are created with software also would be considered as unknown when a driver tries to use the InstallShield installation program or a similar method and the device was removed in Device Manager, but still may have entries left over in the registry. To determine if an unknown device is being created by software, try starting Windows in safe mode. In addition, click on the Start button, select the Programs option, and select the Administrative Tools and then select Computer Management. In the Computer Management console, click the System Information folder, double-click the Software

Environment folder, and double-click the Startup Programs folder. You should then check the event log for errors relating to any of these programs to see if one is not working properly. If you find a related event, uninstall the associated program. In addition, look at the Components folder in the System Information folder. The Components folder lists the common name for the device and the name of the device driver associated with it. In the PNP Device ID column, it will list the device IDs such as the PCI ID, ISA ID, an ID for some other bus type or unknown type. The Error Code column lists the error code associated with a specific problem such as a bad or incompatible device driver.

The unknown device can also be caused by faulty hardware or firmware. To isolate the correct hardware device, remove the hardware devices from the Windows computer one at a time until the unknown device is no longer listed in Device Manager. In addition, check if the device driver is digitally signed. If Windows detects that a device driver is not digitally signed, a Not Digitally Signed message is displayed.

To see hardware in a category, click on the plus (1) sign next to the hardware type. To see information about a piece of hardware, double-click on the hardware device icon or select the hardware device and click on the Properties button. The Properties will usually contain several tabs indicating if the device is working properly and what drivers are loaded, and it gives you an option to update them and to view and change the device resources (if it is a plug-and-play device).

Within the Advanced tab of the System Properties dialog box, you will find the Performance Options, Environment Variables, and Startup and Recovery buttons. See Figure 9.16.

The Performance Options allows you to adjust how the microprocessor resources are distributed between running programs. Selecting Applications assigns more resources to the foreground applications, whereas the Background Services assigns an equal amount of resources to all programs. Select the Background Services if it is a server with network resources/services or Applications if you want the server to act more like a desktop machine. See Figure 9.17.

The Virtual Memory area allows you to configure the paging file size (virtual memory) and the maximum size of the registry. The minimum paging file is 2 MB. For Windows 2000 Professional, the default size of the file is equal to the total amount of RAM plus 12 MB, not to exceed the amount of available disk space. For Windows XP and Windows Server 2003, the default size of the file is 1.5 times

Figure 9.16   Advanced tab in the System Properties dialog box

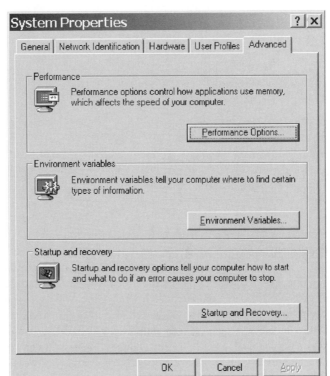

Figure 9.17 Performance Options within the System Properties dialog box

Figure 9.18 Changing the Virtual Memory Settings

the amount of RAM. Usually the size of the paging file can stay at the default value assigned during installation, but the recommended size for the paging file should be 1.5 times the amount of RAM available on your system and it should not exceed 2.5 times the amount of RAM installed. On computers with 4 GB or more of RAM, this is an ineffective use of disk space. A paging file size of 2060 MB is the recommended size for computers with 4 GB or more of physical memory. When changing the virtual memory settings, be sure to click on the OK button and not the Cancel button. See Figure 9.18.

Virtual memory is much slower than physical RAM, because the memory is on the hard drive, which is a mechanical device. If you want to enhance system performance and you have several physical hard drives (not necessary partitions/logical drives), you can create a paging file on each disk by moving the paging file off the boot partition (the partition with the WINNT or WINDOWS directory).

This step is possible because the hard disk controller can read and write to multiple hard disks simultaneously and the Virtual Memory Manager (VMM) tries to write the page data to the paging file on the disk that is the least busy.

To enhance system performance, you can set the initial size of the paging file to the value displayed in the Maximum Size box in the Virtual Memory dialog box. This occurs because when the system needs more RAM beyond what it already has, it will increase the size of the paging file. If the file is already set to its maximum size, then it eliminates the time required to enlarge the file from the initial size to the maximum size. The maximum size of the file is determined by the largest contiguous (continuous) space of disk space. The disk defragmenter utility in the Accessories system tools also is important because it ensures that a maximum amount of the drive is contiguous and available for page file use.

The Environment Variables dialog box allows you to change system and user environment variables such as the TEMP and TMP variables. System environment variables are applicable to all users, whereas user environment variables are different for each user. The environment variables are set by first using the AUTOEXEC.BAT file, then by using the system environment followed by the user environment variables. You can prevent Windows from searching the AUTOEXEC.BAT file by editing the \HKEY_CURRENT_USER\SOFTWARE\Microsoft\WindowsNT\CurrentVersion\ Winlogon\Parseautoexec and setting it to zero.

The last option under the system properties dialog box is Startup and Recovery settings. The System Startup section allows you to determine the default operating system listed in the BOOT.INI file and the time in seconds that the boot menu is displayed on the screen before automatically selecting the default operating system. Note that when these values are changed using this dialog box, the BOOT.INI file is changed. The Recovery section provides options to assist in troubleshooting Stop errors. You must be logged on as a member of the Administrator group to change these options. See Table 9.2.

To help diagnose Stop errors, you can create a memory dump containing debugging information. The debugging information can then be used by support engineers to resolve these errors. To write the debugging information, a paging file must be on the system partition (the partition with the WINNT directory), the paging file must be at least 1 MB larger than the amount of physical RAM in your computer, and you must have enough disk space to write the file in the location you specify.

A **hardware profile** is a set of instructions that tells Windows which devices to start upon computer start-up or what settings to use for each device. For example, if you have a notebook computer, you might create two different hardware profiles, one for when the computer is docked in a docking station and one for when it is not or if you work from two locations.

To create or modify a hardware profile, use the System Properties dialog box (double-click on the System applet of the Control Panel or use the secondary mouse button on the My Computer icon and select the Properties applet), select the Hardware tab, and click on the Hardware Profile button.

To create a new profile, select one of the profiles listed and click on the Copy button to create a copy of the selected profile. The first profile listed is the default profile. If you want to change the order of the profiles, you can select a profile and use the up and down arrows on the sides to move it (or them) up or down on the list.

Table 9.2   Recovery options

Option	Description
Write an Event to the System Log	If enabled, it writes an event to the system log when the system Stops unexpectedly.
Send an Administrative Alert	If enabled, it sends an administrative alert to administrators when the system stops unexpectedly.
Write Debugging Information to	If enabled, it will write debugging information to the specified file name. This file can then be used by support engineers to diagnose problems.
Automatically Reboot	If enabled, it allows Windows 2000 to reboot whenever the system stops unexpectedly.

One of the leading causes of instability in Windows NT is device drivers with bugs. While you should only use hardware that is on the HCL, there is no guarantee that the driver is bug-free. If the drivers are on the HCL, however, there is a better chance that they have no bugs.

To keep your system loaded exclusively with drivers from the HCL, Microsoft introduced **driver-signing technology** starting with Windows 2000. To configure the device driver signature verification system, click on the Driver Signing button in the hardware tab of the System applet. In the Driver Signing Options dialog box, you can disable this feature by selecting the Ignore option, which displays a warning if a driver is being loaded that does not have the signature or blocks the driver with the signature all together.

9.5.2 Display Applet

The Display applet used in Windows 2000 allows you to configure the Windows environment, including menus, windows, icons, the desktop, and the screen saver. See Figure 9.19. In addition, it allows you to configure your video system, install or upgrade video drivers, and choose the video resolution and number of colors. See Figure 9.20. Access is through the Control Panel or the Properties option on the shortcut menu of the desktop.

Originally, screen savers were used to prevent burn-in to a monitor. Burn-in occurred when a monitor displayed the same screen for such a long period of time that the screen image remained even after that screen had changed. Although they are no longer needed to prevent burn-in, screen savers have grown into a form of entertainment.

Although most people who are using Windows 9X are already familiar with screen savers, some may not be aware of the password-protected feature. When you enable password protection, you add a level of security to your system if you leave the system and forget to log off. When the screen saver activates and you press any key or move the mouse, you must specify the login password to be able to continue.

In addition, if you wish to use a screen saver, be sure to select a simple one, not a 3-D variety, especially OpenGL screensavers. 3-D screen savers have a tendency to take up too much processing.

If you have video problems, there are several tools available for troubleshooting. First, if you choose the wrong driver or you select the wrong resolution or refresh rate and thus cannot see anything on the screen, you can reboot the computer, press F8 during the boot menu, and select the VGA mode. Another tool is the troubleshooting tool tab which reduces the hardware acceleration of the video card. If you suspect a video problem, reduce the hardware acceleration to see if the problem goes away.

Figure 9.19 The Appearance and Effects tabs within the Display Properties allow you to change the appearance of Windows

Figure 9.20   The Settings tab of the Display Properties dialog box can be used to adjust the number of colors and the resolution rate of the display system. By clicking on the Advanced button you can adjust the monitor refresh rate

The Display applet in Windows XP and Windows Server 2003 is a little different from the one used in Windows 2000. The menus that appear include Themes, Desktop, Screen Saver, Appearance, and Settings. The Desktop applet is very similar to the Background applet in Windows 2000. You can click on the Customize Desktop button to add or remove My Computer, My Document, My Network Places, and Internet Explorer icons from the desktop.

Different from Windows 95—original version of Windows 98 and Windows NT 4.0—Windows 2000, Windows XP, and Windows Server 2003 support the use of up to 10 monitors. To support multiple monitors, use peripheral component interconnect (PCI) or accelerated graphics port (AGP) devices.

If one of the video cards is built into the motherboard, it must be a multiple-display-compatible card. In addition, the motherboard adapter becomes the secondary adapter. If your motherboard has a built-in video card, you must install Windows before installing the additional video cards. If not, Windows Setup will disable the motherboard adapter.

To configure your display in a multiple environment, follow these steps:

1. Open the Display Properties dialog box by double-clicking on the Display applet of the Control Panel or by using the shortcut menu of the desktop and selecting the Properties option.
2. Click on the Settings tab.
3. Click the monitor icon for the primary display device.
4. Select the display adapter for the primary display and select the color depth and resolution.
5. Click the monitor icon for the secondary display device.
6. Select the display adapter for the secondary display and then select the Extend My Windows Desktop Onto This Monitor check box.
7. Select the color depth and resolution for the secondary display.
8. Repeat the last three steps for each additional display.

The positions of the display can then be changed by clicking the Settings tab and dragging the displays to their desired position. See Figure 9.21.

If you have problems with the multiple displays, review Table 9.3.

9.5.3   Add/Remove Hardware Applets and Add/Remove Software

Unlike Windows NT 4.0, the Windows 2000 and Windows Server 2003 operating system families support plug-and-play (PNP) hardware. This means that by physically installing or connecting a PNP

Figure 9.21   Configuring multiple monitors

Table 9.3   Multiple Display Problems

Problem	Solution
The output on the secondary displays is not visible.	Check if the correct video driver is installed and check the status of the video adapter in the Device Manager. You can also try to switch the order of the adapters in the slots.
The Extend My Windows Desktop Onto This Monitor check box is unavailable.	Select the secondary display instead of the primary display in the Display Properties dialog box. In addition, make sure that the hardware supports multiple hardware and that the Windows 2000 can detect the secondary display.
An application fails to display on the secondary display.	Run the application on the primary display. If it is a DOS program, switch the application to full-screen mode and if it is a Windows application, maximize the application. Lastly, disable the secondary display to determine whether the problem is specific to multiple display support.

device, Windows will automatically configure the device (including the system resources such as I/O addresses, IRQs, and DMAs) and load the appropriate driver. Occasionally, you will need to use the Add/Remove Hardware wizard to discover a PNP device. If the PNP device causes a resource conflict, you can often use Device Manager to resolve such conflicts.

For non-PNP devices, configure the device by using jumpers or dip switches or by running a setup utility that comes with the device. To find out what the free resources are (I/O addresses, IRQ, DMA, and memory addresses), use Device Manager. After the card is configured and physically installed, Windows can often identify the hardware and install the appropriate drivers to activate the driver. If not, you will have to use the Add/Remove Hardware wizard. You may need to provide configuration information such as the resources of the device. See Figure 9.22.

The Add/Remove Programs applet helps you manage programs on your computer. It prompts you through the necessary steps to add a new program, change or remove an existing program, or add or

Figure 9.22   Using Add/Remove Hardware applet

Figure 9.23   The Add/Remove Programs applet can be used to change or remove programs that are already installed on your program

remove Windows 2000 components that were not installed during the original installation. See Figures 9.23 and 9.24.

Under rare circumstances, you may need to uninstall Windows XP and return to your original operating system. To do this, follow these steps:

1. Open Add or Remove Programs in Control Panel.
2. In the list of programs, click Windows XP, then click Change/Remove.
3. Click Uninstall Windows XP, then click Continue.
4. If any programs have been modified since the upgrade to Windows XP, you will receive a warning message. Review the warning; if you want to continue with the uninstall process, click Continue.
5. Click Yes to confirm that you want to start uninstalling Windows XP.
6. Your computer will restart automatically. Be sure that any floppy disks are removed before you click Yes.

Figure 9.24 The Add/Remove applet can be used to add or remove Windows Components without reinstalling Windows

You cannot uninstall Windows XP Professional if you

- Changed your hard disk configuration; for example, if you converted from FAT to NTFS or have created new partitions
- Upgraded from Windows NT 4.0 or Windows 2000 Professional

Programs that have been modified since the upgrade to Windows XP will not be consistent after the uninstallation:

- If you remove a program and then uninstall Windows XP, parts of the program (such as Start menu links) will be restored by the uninstallation process, but other parts of the program (such as its program files) will not be restored.
- If you add a program and then uninstall Windows XP, parts of the program (such as its registry settings) will be lost.
- Changes to programs can result in error messages after the uninstallation process is complete.

9.5.4   Folder Options

The Folder Options dialog box is used to configure if Windows will display hidden files in a window. See Figure 9.25. The File Types tab shows the file name extensions for known file types, and the View tab can be used to hide the protected operating system files, show system folders (such as Windows, WINNT, or System32), add My Documents to the desktop (Windows 2000), add Control Panel to the My Computer window (Windows XP and Windows Server 2003), and show encrypted or compressed files in a different color on NTFS partitions.

The Folder Options box also allows you to enable or disable simple file sharing for Windows XP machines. **Simple file sharing** lets you share folders with everyone on your workgroup or network and make folders in your user profile private. However, if simplified sharing is enabled, you cannot prevent specific users and groups from accessing your shared folders. Clear the check box (see Figure 9.25) if you want to set folder permissions for specific users and groups.

9.5.5   Power Options and the UPS

Advanced configuration and power interface (ACPI) is a powerful management specification developed by Intel, Microsoft, and Toshiba, which enables the operating system to control the amount of power given to each device attached to the computer. With ACPI, the operating system can turn off peripheral devices, such as CD-ROM players, when they're not in use. ACPI enables manufacturers to produce computers that automatically power up as soon as the user touches the keyboard.

Figure 9.25   Folder Options

Another Control Panel item is the Power Option applet. This option allows you to configure Windows to conserve power when not in use. For example, you configure the computer to automatically shut off the monitor or hard drive after a set time limit of nonuse. For servers, it is recommended that you disable power-saving features so that your server can be working at full capacity at all times. Instead, use a simple screen saver.

For notebook computers, Windows supports Hibernate mode and Standby mode to extend battery life. When a computer hibernates, it stores whatever it has in memory on your hard disk and then shuts down. When your computer comes out of hibernation, it returns the content saved to the hard disk back to RAM. In other words, it maintains the state of open programs and connected hardware while it hibernates.

In Standby mode, also known as Suspend mode, the computer switches to a low power state where devices, such as the monitor and hard disks, turn off while there is enough power to maintain the content of the RAM. When you want to use the computer again, it comes out of Standby mode quickly and your desktop is restored exactly as you left it. Since Standby mode does not save your desktop state to disk, a power failure while in Standby mode can cause you to lose unsaved information. Of the two modes, Standby mode returns to a ready state faster than Hibernate mode. Of course, it does need some power to maintain itself.

To enable Standby mode, use the System Standby option in the Power Schemes tab, where you specify the minutes of inactivity before going into Standby mode. To enable Hibernate mode, select the Hibernate option in the Hibernate tab. You can then go into Hibernate mode or Standby mode by clicking on the Start button, selecting the Shutdown option, and selecting the appropriate mode.

Since Hibernate mode is an ACPI feature, if your BIOS requires an upgrade to enable hibernation and you have already installed Windows 2000, Windows XP, or Windows Server 2003, you need to upgrade the HAL. Unfortunately, unlike changing the HAL when upgrading a single-processor system to a multiprocessor system, you must reinstall the operating system.

An uninterruptible power supply (UPS) provides power from internal batteries when the AC power fails. It is usually rated to provide a specific amount of power for a specified time. Many UPS devices can communicate with the operating system of the pending shutdown when the power from the UPS is spent. The UPS service within Windows pauses the server service to prevent any new connections and sends a message to notify users of the power failure. The UPS service then waits a specified time before notifying users to save their work and quit their sessions. The server itself will eventually shut down to protect the integrity of the information stored there. If power is restored before shutdown of the server, another message is sent to inform users that power has been restored and normal operations have resumed.

The UPS typically connects through a serial port to communicate, when a power failure occurs, that the battery power is low and a remote shutdown will occur by the UPS device. You can set options for the operations of the UPS using Power Options in the Control Panel. After installing the UPS and configuring Windows to communicate with the UPS, perform a test of the UPS by disconnecting the power. Remember: To configure the UPS settings, you must be an Administrator or a member in the Administrators group.

9.5.6 Regional and Language Options

With Regional and Language Options in the Control Panel, you can change the format Windows uses to display dates, times, currency amounts, large numbers, and numbers with decimal fractions. You can also choose from a large number of input languages and text services, such as different keyboard layouts, Input Method Editors, and speech and handwriting recognition programs. When you switch to another input language, some programs offer special features, such as font characters or spelling checkers designed for different languages.

If you work in more than one language or communicate with speakers of other languages, you might want to install additional language groups. Each language group you install allows you to type and read documents composed in languages of that group, such as Western Europe and United States, Central Europe, Baltic, and more. Each language has a default keyboard layout, but many languages have alternate layouts. Even if you work mainly with one language, you may want to try other layouts. In English, for example, typing letters with accents might be simpler with the U.S.-International layout. To switch to another input locale, on the taskbar, click the indicator representing the current input locale, then click the input locale you want to use.

Switch to another input locale so that you can compose documents in a different language using the keyboard layout or Input Method Editor designed for that language. You can use a different input locale for each program you use. For example, you can use one input locale to create documents using WordPad and another input locale at the command prompt. To set this up, open the program you want and select the input locale to be used for that program. Each time you switch to that program while it is running, the input locale you selected is active. Once you close the program, however you will need to select the input locale again for that program the next time you start it. If the indicator does not appear on the taskbar, click Start, point to Settings, and then click Control Panel. Double-Click Regional Options, click the Input Locales tab, and then click Enable indicator on taskbar. This option is disabled if you have only one input locale installed.

You can increase the available input locales by installing additional language groups. Multiple input languages can be enabled on a Windows computer. To enable an additional input language click on the Regional Options applet in the Control Panel, select the Input Locale tab, press the Add button, and select the desired input language from the drop-down list.

To change the keyboard layout for an installed input locale, follow these steps:

1. Open Regional Options in the Control Panel.
2. On the Input Locales tab, under Input language, click the language whose keyboard layout or Input Method Editor you want to change, then click Properties.
3. In the Input Locale Properties dialog box, click the keyboard layout or Input Method Editor you want to use, then click OK.

If you have the Windows Multilanguage version, you can change the language used for menus and dialogs by opening the Regional Options in the Control Panel. On the General tab, under Menus and dialogs, select the language you want.

9.5.7 Accessibility Tools

The accessibility tools that ship with Windows are intended to provide a minimum level of functionality for users with special needs. You can adjust the appearance and behavior of Windows to enhance accessibility for some vision-impaired, hearing-impaired, and mobility-impaired users without requiring additional software or hardware. Windows includes the following programs to enhance accessibility, even if you choose not to install accessibility services:

- **Magnifier**—Enlarges a portion of the screen for ease of viewing
- **Narrator**—Uses text-to-speech technology to read the contents of the screen aloud. This is useful for people who are blind or who have low vision
- **On-Screen Keyboard**—Provides users with limited mobility the ability to type on-screen using a pointing device
- **Utility Manager**—Enables users with administrator-level access to check an Accessibility program's status, start or stop an Accessibility program, and designate to have the program start when Windows starts

The accessibility tools available in Accessibility Options in the Control Panel perform various functions:

- Sticky keys enable simultaneous keystrokes while pressing one key at a time.
- Filter keys adjust the response of your keyboard.
- Toggle keys emit sounds when certain locking keys are pressed.
- Sound sentry provides visual warnings for system sounds.
- Show sounds instructs programs to display captions for program speech and sounds.
- High contrast improves screen contrast with alternative colors and font sizes.
- Mouse keys enable the keyboard to perform mouse functions.
- Serial keys allow the use of alternative input devices instead of a keyboard and mouse.

A wide variety of hardware and software products are available to make personal computers easier to use for people with disabilities. Among the different types of products available for MS-DOS and the Microsoft Windows operating systems are these:

- Programs that enlarge or alter the color of information on the screen for people with visual impairments
- Programs that describe information on the screen in Braille or synthesized speech for people who are blind or have difficulty reading
- Hardware and software utilities that modify the behavior of the mouse and keyboard
- Programs that enable the user to type using a mouse or his or her voice
- Word or phrase prediction software that allows users to type more quickly and with fewer keystrokes
- Alternate input devices, such as single switch or puff-and-sip devices, for people who cannot use a mouse or a keyboard

Most users with disabilities need utility programs with higher functionality for daily use. For a list of Windows-based accessibility utilities, see Microsoft Accessibility on the Microsoft website.

9.6   ADMINISTRATIVE TOOLS

Several utilities that are used to control and configure the many network services are grouped into the Administrative Tools folder, which can be accessed from within a Control Panel applet or by clicking on the Start button and clicking on the Programs option. While this book will discuss these utilities throughout, this chapter introduces the Microsoft Management Console (MMC) and the Event Viewer.

9.6.1   Microsoft Management Console

The **Microsoft Management Console (MMC)** is a primary administrative tool that is used to manage Windows. See Figure 9.26. It provides a standardized method to create, save, and open the various administrative tools provided by Windows, BackOffice products, and third-party services. Some of the Windows snap-ins (i.e., pluggable modules) include the following:

- System tools—container for managing local users and groups
- System information—container for managing hardware resources, monitoring the software environment, and controlling system services

Figure 9.26 Computer Management console is a prebuilt MMC

- Storage—container for a disk defragmenter tool, a removable storage control panel, and an optional archive manager
- Server applications and services—DHCP, DNS, RAS, and IIS services
- Links to shared directories, web links, and resource kits

Note that most snap-ins can be used on remote computers.

To start the Microsoft Management Console, follow these steps:

1. Click on the Start button.
2. Click on the Programs option.
3. Click on the Administrative Tools option.
4. Select the Computer Management option.

To start an empty MMC, go to the command prompt and type MMC.EXE. Every MMC has a console tree, which displays the hierarchical organization of snap-ins and extensions (snap-ins that require a parent snap-in). The adding and deleting of the snap-ins and extensions allows each user to customize the console. The console settings can then be saved to an MMC file (file with an .MSC extension) and can be used later, shared by others, and even e-mailed on other computers. By default, MMC stores snap-ins in the *%systemroot%*\system32 folder, the folder into which Windows is installed. By default, the Windows 2000 directory is C:\WINNT and the directory for the Windows Server 2003 family is C:\WINDOWS.

When building a custom console, assign various console modes (access options), as listed in Table 9.4. By default, all new MMCs are saved in author mode. To change the console mode, open the Console menu, select the Option option, and click on the Console tab. See Figure 9.27.

To add snap-ins, follow these steps:

1. Open the MMC.
2. Select the Add/Remove Snap-in from the Console menu.
3. Click on the Add button from within the Add Standalone Snap-in dialog box.
4. Click the snap-in that you want and click on the Add button.
5. Repeat steps 3 and 4 as needed.

Table 9.4   MMC modes

Console Mode	Description
Author Mode	Used to add or remove snap-ins, create new windows, view all portions of the console tree, and save the MMCs
User Mode—Full Access	Primarily used to distribute an MMC console to other administrators. Users cannot add snap-ins, remove snap-ins, or save the MMC console.
User Mode—Limited Access, Multiple Windows	Users cannot add snap-ins, remove snap-ins, or save the MMC console. While users can view the console in multiple windows, they cannot open new windows or gain access to a portion of the console tree.
User Mode—Limited Access, Single Window	Users cannot add snap-ins, remove snap-ins, or save the MMC. Users cannot view the console in multiple windows, open new windows, or gain access to a portion of the console tree.

Figure 9.27   Changing the MMC mode

To remove a snap-in, follow these steps:

1. Open the MMC.
2. Select the Add/Remove Snap-in from the Console menu.
3. Click on the snap-in that you want to remove.
4. Click on the Remove button.
5. Repeat steps 3 and 4 as needed.

9.6.2   Event Viewer

Event Viewer is a utility that is used to view and manage logs of system, program, and security events on a computer. Event Viewer gathers information about hardware and software problems and monitors Windows security events. Event Viewer can be executed by clicking on the Start button, clicking on

Programs, clicking on Administrative Tools, and then clicking on Event Viewer, or by adding it to the MMC. See Figure 9.28.

Windows Event Viewer starts with three kinds of logs:

- **Application log**—The application log contains events logged by programs. For example, a database program might record a file error in the programs log. Program developers decide which events to monitor. The application log can be viewed by all users.
- **Security log**—The security log contains valid and invalid logon attempts as well as events related to resource use such as creating, opening, or deleting files or other objects. For example, if you have enabled logon and logoff auditing, attempts to log on to the system are recorded in the security log. By default, security logging is turned off. To enable security logging, use Group Policy to set the audit policy or change the registry. To audit files and folders, you must be logged on as a member of the Administrators group or have been granted the Manage auditing and security log right in Group Policy. See Chapter 13 for policies and rights.
- **System log**—The system log contains events that are logged by the Windows system components. For example, the failure of a driver or other system component to load during start-up is recorded in the system log. The event types logged by system components are predetermined by Windows. The application log can be viewed by all users.

All BackOffice family applications (Microsoft applications designed to work on Windows servers) can post security events to the Windows event log. Several servers also make their own logs, which can be viewed by the Windows Event Viewer as well.

The five types of events are error, warning, information, success audit, and failure audit. They are shown in Table 9.5.

When you double-click on an event, the Event Properties window appears. The Event Properties can be divided into two parts, event header and event description. The event header information is shown in Table 9.6. The description of the event is the most important information within the Event Properties window, and it usually indicates what happened or the significance of the event.

Figure 9.28   Event Viewer

Table 9.5   Event Viewer event types

Event Type	Description
Error	A significant problem occurs, such as loss of data or loss of functionality, for example, when a service fails during start-up.
Warning	An event that is not necessarily significant, but may indicate a possible future problem. For example, when disk space is low, warning will be logged.
Information	An event that describes the successful operations of an application, driver, or service. For example, when a network driver loads successfully, an information event will be logged.
Success Audit	An audited security access attempt that succeeds. For example, a user's successful attempt to log on the system will be logged as a success audit event.
Failure Audit	An audited security access attempt that fails. For example, if a user tries to access a network drive and fails, the attempt will be logged as a failure audit event.

Table 9.6   Event header information

Information	Meaning
Date	Date the event occurred
Time	Local time the event occurred
User	User name on whose behalf the event occurred
Computer	Name of the computer where the event occurred. The computer name is usually your own, unless you are viewing an event log on another Windows computer.
Event ID	Number identifying the particular event type. The first line of the description usually contains the name of the event type.
Source	Software that logged the event, which can be either a program name, such as SQL Server, or a component of the system or of a large program, such as a driver name.
Type	Classification of the event severity: error, information, or warning in the system and application logs; and success audit or failure audit in the security log. In Event Viewer's normal list view, these are represented by a symbol.
Category	Classification of the event by the event source. This information is primarily used in the security log. For example, for security audits, this corresponds to one of the event types for which success or failure auditing can be enabled in Group Policy.

9.6.3   Services

A **service** is a program, routine, or process that performs a specific system function to support other programs. To manage the services, use the Services console (located under Administrative Tools) or the MMC with the Services snap-in. To start, stop, pause, resume, or restart services, right-click on the service and click on the desired option. Figure 9.29 shows the many services. On the left of the service name is a description.

To configure a service, right-click the service and click on the Properties option. On the General tab, under the start-up type pulldown option, set the following options:

- Automatic—specifies that the service should start automatically when the system starts
- Manual—specifies that a user or a dependent service can start the service. Services with manual start-up do not start automatically when the system starts.
- Disable—prevents the service from being started by the system, a user, or any dependent service

Figure 9.29 Services Console

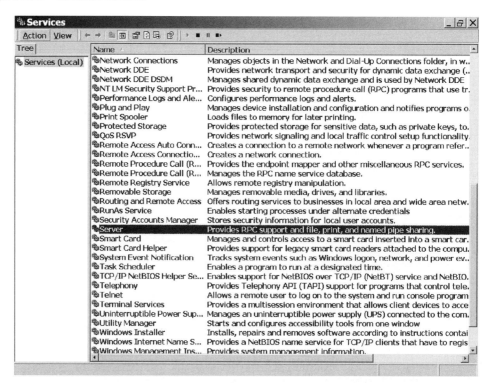

The Workstation service allows a user who is sitting at the computer to access the network to then access network resources such as shared folders. The workstation is also known as the redirector.

The Server allows a computer to provide network resources. When you pause the Server service, only users in the computer's Administrators and Server Operators groups will be able to make new connections to the computer. When you stop the Server service, all users who are connected over the network to the computer will be disconnected. If you stop a Server service, the affected computer can no longer be administered remotely and you must start the Server service locally; therefore, it is a good idea to warn connected users before stopping the Server service.

9.6.4 Task Scheduler

Task Scheduler is a program that comes with Windows which will schedule programs, batch files, and documents to run once, at regular intervals or at specific times. Task Scheduler starts each time you start Windows and runs in the background.

To use the scheduling service, double-click on the Scheduled Tasks applet in the Control Panel. You can schedule new tasks by double-clicking Add Scheduled Tasks, which starts the Scheduled Task wizard. From the wizard, you can then choose when you want the program to run and which program you want to run. After an item has been scheduled, you can manage the item by opening the item listed within the Add Scheduled Tasks applet.

When scheduling a task, you must provide a user name and a password, thereby setting the security context in which the task can run. Once a user name and password are set, another user cannot cancel or delete the task unless that user has the correct permissions. Note: Task Scheduler service must be set to log on using the Local System Account and not a user account. The Task Scheduler is a service and requires "Log on as a service" rights, which allow a security principal to log on as a service, as a way of establishing a security context. The Local System account on the Windows computer always retains the right to log on as a service. Any service that runs under a separate account must be granted this right.

In Windows, tasks are scheduled and performed based on standard Windows security permissions. You can set permissions for which users or groups can view, delete, modify, or use a task. In addition, the items that make up the task (the scripts, programs, and documents) are controlled by whatever ACLs are present for those individual items.

To configure security for a scheduled task, add or remove a user on the Security tab. Once a user name is added to a scheduled task, you can set permissions for that user's involvement with the task.

9.7   THE REGISTRY AND REGISTRY EDITOR

The **registry** is a central, secure database in which Windows stores all hardware configuration information, software configuration information, and system security policies. Components that use the registry include the Windows NT Kernel, device drivers, setup programs, NTDETECT.COM, hardware profiles, and user profiles. These items are discussed throughout the book, so do not worry if some sound unfamiliar.

The data kept in the registry are added and modified by a variety of system modules that start during boot-up and are modified by various configuration tools such as the Control Panel, Windows Setup program, User Manager, adding or removing a hardware device, adding or removing a printer, and other administrative utilities.

In addition, data are added and modified when installing software that uses a single application programming interface (API). You can think of an API as having a set of standard commands that can be used by any software package to access the registry. For example, a software package can find out what type of hardware is installed (including type of processor, resolution, and number of colors of the video system and the IRQ and DMA settings for a device) and the version of drivers and other software modules.

Since Windows is a multiuser system, it records and preserves security and graphical desktop information on an individual basis. Therefore, it contains a permanent record of per-user, per-application, per-machine configuration information. To keep the entire system secure, the key or setting within the registry is protected with an access control list (ACL), which allows selected users to modify the contents of the registry and grants to others read-only access to that data.

9.7.1   Registry Editor

If the need arises to view or change the registry, you can use the **Registry Editor (REGEDIT.EXE or REGEDT32.EXE)** utilities. REGEDT32.EXE is automatically installed in the WINNT\SYSTEM32 folder. REGEDIT.EXE is automatically installed in the WINNT folder. REGEDIT.EXE is easier to use because of its Explorer-style interface. See Figure 9.30. The REGEDT32.EXE is the Windows NT 4.0 version of the Registry Editor that provides access to Windows 2000 security permissions and auditing. See Figure 9.31.

Occasionally you may have the need to view or edit the registry to add or change a value that cannot be changed in the Control Panel or other utility or to add, view, and change hardware settings that cannot be done with Device Manager. You should only make changes when following directions in a magazine article, book, manual, or with a support person. If you make the wrong changes, Windows may not run properly or may not boot at all.

9.7.2   Structure of the Registry

The registry is organized in a hierarchical structure. It is first divided into five **subtrees.** See Table 9.7. Subtrees have names that begin with the string HKEY, which stands for "**handle to a key.**" A subtree is similar to a root directory of a disk.

Of the different subtrees, the two main ones are the HKEY_LOCAL_MACHINE and the HKEY_USERS. The HKEY_LOCAL_MACHINE contains information about the type of hardware installed, drivers, and other system settings. The HKEY_USERS contains information about all users who log on to the computer, including the DEFAULT generic user settings. The DEFAULT user serves as a template for any new users.

Figure 9.30 REGEDIT.EXE

Figure 9.31 REGEDT32.EXE

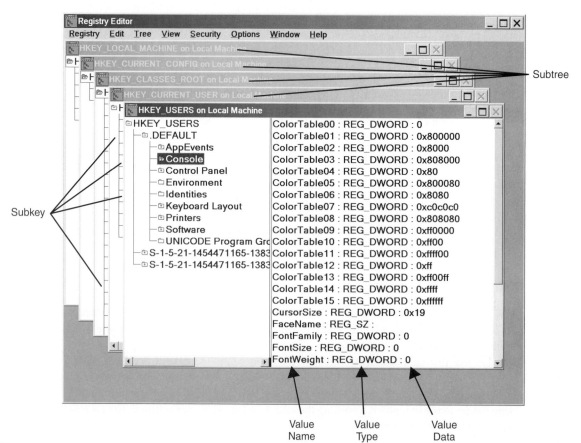

Table 9.7   Windows Registry subtrees

Subtrees	Description
HKEY_CLASSES_ROOT	Contains file associations and OLE information
HKEY_CURRENT_USER	Contains settings for applications, desktop configurations, and user preferences for the user currently logged on. The information retrieves a copy of each user account that is used to log on to the computer from the NTUSER.DAT file and stores it in the systemroot\PROFILES\username key. This subkey points to the same data contained in HKEY_USERS\SID_currently_logged_on_user. Note: This subtree takes precedence over HKEY_LOCAL_MACHINE for duplicated values.
HKEY_LOCAL_MACHINE	Contains information about the type of hardware installed, drivers, and other system settings. Information includes the bus type, system memory, device drivers, and start-up control data. The data in this subtree remain constant regardless of the user.
HKEY_USERS	Contains information about all users who log on to the computer including the DEFAULT generic user settings. The DEFAULT user serves as a template for any new users.
HKEY_CURRENT_CONFIG	Contains information about the current running hardware configuration. This information is used to configure settings such as the device drivers to load and the display resolution to use. This subtree is part of the HKEY_LOCAL_MACHINE subtree and maps to HKEY_LOCAL_MACHINE\SYSTEM\CurrentControlSet\Hardware Profiles\Current.

The root keys are then divided into **subkeys,** which may contain other subkeys. Think of the subkeys as folders within the subtree. Within the subkey is a value entry, which consists of three parts: the name of the value, the data type of the value, and the value itself. Data types describe the format of the data. The data types of the values are shown in Table 9.8.

9.7.3   HKEY_LOCAL_MACHINE Subtree

The **HKEY_LOCAL_MACHINE** subtree is one of the two main trees from which the other trees are made. Its structure is similar to the others. It has five subkeys, which are shown in Table 9.9. The HARDWARE key contains a detailed description of the installed hardware such as the type of motherboard, video adapter, SCSI adapters, serial ports, parallel ports, sound cards, and network adapters. Data in the HARDWARE key are volatile and computed at boot time. When your hardware configuration changes, the changes are reflected in the HARDWARE key at the next boot.

The next two keys, SAM, which stands for Security Accounts Manager, and SECURITY have no visible information, as they point to security policies and user authentication information. The values in these two keys are created, modified, and removed with either the User Manager or the User Manager for Domains. To keep the Windows secure, the Registry Editor does not display these data.

The SOFTWARE key contains a list of file extensions and associated applications—one key for each application that follows the configuration database registration procedure and one key for each loaded network driver. The SYSTEM key describes bootable and non-bootable configurations in a group of ControlSet, where each ControlSet represents a unique configuration. Within each ControlSet, two keys describe operating system components and service data for that configuration. This key also records the configuration used to boot the running system (CurrentControlSet), along with any failed configurations and the Last Known Good Configuration. Finally, the Setup key records the command used to install Windows and the boot disk and provides a list of the OEMSETUP files required to install hardware components.

Table 9.8 Windows Registry data types

Data Type	Description
REG_DWORD	Data represented by a number that is 4 bytes (double word) long. Many parameters for device drivers and services are this type and are displayed in Registry Editor in binary, hexadecimal, or decimal format.
REG_SZ	A fixed-length text string
REG_EXPAND_SZ	A variable-length data string. This data type includes variables that are resolved when a program or service uses the data.
REG_BINARY	Raw binary data represented as a string of hexadecimal digits. Windows interprets every two hexadecimal digits as a byte value.
REG_MULTI_SZ	A multiple string. Values that contain lists or multiple values in a form that people can read are usually this type. Entries are separated by spaces, commas, or other marks.
REG_FUL_RESOURCE_DESCRIPTOR	Stores a resource list for hardware components or drivers. You cannot add or modify entries with this data type.

Table 9.9 HKEY_LOCAL_MACHINE subkeys

Subkey	Description
HARDWARE	Contains type and state of physical devices attached to the computer. Much of this information is collected and built during boot-up. Therefore, it does not point to a specific file on a disk.
SAM	The directory database for the computer. The SAM subkey points to the SAM and SAM.LOG files in the systemroot\SYSTEM32\CONFIG directory.
SECURITY	The security information for the local computer. It maps to the SECURITY and SECURITY.LOG files in the systemroot\SYSTEM32\CONFIG directory. Applications query information by using security APIs.
SOFTWARE	Information about the local computer software that covers all users. IT points to the SOFTWARE and SOFTWARE.LOG files in the systemroot\SYSTEM32\CONFIG directory. It also contains the association and OLE information.
SYSTEM	Information about system devices and services. When you install or configure device drivers or services, they add or modify information under this hive. The SYSTEM hive maps to the SYSTEM and SYSTEM.LOG files in the systemroot\SYSTEM32\CONFIG directory. The registry keeps a backup of the data in the SYSTEM hive in the SYSTEM.ALT file.

Example 1:

Consider the following value:

HKEY_LOCAL_MACHINE\HARDWARE\DESCRIPTION\System\ CentralProcessor\0\ ~MHz

See Figure 9.32. Within the HKEY_LOCAL_MACHINE, you will find the HARDWARE subkey. By clicking on the plus (+) sign next to the HARDWARE subkey, you will open it to show the DE-SCRIPTION subkey. In the System subkey, you will find the CentralProcessor subkey and under that you will find the 0 subkey. In the 0 subkey you will find the ~MHz value, which is shown on the left pane. Next to the ~MHz value, you will find the data type of REG_DWORD, which means that we expected eight hexadecimal digits (4 bytes of information). Lastly, the value is set to 0x000001F5 (hexadecimal), which is equivalent to 501 MHz (decimal).

Windows XP and Window Server 2003 include System Configuration Utility (MSCONFIG.EXE), which allows you to easily enable or disable services and programs that automatically start up during the

Figure 9.32   HKEY_LOCAL_MACHINE values

Table 9.10   Windows hives

Hive	Hive Support Files
HKEY_LOCAL_MACHINE\SAM	SAM, SAM.LOG, and SAM.SAV
HKEY_LOCAL_MACHINE\Security	SECURITY, SECURITY.LOG, and SECURITY.SAV
HKEY_LOCAL_MACHINE\Software	SOFTWARE, SOFTWARE.LOG, and SOFTWARE.SAV
HKEY_LOCAL_MACHINE\System	SYSTEM, SYSTEM.ALT, SYSTEM.LOG, and SYSTEM.SAV
HKEY_CURRENT_CONFIG	SYSTEM, SYSTEM.ALT, SYSTEM.LOG, and SYSTEM.SAV
HKEY_USERS\DEFAULT	DEFAULT, DEFAULT.LOG, and DEFAULT.SAV
HKEY_CURRENT_USER	NTUSER.DAT and NTUSER.DAT.LOG

booting of Windows. If you have Windows 2000, services can be shut off in Windows using the services applet located under administrative tools, and shutting off the programs from loading automatically during the booting of Windows would be done by using the Registry Editor and deleting the key located in the HKEY_LOCAL_MACHINE\SOFTWARE\ Microsoft\Windows\Current Version\Run subtree.

9.7.4   Hives

The registry stores most of its information in sets of files called hives. A **hive** is a discrete body of keys, subkeys, and values. Each hive has a corresponding registry file and .LOG file located in the WINNT\SYSTEM32\CONFIG folder. Windows uses the .LOG file to record changes and ensure the integrity of the registry. When you work with the registry, you view and edit subtrees and their contents; when you back up and restore the registry, you work with hives.

Files without extensions contain a copy of the hive. Files with the .LOG extension contain a record of any changes to the hive. The files with the .SAV files contain copies of the hives at the end of Setup's text mode step. The .ALT file contains the Last Known Good information, in case anything happens to the system hive. The .DAT files contain user profile information. Table 9.10 lists the Windows hives.

Under normal circumstances, your system will reference the files without extensions. When writing changes to a hive file, the system will note the changes in the hive's log, so that it can cancel any unfinished changes in case the hive's updating process is interrupted. If something happens to the critical system hive, the .ALT version replaces it during the boot process. The .ALT then makes itself the new system hive and creates another backup .ALT file.

By default, most hive files are stored in the *%systemroot%*\SYSTEM32\CONFIG folder. The *%systemroot%* indicates the name of the directory that is holding the Windows files. The location of user profile information for each user of a computer, including the NTUSER.DAT and NTUSER.DAT.LOG, may depend on whether the installation of the operating system was a fresh installation or was installed as an upgrade from Windows 9X or Windows NT. In fresh installations and upgrades from Windows 9X, the NTUSER.DAT and NTUSER.DAT.LOG files are stored in the *%systemdrive%*:\DOCUMENT AND SETTINGS*Username* folder. In installations that are upgrades from Windows NT, the NTUSER.DAT/NTUSER.DAT.LOG files are stored in the *%systemroot%*\PROFILES*Username* folder.

9.7.5   Registry Size Limits

When Windows is running, the registry is stored in the paged pool, which is a portion of virtual memory. A value called the *registry size limits* prevents programs from completely filling the paged pool with registry data.

You can view and set the size of the registry by using System in the Control Panel. On the Advanced tab, click Performance Options and then click Change. For more information about setting the registry size, see "To change the maximum size of the computer's registry" and "To change the size of the virtual memory paging file."

By default, for Windows 2000 the registry size limit is 33% of the size of the paged pool. A registry size limit of up to 80% of the size of the paged pool is allowed. The minimum registry size is 16 MB. If you attempt to set the registry size to anything smaller, the system resets this value to 16 MB. Note: In Windows XP and Windows Server 2003, the registry size limit has been removed.

You should change the registry size only if the computer is a domain controller for a large network or if you receive an error message warning that the registry is too small. A large value for the registry size limit does not cause the system to use that much space unless it is actually needed by the registry. In addition, a large value does not guarantee that the maximum space is actually available for use by the registry.

9.7.6   Best Practices of the Registry

Before you make changes to the registry, make a backup copy by using a program such as Windows Backup. After you make changes to the registry, update your emergency repair disk (ERD) and automated system recovery (ASR) disk and tapes. For troubleshooting purposes, keep a list of the changes you make to the registry. Note: Do not replace the registry with the registry of another version of Windows. If you decide to use a registry from another computer, make sure that the computer is identical in every way.

Incorrectly editing the registry may severely damage your system. When possible, use the Control Panel, tools, and programs other than Registry Editor to edit the registry. Limit the number of people who have access to the registry. For example, because members of the Administrators group have full access to the registry, add only users who need Administrator rights to this group. You also can use Group Policy to restrict the use of Registry Editor (both REGEDT32.EXE and REGEDIT.EXE) for users who do not need access to the registry, or you can simply remove Registry Editor from the computers of these users.

If you use REGEDT32.EXE, make sure Read Only Mode on the Options menu is checked until you are ready to make changes. When you are done making changes and have saved your edits, recheck Read Only Mode. Alternatively, be sure to check Confirm on Delete on the Options menu. Never leave Registry Editor running unattended.

9.7.7   Troubleshooting Registry Problems

A corrupt or damaged registry can manifest itself in a number of ways: You may notice that files are missing or that components are not behaving as expected, you may receive an error message or a Stop error, or you may even be unable to start the operating system.

If you suspect a problem with the registry, try the following suggestions:

- If you have kept a record of the changes made to the registry, try undoing the most recent change.
- If you know which components have been affected, determine what the correct registry settings are for those components.
- Try using the Last Known Good Configuration for your computer.
- If you have a backup copy of the registry (as part of your backup of System State data) and can open Windows Backup, try to restore your registry settings. If you cannot start Windows, try repairing the operating system with your ERD. For more information, see Chapter 10.

In a worst-case scenario, reinstall Windows and all of its applications. If you have backed up your entire system, this job will be much easier and quicker.

9.8 WINDOWS SECONDARY LOGON SERVICE

Windows secondary logon allows administrators to log on with a nonadministrative account and still be able to perform administrative tasks (without logging off) by running trusted administrative programs in administrative contexts. In this scenario, system administrators require two user accounts: a regular account with basic privileges, and an administrative account (this can be a different administrative account for each administrator or a single administrative account shared among administrators).

Secondary logons address the security problems presented by administrators running programs that may be susceptible to "Trojan Horse" attacks (such as running Microsoft Internet Explorer in the administrative context while accessing a nontrusted website). Even though secondary logon is primarily intended for system administrators, it can be used by any user with multiple accounts to start programs under different account contexts without the need to log off.

To start a command shell in local computer administrative context while logged on as a normal user, follow these steps:

1. Click the Start button and select the Run option.
2. Type: runas /user:*machine_name*\administrator cmd. The *machine_name* is the name of your computer. Click on OK.
3. When a console window appears and prompts you for a password, type the password for the administrator account and press the Enter key.
4. A new console will appear running in the administrative context with the title of the console stating running as machine_name\administrator. You can then run any command-based administrative programs.

To start a Control Panel tool in Administrative Context while logged on as a normal user, follow these steps:

1. Click the Start button, select the Settings option, and select the Control Panel option.
2. Select the particular tool you want to run in administrative context (for example, Add/Remove Hardware).
3. Highlight the selected tool by using a single left-click on the icon.
4. Hold down the Shift key and right-click on the icon. You will notice the Run As command that appears in the command list.
5. Select the Run As command. You will be prompted with a dialog box titled, "Run program as other user."
6. Type the administrator account name and password in the appropriate fields. Please note that the domain name can also be changed.
7. After entering the credential for the administrator account, click on OK and the program associated with the tool will start in the administrative context.

The following example uses a shortcut to the Computer Management program, but this method will work on shortcuts of .EXE files and shortcuts of registered file types like .TXT, .DOC, and .MSC files.

While logged on as a normal user, follow these steps:

1. Use Windows Explorer to create a shortcut on your desktop for the file COMPMGMT.MSC. COMPMGMT.MSC can be found in the \%WINDIR%\SYSTEM32 directory. By default, this is the \WINNT\SYSTEM32 directory, located on the boot partition.
2. Highlight the Shortcut to Compmgmt icon on your desktop using a single left-click.
3. Hold down the Shift key while right-clicking on the Shortcut to Compmgmt icon on the desktop.
4. Select the Run As command. You will be prompted with the "Run program as other user" dialog box.
5. Type the name and password for the administrator account in the appropriate fields. Click on OK.

This will start an MMC console with the Computer Management snap-in loaded. This snap-in is now running in administrative context.

You can also configure a shortcut to always run using alternate credentials when opened by configuring the Properties for the shortcut as follows:

1. Close and open MMC consoles and highlight the Shortcut to Compmgmt icon on your desktop using a single left-click. Right-click on the icon and select Properties.
2. In the center area of the Properties dialog box find the checkbox labeled, "Run as different user." Select the checkbox and click on OK to close the Properties dialog box.
3. Double-click on the Shortcut to Compmgmt icon to start the console.
4. You will be prompted with the "Run program as other user" dialog box. Enter the credentials in the appropriate fields and click on OK.

To start an MMC in Administrative Context Using a Saved MSC file while logged on as a normal user, follow these steps:

1. Use Windows Explorer to copy the file MSC file to your desktop.
2. Highlight the MSC icon on your desktop by using a single left-click.
3. Hold down the Shift key and right-click on the Compmgmt icon on the desktop.
4. Select the Run As command. You will be prompted with the "Run program as other user" dialog box.
5. Type the name and password for the administrator account in the appropriate fields. Click on OK.

A new MMC console will now appear with the Computer Management snap-in loaded. This snap-in is now running in the administrative context. In a similar fashion, a system administrator can create custom MMC containing frequently used administrative snap-ins and run them in administrative context using secondary logon.

To run the Windows Explorer shell in administrative security context while logged on as a normal user, use these procedures:

1. To start Task Manager, right-click on the taskbar and select Task Manager.
2. Select the Processes tab.
3. Select EXPLORER.EXE. Click on End Process. Click Yes on the warning pop-up message. The entire desktop will disappear. You will still have any programs that you started, including Task Manager.
4. Select the Programs tab.
5. Click on New Task.
6. Type: runas/user:machine/domain name\administrator explorer.exe. Click on OK.
7. A console window will appear and prompt for the password. Minimize Task Manager, type the password, and press Enter. The desktop will return including the taskbar, shortcuts, Startup folder items, etc.
8. Perform necessary administrative tasks. For example, clicking on Start, Settings, and Control Panel will bring up control panel in administrative context.
9. When finished, log off Administrator. A new shell will automatically start, running in the originating user context.

SUMMARY

1. The Windows 2000 interface is based on the desktop, where you do all of your work. On the desktop you will find the My Computer icon, the Recycle Bin, the My Documents shortcut, and the taskbar (with the Start button). Windows XP and Windows Server 2003 use a newer interface designed for the desktop and taskbar to be less cluttered.

2. The My Computer icon represents your computer. It includes all disk drives and the Control Panel.

3. The Recycle Bin is used as a safe delete.

4. By default, the My Documents folder is stored in the C:\Documents and Settings*user_login_name* folder.

5. Disk and file management is usually done with My Computer or Windows Explorer.

6. There are several utilities used to configure Windows. The main ones are the Control Panel and Registry Editor.

7. The Device Manager lists all hardware devices on your computer and allows you to change the properties of any device.

8. The default size of the paging file (virtual memory) is equal to the total amount of RAM plus 12 MB, not to exceed the amount of available disk space.

9. The recommended size for the paging file should be 1.5 times the amount of RAM available on your system.

10. A hardware profile is a set of instructions that tells Windows which devices to start upon computer start-up or what settings to use for each device.

11. To keep your system loaded exclusively with drivers from the Hardware Compatability List (HAL) Microsoft introduced driver-signing technology into Windows 2000.

12. The Display applet allows you to configure the Windows environment including menus, windows, icons, the desktop, and the screen saver.

13. If you enable password protection, when the screen saver activates, then you must specify the login password to be able to continue.

14. Windows 2000 and Windows Server 2003 support the use of up to 10 monitors.

15. Windows 2000 and Windows Server 2003 support plug-and-play (PNP) hardware.

16. Several of the utilities used to control and configure the many network services are grouped into the Administrative Tools folder, which can be accessed from within a Control Panel applet or by clicking on the Start button and clicking on the Programs option.

17. The Microsoft Management Console (MMC) is a primary administrative tool used to manage Windows 2000 and Windows Server 2003.

18. The Event Viewer is a useful utility that is used to view and manage logs of system, program, and security events on a computer.

19. A service is a program, routine, or process that performs a specific system function to support other programs.

20. The registry is a central, secure database in which Windows 2000 and Windows Server 2003 store all hardware configuration information, software configuration information, and system security policies.

21. The data kept in the registry are added and modified by a variety of system modules that start during boot-up and are modified by various configuration tools such as the Control Panel, Windows Setup program, User Manager, adding or removing a hardware device, adding or removing a printer, and other administrative utilities.

22. If the need arises to view or change the registry, use the Registry Editor (REGEDIT.EXE or REGEDT32.EXE) utilities.

23. The registry is first divided into five subtrees. The subtrees have names that begin with the string HKEY, which stands for "handle to a key."

24. The root keys are then divided into subkeys, which may contain other subkeys.

QUESTIONS

1. You just installed a Windows application in Windows 2000. Typically to start the program, you would usually _____ .

   a. find the executable file using My Computer and double-click on it
   b. find the executable file using Windows Explorer and double-click on it
   c. click on the Start button, click on the Programs options, and click on the program in the appropriate folder
   d. click on right mouse on the desktop and select the program from the shortcut menu

2. When you delete a file by mistake, the file can be undeleted using _____.

   a. Recycle Bin
   b. Trash Can
   c. Swap File
   d. Paging File
   e. C drive

3. Which of the following will you *not* find in the My Computer icon?

   a. drive
   b. C drive
   c. Control Panel
   d. Recycle Bin
   e. printer folder

4. You have a program that follows the API specification. While removing the program, you want to make sure that the registry settings and program files are removed. Which applet would you use in the Control Panel?

   a. System applet
   b. Add/Remove Programs applet
   c. Add New Hardware applet
   d. Administrative Tools

5. How do you modify the appearance of the Windows 2000 desktop? (Choose all that apply.)

   a. Double-click on the Display applet in the Control Panel.
   b. Double-click on the System applet in the Control Panel.

c. Double-click on the Add/Remove Hardware applet in the Control Panel.

d. Right-click the My Picture folder.

e. Right-click the desktop and choose the Properties option.

6. To change the video card driver, you would _____ .

a. use the Add/Remove applet in the Control Panel and select the Video tab

b. use the Display applet in the Control Panel and select the Settings tab

c. modify the registry

d. modify the SYSTEM.INI file using a text editor

7. Which tool(s) can be used to install an updated driver for a Windows 2000 device? (Choose all that apply.)

a. Registry Editor

b. SETUP.EXE program

c. Add/Remove Program applet

d. Add/Remove Hardware applet

e. Device Manager

8. What happens when you use your mouse to right-click on an object in Windows 2000?

a. The properties sheet for that object will open.

b. A special Windows 95 property sheet will open that allows you to configure the Windows 95 environment.

c. A shortcut menu pertaining to that object will open.

d. You copy the object into the clipboard.

e. You open the Explorer for that object.

9. All of the devices are shown in the Device Manager. What does it mean when one of the devices has a circled exclamation point?

a. The hardware has a problem.

b. The hardware is disabled.

c. The device is a high-priority device.

d. The device is currently being used and cannot be removed at this time.

e. The hardware was never installed.

10. You have an MS-DOS–based game that has to be run in a full screen. How do you make sure the program will always start in a full screen?

a. Use the PIF editor to create a PIF file for the game.

b. Using the shortcut menu of the DOS program, select the Properties shortcut.

c. Press the Alt+Enter keys.

d. Right-click the icon for the program and choose Full screen.

11. You want to make sure deleted items are removed from the Recycle Bin immediately. How do you configure the Recycle Bin?

a. Select the Display applet in the Control Panel.

b. Select the System applet in the Control Panel.

c. Right-click the Recycle Bin and select the Properties options.

d. Delete the Recycle Bin from the desktop.

12. What files make up the registry?

a. REGISTRY.DAT   d. SYSTEM.INI

b. BOOT.INI   e. WIN.INI

c. SYSTEM.DAT   f. hives

13. How can you copy a file to a floppy disk from Windows Explorer? (Select two answers.)

a. Right-click the file name and choose Send To.

b. Drag the file to the floppy disk drive icon on the taskbar.

c. Drag the file to the desktop.

d. Right-click the file name and choose Copy To.

e. Drag the file to the A drive icon within My Computer.

14. You installed a modem on your computer, but the system does not recognize the modem. What do you do next?

a. Run the Add/Remove Hardware applet in the Control Panel.

b. Reinstall Windows 2000 and let Setup automatically install all necessary drivers.

c. Copy the required driver from the installation CD to the hard drive.

d. Use the Add/Remove Programs applet in the Control Panel.

15. The Device Manager can be found by _____ .

a. double-clicking the System applet in the Control Panel

b. clicking on the Start button and selecting the Settings option

c. double-clicking on the DEVMAN.EXE file

d. double-clicking on the Device Manager icon on the taskbar

16. What utility is used to perform common file and disk management functions?

a. Explorer   c. System Editor

b. File Manager   d. PIF Editor

17. Most of the Windows 2000 configuration information is kept in _____ .

a. initialization files (*.INI)

b. system files (*.SYS)

c. Windows 2000 Registry

d. configuration files (*.CFG)

e. dynamic link files (*.DLL)

18. All of the devices are shown in the Device Manager. What does it mean when one of the devices has a red X?

a. The hardware has a problem.

b. The hardware is disabled.

c. The device is currently being used and cannot be removed at this time.

d. The hardware was never installed.

e. The device is not on or does not have power.

19. You want to increase the initial paging file size. How do you configure the paging file?

a. Edit the registry.

b. Click the Change button on the Performance tab in System Properties.

c. Click the Virtual Memory button on the General tab in System Properties.

d. Click the Paging File button on the Hardware Profiles tab in System Properties.

20. Pat, a member of the users group, would like to view the application, security, and system logs on his Windows 2000 Professional computer using Event Viewer. What must he do to accomplish this?

a. Nothing, provided Pat has a functioning account on the workstation, because he will be able to view all of these logs.

b. Pat must ask the Administrator of the computer to grant the proper NTFS permissions for viewing the logs to him.

c. Pat must ask the Administrator of the computer to add his account to the Administrators local group.

d. Pat must ask the Administrator of the workstation to grant him access to Event Viewer.

21. Pat uses his portable computer both at home and in his office. He has a docking station at the office so that he can connect to the company's network. However, Pat does not want to start any network services while he is using his computer at home. How would Pat configure his computer?

a. Create two different user profiles.

b. Create two different hardware profiles.

c. Create two different roaming user profiles.

d. Create two different BOOT.INI files.

22. Pat wants to optimize the paging file on his computer. His computer has three physical disks and each has only one partition. The boot partition is located on the first physical disk. How would Pat optimize the paging file on his computer?

a. Create one paging file and put it on the disk that contains the boot partition.

b. Create one paging file and put it on any disk other than the one that contains the boot partition.

c. Create three paging files, one for each of the three physical disks.

d. Create two paging files, one for each physical disk except for the physical disk that contains the boot partition.

23. You want to connect an uninterruptible power supply (UPS) device to your Windows NT Workstation computer. How would you install the UPS device? (Select all that apply.)

a. Connect the UPS device to a serial port.

b. Connect the UPS device to a parallel port.

c. Configure the UPS using the Devices option in Control Panel.

d. Configure the UPS using the UPS option in Control Panel.

24. When Windows XP encounters data loss or failure of major functions, it produces kernel Stop errors. Which program would you use to view Stop errors and the time that they occurred?

a. Event Viewer   c. Disk Administrator

b. Server Manager   d. Kernel Debugger

25. Which one of the following log files on a Windows 2000 computer can only be viewed by members of the Administrators local group?

a. application log file   c. security log file

b. Device. Log file   d. system log file

26. How would you ensure that your workstation is locked automatically if you leave for more than 15 minutes?

a. Select a password-protected screen saver.

b. Enforce a system policy that locks the workstation if there is no activity for 15 minutes.

c. Schedule periodical shutdowns of the workstation.

d. Enable locking of the workstation on the Startup/Shutdown tab of System Properties.

27. Your Windows 2000 workstation is continually logged on to the Internet. You are also connected to a departmental domain. You want to ensure that sensitive information on your computer cannot be accessed by unauthorized users who are browsing the Internet. Which one of the following

security precautions should you implement on your computer?

a. Enable IP forwarding.

b. Disable the Workstation service on your machine.

c. Disable the Server service on your machine.

d. Enable the Computer Browser service on your machine.

28. Which utility would you use to search for a particular value in the registry?

a. REGEDIT.EXE   c. RDISK.EXE

b. REGEDT32.EXE   d. POLEDIT.EXE

29. Which tool would you use to run maintenance utilities at a specific time?

a. Task Scheduler   c. Job Manager

b. Task Manager   d. VMM

30. The primary Windows 2000 Administrative Tool is the

_____ .

a. MAT—Microsoft Admin Tool

b. MMC—Microsoft Management Console

c. MZA—Microsoft Zero Administration

d. IEA—Internet Explorer Administration

31. Which registry subtree contains data for the computer including hardware information?

a. HKEY_CURRENT_USER

b. HKEY_HARD_CONFIG

c. HKEY_LOCAL_MACHINE

d. HKEY_DEFAULT

32. Which one of the following user mode MMC types allows the creation of a new MMC window?

a. delegated access, single window

b. full access

c. delegated access, multiple windows

d. author

33. You have just opened an MMC tool in author mode. Which of the following actions can you perform in this MMC? (Select all that apply.)

a. Save MMC console settings.

b. Open additional windows.

c. Remove snap-ins.

d. Add snap-ins.

34. Which of the following are user mode MMC types? (Choose all that apply.)

a. limited access, single window

b. delegated access, double windows

c. full access

d. delegated access, multiple windows

35. You have just opened an MMC tool in user mode with full access. Which of the following actions can you perform in this MMC? (Choose all that apply.)

a. Save MMC console setting.

b. Add snap-ins.

c. Create windows.

d. Remove snap-ins.

36. What are the valid MMC modes? (Choose the two applicable answers.)

a. read-only   c. user

b. author   d. admin

37. Which service allows you to access network resources?

a. PNP   c. Server

b. Workstation   d. Print Spooler

38. To stop new users from logging in but still allow the current users to stay connected, you would _____ .

   a. stop the Server service

   b. pause the Server service

   c. stop the Workstation service

   d. pause the Workstation service

39. You are the desktop administrator for the Acme Corporation. You have recently installed Windows XP Professional on a portable computer that meets the minimum installation requirements for the operating system. After the installation, you attempt to configure the Hibernate mode but this option is unavailable. To ensure that the option becomes available, you update the BIOS on the computer. After the update, the computer displays a Stop error every time you attempt to restart the computer. You cannot successfully start the computer. You need to start the computer and enable hibernation. What should you do?

   a. Use System Restore to restore the last restore point.

   b. Restart the computer with the last known good configuration.

   c. Use the Recovery console to add the correct advanced configuration and power interface (ACPI) HAL to the computer.

   d. Reinstall Windows XP Professional to enable the advanced configuration and power interface (ACPI) and power management support.

40. Five of your company's employees have Windows 2000 Professional portable computers. The employees use their portable computers in a network-enabled docking station when they are at their desks. When the employees are working outside of the office, they use the portable computers without network connectivity. You have just installed wireless PC card network adapters in the portable computers so that the employees can access the network when they are in conference rooms in the office building. You need to configure the portable computers for optimum performance in all of the working environments. What should you do?

   a. Configure the wireless PC card network adapters to use DHCP to obtain their IP addresses.

   b. Configure three different hardware profiles on each portable computer.

   c. Configure the wireless PC card network adapters to use automatic private IP addressing when they cannot detect a DHCP server.

   d. Instruct each employee to unplug the wireless PC card network adapter whenever the portable computer is attached to a network-enabled docking station.

41. You are the administrator of a Windows 2000 Professional computer. You schedule a task to run after 15 minutes. One hour later, the task still has not run. You notice that your Event Viewer system log has the following error message: "The task scheduler service failed to start due to the following error. The service did not start due to login failure." You want to run the scheduler task again. What should you do before restarting the Task Scheduler service?

   a. Set the Task Scheduler service to log on using a local system account.

   b. Set the Task Scheduler service to allow the service to interact with the desktop.

   c. Restart the remote producer call service.

   d. Log off and then log on to an account in power users group.

42. You are the administrator of your company's network. You attempt to install a printer driver on a Windows 2000 computer for user Linda. You receive the following error message: "Error 11—Cannot install printer driver." The driver was originally downloaded from the printer manufacturer's website. You have successfully used the driver in the past on its Windows 2000 Professional computers. You want to configure Linda's computer to check for driver integrity and to allow you to install this printer driver. What should you do?

   a. Configure driver signing to display a message before installing an unsigned driver.

   b. Configure driver signing to ignore file signature verification. Create a local computer policy to enable Windows file protection.

   c. Use the Add Printer driver wizard to install the driver. Create a local computer policy to enable Windows file protection.

   d. Use the print troubleshooter. Configure the computer to prevent the installation of unsigned drivers.

43. Users report that some shortcuts on the Start menu of their Windows 2000 Professional computers are hidden. They want to access their shortcuts without having to click a scroll arrow. How must you configure the client computers to always display all Start menu shortcuts?

   a. In the Folder Options dialog box, clear the Enable web content check box in My Desktop Properties.

   b. In the Display Properties dialog box, clear the Transaction effects for menus and tool tips check box.

   c. In the Folder Options dialog box, clear the Hide file extensions for known File Types check box.

   d. In the Taskbar and Start Menu Properties dialog box, clear the Use personalized menus check box.

44. You are the administrator of your company's network. Your company is based in Russia and conducts the majority of its business in Russian. Users in your company create, view, and edit documents in English (U.S.), French, and Spanish to communicate with vendors internationally. Users run the Russian localized edition of Windows 2000 Professional on their desktop and portable computers. A user named Katrina wants to create word processing documents in both English and Spanish by using Notepad in Windows 2000 Professional. She requests your assistance in enabling English and Spanish on her computer. What should you do?

   a. Instruct Katrina to select the desired input locale for either English or Spanish within Notepad.

   b. Instruct Katrina to select the input locale indicator on the taskbar and select either English or Spanish.

   c. Instruct Katrina to use Regional Options in the Control Panel to add input locales and keyboard layouts /Input Method Editors for both English and Spanish.

   d. Create a local computer policy for Katrina's computer to include both English and Spanish.

45. You are the network administrator for your company. An employee named Bruno uses a Windows 2000 Professional portable computer. When he starts the computer, Windows

2000 prompts him to select either a docked or an undocked mode. Bruno primarily works out of the office and does not use a docking station. What should you do?

a. Modify the portable computer's BIOS settings, and disable support for the docking station.

b. Modify the portable computer's hardware profiles to remove the Docked hardware profile.

c. Modify the portable computer's device settings to disable the Unplug devices icon in the system tray.

d. Modify the portable computer's hardware profiles, and move the Docked hardware profile to the top of the list of hardware profiles.

46. You are the administrator of your company's network. A user named Michael has limited dexterity, which prevents him from using a standard keyboard to complete his daily computing tasks. You want to configure his Windows 2000 Professional computer to use the appropriate accessibility tools. You log on to Michael's computer by using his user account, which is a member of local users group. You configure the Stickykeys, Filterkeys, and Togglekeys. You then log off. Michael logs on to the computer by using this user account. He is able to use the accessibility tools, that you have configured. However, when he returns from lunch, the Accessibility Options are automatically turned off. What should you do?

a. Use Accessibility options in the Control Panel to reconfigure accessibility idle time settings.

b. Use Accessibility options in the Control Panel to enable the Filterkeys option to reconfigure the time setting.

c. Use Utility Manager to configure the Accessibility Options to start automatically when Windows 2000 Professional loads.

d. Use Utility Manager increase accessibility idle time setting for Accessibility Options, and save the settings

47. You attach a USB camera to your Windows 2000 Professional computer. Your Windows 2000 Professional detects the camera and prompts you to install the manufacturer's device driver. You insert the manufacturer-provided floppy disk. After installing the device drivers, you restart the computer. When Windows 2000 Professional loads, you notice that your USB board does not respond. You suspect that the camera drivers are not certified for Windows 2000 Professional. You want to configure your computers to enable your USB keyboard and to prevent uncertified drivers from being installed in the future. What should you do? (Choose two answers.)

a. Configure Windows 2000 Professional to enable driver signing.

b. Configure Windows 2000 Professional to disable driver signing.

c. Start the computer by using the Recovery Console. Restore system state data.

d. Start the computer in Safe mode. Replace the camera driver with Windows 2000 Professional certified driver by using Device Manager.

e. Start the computer in debug mode. Replace the camera driver with Windows 2000 Professional certified drivers by using the Device Manager.

48. You are the network administrator for your company. A user reports that the USB ports on his Windows 2000 Professional portable computer function only when the portable computer is in its docked position at the office. He asks you to configure the computer so that the USB port works when the portable computer is docked and when it is undocked and running on battery power. You verify that the portable computer supports ACPI power management. What should you do?

a. Modify the portable computer's power management settings to ensure the USB ports are not shut down when the computer is running on battery power.

b. Modify the portable computer's BIOS settings to disable ACPI when the computer is running on battery power.

c. Modify the portable computer's undocked hardware profile and enable the USB root hub.

d. Disable the BIOS power management features in the portable computer's BIOS settings.

e. Obtain external power supplies for the user's USB devices. Ensure that these power supplies are connected when the portable computer is undocked.

f. Undock the portable computer and reinstall the drivers for the USB port.

49. You are the administrator of a Windows 2000 network. You use a user account named user 1 to log on to a Windows 2000 Professional computer. The computer is used by different students in a classroom. User 1 does not have administrative rights. However, you prefer to use this account of your daily activities, because it is not a security breach if you fail to log off. You want to schedule a task to run on the command file named AddUser.cmd that automatically adds six more student user accounts. What should you do?

a. Schedule the task to run under the administrative account.

b. Log on by using the local administrator account. Then schedule the task to run under User1.

c. Take ownership of AddUsers.cmd. Then schedule the task to run under User 1.

d. Grant User1 read and execute permission for AddUsers.cmd. Then schedule the task to run under User1.

50. You are the administrator of 20 Windows XP Professional computers. Each computer has one hard disk that has three volumes named C, D, E. Each volumes is 4 GB in size and has approximately 1 GB of available space. The total physical memory of each computer is 196 MB. The paging file on each computer is located on drive D. A user named Andrea reports that every day 1 hour after she starts her Windows XP Professional computer, the computer appears to perform very slowly for 15 seconds. This always happens after she receives an error message stating that the system is low on virtual memory. You want to improve the performance of Andrea's computer. You do not want to install additional memory. What should you do?

a. Increase the initial size of the paging file.

b. Move the current paging file to the system drive.

c. Increase the Buffers setting in the config.sys. file.

d. Enable this option: Adjust for best performance of: System cache memory usage.

HANDS-ON EXERCISES

Exercise 1: Introduction to the Windows Interface

1. Start Windows 2000 Professional or Windows XP and log in.
2. If any windows are open, close them.
3. Start the Calculator by clicking on the Start button, clicking on Programs, clicking on Accessories, and selecting the Calculator. Close the Calculator by clicking on the Close button on the top right corner of the Calculator.
4. Start the Calculator by double-clicking on My Computer, double-clicking on the C: drive, double-clicking on the WINNT or Windows directory, double-clicking the SYSTEM32 folder, and then double-clicking on the CALC file. In the WINNT (or Windows) and SYSTEM32 folder, you will probably have to click on the Show All Files option on the left of the window.

    Note: Remember that Windows 2000 default system directory is C:\WINNT and the Windows XP and Windows Server 2003 is C:\WINDOWS.

5. Start the Calculator by using Windows Explorer. Close the Calculator by double-clicking on the small calculator icon at the top left of the Calculator.
6. Start the Calculator by using the Run option under the Start button and specifying the path of C:\WINNT\SYSTEM32\CALC.EXE. if you are using Windows 2000 or C:\WINDOWS\SYSTEM32\CALC.EXE or if you are using Windows XP. Close the Calculator.
7. Start the Calculator by using the Run option under the Start button and using the Browse button to find the CALC.EXE. Close the Calculator.
8. Open a window for the C:\Documents and Settings*user_login_name* folder (where *user_login_name* is the name used during the login) and notice the contents of the desktop directory.
9. Create a shortcut for the Calculator (C:\WINNT\SYSTEM32\CALC.EXE or C:\WINDOWS\SYSTEM32\CALC.EXE) program. You can do this by using the shortcut menu (right mouse button on the desktop) and select the New option followed by the Shortcut option. Try to determine what distinguishes a shortcut.
10. Test the Calculator shortcut. Close the Calculator.
11. Right-click the desktop, select the New option, select the Text Document option. Double-click the New Text Document.txt file. Use Notepad to create a text file called NAME.TXT located in the C:\ folder. Include your first and last name in the file. Close Notepad.
12. Double-click on the NAME file under the C drive. Notice that Notepad automatically started. Close Notepad.
13. On the desktop, make a shortcut to the NAME file. This can be done by accessing the shortcut menu (clicking on the desktop with the right mouse button—secondary mouse button), clicking on the New option, and clicking on the Shortcut option.
14. Test the shortcut to name.txt file. Close Notepad.
15. Create a new folder called COMMON APPS.
16. In the COMMON APPS group, create icons for the Calculator (CALC.EXE) and Notepad (NOTEPAD.EXE). CALC.EXE is located in the C:*Systemroot*\SYSTEM32 directory and Notepad is located the C:*Systemroot*\folder.
17. Test the newly created shortcuts.
18. Open the desktop folder again and notice the contents of the DESKTOP folder. It should be easy to see the purpose of the Desktop folder.
19. Delete the COMMON APPS folder, the Calculator shortcut, and Names shortcut.
20. Open a window for the C:*Systemroot* directory.
21. Select the Large Icons (or Tiles option) option under the View menu.
22. Select the Small Icons (or Icons option) option under the View menu.
23. Select the List option under the View menu.
24. Select the Details option under the View menu.
25. Open the View menu, click on the Arrange Icons option under the By Type option. "By type" means that it will sort by file name extension.
26. In the *Systemroot* window, open the shortcut menu by clicking on right mouse button without clicking on an icon click on the Arrange Icons option and click on the By Name option.
27. Make sure the Windows window does not auto arrange its icons. This can be done by opening the View menu and clicking on the Arrange Option menu. If there is a check mark on the Auto Arrange option, click on it to shut it off. If there is not a check mark on the Auto Arrange option, click somewhere on the desktop to close the menu.
28. Move some of the files around without putting one on top of another.
29. Enable the Auto Arrange feature for the Windows window.

30. Close all windows.
31. Double-click on the My Computer icon if it is on the desktop. If not, click the Start button and select the My Computer option.
32. Double-click on the C: drive.
33. Open Windows for the C:*Systemroot,* C:*Systemroot*\FONTS, and C:*Systemroot*\SYSTEM32 folders.
34. Close all windows.
35. Double-click on My Computer icon.
36. Select the Folder Options option under the Tools menu.
37. Under the General tab, select the "Open each folder in the same window" and click on OK.
38. Double-click on the C drive, double-click on the *Systemroot* folder, and double-click on the SYSTEM32 folder. Notice how many windows are open.
39. Click on the Up One Level button. Keep clicking on this button until you get back to the My Computer window.
40. Select the Folder Options option under the Tools menu. Under the General tab, select the "Open each folder in its own window" option and click on OK.
41. Select the View tab.
42. Select the "Display the full path in title bar" option.
43. Select the "Show hidden files and folders" option.
44. Deselect the "Hide file extensions for known file types" option.
45. Deselect the "Hide protected operating system files" option.
46. If you are running Windows XP, make sure that the "Show Control Panel" option is selected.
47. Click the OK button.
48. Close all windows.

Exercise 2: File Management

1. Insert a disk in drive A. Under My Computer, use the shortcut menu of the A drive and format the disk.
2. Open a window for the A drive.
3. Create a folder called COMMAND on the A drive using the shortcut menu.
4. Open the A:\COMMAND folder.
5. Open a window for the C:*Systemroot*\SYSTEM32.
6. Close all windows except for the two COMMAND and SYSTEM32 windows.
7. Copy the FORMAT.COM, ATTRIB.EXE, and DISKCOPY.COM files from the C:\ *Systemroot*\SYSTEM32 folder to the A:\COMMAND folder.
8. Create a DATA folder in the A:\ folder.
9. Move the FORMAT.COM file from the A:\COMMAND folder to the A:\DATA folder.
10. Copy the FORMAT.COM file from the A:\DATA folder to the A:\COMMAND directory.
11. Using the shortcut menu of the A drive, perform a disk copy to another disk. A disk must be in the disk drive before the Copy Disk option will appear.
12. Rename the FORMAT.COM file to DESTROY.COM in the A:\DATA folder.
13. Hide the DESTROY.COM file by using the shortcut menu of the DESTROY.COM file and selecting Properties.
14. If you cannot see hidden files, select Options under the View menu, click on the View menu, select Show all Files, and click on the OK button.
15. Use the COPY option from the shortcut menu of XCOPY.EXE file in the C:*Systemroot*\SYSTEM32 directory.
16. Make the A:\ window active. On the A:\ windows, select the Paste option from the shortcut menu.
17. Delete the DESTROY.COM file.
18. Using the A:\ window, highlight both folders at the same time and delete them.
19. Start Windows Explorer.
20. Using the shortcut menu of the A drive shown in Windows Explorer, format the disk.
21. Create a folder called COMMAND on the C drive using the shortcut menu of the C drive window.
22. Click on the DOS COMMAND folder. Notice the right side of the windows should show no files.
23. Click on the plus (+) next to the C:\WINNT folder in Explorer to show the subdirectories under WINNT.
24. Click on the SYSTEM32 folder under the WINNT directory.
25. Copy FORMAT.COM, ATTRIB.EXE, and DISKCOPY.COM files from the C:*Systemroot*\SYSTEM32 folder to the C:\COMMAND folder.
26. Delete the FORMAT.COM and ATTRIB.EXE file from the C:\COMMAND directory.
27. Double-click on the Recycle Bin. These are the files that you deleted in the GUI interface.
28. Drag the FORMAT.COM file to the desktop.
29. Highlight ATTRIB.EXE file and select Restore from the Shortcut menu or click on the Restore button on the left side of the Recycle Bin window.
30. Look in the COMMAND folder and notice that the ATTRIB.EXE file is back.

31. Select the Empty Recycle Bin option from the File menu.

32. Close the Recycle Bin window.

33. Access the shortcut menu of the Recycle Bin and select Properties. Notice the maximize size of the Recycle Bin.

34. Click on the OK button.

Exercise 3: DOS Applications

1. Open a window for the C:*Systemroot*\SYSTEM32 folder.

2. Right-click inside the window (not a file or folder), select the New option followed by the Text File option.

3. Type in the following:

MEM
PAUSE

4. Save the file as GO.BAT and close Notepad. Be sure to save it in the C:*Systemroot*\SYSTEM32 folder.

5. Double-click the GO.BAT file to run it. Record the numbers for extended memory.

6. Select the Properties option in the shortcut menu of the SHOW MEMORY shortcut. Notice the extra tabs for a DOS program compared with a Windows program.

7. Change the properties so that you have 4096 KB of extended memory and change the working directory to C:*Systemroot*\SYSTEM32. In addition, configure the shortcut to run in Windows. Hint: Use the memory and screen tabs.

8. Run the GO.BAT file again and compare the amounts of extended memory with those recorded.

9. Delete the GO.BAT file.

Exercise 4: Control Panel

System Applet

1. Open the Control Panel. If you are running Windows XP, click the switch to the Classic View option.

2. Double-click on the System applet. Record the Windows version, the processor ID listed under Computer, and the amount of physical RAM.

3. Click on the Hardware tab, then the Device Manager button.

4. Open the View menu and select the Resources by Type option.
   a. Find what device is using IRQ 5.
   b. Find which IRQ is being used for COM2 and the hard drive.
   c. Find which IRQs are free.
   d. Find what device is using I/O address 300.
   e. Find what device is using DMA 2.
   f. Find what DMAs are being used by the sound card.

5. Open the View menu and select the Devices by Type option.

6. On the device tree, find and double-click on COM2.
   a. Find and record the device status.
   b. Find and record the bits per second, the number of data bits and stop bits, the type of parity, and the type of flow control.
   c. Find and record the resources used by COM2.
   d. Find and record the entries in the Conflicting Device List.

7. Disable the COM2 by using the Device Usage option in the General tab.

8. If you have a sound card loaded, find it and delete the sound card from the device tree.

9. Close the Device Manager.

10. Click on the Hardware wizard (or Add Hardware wizard) button. You also can use the Add Remove Hardware applet in the Control Panel. Click on the Next button.

11. Select the Add/Troubleshoot a Device option (or "Yes, I have already connected the hardware" option) and click the Next button. The sound card should automatically be detected and the drivers loaded. If not, manually load the drivers by either specifying the type of card or the location of the drivers. When done, click on the Finish button.

12. If you are running Windows 2000, click on the Advanced tab followed by the Performance option. If you are running Windows XP, click the Settings button in the Performance section and select the Advanced tab. If the computer is going to be used as a production server by many people, optimize for Background services. If it is used primarily by you to run applications, optimize for Applications.

13. Click on the Change button under Virtual Memory.

14. Notice the initial size and maximize size. Add 20 MB to the initial size by typing the number and clicking on the Set button.

15. Select the D drive. Type in 384 MB for the initial size and 768 MB for the maximize size. Click on the Set button. Remember, you should not create two paging files on the same physical driver. It is better to put them on two or more physical drivers, not logical drives. In addition, do not use the drive that has the boot volume.

16. Remove the entry for the D drive by putting in zero for the initial size and maximize size. Click on the Set button. Click on OK to close the Virtual Memory dialog box and then click on OK to close the Performance Option dialog box.

17. Click on the Startup and Recovery button. Change the time to display the operating systems to 20 seconds. Click on OK.

18. Open the BOOT.INI file and see that the new time is 20 seconds.

Display Applet

19. Using the Display applet, change the background pattern to feather texture. Note: If you are running Windows XP, you will need to select the Desktop tab.

20. Select the Screen Server tab. Enable the Star Field screen saver and have it activate after 2 minutes of inactivity.

21. If you are using Windows 2000, select the Appearance tab and select the Item options. If you are using Windows XP, select the Appearance tab, click on the Advanced button and select the Item options. Increase the horizontal icon spacing to 75 pixels.

22. Change the icon text to bold, 15-point Arial.

23. Click on the Settings tab.

24. Record the current resolution and number of colors or color quality.

25. Change the screen resolution to 640×480 and the number of colors to 16. Click on OK.

26. Change the screen resolution to 800×600, number of colors to 256 colors, and small fonts. Click on OK.

27. Change the screen resolution to 800×600, number of colors to high color, and large fonts. Click on OK.

28. Change the display back to the recorded resolution and number of colors.

29. Click on the Advanced Properties button.

30. Record the manufacturer and type of video card and monitor.

31. Close the Display dialog box.

Add/Remove Programs

32. Go to the WWW.ADOBE.COM site and download the Adobe Acrobat Reader. Install Acrobat Reader.

33. Double-click the Add/Remove Programs applet in the Control Panel.

34. Under Change or Remove Programs, find Acrobat Reader and click on it. Then click on the Change/Remove button to remove the program.

35. Click on the Add/Remove Windows Components, click on the Other Network File and Print Services option, click on the Details button and select the Print services for Unix. Click on OK.

36. Click on the Next button. Use the wizard to finish the installation.

37. Close the Add/Remove Programs dialog box.

Exercise 5: MMC Console

Computer Management Console

1. If you are running Windows 2000, right-click the taskbar and select the Properties option, select the Advanced tab option, and select Display Administrative Tools option. Click the OK button. If you are running Windows XP, right-click the taskbar and select the Start menu option. Click the Customize option, select the Advanced tab option, and select "Display on the All programs menu and the Start menu" option under the System Administrative Tools section. Click the OK button.

2. Click on the Start button, select the Programs option, select the Administrative Tools option, and select the Computer Management option.

3. Open the Event Viewer. Click on the System option under Event Viewer. Look for any errors. If you find one, double-click to view it.

4. Go back to the Event Viewer and click on the Application option under the Event Viewer. Look for any errors. If you find one, double-click to view it.

5. Close the Event Viewer branch.

6. Click on the Services option located under Services and Applications. This will display all of the services loaded on your system.

7. To get a better view of the services, open the View menu and select the Detail option. Record the status of the service, workstation, and print spooler service.

8. Right-click the Server option and select the Stop option.
9. Right-click the Server option and select the Start option.
10. Right-click the Server option and select the Properties option.
11. Record the start-up type.
12. Close the Computer Management console.

Adding and Removing Components to the MMC

13. Click on the Start button and select the Run option. Execute the MMC command.
14. Open the Console menu and select the Add/Remove Snap-in option. Click on the Add button.
15. Double-click on the Disk Defragmenter and the Event Viewer. If the Select Computer dialog box comes up, select local computer. The Select Computer dialog box allows you to remotely administer to other computers. Click on the Close button. Click on OK.
16. Click on the Defragmenter. Double-click on Event Viewer.
17. Open the Console menu and select the Save option. Save the MMC console as MISC.MSC on the desktop. Close the Console.
18. From the Desktop, double-click on the MISC.MSC file. Close the console.
19. Right-click the MISC.MSC file and select the Copy option.
20. Right-click the taskbar and select Properties option. Select the Advanced tab, followed by the Advanced button.
21. The Start menu should already be highlighted. In the right pane, right-click and select the Paste option.
22. Close the Start menu dialog box. Close the Taskbar dialog box by clicking on the OK button.
23. Click on the Start button and run the MISC.MSC program.
24. Right-click on the System Event Viewer and select the New Window from Here option. Open the View menu and select the Tile Horizontally option.
25. Open the Console menu and select the Options option. Change the Console mode to "User mode—limited Access, single window." Click on the OK button.
26. Close the console and save the settings. When a warning appears asking if you are sure that you want to display a single window, click Yes.
27. Start the MISC.MSC file. If you right-click on any of the components, you will notice the New Window from Here option.
28. Close the console.

Exercise 6: Working with the Registry

1. Start the Display applet in the Control Panel.
2. Set the Wallpaper to Water Color and tile it.
3. Set the screen saver to flying windows and set the wait time to 3 minutes.
4. Start REGEDIT.EXE.
5. Find the following value:

   `HKEY_CURRENT_USER\Control Panel\Desktop\ScreenSaveTimeOut`

   Notice the value and compare it with the wait time of the screen saver. (Remember 1 minute equals 60 seconds.)
6. Change the ScreenSaveTimeOut value to 120 seconds.
7. Find the following value:

   `HKEY_CURRENT_USER\Control Panel\Desktop\TileWallPaper`

   Although the TileWallPaper value is a string, it only uses a 1 or 0 value. 1 indicates to tile the wallpaper and 0 indicates not to tile the wallpaper.
8. Find the following value:

   `HKEY_CURRENT_USER\Control Panel\Desktop\WallPaper`

9. Find the following value:

   `HKEY_LOCAL_MACHINE\hardware\description\system`

   Record the BIOS and BIOS date.
10. Find the following value:

    `HKEY_LOCAL_MACHINE\hardware\description\system\centralprocessing\0`

    Record the processor identifier and the speed.
11. Click on My Computer listed at the top of the tree.
12. Open the Edit menu and select the Find option. Search for the processor until you get to HKEY_LOCAL_MACHINE\hardware\description\system\centralprocessor\0 parameters.
13. Exit REGEDIT.EXE

CHAPTER 10

Networking with Windows

Topics Covered in This Chapter

Introduction

Before considering the advance network features of the TCP/IP protocol and Windows, you need to know the basics of network connectivity. Although some of this chapter may seem like a review of previous material (e.g., connecting Windows 9X to a network), more details are presented here.

Objectives

- Install, configure, and troubleshoot network adapters.
- Given a Windows 2000, Windows XP, or Windows Server 2003 computer, install and configure common network clients, network services, and network protocols.

- Given a Windows 2000, Windows XP, or Windows Server 2003 computer, optimize the computer for data throughput depending on function.
- When a Windows 2000, Windows XP, or Windows Server 2003 computer is connected to the network, test its connection by using common network commands such as PING, TRACERT, and ARP.

10.1   WINDOWS NETWORK ARCHITECTURE

As discussed in Chapter 3, the OSI model is a modular approach to networking. The OSI model is made of layers, each with specific tasks to perform. Although the OSI model is a common learning tool, it does not correspond to any common network architecture. Windows network architecture is arranged in a similar fashion, in that its components are arranged in layers and each has specific tasks to perform within its assigned layer. See Figure 10.1.

Figure 10.1   Windows network architecture

The **network driver interface specification (NDIS)** layer provides a communication path between two network devices. It is similar to the network layer in the OSI model as it acts as the link between the network adapters and the network protocols above it and manages the binding of network interface connections to the protocol. When a packet gets to the card, the NDIS routes it to the appropriate protocol. These protocols could be connection-oriented protocols such as ATM or TCP/IP, or it could be a connectionless protocol such as IPX. This layer contains the network media, including Integrated Services Digital Network (ISDN) lines, Ethernet, token ring, FDDI, and other fiber optic pathways. It also includes the **miniport drivers** that control the network interface adapter and connect the hardware device to the protocol stack.

Windows NDIS is implemented by a file called NDIS.SYS. It is also referred to as the NDIS wrapper because the code surrounds all NDIS device drivers. When a protocol is bound to a network component **(binding),** it is linked to a protocol stack. NDIS allows an unlimited number of network adapters in a computer and an unlimited number of protocols bound to one or more network adapters.

The **network protocol layer,** similar to the data and network layer of the OSI model, consists of the protocols that allow clients and applications to send data over the network. It includes TCP/IP, NWLink (IPX/SPX), NetBEUI, Infrared Data Association (IrDA) protocol, AppleTalk, and Data Link Control (DLC) protocol.

The **transport driver interface layer** provides a standard interface between network protocols and the network services (network applications, network redirectors, and network application programming interfaces (APIs). The network API provides standard programming interfaces for network applications and services including WinSock, NetBIOS, telephony API (TAPI), messaging API (MAPI), and others. The **interprocess communications layer** is the protocol that manages communications between clients and servers, including RPC, DCOM, named pipes, and mailslots. See Chapter 8.

The top layer is the **basic network services layer.** It supports network user applications by providing needed services such as file services, print services, network address management, and name services.

10.2   NETWORK COMPONENTS

You can add, remove, or configure the network components of Windows using the Network and Dial-up Connections applet in the Control Panel or by using the My Network Places icon on the desktop. When opening the Network and Dial-up Connections applet, you will find the Make New Connection and Local Area Connection icons. See Figure 10.2.

On the left side of the window are Network Identification and Add Network Components hyperlinks. The Network Identification hyperlink opens the Network Identification tab of the System Properties dialog box. From there, you can change the full computer/DNS name and the domain name/NetBIOS name. If the computer is a domain controller, however, you cannot change the computer and domain names. See Figure 10.3.

10.2.1   Add Network Components

The Add Network Components hyperlink opens the Windows Optional Networking Components Wizard dialog box. You can then add or remove components within the following three categories:

- Management and Monitoring Tools—includes the Connection Manager components, Directory Service Migration Tool, Network Monitor Tools, and Simple Network Management Protocol (SNMP) utilities
- Networking Services—includes DNS, DHCP, and WINS services
- Other Network File and Print Services—includes file and print services for Macintosh and print services for UNIX

The individual utilities are listed by clicking on the Details button. See Figures 10.4, 10.5, and 10.6.

10.2.2   Make New Connection

The Make New Connection icon starts the Network Connection Wizard so that you can establish a network connection. The network connections include connecting to a private network or the Internet using

Figure 10.2 Network and Dial-Up Connections dialog box

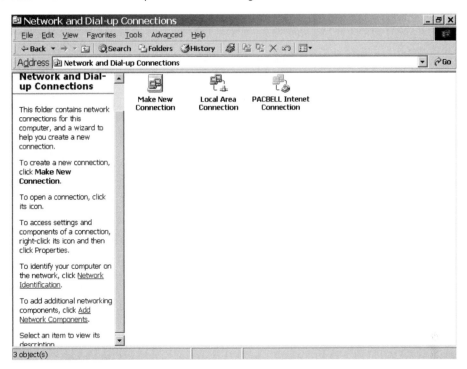

Figure 10.3 Network identification tab

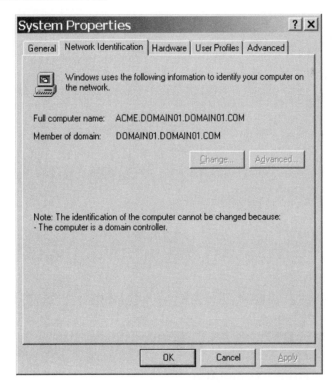

Figure 10.4 Windows Optional Networking Components Wizard dialog box

Figure 10.5 Management and Monitoring Tools dialog box

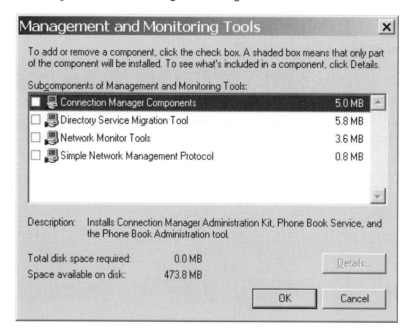

a phone line and connecting to a private network using the Internet (creating a tunnel). In addition, you can set up to accept incoming connections using the phone line or the Internet and to connect directly to another computer using a serial port, parallel port, or infrared port. See Figure 10.7.

10.2.3   Local Area Connection

To view your network connections, double-click the Network Connections applet in the Control Panel. A double-click on a Local Area Connection will show the computer's status on the network. Note: If a local connection does not show for a network interface, make sure the driver is loaded and enabled for

Figure 10.6   Networking Services dialog box

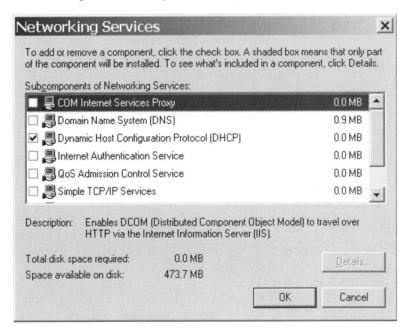

Figure 10.7   Network connection types

the network drive. Status indicates how long the computer has been connected, the speed of the connection, the number of packets that have been sent and received, and an option to disconnect from the network. See Figure 10.8.

For a single-link connection and for individual links in a multilink connection, the speed is negotiated and fixed at the time the connection or link is established. For multilink connections, this speed is equal to the sum of the speeds of the individual links. These speeds will vary as links are added or deleted. A multilink connection is a combination of two or more physical communications links' bandwidth into a single logical link used to increase the remote access bandwidth and throughput.

Figure 10.8   Local Area Connection Status dialog box

The Properties button is used to install and configure the network card, client software, network services, and protocols. The default client is Client for Microsoft Networks with an option to add Gateway (and Client) Services for NetWare. The default service loaded is the File and Print Sharing for Microsoft Networks, which allows other users to connect to the shared drives, directories, and printers on the computer. See Figure 10.9. Clicking the configure button will bring up the Properties dialog box for the network card adapter. The parameters located within the dialog box will vary depending on the network adapter manufacturer and model. See Figure 10.10. If the card and driver are ACPI-compatible, then there may be a tab for Power Management.

On servers, if you click to highlight the File and Printer Sharing Microsoft Networks and click on the Properties button, you can optimize the server depending on its function. For example, if the server is to be a domain controller or a file/print server, you would select "Maximize throughput for file sharing." See Table 10.1 and Figure 10.11. If it is an application server such as an SQL server, choose "Maximize throughput for network applications." The default is "Maximize throughput for file sharing."

10.2.4   TCP/IP Networks

The default protocol is the Internet Protocol (TCP/IP). If you access the properties of the TCP/IP protocol, you can select Obtain an IP address automatically, which is handed to the computer using a DHCP server, or you can manually set the IP address, the subnet mask, and the default gateway.

The IP address identifies the computer on the IP network, while the subnet masks specify which bits of the IP address is used as the network address and which bits are used for the host address. Of course, to communicate on a TCP/IP network, you must use an IP address and a subnet mask. The default gateway is the gateway or router address that connects your local area network to another network. Therefore, if you need to connect to another subnet or network, use the default gateway. At the bottom of the Internet Protocol (TCP/IP) Properties dialog box, you can specify the DNS server address. See Figure 10.12. The DNS server is for name resolution to resolve DNS names such as MICROSOFT.COM or MIT.EDU to an IP address.

If the computer is set to accept a DHCP server and one does not respond, the computer will use **Automatic Private IP Addressing** (also available in Windows 98), which generates an IP address in the form of 169.254.x.y (where *x.y* is the unique host address) and the subnet mask as 255.255.0.0. After the computer generates the address, it broadcasts this address until it can find a DHCP server. When you

Figure 10.9 Local Area Connection Properties dialog box

Figure 10.10 Network adapter properties

FIGURE 10.11   Server optimization dialog box

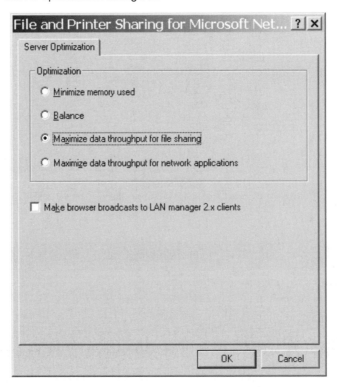

Table 10.1   Server optimization

Options	Environment
Minimize memory used	Choose this if using the server mainly as a workstation and will have fewer than 10 connections to the server.
Balance	Choose this if using the server as a workstation and a server will support between 10 and 64 connections.
Maximize throughput for file sharing	Choose this if using the server as a domain controller or a file-and-print server. If you have at least 128 MB of RAM, this option will result in a good-size system cache.
Maximize throughput for network applications	Choose this if using the server as an application server such as SQL server exchange or IIS. This is typically best used by distributed applications that do their own memory caching.

have an Automatic Private IP address, you can only communicate with computers on the same network/ subnet that have an Automatic Private IP address. By default, the Automatic Private IP Addressing feature is enabled. To disable this feature, change the HKEY_LOCAL_MACHINE\SYSTEM\CurrentControlSet\ Services\TCPIP\Parameters\Interfaces*Adapter*\ IPAutoconfigurationEnabled to zero in the registry.

By clicking on the Advanced button you can add additional gateways, DNS servers, and WINS servers. These additional gateway addresses, DNS servers, and WINS servers are only accessed when the first address is inaccessible, however. See Figure 10.12.

Like most TCP/IP implementations, the TCP/IP connection can be tested with the IPCONFIG, PING, ARP, and TRACERT utilities. The IPCONFIG will display addressing and settings of the TCP/IP protocol. The PING utility can be used to verify a TCP/IP connection while the TRACERT will show all router

Figure 10.12   TCP/IP properties

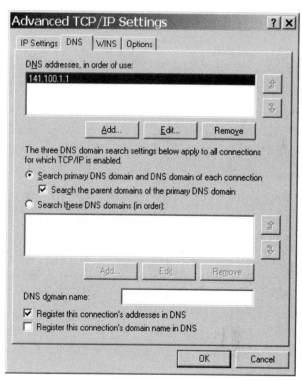

addresses as it connects to another computer. Lastly, the ARP protocol can be used to display the MAC address. For more information on the IPCONFIG, PING, and TRACERT commands, see Chapter 6.

The PATHPING command is a route tracing tool that combines features of the PING and TRACERT commands with additional information that neither of those tools provides. The PATHPING command sends packets to each router on the way to a final destination over a period of time, and then computes results based on the packets that are returned from each hop. Since the command shows the degree of packet loss at any given router or link, it is easy to determine which routers or links might be causing network problems. A number of switches are available, as shown in Table 10.2 and Figure 10.13.

The **NetDiag** command is a command line, diagnostic tool that helps isolate networking and connectivity problems by performing a series of tests to determine the state of the network client. Net-Diag diagnoses network problems by checking all aspects of a host computer's network configuration and connections. In addition to troubleshooting TCP/IP issues, it examines a host computer's internetwork packet exchange (IPX) and NetWare configurations. NetDiag is included in the \Support\Tools\ Support cab folder on the Windows Server compact disk. For information about installing and using Windows Support Tools and Support Tools Help, see the file Sreadme.doc in the \Support\Tools folder on the Windows Server CD.

10.2.5   Other Network Protocols

Two common network protocols are NWLink (IPX/SPX) and NetBEUI, both of which are much simpler to configure than the TCP/IP network protocol. For the NetBEUI protocol, nothing has to be done because it is nonroutable.

For the NWLink, specify the internal network number (eight-digit hexadecimal number) that identifies the server. In addition, specify the frame type and external number that identifies the subnet. If you select the auto frame type detection, it will automatically detect the frame type used by the network adapter to which it is bound. If NWLink detects no network traffic or if multiple frame

Table 10.2 Options of the PATHPING command

Switch	Name Function
–h	Does not resolve addresses to host names
–h *Maximum hops*	Maximum number of hops to search for target. The default number of hops is 30, and the default wait time before a timeout is 3 seconds.
–g *Host-list*	Loose source route along host list
–p *Period*	Number of milliseconds to wait between pings. The default period is 250 milliseconds.
–q *Num_queries*	Number of queries per hop. The default number of queries to each router along the path is 100.
–w *Timeout*	Waits this many milliseconds for each reply. Default is 100.
–T	Attaches a layer-2 priority tag (e.g., for IEEE 802.1p) to the packets and sends it to each of the network devices in the path. This helps in identifying the network devices that do not have layer-2 priority configured properly. The –T switch is used to test for quality of service (QoS) connectivity.
–R	Checks to determine whether each router in the path supports the resource reservation protocol (RSVP), which allows the host computer to reserve a certain amount of bandwidth for a data stream. The –R switch is used to test for quality of service (QoS) connectivity.

Figure 10.13 PATHPING command

```
c:\>pathping -n acme

Tracing route to acme [7.54.1.196]
over a maximum of 30 hops:
  0  172.16.87.35
  1  172.16.87.218
  2  192.68.52.1
  3  192.68.80.1
  4  7.54.247.14
  5  7.54.1.196

Computing statistics for 125 seconds . . .
                  Source to Here      This Node/Link
Hop   RTT      Lost/Sent = Pct     Lost/Sent = Pct     Address
  0                                                    172.16.87.35
                                   0/ 100 =   0%  |
  1   41ms     0/ 100 =   0%       0/ 100 =   0%       172.16.87.218
                                  13/ 100 =  13%  |
  2   22ms    16/ 100 =  16%       3/ 100 =   3%       192.68.52.1
                                   0/ 100 =   0%  |
  3   24ms    13/ 100 =  13%       0/ 100 =   0%       192.68.80.1
                                   0/ 100 =   0%  |
  4   21ms    14/ 100 =  14%       1/ 100 =   1%       7.54.247.14
                                   0/ 100 =   0%  |
  5   24ms    13/ 100 =  13%       0/ 100 =   0%       7.54.1.196

Trace complete.
```

Figure 10.14   NWLink IPX/SPX NetBIOS dialog box

Table 10.3   IPXROUTE command

Command	Description
IPXROUTE CONFIG	Displays the current IPX status including the network number, media access control (MAC) address, interface name, and frame type. See Figure 10.15.
The **IPXROUTE RIPOUT** *network_number*	Uses RIP to determine if there is connectivity to a specific network

types are detected in addition to the 802.2 frame type, NWLink sets the frame type to 802.2. See Figure 10.14.

To help troubleshoot the IPX protocol in Windows, use the **IPXROUTE** command to determine computer settings and perform diagnostic tests to resolve communication problems. See Table 10.3 and Figure 10.15.

10.2.6   Bindings

There are several ways to enhance network performance. First, when choosing which protocols to install, only install and enable the network protocols that you need. This will also reduce network traffic. Second, open the Network and Dial-up Connections folder, open the Advanced menu, and select the Advanced Settings option. This process enables you to use multiple protocols and to select the order of the protocols that are used. For example, if you are connecting to both the Microsoft Windows network and NetWare network using both TCP/IP and IPX protocols, you can set the TCP/IP protocol as the primary protocol for the Microsoft Windows network and IPX for the NetWare protocol by changing the binding order. Simply click on the protocol and use the arrows on the right side to adjust the position of the protocol. See Figure 10.16.

Figure 10.15 IPXROUTE CONFIG command

```
NWLink IPX Routing and Source Routing Control Program v2.00

Num  Name                    Network    Node           Frame
=============================================================
1.   IpxLoopbackAdapter      1234cdef   000000000002   [802.2]
2.   Local Area Connection   00000000   00c0f056bb98   [802.2]
3.   Local Area Connection 2 00000000   00a0c9e73b65   [802.2]
4.   NDISWANIPX              00000000   7ab920524153   [EthII]-

Legend
======
- down wan line
```

Figure 10.16 Advanced Settings where you can change the binding order of the protocol

10.2.7 802.1X Authentication

IEEE 802.1x is a draft standard for port-based network access control, which provides authenticated network access to 802.11 wireless networks and to wired Ethernet networks. Port-based network access control uses the physical characteristics of a switched local area network (LAN) infrastructure to authenticate devices that are attached to a LAN port and to prevent access to that port in cases where the authentication process fails.

During a port-based network access control interaction, a LAN port adopts one of two roles: authenticator or supplicant. In the role of authenticator, a LAN port enforces authentication before it allows user access to the services that can be accessed through that port. In the role of supplicant, a LAN port requests access to the services that can be accessed through the authenticator's port. An authentication server, which can be a separate entity or can be co-located with the authenticator, checks the supplicant's credentials on behalf of the authenticator. The authentication server then responds to the authenticator, indicating whether the supplicant is authorized to access the authenticator's services.

The authenticator's port-based network access control defines two logical access points to the LAN, through one physical LAN port. The first logical access point, the uncontrolled port, allows data exchange between the authenticator and other computers on the LAN, regardless of the computer's authorization state. The second logical access point, the controlled port, allows data exchange between an authenticated LAN user and the authenticator.

IEEE 802.1x uses standard security protocols, such as RADIUS, to provide centralized user identification, authentication, dynamic key management, and accounting. In Windows XP and Windows Server 2003, to set up 802.1x authentication, follow these steps:

1. Open Network Connections and right-click the connection for which you want to enable or disable IEEE 802.1x authentication; then click Properties.
2. On the Authentication tab, do one of the following:
   - To enable IEEE 802.1x authentication for this connection, select the Network access control using IEEE 802.1X check box. This check box is selected by default.
   - To disable IEEE 802.1x authentication for this connection, clear the Network access control using IEEE 802.1X check box.
3. In the EAP type list, select the Extensible Authentication Protocol type to be used with this connection.
4. If you select Smart Card or Other Certificate in the EAP type list, you can configure additional properties if you click Properties and, in Smart Card or Other Certificate properties, do the following:
   - To use the certificate that resides on your smart card for authentication, click Use my smart card.
   - To use the certificate that resides in the certificate store on your computer for authentication, click Use a certificate on this computer.
   - To verify that the server certificate presented to your computer is still valid, select the Validate server certificate check box, specify whether to connect only if the server resides within a particular domain, and specify the trusted root certification authority.
   - To use a different user name when the user name in the smart card or certificate is not the same as the user name in the domain to which you are logging on, select the Use a different user name for the connection check box.
   - Certificates are discussed in Chapter 23.
5. To specify whether the computer should attempt authentication to the network if a user is not logged on, and/or if the computer or user information is not available, do the following:
   - To specify that the computer attempt authentication to the network if a user is not logged on, select the Authenticate as computer when computer information is available check box.
   - To specify that the computer attempt authentication to the network if user information or computer information is not available, select the Authenticate as guest when user or computer information is unavailable check box. This check box is selected by default.

For wired and wireless network connections, the settings in the Authentication tab apply to the network to which you are currently connected. If you are currently connected to a wireless network, you can verify the name of the network by clicking the Wireless Networks tab. The name of the network will appear in Visible networks and Preferred networks, and it will be preceded by an icon with a circle around it.

10.2.8   Internet Connection Firewall

A firewall is a security system that acts as a protective boundary between a network and the outside world. Internet Connection Firewall (ICF), which is available in Windows XP and Windows 2003, is firewall software that sets restrictions on what information is communicated from your home or small office network to the Internet and from the Internet to your network.

If your network uses Internet Connection Sharing (ICS) to provide Internet access to multiple computers, ICF should be enabled on the shared Internet connection. However, ICS and ICF can be enabled separately. Enable ICF on the Internet connection of any computer that is connected directly to the Internet.

ICF also protects a single computer connected to the Internet. If you have a single computer connected to the Internet with a cable modem, a DSL modem, or a dial-up moderm, ICF protects your Internet connection. You should not enable ICF on virtual private network (VPN) connections, because they will interfere with the operation of file sharing and other VPN functions. (VPNs will be explained in Chapter 19.)

In addition, do not enable ICF on any connection that does not directly connect to the Internet. If the firewall is enabled on the network adapter of an ICS client computer, it will interfere with some communications between that computer and all other computers on the network. Similarly, the Network Setup Wizard does not allow ICF to be enabled on the ICS host private connection, the connection that connects the ICS host computer with the ICS client computers, because enabling a firewall in this location would completely prohibit network communication. Note: Firewall is not needed if your network already has a firewall or proxy server.

ICF is considered a "stateful" firewall. A stateful firewall is one that monitors all aspects of the communications that cross its path and inspects the source and destination address of each message that it handles. To prevent unsolicited traffic from the public side of the connection from entering the private side, ICF keeps a table of all communications that have originated from the ICF computer. In the case of a single computer, ICF tracks traffic originated from the computer. When used in conjunction with ICS, ICF tracks all traffic originated from the ICF/ICS computer and all traffic originated from private network computers. All inbound traffic from the Internet is compared against the entries in the table. Inbound Internet traffic is only allowed to reach the computers in your network when there is a matching entry in the table that shows that the communication exchange began from within your computer or private network.

Communications that originate from a source outside ICF computer, such as the Internet, are dropped by the firewall unless an entry in the Services tab is made to allow passage. Rather than sending you notifications about activity, ICF silently discards unsolicited communications, thereby stopping common hacking attempts such as port scanning. Such notifications could be sent frequently enough to become a distraction. Instead, ICF can create a security log to view the activity that is tracked by the firewall.

Services can be configured to allow unsolicited traffic from the Internet to be forwarded by the ICF computer to the private network. For example, if you are hosting an HTTP web server service, and have enabled the HTTP service on your ICF computer, unsolicited HTTP traffic will be forwarded by the ICF computer to the HTTP web server. Operational information, known as a service definition, is required by ICF to allow the unsolicited Internet traffic to be forwarded to the web server on your private network.

10.2.9 My Network Places

If the **My Network Places** is on the desktop, bring up the shortcut menu by using the secondary mouse button on the icon and clicking on the Properties option to bring up the Network and Dial-up Connections dialog box. If you double-click the My Network Places icon, you will find Add Network Place, Computers Near Me, and Entire Network icons. The Add Network Place helps you add a link to the network where you can store your documents such as a shared folder, a web folder, or an FTP site. The Computers Near Me icon shows the computers in your workgroup or network domain. The Entire Network shows all domains and workgroups.

10.2.10 ARP Utility

The Address Resolution Protocol (ARP) is the TCP/IP protocol that provides resolution of IP addresses to MAC addresses. To help manage the ARP protocol, you can use the ARP utility. See Figure 10.17.

To minimize the ARP broadcasts on the network, Windows maintains a cache of hardware-to-software addresses or MAC addresses to TCP/IP addresses for future use. This cache contains the dynamic ARP cache entries and static ARP cache entries. Dynamic ARP cache entries are added and deleted automatically during normal use of TCP/IP sessions with remote computers. Dynamic entries age and expire from the cache if not reused within 2 minutes. If a dynamic entry is reused within

Figure 10.17   ARP utility

```
ARP -a [inet_addr] [-N if_addr]
-a           Displays current ARP entries by interrogating the current
             protocol data. If inet_addr is specified, the IP and Physical
             addresses for only the specified computer are displayed. If
             more than one network interface uses ARP, entries for each ARP
             table are displayed.
-g           Same as -a.
inet_addr    Specifies an Internet address.
-N if_addr   Displays the ARP entries for the network interface specified
             by if_addr.
-d           Deletes the host specified by inet_addr.
-s           Adds the host and associates the Internet address inet_addr
             with the Physical address eth_addr. The Physical address is
             given as 6 hexadecimal bytes separated by hyphens. The entry
             is permanent.
eth_addr     Specifies a Physical address.
if_addr      If present, this specifies the Internet address of the
             interface whose address translation table should be modified.
             If not present, the first applicable interface will be used.
Example:
  > arp -s 157.55.85.212  00-aa-00-62-c6-09 .... Adds a static entry.
  > arp -a                                     .... Displays the arp table.
```

Figure 10.18   Display the contents of the ARP cache

```
C:\>ARP -A

      Interface: 141.3.12.4 on Interface 0x1
        Internet Address      Physical Address   Type
         141.3.12.4           00-a0-04-67-7d-a4  dynamic
```

2 minutes, it may remain in the cache and age up to a maximum cache life of 10 minutes before being removed or requiring cache renewal by using the ARP broadcast process. Static entries are added manually by using the ARP command with the –s option and will remain in the ARP cache until the computer is restarted.

To view the address resolution protocol cache, type ARP–A at the command prompt. See Figure 10.18. In this example, the cache entry indicates that the remote host computer at 141.3.12.4 resolved to a MAC address of 00-a0-04-67-7d-a4 assigned in the remote computer's network adapter hardware. Remember that you can use IPCONFIG/ALL or WINIPCFG on the machine they want, to identify the MAC address. If you recently used the PING command to a host computer, you can then access the ARP cache to view the MAC address.

To establish a static address, use the –S option. For example, to assign the MAC address of 00-a0-04-67-7d-a4 to the TCP/IP address of 141.3.12.4, type in the following command:

```
arp -s 157.55.85.212 00-aa-00-62-c6-09
```

SUMMARY

1. Windows network architecture is similar to the OSI model, in that the Windows network components are arranged in layers and each has specific tasks to perform within its assigned layer.
2. The network driver interface specification (NDIS) layer provides a communication path between two network devices.
3. The miniport drivers control the network interface adapter and connect the hardware device to the protocol stack.
4. When a protocol is bound to a network component (binding), the protocol is linked to a protocol stack.
5. The default client is Client for Microsoft Networks with an option to add Gateway (and Client) Services for NetWare.
6. The default service loaded is the File and Print Sharing for Microsoft Networks, which allows other users to connect to the shared drives, directories, and printers on the computer.
7. Like most TCP/IP implementations, the TCP/IP connection in Windows can be tested with the IPCONFIG, PING, ARP, and TRACERT utilities.

QUESTIONS

1. To add or configure the network components, use_____.
   a. Network and Dial-up Connections
   b. Device Manager
   c. Add/Remove Hardware
   d. System
   e. Network Neighborhood
2. If you have a domain controller, you cannot change the_____.
   a. IP address
   b. network card driver
   c. computer name
   d. subnet mask
3. Doing which one of the following will show the connection speed of an interface?
   a. right-click My Network Places
   b. double-click My Network Places
   c. right-click the Local Area Connection
   d. double-click the Local Area Connection
4. Which is the default client for Windows?
   a. Client Services for Microsoft
   b. Client Services for NetWare
   c. File and Print Sharing for Microsoft Networks
   d. File and Print Sharing for NetWare
5. Which services are loaded by default in Windows? (Choose all that apply.)
   a. Client for Microsoft Networks
   b. Client Services for NetWare
   c. File and Print Sharing for Microsoft Networks
   d. File and Print Sharing for NetWare
6. To specify "Maximize data throughput for file sharing" or "Maximize data throughput for network applications," you would click to highlight _____ .
   a. TCP/IP and click on the Properties button
   b. File and Printer Sharing Networks and click on the Properties button
   c. My Network Place and click on the Properties button
   d. File and Printer Sharing for Microsoft Networks
7. Which one of the following options would you choose if your server is a domain controller?
   a. Minimize memory used
   b. Balance
   c. Maximize data throughput for file sharing
   d. Maximize data throughout for network applications

8. What is the default protocol or protocols loaded in Windows? (Select all that apply.)
   a. TCP/IP
   b. IPX/NWLink
   c. NetBEUI
   d. DLC
   e. AppleTalk
9. Automatic Private IP Addressing can provide an IP address in which range?
   a. 169.254.0.0 to 169.254.255.255
   b. 150.101.0.0 to 150.101.255.255
   c. 130.0.0.0 to 130.255.255.255
   d. 127.0.0.0 to 127.255.255.255
10. If you load NWLink, you need to specify what? (Select two answers.)
    a. gateway
    b. subnet mask
    c. internal network number
    d. frame type
11. How do the binding orders of client machines affect system performance?
    a. Client binding order has no effect on system performance.
    b. You should move slower protocols to the top of the binding order on client machines to improve performance.
    c. You should move frequently used protocols to the top of the binding order on client machines to improve performance.
    d. Client binding order has no effect on system performance, but it is usually possible to improve system performance by reordering server binding orders.
12. In Windows, to see all domains, you would use _____ .
    a. Add Network Place
    b. Computers Near Me
    c. Entire Network
    d. Network Neighborhood
13. The Add Network Place _____ .
    a. helps you add a link to the network where you can store your documents such as a shared folder, a web folder, or an FTP site

b. creates a network share

c. creates a web share

d. sets up a private network connection

14. You want to examine the resolution of IP address to MAC address of outgoing packets on your Windows server computer. Which of the following should you use?

a. TRACERT

b. ARP

c. PING

d. NBTSTAT

15. You are a help desk technician for your company. Pat is an executive. Because Pat travels frequently, she uses a Windows XP Professional portable computer that has a smart card reader. Pat asks you to configure her computer so that she can dial in to the company network when she is out of the office. Company security policy states that dial-in users must use a smart card when they connect to the network, and that the users must use the strongest form of data encryption possible. Company security policy also states that client computers must disconnect if the routing and remote access server do not support both smart card authentication and the strongest possible authentication. You need to configure the dial-up connection properties on Pat's computer to dial in to the company network. Your solution must ensure that company security policies are enforced. Which three actions should you perform? (Each correct answer presents part of the solution. Choose three.)

a. Select "Advanced (custom settings)" security option.

b. Select "Require data encryption" check box.

c. Select "Typical (recommended settings)" security option.

d. Select "Use smart card" item from "Validate my identify as follows" list.

e. Select "Maximum strength encryption" item from the "Data encryption" list.

f. Select "Allow these protocols" option, and select "MS-CHAP v2" check box.

g. Select "Extensible Authentication Protocol (EAP)" option, and select "Smart Card or Other Certificate" from the EAP list.

HANDS-ON EXERCISES

Exercise 1: Using the TCP/IP Network

1. Start a DOS prompt by clicking on the Start button, selecting the Programs option, selecting the Accessories option, and selecting the Command prompt option.

2. Execute the IPCONFIG command and record the following settings:

   IP address
   subnet mask
   default gateway

3. Use the IPCONFIG /ALL command and record the following settings:

   MAC address
   WINS server (if any)
   DNS server (if any)
   DHCP enabled?

4. Ping the loopback address of 127.0.0.1.

5. Ping your IP address.

6. Ping your instructor's computer.

7. Ping your partner's computer.

8. If you have a router on your network, ping your gateway or local router connection.

9. If your network has a DHCP server, right-click My Network Places and select the Properties option. If My Network Places B not on the desktop, you can open the same window by double-clicking the Network Connections applet located in the Control Panel.

10. Click on the Internet Protocol (TCP/IP) and then click on the Properties button.

11. In the Internet Protocol (TCP/IP) Properties dialog box, select "Obtain an IP address automatically." Click on the OK button.

12. Execute the IPCONFIG command at the Command prompt and record the following settings:

    IP address
    subnet mask
    default gateway
    WINS server (if any)
    DNS server (if any)
    DHCP enabled?

13. Ping the loopback address of 127.0.0.1.
14. Ping your IP address.
15. Ping your instructor's computer.
16. Ping your partner's computer.
17. If you have a router on your network, ping your gateway or local router connection.
18. At the Command prompt, execute the IPCONFIG /RELEASE to remove your values specified by a DHCP server.
19. At the Command prompt, execute the IPCONFIG command and compare the recorded values from number 4.
20. At the Command prompt, execute the IPCONFIG /RENEW command.
21. At the Command prompt, execute the IPCONFIG command and compare the recorded values from number 4.
22. Have your instructor stop the DHCP server (or DCHP service).
23. At the Command prompt, execute the IPCONFIG /RELEASE command followed by the IPCONFIG / RENEW. (There will be a pause while Windows attempts to locate a DHCP server.)
24. At the Command prompt, execute the IPCONFIG prompt. Record the address and try to determine from where this address originated.
25. Try to ping your instructor's computer and the local gateway. You should not be able to ping the IP addresses (and subnet mask) to indicate that the two computers are on two different networks.
26. After your partner has acquired an Automatic Private IP address, try to ping each other. Since these addresses are on the same network (physically and logically), it should work.
27. Go back into the TCP/IP dialog box and enter the static addresses that you recorded in steps 3 and 4.
28. Test your network by pinging your partner, instructor's computer, and gateway.
29. Disconnect the network cable from the back of the computer.
30. Look at the taskbar in the notification area (near the clock) and find the red X.
31. From the Command prompt, type in IPCONFIG.
32. Go into the Network and Dial-up Connection dialog box by right-clicking My Network Places and selecting Properties. Note the red X.
33. Connect the cable back into the network card. Note that the red X in both places goes away. In addition, note that the icon disappears altogether from the notification area.
34. Right-click Local Area Connection and select Properties.
35. Select "Show icon in taskbar when connected." Click on the OK button. Close the Local Area Connection dialog box.
36. Go to the notification area and note the new icon representing the network connection.
37. Without clicking on the new icon, move the mouse pointer onto the icon. Without moving the mouse, note the information given.
38. Double-click the icon to bring up the Local Area Connection dialog box.
39. From the Command prompt, execute the ARP–A.
40. Close all windows.

Exercise 2: Navigating the Network

1. Right-click the desktop and create a folder called Shared.
2. If you have Windows XP, double-click the Shared folder. Open the Tools menu and select the Folder option. Select the View tab and deselect the "Use Simple file sharing" option. Click the Off button and close the shared window.
3. Right-click the Shared directory and select the Sharing option.
4. Select the "Share this folder option" and click the OK button. A hand should appear underneath the Shared directory.
5. Open the Shared directory and create a text file with your name. To create a text file, right-click the Open folder, select the New option, and select the Text Document option.
6. Close all windows.
7. Double-click My Network Places to open it.
8. Double-click Computers Near Me.
9. Double-click your computer to see all shared resources.
10. Double-click the Shared directory to see the text file that you created.
11. Click the Up button twice on the toolbar to go back to the Computers Near Me window.
12. Double-click your partner's computer. Double-click the Shared directory to see your partner's text file.
13. Click the Up button three times on the toolbar to go back to the Computers Near Me dialog box.
14. Double-click the Entire Network icon, then click on the entire contents hyperlink on the left side of the window.
15. Double-click the Microsoft Windows Network icon. You should see your workgroup and any domains that might be out there.
16. Double-click your workgroup to see all computers assigned to the workgroup.

17. Use the Up arrow button on the toolbar to go back to the My Network Places window.
18. Double-click the Add Network Place icon.
19. In the "Type the location of the Network Place" text box, type the following: *partnercomputername*\SHARED.
20. Click on the Next button, then click on the Finish button.
21. Close the Shared window.
22. Note the new icon in the My Network Places. Double-click on it.
23. Close all windows.

Exercise 3: Using IPX Protocol

1. Bring up the Network and Dial-up Connection window again.
2. Double-click on the Local Area Connection and click on the Properties button.
3. Click on the Install button. In the Select Network Component Type dialog box, click the Protocol option and click on the Add button. In the Select Network Protocol dialog box, click "NWLink IPX/SPX/NetBIOS Compatible Transport Protocol," and then click OK.
4. In the Local Area Connection Properties dialog box, click the "NWLinkIPX/SPX/NetBIOS Compatible Transport Protocol" and then click Properties. Note which type of frame detection is selected by default.
5. Close the Local Area Connection Properties dialog box.
6. In the Network and Dial-up Connections window, open the Advanced menu and select the Advanced Settings option.
7. In the Advanced Settings dialog box, under Client for Microsoft Networks, unbind TCP/IP by clearing the Internet Protocol (TCP/IP) check box. Click the OK button and close the Network and Dial-up Connections window.
8. Restart the computer.
9. Open a Command prompt window.
10. At the prompt, type in IPXROUTE CONFIG and press Enter. Note the frame type, network address, and MAC address.
11. Close the Command prompt window.
12. Try to access the share that you set up in Exercise 2.
13. Open the Network and Dial-up Connections window.
14. Double-click the Local Area Connection and click on the Properties button.
15. In the Local Area Connection Properties dialog box, click "NWLinkIPX/SPX/NetBIOS Compatible Transport Protocol" and click the Uninstall button. Click on the Yes button to uninstall NWLink.
16. When it attempts to restart your computer, click the No button. Close all windows and reboot the computer.

UNIT III

WINDOWS SERVER BASICS

CHAPTER 11

Advanced TCP/IP Topics

Topics Covered in This Chapter

Introduction

Before you can navigate your network, you need some type of name resolution. Both a DNS and a WINS server are used to resolve names and return IP addresses. This chapter deals with installing and configuring these types of servers. In addition, you will learn to install and configure DHCP servers, so that you can automatically assign IP addresses and other IP parameters to your clients.

Objectives

- Given a name, specify which method of name resolution would be used to resolve the name to an IP address.
- Implement a DNS and NetBIOS naming scheme for all computers on a given network.
- Given a fully qualified domain name, identify each component of the name.
- Explain how a DNS zone relates to a domain and subdomain.
- List and describe each type of zone.
- Configure a root name server.
- Install and configure a DNS server in Windows 2000 or Windows Server 2003.
- Configure a DNS client.
- Configure zones for dynamic updates.
- Test the service of a DNS server.
- Implement a delegated zone for DNS.
- Manually create DNS resource records.
- Manage and monitor DNS.
- Create a zone or subzone in a DNS name space using Windows 2000 or Windows Server 2003.

- Install and configure a WINS server.
- Install and configure a WINS proxy server.
- Given a problem in name resolution, troubleshoot and fix the problem.
- Install and configure a DHCP server in Windows 2000.
- Configure a scope and common DHCP parameters on a Windows 2000 or Windows Server 2003 DHCP server.
- Install and configure a DHCP relay agent.
- Configure a superscope and multicast scopes on a Windows 2000 or Windows Server 2003 DHCP server.
- Configure DHCP for DNS integration.
- Authorize a DHCP server in Active Directory.
- Explain how SNMP agents and managers communicate with each other.
- Install and configure Windows 2000 or Windows Server 2003 as an SNMP agent or manager.

11.1   INTRODUCTION TO DOMAIN NAME SYSTEM NAME RESOLUTION

Two services can be used to find and provide IP addresses, the WINS service and the Domain Name System (DNS) service. If a computer knows the destination's NetBIOS name, it can send the NetBIOS name to the WINS service and the WINS service will send back the corresponding IP address of the destination. Since only Microsoft operating systems uses NetBIOS names, WINS only works with Microsoft products. If a computer knows the fully qualified domain names (FQDNs), it can send that to a DNS service and the DNS service will return the corresponding IP address. Most modern operating systems and programs can use FQDNs.

Domain Name System (DNS) is a hierarchical client-server–based distributed database management system that translates Internet domain names such as MICROSOFT.COM to an IP address. Domain names are easier to remember than IP addresses. The DNS clients are called **resolvers** and the DNS servers are called **name servers.**

DNS can be thought of as its own little network. If one DNS server cannot translate a particular domain name, then another one tries, and so on, until the correct IP address is returned. DNS is

Table 11.1 RFC Documents that Describe DNS

RFC	Title
974	Mail Routing and the Domain System
1034	Domain Names—Concepts and Facilities
1035	Domain Names—Implementation and Specification
1123	Requirements for Internet Hosts—Application and Support
1886	DNS Extensions to Support IP Version 6
1912	Common DNS Operational and Configuration Errors
1995	Incremental Zone Transfer in DNS
1996	A Mechanism for Prompt DNS Notification of Zone Changes
2136	Dynamic Updates in the Domain Name System (DNS UPDATE)
2181	Clarifications to the DNS Specification
2182	Selection and Operation of Secondary DNS Servers
2219	Use of DNS Aliases for Network Services
2308	Negative Caching of DNS Queries (DNS NCACHE)

most commonly associated with the Internet, but private networks can also use DNS to resolve computer names and to locate computers within their local networks without being connected to the Internet.

The first TCP/IP networks used HOSTS files to translate from domain names (such as MICROSOFT.COM, ACME.COM, or MIT.EDU) to IP addresses. As some networks grew so quickly, manually updating and distributing the HOSTS file was not effective. For the Internet (the largest network that uses DNS), no single organization is responsible for keeping the DNS system updated. Instead, a distributed database exists on many different name servers around the world, with no one server storing all the information; thus, DNS allows for almost unlimited growth.

The most popular implementation of the DNS protocol is the Berkeley Internet Name Domain (BIND), which was developed for the University of California Berkeley's BSD UNIX operating system. The primary specifications for DNS are defined in Requests for Comments (RFC) 1034 and 1035. DNS uses either UDP port 53 or TCP port 53 as the underlying protocol. See Table 11.1.

11.1.1 Domain Name Space

The **DNS name space** describes the hierarchical structure of the DNS database as an inverted logical tree structure. Each node on the tree is a partition of the name space called a **domain.** Domains can be further partitioned at node points within the domain into subdomains. Names of the domains and subdomains can be up to 63 characters long. See Figure 11.1.

The top of the tree is known as the **root domain.** It is sometimes shown as a period (.) or as empty quotation marks (" "), indicating a null value. Immediately below the root domain are the **top-level domains.** The top-level domains indicate a country, region, or type of organization. Three-letter codes indicate the type of organization. See Table 11.2. For example, COM indicates commercial (business) and EDU stands for educational institution.

Two-letter codes indicate countries, which follow International Standard 3166. For example, CA stands for Canada, AU for Australia, FR for France, and UK for United Kingdom. For a list of two-letter codes, go to this website: http://www.din.de/gremien/nas/nabd/iso3166ma/codlstp1/index.html.

Figure 11.1 DNS name space

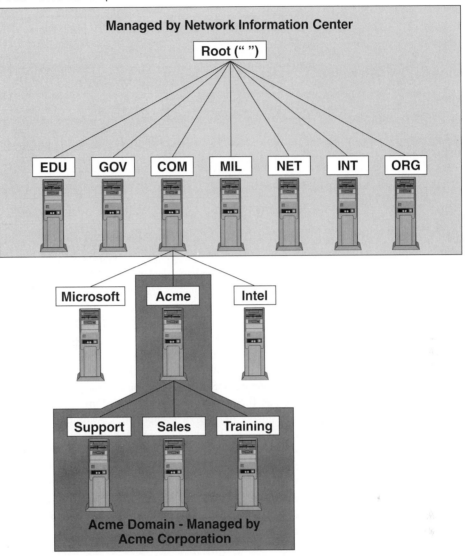

Table 11.2 Top-level domain codes indicating type of organization

Traditional Top-Level Domains		New Top-Level Domains	
Code	**Meaning**	**Code**	**Meaning**
com	Commercial	**aero**	Airline-related services
edu	Educational	**biz**	Businesses
gov	Government	**coop**	Cooperatives
int	International Organization	**info**	Websites providing information
mil	Military	**museum**	Museums
net	Network related	**name**	Personal websites and email addresses
org	Miscellaneous Organization	**pro**	Professionals such as doctors and lawyers

Example 1:

Domain Name	Second-Level Domain Name
MICROSOFT.COM	Microsoft Corporation
CISCO.COM	Cisco Corporation
MTI.EDU	MTI University
ED.GOV	United States Department of Education
ARMY.MIL	United States Army
W3.ORG	World Wide Web Consortium
NATO.INT	North Atlantic Treaty Organization
PM.GOV.AU	Prime Minister of Australia

The **second-level domain names** are variable-length names that are registered to an individual or organization for use on the Internet. These names are almost always based on the appropriate top-level domain, depending on the type of organization or geographical location where a name is used.

Second-level domain names must be registered by the authorized party. For example, for years, Network Solutions, Inc. (http://www.netsol.com/) ran a government-sanctioned monopoly on registrations for .COM, .NET, and .ORG domain names. But as the U.S. government handed the control of the Internet to an international body, several companies, including Network Solutions, Inc., now handle the registration of these three-letter codes. Since most of the common top-level domain names are already taken. Some countries such as Tonga (TO) are selling their domain names. Therefore, some commercial and user sites may be using one of these two-letter codes. Another sale was the domain name ".TV," which belonged to the island nation, Tuvalu. The .TV web address symbolizes rich media, streaming video, and broadband content. To register .TV domain names, as well as .COM, .NET and .ORG domain names, use www.register.com.

Subdomain names are additional names that an organization can create from the registered second-level domain name. The subdomain allows an organization to divide a domain into a department or geographical location, which makes the partitions of the domain name space more manageable. A subdomain must have a contiguous domain name space; that is, the domain name of a zone (child domain) is the name of that zone added to the name of the domain or parent domain.

A **host name** is a name assigned to a specific computer within a domain or subdomain by an administrator to identify the TCP/IP host. Multiple host names can be associated with the same IP address, although only one host name can be assigned to a computer using the Windows Control Panel/Network applet. If the DNS is seen as a tree, the host name represents the leaf or object of the tree. Much like a subdomain, it is the left-most label of the DNS domain name. The host name can then be used in place of an IP address such as PING or other TCP/IP utilities. Total length of an FQDN cannot exceed 255 characters. The host name does not have to be the same as the NetBIOS (computer) name. By default, TCP/IP setup uses the NetBIOS name for the host name and replaces illegal characters, such as the underscore, with a hyphen (-).

A **fully qualified domain name (FQDN)** describes the exact position of a host (computer) within the domain hierarchy, and it is considered to be complete. When used in a DNS domain name, it is stated by a trailing period (.) to designate that the name of the host is located off the root or highest level of the domain hierarchy.

Example 2:

SERVER1.SALES.ACME.COM

COM indicates a commercial business
ACME is the domain name
SALES is the subdomain name
SERVER1 is the name of the server located within the SALES subdomain

---

REGISTERING YOUR DOMAIN

The quickest and easiest way to register your domain name is through your ISP. If that method is not possible, use the following steps:

1. Find the company to register the domain name. For domain names with the .COM, .ORG, and .NET domain suffixes, go to WWW.NETSOL.COM, WWW.REGISTER.COM or WWW.VERISIGN.COM.
2. Pick a name and ensure its availability. At the website you can search for a name without any obligation. Try to select a name that indicates your company or business, although the task may be difficult because most easily identifiable domain names are already taken.
3. Arrange your domain name, either through your ISP or by setting up your own DNS server.
4. Complete the registration form at the company where you are registering the domain name. Follow the company's instructions. During the entire registration period, keep checking for small errors and omissions, as these can delay the processing of the registration form. The registration form will usually need three contacts—admin, technical, and billing. You will usually receive an acknowledgement, which will contain a tracking number. Be sure to keep that tracking number for future inquiries.
5. You will receive a message telling you the date your domain will be activated in the root name servers. It may take a few hours to a few days after the activation date because of the time required for the distributed database to be replicated throughout the Internet with the added address. Note that there is a fee to activate the domain name.

When you create a domain name space, consider the following domain guidelines and standard naming conventions:

■ To minimize the level of administrative tasks, limit the number of domain levels.
■ If possible, each subdomain should have a unique name throughout the entire domain to ensure that the subdomain name is unique.
■ Use simple, yet meaningful domain names that are easy to remember and navigate.
■ Use standard DNS characters including A–Z , a–z, 0–9, hyphen, and unicode characters, which include the additional characters needed for foreign languages such as French, German, and Spanish.
■ Keep names of the domain and subdomains to 63 characters long.
■ Keep total length of an FQDN at or below 255 characters.

11.1.2   DNS Zones

A **DNS zone** is a portion of the DNS name space whose database records exist and are managed in a particular DNS database file. Each zone is based on a specific domain node, or root domain, which is the authority source for that node. Zone files do not necessarily contain the complete DNS name since subdomains may have their own zone. If subdomains are added below the domain, they can be part of the same zone or belong to another zone.

The computer that maintains the master list for a zone is the primary name server for that zone and is considered the authority there. A DNS server might be configured to manage one or more zones.

Example:

Question: Why would you take a domain and partition it into several subdomains (zones), so that they can be controlled by separate DNS name servers?

Answer: By breaking up domains across multiple zone files, the zone files can be stored, distributed, and replicated to other DNS servers. This enables the system to do the following:

■ To delegate management of a domain/subdomain as it relates to its location or department within the organization
■ To divide one large zone into smaller zones so that the traffic load can be distributed among multiple servers for better DNS name resolution performance and for fault tolerance

Table 11.3 Zone Types

Zone Type	Description
Standard Primary	The master copy of a new zone.
Standard Secondary	A replica of an existing zone. Standard secondary zones are read only.
Active Directory Integrated	A zone that is stored in Active Directory (Windows 2000 or Windows Server 2003 only). Updates of the zone are performed during Active Directory replication.

When choosing how to structure zones, use a DNS structure that reflects the structure of your organization.

In Windows 2000 and Windows Server 2003, there are three types of zones to configure. They are the standard primary zone, the standard secondary zone, and the Active Directory integrated zone. See Table 11.3.

The **primary name server** stores and maintains the zone file locally. Changes to a zone, such as adding domains or hosts, are done by changing files at the primary name server. A **secondary name server** gets the data from the zone of another name server—either a primary name server or another secondary name server—for that zone across the network. The process of obtaining this zone information across the network is referred to as a **zone transfer.** Zone transfers occur over TCP port 53. The **Active Directory integrated zone,** which is only found in Windows 2000 and Windows Server 2003, has the zone defined using the Active Directory, not the zone files.

The source of the zone information for a secondary name server is referred to as a master name server. A master name server can be either a primary or secondary name server for the requested zone.

Example:

Question: Why would a user want a secondary name server?

Answer: There are three reasons to have a secondary name server. The first reason is for fault tolerance. You should have at least two DNS name servers serving each zone. In each client's configuration, both name servers should be listed. If the first server listed cannot be contacted, the client contacts the second name server. The second reason is to divide the load between different name servers so that the performance for name resolution will be increased. Lastly, the DNS servers can be used to service computers that are located in remote locations so that they would not have to use a slow WAN link.

11.1.3 Active Directory Integrated Zones

Chapter 12 of this book discusses the Active Directory (AD). Basically, it is a directory service that stores all information about the network resources and services, such as user data, printers, servers, databases, groups, computers, and security policies. In addition, it identifies all resources on a network and makes them accessible to users and applications.

Rather than maintaining two separate naming services (Active Directory and a DNS-based name space), AD integrated zones store the zone data as an AD object and replicate zone data as part of the domain replication. In addition, since AD integrated zones are stored in the Active Directory, there is no zone database file on a primary server. When you store a zone in Active Directory, the zone database file is copied into the Active Directory and deleted on the primary server for the zone.

You cannot install Active Directory without having DNS on your network, because Active Directory uses DNS as its location service. However, you can install DNS separately, without Active Directory. If you install DNS on a domain controller, you can also choose whether to use Active Directory to provide storage and replication for DNS. Using Active Directory for storage and replication provides the following benefits:

- Increased fault tolerance
- Easier management
- Minimal traffic for zone replications
- Security

With primary and secondary servers, clients can only be registered at the primary server. With Active Directory DNS servers, clients can register themselves dynamically on any of the servers. If you have several domain controllers with AD integrated zones, each of these domain controllers holds a write-able copy of the zone database. When the database on one DNS server gets modified, it is replicated to the other DNS servers, which eliminates a single point of failure since these zones automatically replicate to the other zones.

The dynamic DNS update protocol allows computers to automatically register themselves with the DNS server. Thus, management is easier because you do not have to input all of the addresses for your clients.

To minimize zone replication traffic, AD integrated zones replicate on a per-property basis; they propagate only relevant changes, which is more efficient then full-zone transfers. Compression is also used.

Active Directory integrated zones allow you to implement secure dynamic updates. The DNS server only accepts record registration from clients with accounts in Active Directory, so an unknown computer cannot register with the DNS server. In addition, replications between standard and secondary DNS zones are unencrypted. By creating an AD integrated zone, DNS zone transfers are included in Active Directory replication, which has secure channels because of encryption.

11.1.4   Zone Files

A **zone file** is a file that defines a zone. All files are kept on the DNS name server. While most DNS systems such as UNIX must be configured by editing these text files, Microsoft DNS uses a user-friendly interface (DNS console). The zone database files are traditionally maintained on computers that are running the DNS server service. Remember that in Windows 2000 or Windows Server 2003 a zone can be stored in Active Directory rather than in a zone database file.

The primary file, known as the zone database file (*%systemroot%*\SYSTEM32\DNS\ *domain_name.* DNS), contains the resource records (RRs) for that part of the domain for which the zone is responsible. See Figure 11.2 for a sample zone file. There are various resource record types that are defined for the DNS database. Table 11.4 lists some of the more common types of resource records. For more information on resource records, refer to RFC 1034, RFC 2052, and RFC 2065.

The start of authority (SOA) record indicates the starting point or original point of authority for information stored in a zone. The value of the refresh interval in the SOA record, which has a default value of 15 minutes, decides how often the destination server should request to renew the zone. Increasing this value causes fewer zone transfers; however, the danger of increasing the refresh interval is DNS inconsistencies in the network. Configuring the Notify List on the external DNS server to notify the secondary server forces changes to be transferred and thus avoids inconsistencies. The two most common record types are host (A) records and pointer (PTR) records. Host records are used to resolve host names to IP addresses, while pointer records are used to resolve IP addresses to host names.

When a Windows client needs to find a domain controller (e.g., to log on to the domain), the client queries the DNS server to access the service (SRV) resource records in order to locate the logon server for accessing domain controller names. If you are using a UNIX DNS server, the DNS must use BIND 8.2 or later to support SRV resource records and dynamic DNS (DDNS).

11.1.5   Name Resolution

When a client computer needs an IP address, it sends a name query to the DNS client service (resolver) located on the client. The DNS client service then checks the locally cached information and local HOSTS file (if present). Be aware that the cache area is not the cache inside the processor, but rather

Figure 11.2 Sample zone database file

```
;
;   Database file acme.com.dns for acme.com zone.
;       zone version: 6
;
@   IN SOA SERVER1.ACME.COM.
ADMINISTRATOR.ACME.COM.(
                                6           ; serial number
                                900         ; refresh
                                600         ; retry
                                86400       ; expire
                                33600)      ; minimum TTL
;
;   Zone NS records
;
@   NS server1.acme.com
;
;   Zone records
;
server2000-01a     A   132.132.60.45
server1            A   132.132.20.1
testserver         A   132.132.20.20
```

Table 11.4 Common resource record types

Resource Record	Purpose
SOA (Start of Authority)	Identifies the name server that is the authoritative source of information or data within a domain. An SOA record is created automatically when you create a new zone. A primary server for a given zone lists itself in an SOA record to show that it is the source for this zone. The first record in the zone database file must be the SOA record.
NS (Name Server)	Provides a list of name servers that are assigned to a domain.
A (Host Address)	Provides a host name to an Internet Protocol (IP) version 4, 32-bit address. For more information, see RFC 1035.
PTR (Pointer)	Resolves an IP address to a host name (reverse mappings). For more information, see RFC 1035.
CNAME (Canonical Name)—Alias	Creates an alias or alternate DNS domain name for a specified host name. The most common or popular use of an alias is to provide a permanent DNS-aliased domain name for generic name resolution of a server-based name such as www.acme.com and ftp.acme.com to more than one computer or IP address used in a web server. In this way, you can assign acme.com to one server, www.acme.com to a second server, and ftp.acme.com to a third server. If you do use the same server for all three entries and you decide to split the services, simply change the CNAME resource record to point to the new server.
SRV (Service)	Locates servers that are hosting a particular service. Note: SRV records are new in Windows 2000 DNS server services. This record enables you to maintain a list of servers for a well-known server port and transport protocol type ordered by preference for a DNS domain name. For more information, see the Internet draft "A DNS RR for specifying the location of services (DNS SRV)."
MX (Mail Exchanger)	Identifies which mail exchanger to contact for a specified domain and in what order to use each mail host.

an area of memory in RAM set aside to hold DNS entries. The entries in the cache come from the preloaded entries of the HOSTS file or from previous answered responses. When previous queries are cached, data are kept for a preset time, known as the time to live (TTL). If the query does not match an entry in the cache, then the resolution process continues with the client querying a DNS server to resolve the name.

When the resolver queries a DNS server, it will perform a recursive query. A **recursive query** asks the DNS server to respond with the requested data or with an error stating that either the requested data or the specified domain name does not exist. Note that the name server does not refer the query to another name server unless it is configured as a forwarder, in which case it will forward the DNS request as a recursive query.

When the DNS server receives a request, it checks if the host name is located in its own zone database file, in which it is an authority. If it is not listed in the zone file, it checks the cache area. From then on, the DNS server uses iterative queries to resolve the name. An **iterative query** gives the best current answer back as a response. The best answer will be the address being sought or an address of a server that would have a better idea of the address.

Example 3:

A program needs to find the address of SERVER.SUPPORT.ACME.COM. The program will send the request to the resolver. The resolver will look in its cache area and its HOSTS file. If no address is found, the resolver will forward the query to its preferred DNS name server.

The DNS server will check if it knows the address of SERVER.SUPPORT.ACME.COM. If not, it will ask the root server if it knows the address of SERVER.SUPPORT.ACME.COM. The root server will not know the address, so it will respond with the best answer by providing the address of the COM root server. The DNS server will then ask the COM root server for the address of SERVER.SUPPORT.ACME.COM. The COM root server will respond back with its known best answer of the ACME.COM name server address. The DNS server will query the ACME.COM name server for the address of SERVER.SUPPORT.ACME.COM. The DNS server will then respond back to the resolver with the address of the SUPPORT.ACME.COM. The DNS server will query the SUPPORT.ACME.COM name server for the address of SERVER.SUPPORT.ACME.COM and will respond back with the address.

The preferred server will then respond back to the client with the correct address. The program will then use the IP address to communicate its needs.

As shown by this example, the resolver queried its DNS server using a recursive query, while the DNS server queried other DNS servers using iterative queries. See Figure 11.3.

Although the recursive query process can be resource intensive, it has some performance advantages for the DNS server. When the recursion process is complete, the information is cached by the server. The cache information can be used again to help speed the answering of subsequent queries. Over time, the cache information can grow to occupy a significant portion of the server memory resources.

Typically, the process of domain name resolution occurs very quickly. Occasionally, it may be delayed. If the delay is too long, the browser will come back and say that the domain does not exist, even though you know that is true, because your computer got tired of waiting and timed out. Yet, when you try again, there is a good chance it will work because the authoritative server has had enough time to reply and the name server has stored the information in its cache.

DNS servers can be configured to send all recursive queries to a selected list of servers, known as **forwarders.** Servers used in the list of forwarders provide recursive lookup for any queries that a DNS server receives that it cannot answer based on its own zone records. During the forwarding process, a DNS server that is configured to use forwarders essentially behaves as a DNS client to them. Typically, forwarders are used on remote DNS servers that use a slow link to access the Internet.

Another possibility is to set up a DNS server for your company but have your ISP provide DNS services for the Internet. When a computer needs to communicate with hosts on your company's network, it will use your company's DNS server. If a computer needs to communicate with hosts on the

Figure 11.3 A DNS client will use recursive query with the preferred server to find out an IP address, whereas the preferred server will typically use iterative query to discover the IP address

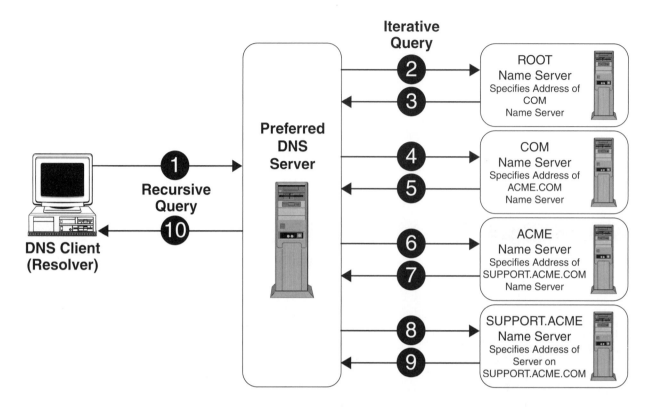

Internet, it will first check with the company's DNS server; then, that DNS server will forward the request to your ISP's DNS server.

If you have machines that serve as duplicates for each other, so that they can be used to split the work load and to provide fault tolerance, you will need to map the same host name (A record) to three different IP addresses. Then enable round-robin or net-mask ordering (see following paragraphs).

DNS servers use a mechanism called **round-robin,** or **load sharing,** to share and distribute loads for network resources. Round-robin rotates the order of resource records data that are returned in a query answer, in which multiple resource records exist of the same type for a queried DNS domain name. Since the client is required to try the first IP address listed, a DNS server that is configured to perform round-robin rotates the order of the A resource records when answering client requests.

Net-mask ordering occurs when a DNS client requests name resolution for a resource name that has multiple A (host) resource records. The DNS server tries to identify a host with the shared DNS name that resides on the same subnet as the requesting client. If the DNS server is successful in identifying such a host, it places that host's IP address at the top of the list of IP addresses that is returned to the requesting client.

By default, all Windows-based DNS servers use a fast zone transfer format, which includes compression and can include multiple records per TCP message during a connected transfer. This format is compatible with more recent BIND-based DNS servers that run versions 4.9.4 and later. If you have an ISP DNS server that is running Legacy BIND implementations and that does not support fast zone transfer format, you need to enable the BIND Secondaries option so that Windows 2000 DNS does not use fast zone transfers.

11.1.6 Reverse Queries

Occasionally, the resolver may perform a **reverse query,** in which a resolver knows an IP address and wants to know the host name. To prevent the searching of all domains for an inverse query,

Figure 11.4 Sample reverse zone database file

a special domain called "in-addr.arpa" was created. Nodes in the in-addr.arpa domain are named after the numbers in the IP address. Since IP addresses get more specific from left to right, the order of IP addresses is reversed when building the in-addr.arpa domain. Once this domain is built, special resource records called pointer records (PTR) are added to associate the IP addresses to the corresponding host names. To find a host name for an IP address, the resolver queries the DNS server for a PTR record for address.in-addr.arpa. For example, to find the IP address of 1.2.3.4, the resolver would query the DNS server for a PTR record of 4.3.2.1.in-addr.arpa. See Figure 11.4 for a sample reverse zone database file.

In addition to reverse lookups, some DNS servers support an **inverse query.** Like the reverse lookup, a client making an inverse query provides the IP address and requests an FQDN. Instead of using the in-addr.arpa domain to find the answer, it checks its own zone for the answer. If the answer is not in the zone, an error message is returned. Inverse queries are not as thorough as reverse queries and so are not used often.

11.2   WINDOWS DNS SERVICES

Microsoft Windows 2000 and Windows Server 2003 include an RFC-compliant DNS name server that is implemented as in Windows NT. Because the Microsoft DNS is an RFC-compliant DNS server, it creates and uses standard DNS zone files and supports all standard resource record types. While being RFC compliant, it offers integration with other Windows services including Active Directory, WINS, and DHCP. Windows also offers DNS dynamic update that enables DNS client computers to register and dynamically update their resource records with a DNS server whenever changes occur. This reduces the need for manual administration of zone records, especially for clients who frequently move or change locations and use DHCP to obtain an IP address.

11.2.1   Installing Windows DNS Services

Before installing a DNS server, be sure that the TCP/IP protocol is installed, a static IP address is assigned, and the appropriate DNS domain name is specified. During the DNS server service installation process, the Windows server does the following:

- Installs the DNS server service and starts the service automatically without restarting the computer
- Installs the DNS snap-ins and adds the DNS Management shortcut to the Administrative Tools menu
- Adds the following key for the DNS server service to the registry: HKEY_LOCAL_MACHINE\ System\CurrentControlSet\Services\Dns
- Creates the *%systemroot%*\SYSTEM32\DNS folder, which contains the DNS database files including the zone database file (*domain_name*.DNS), the reverse lookup file (*z.y.w.x*.IN-ADDR.ARPA), the cache file (CACHE.DNS), and an optional boot file (a BIND-specific implementation that controls how the DNS server service starts)

To install a DNS server, follow these steps:

1. Open the Add/Remove Programs applet in the Control Panel.
2. Click on the Add/Remove Windows Components.
3. Click on the Next button.
4. Click to highlight the Networking Services option.
5. Click on the Details button.
6. In the Subcomponents of Networking Services, make sure that there is a check mark in the box next to the Domain Name System (DNS). See Figure 11.5.
7. Click on the OK button.
8. Click on the Next button.
9. If the Insert Disk dialog box appears, insert the Windows installation CD, ensure that the path to the source files is correct, and click on the OK button.
10. Click on the Finish button.

The primary tool used to manage local and remote Windows DNS servers is the DNS console, which can be accessed from within the Administrative Tools folder or by using the Microsoft Management Console (MMC) snap-in. See Figure 11.6.

When you open the DNS console for the first time, the right pane will state that the DNS server has not been configured yet and to configure the server you need to open the Action menu and select the

Figure 11.5   Installing DNS server using the Add/Remove Programs applet in the Control Panel

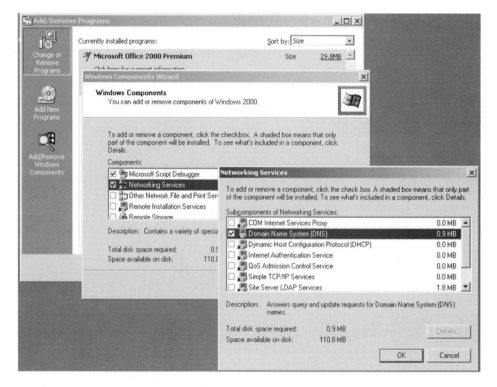

Figure 11.6   DNS Console gives a GUI interface to show the resource records of a zone file

Configure the Server option. When this occurs, the DNS Server Configuration wizard will guide you through the process to configure the name server.

11.2.2   Root Name Servers and Resource Records

When starting the DNS server for the first time, do the following:

1. Configure the root name server.
2. Configure the forward lookup zone.
3. Configure the reverse lookup zone.
4. Create resources records (RRs).

The **root name server** contains the resource records for all top-level name servers in the domain name space, such as the COM and EDU domain. By default, the DNS service implements **root hints** using a file, CACHE.DNS, stored in the *%systemroot%*\SYSTEM32\DNS folder on the server computer. This file normally contains the name server and A resource records for the Internet root servers. See Figure 11.7.

If you are using a DNS service on a private network that is not connected to the Internet, you can edit or replace the CACHE.DNS file with similar records that point to your own internal root DNS servers. In addition, the root name server would use a root domain, which is a standard primary forward lookup zone represented by a period (.). You should then delete the CACHE.DNS files for the root servers. See Figure 11.8.

A **forward lookup zone** is that part of the DNS system that allows you to perform name-to-address resolution (forward lookup queries). On name servers, configure at least one forward lookup zone in order for the DNS service to work. The forward lookup zone can be created by using the DNS Server wizard or starting the Create New Zone wizard by right-clicking the Forward Lookup Zone folder and selecting the Create a New Zone.

A **reverse lookup zone** allows you to perform address-to-name resolution (reverse lookup queries). The reverse lookup zone differs from forward lookup zones in that it is required only to run some troubleshooting tools such as NSLOOKUP and to record a name instead of an IP address in Internet

Figure 11.7   Root hints of a DNS server

Figure 11.8   For a private network, create a root domain (standard primary forward lookup zone) represented by a period (.).

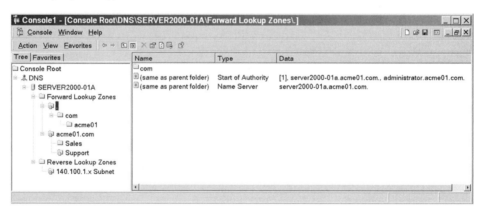

information services (IIS) log files. The reverse lookup zone can be created by using the DNS Server wizard or starting the Create New Zone wizard by right-clicking the Reverse Lookup Zone folder and selecting the Create a New Zone.

Once you create your zones, you can then create resource records (entries in the database file). To add a resource record, right-click the zone to which you want to add the record, and select the type of new record that you want to create.

11.2.3   Creating Zones and Zone Transfers

To configure the standard primary zone or to create a standard secondary zone, right-click the appropriate DNS server and click Create a New Zone option to start the New Zone wizard. The New Zone wizard will then create a standard primary, a secondary primary, and an integrated zone. A fourth type of server, a **caching-only name server,** performs name resolution for the clients and then caches or stores the results, allowing for fast name resolution and reduced WAN traffic. Different from the other servers, it does not contain any zone files and is therefore not an authority for any zone. Of course, the cache is populated with the most frequently requested names and their associated IP addresses. To configure a caching-only server, install the DNS service on a computer that is running Windows servers and do not configure any forward or reverse lookup zones.

If you select the standard secondary zone, you must specify a name server from which to obtain the zone information. The name server from which the information is being copied is known as the master server, which can be a standard primary server or another standard secondary server. To add a secondary server for an existing zone, you need to have network access to the server acting as the master server, since it is the source of the zone data. In addition, if you are accessing the DNS server remotely, you may need to add the applicable DNS server to the console first before you can manage it.

To distribute the load of the DNS database, improve name resolution, improve performance, and provide fault tolerance, additional servers are used to host a zone file. To replicate and synchronize all copies of the zone files, a zone transfer is required between the various DNS servers. When a new DNS server is added to the network and is configured as a new secondary server for an existing zone, it must perform a **full initial transfer (AXFR)** to obtain a full copy of the zone files.

After the Windows DNS servers are replicated and synchronized, they will keep the zone files synchronized by performing an **incremental transfer (IXFR),** in which the secondary server pulls only those zone changes it needs to synchronize its copy of the zone with its source. To keep track of the changes, each version of the zone file includes a serial number in the start of authority (SOA) resource record. If the serial number is the same between two zone files, no transfer is made. If the serial number at the source is greater than at the requesting secondary server, a transfer is made of only those changes to RRs for each incremental version of the zone.

The zone transfer is always initiated at the secondary server for a zone by sending an SOA query to the configured master server. The query includes the following:

- The refresh interval expires for the zone as specified in the SOA resource record (default 900 seconds/15 minutes).
- A secondary server is notified of zone changes by its master server.
- A DNS server service is started at a secondary server for the zone.
- The DNS console is used at a secondary server for the zone to manually initiate a transfer from its master server.

The source server answers the query for its SOA record. The destination server checks the serial number of the SOA record in the response.

Windows DNS servers support DNS Notify (RFC 1996), which permits a means of initiating notification to secondary servers when zone changes occur. DNS notification implements a push mechanism for notifying a select set of secondary servers for a zone when it is updated. Servers that are notified can then initiate a zone transfer. For secondary servers to be notified by the master DNS server, each secondary server must first have its IP address in the notify list of the master server. This list can be accessed when you right-click on the zone and choose the Properties option, select the Zone Transfer tab, and select the Notify button.

When a secondary name server starts up, it contacts the master name server and initiates a zone transfer for each zone for which it is acting as a secondary name server. If the data on the master name server have changed, zone transfers can occur periodically as set by the refresh parameters in the SOA record of the zone file.

When a zone is updated at the master or source server, the serial number field in the SOA RR is also updated, indicating a new local version of the zone. The master server then sends a DNS notify message to the other servers that are part of its configured notify list so that it knows that a zone transfer has to be completed.

For Windows 2000 and Windows Server 2003 use DNS notification only to notify servers that are operating as secondary servers for a zone. For replication of directory-integrated zones, DNS notification is not needed, because any DNS servers that load a zone from Active Directory automatically poll the directory approximately once every 15 minutes to update and refresh the zone. If you configure a notify list, you can actually degrade system performance by causing unnecessary additional transfer requests for the update zone.

To change a zone type, left-click on any zone to highlight it and select the Properties option from the shortcut menu. On the General tab, click on the Change button, select the zone type, and click on the OK button.

11.2.4   Creating a Subdomain

To create a subdomain from within the DNS console, click to highlight the name of the zone in which you want to create the subdomain. Right-click the zone name to bring up the shortcut menu and click on the New Domain option. Type the name of the subdomain in the New Domain dialog box and click on the OK button.

After creating a subdomain, you can delegate authority of it to another DNS server/zone. This allows you to distribute the load of the DNS database and improve name resolution performance. When a query is being done on a zone, it will refer to the NS (name server) resource records to find the name server for the target zone being queried.

To delegate authority for a subdomain, click to highlight the name of the domain to which you want to delegate authority (typically the domain, not the subdomain), right-click the domain name to bring up the shortcut menu, and select the New Delegation option. Follow the Add New Delegation wizard to guide you through the rest of the process, including specifying the name of the domain to which you are delegating authority and adding the names and IP address of the server(s) that will host the delegated zone.

11.2.5   Dynamic DNS Updates

Since DNS has become the primary naming resolution tool for Windows, every computer that holds a network service such as file or print sharing has to be registered. A large network that has many computers using DHCP to obtain a new IP address needs to dynamically register and update the DNS server's resource records. Windows 2000 and Windows Server 2003 provide client and server support for the use of dynamic updates, as described in RFC 2136.

Computers that register with a DNS server follow these rules:

- If Windows 2000, Windows XP, or Windows Server 2003 is operating as a DHCP client, it will register and update its own host (A) resource with the DNS server.
- When a DHCP server issues an address to a client, the DHCP server will update the pointer (PTR) record with the DNS server.
- A Windows 2000, Windows XP, or Windows Server 2003 computer with a static IP address will register and update the host (A) record and the pointer (PTR) record.

Computer that are running Windows 9X or Windows NT cannot update their own resource records with the DNS server. By default, the DHCP server will register the pointer (PTR) record automatically for all DHCP clients, but it does not register the host (A) record. To support these Legacy clients, you can enable the DHCP server to update the host (A) records by configuring the Property on the DNS tab for the DHCP server to "Enable updates for DNS clients that do not support dynamic update."

Dynamic updates can be sent for any of the following reasons or events:

- At start-up time, when the computer is turned on
- When an IP address is added, removed, or modified in the TCP/IP properties configuration for any one of the installed network connections
- When an IP address lease changes or renews with the DHCP server any one of the installed network connections. For example, when the computer is started or if the IPCONFIG /RENEW command is used
- When the IPCONFIG /REGISTERDNS command is used to manually force a refresh of the client name registration in DNS

Dynamic updates are sent or refreshed periodically. By default, Windows sends a refresh once every 24 hours. Unfortunately, the names are not removed from DNS zones if they become inactive or are not updated within the refresh interval (24 hours). DNS does not use a mechanism to release or tombstone names, although DNS clients attempt to delete or update old name records when a new name or address change is applied. The Windows DNS service allows dynamic update to be enabled or disabled on a per-zone basis at each server configured to load either a standard primary or directory-integrated zone. Standard secondary zones are not supported because they get the information from the standard primary zone through zone transfers.

To enable DNS dynamic updates for clients, open the DHCP console and right-click on the applicable DHCP server. In the shortcut menu, pick the Properties option and click on the DNS tab. Then put a check in the "Automatically update DHCP client information in DNS" check box.

If you are using Active Directory integrated zones, use secure dynamic update to automatically update a zone file. Secure dynamic update allows only the computers that you specify to make new entries or modify existing entries in a zone. By default, all authenticated computers in a forest (multiple Windows domains connected together) can make new entries in a zone, and only the computer that created a name is allowed to modify the data associated with that name.

When a client registers a resource record, that specific client becomes the owner of that entry in the zone database, so only that client may update the record. This is true not only for the DHCP client that registers its own host (A) record, but for the DHCP server that registers the pointer (PTR) records for all the DHCP clients to which it leases IP addresses. Since there can only be one owner to a record, and each computer has a unique identifying number called a SID, a problem may exist if you have multiple DHCP servers. To eliminate this problem, when implementing secure dynamic updates, make the DHCP servers members of the DNS update proxy group. DNS registrations performed by computers that are members of the DNS update proxy group are not owned by the registering computer; this allows another computer to later modify the registration. If the computer that later modifies the registration is not a member of the DNS update proxy group, then that computer becomes the owner of the registration.

To allow only secure dynamic updates, right-click on the applicable zone and select the Properties option. On the General tab, verify that the zone type is Active Directory integrated and that the "Allow dynamic update?" dropdown list is set to "Only secure updates." By default, Windows 2000, Windows XP, and Windows Server 2003 clients will try to use unsecured dynamic updates first. If that request fails, then they use secure updates. Unless the DNS server prohibits the clients, the clients try to overcome their previous registered resource records.

DNS service also provides the ability to use WINS servers to look up names not found in the DNS domain name space by checking the NetBIOS name space managed by WINS. See Figure 11.9. To use WINS lookup integration, two special resource record types are enabled and added to the zone, WINS and WINS-R. Use WINS lookup when you are using a mixed-mode client of Windows and UNIX clients. The UNIX clients and some early-version Microsoft clients can locate your WINS clients by extending DNS host name resolution into the WINS-managed NetBIOS name space. If you use a mixture of Windows DNS servers and other DNS servers to host a zone, enable the "Do not replicate this record" option for any primary zones when using the WINS lookup record. This prevents the WINS lookup record from being included in zone transfers to other DNS servers that do not support or recognize this record. If not, it would cause data errors and failed zone transfers.

11.2.6   DNS Best Practices

To get the best results from a DNS server, do the following:

- If you are using Active Directory, use integrated zones for best results and simplified deployment and troubleshooting.
- If you are not using Active Directory, be aware of the points of failure and configuration issues that apply to using dynamic updates with standard primary zones.
- Enter the correct e-mail addresses of those who are responsible for each zone so that these people can be notified for query errors and security problems. Most Internet e-mail addresses contain the at (@) sign, but this sign must be replaced with a period (.).
- Use secondary or caching-only servers for your zones to assist in off-loading DNS query traffic.

Figure 11.9 DNS service also provides the ability to use WINS servers to look up names not found in the DNS domain name space by checking the NetBIOS name space managed by WINS

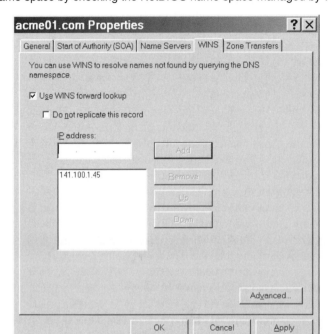

■ If planning a large DNS design, such as for a large Internet service provider (ISP) that supports the DNS name service, read the most current RFCs.

11.2.7   Monitoring and Troubleshooting DNS Services

In Windows, DNS services are essential to the network. Therefore, Windows has several utilities for monitoring and troubleshooting DNS servers:

■ DNS administrative tool is used to test DNS servers and monitor their ability to process and resolve queries. See Figure 11.10.
■ Command-line utilities, such as NSLOOKUP, are used to verify resource records and troubleshoot DNS problems.
■ Logging features, such as DNS server log, can be viewed using Event Viewer.

You can configure the DNS server service to perform queries on a scheduled basis to ensure that the service is operating correctly. In the DNS console, right-click the server that you want to monitor, select the Properties option, and click on the Monitoring tab. From here, you can perform a simple query, a recursive query, or both. The simple query does a query to the local DNS server. If the recursive query fails, the DNS server is unable to contact any of the servers listed in Root Hints or you have zone delegation problems. Such problems can result if the configuration of the root name server is invalid or the root name server cannot be contacted. For more suggestions, see the Windows help files and resource kit.

NSLOOKUP is a diagnostic tool that displays information from the DNS servers. It is only available if the TCP/IP protocol has been installed. NSLOOKUP has two modes, interactive and noninteractive. Use interactive mode when you require more than one piece of data. To run interactive mode, at the Command prompt, type NSLOOKUP. To exit interactive mode, type Exit. Use noninteractive mode when you require a single piece of data. This can be done by typing the NSLOOKUP command at the Command prompt with the proper parameters, and the data then return.

Name resolution problems can occur if a client computer is resolving names incorrectly or if the client computer name is not registered with the DNS servers on your network. If you determine that the client computer is resolving names incorrectly, use the IPCONFIG /FLUSHDNS from the Command

Figure 11.10   The DNS administrative tool is used to test DNS servers and monitor their ability to process and resolve queries

prompt to flush and reset the cache on the client computer. If a client's name records are missing from the servers, use the IPCONFIG/REGISTERDNS to force the client computer to renew its registration.

11.3   INTRODUCTION TO WINDOWS INTERNET NAME SERVICE

If you try to access a computer using its NetBIOS (computer) name, such as using a UNC name to specify a network resource, the computer will need to determine the IP address. Initially, it will broadcast onto the network to ask for the IP address of the computer. Unfortunately, because the broadcast usually does not go across routers, computers on other subnets do not get resolved. In addition, if you have several computers doing these types of broadcasts, then the broadcasts will slow the performance of the network.

Other methods to resolve NetBIOS names are to use either LMHOSTS files or to access a WINS server. Like HOSTS files, it would be extremely difficult to maintain and distribute the LMHOSTS files to all computers in a large network, especially since addresses may change frequently under a network using DHCP servers.

11.3.1   Using a WINS Server

A **Windows Internet Name Service (WINS) server** contains a database of IP addresses and NetBIOS (computer names) that update dynamically. For clients to access the WINS server, they must know its address. Therefore, the WINS server requires a static address—one that does not change. When the client accesses the WINS server, the client sends a message directly to the WINS server instead of doing a broadcast. When the WINS server gets the requests, it knows which computer sent the request and the WINS can reply directly to the originating IP address. The WINS database stores the information and makes it available to the other WINS clients. (The WINS database is located at *systemroot*\System32\WINS\Wins.mdb.) The WINS registration generates little excessive network traffic because it does not use broadcast. The WINS protocol is based on and is compatible with the protocols defined for NetBIOS name server (NBNS) in RFCs 1001/1002.

When a WINS client starts up, it registers its name, IP address, and type of services within the WINS server's database. The type of service is designated by a hexadecimal value, which is placed at the end of the name. For example, when starting a Windows computer called Server2, it will register

Table 11.5 NetBIOS network services

NetBIOS Name Suffix	Network Service/Resource Identifier[1]
\\computer_name[00h]	Workstation service
\\computer_name[03h]	Messenger service
\\computer_name[06h]	RAS
\\computer_name[20h]	Server service
\\computer_name[21h]	RAS client service (on a RAS client)
\\computer_name[BEh]	Network monitoring agent service
\domain_name[1Bh]	The PDC in its role as the domain master browser
\domain_name[1Dh]	The master browser for each subnet
\domain_name[1Ch]	The domain controller (up to 25 IP addresses) within the domain

[1]RAS = remote access server.
PDC = primary domain controller.

three mappings, which are Server2[00h] (workstation), Server2[03h] (messenger), and Server2[20h] (file server). The NetBIOS can be a maximum 15 characters, not counting the hexadecimal value which represents the service. See Table 11.5 for the list of NetBIOS network services.

Since WINS was made only for Windows operating systems, other network devices and services (such as a network printer and UNIX machines) cannot register with a WINS service. Such addresses, then, would have to be added manually.

Names held in the WINS database are given a time to live (TTL) or renewal interval during name registration. A name must be refreshed before this interval ends or it will be released from the database. Names are refreshed by sending a name refresh request to the WINS server by the WINS client. Windows clients will attempt a refresh at one-half the renewal interval and will keep trying to contact the WINS server until the time expires. NetBIOS names are explicitly released when the client performs a proper shutdown or silent when the name is not refreshed within the renewal interval.

When a client node registers a name that already exists in the WINS database and has a different IP address, the WINS server must determine if the name with the old IP address still exists. Therefore, the WINS server sends a name query request to the old IP address. If the old address responds with a positive name query response, then the WINS server rejects the new registration with a negative name registration response. If the old address does not respond to the name query, the new registration is accepted.

11.3.2 WINS Clients

A WINS client can be configured to use one of four NetBIOS name resolution methods. They include B (broadcast) node, P (point-to-point) node, M (mixed) node, and H (hybrid) node. See Table 11.6. In either case, when trying to resolve a computer name, it will always check its own local NetBIOS name cache. Like the DNS name cache, it remembers names and addresses of computers that it recently communicated with. By default, when a system is configured to use WINS for its name resolution, it adheres to H node for name registration. By using DHCP servers or the registry, you can force the client into one of these modes.

Example 4:

The H (hybrid) node first checks if the name is the local machine name. It then checks the NetBIOS cache area for remote names. Resolved names remain in the cache area for 10 minutes. If the name has not yet been resolved, H node tries the WINS server, followed by a broadcast. Lastly, it looks in the LMHOSTS file, if the system has one, followed by the HOSTS file and DNS server if it was configured.

Table 11.6   NetBIOS resolution modes

Node Type	Registry Value	Description
B (broadcast) node	1	A computer doing B-node name resolution relies on broadcasts to convert names into IP addresses. B-node name resolution is not the best option on large networks, because the broadcast will load the network and will usually not go through routers. By default, Microsoft uses B node, which will check the LMHOSTS file after a broadcast.
P (point-to-point) node	2	A computer doing P-node name resolution uses a NetBIOS name server (NBNS)/WINS server to look up NetBIOS names to get IP addresses. All systems must know the IP addresses of the NBNS. The main drawback of P-node name resolution is the NBNS cannot be assessed, there will be no way to resolve names and thus no way to access other systems on the network by using NetBIOS names.
M (mixed) node	4	An M-node computer first tries a broadcast to resolve a name. If that attempt fails, the computer looks up the name in a NetBIOS name server. In other words, an M-node computer first acts as a B node, and if that fails, it tries to act as a P node. M node has the advantage over P node in that if the NBNS is unavailable, systems on the local subnet can still be accessed through B-node resolution. M node is typically not the best choice for larger networks because it uses B-node and thus results in broadcasts. However, when you have a large network that consists of smaller subnetworks connected via slow wide area network (WAN) links, M node is a preferred method as it will reduce the amount of communication across the slow links.
H (hybrid) node (Default)	8	An H-node computer first does a P-node lookup; if that fails, the computer does a broadcast. In either case, the NetBIOS name resolution will try the LMHOSTS file after trying a broadcast and/or WINS server.

11.3.3   WINS Server Replication

To provide fault tolerance, it is recommended to have more than one WINS server with the same WINS database. By having more than one WINS server, a WINS client can go to the second WINS server when the first one is unavailable. To make sure that the WINS server has the same information, replicate the information from one WINS server to the other. These servers are known as replication partners. Windows 2000 and Windows Server 2003 support up to 12 replication partners, in which the first and second WINS servers are the primary and secondary servers, and any remaining servers are backup WINS servers.

A **WINS replication partner** can be added and configured as either a pull partner, a push partner, or a push/pull partner. The push/pull partner is the default configuration and is the type recommended for use in most cases. A **pull partner** is a WINS server that requests new database entries from its partner. The pull occurs at configured time intervals or in response to an update notification from a push partner. A **push partner** is a WINS server that sends update notification messages. The update notification occurs after a configurable number of changes to the WINS database.

Pull partners configure at certain time intervals, so you should use a pull partner across slow links; for example, you could have it replicate every 24 hours beginning at 12:00 midnight, when traffic is at a minimum. A push partner should be used with servers connected across fast links, because push replication occurs when a particular number of updated WINS entries are reached. When you need immediate replication, force the WINS servers to replicate using WINS console.

You can configure a WINS server to automatically configure other WINS server computers as its replication partners, using periodic multicasts to announce their presence. These announcements are sent as Internet Group Management Protocol (IGMP) messages for the multicast group address of 224.0.1.24 (the well-known multicast IP address reserved for WINS server use). With this automatic partner configuration, other WINS servers are discovered when they join the network and are added as replication partners.

Figure 11.11 WINS console

11.3.4 WINS Proxy Agent

A **WINS proxy agent** is a WINS-enabled computer that is configured to act on behalf of other host computers that cannot directly use WINS. WINS proxies help resolve NetBIOS name queries for computers that are located on a subnet where there is not a WINS server, by hearing broadcast on the subnet of the proxy agent and forwarding those responses directly to a WINS server. This keeps the broadcast local, yet gets responses from a WINS server without using the P node. Most WINS proxies are only useful or necessary on networks that include NetBIOS broadcast-only (B-node) clients, and therefore, are typically not needed.

11.3.5 Installing and Managing WINS Server

Before installing a WINS server, ensure that the TCP/IP protocol is installed and a static IP address is assigned. The WINS server is included in the Windows server installation files and is enabled during installation or by using the Control Panel's Add/Remove Software applet.

The primary tool used to manage local and remote WINS servers is the WINS console, which can be accessed from within the Administrative Tools folder or by using the Microsoft Management Console (MMC) snap-in. See Figure 11.11.

The Windows WINS database uses the performance-enhanced Extensible Storage Engine, an updated version of the generic storage engine that serves both Microsoft Exchange 5.5 servers and Windows servers. This database imposes no limit to the number of records that a WINS server can replicate or store. The size of the database depends on the number of WINS clients on the network, but it is not directly proportional to the number of active client entries. As inactive entries proliferate, the WINS database grows and many WINS client entries become obsolete. Eventually, these entries clutter the database.

To recover the unused space, the WINS database is compacted. In Windows 2000, WINS server database compaction occurs as an automatic background process during idle time after a database update. Because the database compaction is also dynamic, you do not need to stop the WINS server to compact the database; this process is also known as online compaction. Although WINS performs regular online compaction, this reduces, but does not eliminate, the need for offline compaction.

Microsoft recommends use of JETPACK.EXE (from the JetPack program) to compact a Jet databse periodically whenever the database grows beyond 30 MB or more in size. Microsoft *Jet Database*, part of the Microsoft Access database system, retrieves data from, and stores data in, user and system databases. To compact a WINS database, you must first stop the WINS server then use JETPACK.EXE. The syntax for JETPACK.EXE is

```
jetpack database_name name_of_the_temporary_database
```

After using this command, you have to restart the WINS database. To compact a WINS database, you could do the following:

```
cd %systemroot%\System32\Wins
net stop wins
```

Table 11.7 NBTSTAT command options

Option	Description
nbtstat –n	Displays the names that were registered locally on the system by programs such as the server and redirector
nbtstat –c	Shows the NetBIOS name cache, which contains name-to-address mappings for other computers
nbtstat –R	Purges the name cache and reloads it from the LMHOSTS file
nbtstat –RR	Releases NetBIOS names registered with a WINS server and then renews their registration
nbtstat –a *name*	Performs a NetBIOS adapted status command against the computer specified by *name*. The adapter status command returns the local NetBIOS name table for that computer plus the media access control address of the adapter.
nbtstat –S	Lists the current NetBIOS sessions and their status, including statistics

```
jetpack wins.mdb tmp.mdb
net start wins
```

11.3.6 NBTSTAT Command

To troubleshoot NetBIOS name resolution over TCP/IP, you can use the NBTSTAT command. Its options are shown in Table 11.7.

11.3.7 WINS Best Practices

Follow these suggestions to get the best results from a WINS server:

- Use the default settings to configure WINS servers. The preconfigured WINS settings provide the optimal configuration for most conditions and should be used in most WINS network installations.
- Schedule consistency checking for an off-peak time such as at night during the weekends. This can be done by clicking on the server using the WINS console and clicking and selecting Verify Database Consistency from the Action menu.
- To provide for the best performance, consider a fast disk system, including using RAID to improve disk-access time.
- For disk defragmentation and improved disk performance, use offline WINS compaction on a regular basis.
- Perform regular backups of the WINS database. This can be done by clicking on the server using the WINS console and clicking and selecting Backup Database from the Action menu.
- Configure clients with more than one WINS server IP address. Thus, when one server is not available, it will contact the second WINS server.
- To refresh the client entries in WINS and replicate them to other replication partners, use the NBTSTAT –RR command.

11.4 INTRODUCTION TO DHCP SERVICES

A **Dynamic Host Configuration Protocol (DHCP)** server maintains a list of IP addresses called a pool. When a user needs an IP address, the server removes the address from the pool and issues it to the user for a limited time. Issuing an address is called leasing. Using a DHCP server to issue an address is more reliable and requires less labor than setting every computer manually, and you can get by with fewer IP addresses, because computers not on the network are not using IP addresses.

Created for diskless workstations, the **Bootstrap Protocol (BOOTP)** enables a booting host to configure itself dynamically. See Table 11.8. DHCP is an extension of BOOTP. It is used to automatically

Table 11.8 Common RFCS for DHCP

RFC Number	Description
RFC 2131	Dynamic Host Configuration Protocol (DHCP)
RFC 2132	DHCP options and BOOTP Vendor extensions
RFC 951	Bootstrap Protocol (BOOTP)
RFC 1534	Interoperation between DHCP and BOOTP
RFC 1542	Clarifications and extensions for BOOTP
RFC 2136	Dynamic updates in the domain name system (DNS UPDATE)
RFC 2241	DHCP options for Novell Directory Services
RFC 2242	NetWare/IP domain name and information

configure a host during boot-up on a TCP/IP network and to change settings while the host is attached. There are many parameters that you can automatically set with the DHCP server. Some of the more common parameters are as follows:

- IP address
- Subnet mask
- Gateway (router) address
- Address of DNS servers
- Address of WINS servers
- WINS client mode

11.4.1   DHCP Requests

A host computer that is configured to get a DHCP address sends a DHCPDISCOVER message on the local IP subnet to find the DHCP server(s). The client does not know the address(es) of the DHCP server, so it uses an IP broadcast address for the DHCPDISCOVER message. All available DHCP servers respond with a DHCPOFFER message. If more than one server is available, the client usually selects the first server to respond, but no rule specifies which server the client has to use. Regardless of how many servers respond, the client broadcasts a DHCPREQUEST message that identifies which server the client will use and implicitly informs all other servers that the client will not use them. The selected server responds to the client with a DHCPPACK message that contains the assigned IP address, any other network parameter assignments, and the lease or amount of time for which the DHCP server assigns the client the IP address. The client sends messages to UDP port 67 on the DHCP server and the server sends messages to UDP port 68 on the DHCP client.

Computers running any of the following operating systems can be DHCP clients.

- Windows Server 2003
- Windows XP
- Windows 2000 Professional or Windows 2000 Server
- Microsoft Windows NT version 3.51
- Microsoft Windows 95 or Windows 98
- Microsoft Windows for Workgroups version 3.11 with Microsoft TCP/IP-32 installed
- Microsoft MS-DOS with the Microsoft Network Client version 3.0 for Microsoft MS-DOS installed, and using the real-mode TCP/IP driver
- Microsoft LAN Manager version 2.2c (LAN Manager 2.2c for OS/2 is not supported)
- UNIX/Linux
- Apple Macintosh

A Windows server that is acting as a DHCP server needs to use a static IP address, but does not need to be a domain controller. To install a DNS server, follow these steps:

1. Open the Windows Component wizard by clicking on the Start button, select the Settings option, and select the Control Panel.
2. Double-click Add/Remove Programs and then click Add/Remove Windows Components.
3. Under Components, scroll to and click Networking Services. Click Details.
4. Under Subcomponents of Networking Services, click Dynamic Host Configuration Protocol (DHCP), then click OK.
5. If prompted, type the full path to the Windows distribution files and click Continue.
6. After the required files are copied to the hard disk and the system is rebooted, manage the DHCP server using the DHCP console. The DHCP console can be opened by clicking on the Start button, selecting the Programs option, selecting the Administrative Tools and then the DHCP option.

11.4.2 DHCP Scope and Options

Traditionally, a DHCP server can have only one scope per subnet per DHCP server. Therefore, you can exclude addresses within the scope. For example, you determine the scope will be between 132.132.20.10 and 132.132.20.110. Let us say that you have a network printer assigned a static IP address of 132.132.20.50 and a UNIX server using a static IP address of 132.132.20.51. You would then have to exclude these two addresses. You cannot use the scopes of 132.132.20.10 to 132.132.20.49 and 132.132.20.52 to 132.132.20.110, because each subnet can have only one scope. When creating a scope, you also provide the scope's subnet mask and the duration of the lease (default is 8 days). See Table 11.9. The DHCP database is stored in the *systemroot*\SYSTEM32\DHCP \DHCP.MDB directory.

To provide fault tolerance, assign two or more DHCP servers for every subnet. With two DHCP servers, if one server is unavailable, the other server can take its place and continue to lease new addresses or renew existing clients. When setting up the two DHCP servers, the scopes of the two servers should include scopes with different addresses to avoid both servers assigning the same address to two different computers.

Before installing a DHCP server, be sure the TCP/IP protocol is installed and a static IP address is assigned to the DHCP server. The DHCP server is included in the Windows server installation files and is enabled during installation or by using the Control Panel's Add/Remove Software applet.

Table 11.9 DHCP scope parameters

Parameter	Description
Name	The name of the scope (optional)
Comment	The comment for the scope, used primarily to describe it (optional)
IP Address Range from Address	The starting IP address of scope or address pool
IP Address Range to Address	The ending IP address of scope or address pool
Mask	The subnet mask assigned to DHCP clients
Exclusion Range Start Address	The starting IP address of the range to exclude within the scope or address pool (optional)
Exclusion Range End Address	The ending IP address of the range to exclude within the scope or address pool (optional)
Lease Duration Unlimited	A parameter that indicates that DHCP leases assigned to clients never expire
Lease Duration Limited to	The number of days, hours, and minutes that a DHCP client lease is available before it must be renewed

Figure 11.12   DHCP console

The primary tool used to manage local and remote DHCP servers is the DHCP console, which can be accessed from within the Administrative Tools folder or by using the Microsoft Management Console (MMC) snap-in. See Figure 11.12.

In Windows 2000 and Windows Server 2003, you must authorize a DHCP server in Active Directory before the server can issue leases to DHCP clients. If this is not done, the DHCP service on a Windows server in the forest will not initialize. This step will ensure that another user does not install another DHCP server, which can cause havoc on the network. To authorize a DHCP server for a domain, a user must be a member of the Enterprise Admins group, which exists in the root domain of the AD forest.

To authorize a DHCP server in Active Directory, perform the following steps

1. From the DHCP console, right-click DHCP and select the Browse Authorized Servers option.
2. In the Authorized Servers in the Directory dialog box, click the Add button.
3. In the Authorized DHCP Server dialog box, enter the name or IP address of the DHCP server to authorize, then click OK.
4. In the DHCP dialog box, click Yes to confirm the authorization.

There are three levels of DHCP scopes that can be configured for DHCP clients: global, scope, and client. Global options are available to all DHCP clients. Use global options (known as Server Options in the Windows DHCP console) when all clients on all subnets require the same configuration information. For example, if you want all clients to use the same DNS or the same WINS server, then use the global options to specify the DNS or WINS server that will preconfigure all scopes with the DNS or WINS address. Any settings used in the scope option or client option will overwrite the global option.

The scope options are available only to those clients within the specific scope. The options are only overwritten by client options such as those set in the TCP/IP properties of Windows 9X.

When you create a scope using the DHCP console, you will be using the New Scope wizard. After inputting the scope using the wizard, you specify the subnet mask and exclusion addresses. After you create a scope, you cannot change the IP address range or subnet mask that is assigned by the scope. Instead, you must delete the scope and create a new scope with the correct information.

After the scope has been defined using the Create Scope wizard, the wizard will ask to configure the DHCP options (default gateway/router, domain name and DNS server, WINS server name and address, and scope activation). If you decide to add DHCP options or change the current DHCP options, then use the DHCP console. See Table 11.10.

After you create a scope, you must activate it to make it available for lease assignments. To activate a scope, in DHCP, right-click the entry for the scope, point to Task, and then click Activate. It is recommended that you finish configuring the scope before activating it, so that clients will receive complete configuration information.

Table 11.10   Common DHCP options

DHCP Options	Description
003 Router	IP address of a router or default gateway address
006 DNS Server	IP address of a DNS server
015 DNS Domain Name	DNS domain name for client resolution
044 WINS/NBNS Servers	IP address of a WINS server available to clients
046 WINS/NBT Node Type	Type of NetBIOS over TCP/IP name resolution to be used by the client. Options are 1 = B node (broadcast) 2 = P node (peer) 4 = M node (mixed) 8 = H node (hybrid)
047 NetBIOS Scope ID	Local NetBIOS Scope ID

If you have a client that must always use the same address, then reserve an address by using client reservation. The DHCP server will assign the reserved address to the computer with the specified MAC address. If multiple DHCP servers are configured with a scope that covers the range of the reserved IP address, then the client reservation must be made and duplicated at each of these DHCP servers. Otherwise, the reserved client computer can receive a different IP address, depending on which DHCP responds.

11.4.3   DHCP Relay Agent

A **DHCP relay agent** is a computer relays DHCP and BOOTP messages between clients and servers on different subnets. This way, you can have a single DHCP server handle several subnets without the DHCP server being connected directly to those subnets. You should enable the DHCP relay agent on those router interfaces that are attached to subnets that contain network client computers and do not contain a DHCP server. When you want to use DHCP to configure TCP/IP information on computers that reside on remote subnets from the DHCP server, you must ensure either that the routers can function as BOOTP/DHCP relay agents or that a server on each remote subnet has a BOOTP/DHCP relay agent installed. A router that has a BOOTP relay agent installed is RFC-1542 compliant.

Windows 2000 Server and Windows Server 2003 include the components to act as a DHCP relay agent; Windows 2000 Professional and Windows XP do not. To enable a server as a DHCP relay agent, you need to use the Routing and Remote Access program.

To add the DHCP relay agent, follow these steps:

1. Click on the Start button, select the Programs option, select Administrative Tools, and select the Routing and Remote Access option.
2. Right-click on the General option and select the New Routing Protocol option. The General option can be found by opening the Server Name option followed by opening the IP Routing option. See Figure 11.13.
3. Select the DHCP relay agent routing protocol and select the OK button.
4. Right-click DHCP Relay Agent, and select the New Interface option.
5. Click the interface you want to add and click on the OK button.
6. If needed, in Hop-Count Threshold and Boot Threshold (seconds), click the arrows to modify the thresholds. The Hop-Count Threshold provides a space for you to type a value for the maximum number of DHCP relay agents that will handle DHCP relayed traffic. You can also click the arrows to select a new setting. The default value is 4 hops. The maximum value is 16 hops. The Boot Threshold (seconds) provides a space for you to type the number of seconds the relay agent waits before forwarding DHCP messages. You can also click the arrows to select a new setting. The default value is 4 seconds. This option is useful when you want a local DHCP server to respond first, but if the local DHCP server does not respond, you want to forward messages to a remote DHCP server. Click on the OK button.

Figure 11.13 Installing a DHCP relay agent

11.4.4 Superscopes

The Windows 2000 and Windows Server 2003 implementations of DHCP support superscopes. A **superscope** allows you to group multiple scopes (child scopes) as a single administrative entity. Using a superscope, the DHCP server computer can activate and provide leases from more than one scope to clients on a single physical network. Superscopes serve the following functions:

■ When running out of addresses assigned to an address pool and more computers need to be added to the network, you can use a superscope to extend the address space for the same physical network segment by adding another range of addresses (scope).

■ If an IP network is renumbered, you can use a superscope to migrate a subnet from one scope to another.

■ You can use two or more DHCP servers on the same subnet to provide scope redundancy and fault tolerance.

■ You can allow two DHCP servers on the same subnet to manage separate logical IP networks.

To create a superscope, click the applicable DHCP server and click New Superscope from the Action menu. The Superscope option is only available when at least one scope is available—when one is not currently part of a superscope. Then use the New Superscope wizard. A superscope can have scopes added to it during or after its creation.

11.4.5 Option Classes

Traditionally, all DHCP clients are treated equally, and the server is unaware of the specific type of clients; thus, the configuration information issued by the DHCP server is the same for all DHCP clients. Starting with Windows 2000, you can use option classes to provide unique configurations to specific types of client computers.

There are two types of option classes, vendor-defined classes and user-defined classes. Vendor-defined classes identify a DHCP client's vendor type and configuration. For example, you can configure a vendor-defined class to provide a custom configuration for computers that are running a specific operating system. User-defined classes allow DHCP clients to differentiate themselves by specifying what type of client they are, such as a desktop or laptop. For example, an administrator can configure the DHCP server to assign different options depending on the type of client receiving them. Since a notebook computer is constantly moved and reconnected to the network, users specify a shorter lease to the notebook computer compared with the desktop clients. Note that a client computer needs to be configured with a user-defined class identifier before it sends this identifier to a DHCP server.

To create a new user or vendor class, do the following:

1. In the DHCP console, click the applicable DHCP server.
2. On the Action menu, choose either Define User Classes or Define Vendor Classes and then click on the Add button.
3. In New Class, type the required information.

For Windows 2000, Windows XP, and Windows Server 2003 DHCP client computers, the IPCONFIG/ SETCLASSID *class* command (where *class* is the unique identity of the user class) can be used to set the specified DHCP class ID string and the IPCONFIG/SHOWCLASSID to confirm that the user class was configured correctly.

11.4.6   Multicast Scopes

IP multicast allows a host to communicate with several hosts simultaneously by transmitting information via one data stream. Multicast can greatly reduce the network traffic that bandwidth-hungry applications such as videoconferencing, software distribution, and Webcast create.

You can create a **multicast scope** so that the DHCP server will issue an IP address to an individual client and a shared multicast address to several clients. For multicasting to work correctly, all routers between the server that is sending packets to the multicast address and the receiving client computers must be configured to recognize the multicast address. See Chapter 20.

To create a multicast scope, follow these steps:

1. In the DHCP console, click the name of the DHCP server for which you want to create a multicast scope, then wait for the server status to update.
2. Right-click the name of the DHCP server, then click New Multicast Scope.
3. In the New Multicast Scope wizard, specify the name and description of the multicast scope, the multicast IP address range, and the number of routers through which multicast traffic can pass.
4. Specify any excluded IP addresses and the lease duration.
5. Activate the multicast scope when prompted.

11.4.7   DHCP Services Best Practices

When deciding how many DHCP servers you need, consider the location of routers on the network and whether you want a DHCP server in each subnet. When extending use of a DHCP server across more than one network, you often need to configure additional DHCP relay agents and, in some cases, use superscopes as well.

Transmission speed between the segments for which DHCP service is provided is another important factor. If you have slower WAN links or dial-up links, you typically need a DHCP server on both sides of these links to service clients locally.

For the best possible DHCP server design in most networks, it is recommended that you have, at most, 10,000 clients per server. This recommendation reflects suggested baseline DHCP server performance monitoring and provides for unusual burst traffic conditions, such as after a large-scale power outage when many DHCP client computers might restart simultaneously.

In addition to observing recommended server capacity baselines, split each of your scopes (e.g., apply an 80/20 rule) between two to three servers to ensure fault tolerance. For two subnets, for example, configure each DHCP server with a superscope consisting of two scopes, one scope for subnet A (scope 1) and one scope for subnet B (scope 2). Make sure that the scopes for DHCP server A and DHCP server B do not overlap. Also make sure that the IP address ranges are split according with the 80/20 (or 75/25) rule, so that the local scope uses 80% (or similar) of the local IP address range, and the remote scope uses 20% (or similar) of the remote IP address range. Of course for this to work, your router has to support DHCP relay.

To obtain the best results from a DHCP server, follow these suggestions:

- Since the DHCP is disk intensive, purchase hardware with optimal disk performance characteristics such as a RAID disk system.
- If routing and remote access service is used on your network to support dial-up clients, reduce the lease time on scopes that service these clients.

- If you have a stable, fixed network where available addresses are plentiful, increase the lease time to reduce DHCP-related broadcast traffic.
- Integrate DHCP services with other services such as WINS and DNS.
- Use the appropriate number of DHCP servers, which depends on the number of DHCP-enabled clients on your network, the transmission speed between network segments, the speed of network links, and if DHCP packets can communicate through routers.
- For dynamic updates, such as DNS dynamic updates performed by the DHCP service, use the default client preference settings.

11.4.8   Monitoring and Troubleshooting DHCP Services

Windows 2000 Server and Windows Server 2003 can assist the DHCP in detecting and flagging duplicate IP addresses by enabling Conflict Detection, which allows the server to be configured to attempt to ping each IP address before issuing a new lease for it. If you enable Conflict Detection it will limit the throughput of the DHCP server because the server must wait several seconds for each retry to time out or respond before servicing clients. Each additional attempt at conflict detection delays the DHCP server response by a second while waiting for the ping request to time out. For improved performance, reduce the number of ping retries. Normally, a setting of 1 or 2 should be adequate. If the DHCP server receives a reply to any of the pings, it will mark the IP address as a "BAD_ADDRESS" and will attempt to lease the next address in the scope. After the offending duplicate address is removed from the network, the "BAD_ADDRESS" can be returned to the pool by deleting it from the scope Active Leases dialog box.

To enable Conflict Detection, follow these steps:

- Open the DHCP console
- In the console tree, click the applicable DHCP server.
- On the Action menu, click Properties.
- Click the Advanced tab.
- For Conflict Detection attempts, type a number greater than 0 (zero), then click OK.

Windows stores the DHCP database in the *systemroot*\SYSTEM32\DHCP directory. By default, the database is automatically backed up every 15 minutes to the *systemroot*\SYSTEM32\DHCP\BACKUP\JET\NEW directory. When DHCP server service starts, DHCP will perform a consistency check of its database and attempt to fix any errors it encounters.

The DHCP server service records service start-up and shutdown events and critical errors in the Windows system log, which can be viewed with the Event Viewer. You can monitor the details of DHCP operations by enabling detailed event logging. If detailed event logging is enabled, it will create detailed log files of its activities in files called DHCPSRVLOG.*xxx,* where *xxx* are the first three letters of the day of the week, which are placed in the DHCP database directory.

To enable logging in DHCP, perform the following steps:

1. From the DHCP console, right-click the server you are configuring, then select the Properties option.
2. In the DHCP Properties dialog box, on the General tab, click Enable DHCP Audit Logging.

If the Event Log contains Jet database messages that indicate a corruption of the DHCP database, first look for disk problems and back up the DHCP database. Then repair the database by using the **JetPack** program from the Windows installation CD. To run the JetPack program, take the following steps:

1. Stop the DHCP server.
2. At the Command prompt, change to the directory where the DHCP database is located (by default *systemroot*\system32\dhcp).
3. Type JETPACK DHCP.MDB *temp* (where *temp* is a file name for a temporary database location that is used during repair), then press Enter.
4. Start the DHCP server.

If JetPack cannot correct the database, you will have to restore it from a backup. The JETPACK DHCP.MDB temp command will also compact the database.

11.5   BROWSING THE NETWORK

Windows uses a computer browser service to easily find network computers and their services. The computer browser service is operating when you use Network Neighborhood, My Network Places, the NET VIEW command, and Windows Explorer to show the available network resources such as shared drives, directories, and printers in a graphical environment.

After installing the appropriate network software (client software, network card driver, and protocol), the Network Neighborhood is automatically placed on the desktop. When you double-click on the icon, it opens a window that displays computers that have network resources available. By double-clicking on one of the computers listed, a new window opens and displays the network resources (mostly shared drives, directories, and printers) provided by that computer.

Windows uses a browser service to discover all shared devices on the network and to compile a database of those resources. A browser is a network computer that tracks the location, availability, and identity of shared devices. Several kinds of browsers exist: a domain master browser, master browser, and backup browser. A domain master browser tracks resources for a group of domains. A master browser maintains a database (called a browse list) of shared resources for its domains. Every time a computer on the network starts, it registers itself with the master browser. In an environment containing two or more domains, each master browser passes along its browse list to the domain master browser. A backup browser keeps a copy of the master browser browse list in case the master browser goes down. Although every server on a Windows NT network has the potential to act as a browser, by default the PDC is the master browser for its domain. In Windows 2000 and Windows Server 2003 networks, Active Directory can provide computer browser service by using global catalogs.

When a Windows client needs to perform NetBIOS name resolution, the client first looks in its local cache to see if it knows its IP addresss from talking to it recently. If not, it then checks the LMHOSTS file. If the entry is not in the file, the client by default, does a broadcast looking for that computer (if the client is a B node) or by checking with a WINS server (if the client is a P or H node). B node broadcasts do not go through routers. So typically, Windows NT4 domains with B nodes that don't have any WINS servers to access have a truncated browse list that features only those workstations on the same side of the router. Additionally, master browser election wars frequently occur when more than one domain is on the same subnet, which causes more confusion. So with Windows NT4, the Network Neighborhood list is created via a highly unreliable network of master browsers on each subnet.

Windows 2000 and Windows Server 2003 domain master browser (the DC with the PDC emulator role) actively queries its configured WINS server for a list of all registered domains. It uses this list to contact the other domain master browsers to coordinate browser lists. This means that the browse list presented to the workstation is more complete than was the case with Windows NT4. All workstations should be represented, assuming that the domain master browser of every domain (or workgroup) is configured to use a central WINS server and that at least one workstation from every domain (or workgroup) on each router segment is able to contact its domain master browser.

11.6   SIMPLE NETWORK MANAGEMENT PROTOCOL

The **Simple Network Management Protocol (SNMP)** has become the de facto standard for internetwork management. It allows the system to configure remote devices, monitor network performance, detect network faults, detect inappropriate access, and audit network usage. Remote devices include hubs, bridges, routers, and servers. Note: SNMP uses the User Datagram Protocol.

SNMP contains two primary elements, a manager and agents. The **SNMP manager** is the console through which the network administrator performs network management functions. The SNMP works by sending messages, called protocol data units (PDUs), to different parts of a network. Agents store data about themselves in **management information bases (MIBs).** The manager, which is the console through which the network administrator performs network management functions, requests the information from the MIB. The **SNMP agent** returns the appropriate information to the manager.

A **trap** is an unsolicited message sent by a SNMP agent to an SNMP management system when the agent detects that a certain type of event has occurred locally on the managed host. The SNMP manage console receives a trap message known as a trap destination. For example, a trap message might be sent when a system restarts or when a router link goes down.

Each SNMP management host and agent belongs to an SNMP community. An **SNMP community** is a collection of hosts that are grouped for administrative purposes. Deciding what computers should belong to the same community is generally but not always determined by the physical proximity of the computers. Communities are identified by the names assigned to them.

Although most networks utilize a user name and a password for authentication, SNMP messages are only authenticated by the community name. A host can belong to several communities at the same time, but an SNMP agent does not accept requests from a management system in a community that is not on its list of acceptable community names. If the community name is incorrect, the agent sends an "authentication failure" trap to its trap destination. Therefore, it is the responsibility of the administrator to set hard-to-guess community names.

Community names are transmitted as clear text, that is, without encryption. Because unencrypted transmissions are vulnerable to attacks by hackers with network analysis software, the use of SNMP community names represents a potential security risk. However, Windows 2000 and Windows Server 2003, IP Security can be configured to help protect SNMP messages from these attacks. For more information about IP security, see Chapter 23.

The SNMP service requires the configuration of at least one default community name. The name Public is generally used as the community name because it is a common name that is universally accepted in all SNMP implementations. You can delete or change the default community name or add multiple community names. If no community names are defined, the SNMP agent will deny all incoming SNMP requests.

When an SNMP agent receives a message, the community name contained in the packet is verified against the agent's list of acceptable community names. After the name is determined to be acceptable, the request is evaluated against the agent's list of access permissions for that community. The types of permissions that can be granted to a community are shown in Table 11.11.

There are two versions of the Simple Network Management Protocol. SNMP 1 reports only whether a device is functioning properly. The industry has attempted to define a new set of protocols, called SNMP 2, that would provide additional information, but the standardization efforts have not been successful. Instead, network managers have turned to a related technology called RMON that provides more detailed information about network usage.

To install the SNMP service, you must be logged on as an administrator or as a member of the Administrators group. To install the SNMP service, do the following:

1. In the Control Panel, double-click the Add/Remove Programs.
2. Click the Add/Remove Windows Components to start the Windows Components Wizard.

Table 11.11 Community permissions

Permission	Description
None	The SNMP agent does not process the request. When the agent receives an SNMP message from a management system in this community, it discards the request and generates an authentication trap.
Notify	This is currently identical to the permission of None.
Read Only	The agent does not process SET requests from this community. It processes only GET, GET-NEXT, and GET-BULK requests. The agent discards SET requests from manager systems in this community and generates an authentication trap.
Read Create	The SNMP agent processes or creates all requests from this community. It processes SET, GET, GET-NEXT, and GET-BULK requests, including SET requests that require the addition of a new object to a MIB table.
Read Write	Currently identical to Read Create.

3. Click to highlight Management and Monitoring Tools, then click Details.
4. Select Simple Network Management Protocol check box and click OK.
5. Click the Next button and finish the Wizard.

To configure agent properties, do the following:

1. In the Control Panel, double-click Administrative Tools, then double-click Computer Management.
2. In the console tree, click Services, which is located under Services and Applications.
3. In the Details pane, click to highlight SNMP Service.
4. Right-click the SNMP Service in the Details pane and select the Properties option.
5. On the Agent tab, in Contact, type the name of the user or administrator for this computer. See Figure 11.14.
6. In Location, type the physical location of the computer or the contact.
7. Under Service, select the appropriate check boxes for this computer, and then click OK. See Table 11.12.

To configure traps, do the following:

1. In the Control Panel, double-click Administrative Tools, then double-click Computer Management.
2. In the console tree, click Services, which is located under Services and Applications.
3. In the Details pane, click to highlight SNMP Service.
4. Right-click the SNMP Service in the Details pane and select the Properties option.
5. On the Traps tab, under Community Name, type the case-sensitive community name to which this computer will send trap messages, then click Add to List. See Figure 11.15.
6. In Trap Destinations, click Add.
7. In Host Name, IP, or IPX Address, type information for the host, and click Add.
8. Repeat steps 5 through 7 until you have added all the communities and trap destinations you want.

Figure 11.14 SNMP agent properties

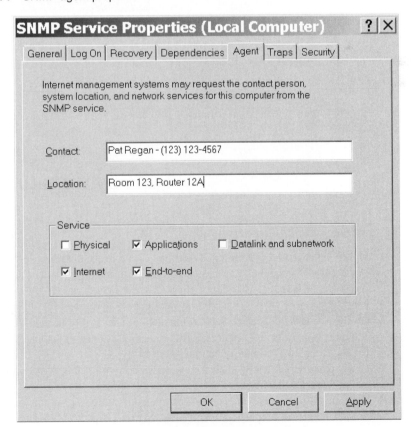

Table 11.12 SNMP service types

Agent Service	Select if this computer:
Physical	Manages physical devices, such as a hard disk partition
Applications	Uses any applications that send data using the TCP/IP protocol suite. This service should always be enabled.
Datalink and Subnet	Manages a bridge
Internet	Is an IP gateway (router)
End-to-end	Is an IP host. This service should always be enabled.

Figure 11.15 SNMP trap properties

To configure security, do the following:

1. In the Control Panel, double-click Administrative Tools, then double-click Computer Management.
2. In the console tree, click Services, which is located under Services and Applications.
3. In the Details pane, click to highlight SNMP Service.
4. Right-click the SNMP Service in the Details pane and select the Properties option.
5. On the Security tab, select Send Authentication Trap if you want a trap message sent whenever authentication fails. See Figure 11.16.
6. Under Accepted Community Names, click Add.
7. Under Community Rights, select a permission level for this host to process SNMP requests from the selected community.
8. In Community Name, type a case-sensitive community name, and then click Add.
9. In SNMP Service Properties, specify whether to accept SNMP packets from a host:

Figure 11.16   SNMP security properties

- To accept SNMP requests from any host on the network, regardless of identity, click "Accept SNMP packets from any host."
- To limit acceptance of SNMP packets, click "Accept SNMP packets from these hosts," click Add, type the appropriate host name, IP, or IPX address, and then click Add again.

You can make changes to an entry by clicking the entry, and then clicking the Edit button. You can delete a selected entry by clicking the Remove button.

11.7   TROUBLESHOOTING ADVANCED TCP/IP SERVICES

Problem: A DNS client received this error message: "Name not found."

Solution: First ensure that the DNS client computer has a valid IP configuration for the network. Verify that the TCP/IP configuration settings for the client computer are correct, including the IP address, subnet mask, gateway, and those settings that are used for DNS name resolution using WINIPCFG or IPCONFIG /ALL. If you are unsure what the IP address is for the preferred DNS server, observe it by using the IPCONFIG command.

Next ensure that the DNS server is running properly by trying to ping it. If you cannot ping the server, the problem lies with the client, the DNS server, or some link between the two. Remember that it can be caused by the client's IP configuration, the DNS server's TCP/IP configuration, the DNS server's network cards, the cable connected to the DNS server, or the routes to the DNS server.

The client of the DNS server does not have authority for the failed name and cannot locate the authoritative server for this name. If the server is the authority, make sure that the record is there.

Lastly, ensure that the DNS server is still running, by bringing up the DNS console, clicking on the zone, and selecting the Properties option from the Action button.

Problem: The DNS client appears to have received a response with stale or incorrect information in it.

Solution: The client of the DNS server does not have authority for the failed name and is using stale information from its local DNS database. Determine whether the DNS server is authoritative for the name and proceed accordingly.

Another option in which dynamic updates are enabled is to force registration and update at the computer that is targeted by the query. If the target computer is running Windows 2000, Windows XP, and Windows Server 2003, you can force it to update the registration of its RRs by using the IPCONFIG /REGISTERDNS command.

If the preferred server is not a direct authority for the queried name, it likely already answered the query based on information obtained and cached during an earlier recursive lookup. In this case, you might consider clearing the server name's cache. This compels the server to use new recursive queries for this RR data and rebuild its cache contents based on current information. If it is a secondary server, then you can initiate a zone transfer at the secondary server to its master server to update the zone.

The name that was queried was specified in error, either through user input or in a stored client configuration. Verify that the name was correctly specified in the application where the name query originated.

For directory-integrated zones, it is also possible that the affected records for the erred query have been updated in Active Directory, but not replicated to all DNS servers loading the zone. By default, all DNS servers that load zones from Active Directory poll it at a set interval (typically every 15 minutes), and update the zone for any incremental changes to it. In most cases, a DNS update takes no more than 20 minutes to replicate to all DNS servers used in an Active Directory domain environment using default replication settings and reliable high-speed links.

Another possibility for the erred data is in whether WINS lookup integration is enabled and used with the zone. If you are using WINS lookup with your zones, verify that WINS is not the source of the erred data.

SUMMARY

1. In Windows, there are two methods to resolve names, Domain Name System (DNS) and Windows Internet Naming Service (WINS).

2. DNS is the primary method for name resolution for Windows.

3. DNS is a hierarchical client-server-based distributed database management system that translates Internet domain names to an IP address.

4. Immediately below the root domain are the top-level domains, which indicate a country, region, or type of organization.

5. Subdomain names are additional names that an organization can create which are derived from the registered second-level domain name.

6. A zone is a portion of the DNS name space whose database records exist and are managed in a particular DNS database file, which is based on a specific domain node.

7. When the resolver queries a DNS server, it performs a recursive query in which the query asks the DNS server to respond with the requested data or with an error stating that either the requested data or the specified domain name does not exist.

8. To prevent the searching of all domains for an inverse query, a special domain called "in-addr.arpa" was created.

9. NSLOOKUP is a diagnostic tool that displays information from the DNS servers.

10. A WINS server contains a database of IP addresses and NetBIOS (computer names) that update dynamically.

11. A WINS client can be configured to use one of four NetBIOS name resolution methods. They include B (broadcast) node, P (point-to-point) node, M (mixed) node, and H (hybrid) node.

12. A WINS replication partner can be added and configured as either a pull partner, a push partner, or a push/pull partner. The push/pull partner is the default configuration and is the type recommended for use in most cases.

13. A WINS proxy agent is a WINS-enabled computer that is configured to act on behalf of other host computers that cannot directly use WINS.

14. Dynamic Host Configuration Protocol (DHCP) is used to automatically configure a host during boot-up on a TCP/IP network and to change settings while the host is attached.

15. A DHCP relay agent is a computer that relays DHCP and BOOTP messages between clients and servers on different subnets.

16. A superscope allows you to group multiple scopes (child scopes) as a single administrative entity.

17. Using a superscope, the DHCP server computer can activate and provide leases from more than one scope to clients on a single physical network.

18. IP multicast allows a host to communicate with several hosts simultaneously by transmitting information via one data stream.

19. You can create a multicast scope so that the DHCP server will issue an IP address to an individual client and a shared multicast address to several clients.

20. The Simple Network Management Protocol (SNMP) has become the de facto standard for internetwork management. It allows the system to configure remote devices, monitor network performance, detect network faults, detect inappropriate access, and audit network usage. Remote devices include hubs, bridges, routers, and servers.

21. A trap is an unsolicited message sent by an SNMP agent to an SNMP management system when the agent detects that a certain type of event has occurred locally on the managed host.

22. Each SNMP management host and agent belongs to an SNMP community. An SNMP community is a collection of hosts that are grouped for administrative purposes.

QUESTIONS

1. Pat installs and configures an Internet Information Server (IIS) web server on a Windows 2000 Server. Pat configures IIS for both WWW and FTP. He wants users to access the same IIS server as either WWW.DATA.ACME.COM or FTP.DATA.ACME.COM. Which resource record type must Pat add?
   a. AFSDB
   b. CNAME
   c. MB
   d. MG
   e. MINFO

2. Pat's network contains four Windows 2000 server computers that set up as web servers. Pat wants to enable Windows 98 and Apple Macintosh computers running Internet Explorer to access each of these web servers by using a host name. What should Pat use?
   a. DHCP
   b. DNS
   c. FTP
   d. WINS

3. Julie has just installed the DNS service on a Windows 2000 Server computer. Julie needs to add a resource record for her domain's mail server. Which resource record must she add?
   a. CNAME
   b. MX
   c. PTR
   d. WKS

4. A _____ is a portion of the DNS name space whose database records exist and are managed in a particular DNS database file.
   a. FQDN
   b. zone
   c. subdomain
   d. host name

5. The top of a DNS name space is referred to as the _____.
   a. root directory
   b. root container
   c. root domain
   d. master domain

6. Which of the following are *not* a second-level domain name? (Choose all that apply.)
   a. COM
   b. " "
   c. EDU
   d. MIL
   e. WWW
   f. FTP

7. _____ names are additional names that an organization can create which are derived from the registered second-level domain name so that they can divide their domain.
   a. Second-level domain
   b. Zone
   c. Subzone
   d. Subdomain

8. What is the maximum length of an FQDN?
   a. 11 characters
   b. 63 characters
   c. 128 characters
   d. 255 characters

9. Windows 2000 has three types of zones. Which is *not* one of these?
   a. self-replicating
   b. standard primary
   c. Active Directory integrated
   d. standard secondary

10. When Windows 2000 uses dynamic update for DNS names, what is the default time before it sends a refresh update?
    a. 1 hour
    b. 12 hours
    c. 24 hours
    d. 8 days

11. When a client does not know the address of a host, it sends what kind of query to its preferred DNS server to find the address?
    a. interactive
    b. iterative
    c. recursive
    d. broadcast

12. When trying to resolve a host name from its IP address, DNS uses a special domain called a _____.
    a. in-addr.arpa
    b. caching only
    c. PTR
    d. conical

13. If a client's name records are missing from a DNS server, what command would you use to force the client to renew its registration?
    a. IPCONFIG /RENEW
    b. IPCONFIG /REGISTERDNS
    c. NSLOOKUP
    d. IPCONFIG /FLUSHDNS

14. From his Windows 98 computer, Pat tries to connect to a Windows 2000 Server using http://support.acme.com. He receives this message: "Internet Explorer cannot open the Internet site http://support.acme.com. A connection with the server could not be established." Pat has no problems when connecting to other remote servers using host names. His computer does not use a HOSTS file for name resolution. Which of the following are the most likely causes of the problem? (Choose all that apply.)
    a. The ARP cache on the Windows 98 computer does not have an entry for support.acme.com.
    b. The DNS server has no entry for support.acme.com.

c. The IP address on the Windows 2000 computer for the default gateway is incorrect.

d. The Windows 98 computer was provided with an incorrect IP address for support.acme.com from the DNS server.

15. Pat has installed a DNS server on his network. To provide for DNS database redundancy, he wants to implement a backup DNS server. Pat should do this by setting up a _____ .

   a. caching-only server
   b. forwarding
   c. replication server
   d. secondary server

16. Which of the following are true of DNS in Windows 2000? (Choose all that apply.)

   a. DNS on Windows 2000 can be integrated into Active Directory.
   b. DNS on Windows 2000 supports dynamic updates.
   c. DNS on Windows 2000 supports both full zone transfer (AXFR) and incremental zone transfer (IXFR).
   d. A DNS server must be available before active directory can be installed.

17. Which file should the DNS root server use to connect to the Internet?

   a. CACHE.DNS
   b. DOMAIN.DNS
   c. HOSTS
   d. HOSTS.DNS
   e. REVERSE-NETID.in-ADDR.ARPA.DNS

18. Pat's Windows 2000 Professional computer resides on a WINS-enabled network. In which order will Pat's computer perform name resolution if his computer is configured to use an LMHOSTS file?

   a. local cache, broadcasting, LMHOSTS file, WINS server
   b. local cache, WINS server, broadcasting, LMHOSTS file
   c. WINS server, local cache, broadcasting, LMHOSTS file
   d. WINS server, local cache, LMHOSTS file, broadcasting

19. Pat manages a TCP/IP network of both Windows-based and UNIX computers with three subnets—Subnet1, Subnet2, and Subnet3—connected by a single router. After installing a WINS server on Subnet1, he configures each Windows-based computer to recognize the WINS server. However, he soon discovers that the UNIX computers on Subnet2 and Subnet3 are not able to use the WINS server for name resolution. What can Pat do to correct this problem?

   a. Install a second router.
   b. On Subnet2 and Subnet3, install BOOTP relay agents.
   c. On Subnet2 and Subnet3, install WINS proxies.
   d. On the WINS server, install DHCP.
   e. On the WINS server, resolve the names of the clients on Subnet2 and Subnet3.

20. Pat wants to see a list of all NetBIOS names currently cached on this Windows 2000 Server. What command should he use?

   a. ARP
   b. NBTSTAT
   c. NETSTAT
   d. Network Monitor
   e. PING
   f. TRACERT

21. At each of his company's two offices, Pat has installed a WINS server. A T1 line connects both offices. He wants both servers to replicate their WINS databases with one another. How does Pat do this?

   a. Make each WINS server a WINS client of the other WINS server.
   b. Set the Directory Replicator Server service to start automatically.
   c. Set up each WINS server as both a push partner and a pull partner of the other WINS server.
   d. Set up each WINS server as the secondary WINS server of the other server.

22. Pat's company is headquartered in Sacramento with a second office in New York. Both offices use TCP/IP as the networking protocol. The Sacramento office has 10 Windows 2000 Server and 800 Windows 2000 Professional computers. The Chicago office has 2 Windows 2000 server computers and 150 Windows 2000 Professional computers. The WINS server in Sacramento is called SERVER1. The WINS server in New York is called SERVER2. Pat wants to set up WINS database replication between the two WINS servers.

Required result:

He must replicate the Sacramento WINS server database to the New York WINS server.

Optional desired results:

1. He must replicate the New York WINS server database to the Sacramento WINS server.
2. He wants to be sure that the Sacramento WINS database is replicated to New York at least once a day.

Proposed solution:

Configure Sacramento to push its WINS database update information to New York once every 1000 updates. Configure New York to pull Sacramento's WINS database update information once every 24 hours.

Which result does the proposed solution produce?

   a. achieves the required result and both optional results
   b. does not achieve the required result but achieves both the optional results
   c. does not achieve the required result but does achieve one of the optional results
   d. achieves the required result but cannot achieve either of the optional results
   e. achieves neither the required result nor either of the optional results

23. You discover that errors in the LMHOSTS file of your Windows 2000 Server computer are creating problems on your network. After correcting the LMHOSTS file, which command will issue to purge the server's NetBIOS name cache?

   a. ARP
   b. NBTSTAT
   c. NETSTAT
   d. PING
   e. ROUTE

24. Pat moves a Windows 2000 Professional computer originally configured at a DHCP client from one subnet to another on a DHCP network. He discovers that the workstation cannot connect to the local Windows 2000 Server. What is the most likely cause of the problem?

   a. The Windows 2000 Professional computer's default gateway address has been manually set.

b. The Windows 2000 Professional computer's default gateway address is set as a local-level option on the DHCP server.

c. The Windows 2000 Professional computer's IP address has been manually set.

d. The workstation's IP address is set as a scope-level option on the DHCP server.

25. You administer a network of 1000 client computers on five subnets. You use DHCP to assign IP addresses to all client computers. You install two DNS servers on the network. Now you want to specify the IP addresses of both DNS servers on each client computer across all five subnets. How do you configure the DHCP option?

a. as a client option   c. as a scope option

b. as a global option   d. as an Internet option

26. Pat uses DHCP to assign IP addresses to all client computers on his network. Pat sets up the DHCP server to assign the IP address of the WINS server to all client computers. What else should Pat do to allow client computers to use WINS?

a. In the DHCP console, specify the NetBIOS resolution mode.

b. On each client computer, enter the IP address of at least one DNS server.

c. On each client computer, enter the IP address of the local gateway.

d. On each client computer, specify the NetBIOS scope ID.

27. Pat has just changed the DHCP configuration on his Windows 2000 server. He wants so see if the client computer has registered the changes. Which command should Pat execute?

a. ARP –S   d. NETSTART –E

b. IPCONFIG /ALL   e. PING –S

c. NBSTART –S

28. You want DHCP to assign IP addresses to all Windows-based computers on your network. Each Windows 2000 server is to be assigned that same unique IP address each time that server is booted up. How should you proceed?

a. Exclude a range of IP addresses that will be assigned to the servers.

b. For each server, create a separate scope that contains that server's IP address.

c. For each server, implement a client reservation.

d. For each server, specify an unlimited lease period.

29. Pat administers several hundred computers on a TCP/IP network with six subnets. Many users have notebook computers that run Windows 98 and Windows 2000. Pat wants to automatically assign IP addresses to these laptop computers each time they connect. Which service must Pat configure?

a. DHCP   d. SNMP

b. DNS   e. WINS

c. FTP

30. On a network with six subnets, all client computers use only one DHCP server. A global option on the DHCP server specifies the IP address of the DNS server that the client computers are to use. A user complains that he cannot connect to other computers using their host names. Running the IPCONFIG utility on the user's computer, you ascertain that all IP settings are correct except for the IP address of the DNS server. What could account for the

difference between the DNS server's IP address as assigned by the DHCP server and its IP address as found on the user's computer? (Choose all that apply.)

a. The client computer is on a subnet other than the one for which the DHCP option was defined.

b. The DHCP scope is not activated for the client's subnet.

c. The IP address for the DNS server has been created for the client computer as a client option.

d. The user's computer is no longer a DHCP client, and the IP address for the DNS server has been manually set at the user's computer.

31. Pat uses DHCP, WINS, and DNS to administer a large TCP/IP network. He wants to reserve the IP addresses of his three domain controllers and his DNS server. What information must Pat have when reserving these servers in DHCP console?

a. MAC addresses   c. lease durations

b. IP addresses   d. subnet masks

32. Pat is designing a TCP/IP network with two subnets: Subnet1 and Subnet2. Pat configures a Windows 2000 Server computer as a static router between the two subnets. He installs a second Windows 2000 Server computer as a DHCP server on Subnet1 and a third Windows 2000 Server computer on Subnet2. Pat wants client computers on Subnet2 to obtain their IP configurations from the DHCP server on Subnet1. Which service must Pat install on the third Windows 2000 Server computer on Subnet2?

a. LLC sublayer   d. DHCP relay agent service

b. proxy service   e. RIP for IP service

c. RAS service

33. Suppose the following situation exists:

Pat administers a TCP/IP network of Microsoft-based computers on five subnets. Pat wants to install two DHCP servers, each on a separate subnet that will automatically assign IP addresses to the host computers.

Required result:
Each DHCP server must act as a backup server if the other DHCP server is down.

Optional desired results:

1. DHCP should provide the same unique IP addresses to each Windows 2000 Server computer when that server initializes.

2. DHCP should assign the IP addresses of the WINS servers and DNS servers to all DHCP clients.

Proposed solutions:

1. On each subnet, install the DHCP relay agent.

2. On one of the DHCP servers, define a DHCP scope for each subnet. In each scope, define the IP address range available to that subnet. Assign half of the available IP addresses on each subnet to each scope.

3. On the other DHCP server, define a DHCP scope for each subnet. In each scope, define the IP address range available to that subnet. Assign the remaining half of the available IP addresses on each subnet to each scope.

4. On the DHCP servers, enable and configure the 044 WINS/NBNS servers, the 046 WINS/NBT node type options, and the 006 DNS server options.

Which result does the proposed solution produce?

a. achieves the required result and both optional results

b. does not achieve the required result but achieves both optional results

c. does not achieve the required result but does achieve one of the optional results

d. achieves the required result but cannot achieve either of the optional results

e. achieves neither the required result nor either of the optional results

34. You manage a network with seven subnets. The network has two DHCP servers, two WINS servers, and three DNS servers. All client computers on the network are Windows based and use DHCP. One user reports receiving a message that he has a duplicate IP address. What is the cause of the problem?

a. DHCP lookup is not enabled on one of the DNS servers.

b. The user's computer is registered with more than one WINS server.

c. DHCP servers have overlapping scopes.

d. WINS lookup is not enabled on one of the DHCP servers.

35. You are setting up a DHCP relay agent on a Windows 2000 Server. What information do you need?

a. DHCP node type

b. DHCP relay agent lease duration

c. IP address of the DHCP server

d. NetBIOS name of the DHCP server

36. Which service must be started on a Windows 2000 Professional computer so that trap messages can be forwarded to various host names on a network?

a. Alerter service   c. SAP service

b. EventLog service   d. SNMP service

37. Pat wants to send TCP/IP protocol statistics from his Windows 2000 computer to a UNIX computer. Both computers are on the same TCP/IP network. What must Pat install on each computer?

a. NETSTAT.EXE on the UNIX computer and Network Monitor Agent on the server

b. Performance Monitor on the UNIX computer and SNMP service on the server

c. Protocol Analyzer on the UNIX computer and Network Monitor Agent on the server

d. SNMP management software on the UNIX computer and SNMP service on the server

38. Pat wants the SNMP service on his Windows 2000 Server computer to send trap messages to an SNMP trap destination. Which of the following must be supplied? (Select two answers.)

a. SNMP management station's community

b. SNMP management station's IP address

c. SNMP management station's scope ID

d. SNMP management station's subnet mask

39. You want to manage and monitor the hosts on your Windows-based network using SNMP. Which of the following do you need to install or configure on your network? (Choose all that apply.)

a. Performance Monitor   c. SNMP manager software

b. SNMP agent   d. TCP/IP

40. Which service automatically registers the domain names to the Windows DNS server using dynamic update?

a. DNS service   c. DHCP service

b. WINS service   d. SNMP service

41. You are the administrator of your company's network. The network consists of one Windows 2000 domain. All servers and client computers are running Windows 2000. To facilitate name resolution and client access to resources on the servers, you have configured your DNS standard primary zone to include the addresses of all of your servers. You later add three new member servers to your network. Users report that they can find these servers in the directory but cannot access these servers. You want to resolve this problem. What should you do?

a. Convert the DNS standard primary zone to an Active Directory integrated zone.

b. Create SRV (service) records for each new server in the DNS zone.

c. Set the Allow Dynamic Updates option for the DNS standard primary zone to Yes.

d. Set the Allow Dynamic Updates option for the DNS standard primary zone to Only Secure Updates.

42. You are the administrator of a Windows 2000 network that consists of three subnets. For load-balancing purposes, each web server on the network is configured to maintain exactly the same content as all the other web servers. You want to configure your DNS server to allow users to type a host name in their browser to connect to a web server that is on the same subnet. The host name that all users type will be identical, regardless of the subnet they are on. How should you configure your DNS server?

a. On the primary DNS server, create three A (host) records that map the same host name to the IP address of the web server on each subnet.

b. On the primary DNS server, create one A (host) record that is located on the same subnet as the DNS server. On the secondary DNS servers on the two remaining subnets, edit the zone file for the domain on each DNS server to include an A (host) record for the web server on each subnet.

c. On the primary DNS server, create three A (host) records that map a different host name to the IP address of the web server on each subnet.

d. On the primary DNS server, create one A (host) record for one web server and two CNAME (canonical name) records for the remaining two web servers.

43. You are the administrator of the blueskyairlines.com domain. You maintain a local DNS server to provide name resolution within your Internet domain. Your DNS server runs on Windows 2000 Server. You have five web servers, which contain company and flight information in addition to the online flight reservation system. For load-balancing purposes, each web server is configured to maintain exactly the same contents as all the other web servers. All the web servers respond to the host name www.blueskyairlines.com. Customer feedback indicates that web server response times are unacceptably slow. You monitor your web servers and discover that only one of the five servers is servicing customer requests, while the others are sitting idle. You want to ensure load balancing and improve response time for

customer web request. What could you do in the DNS management console? (Choose two answers.)

a. Enable round-robin in the DNS server's properties.

b. Disable round-robin in the DNS server's properties.

c. Enable forwarders and configure them to point to each web server.

d. Verify that A (host) records have been created for each web server.

e. Verify that CNAME (canonical name) records have been created for each web server.

44. You are the network administrator of Woodgrove Bank. Srv2 and Srv3 are configured as caching-only servers. Both servers forward requests to Srv1. Srv1 is configured as the primary server for the acme.com domain. Users on networks 10.107.2.0 and 10.107.3.0 frequently use an Internet application that gathers stock quotes from various servers on the acme.com domain. You want to reduce DNS network traffic. What should you do?

a. Increase the time to live for the SOA (start of authority) record on Srv1.

b. Decrease the time to live for the SOA record on Srv2 and Srv3.

c. Set the Server Optimization option on Srv2 and Srv3 to "Maximize data throughput for network applications."

d. Increase the forward timeout seconds on Srv2 and Srv3.

45. You are the administrator of your company's network, which consists of a single subnet. It includes 50 Windows 2000 Professional computers, and four Windows 2000 Server computers, one of which runs DNS. The DNS server is configured to allow dynamic updates. All client computers and servers are configured with static IP addresses and with the address of the DNS server. You add two UNIX database servers named DB1 and DB2 to the network. From your client computer, you can ping both servers by using their IP addresses. However, when you try to ping either server by name, you receive the following error message: "Unknown host." You need to ensure that you can ping DB1 and DB2 by name. Which two actions should you perform? (Each correct answer presents part of the solution. Choose two.)

a. Add A (host) records to the DNS server for DB1 and DB2.

b. Add SRV records to the DNS server for DB1 and DB2.

c. Disable dynamic updates on the DNS server.

d. Run the IPCONFIG/FLUSHDNS command on your client computer.

e. Clear the DNS server cache.

46. You are the administrator of your company's network. The network consists of 10 Windows 2000 Server computers, 100 Windows 2000 Professional computers, and 150 Windows NT Workstation computers. For workgroup collaboration and document sharing, all client computers have file and print sharing services enabled. You are using DHCP to automate the TCP/IP configuration of all client computers.

You want to accomplish the following goals:

• All client computers will be able to be located on the network by the network's fully qualified domain name.

• The A (host) records for all client computers will be automatically added to the DNS zone files.

• PTR (pointer) records for reverse name lookup for all client computers will be automatically added to the DNS zone files.

• The Records, A and PTR, will be automatically removed from the DNS zone files when the DHCP lease expires.

You take the following actions:

• Configure the DHCP server to always update client computer information in DNS.

• Configure the DHCP server to discard forward lookups when the lease expires.

• Configure the DHCP server to update DNS for client computers that do not support dynamic updates.

• Configure the DHCP scope to configure the domain name for all DHCP client computers.

Which result or results do these actions produce? (Choose all that apply.)

a. All client computers are able to be located on the network by the network's fully qualified domain name.

b. The A records for all client computers are automatically added to the DNS zone files.

c. PTR records for reverse name lookup for all client computers are automatically added to the DNS zone files.

d. The A records and PTR records are automatically removed from the DNS zone files when the DHCP lease expires.

47. You are the administrator of one standard primary DNS server and two standard secondary DNS servers in a Windows 2000 domain. There are no other DNS servers on the network. The domain includes Windows 2000 Professional computers and a Windows 98 computer. The DNS zone for the Windows 2000 domain is configured to allow dynamic updates. All three DNS servers are located on domain controllers. You want client computers to be able to register with any DNS server. What should you do?

a. Change the zone type of the DNS zone for the Windows 2000 domain on all three DNS servers to Active Directory integrated.

b. Change the settings on the standard primary DNS server to notify the two standard secondary DNS servers when the zone is updated.

c. Change the settings on the standard primary DNS server to allow zone transfers to only the two standard secondary DNS servers.

d. Change the dynamic update option on the standard primary DNS server to allow only secure updates.

48. You are the administrator of Windows 2000 network. You have three Windows 2000 domain controllers in a single domain. Your primary DNS server is installed on a domain controller named dc1.contoso.com. You have two secondary DNS servers installed on member servers named srv1.contoso.com and srv2.contoso.com. You want to increase fault tolerance for your DNS infrastructure. You also want to optimize and simplify the management of replication and zone transfers on your network. How should you accomplish these goals?

a. Promote the member servers that are hosting the DNS server to domain controllers.

b. Add srv1.contoso.com and srv2.contoso.com to the notify list on the primary DNS server.

c. Remove the DNS server service from the member servers. Install the DNS server service on the domain controller. Convert the zone hosted by dc1.contoso.com to an Active Directory integrated zone.

d. Set the time to live value in the SOA record on the primary DNS server to a low value.

49. You are the enterprise administrator of a Windows 2000 domain. All client computers in the domain are either Windows 98 computers or Windows 2000 computers. Your Windows 2000 users run an Internet application that must access files from a Windows NT computer named WNT_101. None of your Windows 2000 computers can connect to WNT_101, but WNT_101 can connect to every Windows 2000 computer. What should you do?

a. Release and renew the IP address of Windows NT_101.

b. Select "Enable updates for DNS clients that do not support dynamic update" check box.

c. Clear "Discard forward (name-to-address) lookups when lease expires" check box.

d. Set the DNS zone for the Windows 2000 domain to "Active Directory Integrated Primary."

50. You are the administrator for the Acme Corporation. The network consists of one Windows 2000 domain named acme.local. For security reasons, you want to ensure that internal name resolution traffic never passes outside the network. You also want to ensure that external name requests are handled by an external DNS server. What should you do to accomplish these goals?

a. Create a new standard primary zone for your local name space and entry only internal addresses into the host table.

b. Create a new Active Directory integrated zone for your logical name space and enter only internal addresses into the host table.

c. Delete the root zone for your local name space and configure all internal DNS servers to forward name resolution requests to the external DNS server.

d. Create a new root zone for the Internet and configure all internal DNS servers to forward all requests to this zone.

51. You are the administrator of your company's network. The network consists of 10 Windows 2000 Server computers, 200 Windows 2000 Professional computers, and 20 UNIX servers. You are using Windows 2000 as your DNS server. Your DNS zone is considered an Active Directory integrated zone. Your DNS zone is also configured to allow dynamic updates. Users report that although they can access the Windows 2000 computers by host name, they cannot access the UNIX servers by host name. What should you do to correct this problem?

a. Manually enter A (host) records for the UNIX servers to the zone database.

b. Manually add the UNIX servers to the Windows 2000 domain.

c. On the DNS server, manually create the Hosts file that contains the records for the UNIX servers.

d. Configure a UNIX computer to be a DNS server in a secondary zone.

52. You are the administrator of your company's network. Your company has a main office, two branch offices, and two small branch offices. The company's network consists of one Windows 2000 domain. The main office and the two large branch offices are connected by a dedicated T1 line. The two small branch offices use 128-Kbps ISDN lines and routing and remote access over the Internet to connect to the company's internal network. You are designing your DNS name resolution environment. You want to accomplish the following goals:

- DNS name resolution traffic across the WAN links will be minimized.
- DNS replication traffic across the WAN links will be minimized.
- DNS replication traffic across the public WAN links will be secured.
- Name resolution performance for the client computers will be optimized.

You take the following actions:

- Install the DNS server service on one server at each office.
- Create the standard primary zone at the main office.
- Create a standard secondary zone at the four other offices.
- Configure client computers to query their local DNS server.

Which result or results do these actions produce? (Choose all that apply.)

a. DNS name resolution traffic across the WAN links is minimized.

b. DNS replication traffic across the WAN link is minimized.

c. DNS replication traffic across the public WAN links is secured.

d. Name resolution performance for client computers is optimized.

53. You are the administrator of your company's network. The network consists of a single Windows 2000 domain that spans multiple locations. The locations are connected over the Internet by using the routing and remote access program. Resources are located on TCP/IP hosts on your network. To facilitate name resolution for client access to these resources, you implement Windows 2000 DNS servers on your network. You want to ensure that when the zone transfer traffic between your DNS servers crosses the Internet links between the locations, it cannot be compromised by outside parties. What should you do?

a. Select the option to allow zone transfers only to servers listed on the Name Servers tab.

b. Set up an Active Directory integrated zone.

c. Set the Allow Dynamic Updates setting for your zone to No.

d. Set the Allow Dynamic Updates setting for your zone to Only Secure Updates.

54. You are the administrator of your company's network. The network consists of a single Windows 2000 domain that spans multiple locations. The locations are connected over the Internet by using routing and resources located on

TCP/IP hosts on your network. To facilitate name resolution for client access to these resources, you implement Windows 2000 DNS servers on your network. You want to ensure that when the zone transfer traffic between your DNS servers crosses the Internet links between the locations, it cannot be compromised by outside parties. What should you do?

a. Select the option to allow zone transfers only to servers listed on the Name Servers tab.

b. Set up an Active Directory integrated zone.

c. Set the Allow Dynamic Updates setting for your zone to No.

d. Set the Allow Dynamic Updates setting for your zone to only Secure Updates.

55. You are the administrator of a Windows 2000 domain. The domain has six Windows 2000 Server computers, 400 Windows 2000 Professional computers, and 250 Windows NT Workstation 4.0 computers. Three of the Windows 2000 Server computers are DHCP servers. The other three servers are DNS servers. The TCP/IP configuration of all the Windows 2000 Professional computers and Windows NT Workstation 4.0 computers is provided by DHCP servers. For fault tolerance, all three DHCP servers are configured so that they have scopes for all the computers in the network. You configure the DHCP servers to always register and update client computer information on the configured DNS servers. To increase security, you configure the DNS zones on all DNS servers to only allow secure updates. After you perform this configuration of the DNS zones, you discover that the client computer information in the DNS zones is no longer updated correctly when IP address changes occur for Windows 2000 Professional computers and Windows NT 4.0 Workstation computers. You want IP address changes for client computers to appear correctly in DNS zones that only allow secure updates. What should you do?

a. Add the computer accounts of the three DHCP servers to the DnsUpdateProxy global security group.

b. Configure the three DNS servers to use a time-to-live interval on a resource record that is shorter than the lease time used by the DHCP servers.

c. Configure the three DHCP servers to enable updates for DNS client computers that do not support dynamic update.

d. On the Windows 2000 Professional computers and Windows NT Workstation 4.0 computers, configure the DHCP client computers to not release the DHCP lease at shutdown.

56. You are the administrator of your company's network. Your company has a main office, two branch offices, and two small branch offices. The company network consists of one Windows 2000 domain. The main office and the two large branch offices are connected by a dedicated T1 line. The two branch offices use 128-Kbps ISDN lines and routing and remote access over the Internet to connect to the company's internal network. You are designing your DNS name resolution environment. You want to accomplish the following goals:

• DNS name resolution traffic across the WAN links will be minimized.

• DNS replication traffic across the WAN links will be minimized.

• DNS replication traffic across the public WAN links will be secured.

• Name resolution performance for client computers will be optimized.

You take the following actions:

• Install the DNS server service on one domain controller at each office.

• Create an Active Directory integrated zone on each DNS server at each office.

• Configure client computers to query their local DNS server.

• Configure the zone to allow dynamic updates.

Which result or results do these actions produce? (Choose all that apply.)

a. DNS name resolution traffic across the WAN links is minimized.

b. DNS replication traffic across the WAN links is minimized.

c. DNS replication traffic across the public WAN links is secured.

d. Name resolution performance for client computers is optimized

57. You are the administrator of your company's network. The network consists of 10 Windows 2000 Server computers, 200 Windows 2000 Professional computers, 250 Windows 98 computers, and 25 UNIX workstation computers running SMB server software. The network runs only TCP/IP as its transport protocol. You implement WINS in the network for NetBIOS name resolution. Users of the Windows-based client computers report that they cannot access resources based on the UNIX computers by NetBIOS name. There is no problem accessing Windows-based resources by NetBIOS name. What should you do to resolve this problem?

a. Install a WINS proxy agent on one of the UNIX computers.

b. Install a WINS proxy agent on one of the Windows-based computers.

c. On the WINS server, create static mappings for the UNIX computer.

d. On the WINS server, create static mappings for the Windows-based computers.

58. You are the administrator of your company's network. The network consists of a single Windows 2000 domain. The network has Windows 2000 Server computers, Windows 2000 Professional computers, and Windows NT Workstation 4.0 computers distributed across two IP subnets. Two Windows 2000 domain controllers are located on Subnet1. Each domain controller is also a DNS server hosting an Active Directory integrated zone. You implement WINS for NetBIOS name resolution on your network. WINS is installed on a server on Subnet2.

Users of the Windows NT Workstation 4.0 computers on Subnet2 report that they are receiving the following error message, "Domain Controller cannot be located." Subsequently, these users cannot be validated on the network. Windows NT Workstation 4.0 users on Subnet1 are not experiencing this problem. However, they do report that response times for logon requests are extremely slow. None of the Windows 2000 Professional users on either subnet report these problems. You want to ensure that Windows NT Workstation 4.0 users on Subnet2 can be validated. You also want to improve logon request response time for users on Subnet1. What should you do?

a. Configure the router to forward NetBIOS broadcast packets.

b. Configure the Windows NT Workstation 4.0 computers as DNS clients in the existing zone.

c. Configure the Windows NT Workstation 4.0 computers as WINS clients.

d. Configure the Windows 2000 Server domain controller computers as WINS clients.

59. You are the administrator of a Windows 2000 network. The network has four Windows 2000-based WINS servers named NY1, NY2, Bos1, and Bos2. The network has computers in two locations: Boston and New York. The Bos1 and Bos2 WINS servers are at a Boston location. The NY1 and NY2 WINS servers are at the New York location. You want to configure the replication between the WINS servers to accomplish the following goals:

- The NY1 and NY2 WINS servers must replicate changes in the local database each other immediately following each new registration or IP address change registration.

- The Bos1 and Bos2 WINS servers must replicate changes in the local database to each other every 30 minutes.

- The changes in the WINS database in either location should be replicated to the other location every 3 hours.

How should you configure the WINS servers to accomplish these goals? (Choose three answers.)

a. Configure the WINS servers to enable burst handling. Set the number of requests for burst handling to 1.

b. Configure the NY1 and NY2 WINS servers as push/pull partners of each other. Configure both WINS servers to use persistent connections for push replication partners. Set the number of changes before replication to 1.

c. Configure Bos1 and Bos2 WINS servers as push/pull partners of each other. Specify a replication interval of 30 minutes.

d. Configure Bos1 and Bos2 WINS servers as push/pull partners of each other. Configure both WINS servers to enable periodic database consistency checking every 30 minutes.

e. Configure the NY1 and Bos1 WINS servers as push partners of each other. Configure both WINS servers to update statistics every 3 hours.

f. Configure the NY1 And Bos1 WINS servers as push/pull partners of each other. Specify a replication interval of 3 hours.

60. You are the administrator of a Windows 2000 network. The network has seven Windows 2000-based WINS servers, and each is in a separate location. Because network users frequently log on at different locations, you want to configure the seven WINS servers to have a convergence time of less than an hour. How should you configure the seven WINS servers to accomplish this goal?

a. Create a display of the seven WINS servers in a circular arrangement. Configure each WINS server as a push/pull partner with the two WINS servers beside it in the circle. Use a replication interval of 25 minutes.

b. Designate one of the WINS servers as the central WINS server. Configure the other six WINS servers as push/pull partners with the central WINS server. Configure the central WINS server as the push/pull partner with the other six WINS servers. Use a replication interval of 25 minutes.

c. Configure each WINS server to automatically configure the other WINS servers as its replication partners. Use the default interval time for automatic partner configuration.

d. Configure each WINS server to use a renew interval of 50 minutes. Use the default value for verification interval.

61. You are the administrator of a Windows 2000 network. The network has three windows 2000-based WINS servers named Srv1, Srv2, and Srv3. You want to periodically compact the WINS database to reclaim unused space. How should you perform a manual compaction of the WINS database on the Srv1 WINS server?

a. Configure the Srv1 WINS server to block replication of WINS records from the Srv2 and Srv3 WINS servers. Initiate database consistency checking. Allow replication of records from the Srv2 and Srv3 WINS servers.

b. Stop the Srv1 WINS server. Use the JetPack command-line tool to compact the WINS database. Start the Srv1 WINS server again.

c. Stop the Srv1 WINS server. Use the BACKUP DATABASE command to create a backup of the Srv1 WINS database. Compact the backup of the database by using the compact command-line tool. Use the RESTORE DATABASE command to restore the backup of the database. Start the Srv1 WINS server again.

d. In the WINS console, use the SCAVENGE DATABASE command.

62. You are the administrator of your company's network. The network consists of four IP subnets connected by a router. The network contains 12 Windows 2000 Server computers and 100 Windows 2000 Professional computers, evenly distributed across the four subnets. All of the servers are used to serve file and print resources to the client computers. You install WINS server service on one server on one subnet. You configure the WINS option in a DHCP scope to configure all of the other computers on the network to register with and query the WINS server for NetBIOS name resolution. Within 4 hours of the installation and configuration, users on the remote subnets report that they cannot access resources located on the WINS server by NetBIOS name. Other TCP/IP connectivity is not affected. Users located on the same subnet as the WINS server are experiencing no problem accessing these same resources. What should you do to resolve this problem?

a. Install a WINS proxy agent on each remote subnet.

b. Install a WINS proxy agent on the same subnet as the WINS server.

c. Configure the WINS server to include IP addresses of each gateway on the router.

d. Configure the WINS server to include its own IP address as a WINS client computer.

63. You are the administrator of a Windows 2000 network. The network has 300 Windows 2000 Professional computers, 1 Windows 2000-based WINS server, 4 Windows 2000 DHCP servers, and 8 other Windows 2000 server computers. The 300 Windows 2000 Professional computers and the servers are divided over four different locations named North Building, East Building, South Building, and West Building. The WINS server is in the East Building location. The TCP/IP configuration of the WINS client computers is provided by four DHCP servers on the network. Because of a malfunction on the WINS server's hard disk, you replace it and restore the WINS database from a backup that is one week old. After the new WINS server is in place, users report that they cannot browse any of the resources in the other locations. What should you do to enable users to browse resources in other locations again?

a. On the WINS server, use JETPACK.EXE utility on the WINS database.

b. On the WINS server, use the VERIFY DATABASE CONSISTENCY command.

c. On the Windows 2000 Server computer, use the NBTSTAT -RR command to release and refresh the WINS registrations.

d. On the WINS client computers, use the IPCONFIG/REGISTERDNS command to register names and IP addresses.

64. Your network consists of computers running Windows 2000 Server, Windows 2000 Professional, Windows 95, and OS/2 with LAN Manager 2.2c. All are on the same subnet. You want applications on the OS/2 client that use NetBIOS names to be able to resolve the NetBIOS names to IP Addresses from a WINS database. You install WINS on one of the Windows 2000 Servers. What else should you do to enable the applications on the OS/2 computer to resolve NetBIOS names to IP addresses from the WINS database?

a. Configure one of the Windows 2000 Professional computers as a WINS proxy agent.

b. Add static mappings for the OS/2 computer in the WINS database.

c. Configure the OS/2 computer as a WINS client.

d. Configure the OS/2 computer with a static IP address and add a PTR record in the DNS database.

65. You are the administrator of Windows 2000 network. The network contains a Windows 2000 Server computer named Dublin. Dublin has two network interfaces named Side A and Side B. The Routing and remote access option is enabled as a router on Dublin. Only the network segment connected to the SideA interface has a DHCP server. The DHCP server is a Windows 2000 Server named ServerA. You want to allow computers on the segment connected to the SideB interface to receive IP addresses from ServerA. How should you configure Dublin to accomplish this goal? (Choose all answers that apply.)

a. Create an IP tunnel to connect the SideA interface to the SideB interface.

b. Create a static route to the IP address of the SideB interface.

c. Configure the DHCP relay agent routing protocol to run the SideA interface.

d. Configure the DHCP relay agent routing protocol to run the SideB interface.

e. Configure the DHCP relay agent routing protocol to use the IP address of the DHCP server as the server address.

f. Configure the DHCP relay agent routing protocol to use the port number of the DHCP server.

66. You are the administrator of your company's network, which consists of a single Windows 2000 domain. The network includes 10 Windows 2000 Server computers and 2 NetWare 4.1 servers. The Windows 2000 Server computers have static IP addresses and use TCP/IP as their only transport protocol. All client computers run Windows 2000 Professional and use both TCP/IP and IPX/SPX as transport protocols. All clients computers are DHCP clients.

You add 50 client computers to your network. All run Windows 2000 Professional. Many users now report that they experience intermittent connection failures. Connectivity to the NetWare servers remains unaffected, and workgroup resources remain accessible. You inspect the TCP/IP configuration of a client computer that is currently experiencing a connection failure. You discover that this computer uses the IP address 0.0.0.0. How should you correct the connectivity problem?

a. Decrease the lease duration on the DHCP scope to 3 days.

b. Add a sufficient number of new addresses to the DHCP scope to accommodate the new client computers.

c. Create a new scope on the DHCP server to include the new client computers.

d. Add reservations in the DHCP scope for all client computers

67. You are the administrator of your company's network. The network is configured as shown in this exhibit: All client computers on your network receive their IP address information from the DHCP server. The user on Prof4 accesses most of his network resources from computers on segment A. The users on Prof5 and Prof6 access most of their resources from computers on segment C. You want to configure your DHCP server to issue gateway addresses Prof4, Prof5, and Prof6. You want these gateway addresses to offer optimum access time. How should you configure your DHCP server? (Choose two answers.)

a. Create a reservation for Prof4. For this reservation, configure the router option that has the value of 172.16.64.2.

b. Create a reservation for Prof5 and Prof6. For each reservation, configure the router option that has the value of 172.16.64.2.

c. Configure the DHCP server's Predefined Router option so that it has the value of 172.16.64.2.

d. Configure the DHCP server Predefined Router option so that it has the value of 172.16.64.1.

ROUTER 172.16.128.1 | 172.16.64.2   172.16.64.1 | **ROUTER** 172.16.96.1

SEGMENT A   **SEGMENT B**   **SEGMENT C**

Prof 1   Prof 2   Prof 3   Prof 4   Prof 5   Prof 6   Prof 7   Prof 8   Prof 9

DHCP SERVER

e. On the DHCP server's scope for segment B, configure the Predefined Router option so that it has the value of 172.16.64.2.

f. On the DHCP server scope for segment B, configure the Predefined Router option so that it has the value of 172.16.64.1.

68. You are the administrator of your company's network. The network consists of five subnets that are connected by a BOOTP relay-enabled router. There are 50 Windows 2000 Server computers and 1000 Windows 2000 Professional client computers distributed approximately evenly across the five subnets. There are also 25 UNIX servers and 100 DHCP-enabled network printers on the network. You want to accomplish the following goals:

- The correct assignment of IP addresses to each client computer on each subnet will be automated.
- Address conflicts between client computers and servers will be prevented.
- Correct scope options will be applied to each client computer on each subnet.
- Client computers that are not in use will be prevented from keeping an IP address for more than 3 days.
- Each network printer will always receive the same IP address.

You take the following actions:

- Install the DHCP server service on a Windows 2000 Server computer.
- Create five scopes, each containing the address range for a specific subnet.
- In the DHCP console, set optional client configurations for each scope in the Scope Options container.
- Exclude the range of addresses in use by the servers.
- Exclude the range of addresses in use by the network printers.

Which result or results do these actions produce? (Choose all that apply.)

a. The correct assignment of IP addresses to each client computer on each subnet is automated.

b. Address conflicts between client computers and servers are prevented.

c. Correct scope options are applied to each client computer on each subnet.

d. Client computers that are not in use are prevented from keeping an IP address for more than 3 days.

e. Each network printer always receives the same IP address.

69. You are the administrator of your company's network. The network consists of one Windows 2000 domain that has 10 Windows 2000 Server computers and 500 Windows 2000 Professional client computers. You want all client computers to receive their TCP/IP configuration from DHCP. You install the DHCP server service on one of your Windows 2000 Server computers and create and activate a scope of addresses. Users report that they cannot connect to the network. You discover that none of the client computers are receiving TCP/IP configurations from DHCP. What should you do to resolve this problem?

a. Stop and restart the DHCP server on the DHCP server.

b. Restart all client computers.

c. Authorize the DHCP server in Active Directory.

d. Add a DNS host record for the DHCP server.

70. You are the network administrator for Trey Research. Trey Research's network consists of 90 client computers and 50 portable computers, all running Windows 2000 Professional. Only 20 of the users of the portable computers will ever be in the office at the same time. To accommodate the number users on the network, Trey Research purchases a subnetted class B subnet with a 25-bit mask. All users need access to the Internet while in the office. How should you configure DHCP?

a. Create two scopes that have different lease durations.

b. Create manual reservations for all portable computer users.

c. Create one scope that has two user classes, each with a different lease duration.

d. Create one scope that has two vendor classes, each with a different lease duration.

71. You administer the network segment used by your company's sales department. This department employs 50 salespeople, who use portable computers. Each business day, a maximum of 25 salespeople work on-site. The remaining salespeople work remotely. Your network segment includes

IP Address Range	Lease Duration	Conflict Detection Attempts	Enable Dynamic Update of DNS Records?
172.30.20.51 to 172.30.20.101	3 days	0	Yes

one DHCP server running Windows 2000 server. All the portable computers are DHCP clients. The DHCP server is configured with the characteristics shown in the following table.

Your department hires 20 new salespeople and issues portable computers to them. The new salespeople will work on-site for several months, and then begin working remotely. However, none of these new users can connect to the network. They receive an error message indicating that their computers cannot obtain IP addresses. You need to enable the new salespeople to connect to the network. Your solution must prevent the connection problem from happening again. Your solution must also avoid disrupting network communications for existing network users and minimize network traffic associated with DHCP. What should you do?

a. Delete the existing IP address leases from the DHCP server. Increase the setting for conflict detection attempts to 3. Decrease the lease duration to 8 hours.

b. Decrease the lease duration to 1 day. Increase the setting for conflict detection attempts to 2.

c. On the new salespeople's computers, run the IPCONFIG/RELEASE command and then the IPCONFIG/RENEW command.

d. Disable dynamic update of DNS records. Decrease the lease duration to 8 hours. Run the IPCONFIG / RENEW command on the new salespeople's computers.

72. You are the network administrator for your company. For a test lab, you configure a single, dedicated network segment that consists of 5 servers and 40 client computers. The test lab must have connectivity to your production network. You are given an IP address range of 192.168.5.66 to 192.168.5.127 to use for the test lab. You decide to configure one of the test lab servers as a Windows 2000 DHCP server. This server will automatically provide IP addressing information to the other computers in the test lab. You manually configure static IP address and subset mask of 192.168.5.10/24 on the new DHCP server. You create a scope on the DHCP server for the 192.168.5.64/26 subnet. The scope includes an IP address range of 192.168.5.66 to 192.168.5.127. You successfully activate the scope on the DHCP server, but none of the DHCP clients can receive an IP address lease. How should you correct this problem?

a. Edit the network address for the scope to be 192.168.5.0/24.

b. Edit the network address for the scope to be 192.168.5.0/26.

c. Edit the IP address and subset mask of the DHCP server to be 192.168.5.65/26, and configure an exclusion for that IP address in the DHCP scope.

d. Edit the IP address and subnet mask of the DHCP server to be 192.168.5.66/26, and configure an exclusion for that IP address in the DHCP scope.

HANDS-ON EXERCISES

Exercise 1: Installing and Configuring DNS Services

One partner will configure the primary zone, while the other will configure a secondary zone and designate his or her partner's computer as the master server. Record the type of zone you will configure in this exercise.

Configuring the DNS Domain Name of Your Computer

Computers A and B should do the following:

1. Right-click on the My Computer icon and select the Properties option.
2. Click on the Network Identification tab and click on the Properties button. Click on the More button.
3. For the primary DNS suffix, enter ACMExx.COM, where *xx* is your partner number. If you are the first group or are working at home, enter ACME01.COM. Click on the OK button.
4. Notice the full computer name. Click on the OK button.
5. Close the System Properties window and reboot the system.

Installing the DNS services

Computer A should do the following:

6. Open the Add/Remove Programs applet in the Control Panel.
7. Click on the Add/Remove Windows Components.
8. Click on the Next button.
9. Click to highlight the Networking Services option.
10. Click on the Details button.
11. In the Subcomponents of Networking Services, ensure the check box is marked next to the Domain Name System (DNS).
12. Click on the OK button.
13. Click on the Next button.
14. If the Insert Disk dialog box appears, insert the Windows 2000 installation CD, ensure that the path to the source files is correct, and click on the OK button.
15. Click on the Finish button.

Configuring the DNS Server

Computer A should do the following:

16. Open the DNS console by clicking on the Start button, clicking the Programs option, clicking the Administrative Tools option, and selecting the DNS option.
17. The DNS tree is shown in the left pane. Click on the + symbol next to the SERVER2000-01A server. The tree will expand to show Forward Lookup and Reverse Lookup.
18. Right-click the server and select the Configure the Server option. The Configure New DNS Server wizard will begin. Click on the Next button.
19. On the Forward Lookup Zone page, select Yes; create a forward lookup zone and click on the Next button.
20. On the Zone Type page, select the Standard Primary Zone. Click on the Next button.
21. On the Zone Name page, enter the ACMExx.COM, where *xx* represents your partner number. This should be the same domain name that was used in the Identification tab specified previously. Click on the Next button.
22. On the Zone File page, click on the Next button to use the default file name.
23. On the Reverse Lookup Zone page, select Yes; create a reverse lookup zone option and click on the Next button.
24. On the Zone Type page, select the Standard Primary option and click on the Next button.
25. In the Reverse Lookup Zone, enter the first three octets address of the TCP/IP address (192.168.1) and click on the Next button.
26. On the Zone File page, select the Create a New file with this file name and click on the Next button.
27. Click on the Finish button.
28. In the DNS console, expand the entire tree. See Figure 11.17.
29. Right-click the domain name for the forward lookup zone and select the Properties option. If you are the first group, right-click on ACME01.COM.
30. Change the Allow Dynamic Update option to Yes. Click on the OK button.

FIGURE 11.17

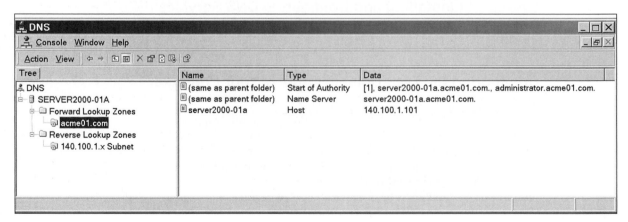

31. Right-click the 192.168.1.X subnet for the reverse lookup zone and select the Properties option.

32. Change the Allow Dynamic Update option to Yes. Click on the OK button.

Computer B should do the following:

33. Start a Command prompt.

34. At the Command prompt, execute PING *address_of_serverA* command, where the *address_of_serverA* is the address of Server A.

35. At the Command prompt, execute PING *computernameA* command, where the *computernameA* is the NetBIOS name of Server A. This command should work because it is finding the computer using broadcast, not DNS.

36. At the Command prompt, execute PING *DNS_name of serverA* command, where the *DNS_name_of_serverA* is the full computer name including the domain name. For example, if you are in group 1, it should be Server2000-01A.acme01.com.

37. Using the properties of the TCP/IP of your Local Area Connection in My Network Place, set the preferred DNS server to the address of Server A.

38. At the Command prompt, execute PING *DNS_name of serverA* command, where the *DNS_name_of_serverA* is the full computer name including the domain name. For example, if you are in group 1, it should be Server2000-01A.acme01.com. It should work now because it is getting the address from the DNS server.

Adding Resource Records

Computer B should do the following:

39. At the Command prompt, execute PING PC.ACMExx.COM command, where *xx* is your partner number.

Computer A should do the following:

40. From the DNS console, right-click the domain name for the forward lookup zone and select the New Host option. If you are the first group, right-click on ACME01.COM.

41. In the Name text box, type in PC. Note that it will automatically attach ACMExx.COM.

42. Specify the address of 192.168.1.253.

43. Select the "Create associated pointer (PTR) record to automatically create a reverse lookup" entry and click on the Add Host button. Click on the Done button.

Computer B should do the following:

44. From the Command prompt, ping PC.ACMExx.COM. Notice that it translated the address with no problem. Because we do not have a computer called "PC" as part of our domain with this specific address, the request will time out.

Computer A should do the following:

45. Right-click the PC Host entry and select the Delete option.

46. From the DNS console, right-click the domain name for the forward lookup zone and select the New Alias option. If you are the first group, right-click on ACME01.COM.

47. Leave the Alias Name text box blank. Note that it will assume ACMExx.COM.

48. In the Full Qualified Name text box, specify the full qualified domain name of your server (SERVER2000-01A.ACMExx.COM).

Computer B should do the following:

49. From the Command prompt, ping your domain name (ACMExx.COM).

50. Click the Start button and select the Run option. Type in MMC and click the OK button.

51. Open the Console menu and select the Add/Remove Snap-in option.

52. Click on the Add button. Select the DNS option and click the Add button. Click on the OK button.

53. At the top of the console tree, right-click DNS and select the Connect to Computer option. Select the "The following computer" option, specify SERVER2000-01A. ACMExx.COM. Click on the OK button.

54. Right-click the domain name under Forward Lookup Zone and select the New Alias option.

55. Specify WWW for the alias name and specify the full qualified domain name for the DNS server. Click on the OK button.

56. Create an alias for FTP, which should also point to the domain server.

57. Add a host record for your instructor's computer.

58. Close the MMC console.

59. Ping WWW.ACMExx.COM and FTP.ACME.xx.COM.

Test the DNS Server

Computer A should do the following:

60. At the Command prompt, execute the NSLOOKUP command.

61. At the NSLOOKUP Command prompt, type in the name of your domain (ACMExx.COM) and press Enter.

62. To set the default server, execute SERVER SERVER2000-xxA.ACMExx.COM at the prompt. For the first group, type in NSLOOKUP SERVER200001A.ACME01.COM.
63. To list the A records, execute ls –t a ACMExx.COM command at the Command prompt. The command is case sensitive.
64. To look at the name servers, execute the set type = ns command at the NSLOOKUP Command prompt and press the Enter key, then type in the domain name, and then press Enter.
65. To look at the SOA records, execute the set type = soa command at the NSLOOKUP Command prompt and press the Enter key, then type in the domain name, and then press Enter.
66. Type in Exit, to go back to the Command prompt.
67. Close the Command prompt window.
68. Double-click My Computer, double-click the C drive, double-click the WINNT or Windows folder, double-click the SYSTEM32 folder, and then double-click the DNS folder.
69. Right-click the Domain Name file and select the Open With option. Select Notepad. View the contents of the file and close it when done.

Create a Secondary DNS Server

Computer B should do the following:
70. Open the Add/Remove Programs applet in the Control Panel.
71. Click on the Add/Remove Windows Components.
72. Click on the Next button.
73. Click to highlight the Networking Services option.
74. Click on the Details button.
75. In the Subcomponents of Networking Services, ensure the check box is marked next to the Domain Name System (DNS).
76. Click on the OK button.
77. Click on the Next button.
78. If the Insert Disk dialog box appears, insert the Windows 2000 installation CD, ensure that the path to the source files is correct, and click on the OK button.
79. Click on the Finish button.
80. Open the DNS console from the Administrative Tools menu.
81. Right-click the server and select Configure the Server option.
82. On the Forward Lookup Zone page, select Yes; the Create a Forward Lookup Zone option is selected. Click the Next button.
83. On the Zone Type page, select the Standard Secondary option and click the Next button.
84. On the Zone Name page, type in your domain name (ACMExx.COM). If you are the first group, it will be ACME01.COM. Click on the Next button.
85. On the Master DNS Servers page, in the IP Address box, type the IP address of your partner's computer, click the Add button and then the Next button.
86. On the Reverse Lookup Zone page, select Yes; the Create a Reverse Lookup Zone option is selected. Click the Next button.
87. On the Zone Type page, select the Standard Secondary option, and then click the Next button.
88. On the Reverse Lookup Zone page, type the first three octets of your IP address (192.168.1) in the IP Address box and click the Next button.
89. On the Master DNS Servers page, type the IP address of your partner's computer. Click the Add button, then the Next button.
90. Click the Finish button.

Creating a Subdomain

Computer A should do the following:
91. Start the DNS console.
92. Right-click the Domain Name and select the New Domain option.
93. For the new domain type, type in "Sales" and click the OK button.

Deleting a Secondary Domain

Computer B should do the following:
94. Right-click the Secondary Domain in your DNS console and select the Delete option. Click on the OK button.

Declaring Delegation of Authority

Computer B should do the following:

95. Click on the Start button. Select the Programs option and select Administrative Tools. Then right-click DNS and select the Run As option.

96. In the Run As Other User dialog box, specify Administrator as the user and Password as the password. Delete the contents of the Domain box. Click on the OK button.

97. Right-click DNS in the console and click Connect to Computer.

98. In the Select Target Computer dialog box, click "The following computer in the text box," type in the name of your partner's computer (SERVER2000-xxA), and click OK.

99. In the console tree, expand the server, expand the forward lookup zones, and expand the domain.

100. Right-click the Domain and select the New Delegation option. Click the Next button.

101. On the Delegated Domain Name page, type the name of your domain in the Domain box and click the Next button.

102. On the Name Servers page, click the Add page.

103. In the New Resource Record dialog box, type the full qualified domain name for your computer and click the Resolve button. Click on the OK button.

104. On the Name Servers page, click the Next button.

105. On the Completing the New Delegation Wizard page, click the Finish button.

Exercise 2: Install and Configure a WINS

Installing the WINS

Computer A should do the following:

1. Open the Add/Remove Programs applet in the Control Panel.

2. Click on the Add/Remove Windows Components.

3. Click on the Next button.

4. Click to highlight the Networking Services option.

5. Click on the Details button.

6. In the Subcomponents of Networking Services, ensure the check box is marked next to the Windows Internet Name Services (WINS).

7. Click on the OK button.

8. Click on the Next button.

9. If the Insert Disk dialog box appears, insert the Windows 2000 installation CD, ensure that the path to the source files is correct, and click on the OK button.

10. Click on the Finish button.

Configuring the WINS Client

Computer A should do the following:

11. To make the WINS server register itself in its WINS database, make the WINS server a client. To make a WINS server a client, right-click My Network Places and select the Properties option. Right-click the Local Area Connection and select Properties.

12. Click Internet Protocol (TCP/IP) and click on the Properties button.

13. In the Internet Protocol (TCP/IP) Properties dialog box, click the Advanced button.

14. In the WINS tab, click the Add button.

15. In the TCP/IP WINS Server dialog box, type the IP address of the WINS server, and click the Add button.

16. Click the OK button to close the Advanced TCP/IP Settings dialog box and click OK to close the Internet Protocol (TCP/IP) Properties dialog box.

17. Click OK to close the Local Area Connection Properties dialog box.

Computer B should do the following:

18. To configure the client to use the WINS server, right-click My Network Places and select the Properties option. Right-click the Local Area Connection and select Properties.

19. Click Internet Protocol (TCP/IP) and click on the Properties button.

20. In the Internet Protocol (TCP/IP) Properties dialog box, click the Advanced button.

21. In the WINS tab, click the Add button.

22. In the TCP/IP WINS Server dialog box, type the IP address of the WINS server, and click the Add button.

23. Click the OK button to close the Advanced TCP/IP Settings dialog box, and click OK to close the Internet Protocol (TCP/IP) Properties dialog box.

24. Click OK to close the Local Area Connection Properties dialog box.

Managing the WINS Server

Computer A should do the following:

25. From the Administrative Tools, start the WINS console.

26. Right-click Active Registration and select the Find by Name option.

27. In the "Find names beginning with" text box, type in an asterisk (*) and click on the Find Now button. Notice all of your entries.

28. To add a static WINS record, right-click Active Registration and select the New Static option.

29. In the Computer Name text box, type in TESTPC. In the IP address, type in 100.100.100.100. Click on the OK button.

30. Use the Find Names option to show all entries in the WINS table. Notice the entries in the WINS table, especially the Static column.

Computer B should do the following:

31. From the Command prompt, ping TESTPC. Since the TESTPC does not exist, PING will respond, "Destination host unreachable." Most importantly, note the address resolution.

Computer A should do the following:

32. Right-click the three entries for TESTPC and select the Delete option.

Setting Up Replication

Computer B should do the following:

33. Open the Add/Remove Programs applet in the Control Panel.

34. Click on the Add/Remove Windows Components.

35. Click on the Next button.

36. Click to highlight the Networking Services option.

37. Click on the Details button.

38. In the Subcomponents of Networking Services, ensure the check box is marked next to the Windows Internet Name Services (WINS).

39. Click on the OK button.

40. Click on the Next button.

41. If the Insert Disk dialog box appears, insert the Windows 2000 installation CD, ensure that the path to the source files is correct, and click on the OK button.

42. Click on the Finish button.

Both Computers should do the following:

43. From the WINS console, right-click Replication Partners and select the New Replication Partner option.

44. In the WINS Server text box, type the IP address of your partner's computer and click on the OK button.

45. In the Details pane, right-click your partner's computer name, and then click the Properties option.

46. In the Advanced tab, verify that the replication partner type is push/pull and that persistent connections are used for both push and pull replications.

Computer A should do the following:

47. Set the start time for pull replication to 18:00 (6 PM) and the replication interval to 12 hours.

Computer B should do the following:

48. Set the start time for pull replication to 21:00 (9 PM) and the replication interval to 12 hours.

Both Computers should do the following:

49. In the "Number of changes in version IS before replication" box, type 250.

50. Click the OK button to close the Properties dialog box for the replication partner.

Computer A should do the following:

51. Right-click Replication Partners and select the Replicate Now option.

52. Click the Yes button to be sure and click on the OK button.

Computer B should do the following:

53. From the WINS console, right-click Active Registration and list all owners. The entries should be the same as your partners. If not, wait another minute and try again.

Exercise 3: Install and Configure a DHCP Server

Installing a DHCP Server

Computer A should do the following:

1. Open the Add/Remove Programs applet in the Control Panel.

2. Click on the Add/Remove Windows Components.
3. Click on the Next button.
4. Click to highlight the Networking Services option.
5. Click on the Details button.
6. In the Subcomponents of Networking Services, ensure the check box is marked next to the Windows Internet Name Services (WINS).
7. Click on the OK button.
8. Click on the Next button.
9. If the Insert Disk dialog box appears, insert the Windows 2000 installation CD, ensure that the path to the source files is correct, and click on the OK button.
10. Click on the Finish button.

Creating a Scope

Computer A should do the following:
11. Open the DHCP console from the Administrative Tools.
12. Right-click the server and click the New Scope option. Click on the Next button.
13. On the Scope Name page, type the name of your server in the Name text box and click on the Next button.
14. Use 192.168.1.XX for the start address and 192.168.1.XX+1 for the end address, where *XX* is your computer number. Change the subnet mask to 255.255.255.0. Click on the Next button.
15. Since we have no exclusions, click the Next button.
16. On the Lease Duration, click the Next button to keep the default of 8 days.
17. On the Configure DHCP Options page, select the "Yes, I want to configure these options now" option and click the Next button.
18. On the Router (Default Gateway) page, type in the address of your gateway or local router. If you do not have one, for now type in 192.168.1.1. Click the Add button and then the Next button.
19. On the Domain Name and DNS Servers page, type in ACMEXX.COM for the parent domain and type in the address of your DNS server. Click the Add button and then the Next button.
20. On the WINS Servers page, type in the address of your primary WINS server address. Click the Add button and then the Next button.
21. Select the "Yes, I want to activate this scope now" option and click the Next button. Click the Finish button.
22. Click on the Scope option and look at the various options that were configured with the wizard.
23. Right-click the new scope that you just created and select Properties.
24. Select the DNS tab. You will notice that the "Automatically update DHCP client information in DNS" option is already selected. Select "Enable updates for DNS clients that do not support dynamic update."
25. Click the OK button.

Making a Client Reservation

Computer A should do the following:
26. From the DHCP console, right-click Reservations and select the New Reservation option.
27. Put in the MAC address of your partner's network card. You can find this out by executing the IPCONFIG /ALL command at your partner's computer.

Testing the DHCP Server

Computer B should do the following:
28. At the Command prompt, execute the IPCONFIG /ALL command.
29. Right-click My Network Places and select the Properties option.
30. Right-click Local Area Connection and select the Properties option.
31. Click the Internet Protocol (TCP/IP) and click on the Properties button.
32. In the Internet Protocol (TCP/IP) dialog box, click the "Obtain an IP address automatically" option.
33. Click the "Obtain DNS server address automatically" option.
34. Click on the Advanced button.
35. In the WINS tab, click the WINS address and click the Remove button.
36. Click the OK button to close the Advanced TCP/IP Settings, click OK to close the Internet Protocol (TCP/IP) Properties dialog box, and click OK to close the Local Area Connection Properties dialog box. Remember, any settings set manually will override settings given by a DHCP server.
37. At the Command prompt, execute the IPCONFIG /ALL command and study the current setting.

CHAPTER **12**

Introduction to Active Directory

Topics Covered in This Chapter

Introduction

One of the biggest changes from Windows NT to Windows 2000 was the introduction of Active Directory, a true directory service. Before you study how to create user and computer accounts and the everyday management activities of a network, it is important to understand what Active Directory is and how it works.

Objectives

- Compare and contrast workgroups and domains.
- Describe the relationships between Active Directory tree, domain, and organizational units (OUs).
- Install the Active Directory.
- Create sites and site links.
- Create global catalog servers.
- Transfer operations master roles.
- Implement an OU structure.
- Explain the purpose of the global catalog.
- Describe the roles of the domain controller, and given a domain controller, identify its role.

- Describe the relationship between sites and domains.
- Move Active Directory objects.
- Control access to Active Directory objects.
- Delegate administrative control of objects in Active Directory.
- Manage and troubleshoot Active Directory replication.
- Install a time sync with a time server.

12.1 INTRODUCTION TO DIRECTORY SERVICES

Directory services is a network service that identifies all resources on a network and makes those resources accessible to users and applications. Resources can include e-mail addresses, computers, and peripheral devices (e.g., printers). Ideally, the directory service should make the physical network, including topology and protocols, transparent to the users on the network. They should be able to access any resources without knowing where or how they are physically connected.

12.2 X.500 DIRECTORY SERVICES AND LIGHTWEIGHT DIRECTORY ACCESS PROTOCOL

There are a number of directory services that are widely used. The most common is the **X.500,** which uses a hierarchical approach in which objects are organized in a similar way to the files and folders on a hard drive. At the top of the structure is the root container with "children" organized under it. X.500 is part of the OSI model; however, it does not translate well into a TCP/IP protocol environment. Therefore, many of the protocols that are based on the X.500 do not fully comply with it.

Windows Active Directory uses **Lightweight Directory Access Protocol (LDAP)** to communicate and perform basic read, write, and modify operations; query an object in the Active Directory; and allow Windows 2000 servers and Windows Server 2003 to communicate with Windows 3.51 and Windows 4.0 servers.

12.3 WORKGROUP

Computers and devices on a peer-to-peer network are usually organized into logical subgroups called **workgroups.** In a workgroup, each computer has a local security database so that it tracks its own user and group account information. The user information is not shared with other workgroup computers;

therefore, you must create users on each workgroup computer if you want to use the other computer's network resources. A workgroup is used more as a basic grouping of the computers and is only intended to help users find objects such as printers and shared folders within that group.

Workgroups have several advantages:

- A workgroup does not require a computer that is running Windows 2000 Server or Windows Server 2003 to hold centralized security information.
- A workgroup is simple to design and implement.
- A workgroup is convenient for a limited number of computers in close physical proximity and should not consist of more than 10 computers.
- Each user manages his or her own computer resources.

There are also disadvantages to workgroups:

- A user must have a user account of each computer to which he or she wants to gain access.
- Any changes to user accounts, such as changing a user's password or adding a new user account, must be made on each computer.
- Workgroups require each user to administer his or her own computer; thus, each user must be relatively proficient for the workgroup to work well.

12.4 WINDOWS NT DOMAIN

The Windows **domain** is a logical unit of computers and network resources that define a security boundary. It is typically found on medium or large networks or networks that require a secure environment. Unlike a workgroup, a domain uses one database to share its common security and user account information for all computers within the domain. Therefore, it allows centralized network administration of all users, groups, and resources on the network.

DOMAIN BENEFITS

- A domain allows centralized administration because all user information is stored centrally.
- A domain provides a single logon process for users to gain access to network resources, and users only need to log on once to gain those resources.
- A domain provides scalability so that it can create very large security databases.

In Windows NT, the Security Accounts Manager (SAM) database (also called the domain database) contains information about all the users and groups within a domain. The system of domains and trusts for a Windows NT server network is known as **Windows NT Directory Service (NTDS).** To manage the users and groups of a domain and to set up trusts with other domains (trusts allow users to access resources in other domains), you use the User Manager for Domains program.

In an NTDS network, Windows NT servers can become loaded and configured to have a copy of the domain database (domain controller). However, only one copy of the database can be considered the master copy. The master copy is on the **primary domain controller (PDC)** and the backup copies are located on **backup domain controllers (BDCs).** Note: You can promote a BDC to a primary PDC without reinstalling the server. But a member server (a server that is not a domain controller and does not have a copy of the domain database) has to be completely reinstalled if you want to change it to a domain controller.

The domain is not limited to a single network or a specific type of network configuration. For example, a domain can consist of computers that are located within a single LAN, or a subsection of a LAN, or on computers that span several LANs connected with any number of physical connections (e.g., Ethernet, token ring, dial-up line, ISDN, fiber optic, and wireless technology).

A trust relationship (or simply trust) is a relationship between domains that makes it possible for users in one domain to access resources in another domain. The domain that grants access to its resources is known as the trusting domain. The domain that accesses the resources is known as the trusted domain. A one-way domain trust relationship is established when domain A allows the users in domain B to access its resources (assuming that the users have the appropriate permissions). In a one-way trust relationship, the domain with the resources to share trusts the domain with the users who want to access those resources—not the other way around.

If users from domain B should be able to access resources on domain A, and users from domain A should be able to access resources from domain B, you need to establish a two-way domain trust relationship. Two-way domain trust relationships are common in WAN situations where two or more locations manage their own domains but need to share information.

Even though trust relationships exist between domains, users and groups within those domains must still be assigned permissions on trusted servers. User and group permissions are assigned only after trust relationships are created between servers.

When you establish trust relationships in Windows NT domains, the trust relationships are non-transitive. For example, if domain A trusts domain B and domain B trusts domain C, domain A does not trust domain C unless you establish a trust between the two.

To configure trust relationships, you need at least two domains. In addition, you must have administrator rights to the domains. To alter trust relationships for a particular domain, click Start, point to Programs, point to Administrative Tools, and click User Manager for Domains. In the User Manager for Domains dialog box, click Policies on the menu bar, then click Trust Relationships. The Trust Relationship dialog box opens, allowing you to add or remove trust relationships between domains.

With Windows NT domains, Microsoft recommends using one of four domain models:

- *Single*—The single domain model is the simplest Windows NT domain model. As its name implies, a single domain model consists of one domain that services every user and resource in an organization. This model works well for small networks.
- *Master*—The master domain model uses a single domain to contain and control user account information. In addition, separate resource domains manage resources such as networked printers and shared files. Each resource domain trusts the master domain. This model suits an environment where each department in an organization controls its files and print sharing, and a central department manages user IDs and groups.
- *Multiple master*—The multiple master domain model user two or more master domains (domains that contain users) that are joined in two-way trusts to manage many resource domains. A multiple master domain provides the options of centrally managing all user IDs, groups, and account information or managing through decentralized administration. Because this model lets you manage complex relationships, it is useful for large corporations or for merged companies.
- *Complete trust*—The complete trust domain model has all domains trust all other domains. To enable domains to communicate with each other, two-way trusts must be established between all domains in the complete trust domain model. Of course, this model is the most difficult to establish. Each domain still administers its resources.

The domain model you select depends on the division of your organization (either by function or geographically), the existing infrastructure, the number of users you support, the site of network administrators, and decisions made by management.

12.5   ACTIVE DIRECTORY

Resources on a network are useless if users cannot find or manage them especially on large networks. Active Directory provides a treelike summary of resources to users and allows users to manage resources from anywhere on the network. It maintains the network information in files that are distributed around the network. This provides fault tolerance and higher performance.

Active Directory is a network directory service that combines domains, X.500 naming services, DNS, X.509 digital certificates, and Kerberos authentication. It stores all information about the network resources and services such as user data, printers, servers, databases, groups, computers, and security policies. Active Directory supports several name formats so that it can be compatible with several standards, as shown in Table 12.1.

The Active Directory database uses a data store to hold all information about the objects. The data store is sometimes referred to as the directory. It is stored on domain controllers and is accessed by network applications and services. The Active Directory uses the **extensible storage engine (ESE),**

Table 12.1   Name format supported by Windows 2000 Active Directory

Format	Description
RFC 822	Internet e-mail addresses that follow a user_name@domain.xxx format
HTTP Uniform Resource Locators (URL)	Hypertext transfer protocol web page addresses that use DNS and follow the http://domain.xxx/path_to_page
Universal Naming Convention (UNC)	A NetBIOS address that follows the \\domainname\sharename
LDAP URL	An address that specifies the server or resource on the Active Directory services tree that follows the LDAP://Domain.xxx/CN=Commonname_of_Resource, OU=Organization_Name, DC=DomainComponentName name

which allows the Active Directory object database to grow to 17 terabytes, giving it the ability to hold up to 10 million objects, although it is best to have no more than 1 million objects.

Active Directory is made of the following files:

- NTDS.DIT is a single file that makes up the Active Directory database. It stores the Active Directory objects on the domain controller. The default location is the *%systemroot%*\NTDS folder.
- The EDB*.LOG files are the transaction log files, with the EDB.LOG being the default log file. Each transaction log file is 10 MB. When the EDB.LOG is full, it is renamed to EDB*nnnnn*.log, where *nnnnn* is an increasing number starting from one.
- The EDB.CHK is a checkpoint file used by the database engine to track the data not yet written to the Active Directory database file. The checkpoint file is a pointer that maintains the status between memory and the database file on disk.
- RES1.LOG and RES2.LOG are reserved transaction log files to reserve disk space to provide sufficient room to shut down if all other disk space is being used.

During the installation of Active Directory, a folder called **System Volume (SYSVOL)** is installed onto the hard drive. In the SYSVOL folder is another folder called SYSVOL, which is shared. The shared folder stores the server copy of the domain's public files, such as the Group Policy and Net Login (logon scripts), which are replicated among all domain controllers in the domain. The contents of SYSVOL are replicated to all domain controllers in the domain.

A handy method for checking SYSVOL replication is to create a file named after the originating computer, such as *%systemroot%*\Sysvol\Sysvol*domain_name**file_name_equals_server_name*. Then observe which other domain controllers receive the new file. Updates to servers in remote sites are governed by a schedule.

The Active Directory, similar to a file system found on your hard drive or DNS, is a structured hierarchy consisting of domains and organizational units that are connected to form a tree of objects (computers, users, and network resources). The top of the Active Directory is called the root domain. Domains that are under the root domain are child domains to the root domain, and the root domain is the parent domain to its child domains. In addition, a child domain could have another domain under it. Therefore, the child domain of the root domain is the parent domain to its child domains.

12.5.1   Windows 2000 Domain

Similar to a Windows NT domain, the Windows 2000 domain is a logical unit of computers and network resources that define a security boundary. When the Active Directory tree is partitioned into several domains, the Active Directory database is broken into smaller parts and stored on different domain controllers. See Figure 12.1. Since the parts are smaller and more manageable, there is a lesser load on the individual domain controllers. Therefore, the Active Directory database can be massive.

Figure 12.1   Active Directory tree

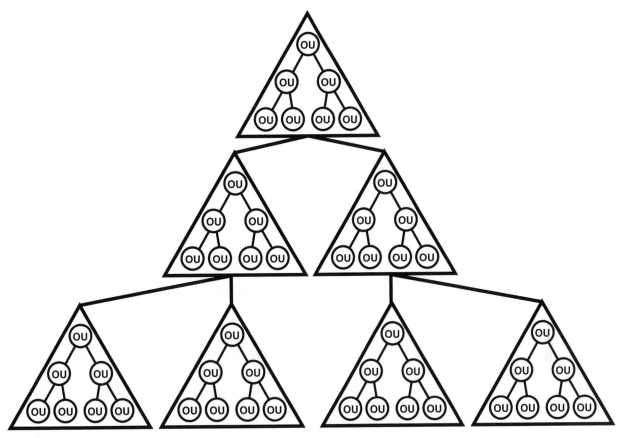

12.5.2   Trust Relationships

Whereas small networks can store accounts and resources in a single domain, large organizations typically establish multiple domains. Windows 2000 Server and Windows Server 2003 Directory Service provide security across multiple domains through trust relationships. Similar to Windows NT, **trust relationship** is a link that combines two domains into one administrative unit that can authorize access to resources on both domains.

The two types of trust relationships in Windows 2000 and Windows Server 2003 domains are as follows:

■ **One-way trust relationship**—One domain trusts the users in the other domain to use its resources. More specifically, one domain trusts the domain controllers in the other domain to validate user accounts to use its resources. The resources that become available are in the trusting domain, as are the accounts that can use them. The one-way trusts are nontransitive, which means that if domain A trusts domain B and domain B trusts domain C, then domain A does not automatically trust C unless another trust is set up between domains A and C. One-way nontransitive trust relationships are typically made between existing domains. Since these types of trust relationships must be created manually, a one-way nontransitive trust relationship requires a large amount of administrative overhead for large networks.

■ **Two-way trust relationship**—Each domain trusts user accounts in the other domain. Users can log on from computers in either domain to the domain that contains their account. Unlike Windows NT trust relationships, two-way trust relationships are transitive, which means that if domain A trusts domain B and domain B trusts domain C, then domain A trusts C. Two-way transitive trust relationships are the default in Windows 2000 and Windows Server 2003. When you create a new child domain, a two-way transitive trust relationship is made between the parent domain and the child domain.

If you want to set up a two-way trust, but you want it to be nontransitive, then you will have to set up two one-way trusts in which domain A trusts domain B and vice versa.

To create an explicit domain trust, follow these steps:

1. On a system that has Active Directory, click on the Start button, select the Programs option, select the Administrative Tools option, and select Active Directory Domains and Trusts.
2. In the console tree, right-click the domain node for the domain you want to administer, then select the Properties option.
3. Select the Trusts tab.
4. Depending on your requirements, click either "Domains trusted by this domain" or "Domains that trust this domain," and then click the Add button.
5. If the domain to be added is a Windows 2000 or Windows Server 2003 domain, type the full DNS name of the domain; or if the domain is running an earlier version of Windows, type the domain name.
6. Type the password for this trust and confirm the password. The password must be accepted in both the trusting and trusted domains.

12.5.3 Organizational Units

To help organize the objects within the domain and minimize the number of domains created to organize objects, the domain can contain organizational units. **Organizational units (OUs)** are used to hold users, groups, computers, and other organizational units. See Figure 12.2. An organizational unit can only contain objects that are located in the domain to which the organizational unit belongs. There are no restrictions on the depth (layers) of the OU hierarchy; however, a shallow hierarchy performs better than a deep one. Therefore, create an OU hierarchy no deeper than necessary, and that mirrors the organization's function or business structure.

Since domains and organizational units are used to contain objects (users, network resources, and other domains), they are sometimes referred to as containers. Containers can be assigned Group Policy settings or be used to delegate administrative authority. Group Policy settings control the work environments for users in the domain or organizational unit. Delegated administrative authority allows assigned users to manage objects within the container.

When you first install Active Directory, there are several organizational units that have already been created. They include computers, users, domain controllers, and built-in OUs. Different from other organizational units that you create, the computer, users, and built-in organizational units do not allow you to delegate control or assign group policies. The domain controller OU is different because it is the container that holds the default domain controllers policy, which is the default domain policy.

12.5.4 Objects

An **object** is a distinct, named set of attributes or characteristics that represents a network resource, including computers, people, groups, and printers. Attributes have values that define specific objects. For example, the attributes of a user account might include the user's first and last names, department, and e-mail address, while printers might include the printer name and location. The most common object types are user account, computer, domain controllers, groups, shared folder, and printers. See Table 12.2.

As new objects are created in Active Directory, they are assigned a 128-bit unique number called a **globally unique identifier (GUID),** sometimes referred to as a security identifier (SID). Whereas objects have several names including a common name, a relative name, or some other identifier and can be moved to another container when so desired, the GUID stays the same. Therefore, it can be used to locate an object regardless of name or location.

The **schema** of the Active Directory contains a formal definition and set of rules for all objects and attributes of those objects. The default schema contains definitions of commonly used objects, such as user accounts, computers, printers, and groups.

To enable the Active Directory to be flexible, the schema allows you to define new objects and attributes for existing objects. For example, you could add badge numbers to the user objects. By default, the Active Directory servers do not allow the schema to be edited without changing the \HKLM\SYSTEM\

Figure 12.2 Organization units (OU) used in the Active Directory tree

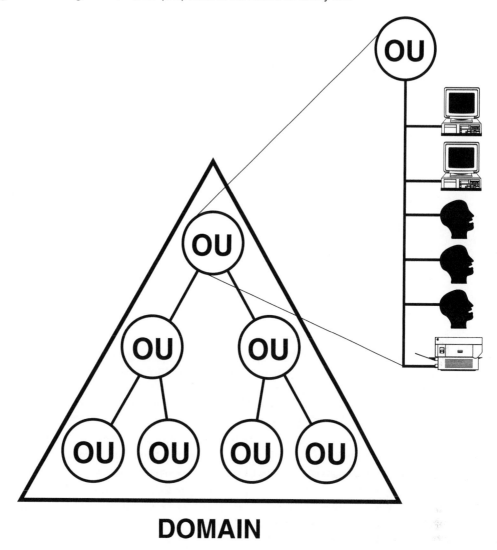

DOMAIN

Table 12.2 Object classes

Object Type	Description
User Account	The information that allows a user to log on to Windows, including the user logon name
Computer Account	The information about a computer that is a member of the domain
Domain Controllers	The information about a domain controller, including its DNS name, the version of the operating system loaded on the controller, the location, and who is responsible for managing the domain controller
Groups	A collection of user accounts, groups, or computers that you can create and use to simplify administration
Organizational Unit (OU)	A container of other objects, including other OUs
Shared Folders	A pointer to a shared folder on a computer (A pointer contains the address of certain data, not the data itself.)
Printers	A pointer to a printer on a computer

CurrentControlSet\Services\DTDS\Parameters\Schema Update Allows value within the registry of the Active Directory to one (1). You can never delete a class or attribute within the Active Directory schema.

A **name space** is a set of unique names for resources or items used in a shared computing environment. A **distinguished name (DN)** for an object uniquely identifies that object by using the actual name of the object plus the names of container objects and domains that contain the object. The distinguished name identifies the object and its location in a tree.

A DNS distinguished name would have a format such as the following:

```
CN = <Object Name>,OU = <Organizational Unit(s)>,
O = <Organization>,C = <CountryCode>
```

For example:

```
CN = pregan,OU = users,OU = support,O = Acme.com,C = US
```

An LDAP distinguished name would have a format such as the following:

```
/O = <Organization>/DC = <DomainComponent(s)>/CN = <Object Name(s)>
```

For example:

```
/O = Internet/DC = Com/DC = Acme/DC = Support/CN = Users/CN = pregan
```

12.5.5   Forests

A **tree** is two or more domains with contiguous name space. If you have two or more existing trees and you need to merge them, then combine them into a grouping called a forest. A **forest** consists of one or more trees that are connected by two-way, transitive trust relationships. In a forest, each tree still has its own unique name space. Therefore, a forest is useful in organizations that need to maintain organizational structures, such as a company that needs distinct public identities for its subsidiaries. By default, the name of the root tree, or the first tree that is created in the forest, is used to refer to a given forest.

Active Directory Tree
- Hierarchy of domains
- Contiguous name space
- Transitive Kerberos trust relations between domains
- Common schema
- Common global catalog

Active Directory Forest
- One or more sets of trees
- Disjointed name spaces between these trees
- Transitive Kerberos trust relationships between trees
- Common schema
- Common global catalog

A domain controller has a replica (copy) of every object in its own domain. If you have more than one domain controller for a domain, ideally, all objects listed in the Active Directory are stored in both servers. Therefore, if one server goes down, you can still access the objects in the database; and if multiple servers are running, performance will be increased because both servers provide access to those objects. If you make changes to an object on one controller, those changes will be duplicated to the other servers in a timely manner.

When you search for an object or retrieve information about an object within a domain, you can retrieve all information from any domain controller. If you need to search for an object or retrieve information about an object in another domain that is part of the forest, access a replica of the global catalog within the current domain to find the object.

The **global catalog** holds replica information of every object in the Active Directory. Instead of storing the entire object, however, it stores those attributes most frequently used in search operations (such as a user's first and last names). It can even be configured to store additional properties as needed. In addition, the global catalog has sufficient information about each object to locate a full replica of the object at its respective domain controller. Since all objects in the forest are listed in the global catalog, all domains within a forest share a single global catalog. The domain controller that contains the global catalog is called the global catalog server. By default, a global catalog is created automatically on the initial domain controller in the forest.

Clients must have access to a global catalog to log on. In addition, a global catalog is necessary to determine group memberships during the logon process. If users are members of the Domain Admins group, they are able to log on to the network even when a global catalog is not available. If your network has any slow or unreliable links, then enable at least one global catalog on each side of the link for maximum availability and fault tolerance.

To enable or disable a global catalog on a domain controller, follow these steps:

1. Click the Start button, select the Program option, select the Administrative Tools option, and select the Active Directory Sites and Services option.
2. In the console tree, double-click the domain controller that is hosting the global catalog.
3. Right-click NTDS Settings, then click Properties.
4. Select the Global Catalog check box.

12.5.6   Planning Your Domain Structure

When deciding between a single domain with organizational units or a forest, it is easy to see why a single domain is the easiest to administer—all users and network resources are located within this domain. If you have a small network or a simple, medium-size network, you should probably use the single domain model.

If you determine that the single domain model no longer meets your needs, then consider using the tree structure based on your organizational structure. The organizational structure could be based on geography or function.

As a general rule, when a network is a far-reaching WAN and you decide to use multiple domains to organize your network resources, organize your domain by geography. Your domain should not span the WAN because of the added traffic that must go back and forth to keep the domain controllers in sync. It is always a good idea to have a local domain controller for all domains at each site so that the users can access the Active Directory database quickly. The exception to this rule is if you have fast links that connect the different sites (256 KB or faster), then organize your domain by function.

Another consideration when designing your domain structure is basing your design on organizational units that allow you to delegate administrative control over smaller groups of users, groups, and resources (decentralized administration). If you are using domains for the various WAN sites, either assign site administrators to each site who have full authority over the site or limited authority. In any case, those site administrators would have no control over the other sites. If you are using a domain design by function, then assign administrator by function. For example, you can have an administrator for all salespeople and an administrator for all researchers.

When choosing your directory structure, consider future growth. This way, you can plan for additional organization units if needed.

12.5.7   Multiple Forest Trusts

Starting with Windows Server 2003, you also have the ability to set up trust among multiple forests so that you can give and limit access to another company through an extranet, and limit access from one forest to the other forest and when a major business unit implements their own forest. A forest trust is one trust link between two forests' root domains. While the forest trust provides cross forest authentication and authorization, it also lets users who have an account in a forest log on to computers in a trusting forest without duplicating accounts.

To establish a forest trust, you must first make sure that both forests are on Windows 2003 forest functional level. This means that every domain controller in both forests must be running Windows Server 2003, each domain must be upgraded to Windows 2003 forest functional level, and both forests' root domains be able to find each other through DNS.

Windows Server 2003 offers two functional levels: domain functional level and forest functional level. Domain functional level is the Windows Server 2003 equivalent of Windows 2000's native mode. When you raise the domain functional level from Windows 2000 to Windows Server 2003, you cannot have any down-level (Windows 2000 or earlier) domain controllers in the domain. Next, you would use the MMC Active Directory Domains and Trusts snap-ins New Trust Wizard to establish the type of trust that you want.

When a user logs on to a computer that is a member of a forest other than the forest that contains the user's user account, the user won't see his or her account domain listed in the logon dialog box. This user will need to enter his or her user principal names (UPN) which are based on the *account @FQDN*. In addition, if you want to add a cross-forest user or group to a resource in your forest, those users won't be able to browse through a list of users and groups to find the resource. Instead, they must enter the UPN.

12.6 PHYSICAL STRUCTURE

Forests, domains, and organizational units are considered logical structures because none of them follow any subnet or network boundary. The physical structure of the Active Directory, which uses subnet/network boundaries, consists of domain controllers and sites.

12.6.1 Domain Controllers

The computer that stores a replica (copy) of the account and security information of the domain and defines the domain is the **domain controller.** A Windows 2000 or Windows Server 2003 domain controller is a Windows 2000 Server or Windows Server 2003 with an NTFS partition running Active Directory services. The directory data (account and security information) are stored in the **NTDS.DIT** file on an NTFS partition on the domain controller. Access to domain objects is controlled by **access control lists (ACLs).** ACLs contain the permissions associated with objects that control which users can gain access to an object and what type of access users can gain to the objects. The domain controller also manages user-domain interactions, including user logon processes, authentication, and directory searches. Note: Windows Server 2003, Web Edition, can participate as a member server in an Active Directory–enabled network but cannot be used as an Active Directory domain controller.

Active Directory uses **multimaster replication,** which means that there is no master domain controller/primary domain controller as in Windows NT. Instead, all domain controllers store writable copies of the directory. When a change is made to one of the domain controllers, it is the job of the domain controller to replicate those changes to other domain controllers within the same domain and within a short time. By adding a domain controller to a domain, the server is automatically configured for replication.

Another type of server on the domain is a member server. A **member server** is used to run applications that are dedicated to specific tasks, such as managing print servers, managing file servers, running database applications, or running as a web server. It does not store copies of the directory database; therefore, it does not authenticate accounts or receive synchronized copies of the directory database.

For each domain, it is recommended to have more than one domain controller. If you only have one domain controller and it goes down for any reason, the users could not use any of the network resources because there is no server to authenticate them and to give the user permissions to use the network resources. The extra domain controllers do not provide fault tolerance for the different network services. They only provide fault tolerance for the Active Directory that contains the account and security information. Whereas Windows NT has primary and secondary domain controllers, in Windows 2000 and Windows Server 2003, domain controllers are all equal to one another. Additional domain controllers also would divide the workload of authentication between the different controllers, thereby allowing for faster network response time.

Because domain controllers store all user account information for a domain, each should be locked in a secure room. Also, only administrators should be allowed to log on interactively to the console of a domain controller. This process will be explained in the next chapter.

To track all changes to an Active Directory, each update is assigned its own 64-bit **unique sequence number (USN).** This number is based on a counter that is incremented whenever a change is made and on what system the changes occurred. When a server replicates an update to other Active Directory servers, it sends the USN with the change. Each domain controller maintains an internal list of replication partners and the highest USN received from them. The domain controller receiving the update requests only those changes with USNs higher than previously received. If two changes occur on two different controllers and are replicated at the same time, a replication collision is detected and is resolved by using the update with the later time stamp. Therefore, it is very important to keep systems time synchronized between Windows servers.

12.6.2   Master Operations

Since Active Directory supports multimaster replication of directory data between all domain controllers in the domain, it is impractical to have certain tasks handled by multiple domain controllers. Therefore, those tasks are assigned to individual domain controllers called operations masters. Because each operations master role can be assumed by another domain controller, Microsoft calls them **flexible single-master operations (FSMO).** There is no automatic failover when an operations master becomes unavailable; each role must be manually assigned to another domain controller in the event of a failure.

In an Active Directory, there are at least five different operations master roles that are assigned to one or more domain controllers. If you have only one domain controller, then it performs all five roles. See Table 12.3. Some of the operations master roles are crucial to the operation of a network. Others can be unavailable for quite some time before their absence becomes a problem. Generally, you will notice that a single operations master is unavailable when you try to perform some function controlled by that particular operations master.

If an operations master is not available due to computer failure or network problems, you can seize the operations master role. This is referred to as forcing the transfer of the operations master role. Do not seize the operations master role if you can transfer it instead. Before forcing the transfer, first determine the cause and expected duration of the computer or network failure. If the cause is a networking problem or a server failure that will be resolved soon, wait for the role holder to become available again. If the domain controller that currently holds the role has failed, you must determine if it can be recovered and brought online.

In general, seizing an operations master role is a drastic step that should be considered only if the current operations master will never be available again. The decision depends on the role and how long the role holder will be unavailable. Note that a domain controller whose schema master role, domain naming master role, or relative ID (RID) master role has been seized must never be brought online. To seize a master role, use the NTDSUTIL command, which will be discussed in the next section.

To identify the RID, PDC and infrastructure roles, follow these steps:

1. Click on the start button, select the Programs option, select Administrative Tools, and select Active Directory Users and Computers.
2. Right-click Active Directory Users and Computers and select the Operations Masters option.
3. Review the roles of operations master in the appropriate tabs. See Figure 12.3.

To transfer the RID, primary domain controller (PDC), and infrastructure roles, follow these steps:

1. Click on the Start button, select the Programs option, select Administrative Tools, and select Active Directory Users and Computers.
2. In the console tree, right-click the domain controller node that will become the new RID, PDC, or Infrastructure role, then click Connect to Domain.
3. Type the domain name or click Browse and select the domain from the list.
4. In the console tree, right-click Active Directory Users and Computers, then click Operations Master.
5. On the appropriate tab, click the Change button.

NOTE: You must be a member of the Domain Admins group or the Enterprise Admins group.

To transfer the domain naming master role, follow these steps:

1. Open Active Directory Domains and Trusts.
2. In the console tree, right-click Active Directory Domains and Trusts, then click Connect to Domain Controller.

Table 12.3 Operations master roles

Operations Master Roles	Scope of Operations Master	Description	Affect of Failure
Schema Master	One per forest	The schema master domain controller controls all updates and modifications to the schema. To update the schema of a forest, you must have access to the schema master.	Temporary loss of the schema master is not visible to network users. It will not be visible to network administrators unless they are trying to modify the schema or install an application that modifies the schema during installation. **Note:** A domain controller whose schema master role has been seized must never be brought online.
Domain Naming Master	One per forest	The domain controller holding the domain naming master role controls the addition or removal of domains in the forest.	Temporary loss of the domain naming master is not visible to network users. It will not be visible to network administrators either, unless they are trying to add a domain to the forest or remove a domain from the forest. **Note:** A domain controller whose domain naming master role has been seized must never be brought online.
Relative ID (RID) Master	One per domain	When a domain controller creates a user, group, or computer object, it assigns the object a unique security ID. The security ID consists of a domain security ID (identifies the domain to which the object belongs) and a relative ID that identifies the object within the domain. The relative ID master allocates sequences of relative IDs to each of the various domain controllers in its domain. To move an object between domains, initiate a move on the domain controllers acting as the relative ID master of the domain that currently contains the object.	Temporary loss of the RID master is not visible to network users. It will not be visible to network administrators either unless they are creating objects and the domain in which they are creating the objects runs out of relative IDs (RIDs). **Note:** A domain controller whose RID master role has been seized must never be brought online.
PDC Emulator	One per domain	If the domain contains computers operating without Windows 2000 client software or if it contains Windows NT backup domain controllers (BDCs), the PDC emulator acts as a Windows NT primary domain controller. It processes password changes from clients and replicates updates to the BDCs. In a Windows 2000 or Windows Server 2003 domain that is operating in native mode, the PDC emulator receives preferential replication of password changes performed by other domain controllers in the domain. If a password was recently changed, that change takes time to replicate to every domain controller in the domain. If a logon authentication fails at another domain controller due to a bad password,	The loss of the primary domain controller (PDC) emulator master affects network users. Therefore, when the PDC emulator master is not available, you may need to immediately seize the role.

Table 12.3   Continued

Operations Master Roles	Scope of Operations Master	Description	Affect of Failure
		that domain controller will forward the authentication request to the PDC emulator before rejecting the logon attempt.	
Infrastructure Master	One per domain	When you rename or move a member of a group (and that member resides in a different domain from the group), the infrastructure master of the group's domain is responsible for updating the group so it knows the new name or location of the member. The infrastructure master distributes the update via multimaster replication. The administrator, when renaming or moving a member of a group, may see that the member of a group notices a temporary inconsistency such as the member not showing up in the group.	Temporary loss of the infrastructure master is not visible to network users. It will not be visible to network administrators either, unless they have recently moved or renamed a large number of accounts.

Figure 12.3   Displaying the domain's Operations Master

3. In "Enter the name of another domain controller," type the name of the domain controller you want to hold the domain naming master role, or click the domain controller in the list of available domain controllers.
4. In the console tree, right-click Active Directory Domains and Trusts, then click Operations Master.
5. Click Change.

NOTE: You must be a member of the Domain Admins group or the Enterprise Admins group.

To transfer the schema master role (GUI interface), follow these steps:

1. Open the Active Directory Schema snap-in.
2. In the console tree, right-click Active Directory Schema, then click change Domain Controller.

3. Click Specify Name, and type the name of the domain controller that you want to hold the schema master role.

4. In the console tree, right-click Active Directory Schema, then click Operations Master.

5. Click Change.

NOTE: You must be a member of the Schema Admins group.

Important Note: Modifying the schema is an advanced operation best performed programmatically by experienced programmers and system administrators, or performed automatically when installing certain programs such as Microsoft Exchange. For detailed information about modifying the schema, see the Active Directory Programmer's Guide at the Microsoft website: http://msdn.microsoft.com/developer/windows2000/adsi/actdirguide.asp.

If the Active Directory Schema snap-in is not available, you will need to do the following:

1. On computers running Windows XP Professional, insert the Windows Server 2003 installation CD into your CD drive, click Browse this CD, double-click the i386 folder, double-click Adminpak, and then follow the instructions that appear in the Administration Tools Setup wizard.

2. On servers running Windows Server 2003, type the following command to register the SCHMMGMT.DLL using the REGSVR32 command-line tool:

```
regsvr32 schmmgmt.dll
```

3. Click Start, click Run, and type:

```
mmc /a
```

Then click OK.

4. On the File menu, click Add/Remove Snap-in, then click Add.

5. Under Snap-in, double-click Active Directory Schema, then click Close.

12.6.3   NTDSUTIL.EXE Command

NTDSUTIL.EXE is a command-line tool that provides management facilities for Active Directory. This command has several purposes: to perform database maintenance of Active Directory; to manage and control single-master operations; to compact, repair, and check the integrity of the Active Directory databases; and to clean up metadata left behind by domain controllers that were removed from the network without being properly uninstalled. It can also be used to do an authoritative restore, which is discussed in Chapter 16. The NTDSUTIL.EXE should be used by experienced administrators. By default, NTDSUTIL.EXE is installed in the *%system%*\System 32 folder.

To transfer or seize a master role at the Command prompt, follow these steps:

1. Open the Command prompt.

2. Type:

```
ntdsutil
```

3. At the NTDSUTIL Command prompt, type:

```
roles
```

4. At the FSMO MAINTENANCE command prompt, type:

```
connection
```

5. At the SERVER CONNECTIONS command prompt, type:

```
connect to server Name_of_Domain_Controller
```

6. At the SERVER CONNECTIONS command prompt, type:

```
quit
```

7. At the FSMO MAINTENANCE command prompt, type one of the following commands:

```
transfer schema master
transfer domain naming master
transfer RID master
transfer PDC
transfer infrastructure master
seize schema master
seize domain naming master
seize RID master
seize PDC
seize infrastructure master
```

NTDSUTIL is the only tool that shows you all the FSMO role owners. To show these roles, you would do the following:

1. Open the Command prompt.

2. Type:

```
ntdsutil
```

3. At the NTDSUTIL prompt, type:

```
domain management
```

4. Type the following command:

```
connections
```

5. At the SERVER CONNECTIONS prompt, type:

```
connect to server Name_of_Domain_Controller
```

6. Type the following command:

```
quit
```

7. Type the following command:

```
select operation target
```

8. Type the following command:

```
list roles for connected server
```

12.6.4   Sites and Active Directory Replication

When domain controllers are linked together through WAN links, the WAN links are usually much slower, less reliable, and more costly than for the equivalent LAN. Therefore, when a domain controller needs to replicate its database to other domain controllers, be sure to define sites and configure replication so that you can make best use of the fast local LAN links and the slower WAN links.

A **site** is one or more IP subnets connected by a high-speed link, typically defined by geographical locations. Sites are based on IP subnets and all subnets can only belong to one site. Multiple subnets can be assigned to a single site. When a user logs on, Active Directory clients locate an Active Directory server in the same site as the user.

Active Directory automatically generates a simple, bidirectional ring topology for replication in the same domain and site with up to seven domain controllers. The ring ensures that if one domain controller goes down, it still has an available path to replicate its information to other domain controllers. When the number of servers grows beyond seven, the number of connections that are needed are estimated so that if a change occurs at any one domain controller, there are as many replication partners as needed to ensure that no domain controller is more than three replication hops from another domain controller. These optimizing connections are created at random and are not necessarily created on every third domain controller.

Note: The replication path, or site topology, within a site is automatically managed by a service called the **Knowledge Consistency Checker (KCC).**

When an update occurs on a domain controller, the replication engine waits for a configurable interval, which is 5 minutes by default. It then sends a notification message to the first replication partner, informing it of the change. Each additional direct partner is notified after a configurable delay, which is 30 seconds by default. Items that are security-sensitive are immediately replicated and partners are notified immediately. If no changes occur during a configuration period, which is 1 hour by default, a domain controller initiates replication with its replication partners to ensure that no changes from the originating domain controller were missed.

When a domain controller replicates to another domain controller in a site, replication information is done without being scheduled. Urgent changes such as password changes, account lockout policy changes, freshly locked accounts, and domain password policies are replicated immediately. In addition, the replication data are sent uncompressed, which keeps the domain controller processing down to a minimum. See Table 12.4.

The default replication pattern used by the Active Directory is optimized for a single location or site with high-speed connectivity. If your network includes multiple locations or sites, however, the replication pattern would have to be configured so that a domain controller will replicate all changes to the domain controllers within a site and have a single domain controller to replicate across a slower WAN link to the other sites.

A bridgehead server is a single server located in each site that is designated to perform site-to-site replication. Bridgehead servers are designated automatically, or they can be assigned manually by an administrator. The bridgehead servers replicate information to other domain controllers at the site. While site replication uses remote procedure call (RPC) transport, intersite replication uses either RPC over IP or Simple Mail Transfer Protocol (SMTP). In addition, the replication traffic between sites in intersite replication is compressed to save bandwidth.

RCP over IP replication is synchronous; thus, a domain controller that sends a replication request does not process any other requests for service until it receives a reply to its replication request. If the site link over which the replication request is sent is broken, the domain controller waits for the site link to be reconnected before it resumes Active Directory replication. RPC over IP should be used on fast, reliable links.

SMTP-based replication is store-and-forward transport. Thus, it can be used with an unreliable connection. SMTP site links are only available between domain controllers from different domains. Consequently, an SMTP site link is the best choice for replication across unreliable or slow communication links.

Table 12.4   Comparing site and intersite replication

Site Replication	Intersite Replication
Replication traffic is not compressed to save processor processing.	Replication traffic is compressed to save bandwidth.
Replication partners notify each other when changes need to be replicated, to reduce replication latency.	Replication partners do not notify each other when changes need to be replicated, to save bandwidth.
Replication partners poll each other for changes on a periodic basis.	Replication partners poll each other for changes on a specified polling interval, during scheduled periods only.
Replication uses the remote procedure called (RPC) transport.	Replication uses the TCP/IP or SMTP transport.
Replication connections can be created between any two domain controllers located in the same site. Connections can be made with multiple domain controllers to reduce replication latency.	Replication connections are only created between bridgehead servers (servers that handle all intersite replication for that domain). Connections between bridgehead servers use the lowest-cost route, according to the site link cost. Connections are only created over higher-cost routes if all domain controllers in lower-cost routes are unreachable.

To optimize traffic between sites, the links between bridgehead servers are assigned time schedules to indicate what times of day they are available to carry replication traffic. The replication interval indicates how often the bridgehead servers poll the other side of the link for replication change. The first site in Active Directory is called "Default-First-Site-Name" which is created automatically for the administrator. This site is a member of the default site link called "DEFAULTIPSITELINK," which also is created automatically for the administrator. If the administrator creates two additional sites, the administrator must define a site link, of which each site is going to be a member, before the sites can be written to Active Directory.

The site replication process works in the background to optimize the replication paths between domain controllers in all sites. Because site links are also bridged by default, replication paths are transitive; that is, if site A is linked to site B and site B is linked to site C, then an implicit replication path exists between sites A and C.

Replication within sites requires little or no planning because the process is fully automatic. When you have multiple sites, however, follow these steps to optimize Active Directory synchronization traffic:

1. Identify sites that are well connected through backbones, and create low-cost site links between them.
2. Identify sites that are interconnected with comparable transport, and create medium-cost site links between them—for example, full-mesh links (remote sites that are connected over telecommunication links), frame-relay cloud links (a point-to-point system that uses a private virtual circuit), and medium-area network links with T1 connections.
3. Identify remaining WAN links.
4. Create a site link for each pair of sites that cross a WAN link.
5. Create a schedule that meets user needs.
6. Avoid high-frequency times.

The most useful tool for monitoring and troubleshooting replication is the Active Directory Replication Monitor, or Replmon. This tool is installed by running the Setup program in the SUPPORT/TOOLS directory on the Windows CD. Another useful tool is the DSASTAT, which allows you to compare the directories on Windows domain controllers. Besides Replmon, you can also use Repadmin (command-line utility) to force replication events.

Avoid confusing trees and forests with sites. Trees and forests are used to manage administration and security in an organization; sites reflect geographical boundaries. You may choose to arrange a site's trees and forests using a geographical or an organizational approach, but doing so does not affect changes to the sites of the domains. In addition, Active Directory does not affect the name space in any way.

Remember to have more than one controller for both fault tolerance and faster authentication. Placing domain controllers and DNS servers at the different physical sites greatly improves the performance of the directory in a WAN, since authentication will be done locally and not through a slow WAN link. Having multiple servers at a site will offer fault tolerance and load balancing for requests. In addition, having multiple global catalog servers is a necessity.

To create a site, follow these steps:

1. Click the Start button, select the Programs option, select the Administrative Tools option, and select the Active Directory Sites and Services option.
2. Right-click the Sites folder, then select the New Site option.
3. In Name, type the name of the new site.
4. Click a Site Link Object, then click OK.
5. Associate a subnet with a site for this newly created site.
6. Move a domain controller from an existing site into this new site, or install a new domain controller.
7. If desired, choose a different licensing computer other than the one automatically selected.
8. Delegate control of the site.

To delete a site, do the following:

1. Open Active Directory Sites and Services.
2. In the console tree, double-click on Sites.
3. Right-click the Site Container, then click Delete.

To bridge all site links, follow these steps:

1. Click the Start button, select the Programs option, select the Administrative Tools option, and select the Active Directory Sites and Services option.
2. Double-click the Sites folder, then double-click the Inter-Site Transports folder.
3. Right-click the appropriate intersite transport folder (such as IP or SMTP), then click Properties.
4. Select the "Bridge all site links" check box.

To create a site link, do the following:

1. Click the Start button, select the Programs option, select the Administrative Tools option, and select the Active Directory Sites and Services option.
2. In the console tree, right-click the intersite transport protocol you want the site link to use, then click New Site Link.
3. In Name, type the name to be given to the link.
4. Click two or more sites to connect, then click Add.
5. Configure the site link's cost, schedule, and replication frequency by right-clicking the site link that you want to configure and select the Properties option.

If you create a site link that uses SMTP, you must have an Enterprise Certification Authority (Enterprise CA) available and SMTP must be installed on all domain controllers that will use the site link.

To create a site link bridge, do the following:

1. Click the Start button, select the Programs option, select the Administrative Tools option, and select the Active Directory Sites and Services option.
2. In the console tree, right-click the intersite transport folder for which you want to create a new site link bridge, then click New Site Link Bridge.
3. In Name, type a name for the site link bridge.
4. Click two or more site links to be bridged, then click Add.

If you have enabled "Bridge all site links," this procedure is redundant and will have no effect.

12.7   INSTALLING AND CONFIGURING DOMAIN CONTROLLERS AND ACTIVE DIRECTORIES

When you install Windows 2000 Server or Windows Server 2003, it defaults to being a member server of the domain. To become a domain controller, install the server and then promote it.

Before installing a domain controller, identify the DNS name space and verify that the computer has an NTFS partition and that the TCP/IP protocol is installed and configured correctly. In addition, make sure that a DNS server is available on the network or you will have to install and configure the DNS service on the domain controller computer.

To install a domain controller, follow these steps:

1. Click Start, point to Programs, point to Administrative Tools, and then click Configure Your Server.
2. Click Active Directory, and click Start Hypertext to start the Active Directory Installation wizard. You must scroll down to get to the Start hypertext.
3. Follow the instructions in the Active Directory Installation wizard.

You can start the Active Directory Installation wizard by clicking on the Start button, then on the Run option, and then executing the DCPROMO command. See Figure 12.4.

The Active Directory Installation wizard will prompt you when the domain controller is used to create the following:

- A new domain or an additional domain controller for an existing domain
- A new tree or to be part of a child domain in an existing tree
- A new forest or to join an existing forest

Figure 12.4   Configure Your Server Wizard can be used to promote a server into a domain controller

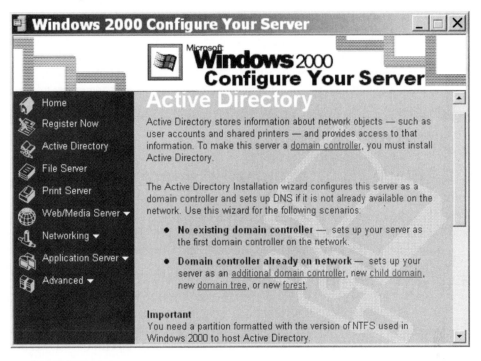

Figure 12.5   (a) Active Directory Sites and Services and (b) Active Directory Domains and Trusts consoles

If you are joining an existing domain, tree, or forest, then the wizard will prompt you for network credentials of a user account with sufficient rights to create objects in the Active Directory.

After the Active Directory has been installed, it can then be configured by using the Active Directory Domains and Trusts console, the Active Directory Sites and Services console, and the Active Directory Users and Computers console, or by using the MMC with the respective snap-ins. See Figure 12.5.

You can also administer Active Directory remotely from a computer that is not a domain controller. To use Active Directory Administrative Tools remotely, you would install Windows 2000 Administrative Tools on a Windows 2000 Professional computer to administer a Windows 2000 Active Directory, or Windows server 2003 Administrative Tools on a Windows XP computer to manage a Windows 2000 or a Windows Server 2003 Active Directory.

When first created, the Active Directory is configured for **mixed mode,** which allows the Windows 2000 or Windows Server 2003 to communicate with Windows 3.51 and 4.0. Unfortunately, when running in mixed mode, Windows 2000 cannot use universal or nested groups. In addition, clients that use operating systems other than Windows 2000, Windows XP, or Windows Server 2003 cannot use the transitive domains that would normally be available through transitive trust relationships.

The default domain mode setting on Windows 2000 and Windows Server 2003 is mixed mode. Mixed mode allows Windows NT and Windows 2000 backup domain controllers to coexist in a domain. Mixed mode does not support the universal and nested group enhancements of Windows 2000 and Windows Server 2003. The domain mode setting can be changed to Windows native mode when all Windows NT domain controllers are removed from a domain.

12.8   UPGRADING TO ACTIVE DIRECTORY

If you are upgrading a Windows NT domain to a Windows 2000 or Windows Server 2003 Active Directory, you must ensure that you have designed a DNS and Active Directory name space and that you have either configured DNS servers or are planning on having the Active Directory Installation wizard automatically install the DNS service on the domain controller. The DNS server should support dynamic DNS and the new resource records (e.g., the SRV resource record).

The first Windows NT 4.0 and earlier server you must upgrade is the primary domain controller (PDC). Upgrading the Windows NT PDC is required for successful upgrade of the domain. If your current PDC does not have the system requirements to load Windows 2000 or Windows Server 2003, you need to promote a BDC that does have the system requirements to a PDC. Or, you can install a new computer as a BDC so that it can have a copy of the domain database. You would then promote it to a PDC and perform the upgrade on the new machine. Use the WINNT32/CHECKUPGRADEONLY command to verify that the system meets the system requirements. Note: As a precaution, take a BDC offline so that it will not be affected by the upgrade. If you can't spare an existing BDC, install a new one and take it offline. Of course, you should also make backups of your servers, especially the domain controllers, before the upgrade.

The promotion process copies the users, global groups, local groups, and computer accounts on the PDC from the Security Accounts Manager (SAM) database to the new AD directory store. Active Directory places local groups in the built-in container, places users and global groups in the users container, and places computer accounts excluding domain controllers in the computers container. It places domain controllers in the domain controllers container. The built-in, users, and computers containers are special containers, and the domain controllers container is an OU.

Password and lockout properties migrate to the Default Domain Account Policy object. User rights and auditing policy migrate to the Default Domain Controllers Local Policy object.

If you migrate to Active Directory from a single domain model, you likely will retain a single domain. By creating OUs in your Windows 2000 single domain, however, you can introduce a degree of administrative delegation that was not possible with the earlier model. If you migrate to Active Directory from the master domain model, you can either dissolve your resource domains to take advantage of Active Directory's granularity, or you can retain the resource domains.

You can migrate a multiple master domain model to either a domain tree or a forest. You can migrate your company's multiple master domain model to one tree. With one tree, you can implement each business unit as a second-level domain below the root domain, and each second-level domain can have child domains. You can also create the second-level domains according to geographical location. A more decentralized approach is to let each business unit create its own domain tree, and join the trees into a forest.

If your Windows NT domain is a complete trust model, you can make a forest of your independent domains after migrating to Active Directory. Alternatively, you can try some domain coordination and migrate the domains to one tree.

After you upgrade all domain controllers, you can raise the domain functional level to Windows 2000 native. When you do this, you get the following results:

- Domain controllers no longer support NTLM replication (replication used by Windows NT domain controllers).
- The domain controller that is emulating the PDC operations master cannot synchronize data with a Windows NT 4.0 and earlier BDC.

- Windows NT and earlier domain controllers cannot be added to the domain.
- Users and computers using previous versions of Windows begin to benefit from the transitive trusts of Active Directory, and with proper authorization, can access resources anywhere in the forest. Although previous versions of Windows do not support the Kerberos protocol, the pass-through authentication provided by the domain controllers allows users and computers to be authenticated in any domain in the forest. This enables users or computers to access resources in any domain in the forest for which they have the appropriate permissions.

Other than the enhanced access to any other domains in the forest, clients will not be aware of any changes in the domain.

If you are upgrading from Windows 2000 Active Directory to Windows Server 2003 Active Directory or you want to add Windows Server 2003 domains to a Windows 2000 Active Directory, you must prepare the forest so that it will update the schema. This is done by running the ADPREP/FORESTPREP command at the command line on the schema operations master. After the changes are replicated to the other domain controllers, you need to prepare the domain. This is done by running the ADPREP/DOMAINPREP command on the infrastructure operations master. The ADPREP.EXE command is available from the i386 directory on the Windows Server 2003 installation CD.

12.9   ACTIVE DIRECTORY CLIENTS

Computers that are running any version of Windows can be configured to participate in either a domain or a workgroup. When setting up one of these computers for networking in a workgroup, specify a computer name and a workgroup name. If the workgroup name matches a domain name, the computer name appears in the Browse list for that domain and can browse computers having shared resources, whether participating in a domain or a workgroup. To determine whether the computer participates in a domain or a workgroup, during setup specify that the computer logs on to either a Windows domain or a workgroup.

For a computer to connect to and make full use of an Active Directory network, it needs to have Active Directory Network Client software installed. A computer configured with the Active Directory Client can locate a domain controller and log on to the network. Computers that are running Windows 2000, Windows XP, or Windows Server 2003, already have Active Directory Client. Computers running Windows 9X need to have add-on Active Directory Client software installed. Computers not running Active Directory Client software will appear just like a Windows NT directory. The Active Directory Client is provided in the Clients folder on the Windows CD.

To log on to an Active Directory network, an Active Directory Client must first locate an Active Directory domain controller for its domain. To locate a domain controller for a specified domain, an Active Directory Client sends a DNS name query with an SRV Query type and ldap._tcp.*domain_name* Query name. For example, to log on to the domain ACME.COM, an Active Directory Client sends a DNS name query of the type SRV for the name_ldap._tcp.acme.com. A DNS server will respond back with the list of DNS names of the domain controllers and their IP addresses. From the list of domain controllers' IP addresses, the client attempts to contact each domain controller. The first domain controller that responds is used for the logon process.

Question: A small company uses a single LAN. How many domain controllers would you recommend?

Answer: Recommend two domain controllers. Although the network could get by with one domain controller, recommend two to allow for fault tolerance and faster network response time.

Question: A small company uses several LANs that are connected to form a WAN through various WAN links. The company's corporate office is located in Sacramento. Other offices in Cleveland, Los Angeles, and Houston need to be part of the network. How many domain controllers would you recommend?

Answer: Recommend two domain controllers located at the corporate office to provide fault tolerance for the corporate office and allow for fast authentication for the corporate users. Next, recommend having a domain controller at each of the different sites to also provide fault tolerance to the network, but allow the users at the remote sites to authenticate locally without sending requests back to the corporate office. This setup would significantly increase the users' response time.

Question: A large company uses several LANs that are connected to form a WAN through various WAN links. The company's corporate office is located in Sacramento. Other offices in Cleveland, Los Angeles, and Houston need to be part of the network. How many domain controllers would you recommend?

Answer: Since this is a large network, it would probably be best to use multiple domains to divide the network resources into smaller, more manageable units. Until you know more about the organization and the WAN links that connect the individual LANs, recommend that the corporate office represent the root domain and the remote sites have their own child domains. Each domain would have two domain controllers to provide fault tolerance.

12.10   TIME SYNCHRONIZATION

Windows uses a time synchronization service to synchronize the date and time of computers running on networks based on Windows 2000 and Windows Server 2003. When a client boots, it contacts a domain controller for authentication. As the two computers exchange authentication packets, the client adjusts its local time based on the time of the domain controller. If the domain controller is ahead of the client's time by less than 2 minutes, then the client immediately adjusts its time to match the target time. If the domain controller is behind the client's time by less than 2 minutes, then the client slows its clock over a period of 20 minutes until the two times are in sync. If the local time is off by more than 2 minutes, then the client immediately sets its time to match the target time. To keep the clients in sync with the time server, the client performs these checks every 8 hours.

To keep the domain controllers in sync with each other, Windows uses a **Windows Time Synchronization Service.** The first domain controller in the forest, which acts as the PDC emulator, becomes the authoritative timekeeper for the entire enterprise. Therefore, the PDC emulator should gather its time from an external source such as an observatory or atomic clock. To configure the PDC emulator, recognize an external SNTP time server as the authoritative timekeeper using the NET TIME /SETSNTP:*server* command from the Command prompt, where the *server* is the IP address or server name that uses the **Simple Network Time Protocol (SNTP).** SNTP defaults to using UDP port 123. If this port is not open to the Internet, you cannot synchronize your server to Internet SNTP servers.

There are many SNTP time servers throughout the world that are satisfactory for this function. Some are as follows:

- ntp2.usno.navy.mil at 192.5.41.209
- tick.usno.navy.mil at 192.4.41.40
- tock.usno.navy.mil at 192.5.41.41
- bitsy.mit.edu at 18.72.0.3
- bonehed.lcs.mit.edu at 18.26.4.105
- clock.isc.org at 192.5.5.250
- clock.nc.fukuoka-u.ac.jp at 133.100.9.2
- ntp.nml.csiro.au at 130.155.98.1
- ntp-p1.obspm.fr at 145.238.110.49
- ntp2.ja.net at 193.63.94.26

Therefore, to set up the PDC emulator to point to the first time server listed, type:

```
NET TIME /SETSNTP:192.5.41.209
```

or

```
NET TIME /SETSNTP:NTP2.USNO.NAVY.MIL
```

For the system to update from a time source, you must have the Windows time service started.

SUMMARY

1. A common directory service is the X.500, which uses a hierarchical approach in which objects are organized in a similar way to files on a hard drive.

2. The Lightweight Directory Access Protocol (LDAP), based on X.500, allows Windows Active Directory to communicate and perform basic read, write, and modify operations; queries an object in the Active Directory; and allows Windows servers and Windows Server 2003 to communicate with Windows 3.51 and 4.0 servers.

3. A workgroup is an organizational unit of computers that is typically found in small peer-to-peer networks. In a workgroup, each computer has a local security database so that it tracks its own user and group account information.

4. Active Directory is a directory service that combines domains, X.500 naming services, DNS, X.509 digital certificates, and Kerberos authentication.

5. NTDS.DIT is a single file located on the domain controller that makes up the Active Directory database.

6. The System Volume (SYSVOL) stores the server copy of the domain's public files, such as the Group Policy and Net Login (logon scripts), which are replicated among all domain controllers in the domain.

7. The Windows domain is a logical unit of computers and network resources that define a security boundary.

8. A trust relationship is a link that combines two domains into one administrative unit that can authorize access to resources on both domains.

9. Organizational units are used to hold and organize users, groups, computers, and other organizational units.

10. An object is a distinct, named set of attributes or characteristics that represents a network resource, including computers, people, groups, and printers.

11. The schema of the Active Directory contains a formal definition and set of rules for all objects and attributes of those objects.

12. A forest consists of one or more trees that are connected by two-way, transitive trust relationships.

13. The global catalog holds a replica of every object in the Active Directory.

14. The computer that stores a replica (copy) of the account and security information of the domain and defines the domain is known as the domain controller.

15. Active Directory uses multimaster replication.

16. The schema master domain controller controls all updates and modifications to the schema.

17. The relative ID master allocates sequences of relative IDs to each of the various domain controllers in its domain.

18. The PDC emulator acts as a Windows NT primary domain controller.

19. When you rename or move a member of a group (and that member resides in a different domain from the group), the infrastructure master of the group's domain is responsible for updating the group so it knows the new name or location of the member.

20. A site is one or more IP subnets connected by a high-speed link (128 Kbps or higher), typically defined by geographical locations.

21. A bridgehead server is a single server located in each site that is designated to perform site-to-site replication.

22. Before installing a domain controller, identify the DNS name space and verify that the computer has an NTFS partition and that the TCP/IP protocol is installed and configured correctly.

23. To start the Active Directory Installation wizard, run the DCPROMO command.

24. For a computer to connect to and make full use of an Active Directory network, it requires network client software.

25. Windows uses a time synchronization service to synchronize the date and time of computers running on a Windows-based network.

QUESTIONS

1. If you combine domain trees, you form a domain _____.
   a. forest
   b. jungle
   c. collective
   d. group

2. _____ is a network service that identifies all resources on a network and makes those resources accessible to users and applications.
   a. Security services
   b. Directory services
   c. Application services
   d. Communication services

3. Which of the following is commonly referred to as a peer-to-peer network that has each computer keep its own security database?
   a. forest
   b. workgroup
   c. domain
   d. replication partner

4. Which of the following uses a centralized security database to authenticate users on the network?
   a. client
   b. workgroup
   c. domain
   d. replication partner

5. If you have performed a default installation of Windows 2000 Server with Active Directory, which folder will be shared as the system volume?
   a. %systemroot%\sysvol\sysvol
   b. %systemroot%\system32\
   c. %systemroot%\system32\system
   d. %systemroot%\sysvol

6. Which of the following are true of a Windows 2000 domain controller? (Choose all that apply.)
   a. A domain controller can be demoted to be a member server and vice versa.
   b. Changes to the Active Directory can be made on any domain controller.
   c. All domain controllers in Windows 2000 are equal status with no primary or master server.
   d. Both Windows 2000 Server and Windows 2000 Professional can be used as a domain controller.

7. Which of the following are true of a global catalog in Windows 2000?
   a. A global catalog contains only the commonly queried objects and all attributes for a single domain only.
   b. A global catalog contains only the commonly queried objects and all attributes for a forest.
   c. A global catalog contains all objects and all attributes for a forest.
   d. A global catalog contains all objects and common attributes for a forest.
   e. A global catalog contains all objects and common attributes for a single domain only.

8. You wish to install Active Directory on a Windows 2000 Server but currently have no DNS server. Which of the following options would allow Active Directory to be installed? (Choose all that apply.)
   a. Install DNS server on a separate computer after installing Active Directory.
   b. Install DNS server on a separate computer before installing Active Directory.
   c. Install both DNS server and Active Directory at the same time on the same server.
   d. Install a WINS server before installing Active Directory.

9. Which server will become the global catalog server in a forest by default?
   a. first domain controller in the first domain in the forest
   b. first domain controller in each domain
   c. every domain controller in the forest
   d. every Windows 2000 Server in the forest

10. The _____ of the Active Directory contains a formal definition and set of rules for all objects and attributes of those objects.
    a. RID master   c. global catalog
    b. GUID   d. schema

11. Which of the following statements are true about trust relationships between domains? (Choose all that apply.)
    a. One-way trust relationships are nontransitive.
    b. Two-way trust relationships are nontransitive.
    c. One-way trust relationships are transitive.
    d. Two-way trust relationships are transitive.

12. Which of the following are containers? (Choose all that apply.)
    a. organizational units   c. groups
    b. domains   d. domain controllers

13. The computer that stores a replica (copy) of the account and security information of the domain and defines the domain is known as the _____ .
    a. member server   c. ACL
    b. domain controller   d. Windows 2000 Advanced Server

14. The Active Directory data (account and security information) are stored in the _____ file.
    a. NTFS.DIT   c. NTFS.DIR
    b. NTDS.DIT   d. NTDS.DIR

15. Which of the following are true of a site with respect to Windows 2000 domains? (Choose all that apply.)
    a. A site must be contained within a single domain.
    b. A site contains one or more IP subnets on a LAN.
    c. A site must contain at least one whole domain.
    d. A site is configured to optimize Active Directory synchronization traffic.

16. Which options are available for site link replication methods? (Choose all that apply.)
    a. IP   c. SMTP
    b. IPX   d. SMB

17. What name is given to the site link created by default on Windows 2000?
    a. DEFAULTIPSITELINK   c. IPLINK
    b. DEFLINK   d. DEFAULTSITE

18. Which of the following statements are true of organizational units (OUs) in a Windows 2000 domain? (Choose all that apply.)
    a. Administrative control of OUs can be delegated to other users.
    b. An OU can contain other OUs.
    c. Administrators have permission to create OUs by default.
    d. Users and computers are two of the built-in OUs in a domain.

19. You have installed Windows 2000 Member Server and now wish to promote it to a domain controller. What should you do?
    a. Run WINNT /U.   c. Run UPDATEAD.EXE.
    b. Run DCPROMO.   d. Reinstall Windows 2000.

20. Which of the following statements are true of a mixed-mode domain in Windows 2000? (Choose all that apply.)
    a. A mixed-mode domain supports group nesting.
    b. A mixed-mode domain supports universal groups.
    c. A mixed-mode domain can contain Windows 2000 domain controllers.
    d. A mixed-mode domain can contain Windows NT 4.0 domain controllers.

21. You are the administrator of a Windows 2000 domain. The domain is in native mode. The domain contains 15 Windows 2000 Server computers that are functioning as domain controllers and 1500 Windows NT client computers. During a power outage the first domain controller that you install suffers a catastrophic hardware failure and will not restart. After the power outage, users report that password changes do not take effect for several hours. In addition users are not able to log on or connect to resources by using their new passwords. What should you do to correct this problem?
    a. Using the NTDSUTIL utility, connect to another domain controller and transfer the PDC emulator role.
    b. Using the NTDSUTIL utility, connect to another domain controller and seize the PDC emulator role.
    c. Using the NTDSUTIL utility, connect to another domain controller and transfer the domain naming master role.
    d. Using the NTDSUTIL utility, connect to another domain controller and seize the domain naming master role.

22. You are the enterprise administrator of a network. The network has eight domains in the domain tree. You add a domain to the domain tree. One of the domain controllers in the root domain becomes unavailable because of a hardware failure. After the hardware failure, you are unable to add an additional domain

to the domain tree. How should you correct this problem?

a. On one of the other domain controllers, seize the domain naming master role.

b. Promote a Windows 2000 Server computer to be a replica controller in the root domain.

c. On one of the other domain controllers, seize the infrastructure master role.

d. In the Active Directory sites and services console, promote a domain controller from the root domain and force replication.

23. You are the administrator of your company's network. The network consists of two Windows 2000 domains. There are 10 Windows 2000 Server computers and 1100 Windows 2000 Professional client computers on the network. Two of the servers in each domain function as domain controllers. Both domains are in native mode. When the initial domain controller is taken offline for maintenance, users receive an error message stating that the domain controller cannot be located. Users are not able to log on to the network, although the other domain controllers are still operating. What should you do to correct this problem?

a. Create a primary DNS zone.

b. Create a secondary DNS zone.

c. Configure at least one other domain controller as the global catalog server.

d. Configure at least one other domain controller as a PDC emulator.

e. Configure at least one other domain controller as a WINS server.

24. Your company's network consists of two Windows 2000 domains: acme.com and sales.acme.com. The acme.com domain contains three domain controllers: dc1.acme.com, dc2.acme.com, and dc3.acme.com. The sales.acme.com domain contains two domain controllers: salesdc1.acme.com and salesdc2.acme.com. You are a member of the Domain Admins group in sales.acme.com. You create 100 new user accounts in sales.acme.com. These new users report they cannot log on to sales.acme.com. What is the most likely cause of this problem?

a. All bridgehead servers in the forest are offline.

b. All global catalog servers in the forest are offline.

c. The server in acme.com that is holding the PDC emulator role is offline.

d. The server in sales.acme.com that is holding the PDC emulator role is offline.

25. You are responsible for implementing a site and replication topology for a Windows 2000 domain named acme.com. The network consists of four offices in four cities that are connected by T1 frame-relay links. Using the Active Directory Sites and Services tool, you have created site and subnet objects for each office, placed domain controller objects in each site, and installed a global catalog server in each site. Because high-priority data are transferred between all offices and the geography of the network spans time zones, it is paramount that you design a site link topology that will maximize the efficiency of your available network bandwidth, optimize Active Directory replication, and provide logon fault tolerance between all four sites. Which of the following methods should you use to connect your sites to maximize the efficiency of your network? (Select the best choice.)

a. Create an IP site link between every site in a mesh topology.

b. Create an SMTP site link between every site in a mesh topology.

c. Connect the four sites with a single IP site link.

d. Connect the four sites with a single SMTP site link.

e. Create an IP site link bridge between every site in a mesh topology.

26. Acme Corporation is an international consulting company with offices located throughout the United States and Europe. The company's enterprise is a Windows 2000 network that is configured as two domains: txglobal.com and europe.acme.com. Each domain includes multiple sites; one site is configured for each office. The sites in the United States are linked by T1 lines. Similarly, the European offices are linked by reliable, high-speed connections. Unfortunately, the link between the United States and Europe is not reliable. What type of link should the Acme Corporation establish between the United States and Europe for Active Directory replication? (Select the best choice.)

a. an IP site link   c. an IP site link bridge

b. an SMTP site link   d. an SMTP site link bridge

HANDS ON-EXERCISES

Exercise 1: Installing Active Directory

Computer A should do the following:

1. To start the Active Directory Installation wizard and to make the stand-alone server into a domain controller, execute the DCPROMO.EXE file. Click on the Start button and select the Run option. Enter DCPROMO in the Open text box and click on the OK button. Click on the Next button.

2. For the Domain Controller Type page, select the "Domain controller for a new domain" option and click on the Next button.

3. For the Create a Tree or Child Domain page, select the "Create a new domain tree" option and click on the Next button.

4. For the Create or Join Forest page, select the "Create a new forest of domain trees" option and click on the Next button.

5. For the New Domain Name page, enter ACMExx.COM in the "Full DNS name for new domain" text box. Click on the Next button.
6. On the NetBIOS Domain Name page, type ACMExx and click on the Next button.
7. On the Database and Log Locations page, leave the default file locations and click on the Next button.
8. On the Shared System Volume page, leave the default location for the SYSVOL folder and click on the Next button.
9. On the Permissions page, select the "Permissions compatible only with Windows 2000 servers" option and click on the Next button.
10. On the Directory Services Restore Mode Administrator Password page, enter the administrator password and click on the Next button.
11. On the Summary page, click on the Next button.
12. Click on the Finish button.
13. After the computer reboots, open the DNS console and notice the SRV records in the form of msdcs and sites folders.

Exercise 2: Adding a Second Domain Controller

Computer B should do the following:

1. To start the Active Directory Installation wizard and to make the stand-alone server into a domain controller, execute the DCPROMO.EXE file. Click on the Start button and select the Run option. Enter DCPROMO in the Open text box and click on the OK button. Click on the Next button.
2. For the Domain Controller Type page, select the "Additional domain controller for an existing domain" option and click on the Next button.
3. For the Create a Tree or Child Domain page, select the "Create a new domain tree" option and click on the Next button.
4. For the Create or Join Forest page, select the "Create a new forest of domain trees" option and click on the Next button.
5. For the New Domain Name page, enter ACMExx.COM in the "Full DNS name for new domain" text box. Click on the Next button.
6. On the NetBIOS Domain Name page, leave the default Domain NetBIOS name and click on the Next button.
7. On the Database and Log Locations page, leave the default file locations and click on the Next button.
8. On the Shared System Volume page, leave the default location for the SYSVOL folder and click on the Next button.
9. On the Configure DNS page, click on the "Yes, install and configure DNS on this computer (recommended)" option and click on the Next button.
10. On the Permissions page, select the "Permissions compatible only with Windows 2000 servers" option and click on the Next button.
11. On the Directory Services Restore Mode Administrator Password page, enter the administrator password and click on the Next button.
12. On the Summary page, click on the Next button.
13. Click on the Finish button.

If you have a DHCP server still running, it will need to be authorized for the domain. To authorize a domain, do the following:

14. From the DHCP console, right-click DHCP and select the "Browse authorized servers" option.
15. In the Authorized Servers in the Directory dialog box, click the Add button.
16. In the Authorized DHCP Server dialog box, enter the name or IP address of the DHCP server to authorize, and then click OK.
17. In the DHCP dialog box, click Yes to confirm the authorization.

Exercise 3: Synchronization with a Time Server

This exercise can only be performed if you are connected to the Internet.

1. Change the date and time to a different value.
2. Start a Command Prompt window and execute the following command:

```
NET TIME /SETSNTP:192.5.41.209
```

3. In the Administrative Tools, start the Services console.
4. Right-click the Windows Time service and select the Start option. Notice the date and time of the system.

CHAPTER 13

Managing Computers, Users, and Groups

Topics Covered in This Chapter

Introduction

Chapter 12 described how Active Directory is installed as a network directory service. Now you are ready to learn how to manage the network by creating and managing users, computers, and groups. In addition, you will learn the first steps to take in securing the network, including setting up passwords and specifying logon times, locations, and Group Policies.

Objectives

- Create a template and use it to create new accounts.
- For a user account, create, configure, and manage user profile and login scripts.
- List and describe the two types of groups.
- List and describe the three types of group scopes.
- Delegate control of an organizational unit to a person or group.
- Move an object from one container to another.
- Implement, configure, manage, and troubleshoot local Group Policy, account settings, and account policies.

- Create and manage local users and groups.
- Implement, configure, manage, and troubleshoot user rights.
- List and describe, in order of priority, the types of group policies.
- Compare and contrast rights and permissions.
- Install applications by using Windows Installer packages.
- Implement, configure, manage, and troubleshoot local user authentication and security configuration.

13.1   USER ACCOUNTS

A **user account** enables a user to log on to a computer and domain with an identity that can be authenticated and authorized for access to domain resources. All users who log on to the network should have their own unique user account and password.

In Windows 2000 and Windows Server 2003, there are two different types of user accounts. The **domain user account** can log on to a domain to gain access to the network resources. A domain controller must authenticate the domain user account. See Figure 13.1. A **local user account** allows users to log on at and gain resources on only the computer where they create such an account. The local user account is stored in the local security database on the computer that the user logs on to. When using a local user account, you will be unable to access any of the network resources except as a peer on a peer-to-peer network. Remember that a local user account is not available to the domain/domain controllers, so, a user cannot log on locally to a domain controller.

13.1.1   Built-In User Accounts

Like Windows NT, Windows 2000 and Windows Server 2003 start with two built-in accounts, the administrator and guest accounts. The administrator account is used to manage the overall computer and domain configuration; create and maintain computers, user accounts, and groups; manage security policies; assign rights and permissions; and create and maintain printers.

Since the administrator account is the most important account within the domain, there should be certain precautions and procedures to follow:

- Since every Windows NT, Windows 2000, and Windows Server 2003 computer begins with having an administrator account, it is a good idea to rename that account. Then, if someone is trying to get into the system, the hacker will have to guess both the name of the administrator and the password. You can only rename the administrator account; you cannot delete it.

459

Figure 13.1   Active Directory Users and Computers console

Figure 13.2   New Object dialog box

■ You should not use the administrator as a general user. Instead, create a second account and use it as a general user and the administrator account for administrative tasks only.

The guest account should be accessible for the occasional users who need to log on and to gain access to resources. The guest account and any other account that performs the same function as the guest account should only be used in low-security networks. Unlike the administrator account, the guest account is disabled by default. If you enable it, you should assign it a password. Similar to the administrator account, you cannot delete it, but you can rename it.

13.1.2   Creating a User Account

To create a domain user account, open Active Directory Users and Computers console and right-click the OU in which you want to create the user account. Click on the New option and click the User option. To create a local user account on a computer, open Computer Management and use Local Users and Groups in System Tools.

In the first dialog box (see Figure 13.2), find the following fields:

- **First name**—User's first name (required)
- **Initials**—User's middle initial
- **Last name**—User's last name (required)
- **Full Name**—User's full name created by combining the first name, initial, and last name. The full name must be unique within the container where you create the user account.
- **User logon name**—The user's unique logon name. The logon name must be unique within the directory.
- **User logon name (pre-Windows 2000)**—The name used in Windows NT domains.

When you click on the Next button, you get to a second dialog box, which defines password requirements. See Figures 13.3 and 13.4. In this dialog box are the following fields:

Figure 13.3   New user's password dialog box

Figure 13.4   Account tab in the User's Properties dialog box

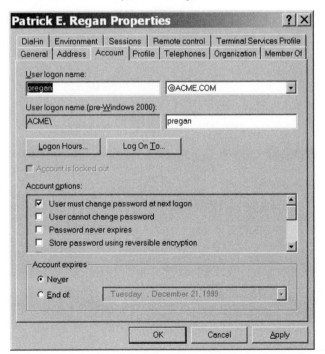

- **Password**—Authenticates the user. Although a password is not required, one should be assigned for greater security. Passwords are case sensitive.
- **Confirm password**—Confirms the password by typing it a second time.
- **User must change password at next logon**—Forces the user to change the password when logging in to authenticate logger use.
- **User cannot change password**—Prohibits any person from a group of people who are using the same user account to change the password. Also allows the administrators to control passwords.
- **Password never expires**—Prohibits a password from being changed, even if a user account is configured to periodically force the user to change the password.
- **Account disabled**—Prevents the use of this account in situations such as when an employee has not yet started or has left the company and no replacement has been assigned.

Under properties of the user are several tabs which can be used for future searches. Use of these fields is recommended. These tabs include the General tab (see Figure 13.5), Address tab, Telephones tab, and Organization tab.

The Account tab is similar to the second dialog box shown during the creation of the user object. From here you can change any of the password requirements and make a password automatically expire on a certain day, for example, a user's last day of work. The logon hours are used to specify when the user can log on during the week. For example, if a user never comes in the middle of the night, then stop the account from logging in during that time. This situation is ideal for temporary workers. The Log On To option is used to specify from which computer the person can log on. See Figure 13.6.

Question: The safety manager of your company was just fired. What should you do?

Answer: Most novice administrator's first reaction would be to immediately delete the account. Although this will prevent the person from accessing the network and causing all kinds of problems, it is probably not the best solution. Prior to making your decision, consider how much time and work goes into maintaining a user account. First, you have to create the account and fill in addresses, phone numbers, and titles. Second, the manager has been assigned to groups and has been given

Figure 13.5 General tab in the User's Properties dialog box

Figure 13.6   (a) User's Logon Hours and (b) Logon Workstations restrictions

rights and permissions to files, printers, and other network resources. It would be a better decision to disable the account, so when a person is hired to replace the safety manager, you can rename the user, reset the password, and reactivate the account. This practice will save time and work, assure managers that they did not miss anything when assigning rights and permissions, and enable the new person to access all old files.

13.1.3   Creating User Templates

Creating multiple user accounts simultaneously can be a long and tedious task. The best method is to create a template and then use it to create the needed accounts. You can only create templates in domains with Active Directory.

Example 1:

Your job is to create 10 users that work for the finance department of your company. The best way is to create a user with the first name of Template and the last name of FinanceUser. You can then preconfigure the Template for FinanceUser with the proper rights, groups, and settings. After the template is finished, you can use the Copy option to create new accounts. Disable the template account when you are finished copying it.

13.1.4   Home Directories

The **home directory** is a folder used to hold or store a user's personal documents. It can be accessed from any Microsoft operating system including DOS and any version of Windows. Although a home directory is typically assigned to an individual user, it can be made available to many users if needed.

The home directory can be stored on the user's computer or in a shared folder on the file server. By having home directories on a file server, users can gain access to their own home directory no matter which computer they are logging in from. In addition, if all home directories are located in one location, it is easy to back up all of the user's data files. Lastly, if the home files are on an NTFS partition, you can further restrict access to the user's personal files. See Figure 13.7.

User Name Guidelines

- User logon domains can contain up to 20 characters (lowercase characters, uppercase characters, digits, and valid nonalphanumeric characters).
- Invalid characters include " / \ [ ] : ; | = , + * ? < and >.
- The user logon name field can accept more than 20 characters, but only the first 20 will be recognized.
- The user logon name is not case sensitive.
- If two employees have duplicate names, add additional letters or numbers to the name to differentiate the two accounts.
- Use a consistent naming convention for all users so that it will be easier to find names that follow a consistent pattern. For example, you can use the first initial, middle initial, and last name or first name and last initial. If you have 100+ employees, however, then perhaps the first name, middle initial, and last name will differentiate all of the users. Create a document stating the naming scheme of user accounts and provide this document to all administrators who create accounts.
- To identify the type of employee, add additional letters at the beginning or end of each name. For example, add a *T* before the name or an *X* at the end to indicate the employee is a temporary or is under contract.

Password Guidelines

- Passwords can be up to 128 characters.
- Set a minimum length of 8 characters.
- Always use passwords that are not obvious. As part of the responsibilities of the administrator, train the employees of your company to not use obvious names.
- Use passwords that combine uppercase characters, lowercase characters, numeral digits, and valid nonalphanumeric characters.
- Invalid characters include " / \ [ ] : ; | = , + * ? < and >.
- Change passwords regularly.

Figure 13.7   Profile tab in the User's Properties dialog box

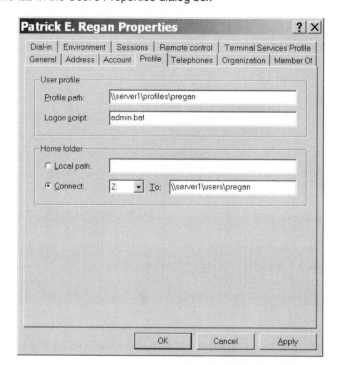

464

From the Active Directory Users and Computers console, right-click the user and click Properties. If the home directory is to be on a file server, then click on the Connect option, specify a drive letter, and enter the UNC path (\\servername\sharename\directory). If the home directory is on the user's computer, however, then click on the Local Path option and enter the drive letter and directory path of the home directory. Note that if you use *%username%* for the last subdirectory in the path, the login user name will be substituted.

To set up a home directory on a network file server, create and share a folder in which to store all home directories on a network server. Typically, this folder is called USERS, but it can be any name that the administrators choose. For the shared folder, remove the default permission Full Control from the Everyone group and assign Full Control to the Users group. This ensures that only users in the Domain Users group can gain access to the shared folder. When you specify the location of the home directory of the user and you specify *%username%* to name a folder on an NTFS volume, the user directory is created with the user's login name, the NTFS Full Control permission is assigned to the user, and all other permissions are removed from the folder including those for the administrator account. For example, if you have just created an account for JGordon and you assign her a home directory of \\SERVER\USERS\%USERNAME%, then a folder\USERS\JGordon will be created on the server disk. (Refer to Chapter 15 for a discussion on NTFS rights.)

13.1.5   User Profiles

A **user profile** is a collection of folders and data that store the user's current desktop environment and application settings. See Table 13.1. A user profile also records all network connections that are established when a user logs on to a computer, such as mapped drives to shared folders on a network server. When users log on to a system, then, they will get the same desktop environment that they had previously on the computer. On computers running Windows 2000, Windows XP, or Windows Server 2003, user profiles are automatically created and maintained on the local computer when users log on to a computer for the first time. See Figure 13.8.

The three types of user profiles are as follows:

- **Local user profile**—Created the first time you log on to a computer and stored on a computer's local hard disk (C:\Documents and Settings*user_logon_name folder*). Any changes made to your local user profile are specific to the computer on which you made the changes.
- **Roaming user profile**—Created and stored on a server. Since the profile is on a server, it can be accessed from any computer. Therefore, this profile is available every time you log on to any computer on the network.
- **Mandatory user profile**—Used as a roaming profile to specify particular settings for individuals or an entire group of users. When the user logs off, Windows does not save any changes that the user made during the session. Mandatory user profile can only be changed by the administrator.

Another important user profile is the default user profile. It serves as the basis for all user profiles. Every user profile begins as a copy of the default user profile, which is stored on each computer running Windows 2000, Windows XP, or Windows Server 2003. To set up the default user profile, follow these steps:

1. Create a user account, which will be used as the default user account template.
2. Log on to the default user account template.
3. Configure the desktop environment in regard to desktop appearance, network connections, applications, shortcuts, and Start menu items. Add printers and map necessary drives. Note: Also add a video system similar to that of the clients that will be using the template.
4. Log off so that Windows creates a user profile on the computer in the login user name profile folder (C:\Documents and Settings*default_user_logon_name)*. This directory will be used for default profile.
5. Click Start, point to Settings, and click Control Panel. Then double-click System.

Table 13.1   Profile Folders

Source	Parameters Saved
Accessories	All user-specific program settings affecting the user's Windows environment, including Calculator, Clock, Notepad, and Paint
Application Data and Registry Hive	Application data and user-defined configuration settings such as a custom dictionary. The program manufacturer decides what data to store in the User profile folder.
Cookies	Cookies store user information and preferences. Cookies are mostly generated when using a browser such as by Microsoft Internet Explorer.
Control Panel	All user-defined settings made in Control Panel
Desktop Contents	Items stored on the desktop including files, shortcuts, and folders
Favorites	Shortcuts to favorite locations on the Internet
Mapped Network Drive	Any user-created mapped network drives
My Documents	User-stored documents. The My Documents shortcut can be redirected to the home directory.
My Network Places	The NetHood folder stores shortcuts to other computers on the network.
My Pictures	User-stored picture items
Online User Education Bookmarks	Any bookmarks placed in the Windows Help system.
Printer Settings	Printhood folder stores shortcuts to defined network printer connections
Screen Colors and Fonts	All user-definable computer screen colors and display text settings
Start Menu	Shortcuts to program items stored in the Start menu. There are several parts to the Start menu (user start menu, all user start menu, and default start menu), which are merged into the Start menu that is shown to the user.
Templates	User template items
Windows Explorer	All user-definable settings for Windows Explorer
Windows 2000–Based Programs	Any program written specifically for Windows can be designed so that it tracks program settings on a per-user basis. If this information exists, it is saved in the User profile folder.

6. If you are using Windows XP or Windows Server 2003, select the Advanced tab and click on the Settings button located in the User Profiles section. If it is Windows 2000, select the User Profiles tab. See Figure 13.9.

7. Click the user profile that you just created, then click Copy To. In the Copy To dialog box, under Copy profile to, click Browse, click the \Documents and Settings\Default User folder, then click OK. Click Yes when you are prompted to continue, then click OK.

8. Under Permitted to use, click Change, click Everyone, and then click OK.

When you create new users, they will automatically start with the settings that you just saved as the default user profile.

Now, to create the roaming profile, follow these steps:

1. You must first set up a directory to hold the roaming profiles. Therefore, you need to create a shared folder to hold the roaming profile. Typically the folder name is Profile, although it can be named anything. Next, share the folder and provide users with the Full Control permission

Figure 13.8   Microsoft Explorer showing a user's profile

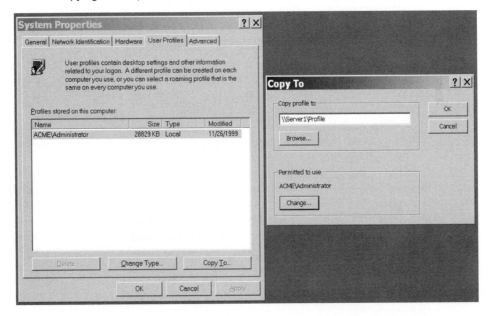

Figure 13.9   Copying a user profile

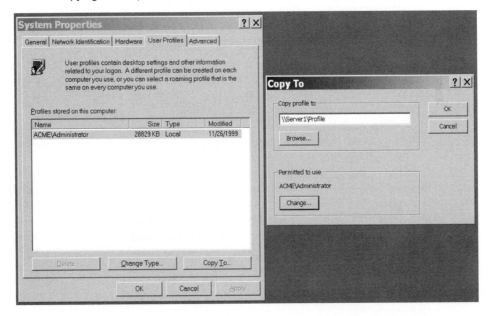

to the folder. Note: The user profile path location can be on any server; it does not have to be a domain controller.

2. From Administrative tools, open the Active Directory Users and Computers console.

3. In the details section, right-click the applicable user account and select the Properties option.

4. In the Properties dialog box, click the Profile tab.

5. In the Profile Path text box, type the *servername**profile_sharename*\\%username%.

When the user logs on, Windows checks the user's account to see if a user profile path exists. If it does, the user profile is located by the system and copied to the local computer. Any changes that you make will be copied back when you log out.

To create a mandatory profile, perform the following steps:

1. On a domain controller, create a template user account that has the same permission as the user or the group for which you want to create the mandatory profile.
2. Use the template user account to log on to a workstation computer. A user profile is automatically created on the local computer in the *Drive:*\Documents and Settings*User_name* folder.
3. Configure the desktop settings that you want to use in the profile, including shortcuts, appearance, and Start menu options.
4. Log off the computer
5. Create a shared folder on the network in which you want to store the mandatory profile; for example, C:\Profiles\Mandatory; then share this folder, for example, create the following share:*servername*\mandatory.
6. Assign at least Read & Execute permissions for users or groups to whom you want to assign the profile.
7. Log on to the domain as an administrator from the workstation computer.
8. Click Start, point to Settings, and click Control Panel. Then double-click System.
9. If you are using Windows XP or Windows Server 2003, select the Advanced tab and click on the Setting button located in the User Profiles section. If it is Windows 2000, select the User Profiles tab.
10. Click the user profile that you just created, then click Copy To. In the Copy To dialog box, under Copy profile to, click Browse, click the \Documents and Settings\Default User folder, and then click OK. Click Yes when you are prompted to continue, then click OK.
11. On the server computer that is holding the profile, start Windows Explorer and locate the shared folder that contains the profile that you copied. Rename NTUSER.DAT to NTUSER.MAN. The NTUSER.DAT file in the user's profile folder is the registry portion of the user profile.
12. Open the Administrative Tolls and open the Access the Active Directory Users and Computers console.
13. Locate the container that contains the user account whose settings you want to modify.
14. In the right pane, right-click the user account that you want to configure, then click Properties.
15. Select the Profile tab.
16. In the Profile path box, type the location of the profile that you want to assign (*servername**sharename*). Click the OK button.
17. On the workstation computer, log on to the domain by using the account to which you have assigned the mandatory profile, then test to make sure that the profile settings have been successfully applied.

In installations that are upgrades from Windows NT, the NTUSER.DAT file is stored in the *systemroot*\Profiles\username folder. You can also create a profile for Windows 9X machines. Instead of NTUSER.DAT, use USER.DAT FILE for a roaming profile and USER.MAN for the mandatory profile. To create the profile on a Windows 9X client, copy the profile folder to the network server.

13.1.6 User State Migration

Let's say that you have been using a computer for a year or so and you decide to purchase a faster computer. Of course, you don't want to lose any information that you currently have on your old machine; instead; you would like to transfer that information to the new machine. Starting with Windows XP, Windows includes two tools to migrate your files and settings:

- **Files and Settings Transfer Wizard**—Designed for home users and small office users. The wizard is also useful in a corporate network environment for employees who get a new computer and need to migrate their files and settings without the support of an IT department or help desk.

■ **User State migration Tool(USMT)**—Designed for IT administrators in performing large deployments of Windows XP Professional in a corporate environment. The USMT provides the same functionality as the wizard, but on a large scale targeted at migrating multiple users. This tool gives administrators command-line precision in customizing specific settings such as unique modifications to the registry.

The Files and Settings Transfer wizard helps you move your data files and personal settings from your old computer to your new one without having to go through much of the same configuration you did with your old computer. For example, you can take your personal display properties, folder and taskbar options, and Internet browser and mail settings from your old computer and place them on the new one. The wizard will also move specific files or entire folders, such as My Documents, My Pictures, and Favorites. To open the Files and Settings Transfer wizard click start, point to All Programs, point to Accessories, point to Systems Tools, and then click Files and Settings Transfer Wizard.

The User State Migration Tool provides the same functionality as the Files and Settings Transfer wizard plus the ability for administrators to fully customize specific settings such as unique modifications to the registry. The USMT is designed for administrators only, not for individual users. In addition, the USMT requires a client computer that is connected to a Windows server domain controller.

The USMTool consists of two executable files, SCANSTATE.EXE and LOADSTATE.EXE, and four migration rule information files, Migapp.INF, Migsys.INF, Miguser.INF, and Sysfiles.INF. SCANSTATE.EXE collects user data and settings based on the information contained in Migapp.INF, Migsys.INF, Miguser.INF, and Sysfiles.INF. LOADSTATE.EXE deposits this user state data on a computer running a fresh (not upgraded) installation of Windows XP Professional. Both of these tools can be found on the Windows XP CD in the \valueadd\msft\usmt\folder.

If you want to modify the default parameters in Sysfiles.INF, follow these steps:

1. Identify which application settings to migrate.
2. Identify which file types, folders, or specific files to migrate.
3. Locate these settings and files and create a migration rule INF file for them.
4. Run SCANSTATE.EXE to copy the user state data to an intermediate store. You can send a shortcut to the script to the users and instruct them to run it when they leave for the evening, or you can deploy the script automatically or on a schedule.
5. Reformat the disk and install Windows XP Professional and any necessary applications. This process can be automated by using disk-imaging software.
6. Run LOADSTATE.EXE as administrator to restore the user settings. (You can do this as a scheduled task running in the administrator context.) When the user logs on, the last of the user state data is reset.

The syntax for the SCANSTATE.EXE command is as follows:

```
Scanstate[/c/i input.inf] [/l scanstate.log] [/v verbosity_level]
[/f] [/u] [/x] migration_path
```

■ /c—Continues past "filename too long" errors. Logs files in Longfile.log.
■ /i—Specifies an INF file containing rules that define which user state data to collect. Multiple INF files can be specified.
■ /l—Specifies a file in which to log errors.
■ /v—Enables verbose output. The syntax is /v # where # is 1 to 7, with 1 being the least verbose, and 7 being the most.
■ /f—Specifies that files will be migrated. This is a switch for troubleshooting only.
■ /u—Specifies that user settings will be migrated. This is a switch for troubleshooting only.
■ /x—Specifies that no files or settings should be migrated.

For example:

```
Scanstate \\fileserver\migration\ pat /i \migapp.inf /i
\migsys.inf /i \miguser.inf /i \sysfiles.inf /i \files.inf
```

By default, user settings, system settings, and files are migrated. Use the /u, /f, and /x flags only for troubleshooting. Multiple migration rule INF files can be specified. If you specify more than one, the Sysfiles.inf migration rule information file must be included.

The syntax for LoadState is as follows:

```
loadstate[/i input.inf] [/l loadstate.log] [/v #] [/f] [/u] [/x]
migration_path
```

- **/i**—Specifies an INF file containing rules to define what state to migrate. Multiple INF files can be specified.
- **/l**—Specifies a file in which to log errors.
- **/v**—Enables verbose output. The syntax is /v # where # is 1 to 7, with 1 being the least verbose and 7 being the most.
- **/f**—Specifies that files will be migrated. This is a switch for troubleshooting only.
- **/u**—Specifies that user settings will be migrated. This is a switch for troubleshooting only.
- **/x**—Specifies that no files or settings will be migrated. This is a switch for troubleshooting only.
- migration_path—A path to the location from which the files should be read.

For example:

```
loadstate \\fileserver\migration\elizabeth /i \miguser.inf
```

By default, user settings, system settings, and files are migrated. The /u, /f, and /x flags should only be used for troubleshooting. Multiple migration rule INF files can be specified.

13.2 GROUPS

A **group** is a collection of user accounts. Groups are tools that help simplify administration. When you assign users, and rights and permissions, to a group, those rights and permissions apply to everyone in the group. Users can be members of multiple groups and groups can belong to other groups. They are, however, not containers of users and other objects. Instead, a group is an object that lists the members. For example, if you delete the group, the members of the group are not deleted, but their rights and permissions that have been assigned to the group are lost.

In Windows 2000, and Windows Server 2003, there are two group types, security and distribution. The **security group** is used to assign permissions and gain access to resources. This group can also be used for nonsecurity purposes such as those that you would find in a distribution group. The **distribution group** is used only for nonsecurity functions such as those used to distribute e-mail messages to many people. Typically, distribution groups are used only for specific applications such as the Microsoft Exchange Mail Server.

The security group can be divided into **group scopes,** which define how the permissions and rights are assigned to the group. In Windows 2000 and Windows Server 2003, there are three scopes—global group, domain local group, and universal group.

13.2.1 Global and Domain Local Group Scopes

Global groups are primarily used to group people within a domain. Thus, user accounts and global groups are listed from their domain. The global group can be assigned access to resources in any domain. Although rights and permissions assignments are valid only within the domain in which they are assigned, by applying groups with global scope uniformly across the appropriate domains, you can consolidate references to accounts with similar purposes.

Using global groups helps to manage directory objects that require daily maintenance, such as user and computer accounts. Because groups with global scope are not replicated outside of their own domain, accounts in a group having global scope can be changed frequently without generating replication traffic to the global catalog.

The **domain local group** is primarily used to assign rights and permissions to network resources that are in the domain of the local group. Different from global groups, domain local groups can list user accounts, universal groups, and global groups from any domain and local groups from the same domain. See Figure 13.10.

Figure 13.10   Users are grouped together in global groups. The global groups are assigned to the domain local groups, and the domain local groups are assigned permissions to the network resources.

Example 2:

Say, for example, that we have a printer and some files to be accessed in the SALES domain. We have users in the FINANCE and SALES domains that need to access these resources.

- First, create two global groups called ANALYSTS and MANAGERS in the FINANCE domain and create a global group called SALESPEOPLE in the SALES domain. Then assign the respective users from the FINANCE domain to the ANALYSTS group and MANAGERS group, and the users from the SALES domain to the SALES-PEOPLE group.
- Next, create a domain local group called SALES_RESOURCES in the SALES domain. Assign rights and permissions to the SALES_RESOURCES group to the printer and directories in the SALES domain.
- You can then assign users from either domain and assign the ANALYSTS group, MAN-AGER group, and SALESPEOPLE group. Since groups consist of many people, it is best to assign the groups first. Then if you still have certain individuals that need different or special access, you can assign them as needed.

As you can see, the global groups are used to group people with common purposes or that have the need for the same rights and permissions. The advantage of using this scheme is that when you add members to the two global groups, they automatically get access to the resources.

13.2.2 Universal Groups

The universal security group was introduced in Windows 2000 and is only available in native mode (not mixed mode), which means there are no Windows NT domain controllers, only Windows 2000 and Windows Server 2003 domain controllers. In a mixed-mode network, the Universal Group option will be grayed out. It can contain users, universal groups, and global groups from any domain and it can be assigned rights and permissions to any network resource in any domain in the domain tree or forest. Thus, the universal group is much easier to use and is more flexible than global and local domain groups.

To avoid unnecessary replication traffic in the global catalog by frequently changing group memberships, nest global groups within universal groups and make membership changes in the global groups. This leaves the universal group membership static (thereby avoiding the need to replicate membership changes in the global catalog) and enables administrators to make changes frequently to global groups (global group membership is replicated only within the domain). To reduce the size of the universal group, instead of putting users in the universal group, assign the users to the global group and assign the global groups to the universal group. Although global and domain local groups are listed in the global catalog, their members are not. As a result, the replication traffic needed to keep the global catalog up-to-date will be reduced.

You can change a global group into a universal group if the global group is not a member of another global group. You can change a domain local group to a universal group if it does not contain another domain local group.

13.2.3 Nesting groups

Having a group listed in another group is called nesting. Nesting consolidates groups, reduces network traffic between domains, and simplifies administration in a domain tree. In domains in mixed mode, nesting is supported only for distribution groups. In domains in native mode, nesting is supported for both distributed groups and security groups.

Nesting can be an efficient way to handle large memberships as well as delegate management of group membership. For example, the top group could be a universal group that contains only global groups. The domain administrators of the domains containing those global groups can manage the membership within their own domains. The enterprise administrator can simply manage the global group membership of the universal group (i.e, adding and removing global groups) and let the domain administrators handle the membership requests from users in their own domains.

When nestings groups, try to minimize the levels of nesting; one level of nesting is the most effective. Tracking permissions and troubleshooting become much more complex with multiple levels of nesting.

13.2.4 Creating Groups

To create a group, use the Active Directory Users and Computers console or the MMC by using the Active Directory Users and Computers snap-in. To create a group, do the following:

1. Open the Active Directory Users and Computers console.
2. Right-click on the organizational unit in which you want to create the group, and click on the New option and then on the Group option. See Figure 13.11.
3. Enter the group name, enter the pre-Windows 2000 group name, and select the group scope and group type. Click on the OK button.
4. To add people to the list or to assign users and groups to a group, right-click on the group and select the Properties option. See Figure 13.12. You can then use the assign rights and permissions to groups. See Figure 13.13.

When choosing a group name, use intuitive names. A name can contain up to 256 uppercase or lowercase characters except for the following:

" / \ [ ] : ; | = , + * ? < >

Figure 13.11   Creating a group

Figure 13.12   Group properties

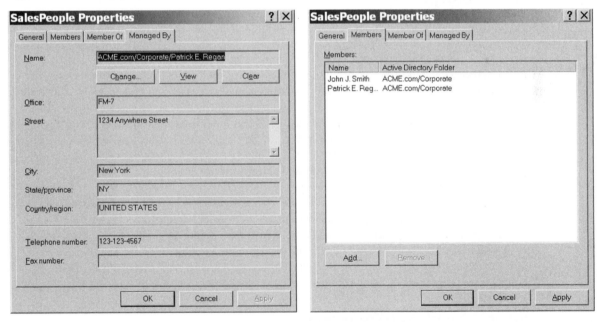

A group name cannot consist solely of periods (.) or spaces. A group name cannot be identical to any other group or user name on the domain. Thus, if you need the domains to have the same name, you must utilize a consistent naming scheme instead. For example, if you need a Managers group for each domain, create the names with the domain name built in, for example, Managers LA and Managers NY.

Figure 13.13   Assign permissions to users and groups

To help identify groups, they are assigned unique security identifiers (SIDs), much like SIDs assigned to domain controllers. If you delete a group and re-create a group with the same name, the second group would have a different SID. Since these are different groups, the users, rights, and permissions will have to be reassigned.

13.2.5   Built-In Groups

Similar to the administrator and guest accounts, Windows 2000 and Windows Server 2003 have default groups called built-in groups. These default groups have been granted a useful collection of rights and permissions. Using built-in groups can save the administrator both time and effort. They have been carefully designed to help users perform common duties such as performing backups or managing printers. There are four categories of built-in groups: global, domain local, local, and system. See boxed material for more information.

Like a global group that you create, a built-in global group is used to group common types of users. In addition, the domain local group is used to assign rights and permissions to various network resources. The only difference is that by default, Windows automatically assigns members to some of these groups and has already assigned rights and permissions to these groups. Therefore, any member of these groups will automatically have these rights and permissions.

Built-in local groups exist for any computer that is running Windows 2000 or Windows Server 2003 (including stand-alone servers, member servers, domain controllers, and workstations). Built-in local groups have rights to perform system tasks on a single computer.

The built-in system groups exist on all computers running Windows 2000 or Windows Server 2003. Unlike the other groups, the membership of the built-in system groups cannot be modified. Therefore, you do not see system groups when you administer groups unless you are adding that group to another group.

13.3   COMPUTER ACCOUNTS

Computers that are running Windows NT, Windows 2000, or Windows Server 2003, are, by design, much more secure than Windows 9X. For example, to use the computer, you must log on to the computer with a user name and password. If you do not log on, you cannot bypass the logon screen by pressing the Escape key and so access the computer's files and programs, or access any network resources.

BUILT-IN GLOBAL GROUP

Domain Admins—Admins can perform administrative tasks on any computer within the domain. By default, the Administrator account is a member.
Domain Guests—Windows automatically adds Domain Guests to the Guests domain local group. By default, the Guest account is a member.
Domain Users—Windows automatically adds each new domain user account to the Domain Users group.
Enterprise Admins—This is used to group administrators that need to have administrative control over the entire network (all domains). For this to happen, the Enterprise Admins must be added to the Administrators domain local groups. By default, the Administrator account is a member.

BUILT-IN DOMAIN LOCAL GROUPS

Account Operators—Members can create, delete, and modify user accounts and groups. Note that members cannot modify the Administrators group or any of the operators groups.
Administrators—Members can perform all administrative tasks on all domain controls and the domain itself. By default, the Administrative user account and the Domain Admins global group are members.
Backup Operators—Members can back up and restore all domain controllers by using Windows Backup.
Guests—Members can perform only tasks for which they have been granted rights. By default, the Guest user account and the Domain Guests global group are members.
Print Operator—Members can set up and manage network printers on domain controllers.
Server Operators—Members can share disk resources and back up and restore files on a domain controller.
Users—Members can perform only tasks for which you have granted rights and gain access only to resources for which you have assigned permissions. By default, the Domain Users group is a member. Use this group to assign permissions and rights that every user with a user account in your domain should have.

BUILT-IN LOCAL GROUPS

Administrators—Members of the Administrator group have full control over the computer. It is the only built-in group that is automatically granted every built-in right and ability in the system so that members can install, upgrade, and configure the operating system.
Backup Operator—Members of the Backup Operators group can back up and restore files on the computer, regardless of any permissions that protect those files. They can also log on to the computer and shut it down, but they cannot change security settings.
Power Users—Members of the Power Users group can create user accounts, but can modify and delete only those accounts they create. They can create local groups and remove users from local groups they have created. They can also remove users from the Power Users, Users, and Guests groups. They can install and remove applications except those reserved for administrators and they can configure printers, Date/Time options, power options, and Control Panel resources. They cannot modify the Administrators or Backup Operators groups, nor can they take ownership of files, back up or restore directories, load or unload device drivers, or manage the security and auditing logs.
Users—Members of the Users group can perform most common tasks, such as running applications, using local and network printers, and shutting down and locking the workstation. Users can create local groups, but can modify only the local groups that they created. Users cannot share directories or create local printers.
Guests—The Guests group allows occasional or one-time users to log on to a workstation's built-in Guest account and be granted limited abilities. Members of the Guests group can also shut down the system.
Replicator—The Replicator group supports directory replication functions. The only member of the Replicator group should be a domain user account used to log on the Replicator services of the domain controller. Do not add the user accounts of actual users to this group.

BUILT-IN SYSTEMS GROUP

Anonymous Logon—Includes any user account that Windows did not authenticate. Primarily used in web and FTP servers.

Continued

> **BUILT-IN GLOBAL GROUP** (continued)
>
> **Authenticated Users**—Includes all users with a valid user account on the computer or in Active Directory. Use the Authenticated Users group instead of the Everyone group to prevent anonymous access to a resource.
>
> **Creator Owner**—Includes the user account for the user who created or took ownership of a resource. If a member of the Administrators group creates a resource, the Administrators group is owner of the resource.
>
> **Dialup**—Includes any user who currently has a dial-up connection.
>
> **Everyone**—All users who access the computer. Be careful if you assign permissions to the Everyone group and enable the Guest account. Windows will authenticate a user who does not have a valid user account as Guest. The user automatically gets all rights and permissions that you have assigned to the Everyone group.
>
> **Interactive**—Includes the user account for the user who is logged on at the computer. Members of the Interactive group gain access to resources on the computer at which they are physically located. They log on and gain access to resources by "interacting" with the computer.
>
> **Network**—Includes any user with a current connection from another computer on the network to a shared resource on the computer.

To use a Windows NT, Windows 2000 or Windows server 2003 computer that is not a domain controller, create a computer account, which is used to uniquely identify the computer on the domain. By having the computer account, you can then audit the computer to ensure that only authorized people who have access to the computer can assign permissions to gain access to network resources.

A computer account, which matches the name of the computer, is an account created by an administrator to uniquely identify the computer on the domain. By being able to identify the computer, a secure communications channel can be created between the client computer and the domain controller. The computer account also allows the administrator to remotely manage the computer user environment and manage the computer user and group accounts.

To create a computer account, do the following:

1. Start the Active Directory User and Computers console or snap-in.
2. Right-click on the container in which you want to create the computer account.
3. Enter the name of the computer.
4. Click on the OK button.

Before you click on the OK button, there is one other option to consider. In Figure 13.14, the following user or group can join this computer to a domain text box which specifies the person(s) who can actually

Figure 13.14 Creating a computer object

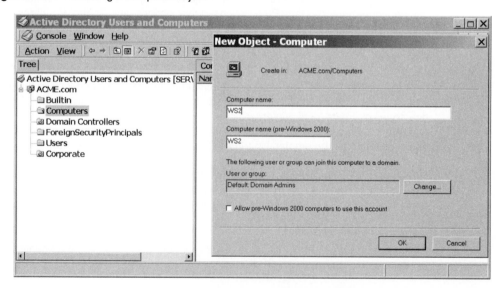

join the computer to the domain. This person will then go to the computer and add the computer to the domain, and would at that time provide a user name and password to make sure that only authorized people can add the computer.

13.4   MOVING OBJECTS

To move an object—including an organizational unit with the same domain, user, or computer—right-click the object and select the Move option. Then select the container where you want to move it and click on the OK button. To move organizational units between domains in the same forest, use MOVETREE, which comes with the Resource Kit. To move an object between two containers, the person performing the move must have the ability to create the object in the destination container and to delete the object from the source container. You can move multiple objects at the same time.

When you move an object, the object is first moved to the LostandFound container, then it is moved to its destination. If you move an object from an OU into another OU, but at another domain controller that destination OU has been deleted, the moved object would remain in the LostandFound container.

When you move the object, permissions that are assigned directly to the object remain the same. Since the object is now in a new OU, it inherits the new permissions from the parent container. In addition, moving a user object, computer object, or a subtree containing user or computer objects can change the Group Policy that is applied to those objects. Note: You must have the proper permissions to move an object. Group policies and permissions are explained later in this chapter.

13.5   MANAGING SECURITY SETTINGS

One important feature of any network is security. The network administrator is ultimately responsible for the network security. Windows 2000 and Windows Server 2003 provide many levels of security:

- User names and passwords
- Account restrictions
- Mandatory user profiles
- Group policies
- Rights and permissions
- Auditing

The user name and password are the first line of defense, as every user requires these to get access to the network and its resources. For the password to be effective, the administrator sets guidelines and policies on how the user should use the network, provides training in these guidelines, and provides frequent reminders. These guidelines include the following:

- Do not give your password to anyone.
- Change your password frequently.
- Do not use obvious or easy passwords.
- Keep people from seeing you type in your password.
- When you leave your computer unattended, log off from the computer.
- Use a password-protected screen saver.
- If you see a security problem or a potential security problem, report it to the network administrator.

Account restrictions, which specify where a user can log on to and which computer a user can log on from, was discussed in Section 13.1.2. Mandatory user profiles, which limit permanently modifying the desktop properties, were discussed in Section 13.1.5. Auditing will be discussed in Chapter 23.

13.6   RIGHTS

A **right** authorizes a user to perform certain actions on a computer, such as logging on to a system interactively or backing up files and directories. Administrators can assign specific rights to individual user accounts or group accounts. Rights are managed with the User Rights policy. Some of the popular user rights are shown in Table 13.2. User rights can be found by opening the Group Policy, opening Computer Configuration, opening Windows Settings, opening Security Settings, opening Local Policies, and then opening User Rights Assignment.

Although rights can be assigned in any group policy (site or domain controller, domain and organizational unit), default rights are assigned at the default domain controller group policy. The other group policies (domain and organizational unit) have no rights assigned by default. For example, the domain controller group policy has the Allow Log on Locally right, which is used to be able to logon directly on the computer, which is assigned to account operator, backup operator, print operator, server operator, and administrators. Yet to Take Ownership of a File or Other Object right is only assigned to the administrators. Note: Windows Server 2003 has a Domain Controller Security Policy console available in administrative tools.

NOTE: To make the changes to rights effective immediately, you must run one of the following commands:

■ Windows 2000:

```
SECEDIT /REFRESHPOLICY MACHINE_POLICY
```

■ Windows server 2003:

```
GPUPDATE /FORCE
```

To simplify the administration of rights, user rights are best administered by using groups. If a user is a member of multiple groups, the user's rights are cumulative, which means that the user has more than one set of rights. The only time that rights assigned to one group may conflict with those assigned to another is in the case of certain logon rights. In general, however, user rights assigned to one group do not conflict with those assigned to another group. To remove rights from a user, the administrator simply removes the user from the group. In this case, the user no longer has the rights assigned to that group.

13.7   PERMISSIONS

A **permission** defines the type of access that is granted to an object or object attribute. The permissions that are available for an object depend on the type of object. For example, a user has different permissions than a printer. When a user or service tries to access an object, its access will be granted or denied by an object manager. Common object managers are shown in Table 13.3.

Computers, users, and groups are assigned a security identifier (SID). Similar to the SID that is assigned to a domain, a SID assigned to a computer, user, or group is a unique alphanumeric structure. The first part of the SID identifies the domain in which the SID was issued and the second part identifies an account object within the domain. Therefore, when a computer, user, or group accesses an object, all three are identified by their SID and not their user name. If the name of the computer, user, or group changes, the SID still identifies the object.

Each object uses an access control list (ACL) to list users and groups. The ACL is divided into discretionary access control lists (DACLs) and system access control lists (SACLs). The DACL contains the access control permissions for an object and its attributes, and the SIDs, which can use the object. The permissions and rights that a user has are referred to as access control entries (ACEs). The SACL contains events that can be audited for an object. The ACEs include Deny Access and Grant Access.

Every object in Active Directory has an owner who controls how permissions are set on an object and to whom permissions are assigned. The person who creates the object automatically

Table 13.2 Windows user rights

User Rights	Description	Groups Assigned This Right by Default
Access this computer from a network	Allows the user to connect to the computer over the network	Administrators, Everyone, and Power Users
Add workstations to domain	Allows the user to add a computer to a specific domain. The user specifies the domain through an administrative user interface on the computer being added, creating an object in the Computer container of Active Directory. The behavior of this privilege is duplicated in Windows by another access control mechanism (permissions attached to the Computer container or organizational unit).	Authenticated Users
Allow logon locally	Allows a user to log on at the computer's keyboard. Since most protection can be bypassed by being able to log on directly to a machine without going through the network, this right should only be given to a few people.	Administrators, Account Operators. Backup Operators, Print Operators, and Server Operators
Back up files and directories	Allows the user to circumvent file and directory permissions to back up the system. Specifically, the privilege is similar to granting the following permissions on all files and folders on the local computer: Traverse Folder/Execute File, List Folder/Read Data, Read Attributes, Read Extended Attributes, and Read Permissions. See also *Restore files and directories.*	Administrators, Backup Operators
Change the system time	Allows the user to set the time for the internal clock of the computer	Administrators, Power Users
Create a page file	Allows the user to create and change the size of a page file. This is done by specifying a paging file size for a given drive in the System Properties Performance options.	Administrators
Debug programs	Allows the user to attach a debugger to any process. This privilege provides powerful access to sensitive and critical system operating components.	Administrators
Enable Trusted for Delegation on user and computer accounts	Allows the user to set the Trusted for Delegation setting on a user or computer object. The user or object that is granted this privilege must have write access to the account control flags on the user or computer object. A server process either running on a computer that is trusted for delegation or running by a user that is trusted for delegation can access resources on another computer. This uses a client's delegated credentials, as long as the client account does not have the Account Cannot Be Delegated account control flag set. Misuse of this privilege or of the Trusted for Delegation settings could make the network vulnerable to sophisticated attacks using Trojan horse programs that impersonate incoming clients and use their credentials to gain access to network resources.	Administrators
Force shutdown from a remote system	Allows a user to shut down a computer from a remote location on the network. See also the *Shut Down the System* privilege.	Administrators
Increase quotas	Allows a process with write property access to another process to increase the processor quota assigned to that other process. This privilege is useful for system tuning, but can be abused, as in a denial-of-service attack.	Administrators

Continued

Table 13.2 Continued

User Rights	Description	Groups Assigned This Right by Default
Load and unload device drivers	Allows a user to install and uninstall plug-and-play device drivers. Device drivers that are not plug-and-play are not affected by this privilege and can only be installed by administrators. Since device drivers run as trusted (highly privileged) programs, this privilege could be misused to install hostile programs and give these programs destructive access to resources.	Administrators
Manage auditing and security log	Allows a user to specify the object access auditing options for individual resources such as files, Active Directory objects, and registry keys. Object access auditing is not actually performed unless you have enabled it in the computerwide audit policy settings under Group Policy or under Group Policy defined in Active Directory. This privilege does not grant access to the computerwide audit policy. A user with this privilege can also view and clear the security log from the Event Viewer.	Administrators
Modify firmware environment values	Allows modification of the system environment variables, either by a user through the System Properties or by a process.	Administrators
Profile a single process	Allows a user to use Windows NT, Windows 2000 and Windows Server 2003 performance-monitoring tools to monitor the performance of nonsystem processes.	Administrators, Power Users
Profile system performance	Allows a user to use Windows NT, Windows 2000 and Windows Server 2003 performance-monitoring tools to monitor the performance of system processes.	Administrators
Restore files and directories	Allows a user to circumvent file and directory permissions when restoring backed up files and directories, and to set any valid security principal as the owner of an object. See also the *Back up files and directories* privilege.	Administrators, Backup Operators
Shut down the system	Allows a user to shut down the local computer.	Administrators, Backup Operators, Everyone, Power Users, and Users
Take ownership of files or other objects	Allows a user to take ownership of any securable object in the system, including Active Directory objects, files and folders, printers, registry keys, processes, and threads.	Administrators

Table 13.3 Common object types

Object Type	Object Manager	Management Tool
Files and Folders	NTFS	Windows Explorer
Shares	Server service	Windows Explorer
Active Directory Objects	Active Directory	Active Directory Users and Computers console or snap-in
Registry Keys	The registry	Registry Editor (REGEDT32.EXE)
Services	Service controllers	Security Templates, Security Configuration, and Analysis
Printer	Print spooler	Printer folder

Table 13.4   Standard permissions

Object Permission	Description
Full Control	Contains all permissions for the object, including take ownership
Read	Users can view objects and object attributes, including the object owner and the Active Directory permissions
Write	Enables users to change all object attributes
Create All Child Objects	Enables Users to add any child object to an OU
Delete All Child Objects	Enables users to delete any child object from an OU

becomes the owner and by default, has full control over the object, even if the ACL does not grant that owner access. If a member of the Administrators group creates an object or takes ownership of an object, then the Administrators group becomes the object group. A member of the Domain Administrator group has the ability to take ownership of any object in the domain and then change permissions.

Standard permissions are the most common and frequently assigned permissions that apply to the entire object. Assigning standard permissions is sufficient for most administrative tasks. The standard permissions are divided into special permissions, which provide a finer degree of control. See Table 13.4.

Explicit permissions are those specifically given to the object when the object is created or assigned by another user. Inherited permissions are those rights that are given to a container and that apply to all child objects under the container. By using inherited permissions, you can manage them more easily and can ensure consistency of permissions among all objects within a given container.

To add or change the permission for an object, do the following:

1. Using the Active Directory Users and Computers console, enable the Advanced Features option.
2. Right-click the object, select the Properties option, and click on the Security tab.
3. To add a new permission, click the Add button and click the user account or group to which you want to assign permissions, click Add, then click on the OK button.
4. In the Permissions box, click on the Allow or Deny check boxes for each permission that you want to add or remove. See Figure 13.15.

The permissions can be allowed or denied for each user or group. To explicitly allow or deny the permission, click the appropriate check box. If a check box is shaded, the permission was granted to the user or group for a container that the object is in and the permission was inherited. If the allow or deny box is not checked for a permission, then the permission may still be granted from a group. You would then have to check which groups the user or group is a member of to determine if the rights are granted or denied.

To view special permissions, do the following:

1. Right-click the object, click on the Security tab, and click on the Advanced button.
2. In the Access Control Settings dialog box on the Permission tab, click the entries that you want to view, and click on the View/Edit button.
3. In the Apply Onto: box, select where the permissions are to be applied.
4. Select or deselect the desired permissions. See Figure 13.16.

Every object, whether in the Active Directory or an NTFS volume, has an owner. The owner controls how permissions are set on the object and to whom permissions are granted. When an object is created, the person creating the object automatically becomes the owner. Administrators create and own most objects in Active Directory and on network servers (when installing programs on the server). Users create and own data files in their home directories, as well as on network servers.

Figure 13.15 Add or change the permission of the user object

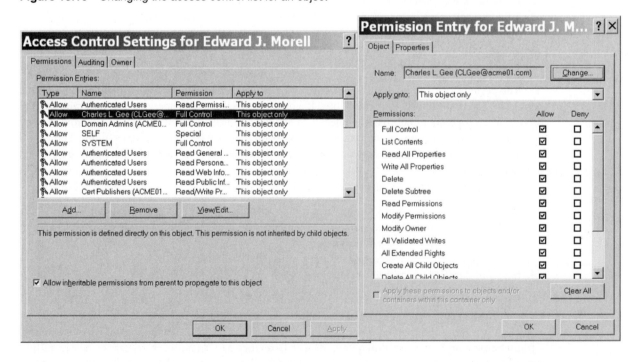

Figure 13.16 Changing the access control list for an object

Figure 13.17   Taking ownership of an object

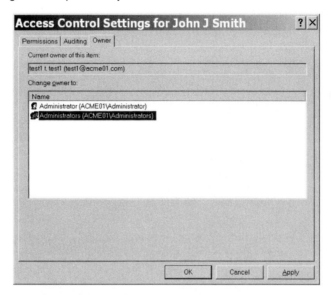

Ownership can be transferred in the following ways:

- The current owner can grant the take ownership permission to other users, allowing those users to take ownership at any time.
- An administrator can take ownership of any object under his or her administrative control. For example, if an employee leaves the company suddenly, the administrator can take control of the employee's files.

Although administrators can take ownership, they cannot transfer ownership to others. This restriction keeps administrators accountable for their actions.

To take ownership of an object, do the following:

1. Right-click the object, select the Properties option, and click on the Security tab.
2. Click on the Advanced button, click the Owner tab, and click your user account. See Figure 13.17.
3. Click on the OK button to close the Access Control Settings dialog box, and click on the OK button to close the object window.

The best way to give sufficient permissions to an organizational unit is to delegate administrative control to the container (decentralized administration), so that the user or group will have administrative control for the OU and the objects in it. To delegate control to an OU, run the Delegation of Control Wizard. To start the Wizard, right-click the desired OU and select Delegate Control. You can then select the user or group to which you want to delegate control, the organizational units and objects you want to grant those users the right to control, and the permissions to access and modify objects. For example, a user can be given the right to modify the Owner of Accounts property, without being granted the right to delete accounts in that OU. See Figure 13.18.

The most obvious way to stop inherited permissions is to change the original permission granted at the container. Other ways are as follows:

1. Select a conflict permission (Allow Deny) at the lower level or object, which will override the inherited permission.
2. Clear the "Allow inheritable permission from parent to propagate to this object" check box. By clearing the check box, you will then have the opportunity to either copy previously inherited permissions to the object or remove them from the object. See Figure 13.19.

Some privileges can override permissions that are set on an object. For example, a user who is logged on to a domain account as a member of the Backup Operators group has the right to perform

Figure 13.18   Using the Delegation of Control Wizard to delegate permissions over a container

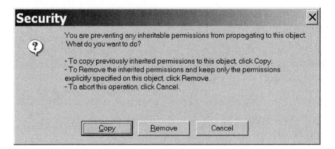

Figure 13.19   Preventing inherited permissions for a container

backup operations for all domain servers. However, this requires the ability to read all files on those servers, even files on which the owners have set permissions that explicitly deny access to all users, including members of the Backup Operators group. A user right—in this case, the right to perform a backup—takes precedence over all file and directory permissions.

13.8   POLICIES

The **IntelliMirror** management technologies are a set of powerful features built into Windows 2000 and Windows Server 2003 that allows users' data, software, and settings to follow them. The features of IntelliMirror increase the availability of a users' data, personal computer settings, and computing environment by intelligently managing information, settings, and software. Based on policy definitions, IntelliMirror is able to deploy, recover, restore, or replace users' data, software, and personal settings in a windows-based environment.

At the core of IntelliMirror are three features:

- User settings management
- User data management
- Software installation and maintenance

IntelliMirror is not a particular service or technology, but several services and technologies including group policies, offline folder synchronization, folder redirection, Windows Installer, roaming user profiles, and remote installation services (RIS).

Policies serve as a tool that is used by administrators to define and control how programs, network resources, and the operating system behave for users and computers in the Active Directory structure. Settings include the following:

- **System settings**—Application settings, desktop appearance, and behavior of system services
- **Security settings**—Local computer, domain, and network security settings
- **Software installation settings**—Management of software installation, updates, and removal
- **Scripts settings**—Scripts for when a computer starts and shuts down and when a user logs on and off
- **Folder redirection settings**—Storage for users' folders on the network

The Active Directory is a structured hierarchy, where different levels of policies enable you to customize your configuration. The different levels of policies are applied in the following order:

1. Windows NT 4.0–style policies
2. Unique local Group Policy object
3. Site Group Policy objects, in administratively specified order
4. Domain Group Policy objects, in administratively specified order
5. Organizational unit Group Policy objects, from the highest to lowest organizational unit and in administratively specified order

Group Policy settings are inherited, cumulative, and affect all computers and user accounts in the Active Directory container with which the Group Policy is associated. If you have settings that are in conflict with each other, the later policies will overwrite the earlier policies. Therefore, settings in the OU Group Policy will overwrite any settings in the other policies. For example, say you have a site Group Policy, two domain Group Policies, and one parent organizational unit and three child organizational unit Group Policies. The site Group Policy will be executed first. Next, the first-listed domain Group Policy will be executed. If any settings from the first domain Group Policy are in conflict with the default domain controller Group Policy, the first domain will overwrite those settings. Then the second-listed domain Group Policy will be executed, again overwriting any settings that conflict. Then the parent organizational unit Group Policy is executed, followed by the child organizational unit Group Policies in the order that they are listed. As they are executed, they overwrite any settings that are in conflict.

> *NOTE:* In the domain Group Policy Object (GPO), Account Policies (Password, Account Lockout, and Kerberos policies) are defined on a domain basis only. This is a very important consideration, because GPOs for account settings defined for lower-level OUs will not work for domain users. Settings at lower-level OUs take effects if users log on locally (i.e., using a local account) to a computer, but not if logging on to the domain. In addition, because domain controllers do not have local accounts like servers and workstation do, account policies that are defined in the default domain controllers organizational unit have no effect. If you need to have different account policies for different computers, you will have to break your network into two or more domains, each domain with its own account policy.
>
> Domain controllers pull some security settings only from the Domain container. Because domain controllers share the same account database for the domain, certain security settings must be set uniformly on all domain controllers, whether the domain controller is in the domain controller organizational unit or not. This ensures that the members of the domain have a consistent experience regardless of which domain controller they use to log on.

13.8.1   Windows NT 4.0—Style Policies

Windows NT 4.0—style policies consist of a set of system registry settings that you create and place on workstations as they log on to the network. These registry entries affect machine and user-specific settings on the workstation. The Windows NT 4.0—style policies control what resources are available to users, including what applications appear on the desktop, which applications appear on the Start menu, what accesses there are to basic system areas including the Control Panel, and what accesses there are to the Command prompt.

Windows 9x system policies are contained in the file CONFIG.POL, whereas Windows NT system policies are contained in the NTCONFIG.POL file. These files are created with the appropriate System Policy Editor such as POLEDIT.EXE and stored in the server's NETLOGON shared folder (\SYSTEM32\REPL\IMPORT\SCRIPTS). The system policies can be defined on a user. Although System Policy Editor (POLEDIT.EXE) has been largely replaced by Group Policy, it is still useful under some special circumstances.

13.8.2   Group Policies

Each computer that is running Windows 2000, Windows XP, or Windows Server 2003 has one local Group Policy object, which can be stored on individual computers regardless if they are part of an Active Directory environment or a networked environment. These settings can be overwritten by any nonlocal Group Policies (sites, domains, and organizational units). The local group policy can be added as a snap-in to the MMC or can be executed as a program in the Administrative Tools. The local Group Policy object resides in SystemRoot\System32\GroupPolicy. Computers that are running Windows NT 4.0 or earlier do not have a local Group Policy object. See Figure 13.20.

The nonlocal group policies are stored on the domain controller as Group Policy templates in the SYSVOL volume and are only available in an Active Directory environment. Different from the local group policies, the nonlocal group policies are stored in Group Policy objects (GPOs). As objects, the GPOs can be assigned to multiple sites, domains, or organizational units; and sites, domains, and organizational units can have multiple Group Policy objects.

There are five major categories under which Group Policies can be configured:

- **Folder Redirection**—Stores users' folders (My Documents, Start menu, Application Data, Desktop, and My Pictures) on the network
- **Security**—Similar to account policies under User Manager in NT 4.0, includes settings for the local computer, the domain, and network security
- **Administrative Templates**—NT 4.0 administrators will recognize this section as system policies, in a more convenient and flexible configuration. Includes desktop, application, and system settings.

Figure 13.20   Selecting Group Policies

- **Software Installation**—Completely new, enables an administrator to have software installed automatically at the client machine, or removed automatically
- **Scripts**—Similar to logon scripts in NT 4.0, but now a **start-up** and a **shutdown** script can be specified for the computer as well as a logon and a logoff script for the user

Group Policy objects other than the local Group Policy object consist of two parts that are stored separately, the **Group Policy container (GPC)** and the **Group Policy template (GPT).** An administrator can create several GPOs in a given GPC and assign the appropriate GPO to the computers or users that need the settings contained in that GPO. Information that is small and infrequently changed resides in the GPT, while information that is large or frequently changed is kept in the GPC. The Group Policy user interface does not expose them separately.

It is possible to disable Group Policy objects without deleting them. If you do this (from Group Policy—Options) it will only disable it for that container and any subcontainers that inherit the settings. If another administrator is "linked" to that GPO from another container, then the GPO is still active in that container.

To create a nonlocal group policy, do the following:

1. Open the Active Directory Sites and Services console or the MMC with the Active Directory Sites and Services snap-in.
2. Right-click the site (Domain Controllers folder), the domain, or the organizational unit and select the Properties option.
3. Click on the Group Policy tab.
4. Click on the New button and name the profile.

If you have multiple group policies assigned to a site, domain, or organizational unit, then specify the order by clicking on the GPO and using the Up and Down buttons. See Figure 13.20.

When a GPO is created and associated with an Active Directory container, the settings from the parent container flow down into the child containers. In other words, the child container inherits those settings from above. Those settings can be overwritten by Group Policies that are executed later. The inheritance or flow down of rights can be stopped or blocked by using the Block Policy Inheritance check box which is located with the properties of the container. This means that when the box is checked, the container does not inherit any policy settings from the parent-level Group Policies.

Sometimes, you may want to block some of the earlier policies from being overwritten by the later executed policies or block the policy inheritance. To maintain these settings, open the Properties of the GPO and select No Override. You would typically use this in one of the higher levels such as the site or domain GPO to make sure that the administrators of the OUs do not overwrite settings that you want to assign to everyone. See Figure 13.21.

The "Disabled: the Group Policy Object is not applied to this container" option is a troubleshooting tool to help isolate a container's origin. For example, if an object is inheriting a setting that is not the desired setting, you may want to see where the setting originated. Since there can be many GPOs, the disable feature allows you to temporarily disable the GPO without removing its link to the container or allows you to delete the GPO. If the settings that are causing the problem go away when you disable it, you know that the setting is involved in the GPO that you disabled.

Figure 13.21   Deleting a GPO

Figure 13.22   To prevent overriding a GPO or to disable a GPO for a container

If you choose to delete a Group Policy object, you will be given two options. You can either remove the association with the GPO to the container or you can remove the link and delete the GPO. If other containers were using the GPO, however, then those containers would also lose these settings. See Figure 13.22.

Because Group Policy can apply settings from more than one Group Policy object to a site, domain, or organizational unit, you can add Group Policy objects that are associated with other directory objects. You can also prioritize how these Group Policy objects affect the directory object to which they are applied.

13.8.3   Group Policy Permissions

The permissions of a Group Policy can be done using the standard access control list (ACL) editor. To use the ACL editor, click a Group Policy object's property sheet, then click the Security tab. The ACL editor can be used by administrators to delegate who can modify the Group Policy object and who is affected by the group policy.

By default, only members of Domain Administrators, Enterprise Administrators, and Group Policy Creator Owners groups can create new Group Policy objects. If the Domain Administrator wants a non-administrator or group to be able to create Group Policy objects, that user or group can be added to the Group Policy Creator Owners security group. When a nonadministrator who is a member of the Group Policy Creator Owners group creates a Group Policy object, that user becomes the creator and owner of the Group Policy object and can edit the object.

For a Group Policy to apply to a person, the person must have Apply Group Policy and Read Permission for the policy. By default, Authenticated Users have read access to the Group Policy object with the Apply Group Policy attribute set.

To edit a Group Policy object, the user must have both read and write access to the Group Policy object. The Domain Administrators, Enterprise Administrators, and Group Policy Creator Owners groups have full control without the Apply Group Policy attribute set. This means that they can edit the Group Policy object, but the policies contained in that Group Policy object do not apply to them. Note: Domain Administrators and Enterprise Administrators are also members of Authenticated Users; therefore, members of those groups are, by default, affected by Group Policy objects unless you explicitly exclude them.

13.8.4   Modifying Policy Settings

To edit a nonlocal group policy, follow these steps:

1. Open the Active Directory Sites and Services console or the MMC with the Active Directory Sites and Services snap-in.
2. Right-click the site (Domain Controllers folder), the domain, or the organizational unit and select the Properties option.
3. Click on the Group Policy tab.
4. Select the desired GPO and click on the Edit button.

Figure 13.23 An MMC showing several policies on the same console

You also can create an MMC with the appropriate snap-ins showing the various Group Profile objects such as that shown in Figure 13.23.

NOTE: Windows Server 2003 has Domain Controller Security Policy and Domain Security Policy consoles available in the administrative tools.

Windows 2000 and Windows Server 2003 periodically refresh Group Policies throughout the network. By default, the client computers are updated every 90 minutes with an offset of +/–30 minutes. The domain controllers are updated every 5 minutes. The settings that belong to the Computer Configuration are applied when the computer boots. The settings that belong to the User are applied during login.

To refresh the Group Policy so that they will go in effect immediately, do the following for Windows 2000:

1. Click on the Start button and select the Run option.
2. To refresh the User Configuration settings, in the Run dialog box, input SECEDIT /REFRESH-POLICY USER_POLICY. To refresh the Computer User Configuration settings, in the Run dialog box, input SECEDIT /REFRESHPOLICY MACHINE_POLICY.

For Windows Server 2003, follow these steps:

1. Click on the Start button and select the Run option.
2. To refresh the User Configuration settings, in the Run dialog box, input GPUPDATE /TARGET: USER /FORCE. To refresh the Computer Configuration settings, in the Run dialog box, input

GPUPDATE /TARGET:COMPUTER /FORCE. To refresh the User and Computer Configuration settings, in the Run dialog box, input GPUPDATE /FORCE.

13.8.5   Computer Security Settings

Computer security settings are used to combat unauthorized access to resources, viruses, theft of data, or disruption of workflow. The computer security settings are subdivided into the following categories:

- **Account policies**—Used to configure password policies, account lockout policies, and Kerberos protocol policies for the domain
- **Local policies**—Include auditing policies, the assignment of user rights and privileges, and various security options
- **Event log**—Used to configure the size, access, and retention parameters for the application logs, the system logs, and security logs
- **System services**—Used to configure security and start-up settings for services running on a computer
- **Registry**—Used to configure security on registry key
- **File system**—Used to configure security on specific file paths
- **Public key policies**—Used to configure encrypted data recovery agents, domain roots, trusted certificate authorities, and so forth. You also can configure public key policies in User Configuration.
- **IP security policies on Active Directory**—Used to configure network Internet protocol (IPI) security (IPSec)

As you open a profile and the various levels of a profile, you will see that the profile stores hundreds of settings. The following section will discuss some of the more important settings. Since the GPO only modifies user settings and no computer settings are altered, you can reduce the time it takes for a client to process the GPO if you disable the computer configuration settings for the GPO.

13.8.6   Password Policy

The password policy determines the password settings for domain and local user accounts. It can be found by opening the Computer Configuration, opening the Windows Settings, opening Account Policies, and clicking on Password Policies. The popular password policy settings are as follows:

- **Enforce password history**—Remembers a specified number of passwords. Therefore, when a user changes a password, you cannot use the same password. For example, if the Enforce password history is set to 3, users would have to change the password three times before they can use the same password again.
- **Maximum password age**—Specifies how often the password must be changed
- **Minimum password age**—Specifies how long a user would have to wait before changing a password. This prevents users from changing their passwords back immediately.
- **Minimum password length**—Specifies the minimum number of characters for a password
- **Complexity requirements**—When enabled, the password contains at least six characters and must contain characters from at least three of the following four classes:

   English uppercase letters (A, B, C, . . . , Z)
   English lowercase letters (a, b, c, . . . , z)
   Westernized Arabic numerals (0, 1, 2, . . . , 9)
   Nonalphanumeric ("special characters") such as punctuation symbols

For a secure network, try setting the Enforce password history to 5 or more, set the maximum password age to between 30 and 45 days, and set the minimum password length to eight characters. Enable passwords to meet complexity requirements.

13.8.7   Account Lockout Policy

The account lockout policy determines when and for whom an account will be locked out of the system. It can be found by opening the Computer Configuration, opening the Windows Settings, opening

Account Policies, and clicking on Account Lockout Policies. The account lockout policy has the following settings:

- **Account Lockout Duration**—When an account is locked out, it specifies the duration of the lockout. If you want the account to be unlocked/reset by an administrator, set the value to 99999.
- **Account Lockout Threshold**—The number of invalid logins within the time specified in the Reset Account Lockout Counter After before the account is locked. This setting will eliminate hackers from trying passwords until one works.
- **Reset Account Lockout Counter After**—The time that the number of invalid logins are counted before the invalid login counter is reset.

For a secure network, set the Account Lockout Duration to either 60 minutes or 99999 depending on your situation, set the Account Lockout Threshold to 5, and reset the Account Lockout Counter After to 30 minutes.

13.8.8   Logon Script

Logon scripts are batch files that run every time the user logs on. Batch files are text files that have a BAT file name extension. They can contain commands, which can be executed at the prompt. You can create logon scripts in Notepad, VBscript, and JScript.

A logon script can be assigned to individual users or groups of users. To assign an individual user account, right-click the User account, select the Properties option, and click the Profile tab. When using group profiles, you can assign logon scripts to an entire site, domain, or organizational unit; logon script can also be activated during shutdown.

With the use of profiles under Windows, logon scripts are not as important as they once were. Yet, logon scripts still come in handy to ensure certain printer and network connections, set environment settings, and auto load applications. Individual logon scripts can be created and assigned to multiple users or containers.

By default, logon scripts are stored and executed from a domain controller's SYSVOL share. If you remember, the SYSVOL directory is replicated among all the domain controllers so that it will be available no matter which domain controller authenticates the user and provides fault tolerance of the logon scripts.

To assign user logon scripts, follow these steps:

1. Open the Group Policy snap-in.
2. In the console tree, click the Scripts node [located in policy_name Policy, User Configuration, Windows Settings, Scripts (Logon/Logoff)].
3. In the Details pane, double-click the Logon icon.
4. In the Logon Properties page, click Add.
5. In the Add a Script dialog box, set the options you want to use, and then click OK. The options are as follows:
   - Script Name: Type the path to the script, or click Browse to search for the script file in the Netlogon share of the domain controller.
   - Script Parameters: Type any parameters you want to use as you would type them on the command line. For example, if your script included parameters called //logo (display banner) and //I (interactive mode), then type //logo //I
6. In the Logon Properties page, specify any of the following options:

   - Logon Scripts For: Lists all scripts currently assigned to the selected Group Policy object. If you assign multiple scripts, they are processed according to the order specified. To move a script up in the list, click it and then click Up; to move it down, click Down.
   - Add: Opens the Add a Script dialog box, where you can specify any additional scripts to use
   - Edit: Opens the Edit Script dialog box, where you can modify script information such as name and parameters
   - Remove: Removes the selected script from the Logon Scripts list
   - Show Files: Select to view the script files stored in the selected Group Policy object.

Figure 13.24 Sample logon script

```
@ echo off
NET USE H: %HOMESHARE%
NET USE G: \\SERVER1\%USERNAME%
NET USE H: \\SERVER1\FINANCE
NET USE I: \\SERVER3\REPORTS
NET USE LPT1: \\SERVER2\HP4-143
IF %USERDOMAIN% = = DOMAIN1 NET USE LPT2: \\SERVER2\HP4-150
IF %USERDOMAIN% = = DOMAIN2 NET USE LPT2: \\TSERVER2\ACCTLASR
NET TIME
```

If the logon script is stored in a subdirectory of the domain controller's logon script path (sysvol\domainname\scripts), precede the file name with that relative path.

The most common command used in logon scripts is the NET command. See Figure 13.24. The NET USE command is used to connect to a shared resource such as a drive, directory, or printer that has been shared or designated for access from clients. This process is called drive mapping.

To access a shared network drive or directory, use the following syntax:

```
NET USE d: \\servername\sharename /Y
```

The d: is the local drive letter so assigned to point to the shared directory. The server name (NetBIOS name) locates where the shared drive or directory resides and the share name is the actual name given by the system administrator when creating the share. The \\servername\sharename is known as the universal naming convention (UNC) name. If the command asks for your confirmation to access, the /Y will automatically respond Yes. For example, to access the shared directory SOFTWARE, which is located on the CLASSROOM server, use the following:

```
NET USE G: \\CLASSROOM\SOFTWARE
```

After this command is executed, as far as the client is concerned, he or she has a G drive. The G drive is actually a pointer that points to the SOFTWARE shared directory on the CLASSROOM server. Therefore, for all practical purposes, the G drive acts like any other local drive. Assuming that you have the proper rights or permissions, you can execute files, access data files, and copy files from or to the G drive. If there already is a G drive, then the computer will ask if you want to overwrite the drive mapping.

Since Windows remembers its previous drive mappings using profiles, and if you try to execute a NET USE command to the same drive letter, the NET.EXE will respond, "System error 85 has occurred. The local drive name is already in use." Therefore, you could delete any drive mappings when they are no longer being used by using the disconnection option (/D):

```
NET USE d: /D /Y
```

where the d: is the local drive letter assigned to the shared drive or directory. If the command asks for your confirmation to access, the /Y will automatically respond Yes. Therefore, to disconnect from the G drive that was pointing to the SOFTWARE share, execute the following command at the prompt:

```
NET USE G: /D /Y
```

The NET USE command can also be used to connect to a network printer. The proper syntax then is as follows:

```
NET USE LPTx: \\servername\printername
```

where the LPTx is the local printer port assigned to the network printer, the servername is the name of the print server, and the printername is the name of the shared printer. For example, to connect to the IPRINTER network printer that is connected to the INSTRUCT print server using your local LPT2, use the following command:

```
NET USE LPT2: \\INSTRUCT\IPRINTER
```

Table 13.5 Variables used in logon scripts

Variable	Description
%HOMEDRIVE%	User's local workstation drive letter connected to the user's home directory
%HOMEPATH%	Full path of the user's home directory
%HOMESHARE%	Share name containing the user's home directory
%OS%	Operating system running on the user's computer
%PROCESSOR_ARCHITECTURE%	Processor type (such as 80386) of the user's workstation
%PROCESSOR_LEVEL%	Processor level of the user's workstation
%USERDOMAIN%	Domain name
%USERNAME%	User name of the user logging on

Thus, all print jobs sent to the LPT2 printer port will be redirected to the IPRINTER, even if you do not really have an LPT2 port.

The NET TIME command can be used to synchronize each client workstation to the server clock. Synchronizing all clients to the same clock is necessary for security and reliability, as you can rely on the time and date stamps of files. For example, to synchronize the client workstation to the server called INSTRUCT, use the following command:

```
NET TIME \\INSTRUCT
```

Variables can be used to customize the logon script by substituting the relevant information during execution. For example, if you use %USERNAME%, the user's name will be substituted, whereas %USERDOMAIN% will substitute the name of the domain where the user is logging on. The variables are listed in Table 13.5. The %USERNAME% will point to an individual home directory; the %HOME-SHARE% will point to the location of the home directory.

Therefore, using

```
NET USE H: %HOMESHARE%
```

will create an H drive that points to the home directory.

To specify a logon script, do the following:

1. Open the Active Directory Users and Computers console.
2. Right-click the user to which you want to assign a logon script.
3. Click on the Profile tab.
4. In the Logon Script text box, enter the name of the logon script you want to assign to the user.

13.8.9 Restricted Groups Policies

Restricted Groups policies are used to manage and enforce the membership of built-in or user-defined groups that have special rights and permissions. Restricted Groups policies contain a list of members of specific groups whose membership is defined centrally as part of the security policy. Enforcement of Restricted Groups policies automatically sets any computer local group membership to match the membership list settings defined in the policy. Changes to group membership by the local computer administrator are overwritten by the Restricted Groups policy defined in Active Directory.

Restricted Groups can be used to manage membership in the built-in groups. Built-in groups include local groups such as Administrators, Power Users, Print Operators, and Server Operators, as well as global groups such as Domain Administrators. You can add groups that you consider sensitive or privileged to the Restricted Groups list, along with their membership information. This allows you to enforce the membership of these groups by policy and not allow local variations on each computer.

13.8.10   Security Templates

In Windows 2000 and Windows Server 2003, User Rights Assignment has been integrated with Group Policy. While it is possible to change security settings for a local machine in a Group Policy object, a better approach is to use a security template. A security template provides a single place where all system security can be viewed, analyzed, changed, and applied to a single machine or to a Group Policy object as shown in Table 13.6.

Security templates do not introduce new security parameters: they simply organize all existing security attributes (account policies, local policies, restricted groups, registry settings, file system settings, and system services) into one place to ease security administration. Security templates can also be used as base configurations for security analysis, when used with the Security Configuration and Analysis snap-in.

Windows comes with preconfigured security templates for common machine configurations, like workstations, secure servers, and domain controllers. The security templates simplify security administration and help to eliminate gaps in security. For servers deployed on the Internet, rather than laboriously going through a checklist to make sure the server is secure, it is now only necessary to apply a security template. This results in a substantial savings of administrators' time.

To import a security template to a Group Policy object, in a console from which you manage Group Policy settings, click the Group Policy object to which you want to import the security template. It can be found by opening the Policy Object Name, Computer Configuration, Windows Settings, Import Policy and selecting the security template that you want to import. The security settings are applied when the computer starts or as the Group Policy settings dictate.

To customize a predefined security template follow these steps:

1. In the Security Templates snap-in, double-click Security Templates.
2. Double-click the default path folder (Systemroot\Security\Templates), and right-click the predefined template you want to modify.
3. Click Save As and specify a file name for the security template.

Table 13.6   Windows 2000 and Windows Server 2003 predefined security template

Security Template	Description
Basic (basic*.inf)	The basic configurations apply the Windows 2000 and Windows Server 2003 default security settings to all security areas except those pertaining to user rights.
Compatible (compat*.inf)	The default Windows 2000 and Windows Server 2003 security configuration gives members of the local Users group strict security settings, while members of the local Power Users group have security settings that are compatible with Windows NT 4.0 user assignments so that local users group can use legacy programs. It is not considered a secure environment.
Secure (secure*.inf)	The secure templates implement recommended security settings for all security areas except files, folders, and registry keys. Besides increasing security settings for account policy and auditing, it also removes all members from Power Users group. These are not modified because file system and registry permissions are configured securely by default.
Highly Secure (hisec*.inf)	The highly secure templates define security settings for Windows 2000 and Windows Server 2003 network communications. The security areas are set to require maximum protection for network traffic and protocols used between computer running Windows 2000 or Windows Server 2003. As a result, such computers configured with a highly secure template can only communicate with other Windows 2000 or Windows Server 2003 computers. They will not be able to communicate with computers running older versions of Windows (Windows 9X or Windows NT).

4. Double-click the new security template to display the security policies (such as Account Policies) and double-click the security policy you want to modify.
5. Click the security area you want to customize (such as Password Policy), then doubleclick the security attribute to modify (such as Minimum Password Length).
6. Check the Define this policy setting in the template check box in order to allow editing.

13.8.11   Resolving Group Policies

If you are using Group Policies and someone is getting an extra permission that you did not expect, or someone is being denied something that you did not expect, you can use the Resultant Set of Policy (RSoP) to help troubleshoot the problem. The RSoP is a query engine that polls existing policies and planned policies and reports the results of all the policies. When policies are applied on multiple levels (site, domain, domain controller, and organizational unit), the RSoP can help resolve conflict by showing the resultant policy and where the policies are set.

RSoP consists of two modes: planning mode and logging mode. With planning mode, you can simulate the effect of policy settings that you want to apply to a computer and user. Logging mode reports the existing policy settings for a computer and the user that is currently logged on. The RSoP wizard helps create an RSoP query.

In Windows Server 2003, the RSoP wizard can be started from the MMC, Active Directory Users and Computers, or Active Directory Sites and Services. You must run the wizard at least once to create an RSoP query. Query results are displayed in the RSoP snap-in in MMC. From here, you can save, change, and refresh your queries. You can create many queries by adding multiple RSoP snap-ins to MMC, one RSoP snap-in per query. See Figure 13.25.

Another program that you can use to view the RSoP logging mode is the command–line tool called GPRESULT, which is available in Windows Tools from the Windows 2000 Server Resource Kit CD and is available with Windows Server 2003. With GPRESULT, you can get detailed information similar to that provided by RSoP logging mode. The syntax for the GPRESULT command is as follows:

Figure 13.25   RSoP console showing the User Right Assignments

```
gpresult [/s computer [/u domain\user /p password]] [/user Targe-
tUserName] [/scope {user|computer}] [/v] [/z]
```

- ◼ /s computer—Specifies the name or IP address of a remote computer. The default is the local computer.
- ◼ /u domain\user—Runs the command with the account permissions of the user that is specified by user or domain\user. The default is the permissions of the currently logged–on user on the computer that issues the command.
- ◼ /p password—Specifies the password of the user account that is specified in the /u parameter
- ◼ /user TargetUserName—Specifies the user name of the user whose RSoP data are to be displayed
- ◼ /scope {user/|/computer}—Displays either user or computer results. Valid values for the /scope parameter are user or computer. If you omit the /scope parameter, GPRESULT displays both user and computer settings.
- ◼ /v—Specifies that the output display verbose policy information.
- ◼ /z—Specifies that the output display all available information about Group Policy.

Because this parameter produces more information than the /v parameter, redirect output to a text file when you use this parameter (e.g., gpresult /z>policy.txt).

13.9   FOLDER REDIRECTION AND OFFLINE SYNCHRONIZATION

Folder Policy, configured using group policies, redirects certain Windows 2000 or Windows Server 2003 special folders located under Documents and Settings such as My Documents and My Pictures to network locations. To individualize a user's redirected folder, it is recommended to incorporate %username% into the path; for example, \\SERVER\SHARE\%USERNAME%\ MY DOCUMENTS.

The benefits of using folder redirection is if a user logs on to various computers on the network, his or her documents are always available. Data stored on a shared network server can be backed up as part of routine system administration.

Offline Files enables users to continue their work with network files and programs even when they are not connected to the network. If you lose your connection to the network or disconnect your notebook computer, you still can view shared network items that have been made available offline as they were when you were connected. You can continue to work with them as you normally would. You have the same access permissions to those files and folders as you would have if you were connected to the network. When the network connection is restored, any changes that you made while working offline are updated to the network. When you or someone else on the network has made changes to the same file, you have the option of saving your version of the file to the network, keeping the other version, or saving both. Note: When the status of your connection changes, an Offline Files icon appears in the status area of the taskbar, and an informational balloon is displayed over the status area to notify you of the change.

To set up your computer to use Offline Files follow these steps:

1. Open My Computer.
2. On the Tools menu, click Folder Options.
3. On the Offline Files tab, make sure that the Enable Offline Files check box is selected.
4. Select "Synchronize all offline files before logging off" to get a full synchronization. Leave it unselected for a quick synchronization.

To make a file or folder available offline, do the following:

1. In My Computer or My Network Places, click the shared network file or folder that you want to make available offline.
2. On the File menu, click on the Make Available Offline option. Note: The Make Available Offline option will appear on the File menu only if your computer was set up to use Offline Files.

To undo making a file or folder available offline, right-click the item and click Make Available Offline again to remove the check mark. To view a list of all of the network files that are available offline, on the Offline Files tab, click View Files.

Synchronization can be initiated manually or Synchronization Manager can be set to control when offline files are synchronized with the network. Synchronization Manager also controls whether a full or a quick synchronization is performed. A full synchronization ensures that you have the most current version of every network file that has been made available offline. A quick synchronization is much faster than a full synchronization, but it may not provide the most current version of every network file that has been made available offline.

13.10   WINDOWS INSTALLER

Windows 2000 and Windows Server 2003 contain a set of new change and configuration management technology features known as IntelliMirror. Using IntelliMirror, you can configure data and applications to follow clients around a network, centrally define client desktop settings for computers and users, and centrally deploy Windows on desktops using remote installation services (RIS), as discussed in Chapter 8.

One important part of IntelliMirror is the Windows Installer. Using Windows 2000 or Windows Server 2003, administrators can control user file systems and registry entries and approve the applications that users can install on their computers. Windows Installer is a service that is responsible for managing installation processes under Windows 2000 or Windows Server 2003 to Windows clients.

Windows Installer uses the .MSI file format, which replaces the setup program (typically SETUP.EXE) that has been used for years to install software. Windows Installer technology consists of two parts:

- The .MSI package file, which contains a relational database of information that stores instructions for installing and removing applications. When you make modifications to a database table, the changes automatically propagate across the database because of its relational nature.
- The MSIEXEC.EXE installer program that runs on the client side, which uses a dynamic link library (DLL) called MSI.DLL to read the .MSI package file. The program copies files to the hard disk, creates shortcuts, modifies registry entries, and performs other tasks. When you install Windows Installer on your computer, Windows automatically configures the file association so that .MSI files associate with Windows Installer and the system runs MSIEXEC.EXE.

With Windows Installer, you can install and uninstall applications without affecting the system state or harming other applications. The tool is smart in that it tracks all modifications made to the system during software installation. If your installation crashes, Windows Installer will roll your system back to its original state.

In addition to installing applications, you can also upgrade applications and apply patches. If you want a user to always use a newer version of an application, you can specify for the upgrade to be mandatory. You must alter the software order listed in the GPO so that the newer version is higher than the older version.

Windows Installer uninstalls applications properly, removing registry entries and deleting application files without harming the shared files that other applications use. You can right-click a Windows Installer package (an .MSI file) in Windows Explorer and select Install, Repair, or Uninstall. Alternatively, you can use the Control Panel's Add/Remove Programs applet to change or remove a Windows Installer package. In addition, when setting up the removal options, specify either an optional removal or a forced removal.

Applications can ask Windows Installer to determine whether any program files are damaged or missing. If so, the tool can repair a program by replacing corrupted or missing files. To repair missing files and correct registry entry problems, choose Detect and Repair from an application's Help menu.

You can also have Windows Installer restore program shortcuts to the Start menu by selecting "Restore my shortcuts while repairing." When you click Start, Windows Installer detects and repairs damaged Microsoft Office 2000 installations. Windows Installer cannot repair your personal data files, but it can repair software that it installed.

If you have installed Microsoft Office, you are already familiar with another feature of Windows Installer—Advertising. Advertising is a feature that lets you install a small subset of applications initially and have additional components install automatically when you use them for the first time. Windows Installer can also remove components that you have not used for a while.

Software Installation works in conjunction with Group Policy and Active Directory. When you deploy software, you can choose to either assign it or publish it. Assigned software can be targeted at users or computers. If you assign an application to a user, the icons show up on the desktop and/or Start menu, but the program is only installed when the user runs it for the first time. The advantage of assigning an application to a user is that it is available wherever the user logs on. If assigned to the computer, the applications are available to all users on that computer and are installed the next time the system is restarted. If you publish the software, the user can install it through Add/Remove Programs, or through a file that requires that particular program (a file association). Published programs cannot self-repair, cannot be published to computers, and are not advertised on the user's desktop or Start menu, but only through Add/Remove Programs. Assigned applications require a Windows Installer file (.MSI); published applications can use Windows Installer files (.MSI) or .ZAP files.

A .ZAP file is used to distribute a legacy application in its native format without using the Windows Installer service. .ZAP files are text files similar to .INI files, and they contain parameters that describe the application that is to be installed and the location of the setup program for that application. Once the .ZAP file has been created, it should be stored in the same folder as the associated application; that folder should be located at the software distribution point. .ZAP files cannot take advantage of .MSI features such as elevated installation privileges, rolling back an unsuccessful installation, or installing on first use of the software.

To customize an installation such as which application features or options that should be installed, you would use a transform file (.MST) along with the .MSI file. Unfortunately, transform files do not allow updating of currently deployed packages. Instead, you must remove the original. MSI file, then redeploy it.

An .MSP file is a type of package that can be used to deploy a patch (bug fixes, service packs, and similar files) for an application that was originally deployed by using an .MSI file. Patches should not be used for major changes. The effects of patches are limited in that they cannot remove components or features, they cannot change product codes, and they cannot remove or change names of shortcuts, files, or registry keys.

To use a GPO to deploy software, perform the following steps:

1. Create or edit a GPO in either User Configuration or Computer Configuration, depending on whether the software is to be assigned to users or computers.
2. Expand Software Settings. Right-click Software Installation, point to New, then click Package. When the File Open dialog box appears, select the package file, then click Open.
3. In the Deploy Software dialog box, select a deployment method, then click OK.

To change the software deployment options for a software package, perform the following steps:

1. In Software Installation, right-click the deployed package, then click Properties.
2. In the Properties dialog box of the application, click the Deployment tab, and set any of the options.

SUMMARY

1. A user account enables a user to log on to a computer and domain with an identity that can be authenticated and authorized for access to domain resources.
2. All users who log on to the network should have their own unique user account and password.
3. The domain user account can log on to a domain to gain access to the network resources.
4. A local user account allows users to log on at and gain resources on only the computer where they create such an account.
5. Like Windows NT, Windows 2000, and Windows Server 2003 start with two built-in accounts, the administrator and guest accounts.
6. To create multiple user accounts simultaneously, it is best to create a template and then use it to create the needed accounts.
7. The home directory is a folder used to hold or store a user's personal documents.
8. A user profile is a collection of folders and data that stores the user's current desktop environment and application settings.

9. The three types of user profiles are local user profile, roaming user profile, and mandatory user profile.

10. A group is a collection of user accounts that is used to simplify administration by assigning rights and permissions to the group. Everyone who is listed in the group will be assigned these rights and permissions.

11. In Windows 2000 and Windows Server 2003, there are two group types, security and distribution.

12. The security group is used to assign permissions and to gain access to resources.

13. The distribution group is used only for nonsecurity functions, such as those used to distribute e-mail messages to many people.

14. The security group can be divided into group scopes (global, domain local group, and universal), which define how the permissions and rights are assigned to the group.

15. Windows 2000 and Windows Server 2003 have default groups, which have been granted a useful collection of rights and permissions.

16. Policies serve as a tool that is used by administrators to define and control how programs, network resources, and the operating system behave for users and computers in the Active Directory structure.

17. A right authorizes a user to perform certain actions on a computer, such as logging on to a system interactively or backing up files and directories.

18. A permission defines the type of access that is granted to an object or object attribute.

19. To delegate control to an organizational unit, run the Delegation of Control wizard.

20. Windows 2000 and Windows Server 2003 contain a set of new change and configuration management technology features known as IntelliMirror.

21. Windows Installer uses the .MSI file format, which replaces the setup program.

22. To move an object, including an organizational unit within the same domain, user, or computer, right-click the object and select the Move option.

QUESTIONS

1. You have recently created some user account objects in an OU in your Active Directory. Later you decide to move these accounts to another OU. Which of the following are true of moving objects in Active Directory? (Choose all that apply.)
   a. Any permissions assigned directly to that object will be moved with the object.
   b. All current permissions on the object will be lost and replaced with the inherited permissions from the new container.
   c. Multiple objects can be moved simultaneously.
   d. Any currently inherited permissions on the object will be lost and replaced with inherited permissions from the new container.

2. Your company has a forest that consists of two domain trees. Each domain tree contains a root domain and two subdomains. You have just created a domain local group and would like to assign permissions to this group of resources within your company. To which resources can permissions be given for this domain local group?
   a. only resources on the same computer as the domain local group
   b. only resources in the same domain as the domain local group
   c. only resources in the same domain tree as the domain local group
   d. any resource in the forest

3. You have just created a global group in a native-mode Windows 2000 domain in a forest. Which of the following can you add to this global group? (Choose all that apply.)
   a. any other global group from the domain
   b. any user account from the domain
   c. any user account from the forest
   d. any global group from the forest

4. Your company has a forest that consists of two domain trees. Each domain tree contains a root domain and two subdomains. You have just created a universal group and would like to assign permissions to this group of resources within your company. To which resources can permissions be given for this universal group?
   a. only resources on the same computer as the universal group
   b. any resource in the forest
   c. only resources in the same domain as the universal group
   d. only resources in the same domain tree as the universal group

5. Where in the Group Policy settings would you configure computer start-up and shut-down scripts?
   a. Client Configuration   c. User Configuration
   b. Start-Up Configuration   d. Computer Configuration

6. You have created a GPO for both a parent and a child OU. The parent OU GPO has the "no override" setting enabled. The child OU has the "block inheritance" setting enabled. Which GPO settings will be applied to the child OU?
   a. parent GPO settings   c. both GPO settings
   b. child GPO settings   d. neither GPO setting

7. Which feature of Windows 2000 and Windows Server 2003 allows an administrator to enforce desktop settings for users?
   a. System Policy   c. User Policy
   b. Group Policy   d. Universal Policy

8. Which two parts compose the contents of a GPO?
   a. GPS   c. GPC
   b. GPT   d. GPA

9. Which of the following objects can have an associated GPO? (Choose all that apply.)
   a. global group   c. domain
   b. site   d. OU

10. You have associated a GPO with both a parent OU and one of its child OUs. Which of the following statements are

true of how the GPO settings will be applied? (Choose all that apply.)
a. If the GPO settings are not compatible, then the parent OU GPO settings take precedence.
b. If the GPO settings are compatible with each other, then *both* GPOs will be applied.
c. If the GPO settings are not compatible, then the child OU GPO settings take precedence.
d. The child OU GPO settings always take precedence.

11. Which one of the following group scopes has its membership listed in the global catalog?
a. domain local group
b. global group
c. universal group
d. all groups

12. You have just created a GPO. Where will the Group Policy container (GPO) for this GPO be stored?
a. DNS database
b. DHCP server
c. SYSVOL share
d. Active Directory

13. You have just created a GPO. Where will the Group Policy template (GPT) for this GPO be stored?
a. DNS database
b. SYSVOL share
c. DHCP server
d. Active Directory

14. Which of the following statements are true of groups in Windows 2000 and Windows Server 2003? (Choose all that apply.)
a. Computer accounts and user accounts can be added to groups.
b. A distribution group can be changed to a security group in native mode.
c. A security group can be changed to a distribution group in native mode.
d. A security group can be changed to a distribution group in mixed mode.

15. By default, which of the following profile folders can be redirected to an alternate location using the Folder Redirection setting in Group Policy? (Choose all that apply.)
a. My Documents
b. Control Panel
c. Start menu
d. Application Data
e. My Pictures
f. Desktop

16. You have just created a GPO for an OU in your enterprise. The GPO only modifies user settings; no computer settings are altered. How can you reduce the time it takes for a client to process this GPO to determine what settings need be applied?
a. Disable the user configuration settings for the GPO.
b. Copy the GPO to every local computer.
c. Split the settings into several GPOs and apply them all.
d. Disable the computer configuration settings for the GPO.

17. Where in the Group Policy settings would you configure user logon and logoff scripts?
a. Client Configuration
b. Computer Configuration
c. User Configuration
d. Start-Up Configuration

18. You would like to redirect a user's desktop folders to an alternate location on the network using Group Policy. You do not, however, want all desktop folders to be redirected to the same location. Which folder redirection option would you choose to enable folders to be redirected to alternate locations?
a. Advanced
b. Custom
c. Basic
d. Manual

19. You have associated GPOs with your site, domain, and OUs. In which order are GPOs processed?
a. site, domain, OU
b. domain, OU, site
c. domain, site, OU
d. OU, site, domain

20. You have created a GPO and allocated it to a particular OU in the Active Directory. You do not want this GPO to be applied to all user objects in this OU. How can you apply the OU GPO settings to only some of the user objects in the OU? (Choose all that apply.)
a. Create a security group that contains only the users that will utilize the GPO settings. Give only this security group both READ and APPLY GROUP POLICY permissions on the GPO.
b. This procedure cannot be done. All GPO settings for an OU will apply to all objects in the OU.
c. Move the user objects that do not require the GPO settings to a sub-OU within the parent OU. Use the Block Inheritance setting on the child OU to stop the parent GPO settings from being applied.
d. Create a security group that contains all the users that will not utilize the GPO settings. DENY the APPLY GROUP POLICY permission on the GPO for this security group.

21. By default, how often will a client computer refresh its Group Policy settings?
a. at user logon only
b. at computer restart only
c. every 90 minutes
d. never

22. You wish to change the scope of a group that you have recently created. Which of the following scope changes can be performed? (Choose all that apply.)
a. A global group can be changed to a universal group.
b. A universal group can be changed to a global group.
c. A domain local group can be changed to a universal group.
d. No changes can be made.

23. Which two of the following are types of user groups in Windows 2000 and Windows Server 2003?
a. distribution groups
b. security groups
c. logon groups
d. access groups

24. You have just created a global group in a native-mode Windows 2000 domain in a forest. Which of the following can you add to this global group? (Choose all that apply.)
a. any other global group from the domain
b. any user account from the domain
c. any user account from the forest
d. any global group from the forest

25. Windows Installer packages can be used to install software on which of the following clients? (Choose all that apply.)
a. Windows Server 2003
b. Windows 98
c. Windows NT 4.0
d. Windows 2000

26. You are investigating ways to automatically remove software on a user's computer using Group Policy. Which two removal options are available?
a. optional removal
b. permanent removal
c. temporary removal
d. forced removal

27. What are the differences between assigning an application to a user and assigning an application to a computer? (Choose all that apply.)

a. Applications cannot be assigned to a computer, as some user interaction is required before the software can be installed.

b. Applications assigned to the user will be available where the user logs on, whereas applications assigned to the computer are available to all users of that computer.

c. Applications assigned to the computer cannot be used interactively as can applications assigned to a user.

d. Applications assigned to a user require the user to either double-click an associated document or click the shortcut to the program, whereas applications assigned to a computer are automatically installed the next time the computer restarts.

28. You have recently published a software upgrade to your users via Group Policy. You have noticed, however, that when a user invokes an associated document, the older version is installed. How can you install the newer version using document invocation?

a. Change the upgrade to be mandatory.

b. Publish the application to the computers rather than the users.

c. Alter the software order listed in the GPO so that the newer version is higher than the older version.

d. Run the SETUP.MSI program with the Run option.

29. When looking at the files on your Windows 2000 Server you notice some with an .MSI extension. What are these files?

a. Multimedia System files

b. Group Policy files

c. Microsoft International Keyboard files

d. Windows Installer files

30. Your job is to deploy a non-Windows installer package to your users by using a .ZAP file. Which of the following are true of deploying non-Windows installer packages? (Choose all that apply.)

a. They can only be assigned.

b. They can only be published.

c. They are resilient.

d. They are not resilient.

31. Which of the following statements are true of assigning an application using Group Policy? (Choose all that apply.)

a. Assigned applications are advertised on the user's desktop.

b. Assigned applications are resilient and can automatically repair themselves.

c. Assigned applications are listed in the Add/Remove Programs applet.

d. Assigned applications can be installed by document invocation.

32. You would like to deploy two different word-processing applications to separate OUs in your company. Users in the first OU require Word 2000 for word processing and those in the second OU require WordPerfect. You have assigned the separate packages to each OU but are concerned that all users would install Word 2000 if they invoked a .DOC file. How can you ensure that document invocation in each OU will install the correct word-processing package?

a. Create two OUs for each department containing only the computers. Publish the correct application to each of these OUs.

b. For each OU, remove the file associations for the unrequired software package.

c. For each OU, modify the file association order so that the required package is higher in the list than the unrequired package.

d. Do not worry, because only the required application is assigned to each OU and installed by document invocation.

33. What are the benefits of using Windows Installer packages to deploy software on your network? (Choose all that apply.)

a. They can be used to deploy software to non-Windows clients.

b. They can be removed cleanly.

c. Packages installed using Windows Installer are resilient and can automatically replace missing or corrupt files.

d. They allow custom installations of the software.

34. You accidentally delete a user's account on a domain controller and you must re-create it with the same permissions and rights. What is the best way to accomplish this task?

a. Assuming that the domain controller has not yet performed synchronization, highlight the deleted user account in Active Directory Users and Computers console and select Undelete from the Console menu.

b. Re-create a new user account with the same name and assign it the security identifier (SID) of the deleted account.

c. Re-create a new user account with the same name and assign it all the permissions and rights of the deleted account.

d. Re-create a new user account with the same name; permissions and rights will be retained since they are contained in the ACLs for domain objects (files, directories, etc.).

35. You are a member of the Enterprise Admin Group at the Acme Corporation. You create and share a printer named HPLaserJ4 on a Windows 2000 Server computer named acme.local. You grant print permission only to a domain local group named CompanySales. Later, you add a child domain named london.acme.local. Pat is a member of the global group named LondonSales in the london.acme.local domain. Pat reports that she is unable to send a print job to HPLaserJ4 printer. You want all the members of LondonSales to be able to print to the HPLaserJ4 printer. What should you do?

a. Add the LondonSales group to CompanySales group.

b. Add the CompanySales group to LondonSales group.

c. Change the CompanySales group to a universal group.

d. Change the LondonSales group to a universal group.

36. You administer a Windows 2000-based network for your company. The forest consists of several domains. A team consisting of users from different domains requires access to documents that reside in shared folders on several file servers in one of the domains. You want to assign permissions to groups rather than to individual users. You want to design a group structure that would not result in an excessive amount of network traffic and that would require the least possible administrative effort to manage. Which of the following should you do? (Select the best choice.)

a. Place all team members into a universal group and assign it the appropriate permissions in the domain where the resources are located.

b. In each domain, place the team members from that domain into a global group. In the domain where the resources are located, create a universal group and assign it the appropriate permissions for the resources. Add the global groups to the universal group.

c. In each domain, place the team members from that domain into a domain local group. In the domain where the resources are located, create a global group and assign it the appropriate permissions for the resources. Add the domain local group to the global group.

d. In each domain, place the team members from that domain into a global group. In the domain where the resources are located, create a domain local group and assign it the appropriate permissions for the resources. Add the global groups to the domain local group.

37. All computers on your company's network run only Windows 2000. You have created a Group Policy object (GPO) and linked it to an organizational unit (OU) named Sales. The GPO contains policies that hide the settings and Appearance tabs of the Display Properties sheet. The Sales OU contains user accounts for all employees in the sales department. You want the accounts of the senior staff in the sales department, who belong to the SeniorSales group, to be restricted from accessing the Settings tab, but not the Appearance tab. Which of the following should you do? (Select the best choice.)

a. Create another GPO and link it to the SeniorSales group.

b. Create another GPO and link it to the domain; assign the Read and Apply Group Policy permissions for the GPO only to the SeniorSales group.

c. Use System Policy Editor to create a system policy for the SeniorSales group and save it to the Netlogon share on a domain controller.

d. Create another GPO, link it to the Sales OU, set the second GPO to be applied after the first GPO, and assign the Read and Apply Group Policy permissions for the second GPO only to the SeniorSales group.

38. You are administrator of 20 Windows 2000 professional computers and 2 Windows 2000 Server computers for your domain. You want to set an account policy that locks any user's account after three consecutive failed logon attempts. You also want to ensure that only administrators will be able to unlock the account. Which two actions should you take?

a. Set the account lockout duration to 0.

b. Set the account lockout duration to 3.

c. Set the account lockout threshold to 0.

d. Set the account lockout threshold to 3.

e. Set the "reset account lockout after" to 0.

f. Set the "reset account lockout after" to 3.

39. You are the network administrator for your company. Your company's main office is in Seattle. Branch offices are in New York, Rome, and Tokyo. The local administrators at each branch office need to be able to control local resources. You want to prevent the local administrators from controlling resources in the other branch offices;

only the administrators from the main office should be allowed to create and manage user accounts. You want to create an Active Directory structure to accomplish these goals. What should you do?

a. Create a domain tree that has a top-level domain for the main office and a child domain for each branch office. Grant the local administrators membership in the Domain Admins group in their child domains.

b. Create a domain tree that has a top-level domain for the main office and a child domain for each branch office. Grant the local administrators membership in the Enterprise Admins group in the domain tree.

c. Create a single domain. Create a group named Branch Admins. Grant the local administrators membership in this group. Assign permissions to the local resources to this group.

d. Create a single domain. Create an organizational unit (OU) for each branch office and an additional OU named CorpUsers. Delegate authority for resource administration to the local administrators for their own OUs. Delegate authority to the CorpUsers OU only to the Domain Admins group.

40. You are the administrator of your company's network. Your company has its main office in Seattle and branch offices in London, Paris, and Rio de Janeiro. The local administrator at each branch office must be able to control users and local resources. You want to prevent the local administrators from controlling resources in branch offices other than their own. You want to create an Active Directory structure to accomplish these goals. What should you do?

a. Create a top-level organizational unit (OU), Delegate control of this OU to administrators at the main office.

b. Create child OUs for each office. Delegate control of these OUs to administrators at the main office.

c. Create child OUs for each office. Delegate control of each OU to the local administrators at each office.

d. Add the local administrators to the Domain Admins group.

e. Create user groups for each office. Grant the local administrators the appropriate permissions to administer these user groups.

41. You are the administrator of Acme Corporation and Daffy Research Facilities. You manage a multidomain Windows 2000 network of 6000 users for the two companies. The network is configured as shown in the exhibit. The two companies have a total of six departments. Each department is an organizational unit (OU) in Active Directory. Each domain and OU has specific Group Policy settings that must be applied to all of its members. All six departments are being reorganized. Some, but not all, of the users in each OU have moved. Many users have changed departments, and some have changed domains. You want to accomplish the following goals in the least possible amount of time:

• Place the user accounts in the appropriate domains.

• Apply the existing policies for each domain or OU to the moved account.

• Avoid disruption of user access to shared resources.

What should you do?

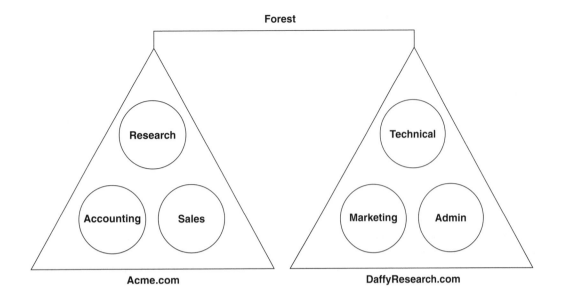

a. For all users, create a new user account in the appropriate OUs. Assign permissions to the accounts to apply Group Policy settings, then delete the old accounts.

b. For users moving between domains, create new user accounts in the appropriate OUs. Assign permissions to the account to apply the Group Policy settings, then delete the old accounts. For the users moving between OUs in the same domain, select the accounts then choose Move from the Action menu, targeting the new OU.

c. For users moving between domains, use the Movetree utility; specify the source and target domains and the OUs. For users moving between OUs in the same domain, select the accounts then choose Move from the Action menu, targeting the new OU.

d. For users moving between domains, create new user accounts in the appropriate OUs. Assign permissions to the account to apply Group Policy settings then delete the old accounts. For users moving between OUs in the same domain, select the accounts then choose Copy from the Action menu, entering the appropriate account information for the new user accounts. Delete the old accounts.

42. You are the administrator of the company network for Arbor Shoes. Arbor Shoes has three domains: arborshoes.com, na.arborshoes.com, and sa.arborshoes.com. All the domains are in native mode. You are going to remove the na.arborshoes.com domain in an effort to consolidate domains. There are 300 users in na.arborshoes.com. You want to move all 300 users at the same time to arborshoes.com. What should you do?

a. At the Command prompt, type the following:

```
Cscroptsidhist.vbs/srcdc:dc1/srcdom:na
.arborshoes.com/dstdc:dc1/dstdom:arbor
shoes.com
```

b. At the Command prompt, type the following:

```
Movetree/start/s
dc1.na.arborshoes.com/d
dc1.arborshoes.com/sdn
cn=users,dc=na,dc=arborshoes,dc=com/
ddn cn=users, dc=arborshoes, dc=com.
```

c. In MMC, use the COPY command in Active Directory Users and Computers.

d. In MMC, use the MOVE command in Active Directory Users and Computers.

43. Your company's network consists of a single Windows 2000 domain named sports.acme.com. You and another employee named Pat are members of the Domain Admins group. Pat creates a domain local security group named Teams. You create three global distribution groups: Bowling, Tennis, and Volleyball. You add these three groups to the Teams group. You create a shared folder named Schedule and grant the Teams group the Change permission for the Schedule shared folder. Users in the Bowling, Tennis, and Volleyball groups report they cannot access the Schedule shared folder. You need to enable users to access the shared folder. What should you do?

a. Grant the Bowling, Tennis, and Volleyball groups the Change permission for the Schedule shared folder.

b. Grant the Bowling, Tennis, and Volleyball groups the Full Control permission for the Schedule shared folder.

c. Convert the Teams group to a global distribution group.

d. Convert the Teams group to a universal distribution group.

e. Convert the Bowling, Tennis, and Volleyball groups to global security groups.

44. Your company's network consists of two domains: contoso.com and sales.contoso.com. The contoso.com domain contains three domain controllers and one member server. The sales.contoso.com domain is a new domain that contains one domain controller and one member server. You

are a member of the Domain Admins group in sales. contoso.com. You want sales.contoso.com to contain two domain controllers. Which two actions can you take? (Each correct answer presents a complete solution. Choose two.)

a. Manually install a new server in sales.contoso.com. During the installation process, install the server as a domain controller.

b. Manually install a new member server in sales.contoso.com. After it is installed, promote the server to a domain controller.

c. Move the domain membership of the member server in contoso.com to sales.contoso.com by using System Properties in the Control Panel.

d. Move the domain membership of the domain controller in contoso.com to sales.contoso.com by using System Properties in the Control Panel.

e. Run DCPROMO.EXE on the member server in sales. contoso.com and provide credentials of a user in the Domain Admins group in sales.contoso.com.

f. Run DCPROMO.EXE on the member server in contoso.com and provide credentials of a user in the Domain Admins group in contoso.com.

45. You are the administrator of the Acme Corporation network. There is one domain containing three sites named Geneva, Milwaukee, and Portland. Each site has two domain controllers from the acme.com domain. Geneva and Portland each have 1000 users; Milwaukee has 500 users. There are two IP site links: Geneva_Portland and Milwaukee_Portland. You want to add another domain controller in each site to handle all replication from each site. What should you do?

a. Configure each new domain controller to be the IP preferred bridgehead server for its site.

b. Create a connection object from each domain controller in each site to the new domain controller in each site.

c. Create a new site link that has a lower cost than the existing site links.

d. Delete the existing connection objects in each site and manually start the Knowledge Consistency Checker (KCC).

46. You are the administrator of your company's network. Your event log shows that hackers are using brute force attacks to attempt to gain access to your network. You do not want user accounts to be easily accessible. You want to strengthen security to protect against brute force attacks. What should you do? (Choose two answers.)

a. Enable the "Users must log on to change the password" setting.

b. Enable the "Store password using reversible encryption for all users in the domain" setting.

c. Enable the "Password must meet complexity requirements" setting.

d. Increase minimum password length.

e. Increase minimum password age.

47. You are the administrator of a Windows 2000 network. The acme.com tree and daffyresearch.com form a forest. The us.acme.com and the eur.acme.com domains, which are child domains of the acme.com domain, are in mixed mode. The acme.com and the daffyresearch.com domains are in native mode. The us.acme.com domain has two Windows NT 4.0 BDCs that supply legacy applications. When users from the us.acme.com domain attempt to access a shared folder in the acme.com domain, they receive an error message stating that access is denied. There is a universal group that has Read permission to the Sales folder. Sales is assigned Read permission for the shared folder. When you log on as a member of the Sales group from the acme.com domain, you are able to access the shared folder. What should you do to correct this problem?

a. Switch the us.acme.com domain to native mode.

b. Add a global catalog server to the us.acme.com domain.

c. Create a global group in the us.acme.com domain. Add the user accounts that need access to the shared folder to the global group. Add the global group to the universal group.

d. Create a universal group in the us.acme.com domain. Add the user accounts that need access to the shared folder to the universal group. Grant Read permissions to the universal group for the shared folder in the litware.com domain.

e. Create a global group in the us.litware.com domain. Add the user accounts from the us.litware.com domain to the global group. Grant Read permissions to the global group for the shared folder.

48. You are the administrator of your company's network. The network consists of one Windows 2000 domain that has several organizational units (OUs). All domain controllers in the domain are in OU1. Resources for two separate office buildings are in OU2 and OU3. Non-administrative users, groups, and computers are in OU4 and OU5. Administrative users, computers, and resources are in OU6. You are designing a domain-wide security policy and you want to accomplish the following goals:

- The same password and account lockout policies will be applied to all users.
- Different security settings will be applied to administrative and nonadministrative computers.
- Strict audit policies will be enforced only for domain controllers and servers.
- The number of Group Policy object (GPO) links will be minimized.

You take the following actions:

- Create a single GPO.
- Create one security template that has all required settings.
- Import the security template into the GPO.
- Link the GPO to the domain.

Which result or results do these actions produce? (Choose all that apply.)

a. The same password and account lockout policies are applied to all users.

b. Different security settings are applied to administrative and nonadministrative computers.

c. Strict audit policies are enforced only for domain controllers and servers.

d. The number of GPO links is minimized.

49. You are the LAN administrator for the Acme Corporation. You hire Pat to be a LAN administrator for the Dublin office. The Acme Corporation has one domain named acme.com. Each office has its own OU. Pat needs to be able to create child OUs under only ou = Dublin, dc = acme,dc = com and verify the existence of the created OUs. Which permissions should you assign to Sophia on the Dublin OU? (Choose three responses.)

a. Full Control

b. List Contents

c. Create Organizational Unit objects

d. Create All Child objects

e. Write

f. Read

50. You are hired by Fabrikam Inc. to secure its Windows 2000 network. You use security templates to create a custom template and save it as securefab.inf. You need to use this template on five domain controllers in fabrikam.com domain. What should you do? (Choose two answers.)

a. Copy the Securefab.inf file to Sysvol shared folder on one domain controller.

b. Create a new security database.

c. Import the Securefab.inf file.

d. Rename Securefab.inf to NTconfig.pol.

e. Create a Group Policy object on domain controllers organizational unit (OU).

f. Configure the file replication service to replicate the template file to all domain controllers.

51. You are the administrator of your company's network. A vendor provides you with an application and four transform files. You need to deploy the application to employees in the sales department. You deploy the application and the transform files. After the deployment is complete, you test the application and discover that the second transform file is unnecessary. You want to deploy the application so that it includes only the direct, third, and fourth transform files. You need to complete this task by using the least amount of administrative effort. What should you do?

a. In the application properties, remove all transform files, then add the required transform files in order.

b. In the application properties, remove the second transform file. Use the Move up and Move Down buttons to order the files.

c. Remove the package definition from Group Policy. Create a new definition for the package. Add the required transform files in order.

d. Remove the package definition from Group Policy. Copy the required transform files to the package source in order. Create a new definition for the package.

52. You are the enterprise administrator of a Windows 2000 domain. The domain is in native mode. You want to implement a policy to disable the SHUTDOWN command for all users in the domain except for the members of the Domain Admins security group. You create a new Group Policy object (GPO) named Shutdown. You configure the Shutdown GPO to disable the Shutdown option. You assign the Shutdown GPO to the domain. You want to ensure that the policy does not apply to the members of the Domain Admins group. What should you do?

a. On the Shutdown GPO, deny the Apply Group Policy permission to the Domain Admins group.

b. On the Shutdown GPO, remove the Apply Group Policy permission from the Authenticated Users group. Grant the Apply Group permission to the Users group.

c. Add the Domain Admins group to the Group Policy Creator Owners group.

d. Create a new OU named No Shutdown. Move the Domain Admins group to the No Shutdown OU. Configure the No Shutdown OU to block policy inheritance.

e. On the computers that the members of the Domain Admins group use to log on, configure the local GPO to enable the Shutdown option.

53. You are the administrator of your company's network. The Network consists of one Windows 2000 domain. Your company has two locations, which are connected by a dedicated T1 line. Users frequently report that logons to the network, file transfers, and directory searches are extremely slow. When you monitor the network, you discover that replication between domain controllers is generating excessive network traffic between the locations. You want to accomplish the following goals:

- Replication traffic between locations will be reduced.
- Logon response time for users will be improved.
- Average file transfer rates for users will be improved.
- Directory search response times will be improved.
- All domain controllers will have up-to-date replicas of the directory.
- Fault tolerance for domain logons and directory searches will be maintained.

You take the following actions:

- Configure a domain controller in each location to be a global catalog server.
- Create a new subnet in Active Directory for each location.
- Modify the location attribute of each domain controller's server object.

Which result or results do these actions produce? (Choose all that apply.)

a. Replication traffic between locations is reduced.

b. Logon response time for users is improved.

c. Average file transfer rates for users are improved.

d. Directory search response times are improved.

e. All domain controllers have up-to-date replicas of the directory.

f. Fault tolerance for domain logons and directory searches is maintained.

54. You are the network administrator of a Windows 2000 network. The network consists of 500 Windows 2000 Professional computers. You recently discovered that users of these computers have been using the same passwords since their accounts were created. You need to correct this problem to maintain security in the network. You create a Group Policy object (GPO) and filter it to the users. You want to configure the GPO to require users to create a different password periodically.

Which two settings should you enable? (Choose two answers.)
a. Minimum password length
b. User logon required to change the password.
c. Enforcement of password history
d. Minimum password age
e. Maximum password age

55. You are the administrator of your company's Windows 2000 network. The password security on a domain controller named DCI has been compromised. You create a new security policy to improve password security. You will deploy the policy by using a Group Policy object. You must force DC1 to apply the new security settings as quickly as possible. What should you do?
a. Restart DC1 and force Active Directory replication from another domain controller.
b. Run SECEDIT.EXE on DC1.
c. Export the configuration of another domain controller, then import the configuration to DC1 by means of the Security Configuration and Analysis snapin.
d. Perform a "Nonauthoritative restore the system state data" on DC1.

56. Your company's network consists of two Windows 2000 domains: contoso.com and sales.contoso.com. You are the network administrator of a Windows 2000 network. Your network contains five Windows 2000 Server computers and 100 Windows 2000 Professional computers. You want to deploy an update for an application that is used on the Windows 2000 Professional computers. You want users to automatically install the update when they log on to the domain. What should you do?
a. Create a distributed file system(Dfs). Place the application update in the root folder of the Dfs.
b. Create a Microsoft Windows Installer package for the application update. Configure RIS to use the package.
c. Create a Microsoft Windows Installer package for the application update. Apply the package to the Local Computer Policy on all of the computers.
d. Create a Microsoft Windows Installer package for the application update. Apply the package to a Group Policy.

57. You are the administrator of a Windows 2000 domain. The domain has a Windows 2000 Server computer named Central. Users in the domain frequently work on different Windows 2000 Professional desktop and portable computers. They use the Windows 2000 Professional portable computers to dial in to the network when they are traveling. All Windows 2000 Professional computers are in the domain. You want to accomplish the following goals:
• All users in the domain will be able to work on all Windows 2000 Professional desktop and portable computers and have their own desktop settings available on all computers.
• All users in the domain will be able to access their documents in the My Documents folder from any computer, including portable computers, when users dial in to the network.

• When users dial in to the network, the logon and logoff times will not be delayed because of the transfer of the contents of the My Documents folder,
    What should you do? (Choose two answers.)
a. Configure a roaming profile for each user in the domain. Use \\Central\Profiles\ % Username % as the profile path.
b. Configure a home folder for each user in the domain. Use \\Central\Home\%Username% as the home folder path.
c. Create a new Group Policy object (GPO) named Offdocs. Assign the Offdocs GPO to the domain. Configure the Offdocs GPO to prevent the use of the Offline Files folder.
d. Create a new Group Policy object (GPO) named Redocs. Assign the Redocs GPO to the domain. Configure the Redocs GPO to redirect the My Documents folder to the \\Central\Docs\%Username% location.
e. Create a new Group Policy object (GPO) named Async. Assign the Async GPO to the domain. Configure the Async GPO to apply Group Policy object settings for users asynchronously when they log on.

58. You are the administrator of a Windows 2000 domain. You want to deploy an application named Travel that will be used by all users in the domain. The vendor of the application did not provide a Microsoft Windows Installer package for the application. When the application is installed, it uses the .tvl file name extension. You want to use Group Policy to deploy the application. You want to accomplish the following goals:
• Users will be able to install the application by using Add/Remove programs.
• Users will be able to install the application by using a Start menu shortcut.
• Users will be able to install the application by using document invocation.
• The application will be automatically reinstalled if key application files are missing.

    You take the following actions:
• Create a zero administration package (.ZAP) text file that specifies how to install the Travel application.
• Copy the .ZAP file to a shared folder on the network.
• Create a new Group Policy object named Install Travel and assign the Install Travel GPO to the domain.
• Configure the Install Travel GPO to publish the travel application to users by using the .ZAP file.

    Which result or results do these actions produce? (Choose all that apply.)
a. Users can install the application by using Add/Remove programs.
b. Users can install the application by using a Start menu shortcut.
c. Users can install the application by using document invocation.
d. The application is automatically reinstalled if key application files are missing.

59. You are deploying new Windows XP Professional computers in your company. All employees will receive new

computers, and their old Windows 98 and Windows 2000 Professional computers will be sold to another company. You must ensure that each employee's documents, personal data, Microsoft Office XP settings, and desktop settings are copied from their old computers to their new computers. You want these data to be copied to the new computer when Windows XP Professional is installed. What should you do?

a. Run the SCANSTATE utility on each employee's computer. Save the information generated by the utility to a shared folder on the network. Run the LOADSTATE utility in the installation script for each employee's new computer, specifying the shared folder on the network as the state source.

b. Start each employee's old computer in the Recovery console. Copy the registry files, documents, and personal data to a removable storage device. In each new computer's installation script, copy the information from the removable storage device to each new computer.

c. Use Windows Explorer to copy all documents and personal data from each employee's old computer to each new computer. Run the REGEDIT command to export the registry to a .REG file. In the installation script for each new computer, copy the documents and personal data to the computer and import the .REG file.

d. Run the SYSPREP utility on each employee's old computer. Use a third-party disk-imaging software utility to create an image of the hard disk. After installing Windows XP Professional, apply the hard disk image to each new computer.

60. You are a network administrator of a Windows 2000 Active Directory domain acme.com. The company has multiple branch offices and multiple Windows 2000 Server computers at each office. A junior administrator is located at each office. This junior administrator is responsible for local server configurations. One junior administrator has applied a new security template to the local file server. Local users running Windows 95 on their computer can no longer communicate with the server. You need to verify that the security settings on the Windows 2000 Server computer at the branch office will allow client computers to connect. What should you do?

a. Use MMC and load the Local Computer Policy snap-in. Examine the Administrative templates in the User and Computer section. Compare the templates against the template settings currently in place on the server.

b. Use MMC and load the security Configuration and Analysis snap-in. Create and open a database. Then choose Import file and specify the basicsv template.

c. Use MMC and load the Computer Management snap-in. Specify the appropriate template file to compare against, then select the Analyze option.

d. Run the SECEDIT/VALIDATE command to display the appropriate template file.

61. You are the administrator of a network that consists of Windows 2000 Server Computers and Windows 2000 Professional computers. You want to configure the deployment of the most recent Windows 2000 service pack so that users of the Windows 2000 Professional Computers receive the service pack automatically when they log on the domain. What should you do?

a. Create a Microsoft Windows Installer package for the service pack. Configure RIS to use the package.

b. Create a Microsoft Windows Installer package for the service pack. Configure the package in Group Policy.

c. Create a Microsoft Windows Installer package for the service pack. Configure the package in Local Computer policy.

d. Place the service pack in a distributed file system.

62. You are a local administrator of a Windows 2000 Professional computer. A secretary named Rena has local administrative rights. Other users report that she has modified their files without permission. You want Rena to be able to install programs, perform backups, and manage printers, but you do not want her to view, change, or read files for which permission has not been granted to her. Applying the least administrative effort, what should you do?

a. Let Rena be a local administrator and limit her rights using a local policy.

b. Let Rena be a local administrator and change the NTFS permissions on other files to deny Rena from viewing or modifying them.

c. Remove Rena's administrative rights. Add her to the Power Users group and Backup Operators group.

d. Remove Rena's administrative rights. Add her to the Power Users group and grant her NTFS permission to the files she will need to back up.

63. You have configured a Group Policy object (GPO) for the marketing organization unit (OU) to prevent users from accessing My Network Places and from running System in Control Panel. You want the Managers Domain Local Group to be able to access My Network Places, but you still want to prevent them from running System in Control Panel. What should you do?

a. Add the managers group to the access control list of the GPO. Disable the permission of the managers group to read and apply the Group Policy.

b. Add the managers group to the access control list of the GPO. Deny the permission of the managers group to read and apply the Group Policy.

c. Create a second GPO in the OU. Add the managers group to the access control list. Allow the managers group to apply the Group Policy. Deny the Authenticated Users group permission to read and apply the Group Policy. Configure the new GPO to deny the ability to run system Control Policy Panel. Give the original GPO a higher priority than the new GPO.

d. Create a Second GPO in the OU. Add the managers group to the access control list. Allow the managers group to apply the Group Policy. Disable the Authenticated Users group permission to read and apply the Group Policy. Configure the new GPO to allow access to My Network Places. Give the original GPO a higher priority than the new GPO.

HANDS-ON EXERCISES

For these exercises, X will represent either A or B depending on if you are computer A or computer B. This will allow both users to perform the exercise.

Exercise 1: Creating Organizational Units

1. Start the Active Directory User and Computers console.
2. To create an organizational unit called SALES, right-click the ACMExx.COM domain, select the New option, and select an Organizational Unit. In the Name text box, input SALES and click on the OK button.
3. Using the same method, create the following organizational units under ACMExx.COM:

```
RESEARCHX
EDUCATIONX
MANUFACTURINGX
```

Exercise 2: Creating Users

1. To create a user in the ACMExx.COM domain, right-click the ACMExx.COM domain, select the New option, and select User. In the New Object–User dialog box, input your first name, middle initial, and last name. For your user logon name, use your first initial, middle initial, and last name without spaces. For example, if your name is Paul G. Rogers, your login name is PGRogers. Click on the Next button.
2. Enter the password of PW (uppercase) and enable the "Password must change password on next logon" option. Click on the Finish button.
3. After your account has been created, right-click on your account and select the Properties option. Input your description as domain administrator and your office as the server room. Input your telephone number, e-mail address, and web page URL if you have one. Click on the Address tab and type in your address. Click on the Telephones tab and input your phone numbers. Click on the Organization tab and input Administrator for the title, IT for the department, and Acme Corporation for the company. Click on the OK button.
4. Create the following users in the appropriate organizational unit.

First Name	Middle Initial	Last Name	User Logon Name	Title	Department	Organizational Unit
Charles	L	Gee	CLGeeX	Sales Mgr.	Sales	Sales
Frank	J	Biggs	FJBiggsX	Sales Rep.	Sales	Sales
Herold	W	Jones	HWJonesX	Sales Rep.	Sales	Sales
Paul	L	Ray	PLRayX	Sales Rep.	Sales	Sales
Juan	O	Hermes	JOHermesX	Sales Rep.	Sales	Sales
Jill	K	Knight	JKKnightX	Sales Admin. Asst.	Sales	Sales
Jean	A	Mao	JAMaoX	Training Mgr.	Education	Education
Edward	J	Morell	EJMorellX	Trainer	Education	Education
Donna	L	Starr	DLStarrX	Manufact. Mgr.	Manufacturing	Manufacturing
Eric	O	Skow	EOSkowX	Manufact. Technician	Manufacturing	Manufacturing
Victor	N	Sloan	VNSloanX	Manufact. Technician	Manufacturing	Manufacturing
Sonny	K	Wong	SKWongX	Research Engineer	Manufacturing	Research
Gina	J	Smith	GJSmithX	Research Engineer	Manufacturing	Research

5. Right-click on the SALES organizational unit, select the New option, and select the Computer option. Enter the name of your partner's Windows 2000 Professional workstation. It should be WS2000-xxy, where *xx* represents your two-digit partner number and *y* represents either A or B. Click on the OK button.

6. Right-click each of these users and input their appropriate departments.

Exercise 3: Home Directories

1. Open My Computer and open the C drive. In the C drive, right-click on empty space within the C drive window, select New, and select the Folder option. Name the folder USERS and press the Enter key. In a real working environment, do not store data files on the system and/or boot partition.

2. Right-click the USERS folder and select the Sharing option. Select the Share This Folder option. Click on the Permissions button. Since Everyone is already highlighted, click on the Remove button.

3. Click on the Add button. Select the USERS group and click on the OK button. In the Permissions section, make sure the check box for Allow Full Control is marked. Click on the OK button to close the Sharing window and click OK to close the Properties windows.

4. Within the Active Directory Users and Computers console, open the Properties window of Charles L. Gee. Click on the Profile tab. Select the Connect To option under Login Scripts, select the Z drive, and in the To: text box enter:

```
\\SERVER2000-xxy.acmeXX.com\Users\%USERNAME%
```

5. Open the Users folder and note the CLGeeX folder.

6. Do the same for Frank J. Biggs, Herold W. Jones, and Paul L. Ray.

Exercise 4: Finding an Object

1. Right-click the ACMExx.COM domain and select the Find option.

2. Under the Users, Contacts and Groups tab, enter Jill in the Name: text box and click on the Find Now button. Notice that it had no problem finding Jill Knight.

3. Double-click on Jill K. Knight at the bottom of the window. Click on the OK button.

4. Click on the Advanced tab. Click on the Field button, select the User option, and then select the Department field. Click on the Condition pulldown menu and look at the various conditions available. For the value, input Sales. Click on the Add button and click on the Find Now button.

Exercise 5: Creating Groups

1. Right-click the ACMExx.COM domain, select the New option, and select the Group option. Click on the Global Group scope and Security Group type. Enter the Managers in the Group Name text box and click on the OK button.

2. Right-click the Managers group and select the Properties option. Click on the Members tab, click on the Add button, click on Charles L. Gee, and then click on the Add button. Click on and add Jean A. Mao and Donna L. Starr. Click on the OK button to close the Select Users, Contacts, or Computers dialog box. Click on the OK button to close the Managers Property window.

3. Right-click the ACMExx.COM domain, select the New option, and then select the Group option. Click on the Global Group scope and Security Group type. Enter the ManagersX in the Group Name text box and click on the OK button.

4. Right-click the ManagersX group and select the Properties option. Click on the Members tab, click on the Add button, click on Charles L. Gee, and then click on the Add button. Click on and add Jean A. Mao and Donna L. Starr. Click on the OK button to close the Select Users, Contacts, or Computers dialog box. Click on the OK button to close the Managers Property window.

5. Right-click the ACMExx.COM domain, select the New option, and select the Group option. Click on the Global Group scope and Security Group type. Enter the Product-StaffX in the Group Name text box and click on the OK button.

6. Right-click the ProductStaffX group and select the Properties option. Add all staff members from the manufacturing department.

7. Right-click the ACMExx.COM domain, select the New option, and select the Group option. Click on the Domain Local Group scope and Security Group type. Enter the ProductResourcesX in the Group Name text box and click on the OK button.

8. Right-click the ProductResourcesX group and click on the Properties option. Add the Managers group, ProductStaffX group, and Jill K. Knight to the group.

9. Create a universal group called SalesX.

The only step remaining is to assign rights and permissions to the Product Resources group. When new employees are added, they only have to be added to the appropriate group and they will automatically inherit these rights.

10. Open My Computer and open the C drive. In the C drive, right-click on empty space within the C drive window, select the New and select the Folder options. Name the folder TestShare and press the Enter key.

11. Right-click the TestShare folder and select the Sharing option. Select the Share This Folder. Click on the Permissions button. Since Everyone is already highlighted, click on the Remove button.

12. Click on the Add button. Select the ProductResourcesX and click on the OK button. Click on the OK button to close the Sharing window.

In this case, we did not need to use the local and global groups because both users and resources are in the same domain. Remember that global groups are intended to group people within a specific domain, whereas domain local groups are to give rights and permissions to objects.

Exercise 6: Disable, Rename, and Delete an Account

1. Paul Ray just got fired. To disable the account, right-click on the Paul Ray account and select the Disable Account option. Note the small x that appears.
2. Right-click the Paul L. Ray account and select the Rename option. While the entire name is highlighted, press the Delete key and then press Enter.
3. Change the name to Tom J. Landers.
   Full name: Tom J. Landers
   First name: Tom
   Last name: Landers
   Display name: Tom J. Landers
   User logon name: TJLanders
   User logon name: (pre-Windows2000): TJLanders
4. Click on the OK button.
5. Right-click on the Tom J. Landers account and select the Reset Password option. Change the password to TEST. Click on the OK button to close the Windows and click on the OK button to close the Confirmation dialog box.
6. Right-click on the Tom J. Landers account and select the Enable Account option.
7. Right-click on the Tom J. Landers account and select the Properties option. Select the Profile tab and note the location of the home folder. Although the account has been changed, Tom Landers was able to get access to everything that Paul Ray had including his home directory, even though his home directory is still called Paul Ray. Eventually, rename the directory and be sure that Tom's profile tab indicates the new name of the home folder.
8. Right-click on the Tom Landers folder and select the Delete option. Say Yes to the Are You Sure? dialog box.
9. Paul Ray got rehired into his original position. Unfortunately, since his account was deleted, a new one will have to be created. Therefore, in the Sales organizational unit, create a new Paul Ray account.
10. Using the Profile tab located within Paul Ray's properties, re-create his home folder.
11. When the "Home directory was not created" warning appears, click on the OK button. Because Paul's old account was created, Paul does not automatically get the same rights that he had before when the new account is re-created. All of Paul's previous rights, permissions, and group memberships will have to be given again.

Exercise 7: Using Templates

1. Right-click the Sales organizational unit and select New User. Specify the following:
   First name: Sales
   Last name: Template
   User logon name: _SALES_TEMPLATE
   Click on the Next button. The reason why you would use the first underscore (_) is it will show first on the list if they are alphabetized by user name.
2. Specify the password of "password" and enable the "User must change password at next logon." Click on the Next button.
3. Click on the Finish button.
4. Right-click the Sales Template and select the Properties option.
5. Put an address and phone number in the Address and Telephones tab.
6. Using the Member Of tab, assign the template to the Sales group.
7. Right-click the Sales template again and select the Copy command to create a new user called Charlie Brown. Use the password of "password" for Charlie Brown.

8. Right-click the Charlie Brown account and select the Properties option. View the various tabs that you modified when creating the _SALES_TEMPLATE.

Exercise 8: User Rights

1. Log out as the Administrator.
2. Try to log in as Charlie Brown. It should not work, because Charlie Brown has not been given the right to log on locally to a domain controller.
3. Log in as the Administrator.
4. In the Administrative Tools, open the Domain Controller Security Policy console.
5. If you open Security Settings, Local Policies, User Rights Assignment, there you will find Logon Locally. Double-click on it.
6. Click the Add button, click on the Browse button, select the Charlie Brown account, click on the Add button, and then click on the OK button twice.
7. Log out as the Administrator and log in as Charlie Brown. When you log in, change the password to PW.
8. As Charlie Brown, try to disable the Frank Biggs account.
9. Log out as Charlie Brown and log in as Administrator.
10. Right-click the Sales organizational unit and select the Delegate Control option. Click the Next button.
11. Click the Add button, select Charlie Brown, and click on the Add button. Click the OK button. Click on the Next button.
12. Select both the Create, Delete, and Manage User Accounts and Modify the Membership of a Group options. Click on the Next button. Click the Finish button.
13. Log out as the Administrator and log in as Charlie Brown.
14. Disable the Frank Biggs account.
15. Log out as Charlie Brown.

Exercise 9: Group Policies

1. Log in as the Administrator.
2. Using the Run option, start a Microsoft Management Console.
3. In the MMC, open the Console menu and select the Add/Remove Snap-in option.
4. In the Add/Remove Snap-in dialog box, click on the Add button.
5. Click on the Group Policy snap-in and then click on the Add button. In the Select Group Policy Object dialog box, click on the Browse button.
6. In the Browse for a Group Policy Object dialog box, click the Domain Controllers.AcmeXX.com. Click the OK button.
7. Click the Default Domain Controllers Policy and click the OK button. Click the Finish button.
8. Click on the Group Policy snap-in again and click on the Add button. In the Select Group Policy Object dialog box, click on the Browse button.
9. In the Browse for a Group Policy Object dialog box, click the Sales.AcmeXX.com. Click the OK button.
10. Click the New Group Policy Object button (next to the Up Folder button). Since the New Group Object is highlighted, rename it to the Sales Group Policy and click the OK button. Click the Finish button.
11. Click on the Group Policy snap-in and click on the Add button. With the Local Computer selected for the Group Policy Object, click on the Finish button.
12. Click on the Close button. Click on the OK button.
13. Under the Default Domain Controllers Policy, open Computer Configuration, Windows Settings, Security Policy, Account Policies, and click on Password Policy.
14. In the Details pane, double-click the Minimum Password Length option.
15. In the Template Security Policy Setting dialog box, enable "Define this policy setting in the template." Specify at least eight characters. Click the OK button.
16. Under Password Policy, click on Account Policy option.
17. In the Details pane, double-click the Account Lockout Duration.
18. Enable "Define this policy setting in the template." Keep the default of 30 minutes and click on the OK button. Click on the OK button.
19. Log out as the Administrator.
20. Log in as Charlie Brown.
21. Log in six times with the password TEST. This should lock out the account.
22. Log in as the Administrator.
23. Using the Active Directory Users and Computers console, right-click Charlie Brown's user account and select the Properties option.

24. In the Account tab, remove the X in the Accounts Locked Out box.
25. Try to change Charlie Brown's password to LETMEIN. Then change the password to PASSWORD.
26. In the Active Directory Users and Computers console, right-click the Sales department and select the Properties option.
27. In the Group Policy tab, click the Add button. Click the Up Folder button and double-click the Domain Controllers.amcexx.com folder. Select the Default Domain Controllers Policy. Click the OK button.
28. Click the Default Domain Controllers Policy and click on the Up button to make the Default Domain Controller Policy have a higher priority than the Sales Policy. Although we will not use the option, note the Block Policy Inheritance. Click the OK button.

Exercise 10: User Profiles

1. Log in as Charlie Brown. Change the background to Solar Eclipse. (The background is changed using the Display applet in the Control Panel.)
2. Log in as the Administrator.
3. Create a PROFILE folder on the C drive.
4. Right-click the PROFILE folder and select the Sharing option.
5. Click on the Share This Folder and click on the OK button.
6. Right-click the My Computer applet and select the Properties option.
7. On the User Profile tab, click the Charlie Brown profile and click the Copy To button.
8. In the Copy Profile to text box, specify \\server2000-XXx\Profile\CBrownx.
9. When it asks if you want to continue, click on the Yes button.
10. Click the OK button.
11. Using the Active Directory Users and Computers console, right-click Charlie Brown and then click the Profile tab.
12. In the Profile Path text box, specify the \\server2000-XXx\profile\CBrownx. Click on the OK button.
13. From your partner's computer, log on as Charlie Brown. Note that the desktop background should be the solar eclipse.

CHAPTER **14**

Introduction to Disk Management

Topics Covered in This Chapter

Introduction

Since all of the user's data are kept on disk, it is easy to see why disk management is essential to managing the server. Having a good understanding of how the disk systems work and how they can be utilized effectively will help you improve the server's performance and reliability. In this chapter you will learn about file systems, about forms of RAID that are available through Windows, and how to set up disks.

Objectives

- Convert from one file system to another file system.
- Configure file systems by using NTFS, FAT32, or FAT.

- Monitor and configure disks.
- Monitor, configure, and troubleshoot volumes.
- Monitor and configure disk quotas.

14.1 DISK STRUCTURE AND FILE SYSTEMS

The **disk structure** does not describe how a hard drive or floppy disk physically works, but how it stores files on the disk. In other words, it describes the formatting of the disk (file system, partitions, the root directory, and the directories). A **file system** is the overall structure in which files are named, stored, and organized. Examples of file systems include FAT, FAT32, and NTFS.

Disks are divided into a circular grid consisting of tracks and sectors. **Tracks** are concentric circles in that they share the same center much like rings in a tree. Tracks are numbered starting with the outside track as track 0. The tracks are then further divided into **sectors,** each typically 512 bytes of useable data. Sectors are numbered on a track, beginning with track 1. See Figure 14.1.

In Windows 2000, Windows XP, and Windows Server 2003, a **volume** is a logical unit of disk space that functions as though it was a physical disk. It can be a portion of a disk, an entire disk, several disks combined, or several portions of a disk combined. Often the volume is assigned a drive letter.

Figure 14.1 Tracks and sectors

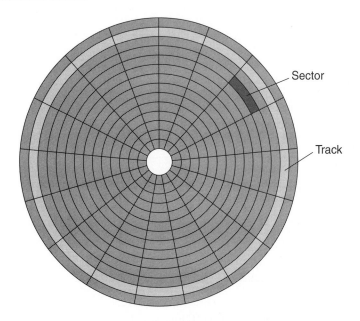

14.1.1   File Allocation Table

When you save a file, it can be stored at the beginning, the middle, or the end of the disk. When you retrieve a file, do not worry about its physical location, because when you specify a name (and sometimes the path), the operating system finds the file. The directory structure, the methods for organizing a volume (partition or floppy disk), and the method of file storage and retrieval are called the file system.

For operating systems, the most basic storage unit is not a sector, but a **cluster.** Another name for cluster is **allocation unit.** It consists of one or more sectors (usually more). The size of the cluster depends on the operating system, the version of the operating system, the file system that the operating system is using, and the size of the volume (partition or floppy disks). See Table 14.1.

The **file allocation table (FAT)** is an index used to remember which file is located in which cluster. It lists each cluster, if the cluster is being used by a file, the name of the file using the cluster, and the next cluster if the file does not fit within the cluster.

Example 1:

Your partition is using clusters of eight sectors (4096 bytes). If you have a file that is 2048 bytes, the file allocation table will have an entry for the cluster and the file belonging to the cluster. Although the file is only half as large as the cluster, the file allocation table can only list one file as part of the allocation unit. Therefore, the 2048-byte file will use the entire 4096 bytes.

Example 2:

Your partition is using clusters of eight sectors (4096 bytes). If you have a file that is 8193 bytes, the file allocation table would have three entries. The first part of the file would be stored in a cluster and listed in the file allocation table. After the first cluster is filled, there are still 4097 bytes remaining, so the entry of the first cluster will list the location of the next cluster. (The cluster may or may not be the next cluster.) The second cluster would then be filled up, leaving 1 byte. Again, the second cluster will list a third cluster, where the last byte would reside. Since the file allocation table can only list one file per cluster, the single byte would take up the entire 4096 bytes of disk space.

Table 14.1   File system default cluster size

Drive Size	FAT	FAT32	NTFS
0 MB–15 MB	8 Sectors (4 KB)		1 Sector (512 bytes)
16 MB–31 MB	1 Sector (512 bytes)		1 Sector (512 bytes)
32 MB–63 MB	2 Sectors (1 KB)		1 Sector (512 bytes)
64 MB–127 MB	4 Sectors (2 KB)		1 Sector (512 bytes)
128 MB–255 MB	8 Sectors (4 KB)		1 Sector (512 bytes)
256 MB–511 MB	16 Sectors (8 KB)		1 Sector (512 bytes)
512 MB–1023 MB	32 Sectors (16 KB)	8 Sectors (4 KB)	2 Sectors (1 KB)
1024 MB–2047 MB	64 Sectors (32 KB)	8 Sectors (4 KB)	4 Sectors (2 KB)
2048 MB–4095 MB	128 Sectors (64 KB)	8 Sectors (4 KB)	4 Sectors (2 KB)
4096 MB–8191 MB		8 Sectors (4 KB)	4 Sectors (2 KB)
8192 MB–16,384 MB		16 Sectors (8 KB)	4 Sectors (2 KB)
16,385–32,767 MB		32 Sectors (16 KB)	4 Sectors (2 KB)
32,768 MB+		64 Sectors (32 KB)	4 Sectors (2 KB)

Note: Windows using NTFS can vary the cluster size from 512 bytes to 4 KB.

14.1.2   Directories, Files, and Attributes

The storage model of the PC is based on an inverted directory tree structure. Every volume has a starting point called the **root directory,** which is located at the top of the tree structure. The root directory holds files and/or directories. The **directories** under the root directory can also be referred to as **subdirectories.** Newer operating systems may even refer to a directory as a **folder.** Each directory can also hold files and/or more subdirectories.

A **file** is a collection of related information that is referenced by name. Each file or directory on a volume can be uniquely identified by using the file name (including the file extension, if any) and the path (or location on the tree). Every file on the system is stored in a directory. The directory itself is a specially marked file or table that contains information about files and subdirectories. Every directory, including the root directory, consists of a small database which stores the file name and extension, the file attributes, and dates and times of when the file was created or last modified.

Files are stored in clusters. Since files are often larger than a cluster, a file will be spread among many clusters. On the last cluster, to indicate the end of the file, a special end-of-file (EOF) character is used. This way, the operating system knows to ignore the rest of the cluster, because it does not have any valid data.

The file allocation table and the directory work closely together. When you open a file, you specify the name. To find the file, the operating system looks in the directory specified. If no directory was specified, it looks in the current directory. After it finds the file name, it looks at the starting cluster. The operating system reads the data in the starting cluster. The operating system then jumps to the file allocation table, specifically the starting cluster to read the next cluster for the file. It then jumps to the next cluster and retrieves the data. It continues jumping between the file allocation table to find the next cluster and the clusters to retrieve the data until it gets to the EOF character.

14.2   FILE SYSTEM

Throughout the history of the PC, there have been a few different file systems. Today, the most common are FAT, FAT32, and NTFS. See Table 14.2.

14.2.1   FAT

The most common file system used is the file allocation table (FAT). FAT is a simple and reliable file system that uses minimal memory. It supports file names of 11 characters, which include the 8 characters for the file name and 3 characters for the file extension.

Table 14.2   Common Microsoft file systems

	FAT	FAT32	NTFS
Operating Systems	Used by DOS, Windows 9X, Windows NT, Windows 2000, Windows XP, and Windows Server 2003	Used by Windows 95B/OSR2, Windows 98, Windows Me, Windows 2000, Windows XP, and Windows Server 2003	Used by Windows NT, Windows 2000, Windows XP, and Windows Server 2003
Volume Size	Floppy disk to 4 GB	512 MB to 2 TB	10 MB to 2 TB
Maximum File Size	2 GB	4 GB	Limited by size of volume
Limit on Entries in Root Directory	Yes	No	No
File and Directory Security	No	No	Yes
Directory and File Compression	No	No	Yes
Cluster Remapping	No	No	Yes

Early versions of DOS used FAT12, which used a 12-bit binary number for each cluster. Therefore, the biggest cluster number that FAT12 could see was 4086. The number would have been 4096, but some clusters were reserved. FAT12 is still used on floppy disks and hard disk partitions that are smaller than 16 MB.

Newer DOS machines use FAT16. Instead of a 12-bit number for the clusters, FAT16 uses a 16-bit number, allowing for 65,526 clusters. It is used for volumes up to 2 GB.

The FAT root directory is fixed in size and so is limited to a specific number of entries. See Table 14.3. Therefore, when you reach the maximum number of files and subdirectories in the root directory, you cannot add more, although there may still be plenty of disk space.

For FAT, a directory entry (see Table 14.4) uses 11 bytes for the entire file name—8 bytes for the file name and 3 bytes for the extension. The file name is meant to identify the file and, thus, should describe the contents of the file. The extension is used to identify the type of file. For example, files that have a DOC extension are usually Microsoft Word documents, and files that have an EXE extension are executable files. To indicate that a file is deleted, the operating system will change the first character to a lowercase sigma (σ). This way, assuming all clusters are intact and have not been used by other files, a file can be undeleted by providing a first character. If the entire eight characters for the file name and the entire three characters for the file extension are not used, then the remaining characters become spaces. Note that the dot separating the file name and the extension is not stored as part of the file allocation table or the directory. It is shown by the operating system to indicate a separation between the two.

Table 14.3 The maximum number of root directory entries under FAT

Volume Type	Maximum Number of Root Directory Entries
360 KB 5¼" floppy disk	112
720 KB 3½" floppy disk	112
1.2 MB 5¼" floppy disk	224
1.44 MB 3½" floppy disk	224
2.88 MB 3⅓" floppy disk	448
Hard disk	512

Table 14.4 FAT/VFAT directory format

Content	Byte Size
File name	8 bytes
File extension	3 bytes
File attributes	1 bytes
Time of creation	3 bytes
Date of creation	2 bytes
Date of last access	2 bytes
Time of last modified	2 bytes
Date of last modified	2 bytes
Starting cluster	2 bytes
Size in bytes	4 bytes

VFAT is an enhanced version of the FAT structure, which allows all Windows operating systems since Windows 95 to support long file names (LFNs) up to 255 characters. If users refer to FAT, they probably mean VFAT. Since it is built on ordinary FAT, each file must have an 8-character name and a 3-character extension to be backward compatible for DOS and Windows 3xx applications. Therefore, programs running in DOS and Windows 3.xxx will not see the LFNs. When running a Win32 program (programs made for Windows 9X, Windows NT, Windows 2000, Windows XP, or Windows Server 2003), they can see and make use of the longer names.

To accomplish the DOS file names and the LFNs, VFAT uses additional directory entries to store the LFNs. Therefore, when an LFN is saved, the first entry will need a truncated name (known as an alias) of the file. It will then use additional directory entries to hold the rest of the LFN. Each entry is 32 bytes in length. Since the root directory has a set number of entries, it is not wise to place too many LFNs in the root directory. To make sure that DOS does not use the directory entries, which hold the LFNs, the entries have the Read-only, Hidden, System, and Volume Label attributes enabled. Having all of these active causes older software to basically ignore the extra directory entries that are being used by VFAT.

A single LFN can use many directory entries (since each entry is only 32 bytes in length), and for this reason it is recommended that LFNs not be placed in the root directory, where the total number of directory entries is limited.

Example 3:

Under Windows 2000, you save a file called *The Budget for 1999 and 2000.DOC*. The first entry will take the first six characters—ignoring the spaces and adding a tilde (~) followed by a number in the directory would be *THEBUD~1.DOC*. Therefore, under a DOS or Windows 3.xx program, you would see *THEBUD~1.DOC*, whereas under Windows 95/98 and Windows NT programs you would see *The Budget for 1999 and 2000.DOC*. It would take several directory entries to store the alias and even more to save the long file name. If you try to save a second file with the name of *The Budget for 2000 and 2001.DOC*, the alias would be THEBUD~2.DOC.

After the file name and file extension, 1 byte is used for attributes. The **file attribute** field stores a number of characteristics about each file. See Table 14.5. Attributes can be either on or off. The most common attributes include Read-only, Hidden, System, and Archive. One of these attributes indicates if the file is a real file or a directory. Since DOS reserves 1 byte for attributes, it can keep track of up to eight attributes. Remember, 1 byte equals 8 bits (on–off switch). To change the attributes, use the ATTRIB command or Explorer (right-click the file and select the Properties option). See Figure 14.2.

Table 14.5   DOS file attributes

Attribute	Abbreviation	Description
Read-only	R or RO	When a file is marked as read-only, it cannot be deleted or modified. The opposite of read-only is read-write.
Hidden	H	When a file is marked as hidden, it cannot be seen during normal directory listings.
System	S or Sy	When a file is marked as system, it should not be moved. In addition, it usually cannot be seen during normal directory listings.
Volume Label		The name of the volume.
Subdirectory		A table that contains information about files and subdirectories.
Archive	A	When a file is marked as archive, the file has not been backed up. Anytime a file is new or has been changed, the archive attribute comes on automatically. When the archive attribute is off, the file has been backed up.
Directory	D	An attribute to indicate a directory listing instead of a file.

Figure 14.2   Properties of a file, including its attributes

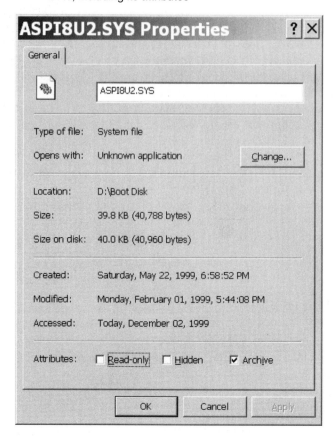

Next, operating systems record the date and time that the file or directory was created, modi-fied, and accessed and the size of the file in bytes. The files are stamped with the date and time from the real-time clock (RTC) on the motherboard. If the RTC clock has an incorrect date and time, then so will the file.

Because files are often larger than one cluster, the cluster that starts the file or subdirectory will be numbered and stored. Then when a file is retrieved from a subdirectory, it reads the directory first to find the starting point of the file. It then goes to the file allocation table to find the location of the sec-ond cluster, the third cluster, and so on, until the file has been retrieved into RAM.

14.2.2   FAT32

FAT32, which uses 32-bit FAT entries, was introduced in the second major release of Windows 95 (OSR2/Windows 95B) and is an enhancement of the FAT/VFAT file system. It supports hard drives up to 2 TB, although Windows 2000, Windows XP, and Windows Server 2003 support volumes up to 32 GB. Note: If you have a drive larger than 32 GB, you must either break the drive into partitions, which are 32 GB or smaller, or use a special program provided by the disk manufacturer. FAT32 uses space more efficiently, such as 4-KB clusters for drives up to 8 GB, which results in 15% better use of disk space relative to large FAT drives.

The root directory is an ordinary cluster chain; thus, it can be located anywhere in the drive. It allows dynamic resizing of FAT32 partitions (without loosing data) and allows FAT mirroring to be dis-abled, which allows a copy of the FAT other than the first to be active. Consequently, FAT32 drives are less prone to failure in critical data areas such as the FAT.

To install FAT32 on a volume, use the Disk Manager or the FDISK utility from the Windows 95—OSR2/Windows 95B or Windows 98 on a hard drive over 512 MB. When running FDISK, it will ask whether to enable large disk support. If you answer yes, any partition you create that is greater than 512 MB will be marked as a FAT32 partition.

Table 14.6   NTFS file system

System File	File Name	Description
Master File Table	$Mft	The file allocation table for the NTFS volume that lists the contents of the NTFS volume
Master File Table2	$MftMirr	A mirror or copy of the Master File Table, used when a Master File Table becomes unreadable
Log File	$LogFile	A list of transaction steps, used by the Log File System for recoverability
Volume	$Volume	The name, version, and other information about the volume
Attribute Definitions	$AttrDef	A table of attribute names, numbers, and descriptions
Root Filename Index	$.	Root directory
Cluster Bitmap	$Bitmap	A representation of the volume showing which allocation units are in use
Partition Boot Sector	$Boot	Includes the bootstrap for the volume, if this is a bootable volume
Bad Cluster File	$BadClus	A location where all the bad clusters in the volume are located
Quota Table	$Quota	Disk quota usage for each user on a volume
Uppercase Table	$Upcase	Used for converting lowercase characters to the matching Unicode uppercase characters

14.2.3   NTFS

NTFS is a file system for Windows NT, Windows 2000, Windows XP, and Windows Server 2003, designed for both the server and the workstation. It provides a combination of performance, reliability, and compatibility. It supports long file names, yet maintains an 8.3 name for DOS and Windows 3.xx programs. Because it is a 64-bit architecture, NTFS is designed to support up to 2^{64} bytes = 18,446,744,073,709,551,616 bytes = 16 exabytes.

When you create (format) a NTFS volume, the high-level format program creates a set of files that contains the metadata used to implement the file system structure. The NTFS uses approximately 1 MB for the metadata files. See Table 14.6.

Since Windows NT, Windows 2000, Windows XP, and Windows Server 2003 include enhanced security, NTFS supports a variety of multiuser security models and allows computers running other operating systems to save files to the NTFS volume on a server. This includes DOS, Windows, UNIX, POSIX, and even Macintosh computers. It does not allow DOS direct access to an NTFS volume directory except through the network (assuming you have the proper permissions or rights to access the volume). It can compress individual files or directories, including infrequently used files or directories.

To make its own volume more resistant to failure, NTFS writes updates to a log area and supports remapped clusters. If a system crash occurs, the log area can be used to quickly clean up problems. If a cluster is found to be bad, it can move the data to another cluster and mark the cluster as bad so that the operating system does not use it.

FAT is simpler and smaller than NTFS and uses an unsorted directory structure. NTFS is generally faster for complex file structures, because it uses a B-tree directory structure, which minimizes the number of disk accesses required to find a file, thus making access to the file faster, especially if it is a larger folder.

NTFS supports volume set and directory/file compression. A volume set combines several hard drives (or parts of hard drives) to be combined into a single volume. If the volume needs to be expanded again, simply add another hard drive and expand the volume. NTFS allows an individual file or directory to be compressed without compressing the entire drive.

The NTFS used on Windows NT 4.0 was known as NTFS4, and the NTFS used on Windows 2000, Windows XP, and Windows Server 2003 is NTFS5. The changes required to update NTFS4 to NTFS5 were implemeted in Windows NT 4.0 server pack 4. Upgrading to a system from Windows NT 4.0

to Windows 2000 or Windows Server 2003 will also update the NTFS4 volumes to NTFS5 volumes. Unfortunately, if a Windows NT computer does not have service pack 4 or higher, it will not be able to directly use the NTFS5 volume.

Some of the updates included with NTFS5 volume include the ability to encrypt files or folders to protect them. NTFS5 has the ability to mount NTFS volumes onto an NTFS folder without assigning additional drive letters. It also has the ability to retain shortcuts and other file information when files are transferred between volumes. In addition, NTFS5 has hard disk quotas to monitor and control disk usage and has full text and property indexing to allow fast retrieval of documents.

NOTE: You can set up a computer to dual-boot between Windows 9X and the newer versions of Windows and have both operating systems access the same files if they are both running VFAT. Remember that Windows 9X cannot read or access NTFS and Windows NT and the original version of Windows 95 cannot read or access FAT32.

14.3   DISK MANAGEMENT

To configure and manage disks in Windows 2000, Windows XP, and Windows Server 2003, use the **Disk Management** console or the Computer Management console (click on the Start button, click on the Programs option, click on the Administrative Tools, and then select the Computer Management option). See Figure 14.3. To use the Disk Management console to configure and manage disks, you must be a member of the Administrators or Server Operators group.

Figure 14.3   Disk Management console

> Data on the system are probably most important on the network and server. Therefore, before making any kinds of changes to the disk systems, back up all important data. Actually, you should back up important data on a regular basis.

After you make changes to your disk configuration, right-click Disk Management or open the Action menu, and use both the Refresh and Rescan Disks options. The Refresh option updates drive letters, file system information, volume information, and removable media information. The Rescan Disks option updates hardware information by scanning all attached disks for disk configuration changes. Be aware that disk rescanning may take several minutes depending on the number of drives.

When you connect a hard drive from another computer, the disks are imported automatically. If the status of the disk appears as Foreign, however, right-click the new disk and use the Import Foreign Disk option. If the status of an imported volume appears as "Failed: Incomplete Volume," you have imported one or more disks that has either a spanned or striped volume and RAID-5 volumes, but is missing one or more disks.

14.3.1   Drive Letters and Paths

Windows 2000, Windows XP, and Windows Server 2003 allow an unlimited amount of volumes, but unfortunately do not allow the user to assign more than 26 drive letters (A–Z). Typically, letters A and B are reserved for the floppy disk. If you do not have a floppy disk drive B, you can use the letter B as a network drive. These drive letters only apply to the local machine, not to network machines that connect to a Windows server.

For many operating systems, drive letters are dynamic, which means that every time you turn on the machine, a drive letter is assigned to each volume. Unfortunately, when you add a drive or create partitions, sometimes the drive letters are remapped. The problem occurs when a program is set to look for or access a particular drive letter only to find that the folder or files are not at the designated location because drive letters have been assigned differently.

Windows also allows the static assignment of drive letters, during which a drive letter can be permanently assigned to a specific hard disk and volume. Then, when a hard disk is added to the existing computer system or partitions and volumes are created, it does not affect statically assigned drive letters.

Windows 2000, Windows XP, and Windows Server 2003 allow you to change drive letters; however, since many DOS and Windows programs refer to specific drive letters, be careful when making drive-letter assignments. You cannot change a drive letter that is assigned to a boot volume or system volume. To assign a drive letter to a volume that currently has no drive letter, do the following:

1. Open the Disk Manager.
2. Right-click the volume that you want to assign a drive letter to.
3. Select Change Drive Letter and Path option and click on the Add button.
4. Select a drive letter and click the OK button.

To remove a drive letter, do the following:

1. Open the Disk Manager.
2. Right-click the volume that you want to remove the drive letter from and click the Remove button.
3. Click Yes to confirm your actions.

To change a drive letter, do the following:

1. Open the Disk Manager.
2. Right-click the volume that you want to change the assigned drive letter to.
3. Select Change Drive Letter and Path option and click on the Edit button.
4. Select a new drive letter and click the OK button.
5. Click Yes to confirm your actions.

14.3.2   NTFS Mounted Drives

A NTFS mounted drive is attached to an empty folder on an NTFS volume, which is assigned a path, not a drive letter. Volumes that are created after the twenty-sixth drive letter have to be accessed as a mounted drive. When you open the drive or directory that holds the mounted drive and then open the mounted drive, you will be automatically redirected to the mounted volume. To the user, the mounted drive acts like a folder or directory at the assigned location.

To create a mounted drive, follow these steps:

1. Create a folder where you want the drive mounted.
2. Open Disk Manager.
3. Right-click the volume that you want to mount and select the Change Drive Letter and Path option.
4. Click on the Add button if it is a volume without a drive letter or is not already mounted, or click on the Edit button if the volume already has a drive letter or is already mounted.
5. Select the Mount in this NTFS Folder option and type or browse the path of the new folder. Click on the OK button. See Figure 14.4.

14.3.3   Formatting Volumes

Before you can store files and directories on a volume or partition, perform a high-level format on it. A high-level format creates the file allocation table and root directory. It can be performed when creating a volume or partitions with Disk Manager or it can be formatted at a later time.

To perform a high-level format, do the following:

1. Open Disk Manager.
2. Right-click on the partition or volume that you want to format, type the volume label if desired, select the file system, and select the allocation unit size. Click on the OK button.
3. If you get a warning that all information will be lost during a format, click on the OK button.

Instead of a normal format, you can perform a quick format. Although a quick format removes the files from the disk, it does not scan the disk for bad sectors. Therefore, its use is not recommended.

14.3.4   Deleting Volumes

Sometimes you may need to delete a volume so that you can reallocate the disk space. You cannot delete the boot volume, however, although you can delete the system volume. To delete the volume, do the following:

1. Open the Disk Management console.
2. Right-click the volume that you want to delete and select the Delete Volume option.
3. At the warning that all data will be lost, click on the Yes button.

Figure 14.4   Mounting a drive

14.3.5   Converting FAT or FAT32 to NTFS

One way to convert a partition or volume to NTFS is to reformat it, but then, all information on the volume is lost. Another way to convert a partition or volume is to open a Command prompt window and use the following command:

```
CONVERT x: /FS:NTFS
```

where *x:* is the drive letter that you want to convert. If the CONVERT command cannot lock the drive, it will offer to convert it the next time the computer restarts, such as the system volume. You cannot, however, convert a NTFS partition or volume to FAT or FAT32.

The Disk Management console displays status descriptions in graphical view and under the Status column of the List View to inform you of the current status of the disk or volume. Use these status descriptions to help you detect and troubleshoot disk and volume failures. The following is a partial list of disk and volume status descriptions:

- **Online**—This is the normal disk status when the disk is accessible and functioning correctly.
- **Healthy**—This is the normal volume status when the volume is accessible and functioning correctly.
- **Healthy (At Risk)**—The volume is accessible; however, underlying I/O errors are detected on the disk. The disk status may display as Online (Errors). To resolve this issue, right-click the disk, then click Reactivate Disk to return the disk to Online status. This action should also return the volume to Healthy status. Note: Only dynamic volumes display the Healthy (At Risk) status.
- **Failed Redundancy**—One or both members of the mirrored volume have failed. The volume is no longer fault-tolerant. The disk status may display as Offline or Missing, or Online (Errors). To resolve this issue, repair any disk, controller, or connection problems and verify that the physical disk is turned on and correctly attached to the computer. Right-click the failed disk, then click Reactivate Disk to return the disk to Online status. This should also return the volume to Healthy status. Note: Only dynamic mirrored or RAID-5 volumes display the Failed Redundancy (At Risk) status.
- **Failed**—The volume cannot be started automatically. Both dynamic and basic volumes display the Failed Status.
- **Missing**—A dynamic disk is corrupted, powered down, or disconnected.

For a complete list of disk and volume status descriptions and troubleshooting procedures, see Disk Management Help (in the Disk Management snap-in or Computer Management window, click Help on the Action menu).

14.4   WINDOWS DISK STORAGE TYPES

Windows 2000, Windows XP, and Windows Server 2003 have two disk storage types, basic disks and dynamic disks. A **basic disk** is a physical disk that contains primary partitions, extended partitions, or logical drives that can be accessed directly using DOS or Windows 9X. Basic disks may contain volume sets, mirrored sets, striped sets, and striped sets with parity if they were created using Windows NT 4.0 or earlier and upgraded to Windows 2000, Windows XP, or Windows Server 2003. Windows 2000, Windows XP, and Windows Server 2003 offer limited support of striped sets and striped sets with parity. You can repair, regenerate, and delete striped sets and striped sets with parity, but you cannot create them.

When you install Windows, your hard disks are automatically initialized as basic. Using Disk Management console in Windows 2000, Windows XP, or Windows Server 2003, you can create, delete, and format partitions without having to restart your computer to make the changes effective.

To create a partition on a basic disk, following these steps:

1. Open the Disk Management console.
2. Right-click unallocated space on the basic disk where you want to create the partition, select the Create Volume option, and select the Next button.
3. Select the partition type and click on the Next button. The default size is the amount of unallocated space.

4. Specify the size for the selected disk and click on the Next button.
5. Assign the drive letter or path and click on the Next button.
6. Select "Format this partition with the following settings"; specify the file system, allocation unit sizes, and volume name; and click on the Next button.
7. Click on the Finish button.

A **dynamic disk** is converted from basic to dynamic storage, which contains simple volumes, spanned volumes, mirrored volumes, striped volumes, and RAID-5 volumes. Unlike basic disks, dynamic disks cannot contain partitions or logical drives or be accessed by DOS. The advantage of dynamic disks is they contain an unlimited number of volumes, and volumes can be extended to include noncontiguous space on available disks.

On a dynamic disk, the disk configuration information is stored on the disk and not in the registry. Therefore, to upgrade a drive successfully from basic to dynamic, you must have at least 1 MB of free space at the end of the disk. To upgrade a basic disk to a dynamic disk, right-click the disk using Computer Manager and select the Upgrade to Dynamic Disk option. When using the Computer Management program to create partitions or volumes on a disk, the program will reserve the free space automatically. In addition, if you upgrade a boot disk or if a volume or partition is in use on the disk, then the computer must be restarted for the upgrade to succeed. Remember that removable media devices can only contain primary partitions, so you cannot upgrade them. Dynamic disks also are not supported on portable computers or Windows XP Home Edition.

After you upgrade a basic disk to a dynamic disk, you cannot change the dynamic volumes back to partitions. Instead, you must delete all dynamic volumes on the disk and then use the Revert to Basic Disk command.

You can install Windows 2000, Windows XP, and Windows Server 2003 on a dynamic volume that was upgraded from a basic disk partition, but you cannot extend either the system volume or the boot volume. In addition, neither can be part of a spanned volume, since Windows considers extended volumes to be the same as spanned volumes.

Windows 2000, Windows XP, and Windows Server 2003 cannot extend a dynamic volume that was a basic volume before the dynamic disk upgrade, and the system and boot volumes (which might be the same volume) are likely the same volumes that existed under basic disk. The upgraded simple volume must match the listing found in the partition table. Extending the dynamic volume changes its size, but the partition table's registration of that volume is not updated to reflect the change. The only dynamic volumes on which you can install Windows 2000, Windows XP, and Windows Server 2003 are simple and mirrored volumes, and since these volumes must be registered in the partition table, they must be upgraded from basic to dynamic.

14.5   RAID

RAID is an acronym for "redundant array of inexpensive disks" or "redundant array of independent disks." It is a category of disk drives that employs two or more drives in combination to improve fault tolerance and performance. RAID disk drives are used frequently on servers but are not generally necessary for personal computers. Ideally, you use a RAID system to ensure that no data are lost and to recover data from failed disk drivers without shutting the system down.

RAID was originally defined as a memory architecture that uses a subsystem of two or more hard disk drives treated as a single, larger logical drive. The purpose of this proposed architecture was twofold: to take advantage of data redundancy inherent in the multiple-drive design and to capitalize on the lower costs of smaller drives. When RAID was first proposed, it was considerably cheaper to buy five 200-MB hard drives than one 1-GB drive. Today, however, this is not true, so the current focus for RAID is data integrity and reliability instead of cost saving.

Originally, RAID had six levels (RAID 0 through RAID 5; see Table 14.7). A few more levels have been added to combine the features of other levels. Although RAID 6 follows the general numbering process, most new levels break with the number sequence, usually for marketing reasons. Not all RAID levels are commercially available, and some are supported by only a few products. Only RAID 0, 1, and 5 are supported by Windows NT 4.0, Windows 2000, and Windows Server 2003 without additional

Table 14.7   RAID levels

Raid Type	Description
Raid 0—Disk Striping	Data striping is the spreading out of blocks of each file across multiple disks. It offers no fault tolerance, but it increases performance. Level 0 is the fastest and most efficient form of RAID.
RAID 1—Disk Mirroring/Duplexing	Disk mirror duplicates a partition onto two hard drives. Information is written to both hard drives simultaneously. It increases performance and provides fault tolerance. Disk duplexing is a form of disk mirroring. Disk mirroring uses two hard drives connected to the same card; disk duplexing uses controller cards, two cables, and two hard drives.
RAID 2—Disk Striping with ECC	Level 2 uses data striping plus error-correcting code (ECC) to detect errors. It is rarely used today since ECC is embedded in almost all modern disk drives.
RAID 3—ECC Stored as Parity	Level 3 dedicates one disk to error correction data. It provides good performance and some level of fault tolerance.
RAID 4—Disk Striping with Large Blocks	Level 4 offers no advantages over RAID-5 level and does not support multiple, simultaneously written operations.
RAID 5—Disk Striping with Parity	Raid-5 level uses disk striping and includes byte correction on one of the disks. If one disk goes bad, the system will continue to function. After the faulty disk is replaced, the information on the replaced disk can be rebuilt. This system requires at least three drives. It offers excellent performance and good fault tolerance.

hardware and software from RAID vendors. Those three levels, though, can be supported by a variety of hard disk and controller combinations.

RAID 0 is the base of RAID technology. RAID 0 stripes data across all drives. With striping, all available hard drives are combined into a single, large, virtual file system, with its blocks spread evenly across all the drives. For example, if you have three 500-MB hard drives, RAID 0 provides for a 1.5-GB virtual hard drive (sometimes referred to as a volume). When you store files, they are written across all three drives. When a large file, such as a 100-MB multimedia presentation, is saved to the virtual drive, part of it may be written to the first drive, the next chunk to the second, more to the third, and perhaps more wrapping back to the first drive to start the sequence again. The exact manner in which the chunks of data move from one physical drive to another depends on the way the virtual drive has been set up, which includes considerations of drive capacity and the way in which blocks are allocated on each drive. No parity control is used with RAID 0; therefore, it is a true form of RAID. RAID 0 has several advantages, however. Most important is that striping provides some increase in performance through load balancing. Windows NT 4.0 and Windows 2000 support RAID 0 with two or more drives.

RAID 1 is known as disk mirroring or disk duplexing. With RAID 1, each hard drive on the system has a duplicate drive that contains an exact copy of the first drive's contents. Since every bit that is written to the file system is duplicated, data redundancy exists with RAID 1. If one drive in the RAID-1 array fails or develops a problem of any kind (such as a bad sector), the mirror drive can take over and maintain all normal file-system operations while the faulty drive is diagnosed and fixed.

Many RAID-1 disk controllers have software routines that will automatically take a faulty drive offline, run diagnostics on it, and if possible reformat the drive and copy all data back from the mirror image—all while the file system proceeds as if nothing has happened. Users are frequently unaware of faults with RAID-1 controllers. Alert messages can be triggered when a fault occurs.

One big disadvantage of RAID 1 is its use of disks. If you have two 2-GB drives, you have a total file system of only 2 GB (the other 2 GB is mirrored). In this situation, then, you are getting only half of the disk space that you are paying for, but you also have fully redundant drives. In case of catastrophic failure of a drive, controller, or motherboard, you can remove a mirror drive and boot on another controller or server.

RAID 1 offers an increase in read performance in most implementations, as the controller card allows both drives (primary and mirror) to be read at the same time, resulting in a faster read operation. Write operations are not faster, though, because data must be written to two drives. In many RAID-1 systems that do not use separate drive controllers for the primary and mirror drives, the speed of writing can even decrease, because the system must perform two complete write operations in sequence.

Implementations of RAID 1 usually require two drives of similar size. If you use a 1.5-GB and a 2-GB drive, for example, the extra 0.5 GB on the second drive is wasted. Some controllers let you combine drives of different sizes, with the extra space used for nonmirrored partitions. Windows NT 4.0 and Windows 2000 support RAID 1 with two drives.

RAID 5 is very similar to RAID 0, but one hard drive is used for parity (error correction) to provide fault tolerance. To increase performance, spread the error-correction drive across all hard drives in the array to avoid having the one drive do all the work in calculating the parity bits. RAID 5 is supported by NT 4.0 and most RAID vendors, because it is a good compromise between data integrity, speed, and cost. RAID 5 has better performance than RAID 1 (mirroring).

RAID 5 usually requires at least three drives, with more drives preferable. The overhead that RAID 5 imposes on RAM also can be significant, so Microsoft recommends at least an additional 16 MB RAM when RAID 5 is used. As with RAID 1, however, drives of disparate capacities may result in much unused disk space, because most RAID-5 systems use the smallest drive capacity in the array for all RAID-5 drives. Extra disk space can be used for unstriped partitions, but these are not protected by the RAID system.

The Microsoft Windows HCL contains numerous hardware RAID configurations for clusters. Many hardware RAID solutions provide power redundancy, bus redundancy, and cable redundancy within a single cabinet and can track the state of each component in the hardware RAID firmware. The significance of these capabilities is they provide data availability with multiple redundancies to protect against multiple points of failure. Hardware RAID solutions also can use an onboard processor and cache.

Because SCSI drives have command queuing and typically a higher throughput, they are the best choice for RAID systems. According to RAID vendors, SCSI subsystems represent more than 95% of the RAID market. Some RAID systems support hot swappable drives where a drive can be removed without powering down the system. SCSI controller cards that support RAID through hardware will allow for better performance, because they will do most of the calculations that would have been done through the processor as instructed by the software. Lastly, if performance is critical on some systems, use a system with a RAID controller card that has a relatively large amount of RAM to be used as cache for the controller card.

14.6 VOLUME DISKS

Windows 2000, Windows XP, and Windows Server 2003 support several types of volumes:

- Simple volume
- Spanned volume
- Mirrored volume
- Striped volume
- RAID-5 volume

Note that you cannot create mirrored volumes or RAID-5 volumes on Windows 2000 Professional or Windows XP.

14.6.1 Simple and Spanned Volumes

A simple volume is made up of disk space from a single physical disk (single region or multiple regions linked together). To create a simple volume, do the following:

1. Open the Disk Management console.
2. Right-click unallocated space on the dynamic disk where you want to create the simple volume, select the Create Volume option, and select the Next button.

3. Select Simple Volume and click on the Next button.
4. Select the disk and the size for the selected disk and click on the Next button.
5. Assign the drive letter or path and click on the Next button.
6. Select the file system to use, select the allocation unit size, and enter the volume label. If you wish, you can also select Quick Format. Click on the Next button.
7. Click on the Finish button.

A spanned volume encompasses multiple disks. It can free drive letters for other uses and allows the creation of extremely large volume for file system use. A spanned volume can be extended up to a maximum of 32 disks and can be used on FAT, FAT32, or NTFS. To create a spanned volume, do the following:

1. Open the Disk Manager.
2. Right-click unallocated space on the dynamic disk where you want to create the spanned volume, click the Create Volume option, and click on the Next button.
3. Select the Spanned Volume and click on the Next button.
4. Select the disks and the size for the selected disks and click on the Next button. (The selected disk size for the different drives can be different.)
5. Assign the drive letter or path and click on the Next button.
6. Select the file system to use, select the allocation unit size, and enter the volume label. Click on the Next button.
7. Click on the Finish button.

To extend or expand an existing volume (simple or spanned), right-click the volume, select the Extend Volume option, and use the Wizard to specify which unallocated space to use and the amount of it. Only NTFS volumes can be extended—you cannot extend a system or boot volume. System and boot volumes are system and boot partitions that were contained in basic disks and upgraded to dynamic disks.

To delete a simple or spanned volume, right-click the volume and select the Delete option. When it asks if you are sure, click Yes and the volume is deleted.

14.6.2   Mirrored Volume

A mirrored volume (RAID 1) is two identical copies of a simple volume on separate hard disks. When data are written to one disk, they are also written to the other. If one hard drives fail, the other hard drive will continue to function without loss of data or downtime. Mirrored volumes also have better overall read performance than simple, spanned, and RAID-5 volumes.

When a disk fails that contains a mirrored volume, you must break the mirrored volume to separate the working volume with its own drive letters. Note that breaking the mirrored volume does not delete the information. You can then re-create a new mirrored volume with unused free space of the same size or greater on another disk. If the second volume is larger, then the remaining space becomes free space. Any existing volume, including the system and boot volumes, can be mirrored onto another volume of equal or greater size on another disk. When creating mirrored volumes, it is best to use disks that are the same size and model, and from the same manufacturer.

To create a mirror set, do the following steps:

1. Open the Disk Management console.
2. Right-click unallocated space on the dynamic disk where you want to create the spanned volume, click the Create Volume option, and click on the Next button.
3. Select the Mirrored Volume and click on the Next button.
4. Select the disks and their sizes and click on the Next button.
5. Assign the drive letter or path and click on the Next button.
6. Select the file system to use, select the allocation unit size, and enter the volume label. Click on the Next button.
7. Click on the Finish button.

If a basic disk that contains part of a mirror set is disconnected or fails, the status of the mirror set becomes Failed Redundancy and the status of the disk remains Online. To repair a basic mirrored set, open Disk Management, right-click the mirrored volume you want to repair, select the Repair Volume option, and follow the instructions on the screen. The mirrored volume's status should change to Regenerating, then to Healthy. If the volume does not return to the Healthy status, right-click the volume and then click Resynchronize Mirror. If this does not work, right-click the volume and select the Remove Mirror option to delete one of the mirrors. Then rebuild the mirror by right-clicking the volume and selecting the Add Mirror option.

To delete a mirror set, right-click the mirror set and select the Delete the Volume option. To create two independent partitions or logical drives, right-click the mirror set and select the Break Mirror. If you want to make the system and boot volume fault tolerant, mirror the volume. As mentioned in Chapter 8, create two different boot disks that point to both the boot partitions by using the appropriate advanced RISC computing (ARC) name. First test each boot disk to make sure that they start Windows by booting the system with the boot disk.

14.6.3   Striped Volume

A striped set is similar to a volume set in that it is the combining of areas of free space on 2 to 32 disks onto one logical volume. The difference is that a striped volume has the data allocated alternately and evenly in 64-KB stripes through the various drives. Therefore, when data are read or written, it writes to all drives simultaneously. Striped volumes offer the best performance of all volumes available in Windows, since the hard disks are working simultaneously. Like a volume set, if one disk in the striped volume fails, then the entire volume is lost. Striped volumes cannot be mirrored or extended.

To allocate striped volumes, follow these steps:

1. Open Disk Management.
2. Right-click unallocated space on the dynamic disk where you want to create the spanned volume, click the Create Volume option, and click on the Next button.
3. Select Striped Volume and click on the Next button.
4. Select the disks and the size for the selected disks and click on the Next button. (The selected disk size for the different drives can be different.)
5. Assign the drive letter or path and click on the Next button.
6. Select the file system to use, select the allocation unit size, and enter the volume label. Click on the Next button.
7. Click on the Finish button.

14.6.4   RAID-5 Volume

RAID-5 volumes are fault-tolerant striped volumes, except they use an extra drive to store parity information. In Windows NT, RAID-5 volume is very similar to stripe set with parity. See Table 14.8.

Table 14.8   Comparison between RAID-5 and mirrored volumes

Mirrored Volume	RAID-5 Volume
Supports FAT and NTFS	Supports FAT and NTFS
Can mirror system or boot volumes	Cannot stripe system or boot volumes
Requires 2 hard disks	Supports 3 to 32 hard disks
Has higher cost per megabyte (50% utilization)	Has lower cost per megabyte
Has good read and write performance	Has moderate write performance and excellent read performance
Uses less system memory	Requires more system memory

A RAID-5 volume can use between 3 and 32 drives. If a drives fail, Windows uses the parity information in the stripe to reconstruct data, thus allowing the system to function. In addition, it still benefits from the performance offered by striping.

When a hard disk fails in a RAID-5 volume, repair or replace the failed hard drive, right-click the unallocated disk space that is the same size or larger than the other members of the RAID-5 volume, and select the Regenerate the Data option. Since the volume must be locked to regenerate, all network connections to the volume are lost and it may require a reboot.

14.7   DISK UTILITIES

Several utilities or built-in functions can be used to help maintain and optimize disks and their data. These include scanning for disk errors, defragging a volume, and backing up the data. These functions can all be accessed by right-clicking the drive, selecting the Properties option, and clicking on the Tools tab. See Figure 14.5. Try to run the disk error-checking tool and the defragmentation tool during the night or during some other period of low usage, using the Task Scheduler.

14.7.1   Disk Error-Checking Tool

The disk error-checking tool checks the selected physical drive for damage. This includes invalid entries in the file allocation table, invalid directory entries, lost clusters, cross-linked files, files left in an open status, and bad sectors.

During this time, the disk is not available for use. To run the Check Disk tool, all files must be closed. If a volume is currently in use, a message will ask if you want to reschedule the disk checking for the next time you restart your computer. The disk-checking process can take a long time for large drives or drives with a large number of files. See Figure 14.6.

Figure 14.5   Disk tools

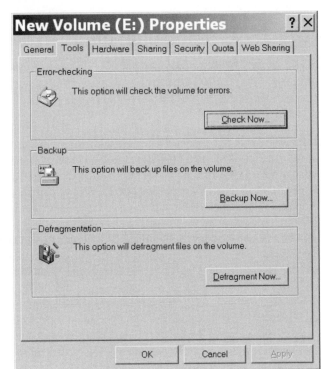

Figure 14.6 Check Disk utility

Figure 14.7 Disk Defragmenter

14.7.2 Disk Defragmenter

When a file is created, it is assigned a certain number of clusters which hold the data. After the file is saved to the disk, other information is usually saved to the clusters following the saved file. Therefore, if you change the original file, add more information to it, and save it back to the disk, then the bigger file will not fit within the allocated clusters. Therefore, part of the file will be saved in the original clusters and the remaining amount will be placed elsewhere on the disk.

Over time, files become fragmented as they are spread across the disk. The fragmented files are still complete when opened, but the computer takes longer to read them. Opening them also causes more wear and tear on the hard disk. Defragging the drive fixes this fragmentation problem by reorganizing the drive, that is, gathering all parts of a file and placing them in continuous sectors.

The Disk Defragmenter can be started using the Tools tab or by using the MMC with the Disk Defragmenter snap-in. If the drive is badly fragmented or is extremely large, then the program may take several hours to finish. In addition, when the defragmenting occurs, it will affect server performance, particularly when accessing the drive with the volume that you are defragging. Therefore, defrag only during periods of low usage. Lastly, defrag busy file servers more often than those on workstations and after deleting large numbers of files. See Figure 14.7.

SUMMARY

1. The disk structure describes how files are stored on the disk.
2. Disks are divided into a circular grid consisting of tracks and sectors.
3. A volume is a logical unit of disk space that functions as though it was a physical disk.
4. For operating systems, the most basic storage unit is not a sector, but a cluster. Another name for cluster is allocation unit.
5. The file allocation table (FAT) is an index used to remember which file is located in which cluster.
6. Every volume has a starting point called the root directory, which is located at the top of the tree structure. The root directory holds files and/or directories.
7. The directories under the root directory can also be referred to as subdirectories. Newer operating systems may refer to a directory as a folder. Each directory can also hold files and/or more subdirectories.
8. A file is a collection of related information that is referenced by name. Each file or directory on a volume can be uniquely identified by using the file name (including the file extension, if any) and the path (or location on the tree).
9. The most common file systems are FAT, FAT32, and NTFS.
10. FAT is a simple and reliable file system, which uses minimal memory. It supports file names of 11 characters, which include the 8 characters for the file name and 3 characters for the file extension.
11. VFAT is an enhanced version of the FAT structure, which allows Windows to support long file names (LFNs) up to 255 characters.
12. FAT32, which uses 32-bit FAT entries, was introduced in the second major release of Windows 95 (OSR2/Windows 95B) and is an enhancement of the FAT/VFAT file system.
13. NTFS is a file system for Windows NT, Windows 2000, Windows XP, and Windows Server 2003, designed for both the server and workstation. It provides a combination of performance, reliability, and compatibility. Windows 2000, Windows XP, and Windows Server 2003 use NTFS5. Windows NT needs to have service pack 4 or higher to support NTFS5.
14. In Windows 2000, Windows XP, and Windows Server 2003, to configure and manage disks, use the Disk Management console or the Computer Management console.
15. Windows allows as many volumes as you wish. Unfortunately, you cannot assign more than 26 drive letters (A–Z).
16. An NTFS mounted drive is attached to an empty folder on an NTFS volume, which is assigned a path, not a drive letter.
17. Before you can store files and directories on a volume or partition, perform a high-level format on it.
18. When converting a partition or volume, open a Command prompt window and use the CONVERT *x:* /FS:NTFS command.
19. Windows 2000 and Windows Server 2003 have two disk storage types, basic disks and dynamic disks.
20. A basic disk is a physical disk that contains primary partitions, extended partitions, or logical drives.
21. A dynamic disk is converted from basic to dynamic storage that contains simple volumes, spanned volumes, mirrored volumes, striped volumes, and RAID-5 volumes.
22. RAID is an acronym for redundant array of inexpensive disks, or redundant array of independent disks. It is a category of disk drives that employs two or more drives in combination to improve fault tolerance and performance. RAID disk drives are used frequently on servers but are not generally necessary for personal computers.
23. Only RAID 0, 1, and 5 are supported by Windows NT 4.0, Windows 2000, and Windows Server 2003 without additional hardware and software from RAID vendors.
24. A simple volume is made up of disk space from a single physical disk (single region or multiple regions linked together).
25. A mirror volume (RAID 1) is two identical copies of a simple volume on separate hard disks.
26. A striped set is similar to a volume set in that it is the combining of areas of free space on 2 to 32 disks onto one logical volume.
27. RAID-5 volumes are fault-tolerant striped volumes, except they use an extra drive to store parity information.
28. Several utilities or built-in functions can be used to help maintain and optimize disks and their data. These include the disk error-checking tool and the defragmentation tool.

QUESTIONS

1. Pat wants to convert one of the NTFS volumes on his computer to FAT so it can be accessed by workstations running Windows 98. The NTFS partition does not contain system or boot files. How can Pat convert the NTFS partition to a FAT partition using the least amount of administrative effort?
   a. Use the CONVERT.EXE program at the command prompt.
   b. Select the NTFS partition and choose Convert on the Partition menu in Disk Administrator.
   c. Select the NTFS partition and choose Reformat on the Partition menu in Disk Administrator.
   d. Right-click on the volume in Disk Administrator and select the Format option to change the format of the partition to FAT and restore all data from tape backup.
2. You want to convert one of the FAT partitions on your computer to NTFS while preserving all of the data currently contained on the partition. What is the best way to accomplish this?
   a. Use the CONVERT.EXE program at the command prompt.
   b. Select the FAT partition and choose Convert on the Tools menu in Disk Administrator.

c. Select the FAT partition and choose Format on the Partition menu in Disk Administrator.

d. Select the FAT partition and choose Convert on the Partition menu in Disk Administrator.

3. What does RAID stand for?
   a. Redundant and inexpensive disks
   b. Readable and interruptible disks
   c. Redundant array of inexpensive disks
   d. Readable array of inexpensive disks

4. Which RAID level has no redundant information and therefore provides no fault-tolerance?
   a. RAID 0   c. RAID 2
   b. RAID 1   d. RAID 5

5. Which RAID levels does Windows 2000 support?
   a. 0, 1, 2, and 5   d. 0, 1, and 5
   b. 0, 1, 2, 3, and 5   e. 0, 1, 2, 3, 4, and 5
   c. 1, 2, 3, and 5

6. You want to implement fault tolerance on your Windows 2000 server and you are most concerned with read performance. There are five hard drives on your Windows 2000 server. Which of the following will best satisfy your requirements?
   a. a volume set   c. disk mirroring
   b. RAID-5 volume   d. disk duplexing

7. You want to combine the free disk space from five hard disks into one logical drive. You are not concerned with providing fault tolerance, but you want to achieve the fastest possible read/write performance. Which of the following disk management strategies would be the best choice?
   a. a volume set   c. a striped volume
   b. a mirror set   d. a RAID-5 volume

8. Your file server contains a database that is accessed by all users in your domain and all trusted domains. Currently, the server only has one physical disk. You want to implement fault tolerance on your file server. Which of the following actions would accomplish this task?
   a. Install one additional physical disk and implement a RAID-5 volume.
   b. Install one additional physical disk and implement a striped volume.
   c. Install three additional physical disks and implement a volume set.
   d. Install three additional physical disks and implement a RAID-5 volume.

9. You want to combine the free disk space from six hard drives into a single logical drive. You are not concerned with providing fault tolerance, and you want to achieve the fastest possible read performance. Which of the following Windows 2000 disk management strategies would you implement?
   a. a volume set   c. a striped set
   b. a mirror set   d. a RAID-5 volume

10. Suppose the following situation exists: Your Windows NT Workstation computer has five 1-GB IDE hard drives. Each drive is formatted with a single FAT partition. The first hard drive contains the system and boot partition. It also contains the paging file. You want to optimize the performance of your computer.

Required result:
• You must speed access to files on your local hard drives.

Optional desired results:
• You want to optimize the paging file.
• You want to optimize network binding orders.

Proposed solution:
Create a second paging file on the drive that contains the system and boot partition. Combine the spaces from the remaining four disks into a volume set. Store all data and program files on the volume set. Move the most frequently used protocols to the top of the network binding order.

Which result does the proposed solution produce?
   a. The proposed solution produces the required result and produces both of the optional desired results.
   b. The proposed solution produces the required result and produces only one of the optional desired results.
   c. The proposed solution produces the required result but does not produce either of the optional desired results.
   d. The proposed solution does not produce the required result.

11. Jeremy's new computer has a 2-GB hard disk drive, and it will be configured with a single partition. The computer will be used mainly to store payroll records and other sensitive information. Which of the following are reasons for using the NTFS file system instead of FAT? Choose all that apply.
   a. Only NTFS supports long file names.
   b. Only NTFS allows permissions to be assigned to individual files and folders.
   c. NTFS generally provides better performance for volumes greater than 400 MB.
   d. NTFS partitions can be used by operating systems other than Windows NT, such as Windows 95 and MS-DOS.

12. The master boot record holds the _____.
   a. partition table   c. volume boot sector
   b. file allocation table   d. root directory

13. Which utility identifies and corrects files that are not contiguous?
   a. SCANDISK   c. disk error-checking tool
   b. defrag   d. backup

14. Which best describes a fragmented hard drive?
   a. The platters are bad or cracked.
   b. The platters are slipping on the spindle.
   c. Data files are corrupted.
   d. Files are not stored in consecutive clusters.

15. The disk error-checking tool can be used to

_____.
   a. locate lost clusters and provide options to save or delete them
   b. look for viruses
   c. reconfigure and optimize programs in RMA
   d. locate a specific program on a disk or drive

16. A hard drive has slowed considerably over time. What should be done to improve the performance of the hard drive?

a. use DriveSpace or DoubleSpace

b. use Fast Disk

c. use Disk Defragmenter

d. use CHKDSK

e. increase the maximum amount of virtual memory

17. Pat must install a busy server with 32 volumes. While Pat is installing all of the drives and is assigning drive letters to all of the volumes, he realizes that he used up all of the drive letters, yet he still has several volumes that require drive letters. What can be done to make the other volumes available to the users?

a. Map these drives to another server.

b. Use NTFS mounted volume.

c. Start using double-letter drive letters, starting with AA.

d. Start using numbers with the drive letters, starting with A2.

e. Do none of the above.

18. You have a hard drive with three partitions. The first partition is a FAT32 and the other two partitions are extended partitions formatted as logical drives with NTFS. You install a second hard drive with a NTFS partition. Which of the following statements are true? Assume the three partitions are assigned C, D, and E drive letters. Choose the one answer that applies.

a. The C drive remains the same, the new partition becomes the D drive, and the other partitions are assigned E and F.

b. The C, D, and E drive letters are still assigned to the three partitions and the drive letter can be assigned to any other drive letter.

c. You need to use Disk Manager to change the D and E drive to E and F and the new partition will automatically be recognized as the D drive.

d. You must use a NTFS mounted volume to use the partition.

19. You want to provide complete redundancy for all data stored on your hardware RAID-5 disk array. You install a second hardware RAID-5 disk array. You want to create a mirror of the original array on the new array. However, when you right-click the free space on the new array in Disk Management, you see no option to create a new volume or a mirrored volume. Before you create a mirrored volume on the new array, what should you do?

a. Convert both arrays to dynamic disks.

b. Create an empty single extended partition on the new disk array.

c. Create a single, unformatted primary partition on the new disk array.

d. Format the new disk array as a single NTFS primary partition.

e. Format the new disk array as a single NTFS logical drive in an extended partition.

20. You are the administrator of a Windows 2000 Server computer that has five hard disks. Four 100-GB hard disks on the server are configured as a single striped volume. You want to reconfigure the four disks so that the volume is fault tolerant and has as much space possible available for storing data. You want to use only existing hardware. What should you do?

a. Convert the disk to dynamic disk. Shut down and restart the server.

b. Back up the data on the striped volume then delete the striped volume. Create a RAID-5 volume on the four disks. Restore the data to the new RAID-5 volume.

c. Back up the data on the striped volume and then delate the striped volume. Create two mirrored volumes. Shut down and restart the server. Restore the data to the new mirrored volumes.

d. Back up the data on the striped volume, then delete the striped volume. Create a spanned volume from the first two disks. Create a second spanned volume from the last two disks. Mount the root of the second spanned volume in the root of the first spanned volume. Restore the data to the first spanned volume.

21. Your Windows 2000 Server computer contains a stripe set with parity on a four-disk array. You convert the stripe set with parity to a dynamic RAID-5 volume. Six months later, users report that disk access on the server is slower than it had been on the previous day. You use Disk Management and discover that the status of the third disk in the array is missing. You want to recover the failed RAID-5 volume. What should you do first?

a. Replace the third disk and restart the server. Use Disk Management to repair the volume.

b. Ensure that the third disk is attached to the server and has power. Use Disk Management to reactivate the disk.

c. Ensure that the third disk is attached to the server and has power. Use Disk Management to repair the volume.

d. Install a new disk and create a single extended partition on the new disk. Restart the computer and allow Windows 2000 to automatically repair the volume on the extended partition.

22. You install the boot volume D on your Windows 2000 Server computer on a dynamic disk 0. You mirror volume D on a dynamic disk 1. One year later, during routine server maintenance, you open Disk Management and find that the status of volume D is Failed Redundancy. The status of disk 1 is Online (Errors). A symbol with an exclamation point appears in the graphical view of the disk. You want to return the status of the boot volume to Healthy. What can you do? (Choose two answers.)

a. Break the mirror, delete the volume on disk 1, and re-create the mirror.

b. Replace disk1, copy the data from the boot volume to the new disk, and use Disk Management to rescan the disks.

c. Replace disk 1, ensure that the new disk is a basic disk, and repair the volume.

d. Reactivate the mirror on disk 1.

e. Convert disk 1 to basic disk, and reconvert it to a dynamic disk.

23. Your domain includes numerous domain controllers. One of the domains controllers is malfunctioning, and a disk with the following ARC path is not responding: multi(1)disk(0)rdisk(1)partition(1). Indicate which drive this is in the following diagram:

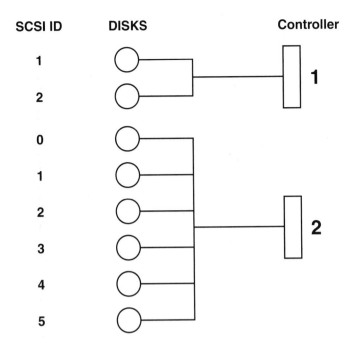

24. You are the administrator of a Windows 2000 Server network. Users report that they are unable to access shared folders on one of your servers. You open My Computer on the server and do not find the volumes on dynamic disk 3 that contains the shared folders. When you open Disk Management, you see that disk 3 is offline. You confirm that the disk has power and it is attached to your SCSI adapter. Other disks connected to the adapter appear to be functioning normally. You want to use Disk Management to resolve the problem. What should you do next?
    a. Rescan the disks on the server.
    b. Reactivate disk 3.
    c. Remove disk 3 by using Disk Administration, and restart the computer.
    d. Convert disk 3 to a basic disk, then convert it back to a dynamic disk.

25. You are the administrator of a Windows 2000 Server computer named Server1. Server1 contains five hard disks. Disks 0 and 1 are configured as a mirrored volume and contain the operating system files. Disk 2, 3, and 4 are configured as a stripe set with parity volume and contain 150 GB of data files. Server1 also contains a tape backup device, which is used to make a full backup of the data files every weekend. Disk 2 fails on Tuesday. You replace disk 2 with a new hard disk. You need to return the stripe set with parity volume to normal operation as quickly as possible. You also need to minimize the amount of data lost. What should you do?
    a. Use the Disk Manager console to delete and re-create the stripe set with parity volume.
    b. Restore the data files from the most recent tape backup to the stripe set with parity volume.
    c. Modify the Boot.ini file so that the ARC path for Windows 2000 Server points to disk 2.
    d. Use the Disk Manager console to repair the volume.

26. You are the network administrator for Acme. You are configuring a new Windows 2000 Server computer. The server contains five physical disks. You plan to implement a Windows 2000 software RAID. You need to ensure that all disk volumes are fault tolerant. You want to minimize disk access time and maximize available storage. What should you do?
    a. Configure the system volume as a simple volume and the other volumes as striped volumes.
    b. Configure the system volume as a simple volume and the other volumes as RAID-5 volumes.
    c. Configure the system volume as a mirrored volume and the other volumes as mirrored volumes.
    d. Configure the system volume as a mirrored volume and the other volumes as RAID-5 volumes.

27. You upgrade a Windows NT Server 4.0 computer to Windows 2000 Server. The computer has two hard disks. The system and boot partitions are located on two primary partitions on disk 0. Both partitions are mirrored on disk 1. One month later, disk 1 fails. You replace the disk with a disk taken from another Windows 2000 computer. When you try to repair the fault-tolerant volumes by using Disk Management, you find that the Repair Volume option is unavailable. You want to repair the mirror set. What can you do? (Choose two answers.)
    a. Delete all volumes on disk 1. Change disk 1 back to basic disk. Repair the fault-tolerant volumes on disk 0.
    b. Create two new volumes on disk 1. Copy all the data from the two disk partitions on disk 0 to the two volumes on disk 1.
    c. Break the mirror set. Convert disk 0 to a dynamic disk. Create a mirror on disk 1.
    d. Create a single volume on disk 1. Copy all the data from disk 0 to the single volume. Convert disk 0 to a dynamic disk.
    e. Restart the computer by using the Windows 2000 Server CD-ROM and choose to repair the installation.

28. You are the administrator of a Windows NT 4.0 Terminal Server edition computer. The server has one hard disk, which is divided into two partitions. The first partition contains the Windows NT 4.0 system files and is formatted as FAT. The second partition contains application data and user data. This second partition is formatted as NTFS. The server currently has service pack 3 installed. You need to upgrade the server to Windows 2000 Server. You want to ensure that no application data or user data are lost during the upgrade. You also want to perform the minimum number of steps necessary to complete the upgrade. What should you do? (Choose all answers that apply.)

    a. Convert the system partition to NTFS.

    b. Install service pack 4 or later on the server.

    c. Use a Windows 2000 Server CD to start the server. In setup, select the option to upgrade.

    d. Replace the Terminal Server installation with a standard Windows NT server 4.0 installation.

HANDS-ON EXERCISES

Exercise 1: Create A Volume

1. Start Computer Management.
2. In the left pane, click on Disk Management.
3. Right-click on Disk 0 and select the Properties option. Do not click on the partitions or volumes.
4. Click on the OK button to close the Disk 0 Properties dialog box.
5. Right-click the C drive and select the Properties option.
6. Click OK to close the Local Disk (C) dialog box.
7. You should have free disk space at the end of the first disk.
8. Right-click the Unallocated Disk Space and select Create Partition.
9. Select the Primary Partition and click on the Next button.
10. Use the entire disk space for the partition and click on the Next button.
11. Assign the M drive to the partition. Click on the Next button.
12. Select to use the FAT32 file system and click on the Next button. Do not select the Perform a Quick Format option. Instead, for a network environment, you would rather have the system perform a more thorough format to find problems with the drive.
13. Click on the Finish button.
14. Right-click the M drive and select to format the drive as a NTFS partition.
15. Right-click the M drive and select the Delete option.

Exercise 2: Convert A Fat Or Fat32 Partition To A NTFS Partition

Note: It is always recommended to perform a backup of all important data before doing a conversion to NTFS.

1. Right-click the unallocated disk space and create a FAT32 partition. Assign the drive letter M to the drive.
2. Start a Command prompt.
3. At the Command prompt, execute the CONVERT M: /FS:NTFS.
4. At the Command prompt, execute the CONVERT C: /FS:NTFS.
5. If the CONVERT command displays a message saying that it has to reboot the computer to finish the conversion, complete a proper shutdown of Windows 2000 and reboot the computer.

Exercise 3: Using NTFS Mounted Volume

1. Right-click the C drive and select Open.
2. In the C drive, create a folder called TestMount.
3. Right-click the M drive and select the Change Drive Letter and Path option. Click on the M drive and click on the Remove button. When it asks if you are sure, click Yes.
4. Right-click the New Volume and select the Change Drive Letter and Path option. Click on the Add button and select the Mount in this NTFS Folder.
5. Either specify C:\TESTMOUNT or use the Browse button to point to the C:\TESTMOUNT folder. Click on the OK button.
6. Right-click the C drive and select the Properties button. Notice the amount of free disk space. Click on the OK button to close the C drive Properties dialog box.

7. Right-click the C drive and select the Open option.
8. Right-click the TESTMOUNT folder and select the Properties option. Click on the Properties button. Notice the amount of free disk space.

Exercise 4: Convert To Dynamic Disks

Note: It is always recommended to perform a backup of all important data before converting to Dynamic Disks.

1. In Disk Management, right-click Disk 0 and select Upgrade to Dynamic Disk.
2. Click OK to accept Disk 0. Click on the Upgrade button. Click the Yes button when it asks if you are sure. On the warning that disks will be forced to dismount, click on the Yes mount and let the computer reboot.
3. Restart Disk Management and right-click the last volume and delete it.
4. Right-click the unallocated disk space and select the Create a Volume option. Click on the Next button. With the simple volume selected, click on the Next button.
5. Since Disk 0 is already selected, specify the size of 500 MB. Click on the Next button.
6. Assign the M drive and click on the Next button.
7. Since the Format this Volume is selected, click on the Next button.
8. Click on the Finish button.
9. Right-click the M drive and select the Extend Volume option. Click on the Next button.
10. Since Drive 0 is already selected, specify 100 MB and click on the Next button.
11. Click the Finish button.
12. Right-click the unallocated disk space and create a 100-MB FAT volume. Assign the next available drive letter.
13. Right-click the M drive and select the Extend option. Use the rest of the disk space to extend the drive.

Exercise 5: Using Error-Checking And Defragmenter Utilities

1. Right-click the C drive and select the Properties option.
2. Click on the Tools tab.
3. Click on the Check Now button.
4. Select the Automatically Fix System Errors option. If you have time in class, enable the "Scan for and attempt recovery of bad sectors." Click on the Start button.
5. From the Computer Management console, click on the C drive and click on the Defragment button.

CHAPTER 15

Directory and File Management

Topics Covered in This Chapter

Introduction

This chapter is the first to focus on enabling and managing a network resource, specifically the directories and files that are located on the hard drive. Because the files on the server need to be kept secure, this chapter will discuss NTFS and Share permissions, the distributed file system (DFS), and encryption. In addition, the chapter describes file compression and quotas.

Objectives

- Monitor, manage, and troubleshoot access to files and folders.
- Configure, manage, and troubleshoot file compression.
- Control access to files and folders by using permissions.
- Optimize access to files and folders.
- Manage and troubleshoot access to shared folders.
- Create and remove shared folders.

- Control access to shared folders by using permissions.
- Manage and troubleshoot the use and synchronization of offline files.
- Connect to shared resources on a Microsoft network.
- Encrypt data on a hard disk by using the encrypting file system (EFS).

15.1   NTFS PERMISSIONS

A primary advantage of NTFS over FAT and FAT32 is that NTFS volumes have the ability to apply NTFS permissions to secure folders and files. By setting the permissions, you specify the level of access for groups and users for accessing files or directories. For example, to one user or group of users, you can specify that they can only read the file; another user or group of users can read and write to the file; and others have no access. No matter if you are logged on locally at the computer or accessing a computer through the network, NTFS permission always applies.

All folder and file NTFS permissions (also known as special permissions) are listed in Tables 15.1 and 15.2. To simplify the task of administration, the permissions have been logically grouped into the standard folder and file NTFS permissions as shown in Tables 15.3 and 15.4. The standard folder permissions include Full Control, Modify, Read & Execute, List Folder Contents, Read, and Write. The standard file permissions include Full Control, Modify, Read & Execute, Read, and Write. The folder permissions are shown in Tables 15.1 and 15.3 while the file permissions are shown in Tables 15.2 and 15.4.

The NTFS permissions that are granted are stored in an access control list (ACL) with every file and folder on an NTFS volume. The ACL contains an access control entry (ACE) for each user account and group that has been granted access for the file or folder as well as the permissions granted to each user and group.

To assign NTFS permissions, right-click a drive, folder, and file (using My Computer or Windows Explorer), select the Properties option, and click on the Security tab. To assign the special permissions, click on the Advanced button within the Security tab and click on the View/Edit button. See Figure 15.1.

15.1.1   Explicit Permission

Permissions are given to a folder or file as either explicit permissions or inherited permissions. In this section we discuss explicit permissions and in Section 15.1.2 we discuss inherited types. **Explicit permissions** are those granted directly to the folder or file. Some of these permissions are granted automatically, such as when a file or folder is created, while others have to be assigned manually.

Table 15.1 NTFS folder permissions

Special Permissions	Full Control	Modify	Read & Execute	List Folder Contents	Read	Write
Traverse Folder/Execute File	x	x	x	x		
List Folder/Read Data	x	x	x	x	x	
Read Attributes	x	x	x	x	x	
Read Extended Attributes	x	x	x	x	x	
Create Files/ Write Data	x	x				x
Create Folders/Append Data	x	x				x
Write Attributes	x	x				x
Write Extended Attributes	x	x				x
Delete Subfolders and Files	x					
Delete	x					
Read Permissions	x	x	x	x	x	x
Change Permissions	x					
Take Ownership	x					
Synchronize	x	x	x	x	x	x

Note: Although List Folder contents and Read & Execute appear to have the same permissions, they are inherited differently. List Folder contents is inherited by folders but not files, and it should only appear when you view folder permissions. Read & Execute is inherited by both files and folders and is always present when you view file or folder permissions.

Table 15.2 NTFS file permissions

Special Permissions	Full Control	Modify	Read & Execute	Read	Write
Traverse Folder/Execute File	x	x	x		
List Folder/Read Data	x	x	x	x	
Read Attributes	x	x	x	x	
Read Extended Attributes	x	x	x	x	
Create Files/ Write Data	x	x			x
Create Folders/Append Data	x	x			x
Write Attributes	x	x			x
Write Extended Attributes	x	x			x
Delete Subfolders and Files	x				
Delete	x				
Read Permissions	x	x	x	x	x
Change Permissions	x				
Take Ownership	x				
Synchronize	x	x	x	x	x

Table 15.3   Standard NTFS folder permissions

NTFS Folder Permissions	Allows the user to:
Read	Display the file's data, attributes, owner, and permissions.
Write	Create new files and subfolders within the folder, write to the file, append to the file, read and change folder attributes, and view ownership.
List Folder Contents	View the names of folders and subfolders in the folder.
Read & Execute	Display the folder's contents and the data, attributes, owner, and permissions for files within the folder and execute files within the folder. In addition, it allows the user to navigate a folder to reach other files and folders, even if the user does not have permissions for these folders.
Modify	Read the files, execute files, write and modify files, create folders and subfolders, delete subfolders and files, and change attributes of subfolders and files.
Full Control	Read the files, execute files, write and modify files, create folders and subfolders, delete subfolders and files, change attributes of subfolders and files, change permissions, and take ownership of the file.

Note: Groups or users who are granted full control for a folder can delete files and subfolders within that folder regardless of the permissions that are protecting the files and subfolders.

Table 15.4   Standard NTFS file permissions

NTFS File Permissions	Allows the user to:
Read	Display the file's data, attributes, owner, and permissions.
Write	Write to the file, append to the file, overwrite the file, change file attributes, and view file ownership and permissions.
Read & Execute	Display the data, attributes, owner, and permissions for file and execute the file.
Modify	Read the file, execute the file, write, modify and delete the files, and change attributes of file.
Full Control	Read the file, execute the file, write, modify and delete the files, change attributes of file, change permissions, and take ownership of the file.

Note: Groups or users who are granted full control for a folder can delete files and subfolders within that folder regardless of the permissions that are protecting the files and subfolders.

To explicitly grant a permission to a folder or file, select the permission by checking the respective box. To remove an explicit permission, deselect the permission to remove the check in the respective box. To remove a user or group from being assigned explicit permissions, click to highlight the user, and click on the Remove button.

Because users can be members of several groups, it is possible for them to have several sets of explicit permissions to a folder or file. When this occurs, the permissions are combined to form the **effective permissions,** which are the actual permissions when logging in and accessing a file or folder. They consist of explicit permissions plus any inherited permissions.

To view effective permissions on files and folders using Windows XP or Windows Server 2003, follow these steps:

1. Open Windows Explorer, then locate the file or folder for which you would like to view effective permissions.
2. Right-click the file or folder, click Properties, then click the Security tab.

Figure 15.1 NTFS permissions

3. Click Advanced, then click the Effective Permissions tab.
4. Click the Select button.
5. In Name, enter the name of a user or group, then click OK. The selected check boxes indicate the effective permissions of the user or group for that file or folder.

Example 1:

USER1 is a member of the local group called MANAGERS.

Question: The MANAGERS group is assigned the Read (R) permission to DOC1.TXT and USER1 is assigned the Write (W) permission to DOC1.TXT. What are the effective rights to the DOC1.TXT file for USER1?

Answer: When USER1 accesses the DOC1.TXT file, the effective rights would be both the Read and Write permissions. Therefore, the user would be able to display the file's data, write to the file, append to the file, overwrite the file, view and change the file's attributes, and view the owner and permissions of the file.

		User1	Managers	Combined
DOC1.TXT	Explicit	W	R	
	Effective	W	R	RW

Windows offers the ability to deny individual permissions (standard or special). The Deny permission always overrides the permissions that have been granted, including when a user or group has been granted full control. For example, if the group has been granted read and write, yet a person has been denied the Write permission, the user's effective rights would be the Read permission.

Example 2:

USER1 is a member of the MANAGERS group.

Question: The MANAGERS group is assigned the Modify (M) permission to DOC1.TXT and USER1 is assigned the Deny Write (W) permission to DOC1.TXT. What are the effective rights to the DOC1.TXT file for USER1?

Answer: In this case, the Deny Write permission will override those rights granted by the Modify permission. If you use Table 15.2, take the special NTFS permissions that are granted for the Modify permissions and remove those permissions that are represented by the Write permission. Therefore, the only permissions that would be granted would be to read and change the - attributes and delete the file. The execute file would also be granted, but the DOC1.TXT file is not an executable file.

DOC1.TXT		User1	Managers	Combined
	Explicit	~~W~~	M	
	Effective	~~W~~	M	See Below

Special Permissions	Modify	Write	Effective
Traverse Folder/Execute File	x		x
List Folder/Read Data	x		x
Read Attributes	x		x
Read Extended Attributes	x		x
Create Files/Write Data	x	x	—
Create Folders/Append Data	x	x	—
Write Attributes	x	x	—
Write Extended Attributes	x	x	—
Delete	x		x
Read Permissions	x	x	—
Synchronize	x	x	—

Example 3:

USER1 is a member of the MANAGERS group.

Question: The MANAGERS group is assigned the Full Control (FC) permission to DOC1.TXT and USER1 is assigned the Deny R (R) permission to DOC1.TXT. What are the effective rights to the DOC1.TXT file for USER1?

Answer: If USER1 is denied access to read the file, it greatly reduces access to the file. Yet, USER1 can still write to the file, append to the file so long as the user does not have to read the file (such as adding information to the end of a log file), change attributes, delete the file, or take ownership of the file.

DOC1.TXT		User1	Managers	Combined
	Explicit	~~R~~	FC	
	Effective	~~R~~	FC	See Below

Special Permissions	Full Control	Read	Effective
Traverse Folder/Execute File	x		x
List Folder/Read Data	x	x	
Read Attributes	x	x	
Read Extended Attributes	x	x	
Create Files/Write Data	x		x
Create Folders/Append Data	x		x
Write Attributes	x		x
Write Extended Attributes	x		x
Delete Subfolders and Files	x		x
Delete	x		x
Read Permissions	x	x	
Change Permissions	x		x
Take Ownership	x		x
Synchronize	x	x	

NTFS file permissions override folder permissions. Therefore, if a user has access to a file, but not the folder that contains the file, the user will still be able to gain access to a file. The user who has no access to the folder cannot navigate or browse through the folder to get to the file. Therefore, the user would have to utilize the universal naming convention (UNC) or local path to open the file.

15.1.2 Inherited Permissions

When you set permissions to a folder (explicit permissions), the files and subfolders created in the folder inherit these permissions (called **inherited permissions**). In other words, the permissions flow down from the folder into the subfolders and files, indirectly giving permissions to a user or group. Inherited permissions ease the task of managing permissions and ensure consistency of permissions among the subfolders and files within the folder.

When viewing the permissions, the check box will be checked, cleared (unchecked), or shaded. If the box is checked, the permission was explicitly assigned to the folder or file. If the box is clear, the user or group does not have that permission explicitly granted to the folder or file. A user may still obtain permission through a group permission or a group may still obtain permission through another group. If the box is shaded, the permission is granted through inheritance from a parent folder. Review Figure 15.1.

Example 4:

On the E drive, you have a DATA folder and under the DATA folder, you have the FINANCE folder. Under the FINANCE folder, you have the DOC1.TXT file.

Question: For USER1, you assign the Modify (M) permission for the DATA folder. What are the effective rights to the DOC1.TXT file for USER1?

Answer: The Modify permission was given to the DATA folder and flows down through the FINANCE folder to the DOC1.TXT file. Therefore, the user will have the modify permission for the DOC1.TXT.

		User1
DATA	Explicit	M
	Effective	M
FINANCE	Inherited	M
	Explicit	—
	Effective	M
DOC1.TXT	Inherited	M
	Explicit	—
	Effective	M

When assigning permissions to a folder, by default, the permissions apply to the folder being assigned and the subfolders and files of the folder. If you show the permission entries, you can specify how the permissions are applied to the folder, subfolder, and files. See Figure 15.2.

To stop permissions from being inherited, clear the "Allow inheritable permissions from parent to propagate to this object" check box. When the check box is clear, Windows will respond with a Security dialog box as shown in Figure 15.3. When you click on the Copy button, the explicit permissions will be copied from the parent folder to the subfolder or file. You can then change the subfolder's or file

Figure 15.2   Selecting how the permissions are applied to a folder and its subfolders and files

Figure 15.3 When you choose to override inherited writes, you have the choice to either stop NTFS permissions from propagating from above or copy the explicit permissions to the object

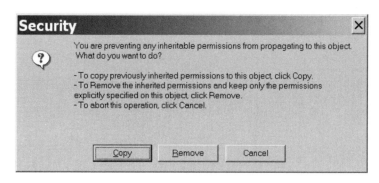

explicit permissions. If you click on the Remove button, it will remove the inherited permissions altogether. Another way to stop a permission from being inherited is to change the parent folder so that the file or subfolder will inherit different permissions or to select the opposite (Allow or Deny) to override the inherited permission.

Example 5:

On the E drive, you have a DATA folder and under the DATA folder, you have the FINANCE folder. Under the FINANCE folder, you have the DOC1.TXT file.

Question: For USER1, you assign the Read (R) permission for the DATA folder. In addition, you assign the Modify (M) permission to the FINANCE folder. What are the effective rights to the DOC1.TXT file for USER1?

Answer: The Read permission was given to the DATA folder and flows down through the FINANCE folder. Assuming that the administrator is selected to overwrite the permissions and not copy, the Read permission is overwritten by the Modify permission, which then flows down to the DOC1.TXT file. Therefore, the user will have the Modify permission for the DOC1.TXT.

		User1
DATA	Explicit	R
	Effective	R
FINANCE	Inherited	R
	Explicit	M
	Effective	M
DOC1.TXT	Inherited	M
	Explicit	—
	Effective	M

Example 6:

On the E drive, you have a DATA folder and under the DATA folder, you have the FINANCE folder. Under the FINANCE folder, you have the DOC1.TXT file. USER1 is a member of the local group called MANAGERS.

Question: For the MANAGER group, you assign the Read (R) permission to the DATA folder. For USER1, you assign the Write (W) permission to the FINANCE folder. What are the effective rights to the DOC1.TXT file for USER1?

Answer: For USER1, the Write permission flows down from the DATA folder to the FINANCE folder, down to the DOC1.TXT file. For the MANAGER group, the Read permission flows down from the DATA folder to the FINANCE folder, down to the DOC1.TXT file. The trick is to keep the permissions granted to USER1 and MANAGERS separate except when combining the writes to determine the effective rights for the object. Therefore, the effective rights for the DOC1.TXT would be to combine the permissions for the user and group; thus, when USER1 logs in, it will have both Read and Write permissions.

		User 1	Managers	Combined
DATA	Explicit	—	R	
	Effective	—	R	R
FINANCE	Inherited	—	R	
	Explicit	W	—	
	Effective	W	R	RW
DOC1.TXT	Inherited	W	R	
	Explicit	—	—	
	Effective	W	R	RW

15.1.3   Folder and File Owners

Every folder and file has an **owner,** a person who controls how permissions are set on a folder or file and who grants permissions to others. When a folder or file is created, either automatically becomes the owner.

To be able to take ownership of a folder or file, the user has to be granted Take Ownership permission or be the administrator. After logging in, the user can take ownership by doing the following:

1. Right-click the folder or file and select the Properties option.
2. Click on the Security tab and then on the Advanced button.
3. Click on the Owner tab.
4. Click on the user who will take ownership.
5. If you want to replace the owner for all subfolders and files, mark the check box.
6. Click on the OK button.

The administrator automatically has the Take Ownership of any folder or directory, which is under his or her administrative control. Therefore, if someone leaves the company or gets fired, the administrator can take control of that person's file. The administrator cannot transfer ownership to others, but can permit the person to take ownership. See Figure 15.4.

15.1.4   Copying and Moving Files

When you copy and move files and folders from one location to another, it is important to understand how the NTFS folder and file permissions are affected. If you copy a file or folder, the new folder and file will automatically acquire the same permissions as the original drive or folder.

Figure 15.4   Taking ownership of an NTFS folder

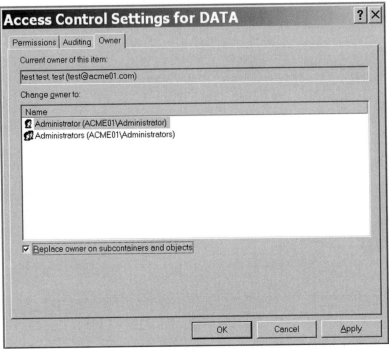

If the folder or file is moved within the same volume, either will retain the originally assigned permissions. When the folder or file is moved from one volume to another, either will automatically acquire the permissions of the original drive or folder and file. An easy way to remember the difference is when you move a folder or file from within the same volume, the folder or file is not physically moved but the Master File Table is adjusted to indicate a different folder. When you move a folder or file from one volume to another, it copies the folder or file to the new location and then deletes the old location. Therefore, the moved folder and files are new to the volume and acquire the new permissions.

NOTE: When copying and moving folders and files, the encryption and compression attributes on the folders and files act the same as NTFS permissions.

15.2   SHARED FOLDERS

A **shared folder** on a computer makes the folder available for others to use on the network. A shared drive on a computer makes the entire drive available for others to use on the network. Shared drives and folders can be used on FAT, FAT32, and NTFS volumes. If used on an NTFS partition, the user will still need NTFS permissions before accessing the share. When the drive or directory is shared, it is indicated with a hand underneath the drive or folder.

To share a folder or drive, do the following:

1. Open Windows Explorer and locate the folder or drive that you want to share.
2. Right-click the folder or drive and select the Sharing option.
3. Click on the Sharing tab and select the Share This Folder.
4. The name of the folder becomes the default share name. If you wish to change the share name, type the name in the Shared Name text box. MS-DOS and Windows for Workgroups 3.11 machines are restricted to 8.3 characters.
5. To set the shared folder permissions on the shared folder or drive, click the Permissions button (not the Permissions tab).

Figure 15.5   Sharing a folder

If the folder is already shared, click New Share and then type the new share name. To share a folder and drive, you must be logged on as a member of the Administrators, Server Operators, or Power Users group. See Figure 15.5. If the Sharing tab is not visible, try using the Services snap-in to start the server service.

If a Windows computer has limited bandwidth, you may want to use the User Limit option. In Windows 2000 Professional and Windows XP, the maximum user limit is 10, regardless of the number you type in the Allow box.

15.2.1   Connecting to a Shared Folder or Drive

The shared resource can be accessed using Network Neighborhood in Windows 9X, and Windows NT; My Network Places in Windows 2000, Windows XP, and Windows Server 2003; or the universal naming convention (\\servername\sharename). See Figure 15.6. Another way to access a shared drive or folder is to map a network drive. This can be accessed by starting Windows Explorer, opening the Tools menu, and selecting Map Network Drive. Then select the drive letter that will be used to point to the network shared drive or folder and enter the UNC name in the Folder text box. See Figure 15.7. When you copy a shared folder, only the original shared folder is still shared. When you move a shared folder, it is no longer shared.

Example 7:

You have a computer with Windows 2000 Server called SERVER1. On the E drive, you have a DATA folder and under the DATA folder, you have the FINANCE folder. Under the FINANCE folder, you have a GROUP1 folder.

If you share the DATA folder and you want to access the GROUP1 folder, then access the \\SERVER1\DATA\FINANCE\GROUP1 folder. Another way is to access the \\SERVER1\DATA share. From there, open the FINANCE folder, which would then allow you to access the GROUP1 folder. See Figure 15.8.

Figure 15.6 Access a shared folder using Windows Explorer

Figure 15.7 Mapping network drives

Example 8:

You have a computer with a Windows 2000 Server called SERVER1. On the E drive, you have a DATA folder and under the DATA folder, you have the FINANCE folder. Under the FINANCE folder, you have a GROUP1 folder.

If you share the FINANCE folder, you would not have access to the DATA folder and FINANCE remotely. You can still access the folder locally by opening the E drive. To access the GROUP1 share, use \\SERVER1\GROUP1, even though the GROUP1 folder is three levels deep. See Figure 15.9.

Network administrators and authorized users can publish a shared folder as a shared folder object in Active Directory by using the Active Directory Users and Computers snap-in of the Microsoft

Figure 15.8 Accessing a shared folder remotely and locally on a first-level shared folder

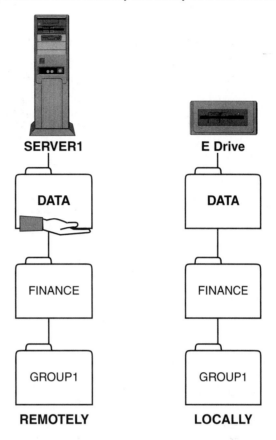

Figure 15.9 Accessing a shared folder remotely and locally on a third-level shared folder

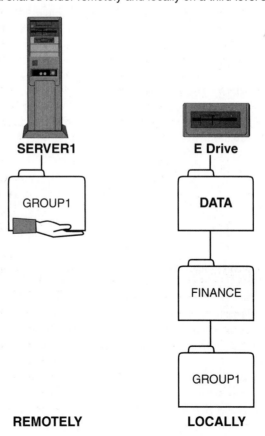

Management Console (MMC). Users can then query Active Directory for a shared folder. To publish a shared folder, follow these steps:

1. Open Active Directory Users and Computers.
2. In the console tree, double-click the domain node.
3. Right-click the folder in which you want to add the shared folder, point to New, and click Shared Folder.
4. Type the name of the folder.
5. Type the UNC name that you want to publish in the directory.

To find a shared folder, follow these steps:

1. Open Active Directory Users and Computers.
2. In the console tree, right-click the domain node, then click Find.
3. In the Find list, click Shared Folders.
4. On the Shared Folders tab, in Named, type the name of the folder you want to find.
5. Click Find Now.

15.2.2 Simple File Sharing

When you first install Windows XP, Windows XP is configured to use simple file sharing. Simplified sharing lets you share folders with everyone in your workgroup or network and make folders in your user profile private. However, if simplified sharing is enabled, you cannot prevent specific users and groups from accessing your shared folders. As a result, the security tab is not available on NTFS partitions. To display the security tab and to disable the simple file sharing, do the following:

1. Open Folder Options in Control Panel.
2. Click Start, then click Control Panel.
3. Double-click Folder Options.
4. On the View tab, under Advanced settings, clear "Use simple file sharing [Recommended]".

See Figure 15.10.

15.2.3 Shared Folder Permissions

To control how users gain access to a shared folder, assign Shared Folder permissions. These permissions are neither required nor utilized if the user is accessing the directory locally (logged on to the computer that has the shared drive or directory). The Shared Folder/Drive permissions are shown in Table 15.5.

To grant or change share permissions to a shared folder, right-click the shared folder or drive, select the Sharing option, and click on the Permissions button. To add a user or group, click on the Add button. To remove a user or group, click to highlight the user or group and click on the Remove button. To specify which permissions to grant, click to highlight the user or group and select or deselect the Allow and Deny options.

Different from NTFS permissions, a shared folder has only one level of permissions assigned to it. For example, on the SERVER1 server, you share a folder called FOLDER1 and assign the Full Control permission. In the FOLDER1 folder, you share a folder called FOLDER2 and assign the Modify permission. Therefore, if you access the \\SERVER1\FOLDER1 folder, you use the Full Control share permission, even when accessing the \\SERVER1\FOLDER1\FOLDER2 folder. If you access the \\SERVER folder, you use the Change Share permission. The permissions assigned to FOLDER1 are not an issue.

Since a user can be a member of several groups, it is possible for the user to have several sets of explicit permissions to a shared drive or folder. The effective permissions are the combination of all user and group permissions. For example, if the user has a Write permission to the user and a Read permission to the group, of which the user is a member, the effective permission would be

Figure 15.10   Windows XP's simple file sharing

Table 15.5   Share permissions

Share Permissions	Description
Read	Allows the user to view folder names and file names, open and view subfolder files and their attributes, and navigate the tree structures
Change	Allows all permissions granted by the Read permission and it also allows the user to create folders, add files to folders, change data in files, append data to files, change file attributes, and delete folders and files
Full Control	Allows all permissions granted by the Change permission and it also allows the user to change file permissions and take ownership of files

the Write permission. See Figure 15.11. Like NTFS permissions, Deny permissions override the granted permission.

15.2.4   Special Shares

Windows 2000, Windows XP, and Windows Server 2003 have several special shared folders that are automatically created by Windows for administrative and system use. See Table 15.6. Different from regular shares, these shares do not show when a user browses the computer resources using Network Neighborhood, My Network Places, or similar software. In most cases, special shared folders should

Figure 15.11   Share permissions

Table 15.6   Special shares

Special Share	Description
Drive letter$	A shared folder that allows administrative personnel to connect to the root directory of a drive, also known as an administrative share. It is shown as A$, B$, C$, D$, and so on. For example, C$ is a shared folder name by which drive C might be accessed by an administrator over the network.
ADMIN$	A resource used by the system during remote administration of a computer. The path of this resource is always the path to the Windows system root (the directory in which Windows is installed, e.g., C:\Winnt).
IPC$	A resource sharing the named pipes that are essential for communication between programs. It is used during remote administration of a computer and when viewing a computer's shared resources.
PRINT$	A resource used during remote administration of printers
NETLOGON	A resource used by the Net Logon service of a Windows server computer while processing domain logon requests. This resource is provided only for Windows server computers. It is not provided for Windows 2000 Professional and Windows XP computers.
FAX$	A shared folder on a server used by fax clients in the process of sending a fax. The shared folder is used to temporarily cache files and access cover pages stored on the server.

not be deleted or modified. For the Windows 2000 Professional and Windows XP computers, only members of the Administrators or Backup Operators group can connect to these shares. For Windows servers, members of Administrators, Backup Operators, and Server Operators groups are the only members who can connect to these shares.

An **administrative share** is a shared folder, typically used for administrative purposes. To make a shared folder or drive into an administrative share, the share name must end with a $. Since the share folder or drive cannot be seen during browsing, you would have to use a UNC name, which includes the share name (including the $). Access the shared folder using the Start button, selecting the Run option, and typing the UNC name and clicking the OK button. By default, all volumes with drive letters automatically have administrative shares (C$, D$, E$, and so on). Other administrative shares can be created as needed for individual folders.

The IPC$ is used for remote administration of a computer and when viewing a computer's shared resources. Windows uses it to exchange information directly between applications on two different computers, without having to write to or read from the file system. If you do not have the guest account enabled, you have not connected to the IPC$ share. If you are trying to access a shared folder or shared printer on a remote system of which you are not a member, the remote computer's domain or local user account Windows will ask you for the password for the IPC$ share, as shown in Figure 15.12.

Following are two ways to overcome this problem:

■ Enable the guest account. This is typically not recommended for security reasons. To access any network resource, you must be logged in with a user name and password (the password may be blank). It does not matter if you are logging into the same domain, another domain, or logging in locally.

■ Connect to the IPC$ share or the remote system using an account and password that exist in the remote system's domain or local user accounts. To connect to the remote IPC$ share, use the following command at the Command prompt:

```
NET USE \\computername\IPC$ /USER:accountname password
```

or run (execute) the following command in the Run dialog box:

```
\\computername\IPC$ /USER:accountname password
```

15.2.5   Volume Shadow Copy Service

A new feature of Windows Server 2003, Volume Shadow Copy Service (VSS) creates a copy of files stored in a shared network folder at regular intervals, even files that are open or locked. While the shadow copy process occurs, applications can continue to write data to the disk volume.

To configure VSS, right-click the volume on which the network shares reside, then select Properties to open the configuration window. Click the Shadow Copies tab, followed by clicking the volume you want to back up. Click Enable to enable a shadow copy of all shares on the volume and create the first backup. To create additional copies, click Create Now. You can stop the shadow copy creation process by clicking Disable; however, be aware that when you do this, it will delete any copies that you have already created.

To configure other VSS settings, click Settings on the Shadow Copies tab. On the Settings dialog box, you can configure the maximum disk space for the shadow copies. Click Schedule to specify when VSS runs. By default, VSS runs twice every weekday, at 7:00 am and 12:00 pm. Click Schedule to open

Figure 15.12   Windows will ask you to log in to the IPC$ if you are not connected to the IPC$ share or to the remote system using an account and password that exist in the remote system's domain or local user accounts, while the guest account is disabled.

Figure 15.13 Shared folders console

the scheduled backup times and configure new backup times. Click New to add new backup times, click Delete to remove scheduled times, and click Advanced to configure advanced schedules.

If users have the client software installed (located in the \windows\system32\clients\twclient\x86 folder), they can access previous versions of files by right-clicking the applicable network share and selecting Properties. Then select the Previous Versions tab, select a volume copy, and click View to see the contents of the backup. The backup file opens in a Windows Explorer window, where you can choose the files that you want to reinstate and copy them to the appropriate network share. You can also select Copy to copy the entire backup to another location, or click Restore to restore the entire network share backup.

15.2.6 Managing Shares

By using the Shared Folders snap-in (included in the Computer Management console), you can manage the server's shared folders. See Figure 15.13. With the Shared Folder snap-in, you can do the following:

- Create, view, and set permissions for shares, including shares on Windows 2000, Windows XP, or Windows Server 2003 computers.
- View a list of all users who are connected to the computer over a network and disconnect one or all of them.
- View a list of files opened by remote users and close one or all of the open files.

15.3 COMBINING SHARED FOLDER PERMISSIONS AND NTFS PERMISSIONS

NTFS permissions apply if you are logged on locally or if you connect to the computer using a network connection. Share permissions are the only protection for FAT and FAT32 drives. Unfortunately, share permissions only protect the network resource when you connect to the computer using a network connection. If you log on locally to the computer, share permissions do not matter. Remember that you help protect the local files by only allowing a small group of people to log on locally.

When accessing a shared folder on an NTFS volume, the effective permissions that a person can do in the share folder are calculated by combining the shared folder permissions with the NTFS permissions. When combining the two, first determine the cumulative NTFS permissions and the cumulative shared permissions and apply the more restrictive permission—the one that gives the fewest permissions.

Example 9:

On the E drive (NTFS partition), you have a DATA folder and under the DATA folder you have a FINANCE folder. In the FINANCE folder, you have the DOC1.TXT file. The DATA folder is shared.

Question: For USER1, you assign the Read (R) NTFS permission to the DATA folder and Full Control (FC) Share permission to the DATA folder. What are the effective rights to the DOC1.TXT file for USER1?

Answer: To determine the effective rights when accessing the server remotely, take the more restrictive permission, or the more limiting permission. Since the Read permission is more limiting than the FC permission, the effective rights when USER1 is accessing the DATA folder over the network are those granted by the Read permission. As the rights flow down to the FINANCE folder, again the R is more limiting than the FC. Therefore, the effective rights when USER1 is accessing the DATA folder over the network are those granted by the Read permission. Lastly, the rights flow into the DOC1.TXT file and again the effective permission is Read.

Remote Access Effective Permissions

		NTFS	Shared	Combined
DATA	Explicit	R	FC	
	Effective	R	FC	R
FINANCE	Inherited	R	FC	
	Explicit	—	—	
	Effective	R	FC	R
DOC1.TXT	Inherited	R	FC	
	Explicit	—	—	
	Effective	R	FC	R

If USER1 logs on locally to the server, the share permissions do not matter and the only permission worth looking at is the Read permission.

Local Access Effective Permissions

		NTFS	Shared	Combined
DATA	Explicit	R	FC	
	Effective	R	NA	R
FINANCE	Inherited	R	NA	
	Explicit	—	—	
	Effective	R	NA	R
DOC1.TXT	Inherited	R	NA	
	Explicit	—	—	
	Effective	R	NA	R

Example 10:

On the E drive (NTFS partition), you have a DATA folder and under the DATA folder you have a FINANCE folder. In the FINANCE folder, you have the DOC1.TXT file. The DATA folder is shared. USER1 is a member of the local group called MANAGERS.

Question: For USER1, you assign the Modify (M) NTFS permission to the DATA folder and Read and Execute (R&E) permission to the FINANCE folder. For the MANAGERS group, you assign the Write permission to the FINANCE folder. In addition, for the Managers group, you assign Full Control (FC) Share permission to the DATA folder. What are the effective permissions to the DOC1.TXT file for USER1 when USER1 logs on remotely?

Answer: To determine the effective rights when accessing the server remotely, take the more restrictive permission, or the more limiting permission. For the USER1 NTFS permission, the R&E permission will stop the FINANCE folder from inheriting the Modify permission from the DATA folder. The DOC1.TXT file will inherit the R&E permission. For MANAGERS, DOC1.TXT file will inherit the Write permission from the FINANCE folder. When you combine all NTFS permissions for the DOC1.TXT file, USER1 will have Read & Execute and Write permissions.

For the shared permissions, the MANAGERS were assigned Full Control to the shared Data folder. Therefore, the effective shared permission is the Full Control permission.

When you combine the two at the DOC1.TXT level, you must take the permissions that are the most restrictive. Since the R&E and Write permissions are more restrictive than Full Control, USER1 will have those permissions when accessing the DOC1.TXT file.

Remote Access Effective Permissions

		USER1 NTFS	MANAGERS NTFS	Combined NTFS	USER1 Shared	MANAGERS Shared	Combined Shared	Combined Overall
DATA	Explicit	M	—	██	—	FC	██	██
	Effective	M	—	M	—	FC	FC	M
FINANCE	Inherited	R&E	—	██	—	FC	██	██
	Explicit	—	W	██	—	—	██	██
	Effective	R&E	W	R&E & W	—	FC	FC	R&E & W
DOC1.TXT	Inherited	R&E	W	██	—	FC	██	██
	Explicit	—	—	██	—	—	██	██
	Effective	R&E	W	R&E & W	—	FC	FC	R&E & W

15.4 DISTRIBUTED FILE SYSTEM

The **distributed file system (DFS)** groups and organizes shared folders that reside on the same or different computers into a single hierarchical tree structure. By using DFS, a user can easily gain access to network resources without knowing the actual location of the underlying resources. To create a DFS share, you must first create a DFS root and then create child nodes that represent the shared folders, which can be physically located on different servers. See Figure 15.14. Note that any Windows 2000 Server or Windows Server 2003 can host one DFS root that is located in a FAT or NTFS volume; however, NTFS would be a better choice because of its extra security features.

The two types of DFS are as follows:

Figure 15.14   Distributed file system

DFS Type	Description
Stand-alone DFS	Stores the DFS topology on a single computer. It does not provide any fault tolerance if the computer that stores the DFS topology or any of the shared folders fails.
Domain DFS (Fault Tolerance)	Provides fault tolerance by having the child nodes point to multiple, identical shared folders. Different than the stand-alone DFS, the domain DFS stores its topology in the Active Directory. By using Active Directory, it supports DNS. Each child node can have up to 32 replicas.

To create the stand-alone DFS root, follow these steps:

1. On the Action menu, click the New DFS Root and click on the Next button.
2. Select Create a Stand-alone DFS Root and click on the Next button.
3. Type in the name of the host server for the DNS root and click on the Next button.
4. Select an existing share or select the Create a New Share and specify the path to share and the share name and click on the Next button.
5. Specify a unique DFS share name and click on the Next button.
6. Click on the Finish button.

To create the domain (fault-tolerant) DFS root, follow these steps:

1. On the Action menu, click the New DFS Root and click on the Next button.
2. Select Create a Domain DFS Root and click on the Next button.
3. Type in the name of the host domain for the DFS root and click on the Next button.
4. Type in the name of the host server for the DNS root and click on the Next button.
5. Select an existing share or select the Create a New Share and specify the path to share and the share name and click on the Next button.
6. Specify a unique DFS share name and click on the Next button.
7. Click on the Finish button.

Replicating the DFS root to another server in the domain ensures that if the host server becomes unavailable for any reason, the distributed file system that is associated with that DFS root is still available to domain users. To set up a replication of the root, right-click the root, select the New Root Replica, and use the Wizard.

Replicating a DFS shared folder stores a duplicate copy of the contents of the original shared folder into another shared folder. To replicate a DFS shared folder, right-click the DFS Link and select the New Replica option. Then specify an alternate shared folder that will act as a replication partner to the original shared folder, select the type of replication policy, and click on the OK button. If Automatic

Figure 15.15 Setting up replicas in DFS

Replication is selected, it automatically will replicate the files from the one share to the other. Automatic Replication can only be used, however, for files stored on NTFS volumes on Windows servers. When manual replication is selected, you must manually copy the files. Also, when using stand-alone DFS, you can only select manual replication. See Figure 15.15.

To remove a link, right-click the link and select the Remove DFS Link option and click on the Yes button. To delete a DFS root share, right-click the DFS root share, select the Delete DFS Root option, and click on the Yes button.

To access DFS resources, the operating system must include DFS client software. This software is included in operating systems since Windows 98 and Windows NT 4.0. If you have a Windows 95 computer, you must download and install a DFS client. If your system has the DFS client, then access it like you would a shared folder or directory.

15.5 DEFAULT PERMISSIONS AND GUIDELINES

By now, it is probably obvious that NTFS is a much better choice than FAT or FAT32. The only reason to use FAT or FAT32 is if you need to dual boot between two different operating systems, such as Windows 2000 and Windows 98.

When you format a volume with NTFS, or create a share, the Full Control permission is assigned to the Everyone group. Therefore, to make the server a secure system, either remove the Everyone group and assign groups and individuals to the drive and directories with the appropriate permissions or change the Full Control permission to something more appropriate.

When planning a directory structure, attempt to group files into application, public data folders, and home folders. See Table 15.7. Then you can assign the appropriate rights to the folder instead of the different files and the task of performing backups is simpler. Next, try to create groups according to their access, and assign only the level of access that the users need by first assigning rights to the group followed by assigning rights to the individual users who do not fit into the groups.

15.6 TROUBLESHOOTING FILE ACCESS PROBLEMS

When a user cannot gain access to a folder or file, the problem is usually caused by insufficient permissions (either NTFS or shared). Make sure that the user or group is assigned the proper permission and that the user is assigned to the proper group. In addition, when checking the permissions of the user and the group, of which the user is a member, check for denied permissions. Lastly, if you just added permissions to a user or group or just added a user to a group and the user still cannot access the folder or file, have the user log off and log on so that the person will get a new token that allows access to the folder or file.

Table 15.7 Recommended folder rights

Directory Purpose	Description	Recommended Rights
Application Folder	Contains the programs that the user needs to run	If the user needs to read the files and run the applications, assign NTFS Read & Execute permission to the users/groups and the Read permission to the share.
		If the user needs to upgrade and troubleshoot the applications, assign NTFS Read & Execute and write permissions to the users/groups and the Modify permission to the share.
		If the user needs to administer the application folder, assign NTFS Full Control permission to the users/groups and Full Control permission to the share.
Public Data Folder	Used to store data files that belong to a group of people. For example, you may have a folder for an administrative group or a project.	If the user needs to make changes to the file or create new files, assign NTFS Read & Execute and Write permissions to the users/groups that need it and the Modify permission to the share.
		If the user needs to read the files without making changes or creating new files, assign NTFS Read & Execute to the users/groups that need it and the Read permission to the share.
		If the user needs to manage the public data folder, assign NTFS Full Control permission to the users/group and Full Control permission to the share.
Home Folder	Used to hold the individuals' data directories	Assign the Full control permission for the individual to the individual's home folder.
		Refer to Section 13.1.4 on setting up user home directories.

15.7   FILE ENCRYPTION

Encryption is the process of converting data into a format that cannot be read by another user. Once a user has encrypted a file, it automatically remains encrypted when the file is stored on disk. **Decryption** is the process of converting data from encrypted format back to its original format. Once a user has decrypted a file, the file remains decrypted when stored on disk.

Windows 2000, Windows XP and Windows Server 2003 include the **encrypting file system (EFS),** which allows a user to encrypt and decrypt files that are stored on an NTFS volume. By using EFS, folders and files are still kept secure against those intruders who might gain unauthorized physical access to the drive, for example, as by stealing a notebook computer or a removable drive. EFS is not intended to support the accessing of an encrypted file by multiple users nor does it decrypt or encrypt files that are transmitted over the network. Instead, another protocol would have to be used to secure the data sent over the network.

When EFS is enabled, the process of encrypting and decrypting a file is transparent to the user. As a file is encrypted, each file has a unique file encryption key, which is later used to decrypt the file's data. The file encryption key is also encrypted by the user's public key. When decrypting files, the file encryption key must first be decrypted. The file encryption is decrypted when the user has a private key that matches the public key. When a user who does not have the right private key tries to open, copy, move, or rename an encrypted file, the user will get an access denied message.

Be aware of the following guidelines when using EFS:

- You cannot encrypt files or folders that are compressed.
- An encrypted file can become decrypted if you copy or move the file to a volume that is not an NTFS volume.

- Use cut and paste to move files into an encrypted folder. If you use a drag-and-drop operation to move the files, they will not automatically be encrypted in the new folder.
- System files cannot be encrypted.
- Encrypting a folder or file does not protect against deletion. Anyone with delete permission can delete encrypted folders or files.
- Temporary files, which are created by some programs when documents are edited, are also encrypted as long as all the files are on an NTFS volume and in an encrypted folder. It is recommended that you encrypt the Temp folder on your hard disk for this reason.
- Encrypt the My Documents folder, if this is where you save most of your documents, to ensure that your personal documents are encrypted by default.

15.7.1 Encrypt Attribute

To encrypt a folder or file, do the following:

1. Right-click the folder or file and select the Properties option.
2. Click on the Advanced button. See Figure 15.16.
3. Select the Encrypt Contents to Secure Data option.

Note that when a folder is encrypted, the folder itself is not encrypted, but all files in the folder are encrypted. To decrypt the folder or file, unselect the Encrypt Contents to Secure Data option. You also can encrypt or decrypt a file or folder by using the CIPHER command. For more information on the CIPHER command, type CIPHER /? at the Command prompt. See Figure 15.17.

15.7.2 Recovering Encrypted Files

For EFS to work, an EFS recovery policy must be defined, which enables an authorized data recovery agent to decrypt encrypted files. Recovery agents can use EFS to recover encrypted files if users leave the organization or lose their encryption credentials. EFS requires at least one recovery agent.

Before you can add a recovery agent for a domain, you must ensure that the recovery agent has been issued a **digital certificate** (namely, a X.509v3 certificate). See Figure 15.18. EFS can use certificates issued by a certificate authority (CA) but does not require them. If no CA is available, then EFS issues its own certificates. Encrypted files can only be unencrypted by the user that encrypted the

Figure 15.16 Encryption and compression attributes

FIGURE 15.17 CIPHER command

```
C:\>cipher /?
Displays or alters the encryption of directories [files] on NTFS
partitions.

    CIPHER [/E | /D] [/S:dir] [/A] [/I] [/F] [/Q] [/H] [/K]
[pathname[...]]

    /E     Encrypts the specified directories. Directories will be marked so
           that files added afterward will be encrypted.
    /D     Decrypts the specified directories. Directories will be marked so
           that files added afterward will not be encrypted.
    /S     Performs the specified operation on directories in the given
           directory and all subdirectories.
    /A     Performs the operation for files and directories. The encrypted
           file could become decrypted when it is modified if the parent
           directory is not encrypted. It is recommended that you encrypt
           the file and the parent directory.
    /I     Continues performing the specified operation even after errors
           have occured. By default, CIPHER stops when an error is
           encountered.
    /F     Forces the encryption on all specified objects, even those that
           are already encrypted. Already-encrypted objects are skipped by
           default.
    /Q     Reports only the most essential information.
    /H     Displays files with the hidden or system attributes. These files
           are omitted by default.
    /K     Creates a new file cncryption key for the user who is running
           CIPHER. If this option is chosen, all other options will be
           ignored.
pathname   Specifies a pattern, file, or directory.

Used without parameters, CIPHER displays the encrytion state of the current
directory and any files it contains. You may use multiple directory names
and wildcards. You must put spaces between multiple parameters.
```

files or by a recovery agent. By default, the domain administrator is a recovery agent and can, therefore, remove the file's encryption attribute. See Chapter 23 for information about digital certificates.

By default, the EFS issues EFS recovery certificates to the Domain Administrator account as the recovery agent for the domain. For stand-alone computers that are not joined to a domain, the EFS issues EFS recovery certificates to the local Administrator user account as the recovery agent for that computer. Many organizations might want to designate other EFS recovery agents to centrally administer the EFS recovery program. For example, you can create organizational units (OUs) for groups of computers and designate specific recovery agent accounts to manage EFS recovery for specific OUs.

If a person leaves the company and his or her data are encrypted, the data will have to be decrypted before someone else can use the information. One way to do this is to reset the password for the account, so that you can have the same permissions and privileges as the original user and have the user's EFS certificate. Alternatively, if you are a recovery agent, you can back up the file to your computer where your EFS certificate is installed, restore the backup, and decrypt the file. If no one except the user has been using the EFS, and all EFS-related settings are at the user's defaults, then you should restore the

Figure 15.18 File recovery certificate

backup on the first domain controller in the domain and log on to the domain controller by using the built-in Administrator account.

If you are the recovery agent, be sure to use the EXPORT command in the Certificates snap-in in Microsoft Management Console (MMC) to back up the recovery certificate and the associated private key and store them in a secure location. After backing them up, use Certificates to delete the recovery certificate. Then, when you need to perform a recovery operation for a user, first restore the recovery certificate and associated private key using the IMPORT command in Certificates. After recovering the data, again delete the recovery certificate. You do not have to repeat the export process.

EFS works only if at least one recovery agent is designated. If your EFS causes a problem with one or more applications, or data are becoming too easily corrupted, or you do not wish users to use encryption, remove all recovery agents from the Encrypted Data Recovery Agents policy in all Group Policy objects (GPOs) that are linked to the domain and you will disable EFS. A recovery policy that has had all of the recovery agent certificates deleted is referred to as an empty policy. To prevent organizational units in the domain from overriding this empty policy, specify the No Override option.

To add a recovery agent for a domain, follow these steps:

1. Open Active Directory Users and Computers.
2. Right-click the domain whose recovery policy you want to change, then click Properties.
3. Click the Group Policy tab.
4. Right-click the recovery policy you want to change, then click Edit.
5. In the console tree, click Encrypted Data Recovery Agents:
   - Computer Configuration
   - Windows Settings
   - Security Settings
   - Public Key Policies
   - Encrypted Data Recovery Agents
6. In the details pane, right-click, then click Add, and follow the instructions.

15.8   COMPRESSION

NTFS compression is the ability to selectively compress the contents of individual files, entire directories, or entire drives on an NTFS volume. NTFS compression uses file compression that works by substitution. It starts by locating repetitive patterns and replaces the repetitive data with another pattern, which is shorter. Windows tracks which files and folders are compressed via a file attribute. As far as the user is concerned, the compressed drive, folder, or file is simply another drive folder or file that works like any other. Although you expand the amount of space for a volume, the performance of the PC will be slower because it has to process the compression and decompression of files. Therefore, do not use compression unless you are compressing files that are rarely used or when disk space is critical. If disk space is critical, use this as a temporary solution until you can delete or move files from the drive or can extend the volume.

To compress a file or folder on an NTFS drive, do the following:

1. Open Windows Explorer.
2. Right-click the file or folder that you want to compress and select the Properties option.
3. Select the Advanced button.
4. Select the "Compress contents to save disk space" check box.
5. Click on the OK or Apply button.
6. If you select to compress a folder, select "Apply changes to this folder only" or "Apply changes to the folder, subfolder and files" and click on the OK button.

To compress an NTFS drive, do the following:

1. Open My Computer.
2. Right-click the drive that you want to compress.
3. Select the "Compress drive to save disk space" check box.

To uncompress a drive, folder, or file, unselect the option.

To display compressed files and folders in a different color, do the following:

1. Open the Control Panel.
2. Double-click the Folder Options applet.
3. Click the View tab.
4. Select the "Display compressed files and folders with alternate color" check box.
5. Click on the OK or Apply button.

When you copy and move files and folders from one location to another, it is important to understand how the NTFS folder and file compressions are affected. If you copy a file or folder, the new folder and file will automatically acquire the compression attribute of the original drive or folder. If the folder or file is moved within the same volume, either will retain the originally assigned compression attribute. Thus, if it was compressed, it will remain compressed at the new location; if it was uncompressed, it will remain uncompressed at the new location. When the folder or file is moved from one volume to another, either will automatically acquire the compression attribute of the original drive or folder and file. An easy way to remember the difference is when you move a folder or file from within the same volume, the folder or file is not physically moved but the Master File Table is adjusted to indicate a different folder. When you move a folder or file from one volume to another, it copies the folder or file to the new location and then deletes the old location. Therefore, the moved folder and files are new to the volume and acquire the new compression attribute.

15.9   QUOTAS

When working as a network administrator, you will find that typical users will think of their network drives as their own personal drives. Therefore, as they receive files from a friend or find something they like on the Internet, they will save the files in the network drive. Unfortunately, after a period of time, a volume will become full.

Figure 15.19   Disk quotas

To manage this type of situation, Windows 2000 introduced **disk quotas,** which track and control disk space usage for an NTFS volume. When you enable disk quotas, you can set both the disk quota limit and the warning level. The limit specifies the user's allowable amount of disk space. The warning level specifies when it will log a system event when the warning level is met. Disk quotas are based on file ownership, not on where the file is located on the volume. In addition, file compression does not affect the quota statistics.

As soon as disk quota is activated on your volume, it will track all disk usage by the user. When users exceed their disk quota, you can deny them the ability to save any more files to the volume. Enabling quotas, not limited disk space use, is useful when you do not want to deny users access to a volume, but want to track disk space use on a per-user basis. See Figure 15.19.

To administer quotas on an NTFS volume, follow these steps:

1. Open My Computer.
2. Right-click the NTFS volume on which you want to enable disk quotas. See Figure 15.19.
3. Select Enable Quota Management check box.
4. If you want users to be denied access when they have exceeded their disk quota, select the "Deny disk spaces to users exceeding quota limit" check box.
5. If you wish, under the "Select the default quota limit for new users on this volume" option, specify the default limit disk space and the warning level for the new users. Note that the default value is in kilobytes.
6. Select the appropriate logging options.
7. Click on the OK or Apply button.

To administer quotas on a volume, you must be a member of the Administrators group on the computer where the drive resides. If you are not a member of the Administrators group or the volume is not an NTFS volume, the Quota tab will not be displayed. Lastly, new members are those who write to a disk for the first time after the disk quotas have been enabled.

Figure 15.20   Managing disk quotas

Status	Name	Logon Name	Amount Used	Quota Limit	Warning Level	Percent Used
OK	Frank J. Biggs	FJBiggs@acme01.com	0 bytes	100 KB	80 KB	0
OK	Charles L. Gee	CLGee@acme01.com	0 bytes	200 KB	200 KB	0
OK		BUILTIN\Administrators	0 bytes	No Limit	No Limit	N/A

3 total item(s), 0 selected.

To manage the quota, do the following:

1. Open My Computer.
2. Right-click the NTFS volume on which you want to enable disk quotas. See Figure 15.20.
3. Select the Quota Entries button.

To change a quota limit or warning level, double-click on the user. To create a quota entry, open the Quota menu and select the New Quota entry. To delete an entry, right-click the entry and select the Delete option.

SUMMARY

1. One primary advantage of an NTFS volume is its ability to apply NTFS permissions to secure folders and files.
2. The standard folder and file permissions consist of special permissions that are grouped logically.
3. The NTFS permissions that are granted are stored in an access control list (ACL) with every file and folder on an NTFS volume.
4. Explicit permissions are those granted directly to the folder or file.
5. The effective permissions are the actual permissions when logging in and accessing a file or folder.
6. NTFS file permissions override folder permissions.
7. The deny permission always overrides the permissions that have been granted, including when a user or group has been granted full control.
8. Every folder and file has an owner, the person who controls how permissions are set on a folder or file and who can grant permissions to others. When a folder or file is created, the folder or file automatically becomes the owner.
9. If you copy a file or folder, the new folder and file will automatically acquire the permissions of the original drive or folder.
10. If the folder or file is moved within the same volume, the folder or file will retain the same permissions that were already assigned. When the folder or file is moved from one volume to another, the folder or file will automatically acquire the permissions of the original drive or folder.
11. A shared folder on a computer makes the folder available to others on the network. A shared drive on a computer makes the entire drive available to others on the network.
12. To control how users gain access to a shared folder, assign Shared Folder permissions.
13. An administrative share is a shared folder typically used for administrative purposes. It does not show when a user browses the computer resources using Network Neighborhood, My Network Places, or similar software.
14. NTFS permissions apply if you log on locally or if you connect to the computer using a network connection.
15. The distributed file system (DFS) groups and organizes shared folders that reside on the same or different computers into a single hierarchical tree structure.
16. A stand-alone DFS stores the DFS topology on a single computer.
17. Domain DFS provides fault tolerance by having the child nodes point to multiple, identical shared folders.
18. Different than the stand-alone DFS, the domain DFS stores its topology in the Active Directory.
19. Once a user has encrypted a file, it automatically remains encrypted when the file is stored on disk.
20. When EFS is enabled, the process of encrypting and decrypting a file is transparent to the user.
21. You also can encrypt or decrypt a file or folder by using the CIPHER command.
22. NTFS compression is the ability to selectively compress the contents of individual files, entire directories, or entire drives on an NTFS volume.
23. If the folder or file is moved within the same volume, either will retain the same compression attribute that was already assigned.
24. When the folder or file is moved from one volume to another, either will automatically acquire the compression attribute of the original drive or folder and file.
25. Windows 2000 introduced disk quotas, which track and control disk space usage for an NTFS volume.

QUESTIONS

1. You have created an uncompressed file called REPORT.DOC in the Documents folder on an NTFS partition. The Documents folder is not compressed. Now you move the file REPORT.DOC to a compressed folder called SCHOOLWORK on a different NTFS partition. Which of the following will occur?
   a. The file will stay uncompressed.
   b. The file will inherit the compression attribute from the target folder.
   c. The file will inherit the compression attribute from the target partition.
   d. A dialog box will appear, asking you whether you want to compress the file in the target folder.

2. What will occur if you copy a file from one folder to another folder within the same NTFS partition?
   a. The file will retain its permissions.
   b. The file will inherit the permissions of the source folder.
   c. The file will inherit the permissions of the target folder.
   d. All file permissions will be lost.

3. You want to control the permissions of files and directories on an NTFS drive on the network. Which application must you use?
   a. Windows Explorer
   b. Active Directory Users and Computers console
   c. Computer Management console
   d. Disk Administrator console

4. What will occur to the permissions and the long file name for a file when it is copied from an NTFS partition to a FAT partition on a Windows 2000 Server computer?
   a. Both the permissions and the long file name for the file will be lost.
   b. The permissions for the file will be lost, but the long file name will be retained.
   c. The permissions for the file will be retained, but the long file name will be lost.
   d. Both the permissions and the long file name for the file will be retained.

5. You have created an uncompressed file called MyPaper.doc in the Documents folder on an NTFS partition. The Documents folder is not compressed. Now you move the file MyPaper.doc to a compressed folder called TermPaper on a different NTFS partition. Which of the following will occur?
   a. The file will stay uncompressed.
   b. The file will inherit the compression attribute from the target folder.
   c. The file will inherit the compression attribute from the target partition.
   d. A dialog box will appear, asking you whether you want to compress the file in the target folder.

6. Pat was a member of the Research group. Now he has been reassigned to the Design team. As a result, he needs access to program source files in the \DATA directory on the file server. The Design Administrators group has Full Control permissions to the \DATA directory. The Everyone group has Read permission and the Research group has been denied access to the DATA. After logging on as a member of the Design group, Pat notices that he still cannot access the files in the \DATA directory on the file server. What is the best way for Pat's domain administrator to grant him the required access to the \DATA directory?
   a. Remove Pat's user account from the Research group.
   b. Remove Pat's user account from the Research group and the Everyone group.
   c. Grant all permissions for the \DATA directory to Pat's user account.
   d. Add Pat's user account to the Administrators group.

7. What will occur if you copy a file from one folder to another within the same NTFS partition?
   a. The file will retain its permissions.
   b. The file will inherit the permissions of the source folder.
   c. The file will inherit the permissions of the target folder.
   d. All file permissions will be lost.

8. What will occur if you move a file from one folder to another within the same NTFS partition?
   a. The file will retain its permissions.
   b. The file will inherit the permissions of the source folder.
   c. The file will inherit the permissions of the target folder.
   d. All file permissions will be lost.

9. Which of the following are features of the NTFS file system on Windows 2000? (Choose all that apply.)
   a. support for on-disk compression
   b. support for file and folder-level security
   c. support for disk quotas
   d. support for on-disk file encryption

10. You have just modified the permissions on an NTFS folder. By default, which permissions will be changed?
   a. permissions on the folder and files in the folder, but not on subfolders
   b. permissions on the folder only
   c. permissions on the folder, files, and subfolders
   d. permissions on the folder and subfolders, but not on any files

11. You have created a DFS tree on your Windows 2000 servers. Which of the following network clients can utilize this DFS tree by default?
    a. Windows 98   c. Windows NT 4.0
    b. Windows 3.11   d. Windows 95

12. There are two domains in your company—Sales and Development—on a mixed domain forest. Five members of the Sales team are now assisting the Development team with verifying beta testing results. For support with this task, these individuals need access to the shared NTFS folder \RESULTS on a server named BETA, residing in the Development domain. What is the recommended approach to grant the five members of the Sales team Full Control permission to the \RESULTS folder?

a. Create a global group in the Sales domain called SALES_TESTERS. Assign each of the five individuals to this global group. Create a domain local group on BETA in the Development domain called BETA_RESULTS. Assign Full Control permission for the \RESULTS folder to this domain local group. Include the SALES_TESTERS global group in the BETA_RESULTS local group.

b. Create a global group in the Sales domain called SALES_TESTERS. Assign each of the five individuals to this global group. Create a global group in the Development domain called BETA_RESULTS. Assign Full Control permission for the \RESULTS folder to the BETA_RESULTS global group. Include the SALES_TESTERS global group in the BETA_RESULTS global group.

c. Remove the existing trust relationship. Establish a new trust relationship where the Sales domain trusts the Development domain. Create a global group in the Sales domain called SALES_TESTERS. Assign each of the five individuals to this global group. Create a local group on BETA in the Development domain called BETA_RESULTS. Assign Full Control permission for the \RESULTS folder to this local group. Include the SALES_TESTERS global group in the BETA_RESULTS local group.

d. Remove the existing trust relationship. Establish a new trust relationship where the Sales domain trusts the Development domain. Create a global group in the Sales domain called SALES_TESTERS. Assign each of the five individuals to this global group. Create a global group in the Development domain called BETA_RESULTS. Assign Full Control permission for the \RESULTS folder to the BETA_RESULTS global group. Include the SALES_TESTERS global group in the BETA_RESULTS global group.

13. Two of your users have connected to their home folders on the same file-and-print server. When the users query the amount of free disk space on the server, they receive different answers. What is the reason for this?

a. One of the users has a compressed home folder.

b. The users have different local hard disk sizes. The local hard disk size determines the disk cluster size, which, in turn, affects the calculation of the free disk space on the server.

c. One user has no access to some of the folders. These folders will not be included in the free disk space calculation.

d. The users have different amounts of unused disk quota on the server.

14. You have several shared folders on your network containing vital company information. Your users are complaining that having to navigate between these servers is confusing and time consuming. You would like to make it easier for your users to navigate around these shared folders. Which feature of Windows 2000 allows this?

a. DNS

b. RIS

c. DFS

d. IntelliMirror

15. Pat is a user in the Corp domain. He needs to access the \Management folder on a file server that is located in another domain called Sales. Both the Corp and Sales domains are part of the same forest. Pat belongs to the Managers global group in the Corp domain. You assign Read permission for the NTFS folder, \Management, on the file server in the Sales domain to the Managers global group. However, Pat is still not able to access the folder. What is the most likely cause of the problem?

a. The trust relationship is not set up correctly.

b. Permissions to resources located in another domain cannot be assigned to global groups.

c. There are overriding share permissions on the folder.

d. NTFS permissions do not apply when a user tries to access the resource remotely.

16. Pat is about to access a Word document from a shared folder in another domain that belongs to the same forest. The folder's share name is FINANCE. The Domain Accountants group of the trusted domain has Change permission to the folder and its Word document files. The folder is stored on an NTFS partition. Pat's user account only has Read permission for the FINANCE share, and the Accountants group has Full Control permission for the FINANCE share. Assuming Pat is not logging on locally to the server that contains the Word document files, what will be his level of access?

a. No Access

c. Change

b. Read

d. Full Control

17. A user moves a folder from an NTFS partition on his Windows 2000 Server to a shared NTFS folder on a remote Windows 2000 Server. What will be the permissions of the moved folder?

a. No Access permission

b. Full Access permission

c. same permissions as its original, residing on the user's workstation

d. same permissions as the folder to which it was copied

18. A Windows 2000 Server contains a shared folder on an NTFS partition. Which one of the following statements concerning access to the folder is correct?

a. A user who is accessing the folder remotely has the same or more restrictive access permissions than if she accesses the folder locally.

b. A user who is accessing the folder remotely has less restrictive access permissions than if she accesses the folder locally.

c. A user who is accessing the folder remotely has the same access permissions as when accessing the folder locally.

d. A user who is accessing the folder remotely has more restrictive access permissions than if she accesses the folder locally.

19. Pat is a member of the Manager group. There is a shared folder called DATA on an NTFS partition on a remote server. Pat is given the Write NTFS permission, the Manager group is given the Read & Execute NTFS permissions, and the Everyone group has the Read NTFS permission to the DATA folder. In addition, Pat, Manager, and Everyone are assigned the shared Change permission

to the DATA folder. When Pat logs on his client computer and accesses the DATA folder, what would be Pat's permissions? (Choose all that apply.)

a. Read the files in the folder.
b. Write to the files in the folder.
c. Execute the files in the folder.
d. Delete the files in the folder.
e. Have no access to the files in the folder.

20. Pat is a member of the Manager group. There is a shared folder called DATA on an NTFS partition. Pat is given the Write NTFS permission, the Manager group is given the Read & Execute NTFS permission, and the Everyone group has the Read NTFS permission to the DATA directory. In addition, Pat, Manager, and Everyone are assigned the shared Change permission to the DATA folder. When Pat logs on at the server, what would be Pat's permissions? (Choose all that apply.)

a. Read the files in the folder.
b. Write to the files in the folder.
c. Execute the files in the folder.
d. Delete the files in the folder.
e. Have no access to the files in the folder.

21. Pat is a member of the Manager group. There is a shared folder called DATA on an NTFS partition on a remote server. Pat is given the Write NTFS permission, the Manager group is given the Deny All NTFS permissions, and the Everyone group has the Read NTFS permission to the DATA folder. In addition, Pat and Everyone are assigned the shared Change permission to the DATA folder and the Manager group is assigned the Full Control shared permission. When Pat logs on his client computer and accesses the DATA folder, what would be Pat's permissions? (Choose all that apply.)

a. Read the files in the folder.
b. Write to the files in the folder.
c. Execute the files in the folder.
d. Delete the files in the folder.
e. Have no access to the files in the folder.

22. You are sharing a directory called DOWNLOAD. You want the share to be hidden from the Network browse list. What should be the name of your share?

a. DOWNLOAD   c. DOWNLOAD$
b. %DOWNLOAD   d. %DOWNLOAD%

23. You are the administrator of a Windows 2000 Server computer. A folder named HR-Data on the system partition of the server is shared on the network as HR-Data. The owner of the HR-Data folder is Administrators. The shared permissions and NTFS permissions are shown in the following table:

HR-Data Folder Shared Permissions	HR-Data Folder NTFS Permissions
Everyone: Full Control	Domain Admins: Read Katrina: Full Control

Katrina creates a file in the HR-Data folder. She sets the NTFS permissions for the file to list only herself on the access control list, with Full Control permission. Katrina then leaves on vacation and cannot be contacted. Later, you discover that the file contains sensitive information and must be removed from the server as soon as possible.

You want to delete the file without modifying any of the permissions of other files in the HR-Data folder. You want your actions to have the least possible impact on users who may be using other files in the HR-Data folder. You want to use the minimum amount of authority necessary to delete the file. What should you do?

a. Grant yourself Full Control permission for only the HR-Data folder and not its files and subobjects. Delete the file. Then remove Full Control permission for the HR-Data folder.
b. Take ownership of the HR-Data folder. When prompted, take ownership of existing files. Grant yourself Full Control permission for the file. Delete the file.
c. Take ownership of the file. Grant yourself Modify permission for the file. Delete the file.
d. Grant yourself Modify permission for the HR-Data folder and its subobjects. Delete the file. Then remove Modify permission for the HR-Data folder.

24. You create a stand-alone DFS root on a computer running Windows 2000 Server. You want to attach links to the DFS root. What share-level permission must you have for each shared folder that you use to define a DFS link?

a. Change   c. Read
b. Full Control   d. No permission needed

25. You are administrator of a Windows 2000 network. The network includes a Windows 2000 Server computer that is used as a file server. More than 800 of your company client computers are connected to this server. A shared folder named DATA on server is on an NTFS partition. The DATA folder contains more than 200 files. The permissions for the DATA folder are shown in the following table:

Type of Permission	Account	Permission
Share	Users	Change
NTFS	Users	Full Control

You discover that users are connected to the DATA folder. You have an immediate need to prevent 10 of the files in the DATA folder from being modified. You want your actions to have the smallest possible effects on the users who are using other files on the server. What two actions should you take?

a. Modify the NTFS permissions for the 10 files.
b. Modify the NTFS permissions for the DATA folder.
c. Modify the shared permissions for the DATA folder.
d. Log off the users from the network.
e. Disconnect all users from the DATA folder.

26. You are the administrator of a Windows 2000 Server computer named Server1. You create a DFS root named Public. You add a shared folder named Docs as a DFS node under the root. The shared permissions and NTFS permissions for Public and Docs are shown in the following table:

Folder	Shared Permissions	NTFS Permissions
Public	Everyone: Read	Everyone: Read
Docs	Users: Read	Training: Full Control
	Domain Admins: Full Control	Domain Admins: Full Control

A user named Maria is a member of the Users and Training user groups. When Maria attempts to save the file \\Server1\Public\Docs\memo.doc, she receives the following error message: "Access denied." You want Maria to be able to change and delete all files in the Docs folder. You do not want her to have more access than necessary. What should you do?

a. Add Maria to the Domain Admins group.

b. Add Maria to the local Administrators group.

c. Set the shared permissions for the Public folder to grant Maria Full Control permission.

d. Set the shared permissions for the Docs folder to grant Maria Change permission.

e. Set the NTFS permissions for the Public folder and its subobjects to grant Maria Modify permission.

f. Set the NTFS permissions for the Docs folder and its subobjects to grant Maria Full Control permission.

27. You manage a computer running Windows 2000 Server. You create a folder named DATA on a volume that is formatted as FAT32. You set these shared permissions:

• The user account Pat is assigned the Read permission.

• The local group DataUpdate is assigned the Change permission.

• The local group DataManage is assigned the Full Control permission.

• The local group DataLimited is denied the Full Control permission.

The user account Pat is assigned to the global group Acct. Acct is a member of DataUpdate and DataManage. The user account Pat is also assigned to the global group Clerks. Clerks is a member of DataLimited. What is Pat's effective permission for the folder DATA when he accesses it from his computer running Windows 2000 Professional?

a. No access   c. Full control

b. Change   d. Read

28. A user named Pat belongs to four global groups in Corp, a Windows 2000 domain that you manage. The global groups are GGApps, GGData, GGMgr and GGDB. The group GGApps is a member of the domain local group Apps. The group GGData is a member of the domain local group Data-Access. The group GGDB is a member of the domain local group DB-Access. You create and share a folder on a member server of the domain. You allow the share permission Full Control for the group DB-Access, the share permission Read for the group Apps, and the share permission Change for the group Data-Access. Pat uses a computer running Windows 2000 Professional that is a member of Corp. What is the effective permission for Pat when she connects to the shared folder from her computer?

a. Access is denied   c. Change

b. Read   d. Full Control

29. You are the administrator of Windows 2000 Server computer. Volume D is formatted as NTFS. Volume D contains folders that are shared by departments within your company. You want to limit the amount of disk space that the shared folders can store. A user named Pat has stored 10 GB of files in the shared folders. Pat's files are using more disk space on the shared folders than any other user's files. You enable disk quotas on Volume D and create a default quota entry. You set the quota limit to 1.1 GB and select "Deny disk space to users exceeding quota limit." When Pat attempts to encrypt the files in his home folder using the encrypted file system, he receives the following error message: "There is insufficient disk space to complete the operation". You need to allow Pat to encrypt the files in his home folder. You also need to maintain the disk quota restrictions. Which *three* actions must you perform?

a. Create a quota entry for Pat, and select "Do not limit disk space."

b. Instruct Pat to encrypt the files in his home folder.

c. Run the CIPHER EXE/d command.

d. Enable the compression attribute on Pat's home folder.

e. Set Pat's quota limit to equal the amount of disk space used by the files in his home directory.

f. Set the default quota entry on volume D to 12 GB, and clear "Deny disk space too users exceeding quota limit."

30. Your company, the Acme Corporation, has a human resources (HR) manager named Pat. She keeps the confidential HR files in a shared folder. To increase the security of the HR files, Pat set the folder to encrypt the files. Pat leaves the company without resetting the permissions and encryption settings for the HR files. The files must be made accessible to the new HR manager. Which *two* actions should you take to allow this access?

a. Select the file permissions on the HR files to allow access to the new manager.

b. Back up the shared folder to tape and restore the files to a different folder.

c. Log on as an administrator and remove the encryption attribute from the HR files.

d. Log on the new manager, connect to the shared folder, and run the CIPHER/E/S*.* command.

e. Configure the new manager's account to be an encrypted data recovery agent for Pat's account.

31. You are the administrator of your company's network. Your network has 200 Windows 2000 Professional computers and 15 Windows 2000 Server computers. Users on the network save their work files in home folders on a network server. The NTFS partition that contains the home folders has EFS enabled. A user named Pat leaves the company. You move all of the files from Pat's home folder to his manager's folder. When the manager attempts to open any of the files, access is denied to her. You want the manager to be able to access the files. What should you do?

a. Grant the manager NTFS Full Control permission to the files.

b. Grant the manager NTFS Take Ownership permission to the files.

c. Log on to the network as a recovery agent. Decrypt the files for the manager.

d. Log on to the network as a member of the Backup Operators group. Decrypt the files for the manager.

HANDS-ON EXERCISES

Exercise 1: Understanding NTFS Rights

1. Delete the M drive and create a new FAT32 volume. Assign the M drive.
2. On your C drive (which should be NTFS volume), create a folder called DIRN1.
3. In the DIRN1 folder, create a DIRN2 folder.
4. In the DIRN2 folder, create a DIRN3 folder.
5. In the DIRN3 folder, create a text file called FILE1.TXT. To create a text file, open the DIRN3 folder and right-click the empty space and select New Text file. In the FILE1.TXT file, type your first name.
6. Right-click the DIRN1 folder and select the Properties option. Click on the Security tab.
7. Click on the Add button. Pick Charlie Brown and click on the Add button. Click on the OK button.
8. Log out as Administrator and log in as Charlie Brown.
9. Try to open the FILE1.TXT file.
10. Try to add your last name to the FILE1.TXT file, save the changes, and exit the program.
11. Try to delete the FILE1.TXT file and try to delete the DIRN2 folder.
12. Try to create a new text file called FILE2.TXT in the DIRN1 folder.
13. Log out as Charlie Brown and log in as the Administrator.
14. Right-click the DIRN1 folder and click the Properties options.
15. From the Security tab, click to highlight Charlie Brown. Give Charlie Brown the Write right.
16. Try to open the FILE1.TXT file.
17. Try to add your last name to the FILE1.TXT file, save the changes, and exit the program.
18. Try to delete the FILE1.TXT file and the DIRN2 folder.
19. Try to create a new text file called FILE2.TXT in the DIRN1 folder.
20. Log out as Charlie Brown and log in as Administrator.
21. For the DIRN1 folder, assign the Modify right also to Charlie Brown.
22. Try to open the FILE1.TXT file.
23. Try to add your last name to the FILE1.TXT file, save the changes, and exit the program.
24. Try to delete the FILE1.TXT file and try to delete the DIRN2 folder.
25. Try to create a new text file called FILE2.TXT in the DIRN1 folder.
26. Log out as Charlie Brown and log in as Administrator.
27. In the DIRN1 folder, re-create the DIRN2 folder. In the DIRN2 folder, re-create the DIRN3 folder. In the DIRN3 folder, re-create the FILE1.TXT file.
28. Right-click the DIRN2 and select the Properties option. From the Security tab, specify Charlie Brown to have the Read permission.
29. Log out as the Administrator and log in as Charlie Brown.
30. Open the FILE1.TXT file and try to add your last name to it. Again try to save it.

Exercise 2: Share Rights

1. Log in as Administrator.
2. In the M drive, create a folder called DIRS1.
3. In the DIRS1 folder, create a folder called DIRS2.
4. In the DIRS2 folder, create a text file called FILE1.TXT, with your first name listed in the file.
5. Right-click the DIRS1 folder and select the Sharing option.
6. Click the Share This Folder option. Keep the default share name and click on the Permissions button to set the share rights.
7. With the Everyone account highlighted, click on the Remove button.
8. Click on the Add button and add Charlie Brown.
9. For Charlie Brown share rights, assign only the Read permission. Click on the OK button.
10. From your partner's computer, log in as Charlie Brown and access the DIRS1 share through the My Network Places.
11. Close the DIRS1.
12. Click on the Start button, select the Run option, and execute \\SERVER2000-XXx\DIRS1.
13. Try to open the FILE1.TXT file.
14. Try to add your last name to the FILE1.TXT file, save the changes, and exit the program.
15. Try to delete the FILE1.TXT file.
16. Try to create a new text file called FILE2.TXT in the DIR1 folder.

17. As the Administrator back at your own computer, change the share rights to include Read and Change permissions for Charlie Brown.
18. From your partner's computer, try to open the FILE1.TXT file.
19. Try to add your last name to the FILE1.TXT file, save the changes, and exit the program.
20. Try to delete the FILE1.TXT file.
21. Try to create a new text file called FILE2.TXT in the DIR1 folder.
22. As the Administrator back at your own computer, change the rights to "Deny all rights for Charlie Brown."
23. From your partner's computer, try to access the shared folder.
24. Back at your own computer, log out as the Administrator and log in as Charlie Brown.
25. Try to delete the FILE2.TXT file. Try to figure out why Charlie Brown was able to delete the folder.

Exercise 3: Groups and Permissions

1. Log in as the Administrator. Make sure that Charlie Brown is a member of the Sales group.
2. In the C drive, create a folder called GROUP1.
3. In the GROUP1 folder, create a GROUP2 folder.
4. In the GROUP2 folder, create a new text file with your name on it.
5. Assign the NTFS Read & Execute and List Folder Contents to the Sales group for the GROUP1 folder.
6. Assign the NTFS Modify to Charlie Brown for the GROUP1 folder.
7. Assign the NTFS List Folder Contents to Everyone for the GROUP1 folder.
8. Right-click the text file and select the Properties option. Click on the Permissions tab. Note the rights assigned to Charlie Brown. Of those rights, note those that are grayed out.
9. Assign Full Control to Charlie Brown for the GROUP1 folder.
10. Assign Full Control to Sales for the GROUP1 folder.
11. Deny all rights to Everyone for the GROUP1 folder.
12. Share the GROUP1 folder and assign Full Control share permissions to Charlie Brown, Sales group, and Everyone.
13. From your partner's computer, log in as Charlie Brown and try to access the text file.
14. Back on your own computer, log out as Administrator and log in as Charlie Brown. Try to access the text file in the GROUP2 folder.
15. Log out as Charlie Brown and log in as Administrator.
16. Remove Everyone from the NTFS permissions for the GROUP1 folder.
17. Log out as Administrator and log in as Charlie Brown. Try to access the text file.
18. Back on your partner's computer, log in as Charlie Brown, try to access the text file.

Exercise 4: Taking Ownership of a Directory

1. Log in as Charlie Brown.
2. Create a folder called OWNER in the C drive.
3. Inside the OWNER folder, create a text file.
4. Right-click the OWNER folder and assign Charlie Brown all NTFS permissions.
5. Note that the checkmarks for the NTFS rights for the Everyone group are grayed out. Click on the Everyone group and click on the Remove button.
6. The error appeared because the rights are inherited from above the folder. Click on the OK button.
7. Disable the "Allow inheritable permissions from parent to propagate to this object" option. Select the Remove button so that the inherited rights cannot flow into the OWNER folder.
8. Click on the OK button.
9. Log out as Charlie Brown and log in as Administrator.
10. Try to access the text file.
11. Right-click the OWNER folder and select the Properties option.
12. Click the Security tab. Read the message and click on the OK button.
13. Click on the Advanced button.
14. Click on the Owner tab. Click on the Administrators and enable the "Replace owner on subcontainers and objects." Click on the OK button. Click Yes to replace all permissions.
15. Click on the OK button.
16. Right-click the OWNER folder and select the Properties option. Click on the Security tab to view the NTFS permissions.
17. Click the OK button to close the OWNER Properties dialog box.
18. Open the OWNER folder.
19. Try to access the text document.

20. Right-click the text document and select the Properties option. Try to figure out why the administrator cannot access the text document.
21. In the Security tab, assign all NTFS permissions to the Administrators group. Click the OK button.
22. Try to access the text document.

Exercise 5: Distributed File System

Creating a Stand-alone DFS Root

1. In Administrative Tools, start the distributed file system (DFS) console.
2. On the Action menu, click the New DFS Root and then the Next button.
3. Select "Create a stand-alone DFS root" and click on the Next button.
4. Type in the name of your server for the DNS root and click on the Next button.
5. Select the GROUP1 share and click on the Next button.
6. Specify a unique DFS share name (if you can) and click on the Next button.
7. Click on the Finish button.
8. Share the DIRN1a directory that you created in an earlier exercise.
9. In the DFS console, right-click the \\SERVER2000-XXX\GROUP1 share and select New DFS Link.
10. In the Link Name text box, type in DIRN1a. Use the Browse button to find your server and specify your DIRN1 share. Click on the OK button.
11. In the DFS console, right-click the \\SERVER2000-XXX\GROUP1 share and select New DFS Link.
12. In the Link Name text box, type in DIRS1a. Use the Browse button to find your server and specify your DIRS1 share. Click on the OK button.
13. In the DFS console, right-click the \\SERVER2000-XXX\GROUP1 share and select New DFS Link.
14. In the Link Name text box, type in DIRN1b. Use the Browse button to find your partner's server and specify his or her DIRN1 share. Click on the OK button.
15. In the DFS console, right-click the \\SERVER2000-XXX\GROUP1 share and select New DFS Link.
16. In the Link Name text box, type in DIRS1b. Use the Browse button to find your partner's server and specify his or her DIRS1 share. Click on the OK button.
17. From either computer, use the Run option under the Start button and execute the \\SERVER2000-XXX\GROUP1.
18. Note that you can browse the shares without being concerned where the shares are located.

Creating a Domain DFS

19. Right-click the DFS Group1 share and delete the DFS root. Click on the Yes button.
20. On the Action menu, click the New DFS Root and click on the Next button.
21. Select "Create a domain DFS root" and click on the Next button.
22. Select your domain for the DFS root and click on the Next button.
23. Type in the name of your server for the DNS root and click on the Next button. Here you can use the Browse button.
24. Select the Create a New Share option. Specify C:\DFSROOT in the Path to Share text box and DFSROOT in the Share Name text box. Click on the Next button. Click on the Yes box to confirm creating the shared directory.
25. Keep the default DFS root name and click on the Next button.
26. Click on the Finish button.
27. Right-click the DFSROOT share in the DFS console and select the Add New Replica option.
28. In the DFS console, right-click the DFSROOT share and select the New Replica option.
29. In the Add a New Replica dialog box, in the Send the User to This Shared Folder box, type \\SERVER2000-XXx\DFSROOT.
30. Select the Automatic Replication option and click the OK button.
31. In the DFS console tree, right-click DFSROOT and select the "Check Status to ensure both replicas" option.
32. Create a text file in one of the shares. Check to see if the text file gets replicated to the other shared directory.

Exercise 6: Compressed Folders

1. Your C and D drives must be NTFS volumes to perform this exercise. If they are not NTFS partitions, use the CONVERT command to convert them to NTFS volumes.
2. In the D drive, create two folders called Uncompressed and Compressed.
3. Open the Compressed folder.
4. Open the Tools menu and select the Folder Options option. Make sure that the "Display compressed files and folders option with alternate color" is enabled. Click on the OK button.

5. In the Compressed folder, create a text file. Note the color of the text underneath the text file icon.
6. Close the Compressed folder.
7. Right-click the Compressed folder and select the Properties option.
8. Click the Advanced button. Select the "Compress contents to save disk space" option and click on the OK button.
9. Open the Compressed folder and note the color of the text underneath the text file icon.
10. Right-click the text file and select the Copy option.
11. Close the Compressed folder.
12. Open the Uncompressed folder.
13. Open the Tools menu and select the Folder Options option. Make sure that the "Display compressed files and folders option with alternate color" is enabled. Click on the OK button.
14. Right-click the background of the Uncompressed folder and select the Paste option. Note whether the file is compressed.
15. Delete the file in the Uncompressed folder.
16. Open the Compressed folder. Right-click the text file and select the Cut option.
17. In the Uncompressed folder, paste the text file. Note whether the file is compressed.
18. In the D drive, create a folder called Uncompress.
19. Open the Tools menu and select the Folder Options option. Make sure that the "Display compressed files and folders option with alternate color" is enabled. Click on the OK button.
20. Paste the text file into the Uncompress folder. Note whether it is compressed.

Exercise 7: File Encryption

1. Log in as Charlie Brown.
2. In the C drive, create a folder called ENCRYPTED.
3. In the ENCRYPTED folder, create a text file with your first and last name in it.
4. Right-click the ENCRYPTED folder in the C drive and select the Properties option.
5. Click on the Advanced button. Select the "Encrypt contents to secure data" option and click on the OK button.
6. Click on the OK button to close the Uncompressed properties dialog box. Select the "Apply Changes to this folder, subfolders and files." Click on the OK button.
7. Log out as Charlie Brown and log in as Administrator.
8. Try to access the text file in the ENCRYPTED folder.

Exercise 8: Quotas

1. Open My Computer. Right-click the C drive and select the Properties option. Note the amount of free disk space.
2. Click the Quota tab.
3. Enable the Enable Quota Management option.
4. Set the default quota limit to 100 MB and the warning to 90 MB. Click the Apply button. Click on the OK button.
5. Click the Quota Entries button.
6. Open the Quota menu and select the New Quota option.
7. Right-click the Administrator user and select the Properties option. Select the "Do not limit disk usage" option. Click on the OK button.
8. Do the same for the Administrators group and Domain Admins group.
9. Close the Quota Entries window.
10. Click the OK button to close the C Drive Properties dialog box.
11. Log out as Administrator and log in as Charlie Brown.
12. Right-click the C drive and select the Properties option. Note the amount of free disk space.

CHAPTER **16**

Printing in Windows

Topics Covered in This Chapter

Introduction

One basic network service that is available in Windows is network printing. Yet, for the users and sometimes the administrators, printing can easily become frustrating, especially if it is poorly planned, executed, and managed. This chapter discusses the basics of using Windows as a print server and allowing the various clients to send print jobs to printers that are connected to a Windows print server.

Objectives

- Manage printers and print jobs.
- Control access to printers by using permissions.
- Connect to an Internet printer.
- Connect to a local print device.
- Connect to network print devices.

16.1   INTRODUCTION TO NETWORK PRINTING

When printing with a network printer, the printer communicates with a print server. The printer can be connected directly to the print server or to the network using a network interface. In Windows NT, Windows 2000, and Windows Server 2003, the printer is known as the **print device.**

When a client prints to the network printer, the print job is sent to the print server. If the print job comes from a Windows application, then the application calls the graphical device interface (GDI), which calls the printer driver that is associated with the target printer. Using the driver, the GDI transforms the data being sent to the printer into a language that is understood by the printer and passes it to the client print spooler. A **print spooler** is software that accepts a document, which is sent to a printer by the user, and then stores it on disk or in memory until the printer is ready for it. The word *spooler* is an acronym for "simultaneous print operations on line." For Windows 9X machines, the client spooler is the Print Manager. If the client is using a non-Windows operating system, a non-Windows application replaces the GDI to perform a similar task.

The client computer sends the print job to the print server. A **print server** can be any computer on a network that manages all printers on that network. For Windows NT 4.0, Windows 2000, Windows XP, and Windows Server 2003 clients, the client spooler makes a remote procedure call (RPC) to the server spooler to send the data to the print server, and the print job is stored on disk. The disk location that stores the print jobs is sometimes referred to as the print spooler or print queue.

On the print server, print jobs from Windows clients are of the **enhanced metafile (EMF)** data type. Most non-Windows applications use the RAM (ready to print) data format.

The print server monitors the printers and when the printer is ready for another print job, the print server sends it to the printer. The printer receives the print job, converts each page into bitmap format, and then prints it. During the entire process, the status of the print job can be reported back to the client so that the user can monitor it.

While the print device is the actual hardware device that produces the printed document, the software interface between the operating system and the print device is the **printer.** The user prints to the printer (software interface or logical printer), which then sends the print job to the print server, which eventually sends the print job to the print device. The printer can be connected to a single print device or multiple print devices (known as a printer pool).

To set up printing on a Windows network, you must have at least one computer to operate the print server (Windows 2000 workstation or server or better). If you have more than 10 concurrent connections, use the Windows server. In addition, if you have a large number of printers or users, then dedicate the server to printing. The Windows computer would need extra RAM beyond the minimum amount required for Windows and sufficient disk space to store all print jobs until they can be printed.

16.2   SHARING A LOCAL PRINTER

To share a local printer so that it can be used on the network, first connect the printer to the computer with a serial port, parallel port, or usb. Windows can sometimes automatically detect the printer and load the appropriate drivers. The steps to sharing a local printer are as follows:

1. Log on as the Administrator.
2. Click on the Start button, select the Settings option, and select the Printers option.
3. Double-click the Add Printer to start the Add Printer Wizard.
4. Click on the Next button.
5. Select the Local Printer option and click on the Next button.
6. If you had the "Automatically detect and install my Plug and Play printer" option from the previous window, it will automatically detect the printer. If not, click on the Next button.
7. Specify the port that you want the printer to use and click on the Next button. See Figure 16.1.
8. Select the printer manufacturer and printer and click the Next button. If the printer is not listed, use either the Windows Update button or the Have Disk button. See Figure 16.2.
9. Then input the name of the printer—a meaningful name that would easily identify the printer.
10. If you want your Windows-based program to use this printer as the default printer, select Yes. In either case, click on the Next button.
11. If you want to share the printer so that it can be available to other users, select the Share As option and provide a meaningful name for the printer. Click on the Next button.
12. Fill in the Location (optional) and Comments (optional) for the printer and click on the Next button.
13. If you want to print a test page, select the Yes option. In either case, click on the Next button.
14. Click on the Finish button.

If you have a printer already installed that is not shared, right-click the printer and select the Sharing option. Then select the Shared As option and give it a meaningful share name. If you want the name to be listed in the Active Directory, click the List in the Directory option.

To enable users to find a shared printer, you can choose one of two methods. First, if the computer with the printer is connected to an Active Directory domain, you can list the printer in the Active Directory. This can be done by selecting the List in the Directory option when you are creating the printer, or by right-clicking the tab and selecting the Sharing tab. Once the printer is published, others users will be able to search for the printer based on location or capability, such as color printing or stapling. The other method is to specify the printer by the UNC (\\servername\printername). The IP address for the server name can be resolved with either a WINS server or by broadcast. Of course, the broadcast normally will not be forwarded to other subnets.

Figure 16.1   Selecting the printer port using the Add Printer Wizard

Figure 16.2   Selecting the printer using the Add Printer Wizard

Figure 16.3   Creating a network printer using the Add Printer Wizard

16.3   ADDING AND SHARING A PRINTER FOR A NETWORK-INTERFACE PRINT DEVICE

In larger companies, most print devices are not connected locally to the print server, which is typically locked in a secure area, especially if the print server provides other network services. Instead, print devices are connected using a network interface such as a built-in or add-in network port. Another reason to connect a printer directly to the network is that the parallel port or serial port is often the bottleneck for printing.

To connect to a network interface print device, follow these steps:

1. Start the Add Printer Wizard and click on the Next button.
2. Select Local Printer and click on the Next button.
3. Select Create a New Port and select the Standard TCP/IP port. When you click on the Next button, it will start the Add Standard TCP/IP Printer Port Wizard. See Figure 16.3.

Figure 16.4   Specifying the IP address of network printer

4. In the TCP/IP Printer Port Wizard, click on the Next button and enter the printer name or IP address and port name. Click on the Next button. See Figure 16.4.
5. From the device type, select the appropriate network interface used by the printer and click on the Next button.
6. Click on the Finish button to close the Add Standard TCP/IP Printer Port Wizard.
7. Finish the Add Printer Wizard.

16.4   PRINTER PRIORITY AND PRINT SCHEDULING

Documents can be sent to a printer with different priorities. Users with a higher priority can bypass other print jobs and thus be printed first. Priorities are assigned to the logical printers, which are associated with the same print device. Windows routes documents with the highest priority level to the printer first.

To set the print priority, follow these steps:

1. Open the Printer folder.
2. Install the printer and the first print driver.
3. Right-click the printer on which you want to set the priority (1–99) and select the Properties option.
4. Click the Advanced tab.
5. In the Priority section, set the priority.
6. Click on the OK button.
7. Install the second print driver that was pointing to the same printer.
8. Right-click the printer on which you want to set the priority and select the Properties option.
9. Click the Advanced tab.
10. In the Priority section, set a higher priority. See Figure 16.5. When loading the driver at the client stations, the normal users are assigned to the first logical printer name and the people with the higher priority use the second logical printer name.
11. Click on the OK button.

Another use for creating two logical printers that point to the same printer is to schedule print jobs. For example, say that when you print letters and small documents, you print to one logical printer that will print immediately to the print device. When you have a large report that will take some time to print, send the data to a second logical printer that is scheduled to print at night.

To schedule printing times, do the following:

1. Open the Printer folder.
2. Right-click the printer you want to set and click the Properties option.
3. Click the Advanced tab and click the Available From option.

Figure 16.5   Setting printer priorities

4. Set the time period that the printer will be available.
5. Click on the OK button.

After you have two logical printers set up, you can load the drivers at the client computers that point to both logical printers. With large print jobs, then, you print to the logical printer that is set to print at night. Be sure to check for sufficient disk space to hold the print jobs so that they can be printed later.

16.5   SETTING CLIENT COMPUTERS TO PRINT TO A NETWORK PRINTER

When a network printer becomes available, set up the clients so that they can access it. For Computers since Windows 95, use the computer's Add Printer Wizard. Instead of selecting Local Printer, select Network Printer. If directory service is enabled, search for the printer, right-click the printer, and select Connect. In other cases, you will need to provide a UNC name (\\printservername\printersharename).

Windows 2000 and Windows Server 2003 have the capability to store drivers for the various operating systems. To add these to the Windows print server, right-click the printer in the Printer folder and select the Sharing option. Then click the Additional Drivers button and select the operating systems that you will be using. See Figure 16.6. You may need the operating system installation CD or disks for the driver for the specific operating system that you are trying to load.

If you have loaded the various operating system drivers on the print server, Windows NT, Windows 2000, Windows XP, and Windows Server 2003, will automatically check the print drivers and configurations each time they connect to the print server. Therefore, if the print driver is newer, it will automatically update the client's driver. The print driver for Windows 9X is not automatically kept current, but is loaded when you use the Add Printer Wizard to load the driver. If you update the Windows 9X drivers on the server, you will have to manually install the driver on the 9X clients. Of course, it will be easier if the clients can install the driver from the print server instead of using floppy disks or CD-ROMs.

When using DOS or Windows for Workgroups, use the NET command to map a printer to a port. In so doing, you are setting up a redirector that takes any print jobs that are sent to the port and redirects them to the network printer. In addition, the Microsoft Network redirector can send jobs using Net-BEUI, NWLink, or TCP/IP protocols.

Figure 16.6   Setting up additional drivers to be handed out by the Windows print server

16.6   PRINTER POOL

A **printer pool** is two or more print devices that use the same driver, are connected to one print server, and act as a single printer. When you print a document to the printer pool, the print job is sent to the first available printer in the pool. The user does not have to determine which printer is free. This is useful in a network with a high volume of printing, because it decreases the time that users wait for their documents. If a print device jams when in the middle of a print job, the job remains in the printer until the jam is fixed. It is not rerouted to the other printers.

The print server checks for an available port and sends documents to ports in the order that they are added. Adding a port to the fastest printer ensures that documents are first sent here before they are routed to slower printers in the printing pool. Since the user does not know which printer in the pool prints a given document, the print devices should be in the same location.

To set up printing to multiple print devices, perform the follow steps:

1. Open the Printer folder.
2. Install a printer and print driver to be used on the network.
3. Right-click the printer and select the Properties option.
4. Click on the Ports tab and select the Enable Printer Pooling check box. See Figure 16.7.
5. Click each port where the printers you want to pool are connected.

16.7   PRINTING VIA WEB BROWSERS AND THE INTERNET

The **Internet Printing Protocol (IPP)** uses the Hypertext Transfer Protocol (HTTP) to send print jobs to printers throughout the world. Windows 2000, Windows XP, and the Windows Server 2003 family support IPP version 1.0, which allows users to print directly to a uniform resource locator (URL) over an intranet or the Internet. In addition, servers that run products in the Windows Server 2003 family can automatically generate print job information in Hypertext Markup Language (HTML) format, so that users can view it in their browsers.

A feature that started with Windows 2000 is Internet printing, when allows you to submit print jobs to a printer across the Internet by using the printer's URL as the name of the printer—such as when you

Figure 16.7   Setting up a printer pool

Figure 16.8   Displaying the shared printers using the HTML interface

use the Add Printer Wizard. See Figures 16.8 and 16.9. For Windows 2000 Server, Windows Server 2003, or Windows XP to process print jobs that contain URLs, they must be running Microsoft Internet Information Services (IIS). For print servers that are implemented on Windows 2000 Professional, use Microsoft Peer Web Service (PWS).

To connect to a printer with a browser, do the following:

1. Start Internet Explorer (version 4.0 or later).
2. In the Address bar, type http://*PrinterServerName*/printers to receive a page listing of all printers and click the printer you want; or, if you know the printer name, type its URL using the format http://*PrintServerName*/*PrinterName*.
3. After you have connected to the printer, it will automatically copy the correct print driver to the client computer.

Figure 16.9 Managing print jobs using the HTML interface

A web page designer can customize this page by displaying a floor plan that shows the location of the print devices.

16.8 PRINTER ADMINISTRATION

On a network, printer problems can lead to headaches and frustration for the user and the administrator. After the printer is set up, you still need to manage the printer permissions, the printers, and the documents and to troubleshoot any print problems that arise.

16.8.1 Printer Permissions

Printer permissions control who can use the printer and which print tasks a user can perform. For example, if you have an expensive color printer, you might want only a handful of people to have access to it. For all printers, you will need someone to delete print jobs, change the printer properties, or change the printer permissions. Therefore, after you have added and shared a printer, assign the appropriate rights to the users.

There are three levels of printer permissions: Print, Manage Printer, and Manage Documents. By default, all users have the Print permission as members of the Everyone group. Administrators, print operators, and server operators on a domain controller have Manage Printer permission. Lastly, the owner of the document has Manage Documents permission for that document only. See Table 16.1.

To set or remove permissions for a printer, do the following:

1. Open the Printer folder.
2. Right-click the shared printer for which you want to set permissions and click the Properties option.
3. Select the Security tab.
4. To change permissions from an existing user or group, click the name of the user or group and select and deselect the appropriate rights. To add a user or group, click on the Add button, select the users or group, and click the OK button. To remove an existing user or group, click its name and click the Remove button.
5. In Permissions, click Allow or Deny for each permission that you want to either allow or deny. See Figure 16.10.

Table 16.1   Print permissions

Print Permission Capabilities	Print	Manage Printer	Manage Documents
Print documents	X	X	X
Pause, resume, restart, and cancel the user's own document	X	X	X
Connect to a printer	X	X	X
Control job settings for all documents		X	X
Pause, restart, and delete all documents		X	X
Share a printer		X	
Change printer properties		X	
Delete printers		X	
Change printer permissions		X	

Figure 16.10   Printer permissions

16.8.2   Printer Device Settings

The processes of managing printers include assigning forms to paper trays, page orientation (portrait or landscape), selecting which tray to print from, configuring the amount of printer memory, and enabling printer duplexing (printing on both sides). The specific type of printer also determines some of the available options.

Many laser printers have multiple trays that hold different types of forms. For example, one tray can be assigned to hold letterhead paper (typically used for the front page of a letter); the second tray, normal white paper; and a third tray, envelopes. Users can then select the form from within the program

Figure 16.11   Device Settings tab found in the Printer Properties window

that is open. When users print a document, the print job is routed to the correct paper tray. Note that the default form setting for a paper tray is letter size ($8\frac{1}{2}'' \times 11''$ paper).

To match a form to a printer tray, do the following:

1. Open the Printer folder.
2. Right-click the printer you are using and click the Properties option. See Figure 16.11.
3. Click on the Device Settings tab.
4. Under the Form To Tray Assignment, click a printer tray.
5. Click one of the available paper sizes for the selected tray.

Laser printers are known as page printers, because they store an entire page in the memory of the printer before printing. Depending on the resolution of the printer, the size of the document, and the complexity of the printer, the printer may require extra memory. After the memory is added to the printer, tell the driver how much memory the printer has. To set the printer memory, do the following:

1. Open the Printer folder.
2. Right-click the printer that you want to configure and select the Properties option.
3. Click on the Device Settings tab.
4. Under the Installable Options, click Printer Memory and specify the amount of memory installed in your printer.

If you specify more or less memory than actually exists in your printer, then you may receive a memory error message or partial printed pages. To check the amount of memory, use the self-test feature of the printer.

16.8.3   Managing the Printer Spooler

Print jobs stored in the spooler are written to a spool (SPL) file, whereas administrative information such as user name, document name, and data type are stored in a shadow (SHD) file. This way, if a power failure or other disaster occurs before all jobs in the queue are printed, the print jobs are protected.

By default, the spooler files are written to the *%SystemRoot%*\System32\Spool\Printers folder. If the hard disk partition containing Windows does not have enough space for these files, you can change the location of the folder. To change the location of the default spool folder for all printers on a server, do the following:

1. In the Printers dialog box, on the File menu, click Server Properties.
2. In the Print Server Properties dialog box, click the Advanced tab.
3. Type the path and name for the new default spool folder, then click OK.
4. The change is effective immediately. You do not need to restart your system.

Do not attempt to spool to a root (such as C:\). This causes the files to revert to the old default.
    To change the location of the spool folder for a specific printer, use the registry, as follows:

1. Create a new spool folder.
2. Start a registry editor (Regedt32.exe or Regedit.exe).
3. Add the following entry to the registry:
Entry name: SpoolDirectory
Path:HKEY_LOCAL_MACHINE\SOFTWARE\Microsoft\Windows
NT\CurrentVersion\Print\Printers\<Printer-name>
Data type: REG_SZ
Value: <path to the new spool folder>
4. Restart the computer to make the change effective.

16.8.4   Printer Preferences and Defaults

To configure the page orientation, page order, pages per sheet, printing on both sides, and the correct tray, use Printing Preferences or Printing Defaults. Default settings apply to all users, but are overwritten by Printing Preferences. To set up personal printing preferences, follow these steps:

1. Open the Printers folder.
2. Right-click the printer you are using and click Printing Preferences.
3. To select the page orientation (portrait versus landscape), page order, pages per sheet, and printing on both sides (if the option is available to the printer), click on the Layout tab. To select the paper source, click on the Paper/Quality tab.
4. Click on the OK button to close the Printing Preferences dialog box.
5. Click on the OK button to close the Printing Properties dialog box.

To set the printer defaults, follow these steps:

1. Open the Printers folder.
2. Right-click the printer on which you want to set the default printer settings and click the Properties option. See Figure 16.12.
3. Click on the Advanced tab.
4. Click the Printing Defaults button.
5. To select the page orientation (portrait versus landscape), page order, pages per sheet, and printing on both sides (if the option is available to the printer), click on the Layout tab. To select the paper source, click on the Paper/Quality tab.
6. Click on the OK button to close the Printing Defaults dialog box.
7. Click on the OK button to close the Printing Properties dialog box.

16.8.5   Separator Pages

A **separator page**, sometimes known as a banner page, separates print jobs and typically states who sent the document to the printer and the date and time of printing. You can use one of the standard separator pages or create a custom page.

Figure 16.12   Printing Preferences options

Table 16.2   Printer separator pages

File Name	Printer Language	Purpose
pcl.sep	Printer Control Language (PCL)	Switches the printer to PCL (Hewlett-Packard printing language standard) printing and prints a separator page before each document. Note: Pcl.sep is compatible with PCL printers, but may not work unless the printer also supports Printer Job Language (PJL).
pscript.sep	PostScript	Switches the printer to PostScript printing, but does not print a separator page before each document. Pscript.sep is compatible with PostScript printers that also support PJL.
sysprint.sep	PostScript	Switches the printer to PostScript printing and prints a separator page before each document. Sysprint.sep is compatible with PostScript printers.

Note: Some printers can support both PCL and PostScript printing. In these cases, the separator page would be used to switch the printer back and forth between the two printer languages.

Windows provides three separator page files, located in the *systemroot*\SYSTEM32 folder. Table 16.2 shows the names of the separator page files, the type of printer with which it is compatible, and the purpose of each page. You can edit or customize any of these separator pages. The separator page files provided by Windows may not work with some printers, however.

To create your own separator file, copy and rename one of the supplied separator files. Table 16.3 shows the escape codes that you can include in a separator file. The first character of the separator page file must always be the escape character. This character is used throughout the separator page file in

Table 16.3   Escape codes used in separator pages

Escape Code	Function
@N	Prints the user name of the person who submitted the job
@I	Prints the job number
@D	Prints the date the job was printed. The representation of the date is the same as the Date Format in the International section in Control Panel.
@T	Prints the time the job was printed. The representation of the time is the same as the Time Format in the International section in Control Panel.
@L*xxxx*	Prints all the characters (*xxxx*) following it until another escape code is encountered
@Fpathname	Prints the contents of the file specified by path name, starting on an empty line. The contents of this file are copied directly to the printer without any processing.
@H*nn*	Sets a printer-specific control sequence, where nn is a hexadecimal ASCII code sent directly to the printer. To determine the specific numbers, see your printer manual.
@W*nn*	Sets the width of the separator page. The default width is 80; the maximum width is 256. Any printable characters beyond this width will be truncated.
@B@S	Prints text in single-width block characters until \U is encountered.
@E	Ejects a page from the printer. Use this code to start a new separator page or to end the separator page file. If you get an extra blank separator page when you print, remove this code from your separator page file.
@*n*	Skips *n* number of lines (from 0 through 9). Skipping zero lines simply moves printing to the next line.
@B@M	Prints text in double-width block characters until \U is encountered.
@U	Turns off block character printing.

escape codes. The separator file interpreter replaces these escape codes with appropriate data, to be sent directly to the printer.

To choose a separator page, do the following:

1. Open the Printer folder.
2. Right-click the printer you are using and select the Properties option.
3. Click on the Advanced tab.
4. Click the Separator Page button.
5. Click Browse and select the separator page located in the *systemroot*\SYSTEM32 folder.

16.8.6   Pausing and Resuming a Printer

Normally you pause a printer if you have a printer problem or need to perform scheduled maintenance. To pause and then resume the printer, you need to have the Manage Printer option. To pause a printer and the printing of all its documents, do the following:

1. Open the Printers folder.
2. Right-click the printer on which you want to pause or resume printing, and select the Pause Printing option.

Note the checkmark that appears next to Pause Printing when the printer is paused. Any documents that are currently printing will finish, but other print jobs in the print queue will be put on hold.

To resume printing on the printer, do the following:

1. Open the Printers folder.
2. Right-click the printer on which you want to pause or resume printing, and select the Pause Printing option to remove the checkmark.

If you want to cancel all print jobs in the print queue, proceed as follows:

1. Open the Printers folder.
2. Right-click the printer on which you want to pause or resume printing, and select the Cancel All Documents option.

16.9 MANAGING DOCUMENTS

As a user or an administrator, at times you may need to manage individual print jobs or documents. To view documents waiting to print, do the following:

1. Open the Printers folder.
2. Double-click the printer on which you want to view the documents waiting to print.

The print queue shows information about a document such as print status, owner, and number of pages to be printed. See Figure 16.13. From the print queue, you can cancel or pause the printing of a document that you have sent to the printer. You also can open the print queue for the printer on which you are printing, by double-clicking the small printer icon in the status area on the taskbar.

To pause a document, do the following:

1. Open the Printer folder.
2. Double-click the printer you are using to open the print queue.
3. Right-click on the document you want to pause and select the Pause option.

To resume printing of a paused document, do the following:

1. Open the Printer folder.
2. Double-click the printer you are using to open the print queue.
3. Right-click on the document you want to pause and select the Resume option.

By default, all users can pause, resume, restart, and cancel printing of their own documents. To manage documents that are printed by other users, however, you must have the Manage Documents permission.

In general, once a document has started printing, it will finish printing even if you pause it. If something happens to the printing of the document such as the wrong type of paper was in the printer, you can restart the print job if it is still in the print queue, as follows:

1. Open the Printers folder.
2. Double-click the printer you are using to open the ping queue.
3. Right-click on the document that you want to restart printing and select the Restart option.

Figure 16.13 Viewing the print queue

Document Name	Status	Owner	Pages	Size	Submitted
Microsoft Word - Ch 15 Printing with Windows 2000.doc	Deleting -...	administrator	8/24	5.25 M...	4:29:30 PM 12/19/1999
Microsoft Word - Document2		administrator	1	3.94 KB	4:31:26 PM 12/19/1999
Microsoft Word - document1.doc		administrator	1	3.94 KB	4:31:35 PM 12/19/1999
Microsoft Word - Ch 15 Printing with Windows 2000.doc	Spooling	administrator	13	11.2 MB	4:32:03 PM 12/19/1999

HP LaserJet 2100 - Paused
Printer Document View Help

4 document(s) in queue

If there is a higher priority document, it will print first.

To cancel a print job, do the following:

1. Open the Printers folder.
2. Double-click the printer you are using to open the print queue.
3. Right-click on the document that you want to stop printing and select the Cancel option.

You can cancel the printing of more than one document by holding down the Ctrl key and clicking on each document that you want to cancel.

To change the printing priority of documents waiting to print, proceed as follows:

1. Open the Printers folder.
2. Double-click the printer you are using to open the print queue.
3. Right-click on the document that you want to move in the print order, and click the Properties option. See Figure 16.14.
4. Click the General tab.
5. Drag the Priority slider to raise or lower the document priority.

Once a document has started printing, any printing priority changes you make will not affect the document.

If a printer fails before printing and cannot be repaired quickly, then you may want to transfer the document to another printer, as follows:

1. Open the Printers folder.
2. Double-click the printer that holds the document(s) you want to redirect.
3. Open the Printer menu and select the Properties option.
4. To send documents to another printer on the same print server, click the port to which the other printer is assigned and click the OK button. To send documents to a printer on a different print server, click the Add Port button, select the Local Port option, and click on the New Port button. Type the name of the other print server and the share name using the UNC name. If you are adding to a network port, you can only add an existing port.

To redirect documents to another printer, you must have the Manage Printers permission on both printers. In addition, since the program has already converted the document into a language that is specific to a particular printer, you must redirect the document(s) that uses the same driver.

Figure 16.14   Viewing the properties of a print job

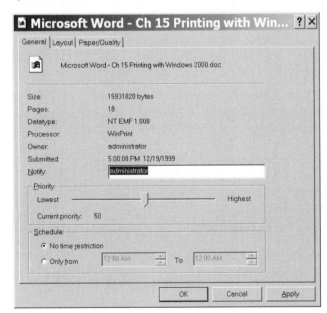

16.10   PRINTING USING LPR AND LPD

To print in a pure TCP/IP network, load the **line printer daemon (LPD)** on a computer designated as the print server. A daemon is a background process or service. The client computer sends print jobs to the **print spooler service** on another computer by using the **line printer remote (LPR)** service. LPR was originally developed as a standard for transmitting print jobs between computers running Berkeley UNIX as published in the RFC 1179. LPR clients are often on UNIX systems, but LPR software exists for most operating systems including Windows NT, Windows 2000, and Windows Server 2003. To view the print queue, then, use the **line printer query (LPQ)**.

For Windows servers to accept LPR client print jobs, load **Print Services** for **UNIX**, as follows:

1. Open the Control Panel.
2. Double-click on the Add/Remove Programs applet.
3. Click on the Add/Remove Windows Components.
4. Click to highlight Other Network File and Print Services and click on the Details button.
5. Select the Print Services for UNIX option.
6. Click on the OK button.
7. Click on the Next button.
8. Click on the Finish button.
9. Click on the Close button to close the Add/Remove Programs dialog box.

To create a LPR port, follow these steps:

1. Open the Printers folder.
2. Double-click Add Printer and click on the Next button.
3. Click Local Printer, clear the "Automatically detect my printer" check box, and click on the Next button.
4. Click the Create a New Port option, select the LPR port in the Type: box, and click on the Next button.
5. Enter the DNS name and the IP address of the server in the "Name or address of server providing LPD."
6. Enter the name of the printer or print queue on the server just listed.
7. Select the printer manufacturer and model and click on the Next button.
8. Enter a printer name. If you want it to be the default printer, click on the Yes option. Click on the Next button.
9. Select the Share As option, provide the share name of the printer, and click on the Next button.
10. Provide an optional location and comment and click on the Next button.
11. Select the Yes option if you want to print a test page. Click on the Next button.
12. Click on the Finish button.

If a printer is already shared, add LPR ports by using the Print Server Properties dialog box.

LPR clients traditionally print with the LPR command. The syntax for the LPR command is as follows:

> **LPR −S** *Server* **−P** *Printer* [**−C** *Class*] [**−J** *Jobname*] [**−O** *option*] *filename*
> **−S** *Server*
> Specifies the name or IP address of the computer that has the printer attached to it
> **−P** *Printer*
> Specifies the name of the printer for the desired queue
> **−C** *Class*
> Specifies the content of the banner page for the class
> **−J** *Jobname*
> Specifies the name of this job
> **−O** *option*
> Indicates the type of file. The default is a text file. Use **−Ol** (lowercase "el") for a binary file (e.g., PostScript).
> *–filename*
> Is the name of the file to be printed

The syntax for the LPQ is as follows:

> **LPQ –S** *Server* **–P** *Printer* [**–l**(el)]
> **–S** *Server*
> Specifies the name of the computer that has the printer attached to it
> **–P** *Printer*
> Specifies the name of the printer for the desired queue
> **–l**
> Specifies that a detailed status should be given

16.11   NETWORK PRINTER HARDWARE

Although Windows handles printing quite well, there are advantages to using printer network cards, such as Hewlett-Packard's **Jetdirect cards**, and print server boxes, such as Intel's **Netport.**

The printer network card is installed into an empty slot located inside the printer, and others are included with the printer as a built-in port. Because these cards/ports connect directly to the network using either UTP cable or coaxial cable, they must have MAC and IP addresses. The MAC address is burned into a ROM chip. The IP address, including the subnet mask and gateway address, is set using the printer controls or by running software on a computer on the same subnet and connecting to the printer by its MAC address. The primary advantage of using a printer network card is to conceal the print server easily in a server room. In addition, the cost is cheaper, because one print server can handle many printers throughout the network, and the network connection is faster than the parallel port.

The print server boxes provide connections to the network, multiple ports to connect printers, and memory to store the print jobs. Because they are similar to a dedicated print server, they also need a MAC and an IP address. Like the printer network card, the MAC address is burned into a ROM chip within the box. The IP address (including the subnet mask and gateway) is configured using a special software program that attaches using the MAC address or by connecting a cable from a computer directly to the box. After the box has an IP address, the print server can be configured using the Telnet program or web pages. The advantage of using a print server box is that the box is cheaper than an entire PC and often has better performance.

16.12   TROUBLESHOOTING PRINTERS

Printing problems occur because of trouble with the following components:

- Printing device
- Connection between the printer and the network
- Other printing components in Windows
- Network, protocols, and other communication components

A quick way to solve most problems associated with printing is to follow these steps:

1. Verify that the physical printer is operational. If other users can print, the problem is probably not with the printer or with the print server.
2. Check that the physical printer is in the ready state (online) and if the printer can print a test page.
3. Verify that the printer or the print server is using the correct print driver. If print clients are using other operating systems, then install all necessary drivers for the other platforms. If the correct print driver is not selected, it will often print garbage.
4. Verify that the print server is operational, that there is enough disk space for spooling, and that the print spool service is running.

SUMMARY

1. When a client prints to the network printer, the print job is sent to the print server.
2. A print spooler is software that accepts a document which is sent to a printer by the user and then stores it on disk or in memory until the printer is ready for it.
3. Documents can be sent to a printer with different priorities. Users with a higher priority can bypass other print jobs and thus be printed first.
4. Another use for creating two logical printers, both pointing to the same printer, is to schedule print jobs.
5. A printer pool is two or more print devices that use the same driver, are connected to one print server, and act as a single printer.
6. Internet printing allows you to submit print jobs to a printer across the Internet by using the printer's URL as the name of the printer.
7. The print server checks for an available port and sends documents to ports in the order that they are added.
8. Printer permissions control who can use the printer and which print tasks a user can do.
9. There are three levels of printer permissions: Print, Manage Printer, and Manage Documents.
10. A separator page, sometimes known as a banner page, separates print jobs and typically states who sent the document to the printer and the date and time of printing.
11. Pause a printer when you have a printer problem or need to perform scheduled maintenance. To pause and then resume the printer, you need to have the Manage Printer option.
12. The print queue shows information about a document such as print status, owner, and number of pages to be printed.
13. To print in a pure TCP/IP network, load the line printer daemon (LPD) on a computer designated as the print server.
14. A daemon is a background process or service.
15. In a pure TCP/IP network, the client computer sends print jobs to the print spooler service on another computer by using the line printer remote (LPR) service.
16. To view the print queue in a pure TCP/IP network, use the line printer query (LPQ).
17. Although Windows handles printing quite well, there are advantages to using printer network cards, such as Hewlett-Packard's JetDirect cards, and print server boxes, such as Intel's Netport.

QUESTIONS

1. There are 50 Windows 2000 Professional computers on your network that print to an HP LaserJet IV SI printer attached to a Windows 2000 print server. You have just obtained an updated print driver. What is the best way to update the driver for all computers that print to this print server?
   a. Update the driver on the print server and do nothing more.
   b. Update the driver on all client computers; there is no need to update the server.
   c. Create a separate printer with the updated driver on the print server, and instruct all client computers to print to the new printer.
   d. Update the driver on the print server and instruct all client computers to download the updated driver from the server.
2. You receive several calls from users who are trying to print to a print server. They complain that they have sent several jobs to the print server, but the jobs have not printed and cannot be deleted. What must you do to resolve the problem?
   a. Delete all files from the spool folder on the print server.
   b. Select Services in the Services console on the print server, stop the spooler service, and then restart it.
   c. Be sure that the Pause Printing option is not checked on the print server.
   d. Delete the stalled printer from the print server and create a new printer.
3. Your boss has asked you to configure network printing so that all documents from the executives will print before other users' documents. What is the best way to accomplish this task?
   a. Create a separate printer for the executives, and set the printer priority to 99.
   b. Create a separate printer for the executives, and set the printer priority to 1.
   c. Create a separate printer for the executives, and configure the printer to start printing after the last page is spooled.
   d. Create a separate printer for the executives, and configure the printer to start printing immediately.
   e. Create a separate printer for the executives, and configure the printer to print directly to the print device.
4. Pat often sends large print jobs to his local printer. His system is running with 128 MB of RAM and a 4-GB hard disk. Pat's hard drive is approaching capacity and he has recently added another 10-GB hard disk. Pat has been experiencing problems when he tries to print large graphics files, because his default spool folder is located on his old hard drive. How can Pat change the location of the spool folder to the new hard drive?
   a. Edit the registry.
   b. Edit the user profile.
   c. Choose the Server option in the Services console.
   d. Choose the System option in the Control Panel.
   e. Choose Printers from My Computer.
5. One print device on your network has failed. There are several jobs waiting to be printed on that print device. How do you redirect the documents to a different print device so that the users do not need to resubmit their print jobs?

a. Add a local port to the faulty printer and type the UNC name of another printer in the Port Name dialog box.

b. Delete the faulty printer, create a new printer attached to another print device, and assign to the new printer the same name as the old printer.

c. Pause the faulty printer first, then drag and drop all print jobs to another printer.

d. Pause the faulty printer first, and choose Redirect Print Jobs from the Printer menu.

6. You have just installed a new printer on your print server. You send a print job to the printer, but it comes out as pages of nonsense words. What is the most likely cause of the problem?

a. The print spooler is corrupt.

b. The correct protocol is not installed.

c. An incorrect printer driver is installed.

d. There is not enough hard disk space for spooling.

7. You are the print operator on your network. You would like to switch the printing mode to PCL for an HP LaserJet print device. What is the easiest way to accomplish this task?

a. Assign a different paper tray for printing in PCL mode.

b. Assign a different printer port for printing in PCL mode.

c. Create a separate printer with PCL drivers.

d. Use a separator page.

8. You are creating a printer pool with four print devices. Which condition must be satisfied for you to create a printer pool? (Select all that apply.)

a. All print devices must be connected to the same print server.

b. All print devices must use the same print driver.

c. All print devices must be located in the same room.

d. All print devices must be able to use the same protocol.

e. All print devices must use the same printer port.

9. You have already created a printer pool consisting of two print devices for the Sales department. What must you do on the print server to add a new print device to the existing printer pool?

a. Enter the print driver and port for the new print device.

b. Enter the name and port for the new print device.

c. Enter the name for the new print device only.

d. Enter the port for the new print device only.

10. Users on your network complained that some large print jobs monopolize the printer, causing unacceptable delays for their small print jobs. The large print jobs are usually not needed on the day they are sent to the printer. How would you improve the situation?

a. Create a separate printer, configure the printer to print directly to the printer port, and direct users to print large documents to the newly created printer.

b. Create a separate printer, configure the printer to start printing immediately, and direct users to print large documents to the newly created printer.

c. Create a separate printer, configure the printer to be available only after hours, and direct users to print large documents to the newly created printer.

d. Create a separate printer, set it to the highest priority, and direct users to print large documents to the newly created printer.

11. You have set up a printer to be available only during off-hours. What will happen to the print jobs sent to the printer during the day?

a. They will be stored in the print spooler.

b. They will be stored in a temporary directory.

c. They will be stored in the print processor.

d. They will be redirected to a functioning printer.

12. You have two printers connected in a printer pool. The first printer is printing a job and the second printer is idle. A paper jam occurs on the first printer. What will happen to the rest of the job that was being printed?

a. The job will be completed on the second printer.

b. The job will be completed on the second printer if the second printer has a higher priority level.

c. The job is held for completion by the first printer until the device is fixed.

d. The job is canceled.

13. You are trying to print a payroll report and the print device jams. The print device is attached to a Windows 2000 print server. Your current application does not allow you to resubmit print jobs. After clearing the paper jam, what would you do to reprint the document?

a. Select the printer from the Printers folder and choose Resume from the Printer menu.

b. Select the printer from the Printers folder and choose Restart from the Printer menu.

c. Select the printer from the Printers folder and choose Resume from the Document menu.

d. Select the printer from the Printers folder and choose Restart from the Document menu.

14. A local group called LaserJet_Users consists of user accounts that are currently accessing a printer in your domain. You have already removed the Everyone special group from the LaserJet_Users group so that only specified users have access to the printer. You would like to tighten security even further by allowing individuals who are using the printer to manage only their own print jobs. However, you want individuals to be able to view all jobs sent to the printer. The LaserJet_Users group currently has Full Control permission for the printer. What is the best way to enact this new security measure?

a. Assign Read permission to the LaserJet5_Users group. Add the user accounts from the LaserJet5_Users group to the Print Operators group on the PDC of the printer's domain.

b. Assign Read permission to the LaserJet5_Users group. Assign Manage Documents permission to the Creator Owner special group on the printer.

c. Assign Read permission to the LaserJet5_Users group. Assign Print permission to the Creator Owner special group on the printer.

d. Assign Print permission to the LaserJet5_Users group.

15. Users from the Accounting domain and the Sales domain share one print device. Users from the Accounting domain often print very large documents which can cause unacceptable delays for small print jobs sent by users in the Sales domain. The large accounting jobs are usually not needed on the day they are sent to the printer. How would you improve the situation?

a. Create a separate printer, configure the printer to print directly to the printer port, and direct users from the Accounting domain to print large documents to the newly created printer.

b. Create a separate printer, configure the printer to start printing immediately, and direct users from the Accounting domain to print large documents to the newly created printer.

c. Create a separate printer, configure the printer to be available only after hours, and direct users from the Accounting domain to print large documents to the newly created printer.

d. Create a separate printer, set the printer to the highest priority, and direct users from the Accounting domain to print large documents to the newly created printer.

16. Which one of the following statements best describes how Print permission and Manage Documents permission differ for a printer?

a. Manage Documents permission allows users to submit jobs to a printer and change the status of their own print jobs. Print permission simply allows users to submit jobs to a printer.

b. Manage Documents permission allows users to change the status of any print job submitted by any user to a printer, but it does not allow users to submit their own jobs to a printer. Print permission allows users to submit their own jobs to a printer.

c. Manage Documents permission allows users to submit jobs to a printer and change the status of any print job submitted by any user. Print permission allows users to submit jobs to a printer and change the status of their own print jobs.

d. Manage Documents permission allows users to submit jobs to a printer and change the status of any print job submitted by any user. Print permission simply allows users to submit jobs to a printer.

17. Pat wants to use a Windows 2000 Server computer as the print server for a TCP/IP network print device. Users will send their documents to the server, which will then forward the documents to the print device. What is the best way for Pat to proceed?

a. Install the TCP/IP printing service on the network print device.

b. Install the TCP/IP printing service on the Windows 2000 Server computer.

c. Use the LPQ utility to redirect all print jobs to a printer port that is mapped to the print device's IP address.

d. Use the LPR utility to redirect all print jobs to a logical printer port that is mapped to the print device's IP address.

18. You configure a UNIX computer as an LPD server. Users on a Windows 2000 Professional computer want to send documents to a print device connected to the UNIX LPD server. How must they send their documents to this print device?

a. Install the TCP/IP printing service on each client computer.

b. Map a logical printer port to the UNC name for the printer.

c. Use the LPR utility.

d. Use the LPQ utility.

19. You are the administrator of a Windows 2000 Server computer at Acme Corporation. You configure a server named print10.marketing.acme.local as a print server at the Los Angeles site. You create and share a variety of printers on the server for use by employees in the marketing acme. local domain. You want to review the configured properties of all the shared printers on the print10.marketing.acme. local. You want to perform this review from a Windows 2000 Professional computer at the London site of Acme Corporation. What should you do?

a. Use your web browser to connect to http://print10.marketing.acme.local/printers.

b. Use your web browser to connect to http://print10.acme.local/printers.

c. Run the NET VIEW\\PRINT 10 command.

d. Run the NET VIEW\\PRINT 10.ACME.COM command.

20. Your network uses TCP/IP as the only protocol. Devices on the network are configured to use IP addresses from the private 10.0.0.0 range. All the client computers on the network use Windows 2000 Professional. The network includes Windows 2000 servers and UNIX servers. Users' print jobs are sent to shared printers on a Windows 2000 Server computer named PrintServ that directs the print jobs to the print devices attached directly to the network. You have a high-capacity print device that is attached to one of the UNIX servers. The UNIX computer uses LPR printing protocol, and its IP address is 10.1.1.99. The name of the printer queue is GIANT. You want users to be able to connect to this printer from their computers. What should you do?

a. Install Microsoft Print Services for Unix on PrintServ. Create a network printer on users' computers, and specify that the printer URL is LPR://10.1.1.99/GIANT.

b. Install Microsoft Print Services for UNIX on user's computers. Create a network printer on users' computers and specify that the printer URL is LPR://10.1.1.99/GIANT.

c. Create a network printer on PrintServ and specify that the printer name is \\10.1.1.99\GIANT. Share this printer and connect to it from users' computers.

d. Create a local printer on PrintServ. Create a new TCP/IP port for an LPR server at address 10.1.1.99 with a queue name of GIANT. Share this printer and connect it from the users' computers.

21. You are the administrator of a Windows 2000 Server network that runs in mixed mode. You install a new Windows 2000 Server computer. You create and share a new HP LaserJet 4L printer. Your Windows 2000 Professional client computer can print to the new printer successfully. However, when users try to connect to the printer from Windows NT Workstation 4.0 client computers, they receive the dialog box showing the following error:

```
The server on which the printer
resides does not have a suitable HP
LaserJet4L printer driver installed.
Click on OK if you wish to install the
driver on your local machine.
```

You want the printer driver to install automatically on the Windows NT Workstation computers. What should you do?

    a. Copy the Windows NT 4.0 printer drivers to the Netlogon shared folders on all Windows NT Server 4.0 computers still configured as BDCs.

    b. Copy the Windows NT 4.0 printer drivers to the Netlogon shared folders on the PDC emulator.

    c. Change the sharing options on the printer to install additional drivers for Windows NT 4.0 or Windows 2000.

    d. Copy the Windows NT 4.0 printer drivers to the Winnt\System32\printers\drivers folder on the Windows 2000 print server.

22. Your network includes Windows 2000 Professional client computers, Windows NT Workstation 4.0 client computers, Windows 95 client computers, and UNIX client computers. Users of the Windows operating systems send print jobs to shared printers on a Windows 2000 Server computer named PrintServ. The UNIX client computers support the LPR printing protocol. You want to make the shared printers on PrintServ available to the UNIX computers. What should you do?

    a. Configure each of the printers to use an LPR port.

    b. Install Microsoft Print Services for UNIX on PrintServ.

    c. Configure each of the printers to support TCP/IP printing.

    d. Use the SRVANY utility from the Windows NT Resource Kit to run the LPR program as a service.

23. You created two shared printers on a Windows 2000 Server computer in your company, the Acme Corporation. One printer is shared as Admin, and the other printer is shared as Executive. Both printers are connected to the same print device. You set the priority of the Admin printer to 90 and the priority of the Executive printer to 50. You want all users at the corporate network to be able to send print jobs to either printer. However, you do not want the Executive printer to appear in the browse list when employees other than executives and administrative assistants create a new printer connection on their client computers. What should you do?

    a. Change the priority of the Executive printer to 99. Change the priority of the Admin printer to 10.

    b. Change the share name of the Executive printer to Executive$. Manually reconfigure client computers that are already connected to the Executive printer.

    c. Deny the Everyone group permission to access the Executive printer. Allow access to the users who are allowed to include the printer in their browse lists.

    d. Install separate device drivers for the Executive printer. Configure NTFS permissions on the device driver files to allow access only to the System account and to users who are allowed to include the printer in their browse lists.

24. You are a network administrator for your company. The network consists of a single Windows 2000 domain. All client computers run Windows 2000 Professional and are members of the domain. Peter is a user in the graphics department. He connects a print device to his computer. He wants other users in the graphics department to be able to find the printer in the directory and to use it to print documents from the network. Peter reports that neither he nor any other users can find the printer in the directory and that no remote users can submit print jobs. Peter can print documents locally. You need to ensure that Peter and other users in the graphics department can find the printer in the directory and can print documents from the network. What should you do?

    a. In the printer properties, share the printer on Peter's computer.

    b. In the printer properties, assign the Everyone group the Allow-Print permission.

    c. In Active Directory Users and Computers, add the printer as a child object to Peter's computer object.

    d. In Active Directory Users and Computers, select the "Trust computer for delegation" check box in Peter's computer properties.

    e. In Active Directory Users and Computers, assign users in the graphics department the Allow-Read Public Information permission for Peter's computer object.

25. You are a desktop administrator for your company. All client computers run Windows 2000 Professional. You are installing a new plug-and-play combination scanner and print device on a user's computer. You connect the print device to the computer's parallel port. However, you discover that Windows 2000 does not detect the new print device. You open Device Manager on the computer and discover that there is no listing for the printer or for any unidentified devices. You run the Scan for hardware changes command in Device Manager, but no new hardware is detected. You want Windows 2000 Professional to detect and install drivers for the new print device. What should you do?

    a. In the system BIOS, enable Enhanced Parallel Port (EPP) Support.

    b. In the Driver Signing Options dialog box, set File Signature.

    c. Use the Add/Remove Hardware Wizard to install the manufacturer's printer driver.

    d. Turn off the computer, turn off the print device, and then turn on the computer.

26. You are the administrator of a Windows 2000 print server named ServerA. ServerA is a member of a Windows 2000 domain. You install a high-speed laser print device on the network. You create and share a printer on ServerA named FastLsr with the default settings. You want all of the users in your company to be able to use to FastLsr. You want the users in the Payroll domain local group to have exclusive use of the print device between the hours of 10:00a.m. and 3:00p.m. and shared use of the print device during all other times. What should you do?

    a. Configure and share FastLsr to be available from 3:00p.m. to 10:00a.m. For the print device, create a second printer that has default availability. For the second printer, assign the Everyone group the Deny-Print permission and assign the Payroll group the Allow-Print permission. Instruct users in the Payroll group to use the second printer.

    b. Configure and share FastLsr to be available from 3:00p.m. to 10:00a.m. For the print device, create a second printer that has default availability. For the second printer, remove permission for the Everyone group and assign the Payroll group the Allow-Print permission. Instruct users in the Payroll group to use the second printer.

c. Create and share a second printer device and configure it to be available from 10:00a.m. to 3:00p.m. For the second printer, assign the Everyone group the Deny-Print permission and assign the Payroll group the Allow-Print permission. Instruct users in the Payroll group to use the second printer.

d. Create and share a second printer for the print device and configure it to be available from 10:00a.m. to 3:00p.m. For the second printer, remove permissions for the Everyone group and assign the Payroll group the Allow-Print permission. Instruct users in the Payroll group to use the second printer.

27. You are a system administrator at the Acme Corporation. The network contains a Windows 2000 Server computer named Server1. You connect a new laser print device to Server1 on the LPT1 port. You configure a printer named Laser1 with the default permissions, and you share the printer as Laser1. Users in a branch office submit large print jobs to Laser1. These print jobs occasionally delay higher-priority print jobs that are submitted by users in the main office. Maria is the manager of the users in the branch office. Maria controls which users in the branch office are allowed to print to Laser1. You find out that Maria is deleting the print jobs that are submitted by the users in the branch office to enable the higher-priority print jobs to print faster. You want to ensure that Maria can control only user access to Laser1. What should you do?

a. Add Maria to the Print Operators group on Server1.

b. Assign Maria the Manage Printers permission for Laser1.

c. Ensure that priority level of Laser 1 is set to 99 on the Advanced tab of Laser1.

d. Run the Delegation of Control Wizard and assign Maria the Read permission for Laser1.

28. You are a domain administrator for your corporate Windows 2000 domain. The network contains two Windows 2000 Server domain controllers, 300 Windows 2000 Professional computers, 40 Windows 95 computers, and 40 Windows NT Workstation 4.0 computers. The domain uses Windows 2000 DNS with a standard primary zone. Several employees create shared printers on their Windows 2000 Professional computers. However, other users report that they cannot locate these shared printers. You want to ensure that all users can locate the shared printers by using the Search command on the Start menu. Which three actions should you take? (Each correct answer presents part of the solution. Choose three.)

a. Implement an Active Directory integrated DNS zone in the domain.

b. Change the domain mode to native mode.

c. Modify the properties in the shared printers to that the List in the Directory check box is selected.

d. Install WINS on a server in the domain. Configure all client computers to use the WINS server.

e. Install the Active Directory client on the Windows NT Workstation computers.

f. Install the Active Directory client on the Windows 95 computers.

29. You implement Internet printing on a computer running Windows 2000 Server. When a user attempts to connect to a printer using Internet Explorer 4.0, what will the client computer use first?

a. Remote Procedure Call (RPC)

b. Server Message Bock (SMB)

c. Internet Printing Protocol (IPP)

d. Hypertext Transport Protocol (HTTP)

HANDS-ON EXERCISES

Exercise 1: Installing a Printer

Note: Most of these exercises can be done even if you do not have a printer connected to your computer.

1. Log in as the Administrator.
2. Click on the Start button, select the Settings option, and select the Printers option.
3. In the Printers window, double-click the Add Printer icon.
4. On the Welcome to the Add Printer Wizard page, click the Next button.
5. On the Local or Network Printer page, verify that Local Printer is selected and click the Next button. If the printer was not automatically detected because it is not a plug-and-play printer, then specify the port that the printer is going to use and select the manufacturer and the printer model.
6. On the Name Your Printer page, type in PRINTER1-XXx, where *XX* is your assigned partner number and *x* is either a or b in the Printer Name box, and click the Next button.
7. On the Printer Sharing page, type the PRINTER1-XXx in the Share As box and click on the Next button.
8. If you add spaces, a warning message will state that the share name may not be accessible from some MS-DOS workstations. In these situations, click the Yes button.
9. On the Location and Comment page, type the room number in the Location box, the row number of your class-room seat, and the actual manufacturer and type of printer.

10. To be sure that the printer is connected properly and functioning, print a test page. On the Print a Test Page page, leave the Yes option enabled and click the Next button. If Windows 2000 asks if the printer page prints out OK, click on the Yes button.
11. On the Completing the Add Printer Wizard page, confirm the summary of your installation choices and click the Finish button.
12. Right-click the printer you have just created and select the Pause Printing option.

Exercise 2: Managing the Printer Documents

The following should be done on your computer.

1. Make sure that the printer is paused.
2. Click on the Start button, select the Programs option, select the Accessories options, and select the WordPad program.
3. Type in your first and last name. Change the font to Arial, the style to Bold, and the font size to 48 points.
4. Print to your printer.
5. Click on the Start button, select the Settings option, and select the Printers option.
6. Double-click your printer icon. Note that your print job is there waiting to be printed.

The following should be done on your partner's computer.

7. Click on the Start button, select the Settings option, and select the Printers option.
8. Double-click the Add Printer icon.
9. When the Add Printer Wizard starts, click on the Next button.
10. Select the Network Printer option and select the Next option.
11. Select Type the Printer Name option, type in the name of your shared printer in the Name text box, and click on the Next button.
12. Select the Yes option to make the printer the default printer. Click on the Next button.
13. Click on the Finish button.
14. Click on the Start button, select the Programs option, select the Accessories option, and select the WordPad program.
15. Type in your first and last name. Change the font to Arial, the style to Bold, and the font size to 48 points.
16. Print to your printer.
17. Click on the Start button, select the Settings option, and select the Printers option.
18. Double-click your printer icon. Note that your print job is there waiting to be printed.
19. Right-click the second print job and select the Cancel option to cancel the print job.
20. Log out as the Administrator and log in as Charlie Brown.
21. In the Printer folder, double-click your printer. As Charlie Brown, try to delete the first print job.

The following should be done at your computer.

22. Right-click your printer, select the Properties option, and select the Security tab.
23. Click the Add button and add Charlie Brown to the list. Give Charlie Brown the Manage Documents and Print permissions. Click on the OK button.

The following should be done at your partner's computer.

24. Logged in as Charlie Brown, try to delete the first print job.

Exercise 3: Scheduling Print Jobs

1. Click on the Start button, select the Settings option, and select the Printers option.
2. In the Printers window, double-click the Add Printer icon.
3. On the Welcome to the Add Printer Wizard page, click the Next button.
4. On the Local or Network Printer page, verify that Local Printer is selected and click the Next button. If the printer was not automatically detected because it is not a plug-and-play printer, then specify the port that the printer is going to use and select the manufacturer and the printer model.
5. The Use Existing Driver page displays because the printer you are installing can use the drivers from a printer that has already been installed on this computer. Therefore, enable the "Keep existing driver" option (recommended) and then click the Next button.
6. On the Name Your Printer page, type PRINTER2-XXx, where *XX* is your assigned partner number and *x* is either a or b in the Printer Name box, and click the Next button.

7. The first printer installed on the computer automatically became the default printer. For printers installed subsequently, change the default printer. Therefore, to keep the first printer as the default, select the No option and click the Next button.

8. On the Printer Sharing page, type PRINTER2-XXx in the Share As box and click on the Next button.

9. If you add spaces, a warning message will state that the share name may not be accessible from some MS-DOS workstations. In these situations, click the Yes button.

10. On the Location and Comment page, type the room number in the Location box, the row number of your classroom seat, and the actual manufacturer and type of printer.

11. To be sure that the printer is connected properly and functioning, print a test page. On the Print a Test Page page, leave the Yes option enabled and click the Next button. If Windows 2000 asks if the printer page prints out OK, click on the Yes button.

12. On the Completing the Add Printer Wizard page, confirm the summary of your installation choices and click the Finish button.

13. Right-click the printer and select the Properties option.

14. In the Advanced tab, select the Available From option and specify "12:00 am to 5 am." Click on the OK button.

15. Create the WordPad document again with your name.

16. Open the File menu and select the Print option.

17. With the General tab, select the second printer.

18. Double-click on the printer icon to view the print queue. Although the printer is not paused, the document will remain until 12:00 a.m. before it starts printing.

19. Cancel the print jobs.

Exercise 4: Connecting a Printer that is Connected Directly to the Network

1. Click on the Start button, select the Settings option, and then the Printers option.

2. In the Printers window, double-click the Add Printer icon.

3. On the Welcome to the Add Printer Wizard page, click the Next button.

4. On the Local or Network Printer page, verify that Local Printer is selected and disable the "Automatically detect and install my Plug and Play printer" option.

5. On the Select the Printer Port page, select the "Create a new port" option and select the Standard TCP/IP Port in the Type box. Click the Next button.

6. When the Add Standard TCP/IP Printer Port Wizard starts, click on the Next button.

7. On the Add Port page, type in 140.100.2XX in the Printer Name or IP Address box, where *XX* is your computer number. Click on the Next button to accept the default port name.

8. Verify the configuration options and click the Finish button.

9. On the Add Printer Wizard page, select the manufacturer for the printer under Manufacturer and select the model of the printer under printers. Click the Next button.

10. On the Name Your Printer page, type in PRINTER3-XXx, where *XX* is your assigned partner number and *x* is either a or b in the Printer Name box, and click the Next button.

11. The first printer installed on the computer automatically became the default printer. For printers installed subsequently, you can change the default printer. Therefore, to keep the first printer as the default, select the No option and click the Next button.

12. On the Printer Sharing page, type the PRINTER3-XXx in the Share As box and click on the Next button.

13. If you add spaces, a warning message will state that the share name may not be accessible from some MS-DOS workstations. In these situations, click the Yes button.

14. Right-click the printer you have just created and select the Pause Printing option.

15. On the Location and Comment page, type the room number in the Location box, the row number of your classroom seat, and the actual manufacturer and type of printer.

16. To be sure that the printer is connected properly and functioning, print a test page. On the Print a Test Page page, leave the Yes option enabled and click the Next button. If Windows 2000 asks if the printer page prints out OK, click on the Yes button.

17. On the Completing the Add Printer Wizard page, confirm the summary of your installation choices and click the Finish button.

CHAPTER 17

Disaster Recovery

Topics Covered in This Chapter

Introduction

For some companies, every minute that the network is down means a loss of thousands of dollars in business and productivity. The loss of data on the network also may be irreplaceable. Although network administrators never hope for disasters to occur, they should be ready to deal with such possibilities. Therefore, this chapter's focus is twofold: first, how to avoid disaster, and second, how to deal with certain kinds of disasters.

Objectives

- Choose a disaster recovery plan for various situations.
- Select the appropriate hardware and software tools to monitor trends in the network.
- Resolve broadcast storms.
- Identify and resolve network performance problems.
- Monitor and configure removable media, such as tape devices.
- Optimize and troubleshoot performance of Windows, including memory performance, processor utilization, disk performance, network performance, and application performance.

- Recover systems and user data by using Windows Backup.
- Troubleshoot system restoration by using safe mode.
- Recover systems and user data by using the Recovery console.
- Implement, configure, manage, and troubleshoot auditing.
- Recover from disk failures.
- Perform an authoritative restore of Active Directory.
- Recover from a system failure of Active Directory.

17.1 FAULT TOLERANCE AND DISASTER-RECOVERY NEEDS

When a computer has a problem, the user's first response is "Oh no, not now!" Any computer user will agree that there is no *good* time for a computer to break down. A network failure can affect many people and can literally cost a company thousands of dollars of business or productivity for every hour the network is down. One primary job of the administrator is to deal with such disasters and to plan ahead to minimize the frequency and degree of failures. The job includes these tasks:

- Establishing a backup plan and then performing the backup
- Documenting the network so that all team members can find information quickly about the network
- Maintaining a log that lists all problems and their solutions, to be used to determine trends, plan network and personnel resources, and provide a quick reference of solutions when the same problem recurs

The cost of server downtime is staggering. If a network of a medium-size business with 300 employees and $100 million of business goes down 24 times a year, 3 hours at a time (less than 1% downtime), the cost can be more than $3 million per year in lost revenues, user salaries, and server outage costs.

In what is called a **hot site**, every computer system and piece of information has a redundant copy. This level of fault tolerance is used when systems must be up 100% of the time. Hot sites are strictly fault-tolerant implementations, not disaster-recovery implementations. You can imagine that these types of systems are costly. To make a system fault tolerant, you must overcome failure points, as shown in Table 17.1.

In a warm site (also called a nearline site), the network service and data are available most of the time (more than 85% of the time). The service and data are less critical than those in a hot site. With hot-site technologies, *all fault*-tolerance procedures are automatic and are controlled by the network operating system. Warm-site technologies require a little more administrative intervention, but they are not as expensive as hot sites.

Table 17.1   Common points of failure in a server

Failure Point	Failure Solution
Network hub and network card	Redundant network cards and hubs
Power problems	Uninterruptible power supply (UPS); redundant power supplies; placement of cluster nodes on separate electrical circuits
Disk	Hardware RAID
Other server hardware, such as CPU or memory	Fail-over clustering[1]
Server software, such as the operating system or specific applications	Fail-over clustering
Wide area network (WAN) links, such as routers and dedicated lines	Redundant links over the WAN, to provide secondary access to remote connections
Dial-up connection	Multiple modems

[1]Clustering is discussed in Section 17.10 (page 635).

The most cost-effective and most commonly used warm-site technology is a duplicate server. A duplicate server is currently not being used and is available to replace any server that fails. When a server fails, the administrator installs the new server and restores the data; the network services are available to users with a minimum of downtime. Use of a duplicate server is a disaster recovery method because the entire server is replaced; however, this recovery takes a shorter time than what is involved if all the components have to be ordered and configured at the time of system failure. Note: Corporate networks do not often use duplicate servers, because of the major disadvantages associated with using them, for example, the need for a current backup of data on the duplicate server and the fact that data since the last backup can be lost.

A cold site does not guarantee server uptime and has little or no fault tolerance. Instead, a cold site relies on efficient disaster recovery methods to ensure data integrity, especially backup of data.

17.2   TAPE DRIVES

Tape drives read and write to a long magnetic tape. They are relatively inexpensive and offer large storage capacities, which makes them ideal for backing up hard drives on a regular basis. To back up a hard drive, insert a tape into the drive, start a backup software package, and select the drive/files you want to back up and it will be done. If a drive or file is lost, the backup software can be used to restore the data from the tape to the hard drive. If the correct tape drive and backup software are chosen, the drive could automatically back up the hard drive at night, when it is used the least. You must remember, however, to replace the tape each day. Also note that tapes do fail and often users fail to properly back up a drive or file. When disaster occurs, users are surprised by their blank tapes. Therefore, it is important to occasionally test the tapes by choosing an unimportant file and restoring it back to the hard drive.

Tapes come in different sizes and shapes and offer different speeds and capacities. As a result, several standards have been developed including the quarter-inch cartridge (QIC) and the digital audio tape (DAT).

In 1972, 3M Company introduced the first **quarter-inch cartridge (QIC)** designed for data storage. The tape cartridge measured 6″ × 4″ × 5/8″. Although the cartridge became the standard, each tape drive manufacturer used different encoding methods, varied the number of tracks, and varied the data density on the tape, thus causing all kinds of compatibility problems.

As a result, in 1982, a group of manufacturers formed the QIC Committee to standardize tape drive construction and applications. The full-size quarter-inch cartridge standardized by the QIC Committee is also referred to as the DC (data cartridge) 6000.

The first tape that the QIC Committee approved was the QIC-24, which used serpentine recording. It had nine tracks and a density of 8000 bits per inch, giving a total storage capacity of 60 MB. It achieved 90 inches per second and offered 720 kilobits per second with the QIC-02 interface.

Through the years, data density was increased and more tracks were added. The last QIC-1000 DC packed 30 tracks across the tape at 36,000 bits per inch, allowing up to 1.2 GB per tape cartridge. Its speed was also increased 2.8 megabits per second. Yet, the QIC-1000 DC drives could read previous QIC tapes.

By 1989, the QIC Committee revamped the original QIC standard by using 1,7 RLL encoding and higher coercivity. This allowed higher bit density, a high number of tracks, and faster transfer rates. By 1995, the QIC introduced the QIC-5210 DC, which had 144 tracks and 76,200 bits per inch, allowing for 25 GB of storage space.

Because the full-size QIC is too large to fit into a drive bay, the committee created the **minicartridge (MC),** which was 3.25″ × 2.5″ × 1.59″. The minicartridges are also called DC 2000 cartridges. The QIC-40 MC was the first standard to be adopted. It fit into the 5.25-inch drive bay and it connected to the computer via the floppy drive controller. As floppy disk drives use MFM encoding, so did the QIC-40 MC. Different from previous tapes, QIC specified the format of the data on the tape, including how sectors were assigned to files and FAT—to list bad sectors. This feature required formatted tapes, which is a time-consuming process. Consequently, you could buy tapes as formatted or unformatted. Another advantage was the tapes could be accessed randomly. Although it had to move the tape to the proper sector, it did not have to read each file sequentially.

The newest type of tape is the **digital audio tape (DAT),** which uses the same technology as VCR tapes (helical scan). The 8-mm DAT allows capacities up to 35 GB. The DAT standard has primarily been developed and marketed by Hewlett-Packard. This company chairs the Digital Data Storage (DDS) Manufacturers Group, which led the development of the DDS standards.

Data are not recorded on the tape in the MFM or RLL formats, but rather, bits of data received by the tape drive are assigned numerical values, or digits. These digits are then translated into a stream of electronic pulses that are placed on the tape. Later, when information is being restored to a computer system from the tape, the DAT drive translates these digits back into binary bits that can be stored on the computer.

The **digital data storage (DDS)** tape is currently the newest standard of the digital audio tape. The DDS-3 can hold 24 GB (or equivalent) of over 40 CD-ROMs and supports data transfer rates of 2 Mbps, all in a space that is slightly larger than a credit card. In a DDS drive, the tape barely creeps along, requiring about 3 seconds to move an inch. The head drum spins rapidly at 2000 revolutions per minute, putting down 1869 tracks across a linear inch of tape which allow 61 kilobits per inch. The main advantage of the DAT is its access speed and capacity.

One of the newest tapes is the **digital linear tape (DLT),** designed for high capacity, high speed, and highly reliable backup. A DLT is 1/2″ wide, has capacities of 35 GB to 70 GB compressed, and a data transfer rate of 5 Mbps to 10 Mbps or more. Unfortunately, the drives are quite expensive and are used primarily for network server backup.

17.3   BACKUP

Data are the raw facts, numbers, letters, or symbols that the computer processes into meaningful information. Examples of data include a letter to a company or a client, a report for your boss, a budget proposal of a large project, or an address book of your friends and business associates. Regardless of the data type, it can be saved (or written to disk) so that it can be retrieved at any time. Data can be printed on paper or e-mailed to someone.

Data stored on a computer or stored on the network are vital to the users and probably the company. Data represent hours of work, which are sometimes irreplaceable. Data loss can be caused by many things including hardware failure, viruses, user error, and malicious users. When disaster occurs, the best method to recover data is backup, backup, backup, because without backup of important files, it is often too late to recover them.

A **backup** of a system is a copy of all data and/or programs. As a technician, consultant, or support person, you need to emphasize at every moment to back up on servers and client systems. In addition, clients should save their data files to a server so that you have a single, central location to store backup. This process may even entail selecting and installing the equipment, doing the backup, or training other people in doing the backup. Having proper equipment and methods will help ensure complete and regular backups; and having good personnel to perform backups is essential in a data protection system.

> THE BEST METHOD FOR DATA PROTECTION IS BACKUP, BACKUP, BACKUP.

When developing a backup, follow these three steps:

1. Develop a backup plan.
2. Stick to the backup plan.
3. Test the backup plan.

When developing a backup plan, consider the following questions:

- What equipment will be used?
- How much data need to be backed up?
- How long will the backup take?
- How often must the data be backed up?
- When will the backup take place?
- Who will do the backup?

Whatever equipment, person, or method is chosen, ensure that the backup is done. If you choose the best equipment, the best software, and the brightest person, but the backup is not done for whatever reason, then you have wasted your resources and put your data at risk.

Backups can be done with floppy disks, extra hard drives (including network drives), compact disk drives, tape drives, and other forms of removable media. The best method of file backup is probably tape drives, which can store 25 + GB.

> **Question:** How often should backup be done?
>
> **Answer:** Frequency of backup depends on the importance of the data. If you have many customers loaded into a database that is constantly changed, or your files represent the livelihood of your business, then you should back them up every day. If you send only a few letters throughout the week with nothing vitally important, then you can back up once a week.

17.3.1   Types of Backups

All types of backups can be arranged into five categories. See Table 17.2.

Example 1:

> You decide to back up the entire hard drive once a week on Friday, using the full backup method. Therefore, you perform a full backup every Friday. If the hard drive goes bad, you use the last backup to restore the hard drive.

Example 2:

> You decide to back up the entire hard drive once a week on Friday, using the incremental method. Therefore, you perform a full backup on week 1. This will shut off all archive attributes, indicating that all files have been backed up. On week 2, week 3, and week 4, you perform incremental backups using a different tape or disk. Since the incremental backup turns off the archive attribute, it backs up only new files and changed files; thus, the four backups comprise the entire backup. It is much quicker to back up a drive using an incremental backup than a full backup. If the hard drive fails, however, you must restore backup 1, backup 2, backup 3, and backup 4 to restore the entire hard drive.

Table 17.2   Types of backup

Category	Description
Normal/Full	The full backup will back up all files selected and shut off the archive file attribute indicating the file has been backed up.
Incremental	An incremental backup will back up the files selected if the archive file attribute is on (files since the last full or incremental backup). After the file has been backed up, it will shut off the file attribute indicating that the file has been backed up.
Differential	A differential backup will back up the files selected if the archive file attribute is on (files since the last full backup). Different from the incremental backup, it does not shut off the archive attribute.
Copy	A copy backup will back up the files selected regardless of the archive attribute and will not shut off the archive attribute after the file has been copied. The copy backup is not typically used as part of a backup procedure. Instead, it would be used as an interim backup in case something goes wrong during major changes or upgrades.
Daily	A daily backup copies all selected files that have been modified on the day that the daily backup is performed. During the backup, files are not marked as having been backed up (archive attribute is not cleared).

Example 3:

You decide to back up the entire hard drive once a week on Friday, using the differential method. Therefore, you perform a full backup on week 1. This will shut off all archive attributes, indicating that all files have been backed up. On week 2, week 3, and week 4, you perform differential backups using a different tape or disk. Since the differential backup does not turn off the archive attribute, it backs up the new files and the changed files since the last full backup; thus, the full backup and the last differential backup comprise the entire backup. It is much quicker to back up a drive using a differential backup than a full backup, but slower than an incremental backup. If the hard drive fails, you only restore backup 1 and the last differential in order to restore the entire hard drive.

After the backups are complete, check if they are working. For example, pick a nonessential file and restore it to the hard drive to check if the backups are empty or a backup/restore device is faulty.

As a manager, keep more than one backup. (Tapes and disks do fail.) One technique is to rotate three sets of backups. If you perform a full backup once a week, then use three sets of backup tapes or disks. For example, during week 1, use tape/disk 1; during week 2, use tape/disk 2; and during week 3, use tape/disk 3. On week 4, begin again with tape/disk 1. If you have to restore a hard drive and the tape or disk fails, you can always go to the tape or disk from the previous week. In addition, perform monthly backups and store them elsewhere. You would be surprised how many times a person loses a file but may not be aware of it for several weeks. If the data are especially important, consider keeping a backup set in a fireproof safe off-site. When Windows is initially installed and you make any major changes to the system's configuration, always make two backups before proceeding. This way, if anything goes wrong, you have the ability to restore everything back to the way it was before the changes. The reason for the two backups is that tapes have been known to go bad on occasion.

After completing a backup, properly label the tape or disk before removing it and then store it in a secure, safe place. Also keep a log of what backups have been done, especially if you need to rebuild the server, so you know what was backed up and when. Keeping a log will also let you know if someone is forgetting to do the backup.

17.3.2   Performing a Backup

To start the backup program, click on the Start button, select the Programs option, select the Accessories option, select the System Tools option, and select Backup. The Backup program can be used to back up and restore files and to create an emergency repair disk. The Welcome tab has buttons to start Backup, Restore, and Emergency Repair Disk wizards. See Figure 17.1.

Figure 17.1   Windows 2000 Backup and Recovery Tools welcome screen

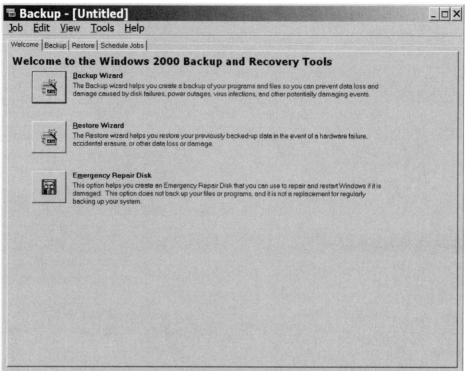

To back up or restore files, you must be an administrator or a member of the Backup Operator group. To back up files to a file or tape, follow these steps:

1. Open the Backup program and click on the Backup tab. See Figure 17.2.
2. Open the Job menu and click New.
3. Select the files and folders that you want to back up by clicking the box to the left of a file or folder. You can back up files on other computers by using the My Network Places located at the bottom of the tree.
4. In Backup Destination, select Tape Device if you want to back up to a tape drive or File if you want to back up to a file. If you do not have a tape device installed on your computer, File is selected by default.
5. In Backup Media or File Name, select the tape that you want to use or the path and file name. Backup files have a BKF file name extension.
6. Open the Tools menu and select the Options menu to select the backup type and log file type.
7. Click on the Start Backup button.
8. After making any changes to the Backup Job Information dialog box, click on the Start Backup button.
9. If you want to set data verification or hardware compression, or change the backup type, click on the Advance button. Click on the OK button to close the Advanced Backup options.
10. Click on the Start Backup button.

If you are attempting a backup and the Backup program indicates that there are no unused media available, you may have to use the Removable Storage console to add your tape to the Backup Media pool. You can access the Removable Storage console by loading the Computer Management console that is located under Administrative Tools.

17.3.3   Scheduling Backup

Because backup is performed on a regular basis and the best time to do a backup is when the network traffic is slow, you can schedule the backup to occur automatically. To schedule an automatic backup, do the following:

1. Start the Backup program.
2. Using the Backup tab, open the Job menu and select the New option.

Figure 17.2   Using the Windows 2000 Backup program

3. Select the files and folders that you want to back up by clicking the box to the left of a file or folder, under "Click to select the check box for any drive, folder or file that you want to back up."
4. In Backup Destination, select File or a tape device in Backup Destination, and then save the file and folder selections by clicking the Job menu and then clicking Save Selections.
5. In Backup Media or File Name, type a path and file name for the backup file or select Tape.
6. If you want to select any Backup options, open the Tools menu and select the Options menu. Click OK to close the Options dialog box.
7. Click Start Backup and make any changes you want to the Backup Job Information dialog box.
8. If you want to set Advanced Backup options such as data verification or hardware compression, click the Advanced button. To close the Advanced Backup options, click the OK button.
9. Click Schedule in the Backup Job Information dialog box.
10. In the Set Account Information dialog box, enter the user name and password that you want the schedule backup to run under.
11. In the Scheduled Job Options dialog box, in Job Name, type a name for the scheduled backup job and then click Properties to set the data, time, and frequency parameters for the scheduled backup. When finished, click twice on the OK button.

If you are scheduling a tape backup, you may have to use the removable storage option to make sure that your tape is available in the Backup Media pool. In addition, you must have the Task Scheduler service running before you can schedule a backup. You can change the settings of a scheduled backup job or delete the job after you schedule it by clicking on the Schedule Jobs tab and then clicking on the job. See Figure 17.3.

Figure 17.3   Scheduling backup jobs

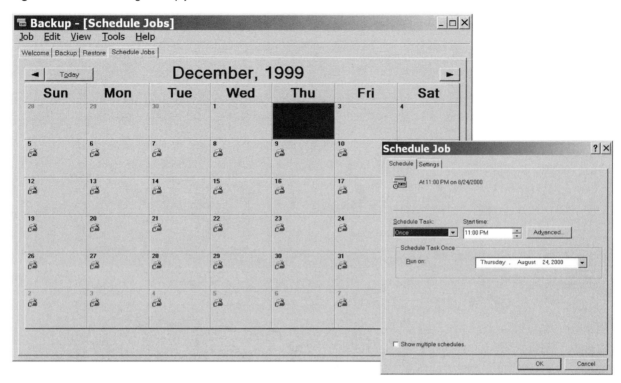

17.3.4   System State

The **System State** data are a collection of system-specific data that can be backed up and restored. For Windows 2000 and Windows Server 2003, the collection includes the following:

- Registry
- COM+ Class Registration database
- System boot files
- Certificate Services database on servers that operate as a certificate server
- Active Directory directory services database on domain controller
- SYSVOL directory on domain controllers

Since the System State components depend on each other, when you choose to back up or restore the System State data, you must back up all of the System State data. To do so, put a check in the System State check box, located after all local drive letters. See Figure 17.4.

When you restore the individual components of the System State components, you can restore the registry files, SYSVOL directory files, cluster database information, and system boot files to an alternate location. When you back up and restore the System State data, you can only back up and restore on a local computer, not on remote computers.

17.3.5   Catalogs

When performing backups, users typically make a catalog. The **catalog** is a summary of the files and folders that have been saved in a backup set. The on-disk catalog is stored on the local disk drive, whereas the on-media catalog is stored on the backup storage media such as the backup tapes.

If you have all the tapes in the backup set and the tapes are not damaged or corrupted, you can speed the cataloging processor if you open the Tools menu, select the Options option, click the General tab, and note if the "Use the catalogs on the media to speed up building restore catalogs on disk" check box

Figure 17.4   Backing up the System State

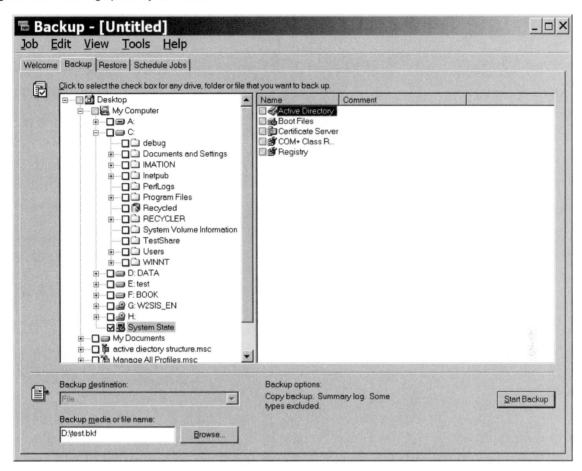

is marked. See Figure 17.5. However, if you want to restore data from several tapes and the tape with the on-media catalog is missing or you want to restore data from media that are damaged, do not select this option. Instead, the Backup program will scan the backup set and build an on-line disk catalog. Unfortunately, if your backup set is quite large, this process could take several hours.

17.3.6   Performing a Recovery

When a Windows 2000, Windows XP, or Windows Server 2003 computer fails and you lose all information, you must first correct any hardware problems and then reinstall Windows. Much like the backup, you can restore the computer using the Restore Wizard or the Restore tab, both of which are located in the Backup program. The restore process will reload the Windows operating system, the Active Directory including database and registry settings, and any other services that were loaded. If you have more than one domain controller, the Active Directory will be replicated throughout the domain controllers. Therefore, if a domain controller goes down, you bring the domain controller up and let the Active Directory replicate to the domain controller.

An advantage of using today's backup programs is you can restore individual files or directories. For example, if someone accidentally deletes a file or a file becomes corrupted, you can restore that file without overwriting the other files.

To restore files, do the following:

1. Open the Backup program.
2. Click on the Restore tab.
3. Click to select the drive, folder, or file that you want to restore.

Figure 17.5 Backup's general options

4. In the Restore Files To: text box, select the location that the files will be restored:
   Original location
   Alternate location
   Single folder
   If you selected Alternate location or Single folder, type a path for the folder under Alternate location, or click the Browse button to find the folder.
5. Click on the Tools menu, click the Options option, click the Restore tab, and select one of the following:
   Do not replace the file on my computer
   Replace the file on disk only if the file on disk is older
   Always replace the file on my computer
6. Click on the Start Restore button.
7. If you want to change any of the advanced restore options, such as restoring security settings, click on the Advanced button. When done, click on the OK button.
8. Click OK to start the restore.

Let us say that you have a Windows 2000 Active Directory object, which has been corrupted. Of course, you can choose to restore the System State data. If you have several domain controllers, they would automatically overwrite the newly restored Active Directory database. To overcome this problem, perform an authorative restore using NTDSUTIL utility so that the Active Directory objects will be replicated to the other domain servers, even though the objects are older than those currently in the Active Directory database.

17.3.7   Backup and Restore at the Command Line

Another way to do a backup is to use batch files that utilize the NTBACKUP command. The advantage of using batch files is you can run the batch file quickly if you need to do a quick backup before making any major changes. With the NTBACKUP command, you can only back up folders, not individual files. In addition, you cannot use wildcards as you can with the Command prompt commands, such as the COPY command.

The syntax for the NTBACKUP command is as follows:

```
ntbackup backup [systemstate] "bks file name" /J {"job name"}
[/P {"pool name"}] [/G {"guid name"}] [/T { "tape name"}] [/N {"media
name"}] [/F {"file name"}] [/D {"set description"}] [/DS {"server
name"}] [/IS {"server name"}] [/A] [/V:{yes|no}] [/R:{yes|no}]
[/L:{f|s|n}] [/M {backup type}] [/RS:{yes|no}] [/HC:{on|off}]
```

NTBACKUP Parameters	Description
systemstate	Specifies that you want to back up the System State data. The backup type will be forced to Normal or Copy.
bks file name	Specifies the name of the backup selection file (.bks file) to be used for this backup operation. A backup selection file contains information on the files and folders you have selected for backup. Create the file using the graphical user interface (GUI) version of Backup.
/J {"job name"}	Specifies the job name to be used in the log file
/P {"pool name"}	Specifies the media pool from which you want to use media. This selection may not be used with the following switches: **/A /G /F /T**.
/G {"guid name"}	Overwrites or appends to this tape. Do not use this switch in conjunction with **/P**.
/T {"tape name"}	Overwrites or appends to this tape. Do not use this switch in conjunction with **/P**.
/N {"media name"}	Specifies the new tape name. Do not use **/A** with this switch.
/F {"file name"}	Logical disk path and file name. You must not use the following switches with this switch: **/P /G /T**.
/D {"set description"}	Specifies a label for each backup set
/DS {"server name"}	Backs up the directory service file for the specified Microsoft Exchange Server
/IS {"server name"}	Backs up the Information Store file for the specified Microsoft Exchange Server
/A	Performs an append operation. Either **/G** or **/T** must be used in conjunction with this switch. Do not use in conjunction with **/P**.
/V:{yes|no}	Verifies the data after the backup is complete
/R:{yes|no}	Restricts access to this tape to the owner or members of the Administrators group
/L:{f|s|n}	Specifies the type of log file: **f** = full, **s** = summary, **n** = none (no log file is created)
/M {backup type}	Specifies the backup type. It must be one of the following: Normal, Copy, Differential, Incremental, or Daily.
/RS:{yes|no}	Backs up the Removable Storage database
/HC:{on|off}	Uses hardware compression, if available, on the tape drive

Example 4:

NTBACKUP BACKUP C:\ /J "JOB1" /A /T "Tape 1" /M COPY
    This example will perform a copy backup type called JOB1 of the entire C drive (logical drive). The back up files and folders will be appended (/A) to the tape called TAPE1.

17.4   EMERGENCY REPAIR

If Windows 2000, Windows XP, or Windows Server 2003 cannot load or start, accessing certain tools may help you solve the problem. These tools are the Advanced Boot menu, Windows Recovery console, and emergency repair disk.

17.4.1   Advanced Boot Menu

As discussed in Chapter 8, if you press F8 while the Windows Boot menu is displayed, it will display the Advanced Boot menu. Safe mode lets you start your system with a minimal set of device drivers and services (PS/2 mouse, monitor, keyboard, mass storage, base video, default system services) with no network connection. Typically, you would use safe mode if you installed a device driver or software that prevents the computer from starting, in the hope that safe mode would remove either from your system.

Using the Enable VGA mode is another option if the wrong video driver is loaded and you need to force the video system into 640 × 480 with 16 colors, and into the Last Known Good Configuration to start Windows using the last saved configuration, which is stored in the registry.

The Directory Service Restore mode is a special version of safe mode that loads all drivers and services, and performs a CHKDSK on all volumes. After logging in, it allows you to restore the Active Directory of the domain controller from Backup Media. After getting into this mode, it will automatically set the computer to have the Active Directory check all indexes next time you boot the domain controller normally.

The Debugging mode has Windows send debug information through a serial cable to another computer. This allows you to monitor the process of a server's boot from another server.

17.4.2   Windows Recovery Console

If your computer fails to boot even in safe mode, the best tool to use is the **Recovery console.** The Recovery console provides a command-line interface that will let you repair system problems using a limited set of command-line commands, including enabling or disabling services, repairing a corrupted master boot record, and reading and writing data on a local drive (FAT, FAT32, or NTFS). Because Recovery console is a powerful tool, it can only be used by advanced users from the Administrators group who have a thorough knowledge of Windows.

There are two ways to start the Recovery console: (1) you can run it from your Windows setup disks or from the Windows installation CD; or (2) you can install it on your computer so it is available in case you are unable to restart Windows. To start the computer and use the Recovery console, follow these steps:

1. Insert the Windows Setup CD, or the first floppy disk you created from the CD, in the appropriate drive. If you cannot boot from the CD drive, you must use a floppy disk, and restart the computer. If you are using a floppy disk, you will be asked to switch disks.
2. When the text-based part of Setup begins, follow the prompts and choose the Repair or Recover option by pressing R. When prompted, choose the Recovery console by pressing C. Again, if you are using a floppy disk, you will be asked to switch disks.
3. If you have a dual-boot or multiple-boot system, choose the Windows installation that you need to access from the Recovery console.
4. When prompted, type the Administrator password.
5. At the System prompt, type the Recovery console commands.
6. To exit the Recovery console and restart the computer, type Exit.

To install the Recovery console as a Startup Menu option, do the following:

1. Insert the Windows Setup CD into your CD-ROM drive.
2. Click No when prompted to upgrade to Windows.
3. At the Command prompt, switch to your CD-ROM drive, and then type the following: \I386\WINNT32.EXE /CMDCONS.
4. When it asks if you want to install the Recovery console, click on the Yes button.
5. Click OK when Setup is complete.
6. To run the Recovery console, restart your computer and select the Recovery Console option from the Boot menu.

To get a list of the commands that are available in the Recovery console, type in Help while in the console. See Table 17.3. To get help about a specific command, type in Help *commandname.* While the console resembles DOS, these commands are very limited. By default, you can copy from removable

Table 17.3   List of commands used in the recovery console

Command	Description
ATTRIB	Changes or displays attributes of files or directories
CD	Changes directory
CHKDSK	Executes a consistency check of the specified disk
CLS	Clears the screen
COPY	Copies a file
DEL	Deletes a file
DIR	Lists Directory contents
DISKPART	Adds and deletes partitions
ENABLE	Starts or enables a system service or a device driver
DISABLE	Stops or disables a system service or device driver
EXTRACT	Extracts a file from a compressed file
FIXBOOT	Writes a new partition boot sector onto the system partition
FIXMRB	Repairs the master boot record of the partition boot sector
FORMAT	Formats a disk
LISTSVC	Lists the services and device drivers available on the computer
LOGON	Logs on to a Windows computer
MAP	Displays the drive letter mappings
MD	Creates a directory
TYPE	Displays a text file
RMDIR	Deletes a directory
REPAIR	Updates an installation with files using the Windows installation CD
REN	Renames a file
SYSTEMROOT	Changes to the installation system root directory (typically \WINNT)

media to hard disk but not vice versa. In addition, wild characters in the copy command don't work, and you cannot read or list files on any partition except the system partition.

17.4.3   Emergency Repair Disk

The **emergency repair disk (ERD)** contains information about your current Windows system settings. You can use this disk to repair your computer if it will not start or your system files are damaged or erased. To create an emergency repair disk, do the following:

1. Open the Backup program.
2. On the Tools menu, click Create an Emergency Repair Disk. Or, you can use the Emergency Repair Disk Wizard.
3. Insert a blank, formatted floppy disk into the drive. Mark the check box if you want a backup copy of the registry copied to the REPAIR folder (highly recommended) and click on the OK button.
4. Click on the OK button when the disk has been created.
5. Label the disk as Emergency Repair Disk and store in a safe place.

When using an emergency repair disk, the disk relies on information that has been saved to the *systemroot*\REPAIR folder. Therefore, do not change or delete this folder. You also should re-create the ERD after each service pack, system change, or updated driver.

To use an emergency repair disk for system repairs, follow these steps:

1. Insert the Windows Setup CD, or the first floppy disk you created from the CD, in the appropriate drive.
2. When the text-based part of Setup begins, follow the prompts; choose the Repair or Recover option by pressing R.
3. When prompted, insert the Windows Setup CD in the appropriate drive.
4. When prompted, choose the Emergency Repair Process by pressing R.
5. When prompted, choose between the following:
   ■ Manual Repair (press M): This should be used only by advanced users or administrators. Use this option to choose whether you want to repair system files, partition-boot sector problems, or start-up environment problems.
   ■ Fast Repair (press F): This is the easiest option, and does not require input. This option will attempt to repair problems that are related to system files, the partition boot sector on your system disk, and your start-up environment (if you have a dual-boot or multiple-boot system).
6. Follow the instructions on the screen and, when prompted, insert the emergency repair disk in the appropriate drive.
7. During the repair process, missing or corrupted files are replaced with files from the Windows CD or from the *systemroot*\Repair folder on the system partition. Be sure to follow the instructions on the screen; you may want to write the names of files that are detected as faulty or incorrect, to help you diagnose how the system was damaged.
8. If the repair was successful, allow the process to complete; it will restart the computer. The restarting of the computer indicates that replacement files were successfully copied to the hard disk.

If you have performed the emergency repair process and the computer still does not operate normally, then use the Windows Setup CD to perform an **in-place upgrade** over the existing installation. This is a last resort before reinstalling the operating system. An in-place upgrade takes the same amount of time as a reinstallation of the operating system. To perform an in-place upgrade of Windows, do the following:

1. Install the Windows Setup CD.
2. Press Enter to install a copy of Windows.
3. When prompted to repair the existing Windows installation, press R.

17.4.4   System Restore

System Restore is a component of Windows XP Professional that you can use to restore your computer to a previous state (including the installation of drivers and applications) if a problem occurs, without losing your personal data files (e.g., Microsoft Word documents, browsing history, drawings, favorites, or e-mail). System Restore monitors changes to the system and some application files, and it automatically creates easily identified restore points. These restore points allow you to revert the system to a previous time. They are created daily and at the time of significant system events (such as when an application or driver is installed). You can also create and name your own restore points at any time, which can come in handy before you make changes to your computer. Note that System Restore does not back up or establish restore points of your data files. Instead, you have to use a backup program to back up your data files.

To create a restore point, follow these steps:

1. Access the System Restore Wizard through Help and Support Center.
2. Click Create a restore point, then click Next.
3. In the Restore point description box, type a name to identify this restore point. System Restore automatically adds to this name the data and time that this restore point is created.
4. To finish creating this restore point, click Create.
5. To cancel restore point creation and return to the Welcome to System Restore screen, click Back.
6. To cancel restore point creation and exit the System Restore Wizard, click Cancel.

Figure 17.6 Using System Restore

Continued

To access the System Restore Wizard, click Start, then click Help and Support. Click Performance and Maintenance, click "Using System Restore to undo changes," then click Run the System Restore Wizard.

To view or to return to a restore point, from the Welcome to System Restore screen of the System Restore Wizard, select "Restore my computer to an earlier time." Then select the data when the restore point was created from the calendar in the Select a Restore Point screen. All of the restore points that were created on the selected date are listed by name in the list box to the right of the calendar. See Figure 17.6.

System Restore is enabled on all drives when you first start your new computer or when the operating system is installed, unless you have less than 200 MB of available space on the hard disk (or the partition that contains your operating system folder). If you do not have enough disk space available when your operating system is installed, you must turn on System Restore after you have made sufficient disk space available. If you run out of disk space, System Restore becomes inactive. When you have made sufficient disk space available, System Restore is automatically activated, but all previous restore points are lost. When System Restore is turned off on a partition or drive, all restore points stored on that partition or drive are deleted. Changes that are made on an excluded partition or drive are not reverted during a System Restore.

To turn on or off System Restore, do the following:

1. Open System Properties from the Control Panel.
2. From the System Restore tab, ensure that the Turn off System Restore check box is selected or deselected appropriately.

Figure 17.6 Continued

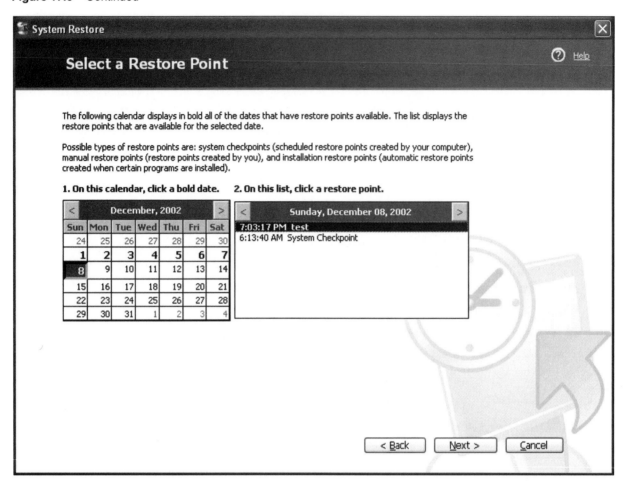

17.4.5 Driver Rollback

Another feature added to Windows XP and Windows Server 2003 is driver rollback. To help ensure system stability, when you update a driver, a copy of the previous driver package is automatically saved in a special subdirectory of the system files. If the new driver does not work properly, you can restore the previous driver by accessing the Driver tab for the device in the Device Manager and clicking Roll Back Driver. Driver rollback permits only one level of rollback (only one prior version can be saved at a time); this feature is available for all device classes, except printers.

To roll back a driver, follow these steps:

1. Log in as Administrator and access the Device Manager. Click Start, then click Control Panel. Click Performance and Maintenance, then click System. On the Hardware tab, click Device Manager.
2. Navigate to the driver you wish to roll back; right click the name of the driver and choose Properties
3. Click the Driver tab, then click Roll Back Driver.

17.5 WINDOWS ERROR MESSAGES

Occassionally, Windows may encounter a program error or a stop error. These errors are similar to Windows 9X general protection errors.

17.5.1 Invalid Page Faults and Exception Errors

A program error or stop error signifies that something unexpected has happened within the Windows environment. This situation usually involves a program that tried to access a memory area which belongs to another program (**invalid page fault**) or an application that tried to pass an invalid parameter to another program (**exception error**). **Dr. Watson** is a program that (1) starts automatically when a program error occurs, (2) detects information about the system and the program failure, and (3) records the information into a log file. Dr. Watson will not prevent errors, but its log file can be used by technical support personnel to diagnose the problem. To open Dr. Watson, click the Start button, select the Run option, and execute the DRWTSN32 program. See Figure 17.7. For more information about the Dr. Watson log file, see Dr. Watson Log File Overview using Windows Help program.

17.5.2 Stop Errors

Applications run in the user mode layer (Intel 386 protection model—ring 3). When an application causes an error, Windows halts the process and generates an illegal operation error. Because every Win32 application has its own virtual protected memory space, this error condition does not affect any other Win32 program that is running. If the application tries to access the hardware without going through the correct methods, Windows takes note and generates an exception error. In these cases, if the application faults, then either Windows or the user can close the offending program and resume work without affecting the other programs.

The Windows kernel runs in the kernel mode layer (Intel 386 protection model—ring 0). When the kernel encounters a fatal error—such as a hardware problem, inconsistencies within data that are necessary for its operation, or a similar error—Windows can display a **stop error** (sometimes known as a "blue screen of death"). During this time, the system is stopped to prevent data corruption. These errors can be caused by hardware errors, corrupted files, a corrupted file system, or a software glitch.

Even though a stop screen may look intimidating, only a small amount of data on the screen is important in determining the cause of the error. At the top of the screen you will find the error code and parameters. In the middle of the screen is the list of modules that have been successfully loaded and initialized. At the bottom of the screen is a list of modules that are currently on the stack. See Figure 17.8.

Figure 17.7 Dr. Watson utility

Figure 17.8 A typical stop error

You can configure Windows to write a memory dump file each time it generates a kernel STOP error. To make a memory dump file, you need sufficient space on a hard disk partition for the resulting file, which will be as large as your RAM memory. For example, if your system has 256 MB of RAM, you need 256 MB of free disk space.

To configure the Windows to save STOP information to a memory dump file, double-click on the System applet in the Control Panel, click on the Advanced tab, and click on the Startup and Recovery button. Within the Startup/Shutdown tab, mark the Write Debugging Information check box in the Recovery section. You can then specify the file location and name. If the "Overwrite any existing file" option is not checked and there is a file with that name, Windows will not overwrite the file.

Since most of the data in the dump file are useless to most support technicians who examine the file to troubleshoot the cause of the crash (instead, it is aimed at programmers), Windows introduced a new option. This new alternative saves only the Windows kernel information, which contains the state of the system at the time of a crash, active applications, loaded device drivers, and the executing code. A kernel-data-only crash dump is much smaller in size compared with the full dump. To choose the type of kernel memory dump, right-click My Computer and select Properties or double-click the System applet in the Control Panel. From the Advanced tab, click the Startup and Recovery button. See Figure 17.9.

Many of the common stop errors are already listed and explained in Windows server Help files. See Appendix G. Other sources of information on stop errors include Microsoft's website and/or Microsoft Technet for possible solutions. In any case, make sure that the system has the most updated system BIOS and the newest Windows service pack.

17.6 VIRUSES

A **virus** is a program designed to replicate and spread, generally without the knowledge or permission of the user. Computer viruses spread by attaching themselves to other programs or to the boot sector of a disk. When an infected file is executed or accessed or the computer is started with an infected disk, the virus spreads onto the computer. Virus forms differ in that some are cute, some are annoying, and others are disastrous. Some of the disastrous symptoms of a virus include the following:

- Computer fails to boot.
- Disks have been formatted.
- The partitions are deleted or the partition table is corrupt.
- Disks cannot be read.
- Data or entire files are corrupt or are disappearing.

Figure 17.9   Configure the memory dump that occurs during a stop error

- Programs no longer run.
- Files become larger.
- System is slower than normal.
- System has less available memory than it should.
- Intercept information is being sent to and from a device.

If a virus gets on a server, it has the potential to infect every computer on the network. See Table 17.4.

Question: How does a virus spread?

Answer: Because viruses are small programs that are made to replicate themselves, they spread quite easily. For example, you are handed an infected disk or you download a file from the Internet or a bulletin board. When the disk or file is accessed, the virus replicates itself to RAM. When you access any files on your hard drive, the virus again replicates itself to your hard drive. If you shut off your computer, the virus in the RAM will disappear. Unfortunately, since your hard drive is infected, the RAM becomes infected every time you boot from the hard drive. When you insert and access another disk, the disk also becomes infected. You then hand the disk or send an infected file to someone else and the cycle repeats itself.

17.6.1   Types of Viruses

Computer viruses can be categorized into several types:

- Boot sector
- File
- Multipartite
- Macro
- Trojan horse

Table 17.4   Virus facts

Viruses cannot infect a write-protected disk.	Viruses can infect read-only, hidden, and system files.
Viruses do not typically infect a document (except macro viruses).	Viruses typically infect boot sectors and executable files.
Viruses do not infect compressed files.	A file within a compressed file could have been infected before being compressed.
Viruses do not infect computer hardware such as monitors or chips.	Viruses can change your CMOS values causing your computer not to boot
You cannot get a virus simply by being on the Internet or a bulletin board. Unfortunately, this fact is beginning to change, because ActiveX and Java controls are being used by today's web pages	You can download an infected file.

Every logical drive (hard drive partition and floppy disk) has a boot sector with both bootable and nonbootable components. The boot sector contains specific information relating to the formatting of the disk and a small program called the boot program, which loads the operating system files. On hard drives, the first physical sector (side 0, track 0, sector 1) contains the master boot record (MBR) and partition table. The master boot program uses the partition table to find the starting location of the bootable partition (active partition). It then tells the computer to go to the boot sector of the partition and load the boot program. A boot sector virus is transmitted by rebooting the machine from an infected disk. When the boot sector program on the disk is read and executed, the virus goes into memory and infects the hard drive, specifically the boot sector or the master boot program.

File viruses attach themselves to or replace executable files (usually files with the COM or EXE file name extension), but they can also infect SYS, DRV, BIN, OVL, and OVY files. Uninfected programs become infected when they are opened, including from the DOS DIR command; or, the virus simply infects all of the files in the directory from which it was run.

A multipartite virus has the characteristics of both boot sector viruses and file viruses. It may start as a boot sector virus and spread to executable files, or start from an infected file and spread to the boot sector.

A macro (or formula language), which are used in word processing, spreadsheets, and other application programs, is a set of instructions that a program executes on command. Macros group several keystrokes into one command or perform complex menu selections. They simplify redundant or complex tasks. The macro viruses are the newest strain and currently the most common type of virus. Unlike previous viruses, macro viruses are stored in a data document and spread when the infected document is accessed or transferred. Currently, the most vulnerable applications are Microsoft Word and Microsoft Excel. Some macro viruses modify the contents of the document, and they can even cause documents to be sent out via e-mail.

The fifth type of virus is the Trojan horse, which, by definition, is not really a virus because it does not replicate itself. The Trojan horse virus is a program that appears to be legitimate software, such as a game or useful utility. Unfortunately, when you run the Trojan horse and the trigger event occurs, the program will do its damage, such as formatting your hard drive.

Some viruses can be characterized as polymorphic viruses or stealth viruses. A polymorphic virus mutates, or changes its code, so that it cannot be as easily detected. Stealth viruses try to hide themselves by monitoring and intercepting a system's call. For example, when the system seeks to open an infected file, the stealth virus uninfects the file and allows the operating system to open it. When the operating system closes the file, the virus reinfects the file.

Table 17.5 lists sources for more information on viruses: how they work, and how they affect your computer.

17.6.2   Worms

A **worm** is a program or algorithm that replicates itself over a computer network and usually performs malicious actions, such as using up the computer's resources and possibly shutting the system down. Typically, a worm enters the computer because of vulnerabilities in the computer's operating system.

Table 17.5   General information about viruses

Source	URL
Virus information library	http://vil.mcafee.com/default.asp
Virus encyclopedia	http://www.symantec.com/avcenter/vinfodb.html
Virus hoaxes	http://vil.mcafee.com/hoax.asp http://www.symantec.com/avcenter/hoax.html
Virus reference area	http://www.symantec.com/avcenter/refa.html

The Computer Emergency Response Team (CERT) Coordination Center was started in December 1988 by the Defense Advanced Research Projects Agency, which was part of the U.S. Department of Defense, after the Morris Worm disabled about 10% of all computers connected to the Internet. CERT studies Internet security vulnerabilities, provides services to websites that have been attacked, and publishes security alerts. CERT Coordination Center's research activities include the areas of WAN computing and developing improved Internet security. The organization also provides training to incident-response professionals.

CERT website

http://www.cert.org/

Microsoft Baseline Security Analyzer

http://www.microsoft.com/technet/security/tools/tools/mbsahome.asp

Symantec Security Advisory List

http://securityresponse.symantec.com/avcenter/security/Advisories.html

---

17.6.3   Virus Hoaxes

A virus hoax is a letter or e-mail message warning you about a virus that does not exist. For example, the letter or warning may tell you that a certain e-mail message may harm your computer if you open it. In addition, the letter or message usually tells you to forward the letter or e-mail message to your friends, which creates more network traffic.

17.6.4   Antivirus Software

Antivirus software detects and removes viruses and helps protect the computer against viruses. Whichever software package is chosen, it should include a scanner-disinfector and an interceptor-resident monitor. The scanner-disinfector software looks for known virus patterns in RAM, the boot sector, and disk files. If a virus is detected, the software typically attempts to remove the virus. The interceptor-resident monitor is a piece of software that is loaded and remains in the RAM. Every time a disk is accessed or file is read, the interceptor-resident monitor software checks the disk or file for the same virus patterns that the scanner-disinfector software does. In addition, some interceptor-resident monitor software detects viruses within the files as you download them from the Internet or bulletin board.

Unfortunately, scanner-disinfector software has three disadvantages. First, it can detect only viruses that it knows about. Therefore, the antivirus software package must be continually updated. The easiest way to do this is through the Internet. Second, scanner-disinfector software cannot always remove the virus. Therefore, the file may need to be deleted, or a low-level format may need to be performed on the hard drive. Third, even if the scanner-disinfector software succeeds in removing the virus, the file or boot sector may have been damaged. Therefore, the infected file still needs to be deleted or replaced, the boot sector may need to be re-created, partitions may need to be re-created, and low-level format may need to be performed on the disk.

If you think a virus is present even though the interceptor software is installed, boot from a clean write-protected disk. This will ensure that RAM does not contain a virus. Without changing or accessing the hard drive, run an updated virus scanner-disinfector from the floppy disk. If a virus is detected and removed, it is then best to reboot the computer when the scanner-disinfector has finished checking the hard drive. (Note: Also boot from a bootable floppy disk and check the hard drive before installing any antivirus software.)

17.6.5   Protecting Against Viruses

To avoid viruses, remember to take the following precautions:

1. Do not use pirated software, since there is more of a chance of such software having a virus.
2. Treat files downloaded from the Internet and bulletin boards with suspicion.
3. Do not boot from or access a floppy disk of unknown origin.
4. Educate your fellow users.
5. Use an updated antivirus software package that constantly detects viruses.
6. Back up your files on a regular basis.
7. Do not use the Administrative accounts for general use.
8. Do not give more rights than are needed.
9. Keep your operating system up-to-date with patches.

17.6.6   Removing a Virus

If you suspect that you have a virus, immediately check your hard drive and disk with a current antivirus software package. If you think that your hard drive is infected, you need to have a non-infected, write-protected, bootable floppy disk or disks that contain the antivirus software. Boot the computer with the noninfected disk without accessing the hard drive. Next, run the software to check the hard drive. If you think that you have a virus on the floppy disk, boot your computer using the hard drive. If you have been using the possibly infected disk on your computer, you need to first check the hard drive for viruses. Lastly, execute the antivirus program to check the floppy drive.

17.7   WINDOWS PERFORMANCE

Performance is the overall effectiveness of how data move through the system. To be able to improve performance, you must determine the part of the system that is slowing down the throughput; check the following functions:

■ Speed of the processor
■ Speed of the memory
■ Speed of the disk system
■ Speed of the network adapter system

The limiting factor is referred to as the bottleneck of the system.

Sometimes relieving one bottleneck causes another. For example, when there are a relatively small number of clients, a configuration of 256 MB of RAM holds its own. But as the number of clients increases the available cache shrinks and the file server starts to rely heavily on the disk subsystem. Adding RAM will increase the available file cache and let the server get the most out of its single microprocessor. If the microprocessor is saturated, you won't see a significant improvement in performance if you add RAM. If the hard drive is causing the bottleneck and you add a second microprocessor, you only make matters worse by inundating the already overworked disk with more requests. No matter how many micro-processors you add and how much RAM you add, you will not be able to increase the server performance until you replace the disk subsystem with a faster one. Note: When a server becomes overworked, another option is to install another server and move some of the services from one server to another server.

Therefore, the questions are how many microprocessors are enough and how much RAM is enough. Unfortunately, too many factors prevent simple answers. Some of these factors are the number of clients, the type of server and type of services offered by the server, and the type of files being accessed and how they are being accessed. So when first installing a server, perform a best-guess on hardware requirements based on your experience. After the server is installed, keep monitoring the performance of the server to determine if any part of it needs to be upgraded. Most servers have intensive utilities that can help you determine the server's performance and identify bottlenecks. For Windows 2000, it is Performance Monitor and Network Monitor, and for Novell NetWare, it is the Monitor NLM and Novell's Lanalyzer.

When choosing the equipment for a server, do not choose the newest or the fastest equipment. Although you want to choose items that offer good performance, it is very important that you choose items that are reliable and have a good track record. Remember that one of the primary goals of a network is to minimize downtime. So reliability is more important than a little bit more performance.

17.7.1   Processor Performance

If the processor has a CPU utilization of approximately 80%, that means that 80% of the time the processor is actually doing work. If the CPU utilization is constantly at 80% or higher, the processor is working too hard. In this case, you need to upgrade your system to a faster processor, increase the number of processors, or decrease the load of the server.

Symmetric multiprocessing (SMP) means a computer uses two or more microprocessors that share the same memory. If software is written to use multiple microprocessors, several programs can be executed at the same time, or multithreaded applications can be executed faster. A multithreaded application is an application that is broken into several smaller parts that are executed simultaneously. For example, a word processor uses a thread to respond to keys typed on the keyboard to place characters in a document. Other threads are used to check spelling, paginate the document as it is being typed, and spool a document to the printer in the background. The ability of an operating system to use additional microprocessors is known as multiprocessing scalability.

To use multiple processors, each processor needs to use the same speed, cache, and steppings (internal version of the processor). In addition, to take advantage of SMP, operating system must support SMP. Most modern network operating systems support SMP. For Microsoft Windows to support SMP, you need to use a HAL (hardware abstraction layer) and for Linux, you have to reconfigure and recompile the kernel.

17.7.2   Memory Performance

To increase performance of the memory system, you must first make sure that you have plenty of RAM. If you do not have enough memory, your system will use virtual memory more often, which will slow performance significantly. As faster processors and new motherboards are released, new forms of memory are also being released. For example, the current standard for memory is SDRAM, which replaced both EDO and FPDRAM. During the past few years, SDRAM was released in three main speeds: PC-66, PC-100, and PC-133. Recently, SDRAM is being replaced with DDR-SDRAM and RDRAM.

Cache memory is a special ultrafast memory that acts as a buffer between the microprocessor and the slower RAM. Data that are stored in the cache are based on an old computer science principle: If the processor recently referred to a location in memory, it is likely that it will refer to it again in the near future. Using a cache to hold recently used memory values saves the processor from going to memory each time to reload them. Today, level 1 (L1) and level 2 (L2) cache are built into the processor.

Significant improvement has occurred in cache memory on workstations and servers that are working with large data sets, such as large databases and heavy graphics applications. For example, moving from 512-KB L2 cache to a 1-MB L2 cache increases performance from 10% to 25%, depending on the application and load. Intel offers processors aimed at the server market; for example, the Intel Pentium II Xeon processor, Intel Pentium III Xeon processor, and Intel Xeon processor, all of which have a large cache memory. In addition, these processors have features that help monitor system performance.

17.7.3   Disk System Performance

For a server, always choose SCSI over IDE or enhanced IDE (EIDE), SCSI hard drives have a higher bandwidth and reduced latency. SCSI hard drives also use command queuing. Command queuing allows a device to accept multiple commands and execute them in an order that is more efficient rather than the order received. Think of command queuing as driving a bus full of people. You can drive to each person's stop in the order that they entered the bus, or you can try to figure out the best way to drop off the people. For example, if two people live in a nearby area, you would drop them off one after the other. For SCSI hard drives, command queuing increases the performance of computers that are running multitasking operating systems and is ideal for servers. Note: RAID is also a way to increase disk performance.

17.7.4 Network Performance

With system monitoring software, you can analyze the packets that are going in and out of your PC. Network monitoring software, such as Network Monitor (Windows NT, Windows 2000 and Windows Server 2003) and Network Lanalyzer (Novell NetWare), enables you to detect and troubleshoot problems on LANs. With network monitoring software, you can identify network traffic patterns and network problems, such as computers that make many more requests than other computers, and identify unauthorized users on your network. In addition, you can capture frames (packets) directly from the network, and display, filter, save, and print the captured frames so that you can analyze them later. For example, you suspect a card is jabbering (i.e., throwing out garbage packets on the network, using up valuable bandwidth); use the network monitoring software to capture these packets and analyze them to determine the MAC address of the offending link.

17.7.5 Performance Monitor

With Performance Monitor, you can measure the performance of your own computer or other computers on the network. When you first start Performance Monitor, you see only a blank screen. You must select the objects, instances, and counters that you want to monitor. An object is any Windows system component that possesses a set of measurable property. It can be a physical part of the system such as the processor, RAM, disk subsystem, or network interface; a logical component such as a disk volume; or a software element such as a process or a thread. An instance shows how many occurrences of an object are available in the system. A counter represents one measurable characteristic of an object. See Figure 17.10.

The computer is centered around the processor. Therefore, the performance of the computer is greatly affected by the performance of the processor. See Table 17.6.

RAM is also an important factor in PC performance. You can typically increase PC performance by adding more RAM. The seven best RAM counters are listed in Table 17.7.

Figure 17.10 Adding counters to the Performance Monitor

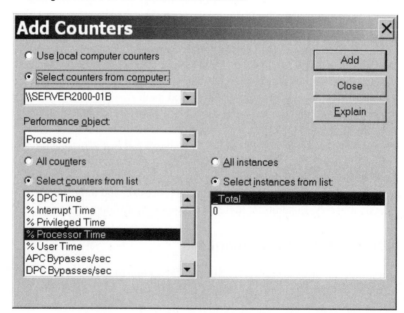

Table 17.6 Specifics of a processor

Processor Counter	Description
Processor: % Processor Time	% Processor Time measures how busy the processor is. Although the processor may jump to 100% processor usage, overall average is still important. If the processor is at 80% all the time, you should upgrade the processor (creating a faster processor or adding a number of processors) or move some of the services to other systems. If you want to see what percentage of the processor utilization each process is using, utilize the Task Manager. Do not use 3-D screen savers, because they can consume 90% of the processor utilization. Instead, use a blank screen saver.
Processor: Interrupts/Second	Interrupts/Second measures how many hardware interrupts per second are occurring. A server that is running 100 interrupts/second can be normal. If the counter is increasing without a corresponding increase in the server load, then the problem may be due to hardware. You should always view this counter when you load a new device driver to make sure that it functions properly. A poorly written device driver can cause huge increases in interrupt activity.
System: Processor Queue Length	The number of threads indicated by the processor queue length is a significant indicator of system performance, because each thread requires a certain number of processor cycles. If demand exceeds supply, long processor queues develop and the system response suffers. Therefore, a sustained processor queue length greater than 2 on a single processor generally indicates that the processor is a bottleneck. This counter is always 0 unless you are monitoring a thread counter as well.

Table 17.7 Best RAM counters

Memory Counter	Description
Memory: Available Bytes	Available Bytes measures the amount of available virtual memory. It is calculated by summing space on the zeroed, free, and standby memory lists. Free memory is ready for use. Zeroed memory involves pages of memory filled with zeros to prevent later processes from seeing data used by a previous process. Standby memory is removed from a process's working set (physical memory) on route to disk, but is still available to be recalled. If it is less than 4 MB, consider adding more RAM.
Memory: Page Faults/Sec	A page fault occurs when a process attempts to access a virtual memory page that is not available in its working set in RAM. Hard page faults must be retrieved from disk, which greatly slows performance. Soft page faults are those that can be retrieved from the standby list, and therefore do not require disk I/O. If this value is high (20) or increasing, it is a sign that you need to add physical RAM to your server.
Memory: Cache Bytes	Cache Bytes monitors the size of the file system cache. When memory is scarce, the system trims the cache; when memory is ample, the system enlarges the cache. Compare this with general memory availability. In addition, track how small the cache gets, and how often that occurs, because this information is useful when associating the size of the cache with its performance.
Memory: Pages/sec	Pages/sec indicates the number of requested pages not immediately available in RAM but read from the disk or written to the disk to make room in RAM for other pages. If your system experiences a high rate of hard page faults, the value for Pages/sec can be high.
Memory: Committed Bytes	Committed Bytes is the amount of committed virtual memory, in bytes. Committed memory is physical memory for which space has been reserved on the disk paging file in case it needs to be written back to disk. This counter displays the last observed value only; it is not an average.
Paging File: % Usage	% Usage of the Paging file is the percentage of space allocated to the page file (virtual memory) that is actually in use. To calculate how much more RAM to add to a server to minimize paging, multiply the percentage by the size of the page file.
Paging File: % Usage Peak	% Usage Peak is the highest percentage usage of the page file. If this value frequently exceeds 90%, allocate more space to the page file and possibly more RAM. A 100% usage peak indicates that the server has, at least momentarily, run out of both physical and virtual memory.

Table 17.8   Hard drive counters

Disk Counter	Description
PhysicalDisk: % Disk Time	% Disk Time measures the percentage of elapsed time that a disk drive is actually occupied in reading data from and writing data to the disk. A value greater than 90% indicates that the disk is the bottleneck.
PhysicalDisk: % Avg. Disk Queue Length	% Avg. Disk Queue Length is the average number of read requests and writes queued for the disk in question. A sustained average higher than 2 queue length indicates that the disk is being over utilized.
LogicalDisk: % Free Disk Space	Free Disk Space reports the percentage of unallocated disk space to the total usable space on the logical volume.
LogicalDisk: Avg. Disk Bytes/Transfer and PhysicalDisk: Avg. Disk Bytes/Transfer	The Avg. Disk Bytes/Transfer measures the size of I/O operations. The disk is efficient if it transfers large amounts of data relatively quickly.
LogicalDisk: Avg. Disk sec/Transfer and PhysicalDisk: Avg. Disk sec/Transfer	Avg. Disk sec/Transfer indicates how fast data are being moved (in seconds). It measures the average time of each data transfer, regardless of the number of bytes read or written. A high value for this counter might mean that the system is retrying requests due to lengthy queuing or, less commonly, disk failures.
LogicalDisk: Disk Bytes/sec and PhysicalDisk: Disk Bytes/sec	Disk Bytes/sec indicates the rate at which bytes are transferred and is the primary measure of disk throughput.
LogicalDisk: Disk Transfers/sec and PhysicalDisk: Disk Transfers/sec	Disk Transfers/sec measures disk utilization by indicating the number of read and writes completed per second, regardless of how much data they involve. If the value exceeds 50 transfers/sec (per physical disk in the case of a striped set), then a bottleneck might be developing.

Table 17.9   Network interface counters

Network Interface Counter	Description
Network Interface: Output Queue Length	Output Queue Length indicates the length of the output packet queue. The value should be low. Queues of one or two items constitute satisfactory performance; longer queues indicate the adapter is waiting for the network and cannot keep pace with server requests.
Network Interface: Bytes Total/Sec	Bytes Total/Sec measures the rate that bytes, including data and framing characters, are sent and received on the network interface. If the value is close to or matching the network capacity, the network may be saturated.
Network Interface: Packets Outbound Errors	Packets Outbound Errors is the number of outbound packets that could not be sent because of errors. If the amount of errors is increasing, then more sophisticated troubleshooting tools are needed to determine the exact problem.
Network Interface: Packet Received Errors	Packet Received Errors is the number of inbound packets that had to be discarded because they contained errors that prevented them from being delivered to the proper destination protocol stack.

One task of a server is to provide file access, thus making a hard drive system an important factor in server performance. Important hard drive counters are listed in Table 17.8.

By default, the system is set to collect physical drive data. Logical drive data are not collected by default—you must enable them specifically. To enable the disk counters, execute the DISKPERF –Y command at the Command prompt and restart the computer.

The network interface counters measure the performance of the network interface cards. The more important counters are listed in Table 17.9.

Figure 17.11   Chart view using the Performance Monitor

Figure 17.12   Report view using the Performance Monitor

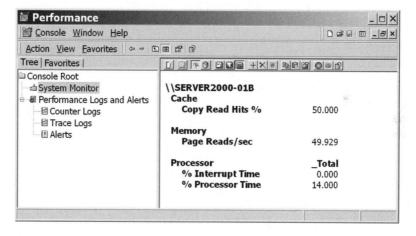

There are several views in Performance Monitor, including chart and report. A real-time activity chart displays the value of the counter over time in a graph. Charts help to investigate why a computer or application is slow or inefficient, to continuously monitor the system to find intermittent performance problems, and to discover why the capacity of a subsystem needs to be increased. See Figure 17.11. A report view allows you to display constantly changing counter and instance values for selected objects. See Figure 17.12.

To add counters, right-click the chart or report pane (right pane) and select the Add Counters option. After you have identified the counters you want to monitor, save the information to reuse later. To save chart settings, right-click the chart or report pane and select the Save As option.

The Performance Monitor supports three types of logs: counter logs, trace logs, and alert logs. **Counter logs** record data from local or remote computers about hardware usage and system service activity. **Trace logs** are event-driven and record monitored data such as disk I/O or page faults. When a traced event occurs, it is recorded in the log. **Alert logs** take trace logs one step further in that they monitor counters, wait for them to exceed user-defined tolerances, and then log the event. You can even set up the alert log to send a message or run an application when a particular value is exceeded.

To create a log, click on the Performance Logs and Alert in the left pane of Performance Monitor, and open the folder for the type of log that you want. Right-click the empty space in the Details window and choose an option from Creating a New Log from the pop-up menu that appears. If you save the file as a binary file (*.BLG), you can use System Monitor to open the log and view it later. If you save the file as a comma-delimited file (*.CSV) or a tab-delimited file (*.TSV), you can open it with Excel to perform your own data analysis.

17.8   MONITORING THE NETWORK

In Windows NT, Windows 2000 and Windows Server 2003, the network monitoring software is Network Monitor. **Network Monitor** reads all data that are transferred over a network at any given time through a network card and passes the data to a temporary capture file. See Figure 17.13. Each frame or packet read contains the source address of the computer that sent the message, the destination address of the computer that receives the frame, the header information of the computer that receives the frame, and the data being sent to the destination computer. See Figure 17.14. To make it easier to analyze the data, isolate certain information by using filters, depending on the basis of source and destination addresses, protocols, protocol properties, and pattern offset. You also can have Network Monitor respond to specific conditions as soon as it detects them and perform specified actions such as starting an executable file.

When analyzing the packets on a network, the number of packets can be quite overwhelming. Therefore, use filters to isolate only the material that you want. Table 17.10 shows the filter items. See Figure 17.15. Whereas capture filters are limited to four address filter expressions, display filters can also utilize AND, OR, and NOT Logic.

To capture all traffic from PREGAN-DESK's computer, except the traffic from CBROWN-DESK computer, use the following capture filter address section:

> include PREGAN-DESK <- - - -> Any
> exclude PREGAN-DESK <- - - -> CBROWN-DESK

The Network Monitor program that comes with Windows servers is a limited software package that only captures the packets that are sent to or from the computer that is running the Network Monitor program. To capture all frames detected on the network, use a network adapter card that supports promiscuous mode and the full version of Network Monitor, which is available with Microsoft Systems Management Server. Promiscuous mode is a state in which a network adapter card copies all frames that pass over the network, regardless of the destination address to a local buffer.

17.9   REDUNDANT NETWORK CARDS AND HUBS

To ensure that the link that connects to your network has fault tolerance, you have several options:

- Adaptive load balancing (ALB)
- Adapter fault tolerance (AFT)
- Link aggregation

Adaptive load balancing (ALB) technology can increase server bandwidth up to 800 Mbits/s over Fast Ethernet, or 8 Gbits/s over Gigabit Ethernet, by automatically balancing traffic across as many as eight network adapters. Essentially, each additional adapter adds another link of 100 Mbits/s or 1000 Mbits/s to the network. Once ALB is configured, all outgoing server traffic is balanced across the adapter team. Incoming traffic is carried by a single adapter. In most environments, this is a highly effective solution, since server traffic is primarily outbound. The distribution of traffic among the adapters is automatic, so there is no need to segment or reconfigure the network.

Figure 17.13   Network Monitor

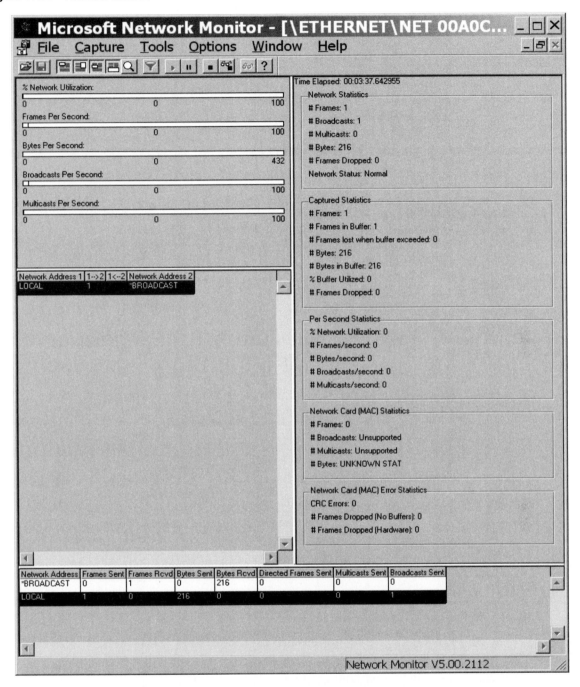

The existing IP address of the server is shared by all of the adapters in the server, and traffic is always balanced between them. All of the adapters in a team must be connected to a switch. Note: All adapters in the team should be the same speed. They can be connected to a single switch or hub, or to two or more switches or hubs, as long as they are on the same network segment. The teamed adapters provide automatic emergency backup links to the network. If one server link goes down due to a broken cable, a bad switch port, or a failed adapter, the other adapter(s) automatically accepts the additional load. There is no interruption in server operation. Some software and drivers also support a network alert to inform IT staff of the problem.

If two or more adapters are installed, adapter fault tolerance (AFT) can be configured to establish an automatic backup link between the server and the network. Should the primary link fail, the

Figure 17.14   Viewing network packets using Network Monitor

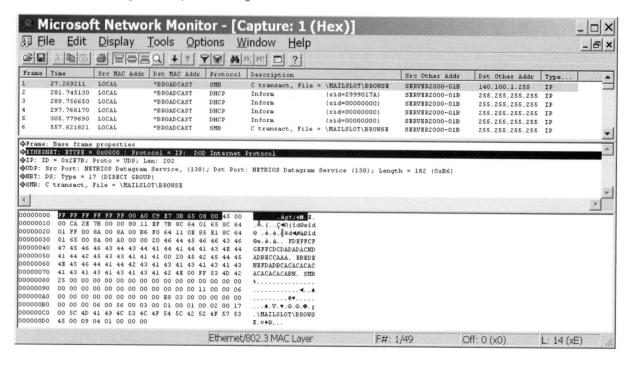

Table 17.10   Network Monitor filters

Filter Item	Description
Protocol	Specifies the protocols or protocol properties
Address Filter (default is ANY <- -> ANY)	Specifies the computer addresses on which you want to capture data. Arrows specify the traffic direction you want to monitor. The INCLUDE or EXCLUDE keyword indicates how Network Monitor should respond to a frame that meets a filter's specifications.
Property	Specifies property instances that match your display criterion

secondary link kicks in within milliseconds, in a manner that is transparent to applications and users. The redundant link that AFT establishes between the server and the network includes a redundant adapter, a cable, and hub or switch port connection. If there is any problem along the primary link, the secondary link immediately takes over. AFT can also initiate a network alert. When the primary link is fixed, the system automatically reverts back to the higher-performance link.

Unlike most redundant-link technologies, AFT supports mixed-speed teaming using any combination of adapters. With this capability, a relatively inexpensive 100-Mbits/s backup link can be used to safeguard a high-speed Gigabit Ethernet connection. The inexpensive backup may not be able to support the full traffic load as effectively, but it allows business critical applications to stay online until the higher-speed link is fixed.

Link aggregation, also referred to as trunking, is a technique that allows parallel physical links between switches or between a switch and a server to be used simultaneously, thereby multiplying

Figure 17.15   Configuring filtering for Network Monitor

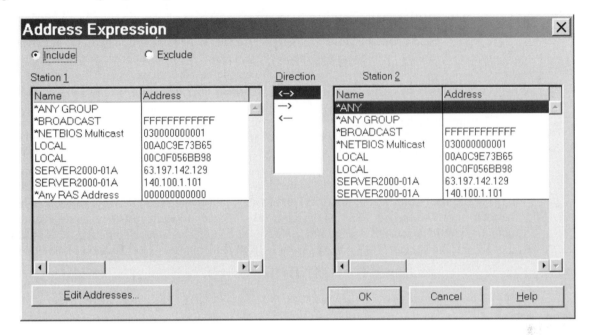

the bandwidth between the devices, and to provide fault tolerance. To meet customer requirements for this type of functionality, several companies support proprietary link aggregation schemes. In 2000, IEEE released 802.3ad as an industry standard for link aggregation. This standard allows for balancing traffic (up to 8 network cards and 16 Gbits/s full duplex of bandwidth) among multiple switches from a single server. Unlike ALB and AFT, link aggregation requires a switch that supports it.

PCI HotPlug and Active PC developed by Compaq and IBM, respectively, allow the adapter to be replaced without interrupting network service. If an adapter fails, AFT automatically moves server traffic onto the redundant link and generates a network alert. Both of these products enable you to replace the failed adapter without bring down the server.

17.10   CLUSTERING

Windows 2000 and Windows Server 2003 have many features to assist in overcoming failure points, as was shown in Table 17.1. One such feature is clustering. **Clustering** means connecting two or more computers, known as nodes, in such a way that they behave like a single computer. Clustering is used for parallel processing, load balancing, and fault tolerance. The computers that form the cluster are physically connected by cable and are logically connected by cluster software. As far as the user is concerned, the cluster appears as a single system.

Network load balancing clusters distribute client connections over multiple servers. Internet clients access the cluster using a single IP address (or a set of addresses for a multihomed host). The clients are unable to distinguish the cluster from a single server. Server programs do not identify that they are running in a cluster; however, a network load balancing cluster differs significantly from a single host running a single server program, because it provides uninterrupted service even if a cluster host fails. The cluster also can respond more quickly to client requests than a single host (for load-balanced ports).

In a **fail-over** configuration, two or more computers serve as functional backups for each other. If one should fail, the other automatically takes over the processing that is normally performed by the failed system, thereby eliminating downtime. If the server is to share common data, the cluster servers are connected to at least one shared SCSI bus with a storage device connected to both servers, and at least one storage device that is not shared. Fail-over clusters are highly desirable for supporting mission-critical applications.

Storage area network (SAN) is a high-speed subnetwork of shared storage devices. A SAN's architecture works in a way that makes all storage devices available to all servers on a LAN. If an individual application in a server cluster fails (but the node does not), the Cluster service will typically try to restart the application on the same node. If that fails, it moves the application's resources and restarts them on another node of the server cluster. This process is called fail-over. The Cluster Administrator can use a graphical console to set various recovery policies, such as dependencies between applications, whether to restart an application on the same server, and whether to automatically rebalance, or fail back, workloads when a failed server comes back online.

Network-attached storage (NAS) is hard disk storage that is set up with its own network address, rather than being attached to a department computer that is serving applications to a network's workstation users. By removing storage access and its management from the department server, both application programming and files can be served faster because they are not competing for the same processor resources. The network-attached storage device is attached to a local area network (typically, an Ethernet network) and assigned an IP address. File requests are mapped by the main server to the NAS file server. Network-attached storage consists of hard disk storage, including multidisk RAID systems, and software for configuring and mapping file locations to the network-attached device. NAS can be part of a SAN. Although low cost may be reason to choose a NAS, NAS devices are not upgradeable.

SUMMARY

1. One primary job of the administrator is to deal with disasters and to plan ahead to minimize the frequency and degree of failures.

2. Data stored on a computer or stored on the network are vital to the users and probably the company.

3. A backup of a system is a copy of all data and/or programs.

4. The best method for data protection and recovery is backup, backup, backup.

5. The System State data are a collection of system-specific data that can be backed up and restored, and include the registry, COM+ class registration database, system boot files, Certificate Services database, Active Directory directory services database (domain controller), and SYSVOL directory (domain controllers).

6. The catalog is a summary of the files and folders that have been saved in a backup set.

7. If you have other domain controllers, they have replicas of the Active Directory, and if you have distributed directories (file replication), the Active Directory data and replicated directories would automatically be updated by the other servers.

8. If Windows cannot load or start, accessing certain tools may help you solve the problem. They are the Advanced Boot menu, Windows Recovery console, and emergency repair disk.

9. If you press F8 while the Windows Boot menu is displayed, it will display the Advanced Boot menu.

10. Using the Enable VGA mode is another option if the wrong video driver is loaded and you need to force the video system into 640 × 480 with 16 colors, and into the Last Known Good Configuration to start Windows using the last saved configuration, which is stored in the registry.

11. The Directory Service Restore mode is a special version of safe mode that loads all drivers and services, and allows

you to restore the Active Directory of the domain controller from backup media.

12. To monitor the process of a server's boot from another server using a serial cable, use the Debugging mode.

13. If your computer fails to boot even in safe mode, the best tool to use is the Recovery console.

14. The Recovery console provides a command-line interface that will let you repair system problems using a limited set of command-line commands, including enabling or disabling services, repairing a corrupted master boot record, and reading and writing data on a local drive (FAT, FAT32, or NTFS).

15. The emergency repair disk (ERD) contains information about your current Windows system settings. You can use this disk to repair your computer if it will not start or your system files are damaged or erased.

16. If you have performed the emergency repair process and the computer still does not operate normally, then use the Windows Setup CD to perform an in-place upgrade over the existing installation.

17. A program error (user mode) or stop error (kernel mode) signifies that something unexpected has happened within the Windows environment.

18. Dr. Watson is a program that starts automatically when a program error occurs, detects information about the system and the program failure, and records the information into a log file.

19. A virus is a program designed to replicate and spread, generally without the knowledge or permission of the user.

20. Performance is the overall effectiveness of how data move through the system. To improve performance, you must determine the part of the system that is slowing the throughput.

21. Network monitoring software enables you to detect and troubleshoot problems on LANs.

QUESTIONS

1. The most important part of the computer is the
   _____ .
   a. microprocessor   c. RAM
   b. hard drive   d. data

2. The best method for protecting data is _____ .
   a. RAID   c. a surge protector
   b. backup, backup,   and UPS
      backup   d. antivirus software

3. Which is ideal for backing up an entire hard drive?
   a. zip drive   c. RAID
   b. second hard drive   d. tape drive

4. After backing up a drive, you should occasionally
   _____ .
   a. restore a nonessential file to the hard drive
   b. reformat the hard drive
   c. shut down the system
   d. reformat the tape

5. The archive attribute indicates whether a file is backed up.
   Which one of the following backups does not shut off the
   archive attribute?
   a. full   c. differential
   b. incremental   d. none of the above

6. Which backup method requires you to provide the full
   backup and a tape for each day you want to go back and
   restore?
   a. incremental   c. full
   b. differential   d. daily

7. How do you save the local registry using Windows NT
   Backup?
   a. Type "NTBACKUP /R" at the Command prompt.
   b. Select the drive and directory containing the registry
      and run Windows NT Backup.
   c. Select the drive containing the registry, check the
      Backup Local Registry box, and run Windows
      Backup.
   d. Select the System State using the Windows Backup
      program and run the Backup program.

8. You have modified some value entries in the registry. Now when you reboot the computer, Windows 2000
   will not start. What is the best way to correct the
   problem?
   a. Boot from the Last Known Good Configuration.
   b. Start the computer from a boot disk and copy Ntldr,
      Ntdetect.com, Ntoskrnl.exe, and Bootsect.dos from a
      coworker's machine.
   c. Start the computer from a boot disk and restore the
      registry from tape backup.
   d. Start the computer from the emergency repair disk
      and let Windows NT automatically attempt to correct
      the problem.

9. Which of the following does the System State include?
   (Choose all that apply.)
   a. registry   d. WINNT folder
   b. system boot files   e. SYSVOL directory
   c. Active Directory files

10. Your Windows 2000 Server has encountered a series
    of stop errors. How do you configure Windows

2000 to save stop error information to a memory dump
file?
a. Specify the recovery option in Dr. Watson.
b. Specify the recovery option in Performance
   Monitor.
c. Specify the proper recovery option on the
   Startup/Shutdown tab in System Properties.
d. Specify the recovery option in Server Manager.

11. Pat wants to use Performance Monitor to view log-
    ical disk object counters on his computer from a
    remote machine. What operations must Pat perform on
    his machine to allow him to monitor these counters
    remotely?
    a. Pat must install Network Monitor Agent on his
       computer.
    b. Pat must run the DiskPerf utility on his computer with
       the −Y switch.
    c. Pat must install Network Monitor Agent on his
       computer and run the DiskPerf utility on his computer
       with the −Y switch.
    d. Pat is not required to do anything more. Simply
       installing Windows NT Server on his machine is
       sufficient to allow other machines to monitor his
       logical disk counters remotely.

12. Which one of the following applications is best suited for
    producing a baseline of all network activities?
    a. Network Monitor   c. Performance Monitor
    b. ARP command   d. TRACERT command

13. Which application is best suited for identifying the com-
    puters on a network that are contributing most to network
    traffic?
    a. Network Monitor   c. Performance Monitor
    b. Packet Monitor   d. Server Manager

14. Your Windows 2000 Server is suffering from poor per-
    formance due to excessive paging. What is the best way to
    alleviate the excessive paging on your server?
    a. Add RAM to your server.
    b. Implement a disk management strategy on your server
       and create multiple paging files.
    c. Upgrade the disk drive containing the paging file to
       one with a faster data access speed.
    d. Upgrade the CPU on your server.

15. You want to use Network Monitor to capture all frames
    being sent from a computer named SERVER1 on your
    network. How must you specify the address inclusion line
    when designing your capture filter?
    a. INCLUDE NetBIOS= =SERVER1
    b. INCLUDE SMB= =SERVER1
    c. INCLUDE ANY <----> SERVER1
    d. INCLUDE SERVER1 <----> ANY
    e. INCLUDE SERVER1----> ANY

16. In planning for the expansion of your company's net-
    work, you want to capture and decode TCP/IP packets
    on your Windows 2000 Server computer. What must
    you use?
    a. ICMP   c. Performance Monitor
    b. Network Monitor   d. UPD

17. Working at his Windows 2000 Server, Pat wants to accumulate and view the TCP/IP protocol statistics on the server. What should he use?
    a. ARP
    b. NBTSTAT
    c. Network Monitor
    d. SNMP
18. What would you call a hard disk assembly that connects directly to the network and is assigned an IP address?
    a. storage area network
    b. network-attached storage
    c. cluster
    d. RAID-6
19. What are the two types of clustering offered by Windows?
    a. fail-over clustering
    b. load balancing clustering
    c. start-up synchronizing clustering
    d. RAID clustering

HANDS-ON EXERCISES

Exercise 1: Performing a Backup and Restore

For this exercise, you will need a blank, formatted floppy disk.

Using the Backup Wizard

1. Log in as the Administrator.
2. On your D drive, create a Data directory.
3. From the C:\WINNT\WEB\WALLPAPER folder, copy all files to the D:\DATA folder.
4. To start the Microsoft Backup program, click on the Start button, select the Programs option, select the Accessories option, select the System Tools option, and select the Backup option.
5. At the Welcome to Windows Backup and Recovery Tools page, click on the Backup Wizard button. Click on the Next button.
6. Select the "Backup selected files, drives, network data" option and click on the Next button.
7. In the Items Backup page, find the DATA folder in the C drive. Click on the Data Drive to show its contents in the box to the right. To select the DATA folder to be backed up, put a checkmark in the box next to the DATA folder. Click on the Next button.
8. In a real-world network, you would typically back up to a tape drive. Because many schools do not have tape drives for every student nor do students have them at home, we will back up to the floppy drive. Therefore, for the Backup Media or File Name text box, keep the A:\BACKUP.BKT and click on the Next button.
9. Before clicking on the Finish button, click on the Advanced button.
10. Open the "Select the type of backup operation to perform" text box and note the options. When done, choose the Normal option and click on the Next button.
11. Select the Verify Data after Backup option and click on the Next button.
12. If the archive media already contains a backup, we will replace the data on media with this backup. Therefore, select this option and click on the Next button.
13. Accept the default labels and click on the Next button.
14. Keep the default of doing the backup now and click the Next button.
15. Insert the blank floppy disk in drive A.
16. Click on the Finish button.
17. When the backup is complete, click on the Close button.
18. When a backup is done, you would typically remove the tape (or disk) and label the name of the backup. It also is recommended to log the backup in a table or notebook or on the disk label. Therefore, remove the disk and write Backup—Data Folder and today's date on the label of the disk.

Using the Restore Wizard

19. Delete the Date folder on the C drive.
20. Back at the Welcome to the Windows Backup and Recovery Tools page, click on the Restore Wizard button. Click on the Next button.
21. Note that because of the catalogs, Windows remembers the backups that were done. Therefore, click on the + sign next to File, click on the next plus sign, and put a checkmark for the C drive. Click on the Next button.
22. Before clicking on the Finish button, click on the Advanced button. This is where you can specify the files to be restored to a different location, if desired. Click on the Next button.
23. In this case, since we no longer have a Data folder, it does not matter which option we choose. Therefore, keep the default option and click on the Next button.
24. Since we have no system or security information to restore, click on the Next button.
25. Click on the Finish button.

26. Click on the OK button to restore from the Default file.
27. Click on the Close button.

Using the Backup Program without the Wizards

28. Click on the Backup tab.
29. To back up the entire C drive, click on the checkbox next to the C drive.
30. Note that while the System State (listed after the drives) is on the C drive, it is not considered normal data. Therefore, it was not included, so select the System State to be backed up.
31. Open the Tools menu and select the Options option. Click the OK button.
32. Click the Backup program.
33. At the bottom of the screen you will find the Backup Media or File Name text box. Type in M:\Backup.bkf in the text box and click on the Start Backup button.
34. Leave the defaults and click the Start Backup button.
35. After the backup is done, click on the Close button.
36. Click on the Restore tab. Note the backups have already been completed as listed by the catalogs on the system.
37. Double-click the first backup listed in the right pane. Double-click the C drive listed in the right pane. Double-click the Data folder listed in the right pane.
38. On the left pane, deselect the Data folder. On the right pane, select the first file listed.
39. Open the Tools menu and select the Options option. On the Restore tab, select "Always replace the file on my computer." Click the OK button.
40. Click on the Start Restore button.
41. Click on the OK button to confirm.
42. Insert the floppy disk from the original backup. Since we did the backup on the A drive, use the Browse button to find the backup file there.
43. After the backup file is selected, click on the OK button to close the Enter Backup File Name dialog box.
44. When the restore is complete, click on the Close button.

Re-creating a Catalog

45. In the Microsoft Backup program, click on the Restore tab.
46. Right-click each of the catalogs listed in the right pane and select the Delete Catalog option.
47. To re-create the catalog, open the Tools menu and select the Catalog a Backup File option.
48. Insert the original backup disk in drive A.
49. Use the Browse button to select the backup file in the A drive. Click the OK button to close the Backup File Name dialog box. Remember, if this is a large tape, the process can take some time.

Exercise 2: Scheduling Backup Jobs

1. Start the Microsoft Backup program and click the Scheduled Jobs tab.
2. To start the Backup Wizard, double-click on today's date in the calendar. Click on the Next button.
3. Select the "Back up selected files, drives, or network data" option and click on the Next button.
4. Select the C:\DATA DIRECTORY. Click on the Next button.
5. Keep the default Backup Media or File Name of the A:\Backup.bkt, and click on the Next button.
6. Keep the default type of backup operation to perform and click on the Next button.
7. On the How to Back Up page, select the Verify Data after Backup option and click on the Next button.
8. Select the "Replace the data on the media with this backup" option and click on the Next button.
9. On the Backup Label page, click on the Next button.
10. If it asks for the Set Account Information dialog box, provide a user account and password and click on the OK button. You can use the Administrator account.
11. On the When to Back Up page, select the Later option, provide the job name of Test, and select the Set Schedule button.
12. On the Scheduled Task option, select the Daily option. Keep the Default Start Time at 12:00 a.m. and the Scheduled Task Daily at every 1 day.
13. Click on the Advanced button. This is where you would specify the start and end dates and how often you want to repeat the task. Click on the Cancel button.
14. Click on the OK button.
15. At the When to Back Up page, click on the Next button.
16. Click on the Finish button.

17. Change the time to 11:58 p.m.
18. Wait 3 minutes and check if the backup is performed.
19. Close the Microsoft Backup program.
20. Reset the clock to its correct time.

Exercise 3: Creating and Using ERD Disks

Create an Emergency Repair Disk

1. Open the Backup program.
2. On the Tools menu, click the Create an Emergency Repair Disk button. Or, use the Emergency Repair Disk Wizard.
3. Insert a blank, formatted floppy disk into the drive. Mark the checkbox to back up the copy of the registry and click on the OK button.
4. Click on the OK button when the disk has been created.
5. Label as Emergency Repair Disk and store in a safe place.

Using the Emergency Repair Disk

6. If you have a computer with a bootable CD-ROM drive, insert the Windows Setup CD. If not, boot with the first installation floppy disk.
7. When the text-based part of Setup begins, follow the prompts and choose the Repair or Recover option by pressing R.
8. When prompted, insert the Windows Setup CD in the appropriate drive.
9. When prompted, choose the Emergency Repair Process by pressing R.
10. When prompted, choose the Fast Repair option by pressing F.
11. Follow the instructions on the screen. When prompted, insert the emergency repair disk in the appropriate drive.
12. During the repair process, missing or corrupted files are replaced with files from the Windows CD or from the *systemroot*\Repair folder on the system partition. Be sure to follow the instructions on the screen; you may want to write the names of files that are detected as faulty or incorrect to help you diagnose how the system was damaged.
13. If the repair was successful, allow the process to complete; it will restart the computer. The restarting of the computer indicates that replacement files were successfully copied to the hard disk.

Exercise 4: Windows Recovery Console

1. Insert the Windows Setup CD into your CD-ROM drive.
2. At the Command prompt, switch to your CD-ROM drive, and then type the following:

   \I386\WINNT32.EXE /CMDCONS

3. When it asks if you want to install the Recovery console, click on the Yes button.
4. Click OK when the setup is complete.
5. Restart your computer and select the Recovery Console option from the Boot menu.
6. When it asks which Windows installation would you like to enter, select the number listed next to the C:\WINNT directory and pass the Enter key. When it asks you for the Administrator password, type in the password and press the Enter key.
7. At the C:\WINNT> Command prompt, execute the Help command. Press the space bar to go back to the prompt.
8. Type in the DIR command. Keep pressing the space bar until you return to the Command prompt.
9. At the Command prompt, execute the FIXBOOT command. When it asks if you are sure, type in a Y and press the Enter key.
10. At the Command prompt, execute the LISTSVC command. Keep pressing the space bar until you return to the Command prompt.
11. At the Command prompt, execute the EXIT command to reboot the computer.

Exercise 5: Performance Monitor

1. Start the Performance console from the Administrative Tools.
2. Right-click the right pane and select the Add Counters option.

3. The % Performance Time option is already selected, so click on the Explain button.
4. Click on the Add button to add % Performance Time Counter to Performance Monitor.
5. Select the Interrupts/sec and click on the Add button.
6. Select the Cache for the Performance Object. Select the Copy Read Hits % from the Counters list and click on the Add button.
7. Select the Paging File for the Performance Object. Select the % Usage from the Counters list and click on the Add button.
8. Select the PhysicalDisk for the Performance Object. Select the % Disk Time from the Counters list and click on the Add button.
9. Click on the Close button.
10. Start the Pinball game and play for 1 minute. Observe the graph.
11. Right-click on the graph and select the Histogram option. Click on the OK button.
12. Play the Pinball game for 1 minute. Observe the histograph.
13. Right-click the graph and select the Report option. Click on the OK button.
14. Play the Pinball game for 1 minute. Observe the report.
15. Close the Pinball game.
16. In the left pane, right-click the Counter Logs. In the New Log Setting dialog box, type in Log1 and click the OK button.
17. Click the Add button and add the % Processor Time Counter.
18. Click the Close button. Click the OK button.
19. Start the Pinball game and play for 1 minute.
20. Right-click the Log1 option in the right pane, and select the Stop option.
21. Click the System Monitor option in the left pane.
22. Right-click the chart and select the Properties option.
23. In the Source tab, click the Browse button and open the C:\PERFLOGS\LOG1_000001.blg file. Click the OK button.
24. Add the % Processor Time Counter.
25. Right-click the Log1 from the left pane of the Performance console and select the Properties option.
26. In the Log Files tab, change the log file type to Text file—CSV. Click on the OK button.
27. Right-click the Log1 from the left pane of the Performance console and select the Start option.
28. Start the Pinball game and play for 1 minute.
29. Right-click the Log1 from the left pane of the Performance console and select the Stop option.
30. If you have access to Microsoft Excel, view the LOG1_000001.CSV file that is located in the C:\PERFLOGS folder.

Exercise 6: Network Monitor

Installing Network Monitor

1. Start the Add/Remove Programs applet in the Control Panel.
2. Click the Add/Remove Windows Components button. Click on the Management and Monitoring Tools option and then click the Details button. Select the Network Monitor Tools and click on the OK button. Click on the Next button and install the Network Monitor software. Click on the Finish button.
3. Close the Add/Remove Programs and Control Panel.

Using Network Monitor

4. In Network Monitor, open the Capture menu and select the Start option.
5. Click the Start button and select the Run option. In the Open text box, type in \\Server2000-XXx to access your partner's computer.
6. In the Network Monitor program, open the Capture menu and select the Stop option.
7. Open the Capture menu and select the Display Captured Data option.
8. Scroll the list of captured frames and view the addresses that are listed in the Src MAC Addr and Dst MAC Addr columns.
9. View the protocols that are listed in the Protocol column.
10. Select a frame and double-click on it.

UNIT IV

ADVANCED NETWORK TOPICS

CHAPTER 18

Understanding WAN Technology

Topics Covered in This Chapter

Introduction

Chapters 3 and 4 briefly described a WAN and the concept of a router. In this chapter we look at the WAN technology that is used to link individual computers or entire networks that cover a relatively broad geographical area. These connections are usually through telephone companies or some other common carrier. Whereas LANs typically are multiple-point connections, WANs are typically made of multiple point-to-point connections.

Objectives

- List the characteristics, requirements, and appropriate situations for WAN connection services, including X.25, ISDN, Frame Relay, and ATM.
- Explain the differences between circuit switching and packet switching.
- Given a scenario, recommend the type of technology that should be used.
- Compare and contrast permanent point-to-point lines and leased lines.

- Compare and contrast cell relay with packet switching.
- Explain how SONET and SDH relate to ATM.
- List and define the three implementations of ATM.
- Compare and contrast xDSL and T1 lines.
- Compare and contrast wireless technology and wire technology.

18.1   DATA SWITCHING TECHNIQUES

Large wide area networks (WANs) can have multiple paths that link source with destination devices, switching information as it travels through the various communication channels. The data switching techniques consist of circuit switching and packet switching.

18.1.1   Circuit Switching

The **circuit switching** technique connects the sender with the receiver via a single path for the duration of a conversation. Once a connection is established, a dedicated path exists (i.e., always consumes network capacity) between both ends, even when there is no active transmission taking place, such as when a caller is put on hold. Once the connection has been made, the destination device acknowledges that it is ready to carry on a transfer. When the conversation is complete, the connection is terminated. See Figure 18.1. Therefore, circuit switching networks are sometimes called connection-oriented networks. Examples of circuit switching include phone systems and data that are transmitted in live video and sound.

18.1.2   Packet Switching

The **packet switching** technique involves messages that are broken into small parts, or packets. Each packet is tagged with source, destination, and intermediary node addresses, as is appropriate. Packets can have a defined maximum length and be stored in RAM instead of on hard disk. Packets can take a variety of possible paths through the network in an attempt to keep the network connections filled at all times. Because the message is broken into multiple parts, however, sending packets via different paths adds to the possibility that packet order could get scrambled. Therefore, each path receives a sequencing number.

Packets are sent over the most appropriate path. Each device chooses the best path at that time for every packet. If one path is too busy, it can send the packet over another path. Because some packets

Figure 18.1   Circuit switching

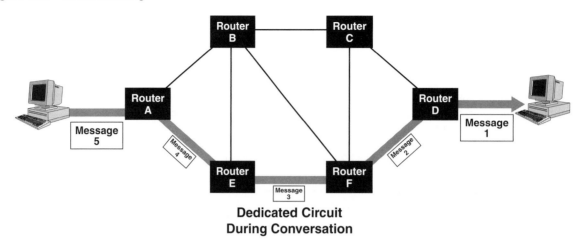

**Dedicated Circuit
During Conversation**

Figure 18.2   Packet switching

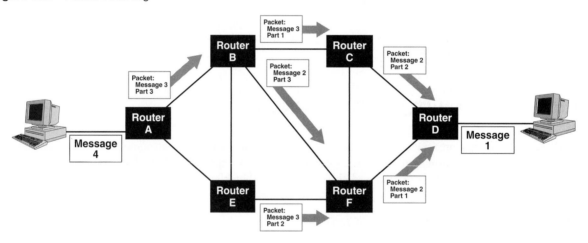

may be delayed, which causes the packets to arrive out of order, the device will reorder them by sequence number to reconstruct the original message. See Figure 18.2. The Internet is based on a packet switching protocol. Other examples include asynchronous transfer mode (ATM), frame relay, switched multimegabit data service (SMDS), and X.25. Message switching is typically used to support services such as e-mail, web pages, calendaring, or workflow information.

18.1.3   Virtual Circuits

A **virtual circuit** is a logical circuit that is created to ensure reliable communications between two network devices. It acts as a direct connection even though it may not be directly connected. It is used most frequently to describe connections between two hosts in a packet switching network. In this case, the two hosts can communicate as though they have a dedicated connection even though the packets may actually travel very different routes before arriving at their destination.

Virtual circuits provide a bidirectional communications path from one device to another and are uniquely identified by some type of identifier. Several virtual circuits can be multiplexed into a single physical circuit for transmission across the network. This capability often can reduce the equipment and network complexity that is required for multiple device connections. A virtual circuit can pass through any number of intermediate devices or switches that are located within the virtual circuit.

> Note: A network switch is a device that filters and forwards packets between LAN segments, which operate at the data link layer of the OSI reference model. In this chapter, a switch will be referred to as a routing switch, which performs routing operations much like a router, although the routing switch also performs many of the functions found in the network layer of the OSI model. The routing switch has its routing capabilities implemented with hardware, not software, so it is faster but not as powerful as a full-fledged router.

Virtual circuits can be either permanent or temporary (or switched). A **permanent virtual circuit (PVC)** is a permanently established circuit that consists of one mode: data transfer. PVCs are used in situations when data transfer between devices is constant. PVCs decrease the bandwidth use associated with the establishment and termination of virtual circuits, but increase costs due to constant virtual circuit availability. PVCs are more efficient than temporary circuits for connections between hosts that communicate frequently, and they play a central role in frame relay and X.25 networks.

A **temporary (switched) virtual circuit (SVC)** is dynamically established on demand and terminated when transmission is complete. Communication over an SVC consists of three phases: circuit establishment, data transfer, and circuit termination. The establishment phase involves creating the virtual circuit between the source and destination devices. Data transfer involves transmitting data between the devices over the virtual circuit, and the circuit termination phase involves tearing down the virtual circuit between the source and destination devices. SVCs are used in situations in which data transmission between devices is sporadic, largely because SVCs increase bandwidth that is used due to the circuit establishment and termination phases, but decrease the cost associated with constant virtual circuit availability.

When leasing a PVC or SVC end-to-end circuit, there is a monthly fee regardless if you send data. If you choose not to lease the line but sign with a network provider, the provider then bills you only for the amount of data packets you send and the distance the packets travel. The cost is also based on the technology used, and there is often a minimum charge per call.

18.1.4   WAN Devices

Typically, when talking about the various WAN connection devices, they can be divided into the following two categories:

- Data terminal equipment (DTE)
- Data circuit-terminating equipment (DCE)

Data terminal equipment (DTE) devices are end systems that communicate across the WAN. They are usually terminals, PCs, or network hosts and are located on the premises of individual subscribers. **Data circuit-terminating equipment (DCE)** devices are special communication devices that provide the interface between the DTE and the network. Examples include modems and adapters. The purpose of the DCE is to provide clocking and switching services in a network and data transmission through the WAN. Therefore, the DCE controls data flowing to or from a computer.

Another term often used when discussing WAN connections is the **channel service unit/data service unit (CSU/DSU).** The DSU is a device that performs protective and diagnostic functions for a telecommunications line; the CSU connects a terminal to a digital line. Typically, the two devices are packaged as a single unit, basically as a high-powered, expensive modem. See Table 18.1 for a summary of the information in this chapter.

18.2   PUBLIC SWITCHED TELEPHONE NETWORK

The **public switched telephone network (PSTN)** is the international telephone system that is based on copper wires (UTP cabling) carrying analog voice data. The PSTN, also known as the **plain old telephone service (POTS),** is the standard telephone service used in most homes. The PSTN is a huge network with multiple paths that link source with destination devices. Because PSTN uses circuit switching when a call is made, the data are switched to a dedicated path throughout the conversation.

Table 18.1 Carrier technology

Carrier Technology	Speed	Physical Medium	Connection Type	Comment
Plain Old Telephone Service (POTS)	Up to 56 Kbps	Twisted pair	Circuit switch	Used by home and small business
Asymmetrical Digital Subscriber Line Lite (ADSL Lite)	Up to 1.544 Mbps downstream Up to 512 Kbps upstream	2 twisted pair	Circuit switch	Used by home and small business
Asymmetrical Digital SubscriberLine (ADSL)	1.5–8 Mbps downstream Up to 1.544 Mbps upstream	2 twisted pair	Circuit switch	Used by small to medium business
High Bit-Rate Digital Subscriber Line (HDSL)	1.544 Mbps full duplex (T1) 2.048 Mbps full duplex (E1)	2 pairs of twisted pair	Circuit switch	Used by small to medium business
DS0 Leased Line	64 Kbps	1 or 2 pairs of twisted pair	Dedicated point-to-point	The base signal on a channel in the set of digital signal levels
Switched 56	56 Kbps	1 or 2 pairs of UTP	Circuit switch	Used by home and small business
Switched 64	64 Kbps	1 or 2 pairs of UTP	Circuit switch	Used by home and small business
Fractional T1 Leased Line	64 Kbps to 1.536 Mbps in 64-Kbps increments	1 or 2 pairs of twisted pair	Dedicated point-to-point	Used by small to medium business
T1 Leased Line (DS-1)	1.544 Mbps (24–64 Kbps channels)	2 pairs of UTP or coaxial or optical fiber	Dedicated point-to-point	Used by medium to large business, ISP to connect to the Internet
T3 Leased Line (DS-3)	44.736 Mbps	2 pairs of UTP or optical fiber	Dedicated point-to-point	Used by large business, large ISP to connect to the Internet or as the backbone of the Internet

Table 18.1 Continued

Carrier Technology	Speed	Physical Medium	Connection Type	Comment
E1	2.048 Mbps	Twisted pair, coaxial cable, or optical fiber		32-channel European equivalent of T1
ISDN—BRI	64 to 128 Kbps	1 or 2 pairs of UTP	Circuit switch	Used by home and small business
ISDN—PRI	23–64 Kbps channels plus control channel up to 1.544 Mbps (T1) or 2.048 (E1)	2 pairs of UTP	Circuit Switch	Used by medium to large business
X.25	Up to 64 Kbps	1 or 2 pairs of twisted pair	Packet switch	Older technology still used in areas where newer technology is still not available
Frame Relay	56 Kbps to 1.536 Mbps (using T1) or 2.048 Mbps using E-1	1 or 2 pairs of twisted pair	Packet switch	Popular technology used mostly to connect LANs
FDDI/FDDI-2	100 Mbps/200 Mbps	Optical fiber	Packet switch	Large, wide-range LAN usually in a large company or a larger ISP
SDH/Sonet	51.84 Mbps and up	Optical fiber	Dedicated point-to-point	Used by ATM
SMDS	1.544 to 34 Mbps using T1 and T3 lines	1 or 2 pairs of twisted pair	Cell relay	Popular growing technology used mostly to connect LANs; is the connectionless component of ATM
ATM	Up to 622 Mbps	T1, T3, E1, E3, SDH, and SONET	Cell relay	The faster network connection up to date
Cable Modems	500 Kbps to 1.5 Mbps or more	Coaxial cable	Leased point-to-point	Used by home and small business

The original concept of the Bell System was a series of PSTN trunks connecting the major U.S. cities. The PSTN originally began with human operators who sat at a switchboard and manually routed calls. Today, the PSTN systems still use analog signals from the end node (phone) to the first switch. The switch then converts the analog signal to a digital signal and routes the call on to its destination. Since the digital signal travels on fiber optic cabling, the signals are switched at high speeds. Once the call is received on the other end, the last switch in the loop converts the signal back to analog, and the call is initiated. The connection stays active until the call is terminated (user hangs up). The active circuit enables one caller to hear the other caller almost instantaneously.

The **subscriber loop**, or **local loop**, is the telephone line that runs from a home or office to the telephone company's central office (CO) or neighborhood switching station (often a small building with no windows). Although its cable length can be as long as 20 miles, it is referred to as the **last mile**, not because of its length, but because it is the slow link in the telecommunications infrastructure as it carries analog signals on a twisted-pair cable. The point where the local loop ends at the customer's premise is called the **demarcation point (demarc)**. Unless you have an agreement with them, phone companies are only responsible for the loop from the central office to the demarc. See Figure 18.3.

The standard home phone communicates over the local loop using analog signals. Therefore, when a PC needs to communicate over the local loop, it must use a modem to convert the PC's digital data to analog signals. Unfortunately, the analog lines can only reach a maximum speed of 56 Kbps due to FCC regulations that restrict the power output, during which time the speed is not guaranteed and is often not reached.

18.2.1   The UART

When connecting a computer to a network using dial-up technology, you typically connect using a serial device. The central part of the serial device, which includes an analog modem, is the **universal asynchronous receiver/transmitter (UART).** The UART is a single integrated chip that is the translator between the serial device and the system bus and is the component that processes, transmits, and receives data.

Inside the computer, data are generated by the processor and moved around in parallel format (system bus). This means that the several bits are being moved from one place to another using several wires. If you have more wires, you can transport more data. As the data come from the system bus, the UART converts the data to a serial signal (bits in a single file), adds the start and stop bits, and adds any error control (such as parity). Then the UART converts the digital (+5 Vdc TTL) signals to a bipolar signal. The data are then sent through the serial device out to the serial cable.

As data come in from the serial port, the UART must reverse the process. First, the UART converts the bipolar signal to +5 Vdc TTL digital signal. It then strips the start and stop bits, checks for errors, and strips the error control information. Finally, it converts the data back into parallel format to the system bus so that data can be processed by the computer.

Early UARTs (8250 and 16450) used a FIFO (first in/first out) buffer. If the computer did not retrieve the data fast enough, the data would be overwritten by new data coming in through the serial

Figure 18.3   Public switched telephone network

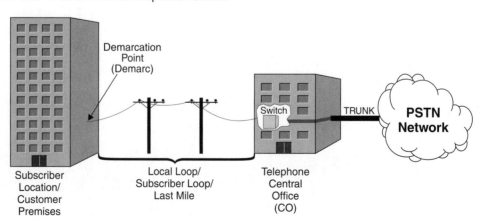

Subscriber
Location/
Customer
Premises

Demarcation
Point
(Demarc)

Local Loop/
Subscriber Loop/
Last Mile

Telephone
Central
Office
(CO)

Switch

TRUNK

**PSTN
Network**

port. Today, newer systems use a 16-byte FIFO-buffer UART, like the 16550. Since the buffer is larger, the processor only has to process the data every 16 bytes before any data are overwritten. Consequently, the serial communication is faster.

18.2.2 Analog Modems

A **modem (modulator-demodulator)** is a device that enables a computer to transmit data over telephone lines. Since computer information is stored and processed digitally, and the telephone lines transmit data using analog waves, the modem converts digital signals to analog signals (modulates) and analog signals to digital signals (demodulates).

Modems can be classified as either an internal modem or an external modem. The internal modem is an expansion card that is plugged into an expansion slot, while the external modem is attached to the computer using a serial port. In either case, the modem has at least one RJ-11 connector that is used to connect the twisted-pair cable between the modem and the wall telephone jack. Some modems include a second RJ-11 jack to connect a phone. See Figure 18.4.

When data need to be sent through the modem, the modem receives the digital data from the computer. The modem then converts the digital signals into analog signals. The UART of the modem then adds the start and stop bits and any error control bits, such as parity. When the data reaches the other modem, the UART strips the start and stop bits, checks for errors, and converts the analog signals to a digital signals, which are then processed by the computer.

As the modem is communicating, it is continuously monitoring the status of the line, the quality of the signals, and the number of errors encountered. When modems detect excessive problems, they interrupt the carrier and reevaluate the line. Consequently, speed may be decreased. If the speed is decreased and the errors have decreased, the line will be reevaluated again to see if the speed can be increased.

When two computers are communicating using a telephone line, both computers must be set to the same number of bits used for data, the length of the stop bit, and the type of error control. If not, the receiving computer would misinterpret the data, and the result would be errors or garbage. Usually, the calling computer is configured to the settings of the receiving computer.

Example 1:

You need to download some technical information, which is not available on the Internet but is available on a bulletin-board service (BBS) computer. You are given the phone number to the BBS computer and the following information: 9600 baud at 7E1. The 9600 baud is the speed of the modem on the other end. The 7 indicates 7 bits are used for data and the E indicates that the computer uses even parity checking (O would indicate odd parity). Lastly, the 1 indicates that the computer has one stop bit.

Baud rate refers to the modulation rate, or the number of times per second that a line changes state. This is not always the same as **bits per second (bps)**. If you connect two serial devices together using

Figure 18.4 RJ-11 connector and jack

direct cables, then the baud rate and the bps are the same. Thus, if you are running at 19,200 bps, the line is changing states 19,200 times per second to represent 19,200 logical 1s and 0s. Much like the data and stop bits, the sending and receiving devices must agree on the baud rate. The speed of a normal serial port is 115.2 kilobits per second.

Different baud rates and bps rates occur when communication is over telephone lines. The telephone lines are actually limited to a maximum of 2400 baud. However, since they use analog signals and not digital signals, the bps can be increased by encoding more bits into each line change. Consequently, the 9600 bps encodes 4 bits at the same time, 14,400 encodes 6 bits, and 28.8 encodes 12 bits. In addition, the bps can be increased by data compression.

When installing a modem, the first step is to configure the resources. If it is an internal modem, you would usually choose a free IRQ, COM port, and I/O address. If it is an external modem, you must then configure the serial port. While the serial port is already assigned an IRQ, COM port, and I/O address, the serial port speed usually has to be configured.

Example 2:

Question: You have a computer running Windows 98 that has two serial ports (COM1 and COM2). COM1 is being used by the mouse and COM2 is not being used at all. You have a proprietary communication software package for your business that will only use COM1 and COM2. Therefore, you purchase an internal modem. How should you configure the modem?

Answer: If you configure the modem to use COM3, the communication software package will not recognize the modem. If you configure the modem as COM1 or COM2, you have a resource conflict. Since you need the mouse (COM1) for Windows 98, you should configure the modem as COM2/IRQ 3. For this to work, you need to disable COM2 using either jumpers, DIP switches, configuration software, or the CMOS Setup program.

The next step is to physically install and connect the modem. The modem is connected to the telephone wall jack using a twisted-pair cable with RJ-11 connectors. Lastly, you must load the modem software drivers and install and configure the communication software. If you have Windows 95/98 or Windows NT, the driver is loaded by using the Add New Hardware icon/applet from the Control Panel.

With the communication software package, you can usually choose the baud rate (up to the speed of the modem), the number of data bits, the number of stop bits, and the parity method. In addition, many of the packages allow you to establish different parameters for different telephone numbers. Therefore, when you call a particular telephone number, the communication software will automatically use the same parameters that were used before.

Although the modem interface is standardized, there are a number of standards and protocols that specify how formatted data are to be transmitted over telephones lines. The International Telecommunications Union (ITU), formerly known as the Comité Consultatif International Téléphonique et Télégraphique (CCITT), has defined many important standards for data communications. Most modems have built-in support for the more common standards. Today, v90 is the most popular standard for 56-K modems.

18.3   LEASED DIGITAL LINES

The **T-carrier system** was introduced by the Bell System in the United States in the 1960s as the first successful system to convert the analog voice signal to a digital bit stream. Although the T-carrier system was originally designed to carry voice calls between telephone company central offices, today it is used to transfer voice, data, and video signals between different sites and to connect to the Internet.

The human voice can produce sounds in the range between 50 Hz and 1500 Hz, while a person can hear in the range between 300 Hz and 3400 Hz. To carry a voice signal on a digital carrier, the analog voice signal needs to be converted to a digital signal. The **Nyquist theorem** states that to ensure accuracy, a signal should be sampled at least twice the rate of its frequency. Therefore, the voice signal is sampled (measured) 8000 times per second. Each measurement is then quantized or converted into an 8-bit number (256 different combinations). As a result,

$$8000 \text{ samples/second} \times 8 \text{ bits/sample} = 64 \text{ Kbps}$$

to represent a digital voice signal.

18.3.1   T-Carrier and E-Carrier Systems

The T-carrier and E-carrier systems are entire digital systems that consist of permanent, dedicated point-to-point connections. These digital systems are based on 64-Kbps channels (DS0 channel, where DS stands for digital signal), and each voice transmission is assigned a channel.

In North America and Japan, you would typically find a T1 line that has 24-Kbps to 64-Kbps channels for a bandwidth of 1.544 Mbps, and a T3 line that has 672-Kbps to 64-Kbps channels for a bandwidth of 44.736 Mbps. In Europe, you will find E1 lines with 32-Kbps to 64-Kbps channels for a bandwidth of 2.048 Mbps, and an E3 line with 512-Kpbs to 64-Kbps channels for a bandwidth of 34.368 Mbps. T1 lines are a popular leased line option for businesses that are connecting to the Internet and for Internet service providers (ISPs) that are connecting to the Internet backbone. T3 connections comprise the Internet backbone and are used by larger ISPs to connect to the backbone. See Table 18.2.

If your company is not ready for a full T1 line, then it can lease a fractional T1 line and thus use only a portion of the 24 channels. Since the hardware already exists to use a full T1 line, you simply call the carrier to increase the number of channels. Therefore, a fractional T1 line leaves room for growth.

The T-carrier system is a bipolar, framed format, time-division digital communication system. It normally uses one of two encoding methods, alternate mark inversion (AMI) or bipolar 8-zero substitution (B8ZS).

AMI bipolar encoding uses no voltage to indicate a digital 0 and uses alternating positive and negative voltages to represent digital 1s. The reason that unipolar encoding (a positive voltage indicates a digital 1 and no voltage indicates a digital 0) was not used is there is no "return to zero," which can lead to lost synchronization of the signal as the system loses track of the many sequential digital 1s. Therefore, the bipolar signal alternates between positive voltage and negative voltage and thus adds redundancy to the timing of the circuit. See Figure 18.5.

Table 18.2   Digital carrier systems

Digital Signal Designator	T-Carrier	E-Carrier	Data Rate	DS0 Multiple
DS0	—	—	64 Kbps	1
DS1	T1	—	1.544 Mbps	24
—	—	E1	2.048 Mbps	32
DS1C	—	—	3.152 Mbps	48
DS2	T2	—	6.312 Mbps	96
—	—	E2	8.448 Mbps	128
—	—	E3	34.368 Mbps	512
DS3	T3	—	44.736 Mbps	672
—	—	E4	139.264 Mbps	2048
DS4/NA	—	—	139.264 Mbps	2176
DS4	—	—	274.176 Mbps	4032
—	—	E5	565.148 Mbps	8192

Figure 18.5   AMI bipolar encoding

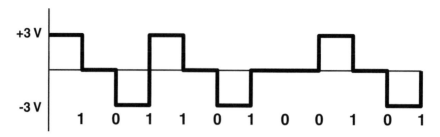

Figure 18.6   B8ZS encoding used by T1 lines

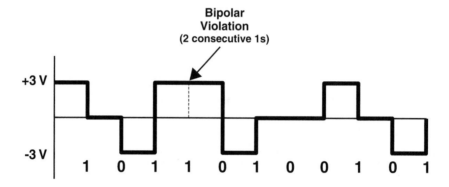

AMI coding suffers the drawback that a long run of zeros produces no transitions in the data stream, which lead to a loss of synchronization. Therefore, successful transmission relies on the user not sending long runs of zeros, but unfortunately, this type of encoding is not transparent to the sequence of bits being sent.

American T1 lines use bipolar 8-zero substitution. B8ZS is like AMI, but to avoid the loss of synchronization with a large number of sequential zeros, B8ZS replaces eight consecutive zeros with a fictional word. To differentiate between a real word and a fictional one, the hardware creates a bipolar violation where it will send two consecutive positive pulses or two consecutive negative pulses. See Figure 18.6. A T3 system uses a bipolar 3-zero substitution (B3ZS), which works the same as B8ZS but modifies any group of three zeros instead of eight. E-carrier systems use high-density bipolar 3 (HDB3), which replaces a four-zero bit pattern with two zeros followed by a bipolar violation.

A T1 line uses a D4 framing format, in which a frame bit prefixes 24 bytes of data, each from one of the 24 channels. The framing bit follows a special 12-bit pattern, called the frame alignment signal. Every 12 frames, the signal repeats, allowing the hardware on either side of the connection to signal changes in line status. This group of 12 D4 frames is called a superframe. The T3 uses a framing called M13, which uses a 4760-bit frame, compared with a 193-bit D4 frame. Of this, 56 bits are used for frame alignment, error correction, and network monitoring.

Traditionally, the T1 system uses two unshielded twisted-pair copper wires to provide full-duplex capability (one pair to receive and one pair to send). Today, the T-carrier system can also use coaxial cable, fiber optic, digital microwave, and other media. See Table 18.3.

While analog signals can travel up to 18,000 feet from the subscriber to the central office or switching station, T1 lines require cleaner lines for the faster speeds. Therefore, repeaters are placed approximately every 6000 feet.

18.3.2   T-Carrier Hardware

To complete the T-carrier connection, you must use a CSU/DSU, and possibly a multiplexer and router. The CSU/DSU physically and electrically terminates the connection to the telephone company, controls timing and synchronization of the signal, and handles line coding and framing. By law, all T1s require that a CSU be connected between the DTE and the T1 line to act as a surge protector and to monitor the line.

Table 18.3   Different media used in T-carrier systems

Media	T-Carrier Capacity
Twisted pair	Up to 1 T1 circuit
Coaxial cable	Up to 4 T1 circuits
Microwave	Up to 8 T3 circuits
Fiber optic	Up to 24 T3 circuits

Figure 18.7   A multiplexer on a T1 line

A multiplexer is used to split the circuit into the various channels, and some can also provide pulse code modulation (PCM) encoding for analog devices such as an analog phone. Remember that most business systems use digital phone systems. The router can connect an Ethernet LAN to a WAN. A router would generally provide one or more RJ-45 connectors for the Ethernet LAN(s) and includes a serial connection for the CSU/DSU, or includes a built-in CSU/DSU. See Figure 18.7.

18.4   CIRCUIT SWITCHED LINES

As you see from the previous information, digital lines are much faster than analog lines. The disadvantages of the leased digital lines are their higher cost and their limitation as a point-to-point connection. If you have multiple sites, then put several lines connecting one site to all other sites.

The advantage of the POTS system is its circuit switching ability, in which it has multiple paths linking many devices together. When one device needs to communicate with another, a circuit is established that consists of a dedicated path. When the conversation is finished, the connection is terminated. This circuit is established on demand. Circuit switch technology can be referred to as **dial-up technology.**

Combining the best features of both systems provides a basic switched digital technology. Examples of such technology are switched 56, switched 64, and ISDN.

18.4.1   Switched 56 and 64 Technology

T-carrier system lines are permanent leased lines. **Switched 56** and **switched 64** lines are digitally switched or "dial-up lines" that provide a single digital channel for dependable data connectivity. While these lines support sporadic high-speed applications, they are typically cheaper than a dedicated DS0 line, and the cost of the termination equipment also is cheaper.

The 56-Kbps value set with the switched 56 technology is based on the DS0 64-Kbps technology. To avoid a loss of synchronization with many consecutive zeros, it uses pulse stuffing, whereby every eighth bit is taken out of the signal and forced to be a pulse.

18.4.2   Integrated Services Digital Network

The **Integrated Services Digital Network (ISDN)** is the planned replacement for POTS to provide voice and data communications worldwide using circuit switching as well as the same wiring that is currently being used in homes and businesses. Because ISDN is a digital signal from end to end, it is faster, more dependable, and has no line noise. ISDN has the ability to deliver multiple, simultaneous connections—in any combination of data, voice, video, or fax—over a single line and allows for multiple devices to be attached to the line.

The ISDN uses two types of channels, a B channel and a D channel. The **bearer channels (B channels)** transfer data at a bandwidth of 64 Kbps for each channel. The **data channels (D channels)** use a communications language called DSS1 for administrative signaling, such as to instruct the carrier to set up or terminate a B-channel call, to ensure that a B channel is available to receive a call, or to provide signaling information for such features as caller identification. Since the D channel is always connected to the ISDN, the call setup time is greatly reduced to 1 to 2 (versus 10 to 40 using an analog modem) as it establishes a circuit. The bandwidths listed here are the uncompressed speeds of the ISDN connections. The compressed bandwidth has a current maximum transmission speed of four times the uncompressed speed. You will probably see a much lower speed, however, as much of the data flowing across the network are already compressed.

Currently, the two well-defined interface standards are the **basic rate interface (BRI)** and the **primary rate interface (PRI).** The BRI defines a digital communications line consisting of three independent channels: two bearer (or B) channels, each carrying 64 KB/s, and one data (or D) channel at 16 Kbps. For this reason, the ISDN basic rate interface is often referred to as **2B + D.** BRIs were designed to enable customers to use the existing wiring in their homes or businesses. This provides a low-cost solution for customers and explains why it is the most basic type of service today for small business or home use.

H channels are used to specify a number of B channels. The following list shows the implementations:

- **H0**—384 Kbps (6 B channels)
- **H10**—1472 Kbps (23 B channels)
- **H11**—1536 Kbps (24 B channels)
- **H12**—1920 Kbps (30 B channels)—Europe

In BRI, ISDN devices use two binary/one quaternary (2B1Q) encoding and time division multiplexing (TDM) to create the 2B + D basic ISDN channels. The 2B1Q means that the input voltage level can be one of four distinct levels, or quaternaries. See Figure 18.8. Each quaternary represents two data bits—since there are four possible ways to represent two bits—and two bits are carried per baud. See Table 18.4.

The PRI is a higher-level network interface defined at the rate of 1.544 Mbps for North America and Japan. The primary rate, used on T1 digital lines, consists of 23 B channels, each at 64 Kbps, and one 64-Kbps D channel for signaling. These B channels can interconnect with the BRI, or carry services to any POTS line. Note that some switches limit B channels to 56 Kbps. European countries support a different kind of ISDN standard for PRI that consists of 30 B channels and one 64-Kbps D

Figure 18.8   Two binary/one quaternary used by BRI ISDN

Table 18.4   Quaternaries

Bits	Quaternary Symbol	Voltage Level
1 1	+1	+0.833
1 0	+3	+2.5
0 1	−1	−0.833
0 0	−3	−2.5

channel for a total of 1984 Kbps. A new technology, nonfacility associated signaling (NFAS), also is available to enable users to support multiple PRI lines with one 64-Kbps D channel.

18.4.3   ISDN Equipment

To use BRI services, subscribe to ISDN services through a local telephone company or provider. By default, you must be within 18,000 feet (about 3.4 miles) of the telephone company's central office. Repeater devices are available for ISDN service to extend this distance, but these devices can be quite expensive. The various ISDN equipment and interfaces are shown in Table 18.5 and Figure 18.9.

The **directory number (DN)** is the 10-digit phone number that the telephone company assigns to any analog line. A **service profile identifier (SPID)** includes the DN and an additional identifier that is used to identify the ISDN device to the telephone network. However, depending on the type of service switch and the utilization of the ISDN service, you may not need a SPID or you may need a SPID for each B channel or each device. Unlike an analog line, a single DN can be used for multiple channels or devices, or up to eight DNs can be assigned to one device. Therefore, a BRI can support up to 64 SPIDs. Most standard BRI installations, however, include only two directory numbers, one for each B channel.

18.4.4   ISDN and Windows

To connect your Windows computer to an ISDN line, physically install your ISDN adapter and start the computer. After you load the appropriate drivers for the adapter, then use the Device Manager to specify the type of switch to which the adapter is connected: ATT (AT&T), NI-1 (National ISDN-1), and NTI (Northern Telecom). If your ISDN adapter is internal to your computer, then it appears in Network adapters; if the ISDN adapter is external to your computer, it appears in Modems.

To connect to the Internet by using an ISDN device, follow these steps:

1. Install the ISDN hardware in your computer.
2. On your desktop, right-click My Computer, click Properties, and on the Hardware tab, click Hardware Wizard.

Table 18.5   ISDN equipment and interfaces

Equipment and Interface Types	Descriptions
U Interface	The U interface is the two-wire interface between the customer premise and the CO. In North America, the customer is responsible for supplying all the equipment from the U interface forward.
NT1	At the customer premise, the ISDN line is terminated by an NT1 at the demarcation (boundary between the customer premise and the phone company's network). It converts the physical wiring interface delivered by the telephone company to the wiring interface needed by your ISDN equipment and provides a testing point for troubleshooting. The NT1 interface combines the B channels and the D channel into a single bit stream at the physical level and is also capable of supporting more than one device attached to an ISDN line, sometimes referred to as a multidrop configuration.
S/T Interface	The S/T interface is between the NT1 and the ISDN networking equipment, which can support up to seven devices. To allow full-duplex interface, the S/T interface uses two pairs of wires, one pair to receive data and the other to transmit data.
TE1	Terminal equipment type 1 (TE1) devices are manufactured from the outset to be completely ISDN compatible. Examples are ISDN phones and integrated video devices.
R Interface	The R reference point provides a non-ISDN interface between equipment that is not ISDN compatible and the rest of the ISDN network.
TA	The terminal adapter allows nonnative ISDN devices (TE2), such as PCs, to connect to the S interface so that it may communicate over the ISDN network.
TE2	All terminal equipment type 2 devices (TE2) are non-ISDN compatible. Therefore, they require a terminal adapter (TA) to provide ISDN functionality to the rest of the network. Examples are personal computers and 3270 terminals.

3. After the ISDN adapter is added and Windows is restarted, verify that the ISDN adapter appears as a port under Ports in Routing and Remote Access.
4. To configure the ISDN port, right-click the port, and then click Properties.
5. In the Port Properties dialog box, click Configure, select the "Demand-dial routing connections (inbound and outbound)" check box, and then click OK.
6. To create a demand-dial interface and configure it to use the ISDN device to dial in to the ISP, right-click Routing Interfaces, and then click New Demand Dial Interface.
7. A default route has a destination of 0.0.0.0, a network mask of 0.0.0.0, and a metric of 1. Add a default route that uses the newly created demand-dial interface. Note, however, because the dial-up connection to the ISP is a point-to-point link, the gateway IP address is not configurable.

18.5   PACKET SWITCHED LINES

Packet switching breaks the messages into small parts, or packets, and sends each packet individually onto the network. Since the packets have their own source and destination addresses, each can travel a different path than the other packets. When the packets reach their destination, they must be assembled. Two well-known examples of packet switched networks are X.25 and Frame Relay.

When a subscriber accesses a WAN network such as X.25, Frame Relay, or ATM, the leased network is sometimes referred to as a cloud. A **cloud** represents a logical network with multiple pathways used with a black box approach. Subscribers who connect to the cloud do not worry about the details inside the cloud, because subscribers know they connect at one edge of the cloud and the data are received at the other edge.

Figure 18.9   Integrated Services Digital Network

18.5.1   X.25

X.25 network is a packet switched network that allows remote devices to communicate with each other across digital links without the expense of individual leased lines. It typically is used in the packet switched network of common carriers, such as the telephone companies that are implemented at speeds below 64 Kbps.

The user end of the network is the data terminal equipment (DTE), and the carrier's equipment is the data circuit-terminating equipment (DCE). Connections occur on logical channels using either switched or permanent virtual circuits.

You can directly access the X.25 data network by using an X.25 smart card or a modem, which dials into a packet assembler/dissembler (PAD). A PAD is used when a DTE device such as a character mode terminal is too simple to implement the full X.25 functionality. The PAD is located between a DTE device and a DCE device, and it performs three primary functions: buffering, packet assembly, and packet disassembly. See Figure 18.10.

Figure 18.10   X.25 network

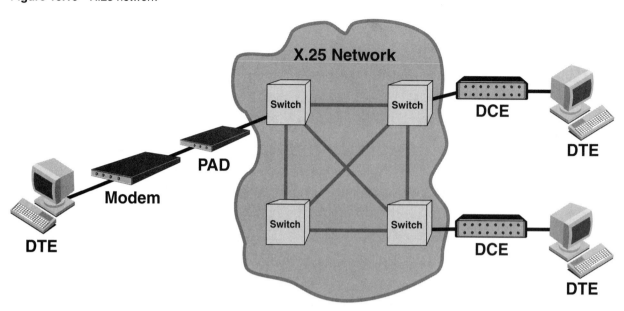

Remote access clients who run Windows can use either an X.25 card or dial in to an X.25 PAD to create connections. To accept incoming connections on a computer that is using X.25 and running Windows, use an X.25 smart card.

Switched virtual circuits (SVCs) are temporary connections used for sporadic data transfers. They require that two DTE devices establish, maintain, and terminate a session each time the devices need to communicate. To establish a connection on a SVC, the calling DTE sends a call request packet, which includes the address of the remote DTE to be contacted. The destination for each packet is identified by means of the logical channel identifier (LCI) or logical channel number (LCN). This allows the network switches to route each packet to its intended DTE.

The calling DCE device examines the packet headers to determine which virtual circuit to use and then sends the packets to the closest switch in the path of that virtual circuit. The X.25 switches pass the traffic to the next intermediate node in the path, which may be another switch or the remote DCE device.

The destination DTE decides whether to accept the call—the call request packet includes the sender's DTE address and other information that the called DTE can use to decide. A call is accepted by issuing a call accepted packet, or cleared by issuing a clear request packet. Once the originating DTE receives the call accepted packet, the virtual circuit is established and data transfer may take place. When either of the DTEs wishes to terminate the call, a clear request packet is sent to the remote DTE, which responds with a clear confirmation packet.

Permanent virtual circuits (PVCs) are permanently established connections used for frequent and consistent data transfers. PVCs do not require that sessions be established and terminated. Therefore, DTEs can begin transferring data when necessary, because the session is always active.

X.21bis is a physical layer protocol used in X.25 that defines the electrical and mechanical procedures for using the physical medium. X.21bis handles the activation and deactivation of the physical medium connecting DTE and DCE devices. It supports point-to-point connections, speeds up to 19.2 Kbps, and synchronous, full-duplex transmission over four-wire media.

Link access procedure, balanced (LAPB) is a data link layer protocol that manages communication and packet framing between DTE and DCE devices. LAPB is a bit-oriented protocol that ensures frames are correctly ordered and error free. See Figure 18.11.

There are three types of LAPB frames: information, supervisory, and unnumbered. The information frame (I-frame) carries upper-layer information and some control information. I-frame functions include sequencing, flow control, and error detection and recovery. I-frames carry send-and-receive sequence numbers. The supervisory frame (S-frame) carries control information. S-frame functions

Figure 18.11   X.25 protocol suite

include requesting and suspending transmissions, reporting on status, and acknowledging the receipt of I-frames. S-frames carry only receive sequence numbers. The unnumbered frame (U-frame) carries control information. U-frame functions include link setup and disconnection, as well as error reporting. U-frames carry no sequence numbers.

Packet layer protocol (PLP) is the X.25 network layer protocol. PLP manages packet exchanges between DTE devices across virtual circuits. PLPs also can run over logical link control 2 (LLC2) implementations on LANs and over the ISDN interfaces that run link access procedure on the D channel (LAPD). The PLP operates in five distinct modes: call setup, data transfer, idle, call clearing, and restarting.

To make a dial-up connection by using X.25 in Windows, follow these steps:

1. Click on Start, select the Settings option, then select the Network and Dial-up Connections option.
2. Double-click the Make New Connection icon, then click the Next button.
3. Select the Dial-up to Private Network option, click on the Next button, and then follow the instructions in the Network Connection Wizard.
4. When the Wizard is finished, right-click the new connection, then click the Properties option.
5. Click on the Options tab and select the Click X.25 button.
6. In Network, click your X.25 network provider.
7. At the X.121 address, type the X.121 address (the X.25 equivalent of a phone number) for the server you want to call.
8. If required by the X.25 host computer, in User Data, type additional connection information.
9. In Facilities, type any additional facility options you want to request from your X.25 provider (e.g., some providers support the /r option to specify reverse charging).

18.5.2   Always On/Dynamic ISDN

Always on/dynamic ISDN (AO/DI) is a networking application that uses the ISDN D-channel X.25 packet service of 16 Kbps to maintain an "always on" connection between an ISDN end user and an information service provider. Low bandwidth requirements, such as sending and receiving simple e-mail, news feeds, automated data collection, and credit card verification, can be met using this constant virtual connection, which accommodates speeds up to 9.6 Kbps. The rest of the 16-Kbps D channel continues to be used for call setup and teardown signaling.

When additional bandwidth is necessary (e.g., to download a graphics-intensive file from the Internet), AO/DI automatically adds circuit switched B channels of 64 Kbps each, for a speed total of 128 Kbps when both B channels are in use. When the additional bandwidth is no longer required, one or both B channels are dropped, leaving the D-channel connection in place. Because the D-channel is an always-available, connectionless packet-oriented link between the subscriber and the central office, it is possible to offer an always-available service that is based on it.

18.5.3   Defining Frame Relay

The Frame Relay protocol is a direct descendant of X.25 and is defined by the ITU standards Q.922 and Q.933. **Frame Relay** is a packet switching protocol designed to use high-speed digital backbone links to support modern protocols for error handling and flow control for connecting devices on a WAN. It only defines the physical and data link layers of the OSI model, which allows for greater flexibility of upper-layer protocols to be run. Frame relay networks are typically found using a switched 56 line, a fractional T1 line, or a full T1 line.

18.5.4   Accessing a Frame Relay Network

The most common use of a Frame Relay network is to connect individual LANs together. Data terminal equipment (DTE) is user terminal equipment that creates information for transmissions such as PCs and routers. Using a Frame Relay network, the cost is typically less than using dedicated point-to-point circuits, since customers can use multiple virtual circuits on a single physical circuit. For example, Figure 18.12 shows how it would take six dedicated point-to-point links to connect four sites. With a Frame Relay network, it would only take four links to connect the same sites. If you have five sites, it would take ten links using dedicated point-to-point links versus five links in a Frame Relay network.

To connect the DTEs to the Frame Relay network, use a **Frame Relay access device (FRAD),** sometimes referred to as a Frame Relay assembler/dissembler. It multiplexes and formats traffic for entering a Frame Relay network. A FRAD is a device that allows non–Frame Relay devices to connect to a Frame Relay network. FRADs can be included in routers or bridges, or they can be stand-alone. You also may need a CSU/DSU to connect to common links such as a T1 line, which may be included with the FRAD.

Frame relay routers are the most versatile of the three FRAD devices as they can handle traffic from other WAN protocols, reroute traffic if a connection goes down, and provide flow and congestion

Figure 18.12   Dedicated point-to-point versus Frame Relay networks

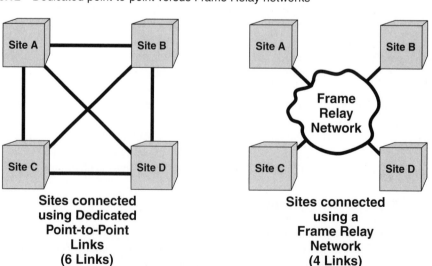

control. Frame Relay bridges, which are used to connect a branch office to a hub, are basically low-cost unintelligent routers. Stand-alone FRADs are designed to aggregate (gather) and convert data, but have no routing capabilities. They are typically used on sites that already have bridges and routers or for sending mainframe traffic. Distinctions between these devices are blurring as vendors combine their functions into a single device.

Initially, the Frame Relay protocal gained acceptance as a means to provide end users with a solution for LAN-to-LAN connections and other data connectivity requirements. Due to advances in areas such as digital signal processing and faster backbone links within the Frame Relay network, end users are beginning to see viable methods being developed that incorporate nondata traffic such as voice or video over the Frame Relay network.

If you have a common, private Frame Relay network and you are using both Frame Relay and non–Frame Relay interfaces (such as phone system), you will need a special multiplexer. The multiplexer will forward the Frame Relay traffic to the Frame Relay interface and on to the data network while non–Frame Relay traffic is forwarded to the appropriate application or service [such as **private branch exchange (PBX)** for telephone service or a video-teleconferencing application]. See Figure 18.13.

To get to a Frame Relay network, first obtain a Frame Relay bearer service (FRBS), which is offered by common carriers such as your telephone company. If you use switched virtual circuit (SVC) as provided by a public carrier, the Frame Relay switching equipment is located in the central offices of a telecommunications carrier. The administering and maintaining of the Frame Relay network equipment and service is provided by the carrier, which relieves the customer of such duties. The majority of today's Frame Relay networks are public carrier–provided networks.

Figure 18.13   Frame Relay network

Today, many organizations worldwide are using PVC to deploy private Frame Relay networks. In such cases, the administration and maintenance of the network is the responsibility of the customer. The customer owns all the equipment, including the switching equipment.

When a packet is being sent on the Frame Relay network, it reaches the first switch. The packet is then switched or forwarded to the next switch toward its final destination, using the PVCs or SVCs. The network is connection oriented, because the originating and terminating ends are programmed into the network switches as identified by data link connection identifiers (DLCIs). DLCI values typically are assigned by the Frame Relay service provider (e.g., the telephone company). Frame Relay DLCIs have local significance, which means that the values themselves are not unique in the Frame Relay WAN. Two DTE devices that are connected by a virtual circuit, for example, may use a different DLCI value to refer to the same connection. See Figure 18.14.

18.5.5   Characteristics of Frame Relay

At the physical layer, all signals in Frame Relay networks are binary and so are represented by a one or a zero. The FRAD is responsible for receiving these binary signals from the telephone carrier. To transmit binary signals on electronic media, voltage is raised or lowered. Most encoding methods are bipolar.

Frame Relay networks are statistically time-division multiplexed; they assign time slots dynamically to make them more efficient by not using empty time slots. As a result, statistical time-division multiplexing uses the bandwidth more efficiently, particularly for bursty data traffic among clients and servers and for inter-LAN links. These networks also use variable-length packets to make efficient and flexible transfers.

Frame Relay networks do not provide any error handling or control. When an error occurs in a frame, typically caused by noise on the line, it is detected upon receipt of the frame using the frame check sequence (FCS), a form of the cyclic redundancy check (CRC), and the frame is simply thrown away. Error handling is left to the destination devices such as the router and the upper protocols (e.g., TCP/IP or IPX). Because the Frame Relay is built on top of an all-digital network, the network discards very few frames, particularly when the networks are operating at well below design capacity. Because the Frame Relay network does not have to perform any error handling and the network automatically preserves the order of data, there are no frame retransmissions, sequence numbers, or acknowledgments. Therefore, the Frame Relay network has low overhead, resulting in a faster network.

Figure 18.14   A single Frame Relay virtual circuit can be assigned different data link connection identifiers on each end of a virtual circuit.

Much like network cards, Frame Relay cards have a buffer or temporary memory that holds the incoming frames until they are processed or holds the outgoing frames until they are sent. Like any other network connection, a Frame Relay network may experience network congestion, such as when a network node or switch receives more frames than it can process or when a network node or switch needs to send more frames across a given line than the speed of the line permits. As a result, the buffer fills up and the node is forced to discard frames. Since LAN traffic is extremely bursty, the probability of congestion occurring occasionally is high. Therefore, it is important that the Frame Relay network have excellent congestion management features, both to minimize the occurrence and severity of congestion and to minimize the effect of the discards when they are required.

When you subscribe to a 56-Kbps, fractual T1 or full T1 line, you will be asked to specify a **committed information rate (CIR)** for each DLCI. This value specifies the maximum average data rate that the network undertakes to deliver under "normal conditions." If you send faster than the CIR on a given DLCI, the network will flag some frames with a **discard eligibility (DE)** bit. The network will do its best to deliver all packets but will discard any DE packets first if there is congestion. Many inexpensive Frame Relay services are based on a CIR of zero, which means that every frame is a DE frame, and the network will throw away any frame when necessary.

Help to provide indications that the network is becoming congested comes from the **forward explicit congestion notification (FECN)** bit and the **backward explicit congestion notification (BECN)** bit, which are embedded within data frames. These are used to tell the application to slow, hopefully before packets start to be discarded. For these bits to be used, the router or bridge would have to recognize and process them.

Frame Relay networks offer bursting, a unique advantage over leased lines. Since the leased line bandwidth is fixed, if a device attempts to send data at a rate higher than the line bandwidth, the packets will not get through and performance will be degraded. Frame Relay networks, however, allow a device to transmit data at a higher rate than the CIR for a few seconds at a time.

Devices using the extra free bandwidth run a risk in that any data beyond the CIR is eligible for discard, depending on network congestion. The greater the network congestion, the greater the risk that frames transmitted above the CIR will be lost. While the risk is typically very low up to the CIR, if a frame is discarded it will have to be resent. Data can even be transmitted at rates higher than the CIR, but doing this has the greatest risk of lost packets. If you find that you consistently need long bursts, then consider purchasing a higher CIR.

18.5.6   Frame Relay and Windows

To connect to the Internet by using the Frame Relay protocol on Windows, do the following:

1. Physically install the Frame Relay adapter in your computer.
2. On your desktop, right-click My Computer, select the Properties option, click on the Hardware tab, then click the Hardware Wizard. Follow the prompts to configure the Frame Relay adapter.
3. After the Frame Relay adapter is added and Windows is restarted, verify that the Frame Relay adapter appears as a routing interface under Routing Interfaces in Routing and Remote Access.
4. The default network route has a destination of 0.0.0.0, network mask of 0.0.0.0, and metric of 1. Add a default network route that uses the Frame Relay adapter. Because the Frame Relay connection to the ISP is a point-to-point link, the gateway IP address is not configurable.

18.6   SYNCHRONOUS DIGITAL HIERARCHY AND SYNCHRONOUS OPTICAL NETWORK

The **Synchronous Digital Hierarchy (SDH)** and the **Synchronous Optical Network (SONET)** are transmission technology standards of synchronous data transmission over fiber optic cables. They provide a high-speed transfer of data, video, and types of information across great distances without regard to the specific services and applications they support. Service providers who must aggregate (combine) multiple T1s to provide connections across the country or around the world typically use both. SDH is an international standard. The ITU coordinates the development of the SDH standard. **SONET** is the North American equivalent of SDH, which is published by the American National Standards Institute (ANSI).

When referring to SONET or SDH, neither apply directly to switches. Instead, they specify the interfaces between switches that are linked by fiber optic cable. A SONET or SDH switch does not actually exist, but instead, an ATM switch or a similar switch (such as FDDI, ISDN, or SMDS) is used. ATM, which we will discuss later in the chapter, can then support a variety of other services including Frame Relay and voice. SDH and SONET map the physical layer of the OSI model.

18.6.1   Building Blocks of SDH and SONET

The basic foundation of SONET consists of groups of DS-0 signals (64-Kbps) that are multiplexed to create a 51.84-Mbps signal, also known as a synchronous transport signal (STS-1). STS-1 is an electrical signal rate that corresponds to the optical carrier line rate of OC-1, SONET's building block. OC-1 has enough bandwidth to support 28 T1 links or one T3 link. Higher rates of transmission are a multiple of this basic rate. So, for example, STS-3 is three times the basic rate, or 155.52 Mbps. OC-12 is 12 times the basic rate, giving a rate of 622 Mbps, and OC-192, which is 9.95 Gbps. The SDH standard is based on the STM-1, which is equivalent to OC-3. Therefore, SDH uses multipliers of 155.52 Mbps. See Table 18.6.

In essence, SONET and SDH are the same technology. There are minor differences in header information, payload size, and framing, but at 155 Mbps and above, the two are completely interoperable.

The basic level of SONET starts at approximately 51 Mbps, but the lower bit rate asynchronous signals are not ignored. The basic STS-1 frame contains 810 DS-0s, 783 of which are used for sending data (including slower asynchronous signals) and 27 of which are overhead. The overhead in this case is information concerning framing, errors, operations, and format identification.

Signals with speeds below STS-1, such as DS-1 and the European E1 (2.048 Mbps) can be accommodated by dividing the STS-1 payload into smaller segments known as virtual tributaries (VTs). The lower data rate signals are combined with overhead information, which leads to the creation of synchronous payload envelopes (SPEs). SPEs allow these signals to be transported at high speeds without compromising integrity. Each VT on an STS-1 signal includes its own overhead information and exists as a distinct segment within the signal.

Table 18.6   SONET/SDH digital hierarchy

Optical Level	SDH Equivalent	Electrical Level	Line Rate (Mbps)	Payload Rate (Mbps)	Overhead Rate (Mbps)
OC-1	—	STS-1	51.840	50.112	1.728
OC-3	STM-1	STS-3	155.520	150.336	5.184
OC-9	STM-3	STS-9	466.560	451.008	15.552
OC-12	STM-4	STS-12	622.080	601.344	20.736
OC-18	STM-6	STS-18	933.120	902.016	31.104
OC-24	STM-8	STS-24	1,244.160	1,202.688	41.472
OC-36	STM-13	STS-36	1,866.240	1,804.032	62.208
OC-48	STM-16	STS-48	2,488.320	2,405.376	82.944
OC-96	STM-32	STS-96	4,976.640	4,810.752	165.888
OC-192	STM-64	STS-192	9,953.280	9,621.504	331.776
OC-768	STM-256	STS-768	39,813.12	38,486.01	1,327.10

Figure 18.15   Carrier SDH/SONET networks use dual rings to provide redundant pathways.

18.6.2   SDH and SONET Lines and Rings

Local SDH and SONET services are sold in two forms: point-to-point dedicated lines or dual fiber rings. Both deliver high speed, but only dual fiber rings guarantee automatic rerouting around outages. Long-distance SDH and SONET connections employ multiple rings within the public network. Some are even using dual ring pairs (four redundant rings on one circuit). See Figure 18.15.

When using dual rings, if one circuit is broken, the traffic reverses and flows in the opposite direction on the same ring, thus avoiding the cut altogether. If the ring is broken in two places, the traffic is automatically rerouted onto the second circuit. This takes a few milliseconds longer than merely reversing direction, but it still happens nearly instantaneously.

Long-distance, point-to-point SDH and SONET services are similar to standard leased lines. A company buys a connection between two points, but its traffic is sent over multiple rings within the public network. Although the customer is not buying rings, he or she gets all the benefits associated with rings within a long-distance portion of the carrier network. Customers who need high reliability end to end should use local access rings.

18.7   CELL RELAY

Data transmission technology is based on transmitting data in relatively small, fixed-size packets, or **cells**. Each cell contains only basic path information that allows switching devices to route the cell quickly. Cell relay systems can reliably carry live video and audio, because cells of fixed size arrive in a more predictable way than systems with packets or frames of varying size. Examples of cell relay are SMDS and ATM.

18.7.1   Switched Multimegabit Data Service

Switched multimegabit data service (SMDS) is a high-speed, cell relay WAN service designed for LAN interconnection through the public telephone network. SMDS can use fiber- or copper-based media. While it mostly supports speeds between 1.544 Mbps and 34 Mbps, it has been extended to support lower and higher bandwidth to broaden its target market. Although SMDS and Frame Relay are both desirable ways of gaining Internet access for a business, Frame Relay is popular for speeds of T1 and below and SMDS is popular for speeds above T1 up to T3. An SMDS circuit is committed at its specified speed. Bursting of the circuit to full bandwidth is never required.

Different from Frame Relay and ATM, SMDS is a connectionless service, in that there is no pre-defined path or virtual circuit setup between devices. Instead, SMDS simply sends the traffic into the network for delivery to any destination on the network. With no need for a predefined path between devices, data can travel over the least congested routes in an SMDS network. As a result, it provides faster transmission for the networks bursty data transmissions and greater flexibility to add or drop network sites. SMDS currently supports only data, and is being positioned as the connectionless part of ATM services.

An SMDS digital service unit (DSU) or channel service unit (CSU) takes frames that can be up to 7168 bytes long (large enough to encapsulate the entire IEEE 802.3, IEEE 802.5, and FDDI frames) from a router and breaks them up into 53-byte cells. The cells are then passed to a carrier switch. Each cell has 44 bytes of payload or data and 9 bytes for addressing, error correction, reassembly of cells, and other control features. The switch then reads addresses and forwards cells one by one over any available path to the desired endpoint. SMDS addresses ensure that the cells arrive in the right order.

Each destination is assigned up to 16 unique SMDS addresses (10-digit numbers similar to a telephone number) as needed. This feature allows the subscribers of SMDS to indicate individual users within a business. This enables you to create the illusion of dedicated access for specific customers when in fact you are using a single SMDS connection.

Another feature is group addressing, in which files or information can be sent to multiple users at one time. This capability allows one member to make last-minute changes and then send all members of the group the updated copy in a matter of minutes.

SMDS implements two security features: source address validation and address screening. Source address validation ensures that the source address is legitimately assigned to the device, which it originated. This helps prevent address spoofing, in which illegal traffic assumes the source address of a legitimate device. Address screening allows a subscriber to establish a private virtual network that excludes unwanted traffic. If an address is disallowed, the data unit is not delivered.

To connect to an SMDS network, communicate with a common carrier to provide T1 connection. To connect to SMDS, use a CSU/DSU (or some other connection device) and router. Often the CSU/DSU and router can be found packaged together.

18.7.2 Introduction to ATM

Asynchronous transfer mode (ATM) is both a LAN and a WAN technology, which is generally implemented as a backbone technology. It is a cell switching and multiplexing technology that combines the benefits of circuit switching and packet switching. The small, constant cell size allows ATM equipment to transmit video, audio, and computer data. Current implementations of ATM support data transfer rates of 25 Mbps to 622 Mbps. The ATM standards allow it to operate in virtually every transmission medium including T1, T3, E1, E3, SDH, and SONET.

Because of its asynchronous nature, ATM is more efficient than synchronous technologies, such as time-division multiplexing (TDM). With TDM, users are assigned to time slots, and no other station can be sent in that time slot. If a station has numerous data to send, it can send only when its time slot comes up, even if all other time slots are empty. If, however, a station has nothing to transmit when its time slot comes up, then the time slot transmits as empty and is wasted. Because ATM is asynchronous, time slots are available on demand.

18.7.3 ATM Overlay Model

The protocol reference model used for ATM is taken from a model that was developed by the ITU for the **Broadband-Integrated Services Digital Network (B-ISDN).** Because ATM is the transport mode used for B-ISDN, this model applies directly to ATM and is often used as the protocol to describe it.

The ATM overlay model is three-dimensional and consists of three planes and four layers. The three planes that span all layers are as follows:

- **Control**—Responsible for generating and managing signaling requests to perform connection administration, such as call setup and call teardown
- **User**—Responsible for managing the transfer of data across the network
- **Management**—Maintains the network and carries out operational functions. This plane is further subdivided into layer management and plane management to manage the different layers and planes.
- **Layer Management**—Manages layer-specific functions, such as the detection of failures and protocol problems
- **Plane management**—Manages and coordinates functions related to the complete system

The ATM reference mode is composed of the following ATM layers:

- **Physical layer**—Analogous to the physical layer of the OSI reference model, the ATM physical layer manages the medium-dependent transmission.
- **ATM layer**—Combined with the ATM adaptation layer, the ATM layer is roughly analogous to the data link layer of the OSI reference model. The ATM layer is responsible for establishing connection and passing cells through the ATM network. To do this, it uses information in the header of each ATM cell.
- **ATM adaptation layer (AAL)**—Combined with the ATM layer, the AAL is roughly analogous to the data link layer of the OSI mode. The AAL is responsible for isolating higher-layer protocols from the details of the ATM processes.

The ATM physical layer has four functions: bits are converted into cells, the transmission and receipt of bits on the physical medium are controlled; ATM cell boundaries are tracked; and cells are packaged into the appropriate type of frame for the physical medium. The ATM physical layer is divided into two parts, the physical medium-dependent (PMD) sublayer and the transmission-convergence (TC) sublayer. The PMD sublayer synchronizes transmission and reception by sending and receiving a continuous flow of bits with associated timing information and it specifies the physical details for the physical medium used, such as cable and connector types. The TC sublayer performs cell delineation, header error-control (HEC) sequence generation and verification, cell-rate decoupling and transmission-frame adaptation. See Figure 18.16.

The ATM layer describes how cells are transported through the network and how quality of service is enforced so that connections provide the necessary bandwidth for the specified service. The ATM layer provides creation of cells, multiplexing and demultiplexing of cells, managing of cell flow and sequencing and handling of dropped cells, and switched-based routing using virtual paths and virtual circuits.

The ATM adaptation layer (AAL) is where user information is created and received as 48-byte payloads. The AAL resolves any disparity between services provided by the cell-based technology of the ATM layer to the bit-stream technology of digital services (such as telephones and video cameras) and the packet-stream technology of traditional data networks (such as Frame Relay and X.25 used in WANs and LAN protocols such as Ethernet and TCP/IP). See Table 18.7.

The ITU first determined the need to provide several standard AALs (classes of service) to satisfy the requirements of encapsulating different information types into ATM layer cells.

The upper layers of the ATM protocol reference model include optional protocol layers that are used to further encapsulate ATM service for use with TCP/IP and other protocols. Some examples of upper-layer protocols include those specified by RFC 1483 (multiprotocol encapsulation over AAL5) and RFC 1577 (classical IP over ATM).

18.7.4   ATM Cell

The ATM cell has a size of 53 bytes. This cell contains 48 bytes of payload or data and 5 bytes to hold the control and routing information. A fixed cell was chosen for two reasons. First, the switching devices that are necessary to build the ATM network require very fast silicon chips to perform the cell switching at such high speeds. These chips can run much faster if they do not vary, but remain a fixed,

Figure 18.16 ATM model

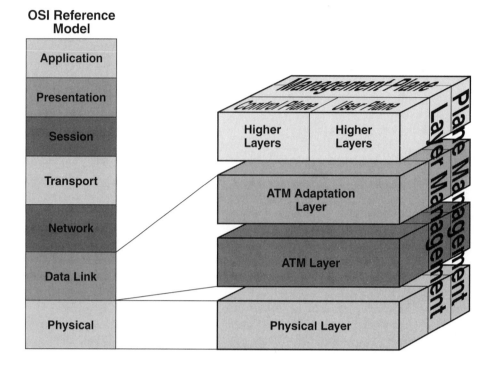

Table 18.7 ATM model layers

Layer	Description
AAL1	Supports circuit emulation using ATM cells for traditional voice, T1, and T3 carrier services. AAL1 uses two methods: structured data transfer (SDT) and synchronous residual time stamp (SRTS). Requirements include a constant bit rate and connection-oriented, isochronous (time-dependent) service.
AAL2	Supports packet-based video and other time-dependent applications that can use variable bit rate. AAL2 is not currently defined by the ATM standards.
AAL3/4	Supports multiplexing of data streams, including connection-oriented and connectionless services. AAL3/4 was used in early ATM implementations but is no longer favored because of additional overhead cost resulting from the segmentation and reassembly (SAR) sublayer. The SAR header and SAR trailer are each 2 bytes long, effectively reducing available cell payload for data to 44 bytes.
AAL5	Designed to support efficient transport of LAN traffic. Widely implemented today in most ATM products. AAL5 is the adaptation layer used most often, offering the best performance when compared to other AALs for LAN traffic.

known value. By using a payload length of 48 bytes for data, ATM offers a compromise between a larger cell size (such as 64 bytes) optimized for data, and a smaller cell size (such as 32 bytes) optimized for voice. See Figure 18.17. Secondly, ATM is designed to carry multimedia communications, composed of data, voice, and video. Unlike data, however, voice and video require a highly predictable cell arrival time for sound and video to appear natural. These cells must arrive one after the other, in a steady stream with no late cells. If the cells varied in size, a very long cell could block the timely arrival of a shorter cell. Therefore, a constant cell size was chosen.

The ISDN data communication discussed earlier in this chapter is known as narrowband ISDN, which was designed to operate over the current communication infrastructure based on the twisted-pair copper cable. With broadband-ISDN (B-ISDN), the end user gets true bandwidth on demand, only

Figure 18.17   ATM cell content

GFC—Generic flow control
    (000 5 uncontrolled access)—4 bits
VPI—Virtual path identifier—8 bits
BCI—Virtual channel identifier— 16 bits
PT—Payload type—3 bits
CLP—Cell loss priority—1 bit
HEC—Header error control—8 bits

paying for the bandwidth used. Bandwidth of B-ISDN is faster than a T1 line (1.544 Mbps), which generally is found on fiber optic cables that are running ATM or SMDS.

18.7.5   ATM Network Operation

An ATM network consists of ATM switches (sometimes referred to as network node interfaces, or NNIs) and ATM endpoints (sometimes referred to as user network interfaces, or UNIs), consisting of PCs with ATM adapter cards, routers, bridges, CSU/DSUs, and video coder/decoders. When a packet initially enters the ATM network, it is segmented into ATM cells, a process known as cell segmentation.

An ATM switch is responsible for moving cells through an ATM network. It accepts the incoming cell from an ATM endpoint or another ATM switch. It then reads and updates the cell header information and quickly switches the cell to an output interface toward its destination. An ATM endpoint (or end system) contains an ATM network interface adapter. Examples of ATM endpoints are workstations, routers, data service units, LAN switches, and video coder/decoders. ATM cells used by UNI and NNI have a slightly different cell format. NNI cells have no generic flow control (GFC) field. Instead, the first 4 bits of the cell are used by an expanded 12-bit virtual path identifier (VPI) space.

On an ATM network, each ATM-attached device (workstations, servers, routers, or bridges) has immediate, exclusive access to the switch. Because each device has access to its own switch port, devices can send cells to the switch simultaneously. Latency becomes an issue only when multiple streams of traffic reach the switch at the same time. To reduce latency at the switch, the cell size must be small enough so that the time it takes to transmit a cell has little effect on the cells waiting to be transmitted. Since each ATM device has immediate, exclusive access to a switch port, device connection to an ATM switch does not require complete media access schemes to determine which device has access to the switch.

On an ATM network, each ATM-attached device (workstations, servers, routers, and bridges) is attached directly to a switch. When an ATM-attached device requests a connection with a destination device, the switches to which the two devices are attached set up the connection. While setting up the connection, the switches determine the best route to take. Therefore, the ATM switch is a routing switch.

Connection setup standards for the ATM layer define virtual circuits and virtual paths. An ATM virtual circuit is the connection between two ATM endstations for the duration of the connection. The virtual circuit is bidirectional, which means that once a connection is established, each endstation can send to or receive from the other endstation.

Whereas a virtual circuit is a connection that is established between two endstations for the duration of a connection, a virtual path lies between two switches and exists all the time, regardless of whether a connection is being made. In other words, a virtual path is a permanent path that all traffic from a single switch can take to reach another switch.

When a user requests a virtual circuit, the switches determine which virtual path to use in order to reach the endstations. Traffic for more than one virtual circuit may travel the same virtual path at the same time. For example, a virtual path with 120 Mbps of bandwidth can be divided into four simultaneous connections of 30 Mbps each.

After the connection is established, the switches between the endstations receive translation tables, which specify where to forward cells based on the port from which the cells enter and the special values in the cell headers that identify the virtual circuit identifiers (VCIs) and virtual path identifiers (VPIs). The translation table also specifies which VCIs and VPIs the switch should include in the cell headers before the switch sends the cells.

ATM can use three types of virtual circuits—permanent virtual circuits (PVCs), switched virtual circuits (SVCs), and smart permanent virtual circuits (SPVCs). The PVCs and the SVCs are the same as discussed earlier in this chapter. The permanent virtual circuits are manually established pathways between two endstations that do not require setup or tear down of the connection. Most early ATM devices supported only PVCs, whereas today's devices support all three.

The SVC is established dynamically when an endstation needs to send data. First, the endstation requests a connection with another endstation. An SVC is established between two endstations on an as-needed basis and expires after an arbitrary amount of time. In ATM, the process of determining whether to establish a connection is called connection admission control (CAC). SVCs are often the preferred mode of operation because they can be dynamically established, thus minimizing reconfiguration complexity. See Figure 18.18.

The **smart permanent virtual circuit (SPVC)** is a hybrid of a PVC and an SVC. Like a PVC, an SPVC is established manually when the network is configured. However, the ATM service provider or network administrator sets up only the endstations. For each transmission, the network determines through which switches the cells will pass.

When the virtual circuits are established, the application or service specifies the average and peak traffic rates, peak traffic duration, and burstiness of the traffic. By setting these parameters, network

Figure 18.18 ATM virtual circuit

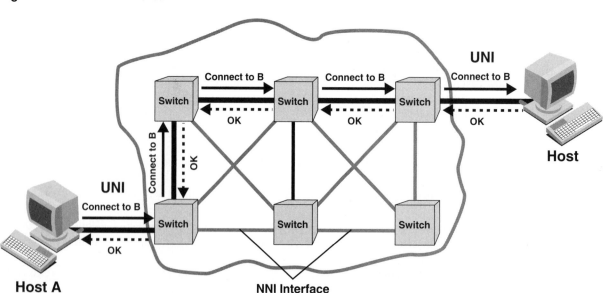

designers can ensure that voice, video, and data traffic get the required quality of service (QoS). For example, the network can respond to traffic burst by automatically allocating additional bandwidth to a particular virtual circuit. Certain types of traffic or calls can be prioritized according to their importance or sensitivity to time delay. The ATM adaptation layer defines the following service categories:

- **Constant bit rate (CBR)**—Specifies a fixed bit rate so that data are sent in a steady stream for applications and services that require a small amount of bandwith at all times and are sensitive to delay and cell loss. Some typical CBR applications are circuit emulation, voice, video, and any type of data that are time defined. CBR applications are not burst. One example is supporting voice traffic connected to a PBX.
- **Real-time variable bit rate (rt-VBR)**—Provides a specified throughput capacity when services and applications require high bandwidth but data are not sent evenly. This is a popular choice for voice and video conferencing data.
- **Non–real-time variable bit rate (nrt-VBR)**—is similar to the rt-VBR except without the latency requirement. An application that may use this category is routers that connect LANs.
- **Unspecified bit rate (UBR)**—Does not guarantee any throughput levels. It is for non–real-time rates with no required service guarantees. UBR gives no guarantee that the cells will even be delivered. Therefore, ATM provides the carrier with the option of dropping certain cells if the network gets congested. This is used for applications such as file transfer and e-mail that can tolerate delays.
- **Available bit rate (ABR)**—Provides a guaranteed minimum capacity but allows data to be bursted at higher capacities when the network is free. This is used for applications such as file transfer and e-mail that can tolerate delays.

Although ATM is connection oriented, many applications such as mail services and other data services are characterized by small amounts of data, sent sporadically. To save time and expense, no connection is established (connectionless service). User information is sent in a message that contains all necessary addressing and routing information, such as those used in local area networks. SMDS provides the connectionless service for ATM networks.

18.7.6   Classical IP Over ATM

Classical IP (CIP) over ATM is a mature standard that enables users to route IP packets over an ATM network or cloud using ATM as either a backbone or a workgroup technology. Classical IP over ATM maps IP network layer addresses to ATM addresses and enables ATM-attached devices to send IP packets over an ATM network.

The IP over ATM client is an endstation (computer, router, or bridge) with an ATM adapter installed and connected to the ATM network. These endstations may be located in physical, separate LANs, but because they are both connected to the ATM network, they are part of the same logical subnetwork, or virtual subnetwork. ATM networks are partitioned into logical IP subnets (LISs) that communicate with each other via routers. Because there is no native broadcast capability in ATM, the traditional broadcast Address Resolution Protocol (ARP) is replaced by a client-server-based ATMARP protocol.

The ATMARP server maintains a database of IP and ATM addresses of all clients on the network, resolving multicast and broadcast IP addresses to ATM addresses. ATMARP only supports unicast traffic, allowing the client to set up point-to-point connections with other endstations. The multicast address resolution server (MARS) maintains a database of broadcast and multicast addresses to all members of the network. The MARS can pass a list of addresses directly to a client so that the client can set up a point-to-point call. If a multicast server is available, the MARS can pass the address of the server to the client. In this case, the client contacts the MARS, and the MARS creates a point-to-multipoint connection and distributes the packets to the endstations. The ATM ARP/MARS server with an integrated multicast server is shipped with Windows servers.

An endstation can use either PVC or SVC connections. If an endstation is using a PVC, the ATM service provider or network administrator manually maps the IP addresses of reachable destination endstations to ATM virtual circuits. To establish a connection using classical IP over ATM, a sending station sends an ATMARP request to the ATMARP server on the logical IP subnet. The server reconciles the IP address of the receiving station with its ATM address and returns the ATM address to the sending client. The sending client then uses the address to establish an ATM link. When the receiving computer receives the first packet, it also sends an ATMARP request to the server to find the location of the sender. Once the server returns the appropriate address, the link is established and the two clients can communicate directly without further involvement by the server. After the PVC or SVC has been established, the sending endstation converts its packets into ATM adaptation layer (AAL) 5 cells and sends them over the virtual circuit to the destination endstation. The destination endstation then converts the AAL 5 cells into IP packets.

A station can have more than one active virtual circuit at a time. A file server or e-mail server may have hundreds of connections within a short period of time, depending on how many client systems it serves. Connections that go unused for a specified amount of time (the default is 15 to 20 minutes) are automatically cleared to recover adapter and ATM network resources. To use classical IP over ATM as a backbone to connect physically separate LANs, route IP packets over ATM by using routers as endstations.

Classical IP over ATM has several disadvantages. Because the ATMARP server can reach only one IP subnetwork, IP hosts can communicate directly with only destination IP hosts in that subnetwork. To send packets to a destination IP host in another virtual subnetwork, a sending IP host must send the packets through a router. The sending IP host uses a virtual circuit to connect to the router, and the router uses another virtual circuit to connect to the destination IP host. Routers create a bottleneck because they are slower than switches.

Another disadvantage is that classical IP over ATM can route only IP. If you want to route other protocols such as IPX, you cannot use classical IP over ATM. Furthermore, it does not solve delay or congestion problems because it cannot take advantage of ATM's qualities of service.

18.7.7   ATM LAN Emulation

The LAN Emulation (LANE) protocol as defined by the ATM Forum, is an ATM standard that emulates an Ethernet or token ring LAN on top of an ATM network. In other words, the LANE protocol makes an ATM network look and behave like an Ethernet or token ring LAN. Since the LANE emulates the media access control (MAC) sublayer of the OSI model, LANE enables any network layer protocol that works with the OSI model (including IPX, IP, and NetBIOS) to travel over an ATM network without modification. Users can then run applications over the ATM network, as they would over an Ethernet or token ring LAN; the ATM network is invisible to LAN users.

An **emulated LAN (ELAN)** consists of a set of LAN emulation clients that reside as ATM endpoints. The ELAN is equivalent to a virtual LAN (VLAN). The end systems (ATM network interface cards and internetworking and LAN switching equipment) have LAN emulation service that is implemented as device drivers, which will resolve MAC addresses to ATM addresses, set up direct connections between the clients, and forward the data. The LANE protocol operates transparently over and through the ATM switches and does not directly impact ATM switches. Endstations on the same physical segment can be part of different emulated LANs, and endstations can be members of more than one emulated LAN.

Each ELAN supports connectivity only between an ATM network and a single traditional (Ethernet or token ring) LAN environment. LANE cannot serve as a gateway between Ethernet and token ring LANs. An ELAN consists of the following components:

- **LAN emulation client (LEC)**—The LEC is implemented in ATM end system computers so that they can forward data between the ATM and LAN environments, process LAN broadcasts, and register MAC addresses with the LAN emulation server (LES). The LEC also provides a standard LAN interface to a high-level protocol on legacy LANs. The LEC is jointly identified by two addresses: its ATM address when communicating to the ATM network and a MAC address when communicating with the Ethernet or token ring LAN. Note that ELANs will have one LEC per ELAN.
- **LAN emulation server (LES)**—The LES provides a central control point for LECs to include registration of MAC addresses for new LECs, resolution of MAC addresses to ATM addresses for existing LECs, and maintenance of a mapped pairing of ATM addresses-to-media access control addresses for all ELAN member devices.
- **LAN emulation configuration server (LECS)**—The LECS is responsible for assigning LAN emulation clients to specific emulated LANs. When a client requests configuration information for

joining an emulated LAN, the LECS supplies the ATM address of the LES for the emulated LAN. Clients are directed to an appropriate LES, based on either their physical location (as interpreted by analyzing the client ATM address) or the identity of a particular destination LAN. The configuration server can, as an option, allow a client to configure and directly assign itself to a specific LES and emulated LAN. Each internetwork has only one LECS that serves all LAN emulation clients within it.

■ **Broadcast and unknown server (BUS)**—The BUS is a multicast server that is used to flood unknown destination address traffic and to forward multicast and broadcast traffic to clients within a particular ELAN. Each client is associated with a single BUS, identified by a unique ATM address, and located within a particular ELAN.

Suppose that you were working on an emulated LAN and wanted to access a file stored on a server that was located on a physically separate LAN. First, you would send the file request, and your LANE client would determine if it knew the ATM address of its LANE server. If your LANE client did not know this address, the client would query the LANE configuration server, asking for the ATM address of the LANE server. Second, after your LANE client received the correct address, your client would query the LANE server for the ATM address of the LANE server on which the file was stored. If the LANE server knew this address, the LANE server would send the address to your LANE client. If the LANE server did not know this address, the server would query the LANE BUS. The LANE BUS, in turn, would ask all LANE clients on the emulated LAN for their ATM addresses. The LANE BUS would then return the correct address to the LANE server, which would return the address to your LANE client. Finally, your LANE client would establish a virtual circuit to the server on which the file was stored. Then the LANE client would convert its Ethernet or token ring frames into cells and send these cells over the virtual circuit to the server.

With LANE, you can also send cells to other LANE clients without establishing a virtual circuit. Every LANE client that joins the emulated LAN establishes a permanent SVC with the LANE BUS. As a result, all LANE clients are connected to the LANE BUS via SVCs. If you want to send cells to another LANE client, your LANE client would forward cells to the BUS via an existing SVC, and the BUS would forward the cells to the destination LANE client. In this way, LANE enables the connection-oriented ATM network to mimic a connectionless network. LANE also allows you to broadcast cells to the entire emulated LAN. Your LANE client sends the cells to the LANE BUS, and the BUS forwards these cells to all other LANE clients.

Since existing LANs mainly support connectionless services, the LAN emulation service uses available bit rate (ABR) service. ABR service is important not only for LAN emulation, but also for applications involving bursty data traffic in which the bandwidth requirements cannot be predicted.

Because the LANE 1.0 standard does not specify a standard way for servers to communicate, each emulated LAN can have only one LANE server. Therefore, you cannot have redundant LANE servers, and the LANE server may become a bottleneck in large emulated LANs. In addition, because the LANE server must use virtual circuits to route traffic and because ATM switches can support only a limited number of virtual circuits (depending on your switches' capacities), using only one LANE server can overburden the switches. The LANE 2.0 standard will solve this problem by defining a way for the components of the LANE services to be distributed and will define the interface between these components, thus allowing up to 20 LANE BUS servers.

LANE has its limitations, however. As with IP hosts on classical IP over ATM subnetworks, an endstation in one emulated LAN must use a router to communicate with an endstation in another emulated LAN. The sending endstation must establish a virtual LAN with a router, which establishes a virtual circuit with the destination endstation. Routers can create bottlenecks because they are slower than switches.

Because LANE is a bridging technology, it limits you to a maximum of 2000 endstations per emulated LANE. Of course, the more endstations you have, the worse your network will perform. More endstations mean more broadcasts and more virtual circuits, which could be a problem since an ATM network can support only a certain number of virtual circuits at one time.

Because LANE is an OSI data link layer technology and is transparent to the higher layers of the OSI model, it cannot take advantage of ATM's quality of service. In addition, the LANE 1.0 standard supports only unspecified bit rate (UBR). LANE 2.0 enables you to specify the type of traffic your emulated LAN will carry: the constant bit rate (CBR), the variable bit rate (VBR), or the available bit rate (ABR). Unfortunately, the LANE 2.0 standard requires all virtual circuits on the emulated LAN to use the specified type of traffic.

18.7.8   Multiprotocol over ATM

Multiprotocol over ATM (MPOA) was developed by the ATM Forum to route protocols such as IP, IPX, and NetBIOS from traditional LANs over a switched ATM backbone. MPOA incorporates LANE to provide bridging capabilities while allowing the MPOA to route between virtual subnetworks without using traditional routers. Using routers in an ATM network significantly slows packet throughput, because each router has to reassemble cells of the OSI network layer packets for routing and then segment the packets into cells again for forwarding.

MPOA consists of route servers and edge devices. Route servers, also known as MPOA servers, maintain routing tables and calculate routes on behalf of edge devices. Route servers also communicate with traditional routers and with outer route servers. Route servers can be one piece of hardware or be built into routers and switches. Edge devices, also known as MPOA clients, can be intelligent switches that forward packets and cells between LANs and ATM networks or network interface boards that forward packets and cells between ATM-attached devices and ATM networks. Together, route servers and edge devices act as distributed routes, in which route servers determine where to send packets and edge devices forward these packets.

If an endstation on a LAN wanted to communicate with an ATM-attached device, the endstation would send a packet to the edge device. This device would check the destination MAC address or the network layer address of the packet. The device would then check its cache to see if it knew the corresponding ATM address. If the edge device did not know the ATM address, this device would query the route server. If the route server knew the ATM address, this server would simply respond with the address. If the route server did not know the ATM address, this server could use one of several routing protocols to communicate with other routers (both traditional routers and other route servers) to determine this address.

When the edge device knew the ATM address, it would establish a virtual circuit with the appropriate destination endstation, convert its LAN packets into ATM cells, and send these cells to the destination endstation. The edge device can establish a virtual circuit even if the destination endstation is on a different subnetwork; the edge device bypasses the route server when sending cells, sending them directly to the destination endstation. This process is called cut-through routing or one-hop routing.

For short transmissions, however, cut-through routing may not be the best approach because connection setup takes a long time relative to the size of the transmission. Using a process called hop-by-hop routing, MPOA can eliminate connection setup. With hop-by-hop routing, edge devices can forward packets to the route server just as LANE clients can forward packets to the LANE BUS. Edge devices can also perform flow detection: They can forward packets to the route server, but if they detect a flow (a long transmission), they can set up a virtual circuit to the destination endstation.

MPOA's biggest disadvantage is its relative newness. ATM Forum has not yet finalized the standard. Depending on the implementation, MPOA can also add complexity to your network; however, MPOA provides many capabilities that neither classical IP over ATM nor LANE provides. Because MPOA is an OSI network layer technology, it has access to important network layer information such as traffic characteristics and ATM's qualities of service. When establishing a connection, the edge device can use this network layer information to chart the best path to a destination endstation based on the QoS that the sending endstation requests.

MPOA also provides routing capabilities that no other ATM interoperability architecture provides. With MPOA, you can route between traditional LANs that are connected by a high-speed ATM backbone, thus creating a high-speed internetwork without the bottleneck of a traditional router. You also can use cut-through and hop-by-hop routing to optimize both short and long transmissions.

18.7.9   ATM and Windows

Windows 2000 and Windows Server 2003 can support a maximum of four ATM network adapters per computer. Most of these are plug-and-play cards. Therefore, after physically installing the card, it is automatically detected during boot-up and the correct driver is automatically installed.

After your ATM adapter is recognized and installed, Windows ATM servers are installed and available. By default, the connection is set up as a LAN emulation client (LEC). To view or configure additional services, do the following:

1. Click the Start button, point to Settings, and select the Network and Dial-up Connections option.
2. Click the ATM connection that corresponds to the ATM network adapter installed on this computer.
3. Open the File menu and select the Properties option.
4. In the list of network components used in this connection, select ATM LAN Emulation and click Properties.
5. If needed, configure the list of emulated LANs available for use with this ATM connection.

To enable a simple TCP/IP-over-ATM connection, do the following:

1. Click the Start button, point to Settings, and select the Network and Dial-up Connections option.
2. Select the ATM connection that corresponds to the ATM network adapter installed on this computer.
3. Open the File menu and select the Properties option.
4. From the list of network components, select Internet Protocol (TCP/IP), then click OK.

18.8   FDDI

Fiber Distributed Data Interface (FDDI) is a metropolitan area network (MAN) protocol that provides data transport at 100 Mbps (much higher data rate than standard Ethernet or IBM Token Ring) and can support up to 500 stations on a single network. Originally, FDDI networks required fiber optic cable, but today they can also run on UTP. Note: The copper part adopted into the FDDI standard is known as Copper Distributed Data Interface (CDDI). Of course, fiber optic cable offers much greater distances than UTP cable. Traditionally, FDDI was used primarily as a backbone to connect several department LANs together within a single building or to link several building LANs together in a campus environment. FDDI has a maximum total ring length of 100 km, or 60 miles (or 200 km, or 120 miles in wrap state, i.e., rings collapse to single ring). The maximum length between stations without repeaters is 2 km, or 1.24 miles.

FDDI communicates all of its information using symbols. Symbols are 4 bits encoded in a 5-bit sequence. To measure a bit in FDDI, as expressed by the change of state of light on the other side, the station takes a sample of the light coming from the other machine approximately every 8 nanoseconds. The light will either be on or off. If it has changed since the last sample, that translates into a bit of one. If the light has not changed since last sample, the bit is a zero.

Like Token Ring, FDDI is a token passing ring that uses a physical star topology. While a Token Ring node can transmit only a single frame when it gets the token, an FDDI node can transmit as many frames as can be generated within a predetermined time before it has to give up the token.

FDDI can be implemented in two basic ways: as a dual-attached ring and as a concentrator-based ring. In the dual-attached scenario, stations are connected directly one to another. FDDI's dual counter-rotating ring design acts as a fail-safe mechanism in case a node goes down. If any node fails, the ring wraps around the failed node. One limitation of the dual counter-rotating ring design is that if two nodes fail, the ring is broken in two places, effectively creating two separate rings. Nodes on one ring are then isolated from nodes on the other ring. External optical bypass devices can solve this problem, but their use is limited because of FDDI optical power requirements.

Another way to implement FDDI is to use concentrators to build networks. Concentrators are devices with multiple ports into which FDDI nodes connect. FDDI concentrators function like Ethernet hubs or token ring multiple station access units (MSAUs). Nodes are singly attached to the concentrator, which isolates failures occurring at those endstations. With a concentrator, nodes can be powered on and off without disrupting ring integrity. Since concentrators make FDDI network more reliable, most FDDI networks are now built with concentrators.

An extension to FDDI, called FDDI-2, supports the transmission of voice and video information as well as data. Another variation of FDDI, called FDDI Full-Duplex Technology (FFDT), uses the same network infrastructure but can potentially support data rates up to 200 Mbps.

18.9   DIGITAL SUBSCRIBER LINE

The **digital subscriber line (DSL)** is a special communication line that uses sophisticated modulation technology to maximize the amount of data that can be sent over plain twisted-pair copper wiring, which is already carrying phone service to subscribers' homes. DSL was originally developed to transmit video signals to compete against cable companies, but soon found use as a high-speed data connection with the explosion of the Internet. DSL is sometimes expressed as xDSL, because of the various kinds of digital subscriber line technologies including ADSL, R-DSL, HDSL, SDSL, and VDSL. See Table 18.8.

18.9.1   DSL Technology

The best quality of DSL technologies is their ability to transport large amounts of information across existing copper telephone lines. This capability is possible because of the DSL modem's leverage signal processing techniques that insert and extract more digital data onto analog lines. The key is modulation, a process in which one signal modifies the property of another.

In the case of digital subscriber lines, the modulating message signal from a sending modem alters the high-frequency carrier signal so that a composite wave, called a modulated wave, is formed. Because this high-frequency carrier signal can be modified, a large digital data payload can be carried in the modulated wave over greater distances than on ordinary copper pairs. When the transmission reaches its destination, the modulating message signal is recovered, or demodulated, by the receiving modem.

Table 18.8   Various xDSL technologies

Technology	Speed	Distance Limitation (24-gauge wire)	Applications
Asymmetrical digital subscriber line lite (ADSL lite)	Up to 1 Mbps downstream Up to 512 Kbps upstream	18,000 feet	Internet/intranet access, web browsing, IP telephony, video telephony
Asymmetrical digital subscriber line (ADSL)	1.5–8 Mbps downstream Up to 1.544 Mbps upstream	18,000 feet (12,000 feet for fastest speeds)	Internet/intranet access, video-on-demand, remote LAN access, VPNs, VoIP
Rate adaptive digital subscriber line (R-ADSL)	1.5–8 Mbps downstream Up to 1.544 Mbps upstream	18,000 feet (12,000 feet for fastest speeds)	Internet/intranet access, video-on-demand, remote LAN access, VPNs, VoIP
ISDN digital subscriber line (IDSL)	Up to 144 Kbps full duplex	18,000 feet (additional equipment can extend the distance)	Internet/intranet access, web browsing, IP telephony, video telephony
High bit-rate digital subscriber line (HDSL)	1.544 Mbps full duplex (T1) 2.048 Mbps full duplex (E1) (uses 2–3 wire pairs)	12,000–15,000 feet	Local, repeated T1/E1 trunk replacement, PBX interconnection, frame relay traffic aggregator, LAN interconnect
Single-line digital subscriber line (SDSL)	1.544 Mbps full duplex (T1) 2.048 Mbps full duplex (E1) (uses 1 wire pair)	10,000 feet	Local, repeated T1/E1 trunk replacement, collaborative computing, LAN interconnect
Very high bit-rate digital subscriber line (VDSL)	13–52 Mbps downstream 1.5–2.3 Mbps upstream (up to 34 Mbps if symmetric)	1000–4500 feet (depending on speed)	Multimedia Internet access, high-definition television program delivery

There are many ways to alter the high-frequency carrier signal that results in a modulated wave. For ADSL, there are two competing modulation schemes: carrierless amplitude phase (CAP) modulation and discrete multitone (DMT) modulation. CAP and DMT use the same fundamental modulation technique—quadrature amplitude modulation (QAM)—but apply it in different ways.

QAM, a bandwidth conservation process routinely used in modems, enables two digital carrier signals to occupy the same transmission bandwidth. With QAM, two independent message signals are used to modulate two carrier signals that have identical frequencies, but differ in amplitude and phase. QAM receivers are able to discern whether to use lower or higher numbers of amplitude and phase states to overcome noise and interference on the wire pair.

CAP modulation is a proprietary modulation of AT&T Paradyne. Income data modulate a single carrier channel that is sent down a telephone line. The carrier is suppressed before transmission and reconstructed at the receiving end. Generating a modulated wave that carries amplitude and phase state changes is not easy. To overcome this challenge, the CAP version of QAM stores parts of a modulated message signal in memory and then reassembles the parts in the modulated wave. The carrier signal is suppressed before transmission, because it contains no information, and is reassembled at the receiving modem (hence the word *carrierless* in CAP). At start-up, CAP also tests the quality of the access line and implements the most efficient version of QAM to ensure satisfactory performance for individual signal transmissions. CAP is normally FDM based.

DMT is actually a form of frequency-division multiplexing (FDM). Because high-frequency signals on copper lines suffer more loss in the presence of noise, DMT discretely divides the available frequencies into 256 subchannels, or tones. As with CAP, a test occurs at start-up to determine the carrying capacity of each subchannel. Incoming data are then broken down into a variety of bits and distributed to a specific combination of subchannels based on their abilities to carry the transmission. To rise above noise, more data reside in the lower frequencies and less in the upper frequencies.

To create upstream and downstream channels, ADSL modems divide the phone line's available bandwidth using one of two methods: FDM or echo cancellation. FDM assigns one band or frequency for upstream data and another for downstream data. The downstream path is further divided by time-division multiplexing (TDM) into one or more high-speed channels for data and one or more low-speed channels, one of which is for voice. The upstream path is multiplexed into several low-speed channels.

Echo cancellation, the same technique used by V.32 and V.34 modems, means that the upstream and the downstream signals are sent on the wire at the same frequencies. The advantage of echo cancellation is that the signals are both kept at the lowest possible frequencies (since cable loss and crosstalk noise both increase with frequency) and therefore achieve greater cable distance for a given data rate. An ADSL receiver will see an incoming signal that is both the incoming signal from the far end and the outgoing signal from the local transmitter. These are mixed over the same frequency range. In other words, the received signal consists of not only the signal to be recovered from the far end but also a local echo due to the local transmitter. The local echo must be accurately modeled by DSP circuitry, and then this replica echo is electronically subtracted from the composite incoming signal. If done properly, all that remains are the incoming data from the far-end ADSL system. Although echo cancellation uses bandwidth more efficiently, the process of modeling the echo is quite complicated and is more costly. Therefore, only a few vendors have implemented the process.

18.9.2   ADSL

Currently, existing POTS data are transmitted over a frequency spectrum that ranges from 0 kHz to 4 kHz. Copper phone lines can actually support frequency ranges much greater than these, and ADSL takes advantage of these ranges by transmitting data in the ranges between 4 kHz and 2.2 MHz. Therefore, ADSL relies on advanced digital signal processing (DSP) and complex algorithms to compress all information into the phone line. In addition, ADSL modems correct errors that are caused by line conditions and attenuation. With this technology, any computer or network can easily become connected to the Internet at speeds comparable with T1 access for a fraction of the cost and it can serve as a suitable medium for video streaming and conferencing.

As its name implies, the asymmetrical digital subscriber line (ADSL) transmits an asymmetric data stream, with much more going downstream to the subscriber than is coming back. The reason for this has less to do with transmission technology than with the cable plant itself. Twisted-pair telephone wires are bundled together in large cables. Fifty pair to a cable is a typical configuration toward the subscriber, but cables coming out of a central office (CO) may have hundreds or even thousands of pairs bundled together. An individual line from a CO to a subscriber is spliced together from many cable sections as they fan out from the CO. (Bellcore claims that the average U.S. subscriber line has 22 splices.) Alexander Bell invented twisted-pair wiring to minimize crosstalk. A small amount of crosstalk does occur, and its amount increases as the frequencies and the length of line increases. Therefore, if you place symmetric signals in many pairs within the same cable, the crosstalk significantly limits the data rate and length of line.

Most people download information as they view web pages and download files, and the amount of information downloaded is far greater than the amount of information that a user uploads or transfers to other computers. This asymmetry, then, combined with always-on access (which eliminates call setup), makes ADSL ideal for Internet/intranet surfing, video-on-demand, and remote LAN access.

ADSL modems usually include a POTS splitter, which enables simultaneous access to voice telephony and high-speed data access. Some vendors provide active POTS splitters, which enable simultaneous telephone and data access. However, if the power fails or the modem fails with an active POTS splitter, then the telephone fails. A passive POTS splitter, on the other hand, maintains lifeline telephone access even if the modem fails (due to a power outage, for example), since the telephone is not powered by external electricity. Telephone access in the case of a passive POTS splitter is a regular analog voice channel, the same as customers currently receive to their homes.

Downstream, ADSL supports speeds between 1.5 Mbps and 8 Mbps; whereas upstream, the rate is between 640 Kbps and 1.544 Mbps. ADSL can provide 1.544-Mbps transmission rates at distances of up to 18,000 feet over one wire pair. Optimal speeds of 6 Mbps to 8 Mbps can be achieved at distances of 10,000 feet to 12,000 feet using standard 24-gauge wire.

Currently, the ADSL lite specification, also known as g.lite, is a low-cost, easy-to-install version of ADSL that is specifically designed for the consumer marketplace. ADSL lite is a lower-speed version of ADSL that will eliminate the need for the telephone company to install and maintain a premises-based POTS splitter. ADSL lite should also work over longer distances than full-rate ADSL, making it more widely available to mass market consumers. It will support both data and voice and provide an evolution path to full-rate ADSL.

18.9.3   HDSL

The **high bit-rate digital subscriber line (HDSL)** derives its name from the high bandwidth that is transmitted in both directions over two copper loops. HDSL has proven to be a reliable and cost-effective means for providing repeaterless T1 and E1 services over two twisted-pair loops. HDSL transceivers can reliably transmit a 1.544- and 2.048-Mbps data signal over two nonloaded, 24-gauge (0.5 mm), unconditioned twisted-pair wire loops at a distance of up to 13,100 feet (4.2 km) without the need for repeaters. Different from ADSL, HDSL does not provide standard voice telephone service on the same wire pair.

Eliminating the need for repeater equipment and removal of bridged taps greatly simplifies the labor and engineering effort to provide the service. This attribute eliminates the need to identify, modify, and verify a controlled environment, with power, secured access, and other factors needed to support repeater equipment. It also reduces the time, cost, and effort of isolating faults and taking corrective action when a failure does occur. Studies by some service providers have indicated that troubleshooting and replacing defective repeater equipment often costs significantly more than the cost of the equipment itself. These attributes translate into increased network uptime and reduced engineering time, thus making possible T1 provisioning in a matter of days as opposed to weeks. Faster service provisioning and greater uptime leads to increased customer satisfaction and increased service revenues. To provision a 12,000-foot (3.6-km) local loop with traditional T1 transmission equipment requires two transceivers and two repeaters. To provision the same loop with HDSL requires only two HDSL transceivers, one at each end of a line.

HDSL2 is the next generation of HDSL, designed to accomplish three primary goals: (1) full T1 rates (1.544 Mbps) on a single pair of copper wires with the same spectral compatibility as traditional HDSL; (2) vendor interoperability, meaning that service providers are no longer tied to proprietary solutions; and (3) a full extension of carrier service area reach to 12,000 feet. HDSL2 can be thought of as offering everything that traditional HDSL offers, but on a single pair of copper wires. HDSL2 has become the DSL of choice for corporations.

18.9.4   Connecting to an ADSL Line

To connect to an ADSL line, either install an ADSL modem via an expansion card or a USB port, or external stand-alone device, connected to a network card. If you are using the expansion card or USB device, assign and configure the TCP/IP. If you are using the external stand-alone device, assign and configure the TCP/IP for the network card.

18.10   CABLE MODEMS

Cable systems were originally designed to deliver broadcast television signals efficiently to subscribers' homes. To ensure that consumers could obtain cable service with the same TV sets that they use to receive over-the-air broadcast TV signals, cable operators re-create a portion of the over-the-air radio frequency (RF) spectrum within a sealed coaxial cable line.

Traditional coaxial cable systems typically operate with 330 MHz or 450 MHz of capacity, whereas modern hybrid fiber/coaxial (HFC) systems are expanded to 750 MHz or more. Logically, downstream video programming signals begin around 50 MHz, the equivalent of channel 2 for over-the-air television signals. Each standard television channel occupies 6 MHz of the RF spectrum. Thus, a traditional cable system with 400 MHz of downstream bandwidth can carry the equivalent of 60 analog TV channels, and a modern HFC system with 700 MHz of downstream bandwidth has the capacity for about 110 channels.

A **hybrid fiber/coaxial (HFC)** network is a telecommunications technology in which fiber optic cable and coaxial cable are used in different portions of a network to carry broadband content (such as video, data, and voice). In a HFC network, a local cable TV company installs fiber optic cable from the cable-head end (distribution center) to serving nodes located close to business and residential users, and from these nodes the cable TV company uses coaxial cable to individual businesses and homes. An advantage of a HFC network is that some of the characteristics of fiber optic cable (high bandwidth and low noise and interference susceptibility) can be brought close to the user without having to replace the existing coaxial cable that is installed to the home and business. Both cable TV and telephone companies are using HFC in new and upgraded networks and, in some cases, sharing the same infrastructure to carry both video and voice conversations in the same system.

While regular cable is analog, digital cable uses digital signals. The digitals signals can be compressed much more than analog signals. Digital cable can provide 200 to 300 channels using the same bandwidth as analog cable.

To deliver data services over a cable network, one television channel in the 50- to 750-MHz range is typically allocated for downstream traffic to homes and another channel in the 5- to 42-MHz band is allocated to carry upstream signals. A cable modem termination system (CMTS) communicates through these channels with **cable modems** located in subscriber homes to create a virtual local area network connection. Most cable modems are external devices that connect to a PC through a 10BaseT Ethernet card, external USB modem, or an internal PCI modem cards.

A single downstream 6-MHz television channel may support up to 27 Mbps of downstream data throughput from the cable using 64-QAM (quadrature amplitude modulation) transmission technology. Speeds can be boosted to 36 Mbps using 256 QAM. Upstream channels may deliver 500 Kbps to 10 Mbps from homes using 16-QAM or QPSK (quadrature phase shift key) modulation techniques, depending on the amount of spectrum allocated for service. This upstream and downstream bandwidth is shared by the active data subscribers connected to a given cable network segment, typically 500 to 2000 homes on a modern HFC network.

An individual cable modem subscriber may experience access speeds from 500 Kbps to 1.5 Mbps or more, depending on the network architecture and traffic load, which is blazing performance compared with dial-up alternatives. When surfing the Web, however performance can be affected by Internet backbone congestion. In addition to speed, cable modems offer another key benefit: constant connectivity. Because cable modems use connectionless technology, much like in an office LAN, a subscriber's PC is always online with the network. That means there's no need to dial-in to begin a session, so users do not have to worry about receiving busy signals. Additionally, going online does not tie up their telephone line.

Similar to DSL routers, cable modems can be replaced with the cable routers. The cable router allows multiple computers to connect to the router, and the router acts as a DHCP server for the clients connected to it.

SUMMARY

1. The circuit switching technique connects the sender with the receiver via a single path for the duration of a conversation.

2. The packet switching technique involves messages that are broken into small parts, or packets.

3. A virtual circuit is a logical circuit created to ensure reliable communication between two network devices.

4. A virtual circuit can be either a permanent virtual circuit (PVC) or a switched virtual circuit (SVC).

5. A PVC is a permanently established virtual circuit that consists of one mode: data transfer.

6. An SVC is a virtual circuit that is dynamically established on demand and terminated when transmission is complete.

7. Data terminal equipment (DTE) devices are end systems that communicate across the WAN.

8. Data circuit-terminating equipment (DCE) devices are special communication devices that provide the interface between the DTE and the network.

9. The DSU is a device that performs protective and diagnostic functions for a telecommunications line. The CSU is a device that connects a terminal to a digital line. Typically, the two devices are packaged as a single unit (CSU/DSU).

10. The public switched telephone network (PSTN) is the international telephone system that is based on copper wires (UTP cabling) carrying analog voice data. The PSTN, also known as the plain old telephone service (POTS), is the standard telephone service used in most homes.

11. The subscriber loop, or local loop, is the telephone line that runs from a home or office to the telephone company's central office or neighborhood switching station (often a small building with no windows).

12. The T-carrier system was introduced by the Bell System in the United States in the 1960s as the first successful system that converted the analog voice signal to a digital bit stream.

13. The disadvantages of the leased digital lines are their higher cost and their limitation as a point-to-point connection.

14. Circuit switch technology can be referred to as dial-up technology.

15. T-carrier system lines are permanent leased lines. Switched 56 and switched 64 lines are digitally switched or "dial-up lines" that provide a single digital channel for dependable data connectivity.

16. The Integrated Services Digital Network (ISDN) is the planned replacement for POTS so that it can provide voice and data communication worldwide using circuit switching as well as the same wiring that is currently being used in homes and businesses.

17. The ISDN uses two types of channels, a B channel and a D channel. The bearer channels (B channels) transfer data at a bandwidth of 64 Kbps for each channel. The data channels (D channels) use a communications language called DSS1 for administrative signaling.

18. Today, the two well-defined standards used are the basic rate interface (BRI) and the primary rate interface (PRI).

19. X.25 network is a packet switched network that allows remote devices to communicate with each other across digital links without the expense of individual leased lines.

20. Frame Relay is a packet switching protocol designed to use high-speed digital backbone links to support modern protocols for error handling and flow control for connecting devices on a WAN.

21. SDH and SONET are transmission technology standards of synchronous data transmission over fiber optic cables. They provide a high-speed transfer of data, video, and types of information across great distances without regard to the specific services and applications they support.

22. A data transmission technology is based on transmitting data in relatively small, fixed-size packets, or cells.

23. Switched multimegabit data service (SMDS) is a high-speed, cell relay, WAN service designed for LAN interconnection through the public telephone network.

24. Asynchronous transfer mode (ATM) is both a LAN and a WAN technology, which is generally implemented as a backbone technology.

25. The digital subscriber line (DSL) is a special communication line that uses sophisticated modulation technology to maximize the amount of data that can be sent over plain twisted-pair copper wiring, which is already carrying phone service to subscribers' homes.

26. Asymmetrical DSL (ADSL) transmits an asymmetric data stream, with much more going downstream to the subscriber than is coming back.

27. The Fiber Distributed Data Interface (FDDI) is a metropolitan area network (MAN) protocol that provides data transport at 100 Mbps and can support up to 500 stations on a single network.

28. Cable modems communicate through the cable system to create a virtual LAN connection.

29. A hybrid fiber/coaxial (HFC) network is a telecommunications technology in which fiber optic cable and coaxial cable are used in different portions of a network to carry broadband content (such as video, data, and voice).

QUESTIONS

1. PSTN is an acronym for _____ .
   a. partial switched telephone network
   b. public switched transmission network
   c. partial switched transmission network
   d. public switched telephone network

2. Which one of the following technologies is intended to replace analog phone lines?
   a. PSTN/POTS   c. Frame Relay
   b. ATM   d. ISDN

3. T1 is a widely used type of digital communication line. What does the T1 technology offer?
   a. transmission speed of up to 1.544 Mbps
   b. transmission speed of up to 45 Mbps
   c. point-to-point, full-duplex transmission
   d. two 64-Kbps B channels and one 16-Kbps D channel per line

4. T1 lines utilize technology that combines signals from different sources onto one cable for transmission. Which one of the following devices can be used to combine multiple data signals onto a single transmission line?
   a. data assembler   c. multiplexer
   b. transceiver   d. redirector

5. How many separate devices can be connected to a basic rate interface (BRI) line?
   a. 1   d. 64
   b. 8   e. no physical limitation
   c. 16

6. What is the maximum number of individual phone numbers that could be assigned to an ISDN BRI?
   a. 1   c. 16
   b. 8   d. 64

7. What is another representation for a standard basic rate interface (BRI) ISDN line?
   a. 64B2+16D   c. 2B+D
   b. B2+D   d. 2B64+D16

8. You decide to implement PPP multilink over multiple ISDN BRI lines. How many BRIs without compression will you need to achieve your minimum-required rate of 384 Kbps?
   a. 1   d. 4
   b. 2   e. You cannot use PPP
   c. 3   multilink with ISDN.

9. What is the compressed theoretical maximum transmission speed you could achieve with compression if you implemented three BRIs to achieve a minimum uncompressed transmission speed of 384 Kbps?
   a. 512 Kbps   c. 1536 Kbps
   b. 768 Kbps   d. 2048 Kbps

10. One of your offices is 2 miles away from a local telephone central office. The other is approximately 5 miles away from the same office. What will you need in order to use an ISDN BRI?
    a. one repeater between the telephone central office and your first office and two repeaters between the telephone central office and your second office
    b. one repeater between the telephone central office and your second office

    c. two repeaters between the telephone central office and your second office
    d. no repeaters

11. Suppose the following situation exists: Your company is based in Sacramento, and it has branch offices in Los Angeles and New York City. Each of the three offices has a 10BaseT network. Users must access resources in all three offices.

    Required result:
    • You must implement a networking solution that will offer WAN communication between the three sites.

    Optional desired results:
    • The WAN connection must support approximately 256 Kbps of data and several analog telephone conversations between sites.
    • The WAN connection must continue operations even if one of the WAN links should fail.

    Proposed solution:
    • Use three T1 connections—one between Sacramento and Los Angeles, one between Los Angeles and New York, and one between New York and Sacramento.
    Which result does the proposed solution produce?
    a. The proposed solution produces the required result and both of the optional desired results.
    b. The proposed solution produces the required result but only one of the optional desired results.
    c. The proposed solution produces the required result but does not produce either of the optional desired results.
    d. The proposed solution does not produce the required result.

12. Suppose the following situation exists: Your company is based in Atlanta, and it has branch offices in Los Angeles and New York City. Each of the three offices has a 10BaseT network. Users must access resources in all three offices.

    Required result:
    • You must implement a networking solution that would offer WAN communication between sites.

    Optional desired results:
    • The WAN connection must support approximately 1.5 Mbps of data.
    • The WAN connection must continue operations at 1.5 Mbps even if one of the WAN links should fail.

    Proposed solution:
    • Use two T1 connection lines—one between Atlanta and Los Angeles, and one between Los Angeles and New York.
    Which result does the proposed solution produce?
    a. The proposed solution produces the required result and both of the optional desired results.
    b. The proposed solution produces the required result but only one of the optional desired results.
    c. The proposed solution produces the required result but does not produce either of the optional desired results.
    d. The proposed solution does not produce the required result.

13. A wide area network requires complex and expensive packet switching equipment. Which one of the following WAN technologies is actually a protocol suite that uses packet assemblers and disassemblers?
    a. X.25
    b. ATM
    c. ISDN
    d. Frame Relay

14. Frame Relay is a form of packet switching technology that evolved from X.25. Which one of the following statements best describes the Frame Relay technology?
    a. It transmits fixed-length packets at the physical layer through the most cost-effective path.
    b. It transmits variable-length packets at the physical layer through the most cost-effective path.
    c. It transmits fixed-length frames at the data link layer through the most cost-effective path.
    d. It transmits variable-length frames at the data link layer through the most cost-effective path.

15. Why is CRC needed in Frame Relay technology?
    a. It helps detect connection failures.
    b. It helps prevent congestion.
    c. It ensures transmission speed.
    d. It ensures frame accuracy.

16. Which one of the following WAN technologies can provide subscribers with bandwidth as needed?
    a. Frame Relay
    b. X.25
    c. ISDN
    d. T1

17. SONET systems are _____ technology.
    a. twisted-pair, copper-based
    b. Thinnet cabling
    c. fiber optic
    d. wireless

18. SONET's base signal (STS-1) operates at a bit rate of _____.
    a. 64 Kbps
    b. 1.544 Mbps
    c. 51.840 Mbps
    d. 155.520 Mbps

19. _____ is the standard for North America, whereas _____ is the standard for the rest of the world.
    a. SONET, SDH
    b. SDH, SONET
    c. ATM, SONET
    d. ATM, SDH

20. In ATM networks, all information is formatted into fixed-length cells consisting of _____ bytes.
    a. 32
    b. 48
    c. 64
    d. 128

21. Packet switching networks divide data into packets and send them over a common transmission line using virtual circuits. Which one of the following is an implementation of a packet switching technology?
    a. T1
    b. ISDN
    c. switched 56
    d. ATM

22. The basic connection unit in an ATM network is known as the _____ .
    a. virtual channel connection
    b. virtual path connection
    c. DSL connection
    d. DS-0 connection

23. CBR is used primarily for _____ .
    a. multimedia e-mail
    b. videoconferencing
    c. data transport
    d. simple e-mail

24. Which service category is most likely to suffer cell loss due to bandwidth constraints?
    a. CBR
    b. ABR
    c. UBR
    d. nrt-VBR

25. ADSL increases existing twisted-pair access capacity by _____ .
    a. twofold
    b. threefold
    c. thirtyfold
    d. fiftyfold

26. A modem translates _____ .
    a. analog signals into digital signals
    b. digital signals into analog signals
    c. both of the above
    d. none of the above

27. A digital subscriber line (DSL) refers to a _____ .
    a. specific gauge of wire used in modem communications
    b. modem enabling high-speed communications
    c. connection created by a modem pair enabling high-speed communications
    d. specific length of wire

28. True or False: T1/E1 and HDSL are essentially equivalent technologies.

29. The practical upper limit of length of ADSL is _____ feet.
    a. 6000
    b. 12,000
    c. 18,000
    d. 36,000

30. What is the major road block to providing full digital service over POTS?
    a. The "last mile" of telephone cable is still copper.
    b. Competition is not strong enough to warrant full digital service.
    c. Fiber optic lines cannot be brought out to rural areas.
    d. It is too expensive for the telephone companies to implement.

31. Name two advantages of xDSL technology.
    a. It runs on fiber optic cables and increased bandwidth.
    b. It is inexpensive and uses commonly available modems.
    c. It provides high-speed digital access and is inexpensive.
    d. It provides fast analog service and always-on Internet access.
    e. It is widely available in rural areas and for a modest cost.

Remote Access

Topics Covered in This Chapter

Introduction

Networks are common in today's workplace. Most people who want to extend their networks away from their offices or to connect to their networks from home or on the road can now access applications and data that are stored on the network. For years, Windows NT has offered remote access and has marketed that fact as a major feature. Windows 2000 and Windows Server 2003 continue to offer remote access with additional features and functions.

Objectives

- Connect to computers by using a virtual private network (VPN) connection.
- Create a dial-up connection to connect to a remote access server.
- Connect to the Internet by using dial-up networking.
- Configure inbound connections.

- Create a remote access policy.
- Configure a remote access profile.
- Configure authentication protocols.
- Configure encryption protocols.
- Configure and troubleshoot IPSec.
- Install, configure, monitor, and troubleshoot Terminal Services.

19.1   REMOTE ACCESS SERVICE

Today, modern networks offer **remote access service (RAS),** which allows users to connect remotely using various protocols and connection types. Current projections call for the number of remote users—telecommuters, road warriors, and other mobile users—to grow to more than 100 million as remote LAN and Internet access continues to grow.

Typically, remote access costs from 63% to 157% more to support than its office-bound counterparts. About one-third of these costs are attributed to incremental charges such as equipment costs and access fees. The remaining costs are devoted to ongoing administration and technical support for the act of keeping remote users connected to the corporate network. These drawbacks are offset by reduced real estate costs and increased productivity. To make remote access a truly sound investment, organizations must find a way to simplify remote desktop management and support while providing the same level of performance and reliability that is currently available with local solutions. There are two types of remote access: dial-up networking and virtual private networking.

Dial-up networking is used when a remote access client makes a nonpermanent, dial-up connection to a physical port on a remote access server by using the service of a telecommunications provider such as an analog phone, ISDN, or X.25. The best example of dial-up networking is that of a dial-up networking client who dials the phone number of one port/modem of a remote access server. A **remote access server** is the computer and associated software that is set up to handle users who are seeking access to the network remotely. Sometimes called a **communication server,** a remote access server usually includes or is associated with a firewall server to ensure security and a router that can forward the remote access: request to another part of the corporate network.

Virtual private networking is the creation of secured, point-to-point connections across a private network or a public network such as the Internet. A virtual private networking client uses special TCP/IP-based protocols, called tunneling protocols, to make a virtual call to a virtual port on a virtual private networking server. The best example of virtual private networking is that of a virtual private networking client who makes a virtual private network connection to a remote access server that is connected to the Internet. The remote access server answers the virtual call, authenticates the caller, and transfers data between the virtual private networking client and the corporate network.

Dial-up networking over an analog phone or ISDN is a direct physical connection between the dial-up networking client and the dial-up networking server. You can encrypt data sent over the connection, but it is not required. In contrast to dial-up networking, virtual private networking is always a logical, indirect connection between the virtual private networking client and the virtual private networking server. To ensure privacy, you must encrypt data that are sent over the connection.

19.1.1   Traditional Remote Access

The typical dial-in session actually consists of six distinct steps or stages, each of which must be completed successfully before the user gains access to centralized resources. Each step is subject to its own unique set of problems or failures that individually could jeopardize the entire connection. These steps are as follows:

1. Modem connection
2. Dial-out
3. Handshake
4. Authentication
5. IP address negotiation
6. Access to resources

During the modem connection, the modem checks the phone line for a dial tone. If the modem fails or cannot detect a dial tone, the connection process fails immediately. A "no dial tone" error can be caused by problems with the phone cable, the phone jack, the modem, the dialer, or any combination of conditions related to these items or devices.

If a dial tone is detected, the remote PC proceeds with the connection process by dialing the remote access number. Any number of events, such as no answer, a busy signal, or no carrier, could cause the connection process to fail. If the call gets through, the remote (dialing) modem will begin negotiating a common data rate and other transmission parameters with the answering modem. This step is referred to as the **handshaking** stage, because both modems must agree on the same parameters before continuing. Technology advancements have produced a variety of ways to encode, compress, modulate, and transfer bits over the phone line, adding complexity—and processing time—to the process. These factors make it critical for IT managers to monitor and measure both the final outcome of the negotiation process and the length of time it takes for the negotiation to be completed. Connection failures and delays are typically the result of the local and remote modems disagreeing on one or more transmission parameters.

Once authentication is complete, the remote PC is assigned a dynamic IP address for identification purposes. The remote PC must agree to use the specified IP address or the local system will refuse to establish the link. The remote PC is also assigned a DNS server at this time; if the assignment is not recorded or is unsuccessful for some reason, attempts to connect will appear as application problems.

Once the previous five stages of the remote connection process have been successfully completed, the dial-in client PC is granted access to the corporate network. At this stage, the user can check e-mail, send messages, copy or transfer files, run application programs, and so forth, but the connection is still not entirely safe: Connectivity problems can occur if the call is abnormally terminated, if the modem speed is too slow, or if the dial-up network has an excessive amount of line noise.

19.1.2   Remote Authentication Dial-in User Service

Adding a remote access point to the centralized corporate network increases the chance of a break-in. Therefore, a secure authentication scheme is required to provide security and protect against remote client impersonation. During the authentication stage, the remote access server collects authentication data from the dial-in client and checks it against its own user database or against a central authentication database server, such as the **Remote Authentication Dial-in User Service (RADIUS).**

RADIUS is the industry standard client-server protocol and software that enables remote access servers to communicate with a central server to authenticate dial-in users and authorize their access to the requested system or service for authenticating remote users. It is defined in RFCs 2138 and 2139, "Remote Authentication Dial-in User Service (RADIUS)" and "RADIUS Accounting." RADIUS allows a company to maintain user profiles in a central database that all remote servers can share. It provides better security, allowing a company to set up a policy that can be applied at a single administered network point. Because it has a central server, RADIUS also makes it easier to perform accounting of network usage for billing and for keeping network statistics.

When a user dials in to a remote access device/server, this server then communicates with the central RADIUS server to determine if the user is authorized to connect to the LAN. The RADIUS server performs the authentication and responds with an "accept" or a "reject." If the user is accepted, the RAS routes the user on to the network; if not, the RAS terminates the user's connection. If the user's login information, user name, and/or password does not match the entry in the RAS, or if the RAS is unable to contact the RADIUS server, then the connection will be denied. Besides being deployed in remote access servers, RADIUS can also be deployed on routers and firewalls.

19.1.3   SLIP and PPP Protocols

The first protocol used to connect to an IP network using dial-up lines was the **Serial Line Interface Protocol (SLIP).** SLIP is simple protocol in which packets are sent down a serial link delimited with special END characters. SLIP does not perform a number of functions that data link protocols perform. First, SLIP only works with TCP/IP; it cannot be used with other protocols such as IPX. It does not perform error checking at the OSI data layer, and it does not authenticate users who are dialing into an access router. Next, with SLIP, you have to know the IP address assigned to you by your service provider. You also need to know the IP address of the remote system you will be dialing into. If IP addresses are dynamically assigned (depends on your service provider), your SLIP software needs to be able to pick up the IP assignments automatically, or you will have to set them up manually. You will have to configure certain parameters of the device such as maximum transmission unit (MTU) maximum receive unit (MRU) and use of compression. Lastly, SLIP does not support encrypted passwords; therefore, it transmits passwords in clear text, which is not secure at all. Typically, you would use SLIP when you are dialing into an older server that does not use PPP connections.

Point-to-Point Protocol (PPP) has become the predominant protocol for modem-based access to the Internet. It provides full-duplex, bidirectional operations between hosts and can encapsulate multiple network layer LAN protocols to connect to private networks. PPP is a fullduplex protocol that can be used on various physical media, including twisted-pair or fiber optic lines and on satellite transmission. PPP supports asynchronous serial communication, synchronous serial communication, and ISDN. Furthermore, a multilink version of PPP can be used to access ISDN lines, inverse multiplexing analog phone lines, and high-speed optical lines. PPP is one of the many variants of an early, internationally standardized data link protocol known as the Highlevel Data Link Control (HDLC) protocol.

To enable PPP to transmit data over a serial point-to-point link, three components are necessary.

- **High-level Data Link Control (HDLC) protocol**—Encapsulates data during transmission
- **Link Control Protocol (LCP)**—Establishes, configures, maintains and terminates point-to-point links (including multilink PPP sessions) and optionally tests link quality before data transmission. In addition, user authentication is generally performed by LCP as soon as the link is established.
- **Network Control Protocol (NCP)**—Configures the different communication protocols including TCP/IP and IPX, which are allowed to be used simultaneously.

One typical IP-specific function of the NCP is the provision of dynamic IP addresses for remote dial-in users. ISPs commonly employ this PPP feature to assign temporary IP addresses to their modem-based customers. Note: The PPP mechanism is not as complete as the DHCP, which can set up a lease period and provide such things as subnet masks, default router addresses, DNS server addresses, domain names, and much more to a newly connected computer. An ISP or other provider of remote connectivity services can use the DHCP as the source of IP addresses that NCP hands out.

There are four distinct phases of establishing a PPP connection. Each of these four phases must complete successfully before the PPP connection is ready to transfer user data:

- PPP configuration
- Authentication
- Callback (optional)
- Protocol configuration

PPP configures protocol parameters using the LCP. During the initial LCP phase, each device on both ends of a connection negotiates communication options that are used to send data. Options include PPP parameters, address and control field compression, protocol ID compression, protocols used to authenticate the remote access client, and multilink options. Note: An authentication protocol is selected but not implemented until the authentication phase.

After the LCP phase is complete, the authentication protocol agreed upon by the remote access server and the remote access client is implemented. The nature of this traffic is specific to the PPP authentication protocol.

19.1.4   Authentication Protocols

When a client dials in to a RAS server, the server must verify the client's credentials for authentication by using the client's user account properties and remote access policies to authorize the connection. If authentication and authorization succeed, the server allows a connection. There are a number of PPP authentication protocols, and each protocol has advantages and disadvantages in terms of security, usability, and breadth of support. See Table 19.1.

Password Authentication Protocol (PAP) is the least secure authentication protocol because it uses **clear-text** passwords. Clear text, also referred to as plain text, is textual data in ASCII format. Two steps are involved in using PAP:

1. The remote access client sends a PAP authenticate-request message to the remote access server containing the remote access client's user name and clear-text password.

Table 19.1   Various security protocols

Protocols	Security	Description	Use When . . .
Password Authentication Protocol (PAP)	Low	Sends passwords across the link as unencrypted plain text. Not a secure authentication method.	the client and server cannot negotiate by using a more secure form of validation.
Shiva Password Authentication Protocol (SPAP)	Medium	Sends password across link in reversibly encrypted form. Not recommended in situations where security is an issue.	connecting to a Shiva LanRover, or when a Shiva client connects to a Windows 2000–based remote access server.
Challenge Handshake Authentication Protocol (CHAP)	High	Uses MD5 hashing scheme. Client computer sends a hash of the password to the RAS, which checks the client hash against a hash it generates with the password stored on the RAS server. CHAP does provide protection against server impersonation.	you have clients that are not running Microsoft operating systems.
Microsoft Challenge Handshake Authentication Protocol (MS-CHAP), version 1 (v1)	High	Similar to CHAP. Provides nonreversible, encrypted password authentication. Does not require the on the server to be in plain text or reversibly encrypted form. It only supports one-way authentication. Therefore, MS-CHAP v1 does not provide protection against remote server impersonation, which means that a client cannot determine the authenticity of a RAS server it connects to. It is more secure than CHAP.	you have clients running Windows.
Microsoft Challenge Handshake Authentication Protocol (MS-CHAP), version 2 (v2)	High (most secure)	An improved version of MS-CHAP v1. It provides stronger security for remote access connections and allows for mutual authentication in which the client also authenticates the server.	you have clients running Windows.

2. The remote access server checks the user name and password and sends back a PAP authenticate-acknowledgment message when the user's credentials are correct, or a PAP authenticate-no acknowledgment message when the user's credentials are not correct.

Therefore, the password can easily be read with a protocol analyzer. In addition, PAP offers no protection against replay attacks, remote client impersonation, or remote server impersonation. To make your remote access server more secure, ensure that PAP is disabled. Another disadvantage of using PAP is that if your password expires, PAP does not have the ability to change your password during authentication.

Shiva Password Authentication Protocol (SPAP), Shiva's proprietary version of PAP, offers a bit more security than PAP's plain-text password with its reversible encryption mechanism. SPAP is more secure than PAP but less secure than CHAP or MS-CHAP. Someone capturing authentication packets will not be able to read the SPAP password, but this authentication protocol is susceptible to playback attacks (i.e., an intruder records the packets and resends them to gain fraudulent access). Playback attacks are possible because SPAP always uses the same reversible encryption method to send the passwords over the wire. Like PAP, SPAP does not have the ability to change your password during the authentication process.

Historically, **Challenge Handshake Authentication Protocol (CHAP)** has been is the most commonly used dial-up authentication protocol. In this protocol, the industry Message Digest 5 (MD5) hashing scheme encrypts authentication. **A hashing scheme** scrambles information in such a way that it is unique and cannot be reversed back to the original format. CHAP does not send the actual password over the wire. Instead, CHAP it uses a three-way challenge-response mechanism with one-way MD5 hashing to provide encrypted authentication without sending the password over the link:

1. The remote access server sends a CHAP challenge message containing a session ID and an arbitrary challenge string.
2. The remote access client returns a CHAP response message containing the user name in clear text and a hash of the challenge string, session ID, and the client's password, using the MD5 one-way hashing algorithm.
3. The remote access server duplicates the hash and compares it to the hash in the CHAP response. If the hashes are the same, the remote access server sends back a CHAP success message. If the hashes are different, a CHAP failure message is sent.

Because standard CHAP clients use the plain-text version of the password to create the CHAP challenge response, passwords must be stored on the server to calculate an equivalent response.

Since CHAP uses an arbitrary challenge string for each authentication attempt, it protects against replay attacks. However, CHAP does not protect against remote server impersonation. In addition, because the algorithm for calculating CHAP responses is well known, it is important that passwords be carefully chosen and sufficiently long. CHAP passwords that are common words or names are vulnerable to dictionary attacks if they can be discovered by comparing responses to the CHAP challenge with every entry in a dictionary. Passwords that are not sufficiently long can be discovered by brute force, that is, by comparing the CHAP response to sequential trials until a match to the user's response is found.

Microsoft Challenge Handshake Authentication Protocol (MS-CHAP) is Microsoft's proprietary version of CHAP. Unlike PAP and SPAP, it lets you encrypt data that are sent using the Point-to-Point Protocol (PPP) or Point-to-Point Tunneling Protocol (PPTP) connections using Microsoft Point-to-Point Encryption (MPPE). The challenge response is calculated with an MD4 hashed version of the password and the network access server challenge. Note: The two flavors of MS-CHAP (versions 1 and 2) allow for error codes, including a "password expired" code, and password changes. Three steps are involved in using MS-CHAP v1:

1. The remote access server sends an MS-CHAP challenge message containing a session ID and an arbitrary challenge string.
2. The remote client must return the user name and an MD4 hash of the challenge string, the session ID, and the MD4-hashed password.
3. The remote access server duplicates the hash and compares it to the hash in the MS-CHAP response. If the hashes are the same, the remote access server sends back a CHAP success message. If the hashes are different, a CHAP failure message is sent.

MS-CHAP v1 supports only one-way authentication. Therefore, MS-CHAP v1 does not provide protection against remote server impersonation; this means that a client cannot determine the authenticity of a RAS server to which it connects.

MS-CHAP v2 provides stronger security for remote access connections and allows for mutual authentication whereby the client also authenticates the server:

1. The remote access server sends an MS-CHAP v2 challenge message to the remote access client that consists of a session ID and an arbitrary challenge string.
2. The remote access client sends an MS-CHAP v2 response that contains the user name, an arbitrary peer challenge string, an MD4 hash of the received challenge string, the peer challenge string, the session ID, and the MD4-hashed versions of the user's password.
3. The remote access server checks the MS-CHAP v2 response message from the client and sends back an MS-CHAP v2 response message containing an indication of the success or failure of the connection attempt. An authentication response is based on the sent challenge string, the peer challenge string, the client's encrypted response, and the user's password.
4. The remote access client verifies the authentication response and if it is correct, uses the connection. If the authentication response is not correct, the remote access client terminates the connection.
5. If a user authenticates by using MS-CHAP v2 and attempts to use an expired password, MS-CHAP prompts the user to change the password while connecting to the server. Other authentication protocols do not support this feature, effectively locking out the user who used the expired password.

If you configure your connection to use only MS-CHAP v2 and the server you are dialing in to does not support MS-CHAP v2, the connection will fail. In Windows NT, the RAS servers negotiate a lower-level authentication if possible. In addition, MS-CHAP passwords are stored more securely at the server than CHAP passwords, but they have the same vulnerabilities to dictionary and brute force attacks as CHAP. When using MS-CHAP, it is important to ensure that passwords are well chosen and long enough that they cannot be calculated readily. Many large organizations require passwords to be at least six characters long with uppercase and lowercase characters and at least one digit.

By default, MS-CHAP v1 for Windows 2000 and Windows Server 2003 supports LAN Manager authentication. If you want to prohibit the use of LAN Manager authentication with MS-CHAP v1 for older Microsoft operating systems such as Windows NT 3.5X and Windows 95, then set Allow LM Authentication (HKEY_LOCAL_MACHINE\SYSTEM\CurrentControlSet\Services\RemoteAccess Policy) zero on the authentication server. Windows 9X supports MS-CHAP v2 only for virtual private network (VPN) connections. Windows 9X does not support MS-CHAP v2 for dial-up connections.

19.1.5   Extensible Authentication Protocol (EAP)

Since security and authentication is a constantly changing field, embedding authentication schemes into an operating system is impractical. To solve this problem, Microsoft has included support for **Extensible Authentication Protocol (EAP),** which allows new authentication schemes to be plugged in as needed. Therefore, EAP allows third-party vendors to develop custom authentication schemes such as retina scans, voice recognition, fingerprint identification, smart cards, Kerberos security, and digital certificates. In addition, EAP offers mutual authentication, which means both computers authenticate each other, so that the client also knows that the server is who it says it is.

Extensible Authentication Protocol Message Digest 5 Challenge Handshake Authentication Protocol (EAP-MD5 CHAP) is an EAP type that uses the same challenge handshake protocol as PPP-based CHAP, but the challenges and responses are sent as EAP messages. A typical use for EAP-MD5 CHAP is to authenticate the credentials of remote access clients by use of user name and password security systems.

EAP-Transport Layer Security (EAP-TLS) is an EAP type that is used in certificate-based security environments. If you are using smart cards for remote access authentication, you must use the EAP-TLS authentication method. The EAP-TLS exchange of messages provides mutual authentication; negotiation of the encryption method; and secured, private, key exchange between the remote access client and the authenticating server. EAP-TLS provides the strongest authentication and key exchange method.

EAP-RADIUS is not an EAP type, but the passing of EAP messages of any EAP type by a remote access server to a RADIUS server for authentication. The EAP messages sent between the remote access client and remote access server are encapsulated and formatted as RADIUS message between the remote access server and the RADIUS server. EAP-RADIUS is used in environments where RADIUS is used as the authentication provider. An advantage of using EAP-RADIUS is that EAP types do not need to be installed at each remote access server, only at the RADIUS server.

In a typical use of EAP-RADIUS, a remote access server is configured to use EAP and to use RADIUS as its authentication provider. When a connection is made, the remote access client negotiates the use of EAP with the remote access server. When the client sends an EAP message to the remote access server, the remote access server encapsulates the EAP message as a RADIUS message and sends it to its configured RADIUS server. The RADIUS server processes the EAP message and sends a RADIUS-encapsulated EAP message back to the remote access server. The remote access server then forwards the EAP message to the remote access client. In this configuration, the remote access server is only a pass-through device. All processing of EAP messages occurs at the remote access client and the RADIUS server.

A new member of the EAP family is the **Protected Extensible Authentication Protocol (PEAP).** PEAP uses TLS to create an encrypted channel between an authenticating EAP client, such as a wireless computer, and an EAP authenticator, such as an Internet Authentication Service (IAS) or RADIUS server. PEAP does not specify an authentication method but provides a secure "wrapper" for other EAP authentication protocols that operate within the outer TLS-encrypted channel provided by PEAP. PEAP is used as an authentication method for 802.11 wireless client computers, but it does not support VPNs or other remote access clients.

You can choose between two built-in EAP types for use within PEAP: EAP-TLS or EAP-MS-CHAP v2. EAP-TLS uses certificates installed in the client computer certificate store or a smart card for user and client computer authentication, and a certificate in the server computer certificate store for server authentication. EAP MS-CHAP v2 uses credentials (user name and password) for user authentication and a certificate in the server computer certificate store for server authentication.

The unauthenticated access method allows remote access users to log on without checking their credentials. It does not verify the user's name and password. The only user validation performed in the unauthenticated access method is authorization. Enabling unauthenticated access presents security risks that must be carefully considered when deciding whether to enable this method.

19.1.6   PPPOE

With the arrival of low-cost broadband technologies in general, and DSL (digital subscriber line) in particular, the number of computer hosts that are permanently connected to the Internet has greatly increased. When a computers connects to the Internet via DSL, which is connected to an Ethernet card, there are no protocols for security. Modem dial-up connection, on the other hand, uses the PPP, which provides secure login and traffic metering, among other advanced features. **PPPOE (PPP over Ethernet)** was designed to bring the security and metering benefits of the PPP to Ethernet connections such as those used in DSL.

19.1.7   Multilink and Bandwidth Allocation Protocol

The **PPP Multilink Protocol (MP)** is an extension that is used to aggregate or combine multiple physical links into a single logical link. Examples are the aggregation of both B channels of an ISDN BRI connection, or connection of two modems to a RAS server that has two modems. The MP fragments, sequences, and reorders alternating packets sent across multiple physical connections so that the end result is a single logical link with the combined bandwidth of all aggregated physical links. MP must be supported on both sides of the connection, however.

In Windows 2000 and Windows Server 2003, **Bandwidth Allocation Protocol (BAP)** and **Bandwidth Allocation Control Protocol (BACP)** enhance multilink by dynamically adding or dropping links on demand. BAP is especially valuable to operations that have carrier charges based on

Figure 19.1 Enabling a multilink connection

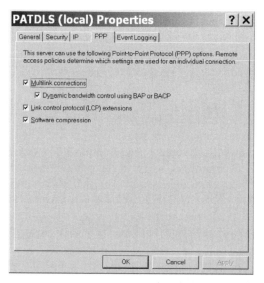

bandwidth utilization. BAP and BACP are sometimes used interchangeably to refer to bandwidth-on-demand functionality. Both protocols are PPP control protocols and work together to provide bandwidth on demand. BAP provides an efficient mechanism for controlling connection costs while dynamically providing optimum bandwidth. For example, a multilink and BAP-enabled remote access client and remote access server create a multilink connection that consists of a single physical link. As the utilization of the single link rises to a configured level, the remote access client uses a BAP request message to request an additional link. The BAP request message specifies the type of link desired, such as analog phone, ISDN, or X.25. The remote access server then sends a BAP response message that contains the phone number of an available port on the remote access server of the same type as specified by the remote access client in the BAP request. When multilink and BAP are used in combination with the callback feature set to always call back to the same number, a concentrator must exist on the caller side that can distribute incoming calls to the same number on various ports. See Figure 19.1

You can enable multilink and BAP protocols on a server-wide basis from the PPP tab of each remote access server's Properties dialog box. Configure BAP settings through remote access policies. Using these policies, specify that an extra line be dropped if link utilization drops below 75% for one group and below 25% for another group. Remote access policies are described later in this chapter.

19.2   WINDOWS REMOTE ACCESS

Windows 2000 and Windows Server 2003 include Routing and Remote Access Service (RRAS), which enables Windows clients to dial other systems for access to remote networks, including the Internet, and enables Windows computers to act as dial-up servers for remote clients. In addition, RRAS enables Windows servers to function as a router. This section will focus on using remote access services. Routing will be introduced in Chapter 20.

Windows RRAS is a mature, full-featured, third-generation service of Windows-based server operating systems. It provides a rich complement of authentication services and protocols that simplify connectivity for clients running Windows, as well as clients using Novell, Apple, and UNIX/Linux. However, only client computers running Windows Professional and Windows XP give remote workers the full spectrum of networking and communication services, technologies, and features.

Remote access enables a client computer to connect to a remote computer or network and access the resources of the remote computer or network as if they were local. For example, users who are out of the office can access the file server's printers, e-mail systems, and other resources from remote locations. Clients also can use remote access services to connect to public networks such as the Internet.

RRAS in Windows provides two primary functions:

- **Dial-up client**—Creates and establishes dial-up connections to remote networks, including the Internet, through a variety of media (e.g., modem, ISDN, X.25, ATM, parallel port, and serial port). Windows dial-up clients support a wide range of authentication protocols and other connectivity options. Support for tunneling protocols enables clients to establish secure connections to remote networks through public networks such as the Internet.
- **Dial-up server**—Allows remote clients to connect to the local server or a local network using a dial-up connection. Windows 2000 and Windows Server 2003 support several authentication protocols and can authenticate users against local or domain user accounts, or they can use RADIUS. Once connected, a remote user can browse, print, access network drives, and perform all functions from the LAN.

Windows servers can use a single authentication mechanism to authenticate users both locally and from remote locations. RRAS can authenticate against the local computer's user accounts or domain accounts, or it can use an external authentication mechanism such as RADIUS. In addition, Windows RRAS is closely integrated with Active Directory.

19.2.1   Common Configurations for Remote Access Servers

When you run the Configure the Routing and Remote Access Service Wizard, the Wizard prompts you to choose the configuration path that most closely resembles the remote access solution that you want to deploy. If none of the Wizard configuration paths meets your needs exactly, you can further configure your server after the Wizard finishes, or you can choose the custom or manual configuration path. However, if you choose the custom configuration path, you must manually configure all elements of RRAS. The most common remote access solutions include dial-up connections, virtual private network (VPN) connections, and secure connections between two private networks.

If you want to establish a remote access (dial-up client), the server running RRAS is configured to allow remote access clients to connect to the private network by dialing into a modern bank or other dial-up equipment. To configure this type of server in the Wizard, click Remote Access, select the Dial-up check box, and follow the steps. After the Wizard finishes, you can configure additional options. For example, you can configure how the server answers the call, how the server verifies which remote access clients have permission to connect to the private network, and whether the server routes network traffic between remote access clients and the private network.

If you choose remote access via VPNs, the server running RRAS is configured to allow remote access clients to connect to the private network across the Internet. To configure this type of server in the Wizard, click Remote Access, select the VPN check box, and follow the steps. After the Wizard finishes, you can configure additional options. For example, you can configure how the server verifies which VPN clients have permission to connect to the private network and whether the server routes network traffic between VPN clients and the private network.

If you choose network address translation (NAT), the server running RRAS is configured to share an Internet connection with computers on the private network and to translate traffic between its public address and the private network. Computers on the Internet will not be able to determine the IP addresses of computers on the private network. To configure this type of server in the Wizard, click Network address translation (NAT) and follow the steps. After the Wizard finishes, you can configure additional options. For example, you can configure packet filters and choose what services to allow on the public interface.

If you choose both VPN and NAT, the server running RRAS is configured to provide NAT for the private network and to accept VPN connections. Computers on the Internet will not be able to determine the IP addresses of computers on the private network. However, VPN clients will be able to connect to computers on the private network as if they were physically attached to the same network. To configure this type of server in the Wizard, click Virtual Private Network (VPN) access and NAT, and follow the steps.

If you want to establish a secure connection between two private networks, you can select one of the following options: router-to-router VPNs, a branch office over the Internet, or a dial-up branch office network.

19.2.2   Windows RAS Server

A RAS server running Windows 2000 or Windows Server 2003 must have a modern or multiport adapter and analog telephones (or other WAN connections). A port is a channel of a device (such as modem) that can support a single point-to-point connection. For single-port devices, the device and the port are indistinguishable. For multiport devices, the port is the subdivision of the device over which a separate point-to-point communication is possible. For example, BRI ISND adapters support two separate B channels. The ISDN adapter is a device. Each B channel is a port, because a separate point-to-point connection occurs over each B channel. If the server provides access to the local network, a separate network adapter card must be installed and connected to the local network. Note: The processor is heavily used by RAS, especially when encryption and routing are implemented.

RAS software is installed automatically when you install Windows 2000 or Windows Server 2003; however, you must enable and configure it for your environment. To initially configure the RAS server, complete the following steps:

1. Click on the Start button, select the Programs option, select Administrative Tools, and select Routing and Remote Access.
2. In the console tree, right-click on your server, and select the Configure and Enable Routing and Remote Access option.
3. When the Routing and Remote Access Server Setup Wizard starts, click on the Next button.
4. Select the Remote Access Server option, then select the Next button. See Figure 19.2 for Windows 2000 systems.
5. Select the appropriate protocols and click on the Next button. Note that to select a protocol, it must already be installed on the system.
6. Remote clients must be assigned to one network for addressing, dial-up purposes, and other purposes, Select the appropriate network connection from the list and click on the Next button.
7. Select the method for which IP addresses will be assigned to the remote hosts. If you select Automatically, then select the Next button.
8. If you want to use a RADIUS server, click on the Finish button.
9. If you select to use a DHCP server for remote access, the Wizard will display a message saying that you have to configure the DHCP relay agent with the IP address of your server. Click on the OK button.

Figure 19.2   Configuring the remote access server

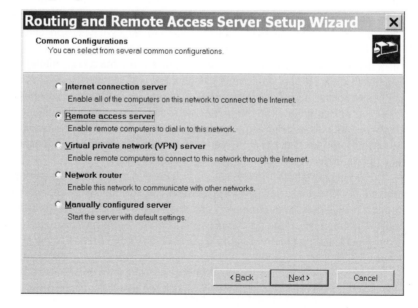

Figure 19.3 Configuring the Routing and Remote Access console

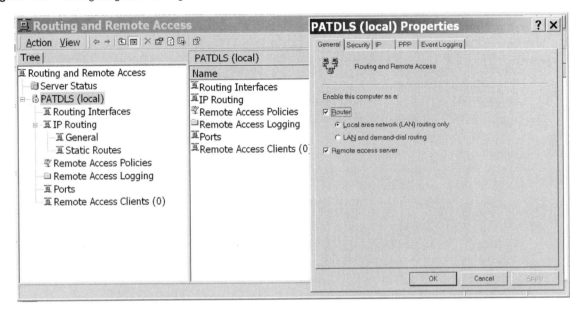

If you want to reset the console so that you can rerun the Wizard, follow these steps:

1. Click on the Start button, select the Programs option, select Administrative Tools, and select Routing and Remote Access.
2. In the console tree, right-click on your server and select the Disable Routing and Remote Access option. When asked to continue, click the Yes button.

To enable the remote access server after it has already been configured, do the following:

1. Click on the Start button, select the Programs option, select Administrative Tools, and select Routing and Remote Access.
2. Right-click the server name for which you want to enable remote access, then click Properties. See Figure 19.3.
3. On the General tab, select the Remote Access Server check box.

19.3 VIRTUAL PRIVATE NETWORKING

A virtual private network (VPN) is the creation of secured, point-to-point connections across a private network or a public network such as the Internet. In other words, a VPN connects the components of one network using another network. The basic technology that defines a VPN is tunneling. **Tunneling** is the method for transferring data packets over the Internet or other public network, providing security and features formerly available only on private networks. A tunneling protocol encapsulates the data packet in a header that provides routing information to enable the encapsulated payload to securely traverse the network. The entire process of encapsulation and transmission of packets is tunneling, and the logical connection through which the packets travel is the tunnel.

As a comparison, tunneling is similar to sending a letter from one company's building in Los Angeles to the same company's building in Chicago. The letter is initially sent through the corporation's mail services. When the letter gets to the mail room, it will then be sent to Chicago via the U.S. mail. The U.S. mail carrier then delivers it to the second building. The letter is then sent through the corporate mail service to the correct office.

19.3.1 Point-to-Point Tunneling Protocol

Remote users who can gain access to their networks via the Internet are probably using the **Point-to-Point Tunneling Protocol (PPTP).** PPTP, developed by Microsoft and Ascend Communications, uses the Internet as the connection between remote users and a local network, as well as between local networks. It is easy to see why the PPTP is the most popular implementation of the VPN, as it is an inexpensive way to create WANs with PSTN, ISDN, and X.25 connections. PPTP wraps various protocols inside an IP datagram, an IPX datagram, or a NetBEUI frame. This process lets the protocols travel through an IP network tunnel, without user intervention. In addition, PPTP saves companies the work of building proprietary and dedicated network connections for their remote users and instead lets them use the Internet as their conduit.

PPTP is based on the point-to-point protocol. The difference between PPP and PPTP is that PPTP allows Internet access as the connection medium, rather than requiring a direct connection between the user and the network. In other words, instead of having to dial up the corporate network directly, a remote user could log in to a local Internet service provider, and PPTP will make the connection from that provider to the corporate network's Internet connection. From there, it continues into the corporate network the same as if the user dialed in directly. The process is as follows:

1. The remote client makes a point-to-point connection to the front-end processor via a modem.
2. The front-end processor connects to the remote access server, establishing a secure "tunnel" connection over the Internet. This connection then functions as the network backbone.
3. The remote access server handles the account management and supports data encryption through IP, IPX, or NetBEUI protocols.

PPTP has certain drawbacks. PPTP has weak encryption technology, so it is not a good choice for highly secure transmission over the Internet. Its authentication features (the same used by PPP) are also weak. Therefore, big corporations tend to prefer IP security.

19.3.2   IP Security

Although the Internet is inherently insecure, businesses still need to preserve the privacy of data as they travel over the network. To help, the Internet Engineering Task Force has developed a suite of protocols called **Internet Protocol Security (IPSec).** IPSec creates a standard platform to develop secure networks and electronic tunnels between two machines. It also encapsulates each data packet in a new packet that contains the information necessary to set up, maintain, and tear down the tunnel when it is no longer needed.

Networks that use IPSec to secure data traffic can automatically authenticate devices by using digital certificates, which verify the identities of the two users who are sending information back and forth. IPSec can be an ideal way to secure data in large networks that require secure connections among many devices.

Users who are deploying IPSec can secure their network infrastructure without affecting the applications on individual computers. The protocol suite is available as a software-only upgrade to the network infrastructure, which allows security to be implemented without costly changes to each computer. Most important, IPSec allows interoperability among different network devices, PCs, and other computing systems. The process is as follows:

1. Send message—Data within an application are sent to a message authentication and integrity function with optional digital signature provision.
2. Data encryption—Data are encrypted with algorithms using a public key.
3. Secure packets—Data are sent over the Internet as encrypted packets in a secure tunnel.
4. Session key—Data are encrypted again in the tunnel using a session key.
5. Data decryption—At the end of the tunnel, data are decrypted using a private key.
6. Verification—When the data hit the receiver's PC, they are checked and the sender is verified using a message integrity function and an authentication provision.
7. Message received—The receiver can now read the text.

Rather than using applications or the operating system, use IPSec policies to configure IPSec security services. The policies provide variable levels of protection for most traffic types, in most existing networks. Your network security administrator can configure IPSec policies to meet the security requirements of a user, group, application, domain, site, or global enterprise. Windows 2000 and Windows Server 2003 provide an administrative interface, IP Security Policy Management, to create and manage IPSec policies (centrally at the group policy level for domain members, or locally on a non-domain computer). IP Security Policy Management is a snap-in that you can add to any Microsoft Management Console (MMC).

To configure TCP/IP to use an IPSec, do the following:

1. Click on the Start button, select the Settings option, and select the Network and Dial-up Connections.
2. Right-click the network connection that you want to configure, then click Properties.
3. On the General tab (for a local area connection) or the Networking tab (for all other connections), click Internet Protocol (TCP/IP), then click Properties.
4. Click on the Advanced button.
5. On the Options tab, click IP Security, then click on the Properties button.
6. To enable IP security, click Use This IP Security Policy, then click the name of a policy.
7. To disable IP security, click Do Not Use IPSec.

The Intel Corporation has developed network adapter cards, which include an encryption coprocessor that offloads IPSec encryption and authentication from the processor in Windows 2000, Windows Server 2003, and Windows NT 4.0 machines. As a result, machine performance and connection speed will be better than when doing IPSec encryption and authentication with the processor doing all the work.

19.3.3   Layer Two Tunneling Protocol

To compete against the PPTP protocol, Cisco developed the Layer 2 Forwarding (L2F) protocol, which allows a server to frame dial-up traffic using PPP and transmit it over WAN links to an L2F server or router, which then unwraps the packets before releasing them to the network.

The **Layer 2 Tunneling Protocol (L2TP)** is a combination of the L2F and PPTP, and enables remote users to access networks in a secure fashion. Therefore, L2TP represents the next generation of tunneling protocols. L2TP provides tunneling and supports header compression, but it does not provide encryption. Instead, it provides a secure tunnel by cooperating with other encryption technologies such as IPSec. IPSec does not require L2TP, but its encryption functions complement L2TP to create a secure VPN solution. Since the L2TP-based VPN connections are a combination of L2TP and IPSec, both L2TP and IPSec must be supported by both routers. L2TP is installed with the routing and remote access service and, by default, is configured for five L2TP ports.

19.4   CONFIGURING OUTBOUND CONNECTIONS

You can configure all outbound connections in Windows 2000 and Windows Server 2003 with the Network Connection Wizard. Much of the work of configuring protocols and services is automated when you use this process. There are three basic types of outbound connections:

- Dial-up connections, which include connections to a private network, private server, stand-alone computer in someone's home, modem pool in a corporate intranet, or connection to an Internet service provider (ISP)
- Connections to a VPN
- Direct connections to another computer through a cable

19.4.1   Creating a Dial-up Connection to a Private Network

To create and configure an outbound dial-up connection to a private network using a phone, ISDN, or X.25 connection, use the Network Connection Wizard. To connect to a private network, perform the following steps:

1. Click on the Start button, select the Settings option, select the Network and Dial-up Connections option, and select the Make New Connection option.
2. The Network Connection Wizard will appear. Click on the Next button. Select the Dial-up to Private Network option and click on the Next button.

3. Enter the phone number of the computer to which you are connecting and click on the Next button. This may be an ISP for an Internet connection or the modems for your private network. If you need to use an area code or select the country/region code, enable Use Dialing Rules.

4. If you want this connection to be made available to all users of this computer, click For All Users, and then click the Next button. If you want to reserve the connection for yourself, click Only for Myself, and then click on the Next button.

5. If you select the For All Users option, and you want to let other computers gain access to resources through this dial-up connection, select the "Enable shared access for this connection" check box. In either case, click on the Next button.

6. If you enable Internet connection sharing, the LAN adapter will use an IP address of 192.168.0.1. Click on the Yes button. Select the local network connection that will access resources through this connection. Click on the Next button.

7. Type a name for the connection and click the Finish button.

19.4.2   Creating a Dial-up Connection to an ISP

To create and configure an outbound dial-up connection to an Internet service provider (ISP) or other private network using a phone, ISDN, or X.25 connection, use the Network Connection Wizard. To connect to a private network, perform the following steps:

1. Click on the Start button, select the Settings option, select the Network and Dial-up Connections option, and select the Make New Connection option.

2. The Network Connection Wizard will appear. Click on the Next button. Select the Dial-up to the Internet, and click on the Next button.

3. The Internet Connection Wizard will start. If you have an account, choose either "I want to set up my Internet connection manually," or "I want to connect through a local area network (LAN)" option. Click on the Next button.

4. If you are connecting using the phone, select the "I want to connect through a phone and a modem" option. Click on the Next button.

5. Enter the phone number of the ISP and click on the Next button. If you need to use an area code or select the country/region code, enable Use Dialing Rules. In addition, the default dial-up protocol is PPP. If you specify the SLIP or C-SLIP protocol or specify an IP address for your system, click on the Advanced button.

6. Type in the user name and password used to log on to the ISP.

7. Type a name for the connection and click the Next button.

8. If you have an e-mail account through the ISP, select the Yes option and click on the Next button.

9. Select the "Create a new Internet mail account" option and click the Next button.

10. Specify the name that will show in the e-mail when you send messages and click on the Next button.

11. Specify your e-mail addresses so that other people reply to you and click on the Next button.

12. Specify the type and name of the incoming mail server and click on the Next button.

13. Type the account name and password for your e-mail account. Click on the Next button.

14. Click on the Finish button.

19.4.3   Configuring Virtual Private Network Connections

To set up a virtual private network connection, do the following:

1. Click on the Start button, select the Settings option, select the Network and Dial-up Connections option, and select the Make New Connection option.

2. The Network Connection Wizard will appear. Click on the Next button. Select the "Connect to a private network through the Internet" option and click on the Next button.

3. Specify the host name (such as Microsoft.com) or an IP address and click on the Next button.

4. If you want this connection to be made available to all users of this computer, click For All Users, and then click the Next button. If you want to reserve the connection for yourself, click Only for Myself, and then click on the Next button.

Figure 19.4   Configuring a VPN port

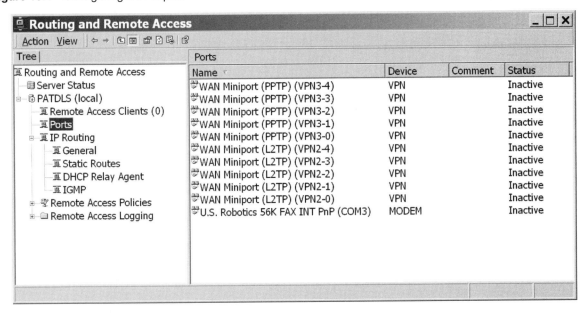

5. If you select the For All Users option, and you want to let other computers gain access to resources through this dial-up connection, select the "Enable shared access for this connection" check box. In either case, click on the Next button.
6. If you enable Internet connection sharing, the LAN adapter will use an IP address of 192.168.0.1. Click on the Yes button. Select the local network connection that will access resources through this connection. Click on the Next button.
7. Type a name for the connection and click the Finish button.
8. The Connect Virtual Private Connection dialog box appears. Type a user name and password. To specify the virtual private connection parameters, click on the Properties button and click the Security tab. Click Advanced (custom) settings following by the Settings button to specify the authentication protocol. When complete, click on the Connect button.

In Windows 2000 and Windows Server 2003, five PPTP and five L2TP ports are created when the routing and remote access service is started for the first time. In addition, Windows automatically detects any modems that are installed and creates modem ports for them. Windows also creates ports for each parallel or serial cable that it detects.

To configure the VPN ports, do the following:

1. Click on the Start button, select the Program option, select the Administrative Tools option, and select the Routing and Remote Access program.
2. In the console tree, right-click Ports, then select the Properties option.
3. In the Ports Properties dialog box, select the device you want to configure and click on the Configure button.
4. In the Configure Ports dialog box, select the Remote Access (inbound) check box to enable inbound VPN connections. In addition, set the number of virtual ports available on the server. Click on the OK button to close the Configure Ports dialog box. See Figure 19.4.
5. Click OK to close the Ports Properties dialog boxes.

19.5   CONTROLLING REMOTE ACCESS

In Windows 2000 and Windows Server 2003, remote access connections are granted based on the dial-in properties and remote access policies. **Remote access policies (RAPs)** are a set of conditions and connection parameters that allow network administrators more flexibility in granting remote access permissions and usage. Some examples of conditions are time of day, group, and type of connection (dial-up or VPN). Connection parameters may include authentication and encryption requirements, use of multilink, and length of session. Remote access policies are stored on the local computer and are shared between Windows RRAS and Windows 2000 Internet Authentication Service (IAS). The RAP option is configured from the Internet Authentication Service console or from the Routing and Remote Access console.

19.5.1   Remote Access Permissions

To grant remote access permission to a user, follow these steps. If the remote access server is part of a Windows 2000 or Windows Server 2003 domain:

1. In Administrative Tools, open the Active Directory Users and Computers console.
2. In the console tree, open Domain and click Users.
3. In the Details pane, right-click a user name, select the Properties option.

If the remote access server is a stand-alone server, which is not a part of a Windows domain or is a member server and you want to use a local user account:

1. In Administrative Tools, open the Computer Management console.
2. In the console tree, open System Tools and Local Users and Groups and click on Users.
3. In the Details pane, right-click a user name, then click Properties.
4. On the Dial-in tab, under Remote Access Permission (Dial-in or VPN), click either Allow Access or Control Access through Remote Access Policy, and then click OK. See Figure 19.5.

If the remote access server is a member of a Windows NT 4.0 domain or a Windows mixed-mode domain, use the Windows NT 4.0 User Manager for Domains administrative tool to grant or deny dial-in access for user accounts.

In the first part of the dialog box, specify if a user is to be allowed access, denied access, or if the access will be controlled through the remote access policy. The Verify Caller-ID option specifies whether this user is required to dial in from a particular number. If access is explicitly allowed, remote

Figure 19.5 Configuring a user to access a remote access server

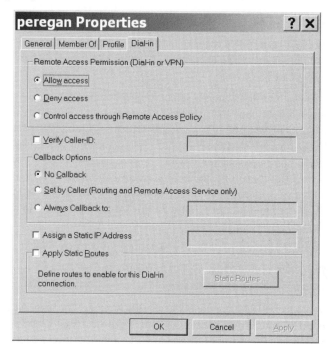

access policy conditions, user account properties, or profile properties can still deny the connection attempt. The Control Access through Remote Access Policy option is only available on user accounts for stand-alone Windows 2000 or Windows Server 2003 remote access servers or members of native Windows domain.

If the Verify Caller-ID option is enabled, the server verifies the caller's phone number. If the caller's number does not match the configured phone number, the connection attempt is denied. For this to work, all parts of the connection must support caller ID. Caller ID support on the remote access server consists of caller ID answering equipment and the driver that passes caller ID information to routing and remote access. If you configure a caller ID phone number for a user and you do not support for the passing of caller ID information from the caller to routing and remote access, then the connection attempt is denied.

In the Callback options, you may determine if the server calls back a specific phone number. If the No Callback option is selected, the remote access server establishes a connection as soon as the connection attempt has been accepted. The Set by Caller option is useful for clients who call from various locations and phone numbers. It also minimizes telephone charges for these users. When the Always Callback To option is selected, it provides additional security by calling back to the preset number. Set this option for stationary remote computers, such as those used by telecommuters that do not move around.

19.5.2   Remote Access Policies

To create a new remote policy, start the RRAS consosle, open the server, and then open the Remote Access Policy branch. Next, right-click the right pane and choose New Remote Access Policy to start the Remote Access Policy Wizard. The Wizard will prompt you for the following information:

- **Policy friendly name**—Specify a name that identifies the purpose of the policy or affected users. This is the policy name as it appears isn the RRAS console.
- **Conditions**—Use the Conditions page of the Wizard to specify the criteria by which the policy grants or denies access.
- **Grant/deny**—Select which action is applied to the selected criteria.
- **Edit profile**—Click the Edit Profile button to edit the other properties for the remote access policy or simply click Finish to complete the Wizard. The properties you can change by clicking Edit Profile are the same as those made available by doubleclicking the policy in the console.

To configure a RAP to grant or deny access, follow these steps:

1. Do one of the following:
   - In the Administrative Tools, open the Routing and Remote Access console and, if necessary, double-click Routing and Remote Access and the server name.
   - Open Internet Authentication Service and, if necessary, double-click Internet Authentication Service.
2. In the console tree, click Remote Access Policies.
3. In the Details pane, right-click the policy you want to configure, then click Properties.
4. Under "If a user matches the conditions,"
   - To grant dial-up permission to these users, click "Grant remote access permission."
   - To deny dial-up permission to these users, click "Deny remote access permission."

Remote access policy conditions are assigned attributes that are compared with the settings of a connection attempt. If there are multiple conditions in a policy, then all conditions must correspond to the settings of the connection attempt to result in a match.

You can create a RAP and an associated profile under the Remote Access Policies node of the Routing and Remote Access console tree. To add a remote access policy, perform the following steps:

1. Open Routing and Remote Access.
2. Right-click Remote Access Policies, then select the New Remote Access Policy.
3. In the Policy Properties dialog box, type the name of the profile in the Policy Friendly Name text box.
4. To configure a new condition, click Add, and then do the following:

Figure 19.6   Selecting attributes that will be used for granting remote access

- In the Select Attribute dialog box, click the attribute to add, and then click OK. See Figure 19.6.
- In the Attribute dialog box, enter the information required by the attribute, and then click OK.

5. If a user matches the conditions section, do the following:

- To grant access to these users, click "Grant remote access permission."
- To deny access to these users, click "Deny remote access permission."

To edit the policy's profile, perform the following steps:

1. In the Policy Properties dialog box, click Edit Profile.
2. In the Edit Dial-in Profile dialog box, configure the settings on any of the six tabs, then click OK.
3. Click OK to close the Policy Properties dialog box.

The profile specifies what kind of access the user will be given if the conditions match. This access will only be granted if the connection attempt does not conflict with the settings of the user account or the profile. See Figure 19.7. Six different tabs can be used to configure a profile as follows:

- **Dial-in Constraints**—These options include settings for idle-time disconnect, maximum session time, day and time, phone number, and media type (ISDN, VPN, etc.).
- **IP**—These settings configure client IP address assignments and TCP/IP packet filtering. Separate filters can be defined for inbound or outbound packets.
- **Multilink**—These settings configure multilink and BAP. A line can be dropped if bandwidth drops below a certain level for a given length of time. Multilink can also be set to require the use of BAP.
- **Authentication**—These settings define the authentication protocols that are allowed for connections using this policy. The protocol selected must also be enabled in the server's properties.
- **Encryption**—These settings specify that IPSec or Microsoft Point-to-Point Encryption (MPPE) is prohibited, allowed, or required.
- **Advanced**—This tab allows for the configuration of additional network parameters that could be sent from non-Microsoft RADIUS servers. You can create a remote access profile from the Policy Properties dialog box.

You can set authentication properties to enable the types of authentication that are allowed for a connection and specify and configure the EAP type that must be used. By default, Microsoft encrypted authentication (MS-CHAP v1) and (MS-CHAP v2) are enabled.

Figure 19.7   Configuring a dial-in profile

Depending on how you connect to the VPN server you will either use Microsoft Point-to-Point Encryption (MPPE) or IPSec encryption. If you connect to a PPTP server, you will use MPPE; if you connect to an L2TP server, you will use IPSec. By default, the VPN is configured for an automatic server type, which means that L2TP with IPSec encryption is tried first, before PPTP with MPPE is attempted.

VPN server encryption settings are configured from the Encryption tab on the profile settings of the remote access policy that matches the VPN connection. you can set encryption properties for the following encryption strengths:

- **No encryption**—When selected, this option allows a nonencrypted connection. To require encryption, clear the No Encryption option.
- **Basic**—For dial-up and PPTP-based VPN connections, MPPE with a 40-bit key is used. For L2TP over IPSec-based VPN connections, 56-bit Data Encryption Standard (DES) is used.
- **Strong**—For dial-up and PPTP-based VPN connections, MPPE with a 56-bit key is used. For L2TP over IPSec-based VPN connections, 56-bit DES encryption is used.
- **Strongest**—For dial-up and PPTP-based VPN connections, MPPE with a 128-bit key is used. For L2TP over IPSec-based VPN connections, triple DES (3DES) encryption is used. This option is only available on North American versions of Windows 2000 and Windows Server 2003.

On the Encryption tab, you can separately enable No encryption, Basic, Strong, or Strongest. The Strongest check box is only available if you install the High Encryption Pack, which can be downloaded from Windows Update on Microsoft's website. To require encryption, clear the No encryption check box.

Each remote access policy has a unique order number, and policies are evaluated and applied in the order of priority. The order of the policies in the list is important, because all connection attempts are evaluated against the first policy that matches the conditions of the call or connection. If no matching policy is found the connection attempt will be rejected. If a matching policy is found, the permission and profile are evaluated to determine whether the connection should be accepted. You can change the order to define the way policies are applied, which determines the final applied result. To change the order, right-click a policy and choose either Move Up or Move Down to change its position and order number.

Example 1:

You are the administrator of a Windows 2000 domain. The domain has a Windows 2000 member server computer named RASSERVER. The Routing and Remote Access option is enabled for remote access on RASSERVER. The domain is in native mode. For all user accounts, the RASSERVER-in permission option is set to control access through remote access policies. You want to allow all users in the domain to dial in during the workday. You also want to allow only members of the global security group named support staff to be able to dial in between 6:00 P.M. and 8:00 A.M. However, you do not want to allow the support staff members to be able to dial in when the log files are made each day between 7:00 A.M. and 8:00 A.M. You create four remote access policies on RASSERVER as shown in the following table.

Policy Name	Condition	Permission	Profile
Domain users all	Windows-group = Domain users	Access	(default)
Support staff all	Windows-group = Support staff	Access	(default)
Domain users 6–8	Day-and-Time = 6 P.M.–8 A.M. Windows-group = Support staff	Deny	(default)
Support staff 7–8	Day-and-Time = 7 A.M.–8 A.M. Windows-group = Support staff	Deny	(default)

Since the remote access policies are applied in order, the first policy which meets the conditions is applied. Only one policy can be applied. Support staff policies must be applied before the domain users policies, since the support staff members also are domain users, and support staff members need access at 6 P.M. to 7 A.M. The Deny policies must be applied before the Allow policies. If not, the Deny policies would never be applied. Therefore, the order should be:

1. Support staff. 7–8 Deny
2. Support staff all
3. Domain users 6–8 Deny
4. Domain users all

A connection is authorized only if the settings of the connection attempt match at least one of the remote access policies (subject to the conditions of the dial-in properties of the user account and the profile properties of the remote access policy). If the settings of the connection attempt do not match at least one of the RAPs, then the connection attempt is denied regardless of the dial-in properties of the user account. The list of parameters checked are time of day, user groups, caller IDs, or IP addresses, matched to the parameters of the client connecting to the server.

If you set the dial-in permission on every user account to "Control access through Remote Access Policy," and if you do not change the default remote access policy, then all connection attempts will be rejected. However, if one user's dial-in permission is set to "Allow access," then that user's connection attempts will be accepted. If you change the permission setting on the default policy to "Grant remote access permission," then all connection attempts are accepted.

19.6   THE DEFAULT REMOTE ACCESS POLICY

A default remote access policy named "Allow access if dial-in permission is enabled" is created when you install the RRAS. The default policy has the following configuration:

- The Day-and-Time-Restrictions condition is set to all times and all days.
- Permission is set to Deny remote access permission.
- All profile properties are set to default values.

If you delete the default remote access policy and want to re-create it, follow these steps:

1. Open Routing and Remote Access console.
2. In the console tree, click Remote Access Policies.

3. Right-click Remote Access Policies, then click New Remote Access Policy.
4. In the Add Remote Access Policy Wizard, type a default name in the policy friendly name and click the Next button. When the Routing and Remote Access service is installed, the default remote access policy name is "Allow access if dial-in permission is enabled," although you do not need to use this name.
5. On the Conditions page, click Add, click Day-and-Time-Restrictions, click Add, and configure the attribute to permit all times on all days. Click OK, then click the Next button.
6. On the Permissions page, click Deny remote access permission, then click the Next button.
7. On the User profile page, click the Finish button. Do not make any changes to the user profile.

19.7   REMOTE ACCESS POLICY ADMINISTRATIVE MODELS

In Windows 2000 and Windows Server 2003, there are three primary models for administering remote access permissions and connection settings: access by user, access by policy in a Windows native-mode domain, and access by policy in a Windows mixed-mode domain.

19.7.1   Access by User

In the access-by-user administrative model, RAPs are determined by the Remote access permission option on the Dial-in tab of the user account. You enable or disable the option on a per-user basis by setting Remote access permission to either Allow access or Deny access. The remote access permission setting on the RAP is effectively overridden if the user permission is set to either Allow access or Deny access. However, you can modify remote access policy conditions and profile properties to enforce connection settings, such as encryption requirements and idle timeouts.

You can administer the access-by-user model with multiple RAPs. Each remote access policy has its own profile settings. You must configure these settings carefully, because a connection attempt may be rejected even when the remote access permission on the user account is set to Allow access. If a connection attempt matches the conditions of a policy but does not match the profile settings or does not match any of the remote access policies, the connection attempt is rejected.

In the access-by-user model, you can control three behaviors:

■ **Explicit allow**—The remote access permission for the user account is set to Allow access, and the connection attempt matches the conditions of a policy subject to the settings of the profile and the dial-in properties of the user account.
■ **Explicit deny**—The remote access permission for the user account is set to Deny access.
■ **Implicit deny**—The connection attempt does not match the conditions of any remote access policies.

In Windows 2000 and Windows Server 2003, the access-by-user model is equivalent to administering remote access on a Windows NT 4.0 RAS server.

The access-by-user model can be used on a stand-alone remote access server, a remote access server that is a member of a Windows 2000 native-mode domain, a remote access server that is a member of a Windows 2000 mixed-mode domain, or a remote access server that is a member of a Windows NT 4.0 domain. You can use the access-by-user model if you have Windows NT 4.0 RAS or IAS servers.

Example 2:

If you want to maintain the same administrative model as Windows NT 4.0, use the dial-in access granted on a per-user basis. This is done by modifying the dial-in properties on the user account. Set the remote access permission to either Allow access or Deny access, which will be the default behavior for remote access policies.

The default policy is named Allow access if dial-in permission is enabled. The settings on this policy are as follows:

■ A single condition that consists of the Day-And-Time-Restrictions attribute is set for all times on all days.
■ The Deny remote access permission option is selected.
■ The profile is set to default settings.

When a user attempts a remote access connection, the following logic is used to accept or reject the connection attempt (assuming the default settings are set on the dial-in properties for the user account):

1. The default policy "Allow access if dial-in permission is enabled" is evaluated.
2. The settings of the connection attempt match the conditions of the policy (the connection attempt is happening at any day or time).
3. On the user account, the setting under Remote Access Permission (Dial-in or VPN) is evaluated.
   - If Allow access is selected, the connection is accepted subject to the settings of the user account dial-in properties and profile properties.
   - If Deny access is selected, the connection is rejected.

   NOTE: If remote access permission on a user account is set to "Control access through Remote Access Policy," the connection attempt is rejected.

19.7.2   Access by Policy in a Windows Native-mode Domain

In the access-by-policy model for a Windows 2000 native-mode domain, the Remote access permission option on every user account is set to "Control access through remote access policy," and RAPs are determined by the permission setting on the policy. Therefore, the Remote access permission setting on the RAP determines whether remote access permission is allowed or denied.

In the access-by-policy model for a Windows 2000 native-mode domain, you can control three behaviors:

- **Explicit allow**—The Remote access permission option on the RAP is set to Grant remote access permission and the connection attempt matches the conditions of the policy subject to the settings of the profile and the dial-in properties of the user account.
- **Explicit deny**—The Remote access permission option on the RAP is set to Deny remote access permission and the connection attempt matches the conditions of the policy.
- **Implicit deny**—The connection attempt does not match the conditions of any RAPs.

If you use the access-by-policy model and you do not add any RAPs and do not change the default remote access policy (named "Allow access if dial-in permission is enabled"), then no users are allowed remote access. By default, the remote access permission on the default RAP is set to Deny remote access permission. If you change the setting to Grant remote access permission, then all users are allowed remote access.

NOTES: The access-by-policy model for a Windows 2000 or Windows Server 2003 native-mode domain also applies to stand-alone remote access servers that are not a member of a domain. In addition, you cannot use the access-by-policy model for a Windows native-mode domain if you have Windows NT 4.0 RAS or IAS servers. If you use the access-by-policy model for a Windows native-mode domain and do not use the Groups option to specify which users get access, then verify that the Guest account is disabled and its remote access permission is set to Deny access.

It is not necessary to have a separate RAP for each group. Instead, you can use nested groups to consolidate group membership and delegate administration of group membership. For a remote access or IAS server in a Windows 2000 or Windows Server 2003 native-mode domain, you can use universal groups. You cannot use the built-in local groups for the Windows Groups attribute.

Example 3:

To allow connection through group membership, use the access-by-policy model in a Windows 2000 or Windows Server 2003 native-mode domain. All user accounts must have the Remote access permission (Dial-in or VPN) option set to "Control access through remote access policy." In this model, you want to allow connections only for those user accounts that belong to a specific set of groups. Once remote access permission is set for all user accounts, the administrator completes the following steps:

1. Delete the default policy named "Allow access if dial-in permission is enabled."
2. Create a new policy named "Accept if member of configured groups."
3. Add the Windows-Groups condition to the new policy, then add the groups that are allowed remote access.
4. Select the Grant remote access permission option on the new policy.

The first policy named "Accept if member of configured groups" is evaluated. If the user account that is used to authenticate the connection is not a member of the configured groups, the connection is rejected because there are no more RAPs to process. If the user account that is used to authenticate the connection is a member of the configured groups, then the Remote access permission (Dial-in or VPN) setting on the user account is evaluated. If "Control access through remote access policy" is selected, then the Remote access permission setting on the policy is checked. Because granting permission is selected, the connection is accepted subject to the settings of the user account properties and profile properties. Note: This all assumes that the default settings are set on the dial-in properties for the user account.

19.7.3 Access by Policy in a Windows Mixed-mode Domain

In the access-by-policy model for a Windows 2000 or Windows Server 2003 mixed-mode domain, the Remote access permission option on every user account is set to "Allow access," the default RAP is deleted, and separate RAPs are created to define the types of connections that are allowed. On a remote access server running Windows 2000 or a Windows Server 2003 that is a member of a Windows mixed-mode domain, the "Control access through remote access policy" option is not available for remote access permission on the user account. If a connection attempt matches the conditions of a policy subject to the profile and user account dial-in settings, then the connection is accepted.

The access by policy model in a Windows 2000 mixed-mode domain also applies to a remote access server running Windows 2000 or Windows Server that is a member of a Windows NT 4.0 domain. In this model, you can control three behaviors:

- **Explicit allow**—The connection attempt matches the conditions of a policy subject to the settings of the profile and the dial-in properties of the user account.
- **Explicit deny**—The connection attempt matches the conditions of a policy but not the settings of the profile. You can do an explicit deny in this administrative model by enabling the "Restrict Dial-in to this number only" constraint and typing a number that does not correspond to any dial-in number being used by the remote access server.
- **Implicit deny**—The connection attempt does not match the conditions of any remote access policies.

If you do not delete the default RAP named "Allow access if dial-in permission is enabled," then all users can obtain a remote access connection. If you have Windows NT 4.0 RRAS servers, you can only use the access-by-policy model in a Windows 2000 or Windows Server 2003 mixed-mode domain if the RRAS servers are configured as RADIUS clients to a Windows 2000 or Windows Server 2003 IAS server. You cannot use the access-by-policy model in a Windows 2000 or Windows Server 2003 mixed-mode domain for Windows NT 4.0 RAS servers.

Example 4:

Let's say that you want to deny connection through group membership using the access-by-policy model in a Windows mixed-mode domain. In this scenario, the network administrator is using the access-by-policy model in a Windows 2000 or Windows Server 2003 mixed-mode domain. All user accounts must have the Remote access permission (Dial-in or VPN) option set to Allow access. The network administrator wants to prevent dial-in access for all vendors. Regular employees have no restrictions on dialing in. All vendor user accounts are a member of the Vendors Windows 2000 group. In this case, two policies are needed: (1) a policy that rejects a connection attempt by a member of the Vendors group; and (2) a policy that accepts a connection attempt from everyone else at any time and day. Once remote access permission is set for all user accounts, the administrator completes the following steps:

1. Verify that the default policy named "Allow access if dial-in permission is enabled" exists.
2. Create a new policy named "Reject vendor connections."
3. Add the Windows-Groups condition to the new policy, then add the Vendors group.
4. Verify that the Deny remote access permission option is selected on the new policy.
5. Modify the profile on the new policy. On the Dial-in Constraints tab, select the "Restrict Dial-in to this number only" check box and type 555-0111. The number 555-0111 is *not* a dial-in number of the remote access server and is deliberately typed so that the properties of the connection attempt do not match the settings of the remote access policy.
6. Move the new policy so that it is the first policy being evaluated.

For this scenario, assume the following:

- All of the Windows 2000 user accounts have the Remote access permission (Dial-in or VPN) option set to Allow access. All other dial-in properties on the user accounts are set at their default values.
- James (account name James) is an employee and Laura (account name Laura) is a vendor.
- The user account Laura is a member of the Vendors group.

When Laura dials in, Laura uses her account name for authentication. The first policy named "Reject vendor connections" is evaluated. The settings of the connection attempt match the conditions of the policy (Laura is a member of the Vendors group). The Remote access permission (Dial-in or VPN) setting on the Laura user account is evaluated and determined to be Allow access. The settings of the user account properties and profile properties are applied: Because the profile properties are set to only allow connections that dial in to the number 555-0111, and the remote access server is not using the dial-in number 555-0111, the connection is rejected.

When James dials in and uses his account name (James) for authentication, the first policy (Reject vendor connections) is evaluated. The settings of the connection attempt do not match the conditions of the policy (James is not a member of the Vendors group). Next, the policy named "Allow access if dial-in permission is enabled" is evaluated. The settings of the connection attempt match the conditions of the policy (the connection attempt is happening at any day or time). The Remote access permission (Dial-in or VPN) setting on the James user account is evaluated and determined to be Allow access. The connection is accepted, subject to the settings of the user account properties and profile properties.

19.8   INTERNET AUTHENTICATION SERVICE (IAS)

A RADIUS server has access to user account information and can check network access authentication credentials. If the user's credentials are authentic and the connection attempt is authorized, the RADIUS server authorizes the user's access on the basis of specified conditions and logs the network access connection in an accounting log. The use of RADIUS allows the network access user authentication, authorization, and accounting data to be collected and maintained in a central location, rather than on each access server.

Internet Authentication Service (IAS), which is available in Windows 2000 and Windows Server 2003, is the Microsoft implementation of a Remote Authentication Dial-in User Service (RADIUS) server and proxy. Note: Windows Server 2003 Web Server Edition does not include IAS. As a RADIUS server, IAS performs centralized connection authentication, authorization, auditing, and accounting for many types of network access such as wireless, authenticating switch, remote access dial-up, and virtual private network connections. As a RADIUS proxy, IAS forwards authentication and accounting messages to other RADIUS servers. You can use IAS to provide authentication for RRAS, IIS, or other services, including non-Microsoft dial-up servers. Any dial-up modem pool that supports RADIUS, for example, can authenticate clients through a Windows 2000 or Windows Server 2003 server running IAS.

When an IAS server is a member of an Active Directory domain, IAS uses the directory service as its user account database and is part of a single sign-on solution. The same set of credentials is used for network access control (authenticating and authorizing access to a network) and to log on to an Active Directory domain.

19.8.1   Components of IAS

A RADIUS authentication, authorization, and accounting infrastructure consists of the following components:

- Access clients
- Access servers (RADIUS clients)
- RADIUS proxies
- RADIUS servers
- User account databases

An access client is a device that requires some level of access to a larger network. Examples of access clients are dial-up or VPN clients, wireless clients, or LAN clients connected to a switch.

An access server is a device that provides some level of access to a larger network. An access server using a RADIUS infrastructure is also a RADIUS client that sends connection requests and accounting messages to a RADIUS server. Examples of access servers are as follows:

- Network access servers (NASs) that provide remote access connectivity to an organization network or the Internet. (e.g., a Windows 2000 computer running the RRAS and providing either traditional dial-up or VPN remote access services to an organization's intranet)
- Wireless access points that provide physical layer access to an organization's network, using wireless-based transmission and reception technologies.
- Switches that provide physical layer access to an organization's network, using traditional LAN technologies such as Ethernet.

A RADIUS proxy is a device that forwards or routes RADIUS connection requests and accounting messages between RADIUS clients (and RADIUS proxies) and RADIUS servers (or RADIUS proxies). The RADIUS proxy uses information within the RADIUS message, such as the User-Name or Called-Station-ID RADIUS attributes, to route the RADIUS message to the appropriate RADIUS server. A RADIUS proxy can be used as a forwarding point for RADIUS messages when authentication, authorization, and accounting must occur at multiple RADIUS servers in different organizations.

A RADIUS server is a device that receives and processes connection requests or accounting messages sent by RADIUS clients or RADIUS proxies. In the case of connection requests, the RADIUS server processes the list of RADIUS attributes in the connection request. Based on a set of rules and the information in the user account database, the RADIUS server either authenticates and authorizes the connection and sends back an Access-Accept message or sends back an Access-Reject message. The Access-Accept message can contain connection restrictions that are implemented by the access server for the duration of the connection.

The user account database is the list of user accounts and their properties that can be checked by a RADIUS server to verify authentication credentials and user account properties containing authorization and connection parameter information. The user account databases that the IAS can use are the local Security Accounts Manager (SAM), a Microsoft Windows NT 4.0 domain, or the Active Directory service. For Active Directory, IAS can provide authentication and authorization for user or computer accounts in the domain in which the IAS server is a member, two-way trusted domains, and trusted forests with domain controllers running Windows 2000 Server or Windows Server 2003.

If the user accounts for authentication reside in a different type of database, IAS can be configured as a RADIUS proxy to forward the authentication request to a RADIUS server that does have access to the user account database. Different databases for Active Directory include untrusted forests, untrusted domains, and one-way trusted domains.

When an access client sends user credentials, a user name is often included. Within the user name are two elements: identification of the user account name and identification of the user account location. For example, for the user name user1@microsoft.com, user1 is the user account name and microsoft. com is the location of the user account. The identification of the location of the user account is known as a *realm*. It can also be loosely defined as the security boundary of a network. With the wholesale adoption of Kerberos authentication, Windows 2000 and Windows Server 2003 domains are, essentially, Kerberos realms. There are different forms of realm names:

■ The realm name can be a prefix (e.g., Microsoft\user1, where Microsoft is the name of a domain)

■ The realm name can be a suffix (e.g., user1@microsoft.com, where microsoft.com is either a DNS domain name or the name of an Active Directory domain)

You can require users to specify the realm name by using the correct syntax when they connect. For example, you can require that the user type the user name (including the user account name and the realm) in User name in the Connect dialog box when making a dial-up or VPN connection in Network Connections. You can also add the realm name automatically to the user account name. For example, you can specify a realm name and syntax when you create a custom dialing package with the Connection Manager Administration Kit, so that the user has to specify only the user account name.

The user name is passed from the access client to the access server during the authentication phase of the connection attempt. This user name becomes the User-Name RADIUS attribute in the Access-Request message that is sent by the access server to its RADIUS server. If the RADIUS server is an IAS server, the Access-Request message is evaluated against the set of configured connection request policies. Conditions on the connection request policy can include the specification of the contents of User-Name attribute. You can configure a set of connection request policies that are specific to the realm name within the User-Name attribute of incoming messages. This allows to you create routing rules that forward RADIUS messages with a specific realm name to a specific set of RADIUS servers when IAS is used as a RADIUS proxy.

Before the RADIUS message is either processed locally (when IAS is being used as a RADIUS server) or forwarded to another RADIUS server (when IAS is being used as a RADIUS proxy), the User-Name attribute in the message might be modified by attribute manipulation rules that are configured on the profile of the first matching connection request policy. Attribute manipulation rules for the User-Name attribute can carry out the following actions:

■ Remove the realm name from the user name (also known as realm stripping). For example, the user name user1@microsoft.com is changed to user1.

■ Change the realm name but not its syntax. For example, the user name user1@microsoft.com is changed to user1@wcoast.microsoft.com.

■ Change the syntax of the realm name. For example, the user name microsoft\user1 is changed to user1@microsoft.com.

Attribute manipulation rules are configured in the Attribute tab on the profile of a connection request policy. After the User-Name attribute is modified according to attribute manipulation rules, additional settings on the profile of the first matching connection request policy are used to determine whether (1) the IAS server processes the Access-Request message locally (when IAS is being used as a RADIUS server), or (2) the IAS server forwards the message to another RADIUS server (when IAS is being used as a RADIUS proxy).

NOTE: When the user name does not contain a domain name, IAS supplies one. By default, the IAS-supplied domain name is the domain for which the IAS server is a member. You can specify the IAS-supplied domain name through the following registry setting: HKEY_ LOCAL_MACHINE\System\CurrentControlSet\Services\RasMan\PPP\ControlProtocols\ BuiltIn\DefaultDomain

19.8.2   Installing and Configuring IAS

To install IAS, use the Add/Remove Programs object in the Control Panel. With the Add/Remove Programs object open, click Add/Remove Windows Components. Open the Networking Services item and select Internet Authentication service, then click OK. Windows installs the Internet Authentication Service console to enable you to manage and configure IAS. Like the RRAS console, the IAS console is located in Administrative Tools. See Figure 19.8. IAS does not have to be installed on the same server as RRAS. You just have to specify the IP address or FQDN of the IAS server when you configure the RAS server to enable RRAS to locate it.

IAS uses certain security measures to restrict which services can connect to a RADIUS server for authentication. Services that use IAS to authenticate remote users are called clients. So, you need to configure IAS to allow specific clients (such as your RRAS server) to connect to a RADIUS server to

Figure 19.8   The IAS console

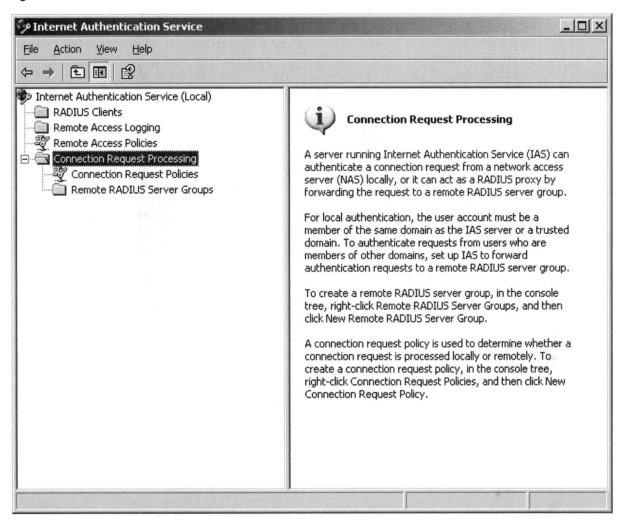

authenticate users. To enable a client to connect, open the IAS console, then open the Clients folder. Right-click Clients, or right-click in the right pane and choose New Client, to start the Add Client Wizard. The Wizard prompts for the following information:

- **Friendly name**—This is the client name as it appears in the IAS console. Select a name that identifies the client.
- **Protocol**—This option specifies the protocol the client will use. By default, RADIUS is the only protocol listed and available.
- **Client address (IP or DNS)**—Specify the client's IP address or FQDN. You can verify an FQDN by clicking Verify, which will attempt to resolve the name to an IP.
- **Client-vendor**—Use this option to specify the client device manufacturer/type. This selection is optional, unless you are using RAPs to restrict access based on vendor type. Select the appropriate type from the list. Select Microsoft for a Windows 2000 (or Windows Server 2003) RRAS server. Select RADIUS Standard if the client is a RADIUS proxy or if the client type does not appear in the list.
- **Client must always send the signature attribute in the request**—Select this option to require the client to send a digital signature attribute in access request packets for PAP, CHAP, or MS-CHAP authentication. IAS always requires the client to include the signature if you are using EAP. Authentication attempts that do not include a signature are discarded if this option is selected.

■ **Shared secret/Confirm shared secret**—A shared secret is a string used as a password to enable the client to gain access to the IAS server. Like any password, the shared secret specified at both the client and server sides must match exactly. You can use any alphanumeric characters and special characters in the string, up to 255 characters. The shared secret is case sensitive. Use a string containing a combination of letters, numbers, special characters, and different cases to help protect against dictionary attacks. You can use the same shared secret for each client or specify a different one for each (for better security).

There are several global options you need to configure for IAS to control the way IAS functions. Open the IAS console, right-click the IAS server's main branch, and choose Properties. This service page contains the following options:

■ **Description**—Specify a friendly name to help differentiate this IAS service from others on the network.

■ **Log rejected or discarded authentication requests**—Select this option to write an event to the Windows Application event log each time the network access server (the client) sends a rejected or discarded authentication request.

■ **Log successful authentication requests**—Select this option to write an event to the Windows Application event log each time a remote access client successfully authenticates.

The RADIUS client must be configured to use the appropriate port, which is done on the RADIUS Properties page. By default, IAS uses ports 1812 and 1645 for authentication and 1813 and 1656 for accounting. Ports 1645 and 1646 are included to support older RADIUS clients.

Surprisingly, IAS does not use realm names. You can configure IAS to strip out the realm portion to authenticate against the domain. So if you have requests that come from another other servers that contain realm names, you will need to strip out the realm name before authenticating the user against the domain.

Like RRAS, IAS can perform logging of accounting requests, authentication requests, and periodic status. You can configure IAS to use one of two formats: IAS compatible or database compatible. While both options create a delimited text file, the database-compatible format allows you to import the log file into a database such as Access or SQL Server. To configure logging through the IAS console, click the Remote Access Logging branch, then double-click the Local File item in the right pane to display its properties. Use the Settings page to configure which events are logged and use the Local File page to control the size of the log, how often the log is replaced, and its location.

To prevent a single IAS server from becoming a single point of failure for authentication, authorization, and accounting, IAS servers are often deployed in pairs (a primary and a backup) to provide fault tolerance, or in multiples to balance the load of large numbers of authentication and accounting requests. When you deploy more than one IAS server computer to provide the same authentication, authorization, and accounting service to RADIUS clients and proxies, you must synchronize the configuration of the IAS server computers.

For more information about IAS, see the following report and others at the website listed. "Internet Authentication Service for Windows 2000"

http://www.microsoft.com/windows2000/technologies/communications/ias/default.asp

---

19.9   CONNECTING TO A RAS SERVER

Chapter 10 introduced how to establish a network connection by using the Make New Connection icon. Access is established by clicking on the Start button, selecting the Settings option, and selecting Network and Dial-Up Connections to open the Dial-Up Connections folder to access the make New Connection icon.

When you start the Network Connection Wizard, you have several options:

■ **Dial-up to private network**—Select this option if you are trying to connect to a private network such as a RAS server at your office or any other non-Internet connection. You will be prompted for a phone number and dialing properties, whether the connection can be used only by you or by all users on the computer, and whether to enable connection sharing for the connection.

- **Dial-up to the Internet**—Select this option to configure a dial-up connection to an Internet Service Provider (ISP) or other RAS that functions like an Internet access server. This option runs the Internet Connection Wizard, which lets you specify how you connect to the Internet (LAN or modem) and configure proxy settings.
- **Connect to a private network through the Internet**—Select this option to create a VPN connection through the Internet to a private network. The Wizard prompts you for the IP address or FQDN of the VPN server, which users can use the connection, and whether to enable connection sharing for the connection.

After the connection has been created, you can right-click the connection and icon to open connection properties, which include several tabs. The Security property tab for a connection lets you specify the authentication method used for the connection. By default, Windows sets up the connection to allow unsecured passwords, which means the client can send the password in plain text, thereby making it susceptible to interception. If you select Require secured password or select from the "Validate my identity as follows" drop-down list, the connection will be forced to require encryption for the password. The encryption will depend on the authentication method negotiated with the remote server. See Figure 19.9.

There also are two other options that work in conjunction with the Require secured password option:

- **Automatically use my Windows logon name and password (and domain if any)**—Select this option to have the connection automatically use your current logon name, password, and domain for logon to the remote server.
- **Require data encryption (disconnect if none)**—Select this option to force data encryption for the connection and to disconnect if the server does not offer a supported encryption method.

Figure 19.9   Configuring security for a remote client

If you want more control, select the Advanced option, then click on the Settings button to open the Advanced Security Settings dialog box. Here you can specify which authentication protocols are allowed and what type of data encryption will be used, or you can configure the EAP protocol.

SMART CARDS

A smart card is a small electronic device about the size of a credit card that contains electronic memory, and possibly an embedded integrated circuit (IC). Smart cards are used for a variety of purposes, including storing a patient's medical records, storing digital cash, and generating network IDs (similar to a token) to help validate someone. To use a smart card, either to pull information from it or add data to it, you need a smart card reader, a small device into which you insert the smart card. Of course, this option must be supported by the remote server for the connection to succeed.

If you want to use multilink connections and the Bandwidth Allocation Protocol (BAP) to dynamically add and drop links as needed to accommodate changes in bandwidth usage, your remote server must support multilink and BAP if you use BAP on the client side. You would, of course, need to first install the multiple devices you will be using to dial out. If you only have one device installed, the multilink options are not shown. If multiple devices are installed but only one is selected for the connection, the multilink options are dimmed.

After installing all connection devices, open the Network and dial-up connections folder, right-click the connection, and choose Properties. On the General page, select all of the devices you want to use to establish the multilink connection. If you need to configure different numbers for each one, make sure that the option "All devices call the same numbers" is deselected, then select each modem from the drop-down list and specify the number to dial through that modem. If the RAS uses a single number with a hunt group to distribute calls, select the option "All devices call the same numbers." Next, click the Options tab to display the Options property page. The drop-down list in the Multiple devices group provides three options:

- Dial only first available device (single device)
- Dial all devices (multiple devices)
- Dial devices only as needed (multiple devices with BAP to manage bandwidth usage)

If you talk with other computers, then potentially other people can gain access to your files. You can prevent that from occurring by disabling the File and Printer Sharing service from the dial-up connection. Open the Network page of the connection's property sheet and deselect the File and Printer Sharing service. Also, deselect any protocols other than TCP/IP if they are enabled and if you don't need them for a specific reason. Lastly, starting with Windows XP and Windows Server 2003, you can use the Internet Connection Firewall to limit or prevent access to your computer from the Internet.

19.10   TERMINAL EMULATION

Telnet is a user command and an underlying TCP/IP protocol for accessing remote computers, as specified in RFC 854. **Terminal emulation (Telnet)** is used to access someone else's computer, assuming that person has given you permission. Such a computer is frequently called a host computer, whereas the client is called a dumb terminal. With Telnet, you log on as a regular user with whatever privileges you may have been granted to the specific applications and data on that computer. You can then enter commands through the Telnet program and they will be executed as if you were entering them directly on the server console; thus, you control the server and communicate with other servers on the network. Telnet is a common way to remotely control web servers.

RFC 854 states: "The Telnet Protocol is built upon three main ideas: first, the concept of a 'Network Virtual Terminal'; second, the principle of negotiated options; and third, a symmetric view of terminals and processes." The default port for Telnet is TCP port 23.

A popular terminal program/brand of terminal from DEC is Visual Terminal 100 (vt100). It was extremely popular with certain companies and universities that ran Berkeley UNIX on their VAXes (also from DEC). Most communication packets support vt100.

Figure 19.10   Using Windows 2000 Telnet client software

To start Telnet server on a Windows 2000 or Windows Server 2003 server, do the following:

1. Open Computer Management.
2. In the console tree, click Services located under Services and Applications.
3. In the Details pane, right-click Telnet, then select the Start option.

To connect to a UNIX computer or Windows with the Telnet server using a Telnet program, Windows computers provide a DOS command called TELNET.EXE. The TELNET command can be used with or without a computer name. If no computer name is used, Telnet provides command mode and provides a prompt to the user. The activation of Telnet results in a TCP connection to the server and to the Telnet daemon, TLNTSVR. After a connection is established, Telnet enters input mode. Depending on the remote computer, typed text is sent from the client either one character at a time or one line at a time. Since Telnet is used for UNIX computers, it does not allow the executing of GUI-based programs. See Figure 19.10.

NOTE: Another program found in Windows to connect to a computer or other host using a terminal emulation program is Hyperterminal. Even though this is a GUI program, it only allows you to execute text commands.

The TELNET command can be used to test TCP connections. You can use the command to test any TCP port to see if it is responding, which is especially useful when checking SMTP and HTTP ports. The syntax for the command is as follows.

```
TELNET hostname port
```

where the host name could be the host name or the IP address. If you do not specify the port number, it will default to port 23. For example, to verify HTTP is working on a computer, type in the following command:

```
TELNET acme.com 80
```

If you connect to a SMTP server, you can further test your e-mail server by actually sending a e-mail message from the Telnet session.

19.11   THIN CLIENTS

A **thin client** is a computer whose characteristics classify it between a dumb terminal and a PC, and is, designed to be especially small so that the bulk of the data processing occurs on the server. Although the term *thin client* usually refers to software, it is increasingly used for computers, such as network computers and PCs that are designed to serve as the clients for client-server architectures.

A **fat client** performs the bulk of the data processing operations. The data are stored on the server. Although the term *fat client* also refers to software, it can apply to a network computer that has relatively strong processing abilities.

A relatively new technology for remote access is the Citrix WinFrame (or MetaFrame) products (including Windows Terminal Services) which use the **Independent Computing Architecture (ICA)** protocol. The Citrix WinFrame allows multiple computers to take control of a virtual computer and use it as if it were their desktop (thin client). The ICA protocol is used by the Citrix or Windows Terminal Services client to communicate with the server. This protocol sends screen shots, mouse movements, and so forth between the client and server. With the WinFrame technology, you can connect to a server and run configuration and administration programs as if you were sitting at the server.

19.11.1   Introduction to Terminal Services

Windows 2000 and Windows Server 2003 **Terminal Services** is a fully integrated component of Windows that enables the latest Windows-based applications to be accessible from any Microsoft-based client operating system. Terminal Services gives you the opportunity to extend remote solutions to your customers that are more efficient and easier to manage.

When a client runs an application on a Terminal Services–enabled Windows server, all client application execution, data processing, and data storage occur on the server. The Terminal Services component in Windows provides a bridging technology for customers who are moving to a Windows 2000 Professional or Windows XP desktop. It allows a homogeneous set of applications to run on a heterogeneous set of desktop hardware through terminal emulation. Since only screen (via the remote desktop protocol, RDP), keyboard, and mouse information is exchanged between the client and server, it is an ideal solution for the remote dial-up network or for using a shared application on a single server that many people need to access from distant locations (across the Internet or dial-up).

There are two main aspects, or modes, of Terminal Services that you can enable: the applications server mode and the remote administration mode. The applications server mode allows end users to log on to Terminal Services from any connected device and access the applications that are installed on the server. The remote administration mode allows up to two concurrent administrators to remotely manage the server. By choosing one mode over the other, users are able to assign a priority to the way Terminal Services operates. When remote administration mode is enabled, memory and CPU utilization settings are unaffected, application compatibility settings are disabled, and there is minimal impact on the server.

Remote administration mode allows end users the ability to manage their server from any location. There are no licensing requirements when using this mode, as only administrator accounts can attach to the server. While in this mode, administrators can view event logs, run commands, check databases such as SQL or Exchange, or upgrade a domain controller. This capability can benefit customers who do not have the budget to upgrade their desktops to run Windows 2000 Professional or Windows XP, as they are still able to utilize advanced applications such as Microsoft Office 2000. Terminal Services also benefits roaming users who do not work on the same computer all the time but need to access their desktop environments and information stored on the server. Companies that require remote management solutions for their networks are another type of potential customer.

19.11.2   Installing and Removing Terminal Services

To add Terminal Services to Windows 2000 Server or Windows Server 2003, follow these steps:

1. Open the Add/Remove Programs applet in the Control Panel.
2. Choose Add/Remove Windows Components.
3. From the list available, check the box next to Terminal Services Click on the Next button. You do not need to install Terminal Services Licensing to run terminal sessions, although you will need to install the licensing tool on some Windows 2000 servers in the network to keep track of terminal license use. If you click the Details button, you will see that you can install either client-created files or files that allow a user to connect to the terminal server and that are needed to enable Terminal Services.
4. As shown in Figure 19.11, in the Terminal Services Setup dialog box, you have two choices for setting up Terminal Services. Choose the desired option and click the Next button.

NOTE: Windows Server 2003, Web Server Edition, does not include Terminal Services.

Windows will then copy the files from an installation source. When the copying is done, you will be prompted to restart the computer to effect the changes. Upgrading from Windows NT Server 4.0,

Figure 19.11   Selecting the Terminal Services mode

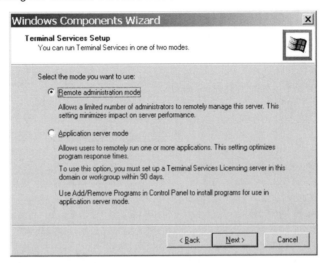

Figure 19.12   Creating Terminal Services Client installation disks

Terminal Server Edition, to Windows 2000 or Windows Server 2003 with Terminal Services will preserve user and applications configuration information. The system will be placed in application server mode and Terminal Server 4.0–based security will be used. Upgrading directly from Citrix WinFrame is not supported; the system must be upgraded to Terminal Server 4.0 as an intermediate step, and then upgraded to Windows 2000 or Windows Server 2003. A clean install is recommended but not required.

To remove Terminal Services from Windows 2000 Server or Windows Server 2003, open the Add/Remove Programs applet in the Control Panel and choose Add/Remove Windows components.

19.11.3   Configuring and Using the Terminal Services Client

Windows 2000 Server and Windows Server 2003 include new clients for Terminal Services, with enhancements to the Remote Desktop Protocol (RDP) and new features. Clients included on the Windows server CD are compatible with the following platforms: 16-bit client (runs on Windows 3.11) and 32-bit client (runs on Windows 9X, Windows NT 3.51, Windows NT 4.0, Windows 2000, Windows XP, and Windows Server 2003). Earlier Windows NT Server 4.0, Terminal Server Edition clients will also work with Windows 2000 Server with Terminal Services enabled; however, some of the new RDP features will not be available unless the new Windows Terminal Services clients are used.

To connect a PC-based client to Terminal Services, run a Terminal Services Client installation program. You can either create installation disks with the Terminal Services Client Creator or share the client files on the network and run the Setup program from the client. The Terminal Services Client Creator can be found in the Administrator Tools program.

As shown in Figure 19.12, the default client types available are Terminal Services for 16-bit Windows (which requires four disks) and Terminal Services for 32-bit x86 Windows (which requires two disks).

Figure 19.13 Connecting a terminal server using the Terminal Services Client software

Figure 19.14 Connecting to a second computer using Windows 2000 Terminal Services

One way to connect to a terminal server is to run the Terminal Services Client found in the Terminal Services Client program group. See Figure 19.13. From the Terminal Services Client dialog box, select the screen area size in resolution and the server. Using a lower resolution will give you a smaller window on the desktop. If the client gets an error message saying that the terminal server is busy, try again later, check the client TCP/IP settings, and make sure the IP address and subnet are valid. After the connection is made, a window will appear that allows you to log in to the server to which you are connecting. After you log on, run programs at the server from your computer. See Figure 19.14.

To create a customized connection, you can use the Client Connection Manager. To define a new connection, open the File menu and select the New option. Then using the Client Connection Manager Wizard, specify the server, the information to do an automatic login, and the session display settings. After the connection has been defined, then choose to create a shortcut in the Programs option using the Start button or by using the Client Connection Manager.

Figure 19.15   Terminal Services Manager

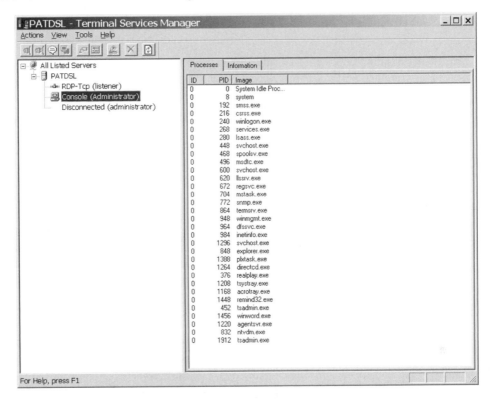

To manage the Terminal Services connection in trusted domains, administrators can use the Terminal Services Manager. The Terminal Services Manager is used to monitor users, sessions, and applications on each terminal server, and allows you to carry out assorted actions to manage the server.

When a user creates a session by connecting to the terminal server from a client computer, the session appears in the Session list in Terminal Services Manager. In addition, the name of the user who logs on using the session appears in the Users list. Any applications run at the user's session can be monitored on the Processes list. Therefore, you can oversee all users, sessions, and processes on a terminal server from one location. See Figure 19.15.

19.11.4   Applications under Terminal Services

If you plan to run a Windows server in the application server mode (a traditional terminal server), then you must install applications correctly in multiuser mode in one of the following two ways:

- Install the applications using the Add/Remove Programs tool in the Control Panel. Using this tool is the easiest option. It will properly install the applications for use in a Terminal Services environment.
- Alternatively, put the server into Install mode manually by using the Change User/Install command-line utility before installing applications on Windows 2000 or Windows Server 2003 with Terminal Services enabled. After installing the application, the server should be put back into execute mode by using the Change User/Execute command-line option.

Note that some programs require an application compatibility script to be run in the Terminal Services environment. Microsoft supplies such a script for Office 2000 in the Office 2000 Resource Kit.

When running applications, you will need to have sufficient processor power and memory. Microsoft states that a quad processor Pentium Pro with 512 MB of RAM will concurrently support about 60 typical users. Of course, the server would typically be dedicated to this task.

19.11.5   Licensing for Terminal Services

The licensing for Terminal Services is a bit more complicated than normal licenses for the server. In a nutshell, each device that initiates a Windows Terminal Services session must be licensed with the following:

- Windows 2000 Professional or Windows XP license, or Windows 2000 or Windows Server 2003 Terminal Services Client Access license
- Windows Server Client Access license or BackOffice Family Client Access license

For more information about the Terminal Services licenses, visit the Microsoft.com website.

19.11.6   Remote Desktop

Starting with Windows XP, Microsoft introduced Remote Desktop and Remote Assistance. Similar to Terminal Services, these features enable you to have access to a Windows session that is running on your computer when you are at another computer. This means, for example, that you can connect to your work computer from home and have access to all of your applications, files, and network resources as though you were in front of your computer at work. You can leave programs running at work and when you get home, you can see your desktop at work displayed on your home computer, with the same programs running. Note: Many work environments may establish a proxy server or firewall that may block this capability.

When you connect to your computer at work, Remote Desktop automatically locks that computer so that no one else can access your applications and files while you are gone. When you come back to your computer at work, you can unlock it by pressing Ctrl+Alt+Del. Remote Desktop also allows more than one user to have active sessions on a single computer. This means that multiple users can leave their applications running and preserve the state of their Windows session even while others are logged on.

With the Fast User Switching feature, you can easily switch from one user to another on the same computer. For example, suppose you are working at home and have logged on to the computer at your office to update an expense report. While you are working, a family member needs to use your home computer to check for an important e-mail message. You can disconnect Remote Desktop, allow the other user to log on and check mail, then reconnect to the computer at your office, where you see the expense report exactly as you left it. Fast User Switching works on stand-alone computers and computers that are members of workgroups.

To use Remote Desktop, you need the following:

- A computer running Windows XP Professional ("remote" computer) with a connection to a LAN or the Internet.
- A second computer ("home" computer) with access to the LAN via network connection, modem, or VPN connection. This computer must have Remote Desktop Connection, formerly called the Terminal Services client, installed.
- Appropriate user accounts and permissions.

To set up the computer to use Remote Desktop, follow these steps:

1. Open System in Control Panel.
2. On the Remote tab, select "Allow users to connect remotely to this computer" check box. See Figure 19.16.
3. Ensure that you have the proper permissions to connect to your computer remotely, and click OK. You must be an administrator or a member of the Remote Desktop Users group on your computer.

You must be logged on as an administrator or a member of the Administrators group to enable the Remote Desktop feature.

To allow other users to connect to your computer, follow these steps:

1. Open System in Control Panel.
2. Click the Remote tab.
3. In the Remote Desktop area, click Select Remote Users . . .
4. On the Remote Desktop Users dialog box, click Add . . .
5. On the Select Users dialog box, click Locations . . . to specify the search location.
6. Click Object Types . . . to specify the types of objects you want to search for.

Figure 19.16   Configuring Remote Assistance and Remote Desktop

7. In the "Enter the object names to select (examples):" box, type the names of the objects you want to search for.
8. Click Check Names.
9. When the name is located, click OK. The name now appears in the list of users on the Remote Desktop Users dialog box.

Again, you must be logged on as an administrator or a member of the Administrators group to add a user to the Remote Users Group.

19.11.7   Requesting Help Using Remote Assistance

Sometimes the best way to fix a problem is to have someone show you how. Remote Assistance is a convenient way for a friend to connect to your computer from another computer running a compatible operating system, such as Microsoft Windows XP, and walk you through your solution. By following the easy steps in Remote Assistance, you can use Windows Messenger Service or an e-mail message to invite a friend to connect to your computer. After he or she is connected, your friend will be able to view your computer screen and chat with you in real-time about what you both see. With your permission, your friend can even use his or her mouse and keyboard to work with you on your computer. To start Remote Assistance, do the following:

1. Click Start, then click Help and Support.
2. Click "Get help from a friend by using Remote Assistance."

Both you and your friend must be using either Windows Messenger Service or a MAPI-compliant e-mail account such as Microsoft Outlook or Outlook Express. You and your friend need to be connected to the Internet while using Remote Assistance.

If for some reason you are unable to send an invitation by using e-mail or Windows Messenger Service, you can create and save an invitation. On the first page of Remote Assistance, click Invite someone to help you, then click the Save option at the bottom of the next page. You can then send the saved invitation file to your friend in the manner you choose, such as copying it onto a floppy disk or a shared network location, sending it over another e-mail service or an FTP connection, and so on.

SUMMARY

1. Modern networks offer remote access service (RAS), which allows users to connect remotely using various protocols and connection types.
2. A remote access server is the computer and associated software that is set up to handle users who are seeking access to the network remotely.
3. Virtual private networking is the creation of secured, point-to-point connections across a private network or a public network such as the Internet.
4. The typical dial-in session actually consists of six distinct steps or stages, each of which must be completed successfully before the user gains access to centralized resources.
5. If the call gets through, the remote (dialing) modem will begin negotiating a common data rate and other transmission parameters with the answering modem. This step is referred to as the handshaking stage, because both modems must agree on the same parameters before continuing.
6. Remote Authentication Dial-in User Service (RADIUS) is the industry standard client-server protocol and software that enables remote access servers to communicate with a central server to authenticate dial-in users and authorize their access to the requested system or service for authenticating remote users.
7. The first protocol used for carrying IP packets over dial-up lines was the Serial Line Interface Protocol (SLIP).
8. The Point-to-Point Protocol (PPP) has become the predominant protocol for modem-based access to the Internet.
9. A client uses an authentication protocol to send either encrypted or unencrypted credentials to the server, depending on the protocol.
10. The Password Authentication Protocol (PAP) is the least secure authentication Protocol because it uses clear-text (plain-text) passwords.
11. Historically, Challenge Handshake Authentication Protocol (CHAP) is the most common dial-up authentication protocol, and it uses an industry Message Digest 5 (MD5) hashing scheme to encrypt authentication.
12. Microsoft Challenge Handshake Authentication Protocol (MS-CHAP) is Microsoft's proprietary version of CHAP, which is the most secure within Windows.
13. Microsoft has included support in Windows for the Extensible Authentication Protocol (EAP), which allows new authentication schemes to be plugged in as needed.
14. Windows 2000 and Windows Server 2003 Routing and Remote Access Service (RRAS) is a mature, full-featured, third-generation service of Windows-based server operating systems.
15. Point-to-Point Tunneling Protocol (PPTP) is the most popular implementation of the virtual private network (VPN) and is an inexpensive way to create wide area networks (WANs).
16. IPSec has stronger encryption and authentication than PPTP.
17. The PPP Multilink Protocol (MP) is an extension that is used to aggregate or combine multiple physical links into a single logical link.
18. In Windows 2000 and Windows Server 2003, Bandwidth Allocation Protocol (BAP) and Bandwidth Allocation Control Protocol (BACP) enhance multilink by dynamically adding or dropping links on demand.
19. In Windows 2000 and Windows Server 2003, authorization is granted based on the dial-in properties of a user account and remote access policies.
20. Terminal emulation (Telnet) is a user command and an underlying TCP/IP protocol for accessing remote computers.
21. A thin client is designed to be especially small so that the bulk of the data processing occurs on the server.
22. Windows 2000 or Windows Server 2003 Terminal Services is a fully integrated component of Windows servers that enables the latest Windows-based applications to be accessible from any Microsoft-based client operating system.
23. In Windows Terminal Services, remote administration mode allows end users the ability to manage their servers from any location.
24. In Windows 2000 and Windows Server 2003, remote access connections are granted based on the dial-in properties and remote access policies.
25. Remote access policies (RAPs) are conditions and connection parameters that allow network administrators more flexibility in granting remote access permissions and usage.
26. Internet Authentication Service (IAS), which is available in Windows 2000 and Windows Server 2003, is the Microsoft implementation of a Remote Authentication Dial-in User Service (RADIUS) server and proxy.
27. The Independent Computing Architecture (ICA) protocol is used by the Citrix or Windows Terminal Services client to communicate with the server.

QUESTIONS

1. Which of the following are dial-up communication protocols? (Choose all that apply.)
   a. PSTN
   b. Telnet
   c. PPP
   d. SLIP
   e. TCP

2. SLIP is an acronym for _____.
   a. Serial Line Internet Protocol
   b. Service Layer Internal Protocol
   c. System Level Information Protocol
   d. Serial Line Information Protocol

3. PPP is an acronym for _____.
   a. Point-to-Present Protocol
   b. Physical Point Protocol
   c. Point-to-Point Protocol
   d. Present Point Protocol

4. What is the most common network protocol that is run over a PPP dial-up connection?
   a. TCP/IP
   b. IPX
   c. NetBEUI
   d. PPTP

5. Which of the following functions does PPP LCP perform? (Choose all that apply.)
   a. establishes link connection
   b. terminates link connection
   c. configures link connection
   d. tests link connection

6. Which of these are authentication protocols for PPP? (Choose all that apply.)
   a. CHAP
   b. PAP
   c. LCP
   d. NCP

7. What is RADIUS used for?
   a. dial-up authentication
   b. WAN-based encryption
   c. remote access compression algorithm
   d. dynamic network configuration

8. Pat has set up a RAS server that connects to an Internet service provider (ISP) using a dial-up connection. Pat wants Windows 98 users on the local network to access the Internet through the RAS server. How should Pat set up the Internet connection?
   a. On the RAS server, leave the default gateway address blank.
   b. On the RAS server, use the subnet mask provided by the ISP.
   c. On the Windows 98 computers, select ISDN as the dial-up networking type.
   d. On the Windows 98 computers, set up the RAS server for multilink.
   e. On the Windows 98 computer, use the subnet mask provided by the ISP.

9. A number of employees at your company have Windows 2000 computers installed on their notebook computers. They need to dial up over the Internet to access client-server applications on your network's Windows 2000 Server computer. You need to provide adequately encrypted security for these connections and prevent unauthorized users from accessing the server. How can you best do this?

   a. Enable IP address filtering on the server.
   b. Implement the point-to-point tunneling protocol (PPTP).
   c. Set up FTP with user-level security.
   d. Set up RAS with SSL security.

10. Your network connects via a RAS server to an Internet service provider (ISP). Employees make a PPTP connection to your network through the ISP. A remote dial-up user calls to say she is having difficulty in connecting to your network. What should you do first?
    a. Have the user run TRACERT.
    b. Have the user try a standard PPP connection.
    c. Reboot the RAS server.
    d. RUN IPCONFIG /ALL on the RAS server to verify the ISP's DNS address.

11. Pat has just set up PPTP on his RAS server, which connects his local network to the Internet. With PPTP filtering enabled, how does the RAS server provide for network security?
    a. The RAS server allows the administrator to set the RAS server port for Dial Out Only, Receive Calls Only, or Dial Out and Receive Calls connections.
    b. The RAS server allows only PPTP packets to enter the local network.
    c. The RAS server allows only PPTP packets to leave the local network.
    d. The RAS server enforces callback security.

12. Over which of the following networks can the point-to-point tunneling protocol (PPTP) support a virtual private network (VPN) using a RAS server?
    a. ISDN only
    b. PSTN (Public Switched Telephone Network) only
    c. ISDN and PSTN only
    d. PSTN, ISDN, and X.25

13. Which one of the following protocols does the Point-to-Point Tunneling Protocol (PPTP) support?
    a. AppleTalk
    b. IP
    c. IPX
    d. NetBEUI

14. You are deciding whether to use PPTP or L2TP to allow network connections to your LAN to be tunneled across the Internet. Which of the following are true of L2TP? (Choose all that apply.)
    a. L2TP provides data encryption.
    b. L2TP requires an IP-based network.
    c. L2TP supports tunnel authentication.
    d. L2TP supports header compression.

15. You are concerned about hackers capturing network packets and reading their contents. Which feature of Windows 2000 and Windows Server 2003 allows you to secure your network traffic so that it cannot be easily read by anyone who may be capturing the packets?
    a. IPSec
    b. Dynamic DNS
    c. PAP
    d. BAP

16. Your remote access server has multiple modems as do your RAS clients. You would like to use the multilink capabilities of this configuration but are concerned that you may be paying for extra phone calls when multilink

connections are unnecessary. Which feature of Windows 2000 and Windows Server 2003 allows you to use the multilink features dynamically, so that extra links are only made when the extra bandwidth is required?

a. BAP
c. L2TP
b. PPTP
d. EAP

17. Pat, a field technician, is required to travel from client site to client site. He does not always have the opportunity to convey his travel itinerary to the network support staff of his company. What is the best way to configure the RAS server at the home office of Pat's company to allow him remote access from various workstations at his client sites while still providing network callback security?

a. Reset the remote access permissions in the Routing and Remote Access console to the default setting.
b. Set the remote access permissions in the Routing and Remote Access console to Preset To and enter his callback number.
c. Set the remote access permissions in the Routing and Remote Access console to Set By Caller.
d. Set the remote access permissions in the Routing and Remote Access console to Preset To, enter a callback number, but invoke the MD5 RAS encryption protocol.
e. Install third-party software that captures Pat's caller ID and configures his Preset To callback number accordingly.

18. Which protocols can be used as dial-out protocols by a Windows 2000 Server using the remote access service?

a. NetBEUI only
b. TCP/IP, NetBEUI, or NWLink
c. TCP/IP and NetBEUI, but not NWLink
d. TCP/IP and NWLink, but not NetBEUI

19. Which dial-up protocol requires that devices on each end know the other's address?

a. SLIP
d. POTS
b. PPP
e. xDSL
c. TCP/IP

20. Which dial-up protocol is capable of passing multiple LAN protocols across the link?

a. SLIP
d. POTS
b. PPP
e. xDSL
c. TCP/IP

21. Which protocol provides an encrypted connection between devices using virtual private networking?

a. PPTP
d. SLIP
b. PPP
e. xDSL
c. TCP/IP

22. Which dial-up protocol is considered self-configuring?

a. SLIP
d. POTS
b. PPP
e. xDSL
c. TCP/IP

23. You are the administrator of your company's network. Your company has branch offices in New York and Paris. Because each branch office supports its own routing and remote access server, you implement a Remote Authentication Dial-In User Service (RADIUS) server to centralize administration. You remove the default remote access policy. You need to implement one company policy that

requires all dial-up communications to use 40-bit encryption. You want to configure your network to require secure communications by using the least amount of administrative effort. What should you do? (Choose two answers.)

a. Create one remote access policy on each routing and remote access server.
b. Create one remote access policy on the RADIUS server.
c. Set encryption to Basic in the remote access policy or policies.
d. Set encryption to Strong in the remote access policy or policies.
e. Enable the Secure Server IPSec policy on the RADIUS server.
f. Enable the Server IPSec policy on the RADIUS server.

24. You are the administrator of your company's network. To allow users to access network resources when they are not in the office, you configure remote access services in their native-mode Windows 2000 domain. Because your company operates 24 hours a day and 7 days a week, and because your users are not running Windows 98 and Windows NT workstation, you do not want to apply any time or authentication restrictions. To accomplish this, you delete the default remote access policy. However, you want to restrict access by unauthorized users. You grant all users in the domain dial-in permission, but you begin to receive reports that users are not able to receive the connection. What should you do to resolve the problem?

a. Create a new remote access policy that has the condition to grant all members of the domain users group dial-in access.
b. Create a new group policy that grants dial-in permissions to the domain user group.
c. Edit the remote access profile to allow the use of encrypted authentication (CHAP) as the only authentication method.
d. Edit the remote access profile to allow the users of unencrypted authentication (PAP, SPAP) as the only authentication method.

25. You are the administrator of your company's network. The network consists of one Windows 2000 domain running in native mode. You are not running Certificate Services in the domain. Your company is a sales organization and has 150 salespeople. When these salespeople are out of office, they require file and print services, e-mail, and access to the company's product and inventory database. These salespeople belong to a group named SalesMobile. Your company has dedicated T1 access to the Internet. Your company also uses a virtual private network (VPN) to reduce the costs and hardware required to support the salespeople. You want to accomplish the following goals:

- Required network resources will be accessible to all salespeople.
- Connections to the network will be made only by salespeople.
- Sensitive company data will be kept confidential over the VPN connections.
- Access to the network will only take place during business hours.
- All salespeople will be able to connect to the network simultaneously.

You take the following actions:

- Install routing and remote access on a Windows 2000 Server computer and configure virtual private networking.
- Grant the salespeople the Allow Access dial-in permission.
- Edit the default remote access policy to grant remote access permission.
- Edit the default remote access profile to require Strong encryption of data.

Which result or results do these actions produce?

a. Required network resources are accessible to all salespeople.

b. Connections to the network are made only by salespeople.

c. Sensitive company data is kept confidential over the VPN connections.

d. Access to the network only takes place during business hours.

e. All salespeople are able to connect to the network simultaneously.

26. You are the administrator of your company's network. You are configuring a Windows 2000 network for dial-up access. Your users need to access their computers from home. To increase security, your company issue smart cards to all users who have dial-up access. You need to configure your routing and remote access server. What should you do? (Choose two answers.)

a. Select the Extensible Authentication Protocol (EAP) check box.

b. Select the Microsoft encrypted authentication version 2 (MS-CHAP v2) check box.

c. Install a computer certificate on the routing and remote access server.

d. Install a smart card logon certificate on the routing and remote access server.

e. Install a computer certificate on the dial-up access client computer.

27. You are the administrator of your company's network. Your company employs account executives who need access to the latest company data when they are traveling. You want to ensure that your company will establish the network connection for your account executives regardless of where the call originates. Your company also allows vendors access to the network by routing and remote access to submit purchase orders. To ensure network security, your company wants to specify the location from which vendors can connect. You want to configure your company's routing and remote access server to facilitate access for account executive and vendors. Which three actions should you take to ensure this configuration?

a. Set the Callback option to "Always callback to" for the account executives.

b. Set the Callback option to "Set by caller" for the account executives.

c. Set the Callback option to "No callback" for the vendors.

d. Set the Callback option to "Always Callback to" for the vendors.

e. Set the Callback option to "Set by Caller" for the vendors.

f. Enable Link Control protocol (LCP) extensions.

g. Enable EAP.

28. You are the administrator of your company's network. You need to implement a remote access solution that is highly available and highly secure. Your company consists of a single location and has a T3 connection to the Internet. Your company has 1000 salespeople who need reliable connectivity to the company network from any remote location. All servers are running Windows 2000 Advanced Server, and all client computers are running Windows 2000 Professional. You want to accomplish the following goals:

- No single point of failure, aside from total loss of the T3, will result in total loss of remote access connectivity.
- No authentication traffic will be carried as clear text.
- No data traffic will be carried as clear text.
- Support for at least 200 remote users accessing the network simultaneously will be available at all times.

You take the following actions:

- Install three virtual private network (VPN) servers at the main office.
- Configure each VPN server to support 150 PPTP connections.
- Configure the client computers to use Password Authentication Protocol (PAP) as the authentication protocol.

Which result or results do these actions produce? (Choose all that apply.)

a. No single point of failure, aside from total loss of the T3, results in total loss of remote access connectivity.

b. No authentication traffic is carried as clear text.

c. No data traffic is carried as clear text.

d. Support for at least 200 remote users accessing the network simultaneously is available at all times.

29. You are the administrator of your company's network. You need to implement a remote access solution that is highly available and highly secure. Your company consists of a single location and has a T3 connection to the Internet. Your company has 1000 salespeople who need reliable connectivity to the company network from any remote location. All servers are running Windows 2000 Advanced Server, and all client computers are running Windows 2000 Professional. You want to accomplish the following goals:

- No single point of failure, aside from total loss of the T3, will result in total loss of remote access connectivity.
- No authentication traffic will be carried as clear text.
- No data traffic will be carried as clear text.
- Support for at least 200 remote users accessing the network simultaneously will be available at all times.

You take the following actions:

- Install a virtual private network (VPN) server at the main office.
- Configure the VPN server to support 250 PPTP connections.
- Configure the client computers to use the Challenge-Handshake Authentication Protocol (CHAP) as the authentication protocol.

Which result or results do these actions produce? (Choose all that apply.)

a. No single point of failure, aside from total loss of the T3, results in total loss of remote access connectivity.

b. No authentication traffic is carried as clear text.
c. No data traffic is carried as clear text.
d. Support for at least 200 remote users accessing the network simultaneously is available at all times.

HANDS-ON EXERCISES

Exercise 1: Remote Access Server

Configure the Remote Access Server

Perform the following on your computer.

1. Log on as the Administrator for your domain.
2. In the Administrative Tools, start the Open Routing and Remote Access console.
3. In the left pane, right-click your server and select the Configure and Enable Routing and Remote Access option. Click on the Next button.
4. On the Common Configurations page, select the Remote Access Server option and select the Next button.
5. On the Remote Client Protocols page, TCP/IP is listed. Keep the default option of "Yes, all of the required protocols are on this list," and click the Next page.
6. On the Network Selection page, select your network connection and click on the Next button.
7. On the IP Address Assignment page, select the "From a specified range of addresses" option and click on the Next button.
8. On the Address Range Assignment page, click the New button.
9. In the Start IP address box, type 10.x.
10. Use 140.100.100.XX for the start address and 140.100.100.XX + 1 for the end address, where XX is your computer number. Click on the OK button. Click on the Next button.
11. On the Managing Multiple Remote Access Servers page, keep the default setting of "No, I don't want to set up this server to use RADIUS now" and click the Next button. Click on the Finish button. Click OK to close the Routing and Remote Access message box.
12. Close the Routing and Remote Access console.

Granting Dial-in Permissions

Perform the following on your computer.

1. In the Administrative Tools, open the Active Directory Users and Computers console from the Administrative Tools menu.
2. In the console tree in the left pane, expand your domain.
3. Click on Users in the left pane and double-click Administrator in the right pane.
4. On the Dial-in tab, select the Allow Access option and click the OK button.
5. Close the Active Directory Users and Computers console.

Configure a VPN Connection

Perform the following on your partner's computer.

1. Right-click My Network Places, then click Properties.
2. In the Network and Dial-up Connections, double-click the Make New Connection icon. Click on the Next button.
3. On the Network Connection Type page, select the "Connect to a private network through the Internet" option and click the Next button.
4. On the Destination Address page, type in the address of your partner's computer and click the Next button.
5. On the Connection Availability page, click the "Only for myself" option. Click the Next button followed by the Finish button.
6. Click on the Cancel button.

Making a VPN Connection

Perform the following on your partner's computer.

1. Right-click My Network Places and select the Properties button.
2. Double-click the Virtual Private Connections icon.

3. Connect as the Administrator with the Connect Virtual Private Connection dialog box.
4. After a message appears indicating that you are connected, you will see an icon in the system tray. Click the OK button.
5. Close Network and Dial-up Connections.
6. At the Command prompt, execute IPCONFIG to verify the IP address for the connection.
7. Double-click the Connection icon in the system tray.
8. Click the Disconnect button.

Exercise 2: Terminal Services

Installing Terminal Services

Perform the following on your server.

1. Open the Add/Remove Programs applet in the Control Panel.
2. Choose Add/Remove Windows Components.
3. From the list available, check the box next to Terminal Services. Click on the OK button.
4. In the Terminal Services Setup page, select Remote Administration Mode and click on the OK button.
5. Windows will then copy the files from an installation source. When the copying is done, click on the Finish button. When you are prompted, restart the computer.

Creating Terminal Services Client Disks

Perform the following on your server. You will need two floppy disks.

1. In the Administrative Tools, select the Terminal Services Client Creator.
2. Select the Terminal Services for 32-bit x86 Windows and click the OK button.
3. Insert the first floppy disk in drive and click on the OK button.
4. When it prompts you, insert the second floppy and click on the OK button.
5. Click the OK button when finished.
6. Click the Cancel button to close the Terminal Services Client Creator.

Installing Terminal Services Client Software

Perform the following on your partner's computer.

1. Insert the first Terminal Services client disks in drive A.
2. Execute the SETUP.EXE in the A drive. Click on the Continue button.
3. Enter your name and organization and click on the OK button. Click on the OK button a second time.
4. Click on the I Agree button to agree to the license agreement.
5. Click on the Large button to start the installation.
6. When it asks if you want all Terminal Services users of this computer to have all the same initial settings, click on the Yes button.
7. When prompted, insert the second disk and click on the OK button.
8. When the installation is complete, click on the OK button.

Note that if you have Terminal Services loaded on your partner's machine, the Terminal Service Client software can be executed from the \WINNT\SYSTEM32\CLIENTS\TSCLIENT\DISKS\DISK1 folder.

Using Terminal Services to Connect to a Terminal Server

Perform the following on your partner's computer.

1. Click the Start button and select the Programs option, the Terminal Services Client option, and the Terminal Services Client option.
2. In Server, type the name or IP address of the terminal server to which you want to connect.
3. Select the Screen Area of 640 × 480.
4. Click the Connect button.
5. In the Terminal Services Client window, log in as the Administrator.
6. In the Terminal Services Client window, execute the Active Directory Users and Computers program located in the Administrative Tools. Note that if the taskbar is set to Autohide, move the mouse pointer to the bottom of the Terminal Services Client window to show the taskbar.
7. Close the Active Directory Users and Computers program.
8. Close the Terminal Services Client window. When it asks to disconnect, click on the OK button.

CHAPTER **20**

Introduction to Routers and Routing

Topics Covered in This Chapter

Introduction

As mentioned in earlier chapters, the router is used to connect different LANs together. This chapter discusses routers and the routing protocols used to connect the various LANs. In addition, it discusses multitasking and introduces Cisco routers.

Objectives

- Compare distant-vector routers with link-state routers.
- Compare RIP and OSPF protocols.
- Define an autonomous system and explain how it relates to exterior and interior gateway protocols.
- Update a Windows-based routing table by means of static routes.
- Manage and monitor border routing.
- Manage and monitor internal routing.
- Manage and monitor IP routing protocols.

20.1   ROUTER OVERVIEW

As local area networks become more and more popular and increasingly vital to the daily operation of an organization, the need to connect multiple LANs has become as crucial as it once was to link individual PCs into a workgroup. Although segmenting the network can solve all kinds of problems—including increasing available bandwidth on the local LANs, linking distant networks, and breaking a large network into smaller, more manageable subnets—you must have a mechanism for the different segments to communicate with each other.

A **router,** which works at the network ISO layer, is a device that connects two or more LANs. As multiple LANs are connected together, multiple routes are created to get from one LAN to another. The primary role of a router is to transmit similar types of data packets from one wide area communications link (such as a T1 line or fiber link) to another T1 line or fiber link. The second role of a router is to select the best path between the source and destination.

When you send a packet from one computer to another computer, the computer first determines if the packet is sent locally to another computer on the same LAN or if the packet is sent to a router so that it can be routed to the destination LAN. If the packet is meant to go to a computer on another LAN, it is sent to the router (or gateway). The router determines what is the best route to take and forwards. the packets to that route. The packet then goes to the next router and the entire process repeats itself until it gets to the destination LAN. The destination router then forwards the packets to the destination computer.

Determining the best route requires complex routing algorithms, which consider a variety of factors including the number or fastest set of transmission media, the number of network segments, and the network segment that carries the least amount of traffic. Routers then share status and routing information to other routers so that they can provide better traffic management and bypass slow connections. In addition, routers provide additional functionality, such as the ability to filter messages and forward them to different places based on various criteria. Most routers are multiprotocol routers, because they can route data packets using many different protocols.

A **metric** is a standard of measurement, such as hop count, that is used by routing algorithms to determine the optimal path to a destination. A **hop** is the trip a data packet takes from one router to another router (or another intermediate point). On a large network, the number of hops that a packet has taken toward its destination is called the **hop count.** When a computer communicates with another computer via four routers, then the computer would have a hop count of 4. With no other factors considered, a metric of 4 would be assigned. If a router had to choose between a route with 4 metrics and a route with 6 metrics, it would choose the route with the least amount of metrics. If you want to force the router to choose the route with 6 metrics, then overwrite the metric for the route with 4 hops in the routing table to one with 6 hops.

To track the various routes in a network, the routers create and maintain routing tables. The routers communicate with one another to maintain their routing tables through a routing update message. This message can consist of all or a portion of a routing table. By analyzing routing updates from all other routers, a router can build a detailed picture of network topology.

20.2 CHARACTERISTICS OF ROUTER PROTOCOLS

There are various types of routing algorithms, each one having a different impact on network and router resources. Routing algorithms use a variety of metrics that affect calculation of optimal routes.

Routing algorithms can be differentiated based on several key characteristics. First, the capability of the routing algorithm to optimally choose the best route is important. One routing algorithm may use the number of hops and the length of delays, but may weigh the length of delay more heavily in the calculation. To maintain consistency and predictability, routing protocols use strict metric calculations.

Routing algorithms are designed to be as simple as possible. In other words, the routing algorithm must offer efficiency with a minimum of software and utilization overhead. Aside from being efficient, the routing algorithm must be robust so that it can quickly change routes when a route goes down because of hardware failure or a route has a high load (high amount of traffic). During these types of situations, the routing algorithm must be stable.

Routing algorithms also must converge rapidly. **Convergence** is the process of agreement by all routers to which routes are the optimal routes. When a route goes down, routers distribute the new routes by sending routing update messages. The time that it takes for all routers to get new routes to which they all agree upon should be quick. If not, routing loops or network outages can occur. A routing loop occurs when a packet is forwarded back and forth between several routers without ever getting to its final destination.

A **count to infinity,** which typically happens when a network has slow convergence, is a loop that occurs when a link in a network goes down and routers on the network update their routing tables with incorrect hop counts. For example, a loop can occur if the link to router C goes down. Router B then advertises that the link is down and that it has no route to C. Because router A has a route to C with a metric of 2, it responds to router B and sends its link to C. Router B then updates its table to include a link with metric 3, and the routers continue to announce between the two routers and update their routing entries to C until they reach metric 16, a count to infinity.

To handle the count to infinity problem, networks use either split horizon or poison reverse. **Split horizon** is a route-advertising algorithm that prevents the advertising of routes in the same direction in which they were learned. **Poison reverse** is a process that, used with split horizon, improves RIP convergence over simple split horizon by advertising all network IDs. However, the network IDs learned in a given direction are advertised with a hop count of 16, indicating that the network is unavailable.

20.2.1 Static versus Dynamic Routes

Static routing algorithms are hardly algorithms at all; rather, they are table mappings established by the network administrator prior to the beginning of routing. These mappings do not change unless the network administrator alters them. Algorithms that use static routes are simple to design and work well in environments where network traffic is relatively predictable and where network design is relatively simple.

Because static routing systems cannot react to network changes, they generally are considered unsuitable for today's large, changing networks. The most dominant routing algorithms now are dynamic routing algorithms, which adjust to changing network circumstances by analyzing the incoming routing update messages. If the message indicates that a network change has occurred, the routing software recalculates routes and sends out new routing update messages. These messages flow through to permeate the network, stimulating routers to rerun their algorithms and change their routing tables accordingly.

Dynamic routing algorithms can be supplemented with static routes where appropriate. A router of last resort (a router to which all unroutable packets are sent), for example, can be designated to act as a repository for all unroutable packets, ensuring that all messages are at least handled in some way.

20.2.2   Single-Path versus Multipath Algorithms

Some sophisticated routing protocols support multiple paths to the same destination. Unlike single-path algorithms, these multipath algorithms permit traffic multiplexing over multiple lines where the traffic can be split among the different routes. In addition, multipath algorithms provide redundancy in case one of the routes fails. Networks connected with redundant routes can also be referred to as a spanning-tree algorithm.

20.2.3   Flat versus Hierarchical Algorithms

In a flat routing system, the routers are peers of all others. In a hierarchical routing system, some routers form what amounts to a routing backbone. Packets from nonbackbone routers travel to the backbone routers, where they are sent through the backbone until they reach the general area of the destination. At this point, they travel from the last backbone router through one or more nonbackbone routers to the final destination.

Routing systems often designate logical groups of nodes—called domains, autonomous systems, or areas. In hierarchical systems, some routers in a domain can communicate with routers in other domains, while others can communicate only with routers within their own domain. In expansive networks, additional hierarchical levels may exist, with routers at the highest hierarchical level forming the routing backbone.

The primary advantage of hierarchical routing is that it mimics the organization of most companies and therefore supports their traffic patterns well. Most network communication occurs within small company groups (domains). Because intradomain routers need to know only about other routers within their domain, their routing algorithms can be simplified, and, depending on the routing algorithm being used, routing update traffic can be reduced accordingly.

20.2.4   Distance-Vector versus Link-State Algorithms

Routers use **distance-vector–based routing protocols** to periodically advertise or broadcast the routes in their routing tables, but they send information only to their neighboring routers. Routing information exchanged between typical distance-vector–based routers is unsynchronized and unacknowledged. Distance-vector–based routing protocols are simple, easy to understand, and easy to configure. The disadvantages are as follows: (1) Multiple routes to a given network can reflect multiple entries in the routing table, thus increasing the routing table. (2) If you have a large routing table, network traffic increases as it periodically advertises the routing table to the other routers, even after the network has converged. (3) Distance-vector protocol convergence of large internetworks can take several minutes.

Link-state algorithms are also known as shortest path first (SPF) algorithms. Instead of using broadcast, link-state routers send updates directly (or by using multicast traffic) to all routers within the network. Each router, however, sends only the portion of the routing table that describes the state of its own links. In essence, link-state algorithms send small updates everywhere. Because they converge more quickly, link-state algorithms are somewhat less prone to routing loops than distance-vector algorithms. In addition, link-state algorithms do not exchange any routing information when the internetwork has converged. They have small routing tables since they store a single optimal route for each network ID. Conversely, link-state algorithms require more CPU power and memory than distance-vector algorithms. Link-state algorithms, therefore, can be more expensive to implement and support and are considered harder to understand.

20.2.5   Metrics

The various routing protocols use different metrics, including path length, hop counts, routing delay, bandwidth, load, reliability, and cost. Path length is the most common routing metric. Some routing protocols allow network administrators to assign arbitrary costs to each network link. In this case, path length is the sum of the costs associated with each link traversed. Other routing protocols define hop counts, as described earlier in this chapter.

Routing delay refers to the length of time required to move a packet from source to destination through the internetwork. Delay depends on many factors, including the bandwidth of intermediate network links, the port queues at each router along the way, network congestion on all intermediate network links, and the physical distance to be traveled. Because delay is a conglomeration of several important variables, it is a common and useful metric.

Bandwidth refers to the available traffic capacity of a link. All other things being equal, a 10-Mbps Ethernet link would be preferable to a 64-kbps leased line. Although bandwidth is a rating of the maximum attainable throughput on a link, routes through links with greater bandwidth do not necessarily provide better routes than routes through slower links. If, for example, a faster link is busier, the actual time required to send a packet to the destination could be greater. Load refers to the degree to which a network resource, such as a router, is busy. Load can be calculated in a variety of ways, including CPU utilization and packets processed per second. Monitoring these parameters on a continual basis can also be resource intensive.

Reliability, in the context of routing algorithms, refers to the dependability (usually described in terms of the bit-error rate) of each network link: Some network links may go down more often than others. After a network fails, certain network links might be repaired more easily or more quickly than other links. Any reliability factors can be taken into account in the assignment of the reliability ratings, which are arbitrary numeric values usually assigned to network links by network administrators.

Communication cost is another important metric, especially because some companies may not care about performance as much as they care about operating expenditures. Even though line delay may be longer, some companies will send packets over their own lines rather than through the public lines that cost money for usage time.

20.3   INTERNET ROUTING PROTOCOL

The Internet Protocol (IP) is a connectionless, unreliable protocol that is responsible for addressing and routing between hosts. The term *connectionless* means that a session is not established before exchanging data. Each packet that travels through the Internet is treated as an independent unit of data, which is not affected by other data packets. The term *unreliable* means that the delivery is not guaranteed. IP always makes a best-effort attempt to deliver a packet. An IP packet might be lost, delivered out of sequence, duplicated, or delayed. IP does not attempt to recover from these types of errors. Instead, the acknowledgment of packets delivered and the recovery of lost packets is the responsibility of a higher-layer protocol, such as TCP.

20.3.1   IP Packet

The IP specifies the format of the packets (also called datagrams). An IP packet, or IP datagram, consists of an IP header and an IP payload. The IP header consists of the following packets (see Figure 20.1):

- The IP version indicates the version of IP currently being used.
- The IP header length (IHL) indicates the datagram header length in 32-bit words.
- The type of services specifies how an upper-layer protocol would like a current datagram, and assigns to datagrams various levels of importance.
- The total length specifies the length, in bytes, of the entire IP packet including the data and header.
- The identification section contains an integer that identifies the current datagram. This field is used to help piece together datagram fragments.
- In fragment status, the flags consist of a 3-bit field of which the two least-significant bits control fragmentation. The low-order bit specifies whether the packet can be fragmented. The middle bit specifies whether the packet is the last fragment in a series of fragmented packets. The third bit is not used.
- Fragment offset indicates the position of the fragment's data relative to the beginning of the data in the original datagram. This allows the destination IP process to properly reconstruct the original datagram.

Figure 20.1   IP packet

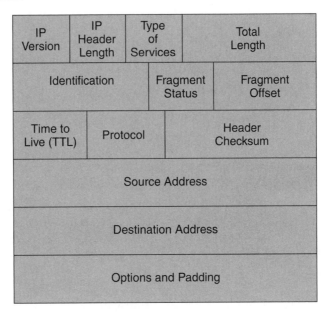

- The time to live (TTL) designates the number of network segments on which the datagram is allowed to travel before being discarded by a router. The TTL is set by the sending host and is used to prevent packets from endlessly circulating on an IP internetwork. When forwarding an IP packet, routers are required to decrease the TTL by at least one.
- The protocol section indicates which upper-layer protocol receives incoming packets after IP processing is complete.
- The header checksum helps ensure IP header integrity.
- The source address is the IP address of the original source of the IP datagram.
- The destination address is the IP address of the final destination of the IP datagram.
- The options section allows IP to support various options, such as security; padding is to help create the datagram in the correct format and maintain a minimum size.

20.3.2   IP Addresses and Routing

TCP/IP hosts use a routing table to maintain knowledge about other IP networks and hosts. As discussed in Chapter 6, networks and hosts are identified with an IP address and a corresponding subnet mask to specify which bits of the address compose the network address and which bits compose the host address.

When a computer prepares to send an IP datagram, it inserts its own source IP address and the destination IP address of the recipient into the IP header. The computer then examines the destination IP address, compares it with a locally maintained IP routing table, and takes appropriate action based on what it finds. The computer does one of three things:

- It passes the datagram up to a protocol layer above IP on the local host.
- It forwards the datagram through one of its attached network interfaces.
- It discards the datagram.

IP searches the routing table for the route that is the closest match to the destination IP address (either a route that matches the IP address of the destination host or a route that matches the IP address of the destination network). If a matching route is not found, IP discards the datagram.

To determine if a packet is to be sent to a host on the local network or to determine if the packet needs to be a remote network via the router, the TCP/IP protocol will complete a couple of calculations. When TCP/IP is initialized on a host, the host's IP address is ANDed (logical bit-wise AND) with its subnet mask at a bit-by-bit level. Before a packet is sent, the destination IP address is ANDed with the same subnet mask. If both results match, IP knows that the packet belongs to a host on the local network. If the results do not match, then the packet is sent to the IP address of an IP router so that it can be forwarded to the host.

When ANDing an IP address and subnet mask, each bit in the IP address is compared with the IP address of the corresponding bit in the subnet mask. If both bits are 1s, the result bit is 1. If there is any other combination, the resulting bit is 0. Be aware that by ANDing the address and subnet mask, you are essentially isolating the network addresses.

Example 1:

You have a host 145.17.202.56 with a subnet mask of 255.255.224.0 with data that must be delivered to 145.17.198.75 with a subnet mask of 255.255.224.0. Are the two hosts located on one local network or are they on two remote networks?

To solve the problem, first convert the addresses and subnet mask to binary.

145.17.202.56	10010001.00010001.11001010.00111000
145.17.198.75	10010001.00010001.11000110.01001011
255.255.224.0	11111111.11111111.11100000.00000000

Next AND the source address and the subnet mask.

145.17.202.56	10010001.00010001.11001010.00111000
255.255.224.0	<u>11111111.11111111.11100000.00000000</u>
	10010001.00010001.11000000.00000000

Then AND the destination address and the subnet mask.

145.17.198.75	10010001.00010001.11000110.01001011
255.255.224.0	<u>11111111.11111111.11100000.00000000</u>
	10010001.00010001.11000000.00000000

If you compare the two results, you will find that they are the same. Therefore, the packet will be sent directly to the host and not the router. If they were different, the host would then send the packet to the router.

20.3.3   Internet Control-Message Protocol

As mentioned, IP does not provide reliable communication, or end-to-end or hop-by-hop acknowledgments. There is no error control for data, other than a header checksum, or error or flow control. There are no retransmissions, as these are left to the higher protocols such as TCP. To report errors and other information regarding IP packet processing, the **Internet Control-Message Protocol (ICMP)** sends notices back to the source. ICMP messages are usually sent automatically in one of the following situations:

- An IP datagram cannot reach its destination.
- An IP router (gateway) cannot forward datagrams at the current rate of transmission.
- An IP router redirects the sending host to use a better route to the destination.

Review ICMP documentation in RFC 792. See Table 20.1.

When you use the PING command, an ICMP echo request message is sent and the receipt of ICMP echo replay messages is recorded. This allows you to detect network or host communication failures and troubleshoot common TCP/IP connectivity problems.

By using its messages, the ICMP can be used by local routers to provide a way for hosts to sense routers that are down and to perform router solicitation and advertisement. Router solicitations are sent by hosts to discover routers on their networks. Router advertisements are sent by routers in response to a router solicitation and periodically to notify hosts on the network that the router is still available. ICMP router discovery is documented in RFC 1256, "ICMP Router Discovery Messages."

Table 20.1   ICMP messages

ICMP Message	Description
Echo request	Determines whether an IP node (a host or a router) is available on the network
Echo reply	Replies to an ICMP echo request
Destination unreachable	Informs the host that a datagram cannot be delivered
Source quench	Informs the host to lower the rate at which it sends datagrams because of congestion
Redirect	Informs the host of a preferred route
Time exceeded	Indicates that the time-to-live (TTL) section of an IP datagram has expired

20.4   INTERIOR GATEWAY PROTOCOLS

As IP provides addressing and connectionless services for packet forwarding, it relies on other protocols for address resolution, dynamic route discovery, and prioritization. Since IP networks can be quite large and complex internetworks, TCP/IP allows the IP internetwork to be divided into logical groups called autonomous systems. The routing protocols that manage routing information within an autonomous system are called **interior gateway protocols (IGPs).** Examples of an IGP are RIP, OSPF, and IGRP (to be discussed in the chapter). Autonomous systems are interconnected using an exterior gateway protocol, such as **Border Gateway Protocol (BGP).** RIP and OSPF protocols are standard TCP/IP routing protocols, which can run as a stand-alone autonomous system or within an autonomous system that belongs to a larger network. See Figure 20.2.

20.4.1   Router Information Protocol

The **Routing Information Protocol (RIP)** is designed for exchanging routing information within a small to medium-size network. The biggest advantage of RIP is that it is extremely simple to configure and deploy.

RIP uses a single routing metric of hop counts to measure the distance between the source and a destination network. Each hop in a path from source to destination is assigned a hop-count value, which is typically 1. When a router receives a routing update that contains a new or changed destination-network entry, the router adds one to the metric value indicated in the update and enters the network in the routing table. The IP address of the sender is used as the next hop.

Since RIP uses only hop count to determine the best path to an internetwork, if RIP finds more than one link to the same remote network with the same hop count, it automatically performs a round-robin load balance. RIP can perform load balancing for up to six equal-cost links. A problem with using hops as the only metric occurs when two links to a remote network have different bandwidths. For example, if you have one link that is a 56-KB switched link and another that is a T1 running at 1.544 Mbps, there would be some inefficiency when sending equal data through both pathways. This is known as pinhole congestion. To overcome pinhole congestion, you would have to design a network with equal bandwidth links or use a routing protocol that takes bandwidth into account.

RIP prevents routing loops from continuing indefinitely by implementing a limit on the number of hops allowed in a path from the source to a destination. The maximum number of hops in a path is 15. If a router receives a routing update that contains a new or changed entry, and if increasing the metric value by 1 causes the metric to be infinity (in this case, 16), the network destination is considered unreachable. Thus, RIP is unable to scale to large or very large internetworks.

Initially, the routing table for each router includes only the networks that are physically connected to it. A RIP router periodically sends announcements that contain its routing table entries so that the other routers can update their routing tables. RIP version 1 uses IP broadcast packets for its announcements. RIP version 2 uses multicast or broadcast packets for its announcements. All RIP messages are sent over UDP port 520.

Figure 20.2   Connecting autonomous systems

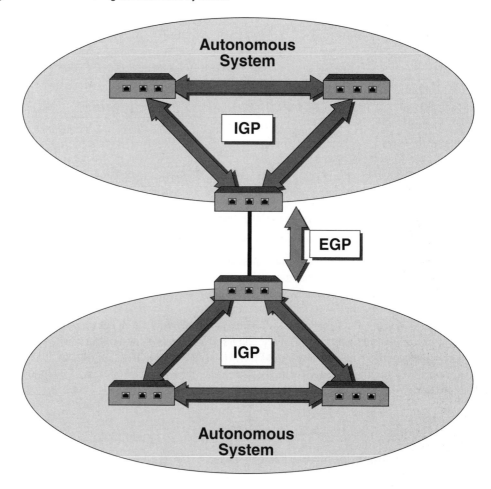

You can configure each RIP router with a list of routers (by IP address) on which RIP announcements are accepted. By configuring a list of RIP peers, you cause RIP announcements from unauthorized RIP routers to be discarded. In addition, to prevent RIP traffic from being received by any node except neighboring RIP routers, you can set up some routers to use unicast RIP announcements to neighboring RIP routers.

Silent RIP means a router processes RIP announcements but does not announce its own routes. Silent RIP could be enabled on nonrouter hosts to produce a routing table with as much detail as the tables of the RIP routers. With more detailed routes in the routing table, a silent RIP host can make better routing decisions.

RIP routers also can communicate routing information through triggered updates, which are set off when the network topology changes. Different from the scheduled announcements, the triggered updates are sent immediately rather than held until the next periodic announcement. For example, when a router detects a link or router failure, it updates its own routing table and sends the updated routes. Each router that receives the triggered update modifies its own routing table and propagates the change to the other routers.

RIP uses three different types of timers to regulate its performance:

- **Route update timer**—Sets the interval (typically 30 seconds) between periodic routing updates in which the router sends a complete copy of its routing table to all neighbors
- **Route invalid timer**—Determines the length of time that must expire (180 seconds) before a router determines that a route has become invalid. It makes this conclusion if it has not heard any updates about a particular route for that time period. When that happens, the router sends out updates to all its neighbors to let them know that the route is invalid.

■ **Route flush timer**—Sets the time between a route becoming invalid and its removal from the routing table (120 seconds). Before it is removed from the table, the router notifies its neighbors of that route's impending doom. The value of the route invalid timer must be less than that of the route flush timer. This is to provide the router with enough time to tell its neighbors about the invalid route before the routing table is updated.

Route filters can be configured on each RIP interface so that the only routes considered for addition to the routing table are those that reflect reachable network IDs within the internetwork. For example, if an organization is using subnets of the private network ID 10.0.0.0, route filtering can be used so that the RIP routers discard all routes except those within the 10.0.0.0 network ID.

Since the RIP is a distance-vector protocol, as internetworks grow larger in size, the periodic announcements by each RIP router can cause excessive traffic. Another disadvantage of RIP is its high convergence time. When the network topology changes, it may take several minutes before the RIP routers reconfigure themselves to the new network topology. While the network reconfigures itself, routing loops may form that result in lost or undeliverable data. To help prevent routing loops, RIP implements split horizon.

To overcome some of the RIP shortcomings, **RIP version 2 (RIP v2)** was introduced to provide the following features:

■ You can use a password for authentication by specifying a key that is used to authenticate routing information to the router.
■ The subnet mask is included in the routing information and supports variable-length subnets. Variable-length subnet masks can be associated with each destination, allowing an increase in the number of hosts or subnets that are possible on your network.
■ The routing table can contain information about the IP address of the router that should be used to reach each destination. This helps prevent packets from being forwarded through extra routers on the system.
■ Multicast packets only speak to RIP v2 routers and are used to reduce the load on hosts that are not listening to RIP v2 packets. The IP multicast address for RIP v2 packets is 224.0.0.9.

NOTE: Silent RIP nodes must also be listening for multicast traffic sent to 224.0.0.9. If you are using silent RIP, verify that your silent RIP nodes can listen for multicasted RIP v2 announcements before deploying multicasted RIP v2.

RIP v1 was designed with forward compatibility in mind. If a RIP v1 router receives a message and the RIP version in the RIP header is not 0x01, it does not discard the RIP announcement but processes only the RIP-v1–defined fields. RIP v2 is supported on most routers and end nodes. Make sure that the mode you configure is compatible with all implementations of RIP on your network.

RIP v2 routers and RIP v1 routers should be used together with caution. Because RIP v1 routers do not interpret the subnet mask field in the route, RIP v2 routers must not announce routes that can be misinterpreted by a RIP v1 router. Variable length subnet masks and disjointed subnets cannot be used in mixed environments.

For an interface using RIP v2 to make announcements such that RIP v1 routers can process the announced routes, the RIP v2 routers must summarize subnet routes when announcing outside a subnetted environment. A specific subnet route announced to a RIP v1 router can be misinterpreted as a host route. Also, the RIP v2 routers cannot announce supernet routes. A RIP v1 router would misinterpret the route as a single network, rather than as a range of networks.

If RIP v2 routers are on the same network as RIP v1 routers, the RIP v2 router interface must be configured to broadcast its announcements. Multicasted RIP v2 announcements are not processed by the RIP v1 routers.

20.4.2   Autonomous Systems Topology

For small or medium networks, distributing data throughout the network and maintaining a route table at each router is not a problem. When the network grows to a size that includes hundreds of routers, the routing table can be quite large (several megabytes) and require significant time to recalculate routes as router interfaces go up or down.

Some protocols, such as OSPF, allow areas (groupings of contiguous networks) to be gathered into an **autonomous system (AS).** See Figure 20.3. Areas that comprise the system usually correspond to an administrative domain such as a department, a building, or a geographical site. An AS can be a single network or a group of networks, owned and administered by a common network administrator or group of administrators.

The **backbone** (given an address of 0.0.0.0) of the AS is a high-bandwidth logical area where all areas are connected. The routers that attach an area to the backbone are called **area border routers (ABRs).** Because the ABR is supposed to be a high-bandwidth pathway connecting the areas and to know the autonomous system's overall topology, it requires additional memory and processing power compared with regular routers located within an area. Therefore, do not use a low-end router as an ABR.

Areas that are not backbone OSPF areas can be classified as either a stub area or a transit area. A **stub area** has only one ABR. All routes to the destination outside the area must pass through the single router. Since the ABR is the only router that routes data in and out of the area, the ABR advertises itself as the default router to all external destinations, which reduces traffic and the size of the routing database. A **transit area,** on the other hand, contains more than one ABR.

OSPF routers within an area are not required to maintain a database of routers and networks located inside of the other areas. The topology of an area is invisible from outside of the area and routers internal to a given area know nothing of the detailed topology outside of the area. This isolation reduces the network traffic since not all routing information has to be sent to the routers in other areas.

Routing in the AS takes place on two levels, depending on whether the source and destination of a packet reside in the same area (intra-area routing) or different areas (inter-area routing). In intra-area routing, the packet is routed solely on information obtained within the area; no routing information obtained from outside the area needs to be used. This protects intra-area routing from the injection of bad routing information and helps simplify the routing tables.

When routing a packet between two areas, the packet will travel on the backbone. The path on which the packet will travel can be subdivided into three contiguous pieces: an intra-area path from the source to an area border router, a backbone path between the source and destination areas, and then another intra-area path to the destination.

A **virtual link** is a logical link between a backbone area border router, an unspecified number of routers, and a second border router that is not connected to the backbone. Virtual links are not recommended, because they can cause routing and other problems, and can be difficult to configure. Instead, always make an effort to connect new areas in your AS directly to the backbone by planning ahead before your AS is implemented.

To connect autonomous systems to other autonomous systems, use an **autonomous system boundary router (ASBR).** An ASBR exchanges routing information with routers belonging to other autonomous systems. The ASBR accesses its routing information from the Internet using EGP and accesses routing information about the corporate network (autonomous system) from OSPF. For further information regarding OSPF routers, see Table 20.2. EGP will be explained later in this chapter.

20.4.3 Open Shortest Path First Protocol

The **Open Shortest Path First (OSPF)** protocol is a link-state routing protocol used in medium-sized and large networks. It calculates routing table entries by constructing a shortest-path tree. The OSPF protocol is designed to be run as an interior gateway protocol to a single AS. In a link-state routing protocol, each router maintains a database of router advertisements called link state advertisements (LSAs). LSAs for routers within the AS consist of router, its attached networks, and their configured costs. An OSPF cost is a unitless metric that indicates the preference of using a link. There are also LSAs for summarized routes and routes outside of the AS.

The router distributes its LSAs to its neighboring routers. LSAs are gathered into a database called the link state database (LSDB). By synchronizing LSDBs between all neighboring routers, each router has each other router's LSA in its database. Therefore, every router has the same LSDB. From the LSDB, entries for the router's routing table are calculated using the Dijkstra algorithm to determine the

Figure 20.3 Autonomous system

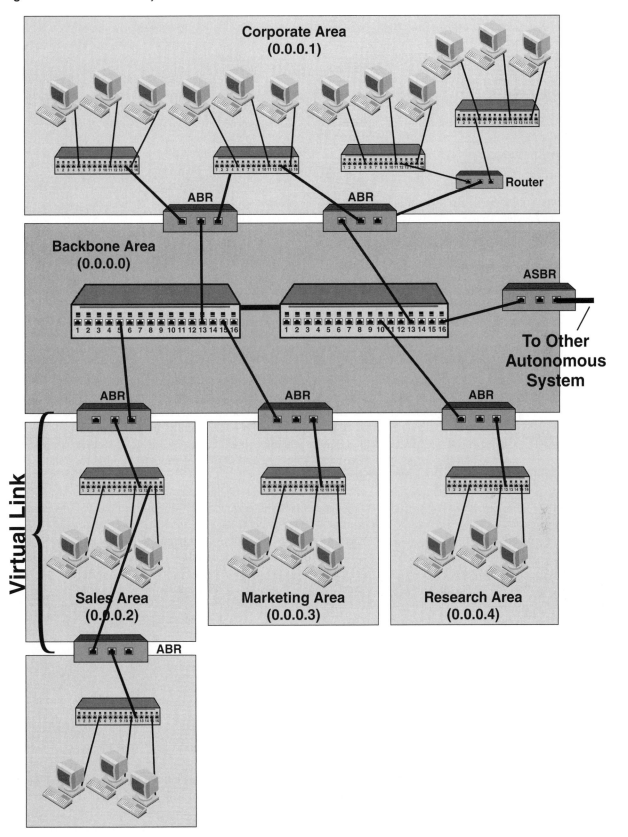

Table 20.2 OSPF routers

Router Type	Description
Internal router	Internal routers send packets only within a single area. The internal router can also be a backbone router if it has no interfaces to other areas.
Area border router (ABR)	Area border routers have interfaces in multiple areas, and route packets between these areas. Area border routers condense topological information before passing it to the backbone, which reduces the amount of routing information that is passed across the backbone.
Backbone router	A backbone router has an interface on the backbone area. This includes all routers that interface to more than one area (i.e., area border routers). However, backbone routers do not have to be area border routers. Routers with all interfaces connected to the backbone are considered to be internal routers.
AS boundary router (ASBR)	AS routers exchange routing information with other autonomous systems. A router boundary exchanges routing information with routers belonging to other autonomous systems. Such a router has AS external routes that are advertised throughout the autonomous system. The path to each AS border router is known by every router in the AS. This classification is completely independent of the previous classifications: AS border routers may be internal or area border routers, and perhaps participate in the backbone.

least cost path (i.e., the path with the lowest accumulated cost) to each network in the internetwork. Unlike the RIP in which metric is based on hops, OSPF metric is based on bandwidth.

The OSPF protocol is considered superior to RIP for the following reasons:

- It is a more efficient protocol than RIP and does not have the restrictive 16-hop-count problem, which causes data to be dropped after the sixteenth hop. An OSPF network can have an accumulated path cost of 65,535, which enables you to construct huge networks (within the maximum TTL value of 255) and assign a wide range of costs. An OSPF network is best suited for a large infrastructure with more than 50 networks.
- OSPF networks can detect changes to the network and calculate new routes quickly (rapid convergence). The period of convergence is brief and involves minimal overhead. The count-to-infinity problem does not occur in OSPF internetworks.
- Less network traffic is generated by OSPF than by RIP, which requires each router to broadcast its entire database every 30 seconds. OSPF routers only broadcast link-state information when it changes.
- Link-state advertisements (LSAs) include subnet mask information about networks. Assign a different subnet mask for each segment of the network (variable-length subnetting) to increase the number of subnets and hosts that are possible for a single network address.

The SPF algorithm is the basis for OSPF operations. When an SPF router is started, it initializes its routing-protocol data structures and then waits for indications from lower-layer protocols that its interfaces are functional.

After a router is assured that its interfaces are functioning, it uses the OSPF hello protocol to acquire neighbors, which are routers with interfaces to a common network. The router sends hello packets to its neighbors and receives their hello packets. In addition to helping acquire neighbors, hello packets also act as keep-alives to let routers know that other routers are still functional.

Adjacency is a relationship formed between selected neighboring routers for the purpose of exchanging routing information. When the link-state databases of two neighboring routers are synchronized, the routers are said to be adjacent. Not every pair of neighboring routers becomes adjacent. From the topological database generated from these hello packets, each router calculates a shortest-path tree, with itself as root. The shortest-path tree, in turn, yields a routing table. To maintain the table, the established adjacencies are compared with the hello messages sent out so that the router can quickly detect failed routers and the network's topology can be altered appropriately.

An LSA from a given router is flooded across the AS so that each other router contains that router's LSA. Although it may seem that the flooding of LSAs across the AS causes a large amount of network traffic, OSPF is very efficient in the propagation of LSA information. To keep track of LSAs in the LSDB, each router is assigned a router ID, a 32-bit dotted decimal number that is unique to the AS. The router ID identifies the router in the AS, not the IP address of one of the router's interfaces. The router ID is not used as a destination IP address for sending information to the router. It is a common industry convention to use the largest or smallest IP address assigned to the router as the router ID. Because IP addresses are unique, this convention ensures that the OSPF router IDs are also unique.

OSPF message addresses are determined by the type of network to which the OSPF interface is connected. One of the following OSPF network types must be selected when configuring an interface on an OSPF router:

- **Broadcast**—A network that can connect more than two routers with a hardware broadcast facility in which a single packet sent by a router is received by all routers attached to that network. Ethernet, Token Ring, and FDDI are broadcast networks. OSPF messages sent on broadcast networks use IP multicast addresses (224.0.0.5 and 224.0.0.6).
- **Point-to-Point**—A network that can connect only two routers. Leased-line WAN links such as Dataphone Digital Service (DDS) and T-Carrier are point-to-point networks. OSPF messages sent on point-to-point networks use IP multicast addresses (224.0.0.5).
- **Nonbroadcast Multiple Access**—A network that can connect more than two routers but has no hardware broadcast facility. X.25, frame relay networks, and ATM are nonbroadcast multiple access (NBMA) networks. Because multicasted OSPF messages do not reach all the OSPF routers on the network, OSPF must be configured to unicast to the IP addresses of the routers on the NBMA network.

20.4.4   Interior Gateway Routing Protocol

The **Interior Gateway Routing Protocol (IGRP)** is an extension of the open RIP standard, which was developed in the mid-1980s by Cisco Systems, Inc. Cisco's principal goal in creating IGRP was to provide a robust protocol for routing within an AS having arbitrarily complex topology and consisting of media with diverse bandwidth and delay characteristics. Cisco developed enhanced IGRP in the early 1990s to improve the operating efficiency of IGRP.

IGRP is a distance-vector protocol that allows gateways to build up their routing table by exchanging information with other gateways. The metric used by IGRP includes the topological delay time, the bandwidth of the narrowest bandwidth segment of the path, the channel load of the path, and the reliability of the path. To get the most out of the network, it splits traffic between two or more paths that are proportional to its bandwidth. Therefore, if you have a 10-Mbps pathway and a 20-Mbps pathway, the 20-Mbps path will get roughly twice as much traffic as the 10-Mbps pathway.

Periodically, each gateway broadcasts its entire routing table (with some censoring because of the split-horizon rule) to all adjacent gateways. When a gateway gets this broadcast from another gateway, it compares the table with its existing table. Any new destinations and paths are added to the gateway's routing table. Paths in the broadcast are compared with existing paths. If a new path is better, it may replace the existing one. Information in the broadcast is also used to update channel occupancy and other information about existing paths.

In 1994, Cisco augmented IGRP with a product called **Enhanced Interior Gateway Routing Protocol (EIGRP).** EIGRP combines the advantages of link-state protocols with those of distance-vector protocols. The key features include the diffusing update algorithm (DUAL) finite-state machine, variable-length subnet masks, partial routing table updates rather than full updates, and bounded updates. DUAL allows routers to synchronize route changes and does not involve routers unaffected by the change. Different from IGRP, DUAL stores all of the neighbors' routing tables so that they can more intelligently recalculate alternate paths in order to speed convergence. Bounded updates is a method whereby routing update messages are sent only to those routers affected by the topology change, which saves overhead and helps speed convergence.

20.5   GATEWAY PROTOCOLS

As mentioned earlier, autonomous systems are interconnected using an exterior gateway protocol. Two common types are the Border Gateway Protocol (BGP) and the Exterior Gateway Protocol (EGP). BGP is an enhancement of EGP and is one of several new interdomain routing protocols designed to give administrators more control. These newer protocols also handle large networks with minimum effort.

20.5.1   Exterior Gateway Protocols

Most companies and organizations group all their routers into one AS, but some large companies use more than one AS. The local routing information of an autonomous area is gathered using an internal gateway protocol such as RIP or OSPF. In these autonomous areas, one or more routers are chosen to use **Exterior Gateway Protocol (EGP)** to talk to other autonomous areas by providing a way for two neighboring routers that are located at the edges of their respective autonomous area to exchange routing information. EGP routers only forward routing table information to routers on the edge of their own autonomous area.

The first step that EGP takes to establish communication between exterior routers is to perform neighbor acquisition. During neighbor acquisition, one exterior router makes a request to another exterior router to agree that they share router table information. After communications have been established, the router then continually tests if the EGP neighbors are responding. Periodically, routing table information is exchanged at intervals between 120 and 480 seconds between EGP neighbors using routing update messages. The neighbor responds by sending its complete routing table.

EGP restricts exterior gateways by allowing them to advertise only those destination networks reachable entirely within that gateway's autonomous system. Thus, an exterior gateway using EGP passes along information to its EGP neighbors, but does not advertise itself to routers outside the autonomous system.

EGP has one major limitation: The distance indicated for a particular destination does not specify the cost to the destination. EGP only reports whether a destination is reachable. Because of this limitation, EGP can only be used in a tree-type network. All routing protocol domains must connect to the same central network; thus, EGP cannot support a looped topology. EGP can advertise only one route to a given network. There can be no load sharing for traffic between any given pair of machines, and packets can take nonoptimal paths when certain traffic conditions cause congestion in the selected route. As a result, it is difficult for EGP to switch to an alternate route if the primary route fails. The newest version of EGP is EGP-2.

20.5.2   Border Gateway Protocol

Because of its limitations, EGP has been made obsolete by **Border Gateway Protocol (BGP).** BGP version 4 (BGP-4), documented in RFC 1771, is the current exterior routing protocol used on the Internet. Other BGP-related documents are RFC 1772 (BGP Application), RFC 1773 (BGP Experience), RFC 1774 (BGP Protocol Analysis), and RFC 1657 (BGP MIB). BGP uses TCP as its transport protocol, on port 179.

BGP is a distance-vector protocol, but unlike traditional distance-vector protocols such as RIP in which there is a single metric, BGP determines a preference order by applying a function that maps each path to a preference value and selects the path with the highest value. Where there are multiple viable paths to a destination, BGP maintains all of them but only advertises the one with the highest preference value. This approach allows a quick change to an alternate path, should the primary path fail. BGP-4 supports CIDR, IP prefixes, and path aggregation.

20.6   IP MULTICAST

IP multicast allows a host to communicate with several hosts simultaneously by transmitting information via one data stream. Multicast can greatly reduce the network traffic that bandwidth-hungry applications such as videoconferencing, software distribution, and Web cast create. Network vendors widely support IP multicast in their routers. Internet service providers (ISPs) now offer multicast service in their backbones.

The purpose of IP multicast is to deliver a data stream from a source to a group of receivers. Receivers interested in a particular multicast application join the application's multicast group. Receivers can join and leave the group at will, and the group disappears when no receivers remain. Group members listen to and receive data that the source delivers to the group's IP multicast address. Individual class D IP addresses in the range from 224.0.0.0 to 239.255.255.255 represent all multicast groups. The multicast's source does not need to join its group, nor does the source know who and where its receivers are. The source simply transmits multicast streams to the IP multicast address of its multicast group, then lets the network handle multicast data delivery. An IP multicast-enabled network can efficiently forward and route multicast data to receivers.

20.6.1   Multicast Scoping

Multicast scoping determines how far a multicast stream can travel from its source. Limiting the range of a multicast can prevent business data from reaching outside a network, thereby providing security. In multicast group management, multicast-enabled routers track multicast group membership through subnets to which the routers directly attach. The multicast-enabled routers forward multicast data only to the subnets that have group members, thereby saving network bandwidth. Multicast distribution trees define data delivery from a source to a multicast group, then build an optimized distribution tree that contains a set of routers and links to let group members receive data from the source.

Traditionally, IP multicast uses a time-to-live (TTL) parameter in an IP multicast application and multicast routers to control the multicast distribution. When you define the TTL value in an IP multicast application, contents do not transmit beyond the TTL value. For example, if you set Site Server's Active Channel Multicaster TTL value to 16, you ensure that Site Server's web contents do not multicast beyond 16 router hops. Each multicast packet carries a TTL value in its IP header. Just as in unicast, every time a multicast router forwards a multicast packet, the router decreases the packet's TTL by 1. By default, a router will not forward packets with a value of TTL = 1. You can modify the default TTL threshold to another value on each interface in a multicast router. For example, if you set the TTL threshold to 10 on a router interface, only packets with a TTL value greater than 10 can pass that router interface.

TTL-based multicast scoping has two shortcomings. First, defining a proper TTL value in a multicast application can be difficult. If the value is too large, your multicast data may leave your network. If the TTL value is too small, your multicast data may fail to reach interested receivers beyond the multicast scope. Second, if someone sets custom TTL thresholds in certain router interfaces, your multicast range can be unpredictable. For example, you would not be able to divide your network into multicast regions to limit multicast applications to those regions, because if one router has an interface TTL threshold that is lower than a packet's TTL value, the router will forward the packet.

To overcome these limitations, the Internet Engineering Task Force (IETF) proposed Administratively Scoped IP Multicast as an Internet standard in RFC 2365 in July 1998. Administrative scoping lets you scope a multicast to a certain network boundary (e.g., within your organization) by using an administratively scoped address. IETF has designated IP multicast addresses between 239.0.0.0 and 239.255.255.255 as administratively scoped addresses for local use in intranets. You can configure routers that support administratively scoped addressing on the border of your network to confine your private multicast region. You also can define multiple isolated multicast regions in your network so that sensitive multicast data will travel only within a designated area.

A multicast network forwards multicast data only to network subnets that have receivers in the corresponding multicast group in a scoped multicast region. To forward multicast data to receivers in a scoped multicast region, routers need information about group membership on their local subnets. One router on each subnet periodically multicasts membership query messages to all computers on the local subnet. Computers on the local subnet who are group members respond to the router's query message with a membership report about the group to which they belong. The router keeps this membership information in its group database. The local subnet computers also multicast membership reports to their own groups. When other group members receive a member computer's report, the group members postpone their membership reports and wait for a variable period of time. This waiting period reduces membership report traffic and router processing time. As long as a router knows one group member on the local subnet, the router forwards multicast data to that subnet, and other group members will receive the multicast data. When a new member joins a group, the member does not have to wait for the next membership query from the router. Instead, the new member immediately sends a membership report as if in response to a membership query. When the router receives this report, it immediately forwards multicast data to the subnet on which the new member resides, if the new member is the first member of that subnet's multicast group.

20.6.2 Internet Group-Membership Protocol

Routers and computers use the **Internet Group-Management Protocol (IGMP)** to exchange membership information. IGMP is an integral part of IP. The two standard versions of IGMP are IGMP v1 (RFC 1112) and IGMP v2 (RFC 2236). IETF released IGMP v2 as an enhanced version of IGMP v1 in 1997. Today, many routers and operating systems support IGMP v2 including Windows Server 2003, Windows 2000, Windows NT with service pack 4, Windows 98, and Windows 95 with WinSock 2.

IGMP v2's biggest enhancement is a group notification feature. In IGMP v1, a receiver that leaves a multicast group does not automatically notify the router. Rather, the router assumes no group member is on the local subnet if the router does not receive a membership report after several queries and waiting intervals. Several minutes or more can then pass before the router stops forwarding data to that subnet. In IGMP v2, receivers leaving a group directly inform the router. The router then queries the subnet to see whether any other group members remain. If the router does not receive a response, it assumes that no other group members exist on that subnet and stops multicast forwarding to that subnet.

IGMP v3 allows more efficient broadcasting of multirecipient information in real-time. It also lets a computer specify the sources in a specific group from which it receives data.

20.6.3 Multicast Routing Protocols

Five multicast routing protocols currently exist, and you can classify each into either the source-based tree (dense mode) or shared-tree (sparse mode) protocol. The three dense-mode protocols are the Distance-Vector Multicast Routing Protocol (DVMRP), Multicast Open Shortest Path First (MOSPF), and Protocol Independent Multicast–Dense Mode (PIM–DM).

20.7 ROUTING IN WINDOWS

For two hosts to exchange IP datagrams, they must both have a route to each other, or they must use a default gateway that knows a route between the two. Normally, routers exchange information using a protocol such as RIP or OSPF. RIP listening service is available for Microsoft Windows 2000 Professional and Windows XP, and full routing protocols are supported by Windows 2000 Server and Windows Server 2003 in the RRAS.

20.7.1 ROUTE Command

The ROUTE command is used to view and modify the network routing tables of an IP network. The ROUTE PRINT command displays, a list of current routes that the host knows. See Figure 20.4.

Routes added to a routing table are not made persistent unless the –p switch is specified. Nonpersistent routes last only until the computer is restarted or until the interface is deactivated. The interface can be deactivated when the plug-and-play interface is unplugged (such as for laptops and hot swap PCs), when the wire is removed from the media card (if the adapter supports media fault sensing), or when the interface is manually disconnected from the adapter in the Network and Dial-up Connections folder.

The usage for the ROUTE command is as follows:

ROUTE [–f] [–p] [command [destination]] [MASK netmask] [gateway] [METRIC metric]

The commands usable in the syntax above are PRINT, ADD, DELETE, and CHANGE.

Figure 20.4   Using the ROUTE command to display the current routing tables on the Windows 2000 multihomed computer

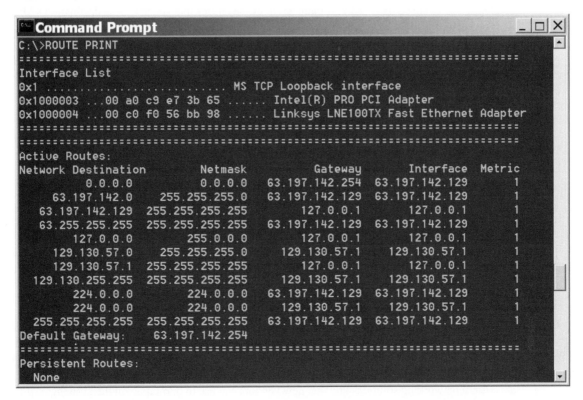

–f   Clears the routing tables of all gateway entries. If this is used in conjunction with one of the commands, the tables are cleared prior to running the command.

–p   When used with the ADD command, this makes a route persistent or permanent, even if you reboot the system. By default, routes are not preserved when the system is restarted. When used with the PRINT command, it displays the list of registered persistent routes. It is ignored for all other commands, which always affects the appropriate persistent routes. Note: Persistent routes are stored in this registry location: HKEY_LOCAL_MACHINE\SYSTEM\CurrentControlSet\Services\Tcpip\Parameters\PersistentRoutes.

Commands

PRINT	View or display a route
ADD	Adds a route
DELETE	Deletes a route
CHANGE	Modifies an existing route
Destination	Specifies the computer to send a command.
MASK netmask	Specifies a subnet mask to be associated with this route entry. If a netmask value is not specified, it defaults to 255.255.255.255.
Gateway	Specifies gateway or router.
METRIC metric	Assigns an integer cost metric (ranging from 1 to 9999) to be used in calculating the fastest, most reliable, and/or least expensive routes.

All symbolic names used for destination or gateway are referenced in both the network database file called Networks, and the computer name database file called Hosts. If the command is PRINT or DELETE, wildcards may be used for the destination and gateway; or the gateway argument may be omitted.

For example, to create a static route, type in the following:

route ADD 132.133.200.0 MASK 255.255.255.0 63.197.142.1 METRIC 2

After this command is executed, any packet that is sent to the 132.133.200.0 network or host with an IP address ranging between 132.133.200.1 and 132.133.200.254 will be forwarded to the router with a local host address of 63.197.142.1. If there are multiple entries that specify these destination addresses, this route has a metric of 2 hops.

20.7.2   Routing and Remote Access Service

The Routing and Remote Access Service (RRAS) for Windows 2000 Server and Windows Server 2003 continues the evolution of multiprotocol routing and remote access services for the Microsoft Windows platform. New features of the RRAS for Windows include the following:

- Internet Group Management Protocol (IGMP) and support for multicast boundaries
- Network address translation with addressing and name resolution components that simplify the connection of a small office/home office (SOHO) network to the Internet
- Integrated AppleTalk routing
- Layer 2 Tunneling Protocol (L2TP) over IP Security (IPSec) support for router-to-router VPN connections
- Graphical user interface program as the routing and remote access administrative utility, a Microsoft Management Console (MMC) snap-in. The command-line equivalent utility is Netsh.

The combined features of the Windows RRAS make a Windows server-based computer function as shown in Table 20.3.

An advantage of RRAS is its integration with the Windows server operating system. The service works with a wide variety of hardware platforms and hundreds of network adapters; the result is a lower-cost solution than many mid-range dedicated router or remote access server products. RRAS is extensible with application programming interfaces (APIs) that third-party developers can use to create custom networking solutions and that new vendors can use to participate in the growing business of open internetworking. See Figure 20.5.

To enable a routing protocol such as RIP or OSPF to an interface, do the following:

1. Open the Routing and Remote Access console (see Figure 20.6).
2. In the console tree, click IP Routing which is located under the server.
3. Right-click General in the details pane and select the New Routing Protocol option.
4. Click to select the protocol that you want to enable and click on the OK button.

20.7.3   Creating Static Routes

To add a static route to a Windows 2000 or Windows Server 2003 multihomed computer, use the Routing Access and Remote Access program located under Administrative Tools or use the appropriate MMC snap-in. Next, right-click Static Routes, and select "New Static route for IP networks" or "New route for IPX routes." See Figure 20.7.

Table 20.3   Windows Routing and Remote Access Service features

Feature	Description
Multiprotocol router	A RRAS computer can route IP, IPX, and AppleTalk simultaneously. All routable protocols and routing protocols are configured from the same administrative utility.
Demand-dial router	A RRAS computer can route IP and IPX over on-demand or persistent WAN links, such as analog phone lines or ISDN, or over VPN connections using either PPTP or L2TP over IPSec.
Remote access server	A RRAS computer can act as a remote access server providing remote access connectivity to dial-up or VPN remote access clients using IP, IPX, AppleTalk, or NetBEUI.

Figure 20.5   Using the Routing and Remote Access console to configure a multihomed router

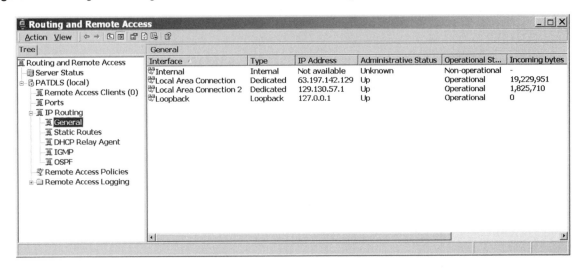

Figure 20.6   Adding a new network routing protocol using the Routing and Remote Access console on a multihomed computer

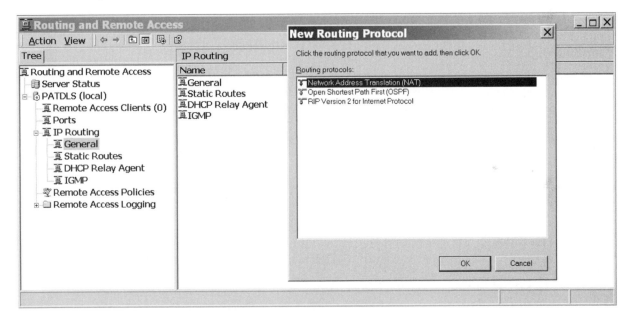

For a static IP route in Destination, Network mask, Gateway, Interface, and Metric, enter the corresponding information into each route. If this is a demand-dial interface, Gateway is unavailable. You can also select the "Use this route to initiate demand-dial connections" check box to initiate a demand-dial connection for traffic that matches the route. For a static IPX route in Network Number (hex), Next Hop MAC Address (hex), Tick Count, Hop Count, and Interface, enter the corresponding information. To delete the static route, right-click the appropriate route, then select the Delete option. To make changes to a static route entry, double-click the correct static route in the Detail pane.

For IP static addresses, the destination provides a space to type a destination for the route. The destination can be a host address, subnet address, network address, or the destination for the default route (0.0.0.0). The subnet mask provides a space to type the network mask for the static route. The network mask number is used in conjunction with the destination to determine when the route is

Figure 20.7   Configuring a static route using the Routing and Remote Access console on a Windows multihomed computer

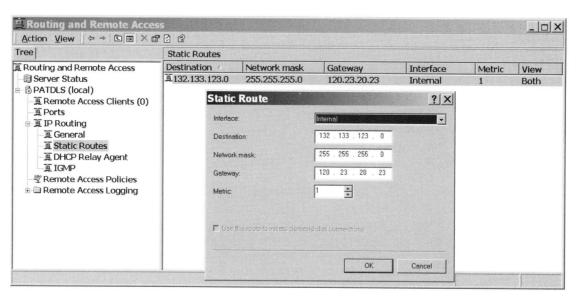

used. The mask of 255.255.255.255 means that only an exact match of the destination number can use this route. The mask of 0.0.0.0 means that any destination can use this route. The gateway provides a space to type the forwarding IP address for this route. For LAN interfaces, the gateway address must be configured and must be a directly reachable IP address for the network segment of the selected interface. Again, for demand-dial interfaces, the gateway address is not configured or used. The metric provides a space to type the cost associated with this route to reach the destination. The metric is commonly used to indicate the number of routers (hops) to the destination. When deciding between multiple routes to the same destination, the route with the lowest metric is selected as the best route.

20.7.4   Planning a Static Route

If appropriate for your IP internetwork, perform the following steps to deploy static routing:

1. Draw a map of the topology of your IP internetwork to show the separate networks and the placement of routers and hosts.
2. For each IP network, assign a unique IP network ID (also known as an IP network address).
3. Assign IP addresses to each router interface. It is a common industry practice to assign the first IP addresses of a given IP network to router interfaces. For example, for an IP network ID of 192.168.100.0 with a subnet mask of 255.255.255.0, the router interface is assigned the IP address of 192.168.100.1.
4. For peripheral routers, configure a default route on the interface that has a neighboring router. The use of default routes on peripheral routers is optional.
5. For each nonperipheral router, compile a list of routes that need to be added as static routes to the routing table for that router. Each route consists of a destination network ID, a subnet mask, a gateway (or forwarding) IP address, a metric (number of router hops to reach the network), and the interface to be used to reach the network.
6. For nonperipheral routers, add the static routes compiled in step 5 to each router. You can add static routes by using the Routing and Remote Access program or the ROUTE command. If you use the ROUTE command, use the –p option to make the static routes persistent.
7. When your configuration is complete, use the PING and TRACERT commands to test connectivity between host computers so that all routing paths are checked.

20.7.5   RIP

Windows RIP for IP is compliant with RFC 1058 and 1723 and has the following features:

- Split horizon, poison reverse, and triggered updates convergence algorithms
- Ability to modify the announcement interval (default is 30 seconds)
- Ability to modify the routing table entry timeout value (default is 3 minutes)
- Ability to be a silent RIP host
- Peer filtering: ability to accept or discard updates of announcements from specific routers identified by IP address
- Route filtering: ability to accept or discard updates of specific network IDs or from specific routers
- RIP neighbors: ability to unicast RIP announcements to specific routers to support nonbroadcast technologies such as Frame Relay (A RIP neighbor is a RIP router that receives unicasted RIP announcements.)
- Ability to announce or accept default routes or host routes

When a Windows router advertises a non-RIP learned route, it advertises it with a hop count of 2. Non-RIP learned routes include static routes (even for directly attached networks), OSPF routes, and SNMP routes.

To enable a router with RIP, follow two basic steps: select the routing protocol and identify the networks to which the router is directly connected. To configure RIP version 2, do the following:

1. Open the Routing and Remote Access console.
2. In the console tree, click RIP.
3. In the details pane, right-click the interface you want to configure for RIP version 2, and then click Properties. Figure 20.8 shows what appears in Properties.

20.7.6   OSPF

To create an OSPF area, do the following:

1. Start the Routing and Remote Access console.
2. In the console tree, click OSPF.
3. Right-click OSPF, then click Properties.
4. On the Areas tab, click Add.
5. On the General tab, in Area ID, type the dotted decimal number that identifies the area.
6. To use a plain-text password, verify that the "Enable plaintext password" check box is selected.
7. To mark the area as a stub, select the Stub Area check box. You cannot configure the backbone area (area ID 0.0.0.0) as a stub area or virtual links through stub areas.
8. In Stub metric, click the arrows to set the stub metric.
9. To import routes of other areas into the stub area, select the "Import summary advertisements" check box. See Figure 20.9.

To configure ranges for an OSPF area, do the following:

1. Start the Routing and Remote Access console.
2. In the console tree, click OSPF.
3. Right-click OSPF, then click Properties.
4. On the Areas tab, click Add.
5. On the Ranges tab, in Destination, type the IP network ID for the range.
6. In Network mask, type the associated mask for the range, then click Add.
7. To delete a range, click the range you want to delete, then click Remove. See Figure 20.10.

To configure an autonomous system boundary router, do the following:

1. Open the Routing and Remote Access console.
2. In the console tree, click OSPF.
3. Right-click OSPF, then click Properties.

Figure 20.8 Configuring the RIP protocol on a Windows multihomed computer

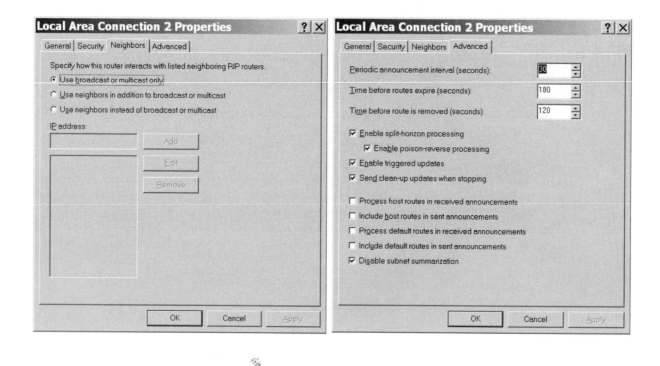

4. On the General tab, click "Enable autonomous system boundary router."
5. To configure external route sources, do the following:
   - On the External Routing tab, click either "Accept routes from all route sources except those selected" or "Ignore routes from all route sources except those selected."
   - Select or clear the appropriate check boxes next to the route sources.
6. To configure external route filters, do the following:

Figure 20.9   Configuring the OSPF protocol on a Windows multihomed computer

- On the External Routing tab, click Route Filters.
- In Destination and in Network mask, type the route you want to filter, then click Add.
- Repeat the preceding step for all the routes you want to filter.
- Click either "Ignore listed routes" or "Accept listed routes" depending on the appropriate filtering action, then click OK.

20.7.7   EGP and BGP

Windows routers do not provide EGP and BGP, but Windows 2000 and Windows Server 2003 do have an application programming interface (API) support that provides a platform to support additional routing protocols such as the BGP for IP. Therefore, an EGP and BGP can be written by third-party independent software vendors.

20.7.8   IP Forwarding

A multihomed system has two network interface cards so that it can route traffic between two networks. The configuration is possible on Windows 2000 Professional or Windows XP systems only if you turn on IP Forwarding. In Windows NT 4.0, you enable IP Forwarding by selecting the Control Panel network applet, highlighting TCP/IP Protocol on the Protocols tab, clicking Properties, then selecting the Enable IP Forwarding check box on the Routing tab. In Windows 2000 Professional and

Figure 20.10   Configuring OSPF area on a multihomed computer

Windows XP, this option does not exist, but the functionality still exists. To turn on IP Forwarding in Windows, use a registry editor to open the registry. Under the HKEY_LOCAL_MACHINE\SYSTEM\ CurrentControlSet\Services\Tcpip\Parameters subkey, change the value of the IPEnableRouter entry from the default value of 0 to 1.

20.8   INTRODUCTION TO CISCO ROUTERS

Cisco Systems is a leading manufacturer of network equipment including routers, bridges, and switches. Cisco routers are able to build routing tables, execute commands, and route packets across network interfaces using routing protocols; thus, the router must have processing power, storage capacity, and RAM. Appropriate software such as an operating system that can be used to configure routed and routing protocols is also necessary.

20.8.1   Hardware Components

Cisco routers come with different processors depending on the router model. For example, the Cisco 2505 router contains a 20-MHz Motorola 68EC030 processor, and a higher-end router such as the Cisco 7010 router contains a 25-MHz Motorola MC68040 CPU.

Cisco routers need a place to store configuration information, a place to boot the router internetwork operating system (IOS), and memory that can be used to hold dynamic information as the router does its job of moving packets on the internetwork. Cisco routers actually contain different types of memory components that provide the storage and dynamic caching required. The different memory components found in a Cisco router are as follows:

- **ROM**—Contains the power-on self-test (POST) and the bootstrap program for the router. The ROM chip also contains either a subset or the complete router IOS.
- **NVRAM** (nonvolatile RAM)—Stores the start-up configuration file for the router. NVRAM can be erased and can copy running configuration on the router to NVRAM. The great thing about NVRAM is that it retains information even if the router is powered down.

■ **Flash RAM**—Flash is a special ROM that can actually erase and reprogram. Flash is used to store the Cisco IOS that runs on your router. You can also store alternative versions of the Cisco IOS on the Flash such as an upgrade of your current IOS, which makes it easy for you to upgrade the router. Flash RAM actually comes in the form of a single in-line memory module (SIMMS), and depending on which router you have, additional Flash RAM may be installed.

■ **RAM**—Similar to the dynamic memory on your PC, RAM provides the temporary storage of information. Packets are held in RAM when their addressing information is examined by the router. In addition, RAM also holds the current routing table and current-running router configuration.

20.8.2   Router Interfaces

Cisco routers can support LAN and WAN interfaces. The most common LAN router interfaces are Ethernet, Fast Ethernet, IBM Token Ring, and FDDI. WAN interfaces, sometimes called serial router interfaces, are connected via leased lines and other third-party connectivity technologies. Some of the commonly used WAN data link layer technologies are HDLC, X.25, Frame Relay, ISDN, and PPP.

Cisco routers such as those in the 2500 Series family basically are off-the-shelf routers that come with a predetermined number of LAN, WAN, and serial ports. Higher-end routers such as the Cisco 4500 are modular and contain empty slots that can be filled with several different interface cards. Built-in ports are designed by their connection type, followed by a number. For example, the first Ethernet port on a router is E0; the second Ethernet port on a router is E1, and so on. Serial ports are designated the same way with the first serial port being S0. Modular routers designate their ports by connection type, followed by slot number, and then port number. For example, the first Ethernet port on an Ethernet card that is placed in the router's first slot would be designated as Ethernet 1/0. The slot is designated first, followed by the port number.

20.8.3   Router Boot Sequence

When you power the router on, the ROM chip runs a POST that checks the router's hardware such as the processor, interfaces, and memory. The next step in the router boot-up sequence is the execution of a bootstrap program that is stored in the router's ROM. This bootstrap program searches for the CISCO IOS. The IOS can be loaded from the ROM itself, the router's Flash RAM, or from a Trivial File Transfer Protocol (TFTP) server on the network. The IOS is typically stored in the router's Flash RAM.

After the router's IOS is loaded, the router searches for the configuration file, which is normally held in NVRAM. As with the IOS, however, the configuration file can be loaded from a TFTP server. After the router loads the configuration file, the information in the file enables the interfaces and provides parameters related to the routing protocols.

20.8.4   Communicating with the Router

Every Cisco router has a console port on its back, which is there to provide a way to hook up a terminal to the router to work on it. The console port, which is sometimes referred to as a management port, is used by administrators to log in to a router directly without using a network connection. A stand-alone CRT, PC, or workstation can be used as a console. Console terminals must run a character-based user interface. They cannot directly use a graphical user interface (GUI). Instead, you must use a PC or workstation as a console, and terminal emulator software such as the HyperTerminal.

Most Cisco routers have an auxiliary port. The auxiliary port is sometimes referred to as the AUX port. Like the console port, the AUX port makes possible a direct, non-network connection to the router.

Once a router is installed on a network, access to it is almost always via Telnet sessions, not via the console or AUX ports. Telnet is a way to log in to a router as a virtual terminal. Telnet connections are instead made through the network. In the most basic terms, a virtual terminal session is composed of IP packets being routed over a network, pretending to be bits streaming over a serial line.

When using Telnet to access a router, do so over a virtual line provided by the Cisco IOS software. These are called VTY lines. IOS supports up to five virtual terminal sessions running simultaneously on a router. It is rare that you will have more than one virtual terminal session running on a router at the same time.

A more recent router access method is the HTTP server. Do not be misled by the name; no computer server is involved in using HTTP server. The term *server* in HTTP server refers to a small software application running inside the Cisco IOS software. HTTP server first became available with IOS release 10.3. HTTP server makes it possible to interact with the router through a web browser.

20.8.5   Internetworking Operating System

Cisco's **internetworking operating system (IOS)** is software that provides the router hardware with the capability to route packets on an internetwork. The IOS, like any operating system, provides the command sets and software functionality that you use to monitor and configure the router, and it also provides the functionality for the various protocols that make the internetwork a reality.

After the router contains a basic configuration, you can then begin to examine the different router modes available. The router supplies you with three basic levels of access: user mode, privileged mode, and configuration mode, as defined in the following list:

- **User mode**—This modes provides limited access to the router. You are provided with a set of non-destructive commands that allow examination of certain router configuration parameters. You cannot, however, make any changes to the router configuration.
- **Privileged mode**—This mode (also known as the enabled mode) allows greater examination of the router and provides a more robust command set than the user mode. After you enter the privileged mode using the secret or enable password, you have access to the configuration commands supplied in the configuration mode, meaning that you can edit the configuration for the router.
- **Configuration mode**—This mode (also known as the global configuration mode) is entered from the privileged mode and supplies the complete command set for configuring the router.

Configuring the router means that you enable the various interfaces and protocols on the router. You must use commands that bring your various hardware interfaces such as Ethernet or serial interfaces to life. You must provide configuration information for the protocols that are routed, such as IP or IPX; and you must configure routing protocols such as RIP, OSPF, and IGRP. After the router is configured, then mange your configuration files.

Cisco provides a **command-line interface (CLI)** that you can use to configure and maintain your router. You can access the CLI using a router console or by Telnetting to a router using a virtual terminal. The IOS has hundreds of commands, some of which can be used anywhere in IOS, whereas others can be used within a specific area only. A few major root commands handle most tasks that are associated with configuring routers, as follows:

show—Examine router status.
configure—Make changes to config file parameters.
no—Negate a parameter setting.
copy—Put configure file changes into effect.

SUMMARY

1. A router, which works at the network ISO layer, is a device that connects two or more LANs.
2. The primary role of a router is to transmit similar types of data packets from one wide area communications link (such as a T1 line or a fiber link) to another T1 line or fiber link. The second role of a router is to select the best path between the source and destination.
3. To determine the best route, the routers use complex routing algorithms, which take into account a variety of factors including the number of the fastest set of trans-

mission media, the number of network segments, and the network segment that carries the least amount of traffic.

4. A metric is a standard of measurement, such as hop count, that is used by routing algorithms to determine the optimal path to a destination. A hop is the trip a data packet takes from one router to another router or a router to another intermediate point to another in the network.

5. To track the various routes in a network, the routers create and maintain routing tables.

6. Routing algorithms must converge rapidly. Convergence is the process of agreement by all routers about which routes are the optimal routes.

7. Static routing algorithms are hardly algorithms at all: rather, they are table mappings established by the network administrator prior to the beginning of routing. These mappings do not change unless the network administrator alters them.

8. Because static routing systems cannot react to network changes, they generally are considered unsuitable for today's large, changing networks.

9. Most dominant routing algorithms today are dynamic routing algorithms, which adjust to changing network circumstances by analyzing incoming routing update messages.

10. Routers use distance-vector-based routing protocols to periodically advertise or broadcast the routes in their routing tables, but they only send information to their neighboring routers.

11. Link-state algorithms are also known as shortest path first algorithms. Link-state routers send updates directly (or by using multicast traffic) to all routers within the network. Each router, however, sends only the portion of the routing table that describes the state of its own links.

12. The various routing protocols use different metrics, such as path length, hop counts, routing delay, bandwidth, load, reliability, and cost.

13. To report errors and other information regarding IP packet processing, the Internet Control-Message Protocol (ICMP) sends notices back to the source.

14. The Routing Information Protocol (RIP) is designed for exchanging routing information within a small to medium-sized network.

15. To overcome some of the RIP shortcomings, RIP version 2 (RIP v2) was introduced.

16. Some protocols, such as OSPF, allow areas (groupings of contiguous networks) to be gathered into an autonomous system (AS).

17. The backbone (given an address of 0.0.0.0) of the AS is a high-bandwidth logical area where all areas are connected.

18. Areas that are not backbone OSPF areas can be classified as either a stub area or a transit area.

19. A stub area has only one area border router (ABR). All routes to the destination outside the area must pass through the single router.

20. A transit area contains more than one ABR.

21. The Open Shortest Path First (OSPF) protocol is a link-state routing protocol used in medium and large networks and calculates routing table entries by constructing a shortest-path tree.

22. The Interior Gateway Routing Protocol (IGRP) is a distance-vector protocol that allows gateways to build up their routing table by exchanging information with other gateways.

23. The local routing information of an autonomous area is gathered using an internal gateway protocol such as RIP or OSPF.

24. In these autonomous areas, one or more routers are chosen to use an exterior gateway protocol to talk to other autonomous areas by providing a way for two neighboring routers that are located at the edges of their respective autonomous area to exchange routing information.

25. IP multicast allows a host to communicate with several hosts simultaneously by transmitting information via one data stream.

26. Routers and computers use the Internet Group Management Protocol (IGMP) to exchange membership information.

27. Cisco Systems is a leading manufacturer of network equipment such as routers, bridges, and switches. Cisco routers are able to build routing tables, execute commands, and route packets across network interfaces using routing protocols.

QUESTIONS

1. Which one of the following communications devices would be used to transport packets between autonomous systems that are over 1000 km apart?
   a. concentrator
   b. hub
   c. router
   d. transparent bridge

2. Your company is based in Atlanta. It has one branch office in Los Angeles and one in New York City. Each office is networked. The WAN uses three T1 connections to connect the three sites. Which one of the following connectivity devices should be used to connect the LANs to the multiple paths in the WAN?
   a. routers
   b. bridges
   c. repeaters
   d. gateways

3. Which one of the following is the smartest network device?
   a. bridge
   b. gateway
   c. concentrator
   d. router

4. How does a router determine where a packet should be delivered?
   a. It examines the MAC address.
   b. It examines the source network address.
   c. It examines the telephone number.
   d. It examines the destination network address.

5. What are the two types of routers? (Select two answers.)
   a. passive
   b. active
   c. static
   d. dynamic

6. Routes and routing tables are built by routing algorithms using _____ .
   a. cost of the router
   b. speed of the router
   c. metrics
   d. whichever router is available first

7. Pat has four multihomed Windows 2000 servers that are functioning as routers on his network. He wants to configure the routing tables on these servers with the least amount of administrative effort possible. How should Pat proceed?
   a. Install DHCP relay agent.   c. Run NETSTAT.EXE.
   b. Install RIP for IP.   d. Run ROUTE.EXE.

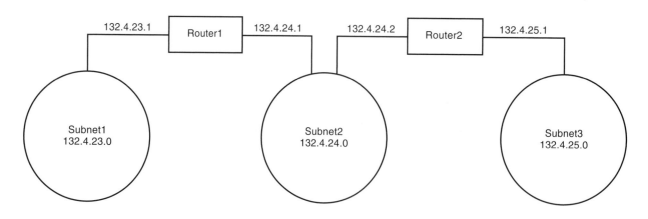

8. What type of packets does TRACERT send out?
   a. ICMP echo packets   c. TCP packets
   b. UDP packets   d. IP packets

9. Pat has been asked to set up a small network with three subnets as shown in the following figure. He plans to connect the subnets with two multihomed gateways. The subnet mask on the network is 255.255.255.0. What command would be used to configure the two routers? (Choose two answers.)
   a. On Router1: ROUTE ADD 132.4.25.0 MASK 255.255.255.0 132.4.24.2
   b. On Router2: ROUTE ADD 132.4.23.0 MASK 255.255.255.0 132.4.25.2
   c. On Router1: ROUTE ADD 132.4.25.0 MASK 255.255.255.0 132.4.24.1
   d. On Router2: ROUTE ADD 132.4.23.0 MASK 255.255.255.0 132.4.23.1

10. _____is the process of agreement by all routers about which routes are the optimal routes.
    a. Coordinating   c. Convergence
    b. Synchronization   d. Ripping

11. _____is a distant-vector routing protocol.
    a. RIP   c. ICMP
    b. OSPF   d. Static route

12. _____is a link-state routing protocol.
    a. RIP   c. ICMP
    b. OSPF   d. Static route

13. You just added 10 routers to your network and suddenly the network performance has dramatically decreased. What is the problem?
    a. The network is probably using static routes.
    b. The network is probably using RIP.
    c. The network is probably using OSPF.
    d. One of the routing links is down.

14. What type of protocol connects autonomous systems together?
    a. exterior gateway   c. RIP
    b. interior gateway   d. OSPF

15. _____allows a host to communicate with several hosts simultaneously by transmitting information via one data stream.
    a. Multicasting   c. Multiplying
    b. Multibroadcasting   d. Converging

16. What is the address of the backbone of an OSPF network?
    a. 0.0.0.0   c. 240.0.0.0
    b. 127.0.0.1   d. 255.255.255.255

17. You are the administrator of Windows 2000 network. The network consists of 10 segments. These segments are connected by four Windows 2000 server-based routers named Router1, Router2, Router3, and Router4. RRAS is enabled as a router on these four servers. To exchange routing information, the four servers use RIP v2 for IP. There are two other routers on the network that use RIP v2 to exchange routing information. These other routers might have been erroneously configured and, consequently, contain incorrect routing information. You want to ensure that Router1, Router2, Router3, and Router4 do not process routes received from any other router than Router1, Router2, Router3, and Router4. How can you configure the four routers to accomplish this goal? (Choose all that apply.)
    a. Configure the RIP routing protocol on the four routers to RIP peer filters. List the other three routers as RIP peers.
    b. Configure each RIP interface on the four routers to unicast announcements to RIP neighbors. List the other three routers as RIP neighbors.
    c. Configure each RIP interface on the four routers to use password authentication. Use the same password on all four routers.
    d. On each RIP interface on the four routers, configure routes for outgoing routes. Announce only routes in the route ranges of the network IDs that are connected to the four routers.

18. You are the desktop administrator of your company. You are responsible for ensuring that your company's Windows 2000 Professional client computers have connectivity to the network and the Internet. All client computers use DHCP for their TCP/IP configuration. The network administrators install a new T1 line and router for Internet access. This router must be used only by administrative staff. You want to configure the administrative staff's client computers to use this new router. You want to ensure that nonadministrative staff users cannot gain access to the Internet through this router. You want to ensure that each targeted client computer will only need to be configured once. What should you do to achieve these goals?
    a. At each administrative client computer, use the route ADD –f command to enter the new router information.
    b. At each administrative client computer, use the route ADD –p command to enter the new router information.

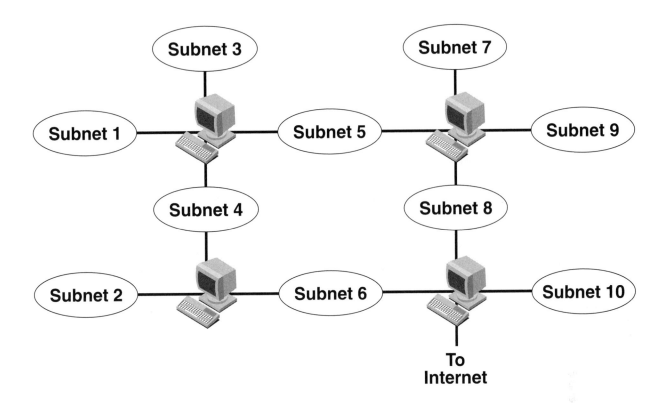

c. Enable the Perform Router Discovery option in the scope options for DHCP.

d. Enter the new router's address in the Router Solicitation Address option in the scope options for DHCP.

19. You are the administrator of your company's WAN. The network consists of 10 internal subnets in two physical sites connected by routes as shown in the exhibit.

You have an additional subnet that is configured for access to the Internet. The routers on the network will be multi-homed Windows 2000 server computers running RRAS. You want to accomplish the following goals:

- Administrative overhead for configuration of routing tables on each router will be minimized.
- Broadcast traffic for configuration of routing tables on each router will be minimized.
- In the event of a router failure, link redundancy within 10 minutes will be ensured.
- Convergence time of less than 1 minute for all known routes on all routers will be ensured.
- Internal routing information will never be exposed to external routers.

You take the following actions:

- Install RIP v1.
- Configure RIP to use all interfaces on all multihomed computers.
- Enable RIP authentication by specifying a password on each interface.

Which result or results do these actions produce? (Choose all that apply.)

a. Administrative overhead for configuration of routing tables on each router is minimized.

b. Broadcast traffic for configuration of routing tables on each router is minimized.

c. In the event of a router failure, link redundancy within 10 minutes is ensured.

d. Convergence time of less than 1 minute for all known routes on all routers is ensured.

e. Internal routing information is never exposed to external routers.

20. You are the administrator for your company's Windows 2000 routed network. Your network has grown considerably over the past year and includes 15 subnets and routers. To accommodate new growth you install 2 new subnets and routers. You also install a RRAS server and configure it as a RIP v2 router on Subnet_17. All subnets are referred as Subnet_A through Subnet_Q, inclusive. All routers are referred to as Router_1 through Router_17, inclusive. However, users on Subnet_R report that they cannot access resources on Subnet_A. After further investigation you find that Subnet_R users cannot access resources on Subnet_A either. What's wrong?

a. RIP has a maximum hop count of 15.

b. RIP has a maximum time to live of 15.

c. The metric count for the routing tables of Router_1 and Router_17 is not set correctly.

d. Router_1 needs a static route configured for Router_17 and Router_17 needs a static route configured for Router_1.

21. You are the network administrator for a large Windows 2000 multidomain network. All servers on the network are configured with Windows 2000 Advanced Server. The network uses TCP/IP and the OSPF routing protocol. You want to increase network speed and efficiency of your

internal routers and area border routers (ABRs). What should you do? (Choose all that apply.)

a. Do *not* connect ABRs to the network backbone.

b. Configure the ABRs to be connected to the network backbone.

c. Do *not* configure source and route filtering because it is too restrictive.

d. Configure the ABRs with correct destination and network mask pairs.

e. Ensure that the computer configured as the router contains only one network card.

f. Use back-door routers to complement the ABRs.

22. You are an administrator for your company's Windows 2000 network. Your network consists of 5 Windows 2000 Server computers, and 150 Windows 2000 Professional client computers. Three of the Windows 2000 Server computers are configured as RIP routers. A fellow company administrator reports that the RIP routers are not receiving routes. What network services or options should you ensure? (Choose all that apply.)

a. Ensure that RIP authentication is enabled.

b. Ensure that you have configured RIP peer filtering.

c. Ensure that you are not deploying variable length subnet masks.

d. Ensure that IP packet filtering is not preventing input or output of RIP announcements.

23. Which of the following protocols is referred to as a hybrid routing protocol because it has features of both distance-vector and link-state protocols?

a. RIP   c. EIGRP
b. OSPF   d. IGRP

24. You are suggesting that your company uses IP RIP as its routing protocol. Your boss would like you to list some facts about IP RIP before he approves your request. Which of the following statements about IP RIP are true? (Choose two answers.)

a. It limits hop counts to 31.

b. It is a link-state routing protocol.

c. It uses autonomous system numbers.

d. It is capable of load sharing over multiple paths.

e. It uses bandwidth as the metric for path selection.

f. It broadcasts updates every 30 seconds by default.

25. You are the network administrator for a small company. You plan to use two machines running Windows 2000 Server with multiple network cards as routers for your network. You would like to have the ability to do classless inter-domain routing as well as institute variable length subnet masks. Which of the following routing protocols can you use to support these features? (Choose all that apply.)

a. EIGRP   c. RIP v1
b. OSPF   d. RIP v2

26. You are the administrator of your company's network, which consists of a LAN with 5000 computers on 15 sub-nets. Each subnet is a separate network segment. You anticipate that the number of hosts on your network will increase by 10% each year for the next 3 years. The network includes three Windows 2000 Server computers configured as routers. The relevant portion of your existing network con-figuration is shown in the exhibit.

You need to configure the routers so that existing hosts on all subnets can communicate with existing hosts on all other subnets. Your solution must minimize network protocol traf-fic, and it must allow the subnets to be reconfigured to accommodate the anticipated growth. What should you do?

a. Create two additional subnets for each router. Enable routing and remote access on each router and add the OSPF protocol in a default configuration. Add each network interface on each router to the OSPF protocol.

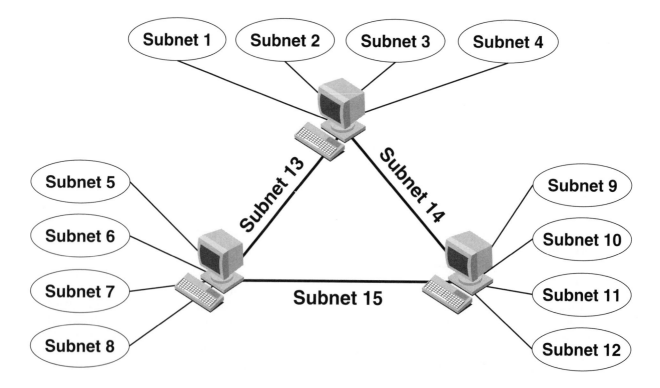

b. Reconfigure the routers and network segments in a backbone configuration. Add two additional subnets for each router. Enable routing and remote access on each router and add the OSPF protocol in a default configuration. Add each network interface on each router to the OSPF protocol.

c. Enable routing and remote access on each router and add RIP in a default configuration. Add each network interface on each router to RIP.

d. Enable routing and remote access on each router and add RIP, configured to use RIP neighbors instead of broadcast or multicast routing. Add each network interface on each router to RIP.

CHAPTER **21**

Introduction to Web Servers

Topics Covered in This Chapter

Introduction

Internet and web servers are essential to many businesses. Microsoft's web server is called Internet Information Services (IIS), which has been available for Windows NT. Since the Internet has grown so popular during the past few years, IIS is now included with Windows 2000 and Windows Server 2003. It is also included with Windows XP. This chapter discusses how to configure IIS.

Objectives

■ Monitor, configure, troubleshoot, and control access to files and folders via web services.

■ Manage and troubleshoot web server resources.

■ Monitor, configure, troubleshoot, and control access to websites.

21.1 INTRODUCTION TO WEB PAGES AND SERVERS

The terms *Internet* and *World Wide Web* are often used interchangeably, but they do have different meanings. The **Internet** refers to the huge global WAN. Until the early 1990s, a person who wanted to use a computer to communicate with another computer via the Internet needed a good deal of knowledge and the ability to understand and use some fairly unfriendly commands. The **World Wide Web (WWW)** was created in 1992, and refers to the means of organizing, presenting, and accessing information over the internet.

To access the Web, a user needs the following technologies:

■ HTML
■ web server
■ web browser
■ http and ftp

Web pages are written using the **Hypertext Markup Language (HTML).** This language is fairly simple and is implemented as special ASCII tags or codes that you embed within your document to give the browser a general idea of how the information should be displayed. The browsers understand the standard HTML tags, although they may display the same document a little differently. If you want your documents to be accessible by people using different browsers, you should stick with the standard tags. The HTML standard is still actively evolving, so new tags are constantly becoming available to support new browser features.

A **web server** is a computer that is equipped with the server software that uses Internet protocols such as Hypertext Transfer Protocol (HTTP) and File Transfer Protocol (FTP) to respond to web client requests on a TCP/IP network via web browsers. One server can service a large number of clients. There are several free server programs available on the Internet. Most web browsers are built to process two basic types of requests: file server and database server requests. New features are always being added to provide additional support for new technology. A web server acting as a file server simply accepts a request for a document, validates the request, and sends the requested files back to the browser. In addition, the browser can act as a front-end tool or interface to collect data and feed it in a database or script. The database can be located either on the same server as the web server or on a different server. When the database responds with the results, it then sends the results back to the browser.

The **web browser** is the client program/software that you run on your local machine to gain access to a web server. It receives the HTML commands, interprets the HTML, and displays the results. It is strictly a user-interface/document presentation tool. It knows nothing about the application to which it is attached and only knows how to take the information from the server and present it to the user. It is also able to capture data entry made into a form and get the information back to the server for processing. The most common browsers are Microsoft Internet Explorer and Netscape Communicator. Both of these tools are available for little or no charge on the Internet.

The application protocol that makes the Web work is **Hypertext Transfer Protocol (HTTP).** Whereas the HTML is the language used to write web pages, HTTP is the protocol that web browsers and web servers use to communicate with each other over the Internet. It is an application level protocol, because it sits on top of the TCP layer in the protocol stack and is used by specific applications to talk to one another. In this case, the applications are web browsers and web servers.

HTTP is a text-based protocol. Clients (web browsers) send requests to web servers for web elements such as web pages and images. After the request is serviced by a server, the connection between client and server across the Internet is disconnected. A new connection must be made for each request. Most protocols are connection oriented, which means that the two computers communicating with each other keep the connection open over the Internet—HTTP does not. Before an HTTP request can be made by a client, a new connection must be made to the server. Another common protocol is the **File Transfer Protocol (FTP),** which is used on the Internet to send files.

Currently, most web browsers and servers support HTTP 1.1. One main feature of HTTP 1.1 is that it supports persistent connections, which means that once a browser connects to a web server, it can receive multiple files through the same connection. This protocol should improve performance by as much as 20%.

HTTP is called a stateless protocol because each command is executed independently, without any knowledge of the commands that came before it. This explains why it is difficult to implement websites that react intelligently to user input. This shortcoming of HTTP is being addressed in several new technologies, including ActiveX, Java, JavaScript, and cookies.

Typically when accessing a web page, you specify the web page location by using a **uniform resource locator (URL).** The first part of the address indicates what protocol to use; the second part specifies the IP address or the domain name where the resource is located; and the last part indicates the folder and file name. See Figure 21.1 and the other URL examples listed here.

```
ftp://www.acme.com/files/run.exe
http://www.acme.com/index.html
```

When you type a URL into a web browser, the following occurs:

1. If the URL contains a domain name, the browser first connects to a DNS server and retrieves the corresponding IP address for the web server.
2. The web browser connects to the web server and sends an HTTP request (via the protocol stack) for the desired web page.
3. The web server receives the request and checks for the desired page. If the page exists, the web server sends it. If the server cannot find the requested page, it sends an HTTP 404 error message (404 means "Page Not Found," as anyone who has surfed the Web probably knows).
4. The web browser receives the page back and the connection is closed.
5. The browser then parses through the page and looks for other page elements it needs to complete the web page, including images, applets, and so forth.
6. For each element needed, the browser makes additional connections and HTTP requests to the server for each element.
7. When the browser has finished loading all images, applets, and so on, the page will be completely loaded in the browser window.

Figure 21.1 Typical URL

A **gopher** was an early system that predates the World Wide Web for organizing and displaying files on Internet servers. A gopher server presents its contents as a hierarchically structured list of files. Gophers are basically obsolete, as they have primarily been replaced by search engines.

Since the Internet is so vast, consisting of countless web pages, it is often difficult to know the URL that a person wants. Therefore, the World Wide Web has several search engines that can be used to locate desired documents. A **search engine** is a program that searches documents for specified keywords and returns a list of the documents where the keywords were found. Typically, a search engine works by sending out a "spider" to fetch as many documents as possible. Another program, called an indexer, then reads these documents and creates an index based on the words contained in each document. Each search engine uses a proprietary algorithm to create its indexes such that, ideally, only meaningful results are returned for each query.

> For more information on the HTTP protocol, go to W3C Architecture Domain Web site located at http://www.w3.org/Protocols/

21.2   INTRODUCTION TO HTML LANGUAGE

To create or modify a web page, use a text editor such as DOS's EDIT or Windows Notepad. The text file begins with the <HTML> tag and end with the </HTML> tag. Web browsers can identify an HTML file by the file extension, and many browsers display pages that do not carry the <HTML> tag. When viewing your document with your own browser, you may be able to get away without the tag, but you cannot be sure that everyone who wants to view your page will be using the same browser that you use. It is best to stick with good programming habits and avoid the temptation to take shortcuts.

The HTML document is divided into two sections: the head and the body. The head begins with the <H> tag and ends with the </H> tag, and the body begins with <BODY> and ends with </BODY>. Although these tags are not case sensitive, try to type them in uppercase so that they are easy to identify. Most HTML tags are used in pairs, with an opening tag and an ending tag to delineate which text you want handled in a particular way. Ending tags are the same as opening tags, but with the addition of a forward slash (/).

21.2.1   The Head

The head includes the title, which is defined with the <TITLE> </TITLE> tags. The information enclosed within the title tags will be displayed by your browser at the top of the web page in the title bar. Beside the title, the head can also include META tags, which are used for including information about the document. This can be valuable when listing the contents of the page in either a series of keywords or a description that can be targeted by search engines. The <META> tag is a singlet with no closing tag. See Figure 21.2.

Figure 21.2   HTML web page that defines the title and body

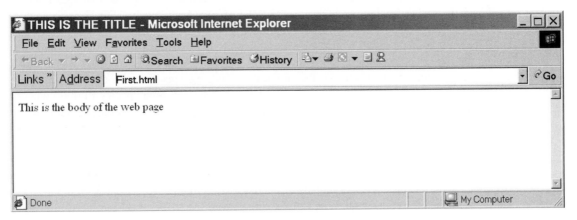

```
<HTML>
<HEAD>
<TITLE>THIS IS THE TITLE</TITLE>
<META NAME="KEYWORD" CONTENTS="HOT,IMPORTANT">
<META NAME="DESCRIPTION" CONTENTS="This is a sample website">
</HEAD>

<BODY>
This is the body of the web page
</BODY>
</HTML>
```

21.2.2   The Body

Everything that shows up on the web page itself is found in the body of the HTML document. The HTML equivalent to hitting the Return key in a word-processing program is the use of the paragraph<P> </P> tags or the break tag <BR>. The paragraph tag <P> </P> is like hitting the Return key twice, creating a blank line and a break. The break tag <BR> is like hitting the Return key once.

To center the text on the screen, use the <CENTER> </CENTER> tag. One excellent way to organize materials on a web page is through the use of a list. There are two types of lists: ordered lists and unordered lists. Ordered lists are usually numbered and often used when items are listed in some kind of sequence. Unordered lists are not numbered and are usually bulleted. The tags <OL> </OL> are used to create an ordered list, and <UL> </UL> are used to indent the text. To make the list into a bulleted list or a numbered list, add the list tag <LI> in front of each item on the list. A <BLOCKQUOTE> </BLOCKQUOTE> is used when you want to set off a quotation or any paragraph by indenting on the left and the right.

Standard text in a browser will usually appear as 12-point text. The font that will appear depends on which font is the default font for the browser. To vary the size of the text on the web page, use the heading tab <H> </H> The heading tab always includes a number 1 through 6, which identifies the size of the text: <H1> </H1> is the largest, <H6> </H6> is the smallest.

The font tags <FONT> </FONT> can also be used to change the size of the text, specify the font, and change the color of the text. Unlike the <H> </H> tag, the font tag does not force a break after the text that it encloses. By itself, the font tag does nothing. It must be given attributes for size, color, or font. An **attribute** is an option that can be used within the tag, and is usually followed by a value, indicating a specific choice within the range of choices for that attribute. All font attributes can be nested within a single font tag.

To change the size of text, enclose it with the font tags. After the word FONT in the opening tag, leave a space and include SIZE=N where N is any number between 1 and 7. The number 1 is the smallest text size and 7 is the largest text size. The default text size is about 3 on the font scale.

To change the font, include a <FONT FACE="name of font"> inside the font tags. For example, to change the font to Arial, use <FONT> <FONT FACE="Arial">text</FONT>. To do this exercise, you must have the font Arial on your computer.

Changing the text color is a bit more complicated than changing the size and font of the text. Inside the font tags, the color is specified with the <FONT COLOR= "rrggbb"> where rr is two hexadecimal numbers that specify the amount of red; gg specifies the amount of green; and bb specifies the amount of blue. If you want the text to be red, then specify FF0000 where FF is the hexadecimal equivalent to 255. If you want black text, then use 000000, and for white use FFFFFF. To change the background color of the page, use the <BODY BG COLOR="rrggbb"> inside the body tag. To change the default text color, use <BODY TEXT="rrggbb"></BODY>. See Figure 21.3.

Many colors can be indicated by entering the name of the color rather than its hexadecimal number value. Some samples of colors include black, navy, silver, blue, maroon, purple, red, fuchsia, green, teal, lime, aqua, olive, gray, yellow, and white.

Figure 21.3   HTML web page with a centered text, ordered list, and colors

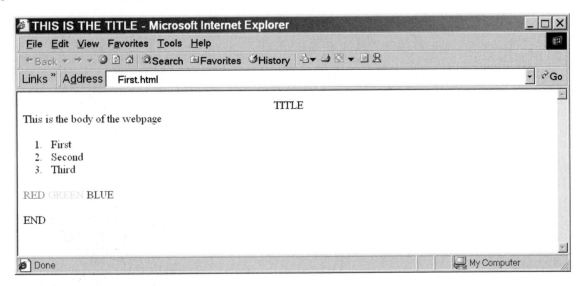

21.2.3   Adding Hyperlinks

Links on a web page are most often achieved through the use of hypertext. Hypertext is text that is connected or hyperlinked to other information on the WWW. When you click on Hypertext, it will take you to the information where the link is anchored. Hypertext is colored and underlined to set it off from the rest of the text. The default color for hypertext is blue, but it can be changed.

```
<HTML>

<HEAD>
  <TITLE>THIS IS THE TITLE</TITLE>

  <META NAME="KEYWORD" CONTENTS="HOT,IMPORTANT">
  <META NAME="DESCRIPTION" CONTENTS="This is a sample website">
</HEAD>

<BODY>
  <CENTER>TITLE</CENTER>
  This is the body of the webpage  <OL>
    <LI>First
    <LI>Second
    <LI>Third
  </OL>

  <FONT COLOR="FF0000">RED
  <FONT COLOR="00FF00">GREEN
  <FONT COLOR="0000FF">BLUE

  <BR><BR>
  <FONT COLOR="000000">END
</BODY>
</HTML>
```

Essential to creating hypertext links are the anchor tags <A> </A>. The anchor tags enclose text that will become the hypertext link. For example, if you want to create a hypertext link to the Acme Toy Company, start by enclosing the text with the anchor tabs. By themselves, the anchor tags do nothing; they must contain information that indicates where the Acme home page is located. We need to add an attribute to the tag that has the address. This attribute is called the hypertext reference, or HREF. For example, to have the Acme Toy Company link to the Acme home page, use

```
<A HREF= "http://www.acme.com\list.htm">Acme Toy Company</A>
```

When links are made between files that recode on the same server and in the same directory, only a partial address or URL is required. The partial address is called a relative URL address. For example, if you have a file called LIST.HTM in the same directory, you can then use

```
<A HREF= "list.htm">Acme Toy Company</A>
```

21.2.4   Adding Pictures

Using pictures helps create an attractive web page. To add a picture (either a GIF or JPG file), use the <IMG tab>, which is another singlet. Inside the <IMG> tag, preceded by a space, include the attribute SRC, which refers to the source or location of the image. The SRC attribute is followed by an equal sign (=) and the URL, in quotations, for the location of the graphic file. For example, to add a picture of the LOGO.JPG, use

```
<IMG SRC=   "LOGO.JPG">
```

or

```
<IMG SRC=   "PICTURES\LOGO.JPG">
```

if the LOGO.JPG is located in the PICTURES directory, which is located underneath the directory of the current web page that you are viewing or using.

Here we assume that the LOGO.JPG is located in the same directory as the current page. The web page does not have the picture embedded into the web page, but rather, it is a separate file shown by a link. Therefore, if you copy a web page, you also need to copy the individual pictures.

Hyperlinks are not limited to text; they can also be images. The following shows how to display the LOGO.JPG which is linked to the ACME.COM home page.

```
<A HREF="http://www.acme.com"> <IMGSRC="LOGO.JPG"></A>
```

21.2.5   Forms and Common Gateway Interface

The common gateway interface (CGI) is a standard for interfacing external applications with web servers. A plain HTML web page is a static document because it does not change. A CGI program, on the other hand, is executed in real-time, so that it can output dynamic information. For example, say that you wanted to "hook up" your server database to the World Wide Web, to allow people from all over the world to query it. Basically, you need to create a CGI program that the PC with the web page will execute to transmit information to the database engine, receive the results back, and display them to the client.

When a web server executes a CGI program, it typically begins with displaying the HTML form on the screen. The form provides space for specific data items in text boxes, pulldown boxes, check boxes, radio buttons, and so on. The form typically has a Submit button that a user can click to submit the entry, and some will have a Clear button to reset the data values to their default values. The FORM tag in the HTML web page specifies a form to complete. More than one fill-out form can be in a single document, but forms cannot be nested (one inside of another).

To create a form, use the </FORM></FORM> tags. Inside the form, identify inputs using the <input> tag. The <input> tag has several inputs including the type, value, size, and maximum length. See Table 21.1.

Table 21.1   Input tag

Attribute	Description
Type	Specifies the type of input. Choices include Text, Checkboxes, and Radio (radio buttons). The default type is Text.
Value	Inserts labels on the form to indicate the input
Size	Specifies the size of the input
Maximum Length	Specifies the maximum length of the input

To create a Submit Query button, use <INPUT TYPE="SUBMIT">, which will submit the data into the specified database. To create a Reset button, which will reset all values back to their default values, use <INPUT TYPE="RESET">. See Figure 21.4.

```
<html>

<FORM action= "http://www.acme.com/script/"
method="GET">

  Name: <INPUT TYPE="TEXT" NAME="Name"
  Size="35"><BR>
  <BR>

  E-mail: <INPUT TYPE="TEXT" NAME="E-mail"
  SIZE="35"><BR>
  <BR><BR>

  Sex: <BR>
  Male<INPUT TYPE="RADIO" NAME="sex">
  Female<Input Type="RADIO": NAME="sex">
  <BR><BR>

  Check if you want to be added to our mailing list:
  <Input Type="checkbox" NAME="mailinglist">
  <BR><BR><BR>

  <INPUT TYPE="SUBMIT">
  <INPUT TYPE="RESET">
</FORM>

</html>
```

The METHOD attribute, which is entered into the <FORM> tag, specifies what to do with the data that are entered into the form. The <FORM METHOD=POST> sends the information to the database. For example:

<FORM ACTION="http://www.acme.com/script" METHOD=POST>

The Practical Extraction and Report Language (PERL), is a programming language especially designed for processing text. Because of its strong text-processing abilities, PERL has become a popular language for writing CGI scripts. PERL is an interpretive language and so makes it easy to build and test simple programs.

21.2.6   Dynamic HTML and Active Server Pages

For the most part, HTML creates static and unanimated documents. Once a web page is loaded into a browser window, it does not change in content or form without being reloaded. This truly limits

Figure 21.4   HTML web page acting as a form

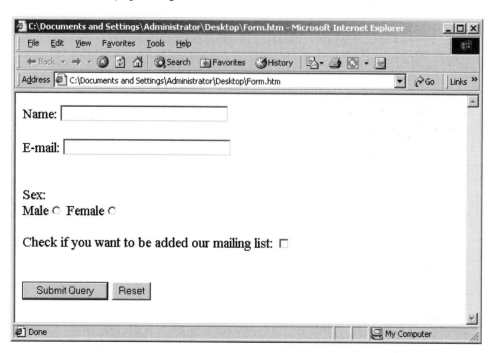

HTML's potential as an interactive multimedia format. To make the Web a more compelling medium, HTML must provide web authors with the ability to dynamically update content; change the appearance of content; and hide, show, and animate content.

Active server page (ASP) is a specification for a dynamically created web page with an .ASP extension that utilizes ActiveX scripting. When a browser requests an ASP, the web server generates a page with HTML code and sends it back to the browser. Thus, ASPs are similar to CGI scripts, but they enable Visual Basic programmers to work with familiar tools.

Control over page layout is one of HTML's most obvious limitations. Even with today's third-generation HTML specifications, web authors do not have the ability to lay out pages with the pixel-level accuracy that is available to the traditional desktop publishing author. A standard HTML document cannot specify that text and images be located at exact coordinates, on top of each other, or even that the text be displayed in a particular point size. Since the beginning of HTML's existence, web authors have struggled to get browsers to display HTML content exactly the way they want it.

Dynamic HTML (DHTML) allows content to be displayed with more design flexibility and accuracy through the use of a cascading style sheet (CSS). Using CSS, a standard from the World Wide Web Consortium (W3C), web authors can define fonts, margins, and line spacing for different parts of an HTML document. In addition to these stylistic improvements, CSS allows the absolute positioning of content by specifying x,y coordinates (and even a z index, which allows different elements to overlap).

The Microsoft implementation of DHTML also adds built-in multimedia and data objects (treated as properties of CCS) that can be controlled through scripting languages, allowing for stereo sound, dynamic image manipulation, and even access to serverside databases.

21.2.7   ActiveX, VBScript, and JavaScript

An ActiveX control can be automatically downloaded and executed by a web browser. ActiveX is not a programming language, but rather a set of rules for how applications should share information. Programmers can develop ActiveX controls in a variety of languages, including C, C++, Visual Basic, and Java.

An ActiveX control is similar to a Java applet. Unlike Java applets, however, ActiveX controls have full access to the Windows operating system, which gives them more power than Java applets. With this power, however, comes a certain risk that the applet may damage software or data.

To control this risk, Microsoft developed a registration system so that browsers can identify and authenticate an ActiveX control before downloading it. Another difference between Java applets and ActiveX controls is Java applets can be written to run on all platforms, whereas ActiveX controls are currently limited to Windows environments.

Related to ActiveX is a scripting language called VBScript that enables web authors to embed interactive elements in HTML documents. Just as JavaScript is similar to Java, so VBScript is similar to Visual Basic. Currently, Microsoft Internet Explorer supports Java, JavaScript, and ActiveX, whereas Netscape Navigator browsers support only Java and JavaScript (though plug-ins can enable support of VBScript and ActiveX).

VBScript is an abbreviated version of Visual Basic Scripting Edition, a scripting language developed by Microsoft and supported by Microsoft's Internet Explorer web browser. VBScript is based on the Visual Basic programming language, but is much simpler. It enables web authors to include interactive controls, such as buttons and scroll bars, on their web pages.

JavaScript is a programmable API that allows cross-platform scripting of events, objects, and actions. It allows the page designer to access events such as start-ups, exits, and users' mouse clicks. JavaScript extends the programmatic capabilities of Netscape Navigator (and to a slightly lesser extent, Microsoft's Internet Explorer) to a wide range of authors, and is relatively easy for anyone who can compose HTML.

21.2.8 Extensible Markup Language

XML is an acronym for Extensible Markup Language. Whereas HTML programs are written using tags that are predefined in the language standards, XML is more of a metalanguage. As a metalanguage, it allows users to create their own collection of tags, elements, and attributes, as needed, and in so doing to accurately describe the physical contents of a document. In effect, XML lets you design your own customized markup language for limitless different types of documents. You will notice more use of XML on web pages, especially as Microsoft's implements its .NET initiative, and more applications will support the XML format (e.g., Open Office and future versions of Microsoft Office).

21.2.9 Web Page Editors

Today, many web pages are created using a web page editing program such as Microsoft Front Page. Using these programs, you can create a web page similar to one in Microsoft Word or Microsoft PowerPoint. In fact, both of these programs also have the capability to save as an HTML format, but they do not have the full capability of creating a web page as web page editors do.

21.3 SECURE COMMUNICATION OVER THE INTERNET

Most companies with connections to the Internet have implemented firewall solutions to protect the corporate network from unauthorized users coming in—and unauthorized Internet sessions going out—via the Internet. Although firewalls do guard against intrusion and unauthorized use, they cannot guarantee the security of the link between a workstation and server on opposite sides of a firewall nor the security of the actual message being conveyed.

To create this level security, two related Internet protocols, Secure Sockets Layer (SSL) and Secure Hypertext Transfer Protocol (S-HTTP), ensure that sensitive information passing through an Internet link is safe from prying eyes. Whereas SSL is designed to establish a secure connection between two computers, S-HTTP is designed to send individual messages securely. SSL and S-HTTP have very different designs and goals, so it is possible to use the two protocols together.

The **Secure Socket Layer (SSL)** protocol operates at the transport layer, such as at the HTTP, FTP, NNTP, and SMTP levels. When both a client (usually in the form of a web browser) and a server support SSL, any data transmitted between the two become encrypted. Microsoft Internet Explorer and Netscape Navigator both support the SSL protocol at the browser level.

When an SSL client wants to communicate with an SSL-compliant server, the client initiates a request to the server, which in turn sends a X.509 standard certificate back to the client. The certificate includes the server's public key and preferred cryptographic algorithms, or ciphers.

The client then creates a key to be used for that session, encrypts the key with the public key sent by the server, and sends the newly created session key to the server. After it receives this key, the server authenticates itself by sending a message encrypted with the key back to the client, proving that the message is coming from the proper server. After this handshake process, which results in the client and server agreeing on the security level, all data transfer between that client and that server for a particular session is encrypted using the session key. When a secure link has been created, the first part of the URL will change from http:// to https://. SSL supports several cryptographic algorithms to handle the authentication and encryption routines.

Secure Hypertext Transfer Protocol (S-HTTP) is simply an extension of HTTP, and is created by SSL running under HTTP. The protocol was developed as an implementation of the RSA encryption standard. While SSL operates at the transport layer, S-HTTP supports secure end-to-end transactions by adding cryptography to messages at the application layer. Whereas SSL is application independent, S-HTTP is tied to the HTTP protocol.

An S-HTTP message consists of three parts:

- HTTP message
- Sender's cryptographic preferences
- Receiver's preferences

The sender integrates both preferences, which results in a list of cryptographic enhancements to be applied to the message.

S-HTTP, like SSL, can be used to provide electronic commerce without customers worrying about who might intercept their credit card numbers or other personal information. To decrypt an S-HTTP message, the recipient must look at the message headers, which designate which cryptographic methods were used to encrypt the message. Then, to decrypt the message, the recipient uses a combination of his or her previously stated and current cryptographic preferences and the sender's previously stated cryptographic preferences. S-HTTP does not require that the client possess a public key certificate, which means that secure transactions can take place at any time without needing individuals to provide a key (as in session encryption with SSL).

21.4   INTRODUCTION TO INTERNET INFORMATION SERVICES

Internet Information Services (IIS) 5.0 is a built-in web server found in the Windows 2000 Server, and IIS 6.0 is found in Windows Server 2003. IIS makes it easy to share documents and information across a company intranet or the Internet. IIS, the fastest web server for Windows 2000 Server and Windows Server 2003, is completely integrated with Microsoft Active Directory directory service. This combination of the Web and operating system services makes it possible to deploy scalable and reliable Web-based applications.

The standard Internet services (the Web and FTP servers) reside in a process called Inetinfo. In addition to these Internet services, this process contains the shared thread pool, cache, and logging services of IIS. IIS includes the following components:

- WWW server—Supports HTTP, allowing users to publish content to the Internet.
- File transfer protocol (FTP) server—Supports the FTP protocol to transfer files between computers on a TCP/IP network.
- Simple Mail Transfer Protocol (SMTP) server—Allows IIS to be an e-mail client so that users can access their e-mail using web-based applications.
- Network News Transfer Protocol (NNTP) server—Allows a commercial-grade electronic discussion group or forum. (The NNTP is beyond the scope of this book.)

By sharing the same security model (user accounts) as Windows 2000 Server and Windows Server 2003, IIS eliminates the need for additional user-account administration. IIS administration also borrows existing Windows server tools such as System Monitor, Event Viewer, and MMC to conduct similar administrative procedures.

Microsoft World Wide Web (WWW) Service supports HTTP, allowing users to publish content to the Internet. The Web is the most graphical service on the Internet and has the most sophisticated linking capabilities. Whether your site is on the intranet or on the Internet, the principles of providing content are the same. You place your files in directories on your website so users can view files with a web browser, such as Microsoft Internet Explorer or Netscape Communicator. The documents include HTML format, which includes text, graphics, animation, or video.

21.4.1   Installing IIS

Internet Information Services is installed on Windows 2000 Server by default. To reduce the attack of the system, IIS 6.0 is not installed by default in Windows Server 2003. You can remove IIS or select additional components by using the Add/Remove Programs application in Control Panel.

To install IIS, add components, or remove components, follow these steps:

1. Click the Start button, select the Settings option, select the Control Panel option.
2. Double-click the Add/Remove Programs application.
3. Select the Add/Remove Windows Components option.
4. Enable the IIS option by marking the check box next to the IIS option and click on the Next button. If so desired, change the IIS options by clicking on the Details button.
5. Click on the Finish button.

If you upgrade to Windows 2000, IIS 5.0 will be installed by default only if IIS was installed on your previous version of Windows.

The following directories containing user content will remain on your system after you completely uninstall IIS:

\Inetpub
systemroot\Help\iisHelp
systemroot\system32\inetsrv

The online documentation is also available when performing remote administration tasks. To reach the documentation, start a browser and type http://*servername*/iishelp/iis/misc/default.asp, where servername is the name of the computer running IIS. If you are at the IIS server, you can also use http://localhost/iishelp/iis/misc/default.asp.

21.4.2   Administering IIS

The IIS snap-in is an administration tool for IIS that was integrated with other administrative functions of Windows 2000. In previous releases, this tool was called the Internet Service Manager.

To launch the IIS console, do the following:

1. Click the Start button, select the Programs option, select the Administrative Tools option, and select the Computer Management option.
2. Under the Server Applications and Services node, expand Internet Information Services.

Another way to launch the IIS is to start the MMC console and use the Internet Information Services snap-in. See Figure 21.5.

With IIS, you can also manage the sites remotely. You can use either the IIS console or you can use a browser-based Internet Services Manager (HTML). You can also use Microsoft Terminal Services over a network connection to remotely administer IIS. Although Internet Services Manager (HTML) offers many of the same features as the snap-in, property changes that require coordination with Windows utilities, such as certificate mapping, cannot be made with Internet Services Manager (HTML).

Figure 21.5   MMC console with Internet Information Services snap-in

Internet Services Manager (HTML) uses a website listed as Administration Web Site to access IIS properties. When IIS is installed, a port number between 2000 and 9999 is randomly selected and assigned to this website. The site responds to web browser requests for all domain names installed on the computer, provided the port number is appended to the address. If basic authentication is used, the administrator will be asked for a user name and password when the site is reached. Only members of the Windows Administrators group can use the site. Website Operators can also administer websites remotely.

To enable the browser-based Internet Services Manager (HTML), do the following:

1. In the IIS snap-in on the local computer, open the property sheets for the Administration Web Site and note the TCP port number on the Web Site property sheet.
2. In the Directory Security property sheet, click the Edit button under IP address and domain name restrictions to set permissions for computers that will be used to administer IIS remotely.

To start the browser-based Internet Services Manager (HTML), start a browser and type the domain name for the website followed by the assigned port number of the administration site. For example, http://www.acme.com:5453/. See Figure 21.6.

Website Operators are a special group of users who have limited administrative privileges on individual websites. Operators can administer properties that affect only their respective sites. They do not have access to properties that affect IIS, the Windows server computer hosting IIS, or the network. Therefore, each Operator can act as the site administrator and can change or reconfigure the website as necessary. For example, the Operator can set website access permissions, enable logging, change the default document or footer, set content expiration, and enable content ratings features. The website Operator is not permitted to change the identification of websites, configure the anonymous user name or password, throttle bandwidth, create virtual directories or change their paths, or change application isolation. Because Operators have more limited privileges than website Administrators, they are unable to remotely browse the file system and therefore cannot set properties on directories and files, unless a UNC path is used.

To add an Operator, follow these steps:

1. In the Internet Information Services snap-in, select Web Site and open its property sheets.
2. On the Operators property sheet, under Web Site Operators, click the Add button. This opens the Add Users and Groups window.

Figure 21.6   The browser-based Internet Services Manager (HTML)

3. Either select a user or group from the Names list or select another name list from the List Names From box.
4. Select a member from a group of users by clicking the Members button and selecting the member from the window.
5. Search for a user or group on a network by clicking the Search button.

To remove an Operator, do the following:

1. In the Internet Information Services snap-in, select Web Site and click the Properties button to display its property sheets.
2. On the Operators property sheet, under Web Site Operators, select the user or groups and click the Remove button. See Figure 21.7.

Note that Web Site Operator accounts need not be members of a Windows Administrators group.

21.4.3   Home Directories

Each website or FTP site must have one home directory—a central location for published pages. It contains a home page or index file that welcomes customers and contains links to other pages in the site. The home directory is mapped to your site's domain name or to your server name. For example, if your site's Internet domain name is www.acme.com and your home directory is C:\INETPUB\WWWROOT, then browsers use the URL http://www.acme.com to access files in your home directory. If you have an intranet and the server name is ACME, then the browsers would use the http://acme URL to access files in your home directory.

When you install IIS and create a new website, a default home directory is created. The default directory for the World Wide Web server is C:\INETPUB\WWWROOT directory and the default

Figure 21.7   Specifying Web Site Operators

directory for the FTP server is C:\INETPUB\FTPROOT directory. To change the home directory do the following:

1. In the Internet Information Services snap-in, right-click Web Site or FTP Site and select the Properties option.
2. Click the Home Directory tab, and then specify where your home directory is located. You can select any of the following:
   - Directory located on a hard disk on your computer
   - Shared directory located on another computer
   - Redirection to a URL (Browsers requesting this URL are forwarded to a new URL. You cannot redirect an FTP directory.)
3. In the text box, specify the path name, share name, or URL of your directory See Figure 21.8.

If you select a directory on a network share, you may need to enter a user name and password to access the resource. We recommend that you use the *IUSR_computername* account. If you use an account that has administration permissions on the server, clients can gain access to server operations, which would seriously jeopardize the security of your network.

21.4.4   Virtual Servers

Normally, a domain name such as WWW.ACME.COM refers to a single computer host. You can, however, configure a single server to appear as different hosts. You might, for example, create virtual servers, one for each department in your organization, or be an ISP that is hosting several sites for various clients. Each of the sites would be recognized by a different IP address in your DNS server, but all would be hosted on the same server. They are called virtual servers because they are hosted on the same physical server.

To create a virtual server, you must have a unique IP address for the virtual server. If you are acting as your own ISP, simply choose an available IP address from your own subnet. If you connect through an outside ISP, then contact the ISP and request an IP address for each virtual server.

After identifying the IP address of each server, you need to plan how you will create the directory structure to contain the files for the virtual servers. Each virtual server needs its own root directory, which

Figure 21.8 Specifying the folder that will hold the web pages

can be located on the same disk as all other virtual servers' directories or on a separate disk. For example, your primary server web root for www.acme.com may be D:\INETPUB\WWWROOT, and the root directory for CLIENT2.COM may be E:\INETPUB\CLIENT2ROOT; or, if you are placing them on the same disk, you may use D:\INETPUB\WWWROOT for www.acme.com and D:\INETPUB\CLIENT2 for client2.com.

To add new sites to a computer by launching the Site Wizard, do the following:

1. In the Internet Information Services snap-in, select the computer or a site and click the Action button.
2. Click New and then Web Site or FTP Site to launch the Site Wizard. Click on the Next button.
3. Type in the description or name of the web or FTP site.
4. Enter the IP address and TCP port to be used by the web or FTP site. Click on the Next button.
5. Specify the home directory to be used by the site. Click on the Next button.
6. Specify the Access Permissions and click on the Next button.
7. Click on the Finish button.

The default website uses all of the IP addresses that are not assigned to other sites. Only one site can be set to use unassigned IP addresses.

Multiple domain names can be hosted on a single computer that is running Microsoft IIS using virtual servers. The three ways of hosting virtual servers on IIS are as follows:

- IP address
- Port number
- Host header name

To use multiple IP addresses, add the host name and its corresponding IP address to your DNS servers. Then clients need only type the text name in a browser to reach your website. If you use multiple IP addresses, you will need an additional network card for each IP address.

In TCP/IP networking, a **port** is a mechanism that allows a computer to simultaneously support multiple communication sessions with computers and programs on the network. A port directs the request to a particular service that can be found at that IP address. The destination of a packet can be further defined by using a unique port number. The port number is determined when the connection is established. See Table 21.2.

Table 21.2   Default port setting

Service	Port
FTP	21
Telnet	23
SMTP	25
WWW	80
NNTP	119
SSL	443
NNTP with SSL	563

The Internet Assigned Numbers Authority (IANA) defines the unique parameters and protocol values necessary for operation of the Internet and its future development. In the past, these numbers were documented through the RFC document series. Since that time, the assignments have been listed on the IANA Web site (http://www.isi.edu/in-notes/iana/assignments/port-numbers), which is constantly updated and revised when new information is available and new assignment are made. By definition, dynamic ports are randomly assigned; therefore, they cannot be known until they are assigned. Private ports are not registered with the IANA, but are used by software applications.

By using appended port numbers, your site would only need one IP address to host many sites. For clients to reach your site, then, they would append a port number at the end of the static IP address (except for the default website, which uses port 80).

If a visitor attempts to contact your site with an older browser (before Microsoft Internet 3.0 or Netscape Navigator 2.0) that does not support host headers, that visitor is directed to the default website assigned to that IP address (if a default site is enabled), which may not necessarily be the site requested. Also, if a request from any browser is received for a site that is currently stopped, the visitor receives the default website instead. For this reason, carefully consider what the default website displays. Typically, ISPs display their own home page as the default, and not one of their customers' websites. This prevents requests for a stopped site from reaching the wrong site. Additionally, the default site can include a script that supports the use of host header names for older browsers.

You can also use host header names with a single static IP address to host multiple sites. Like the previous method, you would still add the host name to your DNS server. The difference is that once a request reaches the computer, IIS uses the host name passed in the HTTP header to determine which site the clients are requesting.

To change or assign an IP address, port, or host header name, right-click the site and select the Properties option. The IP address and TCP port can be set in the Web Site tab. See Figure 21.9. To specify multiple site configuration, click on the Advanced button of the host header name, then click on the Advanced button. When using SSL, you can assign only one host header name to an IP address because the domain name is specified in the server certificate; however, you can have multiple server certificates, multiple IP addresses, and multiple SSL ports per website.

21.4.5   Virtual Directories

Before installing IIS, you must do a little planning. First, plan the amount of disk space that you anticipate you will need by determining the total size of files to be included in each folder and add an estimated amount for growth. Next, decide where your web and FTP files will be stored. By default, IIS creates a folder named INETPUB on drive C. Create a folder on your data disk that will serve as the root folder for all of your Internet resources. For example, if you are using drive D to store the data, create D:\INETPUB or any other name of your choosing. After you have created the root folder for

Figure 21.9   Website TCP ports

the Internet resources, create root folders within that folder for the web and FTP services. For example, create folders named \INETPUB\WWWROOT and \INETPUB\FTPROOT.

In addition to creating virtual servers, you can create virtual directories. A virtual directory exists as a physical directory on disk, but it appears under the root service directory even if it is located on another disk. In effect, virtual directories are like a mountable file system in which directories from disparate physical directories and disks can appear to be a homogenous directory structure. For example, assume that your web root is D:\INETPUB\WWWROOT and contains the general resources for your website. You also want to host three different product catalogs, but for fault tolerance, you want to place each catalog on a separate physical disk. So, you might create E:\INETPUB\CAT1ROOT, F:\INETPUB\CAT2ROOT, and G:\INETPUB\CAT3ROOT. Then specify each of these three directories as virtual directories under D:\INETPUB\WWWROOT. When the client browses the site, it appears that the three catalog directories are subdirectories of WWWROOT.

An important point to understand about virtual directories, however, is that they do not appear in directory listings. For example, if users connect to your FTP site, they will see the root folder, its contents, and any physical subdirectories of that root directory. Virtual directories, even though they are considered logical subdirectories of that root, do not appear in the directory listing. To access virtual directories, users must enter the resource name. Typically, these virtual directories are accessed by using links. Therefore, moving from one virtual directory to another would be transparent to the user.

To create a virtual directory, follow these steps:

1. In the Internet Information Services snap-in, select the Web or FTP Site to which you want to add a directory.
2. Click the Action button, then point to New, and select Virtual Directory.
3. When the New Virtual Directory Wizard starts, click on the Next button.
4. Provide the alias of the virtual directory and click on the Next button. The alias is the name by which the directory is known under the root home directory.
5. Specify the location of the virtual directory and click on the Next button.
6. Specify the access permissions and click on the Next button.
7. Click on the Finish button.

Figure 21.10 Specifying the default web page

If you are using NTFS, you can also create a virtual directory by right-clicking a directory in Windows Explorer, clicking Sharing, and then selecting the Web Sharing property sheet.

To delete a virtual directory, do the following:

1. In the Internet Information Services snap-in, select the virtual directory you want to delete.
2. Click the Action button and select Delete.

Deleting a virtual directory does not delete the corresponding physical directory or files.

21.4.6   Default Documents

When a URL is entered into a browser that does not specify a file name, the default document is generated automatically by the server or is designated by the administrator. Default documents can be a directory's home page or an index page containing a site document directory listing. To add a new default document, do the following:

1. Right-click the website and select the Properties option.
2. On the Documents tab, click the Add button, specify the default document, and click the OK button. See Figure 21.10.

Since you can specify more than one default document, they are served in the order in which the names appear in the list. To change the search order, select a document and click on the arrow buttons. To remove a default document from the list, click Remove.

21.4.7   IIS Security

Microsoft IIS has multiple security options for keeping a server and its data from possible intruders and hackers. The four methods of security that you can apply to your IIS computer are as follows:

- IP Access
- User Authentication
- Web Permission
- File Security (NTFS)

Figure 21.11 IIS security options

You can configure your web server to prevent specific computers, a group of computers, or an entire network from accessing your web server content. See Figure 21.11. When a user initially tries to access your web server content, the server checks the IP address of the user's computer against the server's IP address restriction settings.

To grant access to computers, groups of computers, or domains, follow these steps:

1. In the IIS snap-in, select a website, directory, or file, and open its property sheets.
2. Select the appropriate Directory Security or File Security property sheet. Under IP Address and Domain Name Restrictions, click Edit.
3. In the IP Address and Domain Name Restrictions dialog box, select the Denied Access option. When you select this option, you deny access to all computers and domains, except those to which you specifically grant access.
4. Click Add.
5. In the Grant Access On dialog box, select Single Computer, Group of Computers, or Domain Name options. For more information about these options, click Help.
6. Click the DNS Lookup button to search for computers or domains by name, rather than by IP address. Type in a name, then click OK to close both dialog boxes.

To deny access to computers, groups of computers, or domains, do the following:

1. In the IIS snap-in, select a website, directory, or file, and open its property sheets.
2. Select the appropriate Directory Security or File Security property sheet. Under IP Address and Domain Name Restrictions, click Edit.
3. In the IP Address and Domain Name Restrictions dialog box, select the Granted Access option. When you select this option, you grant access to all computers and domains, except those to which you specifically deny access.
4. Click Add.
5. In the Deny Access On dialog box, select Single Computer, Group of Computers, or Domain Name options. For more information about these options, click Help.
6. Click the DNS Lookup button to search for computers or domains by name, rather than by IP address. IIS will search on the current domain for the computer, and if found, will enter its IP address in the IP address text box. Click OK to close both dialog boxes.

Figure 21.12   Specifying the IP address and domain name restrictions

A group of computers can be either denied or granted access based on the group's network ID and a subnet mask. The network ID is the IP address of a host computer—usually a router for the subnet. The subnet mask determines which part of the IP address is a subnet ID, and which part is a host ID. All computers in a subnet have the same subnet ID, but their own host ID. By specifying a network ID and a subnet mask, you can select a group of computers. See Figure 21.12.

Example 1:

If the host computer has an IP address of 130.200.16.1 and a subnet mask of 255.255.0.0, all computers in that subnet would have IP addresses that begin with 130.200. Therefore using this IP address and subnet mask, specify all computers from 130.200.0.0 to 130.200.255.255.

Example 2:

If you have a network ID of 200.200.200.128 with a subnet mask of 255.255.255.192, you will be specifying the IP addresses of from 200.200.200.128 to 200.200.200.191.

Example 3:

If you have a network ID of 150.150.64.0 with a subnet mask of 255.255.224.0, you will be specifying the IP address of from 150.150.64.0 to 150.150.95.255.

Example 4:

If you have a network ID of 222.34.42.15 with a subnet mask of 255.255.255.240, you will be specifying the IP address of from 222.34.42.16 to 222.34.42.31.

21.4.8   Authentication

You can require users to authenticate themselves by providing a valid Windows user name and password before accessing any information on your server. For IIS, authentication can be set at the website, directory, or file level. IIS provides the following authentication methods for controlling access to content on your server.

WWW Methods

- Anonymous authentication
- Basic authentication
- Digest authentication
- Integrated Windows authentication
- Certificate authentication

FTP Methods

- Anonymous FTP authentication
- Basic FTP authentication

In most situations, all users who attempt to establish a connection with a web server will log on as an anonymous user. **Anonymous authentication** gives users access to the public areas of your website or FTP site without prompting them for a user name or password. When a user attempts to connect to your public website or FTP site, your web server assigns the user to the Windows user account called IUSR_*computername,* where *computername* is the name of the server on which IIS is running.

By default, the IUSR_computername account is included in the Windows user group called Guests. This group has security restrictions, imposed by NTFS permissions, that designate the level of access and the type of content available to public users.

If you have multiple sites on your server, or if you have areas of your site that require different access privileges, then you can create multiple anonymous accounts, one for each website or FTP site, directory, or file. By giving these accounts differing access permissions, or by assigning these accounts to different Windows user groups, you can grant users anonymous access to different areas of your public web and FTP content.

IIS uses the IUSR_*computername* account in the following way:

1. The IUSR_computername account is added to the Guests group on the computer.
2. When a request is received, IIS will impersonate the IUSR_*computername* account before executing any code or accessing any files. IIS is able to impersonate the IUSR_*computername* account because the user name and password for this account are known by IIS.
3. Before returning a page to the client, IIS checks NTFS file and directory permissions to see if the IUSR_*computername* account is allowed access to the file.
4. If access is allowed, authentication completes and the resources are available to the user.
5. If access is not allowed, IIS will attempt to use another authentication method. If none is selected, IIS returns an "HTTP 403 Access Denied" error message to the browser.

If anonymous authentication is enabled, IIS will always try to authenticate using it first, even if other methods are enabled. In some cases, the browser will prompt the user for a user name and password.

The anonymous account must have the user right to log on locally. If the account does not have the Log On Locally permission, IIS will be unable to service any anonymous requests. The IIS installation specifically grants the Log On Locally permission to the IUSR_computername account. The IUSR_computername accounts on domain controllers are not given to guest accounts by default and must be changed to Log On Locally to allow anonymous logons.

The **basic authentication** method is a widely used, industry standard method for collecting user name and password information. Basic authentication proceeds as follows:

1. The user's web browser displays a dialog box where users can enter their previously assigned Windows account user names and passwords.
2. The web browser then attempts to establish a connection using this information. (The password of Base64 is encoded before being sent over the network).
3. If the server rejects the information, the web browser repeatedly displays the dialog box until the user either enters a valid user name and password or closes the dialog box.
4. When the web server verifies that the user name and password correspond to a valid Windows user account, a connection is established.

The advantages of basic authentication are that it is part of the HTTP specification and that it is supported by most browsers. The disadvantage is that web browsers using basic authentication transmit passwords in an unencrypted form. By monitoring communications on your network, someone could easily intercept and decipher these passwords by using publicly available tools. Therefore, basic authentication is not recommended unless you are confident that the connection between the user and your web server is secure, such as a direct cable connection or a dedicated line. Note that integrated Windows authentication takes precedence over basic authentication. The browser will choose integrated Windows authentication and will attempt to use the current Windows logon information before prompting the user for a user name and password. Currently, only Internet Explorer, versions 2.0 and later, support integrated Windows authentication.

New to IIS 5.0, **digest authentication** offers the same features as basic authentication but involves a different way of transmitting the authentication credentials. These pass through a one-way process, often referred to as hashing. The result of this process is called a hash, or message digest, and it is not feasible to decrypt it; that is, the original text cannot be deciphered from the hash.

Digest authentication proceeds as follows:

1. The server sends the browser certain information, which will be used in the authentication process.
2. The browser adds this information to its user name and password plus some other information and performs a hash on it. The additional information will help to prevent someone from copying the hash value and reusing it.
3. The resulting hash is sent over the network to the server along with the additional information in clear text.
4. The server then adds the additional information to a plain-text copy it has of the client's password and hashes all of the information.
5. The server then compares the hash value it received with the one it just made.
6. Access is granted only if the two numbers are absolutely identical.

The additional information is added to the password before hashing so that no one can capture the password hash and use it to impersonate the true client. Values are added that help to identify the client, the client's computer, the realm or domain to which the client belongs, and a time stamp. Because digest authentication is a new HTTP 1.1 feature, not all browsers support it. If a noncompliant browser makes a request on a server that requires digest authentication, the server will reject the request and send the client an error message. Digest authentication is supported only for domains with a Windows 2000 or Windows Server 2003 domain controller.

Integrated Windows authentication (formerly called NTLM or Windows NT Challenge/ Response authentication) is a secure form of authentication, because the user name and password are not sent across the network. When you enable integrated Windows authentication, the user's browser proves its knowledge of the password through a cryptographic exchange (involving hashing) with your web server.

Integrated Windows authentication can use both the Kerberos v5 authentication protocol and its own challenge/response authentication protocol. If Directory Services is installed on the server, and the browser is compatible with the Kerberos v5 authentication protocol, then both the Kerberos v5 protocol and the challenge/response protocol are used; otherwise only the challenge/response protocol is used.

The Kerberos v5 authentication protocol is a feature of the Windows 2000 and Windows Server 2003 Distributed Services architecture. For Kerberos v5 authentication to be successful, both the client and server must have a trusted connection to a key distribution center (KDC) and be compatible with Directory Services.

Unlike basic authentication, Integrated Windows authentication does not initially prompt users for a user name and password. The current Windows user information on the client computer is used for the integrated Windows authentication. However, if the authentication exchange initially fails to identify the user, the browser will prompt the user for a Windows user account user name and password, which it will process by using integrated Windows authentication. Internet Explorer will continue to prompt the user until the user enters a valid user name and password or closes the Prompt dialog box.

Although integrated Windows authentication is secure, it does have two limitations. Only Microsoft Internet Explorer, version 2.0 or later, supports this authentication method. Integrated Windows authentication does not work over HTTP Proxy connections. Therefore, integrated Windows authentication is best suited for an intranet environment, where both user and web server computers are in the same domain, and where administrators can ensure that every user has Microsoft Internet Explorer, version 2.0 or later.

You can also use your web server's secure sockets layer (SSL) security features for two types of authentication. You can use a server certificate to allow users to authenticate your website before they transmit personal information, such as a credit card number; or you can use client certificates to authenticate users who are requesting information on your website. SSL authenticates by checking the contents of an encrypted digital identification submitted by the user's web browser during the logon process. Users obtain client certificates from a mutually trusted third-party organization. Server certificates usually contain information about your company and the organization that issued the certificate. Client certificates usually contain identifying information about the user and the organization that issued the certificate.

You can associate, or map, client certificates to Windows user accounts on your web server. After you create and enable a certificate map, each time a user logs on with a client certificate, your web server automatically associates that user to the appropriate Windows user account. This way, you can automatically authenticate users who log on with client certificates, without requiring the use of either basic, digest, or integrated Windows authentication. You can either map one client certificate to one Windows user account or many client certificates to one account. For example, if you have several different departments or businesses on your server, each with its own website, then you can use many-to-one mapping to map all client certificates of each department or company to its own website. In this way, each site would provide access only to its own clients.

You can configure your FTP server to allow anonymous access to FTP resources. If anonymous authentication is enabled, IIS will always try to use it first, even if basic authentication is enabled. If you select anonymous authentication for a resource, all requests for that resource will be taken without prompting the user for a user name or password. This is possible because IIS automatically creates a Windows user account called IUSR_*computername,* where *computername* is the name of the server on which IIS is running. This process is similar to web-based anonymous authentication.

To establish an FTP connection with your web server by using basic authentication, users must log on with a user name and password that corresponds to a valid Windows user account. If the FTP server cannot verify a user's identity, the server returns an error message. FTP authentication is not very secure, because the user transmits the password and user name across the network in an unencrypted form.

21.4.9   Web Server and NTFS Permissions

Web server permissions allow you to control how users access and interact with specific websites. You can use these permissions to control whether users visiting your website are allowed to view a particular page, upload information, or run scripts on the site. Different from NTFS permissions, web server permissions apply to all users who access your website.

To change the web server permissions, right-click the directory, select the Properties option, and select the Directory tab. If you select the website, the web server permissions are under the Home Directory tab. See Tables 21.3 and 21.4.

For example, disabling the web server's read permission for a particular file will prevent all users from viewing that file, regardless of the NTFS permissions applied to those user accounts. However, enabling read permission will allow all users to view the file, unless NTFS permissions that restrict

Table 21.3   Web file/directory permissions

Permission	Description
Script Source Access	Allows users to access a source code if either read or write permissions are set. The source code includes scripts in ASP applications.
Read	Allows users to read or download files or directories and their associated properties.
Write	Allows users to upload files and their associated properties to the enabled directory on your server, or changes content in a write-enabled file. Write can only be done with a browser that supports the PUT feature of the HTTP 1.1 protocol standard.
Directory Browsing	Allows the user to see a hypertext listing of the files and subdirectories in this virtual directory. Virtual directories will not appear in directory listings; users must know a virtual directory's alias.

Table 21.4   Web execute permissions

Permission	Description
None	Only static files, such as HTML or image files, can be accessed.
Scripts Only	Only scripts, such as ASP scripts, can be run.
Scripts and Executables	All file types can be accessed or executed.

access have also been applied. After setting NTFS permissions, your web server must be configured with an authentication method to identify users prior to granting access to restricted files.

When you select the Write and Execute check boxes, you enable users to upload and execute programs on your web server. In this case, a user could upload and then run a potentially destructive program on your server. When possible, select the Script option rather than the Execute option, because the Script option limits users to executing programs associated with an installed script engine, not any executable application.

21.4.10   Throttling Bandwidth

If the network or Internet connection used by your web server is also used by other services such as e-mail or news, you may want to limit the bandwidth used by your web server so bandwidth is available for the other services. If you are running more than one website, you can individually throttle the bandwidth used by each site.

To determine how much bandwidth your server is using, use System Monitor to examine the bytes total/per second or current bandwidth counter in the Network Interface object. With a normal load, your server should not use more than 50% of its total available bandwidth of the network connection. The remaining bandwidth is used during peak periods. If your server is subject to large peaks or extreme spikes, it is wise to keep the normal load at even lower than 50%.

To throttle the bandwidth used by IIS, do the following:

1. In the Internet Information Services snap-in, select the computer that is running IIS.
2. On the Internet Information Services property sheet, select the Enable Bandwidth Throttling check box.
3. In the Maximum Network Use box, type the maximum number of kilobytes per second (KB/s) that you want to be used by IIS.

To throttle the bandwidth used by an individual website, do the following:

1. In the Internet Information Services snap-in, select the website and click the Properties button to display its property sheets.
2. On the Performance property sheet, select the Enable Bandwidth Throttling option.
3. In the Maximum Network Use box, type the maximum number of kilobytes per second you want to be used by the site.

21.4.11   IIS and Windows Server 2003

Windows Server 2003 includes Internet Information Services (IIS) 6.0, which offers better performance and enhanced security. IIS 6.0 introduces a new kernel-mode driver for HTTP parsing and caching that is specifically tuned to increase web server throughput and scalability of multiprocessor computers. IIS 6.0 also allows a significant increase in the number of sites that a single server can host.

IIS is not installed by default on Windows Server 2003. Furthermore, when you initially install IIS, the service is installed in a highly secure and "locked" mode. By default, IIS serves only static content; therefore, features such as ASP, Indexing Service, Server-Side Includes, WebDAV publishing, and

FrontPage Server Extensions do not work. To serve dynamic content and "unlock" these features, you must enable them through Web Service Extensions in the IIS Manager.

21.5   WEBDAV

Web-distributed authoring and versioning (WebDAV) extends the HTTP/1.1 protocol to allow clients to publish, lock, and manage resources on the Web. Since it is integrated into IIS, WebDAV allow clients to do the following:

- Manipulate resources in a WebDAV publishing directory on your server.
- Modify properties associated with certain resources.
- Search the content and properties of files in a WebDAV directory.

To set up a publishing directory, follow these steps:

1. On the Windows Desktop, click My Computer.
2. In the Inetpub directory, create a physical directory. You can actually put this directory anywhere you want, except under the Wwwroot directory. Wwwroot is an exception because its default discretionary ACLs are different from those on other directories.
3. In the IIS snap-in, create a virtual directory.
4. Type WebDAV as the alias for this virtual directory, and link it to the physical directory that you created earlier in the second step.
5. Grant read, write, and browsing access permissions for the virtual directory to the users who need to publish and manage those documents. Granting write access does not give clients the ability to modify active server pages (ASPs) or any other script-mapped files. To allow these files to be modified, grant write permission and script source access after creating the virtual directory.

You can access a WebDAV publishing directory through one of the following Microsoft products.

- Windows 2000 or Windows Server 2003 connects to a WebDAV server through the Add Network Place Wizard and displays the contents of a WebDAV directory as if it were part of the same file system as on your local computer. Once connected, you can drag and drop files, retrieve and modify file properties, and do many other file system tasks.
- You can connect to a WebDAV directory through Internet Explorer 5 (or higher version) on the Windows operating systems. From the File menu in Internet Explorer, click Open. In the Open box, type the URL for the desired WebDAV directory. Select the Open as Web Folder box, and click OK.
- Create a document in any Office 2000 or Office XP application. From the File menu, click Save As. In the left column of the Save As dialog box, click My Network Places.

Because WebDAV is integrated with Windows and IIS, it borrows the security features offered by both. These features include the IIS permissions specified in the IIS snap-in and the discretionary access control lists (DACLs) in the NTFS file system.

21.6   HTTP ERROR CODES

HTTP status codes are returned by Web servers to indicate the status of a request. The status code is a three-digit code indicating the particular response. The first digit of this code identifies the class of the status code. The remaining two digits correspond to the specific condition within the response class. Table 21.5 outlines all status codes defined for the HTTP/1.1 draft specification outlined in IETF RFC 2068.

Table 21.5 HTTP error codes (4xx)

Code Number	Code Description	
400	Bad Request	
401	Unauthorized	
	401.1	Logon failed
	401.2	Logon failed due to server configuration
	401.3	Unauthorized due to ACL on resource
	401.4	Authorization failed by filter
	401.5	Authorization failed by ISAPI/CGI application
402	Payment Required	
403	Forbidden	
	403.1	Execute access forbidden
	403.2	Read access forbidden
	403.3	Write access forbidden
	403.4	SSL required
	403.5	SSL 128 required
	403.6	IP address rejected
	403.7	Client certificate required
	403.8	Site access denied
	403.9	Too many users
	403.10	Invalid configuration
	403.11	Password change
	403.12	Mapper denied access
	403.13	Client certificate revoked
	403.14	Directory listing denied
	403.15	Client access licenses exceeded
	403.16	Client certificate untrusted or invalid
	403.17	Client certificate has expired or is not yet valid
404	Not Found	
405	Method Not Allowed	
406	Not Acceptable	
407	Proxy Authentication Required	
408	Request Timeout	
409	Conflict	
410	Gone	
411	Length Required	
412	Precondition Failed	
413	Request Entity Too Long	
414	Request-URI Too Long	
415	Unsupported Media Type	

Table 21.6   HTTP error codes (5xx)

Code Number	Code Description
500	Internal Server Error—An internal server error has caused the server to abort your request. This error condition may also indicate a misconfiguration with the web server. However, the most common reason for 500 server errors is when you try to execute a script that has syntax errors.
501	Not Implemented—This code is generated by a web server when the client requests a service that is not implemented on the server. Typically, nonimplemented codes are returned when a client attempts to POST data to a non-CGI (i.e., the form action tag refers to a nonexecutable file).
503	Service Unavailable—The server is too busy to handle your request or there is some problem along the Internet. Try again later.
502	Bad Gateway—The server, when acting as a proxy, issues this response when it receives a bad response from an upstream or support server.
503	Service Unavailable—The web server is too busy processing current requests to listen to a new client. This error represents a serious problem with the web server (normally solved with a reboot).
504	Gateway Timeout—This code is normally issued by proxy servers when an upstream or support server fails to respond to a request in a timely fashion.
505	HTTP Version Not Supported—The server issues this status code when a client tries to talk using an HTTP protocol that the server either does not support or is configured to ignore.

The 4xx errors indicate that the client has sent bad data or a malformed request to the server. Client errors are generally issued by the web server when a client tries to gain access to a protected area using a bad user name and password. For example, the 403 indicates that the requested resource is forbidden, which generally means you have no privileges to access that page. A 404 indicates that a host server responded to your browser but it cannot find the web page on the server, which usually means that the web page was moved or deleted or that you typed in the wrong URL.

The 5xx errors indicate a server error, which indicates that the client's request could not be successfully processed due to some internal error in the web server. These error codes may indicate something is seriously wrong with the web server. See Table 21.6.

IIS features its own set of custom errors that provide more informative or "friendly" feedback than the default HTTP 1.1 errors which are returned to client browsers. For example, the HTTP 1.1 404 error message, which by default simply reads "Object Not Found" is expanded to read "The Web server cannot find the file/script you asked for. Please check the URL to ensure that the path is correct. Please contact the server's administrator if this problem persists." These friendly custom error messages are set by default in the default website in Internet Service Manager.

To configure friendly error messages in IIS, do the following:

1. In Internet Service Manager, select the website, virtual directory, directory, or file in which you would like to customize HTTP errors and click the Properties button.
2. Select the Custom Errors property sheet. See Figure 21.13.
3. Select the default HTTP error that you would like to change.
4. Click the Edit Properties button.
5. Select URL from the Message Type box.

Figure 21.13   Customizing the standard HTTP errors

6. Type /iisHelp/common/<file name>, where <file name> is the HTML file name of the friendly error message.

7. Friendly error messages are installed by default to the following location: <drive letter>:\WINNT\Help\common. The file names are numbers that correspond to the specific HTTP errors, for example, 400.htm, 401-1.htm, and so on.

21.7   BROWSERS

The most common two browsers are Internet Explorer and Netscape Navigator. In addition to explaining how to use the browser, this section discusses how to configure certain features of the browser that are relevant to managing a network.

21.7.1   Plug-ins

A **plug-in** is a software module that adds a specific feature or service to the browser such as displaying or playing different types of audio or video messages. The two most common plug-ins are Shockwave and RealAudio, but the number of plug-ins available is countless.

Shockwave is a technology developed by Macromedia, Inc. that enables web pages to include multimedia objects. To create a Shockwave object, use Macromedia's multimedia authoring tool called Macromedia Director, and then compress the object with a program called Afterburner. Then insert a reference to the "shocked" file in your web page. To see a Shockwave object, you need the Shockwave plug-in, a program that integrates seamlessly with your web browser. The plug-in is freely available from Macromedia's website. Shockwave supports audio, animation, and video, and it even processes user actions such as mouse clicks. It runs on all Windows platforms and on Macintosh.

Streaming technology is a technique for transferring data such that the data can be processed as a steady and continuous stream. Streaming technologies are becoming increasingly important with the growth of the Internet, because most users do not have fast enough access to download large multimedia files quickly. With streaming, the client browser or plug-in can start displaying the data before the entire file has been transmitted.

For streaming to work, the client side receiving the data must be able to collect and send the data as a steady stream to the application that is processing the data and converting it to sound or pictures.

Thus, if the streaming client receives the data more quickly than required, the client needs to save the excess data in a buffer. If the data do not come quickly enough, however, the presentation of the data will not be smooth.

There are a number of competing streaming technologies emerging. For audio data on the Internet, the *de facto* standard is Progressive Network's RealAudio. RealAudio was developed by RealNetworks and supports FM-stereo-quality sound. To hear a web page that includes a RealAudio sound file, you need a RealAudio player or plug-in. RealVideo is a streaming technology developed by RealNetworks for transmitting live video over the Internet. It uses a variety of data compression techniques and works with both normal IP connections and IP multicast connections.

21.7.2 Cookies

A **cookie** is a message given to a web browser by a web server, which is typically stored in a text file on the PC's hard drive. The message is then sent back to the server each time the browser requests a page from the server.

A command line in the HTML of a document tells the browser to set a cookie of a certain name or value. Here is an example of using a cookie:

```
Set-Cookie: NAME=VALUE; expires=DATE; path=PATH;
domain=DOMAIN_NAME;
```

The main purpose of cookies is to identify users and possibly prepare customized web pages for them. When you enter a website using cookies, you may be asked to fill out a form providing such information as your name and interests. This information is packaged into a cookie and sent to your web browser, which stores it for later use. The next time you go to the same website, your browser will send the cookie to the web server. The server can use this information to present you with custom web pages. So, for example, instead of seeing a generic welcome page, you might see a welcome page with your name on it. Some uses of cookies include keeping track of what a person buys using online ordering systems, personalizing a website, storing a person's profile, storing user IDs, and providing support to older web browsers that do not support host header names.

A cookie cannot be used to get data from your hard drive, get your e-mail address, or steal sensitive information about your person. Early implementations of Java and JavaScript could allow people to do this, but for the most part these security leaks have been plugged. Although a cookie typically makes things easier for the user, the feature is not a necessity.

If you want to disallow cookies, do the following:

If you have Internet Explorer 4.0 or greater:

1. Go to the Tools menu and select the Internet Options menu.
2. Click on the Security tab and click on the Custom Level button.
3. In the "Allow cookies that are stored on your computer" section, select Disable.

If you have Netscape 4.0 or greater:

1. Go to the Edit menu and select the Preferences option.
2. Select the Advanced option.
3. In the Cookies section, select Disable Cookies.

21.7.3 Connection Configuration

For the browser to go through a proxy server, the browser must be configured. These configuration settings include automatic configuration, script configuration, or manual specification. The automatic and script configurations enable you to change settings after you deploy Internet Explorer. By providing a pointer to configuration files on a server, you can change the settings globally without having to change each user's computer. This can help reduce administrative overhead and potentially reduce help desk calls about browser settings.

To use automatic configuration, create an Internet Explorer administration kit (IEAK) profile by using the IEAK Profile Manager. The profile consists of an .ins file and any cabinet (.cab) files generated by the Profile Manager. The profile contains information that is used to configure users' browsers. After creating the profile, place it on a server.

To configure the proxy selection and proxy bypass settings in Internet Explorer, do the following:

1. Open the Tools menu, then click on Internet Options.
2. Click the Connections tab, then click LAN Settings.
3. In the proxy server area, select the Use a Proxy Server check box.
4. Click Advanced, then fill in the proxy location and port number for each Internet protocol that is supported.

In cases when only a single proxy server is used for all protocols, enter the proxy location and port number for the HTTP setting, then select the "Use the same proxy server for all protocols" check box. If you want to manually set the addresses, enable the "Use a proxy server" and specify the address and port number of the proxy server. If you need to specify different addresses and/or port numbers for the various Internet services, click on the Advanced button. See Figure 21.14.

Figure 21.14   Configuring the proxy selection and proxy bypass settings in Internet Explorer

Figure 21.15   Configuring the proxy settings for Netscape

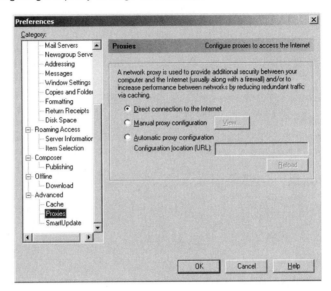

For Netscape, the same basic options are available when you do the following:

1. Open the Edit menu and select the Preferences option.
2. Find and open the Advanced option.
3. Click on the Proxy option. See Figure 21.15.

21.7.4   Internet Explorer Administration Kit

The Internet Explorer administration kit (IEAK) is a software product that makes it easy to create a custom browser that can be deployed across a network or via web download. See Table 21.7 for features and descriptions.

> The IEAK can be downloaded from the following website:
>
> http://www.microsoft.com/windows/ieak/en/default.asp

Table 21.7   Internet Explorer's administration kit

Feature	Description
Customization Wizard	Provides a simple processor for administrators to generate customized versions of Internet Explorer
Custom Browser Settings	To control the cost of managing the browser, customizes and locks down virtually every setting
Enhanced Setup and Deployment Options	Provides greater flexibility and choice about how to distribute your custom browser to your subscribers
On-Demand Install	Lets administrators include components in an IEAK distribution that will not be installed until the user requires them
Easier Remote Connections	The connection manager administration kit (CMAK) allows you to provide a custom dialer and phone book to simplify deployment of preconfigured dial-up/VPN configurations.
Manage Browser Settings	The Internet Explorer Profile Manager makes it easy for administrators to manage browser installations.

SUMMARY

1. Web pages are written using the Hypertext Markup Language (HTML).
2. A web server is a computer that is equipped with the server software that uses Internet protocols such as Hypertext Transfer Protocol (HTTP) and File Transfer Protocol (FTP) to respond to web client requests on a TCP/IP network via web browsers.
3. The web browser is the client program/software that you run on your local machine to gain access to a web server.
4. A gopher was an early system that predates the World Wide Web for organizing and displaying files on Internet servers.
5. The World Wide Web has several search engines that can be used to locate desired documents. A search engine is a program that searches documents for specified keywords and returns a list of the documents where the keywords were found.
6. To create or modify a web page, use a text editor such as EDIT (DOS) or Notepad (Windows).
7. To create network security, two related Internet protocols, Secure Sockets Layer (SSL) and Secure Hypertext Transfer Protocol (S-HTTP), ensure that sensitive information passing through an Internet link is safe from prying eyes.
8. Internet Information Services (IIS) is a built-in web server found in the Windows 2000 and Windows Server 2003 families.
9. You can use either the IIS console or a browser-based Internet Services Manager (HTML).
10. Web site Operators are a special group of users who have limited administrative privileges on individual websites.
11. Each website or FTP site must have one home directory— a central location for published pages.
12. Normally, a domain name such as WWW.ACME.COM refers to a single computer host. You can, however, configure a single server to appear as different hosts.
13. When a URL is entered into a browser that does not specify a file name, the default document is generated automatically by the server or is designated by the administrator.
14. Microsoft IIS has multiple security options for keeping a server and its data from possible intruders and hackers, including restricting IP address, user authentication, web permission, and NTFS file security.
15. Web-distributed authoring and versioning (WebDAV), extends the HTTP/1.1 protocol to allow clients to publish, lock, and manage resources on the Web.
16. HTTP status codes are returned by web servers to indicate the status of a request.
17. A firewall is a system designed to prevent unauthorized access to or from a private network. Firewalls can be implemented in both hardware and software, or a combination of both.
18. A plug-in is a software module that adds a specific feature or service to the browser such as to display or play different types of audio or video messages.
19. A cookie is a message given to a web browser by a web server, which is typically stored in a text file on the PC's hard drive.

QUESTIONS

1. You have created a website for your company on the internet using TCT/IP with both DNS and WINS enabled. Users complain, however, that they can only access the corporate web page by its IP address, 142.33.112.86, not by its domain name, www.acme.com. What is the most likely reason that users cannot connect using http://www.acme.com?
   a. NetBEUI must be installed.
   b. The IP address is not mapped to www.igminc.com in DNS.
   c. The virtual server for the IP address points to the wrong directory.
   d. DHCP is not enabled.
2. You want to create a website to which the general Internet public will be denied access; only company employees with specific IP addresses will be granted access to the site. You open the Advanced tab of the IIS WWW Service Properties page, choose Denied Access, then Add. In the Grant Access On dialog box, you select Group of Computers. You enter the network ID 200.200.200.64 and the subnet mask 255.255.255.224. Which IP addresses will be allowed to access your website?
   a. 200.200.200.32 through 200.200.200.39
   b. 200.200.200.32 through 200.200.200.95
   c. 200.200.200.33 through 200.200.200.64
   d. 200.200.200.64 through 200.200.200.95

3. Pat has no trouble logging on remotely to her company's network with her Windows 2000 user account. However, when she tries to browse the company's website she finds she can access several of the site's virtual directories but not the \WWWROOT directory. What is the best way to correct this problem?
   a. Disable Windows NT challenge/response authentication.
   b. Enable Directory Browsing Allowed on \WWWROOT.
   c. Grant read permission to \WWWROOT.
   d. Add Pat to the Administrators group since access to the \WWWROOT directory is restricted to the Administrators group.
4. You want to block a range of IP addresses from your company's IIS website. Opening the Advanced tab of the WWW Service Properties page, you choose Granted Access, then Add. In the Deny Access On dialog box, you select Group of Computers. Which combination of network ID and subnet mask would you enter to deny access to IP addresses 195.49.200.64 through 195.49.200.95?
   a. network ID: 195.49.200.95; subnet mask: 255.255.255.192
   b. network ID: 195.49.200.64; subnet mask: 255.255.255.224

c. network ID: 195.49.200.95; subnet mask:
   255.255.255.240

d. network ID: 195.49.200.64; subnet mask:
   255.255.255.248

5. One way that Internet browser users can access a virtual web directory is to click on an HTML page link. What other method can Internet browser users utilize to access a virtual web directory?

   a. Enter the appropriate virtual server path in the browser address field.

   b. Enter the appropriate virtual directory path in the browser address field.

   c. Enter the appropriate virtual directory's IP address in the browser address field.

   d. Enter the appropriate URL address in the browser address field.

6. Internet users complain that they cannot access your website. Of the following, which one is the most likely cause of the problem?

   a. They are not accessing port 21.

   b. They are not accessing port 23.

   c. They are not accessing port 70.

   d. They are not accessing port 80.

7. You would assign the same host name to multiple IP addresses in DNS to _____.

   a. allow replication between IIS servers

   b. increase WINS name resolution performance

   c. perform load balancing

   d. maximize available network bandwidth

8. What permissions must you grant so that anonymous users can upload, but not download, files using FTP?

   a. execute   c. read only

   b. read and write   d. write only

9. You enable anonymous user access to your IIS website WEBWORLD. The IUSR_WEBWORLD account is given read permission on the \WWWROOT directory. The Windows NT default permissions are not changed. Who can access the \WWWROOT directory?

   a. everyone

   b. everyone except users with valid Windows NT user accounts

   c. only anonymous users

   d. only guests

10. Paul has an SSL-enabled client laptop that he takes with him on the road to access the Internet. Which one of the following directories can he access?

    a. http:// directories and https:// directories

    b. http:// directories, https:// directories, and httpssl:// directories

    c. only https:// directories

    d. only httpssl:// directories

11. All your company's employees use their Windows 2000 accounts to access files on the corporate FTP site. The FTP site is hosted on an IIS computer named Web on the intranet. What must you do to allow all Internet users to view directories and download files from your corporate FTP site? (Select all that apply.)

    a. In the FTP site's properties, assign the Directory Browsing Allowed permission.

    b. Enable anonymous access for the FTP site.

    c. Assign the NTFS read permission to IUSR_Web user account for the FTP site's content directories.

    d. On the Directory Security tab of the FTP site's properties, grant access to the near-side IP address of the router on the Internet connection.

12. You want to administer websites and FTP sites on an IIS computer in a remote branch of your company. The branch's network is protected by a firewall that does not allow you to use Internet Service Manager. How can you connect to the administration website on the branch's IIS computer?

    a. Specify the remote IIS computer's DNS name and the IISAdmin virtual directory's alias.

    b. Specify the remote computer's DNS name and TCP port 8827.

    c. Specify the remote IIS computer's DNS name and the TCP port that is assigned to the administration website.

    d. Specify the host header name that is assigned to the default website on the remote IIS computer and the TCP port that is assigned to the administration website.

13. Which one of the following statements correctly describes one way that cookies can be used?

    a. Cookies are special viruses that can be used by malicious individuals to cause damage to Internet users' systems through their web browsers.

    b. Cookies can be used to encrypt the contents of web pages without using encryption key pairs.

    c. Cookies are special antivirus programs that can be used by web servers to ensure that client computers that connect to the server's websites do not contain viruses.

    d. Cookies can be used to provide support to older web browsers that do not support host header names.

14. Your website on an IIS computer is experiencing a high volume of user requests. What should you do to provide the best load balancing and fault tolerance?

    a. Install an additional website.

    b. Install an additional virtual server.

    c. Install an additional virtual directory.

    d. Install an additional IIS computer.

15. You are setting up an Internet website for a government agency that has multiple branches nationwide. The information that is published on the website is highly sensitive, and only authorized officials are allowed to access it. Each user must be granted access to only the information that is pertinent to their work duties. All the data transmitted over the Internet must be encrypted. How should you configure the website?

    a. Implement digital signature on the web server to ensure data authenticity.

    b. Grant each user account the appropriate NTFS permissions for the website's files and user client certification to authenticate users; use SSL data encryption.

    c. Use cookies to authenticate users, and instruct all the authorized users to upgrade their web browsers to use 128-bit encryption.

    d. Grant each user account the appropriate NTFS permission for the website's files and use Windows NT challenge/response authentication.

HANDS-ON EXERCISES

Exercise 1: Creating a Web Page

1. Create a folder called ACME on the C drive.
2. Click the Start button, select Programs, select Accessories, and select Notepad.
3. In Notepad, type in the following:

```
<HTML>
<HEAD>
<TITLE>THIS IS THE TITLE</TITLE>
<META NAME="KEYWORD" CONTENTS="HOT, IMPORTANT">
<META NAME="DESCRIPTION" CONTENTS="This is a sample website">
</HEAD>

<BODY>This is the body of the web page</BODY>
</HTML>
```

4. Save the file on the ACME folder and name it DEFAULT.HTM. Ensure that the file is called DEFAULT.HTM. Leave Notepad open.
5. Double-click on the DEFAULT.HTM file. Leave Internet Explorer open.
6. Change back to Notepad and modify the file to the following:

```
<HTML>
<HEAD>
  <TITLE>THIS IS THE TITLE</TITLE>

  <META NAME="KEYWORD" CONTENTS="HOT,IMPORTANT">
  <META NAME="DESCRIPTION" CONTENTS="This is a sample website">
</HEAD>

<BODY>
  <CENTER>TITLE</CENTER>
  This is the body of the webpage
  <OL>
    <LI>First
    <LI>Second
    <LI>Third
  </OL>

  <FONT COLOR="FF0000">RED
  <FONT COLOR="00FF00">GREEN
  <FONT COLOR="0000FF">BLUE
  <BR><BR>
  <FONT COLOR="000000">END
</BODY>
</HTML>
```

7. Save the file in Notepad.
8. Change back to Internet Explorer and notice that the web page has not changed.
9. For Internet Explorer to reread the file, click on the Refresh button.

Exercise 2: Creating a Website

1. Open the Internet Services Manager from the Administrative Tools menu.
2. In Internet Information Services, expand the server in the Console tree.
3. Right-click Default Web Site, then click Stop.

4. Right-click Server, select the New option, and click Web Site. Click the Next button.
5. On the Web Site Description page, type ACMEXX Web Site where XX represents your computer number. Click on the Next button.
6. On the IP address and Port Settings page, verify that the website uses all unassigned IP addresses and TCP port 80. Click the Next button.
7. On the Web Site Home Directory page, in the Path box, type C:\ACME. Verify that the "Allow anonymous access to this Web site" check box is selected, then click the Next button.
8. On the Web Site Access Permissions page, verify that the read and run script permissions check boxes are selected. Click the Next button and click the Finish button.
9. Right-click the ACMEXX Web Site and select Properties.
10. On the Operators tab, verify that only the Administrators group is listed as an operator.
11. On the Documents tab, verify that Default.htm is listed.
12. Click on the OK button.
13. Start Internet Explorer and type in http://localhost.
14. In Internet Explorer, type in http://localhost/iishelp/iis/misc/default.asp.
15. In the Internet Services Manager, right-click the Administration Web Site and select Properties. In the Web Site tab, record the TCP port number.
16. In Internet Explorer, type 3463.

Exercise 3: Configure Basic Security

1. In the Internet Information Services, right-click the AcmeXX Web Site and select Properties.
2. On the Directory Security tab, under Anonymous Access and Authentication Control, click the Edit button.
3. In the Authentication Methods dialog box, clear the Anonymous Access and Integrated Windows Authentication checkboxes. Select the Basic Authentication check box. When the Internet Services Manager dialog box appears, read the warning and click the Yes button.
4. Click on the OK button to close the Authentication Methods dialog box and click the OK button to close the AcmeXX Web Site Properties dialog box.
5. In Internet Explorer, type in http://localhost.
6. In the Enter Network Password dialog box, type ACMEXX\CBROWN for user name and Cbrown's password. Click on the OK button.
7. Minimize Internet Explorer.
8. In Internet Services Manager, right-click the ACMEXX Web Site and select the Explore option.
9. In Windows Explorer, right-click Default.htm and select Properties.
10. On the Security tab, clear the "Allow inheritable permissions from parent to propagate to this object" checkbox. In the Security dialog box, click Remove.
11. Click the Add button. In the Select Users, Computers, or Groups dialog box, under Name, click Administrators, click Add, and then click OK.
12. Allow the Administrators group the full control permission, and then click OK.
13. Close Windows Explorer.
14. Restore Internet Explorer.
15. Click the Refresh button.
16. When Internet Explorer prompts you for your network credentials, try to log in as ACMEXX\CBROWN.
17. Log in as ACMEXX\ADMINISTRATOR with the appropriate password.
18. Close Internet Explorer.
19. Right-click ACME Web Site, then select Properties.
20. On the Directory Security tab, under Anonymous Access and Authentication Control, click Edit.
21. Clear the Basic Authentication check box, then click OK.
22. In the Authentication Methods dialog box, select the Integrated Windows Authentication check box. Click the OK button.
23. Close Internet Information Services.
24. Start Internet Explorer and connect to http://localhost. Note that this worked because you used your current login information to access the website.
25. Close all open windows.

CHAPTER 22

Introduction to E-mail

Topics Covered in This Chapter

Introduction

To make any corporate network complete, you must have an e-mail system. Today's modern e-mail systems are complex software applications and services. For Windows NT, Windows 2000, and Windows Server 2003, you would typically use Microsoft Exchange to host the e-mail system. Unfortunately, because Microsoft Exchange is so complex, this chapter is designed only as an overview of e-mail systems.

Objectives

■ Explain how the e-mail system uses the Internet to deliver messages.

■ Explain the function of MIME and how it relates to the Internet.

22.1   E-MAIL OVERVIEW

Electronic mail (e-mail) is the transmission of messages over communications networks. The messages can be notes entered from the keyboard or electronic files stored on disk. Most mainframes, minicomputers, and computer networks have an e-mail system. Some e-mail systems are confined to a single computer system or network, but others have gateways to several computer systems, enabling users to send electronic mail anywhere in the world. Companies that are fully computerized make extensive use of e-mail, because it is fast, flexible, and reliable. In recent years, the use of e-mail has exploded. By some estimates, there are now 25 million e-mail users sending 15 billion messages per year.

Most e-mail systems include a rudimentary text editor for composing messages, but many allow you to edit your own messages using any editor you want. You then send the message to the recipient by specifying the recipient's address. You also can send the same message to several users simultaneously.

All online services and Internet service providers (ISPs) offer e-mail, and most also support gateways so that you can exchange mail with users of other systems. Usually, it takes only a few seconds or minutes for mail to arrive at its destination. This is a particularly effective way to communicate with a group, because you can broadcast a message or document to everyone in the group at once.

22.1.1   E-mail and the Internet

No matter which e-mail package or service you use to host the e-mail, your e-mail travels the same road as all Internet-based information, including web page downloads. That is, your e-mail traverses the Internet backbone. The sender creates an e-mail message on an application. The client system is the **user agent (UA).** When the user sends the message, it is transmitted to the user's Internet mail server.

Once the message reaches the Internet mail server, it enters the Internet's **message transfer system (MTS).** The MTS relies on other Internet mail servers to act as **message transfer agents (MTAs),** which relay the message toward the receiving UA. Once an MTA passes the message to the recipient's Internet mail server, the receiving UA can access the message.

RFC 822 defines the standard format for e-mail messages, dividing the message into two parts: an envelope and its contents. The **envelope** contains information that is needed to transmit and deliver an e-mail message to its destination. The **contents** is the message that the sender wants delivered to the recipient.

The envelope contains the e-mail address of the sender, the e-mail address of the receiver, and a delivery mode, which in our case states that the message is to be sent to a recipient's mailbox. We can divide the contents of the message into two parts, a header and a body. The header is a required part of the message format, and the sending UA automatically includes it at the top of the message; the user does not input this information. The receiving UA may reformat the header information or delete it entirely to make the message easier for the recipient to read.

The header contains detailed information about who sent the message, who received the message, and how the message got from the sending point to the receiving point. In addition, the header displays the date of the message, the times at which the different MTAs received the message, and the unique ID of the message.

The body of the message contains the actual text that the sender typed and is separated from the header by a "null" line. RFC 822 does not define the message body, because it can be anything the user enters, so long as it is ASCII text.

A standard e-mail address should be set up as follows:

```
<mailbox ID>@<domain name>
```

The mailbox ID is the name of an individual mailbox on a local machine. The domain name is the name of a valid domain registered in the domain name system. The DNS servers are key to Internet e-mail, because they allow MTAs to find the machine specified in the recipient's e-mail address.

22.1.2   Simple Mail Transfer Protocol

The transmission of an e-mail message through the Internet relies on the **Simple Mail Transfer Protocol (SMTP),** which is defined in RFC 821. SMTP specifies the way a UA establishes a connection with an MTA and the way it transmits its e-mail message. MTAs also use SMTP to relay the e-mail from MTA to MTA, until it reaches the appropriate MTA for delivery to the receiving UA.

The interactions that occur between two machines, whether a UA to an MTA or an MTA to another MTA, have similar processes and follow a basic call-and-response procedure. The main difference between a UA-to-MTA transaction and an MTA-to-MTA transaction is that with the latter, the sending MTA must locate a receiving MTA.

To do this, the sending MTA contacts the DNS to look up the domain name specified in the recipient e-mail address. The DNS may return the IP address of the domain name—in which case the sending MTA tries to establish a mail connection to the host at that domain—or the DNS may return a set of mail-relaying records that contain the domain names of intermediate MTAs that can act as relays to the recipient. In this case, the sending MTA tries to establish a mail connection to the first host listed in the mail-relaying record.

When an MTA is sending to an MTA, the sending MTA chooses a receiving MTA, which may be the final destination of the message or an intermediate MTA that will relay the message to another MTA. Next, the sending MTA requests a TCP connection to the receiving MTA. The receiving MTA responds with a server ID and a status report, which indicates whether it is available for the mail transaction. If not, the transaction is over; the sending MTA can try again later or attempt another route. If the receiving MTA is free to handle a session, it will accept the TCP connection.

The sending MTA then sends a HELLO command followed by its domain name information to the receiving MTA, which responds with a greeting. Next, the sending MTA sends a MAIL FROM command that identifies the e-mail address from which the message originated, as well as a list of the MTAs through which the message has passed. This information is also known as a return path. If the receiving MTA can accept mail from that address, it responds with an OK reply.

The sending MTA then sends a RCPT TO command, which identifies the e-mail address of the recipient. If the receiving MTA can accept mail for that recipient (it may perform a DNS lookup to verify this, specifically using the mail exchange, MX records), then it responds with an OK reply. If not, it rejects that recipient. (An e-mail message may be addressed to more than one recipient, in which case this process is repeated for each recipient address.)

Once the receiving MTA identifies the recipient's address, the sending MTA sends the DATA command. The receiving MTA accepts command by responding with OK. It then considers all succeeding lines of data to be the message text. Once the sending MTA gets an OK reply, it starts sending the message. The sending MTA signals the end of the message by transmitting a line that contains only a period (.).

When the receiving MTA receives the signal for the end of the message, it replies with an OK to signal its acceptance of the message. If for some reason the receiving MTA cannot process the message, it will signal the sending MTA with a failure code. After the message has been sent to the receiving MTA and the sending MTA gets an OK reply, the sending MTA can either start another message transfer or use the QUIT command to end the session.

Once the receiving MTA accepts the message, it reverses its role and becomes a sending MTA, contacting the MTA next in line for the relay of the message. The process stops once the message reaches the Internet mail server that services the recipient specified in the Rcpt To e-mail address.

If at any point along the way an MTA cannot deliver the e-mail, it generates an error report, also known as an undeliverable mail notification. The MTA uses MTAs identified in the return path to relay the error report back to the original sender.

22.1.3   MIME

Initially, the Internet e-mail system was limited to simple text messages because SMTP, the protocol used to transport mail across the Internet, could carry only 7-bit ASCII text. In the United States, the main ASCII standard used for e-mail is US-ASCII. This version of ASCII offers only a basic set of characters—128 characters in all, each represented as a 7-bit binary number. This ASCII set was designed to cover the English alphabet, including both uppercase and lowercase letters, and the numbers 0 through 9, as well as some other characters.

If you use e-mail, you know that it is not just simple text anymore. You can use italics, boldface, bullets, and other types of enriched formatting. You can even embed graphics in documents. But because SMTP was developed to handle only basic text messages in a 7-bit format—as laid out by RFC 822, which defines the standard for Internet text messaging—these more sophisticated data formats cannot be sent via e-mail. The problem with the 128-character set is it cannot accommodate rich text. In addition, you cannot use foreign language characters that are not represented in US-ASCII. Therefore, the 7-bit format required by SMPT prevents users from sending other types of data via e-mail, for example, the 8-bit binary data found in many executable files and in files created by applications such as Microsoft Word. For e-mail to handle diverse data such as text, word-processing documents, and images, users could share all sorts of data without having to ship disks or make any actual real-time network connections to copy or download files.

To overcome the limitation of SMPT's 7-bit ASCII format, today's e-mail utilizes the **Multipurpose Internet Mail Extension (MIME).** MIME makes the data appear as standard e-mail messages to the Internet's SMTP servers regardless of the data it contains, even though it did not change the way it handles such data. In other words, the solution did not require that all Internet mail servers be upgraded to a new version of SMTP. In effect, the transport system remained untouched.

As defined in RFC 2045, MIME provides three main enhancements to standard e-mail. First, with MIME, e-mail can contain text that goes beyond basic US-ASCII, including various keystrokes such as different line and page breaks, foreign language characters, and enriched text. Second, users can attach different types of data to their e-mail, including such files as executables, spreadsheets, audio, and images. Third, users can create a single e-mail message that contains multiple parts, and each part can be in a different data format. For example, you can compose a single e-mail message that consists of a plain-text message, an image file, and a binary-based document such as a Word file.

RFC 2045 defines seven types of e-mail contents that MIME can package and pass across the Internet: text, image, audio, video, application, message, and multipart. Each of these data types comes in various formats, or subtypes. (MIME also augments types and subtypes with certain parameters, which are specified in RFC 2045; however, these parameters are too detailed to include in this overview of MIME.)

Obviously the text type of e-mail content supports messages that are carrying text; however, within the text type, MIME also supports the plain subtype, which is usually standard 7-bit ASCII. MIME also supports the rich text subtype, which allows for some simple formatting features such as page breaks.

The image type supports image files, and its subtypes include the graphics interchange format (GIF) and a compressed image format developed by the Joint Photographic Experts Group (JPEG). In the words of RFC 2045, the video type supports "time-varying picture images," and for now, a compressed video format developed by the Motion Picture Experts Group (MPEG) is its only subtype. The audio type support audio data, and its only subtype is basic.

According to the RFC, there is no one ideal audio format in use today, so the developers of MIME tried to define a subtype that would be the lowest common denominator. The basic subtype for audio signifies "single channel audio encoded using 8-bit ISDN mu-law" at a sampling rate of 8 KHz.

The application type supports two types of data: data that are meant to be processed by an application and data that do not fall into any of the other categories. For now, it supports the octet-stream subtype, which means the message can carry arbitrary binary data. It also supports the postscript subtype, meaning the message can be sent to print as a PostScript file. If a mail agent receives a message whose content subtype it does not recognize, then by default it will attempt to pass the message on as an application-type message with a subtype of octet-stream (or, application/octet-stream).

The remaining two content types allow for special handling of an e-mail message. For instance, the message type allows an e-mail to contain an encapsulated message. The external-body subtype allows an e-mail to indicate an external location where the intended body of the message resides. That way, the user can choose whether to retrieve the message body. The message type also allows MIME to send a large e-mail message as several small ones (the subtype for this is partial). The receiving MIME-enabled mail agent can then open the smaller e-mail messages and reassemble them into the original long version.

Finally, the multipart type allows an e-mail message to contain more than one body of data. The mixed subtype allows users to mix different data formats into one e-mail message. The alternative subtype allows a message to contain different versions of the same data, each version in a different format. MIME mail agents can then select the version that works best with the local computing environment. The digest subtype allows users to send a collection of messages in one e-mail, such as the kind used with Internet mailing lists sent in digest form. Finally, the parallel subtype allows mixed body parts, but the ordering of the body parts is not important.

To package the different data formats into the 7-bit ASCII format, MIME uses five different encoding schemes: 7 bit, 8 bit, binary, quoted printable, and base64. As you will soon see, however, only the quoted-printable and base64 schemes actually encode data.

The 7-bit scheme tells mail agents that the message contents are in plain ASCII. For this reason, no encoding is necessary, as all mail systems should support ASCII. The 8-bit scheme indicates that the contents contain 8-bit characters. The mail agents, then, encode this information using their preferred means, if available. Because not all mail agents use the same encoding method for 8-bit characters, there is a good chance the 8-bit characters will not appear correctly when the e-mail is opened. For this reason, the 8-bit scheme currently is not a reliable encoding scheme. The binary scheme, because it is similar to the 8-bit scheme, shares the same problem.

The quoted-printable scheme is used for text that contains a mixture of 7-bit and 8-bit characters. Essentially, it allows 7-bit characters to go unencoded and converts each 8-bit character into a set of three 7-bit characters. As a result, mail servers and mail agents see an e-mail that contains only 7-bit characters.

The base64 scheme is used for data that are not text, such as data that constitute an executable file. Base64 works by breaking the data down into sets of three octets, each containing 24 bits. It then converts each set of 24 bits into a four-character sequence. (In other words, every 6 bits of data are represented by a character.) The characters used in the sequencing come from a set of 65 characters, all of which can be found in any version of ASCII. Because it is in ASCII, data encoded by base64 should be readable by any mail server or mail agent.

Using MIME is simple. If your mail system supports MIME, it automatically chooses the data type and encoding scheme. It then adds MIME headers to the body of the message. These headers tell receiving mail agents that they have received a MIME message and indicate how the mail agents should handle the message.

The main headers are MIME Version, Content Type, and Content Transfer Encoding. The last two headers refer to the data type found in the message and the scheme used to encode the data, respectively. Some other headers are Content Description, which lets you type in a description of the message (much like SMTP's subject header), and Content ID, which is similar to SMTP's Message ID.

22.1.4   Retrieving E-mail

When the e-mail arrives at the recipient's Internet mail server, the user agent can employ different methods to access, or retrieve, its e-mail from the MTA. For instance, the majority of companies rely on proprietary e-mail packages, such as Microsoft Exchange or cc:Mail, to handle e-mail operations on the local network. There are a few different models for this operation and a few different protocols that can handle the task, including proprietary protocols found in commercial e-mail packages and two Internet standards-based protocols, Post Office Protocol 3 (POP-3) and the Internet Message Access Protocol 4 (IMAP-4).

When an e-mail reaches the designated recipient's mail server, the message is placed in a message store, which is also called a post office. In its most basic form, the message store, located on a server, is usually some type of file system that holds delivered mail for access by users. You can think of the message store as one large directory with subdirectories dedicated to each user. These subdirectories are also known as mailboxes. A more advanced form of message store would allow users to create personal folders to store read and unread messages, and it would allow users to create archives for groups of messages. Other advanced features include the ability to perform keyword searches and to create a hierarchy of folders.

The message store component of an e-mail system is usually located on a different machine than the message transport component, which handles the delivery of incoming messages and the transmission of outgoing messages. The reason for their separation is that the transport component usually handles a high volume of operations. So, if both systems were on the same machine, the traffic of inbound and outbound mail would experience slower performance, as would users when they try to retrieve and manipulate mail in their mailboxes.

Once an e-mail message is delivered to the message store, it is ready for retrieval by the recipient. There are three basic models for message access: offline, online, and disconnected.

The offline model is the most basic of the three. In the offline model, a client connects to the mail server and downloads all messages designated for that particular recipient. Once downloaded, the messages are erased from the server. The user then processes, manipulates, and stores the messages locally at the client machine. The offline model has several advantages: (1) it requires a minimal amount of server connect time since the client accesses the server only periodically for mail downloads; (2) because the mail processing is performed at the client, the offline model does not devour server resources; and (3) it requires less server storage space because mail is deleted from the server once it has been downloaded by a client. The offline model also has certain drawbacks: (1) Because mail is downloaded to a particular machine, you must use that machine to access processed mail. Therefore, if you downloaded e-mail to your desktop computer and then went on the road with your laptop, you would not be able to read those same messages off the mail server from your laptop. (2) Because all processing and storage is performed at the client machine, the client must have enough resources to perform the task.

With the online model, all e-mail processing and manipulation is performed at the server. In fact, all the messages remain on the server even after users have read them. In some implementations, users can save e-mail to the local client. As you might expect, the online model requires a constant connection to the server whenever users need to access and work with their e-mail. Consequently, this model's high connect time could mean that more users are sharing bandwidth at any given time. Because the server is burdened with all message processing and storage, you will need a more powerful server to handle an online e-mail system than you would with an offline system. In addition, users cannot work with their e-mail unless they are online, meaning they must be at a client that can access the mail server even to do the simplest task such as reread an old message. Conversely, because all mail is stored and processed at the server, you can access your e-mail from any client that can connect to the server. For the same reason, this model requires fewer resources at the client machine. In addition, online-type systems usually offer enhanced features such as the ability to create a multitude of personal folders to organize e-mail and the ability to create archives for storing messages.

The disconnected model combines elements of both the offline and online models. Using this system, a user connects to a mail server to retrieve and download e-mail. Users can then process the mail on the local client. Once the user is finished with the messages, the user once again connects to the mail server and uploads any changes. With this model, the mail server acts as the main repository of the user's e-mail. The disconnected model's strengths are that users can access e-mail from a variety of clients that have access to the mail server. Users can also process mail offline, which translates to a shorter server connect time. The model does, however, require a sufficient amount of resources on both the server and the client.

The majority of e-mail packages—Microsoft Mail, Microsoft Exchange, and Lotus cc:Mail— follow the online model of e-mail access. These products use their own protocols to retrieve messages from Internet mail servers and store them on local servers. Users can then use the products' client programs to access and work with mail from message stores on the proprietary e-mail servers. The attractiveness of these proprietary packages lies in the added features they offer. For instance, they usually offer advanced mail manipulation such as folders, hierarchical folders, and archives. Some offer the ability to create bulletin board systems for general corporate communications. In addition, some offer message notification when a new e-mail arrives for a particular user. They also usually offer searching abilities, so users can find e-mails with particular headings, or look up the addresses of other users on the system.

One of the first e-mail access protocols developed was the **Post Office Protocol (POP),** the latest version of which is POP-3. In essence, **POP-3** follows the offline model of message access and revolves around send-and-receive types of operation. There have been recent attempts, however, to remodel POP-3 so that it has some online capabilities such as saved-message folders and status flags that display message states; but using POP-3 in online mode usually requires the additional presence of some type of remote file system protocol.

IMAP-4 is the more advanced of the standards-based message access protocols. It follows the online model of message access, although it does support offline and disconnected modes. IMAP-4 offers an array of up-to-date features, including support for the creation and management of remote folders and folder hierarchies, message status flags, new mail notification, retrieval of individual MIME body parts, and server-based searches to minimize the amount of data that must be transferred over the connection.

22.1.5   Messaging Application Programming Interface

Messaging application programming interface (MAPI) is a standardized set of C functions placed into a code library known as a dynamic link library. The MAPI library is also available to Visual Basic application writers through a Basic-to-C translation layer. The functions were originally designed by Microsoft, but they have received the support of many third-party vendors. The standard library of messaging functions allows Windows applications developers to take advantage of the Windows messaging subsystem, supported by default with Microsoft Mail or Microsoft Exchange. By writing to the generic MAPI, any Windows application can become "mail-enabled," in which an e-mail can be sent from within a Windows application with the document you are working on as an attachment. Since MAPI standardizes the way messages are handled by mail-enabled applications, each such application does not have to include vendor-specific code for each target messaging system.

22.1.6   X.400

X.400 is a set of standards relating to the exchange of electronic messages (such as e-mail, fax, voice mail, or telex). It was designed to let you exchange e-mail and files with the confidence that no one besides the sender and the recipient will ever see the message, that delivery is assured, and that proof of delivery is available if desired.

One goal of X.400 is to enable the creation of a global electronic messaging network. Just as you can make a telephone call from almost anywhere in the world to almost anywhere else in the world, X.400 hopes to make that possibility a reality for electronic messaging. X.400 only defines application-level protocols and relies on other standards for the physical transportation of data such as X.25, Frame Relay, or ATM.

The address scheme that X.400 uses is called the originator/recipient address (O/R address). It is similar to a postal address in that it uses a hierarchical format. While a postal address hierarchy is country, zip code, state, city, street, and recipient's name, the O/R address hierarchy consists of countries, communication providers (administrative domain name), companies (private domain name), organization, surname, and given name. For example, while you might use Pat.Regan@acme.com for an Internet e-mail address, X.400 would use

```
G=Pat; S=Regan; OU=acme; PRMD=acme.com; ADMD=mci; C=us
```

22.2   MICROSOFT EXCHANGE

One popular e-mail server is **Microsoft Exchange,** which runs on a Windows NT or a Window 2000 server. Like the ISA server software, the Exchange software does not come with Windows server CD's. Instead, it has a separate program and installation CD. The largest unit, and the one at the top of the Exchange hierarchy, is the organization. All other Exchange structures are contained under this unit. The organization is parent to the sites. This relationship permits an administrator to configure something at the organization level and have it apply or be available at all sites. Because an organization encompasses an entire Exchange system, each company or business should create only one organization.

Sites are logical groupings of one or more Exchange servers. Even though resources reside on different servers in the site, the site groups all those resources without reference to their locations. This grouping makes using resources in the site very easy. For example, say that a certain mailbox physically resides on a site server, called the mailbox's home server. Senders do not need to know the physical location of the mailbox in order to send it a message. The principle applies to public folders in a site. The particular server on which a public folder is stored is of no concern to the users wanting to access it. From the user's perspective, a site creates a transparent messaging environment.

Exchange servers form the final main structure in the Exchange hierarchy. These computers run the Windows NT or Windows 2000 Server operating systems and the Exchange server software. The Exchange servers are the physical location for mailboxes, folders, and other data and information for the site. Individual servers, while inheriting certain configuration parameters from the site, can also be individual configured. All Exchange objects and related processes are created and managed by the software components that comprise the Exchange products.

The Exchange components are executable programs that perform the Exchange functions. Some are in the form of EXE files, while others are in the form of data link libraries. They are referred to as core components because they are necessary for Exchange to be operational. They are also referred to as services, because they run as services on the Microsoft Windows NT or Windows 2000 Server operating systems. The core components include the following:

- Directory service (DS)
- Information store (IS)
- Message transfer agent (MTA)
- System attendant (SA)

22.2.1   Directory Service

The **directory service (DS)** component creates and manages the storage of all information about Exchange objects in an organization. Objects are resources such as mailboxes, distribution lists, public folders, and servers. The database that stores the objects is called the Directory. Objects in the Directory are organized in a hierarchical structure. The main purpose of the Directory is to allow users and administrators the ability to easily locate resources to use or configure. The other Exchange components also reference the Directory for information. The Exchange Directory is patterned after the X.500 standard.

22.2.2   Information Store

The **information store (IS)** creates and manages the message database on an Exchange server. All types of data can be stored in this database, including e-mail messages, electronic forms, word-processing documents, spreadsheets, and graphics. Users access the IS content through their mailbox and folders in their client applications. The IS is the back-end component that makes many of the Exchange features possible.

The **public information store** contains all the public folders of a particular server. Public folders are containers for shared information. In a sense, they are like containers for shared information, or a public mailbox. Different types of data can be stored in a public folder, such as e-mail messages, word-processing documents, and graphic files.

The **private information store** contains all user mailboxes. Security makes mailboxes accessible only to their owners and to others who have been given access permission. By default, a user's messages are stored in their mailbox in this database. Although mailboxes are always located in the private information store on an Exchange server, messages do not have to be stored there. A user can specify a personal location for message storage. This type of folder is called a personal folder and has a PST file extension. A personal folder can be located on a server or on the client computer. When they are sent a message, the message still first goes to their mailbox in the private information store, and then is rerouted to a personal folder. The advantage of storing messages in a personal folder, especially if it is on a local computer, is that the user can access it without logging on to the server. The advantages of keeping message storage in the private information store, which is the default, are centralized backup and fault tolerance.

By default, Exchange servers contain both the public and private databases; but they can be configured to store only one of the two. If only the private information store were configured, that server would act as a dedicated mailbox server. A dedicated folder server would only have the public information store configured. Dedicated servers are created to improve the performance of information access.

22.2.3   Message Transfer Agent and System Attendant Service

The **message transfer agent (MTA)** manages the routing of messages within a site, between sites, and to foreign message systems. The MTA uses other components, called connectors, to manage the transfer of data, while the MTA handles the routing functions. The MTA could be compared with a post office that receives mail and routes it to another post office. The MTA component is based on the X.400 standard.

When an MTA component receives a message to be forwarded, it first stores it, in order to determine a route. It then looks at the message recipients distinguished name (DN). If that address cannot resolve the next route, the MTA looks at the O/R address. In either case, the MTA compares the address with the various locations and paths in the routing table. If the MTA finds a path on which to send the message, it sends it on its way. Because there could be more than one path, the X.400 standard allows an administrator to assign costs to different paths. Costs allow priorities to be given to different routes. When faced with multiple paths, the MTA chooses the lowest-cost path. If the MTA cannot forward a message, a nondelivery report (NDR) is sent to the message originator.

The **system attendant (SA) service** monitors and logs information about the other Exchange services. It also builds and maintains the routing tables for the site.

22.2.4   Optional Exchange Components

Whereas core components are required for normal operations, optional components provide additional servers that might be needed in your Exchange environment. Many of the optional components are connector components.

The **Internet mail service (IMS) connector** enables an Exchange system to interoperate with an SMTP mail system. The IMS permits Exchange users and SMTP mail users to send mail to and receive mail from each other. The IMS connector also permits an organization with geographically disperse locations to use the Internet as a messaging backbone. Messages can be sent from an Exchange user, through the Internet, to the Exchange recipient.

An Exchange system can interoperate with a Microsoft Mail system through the Microsoft Mail Connector. Microsoft Mail is a mail product for PC or AppleTalk networks. The **Microsoft Mail connector** can translate Exchange messages to and from the Microsoft Mail format. This permits Exchange users and Mail users to exchange mail.

A **Lotus cc:Mail connector** permits Exchange to interoperate with the Lotus cc:Mail system. Users of each system can exchange mail with the other system. As with the other connectors, this connector permits organizations to implement Exchange with another messaging system and still have interoperability.

Microsoft Schedule+ performs personal and group calendaring, scheduling, and task management. The group scheduling features allow a user who wants to schedule a meeting to view the schedules of other users. The user who is scheduling the meeting can see if a particular time period is unscheduled for the other users (a free period), or if it is already scheduled (busy period). The **Schedule+ Free/Bus connector** allows Microsoft Exchange with Schedule+ 7.5 and Microsoft Mail with Schedule+ 1.0 to share their incompatible free/busy information.

SUMMARY

1. Electronic mail (e-mail) is the transmission of messages over communications networks.
2. No matter which e-mail package or service you use to host the e-mail, your e-mail travels the same road as all Internet-based information, including web page downloads.
3. The sender creates an e-mail message on an application. When the user sends the message, it is transmitted to the user's Internet mail server.
4. The client e-mail system is the user agent (UA).
5. Once the message reaches the Internet mail server, it enters the Internet's message transfer system (MTS).
6. The MTS relies on other Internet mail servers to act as message transfer agents (MTAs), which relay the message toward the receiving UA.
7. Once an MTA passes the message to the recipient's Internet mail server, the receiving UA can access the message.
8. E-mail messages have two parts, an envelope and its contents.
9. The envelope contains the e-mail address of the sender, the e-mail address of the receiver, and a delivery mode, which states that the message is to be sent to a recipient's mailbox.
10. The header contains detailed information about who sent the message, who received the message, and how the message got from the sending point to the receiving point. In addition, the header displays the date of the message, the times at which the different MTAs received the message, and the unique ID of the message.
11. The body of the message contains the actual text that the sender typed.
12. The transmission of an e-mail message through the Internet relies on the Simple Mail Transfer Protocol (SMTP).
13. To figure out the address of a MTA, the mail system uses the domain name system.
14. Initially, the Internet e-mail system was limited to simple text messages because SMTP, the protocol used to transport mail across the Internet, could carry only 7-bit ASCII text.
15. To overcome the limitation of SMPT's 7-bit ASCII format, today's e-mail utilizes the Multipurpose Internet Mail Extension (MIME), which makes many data types appear as standard e-mail messages.
16. When an e-mail reaches the designated recipient's mail server, the message is placed in a message store, which is also called a post office. In its most basic form, the message store, located on a server, is usually some type of file system that holds delivered mail for access by users.
17. Once an e-mail message is delivered to the message store, it is ready for retrieval by the recipient. There are three basic models for message access: offline, online, and disconnected.
18. One of the first e-mail access protocols developed was the Post Office Protocol (POP), the latest version of which is POP-3. In

essence, POP-3 follows the offline model of message access and revolves around send-and-receive types of operation.
19. Internet Message Access Protocol (IMAP-4) is the more advanced of the standards-based message access protocols. It follows the online model of message access, although it does support offline and disconnected modes.
20. Messaging application programming interface (MAPI) is a standardized set of C functions placed into a code library known as a dynamic link library, which allows Windows applications developers to take advantage of the Windows messaging subsystem, supported by default with Microsoft Mail or Microsoft Exchange. By writing to the generic MAPI, any Windows application can become "mail-enabled," in which an e-mail can be sent from within a Windows application with the document you are working on as an attachment.
21. X.400 is a set of standards relating to the exchange of electronic messages (such as e-mail, fax, voice mail, or telex). It was designed to let you exchange e-mail and files with the confidence that no one besides the sender and the recipient will ever see the message, that delivery is assured, and that proof of delivery is available if desired.
22. One popular e-mail server is Microsoft Exchange, which runs on a Windows NT or a Windows 2000 server.
23. The largest unit, and the one at the top of the Exchange hierarchy, is the organization. Sites are logical groupings of one or more Exchange servers. Even though resources reside on different servers in the site, the site groups all those resources without reference to their locations.
24. The database that stores the objects is called the Directory. Objects in the Directory are organized in a hierarchical structure. The main purpose of the Directory is to allow users and administrators the ability to easily locate resources to use or configure.
25. The information store (IS) creates and manages the message database on an Exchange server.
26. The public information store contains all the public folders of a particular server. Public folders are containers for shared information.
27. The private information store contains all user mailboxes. Security makes mailboxes accessible only to their owners and to others who have been given access permission.
28. The message transfer agent (MTA) manages the routing of messages within a site, between sites, and to foreign message systems. The MTA uses other components, called connectors, to manage the transfer of data, while the MTA handles the routing functions.
29. The system attendant (SA) service monitors and logs information about the other Exchange services. It also builds and maintains the routing tables for the site.

QUESTIONS

1. E-mail can include which of the following? (Choose all that apply.)
   a. text
   b. pictures
   c. video clips
   d. sound clips
   e. executable files

2. Which protocol is responsible for transmitting the e-mail message through the Internet?
   a. MTA
   b. SNMP
   c. SMTP
   d. DNS

3. When you send an e-mail message to PREGAN@ACME.COM, how does the MTA know which server to send the message to?
   a. It looks up the address using the WINS server.
   b. It looks up the address using the domain name system server.
   c. It looks in its internal database to find the address.
   d. It sends it to the router and the router will figure out what to do with it.

4. Which protocol allows the embedding of pictures and video clips into an e-mail message?
   a. SNMP
   b. DNS
   c. IP
   d. MIME

5. Which protocol is responsible to receive an e-mail message and forward it to the appropriate mailbox?
   a. SNMP
   b. MIME
   c. DNS
   d. POP

6. What e-mail server is made to work with Windows NT and Windows 2000?
   a. Microsoft Exchange
   b. IIS
   c. Lotus Mail
   d. NetWare GroupWise

7. What are the two main parts of an e-mail message? (Choose two answers.)
   a. envelope
   b. contents
   c. header
   d. sending address
   e. destination address

8. What component of Microsoft Exchange creates and manages the message database?
   a. Public folder
   b. MTA
   c. X.400 connector
   d. Information store

CHAPTER 23

Network Security

Topics Covered in This Chapter

Introduction

One of the most important features of any network is its security. Modern network operating systems have many levels of security, all of which must be considered. Although the network administrator is ultimately responsible for security, everyone that uses the network must work to keep the network secure—and it is a job that never ends.

Objectives

- Define *threats, vulnerabilities,* and *exploits* and explain how they relate to each other.
- Establish guidelines for user accounts, their passwords, and access to the network.
- Explain how to establish a firewall and/or proxy server to protect a network.
- Describe denial of service attacks and explain how to protect your system against such attacks.
- Compare and contrast private-key and public-key encryption.

- Compare and contrast digital envelopes, digital signatures, and digital certificates.
- Explain how hash encryption protects data.
- Enable and configure auditing for Windows 2000 or Windows Server 2003 computers.
- Explain how patches can improve the security of a system.
- Use the Microsoft Security Analyzer to make your system more secure.

23.1   SECURITY RISKS

Security is a high concern and a major responsibility for network administrators. When you as a network administrator, examine your environment, you need to assess the risks you currently face, determine an acceptable level of risk, and maintain risk at or below that level. Risks are reduced by increasing the security of your network environment.

As a general rule, the higher level of security in an organization, the more costly it is to implement security measures. Unfortunately, at a higher level of network security, the functionality of the network may be reduced. Sometimes, extra levels of security result in systems that are too complex for users. For example, if the authentication process in a system is too complex, some customers will not bother to use the system.

A **threat** is a person, place, or thing that has the potential to access resources and cause harm. Threats can be divided into three categories:

- Natural and physical—Includes fire, flooding, storms, earthquakes, and power failures
- Unintentional—Includes uninformed employees and customers
- Intentional—includes attackers, terrorists, spies, and malicious code

A **vulnerability** is a point where a resource is susceptible to attack. It can be thought of as a weakness. Vulnerabilities are often categorized as follows:

- Physical—Such as an unlocked door
- Natural—Such as a broken fire suppression system or no uninterruptible power supply (UPS)
- Hardware and software—Such as out of date antivirus software
- Media—Such as electrical interference
- Communication—Such as unencrypted protocols
- Human—Such as insecure help desk procedures

An **exploit** is a type of attack on a resource that involves a threat that takes advantage of a vulnerability in an environment. The exploitation of resources can be performed in many ways. When a threat takes advantage of a vulnerability to attack a resource, severe consequences can result.

Figure 23.1   Types of network attacks as they relate to the OSI model

Countermeasures are deployed to counteract threats and vulnerabilities, thereby reducing risk in an environment. For example, an organization that produces fragile electronics may deploy physical security countermeasures, such as securing equipment to the building's foundation or adding buffering mechanisms. These countermeasures reduce the likelihood that an earthquake will cause physical damage to the organization's assets. Residual risk is what remains after all countermeasures have been applied to reduce threats and vulnerabilities.

To analyze all of the ways that a network can be attacked or accessed without proper permission, use the OSI reference model to categorize the various methods See Figure 23.1. Most of the attacks that you hear about in the news occur in the application layer: Attacks are made on web servers and browsers and the information that they access. However, application-layer attacks are also common on open file shares.

Although you can set up an array of defenses against specific threats, any defense can fail the first time that an unanticipated threat shows up. Therefore, you must constantly monitor your network and update your servers. Some excellent resources include the following websites:

- Microsoft Security and Policy
    http://www.microsoft.com/security/default.asp
- HotFix and Security Bulletin Service
    http://www.microsoft.com/technet/security/current.asp
- Security Operations Guide for Windows 2000 Sever
    http://www.microsoft.com/technet/treeview/default.asp?url=/technet/security/prodtech/
        windows/windows2000/staysecure/secops02.asp

23.2   ACCOUNT SECURITY

The user name and password form the first line of defense, since every user needs a password to get access to the network and its resources. For the password to be effective, the administrator should set guidelines and policies on how the user should use the network, provide training in those guidelines, and provide frequent reminders.

23.2.1   User Name Policy

The user name is the name of the account that represents the person or persons who need to access the network. This account receives rights and permissions to resources on the network.

To simplify administration, a consistent naming conventional should be adopted for all users. It will be easier to find names that follow a consistent pattern. For example, use the first initial, middle initial, and last name, or use the first name and last initial. If you have a hundreds of employees, you might need to use the first name, middle initial, and last name to differentiate all of the users. You should create a document stating the naming scheme of user accounts and provide this document to all administrators who might create accounts.

To identify the type of employee, add additional letters at the beginning or at the end of their name. For example, you can add a T in front of the name to indicate a temporary employee or an X at the end of the name to indicate that the employee is under contract.

While standard user names make life easier for the administrator, they also make the hacker's "work" easier. Therefore, to make the network a bit more secure, rename the administrator accounts, if possible. For Windows NT, Windows 2000, and Windows Server 2003 servers, the administrator account name is *administrator*. For NetWare, it is *admin*, and for Linux, it is *root*.

When engaging in everyday activities, you should not be logged in as the administrator of the server. This will help avoid damage that can occur while logged in as that account. For example, if you accessed a virus while logged in as the administrator the virus may spread onto the server and then onto all of the computers in the network. If you are *not* logged in as the administrator, the rights and permissions to many of the files would be read only, and therefore, immune to a virus. If you need to do administrative tasks in Windows 2000 and Windows Server 2003, you could use the RUNAS command at the command prompt, or press and hold the shift key, right-click the program icon, and click Run as.

23.2.2   Password Policies

When it comes to security, the password is more important than the user name. Several important steps can be taken to make the password more secure. First, establish common guidelines for the passwords. Second, educate your users to make sure that they follow the guidelines. Third, keep reminding them about the guidelines. The guidelines should include the following items:

- Remember that user names and passwords are always required.
- Do not give your password to anyone.
- Change your password frequently.
- Avoid people seeing you type in your password.
- Do not write your password down near the computer.
- When you leave your computer unattended, log off from the computer.
- Use a password-protected screen saver.
- Do not use obvious passwords and do not use easy passwords.
- Use strong passwords.
- If you see a security problem or a potential security problem, report it to the network administrator.

Some of these guidelines are commonsense. For example, don't give your password to anyone and avoid typing in your password in front of someone. To prevent people from using your computer when you walk away from you desk, get in the habit of logging off. To protect your computer if you forget to log off, use a password-protected screen saver. When you leave your computer, after a short period of time the screen saver will start. For a person to get past the screen saver, he or she would have to type in a password.

One of the easiest ways for a hacker to get into a network is by exploiting weak passwords. Many people use easy passwords because it is convenient for them and easy to remember. Unfortunately, any good hacker will try these types of passwords first. A weak password might include these elements:

- The word *password*
- The user name
- The person's first name, middle name, or last name

- A pet's name
- A name of a family member
- Birthdates or anniversary dates
- Any text or label on the PC or monitor
- The company's name
- The person's occupation
- A favorite color
- Letters or numerals that follow the order of the keyboard or numeric keypad (e.g., qwerty, asdfgh, 123, or 147)
- Any derivatives of the above, such as spelling backwards

One program that hackers use to break into a server is called a cracker program, which uses a dictionary attack to figure out the password. A dictionary attack initially referred to finding passwords in a specific list, such as an English dictionary. Today, the lists have been expanded to include combination words such as *on-the-fly* and common words with digits. The Cracker program goes through each item in the list until it figures out the password. Depending on system, the password, and the skills of the attacker, such an attack can be completed in days, hours, or perhaps only a few seconds. Because such programs are easily available to anyone who wants them, all users should develop strong passwords.

Strong passwords are difficult-to-crack passwords, but they do not have to be difficult to remember. They can include a combination of numbers, letters (lowercase and uppercase), and special characters. Special characters are those that cannot be considered letters or numbers (e.g., @ # $ % ^ & *). Here is an example of a strong password:

```
tqbf4#jotld
```

Such a password may look hard to remember, but it is not. This password was actually derived from a common typing phrase that includes every letter in the alphabet:

```
The quick brown fox jumped over the lazy dog.
```

By taking the first letter of each word and putting the number 4 and a pound (#) symbol in the middle, you have a strong password.

To make passwords more secure, many network operating systems have password management features, either built into the operating system or installed in an add-on package. One feature is an option to enforce strong passwords. For Windows 2000 and Windows Server 2003, this feature is available with Group Policies, which was discussed in Chapter 13.

Another security option is to require a minimum number of characters for a password. A strong password should be at least 8 characters but not longer than 15 characters, because that would be too difficult for people to create and to remember. By having *at least* 8 characters, a cracker program has to try a substantial number of combinations to discover your password.

To avoid passwords being guessed randomly, some network operating systems offer an automatic account lockout. For example, if the wrong password is tried for an account three times within a 30-minute time period, the account will be disabled for a minimum amount of time or be disabled until a network administrator unlocks the account. In either case, such a failure should be logged somewhere. As the administrator, you should check these logs on a regular basis to see if there are patterns of attempts to hack into a system. Note: If you are the administrator and you accidentally lock yourself out, you will need another administrator to unlock your account. If you are the only administrator, you may not be able to recover.

Another way to avoid passwords being guessed randomly is to set up password expiration dates. In this case, an account expires automatically on a certain date or after a certain amount of days, or it forces users to change their passwords every so often. Most organizations set up passwords to expire every 30 to 45 days. After that, users must reset their passwords immediately or during the allotted grace period. Some systems give the user a few grace logins after the password has expired.

Some systems require unique passwords. In this case, the system remembers a certain number of the past passwords used by a user, and the system is configured so that the user cannot use the same password over and over. When implementing a password history policy, be sure to make the password history large enough to contain at least a year's worth of password changes. For a standard 30-day lifespan for a password, a history of 12 or 13 passwords will suffice.

If a person is having trouble logging in, always have the user check to see if the keyboard's Caps lock function is on. Most of the time, this is the login problem, since passwords, and sometimes user names, are case sensitive. If the person still has problems, change the password for the user and have the user try again. If the problem persists after changing the password, check the encryption scheme. Sometimes passwords are sent in clear text when the program is expecting an encrypted password, or the password is sent encrypted when the program is expecting a clear-text password.

While many of these guidelines are implemented through training and constant reminders some can be managed or enforced with Group Policies. For example, Group Policies allow you to enforce strong passwords, establish how often a person must change his or her password, and establish how often a person can reuse the same password.

23.2.3   User Management

Another step in securing your network involves user management. For example, if you are hiring a temporary employee, most of the network operating systems allow you to create a temporary account and have it automatically disable itself after a certain amount of days or at a certain date. In addition, when someone leaves the company, you should disable or delete the user account. Note: To ensure that the IT department is aware when a person leaves the company, verify that the company has an exit process for employees that includes recovery of all IT equipment and that the IT department has a process to disable or delete the account. Set up a checklist for when people leave the company and be sure to obtain office keys, pagers, cell phones, company software, laptops, badges, and time cards.

If you decide to use anonymous or guest accounts, treat them with extreme care. Typically, such generic accounts are not recommended because they cannot be audited. If you decide to use such as account, however, make sure that you allow only bare minimum access to network resources.

As part of user management, limit the amount of concurrent connections and the number of times that a person can login at one time. For most users, you should allow login on only one machine. Therefore, if the user wants to go to another machine, he or she must first log out of the machine being used. This helps avoid a person leaving a machine unattended.

Some network operating systems allows you to specify which computer a person can log in from and the time at which that person can log in. For example, you can specify that someone cannot log in from 7 A.M. to 6 P.M. If someone tries to hack in during these hours, the person will automatically be denied access, even if he or she has a valid user name and password.

23.2.4   Rights and Permissions

When planning the rights and permissions for network resources, there are two main rules to follow. First, give only the rights and permissions that are necessary for the user to do his or her job. For example, give the user access to the necessary files and only with the rights that he or she needs. If the user needs to read a document but does not need to make changes to the document, give that user only read rights. Second, make sure that the user does have sufficient rights and permissions to do what needs to be done. Even though you want to keep resources secure, must enable users to easily get what they need.

You can secure files that are shared over the network in one of two ways: share-level security or user-level security. In a network that uses share-level security, you assign passwords to individual files or other network resources (such as printers) instead of assigning rights to users. You then give these passwords to all users who need access to these resources. All resources are visible from anywhere in the network; any user who knows the password for a particular network resource can make changes to it. With this type of security, the network support staff have no way of knowing who is manipulating each resource. Share-level security is best used in smaller networks, where resources are more easily tracked. Windows 9X supports share-level security.

In a network with user-level security, rights to network resources (such as files, directories, and printers) are assigned to specific users who gain access to the network through individually assigned user names and passwords. Thus, only users who have a valid user name and password, and have been assigned the appropriate rights to network resources, can see and access those resources. User-level security provides greater control over who is accessing which resources, because users are not supposed to share their user names and passwords with other users. User-level security is, therefore, the preferred method for securing files. Windows NT, Windows 2000, Windows Server 2003, Windows XP, NetWare, UNIX, and Linux support user-level security.

23.3   PHYSICAL SECURITY

Many people forget is to secure computer servers and other key physical components of a network. The server room is the work area of the IT department where the servers and most of the communication devices reside. Only a handful of people should be allowed access to this room. In addition, the server should be secure. Consider implementing the following rules:

- Computers must be physically locked when not in use.
- Computer should have a BIOS password set so that users must enter the password.
- Users must always logout when the server is not being used.
- Passwords must be used on screen savers. Note: Do not select complex screen savers that will take up a lot of processing away from the network services.
- Lock the door into the server room and install camera equipment to monitor the room and/or entrance.

23.4   FIREWALLS AND PROXY SERVERS

To help monitor the network, two approaches are extremely valuable:

- **Packet filters**—Allow you to examine traffic at the network layer, viewing the source and destination addresses. The packet filter can disallow traffic to or from specific addresses or address ranges and can disallow traffic with suspect address patterns.
- **Firewalls**—Allow you to examine traffic as high as the application layer. Firewalls check ports in message addresses and even check the internal content of specific application messages. Traffic that fails any of those tests can be rejected.

23.4.1   Packet Filters

As you may recall, TCP/IP addresses are composed of both a machine address and, within the machine, a port number identifying the program to handle the message. The combined address/port information is available in every TCP/IP message—with the exception of broadcasts and some messages exchanged while a TCP/IP address is being assigned via the DHCP protocol—and is available for both the sender and the receiver of the message.

Packet filters are based on protecting the network by using an **access control list (ACL).** This list resides on the router and determines which machine (IP address) can use the router and in what direction. Typically, the router permits all outgoing traffic but denies any new, incoming connections. If a machine has established a connection with a machine on the outside, the router accepts packets from it. Thus, a router will reject unsolicited connection attempts from the Internet to your computer.

If you have packet filter software that is capable of examining the subnet of the source address based on which physical port delivers the message to the router, you can set up rules to avoid "spoofed" TCP/IP addresses. The idea behind spoofing is for messages from the Internet to appear to have originated from your LAN. The antispoofing filter prevents this by rejecting messages coming from a port with impossible source addresses.

The antispoofing filter is an important part of protecting machines in your network on which you have installed filters to limit particular services to machines on your subnet. For instance, suppose that you have installed software on a Linux machine to act as a Windows network file server. You can configure Linux to reject all network traffic originating outside your subnet, thereby preventing computers on the Internet from seeing the file server. But if an attacker could pretend to be on your LAN, that safeguard would be bypassed. To defeat that attacker, you need to use an antispoofing filter.

The antispoofing filter, also known as egress and ingress filtering, will only route outgoing packets if they have a valid internal IP address. By rule, your routers should disregard and drop any outgoing packets that have not originated from a valid internal IP address. When you follow these guidelines, you effectively prevent your network from becoming a participant in any spoofing attack. Examples of address filters follow:

> Historical low-end broadcast: 0.0.0.0/8
> Limited broadcast: 255.255.255.255/32
> RFC 1918 private networks: 10.0.0.0/8
> RFC 1918 private networks: 172.16.0.0/12
> RFC 1918 private networks: 192.168.0.0/16
> Loop back address: 127.0.0.0/8
> Link local networks: 169.254.0.0/16
> Class D addresses: 224.0.0.0/4
> Class E reserved address: 240.0.0.0/5
> Unallocated address: 248.0.0.0/5

There may be other addresses that need to be blocked by your router. However, blocking the addresses listed above should provide good protection against denial of service attacks and/or spoofing attacks.

One disadvantage of a packet filters is that they generally do not protect against attacks using the user Datagram Protocol (UDP). This is so because there is no formal connection opened with the UDP as there is with TCP; therefore, the filter cannot reject the opening message.

Besides analyzing source and destination TCP/IP addresses, packet filters can examine the source and destination port numbers and the content of packet data. This gives packet filters far more power; for example, they can allow or disallow specific application services such as FTP or web pages, and they can allow or disallow access to services based on the content of the information being transferred. They even allow you to combine functions such as allowing incoming FTP access from the Internet, but only to a specific, designated server.

When you decide which port numbers to block, choose with care. If you decide to block a specific port, any service or application that uses that specific port will not function through the firewall. For example, if you block port 80, you will not be able to contact HTTP web servers that are using the default port 80.

23.4.2   Dynamic Packet Filters

Some firewalls are considered static packet filters while others are considered dynamic packet filters. The static packet filtering mechanism allows you to set rules based on protocol and port number to control inbound and outbound access on the external interface.

The dynamic packet filter is often referred to as **stateful inspection.** It is a firewall facility that can monitor the state of active connections and use the information gained to determine which network packets to allow through the firewall. By recording session information such as IP addresses and port numbers into a dynamic state list (also known as a state table), a dynamic packet filter can implement a much tighter security posture than a static packet filter. For example, assume that you wish to configure your firewall so that all users in your company are allowed out to the Internet, but only replies to users' data requests are let back in. With a static packet filter, you would need to permanently allow in replies from all external addresses, assuming that users were free to visit any site on the Internet. This kind of filter would allow an attacker to sneak information past the filter by making the packet look like a reply (which can be done by indicating "reply" in the packet header). In contrast, by tracking and matching requests and replies, a dynamic packet filter can screen for replies that do not match a request. When a request is recorded, the dynamic packet filter opens up a small, inbound hole so that only the expected data reply is let back through. Once the reply is received, the hole is closed. This process dramatically increases the security capabilities of the firewall; for example, it prevents someone from replaying a packet to get access, because the packet is not part of an active connection.

23.4.3   Circuit-level Gateways

Whereas the application gateway operates on the OSI model's application layer, the circuit-level gateway operates on the network level of the model. A circuit-level gateway translates IP addresses between the Internet and internal systems. The gateway receives outbound packets and transfers them from the internal network to the external network. Inbound traffic is transferred from the outside network to the internal network.

Circuit-level gateways provide a complete break between your internal network and the Internet. Unlike a packet filter, which simply analyzes and routes traffic, a circuit-level gateway translates packets and transfers them between network interfaces. This helps shield your network from external traffic, since the packets that go out of your network appear to have originated from the circuit-level gateway's Internet IP address instead of an address of an internal computer.

Circuit-level gateways often provide network address translation (NAT), in which a network host alters the packets of internal network hosts so they can be sent out across the Internet. (NAT was explained in Chapter 6.)

23.4.4   Application-level Gateways

Application-level gateways take requests for Internet services and forward them to the actual services. Application-level gateways sit between a user on the internal network and a service on the Internet. Instead of talking to each other directly, each system talks to the gateway. Your internal network never directly connects to the Internet.

Application-level gateways help improve security by examining all application layers, bringing context information into the decision process. However, they do this by breaking the client-server model into two connections: one form the client to the firewall and one from the firewall to the server. Unfortunately, since each application gateway requires a different application process, or daemon, you need to add a different application processor (or daemon) to support new applications.

23.4.5   Proxy Server

Recall from Chapter 6 that a proxy server is a server that sits between a client application, such as a web browser, and a real server. It intercepts all requests to the real server to see if it can fulfill the requests itself. If not, it forwards the request to the real server. If the proxy server can fulfill the request itself, the user gets increased performance. In addition, the proxy server provides a means for sharing a single Internet connection among a number of workstations. Even though there are practical limits in performance, the proxy server can still be an effective and inexpensive way to provide Internet services, such as e-mail, throughout an office. Note: Proxy servers typically refer to application gateways, but a circuit-level gateway is also a form of proxy server.

Besides increasing performance, a proxy server sits between a client program (typically a web browser) and some external server (typically another server on the Web), and acts as an application-level firewall. It acts as a type of firewall that manages packet sequence and origin to reduce the chance of hackers hijacking communication sessions. Note: Proxy servers are often used with firewalls, and sometimes they are the same machine or device as a firewall. The proxy server can monitor and intercept any and all requests being sent to the external server coming in from the Internet connection. Therefore, besides improving performance and sharing connections, the proxy server can also filter requests.

Filtering requests is a security function and the original reason for having a proxy server. Proxy servers can inspect all traffic (in and out) over an Internet connection and determine if anything that should be denied transmission, reception, or access. Since this filtering cuts both ways, a proxy server can be used to keep users out of particular websites (by monitoring for specific URLs) or to restrict unauthorized access to the internal network by authenticating users. Before a connection is made, the proxy server can ask the user to log in. To a web user, every site look like it requires a login. Because proxy servers are handling all communications, they can log everything the user does. For HTTP (web) proxies, this includes logging every URL. For FTP proxies, this includes every downloaded file. A proxy server can also examine the content of transmissions for "inappropriate" words or scan for viruses, although this may impose serious overhead on performance.

23.4.6   Advanced Firewall Features

Most firewalls today are a hybrid of stateful inspection, circuit-level gateways, and application-level gateways. Only packets dealing with acceptable activities are allowed in and out of an internal network. Some firewalls provide advanced firewalls features that make them even more effective.

The firewall is a logical place to install an authentication mechanism to help overcome the limitations of the TCP/IP. You can also use a reverse lookup on an IP address to try and verify that the user is actually at his or her reported location. This lookup activity helps identify and prevent spoofing attacks.

Firewalls can also provide user authentication. Some application-level gateways contain an internal user account database or are integrated with UNIX and Windows domain accounts. These accounts can be used to limit activities and services by users or to provide detailed logs of users' activity. Because individual users can be easily identified, more detailed rule sets can be implemented.

Authentication can also be used for remote access. Allowing employees to connect to the internal network form home or while traveling increases productivity, but how can you ensure that the person making the request is who he or she is supposed to be? Most firewalls support third-party authentication methods to provide strong authentication.

Almost every firewall performs some type of logging. Most packet filters do not enable logging by default, because logging degrades performance of traffic analysis. So if you want logging, make sure it is enabled and active. Extensive logging can help you potentially identify a hacker. Since your firewall is the single point of entry to your network, an attacker has to pass through it. Your log files should provide information to show you what the hacker was up to on your systems.

23.4.7   Demilitarized Zone (DMZ)

If you set a firewall between the Internet and your private network, it provides no good place to locate publicly accessible servers. If you place the servers out on the Internet in front of the firewall, they will be unprotected. If you place them behind the firewall, you have to create holes in the firewall protection to permit access to the servers. It is those holes that can be exploited on the rest of the network.

To get around this problem, you need to create **a demilitarized zone (DMZ).** Instead of having two ports, the public network on one port of the firewall and the private network on another port, you have three ports. The third port is the DMZ, which is a less secure area than the private network. The DMZ includes external servers such as the web and FTP servers, and the rest of your computers will be in the private network. See Figure 23.2.

Each segment—the public, the private, and the DMZ—that is connected to the firewall has a different set of security rules. Security for the private and the public segments is no different from what we have already discussed. In the DMZ segment, you need to use antispoofing filters, limit the allowable ports to those used by the servers on the DMZ LAN, and disallow access from known attacking sites. Note: Remember that firewalls themselves are not a guarantee of security. Develop a habit of examining firewall logs for suspicious events and be vigilant about discovering and applying software security patches.

23.4.8   Personal Firewalls

Today, many operating systems offer personal firewalls to protect an individual computer when connecting to the Internet. For example, Windows XP has the Internet Connection Firewall (ICF) (see Figure 23.3) and Linux has GNOME Lokkit. Much like a full-blown firewall, a personal firewall

Figure 23.2   A DMZ in relation to public and private networks

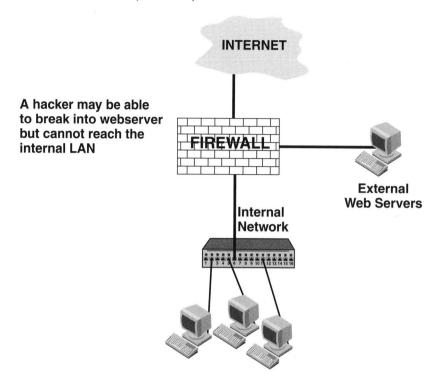

A hacker may be able
to break into webserver
but cannot reach the
internal LAN

Figure 23.3   Internet Connection Firewall (personal firewall) used in Windows XP

restricts what information is communicated from your home or small office network to and from the Internet to your computer.

Most of the personal firewalls are considered "stateful" firewalls. A stateful firewall is one that monitors all aspects of the communications that cross its path and inspects the source and destination address of each message that it handles. To prevent unsolicited traffic from the public side of the connection from entering the private side, the private firewall keeps a table of all communications that have originated from the computer. Some of these firewalls can be used in conjunction with Internet sharing, which in turn keeps track of all traffic originated from computers sharing the Internet link. All inbound traffic from the Internet is compared against the entries in the table. Inbound Internet traffic is only allowed to reach the computers in your network when there is a matching entry in the table that shows that the communication exchange began from within your computer or private network. Communications that originate from a source on the Internet are dropped by the firewall unless an entry is made using the configuration options that allow passage.

Personal firewalls can be configured to allow unsolicited traffic from the Internet to be forwarded by the computer to the private network. For example, if you are hosting an HTTP web server service and have enabled the HTTP service on your ICF computer, unsolicited HTTP traffic will be forwarded by the computer with the personal firewall to the HTTP web server.

23.5   INTERNET SECURITY ACCELERATOR

With Windows NT, Microsoft's firewall and proxy server was Microsoft Proxy Server. For Windows 2000, Microsoft Proxy Server was replaced with the Internet Security Accelerator 2000 (also known as ISA Server).

Whether installed as a dedicated security component or as an integrated firewall and caching server, ISA Server provides a multilayered, enterprise firewall that helps protect networks from attacks by hackers. ISA Server provides several security technologies: unified server management, packet filtering, intrusion detection, and secure publishing. All these features, built on top of Windows 2000, simplify network security management tasks and provide a complete and reliable firewall server.

ISA Server comes in two editions, Standard Edition and Enterprise Edition. Both have the same rich feature set, although Standard Edition is a stand-alone server supporting a maximum of four processors. For large-scale deployments, server array supports multilevel policy, computers with more than four processors, and load balancing and fault tolerance.

Typically, an organization protects itself by installing the ISA Server on the perimeter of its network. The typical deployment scenario is a multihomed system with one connection going to the Internet and the other connection to the internal network. ISA Server provides firewall services, network address translation, and a web proxy for internal network clients. All network traffic should pass through the ISA Server.

Configuration of the network interface cards is essential for proper operation of the ISA Server. The internal interface should be configured with a DNS server address on the internal network. This allows the ISA Server to resolve incoming requests for internal services. Configure the default gatway for the external interface only. Disable bindings on the external interface to improve security. For additional security, disable LMHOSTS lookup and NetBIOS over TCP/IP under the Advanced TCP/IP Settings option.

23.5.1   ISA Server Installation Modes

The ISA Server can be installed in one of three modes: cache only, firewall only, or integrated mode. Cache mode installs the web proxy service and allows storing of web pages locally. This improves network performance and decreases the costs of Internet access. Firewall mode allows internal clients to access the Internet more securely. After an organization decides which mode is best for it, the organization establishes the size and location of the web cache. These decisions are based on hard drive space and number of web users. Next, the internal network address space is defined. Ideally, private network addresses should be used. Private IPs assigned by the Internet Assigned Numbers Authority (IANA) can be found in RFC 1918 at http://www.faqs.org/rfcs/rfc1918.html.

23.5.2   ISA Server Access Policy

After installation of the ISA Server, the next step is to configure the access policy for the firewall. The access policy should be based on an organization's security policy. ISA Server's access policy consists of the following three rules, or filters:

- Protocol rules
- Site and content rules
- IP packet filters

Protocol rules state which protocols clients can use to access the Internet. Protocol definitions are used to create protocol rules. ISA Server comes with all the common Internet protocols predefined. In addition, protocols can be configured as needed. Protocol definitions consist of the following:

- Port number for the initial connection
- Low-level protocol used (TCP or UDP)
- Direction of the connection (inbound or outbound)
- Secondary connections, if needed

Protocol rules must be configured and enabled to allow client access to external network addresses. ISA Server can allow or deny access to all Internet protocols or selected protocols. Furthermore, protocol access can be restricted by user ID, group name, network address, or time of day.

In addition to protocol rules, access policy configuration includes site and content rules. Site and content rules can be configured to allow specific computers access to selected content on specified sites. Destination sets and client sets are policy elements that aid in configuring site and content rules. Destination sets include external sites and/or specific directories that clients can access. Client address sets allow specification of ranges of network addresses that are permitted access to site and content rules.

The final step in configuring access policy is applying IP packet filters. Packet filters block or allow packets from passing through specific ports. By default, no packets can pass through the ISA Server. Once packet filtering is enabled, all packets on the external interface are dropped, unless explicitly allowed. Packets can be filtered by type of service, port number, source address, and destination address. In addition to static packet filtering, ISA Server provides a more secure method of filtering called stateful inspection. Stateful inspection verifies that traffic is behaving as it should. In other words, the state of the connection is known. Another type of filter used by ISA Server is an application filter. Application filters intercept traffic at the application level. These filters inspect the data portion of the packet and can eliminate packets that contains malicious data.

23.5.3   ISA Server Clients

A single, internal-networked system can be configured as three types of clients. Each type of client provides different functions. ISA Server supports the following three types of clients:

- Web proxy clients—All web browser clients that are configured to use ISA Server
- Firewall clients—All computers that have firewall client software installed and active
- Secure NAT clients—All computers that do not have firewall client software installed

A web proxy client is one whose web browser is configured to use the ISA Server. The browser can be configured manually or by downloading the firewall client software from the ISA Server. Web proxy clients use the web proxy service, which is a separate service that manages connections for common HTTPs only.

A firewall client is a computer with firewall software installed on it. The computer must have a Windows-based operating system. The firewall client software can automatically configure web proxy clients, update the local address table, and set the DNS settings for the client. Once the client software is installed and enabled, the client can run WinSock applications that interact with the firewall service. The client can be easily disabled from the Control Panel. The firewall client can pass user credentials to the ISA Server for protocols that require authentication for access, which is a big advantage over secure NAT clients.

Secure NAT clients require no special software. All operating systems can use secure NAT clients. ISA secure NAT provides network address translation (NAT) for the internal network. NAT improves security by hiding the client's network address from the Internet. To configure secure NAT, set the default gateway of the client computer to point to the internal interface of the ISA Server. To ease configuration, it is recommended that a DHCP server be installed on the internal network. In addition, DNS needs configuring, because ISA Server does not provide DNS to secure NAT clients. A protocol rule must be set up to allow DNS queries.

Secure NAT clients have some limitations. First, a protocol definition must exist for each protocol used by a client. The connection cannot pass through a protocol rule that applies to all IP traffic. Unlike firewall clients, secure NAT clients need a protocol rule defined explicitly. A second limitation of secure NAT clients is that application filters are needed for complex protocols. Another limitation is that user-based authentication is not supported for secure NAT clients.

23.5.4   Intruder Detection

ISA Server has built-in intrusion detection that can detect the signature for port scans, Ping of Death, half scans, and Land Attack. Port scans and half scans can lead to system compromise. The Ping of Death and Land Attack are denial of service attacks. Half scans violate the three-way handshake for TCP connections. The attacker can gain valuable information about what ports are open. In addition, the scan is not logged because the TCP connection was not established. The Ping of Death is so named because it uses the ICMP protocol. It denies service to a system by sending fragmented packets greater than 65,535 bytes. Another availability attack, the Land Attack, uses IP spoofing to craft packets with the same source, destination, and port numbers.

Proper configuration of ISA's access policy can prevent some of these attacks. ISA can block access to the ICMP protocol, thereby preventing the Ping of Death attack. To prevent the Land Attack, access policy can deny inbound access to packets whose source address is an internal network address.

The ISA Server users an alerting service for events such as intrusion detections. Alerts can be sent as e-mails or logged to the Windows Event Viewer. The e-mail notification service must be configured correctly. If not, the ISA Server can start a small-scaled denial of service attack on your e-mail client. In addition, alert notification can trigger the stopping of the firewall service, thus cutting off routing to the internal network. These types of attacks exploit security vulnerabilities in the TCP/IP protocol stack. Therefore, security patches must be installed to further protect the internal network.

The ISA Server can also log access, monitor in real-time, provide statistical reports, and send out alerts. Logs are kept for the firewall service, web proxy service, and IP packet filtering. Log files can be transferred to a database or stored as standard text files. The firewall logs and web proxy logs access information from internal clients; the IP packet filtering logs default to showing block packets. ISA Server performs real-time monitoring of alerts, running services and client sessions so that it can distinguish legitimate traffic from illegitimate traffic. ISA Server generates reports at preconfigured intervals. Reports, which can be easily viewed in HTML, include statistics on web usage, application usage, and traffic and utilization. Security reports show numbers of blocked packets and unauthorized access.

ISA Server is a firewall solution for securing internal networks from the Internet. The installation process is troublefree. The ISA Management Console provides administrators with the tools needed to configure access policy and monitor the ISA Server. The ISA Server's access policy must be configured correctly and monitored continuously. Nevertheless, attacks can originate from the internal network or new e-mail macro viruses can penetrate the network. A "defense in depth" strategy is the best way to secure a network. The foundation of such a strategy is a well-written security policy that protects both systems and people. Then to improve network security, enforce a good password policy, and eliminate unneeded services, perform network penetration testing frequently and always apply the latest security patches.

23.6   DENIAL OF SERVICE

An attacker does not necessarily have to gain access to a system to cause significant problems. **Denial of service (DoS)** is a type of attack on a network that is designed to bring the network down by flooding it with useless traffic. Many DoS attacks, such as the Ping of Death and Teardrop attacks, exploit limitations in the TCP/IP protocols. In the worst cases, for example, a website accessed by millions of people can occasionally be forced to temporarily cease operation. A denial of service attack can also destroy programs and files in a computer system. Although usually intentional and malicious, a denial of service attack can sometimes happen accidentally. See Table 23.1. For all known DoS attacks, there are software fixes that system administrators can install to limit the damage. But like viruses, new DoS attacks are constantly being dreamed up by hackers.

Distributed denial of service (DDoS) attacks involve installing programs known as zombies on various computers in advance of the attack. A command is issued to these zombies, which launch the attack

Table 23.1 Forms of denial of service attacks

Attack Name	Description
Buffer Overflow Attack	The most common kind of DoS attack is simply to send more traffic to a network address than the programmers who planned its data buffers anticipated. The attacker may be aware that the target system has a weakness that can be exploited, or the attacker may simply try the attack in case it might work. A few of the better-known attacks based on the buffer characteristics of a program or system include: ■ Sending e-mail messages that have attachments with 256-character file names to Netscape and Microsoft mail programs ■ Sending oversized Internet Control Message Protocol (ICMP) packets (also known as the Ping of Death) ■ Sending to a user of the Pine e-mail program a message with a "from" address larger than 256 characters
SYN Attack	When a session is initiated between the TCP client and server in a network, a very small buffer space exists to handle the usually rapid "hand-shaking" exchange of messages that sets up the session. The session-establishing packets include a SYN field that identifies the sequence in the message exchange. An attacker can send a number of connection requests very rapidly and then fail to respond to the reply. This leaves the first packet in the buffer and other, legitimate connection requests cannot be accommodated. Although the packet in the buffer is dropped after a certain period of time without a reply, the effect of many of these bogus connection requests is to make it difficult for legitimate requests for a session to get established. In general, solutions to this problem depend on the operating system providing correct settings or the network administrator tuning the size of the buffer and the timeout period.
Teardrop Attack	This type of DoS attack exploits the way that the IP requires a packet that is too large for the next router to handle to be divided into fragments. The fragmented packets identify an offset value to the beginning of the first packet since this acts as a numbering system, the receiving system can reorder and reassemble the packet. In the teardrop attack, the attacker's IP puts a confusing offset value in the second or later fragment. If the receiving operating system does not have a plan for this situation, it can cause the system to crash.
Smurf Attack	In this attack, the perpetrator sends an IP ping (or "echo my message back to me") request to a receiving site. The ping packet specifies that it be broadcast to a number of hosts within the receiving site's local network. The packet also indicates that the request is from another site, that is, the target site that is to receive the denial of service. (Sending a packet with someone else's return address in it is called spoofing the return address.) The result will be lots of ping replies flooding back to the innocent, spoofed host. If the flood is great enough, the spoofed host will no longer be able to receive or distinguish real traffic.
WinNuke	WinNuke is a program that sends special TCP/IP packets with an invalid TCP header. Windows will crash when it receives one of the packets because of the way the Windows TCP/IP stack handles bad data in the TCP header. Instead of returning an error code or rejecting the bad data, it sends the computer to the blue screen of death.
Viruses	Computer viruses, which replicate across a network in various ways, can be viewed as DoS attacks where the victim is not usually specifically targeted, but simply a host unlucky enough to get the virus. Depending on the particular virus, the DoS attack can range from hardly noticeable to disastrous.
Physical Infrastructure Attacks	In this type of DoS attack, someone may simply snip a fiber optic cable. This kind of attack is usually mitigated by the fact that traffic can sometimes be quickly rerouted.

on behalf of the attacker, thus hiding the attacker's tracks. The zombies themselves are often installed using worms. The real danger from a DDoS attack is that the attacker uses many victim computers as host computers to control other zombies that initiate the attack. When the system that is overwhelmed tries to trace the attack, it receives a set of spoofed addresses generated by a series of zombies.

The following defensive steps will help you prevent these types of attacks:

- Keep systems updated with the latest security patches.
- Block large ping packets at the router and firewall; stop them from reaching the perimeter network.
- Apply antispoof filters on the router; that is, block any incoming packet that has a source address equal to an address on the internal network.
- Filter the ICMP messages on the firewall and router (although this could affect some management tools).
- Develop a defense plan with your Internet service provider (ISP) that enables a rapid response to an attack that targets the bandwidth between your ISP and your perimeter network.
- Disable the response to directed broadcasts.
- Apply proper router and firewall filtering.
- Use an intruder detection system system to check for unusual traffic, and generate an alert if it detects any. Configure the system to generate an alert if it detects ICMP_ECHOREPLY without associated ICMP_ECHO packets.
- Each week, more DoS attacks are documented and added to bug-tracking databases. Ensure that you remain current on these attacks and how you can guard against them.

The following registry key settings can be implemented on Windows 2000 and Windows Server 2003 to enable protection against DoS attacks:

- `hkey_local_machine\system\currentcontrolset\services\tcpip\`
  `parameters\synattackprotect=1 REG_DWORD`
- `hkey_local_machine\system\currentcontrolset\services\tcpip\`
  `parameters\tcpmaxconnectresponseretransmissions=2 REG_DWORD`
- `hkey_local_machine\system\currentcontrolset\services\tcpip\`
  `parameters\tcpmaxdataretransmissions=3 REG_DWORD`
- `hkey_local_machine\system\currentcontrolset\services\tcpip\`
  `parameters\enablepmtudiscovery=0 REG_DWORD`

For more information about protecting your network system, see the following websites:

HOW TO: Harden the TCP/IP Stack Against Denial of Service Attacks in Windows 2000

http://support.microsoft.com/default.aspx?scid=KB;en-us;315669&

Security Operations Guide for Windows 2000 Server, Chapter 4—Securing Servers Based on Role

http://www.microsoft.com/technet/security/prodtech/windows/windows2000/staysecure/secops04.asp

---

23.7   AUDITING AND INTRUDER DETECTION

Trying to detect intruders can be a daunting task that often requires a lot of hard work and a thorough working knowledge of the network operating system and the network as a whole. Remember to check the logs (especially the Security Log found in Event Viewer) that are available with your network operating system (and firewalls/proxy servers). For example, check the log that lists all of the failed login attempts. If you see that for several days at late hours, the same account has attempted to login but has failed, someone may be trying to figure out the password to login. Sometimes security logging is enabled by default; other times, it has to be enabled. Windows 2000 and Windows Server 2003 have an auditing service (through Group Policies) that allows you to audit a large array of items, including who accesses which files. These auditing features can be arranged to check *everyone*—including the administrators.

Auditing is a feature of Windows 2000 and Windows Server 2003 that monitors various security-related events so that you can detect intruders and attempts to compromise data on the system. Some events that you can monitor are access to an object such as a folder or file, management of user and group accounts, and logging on and off a system. The security events are provided in the Event Viewer. See Figure 23.4. Therefore, auditing is one way to find security holes in your network and to ensure accountability for people's actions.

Events are not audited by default. If you have Administrator permissions, you can specify what types of system events to audit using group policies (Computer Configuration\Windows Settings\Security Settings\Local Policies\Audit Policy). See Chapter 13 for more information on group policies and Figure 23.5.

For files and folders, you can only audit those volumes that are formatted with NTFS. To set, view, or change auditing a file or folder, do the following:

1. Open Windows Explorer and locate the file or folder that you want to audit.
2. Right-click the file or folder and select the Properties option See Figure 23.6.
3. Click the Security tab, click on the Advanced button, and click on the Auditing tab.
   - To set up auditing for a new group or user, click Add and specify the name of the user you want, and click the OK button to open the Auditing Entry dialog box.
   - To view or change auditing for an existing group or user, click the name and then the View/Edit button.
   - To remove auditing for an existing group or user, click the name and then the Remove button.

Figure 23.4   Viewing security log in event viewer

Figure 23.5 Configuring security audit policies

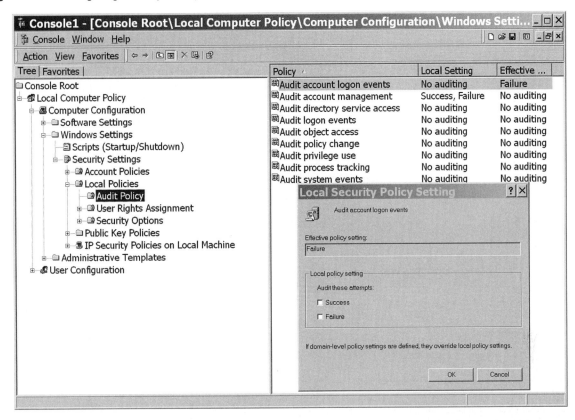

Figure 23.6 Configuring audit policy for directories and files

Figure 23.7 Configuring Security Log Properties

Table 23.2 Audit best practices

Potential Threat	Audit Event
To watch for users who are trying random passwords to bypass security	Failure audit for logon/logoff
To watch for stolen password usage	Success audit for logon/logoff
To watch for misuse of privileges, including those of administrators	Success audit for user rights, user and group management, security change policies, restart, shutdown, and system events
To watch the use of sensitive files	Success and failure audit for file-access and object-access events. File Manager success and failure audit of read/write access by suspect users or groups for the sensitive files.
To watch for the improper use of printers	Success and failure audit for file-access printers and object-access events. Print Manager success and failure audit of print access by suspect users or groups for the printers.
To watch for a virus outbreak	Success and failure write access auditing for program files (.EXE and .DLL extensions). Success and failure auditing for process tracking. Run suspect programs; examine security log for unexpected attempts to modify program files, or create unexpected processes. Perform this when you are actively monitoring the system log.

To perform auditing, you must be logged on as a member of the Administrator group or have been granted the Manage auditing and security log right in Group Policy.

Because the security log is limited in size, select only those objects that you need to audit and consider the amount of disk space that the security log will need. The maximum size of the security log is defined in Event Viewer by right-clicking Security Log and selecting the Properties option. See Figure 23.7.

Taking certain auditing steps helps to minimize the risk of security threats. Table 23.2 lists various events that should be audited, as well as the specific security threat that the audit event monitors.

23.8   ENCRYPTION AND DECRYPTION

In networks, sensitive data are transmitted across the network, sent as e-mail messages, and stored on files on disk. In all cases, the initial unencrypted data are referred to as plain text. **Encryption** is the process of disguising a message or data in what appears to be meaningless data (cipher text) to hide and protect sensitive data from unauthorized access. **Decryption** is the process of converting data from encrypted format back to original format. **Cryptography** is the art of protecting information by transforming it (encrypting it) into cipher text. In data transmission and telecommunications, cryptography is necessary when communication occurs over any untrusted medium. Cryptography not only protects data from theft or alteration, but it can also authenticate users. There are, in general, three types of cryptographic schemes typically used to accomplish these goals:

- **Private-key cryptography** (also known as secret key or symmetric algorithm)—Uses a single key for both encryption and decryption
- **Public-key cryptography** (or asymmetric algorithm)—Uses one key for encryption and another key for decryption
- **Hash encryption**—Uses a mathematical transformation to irreversibly encrypt information

To encrypt and decrypt a file, you must use a key. A **key** is a string of bits used to map text into a code and a code back to text. Think of the key as a super decoder ring that translates text messages to a code and back to text. There are two types of keys: public keys and private keys.

23.8.1   Private-Key Encryption

The most basic form of encryption is **private-key encryption.** In private-encryption, a single key is used for both encryption and decryption. The sender uses the key (or some set of rules) to encrypt the plain text and sends the cipher text to the receiver. The receiver applies the same key (or rule set) to decrypt the message and recover the plain text. Because a single key is used for both functions, private-key encryption is also called the symmetric algorithm.

Each individual must possess a copy of the key; of course, there must be a secure way to transport the key to people. If you must have multiple single keys per person, the process can get cumbersome. Private-key algorithms are generally fast and easily implemented in hardware. Therefore, they are commonly used for bulk data encryption.

There are two general categories of private-key algorithms: block cipher and stream cipher. A block cipher encrypts one block of data at a time. A stream cipher encrypts each byte of the data stream individually. The most common secret-key cryptography scheme used today is the Data Encryption Standard (DES).

23.8.2   Public-Key Encryption

Public-key encryption, also known as the asymmetric algorithm, uses two distinct but mathematically related keys, public and private. The public key is the nonsecret key that is available to anyone you choose, or made available to everyone by posting in a public place. Often it is made available through a digital certificate. The private key is kept in a secure location and is used only by you. When you are ready to send data, you first obtain the intended receiver's public key. With that public key, you encrypt the message. The recipient of your message uses his or her private key to read the data. Since the recipient is the only person who knows the private key, and it is the only item that can decode the message, the message is safe from other eyes.

In addition to encrypting messages (which ensures privacy), the sender can authenticate himself or herself to the receiver (so that the receiver knows who really sent the message) by using his or her private key to encrypt a digital certificate. When the message is received, the recipient can use the sender's public key to decrypt it.

While public keys may be stored anywhere for easy retrieval by computers, your private key should be guarded carefully. Since it is not convenient (or possible) for most of us to commit these keys to memory, they are stored on a personal computer's hard disk, encrypted using conventional

To do this	Use this key
Send an encrypted message	Receiver's public key
Send an encrypted signature	Sender's private key
Decrypt an encrypted message	Receiver's private key
Decrypt an encrypted signature (and authenticate the sender)	Sender's public key

cryptography and a password. Thus, anyone in possession of your computer would still not be able to use your private key, because it is scrambled with your password.

23.8.3   Digital Envelopes, Signatures, and Certificates

A **digital envelope** is a type of security that encrypts data using private-key encryption and that encrypts a key to decode the message using public-key encryption. This technique overcomes the problem that public-key encryption is slower than private-key encryption, because only the key is protected with public-key encryption.

A **digital signature** is a digital code that can be attached to an electronically transmitted message that uniquely identifies the sender. Like a written signature, the purpose of a digital signature is to guarantee that the individual sending the message really is who he or she claims to be.

A **digital certificate** is an attachment to an electronic message used for security purposes, such as to authenticate and to verify that a user sending a message is who he or she claims to be, and to provide the receiver with a means to encode a reply. An individual who wishes to send an encrypted message applies for a digital certificate from a **certificate authority (CA).** The CA issues an encrypted digital certificate containing the applicant's public key and a variety of other identification information. The CA makes its own public key readily available through print publicity or the Internet. The recipient of an encrypted message uses the CA's public key to decode the digital certificate attached to the message, verifies it as issued by the CA, and then obtains the sender's public key and identification information held within the certificate. With this information, the recipient can send an encrypted reply.

23.8.4   Hash Encryption

Hash encryption, also called message digests and one-way encryption, uses algorithms that do not involve a key. Instead, data are converted from a variable length to a fixed length called a hash value. Theoretically, no two data will produce the same hash value. The hash process is irreversible. You cannot recover the original data by reversing the hash process.

People must often use hashes when there is information they never want decrypted or read. Hash algorithms are typically used to provide a digital fingerprint of a file or message contents, to ensure that the file has not been altered by an intruder or virus. Hash functions are also commonly employed by many operating systems to encrypt passwords. Among the most common hash functions in use today are a family of message digest algorithms, all of which are byte-oriented schemes that produce a 128-bit hash value from an arbitrary-length message.

23.8.5   RSA and DES Standard

The **RSA standard** (created by Ron **R**ivst, Adi **S**hamir, and Leonard **A**dleman) defines the mathematical properties used in public-key encryption and digital signatures. The key length for this algorithm can range from 512 to 2048, which makes it a very secure encryption algorithm. The RSA algorithm uses a number known as the public modulus to come up with the public and private keys. This number is formed by multiplying two prime numbers. The security of this algorithm is based on the fact that although finding large prime numbers is relatively easy, factoring the result of multiplying two large prime numbers is not easy. If the prime numbers are large enough, the problem approaches being computationally impossible. The RSA algorithm has become the de facto standard for industrial-strength encryption, especially for data sent over the Internet.

Data Encryption Standard (DES) was developed in 1975 and was standardized by ANSI in 1981 as ANSI X.3.92. It is a popular symmetric-key encryption method that uses block cipher. The key used in DES is based on a 56-bit binary number, which allows for 72,057,594,037,927,936 encryption keys. Of these 72 quadrillion encryption keys, a key is chosen at random. If an encrypted file is being sent from one person (source person) to another person (target person), the source person encrypts the secret key with the target's public key, which was obtained from his or her certificate. Because the target person's key was used to encrypt the secret key, only the target person, using his or her private key, will be able to decrypt the DES secret key and decrypt the DES-encrypted data. Note: Until recently, the U.S. government banned export of DES outside of the United States.

Triple DES is a stronger alternative to regular DES and is used extensively in conjunction with virtual private network implementations. Triple DES encrypts a block of data using a DES secret key. The encrypted data are encrypted again using a second DES secret key. Finally, the encrypted data are encrypted a third time using yet another secret key. Since computers are becoming faster and faster, data protected with DES can be broken with boute force in shorter and shorter times.

The replacement for DES might be the U.S. National Security Agency's recent algorithm called skipjack, officially the Escrowed Encryption Standard (EES). It is defined in FIPS 185, and uses an 80-bit key rather than the DES 56-bit key. Skipjack was supposed to be integrated into a clipper chip. A clipper chip is an encryption chip designed under the auspices of the U.S. government. The government's idea was to enforce use of this chip in all devices that might use encryption, including computers, modems, telephones, and televisions. The government would control the encryption algorithm, thereby giving it the ability to decrypt any messages it recovered. The purported goal of this plan was to enable the U.S. government to carry out surveillance on enemies of state, even if they used encryption to protect their messages. However, the clipper chip created a fierce backlash from both public interest organizations and the computer industry in general. The government eventually retracted its original plan but has since promoted two other plans called Clipper 2 and Clipper 3. The Clipper 3 plan allows the use of any encryption technology, but stipulates that government law enforcement agencies must be able to recover any keys exported out of the country.

Another type of encryption is **Pretty Good Privacy (PGP).** The name is based on the realization that nothing is 100% secure. PGP is one of the most common ways to protect messages on the Internet because it is effective, easy to use, and free. PGP is based on the public-key method, which uses two keys. One key is a public key that you disseminate to anyone from whom you want to receive a message. The other is a private key that you use to decrypt messages that you receive.

23.8.6   X.509 Digital Certificates

X.509 certificates are the most widely used digital certificates. (Note: X.509 is actually an ITU recommendation, which means that it has not been officially defined or approved.) An X.509 certificate contains information that identifies the user as well as information about the organization that issued the certificate, including the serial number, validity period, issuer name, issuer signature, and subject (or user) name. The subject can be an individual, a business, a school, or some other organization, including a certificate authority. The X.509 describes two levels of authentication: simple authentication based on a password to verify user identity and strong authentication based on credentials formed using cryptographic techniques. Of course, strong authentication is recommended to provide secure services. See Figure 23.8.

23.9   SECURITY PROTOCOLS

Authentication, which is an essential part of network security, is the process by which the system validates the user's logon information. Authentication is crucial to secure communication. Users must be able to prove their identity to those with whom they communicate and must be able to verify the identity of others. Typically, after logging on, the user is authenticated for all network resources, that the

Figure 23.8 X.509 certificate

user has permissions to use. The user only has to log on once, even though the network resources may be located throughout several computers.

23.9.1 Interactive Authentication

Windows 2000 and Windows Server 2003 have several forms of authentication. If you are at a computer that is not a domain controller, press Ctrl+Alt+Del to log on, enter a user name and password, specify the individual computer/workgroup, and specify that you are performing a local interactive logon. During a local interactive logon, the steps in authentication are as follows:

1. The user provides the user name and password. The computer forwards that information to the security subsystem of the local computer.
2. The domain controller compares the user name and password to the local Security Accounts Manager (SAM) database.
3. If the information matches and the user account and password are valid, Windows creates an access token for the user.
4. Anytime the user makes a connection to a computer, the user name and password is forwarded to that computer. The computer then authenticates the user and returns an access token.

When you log on as a local user, the local user account is not available to the domain/domain controllers. Note: A user cannot log on locally to a domain controller.

23.9.2 NTLM Authentication

In **NTLM authentication** (NTLM = NT LAN Manager), the client selects a string of bytes, uses its password to perform a one-way encryption of the string, and sends both the original string and the encrypted one to the server. The server receives the original string and uses the password from the account database to perform the same one-way encryption. If the result matches the encrypted string sent by the client, the server concludes that the client knows the user-name password pair. NTLM authentication has been around since the days of LAN Manager (which was part of OS/2 and early Windows NT) and is not very efficient by today's standard. For the most part, it has been replaced by Kerberos authentication, but it remains available so that a Windows 2000 or Windows Server 2003 computer can communicate with a Windows NT computer.

23.9.3   Kerberos Authentication

Kerberos employs a client-server architecture and provides user-to-server authentication rather than host-to-host authentication. The Kerberos authentication process was developed at MIT for the TCP/IP network. Its purpose is to allow users and services to authenticate themselves to each other without allowing other users to capture the network packet on the network and resending it so that they can be authenticated over an insecure media such as the Internet. Therefore, Kerberos provides strong authentication for client-server applications by using symmetric, secret-key cryptography. After a client and server have used Kerberos to prove their identity, they can encrypt all of their communications to assure privacy and data integrity as they go about their business.

With Kerberos, security and authentication are based on secret-key technology in which every host on the network has its own secret key. Clearly, the system would be unmanageable if every host had to know the keys of all other hosts. Therefore, a secure, trusted host somewhere on the network, known as a key distribution center (KDC), knows the keys of all of the hosts (or at least some of the hosts within a portion of the network called a realm). In this way, when a new node is brought on, only the KDC and the new node need to be configured with the node's key. Keys can be distributed physically or by some other secure means.

The Kerberos server/KDC has two main functions, known as the Authentication Server (AS) and Ticket-Granting Server (TGS). When a user requests a service, his or her identity must be established. To do this, a ticket is presented to the server, along with proof that the ticket was originally issued to the user (and is not a captured network packet containing the password or ticket that is resent). The next paragraphs describe how the process works.

When a user logs on, the client transmits the user name to the AS, along with the identity of the service the user desires to connect to, for example, a file server. The TGS constructs a ticket, which contains a randomly generated key, encrypted with the file server's secret key, and sends the ticket to the client as part of its credentials, which include the session key encrypted with the client's key. If the user types the right password, then the client can decrypt the session key, present the ticket to the file server, and use the shared, secret, session key to communicate between them. Tickets are time-stamped and typically have an expiration time of about a few hours.

If the client specifies that it wants the server to prove its identity too, the server adds one of the time-stamped packets the client sent to the AS, encrypts the result in the session key, and sends the result back to the client. At the end of the exchange, the server is certain that the client is who it says it is. If mutual authentication occurs, the client is also convinced that the server is authentic. Moreover, the client and server share a key that no one else knows and can safely assume that a recent message encrypted in that key originated with the other party.

As you can see, through the entire process of getting authentication, the password was never sent on the wire. Therefore, a packet that contains the password cannot be compromised. In addition, many of the tickets and requests are time-stamped to monitor when the packet was made, so that the packet is not captured and resent at a later time. Note that the encryption algorithm is different for every client.

The current shipping version of this protocol is Kerberos v5 (described in RFC 1510), although Kerberos v4 still exists and is being used to some extent. Although the details of operation, functional capabilities, and message formats are different for the two versions, the conceptual overview is basically the same for both. One primary difference, however, is that Kerberos v4 uses only DES to generate keys and encrypt messages, whereas Kerberos v5 allows other schemes to be employed (although DES is still the most widely used algorithm).

23.9.4   SSL and S-HTTP

Most companies with connections to the Internet have implemented firewall solutions to protect the corporate network from unauthorized users coming in, and unauthorized sessions going out via the Internet. Although firewalls guard against intrusion or unauthorized use, they cannot guarantee the security of the link between a workstation and server on opposite sides of a firewall, or the security of the actual message being conveyed. To create this level security, two related Internet protocols, Secure Sockets Layer (SSL) protocol and Secure Hypertext Transfer Protocol (S-HTTP), ensure that sensitive information passing through an Internet link is safe from prying eyes. Whereas the SSL protocol is designed to establish a secure connection between two computers, S-HTTP is designed to send individual messages securely. Since SSL protocol and S-HTTP have different designs and goals, it is possible to use the two protocols together.

The **Secure Sockets Layer (SSL)** protocol operates at the transport layer, as do HTTP, FTP, NNTP, and SMTP. When both a client (usually in the form of a web browser) and a server support the SSL protocol, any data transmitted between the two becomes encrypted. Microsoft Internet Explorer and Netscape Navigator support the SSL protocol at the browser level.

When an SSL client wants to communicate with an SSL-compliant server, the client initiates a request to the server, which in turn sends a X.509 standard certificate back to the client. The certificate includes the server's public key and server's preferred cryptographic algorithms, or ciphers. The client then creates a key to be used for that session, encrypts the key with the public key sent by the server, and sends the newly created session key to the server. After it receives this key, the server authenticates itself by sending a message encrypted with the key back to the client, thereby proving that the message is coming from the proper server. After this handshake process, which results in the client and server agreeing on the security level, all data transfer between that client and that server for a particular session is encrypted using the session key. When a secure link has been created, the first part of the URL will change from http:// to https://. The SSL protocol supports several cryptographic algorithms to handle the authentication and encryption routines.

The **Transport Layer Security (TLS)** protocol is the successor to the Secure Sockets Layer (SSL) protocol. TLS is composed of two layers: the TLS Record Protocol and the TLS Handshake Protocol. The TLS Record Protocol provides connection security with some encryption method such as the DES, but it can also be used without encryption. The TLS Handshake Protocol allows the server and client to authenticate each other and to negotiate an encryption algorithm and cryptographic keys before data are exchanged. The TLS protocol is based on Netscape's SSL 3.0 protocol; however, TLS and SSL are not interoperable. The TLS protocol does contain a mechanism that allows TLS implementation to back down to SSL 3.0. The most recent browser versions support TLS. The TLS Working Group, established in 1996, continues to work on the TLS protocol and related applications.

Secure Hypertext Transfer Protocol (S-HTTP) is simply an extension of HTTP. S-HTTP is created by the SSL protocol running under HTTP. The S-HTTP was developed as an implementation of the RSA encryption standard. While the SSL protocol operates at the transport layer, S-HTTP supports secure end-to-end transactions by adding cryptography to messages at the application layer. Whereas the SSL protocol is application independent, S-HTTP is tied to the HTTP protocol.

An S-HTTP message consists of three parts:

- The HTTP message itself
- Sender's cryptographic preferences
- Receiver's preferences

The sender integrates both preferences, which results in a list of cryptographic enhancements to be applied to the message.

S-HTTP, like the SSL protocol, can be used to provide electronic commerce without customers worrying about who might intercept their credit card number or other personal information. To decrypt an S-HTTP message, the recipient must look at the message headers, which designate which cryptographic methods were used to encrypt the message. Then, to decrypt the message, the recipient uses a combination of his or her previously stated and current cryptographic preferences and the sender's previously stated cryptographic preferences. S-HTTP does not require that the client possess a public-key certificate, which means secure transactions can take place at any time without individuals needing to provide a key (as in a session encryption with SSL).

23.9.5   Security Protocols for Virtual Tunnels

A **virtual private network (VPN)** uses a public or shared network (such as the Internet or a campus intranet) to create a secure, private network connection between a client and a server. The VPN client cloaks each packet in a wrapper that allows it to sneak (or tunnel) unnoticed through the shared network.

When the packet gets to its destination, the VPN server removes the wrapper, deciphers the packet inside, and processes the data.

There are two varieties of VPNs, and they differ primarily in their approach to protecting data: PPTP and L2TP. The oldest and simplest type of VPN uses the Point-to-Point Tunneling Protocol (PPTP). PPTP's data encryption algorithm, Microsoft Point-to-Point Encryption (MPPE), uses the client's login password to generate the encryption key. This is controversial, because hackers are always finding ways to acquire passwords. In addition, early versions of Microsoft PPTP had flaws that could expose tunneled data to inspection by hackers. Microsoft has since patched PPTP for all versions of Windows. To provide authentication, MPPE requires the use of EAP-TLS, MS-CHAP v1, or MS-CHAP v2. MPPE is available on Windows 2000, Windows Server 2003, Windows XP, Windows NT 4.0, and Windows 9X clients.

The more secure alternative to PPTP is Layer 2 Tunneling Protocol (L2TP). Microsoft's L2TP merges elements of PPTP with Layer 2 Forwarding, a Cisco Systems Inc. packet encapsulation scheme. L2TP alone is not secure, so it is almost invariably paired with a fast-growing encryption standard called IPSec (Internet Protocol Security), which supports end-to-end encryption between clients and servers.

IPSec supports end-to-end encryption between clients and servers, whereas MPPE only supports link encryption. If implemented properly, IPSec is virtually impenetrable. Ideally, IPSec encryption employs the triple Data Encryption Standard (3DES) based on ANSI X.509 security certificates. Electronic certificates, issued internally or by a public authority such as Verisign Inc., irrefutably identify the client and server. 3DES encryption (ANSI X9.52) strengthens standard 56-bit encryption keys, which can be broken only with considerable effort, by applying the encryption algorithm three times.

23.9.6   IPSec

IP Security, more commonly known as IPSec, is not a single protocol but a suite of protocols that provide a mechanism for data integrity, authentication, and privacy for the Internet Protocol (and IPSec is part of IPv6). IPSec can provide either message authentication and/or encryption. IPSec is documented in a series of Internet RFCs; the overall IPSec implementation is guided by RFC 2401, "Security Architecture for the Internet Protocol."

IPSec defines a new set of headers to be added to IP datagrams. These new headers are placed after the IP header and before the layer 4 protocol (typically, TCP or UDP). The new headers provide information for securing the payload of the IP packet as follows:

- **Authentication header (AH)**—This header, when added to an IP datagram, ensures the integrity and authenticity of the data, including the fields in the outer IP header. It does not provide confidentiality protection. AH uses a keyed-hash function rather than digital signatures, because digital signature technology is too slow and would greatly reduce network throughput. If any part of the datagram is changed during transit, this will be detected by the receiver when it performs the same one-way hash function on the datagram and compares the value of the message digest that the sender has supplied. The fact that the one-way hash also involves the use of a secret shared between the two systems means that authenticity can be guaranteed. In addition, AH may also enforce antireplay protection by requiring that a receiving host set the replay bit in the header to indicate that the packet has been seen. Without it, an attacker may be able to resend the same packet many times.
- **Encapsulating security payload (ESP)**—This header, when added to an IP datagram, protects the confidentiality, integrity, and authenticity of the data by performing encryption at the IP packet layer. It supports a variety of symmetric encryption algorithms. The default algorithm for IPSec is 56-bit DES. This cipher must be implemented to guarantee interoperability among IPSec products.

AH and ESP can be used independently or together, although for most applications, one of them is sufficient. IPSec also uses other existing encryption standards to make up a protocol suite.

AH and ESP provide the means to protect data from tampering, prevent eavesdropping, and verify the origin of the data. It is the Internet Key Exchange (IKE) protocol, however, that allows nodes to agree on authentication methods, encryption methods, keys to use, and the lifespan of keys. IKE also allows smart, secure, key exchange to provide a secure method of exchanging keys and negotiating protocols and encryption algorithms. The information negotiated by IKE is stored in a security association

(SA). The SA is like a contract laying out the rules of the VPN connection for the duration of the association. An SA is assigned a 32-bit number that, when used in conjunction with the destination IP address, uniquely identifies the SA. This number is called the Security Parameters Index (SPI).

NOTE: IKE is a hybrid protocol which implements the Oakley Key Exchange and Skeme Key Exchange protocols inside the Internet Security Association and Key Management Protocol (ISAKMP) framework. ISAKMP, Oakley, and Skeme are security protocols implemented by IKE.

Perfect forward secrecy (PFS) ensures that no part of a previous encryption key plays a part in generating a new encryption key. Basically, this means that when a new encryption key is generated, the old key does not play any part in that generation. Under normal circumstances, for performance reasons, an old key does play a part in generating a new key. Use of PFS requires a little more overhead time, as PFS requires reauthentication every time a new key is generated.

When IPSec is used, a policy or a collection or rules defines when and how IPSec works. In Windows 2000 and Windows Server 2003, a policy starts out with two sections, the rules section and a general section. You can see this by opening up the Microsoft Management Console (MMC), adding the IP Security Policy MMC snap-in, and opening up any of the preconfigured IPSec policies.

Each rule is composed of five sections: IP filter list, filter action, authentication methods, tunnel settings, and connection type. Each section must be defined to make a rule complete.

- **IP filter list**—An IP filter list can have several IP filters, with each one specifically tailored to a certain IP address, subnet, or specific IP protocol. IP filters can be finely tuned to a company's specific needs.
- **Filter action**—The filter action specifies how the connections in the IP filter list will be treated. All of the connections in the IP filter list receive the following filter action:
    1. Security Methods: Three methods can be applied: permit, block, and negotiate. For example, say you do not want to have DNS requests blocked or to have them negotiate security. You need to create an IP filter list, make an entry for DNS, and create a filter action to specify that the DNS IP filter be permitted.
    2. Negotiated Security: You are able to select the level of security that the IPSec policy will allow for the connections specified in the IP filter list. There are three levels: high, medium, and custom. High and medium are preset settings that can be found in the MMC. If you need or desire to modify these settings, you should customize your security settings.
    3. Customized Security: You can specify your security settings. You can choose to have data and address integrity without encryption, or you can choose to data integrity and encryption. You may also choose to have both. Integrity algorithms used are either Secure Hash Algorithm 1 (SHA1) or Message Digest S. Encryption algorithms are 3DES or DES.
- **Authentication methods**—There are three methods of authenticating when enforcing a rule: applying Kerberos, using a valid security certificate from a certificate authority, or using a pre-shared string of characters.
    1. Kerberos is the default authentication method for IPSec and it is recommended. Using any other method will add another variable to troubleshoot if your IPSec policy does not work correctly.
    2. Using a X.509 security certificate can be another method of authenticating using an IPSec policy, but this method involves more configuration and leaves the policy open to possible problems.
    3. The Preshared key is the least secure method of authentication and the most susceptible to hacking attacks. Although the least secure, this method requires the least amount of infrastructure support.
- **Tunnel setting**—This setting allows for the possible tunneling of IP traffic through unsecured networks, such as the Internet. Tunneling is a method whereby an IP packet is "wrapped" in another IP packet and sent to a tunneling endpoint, where it is "unwrapped" and forwarded on to its destination through a secure or trusted network. The benefit is that the wrapped packet is treated as data by the tunneling packet, thereby gaining possible data encryption and authentication through IPSec policies (if enforced). The wrapped packet also gains anonymity, because the IP packet is sent to the

tunnel endpoint and not the destination. The destination system is unknown until the packet is unwrapped at the tunnel endpoint.

- **Connection type**—You must select the type of connections on which the policy will be enforced: LAN, remote access, or all network connections.

As part of IPSec, you can also specify when new session keys are generated. You can specify that keys are generated after X amount of data have passed over the IPSec connection, or you can specify that keys are generated after X number of seconds. These settings allow you to make your connections more secure by using new keys to defeat possible hacking attempts, but remember performance is always affected when you generate new keys.

Let's look at an example of establishing secure communication. User A wants to send data to user B. User A's router (router A) has a security policy applied with a rule that says all traffic to user B needs to be encrypted. User B's router (router B) will be the other end of the IPSec tunnel. Router A checks to see if an IPSec security association (SA) exists between it and router B. If IKE verifies that an SA exists between the two routers, an IPSec SA is issued. If an SA does not exist, router A requests an IPSec SA from IKE. This association has to be negotiated by the routers exchanging information signed by a third-party certificate authority (CA)—one that both routers trust. Once the IKE SA is agreed upon by the routers, an IPSec SA can be issued, and secure, encrypted communications can begin. This process is transparent to user A and user B.

Windows 2000 and Windows Server 2003 IPSec is implemented transparently to the user. Users do not have to be in the same domain; they can each be in any trusted domain in the enterprise. IPSec management allows administration to be centralized by using group policies. In addition, by default, IPSec policies use the Windows 2000 or Windows Server 2003 default authentication method (Kerberos v5 authentication) to identify and trust communicating computers.

When you configure IPSec for Windows, the initial window displays three predefined policy entries: Client (Respond Only), Server (Request Security) and Secure Server (Require Security). By default, none of these policies are enabled.

- **Client (Respond Only)**—Allows communication in plain text but responds to IPSec requests and attempts to negotiate security. This policy effectively allows clear-text communication but attempts to negotiate security if a security request is made. Uses Kerberos v5 for authentication.
- **Server (Request Security)**—Causes the server to attempt to initiate security communications for every session. If a client who is not aware of IPSec initiates a session, the session is allowed.
- **Secure Server (Require Security)**—Requires Kerberos trusts for all IP packets sent from this computer, with the exception of broadcast, multicasts, and Resource Reservation Setup Protocol (RSVP) and ISAKMP packets. This policy does not allow insecure communications with clients. Therefore, any client who connects to a server with this policy must be aware of IPSec.

Any routers or switches in the data path between the communicating hosts will simply forward the encrypted and/or authenticated IP packets to their destination. However, if there is a firewall or filtering router, IP forwarding must be enabled for the following IP protocols and UDP port for IPSec to function:

- IP Protocol ID of 51: Both inbound and outbound filters should be set to pass AH traffic.
- IP Protocol ID of 50: Both inbound and outbound filters should be set to pass ESP traffic.
- UDP Port 500: Both inbound and outbound filters should be set to pass ISAKMP traffic.

Until recently, IPSec had some problems working with network address translation (NAT). Transport mode IPSec provides end-to-end security between hosts; tunnel mode IPSec protects encapsulated IP packets between security gateways, for example, between two firewalls or between a roaming host and a remote access server. TCP and UDP are involved in transport mode ESP. Since NAT modifies the TCP/UDP packet, NAT must also recalculate the checksum used to verify integrity. If NAT updates the checksum, ESP authentication will fail. If NAT does not update the checksum, TCP/UDP verification will fail. If the transport endpoint is under your control, you might be able to turn off the checksum function. To summarize, ESP can pass through NAT in tunnel mode, or in transport mode if checksums are disabled or ignored by the receiver.

IPSec and NAT can function together when NAT occurs before the packet is encrypted. This typically works fine in gateway-to-gateway communications. Remote access solutions are problematic because the IPSec VPN client on a remote laptop computer encrypts the packet before it travels to the NAT device, subsequently breaking the IPSec VPN connection.

To enable IPSec VPNs to work with NAT devices, some leading technology companies created NAT Traversal. The main technology behind this solution is UDP encapsulation, wherein the IPSec packet is wrapped inside a UDP/IP header, thereby allowing NAT devices to change IP or port addresses without modifying the IPSec packet.

23.10 CERTIFICATE AUTHORITIES

The public-key infrastructure (PKI) provides security for conversations between computers. PKI relies on these components to achieve its purpose:

- **Digital signature (certificate)**—Like a person's cursive signature, the digital signature verifies that a message is actually from the stated source. In a networking computer environment, users, computers, routers, and organizations can use digital certificates to certify their identities. Certificates thus provide authentication.
- **Encryption**—Just as snapping the lid onto a bottle of ketchup verifies that the tasty red contents have not been tampered with, encryption verifies that the message has not been corrupted or viewed. Encryption thus provides privacy as well as integrity to the communicating entities.

A certificate, also known as a digital certificate or public-key certificate, is a digital document that attests to the binding of a public key to an entity. The main purpose of a certificate is to generate confidence that the public key contained in the certificate actually belongs to the entity named in the certificate. The certificate holds the following information:

- User's name
- User's public key
- Serial number
- Expiration date
- Certificate information
- Information about the issuing certificate authority

The certificates are issued by certificate authorities (CAs), which can be any trusted service or entity willing to verify and validate the identities of those to whom it issues certificates and their association with specific keys. The following six steps describe the process of requesting and issuing a certificate:

1. Generating a key pair: The applicant generates a public key and a private key or is assigned a key pair by some authority in his or her organization.
2. Collecting required information: The applicant collects whatever information the CA requires to issue the certificate. The information could include the applicant's e-mail address, birth certificate, fingerprints, or notarized documents, if the CA needs to be certain that the applicant is who he or she claims to be.
3. Requesting the certificate: The applicant sends a certificate request, consisting of his or public key and the additional required information, to the CA. The certificate request may be encrypted using the CA's public key. Many requests are made using e-mail, but requests can also be sent by postal or courier service, for example, when the certificate request itself must be notarized.
4. Verifying the information: The CA applies whatever policy rules it requires to verify that the applicant should receive a certificate. As with identification requirements, the CA's verification policy and procedures influence the amount of confidence generated by the certificate it issues.
5. Creating the certificate: The CA creates and signs a digital document containing the applicant's public key and other appropriate information. The signature of the CA authenticates the binding of the subject's name to the subject's public key. The signed document is the certificate.
6. Sending or posting the certificate: The CA sends the certificate to the applicant or posts the certificate in a directory.

NOTE: A certificate has a default validity period of 2 years. After this period, the certificate expires and the CA must renew the certificate.

Certificate Services, a network service of a Windows server, includes two policy modules that permit two classes of CAs: enterprise CAs and stand-alone CAs. Within these two classes, there can be two types of CAs: a root CA and a subordinate CA. Policy modules define the action that a CA can take when it receives a certificate request, and can be modified if necessary. CAs are usually organized in a hierarchy in which the most trusted CA is at the top.

In the enterprise class, the enterprise root CA is the most trusted CA. There can be more than one enterprise root CA in a Windows domain, but there can be only one enterprise root CA in any given hierarchy. All other CAs in the hierarchy are enterprise subordinate CAs.

An organization should install an enterprise CA if it will be issuing certificates to users or computers within the organization. It is not necessary to install a CA in every domain in the organization. Enterprise CAs have a special policy module that enforces how certificates are processed and issued. The policy information used by these modules is stored in Windows 2000 Active Directory. Note: An Active Directory and a DNS server must be running prior to installing an enterprise CA.

An organization that will be issuing certificates to users or computers outside the organization should install a stand-alone CA. There can be many stand-alone CAs, but there can only be one stand-alone CA per hierarchy. All other CAs in a hierarchy are either stand-alone subordinate CAs or enterprise subordinate CAs. A stand-alone CA has a relatively simple default policy module and does not store any information remotely. Therefore, a stand-alone CA does not need to have Active Directory available.

A root CA is at the top of a hierarchy of CAs and is self-certified. It should be highly secured and, if possible, taken offline to protect its certificate and keys. This way, if a child CA gets "compromised," the child can be disabled and the overall CA hierarchy is still intact; that is, the root CA still contains a clean list of certificates. It communicates with either issuing or intermediate CAs. A subordinate CA is either an intermediate or issuing CA that must communicate with an intermediate or root CA to obtain information about certificates. Moreover, a parent CA certifies a subordinate ("child") CA. A certification path is the trust chain from the certificate all the way up to the root CA. Before the certification path works, the certificate of the root CA must be placed in the Trusted Root Certification Authorities store. For security reasons, a subordinate CA cannot have a certificate expire after a certificate higher up in the hierarchy expires.

When you want Internet users and their browsers to trust executable programs, ActiveX controls, and scripts on your website, you should obtain a Code Signing certificate with which to sign active content. Internet browsers may be configured at security levels that will not allow programs, controls, and scripts to be downloaded unless they are signed. Internet users are more likely to trust a Code Signing certificate that was issued from a well-known commercial CA (such as Verisign) than one that was distributed from your company's own CA.

You may have to revoke a certificate in situations where an employee leaves a company, you suspect a private key has been compromised, or you accidentally issued a certificate when you did not mean to. Revoked certificates are published in the Certification Revocation List (CRL).

A CA can be installed by upgrading from Certificate Server 1.0, during Windows 2000 or Windows Server 2003 installation (including unattended), and after a Windows 2000 installation. In terms of a new installation, add Certificate Services via the Add/Remove Programs (Add/Remove Windows Components) program in the Control Panel. To manage a Certificate Server, use the Certification Authority console which resides in the Administrative Tools folder. See Figure 23.9.

23.11   PATCHES

An important part of security is ensuring that you have the most updated patches for your network operating system. Check with the distributor and vendor of the network operating system (as well as operating system on the network) for security holes and the patches to fix them. Chapter 8 described the Microsoft Update website and installation of service packs. Along with these updates, you will need to find and apply hot fixes and security patches to Windows.

Figure 23.9   Certification Authority console

Quick Fix Engineering (QFE) is a group within Microsoft that produces hot fixes (code patches) for products. These fixes are provided to individual customers when they experience critical problems for which no feasible work-around solution is available. Occasionally, technical documentation refers to hot fixes as QFEs. Hot fixes do not undergo extensive regression testing and are very issue specific; you should apply a hot fix only if you experience the exact issue it addresses and are using the current software version with the latest service pack. Groups of hot fixes are periodically incorporated into service packs, at which time they undergo more rigorous testing, and are made available to all customers.

Security patches are designed to eliminate security vulnerabilities. Attackers who want to break into systems can exploit security vulnerabilities. These patches are mandatory, if the circumstances match, and need to be deployed quickly. Many security updates released are for client-side (often browser) issues. They may or may not be relevant to a server installation. Obtain the client patch to update your current client base and the admin patch to update the client-build area on your server.

HFNETCHK is a command-line utility that allows you to determine if the current configuration on your servers is up to date and has all the appropriate security patches. This tool works by downloading an XML database directly from Microsoft that contains a list of the latest hot fixes to check in order to stay secure. HFNETCHK will use a local XML database if you do not have a connection to the Internet, although the results provided may be out of date. Note: To use HFNETCHK, you must have administrator access to the computer being checked for patches, either local administrator or domain administrator. The tool has a number of command-line switches, which are listed in Table 23.3.

Another aid to security is the Computer Emergency Response Team (CERT) Coordination Center. The center was started in December 1988 by the Defense Advanced Research Projects Agency, which was part of the U.S. Department of Defense, after the Morris Worm disabled about 10% of all computers connected to the Internet. The CERT CC studies Internet security vulnerabilities, provides services to websites that have been attacked, and publishes security alerts. Research activities include the area of WAN computing and development of improved Internet security. The organization also provides training to incident-response professionals.

Table 23.3   HFNETCHK switches

HFNETCHK Switch	Function
–about	Explains HFNETCHK
–h <hostname>	Specifies the NetBIOS machine name to scan. Default is the local host.
–fh <hostfile>	Specifies the name of a file containing the NetBIOS machine names to scan. One name per line, 256 maximum per file.
–i <ipaddress>	Specifies the IP address of a machine to scan
–fip <ipfile>	Specifies the name of a file containing addresses to scan. One IP address per line, 256 maximum per file.
–r <range>	Specifies the IP address range to be scanned, starting with ipaddress1 and ending with ipaddress2. The range is inclusive.
–d >domain_name>	Specifies the domain name to scan. All machine in the domain will be scanned.
–n <network>	Indicates all systems on the local network will be scanned (all hosts in Network Neighborhood)
–history <level>	Not necessary for normal operation.
–t <threads>	Indicates number of threads used for executing scan. Possible values are from 1 to 128; default is 64.
–o <output>	Specifies the desired output format. (tab) outputs in tab delimited format; (wrap) outputs in a word-wrapped format. The default is wrap.
–x <datasource>	Specifies the XML data source containing the hot fix information. Location may be an xml filename, compressed xml cab file, or a URL. The default is mssecure.cab from the Microsoft website.
–s <suppress>	Suppresses NOTE and WARNING messages. 1 = Suppress NOTE messages only, 2 = Suppress both NOTE and WARNING messages. The default is to show all messages.
–z	Indicates not to perform registry checks
–nosum	Indicates not to evaluate file checksum. The checksum test calculates the checksum of files. This can use up large amounts of bandwidth. Using this option will speed up a scan and use less bandwidth. File version checks will still be done.
–b	Displays the status of hot fixes required to meet minimum baseline security standards.
–v	Displays the details for Patch NOT Found, WARNING, and NOTE messages. Enabled by default in tab mode.
–f <outfile>	Specifies name of the file to save the results. Default is to display to screen.
–u <username>	Specifies optional user name for log in to remote computer.
–p <password>	Specifies password to be used with user name.
–?	Displays a Help menu.

For more information about security aids, consult these websites:

CERT

http://www.cert.org/

Symantec Security Advisory List

http://securityresponse.symantec.com/avcenter/security/Advisories.html

23.12   BASELINE SECURITY ANALYZER

As part of Microsoft's Strategic Technology Protection Program, and in response to direct customer need for a streamlined method of identifying common security misconfigurations, Microsoft developed the Microsoft Baseline Security Analyzer (MBSA). The MBSA includes a graphical and command-line interface that can perform local or remote scans of Windows systems. MBSA runs on Windows 2000, Windows Server 2003, and Windows XP systems and will scan for missing hot fixes and vulnerabilities in the following products: Windows NT 4.0, Windows 2000, Windows Server 2003, Windows XP, Internet Information Services (IIS) 4.0 and 5.0, SQL Server 7.0 and 2000, Internet Explorer 5.01 and later, and Office 2000 and 2002. MBSA creates and stores individual XML security reports for each computer scanned and displays the reports in the graphical user interface in HTML. See Figure 23.10.

For more information about Baseline Security Analyzer, consult these websites:

Baseline Security Analyzer Home Page and Download Instructions

http://www.microsoft.com/technet/security/tools/Tools/mbsahome.asp

Baseline Security Analyzer White Paper

http://www.microsoft.com/technet/security/tools/tools/mbsawp.asp

---

Figure 23.10   Baseline Security Analyzer

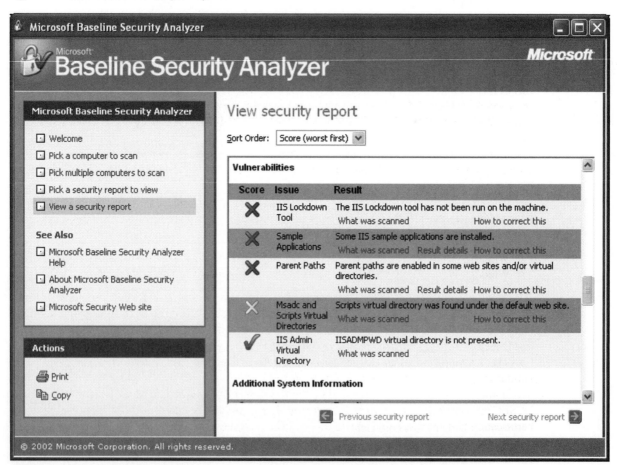

23.13   SECURITY STANDARDS OF THE U.S. DEPARTMENT OF DEFENSE

The U.S. Department of Defense (DOD) gave responsibility for computer security to the National Security Agency (NSA) in 1981 and the National Computing Security Center (NCSC) was formed. The DOD published a series of books dealing with computer and network security issues known as the Rainbow Series.

The NCSC first released Trusted Computer System Evaluation Criteria (TCSEC) in 1983 for stand-alone, non-networked computers; unofficially, the publication containing TCSEC is referred to as the Orange Book. The Orange Book defines the standard parameters of a trusted computer in several classes, indicated by a letter and a number. The higher the letter, the higher the certification. For example, class A is the highest class and class D is the lowest class. According to TCSEC, system security is evaluated at one of four broad levels, ranging from class D to class A1. Each level builds on the previous one by adding security measures at each level and partial level.

- Class D is defined as Minimum Security; systems evaluated at this level have failed to meet higher-level criteria.
- Class C1 is defined as Discretionary Security Protection; systems evaluated at this level meet security requirements by controlling user access to data. Note: C1 has been discontinued as a certification.
- Class C2, defined as Controlled Access Protection, adds to C1 requirements additional user accountability features, such as login procedures.
- Class B1 is defined as Labeled Security Protection; systems evaluated at this level also have a stated policy model, and specifically labeled data.
- Class B2, defined as Structured Protection, adds to B1 requirements a more explicit and formal security policy.
- Class B3, defined as Security Domains, adds stringent engineering and monitoring requirements and is highly secure.
- Class A1 is defined as Verified Design; systems evaluated at this level are functionally equivalent to B3 systems, but include more formal analysis of function to ensure security.

In 1987, the NCSC released enhanced testing criteria based on the Orange Book. The new standard, often referred to as the Red Book, consists of the Trusted Network Interpretation Environment Guidelines. The Red Book also uses the D through A levels. As with the C2 class in the Orange Book, the C2 class is the highest class for generic network operating systems. Higher-level classes require that operating systems be specifically written to incorporate security-level information as the data are input.

The most publicized class is C2, Controlled Access Protection, which requires a unique user account for each person on the network and accountability for the information the user handles. Additionally, the network communications must be secure.

Currently, several network operating systems are under evaluation for class C2 of Trusted Network (Red Book) certification. The following operating systems are C2-level certified for Trusted Computer (Orange Book) certification:

- Windows NT Workstation and Windows NT Server version 3.5 with service pack 3
- Windows NT Workstation and Windows NT Server version 4.0 with service pack 6a and C2 update

If the computer on which Windows NT Server is installed is connected to a network, it loses the C2 Trusted Computer certification. The only currently available network operating system that has achieved C2 Trusted Network certification is Novell IntranetWare [NetWare 4.11 Server] with IntranetWare Support Pack 3A and Directory Services Update DS.NLM v5.90, DSREPAIR.NLM v4.48 and ROLLCALL.NLM v4.10.

The Information Technology Security Evaluation Criteria (ITSEC), developed for Europe, are similar to the TCSEC but have some important differences. The ITSEC emphasize the integrity and availability of products and systems and introduce the distinctions of effectiveness and correctness. The TCSEC are primarily concerned with security policy, accountability, and assurance. Various European certification bodies grant ratings based on the ITSEC. Examples of ITSEC ratings are Level E2, which is a measure of effectiveness, and Class F-C2, which is a measure of functionality. A combined E2/F-C2 evaluation is similar in scope to the Class C2 TCSEC evaluation.

To verify security certification or check out officially released documents, go to the following website:

http://www.radium.ncsc.mil/tpep/epl/index.html

23.14 COMMON CRITERIA

A security standard that is gaining in popularity and importance is called **Common Criteria (CC),** which evaluates the security of computer and network devices. This standard was developed as a joint effort of organizations in the United States, Canada, France, Netherlands, and the United Kingdom. The International Organization for Standardization (ISO) also recognizes the CC standard as ISO 15408. Prior to implementation of the CC standard, the U. S. government used TCSEC. The website for Common Criteria is http://www.commoncriteria.org.

The Common Criteria standard is presented as a set of three distinct but related parts:

- **Introduction and general model**—This part defines general concepts and principles of IT security evaluation and presents a general model of evaluation. Part 1 also presents constructs for expressing IT security objectives, for selecting and defining IT security requirements, and for

Table 23.4 Evaluation Assurance Levels (EALs)

Level	Definition
EAL 0	Inadequate assurance
EAL 1	Functionally tested. Security functions are analyzed using a functional and interface specification of the target of evaluation (TOE) to understand security behavior. Analysis is supported by independent testing of the security functions.
EAL 2	Structurally tested. Security functions are analyzed using a functional and interface specification and the high-level design of the subsystems of the TOE. Analysis is supported by independent testing of the security functions, evidence of developer "black box" testing, and evidence of developer search for obvious vulnerabilities.
EAL 3	Methodically tested and checked. Analysis is supported by "grey box" testing, selective independent confirmation of developer test results, and evidence of developer search for obvious vulnerabilities. Developer environment controls and TOE configuration management are also required.
EAL 4	Methodically designed, tested, and reviewed. Analysis is supported by the low-level design of the modules of the TOE and a subset of the implementation. Testing is supported by an independent search for obvious vulnerabilities. Development controls are supported by a life-cycle model, identification of tools, and automated configuration management.
EAL 5	Semiformally designed and tested. Analysis includes all of the implementation. Assurance is supplemented by a formal model and a semiformal presentation of the functional specification and high-level design, and a semiformal demonstration of correspondence. The search for vulnerabilities must ensure relative resistance to penetration attack. Covert channel analysis and modular design are also required.
EAL 6	Semiformally verified design and tested. Analysis is supported by a modular and layered approach to design, and a structured presentation of the implementation. The independent search for vulnerabilities must ensure high resistance to penetration attack. The search for covert channels must be systematic. Developer environment controls and configuration management controls are further strengthened.
EAL 7	Formally verified design and tested. The formal model is supplemented by a formal presentation of the functional specification and high-level design showing correspondence. Evidence of developer "white box" testing and complete independent confirmation of developer test results are required. Complexity of the design must be minimized.

writing high-level specifications for products and systems. In addition, the usefulness of each part of the CC is described in terms of target audiences.

- **Security functional requirements**—Part 2 establishes a set of functional components as a standard way of expressing the security requirements for targets of evaluation (TOEs). This part also catalogs functional components, families, and classes.
- **Security assurance requirements**—Part 3 establishes a set of assurance components as a standard way of expressing the assurance requirements for TOEs. This part also catalogs assurance components, families, and classes. In addition, part 3 defines evaluation criteria for protection profiles (PPs) and security targets (STs) and presents evaluation assurance levels (EALs) for the predefined CC scale for rating assurance for TOEs.

Version 2.1 of the CC standard outlines a comprehensive set of evaluation criteria. These criteria are broken down into seven EALs, as shown in Table 23.4.

> For more information about EALs, visit the following website:
>
> http://www.commoncriteria.org/docs/EALs.html

The recommended level of certification for commercial systems is EAL 4. Currently, only a few operating systems have been approved at EAL 4, for example, Sun Microsystems' Sun Solaris 8 Operating Environment and Sun Trusted Solaris Version 8 4/01. The Windows 2000 family achieved a rating of EAL 4 + Flaw Remediation. To achieve this rating, Windows 2000 did, the developer/vendor must establish flaw remediation procedures that describe the tracking of security flaws, the identification of corrective actions, and the distribution of corrective action information to customers. The Microsoft Security Response Center fulfills these roles for Windows 2000. For more information, see the following website: http://www.microsoft.com/technet/security/issues/w2kccwp.asp.

SUMMARY

1. The user name and password form the first line of network defense, since every user needs a password to get access to the network and its resources.
2. Because cracker programs are easily available, all users should develop strong passwords (i.e., passwords that are difficult to crack).
3. To make passwords more secure, many network operating systems have password management features, either built into the operating system or installed in an add-on package.
4. Another security option is to require a minimum number of characters for a password.
5. If you decide to use anonymous or guest accounts, treat them with extreme care.
6. Give only rights and permissions that are necessary for the user to do his or her job. In addition, make sure that the user does have sufficient rights and permissions to do what needs to be done.
7. The server room should be secure; only a handful of people should have access to it.
8. The server should also be secure.
9. Packet filters are based on protecting the network by using an access control list (ACL). This list resides on your router and determines which machine (IP address) can use the router and in what direction.
10. Firewalls analyze the source and destination TCP/IP address; they also can examine the source and destination port numbers and the content of the packet data.

11. A demilitarized zone (DMZ) is a solution to placement of publicly accessible servers. Instead of having two ports, the public network on one port of the firewall and the private network on another port, you have three ports. The third port is the DMZ, which is a less secure area than the private network.
12. The proxy server can monitor and intercept any and all requests being sent to the external server or that come in from the Internet connection.
13. Today, many operating systems offer personal firewalls to protect an individual computer when connecting to the Internet.
14. The denial of service (DoS) attack is a type of attack on a network that is designed to bring the network down by flooding it with useless traffic.
15. Encryption is the process of disguising a message or data in what appears to be meaningless data (cipher text) to hide and protect sensitive data from unauthorized access.
16. Decryption is the process of converting data from encrypted format back to original format.
17. Cryptography is the art of protecting information by transforming it (encrypting it) into cipher text.
18. To encrypt and decrypt a file, you must use a key. A key is a string of bits used to map text into a code and a code back to text.
19. The most basic form of encryption is the private-key encryption, also known as the symmetric algorithm. This

type of encryption requires that each individual must posses a copy of the key.

20. Public-key encryption, also known as the asymmetric algorithm, uses two distinct but mathematically related keys, public and private. The public key is the nonsecret key that is available to anyone you choose, or made available to everyone by posting in a public place. The private key is kept in a secure location and is used only by you.

21. A digital envelope is a type of security that encrypts data using private-key encryption and that encrypts a key to decode the message using public-key encryption.

22. A digital signature is a digital code that can be attached to an electronically transmitted message that uniquely identifies the sender. Like a written signature, the purpose of a digital signature is to guarantee that the individual sending the message really is who he or she claims to be.

23. A digital certificate is an attachment to an electronic message used for security purposes, such to authenticate and to verify that a user sending a message is who he or she claims to be, and to provide the receiver with a means to encode a reply.

24. Certificate Authority (CA) issues an encrypted digital certificate containing the applicant's public key and a variety of other identification information.

25. X.509 certificates are the most widely used digital certificates.

26. Authentication, which is an essential part of network security, is the process by which the system validates the user's logon information. Authentication is crucial to secure communication.

27. In NTLM authentication, the client selects a string of bytes, uses its password to perform a one-way encryption of the string, and sends both the original string and the encrypted one to the server.

28. Kerberos is an authentication service. Its purpose is to allow users and services to authenticate themselves to each other without allowing other users to capture the network packet on the network and resending it so that they can be authenticated over an unsecured media such as the Internet.

29. Trying to detect intruders can be a daunting task; often the task requires a thorough working knowledge of the network operating system and the network as a whole.

30. An important part of security is ensuring that you have the most updated patches for your network operating system. Check with the distributor and vendor of the network operating system (as well as operating systems on the network) for security holes and the patches to fix them.

QUESTIONS

1. Which device can prevent Internet hackers from accessing a LAN?
   a. firewall
   b. multistation access unit
   c. gateway
   d. router

2. Pat administers a LAN for the Acme Corporation. Pat recently connected the LAN to the Internet, but Skip, the CEO, is concerned that hackers will infiltrate the LAN and steal important trade secrets. Skip has also noticed that Internet access is extremely slow, and she wants Pat to improve it. What can Pat use to meet Skip's requirements?
   a. a firewall
   b. a router
   c. an IP proxy
   d. a transceiver

3. For what purpose does a network operating system use access control lists?
   a. to determine which users can use resources on the network
   b. to locate hosts on the network
   c. to establish communications between network interface cards
   d. to determine which TCP/IP service receives data packets

4. Which of the following passwords provides the strongest network security?
   a. user1
   b. User1
   c. USER1
   d. uSEr1#

5. Pat administers a network and he wants to implement a strong password policy. How should Pat accomplish this task? (Choose all the correct answers.)
   a. He should configure passwords to expire every 30 days.
   b. He should provide users with password hints.
   c. He should configure the network operating system to lock users out of their accounts after three unsuccessful logon attempts.
   d. He should require users to create passwords that contain only alphabetical characters.
   e. He should require a minimum password length of eight characters.

6. You administer a LAN for your company. A hacker has tried to gain access to the LAN, and you have been directed to increase network security by implementing a password policy. What should you do to increase network security? (Choose two answers.)
   a. Require users to create passwords of 25 or more characters.
   b. Require users to use only alphabetical characters in their passwords.
   c. Require users to change their passwords each month.
   d. Store a password history for each user.

7. You administer a network for a small company. A network user, Pat, cannot access the network through his user account. You successfully access the network with Pat's user name and password. Which of the following could explain why Pat cannot access the network through his user account?
   a. Pat's user account is locked.
   b. Pat's password has expired.
   c. Pat is trying to use a password in the password history.
   d. Pat has activated Caps Lock on his computer.

8. You want to create a strong password to ensure that hackers cannot gain access to the network through your

user account. In this scenario, which password is the strongest?

  a. password   c. 241LaneAve
  b. At#CJo$TM   d. SSN999-99-9999

9. Spoofing is a method of_____.

  a. encrypting a data packet
  b. tracking transactions to verify authenticity
  c. filtering bad packets
  d. fooling a firewall into thinking the packet is friendly
  e. translating one IP address to another.

10. Web servers use what to protect transaction information?

  a. QVP   c. LST
  b. DSL   d. SSL

11. Within your company's private network, you suspect that a user from marketing is trying to hack into the server in the accounting department. You decide to install a firewall between marketing and accounting to stop the unauthorized use of the network. How good a solution is this?

  a. perfect solution
  b. good solution, but there are better options
  c. somewhat helpful, in that network packets can be better monitored
  d. worthless

12. What is DES?

  a. Data-Encoded Subnetwork
  b. Double-Edged Signaling
  c. Dynamic Encoded Synchronization
  d. Data Encryption Standard

13. Which of the following is a public-key encryption utility?

  a. PGP   c. RSA
  b. QSA   d. GPR

14. You manage a small LAN that has a limited bandwidth connection to the Internet. Your users have been complaining of slow access lately. Which of the following could you place on your network to help improve access?

  a. firewall   c. Internet router
  b. multiport switch   d. proxy server

15. Which of the following securely transmits data between corporate sites through the Internet?

  a. CVP   c. NVP
  b. QVP   d. VPN

16. What is the SSL protocol?

  a. Single Socket Layering
  b. Simple Sockets Layer
  c. Simple Socket Layering
  d. Secure Sockets Layer

17. What is IPsec?

  a. Internet Protocol sections
  b. IP secondary protocol service
  c. IP secondaries
  d. IP Security

18. What is L2TP?

  a. Layer 2 Tunneling Protocol
  b. Level 2 Transition Protocol
  c. Level 2 Transport Protocol
  d. Layer 2 Transport Protocol

19. You want users' passwords on the firm's network to be secure. Therefore, you are going to implement a password

policy. Which of the following would probably be *less* of a good idea than the others?

  a. Require the creation of a new password every 90 days.
  b. Set accounts to automatically disable themselves upon three failed login attempts that occur within 30 minutes.
  c. Require passwords to use at least one number in addition to using letters.
  d. Require passwords to be at least 14 characters long.

20. What hardware device prevents unauthorized connections to your internal network?

  a. sniffer   c. fluke
  b. packet wall   d. firewall

21. You are setting up a network and need to decide what type of security you are going to implement to protect the network's resources from use by unauthorized persons. Which do you select?

  a. user level   c. route level
  b. MAC level   d. share level

22. A good rule of thumb is that users should be required to change their passwords every _____.

  a. 90 days   c. 120 days
  b. 60 days   d. 30 days

23. C2 Red Book certification is given by the U.S. Department of Defense when an operating system is trusted to be connected to a network. Which of the following has been given this certification?

  a. Windows 98   c. Unix
  b. Windows 2000   d. Netware 4.11

24. The U.S. Department of Defense has published a series of books dealing with network security issues. Which of the following series is the one they publish?

  a. Bluebook Series   c. Blackbook Series
  b. Redbook Series   d. Rainbow Series

25. You have just fired an employee. At the exit interview, you collect the following items from him/her: office keys, pager, company software, and laptop. What else do you need to get? (Choose two answers.)

  a. badge   c. timecard
  b. cleaning deposit   d. security deposit

26. What is the best place in your network to put your e-mail router, public web server, and FTP server?

  a. PRL   c. TXV
  b. CMA   d. DMZ

27. Users on your company's network are constantly reusing old passwords whenever the system asks them to change their password. You want to put a stop to this. How do you do it?

  a. Set the password history size on all accounts.
  b. Set up user account expiration dates.
  c. Set password length on all accounts.
  d. Set the password expiration date on all accounts.

28. True or False: Your boss is considering replacing one of her company's routers with one that can act as an IP proxy as well as do packet filtering. She believes it will help improve network performance, and she is correct.

29. The U.S. Department of Defense has certified which of the following workstation operating systems as being secure? (Choose all that apply.)

  a. Windows NT 4.0   c. Windows NT 3.5
  b. Windows XP   d. Windows 2000

30. Packet filtering allows a router or firewall to determine if packets being received match preestablished criteria, and to drop packets that do not match or fit the current communication session that is established. A list has to be kept on the router to give it this ability. What is this list known as? (Pick two answers.)
    a. session table
    b. state table
    c. dynamic packet list
    d. dynamic state list

31. What is the practice of sending packets that have fake source addresses?
    a. IP translation
    b. packet hopping
    c. protocol tunneling
    d. IP spoofing

32. The U.S. DOD assigned the role of handling computer security certifications to which federal government agency?
    a. HHS
    b. NASA
    c. FBI
    d. NSA

33. Which of the following is the strongest bit encryption that the United States currently allows to be exported?
    a. 128 bit
    b. 80 bit
    c. 256 bit
    d. 40 bit

34. When abnormally large ICMP packets are sent to a system with the intent to bring it down, what is this called?
    a. Ping of Death
    b. WinNuke
    c. IP spoofing
    d. SYN flood

35. Which of the following are good ways to strengthen users' passwords? (Choose two answers.)
    a. Require them to use their social security number.
    b. Require them to use the names of relatives and pets.
    c. Require them to use passwords that are at least eight characters long.
    d. Require them to use special characters that are neither letters nor numbers.

36. When an employee is fired or quits, what is the best thing to do to his or her network login account?
    a. Delete it.
    b. Terminate it.
    c. Disable it.
    d. Crush it.

37. Windows NT Server is C2 (Orange Book), certified by the U.S. DOD. What would cause a computer running this operating system to lose its C2 certification?
    a. having more than one account with administrative priviledges on it
    b. having an administrative account with a password of less than eight characters
    c. being disconnected from the network
    d. being connected to a network

38. What is skipjack?
    a. a method of counting live network ports
    b. an encryption algorithm
    c. A method of omitting certain unneeded network ports
    d. an extended RJ-45 plug

39. One of your users complains about not being able to login with the same ID and password that worked fine yesterday. What would you check first?
    a. Caps Lock key
    b. workstation's patch-cable
    c. workstation's NIC
    d. User database to see if the account is locked or disabled

40. All of your users are running some version of Windows NT or 2000 on their workstations. For security reasons, what should you require your users to do if they need to leave their workstations, even if only for a few minutes? (Choose two answers.)
    a. turn off their computer
    b. lock their workstation
    c. turn off their monitor
    d. log off

41. You are the network administrator of the Acme Corporation. The network consists of a Windows 2000 Active Directory domain. The domain contains Windows 2000 Server computers and Windows 2000 Professional client computers. From a Windows 2000 Professional client computer in the domain, you want to find out whether the local user accounts on the Windows 2000 member servers and Windows 2000 Professional client computers in the domain use a blank password or a common, simple password, such as "password" or "admin" What should you do?
    a. Run Microsoft Baseline Security Analyzer for the computers in the domain. Ensure that you are a local administrator on the scanned computers.
    b. Run the HFNETCHK.EXE command for the computers in the domain. Ensure that no account lockout policy is defined on the scanned computers.
    c. Run the SIGVERIF.EXE command on the computers in the domain. Ensure that Account Management auditing is turned off on the scanned computers.
    d. Run the QFECHECK.EXE command on the computers in the domain. Ensure that you have the "Log on as a batch job" user right on the scanned computers.

42. You are the network administrator for the Acme Corporation. The network consists of a Windows 2000 Active Directory domain. The domain contains Windows 2000 Server computers and Windows 2000 Professional client computers. From a Windows 2000 Professional client computer in the domain, you want to find out the hot fix status of other computers in the domain. When you use Microsoft Baseline Security Analyzer (MBSA) to scan a Windows 2000 Server computer named Server1, you receive the error message that you are not an administrator on the scanned computer. You want to ensure that you can find the hot fix status of Server1 from the Windows 2000 Professional computer. What should you do?
    a. Run the RUNAS command to start MBSA and specify local administrator credentials for Server1.
    b. Run the NET USE command to specify local administrator credentials for a connection to Server1, then run MBSA.
    c. Run the HFNETCHK command and specify local administrator credentials for Server1 to connect to and scan Server1.
    d. Run the MBSACLI command to connect to and scan Server1.

43. You are the administrator for a Windows 2000 network. Your network consists of one domain and two organizational units (OUs). The OUs are named Corporate and Accounting. A user recently reported that she was not able to log on to the domain. You investigate and find out that the user's account has been deleted. You have been auditing all objects in Active Directory since the domain was created. But you cannot find a record of the

user account deletion. You want to find a record that identifies the person who deleted the account. What should you do?

   a. Search the security event logs on each domain controller for account management events.

   b. Search the security event logs on each domain controller for object access events.

   c. Search the Active Directory Users and Computers console on each domain controller for the user's previous account name.

   d. Search the Active Directory Users and Computers console on each domain controller for the user's computer account.

44. You are the Windows 2000 network administrator for your company. You are implementing the company's network security model. You network has several servers that contain sensitive or confidential information. You want to configure security auditing on these servers to monitor access to specific folders. You also want to prevent users from gaining access to these servers when the security logs become full. What should you do?

   a. Create a GPO that applies to the servers. Configure the GPO to enable auditing for object access. Set up the individual objects to be audited in Windows Explorer, then customize the Event Viewer logs to limit the size of the security log to 1024 KB.

   b. Create a GPO that applies to the servers. Configure the GPO to enable auditing for directory services access. Set up the individual objects to be audited in Windows Explorer, then customize the Event Viewer logs to limit the size of the security log to 1024 KB. Configure the security event log so that it does not overwrite events.

   c. Create a GPO that applies to the servers. Configure the GPO to enable auditing for directory service access. Set up the individual objects to be audited in Windows Explorer. Configure the security event log so that it does not overwrite events. Then configure the GPO to enable "shut down the system immediately if enable to log security audits" setting.

   d. Create a GPO that applies to the servers. Configure the GPO to enable auditing for object access. Set up the individual objects to be audited in Windows Explorer. Configure the security event log so that it does not overwrite events. Then configure the GPO to enable "Shut down the system immediately if enable to log security audits" setting.

45. You are the network administrator for Just Togs. Your Windows 2000 network consists of 15,000 users. Users have recently reported that documents are missing from the servers. You need to track the actions of the users to find out who has been deleting the files. You create a GPO on the justtogs.com domain and assign the appropriate permissions to the GPO. What actions should you audit? (Choose two answers.)

   a. Object access

   b. Process tracking

   c. Privileged use

   d. Delete and Delete subfolders and files

   e. Directory Services access

46. You are the administrator of your company's network. All computers on the network run Windows 2000. Two servers named ServerA and ServerB support a confidential medical records database. ServerA runs the database, and ServerB runs a middle-tier application that employees use to access the database. Your company decides to implement IPSec policies to increase network security. To ensure that all communications on ServerA are secure and encrypted, and to ensure that only ServerB can access resources on ServerA, you assign the default Secure Server IPSec policy on both ServerA and ServerB. However, users report they can no longer access ServerB. How should you correct this problem?

   a. Change the authentication header (AH) algorithm on ServerB to MD5.

   b. Change the encapsulating security payload (ESP) protocol algorithm on ServerB to DES.

   c. Assign a custom IPSec policy on ServerA. This policy will require IPSec authentication headers (AH) and the encapsulating security payload (ESP) protocol for traffic that originates from the IP address of ServerB.

   d. Assign the Client (Respond Only) IPSec policy on ServerB.

HANDS-ON EXERCISES

Exercise 1: Auditing

Enable Auditing

   1. From the Administrative Tools, start the Domain Controller Security Policy console.

   2. In the left pane, open Security Policies, open Local Policies, and click the Audit Policy options.

   3. Double-click the "Audit directory service access" option in the right pane and enable the Success and Failure options.

   4. Double-click the Audit Logon Events option and enable the Failure options.

   5. Close the Domain Console Security Policy console.

Auditing Failed Login Attempts

   6. If the Account Lockout option has not been set, use the Domain Security Policy console to enable the Account Lockout Threshold to four invalid logon attempts. If it asks, set the account logout duration to 30 minutes and the reset account lockout counter after 30 minutes.

7. Log out as the Administrator and incorrectly log in as Charlie Brown three times.
8. Log in as the Administrator.

Audit the Access of a File and Invalid Logons

9. Right-click the C:\DATA folder and select the Properties option.
10. On the Auditing tab, click the Add button.
11. Select Everyone and click on the OK button.
12. Select the following options for successful and failed attempts:
    - Create Files/Write Data
    - Create Folders/Append Data
    - Write Attributes
    - Write Extended Attributes
    - Delete Subfolders and Files
    - Delete
13. Select the "Apply these auditing entries to objects and/or containers within this container only" option and click on the OK button.
14. Click on the OK button again.
15. Delete the Windows 2000 jpg file from the C:\DATA folder.

Using Event Viewer to View Security Log

16. Open the Event Viewer from the Administrative Tools.
17. Select the Security Log option in the left pane.

Appendix

APPENDIX A   USING THE NET.EXE COMMAND

After the DOS client software is loaded, the most common network command is the NET.EXE command, which can be used to log in to servers and access the shared resources located on those servers.

When using the NET.EXE command, you will find that NET.EXE has many options. If you perform NET HELP command at the prompt, you will see the following options.

This book will only discuss the options that are the most useful in connecting to the network that is accessing the common servers.

During boot-up, it will usually ask for your user name and password so that you can log in to the network. The DOS client software can be configured to display a default user name. If you use the wrong user name and/or password, your access will be denied and you will have to log in again before accessing the network resources. If you perform the NET LOGON /? command at the prompt, the following screen will be displayed.

As you can see, to log on, you will use the following command:

```
NET LOGON
```

It will then ask you to input the user name and password. If you need to log on to another domain, you would then use the following command at the prompt:

```
NET LOGON /DOMAIN:domainname
```

where domainname would be the actual name of the domain that you want to log in to.

The NET LOGON command allows you to log on as a user to the network using a user name and password. The user name can be up to 20 characters and the password can be 14 characters. The user name is not case sensitive whereas the password is; and both the user name and password can be up to 8 text characters long and are case insensitive.

You now know how to log on. The command to log off is

```
NET LOGOFF
```

For more information about a specific Microsoft NET
command, type the command name followed by /?
(for example, NET VIEW /?).

NET CONFIG	Displays your current workgroup settings.
NET DIAG	Runs the Microsoft Network Diagnostics program to display diagnostic information about your network.
NET HELP	Provides information about commands and error messages.
NET INIT	Loads protocol and network-adapter drivers without binding them to Protocol Manager.
NET LOGOFF	Breaks the connection between your computer and the shared resources to which it is connected.
NET LOGON	Identifies you as a member of a workgroup.
NET PASSWORD	Changes your logon password.
NET PRINT	Displays information about print queues and controls print jobs.
NET START	Starts services.
NET STOP	Stops services.
NET TIME	Displays the time on or synchronizes your computer's clock with the clock on a Microsoft Windows for Workgroups, Windows NT, Windows 95, or NetWare timeserver.
NET USE	Connects to or disconnects from a shared resource or displays information about connections.
NET VER	Displays the type and version number of the workgroup redirector you are using.
NET VIEW	Displays a list of computers that share Resources or a list of shared resources on a specific computer.

Identifies you as a member of a workgroup.

NET LOGON [user [password | ?]] [/DOMAIN:name] [/YES] [/SAVEPW:NO]

User	Specifies the name that identifies you in your workgroup. The name you specify can contain up to 20 characters.
Password	The unique string of characters that authorizes you to gain access to your password-list file. The password can contain up to 14 characters.
?	Specifies that you want to be prompted for your password.
/DOMAIN	Specifies that you want to log on to a Microsoft Windows NT or LAN Manager domain.
name	Specifies the Windows NT or LAN Manager domain you want to log on to.
/YES	Carries out the NET LOGON command without first prompting you to provide information or confirm actions.
/SAVEPW:NO	Carries out the NET LOGON command without prompting you to create a password-list file.

If you would rather be prompted to type your user name and password
instead of specifying them in the NET LOGON command line, type
NET LOGON without options.

The NET USE command is used to connect or disconnect to a shared resource or to display information about your connections. A shared resource is typically a drive, directory, or printer that has been shared or designated for access from clients.

To access a shared network drive or shared network directory, use the following syntax:

```
NET USE d: \\servername\sharename
```

where d: is the local drive letter that you wish to assign which will point to the shared directory; servername (NetBIOS name) is the name of the server where the shared drive or directory resides; and sharename is the actual name given by the system administrator when creating the share. The \\servername\sharename is known as the Universal Naming Convention (UNC). For example, to access the shared directory called SOFTWARE, which is located on the CLASSROOM server, type in

```
NET USE G: \\INSTRUCT\SOFTWARE
```

After this command is executed, as far as the client is concerned, he or she has a G drive. The G drive is actually a pointer that points to the SOFTWARE shared directory on the INSTRUCT server. Therefore, for the most part, the G drive acts just like any other local drive. Assuming that you have the proper rights or permissions, you can execute files, access data files, copy files from, or copy files to the G drive.

Another option within the NET USE command is the /HOME option, which points to the user's home directory. A home directory is designated by the network administrator and used for personal files. For example, to point the H to a person's home directory, type in the following command at the prompt:

```
NET USE H: /HOME
```

To disconnect from the shared resource, use the following syntax:

```
NET USE d: /D
```

where d: is the local drive letter assigned to the shared drive or directory. Therefore, to disconnect from the G drive that was pointing to the SOFTWARE share, execute the following command at the prompt:

```
NET USE G: /D
```

The NET USE command can also be used to connect to a network printer. The proper syntax to connect to a network printer is

```
NET USE LPTx: \\servername\printername
```

where LPTx is the local printer port that is assigned to the network printer; servername is the name of the print server; and printername is the name of the shared printer. For example, to connect to the IPRINTER network printer that is connected to the INSTRUCT print server using your local LPT2, use the following command at the prompt:

```
NET USE LPT2 \\INSTRUCT\PRINTER
```

Thus, every print job that you send to the LPT2 printer port will be redirected to the IPRINTER, even if you do not actually have an LPT2 port.

To disconnect from a network printer, still use the /D option. Therefore, to disconnect from the IPRINTER, use the following command at the prompt:

```
NET USE LPT2 /D
```

Lastly, the NET USE command can be used to display all connected shared directories, drives, and printers. The syntax to show the connected shared resources is

```
NET USE
```

The NET VIEW command is used to list the shared resources available on a specified computer. The syntax to do this is

```
NET VIEW \\servername
```

Therefore, to show all network resources on the INSTRUCT server, perform the following command at the prompt:

```
NET VIEW \\INSTRUCT
```

```
Displays a list of computers in a specified workgroup or the shared
resources available on a specified computer.

NET VIEW [\\computer] [/YES]
NET VIEW [/WORKGROUP:wgname] [/YES]

computer      Specifies the name of the computer whose shared resources
              you want to see listed.
/WORKGROUP    Specifies that you want to view the names of the computers
              in another workgroup that share resources.
wgname        Specifies the name of the workgroup whose computer names
              you want to view.
/YES          Carries out the NET VIEW command without first prompting
              you to provide information or confirm actions.

To display a list of computers in your workgroup that share resources,
type NET VIEW without options.
```

APPENDIX B   COMMON DOS COMMANDS

Regardless of the operating system (DOS/Windows 3.xx, Windows 95/98, Windows NT, Windows 2000, or Windows Server 2003) that you are using, there are certain DOS commands that you should know to set up Windows or to troubleshoot certain problems.

When performing DOS commands, there is always confusion as to when to use the back slash (\) and the forward slash (/). The back slash is always used to designate a location, whereas the forward slash is used to designate a switch (which has nothing to do with location). The backward slash is always in the same direction as the backslash in the prompt shown on the screen, because the prompt is showing the current drive and directory (location).

FORMAT A:/S	Makes a disk bootable (switch)
CD\DOS	Changes the current directory (location)
COPY C:\DOS\FORMAT.COM A:\DOS	Copies files from one location to another
XCOPY C:\DATA*.* C:\DOS /S	Copies files from one location to another, but also includes subdirectories (switch)

DIR and CD Command

The DIR command, which displays the list of the files and subdirectories, is probably the most commonly used DOS command. When you use the DIR command without any parameters or switches, it displays the following:

1. Disk's volume label and serial number
2. File name/directory name and their extensions
3. Date and time the file was created or last modified, and date and time of when a directory was made
4. File size in bytes
5. Total number of files listed, their cumulative size, and free space in bytes remaining on the disk

The DIR command has many switches. Some of the more common ones used for a technician are shown in Table B1. Many of the DIR command switches can be combined.

Table B1   Helpful DIR command switches

Command Switch	Description
/P	Displays one screen of the DIR listing at a time. This comes in handy when there are too many files to be shown on the screen at once.
/W	Displays the listing in wide format (five columns). This comes in handy when there are too many files to be shown on the screen at once. It does not show the dates, times, and byte size of the files. Note: Directories are indicated with brackets [ ].
/ON	O stands for order; N stands for name. Therefore, when used with the DIR command, the files will be listed in alphabetical order by file name. This comes in handy when looking for a certain file.
/AH	A stands for attribute; H stands for hidden. Therefore, when used with the DIR command, it will show all hidden files. This comes in handy when verifying the boot files on a disk.
/AD	A stands for attribute; D stands for directories. It shows directories only.
/S	S stands for subdirectory. Therefore, when used, it will list every occurrence in the specified directory and all subdirectories. It comes in handy when looking for the location of a certain file or when trying to get the total byte size of a directory (including all subdirectories and files within the directory).

```
C:\>dir

Volume in drive D has no label
Volume Serial Number is 1CE8-1C7A
Directory of C:\

DOS                   <DIR>                  06-10-98           7:32p
WINDOWS               <DIR>                  06-10-98           7:32p
COMMAND     COM                  93,812     08-24-96          11:11a
CONFIG      SYS                      91     06-06-98          11:03a
AUTOEXEC    BAT                     183     06-06-98          10:44a
DATA                  <DIR>                  06-10-98           7:33p
3 file(s)                  94,086 bytes
3 dir(s)          179,634,176 bytes free
The DIR command
```

Example 1:

To show all files one screen at a time, perform the following command:

    DIR /P

To show all files in alphabetical order, one screen at a time, perform the following command:

    DIR /ON /P

To show the hidden files in the current directory, perform the following command:

    DIR /AH

To show all files that have a GIF file name extension, perform the following command:

    DIR *.GIF

To change the current drive, type in the drive letter followed by a colon (:) and press Enter. To change the current directory, use the CD command. To go up to the root directory, specify the backslash (\); and to go up to the parent directory (up one directory), specify the double dot (..).

Example 2:

To change to the TEST directory, which is located under the directory that you are currently in, perform the following command:

```
CD TEST
```

To change to the root directory, regardless of how many directories deep you are, perform the following command:

```
CD \
```

To change to the parent directory (one directory up), perform the following command:

```
CD..
```

To change to the SYSTEM directory under the WINDOWS directory (located off the root directory) regardless of what directory you are in, use the following command:

```
CD \WINDOWS\SYSTEM
```

MD and RD Commands

The MD command is used to create directories; the RD command is used to delete empty subdirectories.

Example 3:

To create a TEST directory, type in the following command:

```
MD TEST
```

If the TEST directory is empty (no files or subdirectories), then use the following command to delete it:

```
RD TEST
```

DEL Command

The Del command is used to delete files. To delete the test.doc file, use

```
DEL TEST.DOC
```

The Copy Commands (COPY and DISKCOPY)

The two primary COPY commands used in DOS are COPY and DISKCOPY. Regardless of which command you use, they use the same three parts—command, source, and target. The source is what you are copying and the target is the location of where the copy is going.

The COPY command makes an exact duplicate of the file or files specified. The COPY command will not copy hidden or system files.

Example 4:

To make a copy of the RESUME.DOC file and call the copy JOB.DOC, perform the following command:

```
COPY RESUME.DOC JOB.DOC
```

To copy the AUTOEXEC.BAT file (located in the current directory) to the A drive, perform the following command at the prompt.

```
COPY AUTOEXEC.BAT A:
```

To copy the README.TXT file located in the C:\DOS directory, while you are in another directory, to the A:\DOS directory, perform the following command:

```
COPY C:\DOS\README.TXT A:\DOS
```

The command is COPY, the source is C:\DOS\README.TXT, and the target is A:\DOS.

To copy the README.TXT file located in the C:\DOS directory, while you are in another directory, to the A:\DOS directory and name the copy INFO.TXT, perform the following command:

```
COPY C:\DOS\README.TXT A:\DOS\INFO.TXT
```

Notice that all examples have three parts divided by two spaces.

Example 5:

To make an exact duplicate of a disk using the A drive, perform the following command at the prompt.

```
DISKCOPY A: A:
```

The REN and MOVE commands are similar to the COPY command, but not the same as the COPY command. The REN command allows you to rename a file and the MOVE command allows you to move a file from one location to another to rename a directory. Unlike the COPY command which leaves you with two files (the source and the target), the REN and MOVE commands leave you with only one.

Example 6:

To rename the README.TXT file to the INFO.TXT file, perform the following command:

```
REN README.TXT INFO.TXT
```

To move the README.TXT file (located in the C:\DOS directory) to the root directory of the C drive, perform the following command:

```
MOVE C:\DOS\README.TXT C:\
```

To rename the TEST directory to JOB directory, perform the following command:

```
MOVE TEST JOB
```

FORMAT and SYS Commands

The FORMAT command is used to prepare a disk for use or to erase everything on a disk. It creates the root directory (starting point on the disk) and the file allocation table (an index of files and directories on the disk and their location). In addition, if you use the /S parameter it makes the disk bootable. To perform an unconditional format in which the disk cannot be unformatted or if you have received read and write errors, then use the /U switch.

Example 7:

To format the D drive, perform the following command:

```
FORMAT D:
```

To make a bootable floppy disk using drive A, perform the following command:

```
FORMAT A: /S
```

To make a disk bootable without reformatting the disk, use the SYS command. This will copy the IO.SYS, MSDOS.SYS, and COMMAND.COM and place them in the correct place, assuming that there is enough room for them to fit on the disk.

Example 8:

To make an important software diagnostic disk bootable using drive A, perform the following command (assuming you are not in the A drive):

```
SYS A:
```

The ATTRIB Command

The ATTRIB command displays, sets, or removes the read-only (R), archive (A), system (S), and hidden (H) attributes assigned to a file or directory. For more information on attributes, see Chapter 14. The archive attribute indicates whether a file has been backed up. To turn on an attribute, use a plus (+) sign and to turn off an attribute, use a minus (–) sign.

Example 9:

To show all files and their attributes, perform the following command:

```
ATTRIB
```

To make the AUTOEXEC.BAT read-only, perform the following command:

```
ATTRIB +R AUTOEXEC.BAT
```

or

```
ATTRIB AUTOEXEC.BAT +R (only on recent versions of DOS)
```

To turn off the read-only, system, and hidden attributes of the BOOT.INI file, perform the following command at the prompt. You must include spaces between each of the attributes.

```
ATTRIB -R -S -H BOOT.INI.
```

AUTOEXEC.BAT and CONFIG.SYS

The CONFIG.SYS is a special text file that executes special configuration commands that cannot be executed at the prompt. These commands configure your computer's hardware components so that MS-DOS and applications can use them and to activate and manage the various memory areas.

The HIMEM.SYS is the DOS's extended memory manager (RAM above 1 MB found on any newer machine), which makes the extended memory available to DOS programs. In addition, its purpose is to prevent two programs from using the same memory area in the extended memory. To load the HIMEM.SYS, use the DEVICE command in the CONFIG.SYS file. Any time that the DEVICE command is used to load a driver, always include the entire path (location) of the file specified and its file name extension. Since Windows 3.xx requires extended memory to run, Windows requires HIMEM.SYS to be loaded. In addition, if you add the /TESTMEM:OFF to the end of the HIMEM.SYS line, DOS will activate the extended memory but will skip the memory test.

The AUTOEXEC.BAT file is a special batch file that automatically executes during boot-up. It has a BAT file extension and it contains commands that you would normally perform at the prompt. In the AUTOEXEC.BAT files, you will usually find the PATH, PROMPT, and SET commands.

To enable hardware and to load useful utilities, you should know how to load device drivers and TSRs. A device driver controls how DOS and applications interact with specific items of hardware. They can be identified with a SYS file name extension, which is loaded in the CONFIG.SYS file.

The terminate-stay resident (TSR) loads instructions into the RAM to control some hardware device or to provide some useful function and give control back to the operating system. The TSR then performs its function quietly in the background while you can load other programs. A program that is not a TSR (e.g., EDIT or a word processor) is loaded in the RAM but typically does as not allow you to perform any other commands at the prompt until you exit the program. Since TSRs have a COM or EXE file name extension, they are loaded in the AUTOEXEC.BAT. Remember that the AUTOEXEC.BAT file is a batch file that can contain commands which you can execute at the prompt.

Most of the time when loading CD-ROM drivers, you insert the floppy disk into a floppy drive and you execute the SETUP.EXE, INSTALL.EXE, or similar file to automatically install and configure the drivers. For DOS, the EIDE CD drives require a device driver to be loaded in the CONFIG.SYS while SCSI drives usually require a device driver for the controller card and a device driver for the CD-ROM drive. The driver for the MITSUMI IDE CD-ROM drive is shown as

```
DEVICE = C:\CDROM\ATAPI_CD.SYS /D:CD0001
```

where /D: is the drive signature to identify the drive.

In addition to the driver, DOS requires the Microsoft Compact Disk Extension (MSCDEX.EXE) to be loaded in the AUTOEXEC.BAT so that DOS can read the CD file system.

```
C:\DOS\MSCDEX /D:CD0001 /M:12 /L:E
```

where /D: indicates the drive signature, which must be the same as the one specified in the device driver loaded in the CONFIG.SYS. The /M: specifies the number of sector buffers and the /L: specifies the drive letter assigned to the CD-ROM drive.

SMARTDRV.EXE, a software disk cache that caches or buffers between the hard drive and the RAM, creates a buffer area called a cache area in the extended memory. The software controlling the cache area tries to anticipate what the microprocessor needs next. One method is to keep a copy of information that has been recently accessed. If it has already been accessed, there is a good chance that it will be accessed again. Another method is read ahead the additional sector after the one that has been accessed. In whatever method(s) used, when the disk needs to be accessed, it will look in the cache area first. If it cannot get what is needed, it will access the slower hard drive. The time to search the cache area (RAM) is almost negligible compared with the time it takes to access the hard drive. Therefore, if it finds the needed information in the RAM, the overall performance of the PC is also increased. Since SMARTDRV.EXE has an EXE file name extension, it is loaded in the AUTOEXEC.BAT file. SMART-DRV.EXE automatically loads into upper memory, if available.

Example 10:

To create a disk cache with the default values, use the following command in the AUTOEXEC.BAT:

```
SMARTDRV
```

To create a 4096-KB cache area (overriding the default values), use the following command in the AUTOEXEC.BAT:

```
SMARTDRV 4096
```

CONFIG.SYS

```
DEVICE=C:\DOS\HIMEM.SYS
DEVICEHIGH=C:\CDROM\ATAPI_CD.SYS /D:CD0001
```

AUTOEXEC.BAT

```
C:\DOS\MSCDEX /D:CD0001 /M:12 /L:E
SMARTDRV 4096 128
```

APPENDIX C   APPLE COMPUTERS ON THE NETWORK

A computer running Windows 2000 Server or Windows Server 2003 with AppleTalk network integration can store files so that users of both Intel-based and Macintosh computers can gain access to them. Users of Intel-based computers (including users of the MS-DOS, OS/2, Windows, Windows for Workgroups, Windows NT Workstation, Windows NT Server, Windows 2000 Professional, Windows 2000 Server, Windows XP, and Windows Server 2003 operating systems) look for shared files in a shared folder on the computer running Windows 2000 Server or Windows Server 2003. Macintosh users look for shared files in the same folder; however, they see the folder as a volume, with familiar folders and files.

A Macintosh user shares a file with users of Intel-based computers by storing that file in a Macintosh accessible volume on the computer running the Windows server. Likewise, a Macintosh user can mount a Macintosh-accessible volume on the desktop to use files stored in shared folders by users of Intel-based computers.

All Macintosh-accessible volumes must be created on an NTFS partition or on a CD file system (CDFS) volume. If you specify a CDFS volume, the Macintosh-accessible volume will provide read-only access. (In this case, CDFS volume refers to a hard disk volume.)

To install File Server for Macintosh, do the following:

1. Open the Windows Components Wizard.
2. In Components, click Other Network File and Print Services (but do not select or clear its check box), then click Details.
3. Select the File Services for Macintosh check box.
4. To install the print server for Macintosh, also select the Print Services for Macintosh check box.
5. Click OK, and then click Next.

You must have an NTFS partition installed before you install the file server for Macintosh. When File Server for Macintosh and TCP/IP are installed, the Apple filing protocol (AFP) over TCP/IP is enabled automatically. If you have not already installed the AppleTalk protocol, it is installed automatically when you install File Server for Macintosh.

To install the authentication files on the Macintosh client, do the following:

1. Open Chooser, click AppleShare, select the AppleTalk zone where the Windows server is located, and then select that file server. Continue to connect and select the Microsoft UAM volume as the item you want to use.
2. On the Macintosh desktop, double-click the Microsoft UAM Volume to open it.
3. Double-click MS UAM Installer.

To create a Macintosh-accessible volume, do the following:

1. Open Computer Management.
2. In the Console tree, double-click the Shared Folders option, right-click Shares, and then click New File Share.
3. In Folder to Share, type the drive and path to the folder you want to make Macintosh accessible, or click Browse to find the folder.
4. In Share Name, type the name and, optionally, in Share description, type a description of the Windows server share.
5. Select the Apple Macintosh check box, click Next, and then follow the instructions in the Create Shared Folder Wizard.

A Macintosh-accessible volume is a folder on a computer that is running Windows server and that is made available to Macintosh clients. Once a Macintosh-accessible volume has been created for Macintosh users and a share created for users of Intel-based computers, both types of users can exchange files. Macintosh clients need to run AppleTalk to access Macintosh volumes and AppleTalk printers. All Macintosh-accessible volumes must be created on an NTFS partition or on a CDFS volume. If you specify a CDFS volume, the Macintosh-accessible volume will provide read-only access. (In this case, CDFS volume refers to a hard disk volume.)

To install Print Server for Macintosh, do the following:

1. Open the Windows Components Wizard.
2. In Components, click Other Network File and Print Services (but do not select or clear its check box), then click Details.
3. Select the Print Services for Macintosh check box.
4. To install File Server for Macintosh, you can also select the File Services for Macintosh check box.
5. Click OK, then click Next.

If you have not already installed the AppleTalk protocol, it is installed automatically when you install Print Server for Macintosh.

To create a printer, do the following:

1. Open Printers.
2. In the Printers dialog box, double-click Add Printer.
3. Follow the Add Printer Wizard instructions and select Local Printer (select the "Automatically detect my printer" check box if the printer is directly attached to the Windows server), then click Next.
4. Click Create a New Port, click AppleTalk Printing Devices, and then click Next.
5. Expand the AppleTalk zone where the printer you want to connect to is located, then select the printer.
6. Complete the Add Printer Wizard.

If the printing device is on a network, click Add Port. In the Printer Ports dialog box, click AppleTalk Printing Devices, then click OK. In the Available AppleTalk Printing Devices dialog box, select a zone and a printer, and then click OK.

APPENDIX D   CONNECTING TO A NOVELL NETWORK

To connect to a Novell NetWare network on a Windows 2000 Professional or Windows XP computer, install the NWLink protocol and Client Services for NetWare. If you are running Windows 2000 Server or Windows Server 2003, install the NWLink protocol and Gateway (and Client) Service for NetWare.

When you install Gateway (and Client) Service for NetWare or Client Service for NetWare, the NWLink protocol is installed automatically. NWLink supports Novell network routing and can support NetWare client-server applications. In networking environments that use IPX/SPX, the NWLink protocol allows computers running Windows to communicate with other computers or network devices that are using IPX/SPX. NWLink also provides client computers that are running IPX/SPX with access to applications that are designed for a Windows 2000 server, such as Microsoft SQL Server and SNA Server.

The process for installing and configuring Gateway (and Client) Service for NetWare and Client Service for NetWare is the same except for the gateway service. You install Gateway (and Client) Service for NetWare on Windows 2000 Server and Client Service for NetWare on Windows 2000 Professional or Windows XP.

NWLink and Client Services for NetWare are two key components of Microsoft networking and Novell NetWare networking interoperability. NWLink is a protocol that allows Windows clients to communicate with applications running in a Novell NetWare environment. Client Services for NetWare is the service that allows Windows clients to connect to network resources such as file and print resources on a NetWare server.

Client Services for NetWare also allows Windows clients to be authenticated by a NetWare server. Client Services for Netware is the implementation provided by Microsoft for the NetWare redirector. The redirector in both Windows and Novell NetWare environments is the service installed on the client that allows the client computer to communicate with the server service.

Gateway (and Client) Services for NetWare allows a Windows server to act as a gateway for Windows clients who want to access NetWare servers via the Windows server. Windows clients use this service for occasional or low usage to a NetWare server. Gateway (and Client) Services for NetWare creates a bridge through the Windows server for the Windows server and clients to access NetWare resources. This service allows a Windows server to access a NetWare share and make it accessible to Windows clients.

The procedure for installing NWLink is the same as that used to install any network protocol in Windows. To install NWLink, perform the following steps:

1. Right-click My Network Places, then click Properties.
2. In the Network and Dial-up Connections window, right-click the icon that represents the local area connection that you want to configure, then click Properties.
3. In the Local Area Connection Properties dialog box, click Install.
4. In the Select Network Component Type dialog box, click Protocol, then click Add.
5. In the Select Network Protocol dialog box, in the Network Protocol list, click NWLink IPX/SPX/NetBIOS Compatible Transport Protocol, then click OK.

6. In the Local Area Connection Properties dialog box, click Close. Install and configure Gateway (and Client) Service for NetWare (GSNW) to enable computers running Windows 2000 or Windows XP to make direct connections to file and printer resources on NetWare servers. GSNW installs NWLink by default when installed. However, it is recommended that you install, and if necessary configure, NWLink prior to installing GSNW.

To install Gateway (and Client) Service for NetWare, perform the following steps:

1. Double-click Network and Dial-up Connections in the Control Panel.
2. Right-click any local area connection, then click Properties.
3. On the General tab, click Install.
4. In the Select Network Component Type dialog box, click Client, then click Add.
5. In the Select Network Client dialog box, click Gateway (and Client) Services for NetWare, then click OK.
6. In the Select NetWare Logon dialog box, choose either a preferred server from a list of NetWare servers or enter a default tree and context, then click OK.
7. On the Local Network dialog box, click Yes to restart your computer.

When you install Gateway (and Client Services) for NetWare, it is installed for all connections. If you do not want Client Services for NetWare installed for a certain connection, view the properties of that connection and then clear the Client Service for NetWare check box. If you want to change the preferred server or the default tree and context, then you may do so with the GSNW icon in the Control Panel. Here you can also configure Print Options and Run Login Script. You can test that Gateway (and Client Services) for NetWare is initialized properly by running the NET VIEW /NETWORK:NW command. You should be able to see a list of available NetWare servers.

As with connecting to a Windows server, connecting to a NetWare server can be done in several ways once CSNW/GSNW have been installed. You can access the server through Windows Explorer, map a network drive, or view the NetWare server through My Network Places.

APPENDIX E   SERVICES FOR UNIX

UNIX, including variations of Linux, use the Network File System (NFS). The NFS is an open operating system designed by Sun Microsystems that allows all network users to access shared files stored on computers of different types. NFS provides access to shared files through an interface called the Virtual File System (VFS) that runs on top of TCP/IP. Users can manipulate shared files as if they were stored locally on the user's own hard disk.

The Services for UNIX 2.0 includes the following:

■ Server for NFS allows NFS clients such as UNIX and Linux to access files on a Windows 2000 Professional or Server, Windows XP, or Windows Server 2003 computer. To manage the server for NFS, use the UNIX Admin Snap-in (sfumgmt.msc).
■ Gateway for NFS (available in Windows 2000 Server and Windows Server 2003 only) allows non-NFS Windows clients to access NFS resources by connecting through an NFS-enabled Windows server to NFS resources. It acts as a gateway/translator between the NFS protocol used by UNIX/Linux and the CIFS protocol used by Windows.
■ Server for PCNFS provides authentication services for NFS clients needed to access NFS files.
■ Server for NIS allows the server to act as the NIS master for a particular UNIX domain as it authenticates requests for NFS shares. The server for NIS must be installed on a Windows 2000 Server or Windows Server 2003 that is configured as a domain controller.

Microsoft Windows Services for UNIX is designed to facilitate interoperability between Windows-based and UNIX-based operating systems. To allow UNIX and Windows machines to communicate with each other, Windows uses the Common Internet File System (CIFS), which is an enhanced version of the Server Message Block (SMB) protocol. Client for Network File Systems integrates Windows Explorer so that you can browse and map drivers to NFS volumes and access NFS resources through My Network Places. Microsoft recommends this over installing Samba (SMB files services for Windows clients) on your UNIX server. The NFS shares can be accessed using standard NFS syntax or UNC syntax:

NFS share syntax	*servername:/pathname*
UNC syntax	*\\servername:/pathname*

If users' UNIX user name and password differ from Windows user name and password, click Connect Using a Different User Name option and provide new credentials.

Services for UNIX version 2.0 includes more than 60 of the most common and important UNIX command-line utilities to provide a familiar environment for UNIX users and administrators. Some of the more popular UNIX utilities are installed along with the Client for NFS:

Utility	Description
grep	Searches files for patterns and displays results containing that pattern
ps	Lists processes and their status
sed	Copies files named to a standard output; edits according to a script of commands
sh	Invokes the Korn shell
tar	Used to create tape archives or add/extract files from archives
vi	Invokes IV text editor

The nfsadmin command-line utility is used for configuration and administration of the Client for NFS. Its options include:

Option	Description
fileaccess	UNIX file permission for reading, writing, and executing
mapsvr	Computer name of the mapping server
type	Mount type, HARD or SOFT
perf	Method for determining performance parameters (MANUAL or DEFAULT)
prefer TCP	Indicates whether to use TCP (YES or NO)
retry	Number of retries for a soft mount—default value is 5
rsize	Size of read buffer in KB
timeout	Timeout in seconds for an RPC call
wsize	Size or write butter in KB

APPENDIX F   ADMINISTERING MICROSOFT OFFICE 2000/XP

Microsoft Office 2000/XP provides the flexibility to customize and install Office in a number of different ways. The simplest methods of installing a customized version of Office include creating an administrative installation point on the network, or distributing a customized version of Microsoft Office 2000/XP Disc 1.

How to Install Office from a Network Server

The most common method of deploying a customized version of Microsoft Office 2000/XP to a large number of users is to create a central copy of Office on a network server. Then users can install Office on their computers over the network. This method provides several advantages over having users install Office individually from the CD:

- You can manage one set of Office files from a central location.
- You can create a standard set of Office features and options for all users.
- You can take advantage of flexible installation options, such as setting features to be installed on first use.

- You have more control when you upgrade Office in the future.
- When you install Office from a network server, you first create an administrative installation point and customize your version of Office Setup. Then you run Setup on users' computers.

The administrative installation point is a server share that contains all Office files. Users connect to the share and run Setup to install Office on their computers.

To create an administrative installation point for Office, do the following:

1. Create a share on a network server for the administrative installation point. The network share must have at least 550 MB of available disk space.
2. On a computer running Windows 95, Windows 98, Windows NT, Windows 2000, Windows Server 2003, or Windows XP that has write access to the share, connect to the server share.
3. On the Start menu, select the Run option and click on the Browse button.
4. Insert the Office Disc 1 in the CD-ROM drive and select the SETUP.EXE file and click the Open button.
5. On the command line following SETUP.EXE, type /A DATA1.MSI and click OK, for example: D:\SETUP /A DATA1.MSI.
6. When prompted by Setup, enter the organization name that you want to define for all users who install Office from this location.
7. When prompted for the installation location, enter the server and share you created.
8. Setup will copy all the files from Office 2000/XP Disc 1 to the network server, creating a hierarchy of folders in the root folder of the share. Setup also modifies the Windows installer package for Office (Data1.msi), identifying the network share as an administrative installation point. After creating the administrative installation point, make the share available to users by providing them with read access.

Customizing the Office Setup Files

Before users run Setup to install Office, modify the administrative installation point to customize the installation process and default settings. Following are three options for customizing Setup:

- Create a custom command line
- Edit the Setup settings file
- Create a Windows installer transform (MST file) by using the Microsoft Custom Installation wizard

Setup command-line options allow you to define properties that Setup uses to control the installation process. You also can specify whether Setup runs interactively or in quiet mode (without user interaction). Users install Office on their computers by running Setup with your command-line options.

The Setup settings file (Setup.ini) is a text file in which you enter properties and values. You can edit the Setup settings file to specify the same properties as you do on the Setup command line—every command-line option has a corresponding setting in the settings file. The advantage of modifying the Setup settings file is that your custom values are used whenever a user runs Setup from the administrative installation point with no command-line options.

You can create more than one settings file with different values, and then you can specify which settings file you want to use with the /settings command-line option. For example:

```
SETUP.EXE /SETTINGS NEWSETUP.INI
```

The Custom Installation wizard allows you to specify the same property settings that you can define on the command line or in the settings file, but the wizard also allows you to make many more customizations. For example, you can select the Office features that you want to install, modify shortcuts, customize options for Microsoft Internet Explorer 5 and Microsoft Outlook, and even add your own custom files to the installation. The wizard saves your selections in a transform.

When you run Setup, specify the transform that you want Setup to use. You can specify an MST file on the Setup command line, or you can set the TRANSFORMS property in the Setup settings file. For example, this command line specifies the transform Custom.mst:

```
SETUP.EXE TRANSFORMS="CUSTOM.MST"
```

After you create and customize the administrative installation point, users can install Office by running Setup from the root folder of the server share. Users can run Setup themselves by using the command-line options, settings file, or transform that you have chosen. For a more controlled installation, run Setup for them through a network logon script or systems management software, such as Microsoft Systems Management Server.

APPENDIX G   WINDOWS STOP ERRORS

STOP 0x0000000A (0xA) IRQL_NOT_LESS_OR_EQUAL

Parameters:

1. Memory referenced
2. IRQL
3. Value: 0 = read operation, 1 = write operation
4. Address that referenced memory

An attempt was made to touch pageable memory at a process internal request level (IRQL) that is too high. In other words, the A driver is using improper memory addresses. This error is usually caused by a bad device driver or by using a 4.0 driver on a Windows NT 3.51.

To isolate the cause of the error, do the following:

- Make sure that you have the most current BIOS.
- Make sure that you have the newest Windows service pack.
- Turn your PC off and take out all cards except the video card and SCSI card if you are booting from the SCSI drive. After the operating system is installed, shut down the computer and plug in one card at a time, boot the operating system, and install the drivers for that card. If you get the error message again, try to update the driver.

STOP 0x0000001E (0x1E) KMODE_EXCEPTION_NOT_HANDLED

Parameters:

1. Exception code that was not handled
2. Address at which the exception occurred
3. Parameters 0 of the exception
4. Parameter 1 of the exception

Although typically this is not a processor stop error, it is one of the most common bug codes. Usually the exception address pinpoints the driver or function that caused the problem. Other causes includes bad processor, bad memory, bad cache, or bad or outdated BIOS. Always note this address as well as the link date of the driver or image that contains this address. A common error is exception code 0x80000003. This error means a hard-code breakpoint or assertion was hit, but the system was booted with the/NODEBUG switch. This problem should not occur often. If it occurs repeatedly, make sure a debugger is connected and the system is booted with the /DEBUG switch.

To isolate the cause of the error, do the following:

- Make sure that you have adequate disk space, especially for new installations.
- Make sure that you have the most current BIOS.
- Make sure that you have the newest Windows service pack.
- Update the offending driver or reinstall the offending driver/software package. You may need to use Last Known Good Configuration or Safe mode.
- If the motherboard and hard drive support Ultra DMA-66 or faster, enter the BIOS CMOS Program, disable the Ultra DMA, and set the PIO to mode 4 for that channel. Then after Windows is installed, try the Ultra DMA to see if Windows is stable. Be sure to use the 40-pin, 80-conductor cable.
- Replace the memory.
- Replace the cache (if on the motherboard).

- Replace the motherboard.
- Replace the processor.

STOP 0x00000023 and 0x00000024 FAT_FILE_SYSTEM or NFTS_FILE SYSTEM

This error is usually caused by heavily fragmented drives, heavy file I/O, some types of drive-mirroring software, or some types of antivirus software. To isolate the error, do the following:

- Disable any antivirus programs, backup programs, and defragmentation utilities.
- Check for hard drive corruption by running Scandisk.
- Try Safe mode and Last Known Good Configuration.
- Delete all partitions, then repartition and reformat your system.

STOP 0x0000002E (0x2E) DATA_BUS_ERROR

Parameters:

1. Virtual address that caused the fault
2. Physical address that caused the fault
3. Processor status register (PSR)
4. Faulting instruction register (FIR)

This bug code is normally caused by a parity error in the system memory. The error can also be caused by a driver accessing a 0x8XXXXXXX address that does not exist. To isolate the cause of the error, do the following:

- Make sure that you have the most current BIOS.
- Make sure that you have the newest Windows server pack.
- Check for viruses.
- If you added a new device driver, start the computer in Safe mode, uninstall the driver, and restart the computer.
- Update the offending driver.
- Run the hardware system diagnostic program. Run a general test for the entire system and an extensive test for memory.
- Replace memory.
- Replace video memory (or video card).
- Replace the cache.
- Replace the hard driver.
- Replace the processor.
- Replace the motherboard.

STOP 0x0000003E (0x3E) MULTIPROCESSOR_CONFIGURATION_NOT_SUPPORTED

The system has multiple processors, but they are asymmetric in relation to one another. To be symmetric, all processors must be the same type and level (same type, cache size, and frequency with compatible stepping). In addition, make sure the processor supports multiprocessing (information is given in the processor specification update guides).

STOP 0x0000003F NO_MORE_SYSTEM PTES

A driver is not cleaning up properly. To isolate the cause of the error, do the following:

- Remove any recently installed software, including backup utilities and disk-intensive applications such as defragmenting and virus protection.

STOP 0x00000058

The failure of a primary drive in a fault-tolerance set. To isolate the cause of the error, do the following:

- Using a Windows start-up disk, start your computer from the mirrored (secondary) system drive.
- Try Last Known Good Configuration.
- Delete all partitions, then repartition and reformat your system.
- If you are using an older machine and the drive is over 8057 GB, you may need to load some special software or update the BIOS.

STOP 0x00000077 (0x77) KERNEL_STACK_INPAGE_ERROR

Parameters:

1. 0
2. 0
3. PTE value at time of error
4. Address of signature on kernel stack

or

1. Status code
2. I/O status code
3. Page file number
4. Offset into page file

The requested page of kernel data could not be read. This error is caused by a bad block in a paging file or a disk controller error; in extremely rare cases, it is caused by running out of resources.

If the first and second arguments are 0, the stack signature in the kernel stack was not found. This error is caused by bad hardware.

If the status code is 0xC000009A, the problem is probably the L2 cache. If the status code is 0xC000009C or 0xC000016A, you have a failing hard drive. If the status code is 0xC0000185 (STATUS_IO_DEVICE_ERROR) and the paging file is on a SCSI disk device, the cabling and termination should be checked. Other items to check include defective L2 cache, defective memory, defective processor, defective motherboard, and defective hard drive.

STOP ERROR 0x00000079 MISMATCHED HAL

- The hardware abstraction layer (HAL) is incorrect for the machine. This usually occurs when one machine mixes single- and dual-processor configuration files. In Windows NT, restart the install and when the message "Windows NT is examining the hardware" appears, press F5. Choose your computer type from the list that appears and continue with the installation. In Windows 2000 or Windows Server 2003 you begin the installation process again and install a clean copy of the operating system.
- Repartition and reformat your hard drive from scratch and install Windows.
- Replace the motherboard.
- Replace the processors.

STOP 0x00000007B INACCESSIBLE_BOOT DEVICE

To isolate the cause of the error, do the following:

- Check for viruses on your computer.
- If you are using a SCSI adapter, obtain the latest Windows driver from the adapter vendor, disable sync negotiation, check termination, and check the SCSI IDs of the devices.
- If you are using IDE devices, define the on-board IDE port to Primary only. Check the Master/Slave/Only settings for the IDE devices. Remove all IDE devices except for the hard disk.

■ Run CHKDSK. The file system could be corrupt. If Windows cannot run CHKDSK, you might have to move the drive to another computer running Windows and run the CHKDSK command on that drive.

■ Restart your computer. At the start-up screen, press F8 for Advanced Startup options, then select Last Known Good Configuration.

STOP 0x0000007F UNEXPECTED_KERNEL_MODE_TRAP

This error means a trap (exception) occurred in kernel mode—either a trap in which the kernel is not allowed to have or catch (a bound trap) or a trap that is always instant death (double fault). This error can be caused by a hardware or software problem, but most commonly it is a hardware failure. The first number in the bug code parentheses is the number of the trap (8 = double fault). To learn more about these traps, consult Intel's *Software Developer Manual*, Volume 3: *System Programming Guide,* Chapter 5. Check for mismatched RAM, bad RAM, bad processor, or outdated BIOS.

To isolate the cause of the error, do the following:

■ Make sure that you have the most current BIOS.

■ Make sure that you have the newest Windows service pack.

■ Run diagnostic software and test the RAM in the computer.

■ Disable memory caching.

■ Turn your PC off and take out all cards except the video card and SCSI card if you are booting from the SCSI drive. After the operating system is installed, shut down the computer and plug in one card at a time, boot the operating system, and install the drivers for that card. If you get the error message again, try to update the driver.

■ Try removing or swapping out controllers, cards, or other peripherals.

■ Check to see if the RAM modules are the same speed and that they are compatible with each other.

■ Make sure that you have sufficient RAM to run Windows.

■ Try different RAM.

■ Try a different motherboard.

■ Try a different processor.

STOP 0x00000080 NMI_HARDWARE_FAILURE

The HAL is supposed to report whatever specific data it has and to tell the user to call his or her hardware vendor for support. To isolate the cause of the error, do the following:

■ Make sure that you have the most current BIOS.

■ Make sure that you have the newest Windows service pack.

■ Check to make sure the system is not using nonparity memory in a parity-based system or mixing of parity/nonparity memory.

■ Try different RAM.

■ Try a different motherboard.

■ Try a different processor.

STOP 0x0000009C Machine_Check_Exception

A fatal machine-check exception has occurred. For Pentium processors, the parameters are

1. Low 32 bits of P5_MC_TYPE MSR
2. Not applicable
3. High 32 bit of P5_MC_ADDR MSR
4. Low 32 bits of P5_MC_ADDR MSR

NOTE: Machine check exceptions are listed in the Intel's *Architecture Software Developer's Manual,* Volume 3: *System Programming Guide*, Chapter 12.

For a processor with a P6 architecture, the parameters are

1. Bank number
2. Address of field of MCi_ADDR MSR for the MCA bank that had the error
3. High 32 bits of MCi_STATUS MSR for the MCA bank that had the error
4. Low 32 bits of MCi_STATUS MSR for the MCA bank that had the error

NOTE: Machine-check exceptions are listed in Intel's *Architecture Software Developer's Manual,* Volume 3: *System Programming Guide,* Chapter 12.

To isolate the cause of the error, do the following:

- Make sure that you have the newest Windows service pack.
- Make sure that you have the most current BIOS update.
- Check memory settings in the CMOS setup program.
- Try different RAM.
- Try a different processor or processors.
- Try a different motherboard.

STOP 0x000000B4 VIDEO_DRIVER_INIT

The video driver is bad, corrupted, missing, or disabled. To isolate the cause of the error, do the following:

- Try starting your computer in Safe mode or Enable VGA mode, and try removing the driver and re-installing the driver.
- Make sure that you have the newest Windows service pack.
- Make sure that you have the most current BIOS update.

STOP 0XC0000185 STATUS_IO_DEVICE_ERROR

To isolate the cause of the error, do the following:

- Make sure the SCSI controller and SCSI cable are connected correctly.
- Check for resource conflicts for your SCSI card.

STOP 0x00000221 STATUS_IMAGE_CHECKSUM_MISMATCH

The installer program found a corrupt driver or DLL file for some hardware device. To isolate the cause of the error, do the following:

- Make sure that you have the most current BIOS.
- Make sure that you have the newest Windows service pack.
- Turn your PC off and take out all cards except the video card and SCSI card if you are booting from the SCSI drive. After the operating system is installed, shut down the computer and plug in one card at a time, boot the operating system, and install the drivers for that card. If you get the error message again, try to update the driver.

Glossary

5-4-3 Rule—Important rule that states an Ethernet network must not exceed five segments connected by four repeaters. Of these segments, only three can be populated by computers. This means that the distance of a computer cannot exceed five segments and four repeaters when communicating with other computers on the network.

10Base2—Also known as Thinnet, is a simplified version of the 10Base5 network. The name describes a 10-Mbps baseband network with a maximum cable segment length of approximately 200 meters (actually 185 meters).

10Base5—Also known as Thicknet, is the original type of Ethernet network. The name is derived because 10Base5 is a 10-Mbps baseband network that can have cable segments up to 500 meters long. It uses a 50-ohm RG-8 and RG-11 as a backbone cable.

10BaseT—A form of Ethernet that uses UTP cabling, which is a physical star topology on a hub.

802.11 standards—Standard for wireless networks.

386 Protection Mechanism—A mechanism used in Intel processors, as the 386 assigns data and instructions to a privilege ring or level. The four privilege levels are 0, 1, 2, and 3. The privilege level 0 is the highest and level 3 is the lowest. Programs in ring 0 can access programs in all rings, but the programs in ring 3 cannot access the programs in ring 0, 1, and 2. Today, some operating systems, such as Windows NT and Windows 2000, assign programs to level 0 and other programs to level 3. If a program becomes corrupt in ring 3, it will not affect the operating system.

A

access control list (ACL)—A table that lists users and groups who have been given permission to an object and their permissions.

access method—The set of rules that defines how a computer puts data onto the network cable and takes data from the cable.

access time—The average amount of time it takes to move the hard drives read/write head to the requested sector. It is the sum of seek time and latency period.

Active Directory (AD)—A directory service that uses the "tree" concept for managing resources on a Windows 2000 or Windows Server 2003 network. It stores all information about the network resources and services such as user data, printers, servers, databases, groups, computers, and security policies. In addition, it identifies all resources on a network and makes them accessible to users and applications.

active server pages (ASP)—A specification for a dynamically created web page with an .ASP extension that utilizes ActiveX scripting.

address bus—Typically used in association with a data bus, is used to define where the data bus signals are going to or coming from.

Address Resolution Protocol (ARP)—A TCP/IP protocol used to obtain hardware addresses (MAC addresses) of hosts located on the same physical network.

administrative share—A shared folder typically used for administrative purposes.

administrator—An individual who is responsible for maintaining the network.

advanced configuration and power interface (ACPI)—A power management specification developed by Intel, Microsoft, and Toshiba, in which the operating system can turn off peripheral devices, such as a controller card or network card, when not in use.

advanced power management (APM)—An older power management specification that has system control power-saving features. See *advanced configuration and power interface.*

Advanced Technology Attachment Packet Interface (ATAPI)—An extension to EIDE (also called ATA-2) that enables the interface to support CD-ROM players and tape drives.

allocation unit—Also known as a cluster, is the most basic storage unit for an operating system.

always on/dynamic ISDN (AO/DI)—A networking application that uses the 16-Kbps ISDN D-channel X.25 packet service to maintain an always-on connection between an ISDN end user and an information service provider.

amplitude—The peak voltage of the sine wave.

analog signal—A signal that has infinite number values that are constantly changing. Analog signals are typically sinusoidal waveforms, which are characterized by its amplitude and frequency.

antivirus software—A software package that detects and removes viruses and helps protect the computer against viruses.

AppleTalk—The Apple network architecture that has been included in Apple Macintosh computers for several years.

application layer—Part of the OSI reference model that represents the highest layer. It is responsible for interaction between operating systems and provides an interface to the system. It provides the user interface to a range of network-wide distributed services including file transfer, printer access, and electronic mail.

application server—A server that is similar to a file-and-print server, except it also does some of the processing.

ARC (advanced RISC computing) path—A string that is used to specify the location (partition) of an operating system.

ARCnet (Attached Resource Computer Network)—An early form of networking technology.

area border router (ABR)—A router that attaches an area to the backbone in an OSPF network.

asymmetrical DSL (ADSL)—A DSL standard that transmits an asymmetric data stream, with much more going downstream to the subscriber than coming back.

asynchronous signals—Intermittent signals, they can occur at any time and at irregular intervals. They do not use a clock or timing signal.

asynchronous transfer mode (ATM)—A LAN and a WAN technology, which is generally implemented as a backbone technology; a cell switching and multiplexing technology that combines the benefits of circuit switching and packet switching.

attenuation—When the strength of a signal falls off with distance over a transmission medium.

auditing—A feature of Windows NT, Windows 2000, and Windows Server 2003 that monitors various security-related events so that you can detect intruders and attempts to compromise data on the system. Some events that you can monitor include access to an object such as a folder or file, management of user and group accounts, and logging on and off a system.

AUI (adapter unit interface) connector—Female, 15-pin D connector used to connect to an Ethernet 10Base5 network. Also known as DIX (Digital-Intel-Xerox) connector.

autonomous system (AS)—A grouping of contiguous networks.

autonomous system boundary router (ASBR)—A router that exchanges routing information with routers belonging to other autonomous systems.

B

backbone—(1) Another term for bus, the main wire that connects nodes. The term is often used to describe the main network connections composing the Internet. (2) The central point that connects multiple networks together. (3) In OSPF, an address of 0.0.0.0 is a high-bandwidth logical area where all areas are connected.

backup—An extra copy of data and/or programs.

backup domain controller—Server that contains duplicate copies of the domain database on Windows NT networks.

band—A contiguous group of frequencies, which are used for a single purpose.

bandwidth—The amount of data that can be carried on a given transmission media. Larger bandwidth means greater data transmission capabilities.

Bandwidth Allocation Protocol (BAP)—Enhances multilink by dynamically adding or dropping links on demand.

baseband—A system that uses the transmission medium's entire capacity for a single channel.

basic authentication method—A widely used, industry standard method for collecting user name and password information for web servers.

basic disk—A physical disk that contains either primary partitions, extended partitions, or logical drives, which can be accessed directly using DOS, Windows 95, or Windows 98. Basic disks may contain volume sets, mirrored sets, striped sets, and stripe sets with parity if they were created using Windows NT 4.0 or earlier and upgraded to Windows 2000 or Windows Server 2003.

basic input/output system (BIOS)—Also known as firmware, ROM chips that control the boot process and hardware.

basic rate interface (BRI)—ISDN communication lines consisting of three independent channels, two bearer (or B) channels, each carrying 64 KB/s and one data (or D) channel at 16 Kbps. It uses T1 digital lines consisting of 23 B channels, each at 64 Kbps, and one 64-Kbps D channel for signaling.

basket systems—Baskets or trays used to hold and hide network cables without using cable ties.

bearer channel (B channel)—An ISDN channel that transfer data at a bandwidth of 64 Kbps.

binary digit (bit)—Piece of information that can represent the status of an on-off switch. When several bits are combined together, they can signify a letter, a digit, a punctuation mark, a special graphical character, or a computer instruction.

binary number system—Simplest number system based on two digits, a zero (0) and a one (1).

bind—When a protocol is logically attached to a network card.

binding—The process when a protocol is linked to a protocol stack.

block cipher—Encrypts one block of data at a time.

Bluetooth—Form of short-range radio technology aimed at simplifying communication among network devices and the Internet. It also aims to simplify data synchronization between network devices and other computers.

BNC barrel—Connector that allows two coaxial cables to be connected together.

BNC connector—Short for British Naval Connector, Bayonet Nut Connector, or Bayonet Neill Concelman. It is a type of connector used with coaxial cables. The basic BNC connector is a male type that is mounted at each end of a cable. This connector has a center pin connected to the center cable conductor and a metal tube connected to the outer cable shield. A rotating ring outside the tube locks the cable to any female connector.

BNC T-connector—Used with the 10Base2 system. They are female devices for connecting two cables to a network interface card.

boot partition—Contains the Windows 2000 or Windows Server 2003 operating system files.

BOOT.INI—A file that provides a Boot Loader Operating System Selection menu, which allows the selection between multiple operating systems.

Bootstrap Protocol (BOOTP)—A protocol, created for diskless workstations, enables a booting host to configure itself dynamically.

Border Gateway Protocol (BGP)—A common exterior gateway protocol.

bridge—A data link OSI layer, is a device that connects two LANs and makes them appear as one or connects two segments of the same LAN. The two LANs being connected can be alike or dissimilar, such as an Ethernet LAN connected to a token ring LAN.

bridgehead server—A single server located in each site that is designated to perform site-to-site replication.

broadband—A system that uses the transmission medium's capacity to provide multiple channels by using frequency-division multiplexing (FDM).

Broadband-ISDN (B-ISDN)—A standard for transmitting voice, video, and data simultaneously over fiber optic telephone lines.

brouter—Short for bridge router, is a device that functions as both a router and a bridge. A brouter understands how to route specific types of packets (routable protocols). For other specified packets (nonroutable protocols), it acts as a bridge, which simply forwards the packets to the other networks.

burst mode—A mode used in data transfers, in which sequential data are transferred faster by specifying one memory address followed by transferring multiple pieces of data.

bus mastering—Similar to direct memory address, which has an expansion card with its own processor, takes temporary control of the data and address bus to move information from one point to another.

bus topology—A topology that resembles a line, and data are sent along this single cable.

C

cable tester—A device specifically made to test a cable. An inexpensive cable tester will typically test for shorts and opens.

cable ties—Small devices used to bundle cables traveling together and to keep cables off the floor so that they will not get trampled or run over by office furniture.

cache—A special high-speed storage mechanism. It can be either a reserved section of main memory or an independent high-speed storage device. Two types of caching are commonly used in personal computers—memory caching and disk caching.

capacitor—A simple electrical device, similar to a battery, which is capable of storing a charge of electrons. When used as memory, the charge or lack of charge represents a single bit of data. If it is charged, it has a logic state of 1; if it is discharged, it has a logic state of 0.

carrier-sense multiple access (CSMA)—The method that has each station listen for network traffic before it attempts to transmit. To avoid collisions, CSMA uses one of two specialized methods of collision management: collision detection (CD) and collision avoidance (CA).

carrier-sense, multiple access with collision avoidance (CSMA/CA)—Access mechanism used in Apple's LocalTalk network. Collision avoidance uses time slices to make network access smarter and avoid collisions.

carrier-sense, multiple access with collision detection (CSMA/CD)—Access method utilized in Ethernet and IEEE 802.3. The collision detection approach listens to the network traffic as the card is transmitting. By analyzing network traffic, it detects collisions and initiates retransmissions.

catalog—A summary of the files and folders that have been saved in a backup set.

CD-ROM file system (CDFS)—The read-only file system used to access resources on a CD-ROM disk. Windows supports CDFS to allow CD-ROM file sharing. Because CD-ROM is read only, you cannot assign specific permissions to files through CDFS.

cell—Relatively small, fixed-size packets.

cell relay—Form of packet switching network that uses relatively small, fixed-size packets called cells.

cellular topology—A topology used in wireless communication. A broadcast device is located at the center, broadcasting in all directions to form an invisible circle (cell). All network devices located within the cell communicate with the network through the central station or hub, which is interconnected with the rest of the network infrastructure. If the cells are overlapped, devices may roam from cell to cell while maintaining connection to the network as the devices.

central processing unit (CPU)—See *microprocessor.*

certificate authority (CA)—A server that issues an encrypted digital certificate that contains the applicant's public key and a variety of other identification information.

Challenge Handshake Authentication Protocol (CHAP)—The most common dial-up authentication protocol used, which uses an industry Message Digest 5 (MD5) hashing scheme to encrypt authentication.

channel—A part of the medium's total bandwidth. In communications, the term refers to a communications path between two computers or devices.

channel service unit/data service unit (CSU/DSU)—The DSU is a device that performs protective and diagnostic functions for a telecommunications line. The CSU is a device that connects a terminal to a digital line. Typically, the two devices are packaged as a single unit.

chipset—A number of integrated circuits located on the motherboard and designed to perform one or more related functions.

circuit switching—A technique that connects the sender and the receiver by a single path for the duration of a conversation. Once a connection is established, a dedicated path exists between both ends (i.e., always consumes network capacity), even when there is no active transmission taking place (such as when a caller is put on hold). Once the connection has been made, the destination device acknowledges that it is ready to carry on a transfer. When the conversation is complete, the connection is terminated.

classical IP (CIP) over ATM—A mature standard that enables users to route IP packets over an ATM network or cloud using ATM as either a backbone technology or a workgroup technology.

classless internetwork domain routing (CIDR)—Used with supernetting, it collapses multiple network ID entries into a single entry.

clear text—Simple text without encryption.

client—A computer that requests services from a network server.

client software—Used on workstations to attach and communicate to the network.

client-server network—Consists of servers and clients.

cluster—Also known as allocation unit, is the most basic storage unit for an operating system.

clustering—Connecting two or more computers, or nodes, in such a way that they behave like a single computer. It is used for parallel processing, load balancing, and fault tolerance.

coaxial cable (coax)—Consists of a center wire surrounded by insulation and then a grounded shield of braided wire. The shield minimizes electrical and radio frequency interference.

Collision—Situation that occurs when two or more devices attempt to send a signal along the same channel at the same time. The result of a collision is generally a garbled message. All computer networks require some sort of mechanism to prevent collisions or to recover from collisions when they do occur.

COM+—An extension of the component object model, is both an object-oriented programming architecture and a set of operating system services. It adds to COM a new set of system services for application components while they are running, such as notifying them of significant events or ensuring they are authorized to run.

command queuing—Used in SCSI devices to accept multiple commands and execute them in an order that is more efficient, rather than in the order received. Consequently, this increases the performance of computers running multitasking operating systems and makes it ideal for servers.

committed information rate (CIR)—The value specifies the maximum average data rate that the network undertakes to deliver under "normal conditions."

common gateway interface (CGI)—A standard for interfacing external applications with web servers.

Common Internet File System (CIFS)—Public, or open, variation of the Server Message Block Protocol used by Microsoft Windows and currently used by Linux with Samba, Novell Netware 6.0, and AppleTalkIP.

communication server—A server that handles data flow and e-mail messages from one network to another network using modems or other dial-up technology.

compact disk (CD)—A 4.72-inch encoded platter, which is read by laser. To read a CD, you need a CD drive. They can hold large amounts of information (680 MB) and are inexpensive.

component object model (COM)—An object-based programming model designed to promote interoperability by allowing two or more applications or components to easily cooperate with one another, even if they were written by different vendors, at different times, in different programming languages, or if they are running on different computers that are running different operating systems.

Computer Emergency Response Team Coordination Center (CERT/CC)—CERT was started in December 1988 by the Defense Advanced Research Projects Agency, which was part of the U.S. Department of Defense, after the Morris Worm disabled about 10% of all computers connected to the Internet. CERT/CC is located at the Software Engineering Institute, a federally funded research center operated by Carnegie Mellon University. CERT/CC studies Internet security vulnerabilities, provides services to websites that have been attacked, and publishes security alerts. Research activities include the area of WAN computing and development of improved Internet Security. The organization also provides training to incident-response professionals.

concentric—Circles that share the same center much like rings in a tree.

contention—The method when two or more devices contend for network access. Any device can transmit whenever it needs to send information. To avoid data collisions (two devices sending data at the same time), specific contention protocols were developed requiring the device to listen to the cable before transmitting data.

Continuity check—Test done with a device such as an ohmmeter. Since a wire or fuse is a conductor, essentially you should measure no resistance (0 ohms) to show that there is no break in the wire or fuse.

Control Panel—A component of Windows that is used for configuration.

convergence—The process of agreement by all routers to which routes are the optimal routes.

cookie—A message given to a web browser by a web server, which is typically stored in a text file on the PC's hard drive. The message is then sent back to the server each time the browser requests a page from the server.

cooperative multitasking—Each program controls the CPU for as long as it needs it. If a program is not using the CPU, however, it can allow another program to use it temporarily.

count to infinity—Typically occurs when a network has slow convergence, is a loop that forms when a link in a network goes down and routers on the network update their routing tables with incorrect hop counts.

crossed pairs—Two wires are connected improperly causing the two wires to be crossed.

crossover cable—Connects one network card to another network card or a hub to a hub; reverses the transmit and receive wires.

crosstalk—Signals induct (law of induction) or transfer from one wire to the other.

cryptography—The art of protecting information by transforming it (encrypting it) into cipher text.

current state method—Periodically measures the digital signal for the specific state.

D

daisy chain—A hardware configuration in which devices are connected one to another in a series.

data—The raw facts, numbers, letters, or symbols that the computer processes into meaningful information.

data bus—Can refer to a bus that carries data in to and out of a device such as the processor or expansion card.

data channels (D channels)—An ISDN channel that uses a communications language called DSS-1 for administrative signaling, such as to instruct the carrier to set up or terminate a B-channel call, to ensure that a B channel is available to receive a call, or to provide signaling information for such features as caller identification.

data circuit-terminating equipment (DCE)—Special communication devices that provide the interface between the DTE and the network. Examples include modems and adapters. Its purpose is to provide clocking and switching services in a network and actually transmit data through the WAN; therefore, it controls data flowing to or from a computer.

Data Encryption Standard (DES)—A popular symmetric-key encryption method that uses block cipher.

Data Link Control (DLC) protocol—A special, non-routable protocol that enables computers running Windows 2000 or Windows Server 2003 to communicate with computers running DLC protocol stack such as IBM mainframes, IBM AS/400 computers, and Hewlett-Packard network printers connected directly to the network using older HP JetDirect network cards.

data link layer—Part of the OSI reference model that is responsible for providing error-free data transmission and establishes local connections between two computers.

data service Unit (DSU)—Device that performs all error correction, handshaking, and protective and diagnostic functions for a telecommunications line.

data terminal equipment (DTE)—End systems devices that communicate across the WAN. They are usually terminals, PCs, and network hosts and are located on the premises of individual subscribers.

de facto standard—The fact standard that has been accepted by the industry because it was the most common.

de jure standard—The bylaw standard that has been dictated by an appointed committee such as the International Organization for Standardization (ISO).

decryption—The process of converting data from encrypted format back to its original format.

demand paging—A feature found in Intel processors which swaps data between the RAM and disk only on the demand of the microprocessor. Since the processor does not try to anticipate what data will be needed from the hard drive, the code and data stored on disk as virtual memory will remain on disk until the code or data are needed.

demand priority—An access method in which a device makes a request to the hub and the hub grants permission.

demarcation point (demarc)—The point where the local loop ends at the customer's premises.

demilitarized zone (DMZ)—Area used by a company that wants to host its own Internet services without sacrificing unauthorized access to its private network. The DMZ sits between the Internet and an Internal network's line of defense, usually some combination of firewalls and bastion hosts. Typically, the DMZ contains devices accessible to Internet traffic, such as web (HTTP) servers, FTP servers, SMTP (e-mail) servers, and DNS servers.

demultiplexing—Technique that occurs when the destination computer receives the data stream and separates and rejoins the application's segments. See *multiplexing*.

denial of service (DoS)—Type of attack on a network that is designed to bring the network down by flooding it with useless traffic.

designator—Keeps track of which drive designations are assigned to network resources.

device drivers—Programs that control a device; serve as a translator between the device and programs that use the device.

Device Manager—A component of Windows that allows users to view and configure the hardware devices on their computers.

DHCP relay agent—A computer that relays DHCP and BOOTP messages between clients and servers on different subnets.

DHCP server—Maintains a list of IP addresses called a pool. When a user needs an IP address, the server removes the address from the pool and issues it to the user for a limited amount of time. Issuing an address is called leasing.

dial-up networking—When a remote access client makes a nonpermanent, dial-up connection to a physical port on a remote access server by using the service of a telecommunications provider such as an analog phone, ISDN, or X.25.

differential SCSI—A SCSI specification that uses differential signaling, where each signal is actually carried by two different wires, each the mirror image of the other. In other words, when one of the two wires is a positive voltage, the other wire is at zero volts. As a result, the signal is much more resilient to interference and allows for a much longer cabling.

digest authentication method—A method similar to the basic authentication method that offers the same features as basic authentication for web servers but

involves a different way of transmitting the authentication credentials. The authentication credentials pass through a one-way process, often referred to as hashing.

digital certificate—An attachment to an electronic message used for security purposes such as for authentication and to verify that a user sending a message is who he or she claims to be and to provide the receiver with a means to encode a reply.

digital envelope—A type of security that encrypts the message using symmetric encryption and encrypts key to decode the message using public-key encryption. This technique overcomes one problem of public-key encryption—being slower than symmetric encryption because only the key is protected with public-key encryption, providing little overhead.

digital signals—Computer language based on a binary signal system produced by pulses of light or electric voltages. The state of the pulse is either on/high or off/low to represent 1s and 0s. Binary digits (bits) can be combined to represent different values.

digital signature—A digital code that can be attached to an electronically transmitted message that uniquely identifies the sender. Like a written signature, its purpose is to guarantee that the individual sending the message really is who he or she claims to be.

digital subscriber line (DSL)—A special communications line that uses sophisticated modulation technology to maximize the amount of data that can be sent over plain twisted-pair copper wiring, which is already carrying phone service to subscribers' homes.

DIP switches—Bank of tiny on-off switches found on many older computers to configure the motherboard or the expansion card.

direct memory access (DMA)—A data transfer mode used by IDE hard drives that uses bus mastering to transfer the data.

direct memory address (DMA) channels—Used by communication devices that must send and receive large amounts of information at high speed (sound cards, some network cards, and some SCSI cards), in which the DMA controller takes over the data bus and address lines to bring data from an I/O device to the RAM without any assistance or direction from the CPU.

directories—Part of a tree structure that can hold directories and files. Newer operating systems may refer to a directory as a folder.

directory number (DN)—The 10-digit phone number that the telephone company assigns to any analog line.

directory service—A network service that identifies all resources on a network and makes those resources accessible to users and applications.

directory services servers—Locates information about the network such as domains (logical divisions of the network) and other servers.

direct-sequence spread-spectrum (DSSS)—A system that generates a redundant bit pattern for each bit to be transmitted. This bit pattern is called a chip (or chipping code). The intended receiver knows which specific frequencies are valid and deciphers the signal by collecting valid signals and ignoring the spurious signals.

disk quotas—A system that tracks and controls disk space usage for a NTFS volume.

disk transfer rate—The speed at which data are transferred to and from the platters; usually measured in bits per second (bps) or bytes per second (B/s).

diskless workstations—Computers that have no floppy drives or disk drives. Since the computer does not have a hard drive, it boots by loading the instructions within a special ROM chip on the network card which connects to the network and loads all necessary files from the network.

distance-vector-based routing protocol—A dynamic routing protocol that periodically advertises or broadcasts the routes in the routing tables, but only sends it to the neighboring routers.

distinguished name (DN)—Uniquely identifies an object (name) in the Active Directory by using the actual name of the object plus the names of container objects and domains that contain the object; identifies the object and its location in a tree.

distributed component object model (DCOM)—A set of Microsoft concepts and program interfaces in which client program objects can request services from server program objects on other computers in a network.

distributed file system (DFS)—A significant improvement to the drive mapping process that allows multiple network locations to be mapped to a single drive; shared folders that reside on the same or different computers joined in a single hierarchical tree structure.

distribution group—Used only for nonsecurity functions such as to distribute e-mail messages to many people.

DIX connector—Digital-Intel-Xerox connector, is a female, 15-pin D connector used to connect to an Ethernet 10Base5 network. Also known as AUI connector.

DNS zone—A portion of the DNS name space whose database records exist and are managed in a particular DNS database file.

domain—A logical unit of computers and network resources that defines a security boundary. It is typically found on medium or large networks or networks that require a secure environment. A domain uses one database to share its common security and user account information for all computers within the domain. There-

fore, it allows centralized network administration of all users, groups, and resources on the network.

domain controller—The computer that stores a replica (copy) of the account and security information of the domain and defines the domain.

domain local group—Primarily used to assign rights and permissions to network resources that are in the domain of the local group. Different from a global group, it can list user accounts, universal groups and global groups from any domain, and local groups from the same domain.

domain name system (DNS)—A hierarchical client-server-based distributed database management system that translates Internet domain names to an IP address. It is used because domain names are easier to remember than IP addresses. The DNS clients are called resolvers and the DNS servers are called name servers.

domain user account—Allows a user to log on to a domain to gain access to the network resources.

double data rate–synchronous DRAM (DDR SDRAM)—A type of SDRAM that supports data transfers on both the rise and fall of each clock cycle, effectively doubling the memory chip's data thoughput.

Dr. Watson—A program that starts automatically when a program error is detected; it records the information about the system and the program failure into a log file.

dual inline memory module (DIMM)—A RAM package type that uses a small circuit board consisting of several soldered DIP memory chips. Compared with SIMMs, DIMMs are larger, typically have a larger capacity, and have a larger data bus.

dumb terminal—A system consisting of a monitor to display the data and a keyboard to input the data used to access a mainframe. Different from a PC, it does not process the data.

duplex volume—A mirror disk that uses multiple controller cards.

dynamic data exchange (DDE)—A component introduced with Windows 3.0 to allow users to copy data between applications while maintaining a link. When data are changed at the source, they are also changed at the target, so DDE maintains this connection.

dynamic DNS—A method that performs automatic registration to a DNS name space.

Dynamic Host Configuration Protocol (DHCP)—Extension of BOOTP. Used to automatically configure a host during boot-up on a TCP/IP network and to change settings while the host is attached. Many parameters can be automatically set with the DHCP server, including IP addresses, subnet masks, DNS servers, WINS servers, and domain names.

dynamic HTML (DHTML)—Allows content to be displayed with more design flexibility and accuracy through the use of a cascading style sheet (CSS).

dynamic RAM (DRAM) chips—Memory chips (RAM) that use a storage cell consisting of a tiny solid-state capacitor and a MOS transistor.

dynamic routing algorithm—An algorithm that determines routes used in a network.

dynamic storage—A disk that is converted from basic to dynamic storage that contains simple volumes, spanned volumes, mirrored volumes, striped volumes, and RAID-5 volumes. Unlike basic disks, dynamic disks cannot contain partitions or logical drives or be accessed by DOS. The advantage of the dynamic storage is that it contains an unlimited number of volumes which can be extended to include noncontiguous space on available disks.

E

E-carrier system—Entire digital system that consists of permanent, dedicated, point-to-point connections. It is typically used in Europe.

effective permissions—The actual permissions when logging in and accessing a file or folder. They consist of explicit permissions plus any inherited permissions.

electromagnetic interference (EMI)—Signals caused by large electromagnets used in industrial machinery, motors, fluorescent lighting, and power lines that cause interference to other signals.

electronic mail (e-mail)—A powerful, sophisticated tool that allows users to send text messages and file attachments (documents, pictures, sound, and movies) to anyone with an e-mail address.

electrostatic discharge (ESD)—Electricity generated by friction (e.g., when your arm slides on a tabletop or when you walk across a carpet). Electronic devices such as network cards and computer components can be damaged by electrostatic discharge.

emergency repair disk (ERD)—Contains information about your current Windows system settings. You can use this disk to repair your computer if it will not start or your system files are damaged or erased.

emulated LAN (ELAN)—A set of LAN emulation clients that reside as ATM endpoints.

encapsulation—Concept of placing data behind headers (and before trailers) for each layer.

encoding—Process of changing a signal to represent data.

encrypting file system (EFS)—A system that allows a user to encrypt and decrypt files that are stored on an NTFS volume.

encryption—The process of disguising a message or data in what appears to be meaningless data (cipher text) to hide and protect the sensitive data from unauthorized access.

Enhanced Interior Gateway Routing Protocol (EIGRP)—Combines the advantages of link-state protocols with those of distance-vector protocols.

enterprise—Any large organization that utilizes computers, usually consisting of multiple LANs.

enterprise WAN—A WAN that is owned by one company or organization.

error checking and correcting (ECC) code—A type of error checking, typically done with memory. It uses a special circuitry for testing the accuracy of data as they pass in and out of memory and can be used to correct some errors in memory.

Ethernet—The most widely used LAN technology today that offers good balance between speed, price, reliability, and ease of installation.

Event Viewer—A utility that is used to view and manage logs of system, program, and security events on the computer. Event Viewer gathers information about hardware and software problems, and monitors Windows security events.

exception error—Occurs when an application tries to pass an invalid parameter to another program.

Exchange—An e-mail server made by Microsoft, which runs on a Windows NT or a Windows 2000 server or on Windows Server 2003.

Executive Services—The component of Windows NT, Windows 2000, and Windows Server 2003 that consists of managers and device drivers.

expansion cards—Circuit boards that are inserted into expansion slots to expand the system.

expansion slot—Also known as the I/O bus, extends the reach of the microprocessor so that it can communicate with peripheral devices.

explicit permissions—Those granted directly to the folder or file.

extended ISA (EISA)—An older bus architecture developed to compete against IBM's MCA slots. Different from the MCA, the EISA was backward compatible with ISA cards; like the MCA, the industry never accepted the new architecture.

Extensible Authentication Protocol (EAP)—A system that allows new authentication schemes to be plugged in as needed. EAP allows third-party vendors to develop custom authentication schemes such as retina scans, voice recognition, fingerprint identification, smart card, Kerberos, and digital certificates.

Extensible Authentication Protocol–Transport Level Security (EAP-TLS)—Used in certificate-based security environments. The EAP-TLS exchange of messages provides mutual authentication, negotiation of the encryption method, and secured private-key exchange between the remote access client and the authenticating server.

Extensible Markup Language (XML)—Pared-down version of SGML, designed especially for web documents. It allows designers to create their own customized tags, thereby enabling the definition, transmission, validation, and interpretation of data between applications and between organizations.

Exterior Gateway Protocol (EGP)—A protocol for exchanging routing information between the neighbor gateway host (each with its own router) in a network of autonomous systems.

external IPX address—An eight-digit (4-byte) hexadecimal number used to identify a network on an IPX network.

F

fast Ethernet—An extension of the 10BaseT Ethernet standard that transports data at 100 Mbps yet still keeps using the CSMA/CD protocol used by 10-Mbps Ethernet.

fat client—Performs the bulk of the data processing operations.

FAT32—A file system that uses 32-bit FAT entries. Introduced in the second major release of Windows 95 (OSR2/Windows 95B), it is an enhancement of the FAT/VFAT file system. It uses space more efficiently, such as 4-KB clusters for drives up to 8 GB, which results in 15% more efficient use of disk space relative to large FAT drives.

fault tolerance—Ability of a system to respond gracefully to an unexpected hardware or software failure. There are many levels of fault tolerance, the lowest being the ability to continue operation in the event of a power failure. Many fault-tolerant computer systems mirror all operations, that is, every operation is performed on two or more duplicate systems, so if one fails the other can take over.

fax server—Manages fax messages sent in to and out of the network through a fax modem.

FDISK—A DOS and Windows 95/98 utility used to partition hard drives.

Fiber Distributed Data Interface (FDDI)—A MAN protocol that provides data transport at 100 Mbps (much higher data rate than standard Ethernet or token ring) and can support up to 500 stations on a single network.

fiber optic cable—Consists of a bundle of glass or plastic threads, each capable of carrying data signals in the form of modulated pulses of light.

file—A collection of related information that is referenced by name. Each file or directory on a volume can be uniquely identified by using the file name (including the file extension, if any) and the path (or location on the tree).

file allocation table (FAT)—(1) An index used to remember which file is located in which cluster. It lists each cluster, if the cluster is being used by a file, the name of the file using the cluster, and the next cluster if the file does not fit within the cluster. (2) The most common file system, FAT is a simple and reliable file system, which uses minimal memory. It supports file names of 11 characters, which include the 8 characters for the file name and 3 characters for the file extension.

file attributes—Several properties of the file. For example, they indicate whether the file is read-only, whether it needs to be backed up, and whether it is visible or hidden.

file server—Manages user access to files stored on a server.

file sharing—Allows users to access files, which are on another computer, without using a floppy disk or other forms of removable media.

file system—The overall structure in which files are named, stored, and organized.

File Transfer Protocol (FTP)—A TCP/IP protocol that allows a user to transfer files between local and remote host computers.

firewall—A system designed to prevent unauthorized access to or from a private network; can be implemented in both hardware and software, or a combination of both. Firewalls are frequently used to prevent unauthorized Internet users from accessing private networks connected to the Internet, especially intranets.

forest—A grouping of one or more trees that are connected by two-way, transitive trust relationships.

forward lookup zone—Part of the DNS system that allows users to perform name-to-address resolution (forward lookup queries).

fox and hound—See *tone generator and probe.*

frame—Structured package for moving data that includes not only the raw data, or "payload," but also the sender's and receiver's network addresses and error checking and control information.

Frame Relay—A packet switching protocol designed to use high-speed digital backbone links to support modern protocols that provide for error handling and flow control for connecting devices on a wide area network.

Frame Relay Access Device (FRAD)—Used to connect the DTEs to the frame relay network. It multiplexes and formats traffic for entering a frame relay network.

frequency hopping—A system used in wireless technology that quickly switches between predetermined frequencies, many times each second. Both the transmitter and receiver must follow the same pattern and maintain complex timing intervals to be able to receive and interpret the data being sent.

full initial transfer (AXFR)—When a DNS server obtains a full copy of the zone files.

full-duplex dialog—Used in communication that allows every device to both transmit and receive simultaneously.

fully qualified domain name (FQDN)—Sometimes referred to as simply domain name; used to identify computers on a TCP/IP network.

G

gateway—A hardware and/or software that links two different types of networks by repackaging and converting data from one network to another network or from one network operating system to another.

gigahertz (GHz)—One billion hertz.

global catalog—Holds replica information of every object in the Active Directory; but instead of storing the entire object, it stores those attributes most frequently used in search operations (such as a user's first and last names).

global groups—Primarily used to group people within a domain. They can list user accounts and global groups from their domain. The global group can be assigned access to resources in any domain.

global WAN—A WAN that is not owned by any one company and could cross national boundaries. The best known example of a global WAN is the Internet, which connects millions of computers.

globally unique identifier (GUID)—A 128-bit unique number used to identify objects in the Active Directory.

gopher—A system that predates the World Wide Web for organizing and displaying files on Internet servers. A gopher server presents its contents as a hierarchically structured list of files.

group—A collection of user accounts; tools that help simplify administration.

group scope—Defines how the permissions and rights are assigned to the group.

H

half-duplex dialog—Allows each device to both transmit and receive, but not at the same time; therefore, only one device can transmit at a time.

handshaking—The process by which two devices initiate communications. It begins when one device sends a message to another device indicating that it wants to establish a communication channel. The two devices then send several messages back and forth that enable them to agree on a communication protocol.

hard drives—Half electronic/half mechanical devices that use magnetic patterns to store information onto rotating platters. They are considered long-term storage devices because they do not forget their information when power is disconnected.

hardware abstraction layer (HAL)—A library of hardware manipulating routines that hide the hardware interface details. It contains the hardware-specific code that handles I/O interfaces, interrupt controllers, and multiprocessor operations so that it can act as the translator between specific hardware architectures and the rest of the Windows 2000 or Windows Server 2003 software. As a result, programs written for Windows 2000 or Windows Server 2003 can work on other architectures, making those programs portable.

Hardware Compatibility List (HCL)—A Microsoft listing that provides approved tested components that will work with Windows 2000 or Windows Server 2003.

hardware profile—A set of instructions that tell Windows 2000 or Windows Server 2003 which devices to start when you start your computer or what settings to use for each device.

hashing scheme—Scrambles information in such a way that it is unique and cannot be reversed to the original format.

hertz (Hz)—A unit of measurement for frequency (cycles per second) of a device or signal. Hertz is typically used to measure the clock speed of a electronic device such as the processor or the bandwidth of a signal. Today in computers, hertz is typically expressed in megahertz and gigahertz.

hexadecimal number system—System based on 16 digits (1, 2, 3, 4, 5, 6, 7, 8, 9, A, B, C, D, E, and F). One hexadecimal digit is equivalent to a four-digit binary number (4 bits or a nibble), and two hexadecimal digits are used to represent a byte (8 bits).

high-bit-rate digital subscriber line (HDSL)—A DSL standard that provides a high bandwidth in both directions over two copper loops. HSDL has proven to be a reliable and cost-effective means for providing repeaterless T1 and E1 services over two twisted-pair loops.

High-level Data-Link Control (HDLC) protocol—Used with Point-to-Point Protocol; encapsulates its data during transmission.

high-level formatting—The process of writing the file system structure on the disk so that it can be used to store programs and data; this includes creating a file allocation table (an index listing all directories and files and where they are located on the disk) and a root directory to begin.

hive—A discrete body of keys, subkeys, and values; each has a corresponding registry file and .LOG file located in the WINNT\SYSTEM32\CONFIG folder.

home directory—A folder used to hold or store a user's personal documents.

HomeRF SWAP—SWAP means Shared Wireless Access Protocol. A Bluetooth standard designed specifically for wireless networks in homes.

hop—Data going through a router. Hop count is the number of a routers that a data packet travels between the source and destination points.

host—(1) A computer system that is accessed by a user who is working at a remote location. Typically, the term is used when there are two computer systems connected by modems and telephone lines. The system that contains the data is called the host, and the computer at which the user sits is called the remote terminal. (2) A network connection to a TCP/IP network, including the Internet. Each host has a unique IP address. Besides computers, hosts may also be network printers and routers. (3) Provides the infrastructure for a computer service. For example, there are many companies that host web servers, which means they provide the hardware, software, and communications lines required by the server, but the content on the server may be controlled by someone else.

HOSTS file—A text file that lists the IP address followed by the host name.

hot swapping—The ability to add and remove devices to a computer while the computer is running and have the operating system automatically recognize the change.

hub—A device that is a common connection point for devices in a network. Hubs, which have multiple hubs, are commonly used to connect segments of a LAN. When a packet arrives at one port, it is copied to the other ports so that all segments of the LAN can see all packets.

hybrid fiber/coaxial (HFC) network—Telecommunications technology in which fiber optic cable and coaxial cable are used in different portions of a network to carry broadband content (such as video, data, and voice).

Hypertext Markup Language (HTML)—Used in web pages that utilize embedded code made of ordinary text to give the browser a general idea of how the information should be displayed.

Hypertext Transfer Protocol (HTTP)—A TCP/IP protocol that is the basis for exchange over the World Wide Web (WWW). WWW pages are written in the Hypertext Markup Language (HTML)—an ACSII-based, platform-independent formatting language.

I

I/O address—Used in the computer to identify a device.

incremental transfers (IXFR)—When a secondary DNS server pulls only those zone changes it needs to synchronize its copy of the zone with its source.

Independent Computing Architecture (ICA)—Protocol that allows multiple computers to take control of a virtual computer and use it as if it were their desktop (thin client).

Industry Standard Architecture (ISA)—The bus architecture used in the IBM PC/XT and PC/AT. The AT version of the bus is called the AT bus and has became a de facto industry standard. The ISA bus is being replaced by the PCI bus.

infrared (IR) system—A form of wireless technology based on infrared light (light that is just below the visible light in the electromagnetic spectrum).

inherited permissions—Those that flow down from the folder into the subfolders and files, indirectly giving permissions to a user or group.

integrated drive electronics (IDE) interface—A fast, low-cost hard drive interface. The IDE hard drive connects to a controller card (is an expansion card or is built into the motherboard) using a 40-pin cable.

Integrated Services Digital Network (ISDN)—A digital network that was a planned replacement for POTS to provide voice and data communications worldwide using circuit switching while using the same wiring that is currently being used in homes and businesses.

Intellimirror—A management tool that replaces the NT 4.0 administration of user profiles and provides more availability and security to user's data applications and settings, and allows for roaming access.

interactive query—Gives the best answer it currently has back as a response to DNS servers. The best answer will be the address being sought or an address of a server that would have a better idea of its address.

interference—When undesirable electromagnetic waves affect the desired signal.

Interior Gateway Protocol (IGP)—The routing protocol that manages routing information within an autonomous system.

Interior Gateway Routing Protocol (IGRP)—An extension of the open RIP standard, which was developed in the mid-1980s by Cisco Systems, Inc. Cisco's principal goal in creating IGRP was to provide a robust protocol for routing within an autonomous system (AS) having arbitrarily complex topology and consisting of media with diverse bandwidth and delay characteristics.

internal IPX network number—An eight-digit (4-byte) hexadecimal number used to identify a server on an IPX network.

Internet Connection Sharing (ICS)—Allows a single dial-up connection to be shared across the network.

Internet Control-Message Protocol (ICMP)—A TCP/IP protocol that sends messages and reports errors regarding the delivery of a packet.

Internet Explorer administration kit (IEAK)—A software product that makes it easy to create a custom browser that can be deployed across a network or via Web download.

Internet Group Management Protocol (IGMP)—A TCP/IP protocol that is used by IP hosts to report host group membership to local multicast routers.

Internet Information Services (IIS)—Built-in web server found in the Windows 2000 Server and Windows Server 2003 families.

Internet Protocol (IP)—A TCP/IP connectionless protocol that is primarily responsible for addressing and routing packets between hosts.

Internet Protocol Security (IPSec)—Creates a standard platform to develop secure networks and electronic tunnels between two machines. It also encapsulates each data packet in a new packet that contains the information necessary to set up, maintain, and tear down the tunnel when it is no longer needed.

internetwork—A network consisting of several LANs, which are linked together.

Internetwork Packet Exchange (IPX)—(1) A protocol suite that was heavily associated with Novell NetWare. (2) A connectionless IPX networking protocol used to interconnect networks.

Internetworking operating system (IOS)—The operating system used on Cisco routers.

interprocess communication (IPC)—A component of Windows NT, Windows 2000, and Windows Server 2003 that allows bidirectional communication between clients and servers using distributed applications. IPC is a mechanism used by programs and multiprocesses. IPC allows concurrently running tasks to communicate between themselves on a local computer or between the local computer and a remote computer.

interrupt request (IRQ)—A signal informing a program that an event has occurred. When a program receives an interrupt signal, it takes a specified action (which can be to ignore the signal) such as causing the program to suspend itself temporarily to service the interrupt.

intranet—A network based on the TCP/IP protocol, the same protocol that the Internet uses. Unlike the Internet, the intranet belongs to a single organization, accessible only by the organization's members. An intranet's websites look and act like any other websites, but they are isolated by a firewall to stop illegal access.

invalid page faults—An error that occurs when a program tries to access a memory area that belongs to another program.

IP next generation (IPng)—See *IPv6*.

IPC$—An administrative shared folder used for remote administration of a computer and to view a computer's shared resources.

IPv6—New TCP/IP standard. It allows for more addresses than previous standards and includes enhancement such as built-in security (IPSec).

J

jumper—A small, plastic-covered metal clip that is used to connect two pins protruding from an expansion card. The jumper (same as an On switch) connects the pins, which closes the circuit and allows current to flow.

K

Kerberos—A security protocol that is used for distributed security within a domain tree or forest. This allows for transitive trusts and a single logon to provide access to all domain resources.

kernel—The central module of an operating system. It is the part of the operating system that loads first, and it remains in main memory. Because it stays in memory, it is important for the kernel to be as small as possible while still providing all the essential services required by other parts of the operating system and applications. Typically, the kernel is responsible for memory management, process and task management, and disk management.

kernel mode—A processing mode used in Windows NT, Windows 2000, and Windows Server 2003 that has programs or software components run in ring 0 of the Intel 386 microprocessor protection model. The kernel mode components are protected by the microprocessor. It has direct access to all hardware and all memory including the address space of all user-mode processes.

key—A string of bits used to map text into a code and a code back to text. To encrypt and decrypt a file, you must use a key.

kill process tree—The utility that has the ability to end all processes related to the one being terminated by the administrator.

Knowledge Consistency Checker (KCC)—The Windows service that automatically creates and manages the replication path or site topology used to replicate Active Directory information.

L

LAN emulation (LANE)—An ATM standard that emulates an Ethernet or token ring LAN on top of an ATM network.

last mile—Also referred to as the local loop and subscriber loop, the cable carries analog signals on a twisted-pair cable.

latency period—The time it takes after the hard drive's read/write heads to move to the requested track, for the requested sector to spin underneath the read/write head. The latency period is usually half of the time for a single revolution of the disk platter.

Layer 2 Tunneling Protocol (LT2P)—Extension to the Point-to-Point Protocol that enables ISPs to operate virtual private networks (VPNs). L2TP merges the best features of two other tunneling protocols: PPTP from Microsoft and L2F from Cisco Systems. Like PPTP, L2TP requires that the ISP's routers support the protocol.

layer 3 switch—Device that combines a router and a switch. It has been optimized for high-performance LAN support and is not meant to service wide area connections.

legacy application—An application in which a company or organization has already invested considerable time and money. Typically, legacy applications are database management systems (DBMSs) running on mainframes or minicomputers. An important feature of new software products is the ability to work with a company's legacy applications, or at least be able to import data from them.

legacy cards—ISA cards, which are not plug-and-play cards.

Lightweight Directory Access Protocol (LDAP)—A set of protocols for accessing information directories. LDAP is based on the standards contained within the X.500 standard, but is significantly simpler; and unlike X.500, LDAP supports TCP/IP, which is necessary for any type of Internet access. Because it is a simpler version of X.500, LDAP is sometimes called X.500-lite.

line conditioner—Device that uses the inductance of transformers to filter out noise and capacitors (and other circuits) to "fill-in" brownouts. Most line conditioners include surge protection.

line printer daemon (LPD)—A protocol that provides printing on a TCP/IP network.

link-state algorithms—Also known as shortest path first algorithms, link-state routers send updates directly (or by using multicast traffic) to all routers within the network. Each router, however, sends only the portion of the routing table that describes the state of its own links. In essence, link-state algorithms send small updates everywhere.

Linux—A freely distributable implementation of UNIX that runs on several hardware platforms.

LMHOSTS—A text file that translates between NetBIOS names and IP addresses.

local area network (LAN)—A network with computers that are connected within a geographical close network, such as a room, a building, or a group of adjacent buildings.

local bus—A data bus that connects directly, or almost directly, to the microprocessor. Although local buses can support only a few devices, they provide very fast throughput.

local loop—See *subscriber loop.*

local procedure calls (LPCs)—A component of IPC, used to transfer information between applications on the same computer.

local user accounts—Allows users to log on at and gain resources on only the computer where you create the local user account.

logical link control (LLC)—A sublayer of the data link layer that manages the data link between two computers within the same subnet and defines service access points (SAPs) or ports.

logical topology—Describes how the data flow through the physical topology or the actual pathway of the data.

M

mail server—Manages electronic messages (e-mail) between users.

mailslot—Connectionless messaging, which means that messaging is not guaranteed. Connectionless messaging is useful for identifying other computers or services on a network, such as the browser service offered in Windows 2000 and Windows Server 2003.

mainframes—Large, centralized computers used to store and organize data.

Management Information Base (MIB)—A database.

Manchester Signal Encoding—The type of encoding used on an Ethernet network.

master boot record (MBR)—Located in the first sector of the disk, contains a small program that reads the partition table (also located in the MBR), checks which partition is active (the partition to boot from), and reads the first sector of the bootable partition.

media access control (MAC) address—Also known as the physical device address, is a unique hardware address (unique on the LAN/subnet) burned on to a ROM chip assigned by the hardware vendors or selected with jumpers or DIP switches.

media access control (MAC) sublayer—Part of the data link layer that specifies the communications directly with the network adapter card.

member server—A server that does not store copies of the directory database and therefore does not authenticate accounts or receive synchronized copies of the directory database. These servers are used to run applications dedicated to specific tasks, such as managing print servers, managing file servers, running database applications, or running as a web server.

memory address—(1) The set of all legal addresses in memory for a given application. (2) A memory area between 640 MB and 1 MB of RAM used as a working area for the expansion card or by the ROM BIOS chips on the card.

mesh topology—Links a computer to every other computer. Although not common in LANs, it is common in WANs where it connects remote sites over telecommunications links.

message transfer agent (MTA)—Part of an e-mail system that manages the routing of messages within a site, between sites, and to foreign message systems.

messaging application programming interface (MAPI)—A system built into Microsoft Windows that enables different e-mail applications to work together to distribute mail.

metadata—Data that describe how and when and by whom a particular set of data was collected, and how the data are formatted. Metadata are essential for understanding information stored in data warehouses.

metric—A standard of measurement, such as hop count, that is used by routing algorithms to determine the optimal path to a destination.

metropolitan area network (MAN)—Designed for a town or city, primarily uses high-speed connections such as fiber optics.

Micro-Channel Architecture (MCA)—An older bus architecture developed by IBM for older PCs to replace the ISA slot. Although it had higher clock speeds, larger data bus, and other performance enhancements, the industry never accepted the new architecture.

Microkernel—The central part of Windows 2000 and Windows Server 2003, which coordinates all I/O functions and synchronizes the activities of the Executive Services. Much like the other kernels in Windows 3.xx and Windows 95/98, it determines what is to be performed and when it is to be performed, while handling interrupts and exceptions. It is designed to keep the microprocessor(s) busy at all times.

microprocessor—Also known as the central processing unit (CPU), is an integrated circuit that acts as the brain of the computer.

Microsoft Challenge Handshake Authentication Protocol (MS-CHAP)—Microsoft's proprietary version of CHAP.

Microsoft Management Console (MMC)—A fully customizable administrative console used as a common interface for most administrative tasks.

miniport driver—A component that controls the network interface adapter and connects the hardware device to the protocol stack.

mirror volume—Also known as RAID-1, is two identical copies of a simple volume on separate hard disks. When data are written to one disk, they are also written to the other disk. If one of the hard drives fail, the other hard drive will continue to function without loss of data or downtime.

modulation—To blend data into a carrier signal. At the receiving side, a device demodulates the signals by separating the constant carrier signals from the variable data signals.

motherboard—Also referred to as the main board or the system board, is the primary printed circuit board located within the PC.

multicast—To transmit a message to a select group of recipients.

multihomed server—Contains multiple network cards that act as the router.

multilink—A combined connection consisting of two or more physical communications links' bandwidth into a single, logical link used to increase remote access bandwidth and throughput.

multimode fiber—A type of fiber optic cable that is capable of transmitting multiple modes (independent light paths) at various wavelengths or phases.

multipoint connection—Links three or more devices through a single communications medium. Because multipoint connections share a common channel, each device needs a way to identify itself and the device to which it wants to send information.

Multiprotocol over ATM (MPOA)—A mechanism to route protocols such as IP, IPX, and NetBIOS from traditional LANs over a switched ATM backbone.

Multipurpose Internet Mail Extension (MIME)—A specification for formatting non-ASCII messages so that they can be sent over the Internet. Many e-mail clients now support MIME, which enables them to send and receive graphics, audio, and video files via the Internet mail system. In addition, MIME supports messages in character sets other than ASCII.

multistation access unit (MSAU)—A token ring network device that physically connects network computers in a star topology while retaining the logical ring structure.

My Computer icon—Represents the computer. It includes all disk drives and the Control Panel. From within the My Computer icon, you can access and manage all files on your drives.

N

named pipe—A connection-oriented messaging via pipes, which set up a virtual circuit between the two points to maintain reliable and sequential data transfer.

name space—A set of unique names for resources or items used in a shared computing environment.

.NET—Microsoft operating system platform that incorporates distributed applications that bring users into the next generation of the Internet by conquering the deficiencies of the first generation and giving users a more enriched experience in using the Web for personal and business applications.

NetBIOS enhanced user interface (NetBEUI)—Provides the transport and network layers for the NetBIOS protocol.

NetWare Core Protocol—An IPX protocol that consists of the majority of network services offered by a Novell NetWare server.

NetWare Directory Services (NDS)—A directory service, consisting of a global, distributed, replicated database that tracks users and resources and provides controlled access to network resources.

network—Two or more computers connected to share resources such as files or a printer. For a network to function, it requires a network service to share or access a common media or pathway, to connect the computers and protocols, and to give the entire system common communications rules.

network address translation (NAT)—Method of connecting multiple computers to the Internet (or any other IP network) using one IP address. With a NAT gateway running on this single computer, it is possible to share that single address between multiple local computers and connect them all at the same time. The outside world is unaware of this division and thinks that only one computer is connected.

network analyzer—See *protocol analyzer.*

network-attached storage (NAS)—Hard disk storage that is set up with its own network address rather than being attached to the department computer that is serving applications to a network's workstation users.

Network Basic Input/Output System (NetBIOS)—A common program that runs on most Microsoft networks (Windows for Workgroups, Windows 95/98, and Windows NT).

network device interface specification (NDIS)—A set of standards for protocols and network card drivers that allow multiple protocols to use a single network adapter card; the layer that provides a communication path between two network devices.

Network File System (NFS)—A TCP/IP protocol that provides transparent remote access to shared files across networks.

network interface card (NIC)—Computers connect to the network by using a special expansion card.

network layer—Part of the OSI reference model that specifies the addressing and routing that is necessary to move data from one network (or subnet) to another. This includes establishing, maintaining, and terminating connections between networks; making routing decisions; and relaying data from one network to another. For the networks to communicate with one another, the network addresses must be unique.

network operating system (NOS)—Includes special functions for connecting computers and devices into a local area network (LAN), to manage the resources and services of the network and to provide network security for multiple users.

network service—Network resources that are offered by a network to multiple users such as files or printers.

node—(1) In networks, a processing location. A node can be a computer or some other device, such as a printer. Every node has a unique network address, sometimes called a data link control (DLC) address or media access control (MAC) address. (2) In tree structures, a point where two or more lines meet.

notification area—A Windows component located on the right side of the taskbar is used for the clock and for any programs running in the background such as printers and modems. The rest of the taskbar is blank or holds the active program buttons, which can be used to switch between open programs.

Novell NetWare—A LAN-based NOS, and a primary player in bringing networking to the PC arena.

NT File System (NTFS)—A file system for Windows NT, Windows 2000, Windows Server 2003, and Windows XP, designed for both the server and workstation. It provides a combination of performance, reliability, and compatibility.

NTLDR—The first Windows 2000 and Windows Server 2003 file read during boot-up, which switches the microprocessor from real mode to protected mode and starts the appropriate minifile system drivers (built into NTLDR) so that it can read the VFAT/FAT16, FAT32, or NTFS file systems.

NWLink—Microsoft's NDIS-compliant, 32-bit implementation of the Internetwork Packet Exchange (IPX), Sequenced Packet Exchange (SPX), and NetBIOS protocols used in Novell networks. NWLink is a standard network protocol that supports routing and can support NetWare client-server applications, where NetWare-aware Sockets-based applications communicate with IPX/SPX Sockets-based applications.

Nyquist theorem—Ensures accuracy by sampling a signal at least twice the rate of its frequency.

O

object—A distinct, named set of attributes or characteristics that represent a network resource including computers, people, groups, and printers in the Active Directory.

object linking and embedding (OLE)—A component of Windows that allows you to create objects with one application and then link or embed objects into another application. Embedded objects keep their original format and links to the application that created them.

ohmmeter—Device that can check wires and connectors and measure the resistance of an electronic device.

open circuit—Conductor with a break in it or wires that are unconnected, which prevents electricity from flowing.

open data link interface (ODI)—A set of standards for protocols and network card drivers that allow multiple protocols to use a single network adapter card.

Open Shortest Path First (OSPF)—A link-state routing protocol used in medium and large networks that calculates routing table entries by constructing a shortest-path tree. Routers using OSPF periodically advertises itself to other routers.

Open Systems Interconnection (OSI) reference model—The world's prominent networking architecture model.

optical time domain reflectometer (OTDR)—Fiber optic equivalent of the TDR that is used to test copper cables. The OTDR transmits a calibrated signal pulse over the cable to be tested and monitors the signal that returns back to the unit. Instead of measuring signal reflections caused by electrical impedance as a TDR does, however, the OTDR measures the signal returned by backscatter, a phenomenon that affects all fiber optic cables.

organization unit (OU)—Used to hold users, groups, computers, and other organization units in the Active Directory.

OS/2—One of the first 32-bit GUI operating systems; originally developed by IBM and Microsoft before Microsoft's Windows NT, but now owned and controlled by IBM. It uses the same domain concept used by Windows NT.

owner—The person who controls how permissions are set on a folder or file and can grant permissions to others. When a folder or file is created, the folder or file automatically becomes the owner.

P

packet—A piece of a message transmitted over a packet switching network. A key feature of a packet is it contains the destination address and the data. In IP networks, packets are often called datagrams.

packet switching—A technique in which messages are broken into small parts called packets. Each packet is tagged with source, destination, and intermediary node addresses as appropriate. Packets can have a defined maximum length and be stored in RAM instead of on hard disk. Packets can take a variety of possible paths through the network in an attempt to keep the network connections filled at all times.

page—A fixed number of bytes recognized by the operating system. It is typically used in memory such as virtual memory.

parity—An error-checking scheme that looks at the number of bits and determines them to be odd and even. When data are checked for integrity, the number of bits would be counted a second time to determine if it is odd or even. Parity error checking is used with older memory and some forms of data communications.

partition—A term used with hard drives, functions as if it were a separate hard disk (logical drive).

partitioning—Defines and divides the physical drive into logical volumes called partitions.

Password Authentication Protocol (PAP)—The least secure authentication protocol because it uses clear text (plaintext) passwords.

patch—Temporary fix to a program bug. A patch is an actual piece of object code that is inserted into (patched into) an executable program.

patch panels—A panel with numerous RJ-45 ports. The wall jacks are connected to the back of the patch panel to the individual RJ-45 ports.

peer-to-peer network—Sometimes referred to as a workgroup, is a network that has no dedicated servers. Instead, all computers are equal, so they both provide and request services.

Pentium processor—The minimum processor needed to load Windows 2000. It is based on an advanced superscalar architecture that allows the processor to execute two instructions at the same time.

peripheral component interconnect (PCI)—A new bus that was developed by Intel to replace the ISA slot with a faster interface.

permanent virtual circuit (PVC)—A permanently established virtual circuit that consists of one mode: data transfer. PVCs are used in situations in which data transfer between devices is constant.

permission—Defines the type of access granted to an object or object attribute. The permissions available for an object depend on the type of object.

personal computer (PC)—Used by one person and contains its own processing capabilities.

phase—The measurement in degrees of two sinusoidals waves.

physical layer—Part of the OSI reference model that is responsible for the actual transmission of the bits sent across a physical media.

physical topology—Describes how the network actually appears.

pipe—Connects two processes so that the output of one can be used as the input to the other.

plain old telephone service (POTS)—The standard telephone service that most homes use. See *public switched telephone network*.

plenum—The space above the ceiling and below the floors that is used to circulate air throughout the workplace.

plenum cable—Special type of cable that gives off little or no toxic fumes when burned.

plug-and-play (PNP)—The ability of a computer system to automatically configure expansion boards and other devices. You should be able to plug in a device and play with it, without worrying about setting DIP switches, jumpers, and other configuration elements.

plug-in—A software module that adds a specific feature or service to the browser such as to display or play different types of audio or video messages.

point to point—A topology that connects two nodes directly together.

Point-to-Point Protocol (PPP)—An advanced version on the SLIP protocol that is commonly used to connect to the Internet using a modem. Provides full-duplex, bidirectional operations between hosts and can encapsulate multiple network layer LAN protocols to connect to private networks.

Point-to-Point Tunneling Protocol (PPTP)—Uses the Internet as the connection between remote users and a local network, as well as between local networks.

poison reverse—A process that, used with split horizon, improves RIP convergence over simple split horizon by advertising all network IDs.

policies—A tool used by administrators to define and control how programs, network resources, and the operating system behave for users and computers in the Active Directory structure.

polling—An access method that uses a single device, such as a mainframe front-end processor, designated as the primary device, which polls or asks each of the secondary devices (or slaves) if they have information to be transmitted.

ports—(1) An interface on a computer to which you can connect a device. (2) In TCP/IP and other protocols, an endpoint to a logical connection. The ports are used to identify the upper-layer protocols and acts as a switchboard to make sure the frames find their way to the right network layer process. (3) To move a program from one type of computer to another. To port an application, rewrite sections that are machine dependent, and then recompile the program on the new computer. Programs that can be ported easily are said to be portable.

POSIX—A set of IEEE and ISO standards that define an interface between programs and UNIX.

Post Office Protocol (POP)—A TCP/IP protocol that defines a simple interface between a user's mail client software and e-mail server. It is used to download mail from the server to the client and allows the user to manage his or her mailboxes.

PPP Multilink Protocol (MP)—An extension that is used to aggregate or combine multiple physical links into a single logical link.

PPPOE (PPP over Ethernet)—Protocol designed to bring the security and metering benefits of the PPP to Ethernet connections such as those used in DSL.

preemptive multitasking—Occurs when the operating system assigns time slices to threads, tasks, and applications; those with a higher priority get a larger time slice. At the end of the time slice, the kernel can regain control of the computer without permission from the thread or program.

presentation layer—Part of the OSI reference model that ensures that information sent by an application layer protocol of one system will be readable by the application layer protocol on the remote system.

primary name server—Stores and maintains the zone file locally. Changes to a zone, such as adding domains or hosts, are done by changing files at the primary name server.

print device—A printer.

print server—Manages user access to printer resources connected to the network, allowing one printer to be used by many people.

print sharing—Allows several people to send documents to a centrally located printer in the office.

print spooler—Software that accepts a document sent to a printer by the user and then stores it on disk or in memory until the printer is ready for it.

printer pool—Two or more print devices that use the same driver which is connected to one print server and acts as a single printer.

private branch exchange (PBX)—A private telephone network used within an enterprise. Users of the PBX share a certain number of outside lines for making telephone calls external to the PBX.

private key—A key kept in a secure location and used only by you.

private-key encryption—The most basic form of encryption, also known as the symmetric algorithm. This encryption system requires that each individual possess a copy of the key. For this to work as intended, you must have a secure way to transport the key to other people. If you must keep multiple single keys per person, this can be very cumbersome. Since private-key algorithms are generally fast and easily implemented in hardware, they are commonly used for bulk data encryption.

processor input/output (PIO)—A data transfer mode used by IDE hard drives that is directly controlled by the processor.

program—An executable outline that follows a sequence of steps. A program consists of code and data initialization, a private memory address space, system resources (such as files, communication ports, and Windows resources), and one or more threads.

Project 802—Set of standards that has several areas of responsibility, including network cards, wide area network components, and media components.

propagation delay—Amount of time that passes between when a signal is transmitted and when it is received at the opposite end of the copper or optical cable.

protocol analyzer—Also known as a network analyzer. Software or a hardware/software device that captures, or receives, every packet on your media, stores it in a trace buffer, and shows a breakdown of each of the packets by protocol in the order that they appeared. It can help you analyze all levels of the OSI model to determine the cause of a problem.

protocol stack—Sometimes referred to as a protocol suite, is a set of protocols that works together to provide a full range of network services.

protocols—Rules or standards that allow the computer to connect to one another and enable computers and peripheral devices to exchange information.

proxy server—Provides local intranet clients with access to the Internet while keeping the local intranet free from intruders.

public key—A nonsecret key that is available to anyone you choose, or made available to everyone by posting it in a public place. It is often made available through a digital certificate.

public-key encryption—Also known as asymmetric algorithm, uses two distinct but mathematically related keys, public and private.

public switched telephone network (PSTN)—The international telephone system based on copper wires (UTP cabling) carrying analog voice data. See *plain old telephone service.*

pull partner—A WINS replication partner server that requests new database entries from its partner. The pull occurs at configured time intervals or in response to an update notification from a push partner.

punch-down block—A device used to connect several cable runs to each other without going through a hub.

push partner—A WINS replication partner server that sends update notification messages. The update notification occurs after a configurable number of changes to the WINS database.

Q

quality of service (QoS)—A networking term that specifies a guaranteed throughput level.

R

RAID-5 volumes—Fault-tolerant striped volumes that also use an extra drive to store parity information.

Rambus DRAM (RDRAM)—RAM based around a Rambus channel, a high-speed 16-bit bus running at a clock rate of 400 MHz.

Rambus inline memory module (RIMM)—A RAM package type that conforms to the standard DIMM form factor, but is not pin compatible. Since it runs at a higher clock speed than SIMMs and DIMMs, RIMMs typically have a heat spreader.

random access memory (RAM)—Electronic memory chips, which store information inside the computer. It is so called because the information is accessed nonsequentially. RAM is volatile memory (loses its contents when the power is turned off).

read-only memory (ROM)—Chips that do not lose their contents when the power is shut off.

Recovery Console—A command-line interface that will let you repair system problems using a limited set of command-line commands, including enabling or disabling services, repairing a corrupted master boot record, or reading and writing data on a local drive (FAT, FAT32, or NTFS).

recursive query—Asks the DNS server to respond with the requested data or with an error stating that the requested data do not exist or that the domain name specified does not exist.

Recycle Bin—An icon in Windows that is used as a safe delete. When you delete a file using the GUI, Windows stores the file in the Recycle Bin.

redirector—A small section of code in the network operating system that intercepts requests in the computer and determines if they should be left alone to continue in the local computer's bus or redirected out to the network to another server.

redundant array of inexpensive (or independent) disks (RAID)—A category of disk drives that employs two or more drives in combination for fault tolerance and performance. RAID disk drives are used frequently on servers but are not generally necessary for personal computers.

register—A high-speed internal storage area that acts as the microprocessors short-term memory and work area.

registry—A central, secure database in which Windows 2000 and Windows Server 2003 stores all hardware configuration information, software configuration information, and system security policy. Components that use the registry include the Windows NT Kernel, device drivers, setup programs, NTDETECT.COM, hardware profiles, and user profiles.

remote access policies (RAPs)—A set of conditions and connection settings that give network administrators more flexibility in authorizing connection attempts for remote access.

remote access server—A computer and associated software that is set up to handle users seeking access to the network remotely. A remote access server usually includes or is associated with a firewall server to ensure security and a router that can forward the remote access request to another part of the corporate network.

remote access service (RAS)—Allows users to connect remotely using various protocols and connection types.

Remote Authentication Dial-In User Service (RADIUS)—An industry standard client-server protocol and software that enables remote access servers to communicate with a central server to authenticate dial-in users and authorize their access to the requested system or service for authenticating remote users.

remote installation service (RIS)—A network service that allows for remote automated installation of Windows 2000 Professional and Windows Server 2003 workstations.

remote procedure calls (RPCs)—A component of IPC, are used to transfer information between applications that are on separate computers.

repeater—A network device used to regenerate or replicate a signal or to move packets from one physical media to another.

Request for Comments (RFC)—A series of documents that specify the standards for TCP/IP.

resource record (RR)—Entries of the DNS server database.

Reverse Address Resolution Protocol (RARP)—TCP/IP protocol that permits a physical address, such as an Ethernet address, to be translated into an IP address.

reverse lookup zone—Part of the DNS system that allows you to perform address-to-name resolution (also known as reverse lookup queries).

reverse query—Used with DNS servers, resolves an IP address and requests the host name.

right—Authorizes a user to perform certain actions on a computer, such as logging on to a system interactively or backing up files and directories.

ring topology—Connects all devices to one another in a closed loop. Each device is connected directly to two other devices.

root directory—Starting point of a volume, which is located at the top of the tree structure; holds files and/or directories.

root domain—Top of the DNS name space.

root hints—A file that normally contains the NS and A resource records for the Internet root servers.

root name server—Contains the resource records for all top-level name servers in the domain name space, such as the COM and EDU domain.

round-robin—A method used in DNS servers, rotates the order of resource records data returned in a query answer in which multiple resource records exist of the same resource record type for a queried DNS domain name.

router—A network OSI layer device that connects two or more LANs. In addition, it can break a large network into smaller, more manageable subnets.

Routing Information Protocol (RIP)—(1) A TCP/IP protocol that is a distance-vector route discovery protocol in which the entire routing table is periodically sent to the other routers. (2) An IPX protocol that is a distance-vector route discovery protocol in which the entire routing table is periodically sent to the other routers.

RSA standard—Created by Ron Rivst, Adi Shamir, and Leonard Adleman, defines the mathematical properties used in public-key encryption and digital signatures. The key length for this algorithm can range from 512 to 2048, making it a secure encryption algorithm.

runt—Frame that is less than 64 bytes with a valid cyclic redundancy check. These frames are typically formed by faulty or out-of-specification LAN drivers. Also known as a short frame.

S

sag—Very short drop in power lasting only a few milliseconds. Usually sags are not a problem.

satellite system—Microwave system that provides far bigger areas of coverage than can be achieved using other technologies. Microwave dishes are aligned to geostationary satellites that can either relay signals between sites directly or via another satellite. The huge distances covered by the signal result in propagation delays of up to 5 seconds.

schema—The formal definition and set of rules for all objects and attributes of those objects in the Active Directory.

search engine—A program used on the Internet that searches documents for specified keywords and returns a list of the documents where the keywords were found.

secondary name server—Gets the data from its zone from another name server, either a primary name server or another secondary name server, for that zone across the network.

second-level domain names—Variable-length names registered to an individual or organization used within a DNS name space.

sectors—The smallest unit that can be accessed on a disk. It is typically 512 bytes.

Secure HTTP (S-HTTP)—A protocol for transmitting data securely over the World Wide Web; designed to transmit individual messages securely.

Secure Sockets Layer (SSL) Protocol—A protocol developed by Netscape for transmitting private documents via the Internet. SSL works by using a private key to encrypt data that are transferred over the SSL connection.

security group—Assigns permissions and gains access to resources.

security identifier (SID)—A hexadecimal string that uniquely identifies the computer, users, and printers.

seek time—The average time it takes the hard drives read/write heads to move to the requested track. It is usually the time it takes the read/write heads to move one-third of the way across the platter.

separator page—Sometimes known as a banner page, separates print jobs and typically states who sent the document to the printer and the date and time of printing.

Sequenced Packet Exchange (SPX) Protocol—An IPX protocol that uses packet acknowledgments to guarantee delivery of packets.

Serial Line Interface Protocol (SLIP)—Sends packets down a serial link delimited with special END characters.

serial line protocols—Used for a computer to connect to a server, such as those used by an Internet service provider (ISP) via a serial line such as a modem to become an actual node on the Internet.

server—A computer that acts as a service provider to provide access to network resources.

server message block (SMB)—A series of commands used to pass information between networked computers using NetBIOS.

server room—The work area of the IT department where the servers and most of the communication devices reside.

service—A program, routine, or process that performs a specific system function to support other programs.

Service Advertising Protocol (SAP)—An IPX protocol used to advertise the services of all known servers on the network, including file servers and print servers.

service pack—A collection of fixes bundled as a single upgrade.

service profile identifier (SPID)—A directory number and additional identifier used to identify the ISDN device to the telephone network.

session—A reliable dialog between two computers.

session layer—Part of the OSI reference model that allows remote users to establish, manage, and terminate a connection (sessions).

shared folder—A folder that is available to clients on the network.

shielded twisted pair—Similar to unshielded twisted pair, but is usually surrounded by a braided shield that serves to reduce both EMI sensitivity and radio emissions.

Shiva Password Authentication Protocol (SPAP)—Shiva's proprietary version of PAP, offers a bit more security than PAP's plain-text password with its reversible encryption mechanism.

signaling—The method for using electrical or light energy to communicate; the two forms are digital signaling and analog signaling.

Simple Mail Transfer Protocol (SMTP)—Helps e-mail messages between servers. Most e-mail systems that send mail over the Internet use SMTP to send messages from one server to another; the messages can then be retrieved with an e-mail client using either POP or IMAP. In addition, SMTP is generally used to send messages from a mail client to a mail server. This is why you need to specify both the POP or IMAP server and the SMTP server when you configure your e-mail application.

Simple Network Management Protocol (SNMP)—A TCP/IP protocol that defines procedures and management information databases for managing TCP/IP-based network devices.

simple volume—Consists of disk space from a single physical disk (single region or multiple regions) linked together.

simplex dialog—Used in communications, allows communications on the transmission channel to occur in only one direction. Essentially, one device is allowed to transmit and all other devices receive.

single inline memory module (SIMM)—A RAM package type that uses a small circuit board consisting of several soldered DIP memory chips.

single-ended SCSI—A SCSI specification that uses a conventional signaling in which a positive voltage indicates a 1 and ground or 0 volt indicates a 0. Each signal is carried on one wire.

single-mode fiber—A type of fiber optic cable that can transmit light in only one mode.

site—One or more IP subnets connected by a high-speed link (128 Kbps or higher), typically defined by geographical locations. Sites are based on IP subnets of which any subnet can only belong to one site.

small computer systems interface (SCSI)—Pronounced "skuzzy," is a high-speed bus capable of supporting multiple devices in and out of the computer.

small office/home office (SOHO)—Small networks used primarily in home offices that might be part of a larger corporation but yet remain apart from it.

smart permanent virtual circuit (SPVC)—A hybrid of a permanent and temporary virtual circuit.

SNMP agent—Client or device that returns the appropriate information to an SNMP manager.

SNMP community—Collection of hosts grouped together for administrative purposes. Deciding what computers should belong to the same community is generally, but not always, determined by the physical proximity of the computers. Communities are identified by the names assigned to them.

SNMP manager—Console through which the network administrator performs network management functions.

software license—The legal permission for an individual or group to use a piece of software.

solid cable—Typically used for the cabling that exists throughout the building, including cables that lead from the wall jacks to the server room or wiring closet.

stranded cable—Typically used as patch cables between patch panels and hubs and between the computers and wall jacks.

source-route bridging (SRB)—Bridging method used on token ring networks in which the responsibility of determining the path to the destination node is placed on the sending node, not on the bridge.

spanned volume—A volume across multiple disks.

spanning tree algorithm (STA)—Method used with Ethernet bridges that designates a loopfree subset of the network's topology by placing those bridge ports that, if active would create loops, into a standby (blocking condition) mode.

split horizon—A route-advertising algorithm that prevents the advertising of routes in the same direction in which they were learned.

spread-spectrum signals—Wireless signals distributed over a wide range of frequencies and then collected onto their original frequency at the receiver.

SQL server—Server that is a database management system (DBMS) that can respond to queries from client machines formatted in the SQL language, a database language.

star topology—The most popular topology, it has each network device connect to a central point such as a hub, which acts as a multipoint connector.

Start button—A component of Windows used to start programs. Using the Start button, you can open recently accessed documents and access the Control Panel and printer folder, find files, and get help for Windows.

static routing algorithms—Table mappings established by the network administrator prior to the beginning of routing.

steppings—Internal version of the processor.

stop error—An error that signifies that something unexpected has happened within the Windows environment.

storage area network (SAN)—High-speed subnetwork of shared storage devices used to make all storage devices available to all servers on a LAN.

straight-through cable—Used to connect a network card to a hub; it has the same sequence of colored wires at both ends of the cable.

straight-tip (ST) connector—Probably the most widely used fiber optic connector. It uses a BNC attach-ment mechanism similar to the Thinnet connector mechanism.

stream cipher—Encrypts each byte of the data stream individually.

strip set—The combining areas of free space on 2 to 32 disks onto one logical volume. The difference is that a striped volume has the data allocated alternately and evenly in 64-KB stripes through the various drives. Therefore, when data are read or written, it writes to all drives simultaneously.

stub area—In OSPF networks, an area with only one ABR. All routes to the destination outside the area must pass through the single router.

subdomain names—Additional names that an organization can create that are derived from the registered second-level domain name of the DNS name space.

subnet—Small networks that comprise a larger network.

subnet mask—Numbers that resemble an IP address used to define which bits describe the network number and which bits describe the host address.

subnetworks—Also known as subnets, smaller LANs that comprise an internetwork.

subscriber (SC) connectors—Sometimes known as the square connector. Typically are latched, which makes it impossible for the connector to be pulled out without releasing the connector's latch (usually by pressing some kind of button or release).

subscriber loop—Also referred to as a local loop, is the telephone line that runs from your home or office to the telephone company's central office (CO) or neighborhood switching station.

supernet—A group of networks identified by contiguous network addresses.

superscalar—The ability of a processor to execute two instructions at the same time.

superscope—A group of multiple scopes (child scopes) as a single administrative entity for a DHCP server. Using a superscope, the DHCP server computer can activate and provide leases from more than one scope to clients on a single physical network.

switched 56 lines—Digitally switched or dial-up lines that provide a single digital channel for dependable data connectivity that is based on the DS-0, 64-Kbps technology.

switched 64 lines—Digitally switched or dial-up lines that provide a single digital channel for dependable data connectivity.

switched multimegabit data service (SMDS)—A high-speed, cell-relay, wide area network (WAN) service designed for LAN interconnection through the public telephone network.

switched virtual circuit (SVC)—A virtual circuit that is dynamically established on demand and terminated when transmission is complete. Communication over an SVC consists of three phases: circuit establishment, data transfer, and circuit termination.

switching hub—Sometimes referred to as a switch, is a fast multiported bridge, which actually reads the destination address of each packet and then forwards the packet to the correct port. A major advantage of using a switching hub is it allows one computer to open a connection to another computer (or LAN segment). While those two computers communicate, other connections between the other computers (or LAN segments) can be opened at the same time. Therefore, several computers can communicate at the same time.

symmetric multiprocessing (SMP)—Involves a computer that uses two or more microprocessors that share the same memory. If software is written to use the multiple microprocessors, several programs can be executed at the same time, or multithreaded applications can be executed faster.

synchronous—Devices use a timing or clock signal to coordinate communications.

Synchronous Digital Hierarchy (SDH)—An international standard for synchronous data transmission over fiber-optic cables.

synchronous dynamic RAM (SDRAM)—A popular form of RAM.

Synchronous Optical Network (SONET)—A standard for connecting fiber-optic transmission systems, mostly used in North America.

system partition—The active partition that contains the NTLDR and BOOT.INI file.

system ROM BIOS—The central ROM chip found on the motherboard. It controls the boot-up procedure and power-on self-test, generates hardware errors during boot-up, and contains the CMOS setup program.

system state data—A collection of system-specific data that can be backed up and restored. For Windows 2000 and Windows Server 2003, it includes the registry, system boot files, Active Directory directory services database, and the SYSVOL directory.

System Volume (SYSVOL)—A special folder that stores the server copy of the domain's public files, such as the Group Policy and Net Login (logon scripts), which are replicated among all domain controllers in the domain.

T

tape drive—A device, typically used to back up data onto long magnetic tape.

Task Manager—A component of Windows NT, Windows 2000, and Windows Server 2003 that provides a list of the current programs that are running and the overall CPU (including number of threads and processes) and memory usage (including the amount of physical memory, size of the file cache, paged memory, and nonpaged memory). You can also use the Task Manager to switch between programs and to stop a program that is not responding.

Task Scheduler—A program that comes with Windows 2000, and Windows Server 2003 that will schedule programs, batch files, and documents to run once at regular intervals or at specific times.

taskbar—A component of Windows 2000 and Windows Server 2003 located at the bottom of the screen, which is used to switch between different programs.

T-carrier system—The first successful system that converted the analog voice signal to a digital bit stream. Although the T-carrier system was originally designed to carry voice calls between telephone company central offices, today it is used to transfer voice, data, and video signals between different sites and to connect to the Internet.

terminal emulation (Telnet)—A program for TCP/IP networks such as the Internet. The Telnet program runs on your computer and connects your PC to a server on the network. You can then enter commands through the Telnet program and they will be executed as if you were entering them directly on the server console. This enables you to control the server and communicate with other servers on the network. To start a Telnet session, log in to a server by entering a valid user name and password. Telnet is a common way to remotely control web servers.

Terminal Services—A fully integrated component of Windows 2000 Server and Windows Server 2003, which enables a client to run a Windows application on a server.

terminating resistor—A device that goes on the end of a cable or daisy chain to stop the signal from bouncing back.

termination—A process in which two ends of a cable or daisy chain have resistors to stop the signal from bouncing back.

thin client—Designed to be especially small so that the bulk of the data processing occurs on the server.

thread—Part of a program that can execute independently of other parts. Operating systems that support multithreading enable programmers to design programs whose threaded parts can execute concurrently. This can enhance a program by allowing multitasking, improving throughput, enhancing responsiveness, and aiding background processing.

time-domain reflectometer (TDR)—A device used to test cables by using a sonarlike pulse along a cable.

Depending on the signal that is bounced back using a TDR, the reflectometer can detect a break or short and inform you how far the break or short is away.

token passing—An access method that uses a special authorizing packet of information to inform devices that they can transmit data. These packets, called tokens, are passed around the network in an orderly fashion from one device to the next. Devices can transmit only if they have control of the token, which distributes the access control among all the devices.

token ring—A type of network that uses token passing and forms a logical ring.

tone generator and probe—Sometimes called a "fox and hound" wire tracer, this type of device consists of a unit connected to a cable with a standard jack or an individual wire with alligator clips, which transmits a signal over the cable or wire. The other unit is a penlike probe that emits an audible tone when touched to the other end of the cable or wire, or even its insulating sheath.

top-level domains—The second level of the DNS name space to indicate a country, region, or type of organization. Three-letter codes indicate the type of organization; for example, COM indicates commercial (business) and EDU stands for educational institution. Two-letter codes indicate countries.

topology—Describes the appearance or layout of the network.

TRACEROUTE—Utility that traces a packet from a computer to an Internet host, showing how many hops the packet requires to reach the host and how long each hop takes. If you are visiting a website and pages are appearing slowly, you can use TRACEROUTE to figure out where the longest delays are occurring.

tracks—Concentric circles used on a disk, numbered starting with the outside track as track 0. The tracks are then further divided into sectors where each sector is typically 512 bytes of usable data.

transceiver—Device that both transmits and receives analog or digital signals.

transit area—In OSPF networks, an area that contains more than one ABR.

transition state—A method that represents data by how the signal transitions from high to low or low to high. A transition indicates a binary 1, whereas the absence of a transition represents a binary 0.

Transmission Control Protocol (TCP)—A TCP/IP protocol that provides connection-oriented, reliable communications for applications that typically transfer large amounts of data at one time or that require an acknowledgment for data received.

transport layer—The middle layer of the OSI reference model that connects the lower to the upper layers.

It is responsible for reliable transparent transfer of data between two endpoints.

Transport Layer Security (TLS) Protocol—Successor to the Secure Sockets Layer (SSL) protocol TLS is composed of two layers: TLS Record Protocol and TLS Handshake Protocol. The TLS Record Protocol provides connection security with some encryption method such as the Data Encryption Standard (DES), but it can also be used without encryptions. The TLS Handshake Protocol allows the server and client to authenticate each other and to negotiate an encryption algorithm and cryptographic keys before data are exchanged.

trap—An unsolicited message sent by an SNMP agent to an SNMP management system, when the agent detects that a certain type of event has occurred locally on the managed host.

trust relationship—A link that combines two domains into one administrative unit that can authorize access to resources on both domains.

tunneling—The method for transferring data packets over the Internet or other public network, providing the security and features formerly available only on private networks.

twisted-pair cable—Consists of two insulated copper wires twisted around each other. Although each pair acts as a single communication link, twisted pairs are usually bundled together into a cable and wrapped in a protective sheath.

U

Uniform Naming Convention—See *Universal Naming Convention*.

uniform resource locator (URL)—A location of a web page or site. The first part of the address indicates what protocol to use, and second part specifies the IP address or the domain name where the resource is located. The last part indicates the folder and file name.

uninterruptible power supply (UPS)—A device used to protect your system against power fluctuations including outages.

unique sequence number (USN)—A 64-bit unique number that is used to track all changes to an Active Directory.

Universal Naming Convention (UNC)—Also known as Uniform Naming Convention. A NetBIOS format for specifying the location of shared resources on a local area network (LAN). UNC uses the following format: \\servername\shared-resource-pathname.

universal security group—A type of group that can contain users, universal groups, and global groups from any domain and it can be assigned rights and permissions to any network resource in any domain in the domain tree or forest. It is only available in native mode.

universal serial bus (USB)—This external port allows you to connect up to 127 external PC peripherals in series (daisy chain) and offers a data transfer rate up to 12 Mbps. The USB allows devices to be attached while the computer is running and requires no rebooting or reconfiguring when a peripheral is added or removed.

UNIX—A popular multiuser, multitasking operation, is the grandfather of network operating systems, which was developed at Bell Labs in the early 1970s.

unshielded twisted-pair cable (UTP)—Uses twisted-pair cable that does not include any additional shielding.

user account—Enables a user to log on to a computer and domain with an identity that can be authenticated and authorized for access to domain resources.

User Datagram Protocol (UDP)—A TCP/IP protocol that provides connectionless communication and does not guarantee that packets will be delivered. Applications that use UDP typically transfer small amounts of data at once. Reliable delivery is the responsibility of the application.

user mode—A processing mode used in Windows NT, Windows 2000, and Windows Server 2003 that has programs running in ring 3 of the Intel 386 microprocessor protection model. These programs are protected by the operating system. It is a less privileged processor mode that has no direct access to hardware and can only access its own address space.

user profile—A collection of folders and data that stores the user's current desktop environment and application settings.

V

value-added network (VAN)—A network with special services such as electronic data interchange (EDI) or financial services such as credit card authorization or ATM transactions.

VFAT—An enhanced version of the FAT structure, which allows Windows 95, Windows 98, Windows NT, Windows 2000, and Windows Server 2003 to support long file names (LFNs) up to 255 characters.

virtual circuits—Establish formal communication between two computers on an internetwork using a well-defined path. This enables two computers to act as though there is a dedicated circuit between two, even though there is not. The path the data take while being exchanged between the two computers may vary, but the computers do not know this nor do they need to. Virtual networks are sometimes depicted as a cloud, because the user does not worry about the path taken through the cloud, only about entering and exiting the cloud.

virtual (or logical) LAN (VLAN)—A local area network with a definition that maps workstations on some other basis than geographical location (e.g., by department, type of user, or primary application). In other words, it is a network of computers that behaves as if the computers are connected to the same wire even though they may actually be physically located on different segments of a LAN.

virtual link—In OSPF networks, is a logical link between a backbone area border router, an unspecified number of routers, and a second border router that is not connected to the backbone.

virtual machine (VM)—A self-contained operating environment that behaves as if it is a separate computer.

virtual memory—Disk space pretending to be RAM, which allows the operating system to load more programs and data. For all programs and data to be accessed, parts are constantly swapped back and forth between RAM and disk. As far as the programs are concerned, the virtual memory looks and acts like regular RAM.

virtual private networking—The creation of secured, point-to-point connections across a private network or a public network such as the Internet. A virtual private networking client uses special TCP/IP-based protocols, called tunneling protocols, to make a virtual call to a virtual port on a virtual private networking server.

virus—A program that is designed to replicate and spread, generally without the knowledge or permission of the user.

volatile—A term typically used with memory chips, meaning the device will lose its contents when the power is turned off.

volume—A logical unit of disk space that functions as though it was a physical disk.

W

web browser—The client program/software that you run on your local machine to gain access to a web server. It receives the HTML commands, interprets the HTML, and displays the results.

Web-distributed authoring and versioning (Web-DAV)—A Windows 2000, and Windows Server 2003 environment that extends the HTTP to allow clients to publish, lock, and manage resources on the Web.

web server—A computer equipped with the server software that uses Internet protocols such as HTTP and FTP to respond to web client requests on a TCP/IP network via web browsers.

wide area network (WAN)—Uses long-range telecommunication links to connect the network computers over long distances and often consists of two or more smaller LANs.

WiFi—Wireless fidelity, and another name for IEEE 802.11b. WiFi is used in place of 802.11b in the same way that Ethernet is used in place of IEEE 802.3.

Win16 on Win32 (WOW)—A component of Windows NT and Windows 2000 which translates, or thunks, 16-bit calls to 32-bit calls.

Windows 2000—Formerly known as Windows NT 5.0, an advanced, high-performance network operating system that is robust in features and services, security, performance, and upgradability. There are four versions of Windows 2000—Windows 2000 Professional, Windows 2000 Server, Windows 2000 Advanced Server, and Windows 2000 Datacenter Server.

Windows Driver Model (WDM)—Driver technology developed by Microsoft to create drivers that are source-code compatible for Windows 98, 2000, Me, and XP. WDM works by channeling some of the work of the device driver into portions of the code that are integrated into the operating system. These portions of code handle all of the low-level buffer management, including direct memory access and plug-and-play device enumeration. The WDM device driver becomes more streamlined with less code and works at greater efficiency.

Windows Explorer—A component of Windows that is used to manage directories and files.

Windows Internet Naming Service (WINS)—System that contains a database of IP addresses and NetBIOS (computer names) that update dynamically. It is used to resolve IP addresses from the computer names.

Windows NT—A high-performance network operating system, which eventually led to Windows 2000.

Windows NT Directory Service (NTDS)—System of domains and trusts for a Windows NT Server network. The User Manager for Domains program manages the users and groups of a domain and sets up trusts with other domains (trusts allow users to access resources in other domains).

Windows Server 2003—Microsoft's newest network operating system that is similar to Windows 2000 Server, yet uses the same interface as Windows XP.

Windows socket (WinSock)—A port that provides the interface between the network program or service and the Windows environment.

Windows XP—Windows operating system that is the client for Windows Server 2003 family. It is based on the Windows 2000 architecture, but has a new, cleaner, more intuitive interface.

WINS proxy agent—A WINS-enabled computer configured to act on behalf of other host computers that cannot directly use WINS.

WINS replication partner—A WINS server that synchronizes with another WINS server.

WINS server—A name server that resolves NetBIOS names to IP addresses.

wired equivalent privacy (WEP)—Form of encryption used by wireless communication.

wireless LAN (WLAN)—A data communication system that uses electromagnetic waves to transmit and receive data over the air, minimizing the need for wired connections.

workgroup—Computers and devices on a peer-to-peer network are usually organized into logical subgroups called workgroups. In a workgroup, each computer has a local security database so that it tracks its own user and group account information. The user information is not shared with other workgroup computers.

Worm—Program or algorithm that replicates itself over a computer network and usually performs malicious actions, such as using up the computer's resources and shutting the system down. Typically, a worm enters the computer because of vulnerabilities available in the computer's operating system.

X

X.25—A packet switched network that allows remote devices to communicate with each other across digital links without the expense of individual leased lines.

X.400—A set of standards relating to the exchange of electronic messages (e.g., e-mail, fax, voice mail, telex).

X.500—A common directory service that uses a hierarchical approach, in which objects are organized similar to the files and folders on a hard drive.

X.509 certificates—The most widely used digital certificates.

XML—See *Extensible Markup Language*.

Z

Zone transfer—Process of obtaining DNS zone information across the network.

Index